DAY BY DAY

The Thirties

Rodney P. Carlisle, Ph.D.

General Editor

Facts On File, Inc.

Day by Day: The Thirties

Facts On File, Inc.
An imprint of Infobase Publishing
132 West 31st Street
New York, NY 10001

Library of Congress Cataloging-in-Publication Data

Day by day : the 1930s / Rodney P. Carlisle, general editor.
   p. cm.
 Includes bibliographical references and index.
 ISBN 0-8160-6664-7 (alk. paper)
 1. Nineteen thirties-Chronology. I. Carlisle, Rodney P. II. Title: 1930s.
 D723.D39 2006
 909.82'30202-dc22

                      2006017697

Facts On File books are available at special discounts when purchased in bulk quantities for businesses, associations, institutions, or sales promotions. Please call our Special Sales Department in New York at (212) 967-8800 or (800) 322-8755.

You can find Facts On File on the World Wide Web at http://www.factsonfile.com

Golson Books, Ltd.

President and Editor	J. Geoffrey Golson
General Editor, The 1930s	Rodney P. Carlisle
Authors, The 1930s	John Barnhill, Joseph Geringer, Kevin G. Golson, Vickey Kalambakal, Pat McCarthy, Luca Prono, Kelly Boyer Sagert
Design Director	Mary Jo Scibetta
Layout Production	Kenneth W. Heller
Copy Editor	Jennifer L. Wallace
Proofreader	Barbara Paris
Indexer	Gail Liss

Photo Credits
Library of Congress: 1930 pages 4–5; 1931 pages 120–121; 1932 pages 232–233: 1933 pages 310–311; 1936 pages 568–569. National Archives and Records Administration: 1934 pages 384–385; 1937 pages 678–679: 1938; pages 814–815; 1939 pages 914–915. National Oceanic and Atmospheric Administration: 1935 pages 486–487.

CONTENTS

VOLUME 2

DAY BY DAY

The Thirties

VOLUME 2

1936 - 1939

1936

A man and two young boys race for shelter in the face of
an oncoming storm on the Great Plains in 1936.

	World Affairs	Europe	Africa & The Middle East	The Americas	Asia & The Pacific
Jan.	The International Labor Office reports a decline in world unemployment, primarily due to increased armaments production.	Edouard Daladier, socialist leader, is elected president of France.	Ethiopians adopt guerilla tactics; Italians take Noghelli (Nogele), a town in southern Ethiopia.	Bolivia and Paraguay sign a treaty ending the Chaco War. . . . Brazil accuses the Soviet Union of helping fund a rebel uprising.	Japanese delegates walk out of the London Naval Disarmament Conference.
Feb.		Britain cedes control of Cyprus to Greece.	Italians take Mount Alaji in Ethiopia, the location of an Italian defeat in 1895.	Brazil and the United States sign a reciprocal trade agreement, part of the U.S. policy of moving from tariffs to such a system of agreements.	Japanese military leaders conduct an attempted coup in Tokyo.
Mar.	At the second London Naval Disarmament Conference, the United States, Britain, and France sign an agreement limiting capital ships.	Germany sends troops into the previously demilitarized Rhineland.	France pressures Ethiopia to work out peace terms with Italy. . . . Italians conduct a large scale air-raid in Ethiopia.	Canada expels the Italian ambassador on grounds of political activity.	In reaction against the attempted military takeover, the Japanese Cabinet is reshuffled with more representation of civilians and moderates.
Apr.			Italians advance to besiege Addis Ababa, the capital of Ethiopia.	President Lázaro Cárdenas of Mexico orders the banishing of former president Plutarco Elías Calles for inciting political unrest. . . . President Franklin Roosevelt issues a call for the convening of a Pan-American Congress.	
May			Addis Ababa falls to Italian troops; Emperor Haile Selassie goes into exile.	National Guard chief Anastasio Somoza leads an uprising against the government in Nicaragua.	
Jun.		Socialist Leon Blum is selected as premier of France. . . . Heinrich Himmler is appointed to head the German Reich Police.	Sporadic but continuing outbursts of violence by Palestinian Arabs result in the increase of British troop presence in the mandated territory.	Anastasio Somoza completes his seizure of power in Nicaragua.	
Jul.	Germany agrees to suspend use of the Nazi salute during the Olympics.	Civil war erupts in Spain with revolt by army generals in Spanish Morocco.		President Franklin Roosevelt conducts an official visit to Canada to improve relations.	
Aug.		Germany, France, and Britain agree to an arms embargo against Spain; Germany later provides arms to Franco's forces there. . . . Soviets accuse Trotsky of complicity in a plot to kill Stalin.	Turkey announces the establishment of a film censorship board.		Japanese-Russian relations worsen over incidents in Manchukuo and Mongolia.
Sept.		Spain complains at the League of Nations of military assistance to the rebels by Italy, Germany, and Portugal.	British forces in Palestine now number about 10,000.		
Oct.		An airraid is conducted in Paris.	A truce is declared in the Palestinian uprising.		Japan nationalizes the electric power industry.
Nov.	Britain leads the world in the arms trade.	The Soviet Union introduces a new constitution.		President Franklin Roosevelt visits Buenos Aires, Argentina, to attend the Pan-American conference.	
Dec.		King Edward VIII abdicates, refusing to abandon plans to marry a divorced American woman, Wallis Simpson.		Mexican President Lázaro Cárdenas offers sanctuary to Leon Trotsky.	In China, President Chiang Kai-shek is briefly kidnapped, then released.

A	B	C	D	E
Includes developments that affect more than one world region, international organizations, and important meetings of world leaders.	*Includes all domestic and regional developments in Europe, including the Soviet Union.*	*Includes all domestic and regional developments in Africa and the Middle East.*	*Includes all domestic and regional developments in Latin America, the Caribbean, and Canada.*	*Includes all domestic and regional developments in Asian and Pacific nations (and colonies).*

U.S. Politics & Social Issues	U.S. Foreign Policy & Defense	Economics & Great Depression	Science, Technology & Nature	Culture, Leisure & Lifestyle	
Governor Alf Landon of Kansas announces his intention to seek the Republican nomination for the presidency.	The 1936 Neutrality Act is introduced and debated in Congress. . . . The Adjusted Compensation Act to provide bonuses to World War I veterans is vetoed by President Franklin Roosevelt; both branches of Congress immediately override the veto.	The Supreme Court declares the Agricultural Adjustment Act unconstitutional.	Dr. Edwin Grant Conklin, a biologist from Princeton University, replaces Dr. Karl T. Compton as president of the American Association for the Advancement of Science.	Avery Brundage, head of American Amateur Athletics, chooses leaders for 30 teams to enter the Summer Olympics in Germany.	Jan.
The Soil Conservation and Domestic Allotment Act is signed into law, replacing the AAA.	The 1936 Neutrality Act is passed, enlarging and extending the 1935 Act to mid-1937.			The Winter Olympics open in Bavaria.	Feb.
Progressive Republican Senator William Borah announces his intent to seek the Republican nomination for the presidency.	Senator William Borah's advocacy of strict neutrality wins him political support.		Johnstown, Pa., suffers a disastrous flood.		Mar.
Amalgamated Clothing Workers leader Sidney Hillman urges the reelection of President Franklin Roosevelt.	British protest against the U.S. refusal to join in an oil boycott of Italy over the Italo-Ethiopian War.			Arturo Toscanini retires from the New York Philharmonic Orchestra.	Apr.
		Congress passes a law establishing the Rural Electrification Administration (REA).	A new wind tunnel, capable of testing speeds up to 500 miles per hour, is opened at Langley Field in Virginia. . . . Mayan influence is discovered in archaeological finds as far north as North Dakota.		May
William Lemke, (R-ND) announces he will run for president on a third-party ticket. . . . Alf Landon is nominated for president and Frank Knox for vice president by the Republican Party; Roosevelt and Garner are given the Democratic nominations.		Congress passes and the President signs the Robinson-Patman Anti-Price Discrimination Act; the 1936 Revenue Act is also enacted.		A total of 53 nations plan to send teams to the Summer Olympics in Germany.	Jun.
		Harold Ickes announces the PWA will fund some $22 million in projects.		The Summer Olympics open in Berlin.	Jul.
Alf Landon mounts criticisms of the New Deal as part of his political campaign; Earl Browder, Communist Party candidate for president, attacks Landon.				African-American athlete Jesse Owens wins four gold medals at the Olympics.	Aug.
In veiled language, the White House criticizes the Hearst newspapers for suggesting that Roosevelt and the New Deal are inspired by un-American, i.e., Communist, ideas. . . . While campaigning, Communist leader Earl Browder is arrested in Terre Haute, Ind.		Republicans charge that New Deal agencies, especially the WPA, have been used for political purposes.			Sept.
Landon warns of dictatorship if Roosevelt is reelected. . . . Al Smith, former Democratic governor of New York and 1928 Democratic candidate for president, asks his supporters to vote for Landon.				Joe Louis defeats Argentina's Jorge Brescia in a prizefight in New York.	Oct.
President Franklin Roosevelt is reelected in a landslide victory; Democrats take both houses of Congress. . . . The rift between the AFL and CIO widens.	Senator Gerald Nye suggests amendments to the Neutrality Act to limit arms exports.	Businesses report profits and employment figures appear to be on the rise.			Nov.
President Franklin Roosevelt hints at plans to expand the Supreme Court.		Rexford Tugwell leaves the Department of Agriculture.			Dec.

F	**G**	**H**	**I**	**J**
Includes elections, federal-state relations, civil rights and liberties, crime, the judiciary, education, healthcare, poverty, urban affairs, and population.	Includes formation and debate of U.S. foreign and defense policies, veterans affairs, and defense spending. (Relations with specific foreign countries are usually found under the region concerned.)	Includes business, labor, agriculture, taxation, transportation, consumer affairs, monetary and fiscal policy, natural resources, pollution, and accidents.	Includes worldwide scientific, medical, and technological developments, natural phenomena, U.S. weather, and natural disasters.	Includes the arts, religion, scholarship, communications media, sports, entertainment, fashions, fads, and social life.

	World Affairs	Europe	Africa & The Middle East	The Americas	Asia & The Pacific
Jan. 1			Six hundred delegates at the 10th Annual College of Surgeons meeting in Cairo find themselves in the center of downtown rioting when a group of students turn out to demonstrate against England.... Imperial Airways' *City of Khartoum*, a flying boat, crashes in the Mediterranean, killing 12 of 13 passengers; an American is among the dead.	The Labor Conference of American States opens in Santiago, Chile. The sessions, introduced by Chilean President Arturo Alessandri, are attended by members of the International Labor Organization and affiliates.	
Jan. 2	France tells visiting U.S. Undersecretary of State William Phillips that it does not agree with the U.S. decision to remain neutral during the present European hostilities.	French ships join British ships already gathered in the Mediterranean Sea as a sign to halt possible territorial trespassing by Italy. Britain and France have pledged each other assistance should Italy retaliate.			
Jan. 3	World unemployment drops for the second year in a row. According to the International Labor Office, many of the returning workers are put to work on the manufacturing of arms—especially in Germany.	The Third Reich responds to the League of Nations' recent chastisement of its treatment of Jews by saying the League should worry about those "minorities" in the countries that belong to the League, and leave others alone. Germany had previously withdrawn from the League.			
Jan. 4		Some 9 million children between the ages of 10 and 18 will be called to participate in Nazi Germany's Reich Youth League, according to Baldur von Schirach, leader of the movement. The league is designed to indoctrinate all children into the Nazi mindset.		Bolivia receives a concession to construct a $250 million hydroelectric power plant to bring electricity to the frontier land. . . . Members of U.S. Congress praise the reciprocal trading pact between the United States and Canada that went into effect last week. Many predict it will not only improve both economies, but will enhance the relationship between the two countries over the next several years.	
Jan. 5	England becomes the latest of several countries to speak up against the U.S. neutrality stance. . . . The Archbishop of Chicago, George Cardinal Mundelein, tells 3,000 members of the Altar and Rosary Society that it will not be long before Nazi Germany totally suffocates the actions of all Catholic churches in Germany.		Lake Tana, which is Ethiopia's source of the Blue Nile and a coveted location centering on others' territories, is watched over by Britain as Italian troops are deployed to battle the Ethiopians. Italy claims Britain is overreacting; Britain says it is merely being cautious.	*La Nacion*, one of Argentina's main newspapers, lauds President Roosevelt for his attention to helping the economy of countries in South America. By abolishing the dollar diplomacy he exhibited true inter-American relationships, says the managing editor of *La Nacion*.	
Jan. 6	Roman newspapers are affronted by U.S. President Franklin Roosevelt's recent neutrality speech. Italian editors call him a dictator with no right to speak on autocracy. . . . The attendees of the London Naval Conference reconvene after a Christmas recess. France puts forth a new proposal to cut naval forces. Like preceding efforts, it meets with trepidation.		Many in the world are shocked by Italy's coldness after accidentally bombing a Swedish Red Cross hospital tent in Dolo, Ethiopia. Italy simply responds that no Swedes were hit, offering no apology to what could have been a tragic event.	After a series of ongoing conferences in Washington, D.C., a "mutually satisfactory" agreement is reached between Mexico and the United States on stabilizing silver.	
Jan. 7	The United States is incensed at the Nazi government's detention of an American traveler whose private letter home, which Nazis opened, made disparaging remarks about Germany. The U.S. General Consul in Germany, Charles Hathaway, promises the release of the American, Paul Herburger.				Japan does not plan to annex Manchukuo in northern China, no matter what the press continues to say, according to an angry Japanese representative, Gen. Jiro Munami, a ranking officer in Japan's army. His views are supported by Tokyo's ambassador to Manchukuo.
Jan. 8		Vickers, Britain's largest private arms manufacturer, denies before a Royal Inquiry that it and other weapons makers have politically conspired to incite the feeling of aggression in order to sell equipment.	Ethiopia's Emperor, Haile Selassie, sends out a request to his troop commanders to cease from fighting the Italian invaders "in a body" and stick to guerilla tactics.	Francis W. Hirst, a noted British economist, sees a gain in the U.S. economy due to its recent trade pact with the Commonwealth of Canada.	

A	B	C	D	E
Includes developments that affect more than one world region, international organizations, and important meetings of world leaders.	Includes all domestic and regional developments in Europe, including the Soviet Union.	Includes all domestic and regional developments in Africa and the Middle East.	Includes all domestic and regional developments in Latin America, the Caribbean, and Canada.	Includes all domestic and regional developments in Asian and Pacific nations (and colonies).

U.S. Politics & Social Issues	U.S. Foreign Policy & Defense	Economics & Great Depression	Science, Technology & Nature	Culture, Leisure & Lifestyle	
Father Philip J. Furlong, professor of history at Cathedral College, New York, asks Catholics to shun newspapers that print crime news and movies that sell sex and low morals.		The U.S. foreign trade income escalated between 1934 and 1935, up to $4.3 billion in 1935 from $3.8 billion in 1934, according to government experts. Britain was the leading trading partner.		An addition to its Pacific passenger route is proposed by Pan-American Airlines. The stretch would island-hop between Honolulu, the Auklands, and New Zealand. . . . Mexican Rodolfo (Babe) Casanova soundly defeats Cincinnati, Ohio's Freddie Miller in a 10-round boxing competition in Mexico City.	Jan. 1
		According to the Westinghouse Electric and Manufacturing Company, increased power demand over the past year is being met by greater electrical units issuing energy for the many new high-powered applications. . . . James D. Mooney, vice president of General Motors, expects U.S. export trade to rise this year, largely due to Secretary of State Cordell Hull's recent reciprocal trade agreement.	The American Association for the Advancement of Science selects Dr. Edwin Grant Conklin, a biologist from Princeton University, as its next president. He replaces the outgoing Dr. Karl T. Compton.	The New York Film Critics Award, recently established to honor top works in the Hollywood media, selects director John Ford's *The Informer* as the best picture of 1934. A close runner-up is Greta Garbo's *Anna Karenina*.	Jan. 2
Dr. James E. West, chief executive of the Boy Scouts of America, which celebrates 25 years of scouting management today, promises to make the Scouts a more "vigorous and militant force" to help defeat national problems throughout 1936.	With the opening of Congress, Secretary of State Cordell Hull finalizes the new Neutrality Bill that will enter debate. The bill is expected to be one of the more controversial items for this session of Congress, as many feel that neutrality can be more of a crutch than a preventative to war.	War veterans compose their own draft of a bonus bill, which they plan to submit to President Roosevelt. The bill is for a multimillion-dollar cash outlay to be disseminated among all living war veterans of America. . . . President Roosevelt, in a speech to the 74th Congress, openly challenges foes of the New Deal to prove that it was not an economically sound avenue to steer the United States out of the Depression.	Recent laboratory tests reveal the existence of the neutrino, a fundamental piece of the atomic structure that scientists have been trying to find for years. The neutrino is 1,800 times lighter than the neutron. The announcement of the discovery is met with excitement by members of the American Association for the Advancement of Science.		Jan. 3
President of Columbia College, Dr. Nicholas Murray Butler, urges U.S. scholars to help stop the persecution of people that is continuing almost wholesale in Germany, Russia, and Italy. He demands campaigns to furnish "leadership toward liberty."					Jan. 4
From Utah, former president Herbert Hoover calls President Roosevelt's speech to Congress in which he challenges all foes of the New Deal to come forward as a "message of ill will." Its tone, he opines, makes everyone who does not agree with his policies sound "wicked and corrupt."				N. Yamaguchi, an official from Tokyo, tells a Los Angeles audience that baseball is quickly becoming Japan's number one sport. Some 50,000 people, he says, attend college games regularly.	Jan. 5
Members of major Jewish leagues in the United States appeal to both the U.S. Congress and the League of Nations to take special steps to help the thousands of Jews trying to find a new home, away from Germany, Poland, Austria, and other nations under Nazi influence.		Washington is stunned by the Supreme Court's decision to ban the Agricultural Adjustment Act, whose focus was farm relief. The Supreme Court claims that the administration held too much power. Proponents of the AAA vow to fight the decision.			Jan. 6
	The Neutrality Bill is introduced in both the Senate and the House of Representatives. A noted element of the bill is that U.S. ships will avoid waters in war zones.	The Westinghouse Electric and Manufacturing Company had a prosperous 1935. Total gross was $122 million, according to Chairman A.W. Robertson. . . . Ford Motor Company announces that it manufactured a record number of automobiles in 1935 with a total of 1,335,865. It is a sign of a recovering economy, company executives attest.			Jan. 7
The insurance industry should avoid getting involved in politics and stick strictly to the development of the insurance business, says New York State's Superintendent of Insurance, Louis H. Pink. A national group of agents at the Life Underwriters Association's dinner applaud his remarks.	Vice Admiral Arthur J. Hepburn is named U.S. Fleet Commander by Secretary of the Navy Claude Swanson. The appointment is part of a wide naval reorganization.				Jan. 8

F	G	H	I	J
Includes elections, federal-state relations, civil rights and liberties, crime, the judiciary, education, healthcare, poverty, urban affairs, and population.	Includes formation and debate of U.S. foreign and defense policies, veterans affairs, and defense spending. (Relations with specific foreign countries are usually found under the region concerned.)	Includes business, labor, agriculture, taxation, transportation, consumer affairs, monetary and fiscal policy, natural resources, pollution, and accidents.	Includes worldwide scientific, medical, and technological developments, natural phenomena, U.S. weather, and natural disasters.	Includes the arts, religion, scholarship, communications media, sports, entertainment, fashions, fads, and social life.

	World Affairs	Europe	Africa & The Middle East	The Americas	Asia & The Pacific
Jan. 9		Unemployment figures in the Reich jumped in December 1935 to the highest in history. Some 522,354 people lost their jobs in one month, due mostly to a production slowdown caused by the lack of raw materials. There are currently 2,506,806 jobless persons in Nazi Germany. . . . Two British college students from Cambridge—Gerald Plunkett and Robert Burtram—are released from a jail in Vienna after paying for a shattered train window that they claim they did not break; they accuse the local constabulary of arresting them because they are British.		Secretary of the Interior Harold L. Ickes receives a rousing ovation from the people of the Virgin Islands when he disembarks his plane for a good-will visit to the islands.	
Jan. 10		Premier Vyacheslaff M. Molotov of the Soviet Union asserts that Japan and Germany are both intent on territorial conquest and he openly announces an increase in Soviet armaments. . . . Fascism has lost much of its support in France, according to the French government. With country-wide elections three months away, all fascist groups have gone silent.			Japan fails to reach consensus with the other members of the naval parley taking place in London. Japan wants to have as large a fleet as the other nations, but the other nations, including the United States, insist on denying Japan parity.
Jan. 11				Peru begins to regulate its wheat prices by taking the first steps to see that its charges conform to the rest of the world market. Its recent wheat trade has not been competitive. . . . At the Pan-American Conference, the delegates from Chile and Brazil shoot down the changes proposed by United States to their textile industry, which includes shorter hours.	
Jan. 12		Russia's military commanders urge their government to increase the defense budget in the face of what they see as ambitious Hitlerism and Japanese aggression. Soviet representatives, in turn, seek an increase in the military budget of 6 billion rubles. Premier Molotov pleads the case before the Central Executive Committee.	A long highway is planned and approved by four powers. It will run through parts of Europe and Turkey, from Tangiers to Cairo. . . . Still convinced that sanctions will fail, Italian Premier Benito Mussolini continues to send more troops into Ethiopia, even though the troops themselves are besieged by incessant torrents during Africa's rainy season.	The Montreal *Gazette* states that year-end figures indicate that Canada showed a stronger economic recovery than the United States did in 1935.	
Jan. 13				Pushing for an across-the-board child labor law, U.S. Rep. Frieda Miller tells attendees of the Pan-American Labor Conference at Santiago that there should be a minimum age of 16 years placed on workers.	
Jan. 14					

A	B	C	D	E
Includes developments that affect more than one world region, international organizations, and important meetings of world leaders.	Includes all domestic and regional developments in Europe, including the Soviet Union.	Includes all domestic and regional developments in Africa and the Middle East.	Includes all domestic and regional developments in Latin America, the Caribbean, and Canada.	Includes all domestic and regional developments in Asian and Pacific nations (and colonies).

U.S. Politics & Social Issues	U.S. Foreign Policy & Defense	Economics & Great Depression	Science, Technology & Nature	Culture, Leisure & Lifestyle	
Dr. Nicholas Murray Butler, Columbia University's president, predicts that because President Roosevelt has failed to live up to "a single item" of his national platform and because he has set the U.S. economy back he will not be reelected. . . . The Democratic Party is looking forward to the opening of its Presidential Convention on June 23 in Philadelphia, which wins the bid to host the convention.			The Scripps Institute of Oceanography recreates a small segment of evolution in its laboratories in La Jolla, Calif., when it transforms living ocean bacteria into land creatures, able to thrive out of water. The process is done by applying slow draughts of seawater to fresh water, a small amount at a time.	The Cincinnati Reds baseball team will conduct their off-season training camp in Puerto Rico. Larry McMurtry, business manager, explains that the Reds are the first team to ever do training outside the contiguous United States. . . . Judges of the upcoming Grand National Steeplechase select five American-bred horses for the competition. Delaneige and Bagatelle II are among the chosen.	Jan. 9
The American Legion disagrees with the Roosevelt administration's proposal for a general pension system for World War veterans. It presses its national commander, Ray Murphy, to urge the President for a better system of pensions. . . . William Hirth, president of the Missouri Farmers' Association and publisher of an extremely popular agricultural newspaper, enters the election for state governor, upsetting the campaign plans of the previously unopposed incumbent, Democrat Lloyd C. Stark.	Professor of law Edward M. Borchard of Yale University sees no sense in the current Neutrality Bill in Congress. He sees it as an "amateurish attempt to change international law" that could do exactly what it means not to do—embroil the country in a war.	The U.S. Department of Commerce reports a rise in exports (38 percent) and imports (14 percent) from 1934. The ongoing trade with Europe accounts for 63 percent of the overall export monetary total of $269,310,247. Of imports, 50 percent are with African shippers. . . . President Roosevelt considers two proposals designed to replace the Agricultural Adjustment Administration (AAA), which the Supreme Court recently declared unconstitutional. The President still envisions the necessity of an ongoing farm-relief law.			Jan. 10
Harper Sibley, president of the U.S. Chamber of Commerce, decries what he refers to as the Roosevelt administration's regulation of free enterprise. . . . Convicted kidnapper and killer of Charles Lindbergh's baby, Bruno Richard Hauptmann, loses his appeal for clemency. The New Jersey Corrections Board maintains his execution will take place. Hauptmann re-appeals.		Bank clearances in the United States rose 13.7 percent in 1935, with the total for a 12-month period reaching the highest point since 1931 at $297,177,288,516.		Samuel Goldwyn, the Hollywood producer known for producing several film classics, announces upcoming features for 1936. They include an adaptation of Edna Ferber's book, Hurricane; Mutiny on the Bounty with Clark Gable; and Pony Boy with Eddie Cantor.	Jan. 11
The American Liberty League calls for a Congressional investigation into "the entire governmental structure," calling President Roosevelt "deceitful" in leading the country into a "spending orgy."		The Chevrolet Company produced 110,000 automobiles in December 1935, and, according to its central offices in Detroit, anticipates an extremely strong year in 1936.	Russia slates 49 separate expeditions in the Antarctic for the upcoming 12 months.	Cats have surpassed dogs as the most favored household pet of the United States, according to a poll of the Atlantic Cat Club, one of the oldest organizations in the nation devoted to love of cats. . . . Spain announces that it is transforming its Costa Brava section below the Pyrenees into another Riviera.	Jan. 12
	Ninety-four percent of the 200,000 polled vote to stay out of any war that erupts in Europe. Many favor a small army for defense but not an armed force designed for open conflict. The poll was conducted by the Council for Social Action of the Congregational Churches of America.				Jan. 13
As part of their election campaign strategy, members of the Republican Party act out an on-the-air parody of President Roosevelt's New Deal. The point of these "follies" is to illustrate how the President's policies will negatively affect the future budget of the nation.		The Senate committee votes 15–20 in favor of the Veterans' Bonus Bill. Because Secretary of the Treasury Henry Morgenthau warns against it because of the $36 billion national debt, President Roosevelt is expected to veto the legislation in its current form.	From the University of Chicago, physicist Dr. Arthur H. Compton oversees a worldwide scientific effort to measure cosmic ray intensity. He has placed meters, which will measure the rays, in various locations across the globe. . . . United Airlines in Chicago establishes the Air Transport Association of America, in which all existing U.S. air companies will participate. Its purpose is to raise quality while cutting redundancy.	British actor and matinee idol Leslie Howard, now playing Hamlet in New York, announces plans to retire soon from the stage.	Jan. 14

F	G	H	I	J
Includes elections, federal-state relations, civil rights and liberties, crime, the judiciary, education, healthcare, poverty, urban affairs, and population.	Includes formation and debate of U.S. foreign and defense policies, veterans affairs, and defense spending. (Relations with specific foreign countries are usually found under the region concerned.)	Includes business, labor, agriculture, taxation, transportation, consumer affairs, monetary and fiscal policy, natural resources, pollution, and accidents.	Includes worldwide scientific, medical, and technological developments, natural phenomena, U.S. weather, and natural disasters.	Includes the arts, religion, scholarship, communications media, sports, entertainment, fashions, fads, and social life.

	World Affairs	Europe	Africa & The Middle East	The Americas	Asia & The Pacific
Jan. 15		While christening the new airplane hangars at Detmold, Germany, Adolf Hitler hints at the possibility of war. He tells fellow countrymen that, because Germany still needs to meet its "goals," there will be many sacrifices ahead for all. . . . The Soviet standing army has doubled its defense budget and its manpower, now totaling 1.3 million people, according to Marshal Mikhail Tukhachevsky, Assistant Commissar for Defense.			Japan, unsatisfied with the proceedings of the second London disarmament conference, walks out.
Jan. 16	Japan is sending out "storm signals for the world's peace," says Nazi Germany, commenting on its recent aggressiveness in China, followed by its departing from the London naval talks.				
Jan. 17	The General Federation of Women's Clubs meets this evening for a World Dinner in Washington, D.C. Among its guests are U.S. First Lady Eleanor Roosevelt, who is a guest speaker, and several wives of international diplomats. They pledge a "will to peace" among their respective countries.	After a series of defiant comments by Adolf Hitler, Britain reminds Germany of the Locarno peace treaty, which holds inviolable the borders of France and Belgium. . . . Joseph Goebbels, Nazi propaganda minister, speaks to an auditorium of 18,000 disciples of Nazism in Berlin, telling them that the day when Germany will be recognized as the greatest power in the world is coming soon.			
Jan. 18		British Foreign Secretary Anthony Eden stresses international unity at a dinner of the Engineering Employers' Association in Warwickshire, England. His plea is for all believers in peace to join together against the aggressors. . . . In Spain, women who hold a very pro-Catholic stance become a deciding factor in elections. With a parliamentarian election nearing, the Conservative Party is expecting victory.		Argentina increases its cotton-growing area by 17 percent. . . . According to Charles H.C. Pearsall, president of the Colombian Steamship Company, the future of U.S. shipping lies in establishing a good trading venue between itself and its neighbors in South America.	Mongol troops march into Changpei, the capital of the Chahar province, claiming autonomy. Their aim is to protect Manchukuo.
Jan. 19		The Radical Socialist Party of France elects Edouard Daladier as president. . . . Doctors say that the health of George V of England is failing fast. His heart weakened, he is not expected to live for many more days.	British-Italian tensions continue to escalate in the Mediterranean, with Italian forces in close proximity. The Palestinians allow the Royal Air Force to use their territory as an air base.		
Jan. 20	World production, which has shown signs of improvement the last several quarters, continues to rise. Output has risen in six nations while prices have, in some corners, become stable. Discrepancies are seen in overall recovery—Germany suffers high unemployment while Britain soars at 176 percent of its 1929 rate.	George V, King of England, passes away of influenza, brought about by heart failure. Britain and all of its territories grieve for their monarch. . . . Germany's foreign trade ends the year on a positive note. A surplus of 111 million marks is a notable figure, especially when contrasted to the 285 million-mark deficit that ended 1934.			Japan's War Office and the Nazi Embassy simultaneously deny that Japan and Germany have united in a war effort. The Soviet Union doubts their integrity and remains dedicated to watching the countries' movements with caution.
Jan. 21		Edward VIII, age 41, heir to the throne of England following the death of his father, George V, is officially proclaimed sovereign in Sandringham. A yearlong mourning period will follow before his eventual coronation.			Japanese Foreign Minister Koki Hirota explains Japan's intention in China. He focuses on a three-point plan for the "readjustment of relationships between Japan, Manchukuo, and China" and expresses hope for the three territories in unifying to banish Communism from the Far East.
Jan. 22		Pressured by radical socialist groups, French Premier Pierre Laval resigns.	In southern Ethiopia, the strategically placed town of Noghelli is claimed by Italian forces under Gen. Rodolfo Graziani. Escaped African forces turn north.		

A	B	C	D	E
Includes developments that affect more than one world region, international organizations, and important meetings of world leaders.	Includes all domestic and regional developments in Europe, including the Soviet Union.	Includes all domestic and regional developments in Africa and the Middle East.	Includes all domestic and regional developments in Latin America, the Caribbean, and Canada.	Includes all domestic and regional developments in Asian and Pacific nations (and colonies).

U.S. Politics & Social Issues	U.S. Foreign Policy & Defense	Economics & Great Depression	Science, Technology & Nature	Culture, Leisure & Lifestyle	
Criticizing President Roosevelt's New Deal economic policies, New York banker James P. Warburg tells "distressed" Chicago bankers to throw their full support behind the Republican candidate in the next election.	The Neutrality Bill is altered to give the United States more freedom of the seas, revising the earlier proposal that U.S. ships would avoid certain "war zones" in the event of an armed European conflict.	Merchant shipbuilding has risen in 1935 throughout the world, with England leading the way and the United States second, says Lloyd's of London's Registry. In total, the sum of tonnage built in the year amounts to 1,543,154. . . . The Wholesale Dry Goods Institute urges grocers to keep in mind three particular aims to improve their business: 1) keep a closer relationship with manufacturers, 2) reduce operating costs, and 3) broaden their programs to assist independent grocers.	Howard Hughes, movie producer, oil baron, and aviator, tells a Hollywood audience that airplanes will soon be spanning the nation coast to coast in less than 10 hours. His own recent triumph of flying from the Pacific to the Atlantic in nine hours and 27 minutes supports his claim.	Leopold Stokowski announces that he and the Philadelphia Symphony Orchestra will embark on a world concert tour. The trip will encompass four continents and is expected to last a four-year period.	Jan. 15
Former president Herbert Hoover outlines his own farm program in opposition to President Roosevelt's to an agricultural audience in Lincoln, Neb. . . . Col. Frank Knox, a candidate in the Republican primary election and publisher of the *Chicago Daily News*, responds to remarks made by Boston entrepreneur Edward A. Filene, who recently intoned that newspapers are "owned by special interest groups."				Horace C. Stoneham, Jr., age 32, becomes the president of the New York Giants baseball team, becoming the youngest baseball magnate in history.	Jan. 16
States in the southwest—Arkansas, Colorado, Kansas, Missouri, New Mexico, Oklahoma, and Texas—propose to legally open their borders to police pursuing criminals who commit crimes near state lines for the sole intention of escaping over boundaries.		William A. Douglas, professor of law at Yale University, is appointed by President Roosevelt as a member of the Securities and Exchange Commission. Douglas will complete the term of Chairman Joseph Kennedy, who recently resigned. . . . A new plan based on the extinct Agricultural Adjustment Administration is being developed for farmers, according to the Roosevelt administration. The revised plan couples soil conservation with crop control.		Governor Harold G. Hoffman of New Jersey grants a reprieve to Bruno Richard Hauptmann, accused of killing the son of Charles Lindbergh. Hoffman expressed doubts that Hauptmann acted alone and asks that the investigation be reopened.	Jan. 17
U.S. Racing Commissioners in 17 states close employment to anyone ever convicted of a drug-related charge. . . . Because "it is right and the right will prevail," the Women's Christian Temperance Union—gathered for Temperance Education Day in New York—say that Prohibition will soon return.	The board of directors of the General Federation of Women's Clubs seeks hard-line neutrality legislation as well as the establishment of an "academy" of public affairs, which would help govern some security measures for the nation, including the changing of certain deportation laws.			Famed author and poet Rudyard Kipling dies of peritonitis in London at age 70. He is the author of such celebrated works as *Gunga Din*, *Captains Courageous*, and *Wee Willie Winkle*.	Jan. 18
Addressing a crowd in Utah, former president Herbert Hoover says he has great faith in the Republican Party for 1936. However, observers note that he sidesteps a response when asked to predict an outcome.			A group of Englishmen establishes the Smell Society. Its function is to study the different aromas and odors in the air, generally to appreciate the more pleasant smells in daily life.	The Ford Motor Company, under the auspices of Henry Ford, is experimenting with a small airplane with a Ford vehicle engine. It is the first time his company has considered manufacturing a "flying machine" for industry use.	Jan. 19
	First Lady Eleanor Roosevelt opens a ladies' conference on "War and Peace." More than 700 female delegates attend the event in Washington, D.C.	In the Great Plains, the effects of the severe drought, which withered the wheat and corn crops, have improved. Some moisture over the last few months has improved the economic outlook for 1936. . . . The Senate passes the Veterans' Bonus Bill, 74–16.	Corning Glassworks in Corning, N.J., has invented a new type of fire-tempered glass ideal for cooking. The glass can be used for skillets, frying pans, and other kinds of pots. Numerous tests have proven their resistance and durability.	Two of Warner Bros. most popular stars, James Cagney and Pat O'Brien, share billing in a photoplay of Frank Wead's Broadway play, *Ceiling Zero*. The movie begins its run in theaters today.	Jan. 20
					Jan. 21
		A Works Progress Administration project counting the number of World War veterans in a dozen major cities, per the request of the Veterans Administration, is completed. Overseeing the project was WPA Administrator Harry L. Hopkins.	A desensitizing medicine becomes available to dentists, who rush to purchase the new anesthetic. The product was invented by Dr. Leroy Hartmann of Columbia University.		Jan. 22

F	G	H	I	J
Includes elections, federal-state relations, civil rights and liberties, crime, the judiciary, education, healthcare, poverty, urban affairs, and population.	Includes formation and debate of U.S. foreign and defense policies, veterans affairs, and defense spending. (Relations with specific foreign countries are usually found under the region concerned.)	Includes business, labor, agriculture, taxation, transportation, consumer affairs, monetary and fiscal policy, natural resources, pollution, and accidents.	Includes worldwide scientific, medical, and technological developments, natural phenomena, U.S. weather, and natural disasters.	Includes the arts, religion, scholarship, communications media, sports, entertainment, fashions, fads, and social life.

	World Affairs	Europe	Africa & The Middle East	The Americas	Asia & The Pacific
Jan. 23				The Soviets respond angrily when Uruguay blames them for helping to fund Brazilian revolutionaries. At the League of Nations conference in Geneva, the Russian Foreign Commissar demands that Uruguay produce proof of alleged bank accounts that would prove payment to Brazil.	
Jan. 24		The British people pay final respects to George V, as he lies in state in Westminster Abbey, London. It is estimated that 10,000 mourners will pass the catafalque of the beloved King between sunup and sundown.		The Chaco Peace Conference, after several previous failed attempts, finally achieves success. Bolivia and Paraguay both sign the pact, bringing to an end a three-year conflict that has killed over 100,000 men.	
Jan. 25		The former secretary of the treasury, Ogden L. Mills, calls for financial aid from Jews and Christians to support the Federation of Polish Jews in America, an organization determined to help Polish refugees evading Nazi takeover. A $1 million rehabilitation fund is the goal.			Japan does not want war any more than the other nations of the earth, says Japanese Christian labor leader Dr. Toyohiki Gedawa, adding that 99 percent of his nation's intellectuals oppose the very idea of war.
Jan. 26		The restored monarch of Greece, George II, promises his people that the poll booths and overall voting process of the upcoming Cabinet elections will be managed honestly and not fouled by the larceny that characterized elections while he was in exile.			As airline travel increasingly transports people between the Pacific islands and the United States, entrepreneurs rapidly build inns and hotels on the islands of Guam, Midway, and Wake. . . . In Bombay, Sir Mohamed Shah, Aga Khan of India, celebrates his 25 years as spiritual head of more than one billion Ismalean Mohammedans.
Jan. 27	Beware "tin soldiers with wooden leaders," advises Rev. Frederick Brown Harris of New York, ruminating over one of two roads the world of the near future could take—toward a straight path of peace or toward a dreadful slope of war.				
Jan. 28		Dr. Heinrich Bruening, former German chancellor who absconded the Nazi government, speaks at the Algonquin Club in Boston. He vows to fight the Nazi way of life as long as "the principles of justice and equality are held in such low regard." . . . The Kremlin demands that the Soviet education system rewrite its history books. Authorities find that the history of Russia as written in most school texts is expressed in a boring manner and is void of the real eloquence that is Russia.			
Jan. 29				Aiming to resume the export sale of grain, Canada calls a grain conference in which all grain powers, dealers, and exporters from around the globe are invited. The symposium is scheduled for February 25 in Winnipeg.	
Jan. 30		Learning that many people in Britain are undernourished despite the country's economic successes in other arenas, the nation's "big five" banks ally to start a government campaign to nourish the needy. . . . Adolf Hitler celebrates his fourth year as absolute head of Germany.			

A	B	C	D	E
Includes developments that affect more than one world region, international organizations, and important meetings of world leaders.	Includes all domestic and regional developments in Europe, including the Soviet Union.	Includes all domestic and regional developments in Africa and the Middle East.	Includes all domestic and regional developments in Latin America, the Caribbean, and Canada.	Includes all domestic and regional developments in Asian and Pacific nations (and colonies).

U.S. Politics & Social Issues	U.S. Foreign Policy & Defense	Economics & Great Depression	Science, Technology & Nature	Culture, Leisure & Lifestyle	
The president of the American Bankers' Association, Robert V. Fleming, insists that there has been "too much dependence upon legislation as a cure-all for our troubles." He urges a new administration to help humanize the relationship between banks and their public.	On a special radio broadcast, British parliamentarian Lady Astor and American suffragette Carrie Chapman Catt unite to underscore the seriousness of the world situation. Terming it "alarming," they make a plea for world amity from international circles, asking women across the sphere to join the peace movement.	Dr. Robert Maynard Hutchins of the University of Chicago asks grocers in the United States to "oppose all price-raising and volume-restricting measures" for a fair and ethical operation. At the same time, he requests that the industry become a stronger advocate for education. . . . Secretary of the Treasury Henry Morgenthau plans to meet the funds required to pay the Veterans' Bonus Bill, which recently passed in Congress.			Jan. 23
	The Adjusted Compensation Act, which provides early payment of World War I bonuses to veterans, is vetoed by President Roosevelt. Both branches of Congress immediately vote to override the veto. The government will issue convertible bonds to some 3 million veterans on June 15.			Sonja Henie, the well-known amateur skater from Norway, announces that after this season she will no longer skate as a competitor, unless in a professional status.	Jan. 24
A farm-relief plan, completely within the scope of the Constitution, is proposed by Franklin O. Lowden, a well-known agricultural expert in Illinois.					Jan. 25
		The president of the Baltimore & Ohio Railroad, Daniel Willard, predicts a glorious future for the rail lines in terms of commerce and travel. Known as the sage of the industry, Willard, now 75 years old, began his career as a young man in a menial job who worked his way up to the highest seat in one of America's most respected railroads.		As the 1936 Olympics draw nearer, the U.S. Amateur Athletic Union president Avery Brundage leaves for Europe, but not before selecting 30 people to chair the teams that will be participating for the United States.	Jan. 26
The greatest roadblock to Communism is the Roman Catholic Church, which stands for everything that Communism does not, says Rev. Edmund J. Walsh, regent of the Foreign Service, Georgetown University. He is one of several guest speakers taking part in a seminar on "The Catholic Answer to Communism."		The Veterans' Bonus Bill becomes law after it passes in Congress by a majority vote, overriding President Roosevelt's veto. The $1.5 billion that will be disseminated as "bonuses" in the form of convertible bonds to military veterans will require a large army of clerks for issuance by a promised June 15, 1936, deadline.			Jan. 27
Governor Oscar Kelly Allen, who succeeded the assassinated Huey Long of Louisiana, dies in Baton Rouge.		S. Sloan Colt, president of the Bankers Trust Company, reminds bankers to utilize those lessons learned from the economic past to create a new banking system that will "stand up in future periods of depression."			Jan. 28
On the 75th anniversary of Kansas's statehood, Governor Alf M. Landon officially enters the Republican presidential primary. . . . Republican candidate Senator William Borah tells his audience that the next man in the White House, be he Republican or Democrat, must be more than a "string puller."	A new naval appropriations bill hints that funds are needed to either build new battleships or refurbish old ones.			Twentieth Century Fox's movie, *The Professional Soldier*, opens today in U.S. theaters. Based on a story by Damon Runyon, it stars Gloria Stuart and Victor McLaglen.	Jan. 29
With words of high praise from President Roosevelt, Surgeon General Hugh S. Cummings announces his retirement, which will be active in February. Cummings, who has been associated with the Public Health Service beginning in 1894, has held his present position since 1920.		Assets of the four groups under the Aetna Insurance banner rose $5,511,442 in 1935.		Remaining unconvinced that the real killers—or at least all of the killers—of Charles Lindbergh's baby have been caught, New Jersey Governor Harold Hoffman demands that the investigation by state police be reopened. In the meantime, the single convicted killer, Bruno Richard Hauptmann, waits on death row.	Jan. 30

F	G	H	I	J
Includes elections, federal-state relations, civil rights and liberties, crime, the judiciary, education, healthcare, poverty, urban affairs, and population.	Includes formation and debate of U.S. foreign and defense policies, veterans affairs, and defense spending. (Relations with specific foreign countries are usually found under the region concerned.)	Includes business, labor, agriculture, taxation, transportation, consumer affairs, monetary and fiscal policy, natural resources, pollution, and accidents.	Includes worldwide scientific, medical, and technological developments, natural phenomena, U.S. weather, and natural disasters.	Includes the arts, religion, scholarship, communications media, sports, entertainment, fashions, fads, and social life.

	World Affairs	Europe	Africa & The Middle East	The Americas	Asia & The Pacific
Jan. 31					Japanese Ambassador Hirosi Saito claims that his country's motive for leaving the recent London Naval Conference was due to neither stubbornness nor aggression, as newspapers say, but because Japan believes it deserves to be treated as an equal by allowing it parity, which the other members of the parley have refused.
Feb. 1	With the opening of the Winter Olympics only five days away, Gustavus T. Kirby, treasurer of the U.S. Olympic Committee, advises Germany to keep its Nazi propaganda away from the games. . . . U.S. and British delegates meet with the National Council for Palestine to help it universally raise $15 million to benefit Jews fleeing Nazi countries.			Provisional President Jose A. Barnet of Cuba limits the sugar crop this year to 2,515,000 long tons, in accordance with Cuba's pre-ruled six-year restriction plan. The quota of export to the United States is 1,434,541 tons, roughly half the amount.	Mongolian rebels kill 10 Japanese soldiers, among them three officers, at the military base of Mishan Station. According to a release from Kwangtung General Headquarters, Russia, which does not want the Japanese army so close to its own borders, is blamed for inciting the Mongols.
Feb. 2			The completion of a road through northern Ethiopia by the Italian army—despite the rainy season beleaguering it daily—now allows for the mobility of Italian vehicles and men to the front lines. . . . Italian troops in Ethiopia are bogged down by foul weather conditions and illness, according to journalistic observers. Troops are huddled in masses along the northern sector, unable to move south as they had planned by this stage of the war.	More than 1,000 conservationists representing Canada, Mexico, and the United States gather in Washington, D.C., at the North American Wildlife Conference. President Roosevelt, who summoned the conference, asks that all three nations consider how to best preserve vanishing species.	
Feb. 3		James G. MacDonald submits his written resignation as Commissioner of German Refugees. He criticizes the Nazis for ignoring every conceivable plan for peace by several world powers and for ignoring the cries against Jewish persecution, "in the name of humanity and the public law of Europe."			Soviet forces and the Far Eastern Red Army scuffle at the Manchukuoan border.
Feb. 4	Insisting that the United States stay neutral, President Roosevelt declines U.S. participation in the oil embargo on Italy outlined by the League of Nations. Diplomats from Britain and France state objections to the U.S. position. . . . U.S. President Franklin Roosevelt's recent words on Nazi Germany—calling it a foreign dictatorship "that drives its people into war"—are met with an onslaught of newspaper responses throughout Germany, accusing the President of bigotry and untruths.				
Feb. 5		Germany reduces train service over the Polish Corridor—the stretch of acreage separating Germany from East Prussia—in an effort to appease the neighboring Poles, who have been complaining of a monopoly of German traffic on its lines.	Deploying his forces south into the Webbe Gestro Valley, Somaliland, Italian Gen. Rodolfo Graziani meets with Ethiopian resistance in the Dawa Parma area. Casualties mount on both sides.	The Canadian Customs Department abolishes the bonding of truckloads between the U.S.-Canadian border and Toronto, Montreal, and other major cities. The purpose of this decision is to diminish competition between the trucking companies and the rail lines.	
Feb. 6				Canadian Governor General Lord Tweedsmuir opens the session of the Canadian Congress with a number of reform issues. Among them is the institutionalization of a nationalized bank and alterations to the central tax rules of the Dominion.	To ease tensions between the United States and Japan, the latter must be given more leeway to participate in the world trade market, according to Sir Frederick Whyte, former federal adviser to China. Other countries, too, must revise their agreements with the Orient to create a more even world market, Whyte advises.

A	B	C	D	E
Includes developments that affect more than one world region, international organizations, and important meetings of world leaders.	*Includes all domestic and regional developments in Europe, including the Soviet Union.*	*Includes all domestic and regional developments in Africa and the Middle East.*	*Includes all domestic and regional developments in Latin America, the Caribbean, and Canada.*	*Includes all domestic and regional developments in Asian and Pacific nations (and colonies).*

U.S. Politics & Social Issues	U.S. Foreign Policy & Defense	Economics & Great Depression	Science, Technology & Nature	Culture, Leisure & Lifestyle	
Calling the Roosevelt administration "New Deal Communists," Georgia Governor Eugene Talmadge promises to stump coast to coast at the grass-roots level for the good of the nation.	The Federation of Jewish Women meet at the 16th Annual Convention in New York City. They ask for the boycott of Nazi-produced goods, condemn the 1936 Olympics taking place in Nazi Berlin, and institute a four-direction plan to enhance society. The plan addresses international relations, youth training, minority rights, and the place of women in civic life.			An express train of the Reading Railway line skips a broken rail and plunges 30 feet into an abandoned canal bed near the Susquehanna River. Immediate reports indicate three dead and 31 injured.	Jan. 31
The United Mine Workers, lead by Assistant Secretary of Labor Edward F. McGrady, celebrate President Roosevelt's support of their industry, as well as the economy and social welfare in general at their convention in Washington, D.C. . . . American socialite John J. Askob announces his determination to build the American Liberty League into a fighting force in U.S. politics. His hope is to "root out the vicious and radical element that threatens the destruction of our government."		After overruling the constitutionality of the NRA and the AAA, the Supreme Court is examining the Tennessee Valley Authority to see if it gives too much power to administrators. A decision is expected soon.			Feb. 1
The Communist Party in the United States announces that it has urged the nation's progressive and radical labor groups—including the American Socialist Group—to join as one organization for the upcoming presidential elections. Their choice for the White House is Tom Mooney, who has been in prison for 20 years, guilty of setting off a bomb in San Francisco at a Preparedness Day Rally in 1916.		The National Youth Administration compiles a report, based on statistics and interviews, about how the Depression has kept the younger generation of the United States from following career goals. . . . Rail line passenger numbers have increased to their highest levels since 1931. An International Commerce Committee statement for 1935 reports that for the 149 Class 1 railroads, earnings totaled $323,526,546.	A British expedition, including one woman, sets off from London en route to Darjeeling, India, to scale Mount Everest for the first time. They hope to find traces of an earlier expedition that vanished without a trace in 1924.		Feb. 2
	Addressing the U.S Congress Against War and Fascism Committee, Smedley D. Butler, a major general in the U.S. Army, acknowledges the reality of a second world war being created overseas—and urges the United States to turn away from being swept into the maelstrom.				Feb. 3
U.S. Attorney General Homer Cummings tightens his focus on crime. He envisions expanded activity by the Department of Justice and closer relationships with local law enforcement troops.		Representatives from railway groups and their respective unions throughout the nation meet in New York City to formulate an overall proposal to protect rail line employees displaced by railroad reorganization and disenfranchisement. . . . The American Woolen Company, Inc., states that it earned $2,740,598 for 1935, amounting to $58 per share.	This year's winners of the $1,000 essay prize offered by the American Association for the Advancement of Science are doctors A.E. Hitchcock and P.W. Zimmerman, both of Boyce Thompson Institute. Their paper explains the effects of hormones in plants.		Feb. 4
		Safeway Stores earned $3,409,755 last year, an increase from the previous year, according to an annual report.			Feb. 5
	The Senate Munitions Investigation Committee takes the first steps toward creating a "monopoly" in all naval construction, effectively having the government manufacture all of its own ships, airplanes, engines, explosives, machine guns, rifles, and side arms. Budget experts forecast a fund of $47 million.			The fourth Olympic Winter Games open in the huge Garmisch-Partinkerchin Stadium in Berlin, Germany, with the participation of 28 nations.	Feb. 6

F	G	H	I	J
Includes elections, federal-state relations, civil rights and liberties, crime, the judiciary, education, healthcare, poverty, urban affairs, and population.	Includes formation and debate of U.S. foreign and defense policies, veterans affairs, and defense spending. (Relations with specific foreign countries are usually found under the region concerned.)	Includes business, labor, agriculture, taxation, transportation, consumer affairs, monetary and fiscal policy, natural resources, pollution, and accidents.	Includes worldwide scientific, medical, and technological developments, natural phenomena, U.S. weather, and natural disasters.	Includes the arts, religion, scholarship, communications media, sports, entertainment, fashions, fads, and social life.

	World Affairs	Europe	Africa & The Middle East	The Americas	Asia & The Pacific
Feb. 7		Austria, Bulgaria, France, Romania, and Yugoslavia are represented by their heads of state at a peace parley in Paris.			The navies of Japan and the United States will never fire upon each other, promises Japanese diplomat Hirosi Saito in Tokyo. He speaks to an assembly of guests gathered for a dinner hosted by the American Council of St. Luke's Medical Center. . . . Japan's Minister of the Navy Mineo Osumi denies that Japan is perpetrating espionage in Alaska, charges leveled by Rep. Sirovitch of Washington after arrests are made off the Alaskan coast.
Feb. 8	A delegation from the Third Reich involved in the study of air flight lands in Washington, D.C., on the German aircraft, *Hansa*. It meets with U.S. officials to discuss partnering on the creation of an airplane that could fly the Atlantic in two days.	Despite the efforts of the naval parley, Britain doubles its defenses as Russia strengthens its naval armament. Germany is also suspected of increasing its soldiery.			
Feb. 9		By interfering with the war in Ethiopia, the British are turning a colonial war into what may yet become "a worldwide disaster," says Premier Benito Mussolini of Italy, countering Britain's latest remarks about Italy's aggression in Africa. . . . Analysts for the League of Nations estimate that, should the rest of the world force an oil embargo on Italy as a penalty for its war efforts against Ethiopia, Italy would not be able to sustain its actions after six months.	The Union of South Africa, in an attempt to centralize the government, takes over all broadcasting in its realm, thus ending the independent system.		
Feb. 10	The topic of this month's meeting of the World Bank is the global stability of the U.S. dollar. The governors of the principal European banks agree that as the fear of inflation wanes the value of the dollar increases, and with it the French franc.	French Foreign Minister Pierre-Etienne Flandin meets today with Czechoslovakia's Premier, Milan Hodza, to discuss strengthening the defenses of central and eastern Europe.			
Feb. 11			The French airplane, *Villa de Buenos Aires*, en route from Paris to Africa, is believed to have gone down somewhere off the coast of Natal, South Africa. The craft, bearing a crew of five and one passenger, lost its communications mid-trip. Search planes scour the area.		
Feb. 12					
Feb. 13		An unusual cold and blizzard strike Britain and parts of Europe, killing more than 100 unprepared people. In Bulgaria, one group of women is found frozen to death, huddled against the wind blasts.			

A	B	C	D	E
Includes developments that affect more than one world region, international organizations, and important meetings of world leaders.	*Includes all domestic and regional developments in Europe, including the Soviet Union.*	*Includes all domestic and regional developments in Africa and the Middle East.*	*Includes all domestic and regional developments in Latin America, the Caribbean, and Canada.*	*Includes all domestic and regional developments in Asian and Pacific nations (and colonies).*

U.S. Politics & Social Issues	U.S. Foreign Policy & Defense	Economics & Great Depression	Science, Technology & Nature	Culture, Leisure & Lifestyle	
		According to the U.S. Department of Commerce, exports rose in December to $223,505,105, up from $170,653,707 in the same month of the prior year. . . . The Chrysler Corporation reports a record year in 1935, with sales bringing in $34,975,837, or $8.07 per share. These figures are 38 percent higher than 1929, the year before the start of the Depression.	Dr. John C. Merriam, president of the Carnegie Institute in Washington, wins the American Institute's Gold Medal for his "discoveries in paleontology, promotion of research and (his) recognition of science in human affairs."		Feb. 7
The U.S. parole system and the administration of the penal system will be jointly studied by a staff under Attorney General Homer Cummings. The aim of the study, which is funded by the Works Progress Administration, is to better understand U.S. efforts at criminal rehabilitation so that they can be made more effective.		Executives of the National Lumber Manufacturers Association adopt a resolution to avoid any legislation that would cost the industry money. Simultaneously, they praise the Roosevelt administration's attention to the maintenance of forestry and wildlife.			Feb. 8
At a gala hosted by Postmaster General James Farley to honor former Democratic mayor of New York Jimmy Walker, the celebrants take the opportunity to hail President Roosevelt. Farley tells 3,000 guests that Roosevelt is not nor will he ever be shaken by his foes' criticism of the New Deal. . . . Senator Royal S. Copeland proposes a bill in Congress to investigate why the tourist trade in the United States is faltering. Over the last year, he says, 160,000 Americans sailed abroad, but only 15,000 Europeans reciprocated.		Newspaper publisher and Republican nominee for the presidency, Col. Frank Knox, blames President Roosevelt for running up a deficit of $14.5 billion. He refers to the entire gamut of New Deal programs as a "waste." . . . Siscoe Gold Mines reports an increase in earnings for 1935 for a total of $2,274,583, an increase from $2,116,603 in 1934.		Representatives from the National Board of Review of Motion Pictures condemn censorship of movies.	Feb. 9
Vast changes are necessary in the way American professors teach law students, according to Columbia University's dean, Young B. Smith. Courses and curriculums should be reconfigured to more accurately teach the public and social impacts of U.S. law, Smith says. . . . Warning against radicals in the United States, Dr. Stephen Wise of the Free Synagogue at Carnegie Hall says that, "Thousands of Americans who call themselves 'Liberty Leaguers' would end democracy here tomorrow…"		A Senate committee on air safety says that the blame for the recent scourge of air crashes in the United States should be put on governmental laxity. The budget has not kept up with the growing industry, causing the upkeep of planes to deteriorate to the point that 90 percent of air companies operate at a loss. . . . The Child's Company restaurant chain reports an increase in its net profit, the best since 1931. In 1935 it netted $117,063, against a loss of more than $34,000 just one year previously.			Feb. 10
Inflation is the real menace, according to former president Herbert Hoover during a speech to the members of the San Jose, Calif., court system. A negative outgrowth of inflation, he adds, is that it is affecting the operation of America's upper educational institutes.	According to Rep. Maury Maverick of Texas, 90 percent of all Americans do not want to get involved in another war. That is why, he says, he does not understand the Roosevelt administration's reticence to commit to a hardline, established neutrality law, calling the current stance "cowardice" on the part of the President.	During Farm & Home Week in Ithaca, N.Y., Cornell University statistician Dr. F.A. Pearson predicts a period coming in the near future of general economic prosperity. . . . The heavy-duty farm machine manufacturer, Caterpillar Tractor Company, announces earnings for 1935, which rose substantially from 1934, totaling $5,949,307, as compared to $3,651,190 for the year prior.	Dietician Dr. Howard W. Haggard warns consumers to beware of many of the diets found in popular magazines, explaining that the ads may promote certain "food fads," but they are actually connected with promoters of get-rich-quick schemes.	Bruno Richard Hauptmann, who was convicted of kidnapping and murdering the child of aviation hero Charles Lindbergh, hears that his appeal for clemency is denied. Hauptmann is slated to go to the electric chair next week at New Jersey State Prison. . . . At the Olympic Games, the only real contender to Norway's Sonja Henie, Constance Wilson Samuel, collapses during the ice skating competition.	Feb. 11
Latest figures show a remarkable decrease in crime where metropolitan police organizations use radio. Arrests in those locations employing the use of "wireless patrols" have skyrocketed due to easier and quicker identification of perpetrators.		The per capita debt of most U.S. cities with a population of over 100,000 was reduced 72 cents between 1934 and 1935, writes the Census Bureau in their latest general communiqué. . . . Guest speakers at the Association of Highway Officials condemn the misuse of funds by some states' highway departments. Many divert funds meant for highway construction and repair to emergency relief, thus cheating the real purpose of the monies.			Feb. 12
		According to James Simpson, chairman of Commonwealth Edison, Chicago's power company, the utility had a net profit of $10,274,000 in 1935, after $12 million paid in taxes.		New York Yankees manager Joe McCarthy signs a promising new outfielder from San Francisco named Joe DiMaggio. . . . Adolf Hitler attends the Olympics in Berlin's Garmisch-Partinkerchin Stadium. His visit is accompanied by great regale, complete with armed guards.	Feb. 13

F	G	H	I	J
Includes elections, federal-state relations, civil rights and liberties, crime, the judiciary, education, healthcare, poverty, urban affairs, and population.	Includes formation and debate of U.S. foreign and defense policies, veterans affairs, and defense spending. (Relations with specific foreign countries are usually found under the region concerned.)	Includes business, labor, agriculture, taxation, transportation, consumer affairs, monetary and fiscal policy, natural resources, pollution, and accidents.	Includes worldwide scientific, medical, and technological developments, natural phenomena, U.S. weather, and natural disasters.	Includes the arts, religion, scholarship, communications media, sports, entertainment, fashions, fads, and social life.

	World Affairs	Europe	Africa & The Middle East	The Americas	Asia & The Pacific
Feb. 14					
Feb. 15		In opening Berlin's National Automobile Show, Adolf Hitler praises U.S. technology and lauds its auto industry for solving many of the problems of the modern road.			Moscow agrees to take part in discussions with the Japanese, Chinese, and Manchukuoans regarding strife at the Manchukuo border. It hopes that a neutral area may be assigned and that a neutral representative be assigned to manage it.
Feb. 16				Brazil and the United States sign a reciprocal trade agreement, which promises to enhance the economies of both countries.	A small Japanese border patrol near Lake Bor, Manchukuo, retreats without injuries from an advancing force of 1,000 Outer Mongolians with armored vehicles, according to press reports. At the same time, Japan calls Russia's latest peace proposal—aimed at ending the ongoing Manchukuoan border rift—a move of insincerity.
Feb. 17		Britain's armed forces ask parliament for more funds to handle what they consider is a necessary precaution—maintaining ships and airplanes in the Mediterranean Sea region—as long as the Italian forces insist on deploying troops to the demilitarized zone.			
Feb. 18	Even though the United States does not fully agree with the regulations suggested on the size of battleships at the London naval parley, it announces it will sign any pact reached between itself and the three other participating nations, Britain, France, and Russia.			Workers of the Southern Pacific Rail Line of Mexico threaten to walk out tomorrow unless the country's president intervenes. The deadline for signing an agreement has passed.	
Feb. 19				An overnight revolution forces the ouster of the Paraguayan dictator, President Eusibio Ayala. Ayala's Cabinet is being detained by rebels and public buildings are used as fortresses.	
Feb. 20	Relations worsen between Russia and Japan with no answer to mending the border disagreements in Manchukuo. Both countries have offered solutions but have yet to find a compromise. The Russian press exacerbates the situation with a strong rebuff of the Japanese in Moscow's central newspaper, *Izvestia*.			Canada adopts a resolution to provide a haven for a "reasonable number" of refugees escaping Nazi Germany. The resolution is adopted in Toronto by representatives from various Canadian churches.	
Feb. 21		Dr. Hugo Eckener of the Third Reich announces that his newest technological wonder of flight, the dirigible called the *Hindenburg*, will soon be completed in Friedrichschafen, Germany, and ready for a world tour. The *Hindenburg* is in fact already scheduled to leave Germany on May 6, bound for a transatlantic flight to the east coast of the United States.			
Feb. 22		Britain cedes the island of Cyprus to Greece. . . . Spain is fighting Bolshevism, purportedly funded by Soviet Russia. A Bolshevistic "united front" has succeeded in placing 3 million of its members in visible civic and government positions. . . . Adolf Seefeld of Schwerin, Germany, receives multiple death sentences for the murders of more than 30 young boys whom he also sexually molested.			

A	B	C	D	E
Includes developments that affect more than one world region, international organizations, and important meetings of world leaders.	Includes all domestic and regional developments in Europe, including the Soviet Union.	Includes all domestic and regional developments in Africa and the Middle East.	Includes all domestic and regional developments in Latin America, the Caribbean, and Canada.	Includes all domestic and regional developments in Asian and Pacific nations (and colonies).

U.S. Politics & Social Issues	U.S. Foreign Policy & Defense	Economics & Great Depression	Science, Technology & Nature	Culture, Leisure & Lifestyle	
Members of the New York chapter of the National Women's Party hear speaker Rebekah Greathouse cite inadequacies rampant in the U.S. Constitution that inadvertently limit the power of women in the country and keep them socially behind men. She asks members to support all legislative change granting females well-deserved equality.	In Washington, D.C., millionaire Harry F. Guggenheim, former ambassador to Cuba, expresses his dissatisfaction with the lack of proper federal regulatory measures governing today's airline industry. Guggenheim has long been one of the leading advocates and developers of aviation in the United States.	The Curtis Publishing Company and its subsidiaries report a net profit for 1935 of $5,576,779, or $7 per share. The amount is a slight loss from the operating year 1934, which totaled $5,906,326.		Decency brings a monetary profit, says Rev. Joseph A. Daley of the College of Mount St. Vincent. He refers to Hollywood's huge profits since adhering to the guidelines under the Hays Office production codes.	Feb. 14
	William Philips, Undersecretary of State, calls equality of trade rights and open trade barriers "the most solid foundation of peace, as well as prosperity."			The two-man bobsled team of the United States wins its first gold medal at the Berlin Olympics—and the first medal for the country.	Feb. 15
A hearing opens today in the Senate to investigate the security and safety of air travel. Because aviation is a fairly new scientific commodity, and because of numerous accidents and near-accidents in the field of late, the session, headed by New York Senator Royal S. Copeland, promises to thoroughly investigate several facets of the industry pertaining to passenger and personnel safety.	Secretary of War George Dern strikes back against critics of the latest War Department appropriation bill who say that the cost of the Army is being wasted on breaking strikes. Dern explains that the Army will not be used for strikes and the cost demanded of the Army is just "small potatoes" to pay in case a war ever threatens America.	Speaking at an open forum at Columbia University, former undersecretary of the treasury Arthur A. Ballantine alleges that President Roosevelt's administration is hiding much of the truth about the mounting federal deficit from the public. . . . Problems with New Deal programs may not be the fault of the programs themselves, but with the administrators running them, according to F.B. Stephens of New Zealand, who is conducting a study of municipal governments in the United States and Britain.		Manufacturers in Detroit, Mich., introduce what they are touting as a "mobile home," an actual residential unit in a trailer to be towed by an auto, designed by William B. Stout. . . . Some 401 libraries across the country are using the Los Angeles Public Library as their model in becoming a source of information on Hollywood films. These centers will be handy to families wanting to be sure their children are not seeing a movie that may include objectionable material.	Feb. 16
In a speech before the Grand Jury Association's eighth annual meeting, H.B. LeQuatte, president of the Advertising Club of New York, praises the newspapers of America as the greatest tool to fight crime that the United States possesses.					Feb. 17
Congress approves an investigation by the Federal Bureau of Navigation and Steamboat Inspection of the tragic burning of the liner, Morro Castle, which took the lives of many passengers on September 9, 1935. The investigation into what caused the blaze is urged by the survivors and by relatives of the 137 people who perished.		A successful financial year is reported by the Goodyear Tire & Rubber Company. Net profit after depreciation was $5,452,240 for 1935, against a sum of $4,553,964 for 1934.			Feb. 18
			The Society of Motion Picture Engineers announces a new process of recording sound photographically on motion pictures via the violet ray. The new process eliminates background static for a clearer sound.		Feb. 19
A law prohibiting the shipment of firearms and ammunition across state lines or to foreign ports is passed. The new law states that only licensed dealers can legally transport weapons from state to state or through commercial channels.		President Roosevelt is compiling a specific and detailed outline of those new taxes that he foresees for the current fiscal year, most notably those required to put into operation the new farm rehabilitation program.			Feb. 20
The warden of San Quentin Prison, James B. Holahan, quits his post in the midst of an investigation checking into the possible existence of a counterfeiting ring operating within the prison.		According to its year-end report, Superior Steel's annual earnings show up as profit this year after having reported several years of losses. Earnings for 1935 are $46,691, versus a loss of $264,865 last year.			Feb. 21
	Senator William Borah of Idaho, who is one of the Republican contenders in the presidential primary election, supports U.S. neutrality in wars to come. In the same speech, he blasts Britain's interference in the Italo-Ethiopian conflict. Borah asserts that interfering with such a situation merely complicates it—and prolongs it.			In New Haven, Conn., Yale University president James F. Angell denounces the rude manners displayed by fans at college football games. At Yale and elsewhere, "mockers" have uprooted goalposts, booed visiting players, and taunted officials.	Feb. 22

F	G	H	I	J
Includes elections, federal-state relations, civil rights and liberties, crime, the judiciary, education, healthcare, poverty, urban affairs, and population.	Includes formation and debate of U.S. foreign and defense policies, veterans affairs, and defense spending. (Relations with specific foreign countries are usually found under the region concerned.)	Includes business, labor, agriculture, taxation, transportation, consumer affairs, monetary and fiscal policy, natural resources, pollution, and accidents.	Includes worldwide scientific, medical, and technological developments, natural phenomena, U.S. weather, and natural disasters.	Includes the arts, religion, scholarship, communications media, sports, entertainment, fashions, fads, and social life.

	World Affairs	Europe	Africa & The Middle East	The Americas	Asia & The Pacific
Feb. 23		The city of London is experiencing a huge up-curve in tourism, much of the trade coming from eastern European nations whose people want to escape the frigid mountains for a more temperate England.		Two Nationalist Party members assassinate Frank E. Riggs, retired U.S. Army colonel and head of the Puerto Rican police for the past three years. The alleged killers are Elias Beauchamp and Hiran Rosado, who have records of anarchy and mayhem.	According to a Tass news agency bulletin, Mongolia, which sits squarely in the middle of the Russian-Japanese border, will now fall under Russian administration. The move is seen as a means to temporarily ease the growing strife between the countries, but Russia remains reserved as to how the government of Mongolia will react to Soviet rule. . . . In Japan, the latest elections of Premier Keisuke Osaka's Cabinet soundly defeat the Fascist Party, unseating all Fascist members and replacing them with representatives of the National and Labor parties.
Feb. 24		The Irish people have a right to determine their own style of government, as well as how to mete out a relationship with the United Kingdom, says Eamon De Valera, president of Free Ireland.			
Feb. 25		In a pamphlet disseminated throughout Germany, War Ministry official and communications chief Major Jost praises the vast military growth that Hitler has made during his reign. The German army has grown faster than that of Russia, Italy, or any other country, claims Jost.			The Japanese military in Tokyo stages a coup, taking over governmental buildings, assassinating certain governmental figures, and seizing police headquarters. Its movement, which surprises the country and even the Emperor, is based on putting the army—not civilians—in control of the country.
Feb. 26	Britain, concerned by the military revolutions in Tokyo, says that if the Japanese army—long known for its territorial ambitions—eventually takes over the Japanese government, there will be no holding back a war with Japan. England's Sir Anthony Eden blames Japanese propaganda for yesterday's tensions in Tokyo.	Leon Trotsky, political refugee from Russia, tells of a "brutal" government existing under Stalin. Citizens who voice their opinions are tortured, and conditions in jail are terrible.		V.F. Boucas, an International Business Machines (IBM) executive in Brazil, points to the recent reciprocal trade with the United States as one of Brazil's top economic triumphs. He advises that the country take similar steps with other countries to keep its export industry thriving and constant.	
Feb. 27		British Prime Minister Stanley Baldwin asks his military for coordinated defenses off the British coast and in major cities. . . . A Soviet-French pact designed to provide mutual assistance in case of war is passed in the French Cabinet, 353–164.			U.S. Secretary of State Cordell Hull telegrams Japan, sending his regrets over the brutal assassinations of four government leaders in Tokyo by an insurgent band of soldiers.
Feb. 28		The Soviet-French pact leaves France divided, with one faction supportive that France has an ally, while the other side is concerned by the alienation of Hitler, who seems to be looking for a reason to start a war. . . . From Dublin, the Catholic Church warns Irish youths to keep clear of political groups preaching Communism, fascism or armed violence.	An Italian infantry takes the town of Mount Alaji, pushing back 3,000 Ethiopians under tribal chieftain Ras Mulugheta. The win is an emotional one for Italy, since the town of Mount Alaji is known as the scene of a spectacular African rout of Italians in 1895.		The Japanese government's pleas to the outlaw army that captured Tokyo have met with no results. Instead, it is learned that the rebels now hold the headquarters of the Diet, Japan's Senate.
Feb. 29		Belgium's premier announces his resignation effective April 1. Paul van Zeeland, who a year ago sought plenary powers to resurrect his government from a low economic period, rehabilitated Belgium through the abandonment of the franc and the stabilization of the sterling.			Members of the Japanese insurgent regiments who attempted to take over the Japanese government in Tokyo surrender under orders from Emperor Hirohito. They turn over their rifles to the loyalist army and return via army transports to their barracks. The Emperor has promised pardons to the noncommissioned ranks. . . . Japan announces Chuji Machida as the new finance minister, replacing the assassinated Korekiyo Takahashi.

A	B	C	D	E
Includes developments that affect more than one world region, international organizations, and important meetings of world leaders.	Includes all domestic and regional developments in Europe, including the Soviet Union.	Includes all domestic and regional developments in Africa and the Middle East.	Includes all domestic and regional developments in Latin America, the Caribbean, and Canada.	Includes all domestic and regional developments in Asian and Pacific nations (and colonies).

U.S. Politics & Social Issues	U.S. Foreign Policy & Defense	Economics & Great Depression	Science, Technology & Nature	Culture, Leisure & Lifestyle	
Four well-known women's rights advocates schedule a special radio broadcast to discuss women's roles internationally and how those roles are recognized by men of many countries. Scheduled speakers are Mary C. Mount, Caroline Hasslett, Mrs. Charles O. Williams, and Lena Madesin Philips, president of the International Federation of Business and Professional Women.			Scientists celebrate the 50th anniversary of commercial aluminum. Both Charles Martin Hall of Oberlin, Ohio, and Paul Heroault of Paris—working independently—discovered its commercial use at the same time.		Feb. 23
The Senate passes the Soil Conservation and Domestic Allotment Act, replacing the Agriculture Adjustment Administration, which the Supreme Court invalidated. The bill provides for payments to farmers to withdraw land from crop production.	Rev. Joseph A. McCaffey, Chaplain of the famous regiment "The Fighting 69th Irishers," says he hopes that the nation is not swept into war for economic reasons, as he claims was the motive in 1917. The United States, he asserts, rushed to a European war to "retrieve and protect" a flood of money owed to the United States by Europe.	A U.S. government press release studying domestic costs of the average U.S. citizen assesses that the office clothing required by a typical working female in a major metropolitan area costs about $77.75 per year.			Feb. 24
				Couture shoemaker Andre Perugia, who has designed shoes for some of Europe's and Asia's most illustrious personalities including the Queen of Manchukuo, states at a designers' conference in the United States that women, searching for what they deem as idyllic footwear, are systematically ruining their arches.	Feb. 25
					Feb. 26
Hearing that some discarded U.S. Army service machine guns had fallen illegally into the hands of Latin American terrorists, Attorney General Homer Cummings sets out on an investigation to determine if some of these same black-market weapons have also found their way into the hands of big-city American gangsters and road bandits.		The $500 million soil conservation bill, touted by President Roosevelt as the new Agriculture Adjustment Administration, passes in Congress by almost a unanimous vote.			Feb. 27
		U.S. export trade for last month was the highest since January 1931, reports the U.S. Department of Commerce. January's $22.2 million increase is attributable mainly to increased sales abroad of cotton, machinery, automobiles, and oil.			Feb. 28
President Roosevelt signs the Soil Conservation and Domestic Allotment Act. The bill provides that some payments for withdrawing land from production will be made to sharecroppers and farm tenants.	The Neutrality Act of 1935 is extended to May 1, 1937. The act is also enforced by prohibiting the extension of loans to belligerents in case of war, regarded as one of the main reasons why the United States was drawn into World War I.	The Coca-Cola Company and subsidiaries report earnings of $15,804,256 in 1935 after depreciation and other charges. The gain is an increase from 1934 earnings, which netted $14,328,668.			Feb. 29

F	G	H	I	J
Includes elections, federal-state relations, civil rights and liberties, crime, the judiciary, education, healthcare, poverty, urban affairs, and population.	Includes formation and debate of U.S. foreign and defense policies, veterans affairs, and defense spending. (Relations with specific foreign countries are usually found under the region concerned.)	Includes business, labor, agriculture, taxation, transportation, consumer affairs, monetary and fiscal policy, natural resources, pollution, and accidents.	Includes worldwide scientific, medical, and technological developments, natural phenomena, U.S. weather, and natural disasters.	Includes the arts, religion, scholarship, communications media, sports, entertainment, fashions, fads, and social life.

	World Affairs	Europe	Africa & The Middle East	The Americas	Asia & The Pacific
Mar. 1		Nazi spokesman Julius Streicher vows that the Nationalist Socialist Party's "campaign for enlightenment," or anti-Semitic campaign, will never end.	Eight accused members of an alleged cabal are freed by a court jury of conspiring to assassinate Turkey's President, Mustapha Kemal Ataturk. Evidence against the eight is sparse and an earlier "confession," says the jury, appears forced.	In the latest Buenos Aires elections, Radical Party hopefuls have gained many government seats, routing Socialists in Argentina.	From all reports, the recent military uprising in Japan—in which a division of Japanese infantry tried to take over Tokyo—has left bitter feuding between civilian statesmen and high-ranking army regulars over the place of military personnel in government decisions.
Mar. 2				Canada's parliament expels Italy's chief ambassador, Consul General Luigi Petrucci, claiming that he had been trying to coerce Italian Canadians to throw their full allegiance behind Premier Mussolini of Italy.	The Japanese Cabinet determines that the military will continue to be represented in government legislation—but its voice will be kept in the background. It is the first major step by civilian lawmakers in Japan to prevent a repeat of the would-be military takeover a week earlier.
Mar. 3		Figures report that it costs Britain £500,000 just to maintain a small fleet of ships and planes to guard the Mediterranean Sea against the threat of Italian power. . . . Army and police personnel face meat rationing as Germany experiences a food shortage. Hitler proclaims that meat will not be served two days a week, until further notice.			
Mar. 4					Russia strongly warns Japan not to attempt a takeover of its ally, Outer Mongolia, saying that if such an action is chosen war will definitely follow.
Mar. 5		Prime Minister Stanley Baldwin's rearmament plan, which calls for an increase in the size of the army—including a 50 percent expansion in the colony of Singapore—will be debated in Parliament over the next few days. . . . Old Heidelberg University's student newspaper, *The Movement*, prints a column signed by the Nazi student league belittling the institution's romantic approach to its 550th anniversary.		Mexican President Lázaro Cárdenas tells teachers and residents of Guadalajara protesting radical mistreatment of the Roman Catholics that it is not the government's desire to cause anti-church sentiment.	
Mar. 6		Third Reich's anti-Jewish newspaper, *Stuermer*, is burned by Dutch Liberals in a demonstration in Amsterdam. Their vehemence is aimed against Nazi-owned shops selling the paper across Holland in an attempt to spread Nazi propaganda.			Japanese Foreign Minister Koki Hirota announces the creation of an all-new Cabinet whose basic political stance is "moderate" and whose aim is "world peace." Military advisers are eliminated. Forced to resign are generals of the Supreme War Council, including Senjuro Hayashi and Jinzaburo Misaki.

A	B	C	D	E
Includes developments that affect more than one world region, international organizations, and important meetings of world leaders.	*Includes all domestic and regional developments in Europe, including the Soviet Union.*	*Includes all domestic and regional developments in Africa and the Middle East.*	*Includes all domestic and regional developments in Latin America, the Caribbean, and Canada.*	*Includes all domestic and regional developments in Asian and Pacific nations (and colonies).*

U.S. Politics & Social Issues	U.S. Foreign Policy & Defense	Economics & Great Depression	Science, Technology & Nature	Culture, Leisure & Lifestyle	
Radio priest Charles E. Coughlin attacks allegations of price gouging by chain stores. He supports the Robinson-Patman bill which, he says, prevents "exploitation from unfair competitors."	New York Democrat Col. Henry Breckenridge, without much fanfare, enters the presidential primary race in Ohio. . . . Countering President Roosevelt's demand for $786 million in new taxes to pay a number of debts, Congress initiates a drive to cut certain expenditures, particularly funds put aside for emergency.	The government pays a record-setting $11 million to 4.4 million federal employees daily across the country, so says a report from Washington, D.C. Mostly, the jobs comprise construction, emergency, and work relief programs.	Archaeologists and oceanographers plan to unearth a treasure from the Spanish ship, Polluce, which sank 130 years ago off Portolongone Bay, near the island of Elba.		Mar. 1
Speaking in New Hampshire, Postmaster General James A. Farley reminds political opponents that it was the New Deal created by President Roosevelt that saved the state from financial ruin.		Statistics show a rise in persons on relief, 3 million more since 1934. However, WPA records indicate that 500,000 of the 3,817,781 employees currently on relief jobs do not constitute "relief employees," but are actually skilled workers hired under exemption orders.			Mar. 2
Republican primary candidate William Borah—one of President Roosevelt's most ardent foes—tells his home state of Idaho that all the President's corporate tax programs are financial "wastes."		The American Tobacco Company, as forecasters predicted, reports a consolidated net income of $23,652,642 for 1935.			Mar. 3
All spying on employees' daily activities by hired detectives at the Fashion Piece Dye Works, Inc., must cease immediately, the National Labor Relations Board mandates. Such subterfuge is not only illegal, but it is causing detrimental gaps in company production. . . . The 18 Republican candidates from Kansas announce that they have already determined to back Governor Alf M. Landon at the upcoming National Convention in Cleveland. . . . A consortium of national manufacturers calls the Wheeler-Rayburn Bill, which expands the Federal Trade Commission's investigative authority, an "unprecedented extension of power" going beyond its decent rights.			Planes in the United States are limited to flying 575 miles per hour after the National Advisory Committee for Aeronautics proves that any speed over that is unsafe. George Lewis, the committee's director, illustrates the reasons why wings cannot endure a faster speed at the New York Museum of Science.	The National Hockey League's board of governors revises elimination rules for playoff games. They apply to those teams battling each other to make the Stanley Cup finals. . . . A new copyright law now makes it possible for a playwright to work directly with the producer of a play or filmed adaptation of his/her work on a straight royalty basis.	Mar. 4
President Roosevelt officially enters the presidential race as a candidate for reelection. . . . Dr. Michael Davis, director of the Julius Rosenwald Medical Service Fund of Chicago, presents a five-point medical health plan for the United States. The crux of his address, which is aired on NBC Radio, is that it opposes social medicine. . . . Republicans buy 200,000 copies of Hell Bent for Election, political author James P. Warburg's scathing anti-New Deal book, to hand out to the public. . . . Earl Browder, secretary of the American Communist Party, proposes the formation of a Farmer-Labor Party to break the power of the nation's ruling money class.		The country will drop 700,000 people from relief payrolls by July 1, says the manager of the Works Progress Administration.	The newly built Norris Dam goes into operation in the Tennessee Valley. Its two huge sluice gates drop, remotely operated by a mechanism set up in President Roosevelt's White House office. The dam, which already brought prosperity to valley families engaged in its construction, will now bring more prosperity through electrical power to hundreds of miles of the valley.	Bette Davis (Dangerous) and Victor McLaglen (The Informer) win Academy Awards for Best Actress and Best Actor for 1935. Best photoplay of the year is MGM's Mutiny on the Bounty.	Mar. 5
A bill waiting passage in the House penalizes any individual or any corporation caught using "fear or intimidation" to sway voting. Individuals will be charged $1,000, corporations $5,000.		The Insurance Company of North America, Inc., publishes its year-end value of assets as $96,762,81; this compares to $83,321 the previous year. At the end of the year, stocks and bonds were held at $82,628,271.			Mar. 6

F Includes elections, federal-state relations, civil rights and liberties, crime, the judiciary, education, healthcare, poverty, urban affairs, and population.

G Includes formation and debate of U.S. foreign and defense policies, veterans affairs, and defense spending. (Relations with specific foreign countries are usually found under the region concerned.)

H Includes business, labor, agriculture, taxation, transportation, consumer affairs, monetary and fiscal policy, natural resources, pollution, and accidents.

I Includes worldwide scientific, medical, and technological developments, natural phenomena, U.S. weather, and natural disasters.

J Includes the arts, religion, scholarship, communications media, sports, entertainment, fashions, fads, and social life.

	World Affairs	Europe	Africa & The Middle East	The Americas	Asia & The Pacific
Mar. 7	Italian Premier Benito Mussolini informs the League of Nations that he is willing to at least listen "in principle" to its latest peace proposal concerning the war in Africa.		Dr. Mary Jobe Akeley, popular African explorer, publishes an article about the ages old traditions and costumes of the tribes of Swaziland and Mozambique in southeast Africa—and about how these peoples resent any intrusion by the white man.	President Arturo Alessandri of Chile raises controversy on two issues—first, over his snubbing of the country's Radical Party in selecting a Cabinet, and now by asking the Chilean Congress for more power to rule.	
Mar. 8	France appeals to the League of Nations to disregard what it deems a hypocritical peace proposal from Germany in light of the latter's marching into the Rhineland—clearly an act not in tune with peaceful overtures.	Germany doubles its current invasion of the Rhineland with Heroes' Memorial Day, mingling both events into a celebration to recognize and honor national pride and growth. Adolf Hitler praises the dead of yesteryear while lauding the brave and loyal men and women of today's Nationalist Socialist movement.			
Mar. 9	Most members of the League of Nations disagree with France's idea of imposing sanctions against Germany for the country's aggression.	Observers describe deployment of German troops in the Rhineland. Currently, "skeleton" troops are spread out throughout the vast area with no barracks, but clearly they are the vanguard of more troops to come.			Japan's realigned Cabinet, under Premier Koki Hirota, commits to "positive" action to erase some of the bad press it has been receiving due to the new military uprising. Military authorities deny that that action was a widespread attempt to turn Japan into a fascist government, as many believe.
Mar. 10		Observers say that the numbers of Hitler's troops in the Rhine have grown, seemingly overnight, to 20 battalions comprising some 50,000 men. German airplanes canvass the area and the dark green uniforms of the "state police" can be seen blending in with the regular troops.			The effects of the military insurgence in Tokyo, which the Japanese government saw as an international embarrassment, are still evident as more army commanders are "asked" to tender their resignations.
Mar. 11		Representatives from Britain, France, Italy, and Belgium meet at Paris's Quai d'Orsay to discuss the Nazi occupation of the Rhineland. Late news confirms that the Germans are moving heavy artillery to the front. . . . Britain sees no alternative to war unless Germany proves itself amenable to peace, not through words, but deeds. France, meanwhile, plans to use a more fastidious tone in dealing with Germany. Observers predict war within two years.		Paraguay, a country long rocked by revolt, meets a single direction under strategist and fascist leader Col. Rafael Franco. He installs a totalitarian government, freezing all political activity and putting all further actions under the auspices of the Officer of the Interior.	
Mar. 12		Gen. Hermann Goering, Hitler's Prime Minister of Prussia, calls upon the Prussians to join the Nazi movement.		Attendees of the Great Lakes-St. Lawrence Waterway Conference, a joint project of the United States and Canada, praise President Roosevelt for his cooperative efforts to bring the event to fruition.	

A	B	C	D	E
Includes developments that affect more than one world region, international organizations, and important meetings of world leaders.	*Includes all domestic and regional developments in Europe, including the Soviet Union.*	*Includes all domestic and regional developments in Africa and the Middle East.*	*Includes all domestic and regional developments in Latin America, the Caribbean, and Canada.*	*Includes all domestic and regional developments in Asian and Pacific nations (and colonies).*

U.S. Politics & Social Issues	U.S. Foreign Policy & Defense	Economics & Great Depression	Science, Technology & Nature	Culture, Leisure & Lifestyle	
A new deportation law is sought by Daniel W. MacCormack, who calls the current system "barbarous" because it separates families. His new Coolidge-Kerr bill, now in Congress, would humanely deport more than 20,000 illegal aliens.	The national commander of the American Veterans Association opposes additional aid to families of soldiers (husbands or sons) whose deaths were not a direct result of military action. Donald Hobart says that such payments are covered by general pensions.	The current total of needy high school students being financially helped by the National Youth Administration is 166,347. Aubrey Williams of the WPA explains that these teenagers receive a $6 monthly stipend for part-time work supervised by local school authorities. . . . Detroit's Economic Club hears Secretary of Commerce Daniel Roper explain that the President would like to turn tax relief burdens back to the local governments, but until they are ready to handle such a responsibility the national government will need to execute such programs.	A U.S. Army representative announces the invention of a radio light phone to be used in military maneuvers. The phone operates on the "electric eye" principle.		Mar. 7
Retail advertising, often full of untruths and "come-ons," will be more factual starting this year, according to Frank Spaeth, sales promotion head of the National Retail Dry Goods Association. . . . The League of Women Voters, angry over the laundry industry's inferior pay to female workers, takes it case directly to the laundromat owners. In the meantime, Attorney General John J. Bennett prepares to take a Minimum Wage Law Act before the Supreme Court.		Manufacturers of electrical household appliances, not content with a campaign that improved sales 30–50 percent in 1934, have united with the Edison Electrical Institute to conduct a campaign to raise sales even higher in 1935. . . . The Liberty League, a hard critic of President Roosevelt's policies, disagrees with his Soil Conservation and Domestic Act—the heir to the Agriculture Adjustment Act—especially since it believes the introduction of the bill is timed strictly at getting the farm vote in the November presidential campaign.		Former director of the national parks, Horace M. Albright, officially protests against the construction of the Grand Lake-Big Thompson Trans-Mountain Water-Diversion Project that would mar the scenic vista of one section of the Grand Canyon. . . . High schools across America are starting to make safe driving courses a part of their ongoing curriculum. This is one response to the nation's ever-rising highway death rate.	Mar. 8
Rev. John Lafarge, well-known Jesuit author and educator, asks Roman Catholics to get involved in issues that will help give African Americans a firmer place in society. . . . The Republican Party invites Democrats dissatisfied with the New Deal to come forward with their support and, in turn, receive the eventual appreciation of the winning Republican president.		Southern planters are supportive of the Roosevelt administration over the recent enactment of the Soil Conservation Act, which they see as a boon to their profession. Delta cotton growers put faith in its method of crop control and envision great yield.			Mar. 9
One-dollar donations—or "participation certificates"—are being sold by the Republican Party in an effort to get "a million dollars from a million Americans," asserts Republican chairman Henry P. Fetcher. The anticipated million dollars would be used as campaign money to unseat President Roosevelt. . . . The Democratic delegation from Massachusetts, consisting of Senators Walsh and Coolidge—two men known for their stand against the New Deal—are ordered by the Democratic Party to nevertheless slate for President Roosevelt.		The Pittsburgh Plate Glass Company doubled its income over 1934—$11,398,739 over $5,763,694—says its annual report, which was disseminated to stockholders today. . . . Chicago's prominent department store, Marshall Field & Co., reports earnings for the first two months of the year of $240,00 over the same period last year.			Mar. 10
Ice cream manufacturers from all parts of the U.S. meeting in New York hear from Dr. John L. Rice, commissioner of health, who explains how the need for safety and quality governs rigid inspections of milk, eggs, and other products that go into the making of ice cream.		The Supreme Court hears arguments from opponents of the Roosevelt administration's Guffey Coal Conservation Act, which, they say, paves the way for the government to further control the economic life of the nation. . . . Republican Senator from Iowa, J.L. Dickinson, visiting Boston, tells its citizens that the New Deal proved to be the worst foe of economic recovery.		Sonja Henie, Norway's gifted ice skater and champion, is reportedly on board the luxury liner, Ile de France, Hollywood bound for a screen test. Producers see in her a possible new big-screen attraction.	Mar. 11
		General Foods Corporation and its subsidiaries declare higher earnings than 1934 at $11,730,768, the best annual income since the early Depression year of 1930. . . . Wool sales, as seen through the merchandising of men's winter suits, take a sharp increase.			Mar. 12

F	G	H	I	J
Includes elections, federal-state relations, civil rights and liberties, crime, the judiciary, education, healthcare, poverty, urban affairs, and population.	Includes formation and debate of U.S. foreign and defense policies, veterans affairs, and defense spending. (Relations with specific foreign countries are usually found under the region concerned.)	Includes business, labor, agriculture, taxation, transportation, consumer affairs, monetary and fiscal policy, natural resources, pollution, and accident.	Includes worldwide scientific, medical, and technological developments, natural phenomena, U.S. weather, and natural disasters.	Includes the arts, religion, scholarship, communications media, sports, entertainment, fashions, fads, and social life.

	World Affairs	Europe	Africa & The Middle East	The Americas	Asia & The Pacific
Mar. 13		Adolf Hitler, in one of his most fiery orations, tells 40,000 cheering citizens gathered at Karlsruhe, Germany, that the nation will never renounce everything it has worked so hard to obtain; he denounces the League of Nations' accusations of rabid ambition and he stands by his occupation of the Rhineland. Yet, he assures neighboring France that he will never turn his bayonets on them. . . . Mining unions from across Europe commit to meeting in London for the purpose of discussing their future in the wake of a possible military conflict. They will examine options the industry might take if a shooting war begins.			
Mar. 14		Dr. Sasse, the Protestant Bishop of Thuringa, Germany, orders all ministers in his diocese to read at service every Sunday a declaration urging the congregation to vote for Adolf Hitler in the upcoming Reichstag elections.		Brazil plans to bring to trial more than 1,000 leftist rebels accused of treason. Special prison camps are in the midst of construction and will be utilized to detain these people, say observers of the situation.	
Mar. 15				The Reciprocal Trade Agreement, formulated recently with the Dominion of Canada, comes under scrutiny by the U.S. Supreme Court. Accusers maintain that the act illegally gives Congress the right to regulate commerce, which, says the Roosevelt administration, is not the case.	
Mar. 16		Adolf Hitler boasts to the press that "no might in the world" could budge Germany from its current goals and that the people of his nation support him and his direction for the country. . . . Germany has forbidden all Poles living in Germany from participating in the Reichstag elections and their property is seized. Polish authorities cannot understand this sudden political backlash against them.			Japan, after consulting with its armed forces, goes on record to pledge peace with the rest of the world. Premier Koki Hirota vows to work on establishing parallel peace with its neighbors across the globe while promising wide reform within its own territories.
Mar. 17	In an international broadcast from London, Viscount Cecil of Chelwood, president of the League of Nations Union, insists that Adolf Hitler should be brought before a global court in The Hague and made to answer for his actions against the world.				
Mar. 18	For the first time since July 1935, world production is slightly down, according to the National Industrial Conference Board. World prices of foodstuffs and raw materials, however, did increase somewhat in January of this year.	Teachers hoping to be assigned to teach at one of Germany's colleges or universities will now be required to first attend and complete two semesters' of propagandistic seminars, as announced today by the Reich's Minister of Education, Dr. Bernard Rust.	Rumors hint at an Ethiopian-generated set of peace terms being sent to Italy for consideration, but this news is unsubstantiated by the League of Nations.	The entire Catholic episcopate in the South American nation of Colombia—as well as the members of the local Conservative Political Party—are in a rage over the Colombian government's exceedingly liberal constitution that allows lifestyles leaning away from conservative and religious teachings and appeal to the president for changes.	

A	B	C	D	E
Includes developments that affect more than one world region, international organizations, and important meetings of world leaders.	Includes all domestic and regional developments in Europe, including the Soviet Union.	Includes all domestic and regional developments in Africa and the Middle East.	Includes all domestic and regional developments in Latin America, the Caribbean, and Canada.	Includes all domestic and regional developments in Asian and Pacific nations (and colonies).

U.S. Politics & Social Issues	U.S. Foreign Policy & Defense	Economics & Great Depression	Science, Technology & Nature	Culture, Leisure & Lifestyle	
Putting a tax on life insurance is playing with a vital entity of American life, says former president Herbert Hoover, who calls President Roosevelt's tax on insurance an act of ill logic. . . . The Democratic Party remains fairly confident that it will carry the state of Pennsylvania during the presidential election, due to the existence of a powerful machine in place and the backing of the state's coal miners.		Allis-Chalmers Manufacturing Company netted $1,935,137 for 1935. This equates to $1.47 per share.		*The Case of Clyde Griffiths*, a dramatic stage adaptation of Theodore Dreiser's *An American Tragedy*, opens at the Ethel Barrymore Theatre. It was written by playwrights Erwin Piscator and Lisa Goldschmidt.	Mar. 13
A bank robber wanted from San Francisco to Vermont is cornered by FBI agents in a home in Brooklyn and forced out by tear bombs. He is one of many Midwest Depression-born holdup men wanted for a Nebraska robbery that brought him more than $1 million.	Army flier Lt. Edgar R. Camp is forced to bail out of his burning airplane over Pennsylvania; while his parachute lands him safely, the smoking craft crashes near Colebrook National Guard Reservation. No one is hurt.	Cost of living for American wage earners has declined one-half of one percent, according to the National Industrial Conference Board. It is the first time since July 1935 that the rate has dropped.			Mar. 14
Mayor Fiorello LaGuardia of New York, a proponent of the Works Progress Administration, says he will not allow any legislation to dampen the great tide of employment that the WPA has nurtured in his state.		The New Deal has violated the Constitution, according to the Republican Party's chairman, Henry P. Fletcher. Asserting that President Roosevelt's welfare laws, in general, not only deride the Constitution but knowingly hurt the principles of the Bill of Rights, Fletcher assumes the President to be a "tyrant." . . . To date, 11,120,925 people are on the federal payroll, estimates the National Industrial Conference Board.	The northeast United States is experiencing a flooding problem brought on by heavy rain. Rivers and streams are overflowing their icy banks. Maine is the state hardest hit; torrents continue with no letup in sight.	Retiring film mogul Carl Laemmle sells his share of Universal Pictures Corp. to Charles R. "Buddy" Rogers, former actor, now executive. Laemmle is a 30-year veteran of moving pictures who witnessed the birth of the industry and helped it to grow.	Mar. 15
Goodyear Tire & Rubber Corp. in Akron, Ohio, awaits the results of the latest bargaining, hoping to bring its 14,000 striking employees back to the assembly line. The strike is four weeks old and, according to Goodyear, the vacant production is hurting company finances. . . . Miss Charl Ormond Williams, president of the National Federation of Business and Professional Women, suggests a "feminine day of rest"—a one-day stoppage of all women in the work world—to show men just how needed women are in day-to-day professional activities.		According to Edmond B. Butler, secretary of America's Emergency Relief Bureau, the cost of the country's relief programs—i.e., WPA, CWA, CCC—is not as much as the effects of a national riot by starving people.	A huge ice jam, caught off Bangor, Maine, threatens the city. Some 20,000 pounds of ice are lodged in the Penobscot River, putting Bangor under the alert of flooding and loss of life.		Mar. 16
An anti-lynching bill, introduced by Senator Frederick Van Nuys of Indiana, is on the calendar for this Congressional season. . . . Praising an "atmosphere of 'friendliness,'" Mrs. Herbert Hoover participates in the Girl Scouts of America's semi-annual directorial meeting. . . . Police uncover a large arsenal of weapons that they believe must belong to gangsters in a private house in New York. Of the 10 people inside the home, three are immediately linked to the recent death of a local racketeer.	In closing its biennial convention, the United Jewish Synagogue calls upon the United States to "reiterate its denouncement of war" as made in the Kellogg-Briand Peace Pact.	The Phelps Dodge Mining Group announces the greatest net income since 1929, with earnings of $6,147,878 after all charges, tax, and depreciation.		Across Ireland, citizens recall their patron saint, St. Patrick, in a day of solemnity. Unlike the raucous fun in the United States, the Irish celebrate with a quiet dinner and church attendance.	Mar. 17
Entrepreneur Charles P. Hull warns members of the metal industry of the Roosevelt administration's attempts (through the Faddis bill) to regulate the tinplate scrap field, a precious commodity in the industry. . . . After first conferring with Congressional leaders and budget experts yesterday, President Roosevelt asks Congress for $1 million to fund relief programs through the coming fiscal year to June 1, 1937.		Those attending the Export Managers Club meeting in New York learn that American goods are now being distributed throughout the world at a record pace, a rhythm unseen since before the start of the Depression. An improved world condition and more open U.S. policies are credited with the success.	During torrential downpours, two flooding streams rolling through Johnstown, Pa., cause waters as high as 14 feet to paralyze the town. An estimated 75,000 citizens of the town, set in the bowl-like Conemaugh Valley, are without power or food. . . . Between the flooding in the northeastern United States and the calamitous flooding in Johnstown, Pa., the entire Red Cross disaster staff is in the field, according to spokesperson Edward H. Powers.		Mar. 18

F	G	H	I	J
Includes elections, federal-state relations, civil rights and liberties, crime, the judiciary, education, healthcare, poverty, urban affairs, and population.	*Includes formation and debate of U.S. foreign and defense policies, veterans affairs, and defense spending. (Relations with specific foreign countries are usually found under the region concerned.)*	*Includes business, labor, agriculture, taxation, transportation, consumer affairs, monetary and fiscal policy, natural resources, pollution, and accidents.*	*Includes worldwide scientific, medical, and technological developments, natural phenomena, U.S. weather, and natural disasters.*	*Includes the arts, religion, scholarship, communications media, sports, entertainment, fashions, fads, and social life.*

	World Affairs	Europe	Africa & The Middle East	The Americas	Asia & The Pacific
Mar. 19		About 6 million men have, to date, joined the Nazi Air Defense in one capacity or another, say government officials. The system of defense, which is explained in the Third Reich's publication, *The Soldier's Friend* for 1936, explains the different tasks and responsibilities that Germany has created to help prevent air attack and survive if an attack occurs. Some 2,200 schools are involved in teaching air warden courses.			
Mar. 20		Thousands of people in the Hamburg Stadium hear Adolf Hitler cry a stop to defamation of Germany by other nations. He calls the League of Nations' plea for peace a "Versailles mentality," outmoded and outdone.	French Prime Minister Flandin tells his deputies that the world, in order to get back to normal, requires a "suspension in hostilities in Ethiopia and of sanctions against Italy." He presses Ethiopia for a manageable peace treaty, one that Italy will accept.		
Mar. 21		The Reichstag elections eight days away, Nazi police are given the order to usher citizens to the polls throughout Germany, dragging in anyone not planning to vote. The order, given by Lt. Col. Kurt Daluege, is aimed at raising the turnout some 8 to 10 percent by making sure the "indifferent and slothful" show up at the polls.			
Mar. 22		In Breslau, Germany, Hitler pledges never to surrender the Rhineland under threats from the League of Nations, France, Britain, or any other entity.		Mexican President Lárzaro Cárdenas's hope for labor unity comes to naught today when the respective four unions representing workers throughout the nation meet in Mexico City seeking their own agendas. Each refuses to yield to the others.	A plan for military conscription is in effect in the Philippine Islands. A call for young males was issued earlier this year.
Mar. 23				Argentina increases the price of corn by 14 percent; a revised bushel minimum, therefore, costs 42.6 cents a barrel.	According to the newspaper *Asahi*, Admiral Osami Nogano, naval minster and commander of the naval fleet, is forming a branch of the Navy Office dedicated to circulating naval news and points of views throughout the government offices.
Mar. 24	The United States, France, and Britain sign the Naval Peace Pact at the rump session of the second London Naval Disarmament Conference, in St. James' Palace, London. The treaty is largely ineffective because of numerous escape clauses. Even though it dropped out of the conference in January, Japan has indicated it will respect the terms of the treaty.	The Federal Council of Churches of Christ in America is in disbelief that Dr. William Zoellner of the Union of Germany Church asks American Christians to stand up against Bolshevism. The Council's foreign secretary, Dr. H.S. Leiper, calls Zoellner's request hypocritical since he is involved with a government that persecutes Jews and other non-Aryan nationalities.			
Mar. 25		Observers say Belgium is growing more nervous daily, apprehensive over Germany's next move. People along the frontier zone, even despite forts that dot the borderland, await invasion by Nazi stormtroopers.	Italy's bombardment of Jijiga and neighboring El Bhai by 20 airplanes has caused the biggest loss of lives yet in the Italo-Ethiopian war. The air raids are believed to have been attempts to cut off a chain of supplies moving from nearby British colonies.	Governors, mayors, council chairmen, and other municipal positions elected in Cuba's general elections of January 10 take their posts today, bringing autonomy to the country. The constabulary, up until now a separate entity, is situated within the structure of the defense department, headquartered in Havana.	
Mar. 26				One thousand Americans in New York rally against Brazilian police for the suspicious murder of an American youth, 21-year-old Victor Barron, who was shot to death by a constable.... Twenty Mexican mine workers die in a blast of a dynamite car in Tulltenango; many others are injured.	

A	B	C	D	E
Includes developments that affect more than one world region, international organizations, and important meetings of world leaders.	Includes all domestic and regional developments in Europe, including the Soviet Union.	Includes all domestic and regional developments in Africa and the Middle East.	Includes all domestic and regional developments in Latin America, the Caribbean, and Canada.	Includes all domestic and regional developments in Asian and Pacific nations (and colonies).

U.S. Politics & Social Issues	U.S. Foreign Policy & Defense	Economics & Great Depression	Science, Technology & Nature	Culture, Leisure & Lifestyle	
Senator William Borah of Idaho officially enters the Republican primary, reaffirming his stand against inflation. He attacks outmoded politics utilized by "old guard" politicians. The day of the political machine should be over, he says, and with it the bureaucracy that limits the power of the people.	U.S. military branches are working side by side with patriotic and lay organizations to establish legislation for national defense, says Maj. Gen. Frank Parker, one of the architects of the plan.		President Roosevelt personally asks Americans to donate to the Red Cross, which is aiding flood victims along the East Coast and in the Middle Atlantic states. The goal is $3 million to feed thousands of people and to find temporary shelter for the 200,000 homeless.	Dorothy Paget's Golden Miller, in the latest poll of bookmakers, is still the horse expected to win the Grand National Steeplechase in Aintree, England, on March 27. Last year's winner, Reynoldstown, is second choice.	Mar. 19
George C. Lucas, president of the Publishers Association and a believer in competition, tells the Traffic Club of New York that intercoastal railroads should be funded and supported with the same zeal as the nation supports intercoastal ship lines. . . . The dress industry and its representing unions are jointly striving to rehabilitate the stale industry for the benefit of its 100,000-plus workers.		As a sign of the public's growing interest in movies, Twentieth Century Fox, the giant film corporation, tripled its earnings from 1934–35. The latest net earnings are $3,563,087, as compared to $1,273,069 one year earlier. The earning is equivalent to $1.24 per share on the common market. . . . Statistics show that there are 22 percent fewer jobless in the factory industry than there were a year ago.			Mar. 20
The problems garnered by relief funding are the major campaign issue for 1936, say politicos. President Roosevelt's latest decrees for relief are the policies that are most attacked by the opposition. . . . The National Guard ends a 10-day strike by WPA workers who seized the Wisconsin state capitol chamber for their demonstration. Several picketers are arrested.		President Roosevelt asks American businesses to take part in a national crusade to reduce unemployment and, simultaneously, help slash relief expenditures. Business, he determines, can take in new employees "by individual and controlled action."			Mar. 21
According to post-NRA industry watchers, child labor has reescalated by 58 percent since the Supreme Court ended the NRA programs. . . . Ninety-one sheriffs from southern states have adjoined their names to a petition disseminated by the Association of Southern Women for the Prevention of Lynching. The petition is signed by 5,638 women from across the southern United States.		In search of constituents' opinions, President Roosevelt issues a survey asking which of his New Deal agencies should be disbanded or revised for continuation. He selects a panel to study the findings and compile them into a report for his examination.		Postmaster General James A. Farley is choosing 15 military heroes from American history, whose visages will appear on a new series of postage stamps honoring the U.S. Army and Navy.	Mar. 22
A New York-based symposium entitled, "Limitations of Political Action" brings Roman Catholics together with politicians to examine the depths to which church and state entwine in political issues.		Henry P. Fletcher, chairman of the Republican Party, says that throughout President Roosevelt's term money has been "squandered." Fletcher is convinced that the President's programs are aimed at prolonging the Depression until they become "frankly socialistic" in nature.			Mar. 23
	Jeannette Rankin, associate secretary for the National Association for Prevention of War, proposes that men running for Congress or the presidency should be forced to state their stand on neutrality so the people they serve are not fooled into electing a warmonger.		A new layer of scientific research, called microchemistry, is created by scientists.	Mexican composer and conductor Carlos Chavez is slated to make his first appearances with American symphonies when he appears with both the Philadelphia Symphony and the Boston Symphony this month.	Mar. 24
Governor Wilbur L. Cross intervenes in a spat that breaks out between the local WPA staff and Hartford Mayor Thomas Spellacy over steps taken to bring the flooded city back to normal. Each faction blames the other for slow response time.		The Federal Communications Commission (FCC) questions telecommunications giant AT&T over its loan of $3,400,000 to a Twentieth Century Fox firm to produce three motion pictures. AT&T explains the money was used to technically enhance the sound quality of the films, thus giving AT&T a technical sponsorship in the finished products.			Mar. 25
The Committee on Government Competition With Private Enterprise would like to see an end of the government's intrusion into private business where competition could foster benefits for the country. George L. Berry, coordinator of industrial cooperation, says that the politicians in Washington, D.C., must protect—not supplant—private enterprise.		The National Association of Manufacturers proffers a seven-point plan to reduce unemployment. It was composed in the wake of rising wages—and prices—and will be presented to lawmakers for their consideration.		Women's clothing suffers a setback, with 30 percent of the wool used for female attire ruined in the flooding of New England mills.	Mar. 26

F	G	H	I	J
Includes elections, federal-state relations, civil rights and liberties, crime, the judiciary, education, healthcare, poverty, urban affairs, and population.	Includes formation and debate of U.S. foreign and defense policies, veterans affairs, and defense spending. (Relations with specific foreign countries are usually found under the region concerned.)	Includes business, labor, agriculture, taxation, transportation, consumer affairs, monetary and fiscal policy, natural resources, pollution, and accidents.	Includes worldwide scientific, medical, and technological developments, natural phenomena, U.S. weather, and natural disasters.	Includes the arts, religion, scholarship, communications media, sports, entertainment, fashions, fads, and social life.

	World Affairs	Europe	Africa & The Middle East	The Americas	Asia & The Pacific
Mar. 27				The Commonwealth of Canada eyes the establishment of a single national director's board for its railroad lines, abolishing a series of directors and trusteeships.	
Mar. 28					
Mar. 29		Nearly 59,000 Jews were exiled from Germany, the American Jewish Distribution Committee alleges. Some 25,000 left for France while 5,837 are now in Holland. Of the remainder, many thousands sailed to North and South America.			
Mar. 30		Adolf Hitler receives almost 99 percent of a plebiscite vote, proclaiming that the German people are wholly behind his policies.			
Mar. 31					
Apr. 1	Hitler tells the peace powers of the League of Nations that he respects their peace offers, but falls short of signing the proposal. He adds that he will soon offer other stipulations.	Austria announces universal service conscription. Chancellor Kurt Schuschnigg explains that all men between 18 and 45 are expected to do their duty, "with or without arms." Observers appraise the move as being a sign of the tension that Austria feels being located next to Germany.			
Apr. 2		The Coronation of Edward VIII, successor to the late George V, is scheduled for May 12, 1937, giving the incoming Regent the necessary time to accustom himself to the duties of the monarch. Edward, in the meantime, promises to work toward world peace and a healthy trade calendar.			
Apr. 3				At the last minute, the country of Nicaragua averts a railway strike. The strike would have been costly, say both sides of the labor table, in terms of lost shipments and job-hours. Business proceeds immediately upon signing of the amendment.	

A	B	C	D	E
Includes developments that affect more than one world region, international organizations, and important meetings of world leaders.	Includes all domestic and regional developments in Europe, including the Soviet Union.	Includes all domestic and regional developments in Africa and the Middle East.	Includes all domestic and regional developments in Latin America, the Caribbean, and Canada.	Includes all domestic and regional developments in Asian and Pacific nations (and colonies).

U.S. Politics & Social Issues	U.S. Foreign Policy & Defense	Economics & Great Depression	Science, Technology & Nature	Culture, Leisure & Lifestyle	
		The financial office of the Stewart-Warner Corporation announces that the company has tripled its earnings in one year with a net of $1,724,313.		Reynoldstown, a nine-year-old thoroughbred jumper owned by Major Noel Furlong, takes the Grand National Steeplechase in Aintree, England. . . . New York City is lauded by the Chicago-based National Safety Council for reducing the number of automobile accidents within its perimeters by 13 percent in one month.	Mar. 27
Pittsburgh's large voter registration turnout indicates that an earlier shift away from the Democrats has swung back heavily in favor of the party.					Mar. 28
Police disperse an angry vigilante mob with tear gas outside a Huntsville, Ala., jail where four African Americans are being detained for the murder of a 19-year-old white girl, Vivian Woodward.					Mar. 29
Nicholas Murray Butler, president of Columbia University and former presidential adviser, predicts a Roosevelt victory in the presidential elections if the Republicans do not find stronger contenders. William Borah and Alf M. Landon cannot carry weight against Roosevelt, he asserts. . . . Governor James M. Curley of Massachusetts proposes a five-day workweek without decrease in salary. He believes it will bring a stability to the workforce.		Free enterprise needs to be recognized and encouraged, says Alfred P. Sloan, Jr., president of the General Motors Corporation. That is why he is against "experiments in economy" offered by the New Deal. The New Deal crippled individual efforts of business to seek a way out of financial slumps, he says, depending too much on bureaucratic programming.			Mar. 30
Rep. Bacharach of New York demands an investigation into allegations of political discrimination within certain Works Progress Administration chapters in the state of New Jersey.		The Federal Reserve proclaims that earnings for 700 representative industrial and mercantile entities increased a dramatic 48 percent over 1934, showing the highest jump since 1930. Though still not as positive as 1929 figures, the results indicate an economy that is good and remains constant.		The safest city award in the United States goes to Evanston, Ill., by the National Safety Council for its precautions to diminish traffic accidents in its area. In all, six municipalities receive trophies, which are presented by General Motors.	Mar. 31
A new organization known as the Labor Nonpartisan League announces it will back President Roosevelt in the presidential elections. The group, founded by coordinator for industrial cooperation, George L. Berry, plans to gather all labor support for the President under one roof. . . . William Borah detours from Milwaukee to Chicago when the entourage is warned of an epidemic of influenza in the Wisconsin city.		Paychecks for 32,000 state employees in Illinois are detained by Treasurer John Stelle, who accuses Governor Homer of "padding the rolls."		In federal court, actor John Barrymore sues the two lawyers who represented him in his recent divorce case for bilking him out of a $100,000 deposit fee. The lawyers deny ever having requested—or seeing—any such fee.	Apr. 1
Friends of New Germany, the American branch of the Nationalist Socialist (Nazi) Party, is renamed the German-American League. Its ruling committee has often stated it plans to gain a "firm foothold" in the United States.		The Aluminum Company of America and its subsidiaries netted $9,571,206 in 1935, nearly doubling earnings from the year before. . . . Businessmen condemn President Roosevelt's new tax program, accusing it as a "promoter of monopolies" and a "direct attack on capitalism." The Manufacturers' Association says the plan benefits larger corporations over small ones.	A lethal tornado whips through five southern states, killing 37 and injuring hundreds; most damage is to parts of North Carolina and Georgia.	The Safeways, an American Athletic Union-sponsored basketball team, returns to the United States after being tossed from the Olympic Games when it is learned they played under the A.A.U. and Y.M.C.A. under different names.	Apr. 2
The National Park Service lashes out at the government's Rocky Mountain Tunnel project, calling it a disfigurement to the scenic beauty of the national preserve. Protestors fear that this project will start a precedent. . . . Senator Wagner introduces a bill for slums to be replaced by low-cost housing, federally assisted by grants and loans to local developers.		Economists and professors address a meeting of the Academy of Political Science, telling members that a credit boom is coming, to be followed by a period of inflation. . . . American Machine Company slightly increases yearly net earnings in 1935, netting $1,120,985 as compared to $1,110,433 in 1934.		Roger William Strauss, an advocate of inter-faith amity, wins the 1935 American Hebrew Medal for the Promotion of Better Understanding Between Christians and Jews in America. . . . Bruno Richard Hauptmann is put to death in the New Jersey State Correctional Facility for the murder of the Lindbergh baby. . . . The National Association of Basketball Coaches kicks off a three-day symposium to look at possibly changing game rules.	Apr. 3

F	G	H	I	J
Includes elections, federal-state relations, civil rights and liberties, crime, the judiciary, education, healthcare, poverty, urban affairs, and population.	Includes formation and debate of U.S. foreign and defense policies, veterans affairs, and defense spending. (Relations with specific foreign countries are usually found under the region concerned.)	Includes business, labor, agriculture, taxation, transportation, consumer affairs, monetary and fiscal policy, natural resources, pollution, and accidents.	Includes worldwide scientific, medical, and technological developments, natural phenomena, U.S. weather, and natural disasters.	Includes the arts, religion, scholarship, communications media, sports, entertainment, fashions, fads, and social life.

	World Affairs	Europe	Africa & The Middle East	The Americas	Asia & The Pacific
Apr. 4		England's Foreign Minister, Anthony Eden, in a communiqué to Paris and Brussels, refuses to admit that talks with Germany are hopeless. In the meantime, Adolf Hitler turns down the latest British plea for further concession toward a legitimate peace.			
Apr. 5		The *London Time's* financial editor says that he believes the economic boon in Germany is quite temporary. Having studied the last report of the Kredit Gesellschaft, he identifies an enormous national debt.	Germany has been vocal about wanting to reclaim colonies "unjustly" mandated to other countries at the end of the world war in 1918. One of these is Tanganyika, Africa, currently administered by Britain. Britain reports that the people of Tanganyika, having heard the German ambition, have made greater strides toward independence.	The Chilean National Library in Santiago officially opens the *Sala Norteamericana* (North American Room) to celebrate the relationship between Chile and the United States. Some 50,000 books and periodicals comprise the new section of the library. . . . Costa Rica votes out many of its once-favored Communist lawmakers in a recent election, signifying the country's latest political transformation.	
Apr. 6				The Banco Cuba sets out to establish a legal lottery, expected to pay $300,000 per annum, money that will be divided among island charities. Supporting the venture are Cuba's governmental Cabinet and its Council of State. . . . Mexican women—5,000 strong—vote for the first time in the National Revolutionary Party primary.	
Apr. 7		The Nazi party is outraged over its well-regarded national prizefighter Max Schmeling's choice of opponent, Joe Louis, who is an African American. The *Reich Sports Journal* calls for a ban on the event, which is scheduled for the months ahead.		Economic conditions in Nicaragua have greatly improved, says economist Dr. C.E. McGuire, chairman of the country's national bank. He expects, with the proper nurturing, that the national budget will be soon balanced.	
Apr. 8		All private schools in Germany are abolished, to be taken over by Nazi-taught institutions that blend Nazi propaganda and lifestyle with math, science, and other basic courses. . . . In what promises to be the beginning of an eventual reciprocal trade between Yugoslavia and Nazi Germany, Germany purchases several items from the other.			Japan's War Minister, Count-General Juichi Terauchi, explains his objectives: to keep discipline, to stock defense supplies, and to adhere to all national policies. He has already forbidden his soldiers to become engaged in political movements. . . . As the ranks of the merchant marine have been littered by unrest and even sabotage, vice president of the National Committee on Safety at Sea Howard S. Cullman requests labor investigations to uncover the reasons for the disorder.
Apr. 9			Twenty-one different peace, social, and religious organizations sign off on a petition to the League of Nations to end Italy's "shocking reported use of gas and bombs against defenseless Ethiopian villagers and the Red Cross."		
Apr. 10				Found guilty of plotting to overthrow the government of Mexico, former Mexican president Plutarco Elias Calles and several aides-de-campe are banished across the border to the United States by current President, Lázaro Cárdenas. Others banished include labor leaders Luis Leon and Luis Morones and the governor of the state of Guanajato, Melchor Ortega.	

A	B	C	D	E
Includes developments that affect more than one world region, international organizations, and important meetings of world leaders.	Includes all domestic and regional developments in Europe, including the Soviet Union.	Includes all domestic and regional developments in Africa and the Middle East.	Includes all domestic and regional developments in Latin America, the Caribbean, and Canada.	Includes all domestic and regional developments in Asian and Pacific nations (and colonies).

U.S. Politics & Social Issues	U.S. Foreign Policy & Defense	Economics & Great Depression	Science, Technology & Nature	Culture, Leisure & Lifestyle	
Helen Varick Boswell, a leader in the Women's Republican Party urges fellow members to avoid getting carried away with the presidential campaigners' "personalities" and listen to how well they address the issues. Otherwise, she says, voters are "eclipsing the American idea." . . . The U.S. government creates a Public Affairs Committee, a commission devoted to cataloguing public and educational resources from universities and civic departments. All information from the latest research institutions will be available to the public eye.	A temporary embargo is placed on tin scrap by Secretary of State Cordell Hull, who is also chief of the National Munitions Control Board. Because he believes that the commodity tin will prove precious in the event of war, exports will cease after July 1; only certain licensed dealers will be allowed to handle it.	The American Bankers Association in Chicago proposes a revision of taxing and of chartering of banks as part of a wider program to maintain overall firmness in the nation's banking industry. Part of the plan also includes building up the public's trust for banking managers. . . . Congress is trying to rush President Roosevelt's new tax plan though the House of Representatives, though the Chamber of Commerce complains that it is still in too much of a "sketchy" form.	Windstorms pummel Georgia, Alabama, and Florida, leaving behind 40 dead and more than 600 injured. Hundreds are without homes and damage is expected to exceed $3 million.	Northwestern University in Chicago and the U.S. auto industry bring traffic policing to school as a graduate course. Northwestern is already known for making accident control an educational study.	Apr. 4
Vacationing gangster Charles "Lucky" Luciano is apprehended by Arkansas Rangers and promptly delivered back to New York City where Special Prosecutor Thomas E. Dewey ordered his arrest for prostitution. According to Arkansas authorities, Luciano—who allegedly runs a vast army of pimps and streetwalkers—resisted arrest.			Doctors H.K. Benson and A.M. Partansky of the University of Washington in Seattle believe that ordinary bacteria contains a previously unrecognized ability to increase human energy.	The National Museum in Athens, Greece, opens an exhibition of ancient pottery fragments discovered below the storied Acropolis Hill by U.S. Minister to Greece Lincoln MacVeagh.	Apr. 5
After a study, William B. Cox of the Osborne Association claims that much of the $125 million that the U.S. government doles out to its penitentiaries, prisons, and reformatories goes to naught. The rehabilitation of convicts and juvenile delinquents has proven futile, he appraises.	The size of the U.S. Army needs to be built up, says Secretary of War George H. Dern, speaking in Chicago. Lauding the Army's history and its fighting potential, he nevertheless worries over a vast force of aggressors sometime in the near future, remarking, "At the present time (the Army) is dangerously small."	According to the magazine, The American Banker, the nation's 20 largest banks, between December 31, 1935, and March 4, 1936, increased their holdings of U.S. government securities by $255,323,000. By March 4, they held $5,970,913,000, or one-fifth of the American debt.	Tupelo, Miss., is ravaged by a vicious 100-mile-per-hour tornado. Early mortality count is 134, but authorities expect the number to rise.		Apr. 6
Transportation Coordinator Joseph Eastman recommends to Congress a large unemployment compensation program for the more than 1.5 million employees in transportation-related industries. . . . American women own 80 percent of all life insurance policies, 65 percent of the nation's savings deposits, 44 percent of utility stocks, 48 percent of railroad securities, and 40 percent of private real estate.		One of the country's most popular department stores, Montgomery Ward & Co., garnered record-breaking monthly sales of $24,844,596 in March—the highest monthly net in the company's history. February results were not far behind, $22,783,089.	The National Geographic Society, members of the National Bureau of Standards, and Georgetown University, together sailing to Russia, announce that they will send back the very first color photographs of an eclipse of the sun, most visible from Siberia. . . . A sum of $2.5 million is set aside from Works Progress Administration funds by President Roosevelt to aid the victims of the recent series of killer tornados in the south. Reviewing the damage, the President allocates this money to supplement that of Red Cross and other relief.		Apr. 7
	Hiding behind neutrality is not the way to prevent war, Sir Arthur Salter of the League of Nations advises the United States. He suggests, instead, that the United States become involved in the peacekeeping activities of Europe and, as part of a collective bargaining unit, he thinks that war can be averted.	Members of the Workers Alliance of America vote 129,958 to 21,114 to merge with other "job relief" organizations—the National Unemployment Councils, the National Unemployment League, and the Work Progress Administration.	An NBC technician, 32-year-old Harry E. Lawrence, is electrocuted on the 58th floor of the Empire State Building while he was in the midst of setting up a transmitter designed for the upcoming experiment of television.		Apr. 8
	Professing that the needs of America's youth are often overlooked in the day-to-day world, Arthur Jones of the University of Pennsylvania recommends the formation of a federal agency to proffer vocation and education guidance across the United States. . . . As alleged price fixing occurs in the oil industry, U.S. Attorney General Homer Cummings promises an investigation.	The Libbey-Owens-Ford Glass Company reports impressive first quarter 1936 earnings of $1,996,967, with shares at 79 cents. . . . On an NBC radio program, Massachusetts Governor James M. Curley and the president of the National Foreign Trade Council Eugene P. Thomas debate the value of the tariff in American economy.		Broadway sees three premieres in the same week: The Mikado at the Majestic Theatre and On Your Toes at the Imperial —both opening today— and Summer Wives, which opens at the Mansfield in two days.	Apr. 9
Speaking before members of the Amalgamated Clothing Workers, president Sidney Hillman speaks on behalf of the Labor Non-Partisan League in urging votes for President Roosevelt. He is one of several labor leaders urging support for the President.		Sales of world-class wool peaked in February, the highest per-month wool sales since 1923. The National Association of Wool Manufacturers states that 23 percent of the consumption was overseas. . . . Government figures report that money in circulation at the end of March 1936 totaled $5,877,042,037.			Apr. 10

F	G	H	I	J
Includes elections, federal-state relations, civil rights and liberties, crime, the judiciary, education, healthcare, poverty, urban affairs, and population.	*Includes formation and debate of U.S. foreign and defense policies, veterans affairs, and defense spending. (Relations with specific foreign countries are usually found under the region concerned.)*	*Includes business, labor, agriculture, taxation, transportation, consumer affairs, monetary and fiscal policy, natural resources, pollution, and accidents.*	*Includes worldwide scientific, medical, and technological developments, natural phenomena, U.S. weather, and natural disasters.*	*Includes the arts, religion, scholarship, communications media, sports, entertainment, fashions, fads, and social life.*

	World Affairs	Europe	Africa & The Middle East	The Americas	Asia & The Pacific
Apr. 11		Hitler receives a landmark grant from the Nationalist Socialist (Nazi) Party to study and rewrite Jewish history; he has already established an institute of authors working under his guidance to rework previous textbooks so that the world will know the real "truth" about the Jewish nationality.	Governor Paul V. McNutt of Indiana, Rep. Schuyler Merritt of Connecticut, Governor Tom Berry of South Dakota, and Governor Harold Hoffmann of New Jersey openly congratulate the chairman of the United Palestine Appeal, Dr. Stephen S. Wise, for his devotion to raising $3.5 million for relief of German and Polish Jews abandoning Nazi Germany.		
Apr. 12					The Philippines are revising their airlines system, bringing all lines under one roof and exacting a fight program for its fliers. . . . Pandit Jawaharlal Nehru, president of the Indian National Congress at Delhi, urges socialism as a political foundation for India. His idea of a strong economic system, he says, is Russia's model, even if it means revolutionary change within India.
Apr. 13		Eight thousand youths sign up for Soviet Russia's aviation program. A.V. Kosarieff, secretary to the Young Communists' League, tells them that whoever controls the skies in the next war will win.			Addressing the National League of American Pen Women, Chinese Ambassador Sao-Ke Alfred Sze says that any global conference truly wishing to solve universal problems should include those experienced by the Far East, which are often overlooked in such world parleys. He professes a clearer agenda for world unity.
Apr. 14	The economy of the world market looks vague, says the *Second Quarter Review*. Conditions are not necessarily bad, but unchanged since last quarter.	Britain and France hold discussions to protect neighboring Belgium from the wrath of Nazi Germany, should it decide to expand outward.	The League of Nations gives an apprehensive Turkey permission to construct a series of forts and defenses on its various islands near Italy.	Brazil and other South American countries reply positively to President Roosevelt's suggestion for a Pan-American Congress. An agenda needs to be approved, but the goal of the conference would be to improve economic relationships between the United States and the Latin American countries.	
Apr. 15	British Labor Party member Herbert Morrison angrily admits that he cannot understand President Roosevelt's refusal to cut off oil shipments to Italy, when the rest of the civilized world recognizes the potency of the sanction. If the United States had stopped oil trade to Italy, he estimates, Mussolini's motorized war on Ethiopia would have ended almost immediately.		Dessye, the last major city before the Ethiopian capital of Addis Ababa, is taken over by Italian troops, who boast they marched 120 miles in five days unopposed.	Secretary of State Cordell Hull, in announcing the Pan-American Congress to be held in Buenos Aires, adds that the event is an example of friendly cooperation and "enlightened internationalism."	
Apr. 16		Germany states that it will introduce over the next couple of months transatlantic air service to the United States. Stopovers will be in either the Azores or Bermuda. . . . In advance of the upcoming meeting of the Reich Cooperative Organization for German Medical Science, its leader, Dr. Gerhard Wagner, publishes an article in a Nazi magazine promoting new methods of treating illnesses and delving into the human body.		In preparation of the forthcoming peace conference set in Buenos Aires, Argentinean Foreign Minister Carlos Saavedra Lamas drafts a trade proposal based on America's Good Neighbor Policy. It bans all elements that might cause political and business friction between the United States and Latin American nations.	
Apr. 17			Ethiopian defenses collapse under the prodding of Italian troops who near the capital city of Addis Ababa. The Italian infantry pauses on the outskirts of town as airplanes bombard it. Regiments of Ethiopian Emperor Haile Selassie's army have already begun evacuation southward.		

A	B	C	D	E
Includes developments that affect more than one world region, international organizations, and important meetings of world leaders.	Includes all domestic and regional developments in Europe, including the Soviet Union.	Includes all domestic and regional developments in Africa and the Middle East.	Includes all domestic and regional developments in Latin America, the Caribbean, and Canada.	Includes all domestic and regional developments in Asian and Pacific nations (and colonies).

U.S. Politics & Social Issues	U.S. Foreign Policy & Defense	Economics & Great Depression	Science, Technology & Nature	Culture, Leisure & Lifestyle	
	The Roosevelt administration asks other nations to review the definitions of their neutrality laws in an effort to understand the U.S. stand and to allow it equal rights to trading if neutrality is imposed. Secretary of State Cordell Hull points out that neutrality does not necessarily mean the United States will not fight, if provoked by an enemy.				Apr. 11
Educators from across the United States lay the cornerstone of a new organization aimed at instilling art programs into public and private grammar schools, high schools, and colleges and universities. The program is called the National Association for Art Education. . . . The City of Toledo, Ohio, creates its own Labor Relations Board to conduct, within its own particular geographic confines, hearings between workers and employers so that problems might be settled before becoming serious issues.				A carrier pigeon—one of many that still serve the U.S. Army, despite more modern communications techniques—wins a medal for outflying other pigeons in Chattanooga, Tennessee's countrywide pigeon race. He clocked 47 miles per hour for 715 miles, faster and farther than the other 1,114 entries.	Apr. 12
Representatives of Catholicism, Judaism, and the Episcopalian Church ask for "religious cooperation" between all faiths in eradicating the definitions of religious and social bigotry from the American idiom.		Howard S. Cullman of the National Committee on Safety at Sea stumps for increases in the operational safety budget of the Bureau of Navigation and Steamboat Inspection	In Kansas City, Mo., Dr. Ernest P. Benger of E.I. duPont de Nemours & Company introduces a new synthetic fiber (nylon) one-third the dimension of natural silk. A one-pound ball of it would, unrolled, stretch from the east to west coast.		Apr. 13
Adversaries of President Roosevelt call his Social Security Act a blanket trying to hide the real problems of unemployment, an idyllic model based on outmoded social structures and ideals.		Between March 1933 and December 1935, the United States increased its working forces by 5,413,000, according to the National Industrial Conference Board.			Apr. 14
After the American Society of Newspaper Editors states that President Roosevelt "is far less concerned with the freedom of the press than an American government should be," the President invites the society's editors to the White House to sit down with him tonight for an "off the record" discussion in the hope that he may change their views of him.		American Telephone & Telegraph reports that it installed 201,000 phones in American homes in the first quarter of 1936, compared with 113,000 of the first three months of 1934.			Apr. 15
The atmosphere in Catholic grade schools has, in many ways, become too secular, voices Father William J. McGucken, regent of education at St. Louis University. He asks institutions that prepare men and women to teach in parochial schools to remain more "Catholic in tone" on every subject. . . . In a speech in Pittsfield, Mass., Postmaster General James A. Farley challenges Republicans to specifically name the reasons they do not like the New Deal—and be ready to argue it.		For the first time since before the Depression, the furniture production industry is showing a profit, according to Dr. A.P. Haake, managing director of the National Association of Furniture Manufacturers, calling it a good omen of times to come for the industry. . . . A high-ranking official of the Washington State WPA administration, George Gannon, is terminated by WPA head Harry L. Hopkins after questions of ill-directed finances surface.		Actor Walter Hampden performs Cyrano de Bergerac for the 991st time tonight at the New Amsterdam Theatre on Broadway.	Apr. 16
The National Association of Furniture Manufacturers, which depends on railroads to ship its products coast to coast, decries the notion of government intervention in the rail industry. The association sees the public and the industry better off if America's railroads are left alone to run as private concerns.	The women's committee of the National Committee for Religion and Welfare Recovery signs a petition to help stop "the rising tide of militarism" in the United States. They urge an embargo on munitions and social justice to avoid armed conflict.	The number of men working in U.S. shipyards rose 50 percent in 1935, says H. Gerrish Smith, president of the Council of Shipbuilders. He attributes this figure to naval contracts out of Washington, D.C., which put many jobless back on productive payrolls. . . . To avoid inflation, says Dr. Edwin Kemmerer of Princeton University, the government should reduce expenditures, balance the budget, and increase both taxes and a statutory gold standard.		The National Federation of Day Nurseries believes that children with behavioral problems are usually the result of parents with emotional imbalances and/or a disagreeable household.	Apr. 17

F	G	H	I	J
Includes elections, federal-state relations, civil rights and liberties, crime, the judiciary, education, healthcare, poverty, urban affairs, and population.	Includes formation and debate of U.S. foreign and defense policies, veterans affairs, and defense spending. (Relations with specific foreign countries are usually found under the region concerned.)	Includes business, labor, agriculture, taxation, transportation, consumer affairs, monetary and fiscal policy, natural resources, pollution, and accidents.	Includes worldwide scientific, medical, and technological developments, natural phenomena, U.S. weather, and natural disasters.	Includes the arts, religion, scholarship, communications media, sports, entertainment, fashions, fads, and social life.

	World Affairs	Europe	Africa & The Middle East	The Americas	Asia & The Pacific
Apr. 18		Plans are in effect for Adolf Hitler's 47th birthday in two days—legions of tanks, marching soldiers, flags, and bunting will enliven the streets of Berlin. Businesses will be closed and all citizens are expected to turn out to celebrate the man who made Germany what it is today. . . . Britain's markets are showing a renewed increase, with the budget nearly even and sales up overseas.			
Apr. 19		Celebrating Adolf Hitler's 47th birthday, Propaganda Minister Joseph Goebbels praises his commander for turning Germany into the greatest nation on earth, civically and militarily. In a broadcast that is aired around the world and translated into many languages, Goebbels predicts that Hitler will be remembered by history as a "world savior" who saved an otherwise "senile" Europe.		According to the U.S. National Association of Credit Men, markets in Latin America show a vast improvement between the first three months of 1936 and the last three months of 1935. Credit, collection, and exchange conditions, says the association, increased markedly.	
Apr. 20		Germany's export and import trades, which have both shown new signs of life thanks to Economic Minister Hjalmar Schacht, continue to escalate. March 1936 export totals are above February totals by 5.5 million marks and the import gauge registers well above 1935 results.	The Italian army's expected easy win of Addis Ababa, the Ethiopian capital city, is challenged as 8,000 Ethiopian volunteers join with conscripts to bar Italy's ingress.		
Apr. 21		Former British labor leader George Lansbury, visiting Washington, D.C., calls for an economic parley between the United States and Britain, hoping that the two nations could effectively lead the rest of the world into an international movement to save global resources. . . . Despite protestations that it is using the Olympics as a Nazi propaganda tool, Germany now circulates its central sports magazine, the *Reich Sports Journal,* worldwide. It professes to focus on the Olympics, but the articles are dedicated to Nazi theory.			
Apr. 22		Members of Britain's House of Commons argue for immediate payment of the war debt owed to the United States, monies owed since 1916. Today, the Liberal Party concurs that the debt serves as a barrier getting in the way of the transatlantic relationship.			
Apr. 23	Experts of wartime technology determine that by 1937 the Nazi Third Reich will be, by far, in the lead as a military air power. Unless the United States begins to upscale its development, it will be ranked sixth, one step ahead of Japan, rated seventh.	Winston Churchill, one of the most outspoken anti-Nazi British Cabinet members, lays out facts, figures and graphs to prove to the House of Commons that Germany is rearming for a major conflict. He predicts that within four years there will be either "a melting of hearts" or a vast "explosion" bringing all nations of the world into a war driven by Hitler.	Ethiopian combatants report that they are slowing down Italy's march to the capital city and that, in several days, the enemy has been able to advance a mere 50 miles from Dessye. They are currently bogged down by mud and gunfire near Ephrata. From the west, the army of Nasibu claims to have staved off Italian troops for four days, resulting in Italian retreat.	Two men who have been lodged in a mine shaft near Moose River in Ontario, Canada, for 10 days are rescued to the applause of a huge group of spectators. Both men are described as being injured, but not critical. . . . A Senate bill that would give Puerto Rico its total independence is introduced by Maryland's Senator Millard E. Tydings, chairman of the Committee of Territories and Insular Affairs.	

A	B	C	D	E
Includes developments that affect more than one world region, international organizations, and important meetings of world leaders.	Includes all domestic and regional developments in Europe, including the Soviet Union.	Includes all domestic and regional developments in Africa and the Middle East.	Includes all domestic and regional developments in Latin America, the Caribbean, and Canada.	Includes all domestic and regional developments in Asian and Pacific nations (and colonies).

U.S. Politics & Social Issues	U.S. Foreign Policy & Defense	Economics & Great Depression	Science, Technology & Nature	Culture, Leisure & Lifestyle	
The Amalgamated Clothing Workers of America, one of the largest unions in the nation, unanimously backs the reelection of President Roosevelt.		For the first time since 1931, national banks in the United States show a net profit. Year 1935 shows a net of $158,491,000 over deficits in 1934, 1933, and 1932. . . . The Johns-Manville Corporation and its subsidiary companies announce a net profit for 1935 of $2,095,044, or $2.09 per share.	An aviation trophy, the coveted Harmon Award, goes to Capt. Edwin C. Musick of Pan-American Airlines for his testing of Clipper ships across the Pacific in 1935.	The Pathé Film Corporation, one of the earliest-born film production companies in France with offices in the United States, announces reorganization. It predicts an agenda of 30 films this year.	Apr. 18
The Roosevelt administration announces the creation of a new health advisory board whose purpose it will be to formulate a standard public health code for the country. Both metropolitan and rural areas will be approached for input by a drafting committee, whose first eight members—all doctors—are appointed today. The program runs under the auspices the U.S. Treasury.		The National Retail Dry Goods Association reports that an excess of $300 million worth of sales taxes are "being lifted from consumers' purses" through state and locally imposed legislation each year.		The Associated Press member group grew in 1935 from 1,340 newspapers to 1,359 newspapers. The AP is in the middle of a project to enhance its state news and wire services to quicken its transmission and reaction time to breaking news. . . . Many large-scale realtors gathering for a convention in Tulsa, Okla., decry the shape of America's cities and urgently call for a beautification of many areas across the United States. They stress the value of an efficient home design and glamour in architecture.	Apr. 19
Charles "Lucky" Luciano awaits his trial, unable to raise $350,000 bail. It is believed that Special Prosecutor Thomas E. Dewey is targeting Luciano, known gangster chief, as an example to other would-be mob bosses.	Four of seven members of the Senate Munitions Committee favor the idea of the United States' manufacturing its own war materials. This could result in a growth of federal "war plants" throughout the United States.		Purdue University of Indiana plans to grant to famous aviator Amelia Earhart her own "flying laboratory," an airplane consisting of all the accoutrements that will allow her to carry on her experiments. The gift is in gratitude to her contribution to the advancement of aviation science, the university explains.	Ellison "Tarzan" Brown, a 22-year-old Narragansett Indian, wins the Boston Marathon, ensuring himself a place in the Olympics.	Apr. 20
Speaking to an accountants' association in New York, the president of the American Bar Association, William L. Ransom, sharply criticizes President Roosevelt's "centralization of power" in government.	Concerned by the growing state of agitation in Europe, retiring Maj. Gen. Dennis E. Nolan of the celebrated Second Corps advises a selective draft of young men in America.	Princeton University professor Edwin V. Kemmerer tells a Chicago audience that the only way to stop the tide of inflation is "an opposition that will result in the prompt repeal of the radical monetary and banking legislation now in our statute books."		The Daughters of the American Revolution are cautioned by one of their leaders, Mrs. George Thatcher Guernsey, to become less rigid and more open in their structure in order to attract young members.	Apr. 21
The Senate approves an increased appropriation for the Justice Department, which wants to widen its base of operations and expand coverage of its law agents, popularly called G-Men. The Senate earlier voted down an attempt to halt the effort by the Appropriations Committee, which did not want to release the money.		The Eastern Gas and Fuel Associates netted $10,007,542 for the 12 months ending February 1936, say administrative offices. It is a slight decline in profits from the same period a year earlier. . . . Reports of increased farm income during the first quarter are released at the same time as predictions of another drought that could plague the Southwest. Secretary of Agriculture Henry Wallace fears that a drought, even smaller than the first, could affect 30 million acres.			Apr. 22
Johnny Torrio, once the kingpin of crime in Chicago before abdicating to Al Capone in 1925, is arrested in White Plains, N.Y., where he has been hiding from what authorities call, "a violation of the Internal Revenue law." His is the second arrest of a big-name gangster in the last few days, the other being Charles Luciano for prostitution racketeering. . . . News must be always free to report and never fettered by regulations and censoring, says Carl W. Ackermann, dean of Columbia University's School of Journalism, addressing the topic of the "newspaper of tomorrow."					Apr. 23

F	G	H	I	J
Includes elections, federal-state relations, civil rights and liberties, crime, the judiciary, education, healthcare, poverty, urban affairs, and population.	Includes formation and debate of U.S. foreign and defense policies, veterans affairs, and defense spending. (Relations with specific foreign countries are usually found under the region concerned.)	Includes business, labor, agriculture, taxation, transportation, consumer affairs, monetary and fiscal policy, natural resources, pollution, and accidents.	Includes worldwide scientific, medical, and technological developments, natural phenomena, U.S. weather, and natural disasters.	Includes the arts, religion, scholarship, communications media, sports, entertainment, fashions, fads, and social life.

	World Affairs	Europe	Africa & The Middle East	The Americas	Asia & The Pacific
Apr. 24		German students planning to study abroad as part of a student-exchange program with other countries must first undergo a training course in National Socialism and the loyalty that is inherent in being a German Nazi. . . . A civil war seems likely in Spain as Marxist advocates and the forces of Premier Manuel Azana verbally clash.		The British parliament in London applauds President Roosevelt's upcoming visit to Canada, a dominion of the British Empire, as a momentous event symbolizing more than 100 years of peaceful cohabitation on the North American continent.	Tokyo is slowly meting out its policy of unification between government entities, allowing the military voice back into council meetings. The premier's Cabinet opens sessions to foreign, war, and navy ministers.
Apr. 25				America's newspapers are warned by the American Newspaper Publishers Association to buy their newsprint from either U.S. or European mills—and avoid Canadian manufacturers currently caught up in a price war with the government.	
Apr. 26		As elections near for the Swedish Riksdag, the central issue is national defense. The present Cabinet sees a need to stay constant and rearm, but the vying Social Democrats reject the notion that an armed conflict is imminent.	More Ethiopian troops arrive from the frontier to protect their capital city of Addis Ababa. Both the forces of Dedjasmatch Moshesha, governor of Kambuta, and Ras Makonnen, governor of Western Wollega, now wait in alert on the ramparts of the city.		As Emperor Hirohito of Japan turns 35 years old, other nations acknowledge his power. He is the supreme ruler of 66 million Japanese citizens and 30 million Koreans and yet, journalists point out, he is the least known of all the world power figures. . . . Observers tell of a Japanese public beginning to show signs of strain over a fear of a possible war with Russia over the rights of entry at the Manchukuoan border. Neither Russia nor Japan is backing down.
Apr. 27		The Russians propose a novel idea to increase taxes—a divorce tax that would be doubled every time a person asks for a dissolution of their marriage.	According to correspondents, there are a total of 10,000 Ethiopians guarding Addis Ababa and its immediate vicinity from an advancing Italian army.		
Apr. 28					
Apr. 29	After several years of trying, China regains a seat on the League of Nations in Geneva, Switzerland. The seat it holds, for now, is considered semi-permanent until China proves itself as a compliant member of the League.		Emperor Haile Selassie, on a radio broadcast from Addis Ababa, surrounded and besieged by Italian Premier Benito Mussolini's army, calls out a final cry for help.		
Apr. 30		As part of its £300 million armament program, Britain announces that it will build 33 new warships for possible emergency defense. Of the 33 new ships, two will be 35,000-ton battleships.			Britain complains to China about the growing smuggling situation and asks it to be more active in routing the smugglers, who are interfering with legitimate trade.
May 1		Reports indicate that May Day celebrations in Austria are tempered by concern over impending *Anschluss*, or union with Germany. . . . Hermann Goering is given control of German finances. The Minister of Economics, Hjalmar Schacht, now reports to Goering.	Correspondents report that the Italian army has reached the gates of Addis Ababa, Ethiopia's capital. The military and the citizens inside prepare for a last stand.	A parade consisting of 60,000 field workers marches through Mexico City in celebration of May Day. Barbo Gonzales, minister of the interior, salutes them as they march past the city palace. . . . The U.S. Senate's recently introduced bill to give Puerto Rico its independence adds confusion to the proceedings of a controversial trial now taking place in Puerto Rican courts. If suddenly given its independence, it is unclear if Puerto Rico would it still have the legal right to try former president Pedro Albizu Campos for attempting to overthrow the U.S. government.	The new Japanese Cabinet under Premier Hirota votes for the largest budget in the country's history—much of it aimed at supplying the army and navy.

A	B	C	D	E
Includes developments that affect more than one world region, international organizations, and important meetings of world leaders.	*Includes all domestic and regional developments in Europe, including the Soviet Union.*	*Includes all domestic and regional developments in Africa and the Middle East.*	*Includes all domestic and regional developments in Latin America, the Caribbean, and Canada.*	*Includes all domestic and regional developments in Asian and Pacific nations (and colonies).*

U.S. Politics & Social Issues	U.S. Foreign Policy & Defense	Economics & Great Depression	Science, Technology & Nature	Culture, Leisure & Lifestyle	
		The Chrysler Corporation celebrates record-breaking income results for three consecutive months. The net profit of $11,453,439 for January through March 1936, is the best first quarter in the company's history, the sum surpassed only by the last quarter of 1935.			Apr. 24
San Francisco docks are in operation again after the settling of a labor dispute that sent 3,300 men on a work stoppage and cost shippers $100,000 a day. . . . An anti-flood bill is prepared for study by the U.S. Senate. The bill authorizes some $420 million to be set aside for assorted costs and damage associated with natural flooding, such as the terrible Johnstown, Pa., flood earlier this month.			The air base at Lakehurst, N.J., is bustling with expectation over the giant German zeppelin, the *Hindenburg*, scheduled to reach American shores early next month. Commander Charles E. Rosendahl says that all mooring procedures are in place for this first-of-a-kind endeavor. Tour buses for the public will bring hundreds to the docking strip to see the new marvel of flight.		Apr. 25
				European conductor Arturo Toscanini, a long-time favorite with American lovers of classical music, conducts his "farewell" symphony with the New York Philharmonic, ending an 11-year association.	Apr. 26
	Critics of Senator Tydings' bill to allow Puerto Rico complete independence ask two main questions: 1) Does the economic makeup of the island promise self-sufficiency? and 2) What does Puerto Rican independence mean to the security of the U.S. outward defenses?	The first quarter of 1936 proved productive for the Monsanto Chemical Company, with a consolidated net profit of $1,071,691, or $3.01 per share.		Bobby Jones, world-famous golfer from Atlanta, Ga., is hired on a no-cash-basis by the Works Progress Administration to advise on the building and beautification of 600 municipal golf courses across America.	Apr. 27
The House of Delegates of the Medical Society of New York condemns health advisers who serve on state and city boards and are also practicing physicians. It is the society's belief that these people cannot serve two masters equally—and sufficiently.		Following up a speech by President Roosevelt asking companies and corporations to help lighten the load of unemployment, Johns-Manville's president, Lewis H. Brown, challenges the President to show them how this can be accomplished. Before an audience of 2,000 business representatives in Washington, D.C., Brown says that it would be impossible for business to pick up the 10 million idle.			Apr. 28
		The Commonwealth and Southern Corporation announce operational results for 1935–36—a net of $9,995,649 through March 31.			Apr. 29
Federal agents arrest a Broadway clothier named Oscar Saffer, accusing him of being the "pay-off man" for top racketeers Louis "Lepke" Buchalter and Jacob "Gurrah Jake" Shapiro. Saffer is arraigned today before Supreme Court Justice Philip J. McCook.		More jobs are opening for college-educated men than those without a college degree, according to statistics. This trend has not been seen since before 1931, with current job availability being often random and infrequent.			Apr. 30
FBI agents capture Alvin Karpis, one of the top "public enemies," in New Orleans. Known as "Old Creepy," Karpis is an alleged motor bandit and kidnapper hailing from the poverty-stricken dust bowls of the southwestern United States. . . . A committee of the National League of Women Voters supports a resolution to expand the government's authority—when and only when the security of the country is at stake.	A Naval Supply Bill is passed in the House of Representatives today. If passed in the Senate, it will give the U.S. Navy $531,068,707 to go toward requisitioning itself. Most of the money will be spent on the construction of two battleships.	National income, says President Roosevelt in a Washington, D.C., speech, has risen from $35 billion in 1932 to the current $65 billion. Experts predict this year's income will be between $50 billion and $65 billion.			May 1

F	G	H	I	J
Includes elections, federal-state relations, civil rights and liberties, crime, the judiciary, education, healthcare, poverty, urban affairs, and population.	*Includes formation and debate of U.S. foreign and defense policies, veterans affairs, and defense spending. (Relations with specific foreign countries are usually found under the region concerned.)*	*Includes business, labor, agriculture, taxation, transportation, consumer affairs, monetary and fiscal policy, natural resources, pollution, and accidents.*	*Includes worldwide scientific, medical, and technological developments, natural phenomena, U.S. weather, and natural disasters.*	*Includes the arts, religion, scholarship, communications media, sports, entertainment, fashions, fads, and social life.*

	World Affairs	Europe	Africa & The Middle East	The Americas	Asia & The Pacific
May 2		The Nazi government, through the Appellate Court at Hamm in the Ruhr Valley, sentences a group of more than 100 Socialists caught handing out anti-Nazi literature. Sentences run from eight to 15 months.		The Chaco Peace pact, having been signed by both factions, Bolivia and Paraguay, begins today with the releasing of prisoners. Between the countries, almost 20,000 men start on their journeys home.	
May 3				The new Pan-American Highway, connecting Laredo, Tex., to Mexico City is almost fully in place with the completion of a bridge over the Tampaon River near Valles, Mexico. All bridges of the route are now in place, according to U.S. highway representative William Harrison Furlong.	
May 4		With the recent election of 61 party members to the Chamber of Deputies, the Conservatives of France now must face the strong Socialist presence in the government.	Italian troops, accompanied by native Askaris, enter the outskirts of Addis Ababa. Britain, which has forces nearby, promises to do what it can to get Americans and other foreign nationals home. Some gunshots and rioting are reported in Addis Ababa. . . . Addis Ababa, the capital of Ethiopia, falls to Italian troops. Few facts are known at this point, except that Haile Selassie, the country's Emperor, has taken a private airplane and escaped from the country.		
May 5		Elated mobs converge on the Piazza Venetia in Rome to cheer on the first of the returning Italian troops of the Ethiopian Campaign, now that Addis Ababa has fallen. The throng hails Premier Benito Mussolini, shouting, "Long live the emperor!"			
May 6					The Japanese decide to take a preventative approach to the uprisings in Manchukuo by Mongols and other Chinese dissidents. The Tokyo government puts army authorities Lt. Col. Itagaki and Col. Sakanishi in charge of increasing armament in that section of China.
May 7		Britain steps forward today with yet another proposal for peace, this time a four-point plan regulating international arms with a built-in check-and-balance system for assuredness. It hopes that all countries will take the time and interest to study it for its value.	Premier Mussolini allows all of Ethiopia's foreign ministers and ambassadors to retain their stations for now. Mussolini's representative, Marshal Pietro Badoglio, pens a release informing them that the status is temporary until a more thorough diagnosis of the political situation is made. . . . Britain intercepts information regarding Mussolini's plan for Ethiopia, now that he has won the war against it. He plans to release all slaves, exile certain settlers, and base Ethiopia's new government on Britain's possession of India.		
May 8	France signs a yearlong trade treaty with the United States, which promises to be lucrative to both parties. Details are forthcoming, but the French and the Americans both express confidence in the arrangement.		A refugee from his conquered kingdom, Haile Selassie appears in Haifa, Palestine, disembarking the British cruiser, Enterprise.		

A	B	C	D	E
Includes developments that affect more than one world region, international organizations, and important meetings of world leaders.	Includes all domestic and regional developments in Europe, including the Soviet Union.	Includes all domestic and regional developments in Africa and the Middle East.	Includes all domestic and regional developments in Latin America, the Caribbean, and Canada.	Includes all domestic and regional developments in Asian and Pacific nations (and colonies).

U.S. Politics & Social Issues	U.S. Foreign Policy & Defense	Economics & Great Depression	Science, Technology & Nature	Culture, Leisure & Lifestyle	
The context of President Roosevelt's new $1.5 billion relief bill is honed down to include only those projects by a resumed Works Progress Administration (WPA). Public Works Administration and Resettlement programs are not included.		Calling Texas "the economic frontier" because of its vast resources, its governor, James V. Allred, urges bankers of the nation to invest in his state where oil, gas, and other natural commodities are "only scratched."		Some 20,000 spectators in Warrenton, Va., see Ghost Dancer win the four-mile Virginia Gold Cup. Ridden by jockey Noel Laing, the horse took the course in seven minutes and 34 seconds.	May 2
		Improved earnings for the first quarter of 1936 greet the American Commercial Alcohol Corporation; earnings were $310,149, compared to $284,125 for the same quarter last year.	Alberta, Canada, sends 20 native buffalo via railroad and steamship to distant Berlin, Germany, which will conduct experiments to try to save the European genus of buffalo. Currently, Canadian buffalo can be seen represented in zoos as far away as Australia. . . . Visitors pour in daily to Colorado to see the newly created man-made Lake Mead, the largest of its kind in the world. It was made as part of the Boulder Dam Construction Project, a conservation and energy project.	The U.S. government is spending $2 million on a beautification project for the nation's capital, all renovations to be completed by spring. A government release promises Americans that groomed lawns, trees, and statues will take the place of dirt roads and broken highways.	May 3
The Southern Women's National Democratic Organization asks citizens of the south for discarded jewelry and trinkets, as well as old gold, to fill a war chest for President Roosevelt's campaign.		The industry magazine *Steel* praises the iron and steel industry for outlasting "unsettling factors of an approaching campaign, impending tax legislation and (a) stock market break." . . . Business representatives participating in the review of President Roosevelt's latest revenue bill say it will force bankruptcies and destroy credit.			May 4
The American Federation of Labor is staunchly behind President Roosevelt, its president, William Green, announces. "We cannot afford to change leadership," he says, at the same time promoting a return of the National Recovery Act. . . . A Senate committee devoted to ensuring the utilization of the country's natural resources urges a corporate power agency, not unlike the Tennessee Valley Authority, to generate water power in the Bonneville-Grand Coulee area on the Columbia River in the west.		The Coca-Cola Company, for the first quarter of 1936, nets $2,660,067, up some $500,000 from a year ago. Price per share is 65 cents. . . . Some 66–80 percent of America's economic recovery is due to "stimulating spending of the federal government," say German economists Dr. Gerard Colm and Dr. Fritz Lewhann, both recently exiled from their homeland.		A mild controversy arises when Civil War generals Robert E. Lee and Thomas "Stonewall" Jackson, two Confederates, join the list of great American military men on a series of stamps issued by the U.S. government.	May 5
Postmaster General James Farley reminds his audience in Hartford, Conn., that many of President Roosevelt's critics are hypocrites, for they once upheld "the policies they denounce now." He speaks at a dinner to raise support for farm legislation.				Promoting its product, the Cigar Progress Board kicks off a new campaign aimed at building awareness of cigar smoking across the United States; it hopes for a 25 percent increase in cigar use.	May 6
The Prohibition Party, whose aim is to restore "dryness" to the country through the banning of alcohol, names Dr. D. Leigh Colvin as its presidential candidate and war hero Alvin C. York as its vice presidential entry. York was never consulted. . . . Only by "its use and not abuse" can radio in America remain unrestricted, assert NBC president Lenox R. Lohr and vice chairman M.H. Aylesworth in a joint statement. Together, they state that radio is a privilege that some people in dictatorial countries cannot enjoy.		According to a report from the Roosevelt administration, there are four states completely debtless: Florida, Ohio, Wisconsin, and Nebraska. The latter possesses a surplus of $21,123,935. . . . After a week of hearings by business concerns—all of whom attack the President's new tax bill—the Senate Finance Committee, which once wholly supported it, is beginning to waver. One of the remaining defenders of the bill is Secretary of the Treasury Henry Morgenthau, who claims it is getting bad publicity.		Prominent concert pianist Ignace Paderewski signs with a Hollywood studio to appear in a motion picture to be shot in London.	May 7
The Commonweal, a Catholic political magazine, blames today's world unrest not on economic or political conditions, but on an "unsettlement of culture"—old cultures being shaken by new ideas, such as Nazism.	The Senate approves the Naval Supply Bill unanimously after slight cuts to its original monetary sum. It passes as an appropriation of $529,125,806, instead of $531,068,707.	Commercial Solvents Corporation earns $617,778 for the first three months of this year, indicating an increase in business from last year at this time when it netted $564,860. . . . Following the trend of the economy, the Federal Reserve System's governing board chief, Marriner S. Eccles, predicts a balanced budget. Revenues are reassuring, he tells a roomful of gathered economists.			May 8

F	G	H	I	J
Includes elections, federal-state relations, civil rights and liberties, crime, the judiciary, education, healthcare, poverty, urban affairs, and population.	Includes formation and debate of U.S. foreign and defense policies, veterans affairs, and defense spending. (Relations with specific foreign countries are usually found under the region concerned.)	Includes business, labor, agriculture, taxation, transportation, consumer affairs, monetary and fiscal policy, natural resources, pollution, and accidents.	Includes worldwide scientific, medical, and technological developments, natural phenomena, U.S. weather, and natural disasters.	Includes the arts, religion, scholarship, communications media, sports, entertainment, fashions, fads, and social life.

	World Affairs	Europe	Africa & The Middle East	The Americas	Asia & The Pacific
May 9		Spain elects Manuel Alzana its president. Alzana, who served four times as the premier of the Spanish Republic, succeeds the deposed Niceto Alcala Zamora. The country, however, continues in an insecure direction, radicals and conservatives both talking of war.		Both workers' representatives and the owners of the Mexican railroads refuse to give in at the bargaining table, despite a rail strike deadline nearing for May 17. Mexico's President Lázaro Cárdenas is expected to take action soon if an agreement is not reached.	In response to last month's military insurrection, Japanese Labor Representative Hishashi writes a pamphlet, *The Principles of National Defense*, which simply yet poignantly underscores "good living"—not the army—as the basis of safe living in Japan.
May 10				Reciprocity must extend beyond treaties, says James S. Carson, former chairman of the Council on Inter-American Relations and one of the architects of Foreign Trade Week in America. Reciprocity must extend deep into the spirit of the relationship between the United States and its "good neighbors" in Latin America, with whom the United States wishes to carry on a successful shipping venture.	Chinese warplanes stage a surprise bombing raid on a Communist community of 7,000 people in the Shansi province. Early reports describe a scene of panic and fire, leaving hundreds dead.
May 11	In spite of Italy's protests, the League of Nations gives a seat to Ethiopia. The Italian representative walks out.	Two young women from Fishback, Bavaria, who refused to join the Nazi's League of German Girls, are sentenced to eight-month prison terms. They are Anna Schreiber, 22 years old, and Cecilie Sternberger, 23. . . . The number of registered jobless people in Germany drops to 1,763,000, but it is a drop of 174,000 from last year, according to the German Labor Office.			
May 12		The German Foreign Minister, Dr. Fritz Reinhardt, tells 1,200 tax officials meeting in Eisenbach that the budget remains unbalanced and national debt continues to deepen.			Japan's Admiral Osami Nagano pushes Japan to strengthen its army while the United States, despite its call for neutrality, builds up its sea power.
May 13	Italy annexes Ethiopia, proclaiming Victor Emmanuel the Emperor over the deposed Haile Selassie. Britain, angry over the outcome but willing to go along with the League of Nations, accepts the situation "under reserve," according to Prime Minister Stanley Baldwin.				
May 14					
May 15		Count Lutz Schwerin von Krosigk, Germany's finance minister, admits to the World Economic Society in Berlin that Germany's quest for colonies is based on its need to recover its dwindling raw materials and enhance its foreign trade situation.		Canada is reworking its nationwide radio programming and, in doing so, contemplates whether it will be controlled by the government or an independent commission (comparable to America's FCC). It also weighs whether or not it will allow advertisers airtime as the United States does or will run without advertisements, as in Britain.	
May 16		In Prague, Czechoslovakia, one of the most notably musical cities in the world and where the country has established the International Society for Musical Education, conductors and educators meet for the first time to discuss music and its place in the world. . . . The Fiat Motor Company of Italy produces a "baby auto" that uses the same amount of gas as a motorcycle.			

A	B	C	D	E
Includes developments that affect more than one world region, international organizations, and important meetings of world leaders.	Includes all domestic and regional developments in Europe, including the Soviet Union.	Includes all domestic and regional developments in Africa and the Middle East.	Includes all domestic and regional developments in Latin America, the Caribbean, and Canada.	Includes all domestic and regional developments in Asian and Pacific nations (and colonies).

U.S. Politics & Social Issues	U.S. Foreign Policy & Defense	Economics & Great Depression	Science, Technology & Nature	Culture, Leisure & Lifestyle	
President William L. Ransom of the American Bar Association announces reorganization. The governing committee has put forth a new constitution mandating changes over various periods of time.		Secretary of the Interior Harold L. Ickes announces he must decrease the 10,000-man administrative staff of the Public Works Administration by 25 percent across the board. He asks directors to submit a list of one-quarter of their staff whose jobs might be terminated.	This year's recipient of the Daniel Guggenheim Medal goes to George William Lewis, one of the directors of the National Advisory Committee for Aeronautics. He wins for "outstanding success in the direction of aeronautical research and for the development of equipment and methods."		May 9
			A team of *National Geographic* writers and photographers, along with members of the National Bureau of Standards, have brought with them to Siberia a huge camera with an astrographic lens customized to take photographs of the sun's corona during a rare total eclipse June 19.		May 10
A strike is foreseen as the United Textile Workers of America—representing 100,000 workers across the United States—announce strike mobilization rules. To date, the workers are begrudged a 20-percent wage increase and a revised working schedule.		Asking for a cease-fire in "unjustifiable political friction," Secretary of Commerce Roper seeks businesses' acceptance of the government's New Deal program on the basis that it is the administration's aim to "assure the perpetuity of our American system."		Managing members of the American Library Association convening in Richmond, Va., ask the government to consider funds allowing them to expand, bringing library services to an estimated 45 million people currently without access.	May 11
The Young Women's Christian Association (Y.M.C.A.) will now include sex education in its agenda, Colorado conference attendees learn. It will be added to courses teaching young ladies to avoid marital problems.					May 12
First Lady Eleanor Roosevelt speaks to the nation on the radio from a house that stands where slums used to be, urging listeners to support better housing programs in America. She particularly addresses all mothers who have "an interest in her own children and in the future of our country." . . . Some Republicans hint that Postmaster General James Farley may have been responsible for the mutilation of thousands of Republican campaign ads sent to the public through U.S. mail.		Profits of $2,255,139 were realized by the Ohio Oil Company during the first quarter ending March 31. This is a dramatic increase from the first quarter of 1935, which netted $622,150.			May 13
In President Roosevelt's first campaign speech after formally accepting the Democratic nomination, he calls for shorter working hours for labor. In doing so, he incites protests from Republicans who accuse him of ignoring earlier Supreme Court rules.		The U.S. Foil Company, parent company of Reynolds Metal and the Reynolds Company, announce sthat its year-end 1935 assets were equal to $23.32 per share on the common market.			May 14
Presidential candidate William Borah of Idaho refuses to go on the air at the last minute in Newark, N.J., when he discovers the station has given him only one-half hour. . . . Former secretary of the treasury Ogden Mills calls President Roosevelt's economic direction unsound. The President's economic policy is the root problem of his administration, says Mills, which he tries to keep afloat with a series of red-tape relief programs.				A gang of people in New York City—two women and four men—who were apprehended tending an arsenal of weapons for gangsters, each receive a seven-year prison term. Some of the confiscated arms were proven ballistically to have been used in gangland murders.	May 15
A business advisory council to the U.S. Commerce Department asks for a $6 million appropriation to promote an air safety campaign for travel in the United States and Alaska. Promotion would include a number of safety aids for crew and passengers.	President Roosevelt signs an authorization allowing the United States to participate in the upcoming Pan-American Peace Conference in Buenos Aires. The date of the conference is forthcoming, pending some technical problems.			Frank Marshall, who has held the title of U.S. chess champion since 1909, stumbles at the national tournament, losing to Polish immigrant Samuel Reshevsky. The latter has been a member of Marshall's personal chess club for 15 years.	May 16

F	G	H	I	J
Includes elections, federal-state relations, civil rights and liberties, crime, the judiciary, education, healthcare, poverty, urban affairs, and population.	Includes formation and debate of U.S. foreign and defense policies, veterans affairs, and defense spending. (Relations with specific foreign countries are usually found under the region concerned.)	Includes business, labor, agriculture, taxation, transportation, consumer affairs, monetary and fiscal policy, natural resources, pollution, and accidents.	Includes worldwide scientific, medical, and technological developments, natural phenomena, U.S. weather, and natural disasters.	Includes the arts, religion, scholarship, communications media, sports, entertainment, fashions, fads, and social life.

	World Affairs	Europe	Africa & The Middle East	The Americas	Asia & The Pacific
May 17		Once a major destination on the tourist trade, France kicks off a campaign to resurrect a former global interest in its art, history, culture, and beauty—all those aspects that until recently lured more vacationers to its shores than to any other country.	Gold proves to be South Africa's boom. The financial year for the Union of South Africa began with a surplus of $3,750,000 and ended with a surplus of $14,820,000, generating its finance department to term 1935 "a wave of prosperity upon which the country is still riding." Customs rates are down and social outlays increase. . . . Arab-Jewish upheavals rock the city of Jerusalem. Sir Arthur Grenfell Wauchope, British high commander, issues a curfew after three Jews are slain in a movie theater.	A 5 p.m. strike deadline is set if Mexico's rail workers and the Mexican National Railway Company do not reach an agreement. . . . A bloodless coup takes place in La Paz today by the Bolivian military, which kicks out President Jose Luis Tejada Sorzano. The ousted government blames the Socialist Party as the real reason for the agitation.	The Philippine Commonwealth, having been given its own system of government by the United States, celebrates its first six months of existence, but reports that problems have come with the transition. Its budget is still unstable and the Japanese are pressuring it for land in which to settle before the natives themselves have obtained a firm grasp of the reality of its real estate.
May 18		Until the Olympic Games are over in Berlin, the publishers of Germany's anti-Semitic publication *Judenkenner* (*Observer of Jews*) say it will not be printed. The magazine is a spiteful chastisement against the Jew, "wherever he may be found."		Since the Tydings bill hit the Senate, making the independence of Puerto Rico a possibility, manufacturers, realtors, and traders come to a standstill, afraid to invest in a country that, with a new government, could lose its stability. . . . Some 50,000 Mexican railway workers walk off their jobs, no agreement having been met with the national rail system that, until the strike ends, is virtually crippled.	
May 19	Nearly 500 political prisoners in Ethiopia are given their freedom by Italian Premier Benito Mussolini after his country begins its official takeover of the country. The exiles will be allowed to return home. At the same time, Mussolini calls for a buildup of his army in Ethiopia, calling all fascists to enroll.			In overture to the Pan-American Peace Conference, scheduled for the near future, the governing board of the Pan-American Union proposes the formation of an ongoing committee to govern the dealings between North and South America. The committee would act as a sort of Junior League of Nations. . . . A strike handicapping Mexico's entire railway system ends today as 50,000 men return to work after a one-day walkout. The government's threat to abolish their contracts altogether proved to be too much of a threat for the thousands of poor who need their jobs to maintain a living.	
May 20		The Ministry of Finance in Romania faces a criminal scandal after it is discovered that the government has been paying its employees with counterfeit money, says the leading newspaper, the *Zorile*. Evidently, many bags of counterfeit 100-lei currency made their way into circulation. . . . Even though Italy's Finance Minister, Count Paolo Thaon di Revel refuses to name the cost of the Italo-Ethiopian war, budget experts appraise its cost at upwards of $1 million.		Havana, Cuba, prepares for the inauguration of its first president under constitutional rule, Miguel Mariano Gomez.	
May 21	Reporting from Geneva, Switzerland, International Labor Office director Harold B. Butler expresses dismay at a possible coming world war, which would, he says, cause a total blight on global trade. He adds that a war would destroy the hopes and dreams of the coming generation.			Twenty thousand citizens riot against an unpopular Venezuelan government; it's the second—and more violent—demonstration in a week with gunfire reported. Several are injured.	
May 22	International Business Machines president Thomas Watson expects a reconfiguration of world trading patterns. Nations are in search of economic justice, he claims, and that quest shall lead the globe into revising its financial relationships.	A well-respected member of the British parliament, Colonial Secretary J.H. Thomas, resigns in scandal, suspected of manipulating a "leak" of budget secrets. He denies any involvement, but quits to minimize political distress to his peers.			

A	B	C	D	E
Includes developments that affect more than one world region, international organizations, and important meetings of world leaders.	Includes all domestic and regional developments in Europe, including the Soviet Union.	Includes all domestic and regional developments in Africa and the Middle East.	Includes all domestic and regional developments in Latin America, the Caribbean, and Canada.	Includes all domestic and regional developments in Asian and Pacific nations (and colonies).

U.S. Politics & Social Issues	U.S. Foreign Policy & Defense	Economics & Great Depression	Science, Technology & Nature	Culture, Leisure & Lifestyle	
The Catholic Hospital Association of the United States announces its upcoming conference, to take place in Baltimore June 15–19. It will convene some 600 nuns from various Orders and from more than 750 hospitals across the United States and Canada who are part of the ongoing health-medical system in the United States. . . . To protect family morals, three former directors of the Citizens Family Welfare Committee introduce a fundraiser aimed at accruing $1.5 million to go toward literature and special home-aid educational programs.		Shippers in the nation strongly protest a request by Class 1 (major) railroads to the Interstate Commerce Commission for renewal of emergency freight surcharges that had been scheduled to end July 1. Because the railroads gained an additional $104.5 million last year due to the surcharges, nonrail shippers cried foul, saying they are averse to the ethics of competition.		The State of California announces that it is severely cracking down on speed demons and other law-breaking motorists, beginning immediately. It is a part of the state's determination to bring safety back to California highways.	May 17
		Eugene P. Thomas, president of the National Foreign Trade Council, foresees a new countrywide prosperity brought about by a boost in world trade. His speech is part of the nation's observance of Foreign Commerce Week.			May 18
Taking aim at the spoils system in politics, the National Civil Service Reform League proposes an anti-spoils "plank" for both the Democratic and Republican campaigns. Copies of the proposal are sent to both national chairmen. . . . A nation headed toward economic self-containment is leaving itself open for socialism to creep in, warns Henry F. Grady of the State Department at Export-Import Day in New York. He speaks of America's lax attitude toward a dissident uprising.		Accountants say that the new Robinson-Patman bill, which is meant to lower merchant distribution prices, is not the fair tool that merchants expected. Small distributors, under its guidelines, will not be able to buy goods at as low a price as the larger distributors. . . . Five hundred southern bankers meeting in Memphis, Tenn., resolve that the "man behind the plow," the farmer, is the entity who, with proper backing, can pull the south away from economic depression.		Accidents and deaths having greatly decreased in the rail lines of America, the National Safety Council's president, C.D. Watson, praises the lines' safety efforts. . . . President Roosevelt proclaims May 22 as Maritime Day, honoring modern sea power beginning with the steamship Savannah in 1819.	May 19
The National Association of Hosiery Manufacturers fails in its attempt to establish a voluntary but unanimous governance of work hours and shifts. Only 66 percent of workers vote for it.		The American Safety Razor Corporation and subsidiaries earned $291,538 in the first quarter of 1936, the equivalent of $1.67 per share. . . . Comparing high and low trends, Harry Tipper, the executive vice president of the Foreign Trade Association, concludes that employment is high when import value is up and employment always sinks when purchases of American goods decline.	A new wind machine testing the effect of airplanes at the air velocity of 500 miles per hour opens today at Langley Field military base in Virginia. Some 300 luminaries in the field of aeronautics are invited to view the first demonstrations.		May 20
Missouri Senator Dewey Short criticizes Postmaster General James Farley for failing his responsibilities, saying that being Postmaster of the United States and serving as the Democratic chairman simultaneously is doing injustice to both positions.			Efforts are under way to ban the drug desomorphine, which the health industry calls even more dangerous than morphine or opium. Leading the movement is Stephen J. Fuller of the U.S. State Department.		May 21
The American Association for Adult Education regards the U.S. newspaper as equal to the best newscasting agency in terms of teaching the American adult the ways of government and the crux of social issues. The Association considers the radio to still be in developmental stages. . . . Some 5,500 workers at the Portsmouth Steel Works in Portsmouth, Ohio, leave their shift in demand for 50 percent higher wages and representation by the Amalgamated Association of Iron, Steel, and Tin Workers.		Yale University professor of economics Dr. Irving Fisher explains that recovery would be hastened if the administration worked more closely with business in getting people on employment instead of wasting time with relief bills.			May 22

F	G	H	I	J
Includes elections, federal-state relations, civil rights and liberties, crime, the judiciary, education, healthcare, poverty, urban affairs, and population.	Includes formation and debate of U.S. foreign and defense policies, veterans affairs, and defense spending. (Relations with specific foreign countries are usually found under the region concerned.)	Includes business, labor, agriculture, taxation, transportation, consumer affairs, monetary and fiscal policy, natural resources, pollution, and accidents.	Includes worldwide scientific, medical, and technological developments, natural phenomena, U.S. weather, and natural disasters.	Includes the arts, religion, scholarship, communications media, sports, entertainment, fashions, fads, and social life.

	World Affairs	Europe	Africa & The Middle East	The Americas	Asia & The Pacific
May 23			Bloody rioting continues in Palestine. In the latest series of outbursts over the past several days, Arab mobs turn their wrath on edifices belonging to the British authorities, breaking windows and starting fires. One such attack in Tulkarem is repulsed only after British soldiers are forced to fire directly into an attacking throng.	In the midst of an ongoing church-state rift between Mexico and the Roman Catholic Church, the Catholics' beloved Archbishop Pascual Diaz dies. His funeral today finds 150,000 mourners lining the hills around Tepeyac, the destined burial place, and another 40,000 following the coffin from the funeral mass to the cemetery.	
May 24		Leftists in Barcelona, Spain, are becoming more vocal than usual, say local newspapers. Over the last couple of days, the movement threatens strikes of hotels, restaurants, and cafes—a strike that would cripple the tourist trade— if certain members of the government are not removed from office.		Brazil signs a trading agreement with Germany allowing each country to trade $46 million worth of goods manufactured in both nations, according to the Federal Council on Foreign Commerce. This guarantees that Germany will get South American cotton that it has long been pursuing.	The political officials of the National People's Republic in Shanghai, China, in trying to revise their simple election rules for delegates to their congress, admit they have created a complex, cumbersome set of rules not understood by the general public.
May 25					
May 26					Japan passes an anti-sedition law to stop the dissemination of controversial literature bent on causing unrest for the government among the armed forces.
May 27		There will be no new world war, states Gen. George Pouderoux, a French division commander and war hero. Neither Germany nor France wish to attack each other nor are politicians across the world ready to sacrifice all for a global conflict. . . . A friar of the Order of St. Francis, Father Bernard Steinhoff, loses all powers of rites for the next eight years while a prisoner of Germany. His charge is "immorality," but critics say it means he spoke up against the Nazis.		Roman Catholics in Mexico, all members of the state of Veracruz, appeal to Minister of the Interior Silvano Barba to reopen 13 Catholic churches closed in the state by despotic powers. Meanwhile, a boycott of goods takes place in Chihuahua until officials rethink their antagonistic attitude toward the Church.	
May 28	A pair of British officers are detained in Ethiopia by the occupying forces of Italy for unspecified reasons. It is the latest in a series of goadings from the Italian fascists, who seemingly want to prod Britain into war, say European observers.			Nicaragua's National Guard under Gen. Anastasio Somoza overthrows the government and, in Managua, have requisitioned governmental buildings as their headquarters.	An angry Chinese government refuses to listen to Japan, which tries to explain the reason it is deploying thousands of additional troops into northern China. Thousands of college students in Tientsin rebel against the enlarged garrison there, calling Japan's excuses lies and demanding that the "invader" leave their country. During a demonstration, one Japanese soldier is killed.
May 29		Adolf Hitler views more than 100 battleships, cruisers, speedboats, and submarines as they take part in a mock battle off Kiel, Germany. The maneuvers, the first such spectacle since the rebuilding of the new Nazi navy, seems to delight the leader, according to observers.			Tokyo complains of bad press out of Britain and the United States. Reports of this alleged defamation come from the Japanese news agency, Domei, which relates "sinister" lies appearing in both United Kingdom and American news gazettes. Both countries deny taking part in any effort "deliberately misrepresenting the facts" about Japan.

A	B	C	D	E
Includes developments that affect more than one world region, international organizations, and important meetings of world leaders.	Includes all domestic and regional developments in Europe, including the Soviet Union.	Includes all domestic and regional developments in Africa and the Middle East.	Includes all domestic and regional developments in Latin America, the Caribbean, and Canada.	Includes all domestic and regional developments in Asian and Pacific nations (and colonies).

U.S. Politics & Social Issues	U.S. Foreign Policy & Defense	Economics & Great Depression	Science, Technology & Nature	Culture, Leisure & Lifestyle	
Walter Clemens Martin of New York pleads guilty in court to grand larceny charges in the fixing of loans while posing as a person of "influence" within the ranks of the Public Works Administration. Sentencing is forthcoming.		The world is at a "crossroad" between free competition and ultimate regulation, and will choose one over the other soon, says General Motors' president, Alfred P. Sloan, Jr. . . . George L. Berry, industrial coordinator for President Roosevelt, forms a committee to inventory the nation's unemployed, saying it is the first step to finding the jobless positions in private industry.		The American Bar Association starts a campaign to change the often celluloid portrayals of lawyers in film. . . . While inspecting the murder of a 32-year-old WPA worker in Detroit, police uncover the existence of an organization calling itself the Black Legion, a Ku Klux Klan-like terrorist organization committing random crimes of hate.	May 23
A pamphlet entitled, *The Married Woman and Her Job*, issued by the National League of Women Voters and distributed throughout the nation, warns brides and prospective brides of a possible jeopardy to their working positions. They are on the firing line, literally, the pamphlet discloses. . . . Speaking before the Young Republican Organization, Republican chairman Henry P. Fletcher describes adherents of the Roosevelt administration as "termites," eating away at the foundation of American institutions.		The Automobile Manufacturers Association asks that a policy approving the nation's reciprocal trade agreement be added to both political parties' platforms.	Mayan artifacts found in North Dakota—including what is assumed to be an astronomical observatory—prove that the Mayans of Mexico extended well into the Northern Great Plains of North America. These discoveries change previous archaeological assumptions.		May 24
The Advertising Federation of America celebrates the 25th anniversary of the Truth-in-Advertising movement, which has eradicated many fraudulent examples of merchant advertising. The celebration takes place over a special program on NBC Radio tonight. . . . Twelve members of the Black Legion in Detroit are held for their alleged part in the murder of a young WPA worker. The Legion is a bigotry-driven hooded terrorist organization operating in Michigan.	Inspired by the plight of the European Jew trying to find a home in Palestine, U.S. President Franklin Roosevelt praises their courage, but at the same time decries the injustices that lead to mistreatment of minorities in Germany and elsewhere. He speaks to 1,000 members of the United Jewish Appeal in Washington, D.C.	One golden key to bringing some of America's jobless back into the work world is by modernizing the nation's industrial plants, opines General Motors' president, Alfred P. Sloan, Jr., speaking in San Francisco. Better jobs can be provided than by the division of the workload being offered by relief programs. . . . Joseph Curran, chairman of striking seamen of New York, tells the International Seamen's Union that he is "willing to go halfway" to bring the strike to a finale. He promises to disempower the strike if union officials agree to a referendum.		Comedian W.C. Fields is signed to appear in a film version of Julian Street's popular novel, *Need to Change*.	May 25
		President Roosevelt tells Democrats of the Senate Finance Committee that their rebudgeting of the much-debated new tax program is insufficient for creating new revenue, which is the essential purpose of the bill.			May 26
The New Jersey State Police Organization in Trenton demonstrates how "talking" motion pictures can help identify runaway criminals and other law dodgers. Their audience is 400 lawmen from across the United States, Canada, and England.		Over the last 21 weeks, small businesses have remained steadier than in years, experiencing fewer closings, according to Dun & Bradstreet. Retail and commercial services are reportedly the strongest. . . . A nationwide survey conducted by George A. Sloan, chairman of the Consumer Goods Industry Committee, indicates that employment levels are nearing those of 1929, before the start of the Depression. Work hours and wages are better than ever, the survey shows.		The newest luxury liner and technological dream ship, Britain's *Queen Mary*, leaves Southampton on her maiden voyage to New York City. The ship is named for England's beloved Queen Mary, who celebrates her 69th birthday with the sailing of her namesake ship.	May 27
In a New York state conference, the Methodist Episcopal Church resolves that all sales of liquor for profit should be banned in the United States.		The Electric Power and Light Corporation of New York earned $3,164,214 in one year, overcoming a deficit in the previous period. Shares are $4.11.			May 28
Members of the steel manufacturers' organizations in the United States band together to voice their dissatisfaction with the Roosevelt administration's bureaucratic approach to the steel industry; they demand a curb on "political control and ruinous taxes."		According to Socony-Vacuum Oil Company's president, J.A. Brown, the company is ahead $7 million in 1936, compared to the same period last year. Total for 1935 was $22,525,892.			May 29

F
Includes elections, federal-state relations, civil rights and liberties, crime, the judiciary, education, healthcare, poverty, urban affairs, and population.

G
Includes formation and debate of U.S. foreign and defense policies, veterans affairs, and defense spending. (Relations with specific foreign countries are usually found under the region concerned.)

H
Includes business, labor, agriculture, taxation, transportation, consumer affairs, monetary and fiscal policy, natural resources, pollution, and accidents.

I
Includes worldwide scientific, medical, and technological developments, natural phenomena, U.S. weather, and natural disasters.

J
Includes the arts, religion, scholarship, communications media, sports, entertainment, fashions, fads, and social life.

	World Affairs	Europe	Africa & The Middle East	The Americas	Asia & The Pacific
May 30				Warning atheists, pagans, Communists, and any other serious force threatening Europe to stay away, Canada's Prime Minister Mackenzie King says they will not be given a foothold in Canada to undermine all that is sacred about the Commonwealth.	
May 31		Poland's Undersecretary of Commerce and Industry, Franciszek Dolezal, arrives in America to discuss the trade of cotton with the United States. He predicts a healthy economic relationship between the two nations.			
Jun. 1		Fed up with subservience and living in fear, a cabal of private trade union representatives have determined to oust dictator Adolf Hitler from Germany, according to British reporter J.C. Little, speaking to the Amalgamated Engineers in London.		President Sacasa of Nicaragua holes up in his palace as rebel National Guards under Gen. Anastasio Somoza besiege the royal grounds in Leon. Loyal troops and citizens fight to save their president, but they are outgunned.	
Jun. 2	Germany, noting America's success with its joint trading programs with other nations, seeks a like trading agreement with the United States.	Premier Benito Mussolini, his daughter Countess Ciano, and more than 450 other emissaries, envoys, and those from the ranks of the privileged from Italy arrive in Berlin, guests of Adolf Hitler. Hitler hopes to demonstrate friendship with Mussolini.		The Grand Presidential Palace in Leon, Nicaragua, falls to Gen. Somoza and his National Guards. President Sacasa is taken into custody by the rebels, but not harmed.	
Jun. 3		In Warsaw, 119 followers of Poland's outlawed Nationalist Socialist (Nazi) Workers' Movement go on trial for conspiring to divide Poland and give the country's Upper Silesia province to Germany. . . . Socialist Leon Blum replaces the resigning Premier Sarraut in a government shift that is meant to revitalize France's ailing economy. The country is in disarray, thousands of citizens suffering shortages of food, water, and gas.	In London, sympathizers cheer exiled Ethiopian Emperor Haile Selassie as he disembarks from a train in Waterloo Station, bound for a private apartment in the West End, loaned to him by a private supporter, the wealthy Oriental merchant, Sir Elly Kadoorie.	Managua turns out in force to applaud conquering rebel Gen. Anastasio Somoza, who returns to Managua today with his triumphant force of 2,500 National Guards. Although he promises to divulge his plans for Nicaragua, now in his control, he so far remains silent.	From Shanghai comes the news that the government of Canton, in south China, is on the verge of declaring war against Japan, whose forces have invaded the north. While no action is yet taken, the war planning seems beyond the point of return.
Jun. 4		As guest of the Jewish Congress, exiled German statesman and author Georg Bernhardt pleads the cause of the German Jew, tossed from his country or made into a servant by Nazi terrorism. Seeing no easing of Hitler's policies, Bernhardt—who once managed the prosperous Ullstein Press in Germany—predicts a world war.		Applying U.S. neutrality policy, Secretary of State Cordell Hull issues a statement informing other Latin American countries that the United States does not plan to interfere in the political transformations that are taking place in Nicaragua.	
Jun. 5		According to journalists in Germany, the last remaining enemies of Nazism in the country are the Catholic and Protestant churches. For now, however, to give Olympic visitors a serene picture of a "happy" Germany, Hitler leaves the Christian churches alone. . . . Realizing that the Nazi regime in Germany seeks unification with Austria, and hoping to remain in power, Chancellor Schuschnigg reportedly befriends the National Socialists.		As citizens of Panama go to the polls today to elect a new president and a National Assembly, current President Harmodio Arias begs for order. The campaign had been bitterly fought, sometimes violently, between Arias of the Doctrinary Liberal Party and Juan Barreati of the National Liberal Party.	

A	B	C	D	E
Includes developments that affect more than one world region, international organizations, and important meetings of world leaders.	*Includes all domestic and regional developments in Europe, including the Soviet Union.*	*Includes all domestic and regional developments in Africa and the Middle East.*	*Includes all domestic and regional developments in Latin America, the Caribbean, and Canada.*	*Includes all domestic and regional developments in Asian and Pacific nations (and colonies).*

U.S. Politics & Social Issues	U.S. Foreign Policy & Defense	Economics & Great Depression	Science, Technology & Nature	Culture, Leisure & Lifestyle	
		Movie industry giant, Paramount Pictures, Inc., drew a first quarter net of $718,921, with some dividends yet to be credited.			May 30
	Twenty-two members of the Grand Army of the Republic—veterans of the American Civil War—ride in New York City's Memorial Day Parade, accompanied by more than 20,000 soldiers and veterans of America's subsequent wars, including the Cuban Uprising of 1898 and World War I. Of the G.A.R. vets, half of them are in their 90s.	Congress passes the Norris-Rayburn Rural Electrification Act, which will bring cheap electrical power to remote farms. A permanent bureau regulating this project out of Pennsylvania has as its head Morris L. Cook of Philadelphia.	Sigismund Levanevsky, a Russian aviator, announces plans to fly from Moscow to San Francisco, linking America to Europe via the Arctic. He hopes to make the flight this summer.		May 31
At their convention, Republicans debate the option of nominating a rogue Democrat for vice president in an effort to capture the independent vote. One name they consider is Lewis W. Douglas, former budget director under Roosevelt. . . . The American Federation of Labor is aghast after the Supreme Court today voids the Minimum Wage Law for Women and Children.	Editors nationwide, members of the American Newspaper Guild, call as a unit for an amendment to the Constitution to protect the rights of the working man. Federal courts, they say, have seized "dictatorial powers over state and federal government" to "threaten newspaper workers and labor."	The Senate passes the latest relief bill—the Deficiency Appropriation Bill—by 62 votes to 14. It allows $1.4 billion for work relief and $300 million for grants and loans on public works to take effect during this fiscal year.		The eight-woman U.S. team of golfers who soundly beat the British to win the Curtis Cup return to the United States on the liner, Queen Mary. A congregation of celebrants and reporters meets them at the wharf. . . . J.M. Orr, general manager of the Equitable Auto Company of Pittsburgh, tells the Society of Automotive Engineers in Pittsburgh that the design of automobiles leaves "much to be desired" in terms of safety. He outlines a six-point driving-safety plan.	Jun. 1
President Roosevelt promises Iowan senators to "earnestly consider" a plank suggested for the convention on a proposal for farm improvement in Iowa and other midwestern states. . . . Commenting on the Supreme Court's voiding of the Minimum Wage Law for Women and Children and other such programs—such as the NRA—an angry President Roosevelt says the Supreme Court is creating a "no-man's land" where neither states nor the federal government have a right to legislate.		The Piano Manufacturers Association celebrates as new financial figures estimate that piano sales have risen 300 percent since 1933, the middle of the Depression. The association credits radio for much of the sales, helping to keep the public's interest in music high.			Jun. 2
Arrested with a dozen others for the murder of a young Detroit man, a member of the infamous Black Legion named Dayton Dean startles the court—and his 12 accomplices—by confessing to the murder. He explains how he and several others shot the man multiple times. The Legion is a vigilante group whose targets are the general public.		General Motors in 1935 raised the salaries of many of its upper staff, a company report states. Some 185 employees already earning $20,000 or more received more wage boosts than they did in 1934. In all, their wages rose $7,031,983 in 1935 as compared to $3,170,215 the previous year.			Jun. 3
Senator William Borah of Idaho, one of the Republican candidates for the presidency, alleges that the Republican Party redirected funds from his home state, meant for his campaign, to the coffers of another candidate. The Republicans deny the charges. . . . The Flavoring Extract Manufacturers Association of America prods the U.S. government to stop all imitation vanilla and lemon extracts being passed off to the public as the real thing.	Lawmakers of the General Synod of the Reformed Church cry out against an "alarming increase in military and naval appropriations," going on record to condemn such action in the United States.	The Thompson-Starrett Company and subsidiaries report a net income of $31,827 for the fiscal year ending April 30. The corporation faced a deficit of $200,000 the previous year.		More than 100 domestic retailers meet in New York to formally ignite a campaign to revive the female interest in homesewing. Present are executives from sewing machine companies and spokespersons from textile organizations. . . . A competitor of RCA, Mackay Radio and Telegraph, is denied circuit access between New York and Oslo, Norway, because the Federal Communications Commission says the preexisting RCA link between locations is adequate.	Jun. 4
Predicting the largest crowd to ever attend a national convention, W. Forbes Morgan, secretary of the National Democratic Committee, arrives in Philadelphia to make final preparations for the convention, which opens June 23. A crowd of 500,000 is expected.		A new set of rules against trade abuses in the rubber industry—such as price discrimination and false advertising—are adopted by the Federal Trade Commission, announces commission member Robert E. Freer. . . . The Senate passes a revised version of President Roosevelt's 1936 Revenue Act by a vote of 38–24, which aims to make up for budget deficiencies caused by the bonus compensations to war veterans and the invalidation of the Agricultural Adjustment Act.			Jun. 5

F	G	H	I	J
Includes elections, federal-state relations, civil rights and liberties, crime, the judiciary, education, healthcare, poverty, urban affairs, and population.	Includes formation and debate of U.S. foreign and defense policies, veterans affairs, and defense spending. (Relations with specific foreign countries are usually found under the region concerned.)	Includes business, labor, agriculture, taxation, transportation, consumer affairs, monetary and fiscal policy, natural resources, pollution, and accidents.	Includes worldwide scientific, medical, and technological developments, natural phenomena, U.S. weather, and natural disasters.	Includes the arts, religion, scholarship, communications media, sports, entertainment, fashions, fads, and social life.

	World Affairs	Europe	Africa & The Middle East	The Americas	Asia & The Pacific
Jun. 6		The French Cabinet under the newly appointed premier, Leon Blum, promises one million hungry strikers food as the first step to getting France back on course. The French Labor Confederation stands firmly behind Blum to also consider an employment program as many Parisian businesses financially collapse. Meanwhile, the head of the Bank of France, Jean Tannery, is replaced by a Blum confrere, Emile Labeyrie.	Col. Hubert Fauntleroy Julian of the now-defunct Ethiopian army, a former ally of deposed Emperor Haile Selassie, considers himself an Italian since Ethiopia's fall. Publicly referring to the Italian banner as "my own national flag," Col. Julian is spotted taking a respite on the Mediterranean cruiser, *Vulcania*, dressed in Italian finery.	Gen. Anastasio Somoza, now in charge of the Nicaraguan government, tells newspapers that debts will be paid and that the country will be brought back to economic security. Details, he promises, will continue to roll out.	Declaring war and seeking the national unity of China, the Cantonese government is in the midst of forming an army sizeable enough to rout the Japanese in north China.
Jun. 7		Socialist Premier Leon Blum of France, meeting for the first time with the parliament, announces that he will create a 40-hour week and improve wages and working conditions for a million people on strike.			Gen. Douglas MacArthur, military adviser to Philippines President Manuel Quezon, says that he has authored a defense plan to make the islands "invasion proof" within a decade.
Jun. 8	The 1,000 representatives of several Jewish organizations meeting in New York vote for a World Congress to take place in the near future. Its purpose would be to honor Jewry and bring world understanding of their plight in Europe.	In Romania, during a celebration honoring the fifth year of the reign of King Carol, a grandstand holding 5,000 celebrants collapses. Twenty people are killed and 700 are injured.			The Nanking government of China admits that a civil war with the south is quite probable. The south is soliciting troops to battle Japanese in the north as well as help from northern generals sympathetic to the rebellion.
Jun. 9		England's Sir Samuel Hoare, First Lord of the Admiralty, upholds his own country as the "model" of the perfect League of Nations member: peace-conscious, highly intelligent, conservative, proud, and self-contained.			
Jun. 10	Premier Benito Mussolini formally annexes Ethiopia and claims Rome has attained the status of capital of an empire.			Admiral Joseph M. Reeves of the U.S. Navy calls the lock system at Panama outmoded and promotes a third set of locks to handle both the busier traffic and the larger ships, which did not yet exist when the locks were initially constructed.	
Jun. 11		Premier Benito Mussolini appoints Marshal Pietro Badoglio, Viceroy of Ethiopia, as Chief of Staff of the Italian army. Replacing Badoglio as Viceroy is Rodolfo Graziani.			
Jun. 12	Britain weighs Premier Benito Mussolini's threat to leave the League of Nations if the sanction against Italy is not removed. The British envoy to Italy, Sir Eric Drummond, reaffirms that Mussolini's threat is serious.			A governmental annual report states that, of 153 corporations, Canada's mines brought in 42.17 percent of the total Canadian income of those businesses during 1935. These mines include base-metal mines, gold mines, and many others.	
Jun. 13		Eduard Benes, president of Czechoslovakia, asserts that his last meeting with the ministers of the "Little Entente" of eastern European countries has "accomplished more than all (our) preceding meetings." The countries think alike on all matters politically and economically, he reports, and concurs that the present safety of Europe is in danger.			

A	B	C	D	E
Includes developments that affect more than one world region, international organizations, and important meetings of world leaders.	Includes all domestic and regional developments in Europe, including the Soviet Union.	Includes all domestic and regional developments in Africa and the Middle East.	Includes all domestic and regional developments in Latin America, the Caribbean, and Canada.	Includes all domestic and regional developments in Asian and Pacific nations (and colonies).

U.S. Politics & Social Issues	U.S. Foreign Policy & Defense	Economics & Great Depression	Science, Technology & Nature	Culture, Leisure & Lifestyle	
As their national convention opens, Republicans find themselves in a dilemma that they did not foresee. They fear that the focal presence of "Lily-White" Republicans from the south will spoil the African-American vote below the Mason-Dixon Line; at the same time, African-American delegates, prominently seated at the convention, might very well kindle a white exodus to the Democrats.		The grocery chain First National Stores, Inc., earns $3,163,329 after taxes and depreciation in the 1935–36 fiscal year ending March 31. Price per share is $3.65.			Jun. 6
The mayor of Ecorse, Mich., comes out of "hiding" after members of the local Black Legion vigilante band who threatened him with death are arrested. A vocal adversary of the Legion, Mayor Bill Voisine had been threatened along with a local steel industry official who commented against them.	An anti-Soviet plank in the Republican National Convention is suggested by Rep. Tinkham, Massachusetts. He demands a severance with Russia over distributed "Red" propaganda in America.	By encouraging reciprocal trading, one also encourages price increases and a curb on small producers, according to George A. Renard of the National Association of Purchasing Agents, addressing national legislators. . . . Although home-building numbers are above those of 1934, the actual number of new homes under construction at this time of the year is lower than last year's totals.	A new, improved blend of fuel for airplanes, which gives planes an estimated 30 percent more power, is described by agents from the Standard Oil Development Company. The fuel blends isopropyl and ether.	In a spectacular and literal "photo finish," the thoroughbred Granville takes the Belmont Stakes in a nose-to-nose vault across the finish line with the horse Mr. Bones. William Woodward, owner of the winner, takes home a $41,000 stake.	Jun. 7
Founders Day activities in Doylestown, Pa., feature guest speaker John B. Kelly, Pennsylvania's revenue authority, who delivers a rousing applause for President Roosevelt's programs for the farmer. Members of a large farm school are in attendance. . . . A survey taken by the National Self Government Committee reports that 70 percent of the 121 teachers who responded are dissatisfied with the standard of teaching civics.		An estimated 1,500 delegates from across the United States arrive in Seattle, Wash., for a four-day American Banking Institute conference. The effect of the latest revenue bill is one topic on the busy agenda.		Overpowering five armed guards, 16 members of the one-time Alvin Karpis-Ma Barker bankrobbing gang escape from a criminal ward of an insane asylum in St. Peter, Minn.	Jun. 8
Author S.G. Blythe asserts that Herbert Hoover's main task in this presidential campaign is to scare Democrats out of voting for President Roosevelt without damaging his own party with a negative campaign.		President Roosevelt invites to the White House members of the conference committee involved in the latest revenue bill to discuss the differences of opinion between members in the Senate and the House—and how to reach a compromise agreement.			Jun. 9
Before 15,000 people at the Republican convention, Herbert Hoover compares Roosevelt's New Deal to what is occurring in Europe—a mixture of "socialism and dictatorship." He says it is now the Republican Party's aim to direct a "holy crusade of freedom" against the New Deal.		Based on shipline bookings and travel agency data, the U.S. Tourist Bureau reports a 50 percent increase in tourist traffic from Europe.			Jun. 10
Representatives of the new Non-Partisan League, which recently built headquarters in Washington, D.C., and which has already vocally hailed President Roosevelt as its candidate, call on the Chief Executive at the White House to promise him the support of 30,000 union officials who have committed their names as sponsors.		Economics professor Carl S. Dakan from the University of Washington, speaking to representatives from the American Institute of Banking, presents arguments putting to rest fears that inflation will cause American banks to plummet in a similar way to the Depression of 1929.		Some 124 athletes of the U.S. Army Academy receive insignia awards for their performance in their respective physical training module—polo, baseball, track, golf, tennis, or lacrosse.	Jun. 11
Since many passenger trains are showing a mild decrease in customers, Federal Coordinator of Transportation Joseph Eastman recommends changes in the operation of the typical passenger line—faster trains, more comfortable cars, and cheaper fares.		A majority of American department stores in 1935 enjoyed a respite from the low sales levels reminiscent of the worst Depression years, cites a survey done by Harvard Business School and issued by the Bureau of Business Research. For the first time since 1929, the majority of stores experience an average 3.4 percent gain in business sales.			Jun. 12
Fifteen men are arrested in Detroit, members of the Black Legion, a continuously growing menace in the Great Lakes area of the United States. A vigilante organization, these 15 men are alleged to have plotted the death of two politicians who sought the Legion's demise. In all, 42 such terrorists now sit in Michigan jails awaiting trials for crimes ranging from arson to murder.					Jun. 13

F	G	H	I	J
Includes elections, federal-state relations, civil rights and liberties, crime, the judiciary, education, healthcare, poverty, urban affairs, and population.	Includes formation and debate of U.S. foreign and defense policies, veterans affairs, and defense spending. (Relations with specific foreign countries are usually found under the region concerned.)	Includes business, labor, agriculture, taxation, transportation, consumer affairs, monetary and fiscal policy, natural resources, pollution, and accidents.	Includes worldwide scientific, medical, and technological developments, natural phenomena, U.S. weather, and natural disasters.	Includes the arts, religion, scholarship, communications media, sports, entertainment, fashions, fads, and social life.

	World Affairs	Europe	Africa & The Middle East	The Americas	Asia & The Pacific
Jun. 14			Bethlehem becomes a scene of political bloodshed today as Arabs and police trade shots in an open market. One Arab sniper is slain on what is the beginning of the eighth week of fighting.	Canada's recent welfare program has affected its North American Indian population, for the better. New census estimates from the Bureau of Indian Affairs show that the once-dwindling tribal population has risen in the last year—from 104,894 to 112,510.	
Jun. 15				Anastasio Somoza is officially elected president of Nicaragua at the convention of the National Liberal Party in Leon two weeks after ousting the former president from office.	
Jun. 16		The death of a Nazi soldier in Danzig sets off a retaliation by Nazi stormtroopers in Poland. The violence escalates as known anti-Nazi groups are beaten to death on the streets and innocent storeowners are yanked from their shops and whipped.			
Jun. 17	The Annalist publication examines the world economic trade situation, reporting that it noticeably improved this last April. Industrial activity grew, and with it international trade, while surplus commodity stocks declined at a faster rhythm.	Notorious anti-Semite Heinrich Himmler is appointed by Adolf Hitler to direct the Reich Police. It is considered by many inside and outside Germany to be one of the strongest political jobs in the world, giving Himmler free license to arrest and imprison anyone at will. . . . Budapest welcomes Germany's economics minister, Dr. Hjalmar Schacht, who will spend the next few days advising the Hungarian National Bank and consulting with top Budapest officials from the financial and political arenas.			
Jun. 18		World-famous Arctic explorer and adventurer Peter Freuchen, on his way to Germany for a speaking engagement, is barred at the border by troops because of his anti-fascist leanings. Freuchen is of Danish descent.		In protest against the Mexican government's recent ban against the railway workers' strike, almost a half-million members of the Confederation of American Workers walk off their jobs for half an hour in the morning and afternoon today. The movement was adopted on June 2 at the Confederation's conference in Mexico City. . . . The Cuban government joins the United States against business interests in Florida that are questioning the validity of the reciprocal trade agreement between both countries.	
Jun. 19		Various Jewish leaders from around the world convene in New York, where they relate tales of Jewish persecution in Germany and eastern Europe. The speakers' mission is to gather rehabilitation and support for homeless Jews forced to leave their homeland.			
Jun. 20		The Republic of Ireland, through President Eamon de Valera, outlaws the Irish Republican Army. It accuses the I.R.A. of terrorism and strong-arm tactics—sometimes used in the name of religion—that only increase hostilities between Free Ireland and Britain. . . . Nazi Germany applauds its prizefighter, Max Schmeling, for defeating African-American boxer Joe Louis in a bout in America. The Nazis had scorned the event, claiming it was below Schmeling to fight Louis—but now that Schmeling has won, they pronounce the feat a world victory.		Wanting to show that he is a man of the people, Cuban President Miguel Mariano Gomez issues a statement today promising an amnesty bill for Cuba. In the background, however, coalition parties grumble over the government's policies.	

A	B	C	D	E
Includes developments that affect more than one world region, international organizations, and important meetings of world leaders.	Includes all domestic and regional developments in Europe, including the Soviet Union.	Includes all domestic and regional developments in Africa and the Middle East.	Includes all domestic and regional developments in Latin America, the Caribbean, and Canada.	Includes all domestic and regional developments in Asian and Pacific nations (and colonies).

U.S. Politics & Social Issues	U.S. Foreign Policy & Defense	Economics & Great Depression	Science, Technology & Nature	Culture, Leisure & Lifestyle	
Long an advocate for preserving the nation's woodlands and natural resources, President Roosevelt once again makes that the subject of his speech in which he simultaneously dedicates a memorial to 18th-century trailblazer and patriot George Rogers Clark in Vincennes, Ind.		In 33 years of operation, the Ford Motor Company sold 24,500,000 automobiles for a total earnings of $12,951,338,028 and paid $12,109,321,884 for labor, materials, and wages. These figures come from Ford executive William Cameron. . . . From across 12 different industries, business leaders report operating and employee levels close to what they were before the Depression says George A. Sloan, chairman of the Consumer Goods Committee.	As a total eclipse of the sun, best viewed from Siberia, is one week away, 25 Soviet and 11 foreign expeditions will converge in Russia to collect scientific data. Among the milieu of scientists will be two groups from the United States.		Jun. 14
Thousands of citizens in and near the farming burg of Grayville, Ill., turn out for a picnic given for First Lady Eleanor Roosevelt, who is stumping for her husband in the Midwest. From all reports, of the many activities on the agenda, she enjoys the hog-calling sessions the best.	In accord with the Adjusted Compensation Act, World War I veterans are issued $1.5 billion in bonds, convertible to cash.	Earnings for the Associated Gas & Electrical Company utility and its consolidated companies for 1935 were $93,215,717, up from $83,973,089 for 1934.			Jun. 15
The Democratic Party takes over Municipal Auditorium in Philadelphia to wire its technology and deploy its huge army of volunteers, all in preparation for its national convention, which opens next week. The hall is already besieged by journalists and photographers from around the country. . . . Alf M. Landon draws the "warm commendation" of the directing staff of the Lord's Day Alliance for his recent decision not to make campaign speeches on Sunday.		Basing their plan on the wage-scale and work-hour standards of the now-defunct NRA, the leaders of the National Coat and Suit Industry Recovery Board from across the country meet to ratify a proposal to form their own mini-NRA for their 1,800 employees. An experiment based on the NRA codes has proven to be well-received by the employee body.	The earth is much older than science initially thought, according to the American Association for the Advancement of Science. Guest speakers, Doctors W.M. Rayton and T.R. Wilkins, estimate that the earth was born from the sun 2.5 billion years ago and that it took some 700 million years to cool off in order for life to begin.		Jun. 16
Before taking charge of the activities at Democrat National Headquarters, Postmaster General James A. Farley pays a quick visit to Philadelphia to review the initial setup and ensure that preparations are on schedule. . . . Advising upward of 100 delegates from assorted labor organizations, the American Federation of Labor's Charlton Ogburn says that employees should work through collective bargaining with their unions and not depend upon legislation to gain what they want.		The U.S. national public debt reaches its highest peak in the country's history—$34,331,355,867—with the financing of the U.S. soldiers' bonus, according to a press release from the U.S. Treasury.	To test the effects of the upcoming solar eclipse on short-wave radio transmission, Soviet engineers begin a five-day series of broadcasting tests to record any frequency changes or any other technical anomalies.		Jun. 17
The National Civil Service Reform League, in its tirade on the Roosevelt administration's spoils system, points out Postmaster General James A. Farley as an example. The League accuses Farley of using postal workers under his employment for political errands, such as campaigning and helping to staff the Democratic convention. . . . Violence erupts when strikebreakers taunt a picket line at the Black & Decker factory in Kent, Ohio. Fourteen men are injured.		A minor employee of the Works Progress Administration gets prison time at Sing Sing for posing as a PWA authority and fraudulently selling political "influence" for pay. Walter Clemens Martin, 49, who has police records in Florida, New Hampshire, North Carolina, and Washington state, gets five years.		The U.S. liner, Manhattan, which will carry the next group of America's Olympic contenders to the games in Berlin, has been specially outfitted with an Olympic-size pool, a running track, and a gymnasium to provide practice time on the voyage across the Atlantic. Workout times and a curfew will be enforced by Olympic chaperones.	Jun. 18
William Lemke, Republican member of Congress from North Dakota, announces that he will be a third-party candidate for the presidency on a Union Party ticket; his candidacy is later officially endorsed by the National Union for Social Justice, headed by Father Charles Coughlin.	In charge of protecting the Philippines from invasion, Gen. Douglas MacArthur presents a defense plan to the government that will "give pause to the most ruthless and powerful." MacArthur, semi-retired, is the former U.S. Chief of Staff.	Reporters reveal that Major Wilfred E. Boughton, who once was in charge of the Works Progress Administration's efforts to place America's jobless into private industry, is now, himself, collecting relief.			Jun. 19
Hundreds of Public Works Administration workers in the United States randomly receive tickets to the Democratic National Convention in Philadelphia. The Los Angeles committee tells its recipients that they can be sold to others who can use them for $1, which they can pocket. . . . President Roosevelt signs the Federal Anti-Price Discrimination Act, also known as the Robinson-Patman Act, empowering the Federal Trade Commission to take action against retailers who use pricing to destroy competition.		Addressing a crowd of 500 at the New York State Bankers Association, financier S. Sloan Colt, president of the Bankers Trust Company, advocates the removal of $2 billion in gold from the Federal Reserve for the purpose of starting a stabilization fund.		The Protestant Church announces that it is sending 1,000 delegates from the United States and Canada to Oslo, Norway, to attend this year's gathering of the World's Sunday School Association. The event features a series of multi-denominational theology courses designed for global participation. . . . Jerome "Dizzy" Dean, one of professional baseball's most popular, and colorful, players, leads the way in the tallying of fan votes on who will take part in the All-Star Game set for July 7. Dean is expected to pitch for the National League at the Boston event.	Jun. 20

F	G	H	I	J
Includes elections, federal-state relations, civil rights and liberties, crime, the judiciary, education, healthcare, poverty, urban affairs, and population.	Includes formation and debate of U.S. foreign and defense policies, veterans affairs, and defense spending. (Relations with specific foreign countries are usually found under the region concerned.)	Includes business, labor, agriculture, taxation, transportation, consumer affairs, monetary and fiscal policy, natural resources, pollution, and accidents.	Includes worldwide scientific, medical, and technological developments, natural phenomena, U.S. weather, and natural disasters.	Includes the arts, religion, scholarship, communications media, sports, entertainment, fashions, fads, and social life.

	World Affairs	Europe	Africa & The Middle East	The Americas	Asia & The Pacific
Jun. 21		Heinrich Himmler's military-style national police in Germany trade their blue tunics for a gray-green uniform, which Himmler deems as looking more "authoritative" and that is reminiscent of the German army. . . . Nineteen workers in the Saar Valley territory are sentenced to long prison terms by the People's Court of Nazi Germany for having affiliations with the Communist Party.			Japan's recent taunting of north China and Siberia should not be underestimated, say members of the League of Nations. Japan's "divide and rule" strategy is not meant for just those two parts of the world, but for whatever land Japan might get the urge to possess. It needs to let grow its suffocating population and wherever that might be done would be appropriate.
Jun. 22				A proposed budget of $73,166,971 for 1936–37 is submitted to his country's Congress by Cuban President Miguel M. Gomez. A good portion of the budget is dedicated to national defense, say budget advisers.	Three thousand Japanese troops dressed in full war regalia march into Peiping, China, startling a morning crowd and, say insiders, dampening plans for a civil war that was on the verge of starting. Despite pleas from northern generals, many dissidents in the south want war against the Japanese.
Jun. 23		Rightist students riot in Bucharest, Romania, burning liberal newspapers, attacking offices of Jewish merchants, and wrecking autos lining the streets. Police restore quiet, but not before much damage to many commercial intersections.	Arab gunfire kills a Jewish passenger on a bus and wounds three other Jews in the small villa of Rosh Pinah, not far from Jerusalem, in a continuance of an Arab uprising in the Middle East. Because of the violence in that area, most business owners refuse to open shop. . . . At a dinner in Hollywood saluting the retired producer, Carl Laemmle, a Jew, funds are raised to aid the founding of a Jewish state in Palestine.	A day after a heated debate between Premier R.B. Bennett and members of parliament over wheat policy, the Canadian parliament closes its Ottawa session on the birthday of the new British King, Edward VIII. Celebrating this session's successful trade treaty with the United States, certain ministers will spend their recess in Europe, laying the ground for other possible treaties.	
Jun. 24		At the Dardanelles Convention, Britain's representative, The Earl Stanhope, remains at odds with Soviet Foreign Commissar Maxim Litvinoff over who controls the Straits of Magellan and intrinsic passage rights to the Black Sea. The argument comes down to whether or not warships will be allowed ingress during a prospective war.			Gen. Chiang Kai-shek of China denies being part of an anti-Japanese pact with Russia. He goes on record to say, "The central government (of China) does not want war," adding that war at this time could weaken the country beyond repair.
Jun. 25	A member of the Italian Senate mocks the League of Nations for its inability to maintain world peace through the understanding of the human drive and spirit, saying its decision makers are "diplomats, not people." Guido C.V. DiMadrone jeers that the League of Nations—"judging by the way civilization is rushing to its doom"—should be replaced.				America, through its embassy in Peiping, demands an answer from Japan as to why Japanese forces there roughed up two American visitors during an army exhibition. The embassy promises an explanation.
Jun. 26			New scrimmages erupt tonight across Palestine, leaving Jews, Arabs, and police dead. Snipers retreat after being fired upon by troops.		

A	B	C	D	E
Includes developments that affect more than one world region, international organizations, and important meetings of world leaders.	*Includes all domestic and regional developments in Europe, including the Soviet Union.*	*Includes all domestic and regional developments in Africa and the Middle East.*	*Includes all domestic and regional developments in Latin America, the Caribbean, and Canada.*	*Includes all domestic and regional developments in Asian and Pacific nations (and colonies).*

U.S. Politics & Social Issues	U.S. Foreign Policy & Defense	Economics & Great Depression	Science, Technology & Nature	Culture, Leisure & Lifestyle	
Since private initiative groups have done nothing to improve the lot of the poor, the federal government must therefore step in and accelerate its housing program for the low-income population, says Harold L. Ickes of the Public Works Administration. He adds that private concerns cannot muster the funds for even one-third of new housing.		The National Association of Purchasing Agents exclaims that economic recovery and, with it, increased public consumption, have prevented manufacturing plants in the middle of large industrial centers in eastern and midwest America from facing their usual slumps in productivity.		Professional football announces its annual fundraiser for September 8 that will pit the top college players for 1936 against the Eastern Champions, the New York Giants. Proceeds will go to national charities.	Jun. 21
African Americans have received better treatment under the Roosevelt administration than they ever have under a Republican regime, attests Rep. Arthur W. Mitchell of Illinois. Supporting him, the Bishops Council of the African Methodist Episcopal Church promotes Roosevelt for 1936. . . . J. Edgar Hoover visits the Washington, D.C., branch of the Hi-Y Clubs of America on a leg of his journey to promote an end to juvenile delinquency in America. Many criminals, he reminds his audience, began a life of crime in boyhood.	A methodical growth of Army forces and a building up of modern, up-to-date equipment are the two current aims of the U.S. War Department, says Chief of Staff Gen. Malin Craig.	The U.S. Department of Commerce strongly recommends the building of 350 commercial ships—double the size of the fleet that the country now possesses—for America to achieve and maintain its commercial shipping presence on the open seas of the world. Also, the department suggests an upscaling of facilities for the storage and transport of shipped goods. . . . Congress passes and Roosevelt signs the 1936 Revenue Act, which increases corporate income tax rates in the highest brackets to 27 percent. Business groups immediately oppose the tax as hampering business expansion.		President Roosevelt writes to the National Parks and Resorts Association, personally thanking it for its efforts on behalf of the tourist industry in the United States. Summer tourism has doubled 50 percent this year. . . . To date, the Olympic games in Berlin have drawn participation by 53 countries, according to the German Olympics Committee, which closes entries tomorrow.	Jun. 22
Five thousand retail grocers meeting in a Dallas convention hall for their annual four-day planning session cheer the passing of the new Robinson-Patman Act that prohibits price gouging and other trade evils. Emcee D.A. Affleck, president of the National Retail Grocers Association, promises that the Association will seek more legislation of that kind to help grocers the world over conduct fairer and more productive business. . . . A strike of steel workers becomes violent when a band of strikers kills one guard and wounds four others on a train trying to bring food and nourishment to wire mill employees who refuse to walk out with the others.	The Air Defense League of the United States meets in New York City, engaged in a proposal to multiply its membership and to broaden its efforts in defense of America. It hopes to do this through an awareness campaign and through political channels.	Republican presidential candidate Alf M. Landon's steps to balance the budget are unrealistic and unworkable—so says Prof. F. Cyril James of the Wharton School of Finance at the University of Pennsylvania. . . . Reports from the Republican camp have President Roosevelt's popularity waning, especially among the farming families of the midwest and west, areas battered by drought and poverty for much of the Depression. In contrast, the Democrats say they have no indication of Roosevelt losing support.			Jun. 23
Publishers of the magazine *Today* advertise an upcoming article by political author and founder of *Newsweek*, Raymond Moley, that examines the reasons why the New Deal has faced a crisis, despite its proven track record. Distrust of government and a slacking in the public interest in reform are two reasons.	Two men are taken into custody in Los Angeles—one a Japanese spy, the other a former U.S. petty officer—on charges that they allegedly tried to give the Japanese government data on U.S. naval bases on the West Coast. Both prisoners will be tried according to the Espionage Act.	American Car & Foundry Company president Charles J. Hardy, while reporting slight losses in railroad car equipment sales in 1935, says that sales for 1936 have already greatly improved. In fact, he predicts that the railway manufacturing business will meet new heights this year.			Jun. 24
John D.M. Hamilton of the National Republican Committee says he "never saw a crowd so scared and so unwilling to admit it," referring to the Democrats. He predicts a nationwide sweep by the Republican Party at election time; Alf Landon may carry all 48 states, he asserts.	Some 2,320 more airplanes will be constructed for the Army Air Corps now that President Roosevelt has signed the Army Plane Bill today. Production of the defense aircraft will begin shortly.	The U.S. Smelting, Refining and Mining Company gained a five-month net of $2,116,934, which is a slight loss from the year before. . . . The Association of Buying Offices fights to have a 3 percent federal tax on fur-trimmed coats included with the price of the garment. The association states that listing the tax separately would disturb prices and cause confusion in the industry, which in turn would be unfair to competition.			Jun. 25
President Roosevelt officially accepts the Democratic Party's re-nomination as president of the United States in 1936 at Municipal Auditorium in Philadelphia, to the standing applause of thousands. The world hears the nomination via radio broadcast.	Humanitarian Dr. Henry Smith Leiper, secretary of the American Section of Universal Council and of the American Christian Committee for German Refugees, pitches for funds to aid thousands of homeless en route from persecution in Europe. He is touring the United States, describing the terrible plight of the displaced minorities.	The Great Atlantic & Pacific Tea Company, according to a press release, netted $16,953,252 last year, equivalent to $7.09 per share.			Jun. 26

F	G	H	I	J
Includes elections, federal-state relations, civil rights and liberties, crime, the judiciary, education, healthcare, poverty, urban affairs, and population.	*Includes formation and debate of U.S. foreign and defense policies, veterans affairs, and defense spending. (Relations with specific foreign countries are usually found under the region concerned.)*	*Includes business, labor, agriculture, taxation, transportation, consumer affairs, monetary and fiscal policy, natural resources, pollution, and accidents.*	*Includes worldwide scientific, medical, and technological developments, natural phenomena, U.S. weather, and natural disasters.*	*Includes the arts, religion, scholarship, communications media, sports, entertainment, fashions, fads, and social life.*

	World Affairs	Europe	Africa & The Middle East	The Americas	Asia & The Pacific
Jun. 27					
Jun. 28	Judging by foreign newspapers, the nations of the world are anxiously watching the presidential campaign in the United States to see if there will or will not be a change in the present neutrality policy.	Poles in the United States speak out against their home country's "deplorable" avoidance of duty by neglecting to stop a growing Nationalist Socialist (Nazi) Union's mistreatment of Jews throughout Poland. One Polish delegate expressed that Poland has "ignominiously surrendered to the forces of anarchy and mob violence."			Japan grows suspicious when it learns that the Chinese have entered into an agreement with Germany; China denies today that the deal has anything to do with the sales of arms or ammunition—just "non-military" goods.
Jun. 29					
Jun. 30		Chancellor Kurt Schuschnigg of Austria ignores the invitation by the League of Nations to join its peace-setting session in Geneva, Switzerland. Britain and France conclude that Austria has become part of what seems to be a German-Italian partnership to make its own policy in western Europe.			The China Society of America hears former minister of foreign affairs Dr. C.T. Wang disparage the Japanese takeover in his country. However, he predicts that the people will rise up militantly to conquer the invading horde by the same means as those "who are trying to destroy us."
Jul. 1		German scientists are now forbidden to spend their time conducting research to "find the truth for truth's sake." From here on, scientific research must be conducted only to advance the knowledge and security of the Third Reich. . . . French military experts study locations along the Swiss border to serve as defense positions in the event of threatened invasion from Germany using Switzerland as ingress. Such fortifications would extend across the Swiss border as an extension to the Maginot Line.		U.S vice president John Garner and Mexican general Eduardo Hay meet midway across the international bridge at Nuevo Leone to officially open the Mexican Highway, which connects Laredo, Tex., to Mexico City. The highway, at a cost of $17 million, is hailed as a true joint effort between the two nations.	
Jul. 2		The Netherlands reports a growing movement among its intellectual base to thwart Nazism. The movement attempts to thwart Nazi agitation through education and intellectual argument.		Col. Fulgencio Batista, head of the army of Cuba, protests the June 30 dismissal of 3,000 government employees by President Gomez. Most of those who lost jobs are government reservists. . . . Brazil's government in Rio de Janeiro estimates that the overabundance of coffee beans must be destroyed—6.6 million bags, which is 30 percent of the estimated total. Growers will receive 5 milreis per bag.	China's central government sends 600,000 men to the provinces of Kwangsi and Kwangtung in order to squelch a revolution by southern Chinese rebels, which seems on the brim of erupting into a full-scale war.

A	B	C	D	E
Includes developments that affect more than one world region, international organizations, and important meetings of world leaders.	Includes all domestic and regional developments in Europe, including the Soviet Union.	Includes all domestic and regional developments in Africa and the Middle East.	Includes all domestic and regional developments in Latin America, the Caribbean, and Canada.	Includes all domestic and regional developments in Asian and Pacific nations (and colonies).

U.S. Politics & Social Issues	U.S. Foreign Policy & Defense	Economics & Great Depression	Science, Technology & Nature	Culture, Leisure & Lifestyle	
Only through a unification of all workers across the globe can true universal peace be achieved, opines Robert Minor, who runs on the Communist ticket for governor of New York State and who criticizes the country's "ruthless war preparations." Workers must come together, he says, regardless of political, racial, or national beliefs. . . . John Nance Garner is nominated to run again as Democratic candidate for vice president.		An agriculture program bringing the work of six different federal agencies together to deliver aid to the drought-stricken southwest is announced today by Secretary of Agriculture Henry Wallace. Efforts of the six groups supplying monies, manpower, equipment, and more will be aligned under the Works Progress Administration. . . . All 24 railroads to report May earnings show nearly a 25 percent increase in net operating income.			Jun. 27
		Barring any unforeseen catastrophe, the south is anticipating a good cotton year. Growers and merchants are determining the volume of their crop to calculate how the new cotton administration programs might affect the outlay and, simultaneously, how cotton might be produced at lower cost to return a living for the people who depend on it.			Jun. 28
At a meeting of the Maryland Bar Association, the former governor of Maryland, Albert C. Ritchie, although a Democrat, relates how "American self-government is being destroyed before our very eyes" by a New Deal mindset. . . . In a true-crime journalism style, the New York District Attorney's Office publishes a magazine entitled, *The Human Side of the People's Case.* In it, Attorney General Homer Cummings pens a factual article detailing the reasons why federal G-Men need more license to pursue the nation's mobile criminals.		Yale University economics professor Ray B. Westerfield fears a "disastrous rise in the price level" which will lead, if not paused now, to serious inflation. He speaks in Johnsburg, N.J., at the Stevens Institute's annual Economics Conference of Engineers.			Jun. 29
Members of the American Federation of are urged by Rep. Thomas R. Amlie of Wisconsin to join the "progressives" in Congress who believe that the country needs a more open-minded "third party." . . . The Walsh-Healy Government Contracts Act is enacted, requiring that government contractors pay minimum wage, limit hours to eight hours per day and 40 per week, and prohibit child or convict labor.		U.S. economists and business watchers laud some very promising statistics for the first half of 1936, which indicate that business conditions in the country have indeed returned to "normal" pre-Depression levels. Stability is even with the early years of 1930, before the effects of the Depression began to jolt the nation. But, most promisingly, the prosperity shown in 1935 has continued into 1936 in most industries.			Jun. 30
Recent reciprocal trade agreements affecting farmers of the nation should be an all-important element in this year's presidential race, asserts candidate Senator William Borah. He points to the Republican farm plank as an example of the party's attention to the American farmer.	A stronghold of 1,000 airplanes will be established in Alaska, according to U.S. War Department sources. Alaska is one of those positions lately deemed vulnerable in its current, unguarded state.	An accounting system for public utility companies begins January 1, 1937, giving such companies until then to conform to the New Federal Power Commission rules. . . . Secretary of the Treasury Henry Morgenthau, in a radio address to the public, is optimistic about the economic situation: incomes are steadily rising, revenues are increasing, expenditures are declining, and business is improving, coast to coast.			Jul. 1
Representatives of several trucking units testify at an Interstate Commerce Commission hearing, explaining how a current plan by several eastern railroads could put them out of business. That plan includes free pickup and delivery of merchandise to customers' locations. This "store-to-door" service could force as high as a 45 percent downsizing in the trucking industry. . . . The chairman of the Republican National Committee, John D.M. Hamilton, says the Democratic convention closely mirrored theirs, quipping that he considers the effort "a sincere flattery of imitation."		Government figures indicate that the country spent one dollar for every 46 cents it collected from July 1, 1935, to June 30, 1936, to create a deficit of $4,763,841.642—the largest deficit ever in peacetime.		Pope Pius XI asks that "right-minded" Roman Catholics boycott all motion pictures that are morally unsound. He believes that a ban on Hollywood decadence will lead the industry toward distributing finer films.	Jul. 2

F
Includes elections, federal-state relations, civil rights and liberties, crime, the judiciary, education, healthcare, poverty, urban affairs, and population.

G
Includes formation and debate of U.S. foreign and defense policies, veterans affairs, and defense spending. (Relations with specific foreign countries are usually found under the region concerned.)

H
Includes business, labor, agriculture, taxation, transportation, consumer affairs, monetary and fiscal policy, natural resources, pollution, and accidents.

I
Includes worldwide scientific, medical, and technological developments, natural phenomena, U.S. weather, and natural disasters.

J
Includes the arts, religion, scholarship, communications media, sports, entertainment, fashions, fads, and social life.

	World Affairs	Europe	Africa & The Middle East	The Americas	Asia & The Pacific
Jul. 3					
Jul. 4		Deriding those who chastise his dictatorship, Adolf Hitler says that he will continue to make decisions first and ask questions later. Nazi power, he adds, is "eternal," and assures his followers that they will never have to answer to a critical world—"for all time."		Responding to criticism in the press, Col. Fulgencio Batista, head of Cuba's army, says his assertive actions do not imply that he is trying to overshadow President Gomez. While he plans to keep the military in the background, at the same time he will continue to very aggressively deal with revolutionary activity.	The Philippines aims to have 40,000 men ready in arms by January 1, 1937, as the first round of citizens' army draftees. It sets a goal to have a force as strong as 500,000 by 1945.
Jul. 5		A popular Nazi newspaper in Berlin, *Angriff*, calls upon every citizen to enact his duty as "host" during the Olympic Games and, while Berlin is crowded with many nationalities, become his or her own master of propaganda for the Third Reich.			
Jul. 6				At a dinner in Mexico City to celebrate the completion of the highway spanning from Mexico to Texas, Mexican President Lázaro Cárdenas thanks U.S. delegates for helping to free poor, uneducated laborers in his country from "ignorance and misery."	
Jul. 7				Cuba's economy is advancing with the help of the United States, with whom it shares a reciprocal trade pact. While still below par, the Cuban economy has had a great boost by America's decision to cut the duty on sugar, to assist it with crop control, and to help its tourist board promote the country. President Gomez says his biggest current problem remains national credit.	Of the turncoat military unit that staged the unsuccessful takeover of Japan several weeks ago in Tokyo, 17 soldiers are condemned to die by a military tribunal. The 17 receive multiple death sentences for the lives of authorities they took during the mutiny.
Jul. 8		Construction begins on what the Third Reich calls the "world's largest" aviation field, near Frankfurt, Germany. . . . Besides its ongoing civil warfare between leftists and rightists, Spain now faces a series of labor disputes that have been badly hurting the country's economy. Today, conflict erupts between major labor parties in Madrid, forcing another round of walkouts. Most labor problems are based on the political friction taking place between the factions.			Thirteen airplanes and 32 pilots desert the rebellious factions of south China and change sides in the conflict. The central government of north China has put a $20,000 reward for any other dissident airmen.
Jul. 9		By withdrawing its warships from the Mediterranean—ships placed there during the hostilities between Italy and Ethiopia—Britain displays a show of trust to Italy and a hope for reconciliation between the nations. . . . Germany and Austria begin diplomatic talks, which have been forthcoming for some time. Critics say that Germany will have full influence over its cautious neighbor.		While Cuba's economy seems to improve, so do its social problems. President Gomez announces that reforms still need to be made, but protective labor laws, better wages, and the apprehension of radicals have greatly added to the leveling out of difficulties.	

A	B	C	D	E
Includes developments that affect more than one world region, international organizations, and important meetings of world leaders.	Includes all domestic and regional developments in Europe, including the Soviet Union.	Includes all domestic and regional developments in Africa and the Middle East.	Includes all domestic and regional developments in Latin America, the Caribbean, and Canada.	Includes all domestic and regional developments in Asian and Pacific nations (and colonies).

U.S. Politics & Social Issues	U.S. Foreign Policy & Defense	Economics & Great Depression	Science, Technology & Nature	Culture, Leisure & Lifestyle	
Visiting his home state of Idaho, presidential candidate Senator William Borah hints to a Pocatello crowd that he may consider running for governor of the state.... Referring to past candidates' presidential election defeats by wide margins, Republican National Chairman predicts, "Roosevelt (will take) the same kind of licking Smith did in 1928 and Hoover did in 1932."		Per instructions of Elaine W. Sheffler, Department of Industrial Relations supervisor, the city of Columbus, Ohio, plans to go ahead with its minimum wage reinforcement despite the Supreme Court's recent outlawing of the minimum wage law for women and children. She determines that the decision should be left up to individual states.			Jul. 3
After a 10-day respite from the campaign trail, candidate Alf M. Landon takes part in rodeo festivities in Greeley, Colo., in front of 10,000 spectators. . . . Speaking at Thomas Jefferson's home, Monticello, President Roosevelt salutes "the spirit of youth," citing examples of great feats performed in the name of liberty by America's men and women while still in their 20s and 30s.			The Guadalupe River overflows its banks during a tremendous downpour to force the evacuation of 200 homes in Victoria, Tex.	A section of woodland in North Carolina's Blue Ridge Mountains is dedicated to the poet and war hero, Joyce Kilmer, whose poem *Trees* is considered a timeless classic. Kilmer was killed in the Battle of Ourcq in 1918, fighting with the famous "New York Irishers."	Jul. 4
		Economic conditions in the machinery industry are the best since 1933, reports the U.S. Department of Commerce. Machinery manufacturers have increased output and improved both payroll and employment, says the report.	Chester Decker, age 21, of New Jersey is the national glider champion, his homemade glider having soared 146 miles. The administrators of the contest plan an international competition for next year.	Hollywood puts a plug in a major project, a bio-epic of the artist and feminist Marie Bashkirtseff, after her estate promises legal action. The film, which had already begun production, starred Katharine Hepburn.	Jul. 5
Siding with six rogue American Federation of Labor unions, John L. Lewis, president of the United Mine Workers of America, says he is determined to organize the steel industry "by accepting the challenge of the omnipresent overlords of steel to fight for the prize of economic freedom and industrial democracy." . . . By campaign's end, the Republicans will have spent $3–$4 million on their national effort to place a Republican back in the White House, estimates party finance manager William Bell.		Amherst College economics professor Colston E. Warne, addressing the Summer Institute of Social Progress, deduces the "most immediate and pressing issue" of this year's presidential campaign is economic relief.		The U.S. Olympic Committee, in realizing it has a deficit of nearly $150,000, announces that it may have to cut the size of certain teams. The first affected is the women's track squad, cut from 17 to four runners.	Jul. 6
Senator L.J. Dickinson of Iowa blames the Democrats' crop-curtailment program for hurting, not helping, the drought-possessed southwestern states, thus causing a severe food shortage in that part of the nation.... New York Senator George Fearon scathingly calls the New Deal a way to centralize power in the White House and President Roosevelt a "despot."		The Roosevelt administration announces a work-relief program (affecting 97 counties) designed solely for farmers in geographic areas affected by drought. The program provides either jobs or subsistence to 100,000 families initially, then to another 30,000 in a second phase. All this is in addition to the 70,000 families now receiving subsistence.	Hundreds of brigades of firemen battle out-of-control forest fires continuing to spread throughout parts of Montana and Wyoming. Thousands of acres of woodland are destroyed.		Jul. 7
For aiding United Mine Workers president John L. Lewis in his effort to take over organization of steel unions, the American Federation of Labor considers terminating eight national and international unions. The decision, to be made in a few days, could affect millions of members.		Architects of a $1.7 million relief fund calculate that the drought across the west and southwest United States seriously hurt the livelihoods of up to 5 million farmers. It asks the Works Progress Administration to assist those people in finding jobs. . . . If rains do not end the dry spell in the Corn Belt by the end of August, the U.S. government may have to purchase some $30 million in drought cattle, says Secretary of Agriculture Henry Wallace.	Unseasonably hot weather in the western plains, hovering at about 95°F, is killing more than crops; fatalities reach 120 people, with 59 dying yesterday. No relief is in sight as the heat wave moves east of the Mississippi to affect Illinois.		Jul. 8
Illustrating the depth of bureaucratic governmental services in the United States, a national resources report states that there are 175,000 separate federal, state, and local government public affairs divisions; some work in close unison while others work independently of each other in "apparent conflict."					Jul. 9

	World Affairs	Europe	Africa & The Middle East	The Americas	Asia & The Pacific
Jul. 10		As sanctions against it come to an end, Italy is hopeful it can resume its trading policies with the rest of the world. The Italian Cabinet refuses to estimate the negative effects the sanctions had on its country's economic health.			
Jul. 11		Police in Madrid announce that they are investigating the possibility of local counterfeiters who may have spread as much as 120,000 bogus pesetas into the Spanish market. The chief of police admits he has no leads as to the source of the fake currency or the perpetrators. . . . Citizens of Vienna and across Austria are stunned to hear, via the radio, that the leaders of their nation have made a pact with Germany. Details are forthcoming, but the tone of the broadcast emanates surrender.			Another life is claimed in rebel-strewn China. This morning a Japanese man named Kosaku Kayau is killed on a Shanghai street while walking down a quiet avenue with his two children. Japanese marines scour the city for the murderer, who is believed to be a Chinese Nationalist. . . . A drought in west China has taken the lives of 5 million people so far. So bad is the situation that the starving have resorted to cannibalism and the selling of their own children for food.
Jul. 12		Near Berlin, construction of the concentration camp Sachsenhausen begins.	Britain considers building a defense base in Cape Town in the Union of South Africa. Having a huge landing strip for British planes and a large collection of warships in its waters, the site would rival the Singapore Station, now one of the largest military depots in the Far East.		
Jul. 13	Members of the Bank for International Settlements in Geneva, Switzerland, in discussing the recent pact between Germany and Austria, fear that it is a pre-war alliance forced by the stronger Germany—allowing Germany now to set its sights on other countries such as France and Belgium without concern over revolution in the Austrian Alps.	The County of Ulster in Northern Ireland draws a celebration of 60,000 Protestants—or "Orangeman"—who mark King William of Orange's victory on the River Boyne in 1690.		Brazil sets up roadblocks along nine international borders—and watches its coastline, the longest in the American continent—for any signs of the outlawed Hungarian Communist, Bela Kun. International news agencies have reported the exiled dissident trying to sneak into Brazil.	
Jul. 14		The Austrian Alliance pact is Germany's first step to sequestering the Balkans and the Danubians, reads an article in the Soviet newspaper *Izvestia* entitled "German Preparations" by journalist Karl Radek. The author argues that Austria is doomed and that Poland will be Germany's next large conquest, adding that there is no European country at this time capable of stopping the Nazis' advance.			Japanese legislators submit a huge armament program to take effect over the next 12 years and to cost some 3 billion yen for the first six years. The plan calls for a renovation and rebuilding of the entire defense program.
Jul. 15					Southwest China clings to hope as it continues to defy north China. In the meantime, two rebel torpedo boats surrender to the central government, only two of many other crews that have defected to the north.
Jul. 16		In Germany, *Voelkisher Beobachter* describes Hitler as "infallible."		When the Mexican Light and Power Company refuses to grant the pay wage requested by the representing union bosses, 3,000 workers walk out of plants around the country. The company is owned by a Canadian concern.	

A	B	C	D	E
Includes developments that affect more than one world region, international organizations, and important meetings of world leaders.	Includes all domestic and regional developments in Europe, including the Soviet Union.	Includes all domestic and regional developments in Africa and the Middle East.	Includes all domestic and regional developments in Latin America, the Caribbean, and Canada.	Includes all domestic and regional developments in Asian and Pacific nations (and colonies).

U.S. Politics & Social Issues	U.S. Foreign Policy & Defense	Economics & Great Depression	Science, Technology & Nature	Culture, Leisure & Lifestyle	
Franklin Roosevelt will lose the presidential election, predicts radio priest Father Charles E. Coughlin, who supports the third-party candidate, William Lemke, whom he helped nominate. . . . A longshoremen's strike is feared on the Gulf of Mexico if workers and dock owners do not come to at least a partial agreement within 24 hours. If a walkout does occur, it will mean that 10,000 longshoremen leave their ports between New Orleans and Florida—and shipping in that part of the country would be frozen.		Consolidated Laundries, Inc., reports a net profit of $42,315 for the first 24 weeks of business this year. The profit is equivalent to seven cents per share.		Helping the Philadelphia Phillies beat the Pittsburgh Pirates today, Phillies player Chuck Klein hits four home runs in one game, the last in the 10th inning bringing home the on-base players for a 9–6 win. Only one other player in baseball history has hit four homers in a game—the Yankees' Lou Gehrig.	Jul. 10
After a lengthy hearing, the National Labor Relations Board finds the Goodyear Tire and Rubber Company at fault in three assaults that occurred on union employees during a recent strike at the plant in Gadsden, Ala. . . . Joseph McDonald, Democratic Senator from Kansas and a harsh critic of presidential aspirant Senator Alf Landon, demands a correction to the latest edition of the *Kansas Legislative Journal*, which lists various Republicans as authors of bills that he introduced.					Jul. 11
Random tests performed on a thousand cars by the National Safety Council show that 60 percent of today's automobiles have some deficient or defective parts. The Council urges Americans to have their cars checked regularly, stressing brakes, steering, and other major operational systems.					Jul. 12
Arthur Besse, president of the National Association of Wool Manufacturers, refuses to negotiate with union heads representing the wool and worsted employees, chancing a walkout of 100,000 people. The workers want a pay raise and improved working conditions. . . . Aggravated at "alarmists and propagandists," Secretary of Agriculture Henry Wallace strikes back against those who say the drought is leaving the country without food. With food aplenty, he condemns those who try "for their own purpose to scare the consumer about food scarcity."		With a deadlock in the Harrisburg State Capitol holding up relief in Pennsylvania, citizens' ire is being roused. The church, corporations, and private businesses are condemning the politicians in charge as a mammoth "hunger parade" is being formed in neighboring towns to march upon Harrisburg.			Jul. 13
The chairman of the Home Loan Bank sends praise to President Roosevelt and his administration during a session of the Institute of Public Affairs at the University of Virginia. He asserts that the New Deal warrants "the unreserved gratitude and support" of all America.	A former naval officer, Lt. Commander John Semer Farnsworth, is arrested by the FBI in Washington, D.C., for serving as a spy for the Japanese navy. Suspected for more than a year, agents have been following him for months.	For the first six months of this year, the Gillette Safety Razor Company earned $2,234,817, according to a press release. That equals $7.21 per share of preferred stock.		Movie star James Cagney, who recently left Warner Bros. Pictures over a contract dispute, reportedly signs a contract to film several motion pictures for the budding Grand National Corporation.	Jul. 14
		The Bell System's three-month earnings of $45,196,739—or $2.42 per share—are the best in six years, a company spokesperson says.		Orchestra leader Paul Whiteman, opera singer Laurence Tibbett, singer Dennis O'Keefe, and other entertainers file joint injunction suits against broadcasters to prevent airing of what they believe are "bootlegged" music and radio shows, altered slightly to sound original.	Jul. 15
Attacking a group of critics who "maliciously distort" reciprocal trade's effect on American farming, Secretary of State Cordell Hull details the Roosevelt administration's success with both trade and agriculture.					Jul. 16

F	G	H	I	J
Includes elections, federal-state relations, civil rights and liberties, crime, the judiciary, education, healthcare, poverty, urban affairs, and population.	Includes formation and debate of U.S. foreign and defense policies, veterans affairs, and defense spending. (Relations with specific foreign countries are usually found under the region concerned.)	Includes business, labor, agriculture, taxation, transportation, consumer affairs, monetary and fiscal policy, natural resources, pollution, and accidents.	Includes worldwide scientific, medical, and technological developments, natural phenomena, U.S. weather, and natural disasters.	Includes the arts, religion, scholarship, communications media, sports, entertainment, fashions, fads, and social life.

	World Affairs	Europe	Africa & The Middle East	The Americas	Asia & The Pacific
Jul. 17					With all guilty parties tried and executed, Japan's Minister of Home Affairs lifts its martial law over Tokyo, imposed since the rebellion of army dissidents 133 days ago.
Jul. 18		Paris, Moscow, and London agree to take part in a meeting to review the situation in Europe now that Germany has turned down the latest peace proposal. Italy refuses to attend unless Germany does, which adds to suspicion that Italy and Germany have been discussing their own pact. . . . The Spanish civil war begins with a revolt of leaders of the Spanish army in Spanish Morocco. The rebel army leaders, supported by the rightwing Falange Party, are opposed by the Socialist-dominated loyalist government, which arms a popular militia.			
Jul. 19	The trade of wool between South Africa and Japan is booming to the extent that both countries are considering a reciprocity act.		With the hostilities now over in Ethiopia, the Vatican dispatches Catholic missionaries to the country to keep the Christian faith constant in the wake of bitterness and despair left from warfare.	The many people left in darkness are again disappointed that the latest attempt to settle the strike of Mexican Light and Power Company employees has failed. The Canadian-owned utility stands firm against union demands. To date, Mexican President Lázaro Cárdenas has remained aloof of the situation, but newspapers have condemned his inactivity.	
Jul. 20		British warplane manufacturers are working overtime to turn out battle craft at an alarming rate. Their main product is the "pursuit plane," able to chase an enemy plane at 300 miles per hour. This is part of Britain's boosted defense program. . . . The exiled King Alfonso of Spain, staying at his brother-in-law's Rausenbach Castle in Slovakia, denies rumors that he is trying to reclaim the throne. He says, however, that he would love to see it rescued from "daily murders and disorders."		Brazil's finance minister, Arthur de Souza Costa, assembles top bankers and businessmen as well as legislators to plan a central reserve bank and, with it, a system for regulating private banking in the nation.	
Jul. 21		Nazi Germany sentences a newspaper reporter to life imprisonment after he is found guilty of treason. Walter Schwertfeger allegedly passed confidential information to foreign correspondents. The international diplomatic corps hints at him being a Nazi scapegoat to ensure other reporters' discretion.			On the day that the Chinese central government takes effective control of south China, dispelling all hopes of the southern rebels, China also signs a loan agreement with the United States for $30.2 million. The huge sum is to be used for arms and defense. Japan, which has troops in northern China, is concerned.
Jul. 22		In the midst of fighting in Guandarrama, near Madrid, an American woman is wounded, accidentally caught in crossfire between rightist and leftist bullets. The American Embassy in Madrid calls all Americans into its walls for protection. . . . Men over the age of 60 and boys under age 18 will be assigned to homeland defense in the event of war, the British press announces after listening to parliamentarian discussion of the possibility of another world war.		Canada's exports are up 35 percent over the past six months to various parts of the world and up 75 percent to British-owned territories.	
Jul. 23		Germany breaks off all relations with the provisional administration of the Protestant Church, raiding its provincial offices to seize funds as well as typewriters and mimeographs in order to put them out of business. . . . A leftist/Communist group seizes Madrid's "gentlemen clubs" as a sign that the aristocratic wealthy of Spain are beginning to lose control of the government.			

A	B	C	D	E
Includes developments that affect more than one world region, international organizations, and important meetings of world leaders.	*Includes all domestic and regional developments in Europe, including the Soviet Union.*	*Includes all domestic and regional developments in Africa and the Middle East.*	*Includes all domestic and regional developments in Latin America, the Caribbean, and Canada.*	*Includes all domestic and regional developments in Asian and Pacific nations (and colonies).*

U.S. Politics & Social Issues	U.S. Foreign Policy & Defense	Economics & Great Depression	Science, Technology & Nature	Culture, Leisure & Lifestyle	
A new Labor Party formed by delegates who represent more than 400,000 employees in New York State endorse the reelection of both President Roosevelt and New York Governor Herbert Lehman. . . . In an effort to prove "favoritism" by the Democratic Party, the Republicans allege to have obtained from the office of Democratic Governor Leslie A. Miller of Wyoming a job application in which Miller asks the candidate to relate his past gifts and contributions to the party.		Charging Harry L. Hopkins, the head of the Works Progress Administration, with neglect in denying vacation time to two WPA employees, the U.S. District Court promises to look into other employees' requests on the same matter. With owed vacation time, the effects could be widespread—and expensive.		Clifton Webb and Helen Gahagan sign to star in the play, *And Stars Remain* for the Theatre Guild. Rehearsals begin in early September.	Jul. 17
Police arrest 11 men for assault and battery after disturbances during a strike outside the Northwestern Barbed Wire Company in Sterling, Ill.					Jul. 18
Vexed by the Roosevelt administration's revenue laws for 1935 and 1936, the Liberty League blames government officials for prostituting constitutional taxing power to "accomplish social and economic ends" fruitful to themselves.	The president of Columbia University, Dr. Nicholas Murray Butler, urges the United States to summon a conference, international in scope, of economists and financiers to waylay fundamental economic problems that might occur if a war breaks out. He makes his plea through the Carnegie Endowment for International Peace.	Heavy downpours inject new hope into the drought-stricken areas of midwestern America. Omaha, Neb., reports heavy winds and some damage, but to most farmers the change in weather appears to be welcome.	A Soviet scientist, Prof. Boris Gerasamovitch, is accused of "servility" after he publishes his astronomical theories first in a foreign—not a Russian—publication. Though the professor claims his intentions were not hostile, the Leningrad newspaper, *Pravda*, denounces him.	The American Motorcycle Championship in New Hampshire has a deadly end when two participants are killed and eight injured during the 200-mile event. One of the dead, a 20-year-old entry from Washington State, rams a curb at 70 miles per hour.	Jul. 19
A Camden, N.J., judge refuses to release 85 persons accused of violence during a recent strike outburst at the local RCA manufacturing plant. Because lawyers have no proof of their innocence, the judge says they must stand trial for the wrongful coercion of which they are accused. . . . Now that Alvin "Old Creepy" Karpis is behind bars awaiting his trial on robbery and kidnapping, FBI chief J. Edgar Hoover names the next Pubic Enemy Number One: Maurice Denning, an alleged thief and gunner for the Kansas City mob.		Throughout the country, U.S. hardware stores report, on the average, a 13 percent gain in sales during the first six months of the year.	An American expedition staffed to survey a total solar eclipse from a focally prominent position in Siberia returns disappointed. Having headed the crew of Georgetown University and National Geographic scientists, the Rev. Dr. Paul A. McNally chagrins the fact that heavy rains on the day of the phenomenon caused the event to be obliterated by thick, low-lying clouds.		Jul. 20
Strikers finally agree to a five-point company plan ending the four-week-old RCA strike in Camden, N.J. This morning, management signed off on the plan and the 4,500 employees ratified it before returning to their shops.		Employees of the steel industry generally earn anywhere from 12–18 percent more than other manufacturing workers, according to pay-scale statistics. In March, steel companies paid $26.38 weekly for a general laborer, compared to $22.21 in other businesses.		Two thousand Civil War reenactors stage the Battle of Bull Run on its 75th anniversary. Here, at Manassas, Va., occurred one of the first—and bloodiest—armed engagements of America's war of rebellion.	Jul. 21
Third-party candidate Walter Lemke, from the Union Party, as a guest speaker at the Union Club of Washington, mocks the Democrats' claims of prosperity and criticizes the New Deal for unrealized promises. . . . Having outstripped the other two Republican primary candidates, Senator Borah and Col. Knox, Kansas Senator Alf M. Landon in Topeka accepts the Republican nomination for the 1936 presidential election.			A four-point program guarding the United States from the harmful effects of future droughts is outlined via a radio broadcast by Secretary of Agriculture Henry Wallace. The plan cites crop loans, crop insurance, normal granary, and land purchases.		Jul. 22
Talladega, Ga., is the site of a bloody demonstration outside a cotton mill. The scuffling ends only with the appearance of the National Guard. Thirty-four people are apprehended after a local sheriff is shot dead and 18 others are injured.	Famed American aviator Charles Lindbergh, now living in Paris with his family, speaks in Germany, warning the world to beware of the airplane—the instrument that shot him to fame. He believes it has inadvertently become the world's greatest technical wonder and, simultaneously, the most deadly weapon of mankind.		Meeting in New York, the American Osteopath Association warns females to watch their posture; a bad posture, it says, can cause a number of illnesses later in life.		Jul. 23

F	G	H	I	J
Includes elections, federal-state relations, civil rights and liberties, crime, the judiciary, education, healthcare, poverty, urban affairs, and population.	Includes formation and debate of U.S. foreign and defense policies, veterans affairs, and defense spending. (Relations with specific foreign countries are usually found under the region concerned.)	Includes business, labor, agriculture, taxation, transportation, consumer affairs, monetary and fiscal policy, natural resources, pollution, and accidents.	Includes worldwide scientific, medical, and technological developments, natural phenomena, U.S. weather, and natural disasters.	Includes the arts, religion, scholarship, communications media, sports, entertainment, fashions, fads, and social life.

	World Affairs	Europe	Africa & The Middle East	The Americas	Asia & The Pacific
Jul. 24		Fighting continues in Madrid, Spain, between the leftwing and rightwing factions, almost nonstop over the last week. President Alzana believes that the rebels are making tactical errors that will cost them the war. In the meantime, special ships depart Barcelona, Managua, and San Sebastian, bringing Americans out of danger.			
Jul. 25		As Gen. Francisco Franco's revolutionist forces surround Madrid, nearly 150 Americans are trapped inside the American Embassy. The Chargé d'Affaires reports that food and water are ample for a week in the event of a siege, but Secretary of State Cordell Hull continues to work with Spanish officials to have them extricated. . . . Franz von Papen, the man credited with pulling off the German-Austria pact that put Germany at the helm of Austria, is honored by Adolf Hitler with a promotion to "Ambassador Extraordinaire" to Vienna.			In an effort to tighten military discipline, Japan's war office commits to several changes, among them cutting down on the circulation of rumors of a political nature. The service intends to "drive home the necessity of stricter discipline to protect military secrets and to unify personnel administration." All changes become effective August 1. . . . Australia's trade prospects are the highest since before the world depression; export outlook is positive as the trading season ripens with fair prices and primary products.
Jul. 26		U.S. representatives at the Olympics have requested that German authorities cease with the out-shot arm salute and "Heil, Hitler!" characteristic of the Nazi soldiery. The German Office replies that it will comply, but only while the games are in session.		President Roosevelt announces a diplomatic tour of Canada; it will be the first time a U.S. President visits a Canadian Governor General (currently Lord Tweedsmuir). The event is symbolic of two neighbor nations solidifying their relationship.	
Jul. 27		Both King Edward VIII of England and his prime minister, Stanley Baldwin, cancel their holidays in light of the poor conditions of world peace at the moment. The King was to have vacationed in Paris, the prime minister in Aixles-Bains.			
Jul. 28		The Nazis forbid boys 14 years old and younger to play sports of any kind—unless they become a member of the Youth Training Corps. It is Reich Sports Manager Hans von Tschammer's attempt to get male children involved in the youth movement, a propaganda concept that is guided by Tschammer's peer, Baldur von Schirach.		Trade relations may resume between Canada and the Soviet Union, whose past relationship proved stormy. Canadian Minister of Trade and Commerce W.D. Euler confers with a delegation of both Canadian and Russian officials.	
Jul. 29				One important item on President Roosevelt's agenda slated for his trip to Canada is the discussion of a hydroelectric-power program to be officiated between the two nations. He meets with Governor General Tweedsmuir and Prime Minister King in two days to kick off a series of formal and informal events.	
Jul. 30		The Nazis oust New Orleans native Ernest Lee Jahncke from the Berlin Olympics Committee with little explanation. He is replaced by Avery Brundage, U.S. Olympic Committee president. Jahncke had tried last year to ban Nazi sponsorship of the Olympic Games.			China's central government has warships and crews ready in case rebellious south Chinese generals Li Tungjen and Pai Chung-hin carry out their secession of the Kwangsi province. Central government boats will blockade all sea traffic so that food, munitions, and reinforcements will not be able to reach the province.
	A Includes developments that affect more than one world region, international organizations, and important meetings of world leaders.	**B** Includes all domestic and regional developments in Europe, including the Soviet Union.	**C** Includes all domestic and regional developments in Africa and the Middle East.	**D** Includes all domestic and regional developments in Latin America, the Caribbean, and Canada.	**E** Includes all domestic and regional developments in Asian and Pacific nations (and colonies).

U.S. Politics & Social Issues	U.S. Foreign Policy & Defense	Economics & Great Depression	Science, Technology & Nature	Culture, Leisure & Lifestyle	
		According to the National Industrial Conference Board, overall business conditions for the first half of 1936 show a substantial gain over figures from the same period in 1935. This includes all phases of production, sales, and distribution. . . . Second quarter earnings for the Union Carbide and Carbon Corporation were $7,936,660 after provision of income and other taxes and associated costs.		Three new films are released to major theaters across America this week. They are *Suzy*, with Jean Harlow; *Earthworm Tractors*, starring Joe E. Brown; and *We Went to College*, featuring Walter Abel.	Jul. 24
	Through general enlistments, the U.S. Army rose by 28,000 over the last 12 months, according to a press release issued today by the War Department. Some 112 men have applied for officer training, aside from the officer training curriculum being taught at West Point Military Academy.	The Works Progress Administration counters opponents who are criticizing it for letting about 750,000 off its rolls during the last quarter, many among them farmers who still face poor prospects. In response, the WPA explains that they are releasing farmers to allow them to tend to their seasonal planting—and that those who are released are not done so randomly, but judiciously.	Transcontinental & Western Air plans freight service between several geographic locations with its new "flying boxcars," trimotor wonders capable of hauling twice the amount of goods than the ordinary cargo plane.		Jul. 25
		Sales figures have increased for nationally distributed refrigerators. Until June, some 216,800 assorted refrigerating appliances have been sold to the public, which has taken a new interest in many of the new freezing features available in late models. . . . Sun Oil Company earnings for the first six months of 1936 are $3,474,811, an increase from the first half of 1934, which was $3,157,863.			Jul. 26
From Topeka, Kans., Republican presidential candidate Alf M. Landon focuses on the drought situation out west, determined to get business involved. A business consortium out east, in turn, asserts that Landon has a very broad business vision on alleviating the drought and other economic problems in the United States. . . . Some 27,000 tickets have already been distributed in Chicago to those wanting to turn out to see the city's own Col. Frank Knox accept the nomination as vice presidential candidate, Landon's running mate.		Schenley's Distillers Corporation announces its first six-month net income—$3,065,948—slightly up from a year ago. Shares are $2.52.			Jul. 27
During the 13 years encompassing the terms of Democratic governors—Al Smith, Herbert Lehman, and Franklin Roosevelt—New York Commissioner of Finance Mark Graves has never seen "more constructive legislation in the interest of agriculture, labor, industry, and finance…than during any like period of the state."		Secretary of the Interior Harold L. Ickes announces a new public works program comprised of 352 separate projects, federal grants of $22,742,345, and secured loans of $2,142,000.		Hans Lessing, who heads the ticket office for the Berlin Olympics, estimates that of the 100,000–250,000 seats that are filled each day at the stadium, at least 40,000 of the spectators are foreign.	Jul. 28
			President Roosevelt allots $1,050,000 for surveys of seven flood control projects as a means to prevent flooding catastrophe in the future. Inspections will include several areas from New York to Pennsylvania, where the heaviest flood disasters took place this past season. . . . The nation's corn yield may be the shortest since 1881 unless precipitation and cooler temperatures visit the Corn Belt, declares Secretary of Agriculture Henry Wallace after touring the west.	A pair of amateur boxers scheduled to take part in the Olympic Games in Berlin decide to head home. They find the Olympic guidelines too overbearing and the conditions of living under Nazi observation even worse. They are featherweight Joe Church and welterweight Howell King.	Jul. 29
		June earnings results for the Jones & Laughlin Steel Corporation of $1,115,773 are well received, since the company had experienced a deficit of $933,729 in the first quarter.			Jul. 30

F	G	H	I	J
Includes elections, federal-state relations, civil rights and liberties, crime, the judiciary, education, healthcare, poverty, urban affairs, and population.	*Includes formation and debate of U.S. foreign and defense policies, veterans affairs, and defense spending. (Relations with specific foreign countries are usually found under the region concerned.)*	*Includes business, labor, agriculture, taxation, transportation, consumer affairs, monetary and fiscal policy, natural resources, pollution, and accidents.*	*Includes worldwide scientific, medical, and technological developments, natural phenomena, U.S. weather, and natural disasters.*	*Includes the arts, religion, scholarship, communications media, sports, entertainment, fashions, fads, and social life.*

	World Affairs	Europe	Africa & The Middle East	The Americas	Asia & The Pacific
Jul. 31				Quebec greets President Roosevelt as he and Governor General Lord Tweedsmuir ride through the city in an open touring car, accompanied by scarlet-coated Canadian troops. Thousands of Canadians line the curbs to applaud the U.S. Chief Executive, who has come to reestablish ties between the neighboring countries.	Forty-two American students representing 18 colleges and universities arrive in Tokyo to participate in the third Japanese-American Student Congress.
Aug. 1		Britain announces restructuring of its national broadcasting system under direction of the British Broadcasting Corporation. New policies, which will roll out over the next 10 years, include guidelines both for radio and for the introduction of television to the viewing public.		Governor Blanton Winship, who is also Education Commissioner of Puerto Rico, assigns $8,000 to be sent to 46 Puerto Rican teachers stranded in France, having escaped the violence in Spain where they had been on a culture tour. The money will allow them passage back home.	The International Olympic Committee awards Japan the right to host the 1940 Olympic Games. The Japanese government and its citizens are reportedly ecstatic.
Aug. 2		While civil war rages in Spain between an assortment of left and right coalitions and its government structure weakens under the chaos, Britain and France lead the way in trying to influence other European powers not to interfere and to ban sales of weapons to both sides in the conflict.		According to a survey conducted by the Foreign Credit Interchange Bureau of the National Association of Credit Men, Latin America, for the first half of 1936, has shown excellent improvement in its credit conditions—solid in the first quarter and better in the second.	
Aug. 3				Just south of Florida, the Bahaman Islands are facing a building boom, say vacation industry watchers. The boom, prompted in part by an interest in real estate by the New England area wealthy, is also aided by the islands' reputation as a sporting haven. Its surrounding waters offer big-game fishing.	
Aug. 4		General Mangada's People's Army storms the little Spanish town of San Rafael, then corners a rebel army beneath San Leone Pass. . . . Local newspapers claim that fascists have been arrested in such huge numbers in Spain as to cause extreme overcrowding in prisons. The estimated number of political prisoners at the moment is 7,000.		Organizers of a plan to increase the cost of newsprint for Canadian distributors to a substantial sum are surprised today when the Great Northern Paper Company, on its own, announces it is raising its cost of newsprint to $1.50 a ton. The protagonists of the plan are disappointed because they had envisioned a much larger increase.	
Aug. 5		Lithuania signs a reciprocal trade pact with Germany, giving Germany the major share of the benefits. Critics say the smaller country was bullied into the deal in hope of preventing hostilities with the stronger power.			

A	B	C	D	E
Includes developments that affect more than one world region, international organizations, and important meetings of world leaders.	Includes all domestic and regional developments in Europe, including the Soviet Union.	Includes all domestic and regional developments in Africa and the Middle East.	Includes all domestic and regional developments in Latin America, the Caribbean, and Canada.	Includes all domestic and regional developments in Asian and Pacific nations (and colonies).

U.S. Politics & Social Issues	U.S. Foreign Policy & Defense	Economics & Great Depression	Science, Technology & Nature	Culture, Leisure & Lifestyle	
By all estimates, the Democrats will not only hold onto the House of Representatives, but will do so in larger numbers, predicts Speaker of the House William B. Bankhead and Democratic Floor Leader John J. O'Connor. . . . With the presidential race heating up, Postmaster General James Farley temporarily resigns from his position to lead the Democratic campaign.		The Electric Bond & Share Company reports net earnings of $9,098,865 for the fiscal year ending June 30. It is a $300,000 decrease from the same period last year.		Maryknoll Missions names Bishop James Edward Walsh of Cumberland, Md., superior general of the Catholic Foreign Mission Society of America.	Jul. 31
The drought paralyzing the farms of the west and southwest becomes a major topic in the current presidential campaign. According to political watchers, farmers' organizations are springing up everywhere either condemning President Roosevelt for ignoring the situation or praising his programs aimed at farm relief. . . . The government allots $78,000 for fire-safety improvements for the White House and the safety of the First Family after an inspection uncovers potential hazards. Improvements will include removal of antiquated wiring and a fire-alarm system.		The American Banking Association says there is nothing to fear in the slight drop this month in buying, expecting a strong recovery that will continue as America heads into the holiday months. . . . The United Gas Improvement Company and subsidiaries gained $28,683,537 for the fiscal year ending June 30, equal to $1.07 per share. . . . Nelson Shipping, one of the West Coast's oldest and most dependable shipping lines of America's goods in the Pacific route, closes its doors today. Cause is inability to maintain rigidity during the Depression years.		Dr. Walter A. Maier, staff member of the Concordia Lutheran Theological Seminary in St. Louis, claims that the oft-controversial Father Charles E. Coughlin, whose radio program is listened to by thousands each week, is merely a puppet of the Catholic Church.	Aug. 1
Attendees of the International Federation of Business and Professional Women, representing some 100,000 women across America, sign a resolution demanding rights and pay equal to men in the work world. . . . Col. Frank Knox, the Chicago newspaper publisher now running alongside Alf Landon for vice president, announces his upcoming campaign schedule, which will start in New Hampshire and include 16 states. . . . From his Hyde Park, N.Y., estate, President Roosevelt summons his Cabinet and others who are working on his reelection campaign. Observers expect a change in direction.		Because of a shortage in the foreign markets for American produce, apple growers are forced to destroy this season's apple crop, says E.W.P. Hearty, an officer of the International Apple Association. The problem will be formally addressed, Hearty adds, at the upcoming World Two-Way Trade Fair. . . . According to the League of Nations book of yearly statistics, the United States sold more beer in 1935 than the country that is known for beer and has some of the finest breweries in the world—Germany.		Midwest motor bandit John Sullivan, allegedly the gunman who robbed $14,000 from a bank in St. Charles, Ill., is captured by FBI agents in Cedar Lake, Ind.	Aug. 2
A session of Catholic Charities in Seattle attributes many of the wayward children of today as products of parents whose lives or lifestyles were ended by the world war of 1917–1918, followed by the haphazard behavior engendered by the "Roaring Twenties." Today's youth, says the organization, are "inheritors of a crazy-quilt civilization."		The automobile industry continues to recover, evidenced by the latest figures published by Detroit manufacturers. From 1932, the worst year of the Depression, through year's end 1936, the industry estimates that it will have sold 13,575,683 vehicles throughout the United States and neighboring Canada. In that number are the 4.6 million cars and trucks that the industry determines it will sell this year.			Aug. 3
Many recent parolees may be heading back to prison after the decision by the U.S. Circuit Court of Appeals, which states that too many federal judges have been allowing convicts early paroles to compensate for prison time. The Parole Board announces that hundreds of men and women will need to complete their assigned sentences.			According to Chicago-based observers, the corn crop around the globe this year falls horrendously below the expected amount based on a five-year average. Barring Argentina, every major corn producer in the world is experiencing great shortages, in particular those growers in the United States. In all, the shortage may exceed 900 million bushels.		Aug. 4
President Roosevelt discounts the suggestion of his political foes that his upcoming tour of the drought-ravaged west is an excuse for a political tour. He calls their linking of the misery encountered by the people there with political stumping a "great disservice" to mankind.		This season's drought, which has terribly affected the output of farms in the west and southwest, is deemed to be the worst in the nation's history. As of today, the Works Progress Administration is aiding 93,500 people affected by the drought in Oklahoma, Kansas, Wyoming, and elsewhere.			Aug. 5

F	G	H	I	J
Includes elections, federal-state relations, civil rights and liberties, crime, the judiciary, education, healthcare, poverty, urban affairs, and population.	Includes formation and debate of U.S. foreign and defense policies, veterans affairs, and defense spending. (Relations with specific foreign countries are usually found under the region concerned.)	Includes business, labor, agriculture, taxation, transportation, consumer affairs, monetary and fiscal policy, natural resources, pollution, and accidents.	Includes worldwide scientific, medical, and technological developments, natural phenomena, U.S. weather, and natural disasters.	Includes the arts, religion, scholarship, communications media, sports, entertainment, fashions, fads, and social life.

	World Affairs	Europe	Africa & The Middle East	The Americas	Asia & The Pacific
Aug. 6		The entertainment of the cinema and radio has cut down on the once popular French habit of drinking at cafes, says a social report by the League of Nations. The change is viewed positively since it has kept many a youth from becoming inebriated and getting into trouble. . . . Adolf Hitler advocates doing away with the League of Nations and replacing it with a committee "of common sense (using) reason and justice" to avert a general worldwide war.			
Aug. 7				In the latest Canadian provincial elections, the Liberal Party, which has enjoyed political prosperity for some time, loses support for not doing enough to counter a fallen economy and job losses. In Manitoba, the Liberal Progressives suffer a harsh setback, and in Quebec's upcoming election the prospects appear worse.	
Aug. 8		After trying to get its unemployment figures down, Germany is encouraged by reports from its Labor Office. The number of citizens registered as unemployed has dropped by another 144,000 people. The total of jobless remaining in the country is 1,170,000.		A drought that has burned much of the U.S. farm output has also affected certain agrarian areas of Canada. According to the Dominion Bureau of Statistics in Ottawa, a lack of rain and a blistering sun have ruined some 45 percent of the prairie provinces.	
Aug. 9	The World Jewish Congress in Geneva, Switzerland, proposes two new governing bodies—one to help direct the global migration of Jews and another to bring them financial relief.	African-American sprinter Jesse Owens from Ohio State University, one of the most able competitors in this year's Olympic Games, wins his fourth gold medal today. Adolf Hitler, who had earlier predicted Germany's triumph in most if not all track events, is irritated that an African American, whom the Nazi Party would consider "inferior," bests the Nazi runners. At the medal presentation, he refuses to shake Owens's hand.	The Union of South Africa promotes the Noxious Weeds Bill in parliament, addressing the growing problems caused by the profuse growth of thistle, Mexican marigold, khaki brush, and other weeds.		
Aug. 10		A new Catalan government is in place in Spain. The new authority is anti-fascist and anti-socialist.			
Aug. 11		Soviet Russia, in wanting to modernize and expand its food industry, announces it is sending Anastas Mikoyan, Soviet Commissar for Internal Supply, and several delegates to America to inspect its machinery for food preparation. The Soviets then plan to purchase such equipment from the United States. . . . Joachim von Ribbentrop, a hard-line Nazi and Hitler's foreign affairs adviser, is personally appointed by Hitler as Germany's new ambassador to Great Britain, replacing Dr. Leopold von Hoesch, who died in April.			Stressing solidarity, Gen. Chiang Kai-shek, speaking at a press conference in the Kiangsi province, calls for a parley between north and south China, believing that amends can be made in their differences without resorting to full-scale war.
Aug. 12				As the League of Nations decides whether or not to recognize Italy's conquering of Ethiopia as a legal action, Argentina—which has been against the Italo-Ethiopian War from the start—readies Foreign Minister Carlos Saavedra Lamas to present its views on the subject. He will leave September 28 to vote against the Italian decision.	With the budget under debate in Tokyo, the Japanese War Ministry bemoans any cost-saving measures that would decrease military expenditures. It is no time for a policy to put the national defense of the country in danger, says the War Minister.
Aug. 13		As an aside to the sporting events, the Berlin Olympics presents a special tribute to Germany's army, navy, and air force in a huge and colorful military display before 100,000 spectators.			

A	B	C	D	E
Includes developments that affect more than one world region, international organizations, and important meetings of world leaders.	Includes all domestic and regional developments in Europe, including the Soviet Union.	Includes all domestic and regional developments in Africa and the Middle East.	Includes all domestic and regional developments in Latin America, the Caribbean, and Canada.	Includes all domestic and regional developments in Asian and Pacific nations (and colonies).

U.S. Politics & Social Issues	U.S. Foreign Policy & Defense	Economics & Great Depression	Science, Technology & Nature	Culture, Leisure & Lifestyle	
Thomas E. Dewey, Special Prosecutor for the State of New York who recently shut down a vast prostitution ring under mobster "Lucky" Luciano, appoints a grand jury to investigate racketeering in the city's garment district. He alleges corrupt union officials have tainted the industry as a personal get-rich-quick scheme.		Liquor imports have increased this fiscal year, evident in the amount of duties paid through the end of June: $33,353,989 on 9,803,235 gallons.			Aug. 6
		American Power and Light Company's report states that the company netted $9,302,104 for the fiscal year ending in June. The net is equal to $5.25 per share.			Aug. 7
Speaking in Connersville, Ind., vice presidential hopeful Col. Frank Knox promises to free the "plain man" from burdensome taxes and shift those taxes to the wealthy. At the same time he will "return millions of unemployed to honest work."		Wheat crop in the United States, despite drought and despite other unfavorable weather conditions, has maintained a steady quantity. According to a U.S. agriculture report, the nation's wheat supply is at 1926, pre-Depression, levels.	Philadelphia's Academy of Natural Sciences announces that it is currently sponsoring some 20 expeditions and archaeological field trips on the North and South American continents and in Africa. Managing director Charles M.B. Cadwalader expects that as the adventurers return, they will be bringing artifacts that will expand the Academy's already impressive exhibit of 5 million specimens.	The Catholic Daughters of America, convening for their conference in Atlantic City, denounce birth control, movie obscenity, and Communism. . . . Growing out of interest garnered in the Olympics, the International Baseball Federation completes its first registration with 16 nations and several states enrolled as participants. The first game is slated for next summer in Tokyo, Japan.	Aug. 8
A commission representing silk workers leads the way to a general strike, demanding better pay—$9 per week instead of the outdated $6—and improved working conditions.			A new system for tracking hurricanes is developed by the University of Florida through the process of "static photos," which help estimate the path a hurricane is taking.	Max Schmeling, the German pugilist who beat African-American prize-fighter Joe Louis last year, visits the latter's training camp in Pompton Lakes, N.J. Because Chancellor Adolf Hitler made the fight a race issue, Schmeling's visit is to ensure that he and Louis—whom the country calls "The Brown Bomber"—remain friends despite Hitler's bigotry.	Aug. 9
			Scientists from around the globe meet in Copenhagen, Denmark, to study recent achievements and explore new areas of inquiry at the International Scientific Congress. The rector of Copenhagen University presides.		Aug. 10
	National Republican Headquarters has assembled a group of political "advertising men" whose charge is to break President Roosevelt and his administration apart, piece by piece, program by program. The committee promises to attack the very roots of the New Deal and bare its inadequacies in terms of how it has negatively affected the average household.	Blaming President Roosevelt's avoidance of issues, broken promises, and unchecked spending, former Assistant War Secretary F. Trubee Davison campaigns to get Republican Alf M. Landon in the White House.			Aug. 11
Imprisoned gangster Charles "Lucky" Luciano waits for his trial on racketeering in a cell at Dennemora Prison. He promises to fight the U.S. government in "legally" freeing himself of a 30- to 50-year sentence promised him from Supreme Court Justice Phillip J. McCook.		U.S. exports for the month of June did exceptionally well, according to the latest report from the Department of Commerce. Valued at $194,908,000, they increased in all divisions except in the southern section of the United States.		Woodlands immediately adjacent to the town of St. Paul, Minn., and for 200 miles around it continue to burn. Firefighters by the thousands turn out from every connecting county and village, large and small. The scene is reminiscent of the blaze in 1918, which caused $60 million in damages to the northern woods.	Aug. 12
Assailing President Roosevelt's tax policies that "attack" the family man, Republican vice presidential candidate Frank Knox says he envisions "a real share-the-wealth environment" in America under a new regime.		Second quarter earnings for the Eastman Kodak Company indicate that the photographic company continues to show gains. A release reports it has netted $8,081,870 over the past three-month period after depreciation and other expenses.			Aug. 13

F	G	H	I	J
Includes elections, federal-state relations, civil rights and liberties, crime, the judiciary, education, healthcare, poverty, urban affairs, and population.	Includes formation and debate of U.S. foreign and defense policies, veterans affairs, and defense spending. (Relations with specific foreign countries are usually found under the region concerned.)	Includes business, labor, agriculture, taxation, transportation, consumer affairs, monetary and fiscal policy, natural resources, pollution, and accidents.	Includes worldwide scientific, medical, and technological developments, natural phenomena, U.S. weather, and natural disasters.	Includes the arts, religion, scholarship, communications media, sports, entertainment, fashions, fads, and social life.

	World Affairs	Europe	Africa & The Middle East	The Americas	Asia & The Pacific
Aug. 14				A Toronto newspaper reports that Canada's Royal Commission is investigating charges by certain Toronto-based anthracite coal companies who claim they were subjected to unfair credit tactics by a number of U.S. concerns. . . . Nicaragua enters into a trade pact with the United States, one that will help boost the exports of both countries.	
Aug. 15		An anonymous woman flaunting a bright red hat breaks through Adolf Hitler's personal guards to kiss his cheek, providing cameramen a rare opportunity of catching him off guard. Who the woman is remains a mystery, but she afterward gives her name as Carla de Uriese, claiming she hails from California.	The country of Turkey announces a new board for the censoring of films. Its main objective is to eradicate all religiously and politically dangerous content from public viewing.	Seventeen Americans are killed when their truck is slammed by a speeding train at a midnight crossing in Louisville, Quebec. The collision involves another series of vehicles, injuring 15 more people, four of whom leap to safety.	
Aug. 16		The British Commonwealth applauds the New Deal, holding it up as a model for good economics. Many nations belonging to the Commonwealth are emulating it, says Oliver L. Lawrence of the British Institute of International Affairs. . . . The 11th modern Olympics closes tonight in Berlin with a light display, the clash of bells, trumpets, booming cannon fire, and a massive choir performing Beethoven.			
Aug. 17	The United States announces that Germany, during the first half of this year, paid off part of its long-standing debt. It remitted 19 million marks, reducing the deficit from 70 million to 50.9 million marks.			Both Canada and the United States are enjoying benefits of their reciprocal trade agreement that went into effect six months ago, according to an Ottawan source. Although Canada enjoys an excess over the United States in the ratio of earnings, the two-way business has wrought an $85 million gain in total trade between both countries.	
Aug. 18		Germany agrees with the request of France and Britain to put an embargo on the delivery of arms and ammunition to Spain, provided that all other countries possessing large armaments also join the union.			
Aug. 19					Japan's naval aide, Capt. Yamaguchi, is transferred to another position after U.S. agents arrest and question a former U.S. naval officer for attempting to sell secret documents to Japan. Tokyo explains that the removal of Yamaguchi—who has denied any association with the accused— has nothing to do with that affair.
Aug. 20		Germany, who has had its merchant ships tampered with beyond the legal "three-mile limit" off the coast of Spain, orders its warships now patrolling those waters to open fire upon the transgressors if such interference occurs again. . . . Josef Stalin learns for the first time that he narrowly missed death during a fumbled assassination attempt, when Valentine Olberg, one of 16 people being tried for terrorist activities in Russia, explains the plot at his trial. He blames Leon Trotsky as the architect of the plan. The trials mark the beginning of a new round of purges in the Soviet Union.			China and Japan unite in an economic plan for North China when Gen. Sun Cheh-yuan, head of the political council in the Chahar province, and Japanese Ambassador Shigeru Kawagoe jointly sign off on a development program.

A	B	C	D	E
Includes developments that affect more than one world region, international organizations, and important meetings of world leaders.	Includes all domestic and regional developments in Europe, including the Soviet Union.	Includes all domestic and regional developments in Africa and the Middle East.	Includes all domestic and regional developments in Latin America, the Caribbean, and Canada.	Includes all domestic and regional developments in Asian and Pacific nations (and colonies).

U.S. Politics & Social Issues	U.S. Foreign Policy & Defense	Economics & Great Depression	Science, Technology & Nature	Culture, Leisure & Lifestyle	
The National Union for Social Justice at its convention in Cleveland, Ohio, nominates William Lemke for president. He has the support of Father Coughlin, Dr. Francis Townsend, and Gerald L.K. Smith, who has inherited the organization established by Huey Long.	In response to his critics who have been saying he is avoiding a verbal stand for or against neutrality, President Roosevelt, speaking in Chautauqua, N.Y., addresses the issue by vigorously condemning war. He chastises those who "violate with impunity" their duties to their country. But, he asserts, if America should be attacked, he will defend "our neighborhood."	President Roosevelt's Agriculture Adjustment Administration, which promises to introduce a new bill in the next session of Congress, explains that it will offer farmers more stability and keep consumer food prices at a medium level.			Aug. 14
		The Republican Party, hoping to win the White House this year, appoints a research team to compile and publish the facts on the Roosevelt administration's tax increases and debt accumulation caused by New Deal programs. Heading the endeavor is Robert Kratky, a St. Louis-based financial attorney.		Oklahoma waits for the return of Carlton B. Chilton, who was discovered living in Ohio 23 years after escaping from a Granite City jail in the middle of a two-year term for bank robbery. Although living an upright life in Cleveland, Ohio, Governor Marland refuses his clemency and prepares to extradite him to Oklahoma. . . . As expected, Germany takes the gold medal in the Olympic boxing tournament, scoring 34 points to Italy's 26 in the final round. Argentina wins the silver and Italy the bronze.	Aug. 15
Alleging that Communists have entered its ranks, as well as desiring to adopt its own brand of educational system in the state, the Socialist Party of Pennsylvania secedes from the National Socialist Party. . . . Third-party candidate for president, William Lemke, a favorite of radio priest Charles E. Coughlin, draws an unexpected 30,000 to his campaign speech at Cleveland's Municipal Stadium.		The Armstrong Cork Company announces earnings for the first six months of the year of $1,876,399 after expenses, including flood loss.	Evidence of a form of organized crime existed 3,500 years ago, say archaeologists who unearth cuneiform texts from a dig in Mesopotamia. The tablets tell of bribery, graft, and intimidation, written during the trial of what appears to have been a corrupt public official.		Aug. 16
"Maintain an organized line of common defense" when dealing with subversive groups such as the Communists, says Martin H. Carmody, Supreme Knight of the Knights of Columbus in Grand Rapids, Mich. He warns Americans to avoid doing business with suspect organizations that undermine the political process and the right to practice one's religion.		As of the end of June, the steel industry is employing 498,000 people, the largest number of employees it has ever had on its payrolls—even though steel mills have been running at 70 percent of their capacity. Hourly wages have also reached full scale in many areas of the industry, according to the American Iron and Steel Institute.			Aug. 17
A presidential holiday cruise down the Mississippi River is cancelled when Roosevelt decides he should stay at home to keep his attention on escalating problems overseas. He does, however, keep on the agenda an investigative tour through the drought areas of the nation, which is scheduled for next week.		Sperry Corporation doubles its income over the past six months, from $809,751 January-June 1935 to $1,657,305 this year. This includes a profit of $1,055,204 made on sales of securities. Shares are 85 cents.			Aug. 18
"There will be no further violent and sudden interferences with the vital implements" of industry, says Col. Frank Knox, Republican nominee for vice president. Economic recovery, he tells a Hagerstown, Md., audience will be a "fact," not an issue.		The Agricultural Adjustment Administration declares its intention to introduce a new soil conservation program next year that will pay farmers a large stipend for repairing land marred by drought.		Reportedly, Joseph Schenck, Hollywood producer, and Robert Rubin, producer of British films, are seriously considering merging Twentieth Century Fox, Gaumont British Pictures Corp., and Loew's, Inc.	Aug. 19
Claiming he will restore "the American way," Republican candidate for president Alf M. Landon begins his train tour east speaking from a train platform in Omaha. He attacks reciprocal trade and "squandering," pledges drought aid and helpful tariffs, and preaches "good government."		The Chesapeake & Ohio Railroad, one of the nation's most prestigious railways, earned $21,000,436 through the first seven months of this year—equal to $2.74 per share.		A long-awaited release from Hollywood opens tonight in theaters in America—*Romeo and Juliet*, starring Leslie Howard and Norma Shearer.	Aug. 20

F	G	H	I	J
Includes elections, federal-state relations, civil rights and liberties, crime, the judiciary, education, healthcare, poverty, urban affairs, and population.	Includes formation and debate of U.S. foreign and defense policies, veterans affairs, and defense spending. (Relations with specific foreign countries are usually found under the region concerned.)	Includes business, labor, agriculture, taxation, transportation, consumer affairs, monetary and fiscal policy, natural resources, pollution, and accidents.	Includes worldwide scientific, medical, and technological developments, natural phenomena, U.S. weather, and natural disasters.	Includes the arts, religion, scholarship, communications media, sports, entertainment, fashions, fads, and social life.

	World Affairs	Europe	Africa & The Middle East	The Americas	Asia & The Pacific
Aug. 21		War maneuvers by six countries are slated for next week, bringing Italy, Germany, Albania, Austria, Hungary, and Poland together as one 200,000-man allied force. The display is not so much for power, explains the Italian consulate hosting the fête, but to exhibit a unity at a time when central European relations seem to be faltering. France and Britain remain unsupportive of the endeavor.	Italian Gen. Graziani, head of the Italian forces in Ethiopia, calculates the division of what was once Emperor Haile Selassie's country. For now, he awaits the end of the rainy season before distributing his 250,000 troops across the land to secure it for Italy. The troops, which expect not to encounter any more resistance, will oversee a pacification period in the respective colonies, followed by a large-scale building program.	From the Buenos Aires press comes word that all of South America is concerned by the bloody civil war in Spain. It does not want to revive bad feelings that existed between Spanish-speaking peoples of Latin America and their neighbor, the United States, during the Spanish-American War of the late 1890s. Many in Brazil, Paraguay, Uruguay, and other Latin American countries express a need for peace among the citizens of their motherland, Spain, and push for a peace pact returning Spain to normalcy.	
Aug. 22		Leaders of the Protestant Church in Germany call for an end to the Third Reich's religious persecution and a return to the days when they could practice their faith without fear of reprisal. They demand to have their church restored and all attempts to replace it with paganism ceased immediately.		According to Canada's Department of Mines, two of the Dominion's oldest gold mining areas, the Porcupine Camp and the Kirkland Lake Camp, are still the richest mines, providing 56 percent of the gold mined. The government expects an increase in gold output this year from these and other mines.	If Japan and China go to war, Japan would have more to lose, say economic observers; it could win the war, but in doing so cripple itself financially. Politicos assert that the two countries have not been so close to intolerance since April 1895, when the Treaty of Shimonoseki ended a fierce rivalry.... From the Institute of Pacific Relations, France and Belgium together react with "strenuous objections" to rumors that Japan may have formed an alliance with Nazi Germany.
Aug. 23		Observers describe a much smoother relationship between Germany and Austria since the signing of the Austro-German agreement last month. While the details of the pact have never really been explained in clarified terms, it is becoming apparent that the German and Austrian governments have melded, with the former in control.			
Aug. 24		Adolf Hitler strengthens his army by enlarging it by another 200,000 men and changing the prescribed conscription period from one to two years. He explains his action is in response to the growing "Red menace" of Soviet Russia.		Agricultural trade between the United States and Canada has increased each country's import/export trade by 24 percent, estimates the Bureau of Agricultural Economics. This includes fruits, vegetables, and ore.	Japan announces that its army in Hsinking, Manchukuo, has executed nine Russian Communists and imprisoned 17 others for conspiring to lead a "stormtrooper" movement of Russian soldiers against public buildings there. Allegedly, there were 300 in the plot, many of whom escaped before being apprehended.
Aug. 25		The Hungarian newspaper, *Esti Ujsaj*, alludes to the Hungarian government's possible strengthening of its armament. Its reasons are twofold: the Nazi menace from Germany as well as a "Red" menace from the Soviet Union. Its geographic position places it in a dangerous position to ignore the threats from either power.			A Chinese mob, seemingly unprovoked, attacks four visiting Japanese men in a hotel in Chengtu, capital of the Szechwan province. Of the four, two are slain, one injured, and one is missing.
Aug. 26		Berlin's skeptical attitude toward a "world peace conference," as suggested by President Roosevelt, in which America would take an active role, is made clear in a quote from a German official who calls the idea "charming naiveté."			For the first time since 1929, visiting Japanese naval ships sail into the Hudson River, where they are met and saluted by a U.S. Navy flotilla. The personnel of the two Nipponese ships, the *Iwate* and *Yakumo*, are on an eight-day naval training tour as guests of the State of New York.

A	B	C	D	E
Includes developments that affect more than one world region, international organizations, and important meetings of world leaders.	Includes all domestic and regional developments in Europe, including the Soviet Union.	Includes all domestic and regional developments in Africa and the Middle East.	Includes all domestic and regional developments in Latin America, the Caribbean, and Canada.	Includes all domestic and regional developments in Asian and Pacific nations (and colonies).

U.S. Politics & Social Issues	U.S. Foreign Policy & Defense	Economics & Great Depression	Science, Technology & Nature	Culture, Leisure & Lifestyle	
FBI agents arrest 22 high-ranking members of the Detroit chapter of the Black Legion, a vigilante-terrorist organization, for suspicion of forming a cabal bent on taking over the federal government.		During the first six months of the year, the General American Transportation Company increased profit over last year, netting $1,030,589 after taxes and assorted expenses.			Aug. 21
Harvard Law School critiques the Massachusetts criminal court system as "antiquated." According to professors Henry B. Cabot and Sam Bass Warner, the system remains the same as it did a half-century ago. Harvard urges reform. . . . Problems such as overpopulation, hunger, and drought, which haunt rural areas such as the Cotton Belt and the southern Appalachian district, cannot be repaired until the natives are relocated to another area, says the University of Pennsylvania Social Department.	Because 95 percent of the people in Europe do not want war, attorney Thomas W. Lamont believes that war will be avoided. Having just returned from an overseas holiday, Lamont, of J.P. Morgan & Co., scoffs at the idea of a world war.				Aug. 22
		In his recently published book, *I'm for Roosevelt*, former Securities and Exchange Commission chairman Joseph P. Kennedy compliments President Roosevelt for keeping the cost of the nation's recovery at a minimum. Kennedy refers to Roosevelt's critics as "ingrates." . . . Economist Bernard Baruch proposes economic stability via international regulation of hours and wages. . . . In its monthly report, the National Association of Purchasing Agents predict a 1936 business volume of 20 percent greater than 1935.	According to Dr. Ewing Adams, chairman of the Optometric Research Institute of Michigan, nearly 60 percent of the nation's drivers have some eyesight deficiency. Visiting the DeSoto automotive manufacturing plant, he adds that most of the eye problems are minor treatable defects.		Aug. 23
		The newly formed Workers Alliance of America, backed by the American Federation of Labor and representing the Works Progress Administration, sends workers' demands for higher wages to President Roosevelt and Deputy WPA Administrator Aubrey Williams for comment.		The Anglican Church in the Western Hemisphere announces that it is hosting a three-day Pan-Anglican Conference in mid-October in Chicago. There, more than 150 archbishops and bishops will reclarify the church's definition of Christian unity and state their stand on America's place in world peace.	Aug. 24
					Aug. 25
		"Cockeyed" is how presidential nominee Alf M. Landon labels President Roosevelt's tax surplus program. Deliberating on the President's "reckless spending" before a huge Buffalo, N.Y., crowd, Landon claims the poor man of today and his children will be forced to pay off a huge deficit in the years to come. . . . The American National Jeweler's Association opts to use a better strategy and a more ambitious advertising plan to regain trade lost to other industries.		Various top production agents from the Hollywood industry, including Columbia Pictures' Jack Cohen, protest against various national radio stations that use their film stars on an ongoing basis, exploiting the success of the film industry.	Aug. 26

F	G	H	I	J
Includes elections, federal-state relations, civil rights and liberties, crime, the judiciary, education, healthcare, poverty, urban affairs, and population.	*Includes formation and debate of U.S. foreign and defense policies, veterans affairs, and defense spending. (Relations with specific foreign countries are usually found under the region concerned.)*	*Includes business, labor, agriculture, taxation, transportation, consumer affairs, monetary and fiscal policy, natural resources, pollution, and accidents.*	*Includes worldwide scientific, medical, and technological developments, natural phenomena, U.S. weather, and natural disasters.*	*Includes the arts, religion, scholarship, communications media, sports, entertainment, fashions, fads, and social life.*

	World Affairs	Europe	Africa & The Middle East	The Americas	Asia & The Pacific
Aug. 27		Austria edits the Berlin Olympic movie, which is scheduled to be shown in German and Austrian movie houses, but draws the wrath of the Nazi party by cutting out scenes of Hitler and other Nazi authorities giving speeches and participating in behind-the-scenes activities. The editors defend their actions by responding that those scenes, being political, had nothing to do with the Olympics.			
Aug. 28				The Newfoundland economy's chief export, seafood, is experiencing a drop-off in exportation, but more countries are buying the country's newsprint. Plans are being made to revive interest in its fish trade.	
Aug. 29				Peru plans to build a huge airplane factory at La Palmas, 10 miles from the heart of Lima. The Sociedad Anonemia Aeroplani Caproni of Milan, Italy, which obtained the $75,000 contract. Employment is expected to surge in the area, due to the new production plant.	The Formosa government approves the appointment of Japanese Admiral Seizo Kobayashi as its Governor General. What makes this move significant is that it is indicative of Japan's "Southward Policy," in which it plans to expand its empire into the South Seas where new raw materials can be found.
Aug. 30		Australian newspaper publisher Sir Keith Murdoch, after observing first-hand the political situation overseas, believes that although Germany has been making overtures of war and other countries have been making warlike preparations, tensions overseas will not necessarily lead to war.	South Africa's real estate and gold mining industries both continue to offer high value as speculators and prospectors continue to see large profits, says a Johannesburg newspaper. Economists signal caution, however, for there have been other such booms before—but little attention is paid to their warnings as investments continue to animate sky-high returns.		
Aug. 31	Five hundred delegates and 200 alternates representing 36 countries converge on Geneva, Switzerland, to open the first World Youth Congress to Prevent War and Organize Peace. The majority of attendees are those who were too young to participate in the world war, but old enough now to fight in the event of another. By sharing ideas and creating international friendships, they hope to override the friction that certain powers in the world are creating.	Premier Benito Mussolini of Italy has reportedly agreed to a meeting at Hitler's personal Alpine getaway at Berchtesgaden. The Third Reich denies the rumors.			
Sept. 1	New Zealand's representative to the League of Nations suggests the formation of an "international force under the League's control," whose purpose would be to protect the League from dissidents and, upon allocation, serve as an auxiliary force for member countries, guarding them "from land, sea, and air."	Nazi propagandist Joseph Goebbels compliments Italy for its aggressive attitude in a speech near Rome. Like Germany, both countries are aiming for peace, he says, by enforcing their own military strength.		President Harmonio Arias of Panama lauds President Roosevelt for suggesting a Pan-American peace conference when the rest of the world seems to be rushing into war. Arias calls Roosevelt's action "a magnificent gesture."	

A	B	C	D	E
Includes developments that affect more than one world region, international organizations, and important meetings of world leaders.	Includes all domestic and regional developments in Europe, including the Soviet Union.	Includes all domestic and regional developments in Africa and the Middle East.	Includes all domestic and regional developments in Latin America, the Caribbean, and Canada.	Includes all domestic and regional developments in Asian and Pacific nations (and colonies).

U.S. Politics & Social Issues	U.S. Foreign Policy & Defense	Economics & Great Depression	Science, Technology & Nature	Culture, Leisure & Lifestyle	
Earl Browder, the Communist Party's choice for president, targets Alf M. Landon, the Republican candidate, as his chief antagonist. Browder refers to him as the "figurehead" for advocates of fascism that will cater to the wealthy and the prosperous once in office.		Members of his appointed Great Plains Drought Area Committee advise President Roosevelt to commission a federal-state board to execute a water and soil conservation program in drought-stricken sections of the United States, as well as a detailed study to examine growing shifts in the whole "Dust Bowl" economy. . . . For the 24 weeks ending July 31, retail giant Sears, Roebuck & Company earned $12,634,285 after depreciation and other costs. It is a large increase from the same period in 1935, which totaled $7,472,512.			Aug. 27
The trial of several people arrested for disorderly conduct during an anti-Nazi demonstration in New York brings to light the issue of Adolf Hitler's Germany. The lawyer for one of the accused explains that his client is speaking out against a war that will affect Americans worldwide.	British parliamentarian A.V. Alexander pleads for the United States to drop its isolationist policies. At the Pacific parley taking place at Yosemite Park, Calif., he expresses concern over the world situation, worried that current events are leading the globe into war for which America should be prepared.		There will come a day in the future, predicts Dr. Philip Drinker of Harvard's School of Public Health, when science will be able to condition the very air, just as it now sterilizes milk and water. He addresses the university's annual health conference.		Aug. 28
	President Roosevelt, in discussing reelection plans, alludes to the possibility of his calling a conference of the world's leaders to Washington for the sole purpose of discussing the maintenance of world peace. While a protagonist of neutrality, the President continually refers to his hope for peace among nations.	The New Deal comes under attack as political campaigning intensifies. In West Virginia, former secretary of war Patrick J. Hurley reminds a crowd that President Roosevelt's policies omit a lot of the promises he made to Americans in 1932. In Rochester, N.Y., Supreme Court Justice William F. Beazley maintains that the people of America "do not want relief, they want work." . . . Pledging to invest in soil conservation, President Roosevelt tells a Pierre, S. Dak., audience that spending $1 million dollars to save $10 million is common sense. He vows to battle the effects of drought in that and other states where crops have withered.			Aug. 29
		Corn, alfalfa, beans, and sugar cane are all crops that are doing well this year, according to industry watchers.			Aug. 30
Leaders representing three different religions—a Jewish rabbi, a Catholic priest, and a Protestant vicar—hold a public meeting in Appleton, Wisc., to discuss forming a "united front" to address social and civic problems, not as three separate entities but as a single group under one God. . . . The U.S. Customs Bureau joins the fight to prevent the distribution of narcotics in the United States by having 570 border agents concentrate on eliminating the importation of smuggled drugs through America's boundaries.		Earnings for W.T Grant's first six months of the year double over those of the same period last year, totaling $1,448,978 in 1936 compared to $669,529 in the same period the year prior. The 1936 figure is equivalent to $1.22 per share.	Sir Arthur Eddington, British physicist, announces that he has completed a long project, calculating the number of electrons—infinitesimal units of matter in the universe—comprising the world. He plans to state his findings in the near future at a seminar that has yet to be scheduled.	Comedian legend turned producer and director, Charlie Chaplin, buys the rights to D.L. Murray's *Regency* as a vehicle for budding actress Paulette Goddard, his protégé. Simultaneously, 1920s cowboy star William S. Hart announces that he has decided not to make a comeback. He leaves the Hollywood Western to newer, younger stars, such as Randolph Scott.	Aug. 31
Organized labor's internal fighting continues as John L. Lewis's Committee for Industrial Organization and its rival, William Green's American Federation of Labor, each call foul. Green charges a "raid" on his organization as Lewis convinces a group of gas and coke unions under the AFL to change homes and move into the CIO.	Two thousand veterans of the Spanish-American War of 1898 hold a reunion at the Saratoga Springs battlefield, where they are joined by the Military Order of the Serpent, a politically minded band of war veterans.	Banks across the nation report a healthy economy. Purchasing power is up, farm prices are advancing, and the upcoming holiday season promises to be a prosperous one. . . . President Roosevelt announces the U.S. Treasury's estimate of the 1936–37 national deficit as $2,096,996,000—nearly $1 million more than had been predicted, but still the lowest deficit under the New Deal.			Sept. 1

F	G	H	I	J
Includes elections, federal-state relations, civil rights and liberties, crime, the judiciary, education, healthcare, poverty, urban affairs, and population.	Includes formation and debate of U.S. foreign and defense policies, veterans affairs, and defense spending. (Relations with specific foreign countries are usually found under the region concerned.)	Includes business, labor, agriculture, taxation, transportation, consumer affairs, monetary and fiscal policy, natural resources, pollution, and accidents.	Includes worldwide scientific, medical, and technological developments, natural phenomena, U.S. weather, and natural disasters.	Includes the arts, religion, scholarship, communications media, sports, entertainment, fashions, fads, and social life.

	World Affairs	Europe	Africa & The Middle East	The Americas	Asia & The Pacific
Sept. 2		French Premier Leon Blum and his Cabinet begin an assertive move to strengthen their country's military defenses on the heels of Nazi Germany's announcement that it is lengthening conscripts' military time. . . . Francisco Franco, Spanish rebel general, deploys a large army of young men from the youth movement to the war front as a shortage of regular troops becomes apparent. Franco himself moves headquarters nearer the action, from Seville to Caceres.		Gen. Anastasio Somoza, who took over the Nicaraguan government last month but who is now running a democratic election, predicts victory at the polls, based on his people's trust in him.	Vice Admiral Zengo Yashida of the Japanese imperial training squadron denies that his country's moves into China and the South Seas are aggressive; rather, they are meant to enhance Japanese trade, he explains.
Sept. 3		Erlangen, Germany, hosts the fourth Reich Congress of Germans Abroad, attended by members of the Nazi party throughout Europe. There, 5,000 disciples of Adolf Hitler pledge their unswerving loyalty to him and the Third Reich. . . . Progressive David Lloyd George of England visits Adolf Hitler in an attempt to persuade him to reconsider any aggression he may be planning against European nations.			
Sept. 4		The United States appoints William C. Bullitt as its Ambassador to France, formerly the Ambassador to the Soviet Union. President Roosevelt contends he is the ideal agent through whom to support democracy at a time when France faces a domestic quarrel between fascism and Communism.			Hopeful that peace will prevail in southern China, Gen. Chiang Kai-shek promises to review peace proposals offered by Kwangsi province leader Li Tsung-jen.
Sept. 5		Gen. Francisco Franco's army makes quick progress to arrive closer to Toledo, Spain, slowly spanning out regiment by regiment to flank the city. His eventual destination is Madrid.		Canada, via Prime Minister Richard B. Bennett, sends its final warning to Japan to remove its 50 percent surtax that it imposed against principal Canadian imports. If Japan fails to remove it, Canada will consider the 1913 trade agreement, which has been guiding the trading regulations, null and void.	
Sept. 6			The *London Times* reports the death of another British soldier as the Arab uprising in Palestine enters its 21st week. To date, 300 people have been slain in the revolt, which may be squelched with the arrival of 10,000 British troops by the end of the week.		
Sept. 7		Speakers at the Nazi party conference at Erlangen, Germany, remind listeners that those of "German blood" living in other parts of the world must be brought to Germany's side and become part of the German psychology. The conference equates being German with being Nazi.			
Sept. 8		More than one million people turn up in Nuremberg, Germany, for the grand opening of the seventh National Socialist (Nazi) Conference. Notable members of the party are expected to attend and further the global direction for the Third Reich. One such figure is Adolf Hitler, whose arrival spawns a brief but potent speech on full arms sovereignty and the evils of Bolshevism.			Tokyo is on alert following rumors of another uprising similar to the military insurgence last month. Police crews are doubled and local army patrols scour sections of the city for troublemakers.
	A *Includes developments that affect more than one world region, international organizations, and important meetings of world leaders.*	**B** *Includes all domestic and regional developments in Europe, including the Soviet Union.*	**C** *Includes all domestic and regional developments in Africa and the Middle East.*	**D** *Includes all domestic and regional developments in Latin America, the Caribbean, and Canada.*	**E** *Includes all domestic and regional developments in Asian and Pacific nations (and colonies).*

U.S. Politics & Social Issues	U.S. Foreign Policy & Defense	Economics & Great Depression	Science, Technology & Nature	Culture, Leisure & Lifestyle	
Realizing the importance of the African-American vote, Republican National Chairman John Hamilton organizes 75 African-American followers into a local governing board to manage the obtaining of votes along the Mason-Dixon Line.	Orders for military planes have put San Diego aircraft manufacturers into overtime mode. Factories reportedly turn out equipment night and day as plants are enlarged to accommodate the pile-up of requisitions. . . . The United States, in deciding not to send 40,000 tons of overage destroyers to the scrap heap, notifies Great Britain that it is "very reluctantly" maintaining tonnage beyond its naval parley agreement.	In trying to depict an out-of-control Democratic bureaucracy, the Republican Party estimates that an average household faces any number of 2,700 "hidden taxes" daily through purchases of food, clothing, furniture, and more.		Housewife D.K. Marlowe from Youngstown, Ohio, arrives in New York City for a paid vacation, compliments of the Democratic Party. Marlowe, 29, won the Democrats' essay contest on "What the New Deal Has Meant to Me." . . . The Grand Opera Artists Association asks the government for a national operatic institution for the development and advancement of this classical form of theater.	Sept. 2
Olympic star Jesse Owens throws his support behind the Republicans. The famous sprinter promises to help set a "fast pace" in bringing in votes for Alf Landon. . . . Organized labor is supporting Franklin Roosevelt in the elections because the working man is not ready to surrender all that he has gained under the New Deal, says New York Senator Robert Wagner.		The National Association of Purchasing Agents, recognizing the possibility of a coal shortage, advises the coal industry to start ordering tonnage now and start stocking up for the interim.			Sept. 3
Earl Browder, presidential candidate of the Communist Party, asks for a ban on the radio station WCAE-Pittsburgh, which, he says, barred his on-the-air appearance because of his political leanings. . . . Rumors that the Vatican has chastised political activist and radio host Father Charles E. Coughlin for his on-air political statements is untrue, says Bishop Michael J. Gallagher of Detroit, Coughlin's superior.	The hostilities in Spain could ignite a wider, more universal war, fears John Thomas Taylor, legislative director for the national American Legion. The Legion has accelerated its influence on government legislators to adopt an army draft measure.	Citizens' income derived from government programs increased by more than 50 percent between the years 1929–34, according to the National Industrial Conference Board, which is examining the thrust of government intervention on Americans during the Depression years. . . . American credit is on "a sounder basis than it has ever been before in our history," declares President Roosevelt before a crowd of 20,000, who greet him at the Springfield, Ill., train depot.			Sept. 4
Attorney Arthur J. Hughes, president of the Notre Dame alumni association of South Bend, Ind., promises Pope Pius XI the assistance of Notre Dame's 10,000 graduates to help combat Communism. . . . Vice presidential aspirant Col. Frank Knox tells a newspaper interviewer in Washington, D.C., that all of New England will go Republican this election year simply because they have "ditched the New Deal."		There are still 11 million people out of work, show government statistics, despite all the work programs. One problem may be that machinery has taken the jobs of human workers in so many facets of industry, say experts.		Paramount Pictures signs the newest sensation, crooner-actor Bing Crosby, to a two-year contract nine months in advance of the end of his current one. In the meantime, Crosby returns to the studios to shoot several retakes for his latest picture, Garden of Allah.	Sept. 5
Calling rogue labor chief John L. Lewis a "radical" and a "menace" to the American Federation of Labor, the Republicans profess that it was only in the last three years that labor began to experience ugly trends—hinting at the Roosevelt administration's inability to maintain good relations between labor and management.	While Austrian Governor General Franz Ritter von Epp and German railroad chief Julius Dorpmueller speak to the German-American Chamber of Commerce in New York, calling for understanding and international amity, a demonstration of American Communist Party members pickets outside.	The number of installment sales continues to grow, accounting for 11 percent of department stores' volume. This is a tremendous increase over the Depression years and a sizable increase over the pre-Depression years. Experts foresee no letup. . . . In one of his popular "fireside chats," President Roosevelt describes his latest relief bill, which will lend "a protecting arm" to the sufferers of the drought areas.	With American and European technicians working independently on their separate plans for television, NBC chief engineer O.B. Hanson worries that there will not be a "standard" home receiver in the near future to offer the anxious public.		Sept. 6
With campaign rhetoric heating up, the Republican Party in Pennsylvania calls the Democrats "debauched." It alleges that the Democrats' have used relief funds for political purposes and that events staged by the Works Progress Administration have actually been political promotions disguised as relief conferences . . . . President Roosevelt is indecisive and Alf M. Landon is inconsistent, says Communist Party presidential candidate Earl Browder of his opponents' labor records over an NBC national broadcast.	At the Third World Power Conference in Washington, D.C., U.S. Secretary of State Cordell Hull describes the "dangerous ambitions" of men like Adolf Hitler who preach peace but crave war. The United States, despite its neutrality aim, is not blind to these people, he informs. The conference attendees, numbering 3,000 people, represent 50 nations.	Due mostly to summer-term help required by the Engineer and Quartermaster's Corp. in the War Department, the roll call of civilian employees in the executive branch of the federal government rose by 6,363 employees in the month of June. The total now is 830,622.	Human nature is going through a case of "critical maladjustment," Dr. Bronislaw Malinkowski diagnoses. Anthropology professor at the University of London, he says that a bad side effect of this kind of psychosis is a taste for war.		Sept. 7
A feud breaks out between the two central political parties, the Republicans and the Democrats, after the Republicans hear that an unnamed source blames presidential candidate Alf Landon of Kansas for closing 700 working schools in his state to balance the budget. Landon calls the insinuation preposterous and "cheap propaganda."		All of the relief acts of 1935 and 1936 combined allocated $276,016,564 in the month of July, according to government reports.		The Chiropractors of America states that women who work at home and do the cleaning, laundry, and other household chores walk nearly eight miles per day, or 3,000 miles per year, the same distance from Boston to San Francisco.	Sept. 8

F	G	H	I	J
Includes elections, federal-state relations, civil rights and liberties, crime, the judiciary, education, healthcare, poverty, urban affairs, and population.	Includes formation and debate of U.S. foreign and defense policies, veterans affairs, and defense spending. (Relations with specific foreign countries are usually found under the region concerned.)	Includes business, labor, agriculture, taxation, transportation, consumer affairs, monetary and fiscal policy, natural resources, pollution, and accidents.	Includes worldwide scientific, medical, and technological developments, natural phenomena, U.S. weather, and natural disasters.	Includes the arts, religion, scholarship, communications media, sports, entertainment, fashions, fads, and social life.

	World Affairs	Europe	Africa & The Middle East	The Americas	Asia & The Pacific
Sept. 9		Hitler's formal speech today at the Nuremberg Nazi Conference is extensive in its aims. In his usual high-energy style, he orates of reclaiming old colonies lost to other nations in the world war, of Germany's ability to repel any nation, of how the Jews are behind the conflict in Spain, and of Bolshevism, the scourge of the world.			
Sept. 10		Concerned over the outcome of the Spanish civil war—and worried that the nation could not at this time afford an armed conflict—the British Trade Union votes for Britain to stay removed from the conflict in Spain. . . . Propaganda Minister Dr. Joseph Goebbels of Nazi Germany decries Bolshevism and bars all accords with Soviet "Reds."		With the nationalization of Canada's railway system, Prime Minister Mackenzie King holds a special session of the Cabinet Council to introduce the directors and the chairman, S.J. Hungerford, of the Canadian National Railway.	
Sept. 11		Violence escalates in Spain to the extent that it experiences its bloodiest encounter today when, at the town of Sietmo, Aragon, loyalists and rebels exchange grenades, then charge each other face-to-face with bayonets.	Britain reports that Arab resistance in Palestine did not diminish to the extent it had predicted with the arrival of an entire army division from England. Snipers and terrorists continue to incite conflict.		Japan sends four more warships from Tsingtao to join the three already off the south China coast when it is learned that south China, despite the recent calm, may be on the verge of a rebellious detonation.
Sept. 12		Soviet Russian authorities in Moscow, hearing of Joseph Goebbels's tirade against them at the National Socialist Congress in Nuremberg, launch an anti-Nazi retort—complete with epithets and threats—in their major newspaper, *Pravda*.		The United States and Panama sign off on a mutually beneficial trade pact while the press of both countries supports the agreement as a boost to good relationship-building between North and South America.	
Sept. 13		Ireland's President Eamon De Valera promises his people that their country's version of the New Deal is working and that it is bringing more economic security to the country. He states that economic security will eventually mean more self-sufficiency from the United Kingdom.			A possible scuffle between Japanese troops and Chinese troops at Pakhoi in southern China is the subject of controversy. Chinese newspapers give vivid details; Japanese papers deny the entire incident.
Sept. 14		According to refugees, the major press outlets in Spain are being censored from reporting the true extent of atrocities taking place, including mass killings of citizens, officials beaten to death, and nightly ambushes.			
Sept. 15		Both Germany and Italy—within a day of each other—back out of the Locarno peace meeting scheduled for the middle of next month, saying that October is far too early and does not afford proper time for diplomatic negotiations. This double postponement, coupled with the fact that Austria's emissary is known to be visiting Italy's Premier Mussolini, is a cause of concern to the British Foreign Office.		Three of Canada's largest mining concerns are merging into one vast enterprise in British Columbia, according to Dominion sources. The companies are the Premiere Gold Mining Co., Ltd.; the British Columbia Silver Mines, Ltd.; and the Sebawke Gold Mining Company.	
Sept. 16	In an unexpected move, Austria's minister of finance, Ludwig Draxler, informs the League of Nations' finance committee that his country will be pulling out of the League. The League sees the action as Nazi motivated.				Japan's Shiunso (Purple Cloud) Society, a peace-conscious organization, asks the government to consider a world parley concentrating on the formation of a nonaggressive, universal global trade relationship with the freedom-loving world.

A	B	C	D	E
Includes developments that affect more than one world region, international organizations, and important meetings of world leaders.	Includes all domestic and regional developments in Europe, including the Soviet Union.	Includes all domestic and regional developments in Africa and the Middle East.	Includes all domestic and regional developments in Latin America, the Caribbean, and Canada.	Includes all domestic and regional developments in Asian and Pacific nations (and colonies).

U.S. Politics & Social Issues	U.S. Foreign Policy & Defense	Economics & Great Depression	Science, Technology & Nature	Culture, Leisure & Lifestyle	
Princeton's professor of jurisprudence, Dr. Edward S. Corwin, claims that the U.S. Constitution needs enlarging; currently the country is heading to a constitutional crisis "of unpredictable gravity." . . . Republican presidential candidate Alf Landon leaves for a multi-city tour over several days. His stops are Indianapolis and many points east, ending in Maine.		Because there has not been a notable increase in men's clothing sales across the nation, the National Association of Wool Manufacturers in the United States is apprehensive for the holiday season. In fact, late figures indicate a 12 percent drop in men's fabrics.			Sept. 9
At the World Power Conference, attendees are warned that this is not a political symposium but a unique opportunity to review the world's electrical and water power and to organize ways to harness it for the benefit of mankind.		The Department of Agriculture predicts a harvest of 1,458,295,000 bushels of corn this season, 1.3 percent better than expected earlier, but still below normal production figures. . . . Addressing the Green Pastures Rally in Charlottesville, President Roosevelt tells an enthusiastic North Carolina audience of 35,000 people that the woes of the Depression are virtually over; he points to improved labor conditions on farms and in manufacturing plants.	Maurice Arnoux, French aviator, sets a new mark by traveling at a speed of 248 miles per hour for over 1,000 kilometers.		Sept. 10
Forty-eight states and the District of Columbia receive $19,606,767 to be divided among them for federal projects for the National Youth Administration. Of that total, $1,118,494 must be used to increase student quotas in those areas where families were affected by the drought.		Indicative of their confidence, Democrats have spent only half as much as the Republicans on the presidential campaign so far. Between June 1 and August 31, the Democrats expended $1,008,840, compared to over $2 million by the Republicans.			Sept. 11
		The government is "rapidly approaching that point where the budget can be balanced," Secretary of Commerce Daniel Roper declares in Tulsa, Okla. With reference to drought response measures, Roper states that the administration has learned to work with nature and not against it, citing improved crop control as the aim for 1937. . . . The National Steel Corporation and its subsidiaries netted a profit of $10,003,171 for the fiscal year ending in June. Price per share is $4.64.			Sept. 12
The Social Justice Commission of the Central Conference of Rabbis condemns the current political system as one that invites despair and destitution to a population. It suggests instead a "thoroughly socialized democracy," free of the threat of fascism and Communism.		The $1 billion spent to improve U.S. railroads over the last five years has directly resulted in the maintenance and increase of business in the United States, says John M. Fitzgerald, public relations vice chairman of the Eastern Railroads.			Sept. 13
Judge Thomas F. Croake refuses a writ of habeas corpus for recently arrested Charles "Lucky" Luciano, king of the New York rackets, meaning he will not get out of Dannemora Prison on bail.		In its stockholders' semi-annual report, Montgomery Ward & Company's president, Sewell L. Avery, pushes a letter-writing campaign to Congress to eliminate "burdensome and inequitable taxes."		Playwright George Bernard Shaw, best known for his works *Pygmalion* and *Man and Superman*, rails the Hollywood community for trying to rewrite his play, *St. Joan*, as a movie script, void of political rhetoric and complicated allusions.	Sept. 14
Dishonest lawyers are largely responsible for creating recidivist felons by supporting their activities through legal chicanery, says Kentucky's chairman of crime prevention, R.V. Bastin. . . . The New York Prison Association lauds the U.S. Department of Corrections for its closing of the ancient Welfare Island penitentiary and replacing it with the up-to-date Rikers Island Prison.		B/G Foods, Inc., turned in a net gain this year after a large deficit last year. This year's profit of $55,750 overshadows the deficit figure of $9,988 last year. Shares this year are 43 cents.		A troubled youth from Atlanta, Ga., recently having finished serving 16 years in a local reformatory, admits under questioning that he wrote a death threat to actress Shirley Temple's mother in an attempt to extort $25,000.	Sept. 15
The National Association of Insurance Brokers pens a harsh letter to the Republican Party after its vice presidential candidate, Col. Frank Knox, publicly states that "no life insurance policy is secure." The Association's Mortimer Nathanson demands a retraction. . . . Republican Senator from New York George R. Fearon, who is running against incumbent governor Herbert Lehman, a Democrat, tells voters that the state needs a new system of rule that is not dictated by the "brain trusters in Washington."		According to a government bulletin, retail collections rose seven percent during the month of August while collections increased 10.7 percent in the United States.	President Roosevelt asks Secretary of Commerce Daniel Roper for his support of the proposed "Air Progress" day—a time for the people of America to stop and meditate on the nation's achievements in aviation. . . . A huge crowd of scientists and evolutionists gather in Blackpool, England, to hear famous anthropologist Dr. H.J. Fleure say that, despite the arrogant claims of some, no one race is superior to the other.		Sept. 16
F	G	H	I	J	
Includes elections, federal-state relations, civil rights and liberties, crime, the judiciary, education, healthcare, poverty, urban affairs, and population.	Includes formation and debate of U.S. foreign and defense policies, veterans affairs, and defense spending. (Relations with specific foreign countries are usually found under the region concerned.)	Includes business, labor, agriculture, taxation, transportation, consumer affairs, monetary and fiscal policy, natural resources, pollution, and accidents.	Includes worldwide scientific, medical, and technological developments, natural phenomena, U.S. weather, and natural disasters.	Includes the arts, religion, scholarship, communications media, sports, entertainment, fashions, fads, and social life.	

	World Affairs	Europe	Africa & The Middle East	The Americas	Asia & The Pacific
Sept. 17		Premier Leon Blum of France, during a radio address to his country, ridicules Adolf Hitler's Nuremberg speech in which he called France "enfeebled," and praises countries such as the United States and Britain that show the world the wonders of true democracy. . . . Adolf Hitler, addressing a military maneuver near Berlin, calls Germany's army the "strong fist" and the watchdogs of "the holy Reich."			
Sept. 18		For the first time in history, labor accords give British merchants on seagoing vessels actual work hours in engine rooms and stokeholds per agreements between Britain and the National Maritime Board.	A correspondent with the *London Daily Herald*, stationed in Jerusalem, accuses Italy of purposely roistering Arab citizens there to revolt against the British as a means of achieving an independent government.		A united political party process is created today in Manchukuo by the Japanese, giving the citizens there some feeling of self-government, according to Gen. Kenkichi Ueda, Japanese ambassador. A local paper, the *Kyokai*, applauds the action.
Sept. 19		A report out of Munich, Germany, admits to the fact that there are 5,000 political prisoners currently incarcerated in Third Reich concentration camps. Since the camps became part of the national penal system in 1933, some 40,000 people have been confined for varying lengths of time on various charges.			
Sept. 20		At the Nuremberg Conference, Hitler notifies the world that Germany wants back those colonies lost in the world war. The Reich will never forget "nor relinquish the solution of her colonial demands," insists the Reichschancelor.	The formation of the first regular army for the Union of South Africa is in progress. Minister of Defense Donald Pirow, who is leading the conscription, has just returned from London where he sought advice on keeping the country's harbors safe from predators.	Mexico offers a free hospital for railway workers across the country. The institution is located in Mexico City and accommodates 1,000 patients.	
Sept. 21	A joint plea is made by the Carnegie Endowment for International Peace and the International Chamber of Commerce to the world's nations to act in unison "for a solution to the world's most urgent political and economic problems."				
Sept. 22			Italian troops announce a plan to march approximately 200 miles south of Ethiopia's capital, Addis Ababa, to crush a growing resurgence there of rebels still dedicated to the exiled Emperor, Haile Selassie.	Uruguay angrily severs diplomatic ties with Spain after the Spanish government in Madrid admits it can no longer vouch for the safety of traveling foreigners, including Uruguayan businessmen and tourists now there.	

A	B	C	D	E
Includes developments that affect more than one world region, international organizations, and important meetings of world leaders.	*Includes all domestic and regional developments in Europe, including the Soviet Union.*	*Includes all domestic and regional developments in Africa and the Middle East.*	*Includes all domestic and regional developments in Latin America, the Caribbean, and Canada.*	*Includes all domestic and regional developments in Asian and Pacific nations (and colonies).*

U.S. Politics & Social Issues	U.S. Foreign Policy & Defense	Economics & Great Depression	Science, Technology & Nature	Culture, Leisure & Lifestyle	
America is oblivious to one of society's worst problems—the housing problem—apprises Dr. Margaret Miller of London. A housing expert, she gives the nation a grade of zero on slum removal after touring the country and studying large metropolitan areas. . . . Opening a drive for the 1936 Mobilization for Human Needs campaign, President Roosevelt pleads with Americans to support private welfare agencies so that they may continue to rehabilitate lives and reinforce the strong character of America.		A scathing accusation that the Democrats destroyed cattle and hogs in 1934 that they had forbidden to be given to the poor is promptly denied by both the Democratic Party and the U.S. Department of Agriculture. A department official asserts that no one from the government ever interfered with relief donations.		Paramount Pictures buys the talking picture rights to Mary Johnston's *To Have and to Hold* for $10,000. Like many other astute authors whose works were already made into silent pictures, Johnston retained the "dialogue rights," giving her leverage in the event the work is ever reproduced for sound.	Sept. 17
				Four men are apprehended by FBI agents for an alleged plot to buy stolen bonds. The quartet, which was led by Minnesota underworld figure Morris Roisner, is indicted today by a federal grand jury.	Sept. 18
The White House issues a press release denouncing a "notorious newspaper owner," which the public recognizes as William Randolph Hearst, for running articles that give a false impression of the President's association with political organizations hostile to American beliefs. . . . Rev. Monsignor Fulton J. Sheen of the Catholic University tells Americans that the best way to combat Communism is by preaching the truth.	President Roosevelt is a man who hates war "with every fiber of his soul," states Acting Secretary of War Harry H. Woodring, addressing the Grand Army of the Republic in Washington, D.C. It is the President's aim, he goes on, to steer America clear of trouble.	The greatest asset to making a sale is personal appearance, say the majority of department store clerks who responded to a poll disseminated by the National Retail Dry Goods Association. The poll had asked what qualities are most beneficial to making a success of one's job. . . . Connecticut Senator Arthur Vandenberg asserts that the Congress under President Roosevelt was "money-dumb" in overspending public funds.			Sept. 19
Federal Bureau of Investigation chief J. Edgar Hoover, addressing a Holy Name Society in New York, says that those who accuse the FBI of "running wild" and shooting "anyone on sight" are "schemers" and a disgrace to American law enforcement. . . . Citing the gains made by Pennsylvania farms, Emma Guffey Miller of the Democratic Business and Professional Women's Organization hails the work done by President Roosevelt and assails the empty promises of his opponents.		By all accounts, retailers are showing high hope for sales for the upcoming holiday cycle. Basing their goals on the year's continuing up-trends and on the Thanksgiving holiday successes of last year, they are going ahead with product-and-delivery campaigns for the 1936 yuletide season.		The National Park Association reminds Americans of the natural reserves open to them for their enjoyment, particularly the 136,959 miles of hiking trails cutting through some of the 48 states' most impressive woodlands and lake lands.	Sept. 20
The Women's Christian Temperance Union commits to raising $1,000 for temperance education, featuring the evil of alcohol use among the "modern" youth. . . . The nomination of Alf M. Landon for president is a turning point in America, a beginning of a "new confidence," asserts John D. Hamilton, Republican campaign chairman. He will usher in a fresh new government, Hamilton adds, which is tired of being "betrayed" by the current president.		Opening today in San Francisco, the American Bankers Association's 62nd Annual Convention lures 4,000 attendees who will hear some of the nation's top bankers and Wall Street luminaries deal out advice and discuss banking problems inherent in today's economy.		On the occasion of his 70th birthday, author H.G. Wells receives an honorary membership from members of the National Association of Science Writers for his novels such as *The Time Machine*, *The Invisible Man*, and *The Shape of Things To Come*, which gave readers an inventive look into the worlds of a scientific wonderlust.	Sept. 21
A huge gathering in New York's Madison Square Garden comprised of nearly 14,000 African Americans and 26 other such meetings in a number of major metropolitan areas are synchronized in order to simultaneously present one massive turnout for the Roosevelt campaign as a grand celebration of African-American support for the present administration. . . . Republicans raise allegations of "graft, payroll padding, and political discrimination" taking place in the Public Works Administration in various midwest and eastern states. Democrats deny such activities and score their opponents' stories as political blarney issued from panicked opponents.		The Phillips Petroleum Company's profits for eight months—January through August—were $2,087,409, a 36 percent increase over the same period in 1935. . . . U.S. Smelting, Refining & Mining Company, however, did not fare so well, experiencing a sizable drop in income over the past eight-month period. Income decreased from $4,173,521 last year to $3,782,769 this year.			Sept. 22

F	G	H	I	J
Includes elections, federal-state relations, civil rights and liberties, crime, the judiciary, education, healthcare, poverty, urban affairs, and population.	Includes formation and debate of U.S. foreign and defense policies, veterans affairs, and defense spending. (Relations with specific foreign countries are usually found under the region concerned.)	Includes business, labor, agriculture, taxation, transportation, consumer affairs, monetary and fiscal policy, natural resources, pollution, and accidents.	Includes worldwide scientific, medical, and technological developments, natural phenomena, U.S. weather, and natural disasters.	Includes the arts, religion, scholarship, communications media, sports, entertainment, fashions, fads, and social life.

	World Affairs	Europe	Africa & The Middle East	The Americas	Asia & The Pacific
Sept. 23		Catholic Bishops in Germany are denounced by Nazism for their stand on sectarian schools; the Reich sees them as a threat to the unity of a single Germany. Nevertheless, the Bishops distribute a letter to all Catholic churches in the nation, explaining and defending the right of the Church to adopt these schools. . . . Sir Austen Chamberlain of Britain warns his country that it should prepare for war, as Hitler seems intent on regaining Germany's "lost" colonies, now under British, South African, French, and Belgian administration.		A delegation from Nazi Germany arrives in Canada today to meet with Prime Minister Mackenzie King and his financial advisers to discuss details of a potential trade agreement. The Dominion of Canada admittedly remains cautious.	
Sept. 24			Gen. Dill of the British army warns Arab rioters in Palestine that a full corps of British troops is on its way and expects a full lay-down of arms and a cessation to the current revolt against the United Kingdom.		
Sept. 25		Leon Jouhaux of France's General Confederation of Labor proposes a wage scale that would escalate with the cost of living, provided that striking Frenchmen close their plants and cease all strike activities until bargaining ends.			
Sept. 26		Lufthansa Airlines' director, Baron von Gablenz, announces that his company will introduce a 48-hour transatlantic mail delivery from Berlin to New York City by late 1937.		Mostly because of the new Pan-American Highway linking Texas to Mexico City, Mexico is experiencing an unprecedented tourist boom. According to a government representative, the trade positively affects other facets of the industry: hotels are being built by demand, restaurants are expanding, and many families are opening their private homes as bed-and-breakfast-type *haciendas*.	
Sept. 27		Adolf Hitler, while introducing a new national highway, speaks of Germany's self-sufficiency which, he claims, puts the Third Reich above the "good or ill will" transpiring between other European countries. . . . By dictating how to run science and education, Nazi Germany is erasing its own *kultur* (culture), says former Heidelberg University professor Dr. Emil Lederer, now in exile.	According to observers in Johannesburg, a trading agreement between the Union of South Africa and Nazi Germany that had been delayed has resumed in full force, prodded by German emissaries who seem to have dictated to Africa what to buy and in what quantities. Great Britain is checking into the allegations.		
Sept. 28		Lawrence Simpson, a 34-year-old American seaman, is sentenced to three years in a German prison after he admits to the Nazi People's Court that he smuggled Communist literature into Berlin.			A list of 21 "mild general principles" for life under Japan, which was given to the Nanking government by Japanese Ambassador Shigeru Kawagoe, seems to diminish China to a puppet state. The laws provide for full-time policing by Japanese troops, emanating vassalage rather than a dominion.
Sept. 29		Delegates at the Lutheran World Convention in Germany express their satisfaction that the Nazi government has not harassed them and that the outlook overall has begun to appear more peaceful.			

A	B	C	D	E
Includes developments that affect more than one world region, international organizations, and important meetings of world leaders.	Includes all domestic and regional developments in Europe, including the Soviet Union.	Includes all domestic and regional developments in Africa and the Middle East.	Includes all domestic and regional developments in Latin America, the Caribbean, and Canada.	Includes all domestic and regional developments in Asian and Pacific nations (and colonies).

U.S. Politics & Social Issues	U.S. Foreign Policy & Defense	Economics & Great Depression	Science, Technology & Nature	Culture, Leisure & Lifestyle	
Alerting store owners of "burdensome laws" instituted by the Roosevelt administration, Clarence O. Sherrill of the American Retail Federation counsels merchants across the nation to remain firm against "laws hostile to retailers' interests."		A policy on old-age security is recommended by the Republican National Committee, based on a "pay-as-you-go" system requiring each generation to pay into it for the benefit of the elderly.			Sept. 23
		During a Senate hearing on strike violence, professional strikebreakers admit that they have been hired by many corporations under the guise of being "security guards." In those positions, they are expected to "incite violence" and to damage and discredit the unions.		The New York Giants clinch the pennant, beating the Boston Bees 2–1 in the 10th inning of the opening game of a doubleheader.	Sept. 24
H.L. Mencken, satirist and author—as well as an independent candidate for the presidency against Harding, Coolidge, Hoover, and Roosevelt—backs Alf Landon in an editorial that appears today in Mencken's own publication, The American Mercury.		With America taking an active financial role in bringing the French franc, the British pound, and the American dollar to an exchangeable stability, U.S. Secretary of the Treasury Henry Morgenthau is jubilant that America has accomplished a nonmilitary feat of helping to promote European harmony.			Sept. 25
Presidential aspirant Alf M. Landon tours five Wisconsin cities today between Milwaukee and Oshkosh, shaking hands and orating about racial tolerance, freedom of education, and the right to worship as one pleases.		Attacking "inequities visited upon business," the U.S. Chamber of Commerce decries the new surtax levied upon "undistributed earnings and profits of corporations" as unfair and dangerous to honest competition. The surtax, approved by the Roosevelt administration, was written into the Revenue Act of 1936. . . . The construction industry, though much improved since the midst of the Depression, has not reached the heights predestined for it 24 months ago. Many exterior forces are to blame, say critics, such as the rising cost of materials, but authorities now consider the prediction to have been overzealous.		Contrary to previous announcements, the United States will offer two, not just one, transatlantic airline routes—one serving a northerly direction, another destined to southern climes—says Assistant Secretary of Commerce J.M. Johnson.	Sept. 26
American Communist Party leader Earl Browder, wanting to respond to Msgr. Fulton J. Sheen's recent remarks about Communism being anti-Catholic, is given equal time by the Monsignor to speak at the Catholic University in Washington.		Dr. Iva Lowther Peters releases "testimony" by 212 women who completed a survey relating to their jobs and the obstacles that they find in fulfilling those jobs. Contributors have found certain elements vital to the success of their careers, with appearance and good speaking habits leading the list. Most say age is "immaterial."		Some 1,200 members of the Congress of American Poets—a society open to 5 million men and women ranging from well-known poets to those still awaiting publication—formalizes a petition to the U.S. Congress to create a department aimed at financially assisting budding bards. . . . Baseball fans in New York City are elated as the Yankees win the American League pennant. This comes on the heels of the Giants winning the National League pennant, which means two New York teams will face each other in the World Series.	Sept. 27
More than 3.5 million women throughout several industries have made employment gains under the New Deal, reports U.S. Secretary of Labor Frances Perkins at a testimonial dinner for Democrats.				The luxury liner, Paris is installing a ski slide on board, an unprecedented feat, for a special cruise to St. Moritz.	Sept. 28
Republicans admit to the press a concern that since their presidential candidate, Alf Landon, has a record of voting for Prohibition—a very unpopular topic among the U.S. populace—the Democrats may use it against him as the elections draw nearer.		Baltimore's Consolidated Gas, Electrical Light and Power Company has slightly increased income from last year in the year ending August 31, totaling $6,499,443 this year as compared to $6,077,025 in 1935.			Sept. 29

F
Includes elections, federal-state relations, civil rights and liberties, crime, the judiciary, education, healthcare, poverty, urban affairs, and population.

G
Includes formation and debate of U.S. foreign and defense policies, veterans affairs, and defense spending. (Relations with specific foreign countries are usually found under the region concerned.)

H
Includes business, labor, agriculture, taxation, transportation, consumer affairs, monetary and fiscal policy, natural resources, pollution, and accidents.

I
Includes worldwide scientific, medical, and technological developments, natural phenomena, U.S. weather, and natural disasters.

J
Includes the arts, religion, scholarship, communications media, sports, entertainment, fashions, fads, and social life.

	World Affairs	Europe	Africa & The Middle East	The Americas	Asia & The Pacific
Sept. 30	At a session of the United Nations, Spain's Foreign Minister, Julio Alvarez de Vayo, accuses Germany, Italy, and Portugal of interfering with and taking part in the Spanish civil war by aiding the rebels' air force. Vayo says these nations are shifting the tide in favor of a faction that could bring down the current government of Spain.		South African aviator Capt. Stanley Halse wins a $50,000 cup air race from Portsmouth, England, to Johannesburg in the Union of South Africa. Halse lands at noon after making the trip in a record-breaking 30 hours.		
Oct. 1		Britain's cautious approach toward Adolf Hitler is ignored today when an angry Cabinet answers Hitler's dictum of demanding "old territories." The Cabinet denies that the Nazis will reclaim any lands rightfully ceded to Britain by the armistice agreements of 1918. . . . The Vatican's Secretary of State, Cardinal Pacelli, and the new Italian ambassador to the United States, Fulvio Suvich, board the *Conte de Savoia* on their way to America to seek its help in an anti-Communist campaign.			Trying to avoid what seems like an inevitable Japanese takeover, China, through proposals and counterproposals, is trying to stall the event. In the meantime, it hopes to convey to the Western powers what a weakened China might mean to the rest of the world.
Oct. 2		Priceless oil paintings and ancient artifacts are destroyed by Spanish marauders at Toledo art museums during a day of fighting between loyalists and rebels throughout the city.	As a large expeditionary relief force arrives in Palestine, the British set out to stifle Arab uprisings and hopefully force its inciters to the bargaining table.		
Oct. 3	Agriculturists from across the world—including the United States—turn out for the 13th assembly of the Institute of Agriculture in Rome. The event gives farmers worldwide a chance to discuss and share experiences concerning problems they face inherent in their business.	A piece of history was saved last night from flames when Parisian firemen quickly responded to a fire at Versailles Palace, the royal court of King Louis XIV. None of the ages-old furnishings or artwork was marred. . . . French Premier Leon Blum ends a two-day session with the League of Nations where he extolls the peace efforts of France and informs the League on many other issues.			Japan signals it has made the last entreaty to current negotiations with the Chinese authorities at Nanking. Their Embassy writes, "Under no conditions will (we) entertain counter-demands from the Chinese government."
Oct. 4		Nazi Germany celebrates Thanksgiving Harvest Festival in the town of Hamelin, where 700,000 country folk take part in a great feast and watch the display of power as the German military enacts a mock battle, complete with airplanes.			China ceases all exportation of cotton and cotton by-products, thus sending Belgium, France, Germany, and Japan out looking for another source of cotton waste, an important ingredient of munitions manufacturing.
Oct. 5		The Soviet Union, which already claims it owns the best foot army in the world, is intent on becoming the supreme naval power as well. Cruisers and gunboats are reportedly being manufactured in Russian shipyards.		The Chaco Peace Agreement between Paraguay and Bolivia, signed several months back, is being tested as Paraguay refuses to evacuate the Villa Montes-Santa Cruz road, an area that it claims territorially.	

A	B	C	D	E
Includes developments that affect more than one world region, international organizations, and important meetings of world leaders.	Includes all domestic and regional developments in Europe, including the Soviet Union.	Includes all domestic and regional developments in Africa and the Middle East.	Includes all domestic and regional developments in Latin America, the Caribbean, and Canada.	Includes all domestic and regional developments in Asian and Pacific nations (and colonies).

U.S. Politics & Social Issues	U.S. Foreign Policy & Defense	Economics & Great Depression	Science, Technology & Nature	Culture, Leisure & Lifestyle	
U.S. Secretary of the Treasury Henry Morgenthau draws Moscow's ire by declaring that the United States saved the British pound from Soviet Russia's intention of driving down its value. While Russian diplomats do not personally respond, several vehement articles appear in Moscow-area newspapers. . . . City fathers in Terre Haute, Ind., toss Communist Party presidential candidate Earl Browder into jail on a charge of "vagrancy" when he arrives to make a campaign speech. The governor of Indiana refuses to intervene.		The Nash Motor Company netted $177,249 for the third quarter, a remarkable sum compared to the same period last year, which recorded a deficit of $161,878.			Sept. 30
At one time a devoted Democrat, Al Smith, former governor of New York, crosses over to the Republican camp, disillusioned with the party that launched him. At a Carnegie Hall rally he tells voters to vote Republican this time around; Alf M. Landon, he says, is a "remedy for all ills." . . . The American Bankers Association, meeting in Atlantic City, lambastes the world of false advertising that plagues the public. One spokesperson calls such dishonest efforts a "stupendous, gorgeous, unbelievable conglomeration of bunk."	The American Legion's new national commander, Harry Colmery, proposes a three-point peace plan for the nation, including adherence to a neutrality policy and honing up of defense in case of an unavoidable war.	Christmas orders—especially for toiletries, toys, and novelties—are already beginning to pick up speed in department stores throughout major American cities. . . . Defending the deficit he created in the country as an "investment for the future," President Roosevelt also chides the Republicans' "boondoggling" economic plans before a vast crowd cramming Pittsburgh's Forbes Field.			Oct. 1
Alf Landon's supporters view rogue Democrat Al Smith's verbal support as a boon to their campaign. They estimate that it improves Landon's chances in states where Smith is well liked, such as Illinois and Pennsylvania, and in New York, Smith's home state. . . . The Church of Latter-day Saints (Mormons) proclaims that national relief efforts are not working and proposes to institute its own plan to take its members off the jobless lists.		Through mid-September 1936, 7 million men and women returned to work in private industry since the Depression struck, estimates John O'Leary of the Chamber of Commerce, who also claims unemployment has been exaggerated by the administration's foes.		Having the honor of throwing the first ball of the second game of the World Series, President Roosevelt arrives at the New York Giants' stadium, the Polo Grounds, in early afternoon. It is an exciting series for New Yorkers as both World Series contenders—the Giants and the Yankees—hail from the city.	Oct. 2
Civilian Conservation Corps (CCC) camps are opening schools where young men can choose to learn varied subjects and trades. With the fall term opening, nearly 200,000 students are taking advantage of the free courses. . . . As the presidential campaign rolls into the last dynamic gears, Republican candidate Alf Landon starts off on a stumping tour of Illinois, Indiana, Michigan, and Ohio.		A major war is erupting between the Roosevelt administration's reciprocal trade pacts and the Landon supporters, who see the pacts as another example of President Roosevelt's economic adversities. The issue promises to heat up through the rest of the campaign, warn observers.			Oct. 3
Extremely well-respected analytical psychologist Carl Jung, visiting Harvard College, tells Tercentenary members that his initial opinion of President Roosevelt has vastly changed—from an "opportunist" to a "strong man" and a great leader. . . . For safety reasons, the United States proposes to the International Labor Board a maximum eight-hour watch on merchant ships at sea.		Defending the President's New Deal policy of "building spending power from the ground up," Secretary of Labor Frances Perkins tells a Democratic women's organization that, "The result has been an improvement in every segment of the economic order."		Max Reinhardt, impresario turned film director who thrilled the cinematic world with his recent version of A Midsummer Night's Dream, is hired by the same studio, Warner Bros., to direct a big-budget historical production, Danton, the Terror of France.	Oct. 4
Due to a letter issued by the National Catechetical Congress of the Confraternity of Christian Doctrine to all Catholic churches warning of Communistic infiltration into everyday life of America, priests in today's pulpits stress a strong revival of basic Catholic instruction for children. . . . The problem of Communism in the United States should be dealt with severely—perhaps deporting all known Communists—says Republican National Chairman John D. Hamilton. President Roosevelt is being too lenient, he insists.		A decade-long trend is changed as the United States announces that for the first six months of this year it has imported more goods than it has exported. Even though it amounts to a mere $9 million ratio at this point, it is foretelling for the future of world trade, says Amos E. Taylor of the Finance Bureau.			Oct. 5

F	G	H	I	J
Includes elections, federal-state relations, civil rights and liberties, crime, the judiciary, education, healthcare, poverty, urban affairs, and population.	Includes formation and debate of U.S. foreign and defense policies, veterans affairs, and defense spending. (Relations with specific foreign countries are usually found under the region concerned.)	Includes business, labor, agriculture, taxation, transportation, consumer affairs, monetary and fiscal policy, natural resources, pollution, and accidents.	Includes worldwide scientific, medical, and technological developments, natural phenomena, U.S. weather, and natural disasters.	Includes the arts, religion, scholarship, communications media, sports, entertainment, fashions, fads, and social life.

	World Affairs	Europe	Africa & The Middle East	The Americas	Asia & The Pacific
Oct. 6		After a day of debate, Britain's Labor Party, meeting in Edinburgh, Scotland, votes by a strong majority to press armament in light of remonstrances from the world's dictators.... Barrage after barrage from the loyalist army under Col. Jose Moscardo fails to dislodge rebel forces from the mountain passes near Madrid. The day's fighting is described as some of the most vicious of the Spanish civil war.			
Oct. 7		With a food shortage currently handicapping Germany, the government declares that prices of food must be kept at a minimum. The Reich promises to deal austerely with any price profiteers or tamperers.			
Oct. 8	Harvard University's Manley O. Hudson is inducted onto the World Court bench. He fills one of two vacancies left by the resignations of former U.S. Secretary of State Frank B. Kellogg and German jurist, Dr. Walter Shucking.	According to German Minister of Education Bernhard Rust and famous German surgeon Dr. Ferdinand Sauerbruch, today's Nazi youth are nothing more than uncontrollable heathens. The National Socialist Student League responds in kind to the two noted elderly statesmen by telling them, in certain terms, to mind their own business.			
Oct. 9					Dr. John R. Mott, president of the Young Men's Christian Association and chairman of the International Mission Society, leaves for several months in India. Mott will attend the World Conference there and follow it up with a scholastic study of Indian society.
Oct. 10		Catholic Bishops in Germany loudly censure the Nazi government's attempts to discredit members of a monastery near Coblenz by charging them with "immoral" conduct. The Bishops disseminate a letter, which they ask to be read Sunday to parishioners, denouncing the action.			Japan's Jigoro Kano, who heads the country's Amateur Athletics Association, promises the International Olympics Committee that the country will make every effort to avoid making ill-fated, controversial decisions that might imperil its chances to host the 1940 Olympics in Tokyo.
Oct. 11		The Gaelic language and ancient Irish folklore are blossoming again in Irish culture, says Michael MacWhite, minister of the Irish Free State, who does not think the old ways should succumb to the advent of the new.	A worried world is watching how Italy, which has ousted the government of Ethiopia and is in the midst of reorganizing it under Italian rule, will handle 50,000 Falashas—or black Jews—who have their own particular society based on their religion. The rampant anti-Semitism in Europe leaves many observers concerned.... Trying to repeat Dr. Ludwig Krapf's feat of 1848, Daniel Brimble of Cape Town plans to climb Africa's Mount Kilimanjaro, one of the highest peaks in the world.		
Oct. 12			Intervention by four Arab chieftains—including Haj Amin el Husseini—convinces Palestine Arabs to end their 24 weeks of rioting today, something even overwhelming British forces have been unable to do. The British infantry remains on alert until the armistice proves authentic.		

A	B	C	D	E
Includes developments that affect more than one world region, international organizations, and important meetings of world leaders.	Includes all domestic and regional developments in Europe, including the Soviet Union.	Includes all domestic and regional developments in Africa and the Middle East.	Includes all domestic and regional developments in Latin America, the Caribbean, and Canada.	Includes all domestic and regional developments in Asian and Pacific nations (and colonies).

U.S. Politics & Social Issues	U.S. Foreign Policy & Defense	Economics & Great Depression	Science, Technology & Nature	Culture, Leisure & Lifestyle	
An array of exporters in New York City unite for the team of Landon & Knox, the first time that this particular group has joined hands for the election of any president and vice president. The consortium's distrust of President Roosevelt stems from what they see as premeditated government control.		If reelected, President Roosevelt promises that he will seek from Congress an extension of his power to devalue the currency more than he has in the current term and will continue to support Secretary of State Cordell Hull, who is achieving success in liberalizing world trade to the benefit of the United States and its world neighbors.			Oct. 6
Speaking at a women's political seminar in Washington, D.C., First Lady Eleanor Roosevelt leads the dialogue on the attitude of females in a speedily changing world. . . . Saying that President Roosevelt sees himself as another theorist like Karl Marx—but is more like a Groucho Marx—Col. Frank Knox, vice presidential hopeful belittles the Chief Executive in front of a tittering Philadelphia crowd.	More than anything else, a world facing a possible war needs to believe in and trust in God, says the Most Rev. Amleto Giovanni Cicognani, Apostolic delegate to the United States, at the conclusion of the National Catechetical Congress of the Confraternity of Christian Doctrine.	Charging that the President is "careless with facts," opponent Alf Landon charges that the $1.5 billion bonus bill paid to U.S. veterans is not "behind us," as President Roosevelt claims, but is still very much a large part of the massive American deficit.		The New York Yankees win their first World Series without Babe Ruth, who left the team several months prior. The Yankees brought in seven runs in the last inning alone to beat the fellow New York sluggers, the Giants, 13–5.	Oct. 7
Helping to ensure a Democratic victory, President Roosevelt conducts a tour of 13 states that he carried in 1932. The tour kicks off in Maryland, then heads directly west to Iowa and Colorado. Ten days, 40 stops, and 18 major speeches later, he will return to Washington.		Al Smith rouses a mob of Republican supporters tonight in Philadelphia by reminding them of President Roosevelt's "broken" campaign promises of 1932 and the negligent way he tried running this country through his New Deal.		*Time* buys *Life Magazine*, planning to turn the basically humorist publication into a weekly photo journal.	Oct. 8
A bellicose James M. Cox, former governor of Ohio, berates those who try to belittle President Roosevelt's achievements. The Chief Executive pulled the nation out from its worst historical episode, says Cox, challenging fate itself to "turn economic night into day."		On his multiple-state stumping tour, President Roosevelt touts reciprocal trade. According to him, the much-debated trade pacts with Canada and other countries did more than boost U.S. agriculture. By forming relationships with the partnering countries, they directly aided the world peace effort.	The dirigible, *Hindenburg*, cruises over several eastern and mid-Atlantic cities today—including Boston and Philadelphia—as a farewell gesture to its first U.S. tour before heading back to Germany for the end of the season.	The theme of the 1939 New York World's Fair will be, "The World of Tomorrow," according to its planning board. Construction will begin this December, set at a predetermined, preapproved cost of $125 million. Millions of visitors from across the globe are expected.	Oct. 9
From Omaha, Neb., President Roosevelt broadcasts the details of his four-point farm program that promises to bring permanent prosperity to the suffering American farmer. Unlike Landon's superficial plan, he asserts, this program will produce a "continuous plenty" to increase buying power. . . . Musicians under the Works Progress Administration have been busy. This year alone, orchestras sponsored by the WPA Music Project have played to 32 million people throughout America.		A New York State Works Progress Administration chapter attracts scandal when it is learned that some 1,500 people were terminated for "continued absence."	A winner of the Nobel Prize for Chemistry, Dr. Irving Langmuir, announces his achievement of recreating a cell wall from dead matter. His audience is the centenary committee of Williams College in Massachusetts.	"The Brown Bomber," African-American boxer Joe Louis, knocks out Argentina's Jorge Brescia two minutes and 12 seconds into the third round of the bout at New York's Hippodrome. . . . An Apache Indian known as Major Smiley, who turned over Geronimo to the U.S. Cavalry many years ago, dies today at age 102.	Oct. 10
	The U.S. Air Corps is adding to the U.S. arsenal by contracting the building of a series of "observation" planes. These specialized craft are designed to stealthily scout and detect approaching enemy bombers.	Col. Frank Knox tells Americans not to sacrifice liberties for fear of economic security, reminding them of President Roosevelt's "failures"—losses in Europe, missed trade opportunities, and a deficit that will be felt by their children and grandchildren.			Oct. 11
At the Pan-American Congress of the Episcopalian Church, set in Chicago this year, Bishop George Craig Stewart describes "a moral collapse that is engulfing mankind." It is up to "the unification of Christians" to defeat it. . . . A Denver audience listens as President Roosevelt describes his economic plan for his upcoming term—based on those policies which have already proven effective—as compared to those proposed by the "two-faced" Republicans.		An effective plan of economic relief would be state—not nationally—directed, explains Alf Landon to an auditorium full of Clevelanders. The bureaucrats and the "shameful machine politicians" will be barred from practice once he is in office, he adds.			Oct. 12

F	G	H	I	J
Includes elections, federal-state relations, civil rights and liberties, crime, the judiciary, education, healthcare, poverty, urban affairs, and population.	*Includes formation and debate of U.S. foreign and defense policies, veterans affairs, and defense spending. (Relations with specific foreign countries are usually found under the region concerned.)*	*Includes business, labor, agriculture, taxation, transportation, consumer affairs, monetary and fiscal policy, natural resources, pollution, and accidents.*	*Includes worldwide scientific, medical, and technological developments, natural phenomena, U.S. weather, and natural disasters.*	*Includes the arts, religion, scholarship, communications media, sports, entertainment, fashions, fads, and social life.*

	World Affairs	Europe	Africa & The Middle East	The Americas	Asia & The Pacific
Oct. 13		Economic experts in Britain grade America's New Deal in a special 23-page section of *The London Times*. They applaud some points and question others, but the overall consensus is that its intention is honest, and that it assisted America at a time when it needed such an economic plan to keep it in a single, forward-going direction.			
Oct. 14		Expatriate German playwright Ernst Toller, on reaching American shores aboard the liner *Normandie*, tells reporters that he is disappointed by the many democratic peoples in his homeland for not banding together against Hitler. He calls the Germans "cowards" for letting Nazism thrive.			
Oct. 15			With quiet coming to the streets of Palestine—as well as a huge British expeditionary force—several of the Arab rioters return to their native lands. One such is Iraq's Fawzi Bey-el-Kaougji, a military trainer.		
Oct. 16		Paris tests its air-raid preparations this evening by going totally dark for 58 minutes. It is the first time it has done so since 1918, when the world was still fighting the Kaiser's low-flying air patrols. . . . A Soviet envoy clarifies Josef Stalin's statement made last night on the radio. Stalin's assertion that Russia is justified in giving aid to the "revolutionary forces of Spain" does not mean that it is going to supply arms. The Soviets are on the side of the loyalist faction in the civil war there.	The British envoy in Jerusalem reports that the atmosphere in Palestine remains tense, even with last week's laying-down of the Arabs' arms.		
Oct. 17		The British Royal Air Force considers constructing an air base on the Isle of Cyprus, a strategic position and another strong link in the United Kingdom's defense chain. . . . Word comes from overseas that Italians are hoping for President Roosevelt's victory. The Republicans' tariff policies frighten them.		A never-before-discovered nickel mine found in Canada's Northwest Territory is already adding to the Dominion's vast nickel output. It produced 19,620 ounces in August alone. . . . Mexico favors President Roosevelt, reads the country's top newspaper, *Excelsior*. Despite its customary shunning of involvement in other nations' politics, in this case, the paper says, Mexico foresees a bad omen in its silver trade in the hands of President Landon.	Japan's refusal to readmit American Baptist missionary Dr. J. Spencer Kennard into the country worries other missionaries who fear that a paranoid Japan suspects missions as being safe harbors for anti-Japanese organizations.
Oct. 18		With Princess Juliana's upcoming wedding scheduled for after the holidays, the people of the Netherlands have renewed hope that the royal line will be kept intact. As the last of the royal family, she must bear a child to keep the long lineage alive.		Capsizing in a 50-mile gale that sweeps across Lake Erie, the 252-foot Canadian sandsucker, *Sand Merchant*, kills 10 people, including one woman passenger. Seven crew members, clinging to the side, are picked up by an American rescue vessel from Cleveland.	
Oct. 19		The Jewish population in Germany has been slashed 21 percent in just three years—January 1933 to July 1936—through intimidation, threats, and imprisonment, according to Dr. Michael Traub, who directs the Palestine Foundation Fund in Germany. In terms of population, this is a drop from 517,000 to 405,000. . . . By appointing Gen. Hermann Goering as Economics Commissar, Adolf Hitler gives him a virtual free hand in managing a four-year economic plan announced recently at the Nuremberg Conference.		Argentina is leading the way in establishing a single Latin American committee whose goal is to work through assorted national embassies to save the lives of hundreds of Spanish refugees hiding in South America from Spanish vendettas.	Chinese newspapers report that the peace talks in Hangchow between Chinese Minister Chang Chun and Japanese Ambassador Shigeru Kawagoe have not produced an agreement.

A	B	C	D	E
Includes developments that affect more than one world region, international organizations, and important meetings of world leaders.	Includes all domestic and regional developments in Europe, including the Soviet Union.	Includes all domestic and regional developments in Africa and the Middle East.	Includes all domestic and regional developments in Latin America, the Caribbean, and Canada.	Includes all domestic and regional developments in Asian and Pacific nations (and colonies).

U.S. Politics & Social Issues	U.S. Foreign Policy & Defense	Economics & Great Depression	Science, Technology & Nature	Culture, Leisure & Lifestyle	
Warning of a dictatorship if President Roosevelt is reelected, Alf Landon promises to fight him at every turn. He vows to a cold Detroit audience at an outdoor rally that he will work with Congress to diminish any autocratic powers the President has adopted or will seek in the future. . . . Automaker Henry Ford invites presidential candidate Alf Landon to his home for dinner and a tour of his antique Dearborn Village.		Delegates speaking at the Institute of American Meat Packers, hosted by the Chicago Stock Yards, predict limited supplies and higher prices of meat for the next several years until the economy levels off.	Attendees of the Society of Motion Picture Engineers convention learn that the medical field has begun shooting colored films of various operations as visual teaching aids for anatomy classes.		Oct. 13
Some 150,000 marchers parade the streets of downtown Chicago tonight, despite the cold, in an organized tribute to President Roosevelt. Police estimate that nearly double that number of spectators line the curbs.		For the first nine months of this year, the Johns-Manville Company and subsidiaries netted $3,093,560, or $3.60 per share, a great increase of $1,573,040 in the same period one year earlier.		M.H. Aylesworth, chairman of R.K.O. Studios., predicts that in the near future, movie admission prices will rise slightly and the double feature will be phased out.	Oct. 14
In St. Louis, Frank Knox warns the President to stop shirking the issue of wages and hours; he demands to know if the President is or is not going to order increases and thus continue to increase the deficit.		The U.S. Steel Corporation is investing in the south by instituting a $29 million development program of its Birmingham, Ala., manufacturing complex. Improvements include a tin mill and ancillary plants, and would increase employment in the poverty-stricken area.			Oct. 15
At the usually politically-active Vassar College, a poll shows that a mere one-third of its student body of 1,400 express a political preference in the upcoming presidential elections. . . . Samuel W. Reyburn, president of the Associated Dry Goods Corporation, quips that a businessman often finds it harder to gain public respect than a politician.		An assembly of the U.S. Building & Loan League fires off a letter to Washington, D.C., demanding an end to bureaucratic intervention in the execution of housing and mortgage loans. . . . Vice president of General Foods Carl Whitman sees a Christmas shopping boom immediately tailing the presidential elections this year.	Jean Batten lands in Auckland, New Zealand, the first woman to fly there solo from England. During her 21-hour flight, which required a gas stopover in Sydney, Australia, she battled storms and darkness.		Oct. 16
Political activist Rev. Charles E. Coughlin receives a strange surprise during his oration to 5,000 members of the National Union for Social Justice: a fellow clad in red leaps to the stage and showers him with feathers from a war bonnet he wears. Police usher the trespasser out. . . . Michigan Senator Arthur H. Vandenberg, whose radio address plans to scorn President Roosevelt by playing back "utterances" he made over the last several months, is thwarted by CBS, which says copyright laws prevent him using pre-recorded material from other shows without absolute permission.	The president of the Jewish Women's Council, Mrs. Arthur Brin, estimates that neutrality laws work only as well as its people, and urges women of the world to develop a "collective responsibility" to ensure peace.	George E. Wallis, president of the Dairy and Ice Cream Machinery and Supplies Association based in Chicago, talks of one of his company's most essential products, skimmed milk powder for infants. An estimated 300 million pounds are sold each year, produced from a half-billion quarts of skimmed milk, dried and powdered. . . . G.C. Pfeiffer, president of the National Council of American Importers and Traders, Inc., contends that reciprocal trade agreements were the only practical way out of the economic mess the country found itself in by 1934.		Clark Gable stars in Caine and Mabel, MGM's new comedy farce, which opens tonight in national theaters. His leading lady is Marion Davies, whose career was made possible, say Hollywood sources, by the smitten publisher, William Randolph Hearst.	Oct. 17
President Roosevelt has 314 electoral votes and Landon has 217, according to a straw vote done by Britain's Reuters News Agency.	Former adviser to the President James Warburg, who turned against him over matters of economy, announces he is again a supporter of President Roosevelt because of his recently played-out foreign policies. These, Warburg explains, have collectively begun building a sound path toward creating a peaceful world.	Industry experts project an expenditure of more that $500 million in office machines over the next 12 months. This includes dictating machines, typewriters, calculators, and more.			Oct. 18
The growing Catholic concern over the spread of Communism is not a phobia, attests Rev. Francis X. Talbot, editor of the Jesuit magazine, America. The priest, who researched the situation, reports that "Reds" have a $6 million American bank account and a staff of 38,000 strategically deployed across the 48 states.		After a recent speech by Herbert Hoover accusing the current administration of "dishonesty and deceit," Secretary of the Treasury Henry Morgenthau laughs at Hoover's references to "double budgets" and "double bookkeeping." There is no such element, the latter explains, and terms such language as political jabberwocky.	Early reports of airplanes afire crashing into St. John's, Newfoundland Bay—and frantic cries about the end of the world having arrived—are proven to be, upon scientific investigation, a shower of meteors.	Sing Sing Prison halts its prisoner football games, which it put on for the benefit of the prison's fund, after the state Commission of Corrections forbids paid admissions at penal institutions.	Oct. 19

F	G	H	I	J
Includes elections, federal-state relations, civil rights and liberties, crime, the judiciary, education, healthcare, poverty, urban affairs, and population.	*Includes formation and debate of U.S. foreign and defense policies, veterans affairs, and defense spending. (Relations with specific foreign countries are usually found under the region concerned.)*	*Includes business, labor, agriculture, taxation, transportation, consumer affairs, monetary and fiscal policy, natural resources, pollution, and accidents.*	*Includes worldwide scientific, medical, and technological developments, natural phenomena, U.S. weather, and natural disasters.*	*Includes the arts, religion, scholarship, communications media, sports, entertainment, fashions, fads, and social life.*

	World Affairs	Europe	Africa & The Middle East	The Americas	Asia & The Pacific
Oct. 20		Six factories in England have been precontracted by the British government to produce airplane parts and engines—but only in the event of war. The contracts do not become authorized until war is declared and manufacturing is approved by the proper authorities.			Japan nationalizes its power industry, placing all communications, commerce, and railway movement under one department.
Oct. 21		Adding to its own manufacturing of airplanes to combat foreign enemies, Britain purchases 1,500 "first-line" fighter planes from the United States to be delivered in whole on or before 1939. Its aim is to keep up with Nazi Germany's ever-growing air force. . . . Edward VIII, the new king of England, is enmeshed in a scandal, being tied to a recently divorced "commoner," Mrs. Wallis Simpson. According to a British magazine, there are no stout laws that could keep him from marrying her—much to the chagrin of the Conservatives.		Ontario's Premier Mitchell F. Hepburn calls the evening's professional bout between fighters Max Baer and Dutch Weimer a "fake. . . . and a disgrace to the sport," immediately replacing the province's Athletic Commissioner who approved the fight.	The Philippines Commonwealth uncovers a plot by five Sakdalistas to torch Manila and overthrow the government. A Japanese refugee is held pilot of the plot.
Oct. 22			Alfred M. Cohen, president of B'nai B'rith, a non-Zionist fraternity, donates $100,000 toward 1,000 acres of land in Palestine to be given to Jewish refugees.		The latest round of government appointments in north China—mainly those of Japanese background or those with much to gain by a Japanese takeover—clearly indicate the extension of Japan's power in the region.
Oct. 23	In a race to rearm fastest and most abundantly, nations of the world expended a collective $9.3 billion, according to the League of Nations. This figure does not include Germany, which refuses to share its costs.	Germany and Italy announce that they are in full agreement, offering a united front toward the resolution and the transformation of European problems. This development represents the melding of two extreme powers whose outlooks are warrior-influenced and whose policies bespeak "survival of the fittest." The announcement was made tonight after a meeting in Adolf Hitler's retreat house in Berchtesgaden between Italian and German representatives.		Boeing Airlines, a U.S. business, gets an order from the British Air Ministry for 300 military-type airplanes to be made at Boeing's Vancouver, Canada, factory.	
Oct. 24		The British navy does not put much credence to rumors hinting that Spain plans to give the Canary Islands to Germany and the Balearic Islands to Italy for services done in the ongoing civil war there. Such plans would upset the British defense positions in the Mediterranean and Indian Ocean. Spain, says London, would not throw away such valuable possessions.			
Oct. 25		Premier Benito Mussolini believes in and cherishes "long periods of peace," he affirms to the roar of 70,000 people listening outside his palace in Rome. However, he adds that "eternal peace" is "absurd and impossible," and that when the "crucial hour approaches" for war—and it will approach—his people will be ready. . . . Loyalist and fascist students clash in Brussels and a leader of the fascist movement, Leon Degrelle, is arrested. Violence is smothered after troops arrive to empty the plazas and streets.	Gershon Agronsky, editor of the Palestine Post of Jerusalem, the only English language newspaper in the nation, sends a caveat to the local people, warning them that the supposed peace accord is not what it might appear to be. He reminds them that Arabs and Jews continue to differ on what is best for the country, and that differential is not something one can change by writing it down onto a piece of paper.		Japan, which has been for so long at odds with Soviet Russia over the Manchukuoan border, now suspects that the Soviets are conducting secret talks with the Chinese concerning a Manchukuo takeover.
Oct. 26		London authorities are taken aback when Joachim von Ribbentrop, the new ambassador to Great Britain, arrives at the Embassy clad in the brown shirt, black tie, and scarlet Nazi arm band of the stormtrooper.			

A	B	C	D	E
Includes developments that affect more than one world region, international organizations, and important meetings of world leaders.	Includes all domestic and regional developments in Europe, including the Soviet Union.	Includes all domestic and regional developments in Africa and the Middle East.	Includes all domestic and regional developments in Latin America, the Caribbean, and Canada.	Includes all domestic and regional developments in Asian and Pacific nations (and colonies).

U.S. Politics & Social Issues	U.S. Foreign Policy & Defense	Economics & Great Depression	Science, Technology & Nature	Culture, Leisure & Lifestyle	
To contest "gigantic government expenses," Clarence O. Sherrill, the American Retail Federation's president, summons a business consortium to curtail government costs. . . . National Biscuit earns $3,659,769 for the third quarter. Shares are up 51 cents from 40 cents last year.					Oct. 20
		Secretary of Commerce Daniel C. Roper anticipates the biggest business upswing in history. It will be the result of a current trend that sees business and government coming together in the interest of public satisfaction.			Oct. 21
		Slamming those who ridicule his tax policies, President Roosevelt, in a speech in Worcester, Mass., declares that his program is a decisive weapon aimed at keeping America upright by giving the country a formidable allowance to pay off all debts created by emergencies in a quick and efficient manner. . . . Secretary of State Cordell Hull's trade pacts win praise from James A, Farrell, chairman of the National Foreign Trade Council, sees global prosperity in open agreements without barriers.			Oct. 22
The Democrats and Republicans will each be given a broadcasting bill of about $800,000 accrued for airtime during this year's presidential campaign, predict NBC executives.		A letter to shareholders from Texas Instruments' chairman, T. Rieber, hails the company's three-quarter net of $28 million, equal to $3.02 per share.	The Burlington Railroad's Denver Zephyr establishes a new speed record for rail distance. It traverses four states—Colorado to Illinois, or 1,017 miles—in 12 hours and 12.5 minutes.		Oct. 23
Stock market expert and former head of the Securities and Exchange Commission Joseph P. Kennedy rushes to President Roosevelt's aid by blasting those who call the Chief Executive a radical. He scorns all such "pernicious" statements as political propaganda by frightened foes.		The biggest-ever outlay of turkeys is estimated for this year's Thanksgiving dinners—some 20 million—by the Bureau of Agricultural Economics. The number is higher than 1935 by one-third.		The government in Dublin reports that 471 Americans who hold an Irish Sweepstakes ticket have earned "the luck of the Irish" by being assured at least $1,250,000 in the first drawing next Wednesday in Newmarket.	Oct. 24
		National Republicans issue a statement claiming that the Democrats' New Deal is responsible for creating a large crowd of idle people dependent on the government for a livelihood. They also claim the policies did little in terms of providing sustainable jobs since, according to statistics, the United States has twice as many jobless people as other nations.			Oct. 25
Even though a parade in his honor is cancelled because of rain, presidential candidate Alf Landon's fire is not dampened as he roars to a crowd of 20,000 in a Philadelphia conference hall that President Roosevelt's "open and impudent use of public money for political purposes" is illegal.	In a letter to Secretary of the Navy Claude A. Swanson on the eve of Navy Day, President Roosevelt calls the U.S. fleet strong but "compatible with the Good Neighbor Policy" and rejoices that America is on good terms "of peace and amity with all nations."	Secretary of Agriculture Henry Wallace says that if President Roosevelt remains in office, America will most assuredly witness a "sufficient" rise in national income in the very near future, a rise which will balance the federal budget. He worries, however, if Republican Alf Landon possesses the gall "to collect a fair share from the taxpayers according to their ability to pay."		The world-traveling team of Mr. and Mrs. Martin Johnson bring back to America one of the many prizes they accrued on their trip to the South Seas, a 300-pound orangutan they captured in Borneo. They will tour the country with photos and stories of their latest expeditions. . . . British playwright Noel Coward and actress Gertrude Lawrence appear together tonight at the Colonial Theater in *Tonight at 8:00*, a sophisticated drawing-room comedy.	Oct. 26
F Includes elections, federal-state relations, civil rights and liberties, crime, the judiciary, education, healthcare, poverty, urban affairs, and population.	**G** Includes formation and debate of U.S. foreign and defense policies, veterans affairs, and defense spending. (Relations with specific foreign countries are usually found under the region concerned.)	**H** Includes business, labor, agriculture, taxation, transportation, consumer affairs, monetary and fiscal policy, natural resources, pollution, and accidents.	**I** Includes worldwide scientific, medical, and technological developments, natural phenomena, U.S. weather, and natural disasters.	**J** Includes the arts, religion, scholarship, communications media, sports, entertainment, fashions, fads, and social life.	

	World Affairs	Europe	Africa & The Middle East	The Americas	Asia & The Pacific
Oct. 27		Five Scandinavian countries—Denmark, Finland, Iceland, Norway, and Sweden—join in celebrating "Day of the North," an on-the-air program featuring goodwill between their governments. Steady economics and support of each other's cultures are topics discussed between leaders. In the meantime, citizens at home sample their country's national foods.		Mexico plans its first Pan-American Chamber Music Festival to take place next year in the month of July. As part of the promotion of the fête, the government announces it is looking for a winning string quartet, which will win $500 and the opportunity to perform at the flagship event.	After three British sailors are taunted and beaten by Japanese soldiers in Tokyo, Britain lends what the Japanese call "an unprecedented snub" in canceling its appearance at a reception to toast Japan's Emperor Hirohito.
Oct. 28		In Belgium, the followers of both Nazism and fascism demand that Premier Paul von Zeeland withdraw his country from the League of Nations, which is vocally against both parties. Belgium's transformation to its more aggressive government has been a steady one, prodded by Hitler and Mussolini.		Brazil, wanting to train pilots for its newly formed air squadron, buys 30 planes from the United States. . . . A majority of Latin Americans back the incumbent in the upcoming U.S. presidential elections. All reports indicate that President Roosevelt's policies and his attempts to befriend the country's southern neighbors have been recognized with earnestness and appreciation.	
Oct. 29		Germany's Propaganda Minister, Joseph Goebbels, turns 39 today. Huge parades of marching infantry and fireworks celebrate the event.	Britain releases an estimate of the number of casualties totaled in the half-year-long insurgence of Arabs in Palestine—314 dead and 1,286 wounded. The rebellion ended in mid-October with the disbandment of its leaders.		
Oct. 30		Italy strongly hints during a broadcast that it will no longer maintain friendly relations with Madrid, but instead will opt to support the rebel army under Gen. Francisco Franco who is besieging the town.			
Oct. 31		The longer the Spanish civil war lasts the more dangerous it is to Europe, say critics. Italy and Germany are already suspected of assisting the fascists, while France and Soviet Russia are aiding the loyalists. . . . Premier Benito Mussolini of Italy announces that he is enlarging his nation's navy by as much as 100,000 men, a move he considers necessary to stave off any British interference in the Mediterranean.			
Nov. 1		Premier Benito Mussolini of Italy suggests to France and England that they should work with him and Germany to set up a peace parley. The League of Nations, he says, can no longer cope with the world situation.	The Turkish Assembly, lately showing stirrings of independence, wildly cheers President Kemal Ataturk when he describes both French-administered Alexandretta and Antioch as "ethnically purely Turkish."	With others attempting to get him to change his coffee trade policy to better accommodate some internal grievances, Brazil's Finance Minister, Arthur de Souza Costa, is firm on continuing the current process, saying that it is good for the economy.	
Nov. 2					The British Embassy alleges that Japanese officers in Shanghai forced an English sailor into admitting to a misdemeanor by forcing a fountain pen tip under his fingernails. Japan promises an investigation into the matter.
Nov. 3		Nazi Germany, even before the election returns are counted, names President Roosevelt the overwhelming winner in the American elections today. In the same announcement, it claims that the United States has made a secret trade pact with the Vatican.			

A	B	C	D	E
Includes developments that affect more than one world region, international organizations, and important meetings of world leaders.	Includes all domestic and regional developments in Europe, including the Soviet Union.	Includes all domestic and regional developments in Africa and the Middle East.	Includes all domestic and regional developments in Latin America, the Caribbean, and Canada.	Includes all domestic and regional developments in Asian and Pacific nations (and colonies).

U.S. Politics & Social Issues	U.S. Foreign Policy & Defense	Economics & Great Depression	Science, Technology & Nature	Culture, Leisure & Lifestyle	
The Daily Princetonian, Princeton University's school newspaper, announces that its faculty supports President Roosevelt over Alf M. Landon, 90–81.				The Works Progress Administration's theater project opens in New York with a production of Sinclair Lewis and John C. Moffitt's It Can't Happen Here. The stage production will play in 21 cities.	Oct. 27
	Beneath the Statue of Liberty, celebrating Lady Freedom's 50th anniversary, President Roosevelt, wired by radio to an audience across America, underscores the importance of defending the nation's liberty. From France, President Albert Lebrun joins him in celebrating the life and liberty of the United States.	Labor leaders in a national radio broadcast tell American workers not to be misled by what their workplaces tell them about employees being responsible for their own old-age pension fund; companies and corporations are required to submit to the fund, also. . . . For the year ending September, the North American Company met a profit of $15,534,833. This is an increase from 1935 figures at the same time of the year, which were $12,414,325.			Oct. 28
Addressing some 3,500 people in the beautiful Mosque Temple in Newark, N.J., Alf Landon reminds them of the advice given by the late labor boss Samuel Gompers—that the true interests of labor should not be tied to any political party. . . . Secretary of the Interior Harold Ickes calls Alf Landon's style of politics "reactionary"—leading eventually to Communism or fascism.		Of the first 57 railroads to report earnings this month, all had achieved a near 20 percent profit increase over September 1935—and a telling 58.6 percent gain over September 1934.			Oct. 29
On the same day that Democratic U.S. Postmaster General James Farley predicts 46 of 48 states for Roosevelt, former mayor of New York Jimmy Walker berates former state governor Al Smith for switching party alliances to the Republicans after so many years.				A musical, Red Hot and Blue, starring Jimmy Durante, opens at Broadway's Alvin Theater. Other cast members are Ethel Merman and a wise-cracking newcomer, Bob Hope. The play is a collaboration of music by Cole Porter, Howard Lindsay, and Russell Crouse.	Oct. 30
Al Smith, the one-time Democratic governor of New York who traded allegiance to the Republicans, asks Americans in Albany to cast their votes for Alf Landon because President Roosevelt and his "crackpot ideas" are setting the stage for "class warfare and revolution" in America.		Earnings for the United Gas Improvement System for the year ending September 30 are $28,656,808, down a little more than $1 million from 1935. . . . Bethlehem Steel experienced the largest third quarter net profit since 1929, according to a corporate report. In this last quarter it netted $4,578,058, an incredible intake.			Oct. 31
Fordham University confers a Doctorate of Law on visiting Eugenio Cardinal Pacelli, the Vatican's Secretary of State, who is on a peace tour.		A report from the U.S. Chamber of Commerce compares the nation's status now to the day when Franklin D. Roosevelt took over the office of president on March 4, 1933, reporting higher payrolls, increased factory production, less bank failures, greater farm income, improvements in transportation and construction, and an expansion in trade.		The course at Hialeah, Fla., becomes the first professional horse-racing track to test the new Australian-type starting gate, allowing for walking or running starts. Installation begins today and this and other improvements will be ready for the January 1937 season.	Nov. 1
Striking members of the Seamen's Union of America decide not to speak to reporters about their plight, except if the reporters are labor-enrolled, card-carrying members of the American Newspaper Guild. . . . Earl Browder, the Communist Party's presidential candidate, reminds Americans that tomorrow's elections will decide if the country will survive or be "dragged down the bloody path of reaction."	Rev. Walter Kellenberg of New York City's St. Patrick's Cathedral says that all Catholics in Spain who are dying for their church at the hands of the Communists and anarchists should be made saints.	For every dollar paid in dividends, taxes ranging from 50 cents to $8.60 are paid to the government, claims a press release from Women Investors in America, Inc., which bases its conclusion on interviews with 41 corporations. . . . Despite the political anxiety caused by the presidential elections, the magazine Steel reports that the steel industry remained at 73 percent production.			Nov. 2
Franklin Roosevelt, only the third Democrat to occupy the White House since the Civil War (1861–65), is re-elected to the U.S. presidency by a huge margin over the Republican contender, Senator Alf M. Landon.		Expenses are down and the deficit is lower, reads a U.S. Treasury report released the day of the national elections. This "daily statement" reports a cost-and-recovery expenditure lowered from $1,166,517,940 to $916,629,959.			Nov. 3

F	G	H	I	J
Includes elections, federal-state relations, civil rights and liberties, crime, the judiciary, education, healthcare, poverty, urban affairs, and population.	Includes formation and debate of U.S. foreign and defense policies, veterans affairs, and defense spending. (Relations with specific foreign countries are usually found under the region concerned.)	Includes business, labor, agriculture, taxation, transportation, consumer affairs, monetary and fiscal policy, natural resources, pollution, and accidents.	Includes worldwide scientific, medical, and technological developments, natural phenomena, U.S. weather, and natural disasters.	Includes the arts, religion, scholarship, communications media, sports, entertainment, fashions, fads, and social life.

	World Affairs	Europe	Africa & The Middle East	The Americas	Asia & The Pacific
Nov. 4		The French Council hails President Roosevelt's victory and joins him in celebrating a momentous time in American history; the French premier calls the triumph a boost to the forces of peace and progress around the world.		Canada reports ongoing success in the Trinidad trade market. The island, which is the largest producer of oil in the British Empire and the source of asphalt for much of the globe, is buying more Canadian vegetables, oats, and paper products than ever before.	
Nov. 5		King Carol of Romania and some court members receive threats from the rebel Corneliu Zelea Codreanu promising death if Romania goes to war against Germany. Codreanu labels himself head of the "Iron Guard," the same allegedly Nazi-supported organization that assassinated other political authorities of the Baltic states, including Liberal Premier Ion Duca. . . . The Nazis publish their new Criminal Code regulations that virtually put all Nazi authorities above the average citizen. Crimes against the Third Reich are usually punishable by death.		Finance Minister Souza Costa of Brazil, to keep the coffee bean industry running at a smooth and constant pace, creates the new position of president of the National Coffee Department in Rio de Janeiro and appoints Luis Piza Sobrinho, former secretary of agriculture, to fill it.	
Nov. 6		Britain, which has been experiencing an economic boom this year, expects the trend to continue. According to the Federation of British Industries, the fourth quarter of 1936 appears to be sustaining a continuation of the prosperity. . . . Londoners are incensed at Germany's new envoy, Joachim von Ribbentrop, for wearing his Nazi uniform while posted in their city. Sidewalk graffiti outside his offices reads, "Ribbentrop must go!"			Tokyo goes on a moral crusade, closing gambling parlors, taxi dance halls, and other places of low repute in order to start cleaning its image in preparation of the Olympic Games slated to take place there in 1940.
Nov. 7		Vincent Auriol, France's finance minister, in addressing the nation's huge deficit, says the budget will be balanced—but it will require honest communication and honest measures.	"Away from the British Empire—South Africa for South Africans," is the rallying phrase for the next elections in Johannesburg. Although two years away, South Africa is showing impatience for its independence.		
Nov. 8		Bucharest's streets are filled with 200,000 anti-Jewish dissenters, mostly nonresidents brought in by the local Fascist Party. The "parade" is headed by local pro-Nazi leaders Octavian Goga and A.C. Cuza.	Liberia, the last remaining independent state of Africa, is beginning to demonstrate some internal unrest, observes Walter F. Walker, Liberian Consul to the United States. He suspects the influence of fascist Italians who, after taking over Ethiopia, have crossed over the Liberian border.	Cuban authorities detain four people for allegedly plotting to assassinate the national police chief, Col. Jose Pedraza. The constabulary also confiscates their getaway car, which bears a Florida license plate.	
Nov. 9		The Nazi Party forbids ovations to Michael Cardinal von Faulhaber of Frauenkirche Cathedral, a popular priest among the Munich congregation. In fact, the Third Reich banishes any such outward praise for any clergy in Germany. . . . Prime Minister Stanley Baldwin of Britain, speaking to Guildhall, compliments America's trade policy and likens it to Britain's. Both, he intones, are attempting to open the seas for unfettered international trade.			

A	B	C	D	E
Includes developments that affect more than one world region, international organizations, and important meetings of world leaders.	Includes all domestic and regional developments in Europe, including the Soviet Union.	Includes all domestic and regional developments in Africa and the Middle East.	Includes all domestic and regional developments in Latin America, the Caribbean, and Canada.	Includes all domestic and regional developments in Asian and Pacific nations (and colonies).

U.S. Politics & Social Issues	U.S. Foreign Policy & Defense	Economics & Great Depression	Science, Technology & Nature	Culture, Leisure & Lifestyle	
Kansas, Alf Landon's home state where he has served as governor for years, turns against him in the elections. Late reports show that the majority of its citizens supported President Roosevelt with a margin of 17,000 votes. Landon has the dubious honor of being the worst-defeated candidate in history.		During the first six months of the year, major toy manufacturers earned a consolidated $584,362—a 30 percent gain over the same months of 1935—and expect a dramatic increase in the last six months, which includes the traditionally prosperous holiday shopping season.	The National Geographic Society campaigns for fire safety, expressing its hope that science invents new and quicker ways to combat the many blazes that cost lives and property by the thousands in America every year. The Society promotes fire alarms and building sprinklers.	Charged with conspiracy to undermine the National Bankruptcy Act, Julius Krompier—the brother of Martin Krompier, lieutenant in the now-defunct Dutch Schultz Gang—is arrested today for attempting to conceal furs for a client filing bankruptcy.	Nov. 4
Election statistics indicate that the Communist Party drew such a low number of votes—far below the required 50,000—that it cannot at this time consider itself an officially recognized competing political party in the United States. . . . Hoping for a return of Prohibition in the United States, the Dry Party's presidential campaign cost it $11,514, greatly aided by the millionaire Nelson Rockefeller's family.		General Electric's president, Gerard Swope, who is also spokesperson for the 1936 Mobilization for Human Needs Campaign, officially kicks it off in Cleveland. The campaign will run in 330 cities nationwide and includes support by many big-name proponents, among them the president of the United States.		British actor Henry Hull is cast to play Edgar Allen Poe in a new stage drama based on his life, Sophie Treadwell's *Plumes in the Dust*, on Broadway.	Nov. 5
Labor organizers and business luminaries meet in Washington, D.C., to plan a conference, which will eye the possibilities of successfully rejuvenating cooperation between government and big business. . . . Back in Topeka, Kans., Governor Alf M. Landon, who lost the bid for the presidency, commits to changing policy for the better and will support President Roosevelt when and where he thinks the direction is the correct one.		Manufacturing leads the way in America's income, contributing as much as 25 percent of the total, according to the National Industrial Conference Board. The Board estimates wages, salaries, dividends, interest, and other payments at $12 billion.			Nov. 6
With the rift in the American Federation of Labor still unmended, members of the two warring camps—the AFL and its rogue brother, the Committee for Industrial Organization—promote the idea of a parley between their organizations' presidents, William Green and John L. Lewis, respectively. . . . Father Charles E. Coughlin, known for his lively radio show that presents dissertations against evildoers in American politics, ends his weekly broadcasts after his own political party, the National Union for Social Justice, fails miserably at the polls. He says the Catholic Church, despite rumors, has nothing to do with his decision.		Second only to the food industry, auto manufacturing has been the quickest to recover since the Depression. The first half of the year shows remarkable sales results, with medium-size cars leading the list. Today, forecasters—basing their statement on upward trends—predict that 1937 will be a record year for the automobile, as 1936 has so far reached a 26 percent increase in auto purchases over 1935. . . . One of President Roosevelt's first priorities in his second term is to get Congress to restore a system of control of crops based on conservation, say Democrats. Initial plans under the Agricultural Adjustment Act were invalidated by the Supreme Court.	This year's recipient of the Chemical Industry Medal is Dr. Walter S. Landis, vice president of the American Cyanamid Company. The medal, which he receives today, cites "valuable application of chemical research to industry."		Nov. 7
Union labor leader John L. Lewis dashes the American Federation of Labor's hopes for a resolution to its infighting, which has been a topic of headlines for weeks. Having initially sought peace with dissident members under Lewis's Committee for Industrial Organization—members who once belonged to the AFL—Lewis now refuses to talk. He may agree to a parley at a later date, he explains, but does not want to rush into negotiations at this point.	With the U.S. Army showing signs of age, Chief of Staff Malin Craig strongly recommends the enlistment of a new, young reserve force that will be ready for any emergency the nation may encounter. He speaks to government authorities in Washington, D.C.	Democrats spent $3.3 million getting President Roosevelt reelected, according to figures released today by the national campaign staff. The Democratic Party, victory aside, now has a $500,000 deficit. . . . Determined agents of the National and Grocery Conference present state legislatures with a "model" statute that eradicates illegal below-cost selling, which hurts the honest majority of the industry. If accepted, the law could go into effect in 1937.			Nov. 8
	A true national peace cannot be established without Christian principles of good fellowship and goodwill, asserts the Young Women's Christian Association general secretary at the association's international conference.	According to a U.S. Treasury report, a total of $6,351,265,033 was in circulation at the end of October. This is a tremendous increase from the October 1935 figure of $638,668,103 and an even bigger leap from that of September 1936, which was $84,725,587.			Nov. 9

F	G	H	I	J
Includes elections, federal-state relations, civil rights and liberties, crime, the judiciary, education, healthcare, poverty, urban affairs, and population.	Includes formation and debate of U.S. foreign and defense policies, veterans affairs, and defense spending. (Relations with specific foreign countries are usually found under the region concerned.)	Includes business, labor, agriculture, taxation, transportation, consumer affairs, monetary and fiscal policy, natural resources, pollution, and accidents.	Includes worldwide scientific, medical, and technological developments, natural phenomena, U.S. weather, and natural disasters.	Includes the arts, religion, scholarship, communications media, sports, entertainment, fashions, fads, and social life.

	World Affairs	Europe	Africa & The Middle East	The Americas	Asia & The Pacific
Nov. 10		From Paris comes word that France has committed to spending $884 million on its defense. The European situation has decayed to such an extent that it sees itself a target of not only Germany, but of the newest Nazi ally, Italy.	According to the Export Managers Club, Japanese buyers are currently focused on Africa in seeking product information and potential new trade opportunities.		
Nov. 11		Madrid, victim of heavy rebel bombing and ground assaults throughout the day, is in flames tonight, say correspondents from Spain. And yet, the loyalists within the town continue to battle the attackers, even repelling them in the west and south. Missiles continue to drop as more and more of Madrid crumbles under the endless firepower. . . . U.S. Ambassador William C. Bullitt meets with France's Agence Econimique et Financiere to discuss world trade and how the United States and Europe can work together to abolish more barriers.			
Nov. 12		Ten German journalists posted in America cannot hope to return to their native soil if they do not resign from the Foreign Press Service, which the director of the Nazi press in Berlin, Max Ammann, condemns. Adolf Hitler does not want his press corps mingling with—and trading news items with—reporters from other countries.			
Nov. 13	The giant global textile industry, assisted by the International Labor Organization in Geneva, Switzerland, proposes a labor conference for April 5 in Washington, D.C. It promises to be the biggest of its kind since the ILO was established in 1919.	Hungary gives a festive welcome to Italian Foreign Minister Galeazzo Ciano, according to observers, suggesting a bonding between the two countries that many of the Western powers already suspected. . . . Incited by one member's verbal insults of the premier, the French Chamber of Deputies erupts when members of the left take on members of the right in a violent fistfight. It is not until the president of the Chamber, Edouard Herriot, adjourns the session that the fighting stops.			
Nov. 14		Dr. Willi Menzel, a professor of armament technique from Berlin Technical Institute of Charlottenburg, is appointed commander of Nazi Germany's research scientists who will devote much of their time, under his guidance, to rearmament and related problems.	In a move that some Britons say extends too much leeway to one of their colonies, Britain gives Egypt its assurance of independence during a three-day parley between the mother country and her subjects. The agreement allows the Egyptian parliament to ratify its existing Anglo Treaty to proclaim itself an independent nation with Britain as its strongest ally.		
Nov. 15		Europe has only two choices left—to either give in to the Nazis and become part of their "Mitteleuropa" or enforce those treaties already in place as a means to limit Adolf Hitler's ambition, says French author Andre Geraux to the diplomatic corps in Washington, D.C., tonight.			Although not an official pact between the two, Germany and Japan sign an agreement together declaring a full-scale war on Communism. Speculators predict that Italy will soon become a third collaborator.

A	B	C	D	E
Includes developments that affect more than one world region, international organizations, and important meetings of world leaders.	Includes all domestic and regional developments in Europe, including the Soviet Union.	Includes all domestic and regional developments in Africa and the Middle East.	Includes all domestic and regional developments in Latin America, the Caribbean, and Canada.	Includes all domestic and regional developments in Asian and Pacific nations (and colonies).

U.S. Politics & Social Issues	U.S. Foreign Policy & Defense	Economics & Great Depression	Science, Technology & Nature	Culture, Leisure & Lifestyle	
Never has the country seen such a vast array of effective labor laws passed in such a short time period than during the three years of the New Deal, boasts Frances Perkins, Secretary of Labor. . . . Foreign countries ordering airplanes from U.S. manufacturers are now facing a two-year wait due to a plan conceived by President Roosevelt that involves safeguarded construction and delivery. The guidelines have been agreed upon by the Navy, Army, and Justice departments.		President Roosevelt assigns several agencies to research the practicality of reintroducing the main reform tenets of the National Industrial Recovery Act back into legislation under new cover. The NIRA was declared unconstitutional by the Supreme Court in 1935. Among those principles that the President wants to see in place are the outlawing of child labor and the maintenance of standard labor conditions overall.		Dr. Frank A. Vizetelly, author of dictionaries and encyclopedias, explains that 200,000 new words have come into existence in America in very recent years. Some are older words whose definitions have greatly changed.	**Nov. 10**
L.J. Taber of the Grange, a venerable farmers' organization, promises to assist President Roosevelt to rebuild the nation's farms if the farmers themselves have a controlling option in the program. The President responds by explaining to the National Grange Convention in Columbus, Ohio, that his goal is to ensure "real equality for agriculture."	Addressing the Jewish War Veterans of the United States, former Supreme Court Justice Joseph M. Proskauer scoffs at the fascist notion that Jews are Communists. He pledges to fight anti-Semitism and other forms of bigotry in the United States and abroad.	Railroads are coming into a new, more progressive, more dynamic period of life, thanks to the Roosevelt administration's support, states Union Pacific's chairman, W.A. Harriman. America's faith in the rail lines, he says, has been restored.		Much of Shakespeare's work is "garbled," attests Dr. Samuel A. Tannenbaum, an expert on the bard. Even though scholars and editors have labored over the texts for centuries, there are many spots still "hopelessly or almost hopelessly corrupt."	**Nov. 11**
	As head of the Senate Munitions Committee, Senator Gerald P. Nye informs thousands attending an Armistice Day peace gathering in Madison Square Garden that he will submit to Congress a proposal for curbing arms in the world. The program would ban credit to any nation engaged in arms distribution and place a high tax on any profits made by war.	Both the Chamber of Commerce and the Federal Reserve Board on the same day address the nation's recovery in reports that lend support to the Roosevelt administration, indicating that, in terms of production, earnings, and world trade activity, the current situation is the best since 1930.		Some 250 major radio stations commit to running a series of highway-safety broadcasts, sponsored by the American Road Builders Association.	**Nov. 12**
	Maj. Gen. Edward M. Markham approves the design of a large seaplane base on Midway Island in the Pacific Ocean.	The businesses of America are showing a more willing attitude to work side by side with bureaucratic agencies since the reelection of President Roosevelt, say industry watchers. For instance, the National Association of Manufacturers suddenly promises to support the administration "in a new era of good feeling between industry and the government."			**Nov. 13**
A proposal filed by George L. Berry, printing press union boss, for arbitration between the American Federation of Labor and the Committee for Industrial Organization is rejected at the AFL convention in Tampa, Fla. The division between the AFL and CIO therefore continues. . . . Disgusted by the mass of "hate propaganda" that appeared in the nation during the presidential elections, the House Immigration Committee proposes an investigation into subversive groups suspected of distributing such racist material.		The Anaconda Copper Mining Company reports earnings for the first nine months of 1936 at $1.15 per share.			**Nov. 14**
Even minor criminals and those guilty of misdemeanors are concerned by Special Prosecutor Thomas E. Dewey's racketeering probes, which have sent police units onto the streets in search of detainees. Many fret of guilt by association.		A letter to shareholders from Russell Brown, president of the American Commercial Alcohol Company, declares record earnings of $924,813 for the first three quarters of this year, or $3.54 per share.			**Nov. 15**

F	G	H	I	J
Includes elections, federal-state relations, civil rights and liberties, crime, the judiciary, education, healthcare, poverty, urban affairs, and population.	Includes formation and debate of U.S. foreign and defense policies, veterans affairs, and defense spending. (Relations with specific foreign countries are usually found under the region concerned.)	Includes business, labor, agriculture, taxation, transportation, consumer affairs, monetary and fiscal policy, natural resources, pollution, and accidents.	Includes worldwide scientific, medical, and technological developments, natural phenomena, U.S. weather, and natural disasters.	Includes the arts, religion, scholarship, communications media, sports, entertainment, fashions, fads, and social life.

	World Affairs	Europe	Africa & The Middle East	The Americas	Asia & The Pacific
Nov. 16		Officials in Germany meet with State Secretary Heydrich, high lieutenant of the secret police, to effect changes in the application of justice in trials dealing with treason or "race pollution." It is predicted that many more trials of a racial nature are slated on the upcoming ministerial calendar.	Patrick Duncan, South African minister of mines, is chosen by King Edward VIII of England to serve as Governor General of the Union of South Africa. This is noteworthy because Duncan is the first South African resident to take that position.	Major D.W. Herridge, Canada's former minister to Washington, speaks today to the Canada Club in Toronto, appealing for new policy on national planning. Observers afterward say he seemed to hint at the creation of a new political party.	
Nov. 17		King Edward VIII personally tours the South Wales coal mining areas—a scene of labor unrest—to proclaim to its workers that the government does understand their plight and has already begun reform to assist them. Accompanying the King are the nation's health and labor ministers.		The government of Canada announces huge expenditures for defense; large orders for airplanes and ground vehicles have been completed.	
Nov. 18		Germany and Italy recognize Gen. Francisco Franco's government in Spain.			
Nov. 19	World production is at an all-time high, says the monthly *Annalist* publication, with world economic conditions boosting through October and November; global trade continues to increase to more than satisfactory levels.	Adolf Hitler of Germany and Benito Mussolini of Italy officially recognize the fascist rebels in Spain against the loyalists. This support incites wild enthusiasm and shouts from the insurgents that they are the "saviors of Spain." The rest of Europe, in the meantime, now strongly suspects that the two factions may be donating military support to create a fascist government in Spain.			
Nov. 20				As Brazil adopts a new law allowing government regulation of freight rates, an American maritime attorney complains that such fixing of rates will serve to encumber the shipping industry.	Japan loads north China with the implements of war—namely, planes and tanks—to suppress any further revolts from dissident members of the provinces. Additionally, 50,000 soldiers in Nanking and elsewhere provide what Japan hopes will be a discouragement to rebels.
Nov. 21		Gen. Francisco Franco, who is besieging Madrid, promises Britain that he has warned his army against bombing or attacking British or American embassies. He makes no mention of the consulate in Barcelona, about which the British also inquired. . . . Germany and Italy's declaration of support for the fascist rebels in Spain counters the Soviets' support for the Communists on the other side of the conflict, but Italy denies the idea of Soviet intervention, saying that Russia would not risk a war with Hitler and Mussolini.		Brazilian authorities allow a large peace gathering of women to meet in Buenos Aires against the wishes of the city police force, which claims they are Communists. The committee—the Popular Conference for Peace—contends that it is converging "in favor of peace," but the chief of constables says the organizers have records of "Red" participation.	Because of its hatred for war, Japan is considering more ways it can expand and nourish economic and social equality, says the nation's minister to the United States, Hirosi Saito, in an address to a corporate dinner in New York City.
Nov. 22			As Portugal institutes an anti-Communist rule for its colonies, it includes Portuguese East Africa. In Lourenco Marquess, announcements appear forbidding members of Communist associations to work for the local state administration under risk of penalty.	From the Pan-American Conference comes news that Latin America is jubilant over the reelection of President Roosevelt. His Good Neighbor policy, which brought new trading opportunities, proves that he is what that the world needs today to ward off global economic distress, according to conference attendees.	

A	B	C	D	E
Includes developments that affect more than one world region, international organizations, and important meetings of world leaders.	Includes all domestic and regional developments in Europe, including the Soviet Union.	Includes all domestic and regional developments in Africa and the Middle East.	Includes all domestic and regional developments in Latin America, the Caribbean, and Canada.	Includes all domestic and regional developments in Asian and Pacific nations (and colonies).

U.S. Politics & Social Issues	U.S. Foreign Policy & Defense	Economics & Great Depression	Science, Technology & Nature	Culture, Leisure & Lifestyle	
An optimistic note from President Roosevelt is sent to attendees at the American Federation of Labor Conference in Tampa. He tells of his hope to help restore prosperity to the American worker. . . . Mayors of eight seaport towns on the Pacific, Atlantic, and Gulf coasts offer a united plea for an end to the longtime Pacific Coast maritime strike that has virtually thrown shipping into idle gear. They suggest a special arbitration board hand-picked by the President to resolve differences before damages to the shipping industry are irreparable.		Shipments of new pianos and organs to America's homes rise 31 percent. . . . Between now and the President's reelection ceremonies in mid-January, a series of conferences will take place among government and business entities for the purpose of absorbing the remaining 4 million jobless into corporations.	The Southern Medical Association meeting in Baltimore announces allantoin for the treatment of ulcers, wounds, and burns. Allantoin is much more effective than other medicines of its type.	One of several main actors are being sought for the male lead in Paramount's *Souls at Sea*; they are George Raft, Lloyd Nolan, Lee Tracy, and John Barrymore.	Nov. 16
Some 4,300 employees of the Bendix Product Corp. stage a "sit-in" strike, locking themselves into the South Bend, Ind., plant, barring nonunion workers from entering. Vice president and works manager J.P. Mahoney orders all to turn in their tools and leave the premises. . . . Eight resolutions offered at the American Federation of Labor Conference in Tampa reject the AFL's proposal to suspend members who joined the dissident Committee for Industrial Organization, presided over by John L. Lewis, but AFL officers still call for ousters.					Nov. 17
		Congress eyes the construction of a seaway connecting the Great Lakes, Montreal, Lake Champlain, and the Hudson River that would save an estimated $1 billion in rail shipping costs.	The main span of the Golden Gate Bridge, under construction in San Francisco, Calif., is joined.		Nov. 18
The director of New York's safety service of the State Insurance Fund, Roger Williams, tells the National Founders Association that he seeks more industry-backed legislation to guide social programs.	Secretary of State Cordell Hull tells 1,000 delegates at the National Foreign Trade Convention in Chicago that it is America's aim to abolish those trade obstacles proffering "economic tensions that set the stage for revolution and war."				Nov. 19
Striking members of the Atlantic Coast seamen's organization, out of work for three weeks, bring their appeal to the Supreme Court. Their initial goal of improved working conditions has grown; they now protest the contract signed by union leaders, which they claim is illegal. . . . The American Federation of Labor bans the purchase of clothes bearing the label of the CIO's Amalgamated Clothing Workers of America.		During the first four months of the current fiscal year, the Internal Revenue Service of the Treasury collected some $1,209,242,231, which is an increase of nearly 17 percent over figures at the same time last year. Simultaneously, the sale of alcoholic products jumped a dramatic 26 percent higher over 1935; the latest income on alcohol sales is $37,120,110.	A scientific expedition under Prof. Herman von Walde-Waldegg of the University Museum of Boston College uncovers a huge stone "calendar," from ca. 300 A.D. The museum says it is probably the oldest-known time-telling device in existence.	More than 300,000 females across the country are summoned to take part in the awareness-building Women's Field Army for "a war to save lives" against cancer, a killer of 150,000 yearly.	Nov. 20
The Daughters of the American Revolution promise to investigate the legality of the Communist Party being allowed to exist in the United States, as well as conduct an official presidential campaign. . . . About 1,000 people attend the 52nd birthday celebration of Norman Thomas, the Socialist leader who just ran an unsuccessful campaign for the presidency. At a dinner speech he says that while he rejects the idea of violence, he does urge "the maximum possible amount of joint action against the forces of reaction."		Major advertising agencies in America offer their 1937 budgets, allowing for a 15 percent rise over 1936. The budgets are planned based on several factors, two of the most important being the dramatic business recovery in the country and the rise in print costs for newspapers and magazines. . . . America's civil service and merit system will be expanded to take in the majority of the 20,000 civil servants hired during the New Deal years, forecasts Luther C. Steward, president of the National Federation of Federal Employees.			Nov. 21
	Visiting America, Spain's Minister to the United States, Fernando de los Rios, tells the American Federation of Labor assembly in Tampa that the results of the Spanish civil war will have long-lasting effects on America. A fascist victory could harm the good relations that President Roosevelt has been trying so hard to establish in Europe.	In the last 12 months, the Caterpillar Tractor Company earned $8,971,420—or $4.77 a share—compared to $5,169,877 net the previous year.			Nov. 22

F	G	H	I	J
Includes elections, federal-state relations, civil rights and liberties, crime, the judiciary, education, healthcare, poverty, urban affairs, and population.	*Includes formation and debate of U.S. foreign and defense policies, veterans affairs, and defense spending. (Relations with specific foreign countries are usually found under the region concerned.)*	*Includes business, labor, agriculture, taxation, transportation, consumer affairs, monetary and fiscal policy, natural resources, pollution, and accidents.*	*Includes worldwide scientific, medical, and technological developments, natural phenomena, U.S. weather, and natural disasters.*	*Includes the arts, religion, scholarship, communications media, sports, entertainment, fashions, fads, and social life.*

	World Affairs	Europe	Africa & The Middle East	The Americas	Asia & The Pacific
Nov. 23		Germany accepts a curb on submarine warfare, a curb that, had it been established 20 years ago, might have saved the British liner *Lusitania*, which was torpedoed by one of Kaiser Wilhelm's submarines.		American delegates attending the all-female Popular Conference for Peace propose to support the economic treaties that are being affected between Washington, D.C., and other countries. Through a strong economy, they say, peace can be obtained. The conference represents 10 million women worldwide.	Japan's budget for 1937 is fixed at 3 billion yen after much deliberation and after the war and navy departments consent to some budgetary maneuvering. The defense budget automatically consumes 46 percent of the total.
Nov. 24		Germany is outraged to learn that a man it once sentenced to 18 months in prison for treason—for preaching against the warlike measures of the Third Reich—wins the Nobel Peace Prize. The Nobel recognition of Prof. Carl von Ossietzky's long list of peace efforts is taken by Adolf Hitler himself as a personal affront.		Uruguay welcomes U.S. Secretary of State Cordell Hull when he lands in Montevideo as a goodwill gesture on his way to the Pan-American Peace Conference in Buenos Aires. The Uruguayan minister at the scene lauds American progress and its firm belief in democracy.	
Nov. 25		At the Congress of Soviets in Moscow, a new constitution for the Soviet Union is introduced tonight by Josef Stalin, general secretary of the Communist Party. No major political changes are expected, but Communism is now the only political party in the Soviet Union. Fascism will not be allowed.			
Nov. 26		Poland and Romania work to form a relationship, despite past misunderstandings. Romanian Foreign Minister Antonescu's visit to Warsaw is a sign of such efforts, but the peacemakers of Europe are concerned by a possible alliance as Poland could be swept into the fascist politics of Antonescu, who has been supportive of Hitler's anti-Semitism.			In reaction to the news that Germany and Japan formed an accord, the Tokyo press announces its apprehension, fretting that the country may have gotten itself into something bigger—and more dangerous—than it anticipates.
Nov. 27		Two Nazi-published magazine newspapers, The *Angriff* and the *Black Corps*, which are mouthpieces for Adolf Hitler, debase a decision by the Leipzig municipal authorities to raise orphans under their care as Christians. . . . Britain pledges to defend Belgium if attacked by Germany while British Foreign Secretary Anthony Eden follows up the promise with a warning to Hitler.		While in South America for the Pan-American Conference, President Roosevelt addresses a special joint session of the Brazilian Congress, vowing U.S. support to Latin America in the event of war from abroad. He also clarifies the U.S. stand on neutrality—that America will remain out of the fray, except if attacked.	
Nov. 28		After a remark made by Austrian Chancellor Kurt von Schuschnigg to a Carinthian audience today, the Nazi authorities are visibly irate. Chancellor Schuschnigg, during his oration, refers to the Nazis as a "great enemy" that Austria needs to fight.	The Union of South Africa's public debt has lowered by $115 million in one year, according to the country's Treasury. The Public Debt Commission's report shows it has been an eventful year of large-scale financing and the raising of over $110 million in loans.		
Nov. 29		Compulsory labor for all German girls—that is, expected participation in the Nazi Youth work groups—will begin in the near future, according to Chief of the Third Reich Labor Service Konstantin Hierl. The service, explains Hierl, who addresses the Central School for Women Labor, readies young ladies for posts under the Labor Service.			
Nov. 30	Traffic of arms from country to country, including purchases between countries, cost the world $72 million in 1935, according to estimates by the League of Nations. Britain leads the rearming race and the United States rests in fourth place. Germany is in sixth place if its reported figures are accurate.			National Broadcasting Company outlets air a scholarly speech by Argentine Foreign Minister and Nobel Prize recipient Dr. Carlos Saavedra Lamas on "The Significance of the Nobel Prize." As a world peace advocate, Dr. Lamas, who is also president of the Pan-American Conference for the Maintenance of Peace, focuses his talk on the values of recognizing the rights of all mankind in a complex world.	According to the theory of author Emil Ludwig, speaking on behalf of the Free Synagogue to a crowd of 2,200 in Carnegie Hall, Japan will be at the center of any future world war due to its territorial ambitions. Once a war begins, he acknowledges, the United States will not be able to avoid it—and will most likely be sucked into the maelstrom.
	A Includes developments that affect more than one world region, international organizations, and important meetings of world leaders.	**B** Includes all domestic and regional developments in Europe, including the Soviet Union.	**C** Includes all domestic and regional developments in Africa and the Middle East.	**D** Includes all domestic and regional developments in Latin America, the Caribbean, and Canada.	**E** Includes all domestic and regional developments in Asian and Pacific nations (and colonies).

U.S. Politics & Social Issues	U.S. Foreign Policy & Defense	Economics & Great Depression	Science, Technology & Nature	Culture, Leisure & Lifestyle	
In an emotional show of support for the American Federation of Labor, a huge majority of the one million members vote down the rogue eight unions that joined the Committee for Industrial Organization, thus suspending them from the Federation. The vote officially marks the separation of the CIO and AFL.		For the year ending in August, the entertainment company Loew's, Inc., netted an impressive $11,076,823, or $6.79 per share.			Nov. 23
	Raymond Leslie Buell, president of the Foreign Policy Association, returns home to America after visiting nine European countries. He wishes that President Roosevelt would become more assertive in his overseas peace-making efforts, believing that America, with proper intervention, could ease the growing tensions in Europe.			Successful movie producer David O. Selznick plans to produce a dozen mainstream films in 1937. One large project that Selznick International Pictures claims is a photoplay of Sir Anthony Hope's The Prisoner of Zenda, starring Ronald Colman in the title role and heartthrob Douglas Fairbanks, Jr., in the uncharacteristic role of the villain.	Nov. 24
Philadelphia's mayor, S. Davis Wilson, irritated by the rising crime rate, summons a press conference where he publicly orders a "war on vice." He demands a reorganization of the police department and immediate results from those squads on the street.		The motion picture company Paramount clears $1,961,789 for the third quarter, as well as a profit of $51,000 in debentures.			Nov. 25
		Compared to 1933, the middle of the Depression years, wholesale business rose an outstanding 41 percent by 1935, only two years later, reports William L. Austin, director of the census. Volume from 1935 amounted to $42 billion. Other comparison estimates show that payrolls increased by 23 percent and average pay rose from $1,397 to $1,608.			Nov. 26
In closing its two-week session in Florida, the American Federation of Labor reelects William Green as its president and proposes a 30-hour workweek.				World champion welterweight Barney Ross faces off tonight with Izzy Jannazzo for 15 rounds at Madison Square Garden. Ross is the strong favorite to win the bout.	Nov. 27
Of America's vast railway system, the first 61 rail lines to report earnings for October 1936 show a collective gain of 17.1 percent in net operating income over the previous month. Owners of the lines reply with enthusiasm to the news, commenting that figures like this prove that the railroads continue to be the major mode of transpiration for passengers and commerce, despite the growing use of the airplane.		The National Industrial Conference Board says that, even though jobs have increased along with weekly pay, weekly working hours for American employees have still not reached the 40-hour maximum—a schedule which is sought by many corporations and industries.	Boston police are now utilizing a two-way radio that allows them to communicate back and forth from their squad cars to the central station. General Electric, which installed the equipment, says the gear makes Boston "the most difficult city in which (criminals can) operate."	Speedster Mauri Rose accepts a trophy from the American Automobile Association after winning the National Automobile Racing Championship in Indiana tonight.	Nov. 28
With "staggering losses" mounting in the shipping industry with shipments of food not being delivered to many locations, the New York Board of Trade pleads with Labor Secretary Frances Perkins to get involved in ending the four-week-old seamen's strike. The effects of the strike have been far-reaching—some places, such as Alaska, have been unable to get materials in weeks and in other areas tourists are stranded, unable to get home.		A study conducted by the well-known German banking institution, the Reich Credit Association—which is highly regarded for the accuracy of its economic and business predictions—claims that unemployment in the United States has given way to a strong recovery evidenced by top wages that meet the cost of living.			Nov. 29
			As part of the Rhodes Memorial Lecture Series, noted astronomer Edwin P. Hubble of the Mount Wilson Observatory delivers a traveling lecture on "Observational Approach to Cosmology" along the East Coast.	Broadway producers George M. Cohan and Sam Harris, who presented many of Broadway's top musicals from 1904–19 before separating on friendly terms, are once again collaborating on a new show, Fulton of Oak Falls by Parker Fennelly, extensively rewritten by Cohan. Cohan, as a songwriter, has composed such hits as Over There, I'm a Yankee Doodle Dandy, and It's a Grand Old Flag.	Nov. 30

F
Includes elections, federal-state relations, civil rights and liberties, crime, the judiciary, education, healthcare, poverty, urban affairs, and population.

G
Includes formation and debate of U.S. foreign and defense policies, veterans affairs, and defense spending. (Relations with specific foreign countries are usually found under the region concerned.)

H
Includes business, labor, agriculture, taxation, transportation, consumer affairs, monetary and fiscal policy, natural resources, pollution, and accidents.

I
Includes worldwide scientific, medical, and technological developments, natural phenomena, U.S. weather, and natural disasters.

J
Includes the arts, religion, scholarship, communications media, sports, entertainment, fashions, fads, and social life.

	World Affairs	Europe	Africa & The Middle East	The Americas	Asia & The Pacific
Dec. 1		France's Premier Leon Blum considers President Roosevelt's personal participation in the Pan-American Conference for the Maintenance of Peace, set in Buenos Aires, as the beginning of a new era of democracy, providing an opposing influence to the rule of dictators.		Mexicans sympathetic to the loyalists' cause in Spain contribute arms, food, and other materials on the first of a series of airplanes that will carry supplies to the loyalist base in Vera Cruz. . . . President Roosevelt delivers an address at the Buenos Aires Conference, also known as the Inter-American Peace Conference. He pledges consultation for mutual safety in the event of war.	
Dec. 2	The League of Nations is surprised, and very encouraged, by the steadfastly neutral President Roosevelt's allusions to the warlike overtures of Germany, Japan, and Italy as an apparent means to shame them before the world for their actions.			Brazilian publishers as a unit praise U.S. attempts at making South America a fielding ground for world peace—first at the Pan-American Congress last month and now at the Inter-American Peace Conference, which begins this week.	
Dec. 3	Italy and Japan deny that they have formed a pact, even though an Italo-Japanese agreement placed with the Foreign Office clearly states that Italy gives Japanese legislators what amounts to first-choice options in commercial and business ventures in Ethiopia.	From all reports coming from Germany, Adolf Hitler shows no sign of interest in the peace conferences taking place in Buenos Aires. The singular reference to it in German newspapers says that President Roosevelt delivered an incoherent opening speech.		On his way home from his South American tour, President Roosevelt is applauded by adoring Uruguayans in the town of Montevideo.	
Dec. 4		Pertaining to the King's romance with Wallis Simpson, the prime minister tells him that the British Cabinet will not allow him to call upon the Morganic Act—the right of some nations' monarchs to marry a commoner as long as they have no claim to the throne. King Edward will have to surrender his romance or abdicate the throne. . . . Catholic Free Ireland denounces the twice-divorced Wallis Simpson and calls the British King "a fallen idol."			Learning of their monarch King Edward VIII's indiscretions with a divorced commoner, Mrs. Wallis Simpson, most Australians want him to give her up and remain with the duty assigned to him by Right of Throne.
Dec. 5		Prime Minister Stanley Baldwin calls an early-morning meeting of his Cabinet at 10 Downing Street; the streets of London buzz with rumors that King Edward VIII is about to abdicate. . . . French and British envoys meet to authenticate their country's pledges of parallel defense—defending each other when and if Hitler and/or Mussolini attack.			Observers wonder at Japan's sudden build-up of submarines and bomber planes. As in the case of Germany, journalists question whether this rash of war equipment might be aimed for assault.
Dec. 6		In a very frank response to questions concerning its naval enforcement program, Germany answers that the real reason is it increasing its fleet is because it needs a navy "formidable enough to keep the Russians bottled up in Leningrad for the duration of any war."		Germany's Nazi-controlled newspaper, *Koelnische Zeitung*, claims that the only reason President Roosevelt is so interested in the Inter-American Conference for Maintenance of Peace, taking place in Argentina, is to begin domination of Latin America.	
Dec. 7		The mortality rate in the Spanish civil war is startling, says the American National Red Cross chairman, Rear Admiral Cary Grayson, who puts the number at 500,000. Most, he said, died not in battle, but a few days after battle from disease and illness as a result of wounds.		While Canada's Prime Minister Mackenzie King refuses to verbally take a stand on the relationship of Edward VIII and Wallis Simpson, most others in the Canadian government say that England, their mother country, should allow the King to marry whom he pleases. . . . All members at the Inter-American Conference do not agree on the neutrality issue as proposed by the United States. Some noncommittals hold back final declaration expected this week, throwing an unexpected pause in the proceedings.	

A	B	C	D	E
Includes developments that affect more than one world region, international organizations, and important meetings of world leaders.	Includes all domestic and regional developments in Europe, including the Soviet Union.	Includes all domestic and regional developments in Africa and the Middle East.	Includes all domestic and regional developments in Latin America, the Caribbean, and Canada.	Includes all domestic and regional developments in Asian and Pacific nations (and colonies).

U.S. Politics & Social Issues	U.S. Foreign Policy & Defense	Economics & Great Depression	Science, Technology & Nature	Culture, Leisure & Lifestyle	
In his opening speech at the Inter-American Conference for the Maintenance of Peace, President Roosevelt calls for the forces of good to join "shoulder to shoulder" for the purpose of bringing the world back from the tear being caused by "new fanaticisms." . . . Speaking in support of the Child Welfare League of America by radio, President Roosevelt asks Americans to help devote time and money in keeping alive those many organizations that help feed, clothe, and house orphans and unloved children.	The U.S. Navy's newest 10,000-ton light cruiser, U.S.S. *Brooklyn*, rolls out of the New York Navy Yard while 12,000 onlookers watch from the wharves. It is one of several warships that the Navy is building to reenforce the U.S. fleet, even under the law of neutrality that governs the current U.S. policy toward war.	With onions unobtainable from Spain because of its civil war, London turns to the United States to replenish its stock. The first two British ships laden with 75,000 pounds of yellow onions leave America headed back to Liverpool.		Actress Ruth Gordon opens tonight on Broadway in the play, *The Country Wife*. Others in the cast are Anthony Quayle and Irene Browne. . . . While the trend of evening games is catching on among the major league baseball park owners, the two New York teams, the Yankees and Giants, refuse to take part. Their stadiums remain without light towers lining the walls.	Dec. 1
The presidential election that just transpired shows a "rather definite" consciousness of America's social and welfare issues, much more than ever experienced before, James Rowland Angell of Yale University attests. He addresses the American Society of Mechanical Engineers meeting at the college hall.	Optical manufacturer Bausch & Lomb refuses more than $1 million in orders for artillery fire-controlled instruments sought by alien countries engaged in warlike activities. A large percentage of business of that nature would ordinarily come from the Nazi government to the Bausch & Lomb plant in Jena, Germany.	To benefit its 220,000 Michigan-based employees, General Motors Corporation announces a change in its overtime payout process; starting today, employees will receive time-and-a-half for every hour worked beyond a 40-hour workweek schedule—not 48 hours as it had been previously.	Members of various industries—such as the railroad, shipping, aviation, and farming industries—gather in New York to celebrate the 40th anniversary of Rudolf Diesel's first diesel engine and create a dialogue on the future of diesel power.		Dec. 2
The National Council of Women asks President Roosevelt and governors of states to consider the appointment of females to positions of esteem and respect in the systems of federal, state, and city governments.	The Right Rev. James E. Freeman of the Protestant Episcopal Diocese in Washington, D.C., wants the President's assurance of America's stand on neutrality; he suggests a meeting with the country's clergy.	According to retailer Marshall Field & Company's chairman, James O. McKinsey, businesses need to adapt to a changing economy by mending their past mistakes and redefining their structures for a more politically- and socially-conscious world. . . . Ice cream sales rose 33 percent over the last six months nationally, according to Peter G. Ten Eyck, agricultural commissioner.			Dec. 3
Incited by the fact that many crimes are committed by criminals out on parole, both Democrats and Republicans from the Illinois state legislature introduce a bill to curb premature prison releases. They cite specific crimes committed in Illinois by "reformed" criminals.			Doctors E.C. Ernst and Otto Glassner win the 1936 Radiological Society of North America medallion to honor their 11 years of research, which culminated in their finding a "yardstick" to measure x-ray doses.		Dec. 4
	At the Inter-American Conference in Buenos Aires, Secretary of State Cordell Hull presents an eight-point plan for peace, which he says also "prepares" the forces allied for peace against the possibility of war. Though it is well-received overall, discussion begins with some representatives contending parts of the plan.	Following an announcement that 175,000 men would be dropped from the Works Progress Administration payrolls on December 1, a delegation is sent to Washington, D.C., in protest. Aubrey Williams, acting WPA administrator, explains that the decision is based strictly on lack of program funds.		Eighty-year-old Pope Pius XI is forced to his bed after several days of illness. The Vatican reports to a concerned world that at this point there is no need for alarm. . . . Movie director Cecil B. DeMille's *The Plainsman* opens in American theaters. This bio of Wild Bill Hickok stars Gary Cooper and Jean Arthur.	Dec. 5
Pleading for the enactment of special trial courts for offenders between the ages 16 and 20, George Z. Medalie seeks the backing of the Jewish Board of Guardians, which he heads, and the Federation for the Support of Jewish Philanthropic Societies.	Great Britain has not done enough to suppress the Arab population's anti-Jewish outbreaks in Palestine, says U.S. Senator Royal S. Copeland at the 25th anniversary of the Mizrachi Organization of America.	Ordway Tead, the economics editor for Harper & Collins Publishers, urges business stability through profit sharing, higher wages, and lower pricing.			Dec. 6
Jeremiah Titus Mahoney, president of the Amateur Athletic Union, warns against government intervention, saying competition should remain free and open. He proposes a wide-ranging plan for the development of the AAU, stressing participation coast to coast but avoiding "athletic nationalism." . . . New York Mayor Fiorello LaGuardia reports some inroads against racketeering in the city, thanks to Police Department and legal efforts, but he openly wonders if the town can eliminate all such vice.		Economic recovery rests on "jittery foundations," opines one-time chief of the National Recovery Act Gen. Hugh S. Johnson. However, he believes the Roosevelt administration is earnest about curbing inflation to avoid another Depression-like setback.			Dec. 7

F	**G**	**H**	**I**	**J**
Includes elections, federal-state relations, civil rights and liberties, crime, the judiciary, education, healthcare, poverty, urban affairs, and population.	*Includes formation and debate of U.S. foreign and defense policies, veterans affairs, and defense spending. (Relations with specific foreign countries are usually found under the region concerned.)*	*Includes business, labor, agriculture, taxation, transportation, consumer affairs, monetary and fiscal policy, natural resources, pollution, and accidents.*	*Includes worldwide scientific, medical, and technological developments, natural phenomena, U.S. weather, and natural disasters.*	*Includes the arts, religion, scholarship, communications media, sports, entertainment, fashions, fads, and social life.*

	World Affairs	Europe	Africa & The Middle East	The Americas	Asia & The Pacific
Dec. 8		The trial of David Frankfurter opens tomorrow, and Nazi party members want to see Frankfurter pay for his crime of killing Swiss Nazi leader Wilhelm Gustloff last February. Despite pressure from the Nazis as high as Adolf Hitler, Switzerland promises a fair and just trial. . . . Latest news from Madrid puts the rebels stalled outside the capital city, having faced defenses greater than anticipated. Rebels seem under-gunned and weary.			
Dec. 9		The British Cabinet is remaining steadfast in its position on the issue of the King's relationship with Wallis Simpson. It does not consider her offer to withdraw from the scandal a realistic and acceptable solution, but demands the King's solemn oath to end the romance once and for all. . . . Germany's Minister of Economics, Dr. Hjalmar Schacht, iterates his country's demand for "lost colonies" in a more virulent fashion than ever before. If Germany does not get what it wants, he says, and is forced to endure its crowded territories, there will come such an explosion as to shoot Europe to its feet.		Feminist leaders from a dozen different countries meet in Buenos Aires to demand that the current Inter-American Conference commit to allowing suffrage for women as a large "next step" toward helping the world meet universal peace.	American planes rush food and vaccines to the heavily flooded Cagayan Valley in the Philippines where rising waters from torrential rains force thousands of people from their homes.
Dec. 10		King Edward VIII abdicates the throne of England rather than give up the woman he loves, Mrs. Wallis Simpson. The news shocks England and the rest of the world, and even Adolf Hitler expresses his amazement. The new King, George VI, is described as a happily married family man.		In Buenos Aires, all parties reach an agreement on the neutrality pact at the Inter-American Conference for the Maintenance of Peace. U.S. Secretary of State Cordell Hull is delighted that the deadlock is broken and the committees may move on to other business.	
Dec. 11		Britons' respect for their new King, George VI, runs high; he is considered to be serious and reserved—but with a steadfast determination and love for his country. The date of the coronation remains May 12, the day that Edward was to have been crowned.		With the finalization of the definition of neutrality, the 21 nations attending the Inter-American Conference in South America sign off on a formula for peace governing the Americas.	
Dec. 12		Soviet Russia's gold output has risen 46 percent over last year by keeping 144 various mines active around the clock to bring in $200 million. Foreign observers widely speculate on Russia's annual output.		Canada, after listening to the broadcast of Edward VIII's outgoing message explaining his abdication, officially proclaims its allegiance to the royal heir apparent, George VI. Prime Minister Mackenzie King and other Canadian officiales, on a nationwide radio address timed with London's own ceremony, welcome the new monarch.	A press release from the U.S. Trade Commissioner informs that the Japan Broadcasting Corporation is increasing its power as part of its 1937 plan to include advanced broadcasting wattage and television research.
Dec. 13		Germany, finding itself one million tons short of wheat and an equal amount short of rye at the end of a depressed crop year, reminds peasants once again of Gen. Hermann Goering's request made two weeks ago for food "donations." In order not to be branded a traitor, all German farmers are required to bring in a fixed amount of bread and grain to the local counting house.	South Africa mandates its objection to National Socialist (Nazi) policies and vows to expel any practitioners from its shores, thus provoking Nazi Germany. . . . Outlandishly high prices of staples, such as bread, milk, and butter, are responsible for bringing malnutrition to Africa, says the Union of South Africa's Chamber of Commerce board.		

A	B	C	D	E
Includes developments that affect more than one world region, international organizations, and important meetings of world leaders.	Includes all domestic and regional developments in Europe, including the Soviet Union.	Includes all domestic and regional developments in Africa and the Middle East.	Includes all domestic and regional developments in Latin America, the Caribbean, and Canada.	Includes all domestic and regional developments in Asian and Pacific nations (and colonies).

U.S. Politics & Social Issues	U.S. Foreign Policy & Defense	Economics & Great Depression	Science, Technology & Nature	Culture, Leisure & Lifestyle	
At the International Labor Committee meeting in Geneva, Switzerland, American labor delegate Prof. Theodore Krets supports a 40-hour workweek for the U.S. chemical industry. . . . Because of changes in the political scene and promises on the economic landscape, industry is now "willing to meet workers half way in their demands," according to Ernest Poole of the National Association of Manufacturers.		The price of wheat advances upward today, the best price for the season. In fact, it reaches the highest level since 1929, according to a report from the Chicago Board of Trade.		RKO Pictures is trying to lure Adele Astaire, sister of dancer Fred Astaire, into the limelight by offering her a role in an upcoming film, *A Lady in Distress*, starring her brother.	**Dec. 8**
As the seamen's strike continues to freeze commerce in the Pacific—and as another compromise is rebuffed—the union accuses Capt. George Fried of the Steamboat Inspection Service and John Daley, U.S. Shipping Commissioner, of being behind "vicious attempts" to break the strike. Both men deny the charges.		Leading business entities, which have long been a thorn in the side to President Roosevelt's reform plans, call a truce at the Congress of American Industry by agreeing to back federal agencies to aid employment and other intrinsic problems created by the Depression. . . . In a speech in Pasadena, Calif., Secretary of State Cordell Hull advises farmers to "accept small increases in the imports of certain agricultural products" to benefit the growth of world trade.			**Dec. 9**
Reese Bailey, age 30, midwest bank robber and killer, gets 20 years for the slaying of an FBI agent in Ohio. In handing out the sentence, Judge Mell G. Underwood withdraws a $10,000 fine so as not to deprive Bailey's poor family of food and clothing.		Kentucky tobacco, the state's chief crop, is at its highest price since 1928 and, according to stock market watchers, approaches the all-time record high of the post-war market of 1919. . . . Stopping short of mentioning a conscription plan—or from deliberating the possibility of a coming war—President Roosevelt and the War Department announce that they will seek from Congress a national industrial mobilization campaign to prepare labor for the event of a full-scale world conflict.			**Dec. 10**
	The Federal Council of Churches of Christ in America "cannot and will not" concede to the nation's expenses on battleships, tanks, airplanes, and other items of war, even in preparation of defense.	Farmers in America are now learning, through a print campaign and a strategic public education program, the details of the nation's agricultural programs for 1937. One of these is the issue of "limits"—such as for the corn crop—where corn growers are not to exceed a growth limit in order to avoid crop surplus and waste. . . . Now in its sixth week, the seamen's strike is beleaguering West Coast businesses. Loss is determined at $7 million per day on the Pacific Coast—some $3 million in San Francisco alone.		Representatives of the arts, the various religions, labor, and other special groups push for more quality airtime on the radio at the National Conference on Educational Broadcasting in Washington, D.C.	**Dec. 11**
Secretary Emeritus of the Council of Churches, Rev. Dr. Charles S. MacFarland, insists that the world is bringing on its own social and economic ailments by "forgetting God," substituting the materialistic for the spiritual view of the world.		President Roosevelt hints that once he returns from the peace conference in Argentina he will turn his attention back to domestic economic matters and concentrate on the jobless and financially depressed. . . . As rumors abound of the demise of the Works Progress Administration, its chief, Harry L. Hopkins, assures the public that it will not disband until most, if not all, of the unemployed are put back to work.			**Dec. 12**
Federal agents arrest a 42-year-old dockworker of French background in New York after learning that he is wanted in his native country for the murder of two people more than 12 years ago. He escaped from the guillotine in 1924.		Warning against inflation, Dr. Joseph J. Goodbar, president of the Society for the Stability in Money and Banking, promotes a detailed study on durable goods construction. "Its true normal (must be) recognized," Goodbar advises, "and held when that point is reached."		As the hurricane season comes to an end, the prosperous tourist and sporting season now begins in the Bahamas, say cruise experts. The time of the year is ideal for fishermen, yachtsmen, and hunters who enjoy plying their craft in tropical sunshine. . . . Seabiscuit, the racehorse that has been taking the tracks by storm, wins the $10,000 purse at the World's Fair Handicap in Bay Meadow, Calif.	**Dec. 13**

F	G	H	I	J
Includes elections, federal-state relations, civil rights and liberties, crime, the judiciary, education, healthcare, poverty, urban affairs, and population.	*Includes formation and debate of U.S. foreign and defense policies, veterans affairs, and defense spending. (Relations with specific foreign countries are usually found under the region concerned.)*	*Includes business, labor, agriculture, taxation, transportation, consumer affairs, monetary and fiscal policy, natural resources, pollution, and accidents.*	*Includes worldwide scientific, medical, and technological developments, natural phenomena, U.S. weather, and natural disasters.*	*Includes the arts, religion, scholarship, communications media, sports, entertainment, fashions, fads, and social life.*

	World Affairs	Europe	Africa & The Middle East	The Americas	Asia & The Pacific
Dec. 14		Adolf Hitler asks that the Nazi Party cease its attacks on religious institutions. Skeptics wonder if the announcement is made because he fears an uprising at a time when he needs the peasants to help deliver the country from its devastating food shortage.			
Dec. 15				Montreal, Canada, celebrates its busiest shipping season since 1928. It credits the reciprocal trade agreement between it and the United States as one of the major reasons for the tremendous upswing.	
Dec. 16		Per an agreement signed today, Britain and Italy concur to keep a balanced presence of men and warships in the Mediterranean Sea. This does not include those Italian volunteers who, on their own, have gone to fight with the fascist side in the Spanish civil war.		Argentina signs off on the neutrality pact agreed at the Inter-American Conference for Maintenance of Peace after the standing committee amends it, deleting minor articles and phrases to Argentina's and the other signers' approval. Argentina's main consideration was its right to export food and raw materials during wartime.	
Dec. 17	According to the world economic barometer, *The Annalist*, trends continue upward on a positive basis; industrial expansion grew faster than in previous years and commodity prices have escalated.	Arriving from overseas, five Spanish nuns burned out of their convent in Burriana in the province of Castilla tell a New York crowd that the shabby civilian clothing they wear is a disguise that got them safely out of the country. . . . Francisco Franco's forces, intent on breaking the defensive lines encircling Madrid, cut an arc around the northeast sector with an obvious plan to enter the city through Guadalajara. Loyalist and rebel artillery test each other's strength in a cannon duel just beyond Taracena, near Guadalajara.		President Lázaro Cárdenas of Mexico offers Russian exile Leon Trotsky asylum in his country. Trotsky, ejected from Stalin's Soviet Russia, considers the opportunity. . . . As the Inter-American Conference enters into its concluding sessions, a poll suggests that the members of the standing committee representing the main players of the conference are equally satisfied with what the event has meant to world trade and peace. Countries all indicate that they were given a chance to speak up and contribute and were well-represented in the sessions.	
Dec. 18		One of the top-selling books in the Netherlands is *Menschliche Erblehreund Rassenhygiene* (*Human Hereditary Doctrine and the Racial Hygiene*), which is a salute to the Jewish race. Its main critic is Adolf Hitler of Nazi Germany who realizes that the book smartly debunks his theories. . . . The rebel warship, *Espana*, fires a shell at the town of Musel, Spain, but barely misses the U.S. gunboat, *Erie*, stationed there as an observer. The Spanish apologize.		A natural gas line, the longest in the world, will be laid between Poza Rica in Veracruz and Mexico City by the Compania de Petrolios de Mexico (the Mexican Petroleum Company). Along the way, says the Mexican government, 26 oil wells will be drilled.	Chinese dictator Chiang Kai-shek, who opposes both the Communists' and the Japanese involvement in the Republic of China, is kidnapped by an opposing force under Chang Hsueh-liang, a warlord with Communistic leanings. The Republic is unsure as to who masterminded the kidnapping—the Communists or the Japanese.
Dec. 19		Britain's Sir Anthony Eden's accusations that Germany, Italy, and Russia are helping to arm their respective sides in Spain rile the German press. The *Boersen Zeitung* replies that Eden misrepresents the situation "against his better knowledge."		Canada ends a record-breaking year in mining production: mineral output is up eight percent to $335 million; gold is up 13 percent to $130 million. Wealth produced, dividends earned and distributed, and manpower utilized are all facets that exceeded past years.	
Dec. 20		James G. McDonald, the former commissioner of refugees for the League of Nations, explains that Nazi Germany is not only against Jews, but anything or anyone that suggests freedom and liberty.			

A	B	C	D	E
Includes developments that affect more than one world region, international organizations, and important meetings of world leaders.	*Includes all domestic and regional developments in Europe, including the Soviet Union.*	*Includes all domestic and regional developments in Africa and the Middle East.*	*Includes all domestic and regional developments in Latin America, the Caribbean, and Canada.*	*Includes all domestic and regional developments in Asian and Pacific nations (and colonies).*

U.S. Politics & Social Issues	U.S. Foreign Policy & Defense	Economics & Great Depression	Science, Technology & Nature	Culture, Leisure & Lifestyle	
Before 200 judges, lawyers, criminologists, and others in the penal profession, Governor Earle of Pennsylvania demands that the state bar eradicate "unethical lawyers and venal judges" who do nothing for their profession but bring shame upon it while supporting the activities of the people they are supposed to be bringing to justice.		For the year ending September 30, Columbia Gas and Electric and subsidiaries report a net of $12,442,512, equal to 47 cents per share on the market.			Dec. 14
While leading an investigation into vote fraud rackets in Kansas City, Mo., in the November presidential election, Judge Albert L. Reeves discloses that he was threatened by an anonymous caller demanding that he dismiss the case. . . . A pitched gun battle between J. Edgar Hoover's "G-Men" and famed bank robber Harry Brunette ends with the latter's arrest. New Jersey police, who were not consulted, accuse Hoover of stealing glory.		Many leaders of the huge textile industry make it clear that they would love to see a restoration of the basic wage and hour policies created under the no-longer-extant National Industrial Recovery Act. However, some business leaders still express their disapproval of such a return of laws ruled unfair by the Supreme Court.			Dec. 15
Gimbel Brothers Department Stores' vice president, Kenneth Collins, states that several managerial positions now held by males could easily be held by women. He predicts that in the near future, women will be occupying at least half the positions in Gimbels' stores.			The habit of cooking flower bulbs for sterilization before interstate shipping is called unnecessary by horticulturalists and members of the Department of Agriculture at a meeting overseen by U.S. Secretary of Agriculture Henry Wallace.		Dec. 16
Florida Governor David Sholtz's strategy to block miscreants and loiterers at Florida's northern border draws both ire and praise. The detractors say he is taking away from the tourist trade through unconstitutional means; his supporters say he has reduced crime caused by the shiftless who are there to freeload rather than contribute.		The Bureau of Agricultural Economics of the Department of Agriculture foresees higher prices for wheat in January after the pause in the holiday season.		The annual Associated Press sports poll names the New York Yankees, winners of the 1936 World Series, as the number one major league baseball team. Of the players' singular performances, Lou Gehrig batted in 152 runs, and DiMaggio, Lazzeri, Dickey, and Selkirk were each above 100.	Dec. 17
Seven participants in an international drug smuggling ring operating between the Port of New York and Boston are given 94 years in prison and a collective fine of $86,500. The U.S. government, in an attempt to stop all such future activity, had the intention of being severe in its judging.					Dec. 18
As the seamen's strike enters its 51st day and the shipping world continues to suffer, both striking members and their employers are given a chance to face off live on the radio in front of a listening America. Both parties are given time to explain their stance and rebut the other's opinions.		Trade editors all seem to agree that a business surge is coming in 1937. It will positively affect many industries, including manufacturing and retailing, and will be sensed mostly in the furniture, food, shipbuilding, and automobile areas. . . . General Motors opens a new Chevrolet commercial body plant in Indianapolis to keep up with the manufacturing of commercial cars and trucks, a market beyond the family automobile.			Dec. 19
World events and changing history seem to be occurring at a much more rapid pace than ever, asserts *Scribner's Magazine*'s 50th-year anniversary issue in an article written by columnist J.T. Adams. . . . Catholic theorist Monsignor Fulton J. Sheen says that a major difference between Christianity and Communism is that Christianity leaves asceticism to one's own choosing, but Communism imposes it.	Secretary of War Harry Hines Woodring estimates a larger armed force for America; in these troubled times, he suggests an Army of 165,000 men and 14,000 officers and a much larger National Guard than what currently serves the country.	American exporters are benefiting from the tense world situation. The war in Spain and threats of war throughout Germany, France, Italy, and across western Europe have turned away many global buyers to seek goods in America, where expectations of an ongoing supply are not in danger. . . . The jewelry industry, which has been showing signs of economic stagnation, indicated signs of recovery in last month's records with sales, payrolls, and jobs up across the nation.		The president of the University of Minnesota, Dr. Lotus D. Coffman, calls for a nationwide program to improve intercollegiate sports; he says the athlete borne by most colleges does not have the acumen or the determination to play professional sports. Notre Dame's president, the Rev. John F. O'Hara, calls the plan "both sensible and practical."	Dec. 20
F *Includes elections, federal-state relations, civil rights and liberties, crime, the judiciary, education, healthcare, poverty, urban affairs, and population.*	**G** *Includes formation and debate of U.S. foreign and defense policies, veterans affairs, and defense spending. (Relations with specific foreign countries are usually found under the region concerned.)*	**H** *Includes business, labor, agriculture, taxation, transportation, consumer affairs, monetary and fiscal policy, natural resources, pollution, and accidents.*	**I** *Includes worldwide scientific, medical, and technological developments, natural phenomena, U.S. weather, and natural disasters.*	**J** *Includes the arts, religion, scholarship, communications media, sports, entertainment, fashions, fads, and social life.*	

	World Affairs	Europe	Africa & The Middle East	The Americas	Asia & The Pacific
Dec. 21	The League of Nations recordkeeping bureau divulges that the world Depression cost the globe $149 billion.	Italy claims that too much attention is being paid to an incident that occurred in occupied Tripoli—the flogging of two Jews who refused to open their shops on Saturday. The unfortunate event, says the Italian regime, does not portray anti-Semitism but an act of two people who disregarded Italian law.	A British Royal Commission arriving in Jerusalem clarifies that its objective—to settle differences between the Arab and Jewish populations—will not be sidetracked by tending to other matters, including inter-political differences between groups of Jewish factions.		
Dec. 22		The Archbishop of York, still reeling from the scandal involving the abdication of Edward VIII, scorns him for causing a "human tragedy" over falling in love with another man's wife. . . . Observers say that Germany is in the midst of a mobilization plan that will prepare it for any war that may come. Males are forbidden to leave the country without permission and females should prepare in case they are quickly summoned to work at the factories.		Havana is in an uproar as news of the impeachment of Cuban President Miguel Gomez reaches the streets. The Cuban Senate voted 111–45 for impeachment proceedings after he was found to have allegedly tampered with the government to defeat a bill that he did not support. . . . The Inter-American Conference, coming to a finale in Buenos Aires, does not adjourn before first calling upon the Bolivian and Paraguayan representatives to ensure that the recent Chaco peace conference between the countries is enduring.	
Dec. 23		Soviet Russia, it appears, will not seek justification on the sinking of its ship, *Komsomol*, off the coast of Spain. No evidence exists that Spain was involved.			According to the Japanese paper, *Nichi Nichi*, Japan's Foreign Minister Hachiro Arita tells the United States that his country is willing to develop a new plan of peace in the Pacific Ocean. The focus will be on the Philippines and other U.S.-owned islands where America has displayed concern for their safety.
Dec. 24		Madrid endures another fierce bombing as the rebels surprise the outer defenses by breaking through from Boadilla del Monte, a rocky terrain that the loyalists had thought would have slowed their advance. This is one of the closest vantage points to the city that the rebel gunners have been able to reach so far.			
Dec. 25		Adolf Hitler, Reichschancelor of Germany, spends his Christmas with his administrative staff and counsel generals behind closed doors. The rest of Europe wonders what will prevail after the holidays.		Correspondents say that the citizens of San Vicente, El Salvador, are maintaining their Christmas Day spirits despite their town having been racked yesterday by a severe earthquake. Christmas celebrants attempt to cheer the otherwise devastated landscape.	
Dec. 26		It is the contention of British journalist and author George Slocombe, who is visiting America, that despite the bravado of men like Hitler, there is no immediate danger of war— if skittish Europe does not force a war by its own hysteria. Slocombe is visiting Chicago and other major U.S. metropolises.			A very weary Gen. Chiang Kai-shek, held in captivity since December 18 by Communist opponent Gen. Chang Hsueh-liang—who sources say is running for his life—is released. He does not reveal the details of his imprisonment or the terms of his release. The people of Shanghai carry him through the streets in celebration while Japan waits to hear what his release now means to them. The dictator has been at war with Japanese policy for months.
Dec. 27		Britain refuses to negotiate on Germany's demand to return its "old colonies." Their stance is that any matters regarding territorial rights be handled peaceably through the League of Nations. . . . Germany will not put too much time and effort into supporting the Spanish fascists, says Britain; the venture would prove too costly against its already aching economy and would interfere with other territorial ventures that Hitler is already contemplating.	It is falsely rumored that France has given the Third Reich lands in Africa that once belonged to Germany before the Treaty of Versailles of 1918, the pact that ended the World War.	Puerto Rican exports and imports gained in the 1936 fiscal year, reports Governor Blanton Winship in a communiqué to U.S. Secretary of the Interior Harold Ickes.	In an open address to his people at the Indian National Congress in Bombay, its president, Pandit Jawaharlal Nehru, urges his country to strike back against British imperialism.

A	B	C	D	E
Includes developments that affect more than one world region, international organizations, and important meetings of world leaders.	Includes all domestic and regional developments in Europe, including the Soviet Union.	Includes all domestic and regional developments in Africa and the Middle East.	Includes all domestic and regional developments in Latin America, the Caribbean, and Canada.	Includes all domestic and regional developments in Asian and Pacific nations (and colonies).

U.S. Politics & Social Issues	U.S. Foreign Policy & Defense	Economics & Great Depression	Science, Technology & Nature	Culture, Leisure & Lifestyle	
Dr. Charles Gordon Heyd, who presides over the American Medical Association, advocates free medical service for the poor and needy, a system that would be supported by each individual state's taxes.	With all naval treaties effectively dissolved, Jane's publication predicts an unprecedented arms race. In demonstration of this opinion, it alludes to Japan's recent protest to America's changing of its naval gun size from 14- to 16-inch bore; Japan asserted that it would follow suit.	Dun & Bradstreet writes that the expected Christmas surge has surpassed expectations by 15–20 percent; this season has, they say, "no parallel to its proportions since 1929."			Dec. 21
		While industry claims there are not enough skilled workers in the United States to assume many jobs, critics point to the 9 million names on government lists and find it hard to believe that among the jobless there are not the professionals and artisans needed to walk into those positions.		Gate receipts for 1936 indicate a rejuvenated interest by the public in college sports. A study conducted by the Associated Press attributes this to college reforms, including the subsidizing and recruiting of athletes.	Dec. 22
		The oil industry showed marked improvement in many areas during 1936, states W.S. Farish, a Standard Oil regional executive. Not only did the demand for gasoline rise 10 percent, but regulations for crude oil were revised for better production. Sales of gas, oil, distillate fuels, and residual fuel oils all increased.		Pope Pius XI may never walk again, say Vatican doctors. An advanced case of varicose veins prevents him from using his legs for mobility. Not discouraged, he goes ahead with his plans to make his annual Christmas message from his bedroom.	Dec. 23
President Roosevelt lights the annual Christmas tree in Lafayette Square, across Pennsylvania Avenue from the White House. On a radio setup, he wishes the country a great holiday and a happy new year, stressing peace and love of mankind throughout 1937.			Bellevue Hospital, in New York, announces that it is conducting tests to determine if insulin—which is normally used to treat diabetes—might alleviate certain types of mental conditions, including insanity.		Dec. 24
		Next year shows high realty interest as builders prepare for a busy year and the FHA predicts a 50 percent increase in home construction. A minimum of 400,000 new units are foreseen.		An ill Pope Pius XI extends his Christmas greetings to the world today, speaking not in Latin as is his custom, but in Italian. He asks the world to pray for peace in this tense era. . . . With 40,000 fans packing Santa Anita Racetrack under a warm Los Angeles sun for its festive Christmas races, three-year-old gelding Goldeneye takes the stakes. He comes in over Sangreal, who many thought would win the event.	Dec. 25
The Committee for Industrial Organization, a rival of the American Federation of Labor, begins a campaign to penetrate the motor industry, much to the latter's disapproval.	In a radio broadcast from Washington, D.C., Mrs. Charl Ormond Williams, president of the National Federation of Business and Professional Women, tells the organization's 60,000 members that their task for the new year is to help devise a long-lasting policy of peace for the nation.	General Motors boasts an increase in employment as more people are hired at all of its six manufacturing plants and 11 assembly plants across the nation. One particular reason for the boost in employment is the introduction of 1937 models, which incited steady buying for the new year.			Dec. 26
The National Trade Women's League introduces a charter aimed at formulating a "basis for common action by women throughout the world to spur an equal rights agenda."		In all, 1936 has been the best year for business since the Depression, relates an article in The Survey, the publication of the Guaranty Trust Company. Based on this, the magazine predicts a solid year in 1937.		After four years on the amateur circuit, popular tennis player Frederick J. Perry—after winning the British Amateur Tournament for four successive years—decides to go professional. He plans to compete in pro events, starting in 1937.	Dec. 27

F	**G**	**H**	**I**	**J**
Includes elections, federal-state relations, civil rights and liberties, crime, the judiciary, education, healthcare, poverty, urban affairs, and population.	Includes formation and debate of U.S. foreign and defense policies, veterans affairs, and defense spending. (Relations with specific foreign countries are usually found under the region concerned.)	Includes business, labor, agriculture, taxation, transportation, consumer affairs, monetary and fiscal policy, natural resources, pollution, and accidents.	Includes worldwide scientific, medical, and technological developments, natural phenomena, U.S. weather, and natural disasters.	Includes the arts, religion, scholarship, communications media, sports, entertainment, fashions, fads, and social life.

	World Affairs	Europe	Africa & The Middle East	The Americas	Asia & The Pacific
Dec. 28			At their convention, members of the Junior Hadassah, the young women's Zionist organization in the United States, resolve to press the British Royal Commission—now investigating the political climate in Palestine between the Arabs and Jews—to recommend "constructive building for all sections of the populace." However, violence and bigotry in and around Jerusalem still threaten any resolution of peace.	Canada experienced an increase in exports by 28 percent in one month for a total of $120,971,304 gained in November. Of that, $46,536,866 was purchased by the United States.	
Dec. 29		Political strife between the Soviet Union and Germany is the cause of a 65 percent drop in trade between the two countries these past 12 months—$20 million as compared to $58 million in 1935.			
Dec. 30		The recent curiosity of Britain and France over whether or not Germany was supplying materials to the Spaniard rebels is answered today when Adolf Hitler turns down their ban on aid to the war in Spain.		Committed to keeping this New Year's Eve safe, Canadian police are warning drivers who drink that they will show no leniency to any motorist with alcohol on his breath or an open bottle in the automobile.	
Dec. 31		On a New Year's Eve broadcast to the people of France, its prime minister stresses unity among all classes in 1937 and unending peace for the world.			

A	B	C	D	E
Includes developments that affect more than one world region, international organizations, and important meetings of world leaders.	*Includes all domestic and regional developments in Europe, including the Soviet Union.*	*Includes all domestic and regional developments in Africa and the Middle East.*	*Includes all domestic and regional developments in Latin America, the Caribbean, and Canada.*	*Includes all domestic and regional developments in Asian and Pacific nations (and colonies).*

U.S. Politics & Social Issues	U.S. Foreign Policy & Defense	Economics & Great Depression	Science, Technology & Nature	Culture, Leisure & Lifestyle	
President Roosevelt's annual message to Congress, which is slated for January 6 after the holidays, is expected to bring the news that revisions to a new NRA proposal have been concluded.		Reducing the national debt as soon as possible, and thus lowering taxes that are a result of the debt, is encouraged by Chicago University economics professor Simeon L. Leland. Such reduction, he tells the American Economic Association, is the key to a stable future.		The central boxing publication, *The Ring*, names Germany's Max Schmeling as the top professional boxer of the past year. It commends his lithesome quickness and cement punch.	**Dec. 28**
Educator and journalist John H. Finley remarks that journalists are as eager to present the truth to the world as any research chemist or scientist.		According to the U.S. Chamber of Commerce, the nation's foreign trade—totaling $3.5 billion—is the result of the most diverse geographical distribution of American goods in history.	Thanks to Dr. Harold C. Urey, Nobel Prize winner, "heavy oxygen" may now be produced on a mass scale, due to chemical experiments he perfected in his labs at Columbia University.	*Alice in Wonderland*, Lewis Carroll's famous fantasy, is bad for children, according to psychiatrist Dr. Paul Schilder of New York University. The tale, he professes, is one of subtly hidden "oral sadistic trends of cannibalism."	**Dec. 29**
Annoyed by the Supreme Court's barring of so many relief plans instituted by the Roosevelt administration, former NRA chief Donald Richburg and dean of law at the University of Wisconsin Lloyd K. Garrison advise U.S. government officials to rework the Constitution, watering down the Supreme Court's ability to tamper.					**Dec. 30**
As he had promised, President Roosevelt begins to reorganize the Agriculture Department. The Assistant Secretary of Agriculture becomes the Undersecretary, replacing Rexford G. Tugwell, who leaves the service to assume an executive position with the American Molasses Company.		Taking part in a New Year's Eve radio broadcast, U.S. Secretary of the Treasury Henry Morgenthau tells the people of America that he does not see any reason why they should not expect a better economy in 1937. . . . American shipbuilding in 1936 increased from the previous year. According to the National Association of American Shipbuilders, 24 vessels or 161,740 tons were built this year, as opposed to 16 ships or 92,070 tons last year.	Dr. Birkhoff of Harvard University closes the gap between the relativity and quantum theories by conceiving a new structure of the atom. Dr. Birkhoff's work, which is explained today at a meeting of the American Association for the Advancement of Science, brings the understanding of the atom—and its potential—into clearer light. . . . Maryse Bastie, French aviator, breaks a flight record as she flies between Senegal and Brazil in 12 hours, five minutes.		**Dec. 31**

F	**G**	**H**	**I**	**J**
Includes elections, federal-state relations, civil rights and liberties, crime, the judiciary, education, healthcare, poverty, urban affairs, and population.	*Includes formation and debate of U.S. foreign and defense policies, veterans affairs, and defense spending. (Relations with specific foreign countries are usually found under the region concerned.)*	*Includes business, labor, agriculture, taxation, transportation, consumer affairs, monetary and fiscal policy, natural resources, pollution, and accidents.*	*Includes worldwide scientific, medical, and technological developments, natural phenomena, U.S. weather, and natural disasters.*	*Includes the arts, religion, scholarship, communications media, sports, entertainment, fashions, fads, and social life.*

1937

A terrified baby was almost the only human being left alive in Shanghai's South Station after Japanese bombing. China, August 28, 1937.

	World Affairs	Europe	Africa & The Middle East	The Americas	Asia & The Pacific
Jan.	The League of Nations Council holds its 96th session in Geneva.	Italy and Britain sign the Mediterranean Treaty, agreeing to respect each others' interests and rights in the region. . . . The Supreme Soviet officially adopts the 1936 Constitution. . . . The Austrian government announces an amnesty for all National Socialists.	Arabs boycott the Peel Commission, which had been sent to Palestine by the British government to investigate the political situation. . . . The French government restores the Lebanese Constitution.	Left-wing parties win the elections for one-third of the seats in the Venezuelan parliament.	Provincial assembly elections across India mark the success of the nationalist All-India Congress Party, whose agenda includes complete independence from Britain. . . . Chinese Nationalist and Communist forces cease hostilities and join to fight against the Japanese.
Feb.	The League of Nations holds its second conference on German refugees in Geneva.	Spanish Nationalists capture the city of Malaga. . . . Austrian Premier Kurt Schuschnigg announces that he is in favor of Habsburg restoration. . . . The Agrarian Party, led by Kyosti Kallio, wins the Finnish national elections with the support of the Social Democrats. Kallio becomes the new prime minister.	The Ethiopians attempt to assassinate the Italian viceroy, Gen. Rudolfo Graziani, in Addis Ababa. . . . The Ethiopian leader Ras Desta Demtu is arrested and executed by Italians.	In spite of the victory of left-wing parties in the January elections, the Venezuelan government arrests and exiles many leftist leaders. . . . Due to heavy losses in the Chaco War and international pressure, Paraguay announces its intention to withdraw from the League of Nations.	
Mar.	Pope Pius XI again condemns Communism in a papal encyclical criticizing the Soviets and their religious repressions.	Col. Adam Koc forms the Camp of National Unity, a nationalist coalition of political organizations that support the Polish government. . . . The Hungarian government exposes a National Socialist plot and arrests party leaders. . . . The Italian and Yugoslav governments sign a five-year nonaggression plan.	Republican forces rebel against Nationalists in Spanish Morocco. The rebellion is quickly repressed. . . . Italian Premier Benito Mussolini conducts a state visit to the Italian colony of Libya.	The Bolivian military junta sets up a monopoly over the oil industry and confiscates the holdings of the Standard Oil Company, a U.S. multinational corporation. . . . The Mexican government announces the nationalization of the oil industry. . . . In Puerto Rico, the police kill 19 at a nationalist parade.	At the congress of the All-India Party, the moderate faction defeats the radicals led by Pandit Jawaharlal Nehru.
Apr.	The League of Nations holds a conference in London to prevent further decline in sugar prices. . . . Representatives of the dominions and colonies of the British Commonwealth meet in London to address the problems of the economic depression.	Austrian Chancellor Kurt Schuschnigg conducts a state visit to Venice to meet with Premier Benito Mussolini. . . . Belgium withdraws from the Treaty of Locarno. Britain and France release the country from its obligations to defend the borders of western Europe. . . . The Spanish Nationalist air force destroys the city of Guernica.	The Yemeni government joins the Saudi-Iraqi Treaty of Non-Aggression and Arab Brotherhood of April 1936.		The Government of India Act establishes the All-India Federation, but the All-India Party refuses to form an administration.
May	The Montreux Conference of countries enjoying capitulary rights in Egypt ends with an agreement abolishing all capitulations. . . . The Permanent Court of International Justice holds its 40th session in The Hague. . . . The League of Nations admits Egypt to the organization.	The prohibition of the veiling of women in southern Albania provokes a Muslim insurrection. . . . The Liberal Democratic Party makes important gains in Dutch national elections, while the National Socialists suffer major losses. . . . Neville Chamberlain becomes the new British prime minister. . . . The Duke of York is crowned King George VI at Westminster Abbey.		After the Chaco War, Bolivia and Paraguay resume diplomatic relations.	
Jun.	The International Labor Organization holds its 23rd session in Geneva.	Purges eliminate Trotskyites and other political threats to Stalin's regime. . . . Spanish Nationalists capture the city of Bilbao. . . . The French coalition government led by Leon Blum resigns. . . . The Irish Parliament passes the draft for the new Constitution of Eire.			Japan's Premier Hayashi resigns.
Jul.	The governments of Turkey, Iraq, Iran, and Afghanistan sign a nonaggression pact in Teheran, setting up an Islamic front to counter Western ambitions in the Middle East.	Rev. Martin Niemoeller, who opposes Nazi influence in religious affairs, is arrested in Germany. . . . Britain signs the Anglo-Russian Naval Agreement and the Anglo-German Naval Agreement to establish naval parity and prevent an international conflict. . . . Irish Premier Eamon De Valera wins the general election.	Kurds rebel in Syria, asking for independence in light of the Franco-Syrian Treaty. The French crush the revolt. . . . The Peel Report on Palestine recommends the division of Palestine into two separate Arab and Jewish states.	The Cuban government announces a Three-Year Economic Plan to reorganize the national economy.	Japanese troops clash with Chinese forces at Lukouchiao, near Peiping, known as the Marco Polo Bridge Incident. The fighting quickly escalates into the Sino-Japanese War. At the end of the month, Japanese forces gain control of Peiping and of the strategic port of Tianjan.
Aug.	The League of Nations accepts the Peel Report as a basis to solve tensions in Palestine. . . . Pope Pius XI formally recognizes the Nationalist government of Francisco Franco in Spain. . . . The Chinese Nationalist and Russian governments sign a nonaggression treaty.	Spanish republicans gain control of the Catalan government. . . . The Buchenwald concentration camp becomes operational.	The World Zionist Congress adopts the Peel report and its suggestion for the partition of Palestine.	El Salvador withdraws from the League of Nations. . . . Canadian Prime Minister Mackenzie King appoints the Rowell Commission to amend the British North America Act.	Japanese troops start their campaign to gain control of Shanghai. . . . The Japanese government establishes a naval blockade over the southern Chinese coast.
Sept.	The League of Nations Assembly holds its 18th session in Geneva.	The Nyon Conference addresses the problem of piracy in the Mediterranean linked to the Spanish civil war. . . . Former Czechoslovak president and founder of the republic Thomas Masaryk dies. . . . A meeting between Italian Premier Mussolini and Hitler in Berlin reaffirms the goals of the Axis.	A Nationalist revolt in French Morocco is quickly repressed by the French. . . . The Pan-Arab Congress rejects the Peel Report on Palestine. . . . Yelland Andrews, the British District Commissioner for Galilee, is murdered.		The Japanese make swift advances in northern China. They also extend their naval blockade to include the entire Chinese coast with the exceptions of Qingdao (Tsingtao), Hong Kong, Macau, and Guangzhou (Canton).

A	B	C	D	E
Includes developments that affect more than one world region, international organizations, and important meetings of world leaders.	Includes all domestic and regional developments in Europe, including the Soviet Union.	Includes all domestic and regional developments in Africa and the Middle East.	Includes all domestic and regional developments in Latin America, the Caribbean, and Canada.	Includes all domestic and regional developments in Asian and Pacific nations (and colonies).

U.S. Politics & Social Issues	U.S. Foreign Policy & Defense	Economics & Great Depression	Science, Technology & Nature	Culture, Leisure & Lifestyle	
	Congress bans the sale of weapons to both Republicans and Nationalists in the Spanish civil war.			Howard Hughes flies from Los Angeles to New York in 7 hours and 22 minutes.	Jan.
President Roosevelt proposes to increase the number of Supreme Court justices. . . . After a strike of 44 days, General Motors agrees to recognize the United Automobile Workers Union.			Wallace H. Carothers invents nylon and receives a patent for the synthetic fiber.		Feb.
William H. Hastie becomes the first black federal judge in the Virgin Islands.		U.S. Steel raises workers' wages to $5 per day.	More than 400 people are killed in a gas explosion at a school in New London, Tex.	H.P. Lovecraft, horror author, dies in Providence, R.I. . . . Jack S. Liebowitz and Harry Donenfeld publish the first issue of Detective Comics.	Mar.
A series of strikes organized by the CIO extends across the United States in the automobile and steel industries.	President Roosevelt appoints the Joint Preparatory Commission on Philippine Affairs to prepare the scenario for the country's independence.			Cartoon characters Daffy Duck, Elmer J. Fudd, and Petunia Pig make their first appearance.	Apr.
Industrialist John Davison Rockefeller dies at 97 years of age. . . . The Golden Gate Bridge is opened to pedestrian traffic. . . . At the South Chicago Republic Steel plant, 10 union demonstrators are killed and 84 wounded when police open fire during a demonstration. The incident becomes known as the Memorial Day Massacre.	Congress passes the Neutrality Act, which aims to keep the United States out of future world wars.		Thirty-six people die when the giant German airship Hindenburg crashes and catches fire at Lakehurst Naval Air Station in New Jersey.	Margaret Mitchell wins the Pulitzer Prize for her novel Gone with the Wind.	May
Henry Ford introduces the 32-hour workweek.	The U.S. government helps Brazil to build a larger naval fleet.		The first total solar eclipse in over 800 years to exceed seven minutes takes place.	A Day at the Races by the Marx Brothers is released. . . . Joe Louis becomes heavyweight champion by defeating Jim Braddock.	Jun.
The Senate rejects President Roosevelt's proposal to increase the number of Supreme Court justices. . . . The state of Alabama drops charges of rape against five African Americans in the so-called Scottsboro case.	The United States protests against the Japanese invasion of China. . . . Congress approves the Pitman Act, which allows the U.S Treasury to exchange Chinese silver dollars for American gold. This gives the Chinese supplementary funds to buy military equipment for their war against the Japanese.		Inventor Guglielmo Marconi dies in Rome. . . . Yale University announces the isolation of the pituitary hormone.	Amelia Earhart and navigator Fred Noonan disappear over the Pacific Ocean while attempting to make the first round-the-world flight at the equator. . . . Composer George Gershwin dies at 38 from a brain tumor.	Jul.
Pullman signs a contract with the Brotherhood of Sleeping Car Porters, one of the first victories for black workers.	The United States signs a trade treaty with the Soviet Union.				Aug.
	The United States bans all shipments of arms to both Japan and China.	President Roosevelt dedicates the WPA project Timberline Lodge at the foot of Palmer snowfield in Mt. Hood National Forest.		The Hobbit by J.R.R. Tolkien is first published. . . . Bessie Smith, the "Empress of Blues," dies in a car crash.	Sept.

F	G	H	I	J
Includes elections, federal-state relations, civil rights and liberties, crime, the judiciary, education, healthcare, poverty, urban affairs, and population.	Includes formation and debate of U.S. foreign and defense policies, veterans affairs, and defense spending. (Relations with specific foreign countries are usually found under the region concerned.)	Includes business, labor, agriculture, taxation, transportation, consumer affairs, monetary and fiscal policy, natural resources, pollution, and accidents.	Includes worldwide scientific, medical, and technological developments, natural phenomena, U.S. weather, and natural disasters.	Includes the arts, religion, scholarship, communications media, sports, entertainment, fashions, fads, and social life.

	World Affairs	Europe	Africa & The Middle East	The Americas	Asia & The Pacific
Oct.	The League of Nations condemns the Japanese invasion of China.	The opposition parties in Yugoslavia close ranks and form the Agrarian-Democratic Party, asking an immediate end to the dictatorship of Milan Stoyadinovich. . . . Spanish Nationalists complete their conquest of northwestern Spain. The Republican government moves from Valencia to Barcelona.	In retaliation for the assassination of the British Commissioner for Galilee, the British government arrests and expels the members of the Arab High Commission. Haj Amin el Husseini, the most influential of Arab leaders, escapes to Syria.	An immigration crisis breaks out between the Dominican Republic and Haiti. . . . Roberto Ortiz is elected president of Argentina.	The Japanese set up an Advisory Cabinet Council to coordinate the war in China.
Nov.	The League of Nations sponsors an international conference on terrorism in Geneva. . . . The signatories of the Nine-Power Pact, except Japan, meet in Brussels to discuss the Sino-Japanese War.	The Osobaya Troika signs death sentences for prisoners of gulags across Russia, leading to the massacre of 9,000 victims. . . . The Italian government officially enters the Anti-Communist Pact with Germany and Japan. . . . The French government exposes a plot by the *Cagoulards* to restore the monarchy.	A British Royal Commission visits Northern Rhodesia, Southern Rhodesia, and Nyasaland to establish closer political and economic ties between the three colonies. . . . Special courts are set up in Palestine to try suspected terrorists. Arab and Jewish forces riot in Jerusalem.	The Mexican nationalization of sub-soil rights of the country, including petroleum, leads to tensions with foreign governments whose multinationals operate in Mexico. . . . President Getulio Vargas proclaims a new Brazilian constitution.	The Japanese government creates an Imperial Headquarters to centralize the Chinese war effort in the hands of military and naval commanders, under the direct authority of Emperor Hirohito. Japanese forces enter Shanghai, pushing out Chinese Nationalist forces.
Dec.	Tensions between Turkey and Syria over the Sanjak of Alexandretta threaten to escalate into a war. The French act as mediators.	Yvon Delbos, the French foreign minister, visits France's allies in eastern Europe to prevent German expansion. . . . The Italian government withdraws from the League of Nations. . . . The Romanian elections lead to the formation of a right-wing government. . . . The Irish Free State adopts its new constitution and becomes Eire.	King Farouk of Egypt dismisses the Wafd government led by Nahas Pasha.		The Japanese bombing of the U.S. *Panay* gunboat results in acute tensions between Japan and the United States. . . . The Japanese take control of Nanking, committing atrocities against civilians. . . . Japan recognizes Franco's government.

A	B	C	D	E
Includes developments that affect more than one world region, international organizations, and important meetings of world leaders.	*Includes all domestic and regional developments in Europe, including the Soviet Union.*	*Includes all domestic and regional developments in Africa and the Middle East.*	*Includes all domestic and regional developments in Latin America, the Caribbean, and Canada.*	*Includes all domestic and regional developments in Asian and Pacific nations (and colonies).*

U.S. Politics & Social Issues	U.S. Foreign Policy & Defense	Economics & Great Depression	Science, Technology & Nature	Culture, Leisure & Lifestyle	
Congress passes the Marijuana Tax Act, which bans the sale of marijuana without a license.	President Roosevelt proposes an international quarantine of aggressors as the only means to preserve global peace.			*To Have and Have Not* by Ernest Hemingway is first published.	**Oct.**
				NBC forms the first full-sized symphony orchestra exclusively for radio broadcasting for Arturo Toscanini. . . . Clifford Odets' *Golden Boy* premieres in New York.	**Nov.**
Former Secretary of State Frank Kellog dies.	The Roosevelt administration accepts the Japanese explanation and apology for the *Panay* incident.			*Snow White*, the first feature-length color and sound cartoon, premieres. . . . Mae West is banned from the radio for her Adam and Eve performance on *Chase & Sanborn Hour*.	**Dec.**

F	G	H	I	J
Includes elections, federal-state relations, civil rights and liberties, crime, the judiciary, education, healthcare, poverty, urban affairs, and population.	Includes formation and debate of U.S. foreign and defense policies, veterans affairs, and defense spending. (Relations with specific foreign countries are usually found under the region concerned.)	Includes business, labor, agriculture, taxation, transportation, consumer affairs, monetary and fiscal policy, natural resources, pollution, and accidents.	Includes worldwide scientific, medical, and technological developments, natural phenomena, U.S. weather, and natural disasters.	Includes the arts, religion, scholarship, communications media, sports, entertainment, fashions, fads, and social life.

	World Affairs	Europe	Africa & The Middle East	The Americas	Asia & The Pacific
Jan. 1		The German cruiser *Koenigsberg* seizes the loyalist Spanish freighter *Soton* in reprisal for Spain's taking of German arms cargo. . . . Britain lays keels for two battleships, first of 30 to be built in 1937.		An assassination attempt against former Mexican president Plutarco Elías Calles in San Diego, Calif., fails when a bomb outside his home is detected. . . . Anastasio Somoza is inaugurated as president of Nicaragua.	
Jan. 2	The Vatican assures Catholics worldwide that Pope Pius XI is not in immediate danger and is rallying.	Great Britain and Italy sign assurances to maintain peace and security in the Mediterranean. . . . The Spanish government terms Germany's firing upon and seizure of the *Soton* an "act of war" and threatens reprisals.			
Jan. 3		Spain's Foreign Minister, Julio Alvarez del Vayo, denounces Germany's aggressive actions at sea and vows resistance. . . . At Cadiz, 5,000 armed Italian troops disembark from Italian warships to join the forces of General Franco. . . . Through representatives in Barcelona, Catalonia declares itself independent of Spain. . . . A British trawler claims to have been fired on by Spanish insurgents.	Arturo Toscanini, touring Palestine, is given the deed to an orange grove in the Jewish settlement of Ramothakovesh, where 60 German refugee families have lived for three years.	Mexico announces it will not ship planes or arms from the United States to Spain. . . . The Venezuelan government seizes all property belonging to two ousted generals, both former governors. . . . In Brazil, the former mayor of Rio de Janiero, Pedro Ernesto Baptista, is tried for abetting a 1935 leftist revolt.	China executes 130 undesirables for violating the morality code.
Jan. 4	The Vatican announces a "cautious" outlook for the Pope's health, acknowledging a serious decline in his heart function. . . . The International Labor Union says global unemployment has declined for four years straight. Austria and Switzerland were the only exceptions in 1936.	The *Koenigsberg*, the German ship that seized the *Soton*, halts another Spanish ship in the Bay of Biscay. Germany denounces Spanish loyalists as "red pirates," calling attention to a December 20 incident in which German ships were fired upon. . . . Two weeks of heavy fighting around Madrid force Leftists to abandon the Escorial Road and other positions. . . . Bombs fall on Madrid, narrowly missing the U.S. Embassy. Most bombs fall in the neutral zone, killing 100 people. . . . Norway fortifies its northern coast against military aggression.	Lieutenant General Dill, commander of the British forces in Palestine, submits a plan for public security to the Royal Commission. . . . France restores the constitution of the Lebanese Republic, which had been suspended.	Artist Diego Rivera announces that Mexican President Lázaro Cárdenas will shelter Soviet exile Leon Trotsky.	Nanking issues an unconditional pardon to Chang Hsueh-liang, who had been sentenced to 10 years in prison for revolt and kidnapping Chiang Kai-shek. The Japanese embassy expresses concern over China's veer toward the left.
Jan. 5		Britain appeals to Germany and Italy, asking for an end to foreign enlistments in the army of Franco. . . . The upcoming nuptials of the Netherlands' Crown Princess Juliana to a German citizen are marred by disagreements over displaying swastikas and playing Nazi songs. . . . Holding two Spanish ships, Germany issues an ultimatum demanding return of its cargo from the ship *Palos* within three days. . . . In Bilbao, Spain, mobs throw grenades and kill over 200 insurgent hostages in retaliation for insurgent bombings of the area.			Hachiro Arita, Japan's Foreign Minister, defends and explains the Tokyo-Berlin Pact in a radio broadcast, calling it an "anti-Comintern" (anti-Communist International) accord, designed to keep communism out of China. He claims the pact implies neither fascism nor hostility toward the United States.
Jan. 6	Spanish Foreign Minister Alvarez del Vayo complains to the League of Nations about Germany's aggressive moves in Spanish waters. . . . President Ataturk of Turkey and his top officials meet as relations with France worsen over both countries' interests in Alexandretta in the south.	Germany fortifies part of its border with Poland. . . . Heavy shelling rocks Madrid. Insurgents capture Mount Cumbre and cut off troops in the mountains from their base in Madrid. Up to 620 government troops have died in the last three days of fighting.	In Jerusalem, the Arab High Committee ends its boycott of the British Royal Commission of Inquiry on Palestine, also called the Peel Commission.		China's armies move against the forces of General Yang Fu-cheng in an attempt to occupy Sian and Lanchow, where a revolt took place last month.
Jan. 7	Turkey threatens to withdraw from the League of Nations, demanding that France separate its administration of Antioch and Alexandretta from Syria. . . . France accuses Germany of invading Spanish Morocco and fortifying Ceuta.	Netherlands Princess Juliana marries Prince Bernhard zu Lippe-Biesterfeld in The Hague. . . . Germany and Italy reject Britain's request to stop the influx of volunteers to Spain, but promise to support non-intervention if all others do the same.	Arturo Toscanini conducts the Palestine Symphony Orchestra in its first foreign concert, in Cairo. . . . David Ben Gurion, chairman of the Palestine Zionist Executive, testifies before the Royal Commission in Jerusalem, citing the Bible as a mandate for a Jewish homeland there.		The Chinese government protests the presence of unauthorized Japanese aircraft over North China. . . . In the Shensi province of northwest China, 250,000 men join forces to create a Communist state.

A	B	C	D	E
Includes developments that affect more than one world region, international organizations, and important meetings of world leaders.	*Includes all domestic and regional developments in Europe, including the Soviet Union.*	*Includes all domestic and regional developments in Africa and the Middle East.*	*Includes all domestic and regional developments in Latin America, the Caribbean, and Canada.*	*Includes all domestic and regional developments in Asian and Pacific nations (and colonies).*

U.S. Politics & Social Issues	U.S. Foreign Policy & Defense	Economics & Great Depression	Science, Technology & Nature	Culture, Leisure & Lifestyle	
			Dr. Wendell Stanley is honored for work on viruses and wins a prize from the American Association for the Advancement of Science.	University of Pittsburgh wins the Rose Bowl over University of Washington. . . . Marquette University loses to Texas Christian University in the first Cotton Bowl. . . . Louisiana State is defeated by Santa Clara in the Sugar Bowl.	Jan. 1
The U.S. Conference of Mayors asks the WPA for $877.5 million in aid through June 1937.		Injunctions naming the unions, but no arrest warrants, are issued against sit-down strikers at General Motors plant in Flint, Mich.		Andrew Mellon gifts $19 million in art and $8–9 million toward building a National Gallery to the United States.	Jan. 2
		Two hundred members of the United Auto Workers meet in Flint, Mich., and authorize a committee to negotiate and call a strike, which could potentially shut down 200 General Motors plants in 14 states.		The death of screen actor Ross Alexander, found dead of a gunshot wound, is ruled a suicide. . . . A comprehensive exhibit of prints made under the auspices of the WPA Federal Art Project opens at the International Art Center in New York City.	Jan. 3
A day before the 75th Congress convenes, Sam Rayburn is chosen House majority leader and William Bankhead of Alabama is reelected Speaker. . . . The Supreme Court unanimously overturns the conviction of Dirk de Jonge, a Communist from Oregon, on criminal syndicalism charges. . . . The NAACP asks Congress to draft an anti-lynching bill. . . . The National Urban League sends a letter to President Franklin Roosevelt asking that Social Security be amended to include benefits for domestic and agricultural workers, so that African Americans are not excluded from recovery.	Congress drafts legislation to plug holes in the Neutrality Act and prevent arms from being shipped to Spanish belligerents. . . . The Army Air Corps has only 1,400 serviceable planes and 1,600 pilots; the Navy has 1,200. The Navy's goal is to have 1,900 planes by 1942.	Shipowners criticize the Federal Maritime Commission for not taking action to end the strike between longshoremen and shipping companies. . . . General Motors President Alfred Sloan refuses to recognize any union as a bargaining unit, while sit-down strikers continue their action in Flint. Nearly 40,000 are out of work due to the strike. . . . In Philadelphia, 1,800 employees of the Electric Storage Battery Company begin a sit-down strike.			Jan. 4
The 75th Congress convenes at noon, and 2,500 bills are introduced in the House. . . . In its annual report, the Interstate Commerce Commission urges Congress to reconsider a surtax on railroads' undistributed profit, part of the 1936 Revenue Act. . . . President Franklin Roosevelt's address to Congress will be broadcast by radio.	Richard Dineley, a munitions merchant in San Francisco, plans to ship $9 million in arms to loyalist forces in Spain. Congress attempts to block the sale by approving resolutions allowing the President to halt shipments of arms to rebels or loyalists. (Civil wars were not covered in the Neutrality Acts of 1935 and 1936.)	The General Motors strike affects other industries; steel furnaces shut down in Ohio. . . . James Dewey, a Labor Department conciliator, tries to arrange a meeting between the company's vice president William Knudsen and union leaders. . . . The Federal Reserve and other agencies call on banks to reveal their financial conditions as of December 31, 1936.	Sub-zero weather moves into the Midwest, with temperatures as low as minus 37°F recorded in Minnesota.	Sergey Rachmaninoff performs two of his own compositions at Carnegie Hall with the visiting Philadelphia Orchestra, Eugene Ormandy conducting.	Jan. 5
In his speech to Congress, President Franklin Roosevelt calls on the courts to take an enlightened view of the Constitution, and make it an instrument for achieving the common good.	In spite of Congress' speed in approving an arms embargo resolution, enforcement is delayed for a day and a shipment of munitions embarked for loyalist Spain. The Neutrality Act passes with wording specifically prohibiting the sale of arms or war material to either side in the Spanish civil strife.	Federal conciliator Dewey meets with General Motors executives, then with union leaders in Flint, Mich. . . . The SEC presents a report to Congress outlining the changes it plans to implement, including the regulation of "pegging."		Young British actor John Gielgud performs Hamlet for the 103rd consecutive time at the St. James Theatre in New York, a record for Broadway.	Jan. 6
The U.S. Post Office announces a deficit of $88 million for the fiscal year ending June 1936, $22 million more than the previous year's deficit. . . . Governor Alfred Landon of Kansas asks Congress for legislation outlawing child labor.		Strikers and non-striking auto workers confront each other at the Chevrolet plant in Flint, Mich., and two men are arrested. Two hundred strikers later storm the jail but police disperse them with tear gas. There are 21 plants and 56,323 workers now idle. . . . The American Bar Association orders an investigation into the actions of Judge Edward Black, who ruled on the strikers in Flint, even though he owns stock in General Motors.	Seismographs worldwide record an intense earthquake at 8:32 a.m., centered near Lhasa, Tibet. . . . The heaviest snowstorm in 20 years hits Arizona.	WPA archive workers find long-lost indictments for treason of Robert E. Lee and others in a basement.	Jan. 7

F	G	H	I	J
Includes elections, federal-state relations, civil rights and liberties, crime, the judiciary, education, healthcare, poverty, urban affairs, and population.	Includes formation and debate of U.S. foreign and defense policies, veterans affairs, and defense spending. (Relations with specific foreign countries are usually found under the region concerned.)	Includes business, labor, agriculture, taxation, transportation, consumer affairs, monetary and fiscal policy, natural resources, pollution, and accidents.	Includes worldwide scientific, medical, and technological developments, natural phenomena, U.S. weather, and natural disasters.	Includes the arts, religion, scholarship, communications media, sports, entertainment, fashions, fads, and social life.

	World Affairs	Europe	Africa & The Middle East	The Americas	Asia & The Pacific
Jan. 8	France lodges a protest over the presence of German troops in Morocco, and War Minister Édouard Daladier plans to visit Morocco within a week. . . . Germany denies the presence of troops in Morocco, calling the reports comic and absurd.	The Soviet Union denies sending any troops to Spain.		The U.S. State Department says nothing as thousands of acres of property belonging to Americans and Europeans are seized by the Mexican government without compensation, in violation of the Mexican Agrarian Law. . . . The first Pan-American Press Conference opens in Valparaiso, Chile, with 155 delegates from 13 nations attending.	
Jan. 9	French and British diplomats exchange information about German activities in Morocco.	Franco's insurgents reach the banks of the Manzanares River near Madrid, capturing bridges and killing at least 1,000 leftist soldiers. . . . Germany makes public an agreement signed with Portugal last June, in which Portugal abrogated all rights to German property won in the Treaty of Versailles. . . . The Danzig Agreement, drafted by the Free City Senate jointly with the Polish government to settle disputes with the League of Nations, is signed.		Leon Trotsky arrives in Tampico, Mexico, on the freighter *Ruth Heat* from Norway. . . . The Pan-American Press Conference passes by acclamation a resolution asking President Franklin Roosevelt to free three Puerto Rican journalists now in jail as well as all patriots fighting for independence, and to liberate Puerto Rico.	
Jan. 10	A riot between Turks and Arabs in Antioch erupts in front of League of Nations officials investigating trouble between Syria and Turkey, causing one death.	Britain invokes an 1870 law to prevent citizens from joining forces in Spain.		Puerto Rico's first sugar cooperative opens, funded by President Franklin Roosevelt's reconstruction financing. . . . Mexican President Lázaro Cárdenas forces labor leaders to forbid their followers to demonstrate against Leon Trotsky.	The Diet of Japan agrees to pass the budget and accept tax increases from Premier Hirota, rather than risk dissension and military interference in the government.
Jan. 11		Tensions lessen between France and Germany as both nations resolve not to interfere with Spain or its possessions, including Morocco. . . . Soviet Finance Commissar Gimko announces the military budget for 1937 will increase by one-third. . . . An insurgent attack by sea and air on Málaga leaves 300 dead and 50 buildings destroyed. In Madrid, the fascist drive to the northwest of the city stops.		Leon Trotsky arrives at the home of artist Diego Rivera in Coyoacan, a suburb of Mexico City.	
Jan. 12	In Mexico, Leon Trotsky accuses Joseph Stalin of sabotaging the Spanish revolution by withholding needed troops in deference to the feelings of his European allies. . . . The Soviet news agency TASS reports a raid by Manchukuo cavalry on Mongolia, possibly with Japanese support.		Haj Amin el Husseini, the Mufti of Jerusalem, testifies on behalf of Palestinian Arabs before the Royal Commission. He calls for an end to Jewish immigration and abandonment of plans for a Jewish homeland in Palestine.		Despite their threats, Chinese leaders in Nanking hesitate to reopen a civil war in the Shensi province.
Jan. 13	An "Empire Trade Agreement" between Canada and Great Britain is reached.	German Air Minister Hermann Wilhelm Goering arrives in Rome for a series of talks with Premier Benito Mussolini. . . . A Spanish insurgent trawler stops a British ship in the Strait of Gibraltar. The ship is released when a British destroyer intervenes. . . . Leftists send 18 tanks from Madrid hoping to regain territory lost to the insurgents. The tanks are repulsed and the crews die when the tanks burst into flames. . . . The Polish parliament debates the emigration of Jews. Foreign Minister Jozef Beck appealed to Jews to cooperate with the administration and leave.	Britain sends a military mission to Egypt to develop an army.	The press reports that President Lázaro Cárdenas of Mexico has silenced foreign criticism by arranging settlements of debts from the seizure of foreign-owned property. . . . The Cabinet of Chilean President Arturo Alessandri resigns, citing the presence of radicals aligned with left-wing groups as a principal reason.	Voting dates are set for provincial elections in India, with over 30 million voters. In different areas, polls will open for a day or up to a week, but all will close by the end of February.
	A *Includes developments that affect more than one world region, international organizations, and important meetings of world leaders.*	**B** *Includes all domestic and regional developments in Europe, including the Soviet Union.*	**C** *Includes all domestic and regional developments in Africa and the Middle East.*	**D** *Includes all domestic and regional developments in Latin America, the Caribbean, and Canada.*	**E** *Includes all domestic and regional developments in Asian and Pacific nations (and colonies).*

U.S. Politics & Social Issues	U.S. Foreign Policy & Defense	Economics & Great Depression	Science, Technology & Nature	Culture, Leisure & Lifestyle	
President Franklin Roosevelt announces that he has written to 19 governors urging their ratification of the child labor amendment.	President Franklin Roosevelt orders construction of two replacement battleships. . . . The President signs the Spanish arms embargo resolution.	President Franklin Roosevelt delivers an optimistic message on the budget to Congress. While the net deficit of 1937 is projected to be $2 billion, a balanced budget is promised by 1939. The stock market reacts favorably to the report, closing strongly. . . . The TVA asks the circuit court to lift a December 12 injunction and allow it to expand, pending a suit brought by 19 power companies testing its constitutionality.	Albert Einstein and Dr. N. Rosen author a paper proving the existence of a new radiation type, consisting of gravitational waves paralleling electro-magnetic waves. The paper is published in the *Journal of the Franklin Institute* of Philadelphia. . . . Thomas Midgely, Jr., receives the Perkin Medal for his work in developing the ethyl gasoline industry.	Paramount Pictures announces a $30 million budget and plans to produce 80 films over the next year.	Jan. 8
The child labor amendment has been ratified by 24 states; Governor Herbert Lehman of New York asks businessmen to push for ratification there. . . . Twenty-five men are indicted in Kentucky for beating and terrorizing their neighbors as members of the Black Leg band. Several have been tried before, and freed by hung juries.		Michigan Governor Frank Murphy and union head Homer Martin meet to discuss the ongoing strike. They talk until 2:30 a.m., but union officials say General Motors rejects "all responsible" solutions. . . . Labor Secretary Frances Perkins lists a five-point program for workers in her annual report, including wage and safety standards and greater cooperation with states. . . . Eight thousand march in New York to ask President Franklin Roosevelt to double the funding for the WPA.	Citrus crops in California are damaged as temperatures in groves drop to below freezing at night.	The first issue of *Look Magazine* goes on sale.	Jan. 9
The President meets with Congressional leaders to discuss reorganization of the executive branch, and will present a plan later this week.		In spite of the strike, General Motors stock rose the first week of 1937. Average stock prices were up 4.5 points.	Smudging continues in an effort to save crops in California. Citrus growers suffer an estimated 15 percent loss so far. . . . In an article in the British journal *Nature*, L.S.B. Leakey describes a new type of skull found in east Africa as a "low type of human," occurring 30,000 years after Neanderthals.		Jan. 10
The beaten body of 10-year-old Charles Mattson is found in the snow in Tacoma, Wash., ending a two-week-long search and requests for ransom.	The State Department announces it will mark all American passports "not valid in Spain."	Rioting breaks out in Flint, Mich., when guards threaten to starve the strikers, who then storm the plant's gates. The conflict continues into the early morning hours. . . . Almost 113,000 auto workers are idled by the strike. . . . The President submits a request for $790 million to continue relief efforts for five more months. . . . The 9th Circuit Court in San Francisco rules against the National Labor Relations Board and finds the Wagner Act unconstitutional in its attempts to "require collective bargaining."			Jan. 11
President Franklin Roosevelt presents a five-part executive branch reorganization plan to Congress, calling for two new Cabinet posts, heading departments of social welfare and public works.		While National Guard troops assemble in Flint, Mich., John Lewis, chair of the Committee of Industrial Organizations, says he will ask for a Congressional investigation into General Motors. . . . At the Fisher Body plant in Flint, 24 men are injured, some by exploding tear gas containers, in five hours of fighting between strikers and police. The police were trying to dislodge 800 strikers in the plant, but were unsuccessful. . . . Special Prosecutor Thomas Dewey subpoenas the books of several electrical workers' unions and executives of Consolidated Edison after a 13-month investigation into a $10 million extortion ring.	The successful use of insulin as a treatment for dementia praecox was reported before several medical associations in New York.	Under a schedule submitted today, the zeppelin *Hindenberg* will make 18 trips to the United States between May and October.	Jan. 12
		The first shipment of gold bullion is delivered to Fort Knox under heavy guard. . . . Representatives of union and company agree to meet with Governor Frank Murphy about the ongoing strike in Flint, Mich. . . . Claiming a tax would aid U.S. and Cuban sugar growers, Secretary of Agriculture Henry Wallace proposes a penny-a-pound levy on sugar processing, which would total $135 million per year. . . . Unsettled conditions in Europe lead creditors to shorten their terms and re-classify the risks of extending credit in some countries.	An electrical psychoglavanometer, or lie detector, is used for the first time on a man suspected of murder. The data gathered is unofficial. The lie detector was invented by Rev. Walter Summers of Fordham Graduate School.	Martin Johnson, an adventurer, author, and filmmaker, is killed in a plane crash near Burbank, Calif. His most well-known work was *Congarilla*, shot over two years in Central Africa. His wife is injured in the crash.	Jan. 13

F	**G**	**H**	**I**	**J**
Includes elections, federal-state relations, civil rights and liberties, crime, the judiciary, education, healthcare, poverty, urban affairs, and population.	*Includes formation and debate of U.S. foreign and defense policies, veterans affairs, and defense spending. (Relations with specific foreign countries are usually found under the region concerned.)*	*Includes business, labor, agriculture, taxation, transportation, consumer affairs, monetary and fiscal policy, natural resources, pollution, and accidents.*	*Includes worldwide scientific, medical, and technological developments, natural phenomena, U.S. weather, and natural disasters.*	*Includes the arts, religion, scholarship, communications media, sports, entertainment, fashions, fads, and social life.*

	World Affairs	Europe	Africa & The Middle East	The Americas	Asia & The Pacific
Jan. 14	The United States and Great Britain register their concern over China's attitude and the lack of planes in the Shensi region, where rebellion is threatened. While Chinese and German nationals have been evacuated, the United States and Britain feel their citizens are ignored.	A force of 20,000 insurgents capture the town of Estepona, 45 miles from Málaga—but leftist forces say the attack was routed. . . . In Rome, Premier Benito Mussolini and German Air Minister H.W. Goering agree that Franco's forces, supported by Germany and Italy, could take over Spain before nonintervention legislation is passed. . . . French Premier Léon Blum introduces a bill empowering his government to stop volunteers from joining the armed forces in Spain.		Two Brazilian army captains tie sheets together to escape a hospital, where they were held pending charges for their involvement in a 1935 rebellion. . . . Authorities in Sao Paulo release 200 prisoners, while police in Rio de Janeiro conduct raids and arrest leaders of another leftist plot. . . . Secretary of State Cordell Hull briefs President Franklin Roosevelt on the Inter-American Peace Conference in Buenos Aires, Argentina.	
Jan. 15		The Supreme Soviet adopts the Constitution of 1936 as the law of the land. . . . To improve relations with Germany, the Austrian government offers a general amnesty to 18,684 National Socialists who participated in a failed coup. . . . Premier Léon Blum is voted the authority to stop French volunteers from fighting in Spain. . . . Twenty-nine French ships set out for the coast of Morocco to participate in war games.			
Jan. 16		The capture of Estepona by insurgents is confirmed, and Franco's troops now move toward Málaga. . . . Yugoslav Premier Milan Stoyadinovitch meets for four hours with Croat leader Vladimir Matchek, leading to hopes of further talks between the two leaders.	The mayor of Jerusalem and other Arabs testify before the Royal Commission, claiming that industrialization and favoritism toward Jews result in denial of self-government and discrimination against the Arabs of Palestine.		
Jan. 17	The fate of over 1,000 Spanish refugees in the Chilean Embassy in Madrid is to be decided soon. Chile has asked the League of Nations to intervene. . . . While no military occupation exists, Germans use Spanish Morocco as a military air base as they support General Franco's troops.	The Soviet government informs the British Ambassador in Moscow that, although it does not send volunteers to Spain, it objects to prohibitions stopping such volunteers.	Egypt invites the United States to participate in the Montreux Conference in April, where Egypt hopes to step closer to full sovereignty.		Averting a potential civil war in the Shensi province of China, the armies of two generals and Marshal Chang Hsueh-liang agree to obey the government in Nanking. . . . A fire sweeps through a train bound from Canton to Hong Kong, killing at least 80 people.
Jan. 18	The condition of pacifist Carl von Ossietzky, winner of the Nobel Peace Prize, has worsened since his release from a concentration camp. Now in a Berlin nursing home, his attorney requests that the $40,000 prize money be transferred to a German bank for him.	Insurgents capture Marbella and head toward Málaga, Spain. . . . The German Reich makes a loan of $40 million to Greece for armaments, following up an earlier $20 million loan for the same purpose. . . . The Nazi secret police seize and suppress the journal of the German Church Ministry.	After hearing more grievances from Arab leaders, the Royal Commission ends its sessions in Jerusalem.		
Jan. 19	Iran threatens to break off diplomatic relations with France over a pun published in a French paper.	Loyalist troops under General Lister of the International Brigade capture Cerro de Los Angeles, a hill eight miles south of Madrid, then retreat to more defensible positions.			General Yang Fu-cheng makes new and rebellious demands of the Nanking government from his position in the Shensi province, reviving fears of revolt. . . . Seven officers and eight civilians are sentenced to prison for their parts in the Tokyo mutiny of February 1936.

A	B	C	D	E
Includes developments that affect more than one world region, international organizations, and important meetings of world leaders.	Includes all domestic and regional developments in Europe, including the Soviet Union.	Includes all domestic and regional developments in Africa and the Middle East.	Includes all domestic and regional developments in Latin America, the Caribbean, and Canada.	Includes all domestic and regional developments in Asian and Pacific nations (and colonies).

U.S. Politics & Social Issues	U.S. Foreign Policy & Defense	Economics & Great Depression	Science, Technology & Nature	Culture, Leisure & Lifestyle	
Seventy men and women are arrested by order of Special Prosecutor Thomas Dewey, from ringleaders and executives to "slip" girls, in a coordinated raid ending one of the largest organized gambling rings in history. . . . Senator McCarron of Nevada proposes that oversight of air transport be taken from the Bureau of Air Commerce and given to the Interstate Commerce Commission. . . . Witnesses tell the La Follette Senate subcommittee of floggings by company men and National Guardsmen. The Senate body is investigating labor espionage.		A federal court in Alabama upholds the constitutionality of taxing employers to pay for Social Security, citing the general welfare clause of the Constitution.	Lt. Gorry, commander of the submarine *Barracuda*, with Dr. Maurice Ewing, reports that the Caribbean Sea floor features a submerged mile-long mountain ridge and three extinct volcanoes. The men conducted underwater exploration of the area for the Navy Department.		Jan. 14
Setting a surprising precedent, a New York judge appoints an African-American attorney, H.C. Lipscomb, to represent Major Green, an African-American porter accused of murder.		At 3 a.m., Governor Frank Murphy announces a truce in the Flint strike; strikers will leave five plants, and joint negotiations will begin in Detroit on January 18. . . . The strike that began October 1 at the Berkshire Knitting Mills in Pennsylvania continues, although a strike of shipmasters and other workers, which began in late November, has been called off. . . . President W.A. Irwin of U. S. Steel Corp. announced that $60 million will be spent on plants in Pennsylvania.		Margaret Sanger receives a medal from the Town Hall Club in New York, honoring her work on birth control. . . . The Union of American Hebrew Congregations, meeting in New Orleans, urges worldwide unity to combat anti-Semitism. . . . Dr. Norman Vincent Peale speaks at the Women's Christian Temperance Union meeting, kicking off their campaign to raise $1 million to combat the repeal of Prohibition. . . . After only two months of marriage, Elaine Barrie files for divorce from John Barrymore in California, charging mental cruelty.	Jan. 15
		Four union organizers are arraigned in Flint, Mich., for their participation in a confrontation with police on January 11. . . . Employees of two gas companies in Toledo, Ohio, go on strike after contract negotiations fail. . . . The steel industry leads stocks to a stronger close than anticipated for a Saturday.			Jan. 16
		Sit-down strikers refuse to evacuate two General Motors plants, and that leads to the cancellation of talks between the company and the union, scheduled to begin on January 18. . . . Bus and streetcar operators in Terre Haute, Ind., stage a one-day strike for higher wages. . . . The ILGWU announces that a strike involving 8,000 workers will be called in Philadelphia. . . . Negotiations continue in a glass workers strike, now in its third month, affecting 17,000 in Pittsburgh.		The Cleveland Indians baseball team trades players to the St. Louis Browns for Moose Solters, an RBI leader, Lyn Lary, and Ivy Andrews. . . . Sam Snead, age 24, takes first place in the Oakland Open Golf Tournament. . . . Richard Boleslawski, film director, dies in Hollywood at age 47. In 1935 he directed *Les Miserables* and *Clive of India*.	Jan. 17
President Franklin Roosevelt names Interior Secretary Harold Ickes head of a committee that will devise a national policy on the generation and distribution of electrical power. . . . Senator Sherman Minton of Indiana announces that the President would soon seek ways to limit the power of the Supreme Court over legislation.	A bill to separate the Army Air Corps from the ground forces of the Army is introduced in the House of Representatives.	Union leaders, but no company representatives, show up for negotiations in Flint, Mich. Governor Frank Murphy leaves by train for Washington D.C., to seek federal intervention. . . . Shipments of gold continue to move from New York to Fort Knox, Ky. . . . In Washington, 1,200 ship workers from the East Coast march, demonstrate, and meet with Cabinet members and Congressional leaders.	Thousands flee the Ohio River Valley in four states, forced away by flooding. . . . Henry Ford and his son drive the 25 millionth Ford produced off the assembly line at the River Rouge plant.	The William Vanderbilts embark from Miami Beach on a 14,000-mile goodwill tour of South America aboard their private airliner.	Jan. 18
The White House denies Senator Sherman Minton's story that the President seeks to curb the power of the Supreme Court.		Steel production reaches a seven-year high. . . . A sit-down strike at the Kelly Tire Plant in Maryland starts just before midnight, and idles 1,800 workers.	Howard Hughes breaks his own record for speed and distance in his 7.5-hour flight from Los Angeles, Calif., to Newark, N.J. His average speed was 332 miles per hour.	Cy Young, Tris Speaker, and Nap Lajoie are voted into the Baseball Hall of Fame. . . . United Airlines begins flights of a luxury airplane, with 14 seats instead of 21, "the nearest thing to a railroad club car yet devised."	Jan. 19

F	**G**	**H**	**I**	**J**
Includes elections, federal-state relations, civil rights and liberties, crime, the judiciary, education, healthcare, poverty, urban affairs, and population.	Includes formation and debate of U.S. foreign and defense policies, veterans affairs, and defense spending. (Relations with specific foreign countries are usually found under the region concerned.)	Includes business, labor, agriculture, taxation, transportation, consumer affairs, monetary and fiscal policy, natural resources, pollution, and accidents.	Includes worldwide scientific, medical, and technological developments, natural phenomena, U.S. weather, and natural disasters.	Includes the arts, religion, scholarship, communications media, sports, entertainment, fashions, fads, and social life.

	World Affairs	Europe	Africa & The Middle East	The Americas	Asia & The Pacific
Jan. 20	The League of Nations mediates talks between France and Turkey about the status of Alexandretta.... A German-Japanese commission will enact provisions of the anti-international Communism pact of last November. . . . A result of Air Minister H.W. Goering's recent trip to Italy is an agreement between Germany and Italy to develop the mineral resources of Ethiopia.	Portugal rejects a plan to allow international observers to prevent arms shipments across its borders with Spain. . . . Bombs explode in several locations in Lisbon, including the War Ministry. They are believed to be the work of radicals.... French sources report that 3,000 German troops passed Trieste three days ago, en route to Spain. . . . Germany announces its exports were up 12 percent in 1936; British exports were up 3 percent that year.		Brazil indicts 60 more people, including four women, in connection with the 1935 revolt.	In China, 200 people, many of them children, die when a ferryboat traveling from Canton to Kongmoon hits rocks and sinks quickly.
Jan. 21	The League of Nations opens its 96th session in Geneva, Switzerland. Haile Selassie, writing from England, protests Switzerland's recognition of Italy's claim over Ethiopia.	To satisfy Paris brokers, the French government says that because of Chancellor Adolf Hitler's habit of making announcements on Saturdays, the Bourse will close for the next six Saturdays. . . . Germany's Foreign Office criticizes the attitude of Czechoslovakia toward Germans, suggesting that the country's situation—and perhaps its existence—is tenuous and subject to change.		Droughts have destroyed sugar crops and shut down mills, leaving over 100,000 people in the Brazilian area of Pernambuco in dire need.	As Japan's Diet meets under unusually heavy guard, Foreign Minister Arita asks for a worldwide "open door" trade policy to give poor nations access to resources. Prime Minister Hirota emphasizes the importance of armaments and defense, especially against Communist nations. Bitter words erupt between War Minister Terauchi and the leader of the Seiyukai Party, ending with a demand that accusations be proved or the Minister kill himself. In Osaka, an agreement is reached between the United States and Japan over textile quotas. . . . Armies move north to Shensi province in China.
Jan. 22		The German government demands that Madrid's gold reserves, reportedly moved to France, be placed under international control.			The Japanese Cabinet votes to dissolve the Diet and will put the matter before the Emperor tomorrow. . . . The Chinese government in Nanking issues an ultimatum to the armies under General Yang Fucheng in Shensi, giving them three days to accept terms or face war.
Jan. 23	Walter Runciman, president of the British Board of Trade, meets with Secretary of State Cordell Hull, then with President Franklin Roosevelt for talks, presumably on armament and trade.	Trials begin in Moscow for 17 followers of Leon Trotsky, accused of plotting to overthrow Joseph Stalin. All plead guilty. Gregory Piatakoff testifies for five hours that Trotsky told him of conspiring with German Rudolf Hess to seize power, and of a plan to reward Germany with the Ukraine for its support. . . . The Bavarian Minister of Education and the Interior limits children's attendance at church services to between 7:00–9:00 a.m. on Sundays, so that they may participate in Hitler Youth Activities.		Leon Trotsky, in an essay printed in U.S. newspapers, calls the trials in Moscow a "cruel fiasco," and compares Stalin's actions to those of Cesare Borgia.	In the latest move in the power struggle in Japan, all members of the Japanese Cabinet resign. The Diet continues in place. The Emperor must appoint a new premier.
Jan. 24		Bulgarian Premier George Kiosseivanoff and Yugoslavian Premier Milan Stoyadinovitch sign a pact of friendship for their kings and countries.... Karl Radek testifies at his trial in Moscow of plots with Japan and Germany to overthrow Stalin. . . . Torrential rain causes the Thames River in London to overflow its banks and flood many areas, including Windsor Castle.	A blizzard between the Black and Aegean seas drops snow on the city of Istanbul and disrupts shipping.		Peace is assured in China; Generalissimo Chiang Kai-shek is rumored to have arranged the details.
Jan. 25		Daily shelling continues in Madrid. . . . In a long-awaited response to Britain's January 5 request, Germany announces it has drafted a law banning its citizens from participating in the Spanish civil war. Italy's Foreign Minister Galeazzo Ciano replies also that legislation to prevent recruitment to Spain has been prepared. . . . Dimitri Navashine, an expatriate and enemy of Stalin, is shot to death in the Bois de Boulogne in Paris. His assassin escapes.		An accidental explosion of dynamite at the Chuquicamata Copper Mine in Antofagasta, Chile, kills 16 workers and injures more than 200 others.	Retired army General Kazushige Ugaki asks to be premier of Japan. Newspapers report that the military will oppose his appointment, but popular support is with Ugaki, a former governor of Korea.... Chinese troops loyal to Nanking travel to Shensi province and skirmish with rebel troops, in spite of the reported truce.

A	B	C	D	E
Includes developments that affect more than one world region, international organizations, and important meetings of world leaders.	*Includes all domestic and regional developments in Europe, including the Soviet Union.*	*Includes all domestic and regional developments in Africa and the Middle East.*	*Includes all domestic and regional developments in Latin America, the Caribbean, and Canada.*	*Includes all domestic and regional developments in Asian and Pacific nations (and colonies).*

U.S. Politics & Social Issues	U.S. Foreign Policy & Defense	Economics & Great Depression	Science, Technology & Nature	Culture, Leisure & Lifestyle	
Franklin D. Roosevelt is sworn in as President for the second time in the first inaugural to take place in January, thanks to the 20th Amendment. His address speaks of the nation's united resolve, and the need for government to find solutions to problems and protect its citizens.		Further strike actions by gas workers in Toledo, Ohio, are postponed for 24 hours. . . . General Motors president Alfred Sloan and other executives spend hours with Secretary of Labor Frances Perkins and Governor Frank Murphy, but the meeting ends with no progress made regarding the Flint, Mich., strike. . . . In Pittsburgh, 6,000 glass workers return to work with pay raises after their strike issues are settled. . . . The Fifth Circuit Court of Appeals upholds the authority of the Federal Mediation Board to settle disputes between unions.	The coldest temperature ever in California is recorded: minus 45°F. . . . An estimated 20,000 persons flee their homes because of flooding in the Midwest and Southeast. The Ohio River is dangerously high in several states, and levees on rivers in Missouri and Arkansas have given way.	The U.S. Junior Chamber of Commerce names Walt Disney the "leading young man of the past year."	Jan. 20
	The President asks to extend for three years the Trade Agreements Act, which empowers him to make reciprocal trade pacts without Congressional approval.	After a closed five-hour meeting, seamen vote to call off their three-month-long strike of East Coast ports, trusting the National Labor Relations Board to negotiate for them. West Coast strikers are unaffected. . . . GM executives leave Washington and both sides are considered deadlocked; 80 percent of Flint's workers are left idle and without income.	Vincent Bendix, head of Bendix Aviation, announces the formation of a new company, Bendix Radio Corp., to develop and market radio compass homing devices for airplanes.		Jan. 21
	Senator Key Pittman of Nevada introduces a resolution giving the president authority to embargo arms and protect U.S. neutrality.	President Franklin Roosevelt refuses to become involved in the General Motors Strike. . . . Chicago is briefly without lights as the city's electrical workers stage a 2-hour strike.	Floods leave 80,000 homeless, 50,000 of them in the Ohio River Valley. Cincinnati and other cities in Ohio, along with Indiana, Kentucky, West Virginia, Illinois, Missouri, Tennessee, and Pennsylvania suffer flood damage. Pittsburgh expects flooding shortly.		Jan. 22
		General Motors says that the Flint strike has idled almost 126,000 workers and 50 plants in 12 states.	Low temperatures in California could cost growers 50 percent of their citrus crops. . . . The rising Ohio River forces 41,500 people in Cincinnati to leave their homes. President Franklin Roosevelt directs the WPA, the CCC, the Coast Guard, and other agencies to work with the Red Cross in providing manpower and assistance to flooded areas. An estimated 300,000 people in 10 states have been evacuated due to flooding. In Kentucky, 50,000 are left homeless. Looting becomes a problem in Indiana, where 40,000 have left their homes. Cold temperatures and lack of drinking water are concerns.	Marie Prevost, silent film actress who worked for Ernst Lubitsch, is dead at age 38 of alcoholism and malnutrition. She died at least two days before her body was discovered.	Jan. 23
Senator La Follette's subcommittee on labor espionage hears from witnesses who connected Army and Navy intelligence to union spying in the National Metals Trade Association. Names of dozens of labor spies are published.		Secretary of Labor Frances Perkins summons both union and company representatives to meet in two days and try to end the strike in Michigan.	Flood evacuees now number 400,000 as the Ohio River reaches its highest point ever. President Franklin Roosevelt mobilizes the Army and Navy to work with other agencies. Gas and oil-fed fires sweep over two square miles of Cincinnati. Indiana is placed under martial law. The Mississippi River is also rising, and recent flood control projects, such as the Birds Point-New Madrid Floodway, will be tested. The flooding has caused 41 deaths.	The WPA Federal Music Project opens its Theatre of Music on West 54th Street.	Jan. 24
Auto companies pay high fees for agents who spy on union activities, the La Follette subcommittee learns.		General Motors president Alfred Sloan informs Secretary of Labor Frances Perkins that his company will not participate in upcoming negotiations in Washington to end the strike in Flint. . . . General Motors recalls 40,000 workers and reopens some plants with limited work schedules. . . . In Toledo, gas workers end their strike and return to work with pay raises ranging from 4–49 percent.	President Franklin Roosevelt installs Harry Hopkins as White House liaison, coordinating federal agencies in their flood relief operations. Flooding between Pittsburgh and Cairo, Ill., is now the worst ever recorded: 300,000 left homeless in Kentucky alone, at least 550,000 homeless overall, and 100 dead.		Jan. 25

F	G	H	I	J
Includes elections, federal-state relations, civil rights and liberties, crime, the judiciary, education, healthcare, poverty, urban affairs, and population.	Includes formation and debate of U.S. foreign and defense policies, veterans affairs, and defense spending. (Relations with specific foreign countries are usually found under the region concerned.)	Includes business, labor, agriculture, taxation, transportation, consumer affairs, monetary and fiscal policy, natural resources, pollution, and accidents.	Includes worldwide scientific, medical, and technological developments, natural phenomena, U.S. weather, and natural disasters.	Includes the arts, religion, scholarship, communications media, sports, entertainment, fashions, fads, and social life.

	World Affairs	Europe	Africa & The Middle East	The Americas	Asia & The Pacific
Jan. 26	Rabbi Dr. Jonah B. Wise, responding to reports that the 3 million Jews of Poland face anti-Semitism on the level of Nazi Germany's, calls for aid to be sent through the Joint Distribution Committee of New York's Central Synagogue.	King George VI of England calls for a new Regency Act to ensure the functions of government if the monarch is ill, away, or—in the case of George's two daughters—too young to act. . . . All German businesses must close for three hours this Saturday so that Chancellor Hitler's speech, broadcast over loudspeakers, may be heard. . . . Negotiations for a new trade agreement between Germany and Austria end. Austria is not able to fulfill all demands for food exports in return for armaments and coal from Germany. . . . One of the 17 defendants in Moscow implicates Alexander Belaborodoff in a 1928 plot. Belaborodoff, believed to have been one of the executioners of the Czar's family, is arrested.		An earthquake in Chilpacingo, Mexico, cracks walls and rings church bells.	
Jan. 27	The 96th Council of the League of Nations ends. Alexandretta will be independent internally, but tied to Syria in foreign affairs. The League withdraws from further decisions on Danzig, and the refugee dispute between Chile and Spain remains unresolved.	French and British ships are lost with all hands as storms wrack the North Sea. Portugal's infrastructure is damaged by cyclonic winds. Snowstorms paralyze the Balkans as far south as Greece. . . . Vice Premier Emile Vandervelde of Belgium, a socialist, resigns. . . . The Vatican lodges a formal complaint with Germany over the Reich's interference in Catholic youth organizations. . . . Austria and Germany sign the Vienna-Berlin Pact, a trade agreement for 1937.		The Cuban Cabinet votes to nominate President Franklin Roosevelt for the Nobel Peace Prize for his work on the Inter-American Conference in Buenos Aires and prepares the nomination.	The Chinese government in Nanking recalls its army, and the Communist, or rebel, forces in Shensi agree to Nanking's compromises, which remain secret.
Jan. 28	In London, the Judicial Committee of the Privy Council rules that Canada's laws on unemployment insurance, minimum wage, and other matters are unconstitutional.	Austrian courts begin accepting "race" as a reason for divorce between Jews and non-Jews, as in Germany. . . . In Poland, Jewish students of Warsaw University are turned away at the gates when they try to attend classes. . . . Italy signs a trade agreement with the Franco government in Salamanca, Spain.		Gen. Pedro Irias surrenders to authorities in Nicaragua after hiding in the jungle for 10 years. He served with the outlaw leader Sandino. . . . A riot between conservatives and liberals in the Colombian state of El Valle kills five men.	The military blocks Gen. Kazushige Ugaki's attempt to form a new government in Japan. Withdrawing his name as premier, Ugaki says the nation must choose between fascism and constitutionalism. . . . A truce agreement in China, signed at Tungkwan, is accepted by Communists and Nationalists.
Jan. 29	Egypt will be admitted to the League of Nations in a special session next May.	Storms cause 74 deaths at sea in northern Europe. High seas inundate roads in Britain and Scotland and tear away a sea wall in Quiberon, Brittany. . . . Police Commander Heinrich Himmler states that some prisoners in Germany's concentration camps will never be released. . . . Poland's Foreign Minister Josef Beck says that economics, not anti-Semitism, is the rationale for urging Poland's "excess" Jews to emigrate.		Cuba sentences a seventh man to die for the kidnapping of a railroad executive in 1935. Enrique Giraud Carreno will face a firing squad within 24 hours. . . . Employees of the Cartagena railroad settle their strike in Colombia, winning pay increases of up to 20 percent and medical services.	
Jan. 30	Chancellor Adolf Hitler forbids acceptance of Nobel prizes by Germans, and terms the recent award to pacifist Carl von Ossietzky—whom Hitler calls a traitor—a "shameful occurrence." A German prize for art and science will be given.	Adolf Hitler speaks for two hours during the festivities marking his fourth anniversary in power. His speech outlines his achievements, rejects any compromise with Bolsheviks, demands the return of colonies taken from Germany, and repudiates the Treaty of Versailles and the war debts it laid upon Germany. Hitler later announces that the Reichsbank and railways would henceforward operate under state control. . . . Sentences are read in the treason trials of 17 Trotskyites in Moscow. Thirteen men are condemned to death; three, including Karl Radek, get prison sentences of 10 years.		Brazil opens a Congressional inquiry into allegations that Congressmen representing Argentinian interests profited from wheat imports.	The Emperor of Japan chooses retired General Senjuro Hayashi, a political neutral, as premier. . . . Conflicting reports of troop withdrawals feed rumors that the Communist forces in North China are ignoring the truce. . . . President Quezon of the Philippines is feted and honored in Japan during a visit.
Jan. 31		The Soviet Union rejects pleas for clemency for the 13 men condemned yesterday. . . . France's Foreign Minister Yvon Delbos responds to Hitler's speeches, pointing out that respecting treaties is a factor in insuring world peace. Delbos says that the Soviet Union, a nation of 200 million, cannot be excluded from the international community. . . . Rain and bad weather subdue much of the fighting around Madrid and Málaga.			

A	B	C	D	E
Includes developments that affect more than one world region, international organizations, and important meetings of world leaders.	Includes all domestic and regional developments in Europe, including the Soviet Union.	Includes all domestic and regional developments in Africa and the Middle East.	Includes all domestic and regional developments in Latin America, the Caribbean, and Canada.	Includes all domestic and regional developments in Asian and Pacific nations (and colonies).

U.S. Politics & Social Issues	U.S. Foreign Policy & Defense	Economics & Great Depression	Science, Technology & Nature	Culture, Leisure & Lifestyle	
		The President and his Labor Secretary publicly rebuke Alfred Sloan of General Motors for refusing to attend the Washington meeting called over the strike. A rally of 8,000 non-strikers demands that Governor Frank Murphy of Michigan put them back to work. . . . The Brooklyn-Manhattan Transit Corp. is hit by a sit-down strike, but a truce is called shortly before 8 a.m. . . . The President ends the studies he ordered of electrical power companies "pools," because of the injunctions holding up the TVA.	For the second time in two days, dynamite blasts levees to speed Ohio River floodwaters into the Mississippi River and floodway. The homeless number 750,000, with over 400,000 in Red Cross shelters. Fires further damage Louisville, Ky. Over 100,000 federal employees aid victims, and all of the previously approved $790 million will go to pay for flood relief.		Jan. 26
The Senate passes a $50 million aid bill to assist flood victims.		Chevrolet plants reopen, and 38,800 return to work. Labor Secretary Frances Perkins asks Congress for further authority, enabling her to compel company and union representatives to meet. . . . The strike of 7,100 workers against Libby-Owens-Ford Glass of Toledo is settled with an across-the-board raise of 8 cents per hour.	The Ohio River slowly starts to drop as floodwaters pour into the Mississippi River.	With Cincinnati's Crossley Field covered in 21 feet of water, Reds pitchers Gene Schott and Lee Grissom row a boat out of the ballpark.	Jan. 27
The Ramspeck Bill, passed by Congress, expands the civil service to include postmasters. . . . Pinkerton detectives posed as NRA agents to get information, according to testimony given before the La Follette Senate subcommittee.	The House Ways and Means Committee approves the extension for three years of the Trade Agreements Act.	General Motors asks a circuit court for an injunction ordering the sit-down strikers out of their premises. . . . The National Labor Relations Board charges General Motors with industrial espionage, coercion, and violation of the civil rights of its employees. . . . In Akron, Ohio, a sit-down strike of 31 workers in a Goodrich Tire plant employing 10,000 stops production.	A million people are homeless as the Ohio River slowly recedes, but near Cairo, Ill., a 62-foot crest is expected in four days. As waters pour south into the Mississippi, the worst flooding will move south as well.		Jan. 28
	Twelve Navy sky cruisers land in Honolulu, completing the biggest nonstop flight ever attempted. The airplanes carried a total of 80 men from San Diego and flew for 21 hours, 43 minutes.	GM president Alfred Sloan meets with the Secretary of Labor, Frances Perkins, to discuss a possible solution to the strike. . . . Michigan Governor Frank Murphy scolds "anti-strikers" for their attempts to embarrass him and provoke the use of force against strikers. . . . The U.S. District Court upholds provisions of the Public Utilities Act of 1935, saying that holding companies of utilities must register with the SEC, and that the Act can be judged provision by provision, rather than as a whole.		Heavyweight Joe Louis defeats Bob Pastor in 10 rounds but is booed in Madison Square Garden because he didn't deliver a knockout. . . . The Book-of-the-Month Club hands out $2,500 to authors whose books received insufficient attention last year. The winners were: Robinson Jeffers for Solstice and Other Poems, Katherine Anne Porter for Flowering Judas, James T. Farrell for Studs Lonigan, and Paul B. Sears for Deserts on the March.	Jan. 29
		GM president Alfred Sloan rejects the proposals made by Secretary Frances Perkins. . . . President Franklin Roosevelt says he approves giving the Labor Secretary the power of subpoena. . . . Congress selects a committee to study the President's reorganization of the Executive Branch. . . . The Federal Reserve Board orders an increase of one-third in the amount of reserves banks must keep on hand, the highest amount allowed by law. . . . Maritime workers on the West Coast call for a vote to end their 93-day strike and send 40,000 back to work.	A force of 115,000 man levees along the Mississippi River as the water rises. From Cairo south, all levees hold, but higher waters are expected over the next few days. Ohio's flood losses alone are estimated at $70 million.	Edward Reilly, defense lawyer of Bruno Hauptmann in the Lindbergh baby kidnapping case, is committed in the Brooklyn State Hospital for the Insane due to a nervous breakdown.	Jan. 30
		John L. Lewis, chair of the CIO, calls financiers J. P. Morgan and Pierre duPont the true powers of the auto industry, and asks them to change their policies so that the strikes can be ended. . . . Father Charles Coughlin exhorts the auto companies to pay a "living, annual raise."	Louisville, Ky., is under quarantine; only emergency vehicles are allowed within five miles of the city.		Jan. 31

F	G	H	I	J
Includes elections, federal-state relations, civil rights and liberties, crime, the judiciary, education, healthcare, poverty, urban affairs, and population.	Includes formation and debate of U.S. foreign and defense policies, veterans affairs, and defense spending. (Relations with specific foreign countries are usually found under the region concerned.)	Includes business, labor, agriculture, taxation, transportation, consumer affairs, monetary and fiscal policy, natural resources, pollution, and accidents.	Includes worldwide scientific, medical, and technological developments, natural phenomena, U.S. weather, and natural disasters.	Includes the arts, religion, scholarship, communications media, sports, entertainment, fashions, fads, and social life.

	World Affairs	Europe	Africa & The Middle East	The Americas	Asia & The Pacific
Feb. 1	A delegation from the Arab National League meets with Secretary of State Cordell Hull in Washington, and asks that the Arabs of Palestine not be "pushed back into the desert" by Zionist supporters.	The Soviet government announces the executions of the 13 condemned Trotskyites sentenced in January. . . . The insurgent army cuts off Málaga from loyalist troops. . . . Vatican newspaper *Osservatore Romano* reports that 40–50 percent of the 33,500 priests in Spain have been killed by Reds in the last year.		Cuba announces that 50,000 Jamaican and Haitian workers will be held in concentration camps, then deported.	General Hayashi accepts Kotara Nakamura as War Minister, along with other nominations for office made by the military. . . . Four days of war games begin in the Straits Settlements, designed to test the $50 million British-built naval base there.
Feb. 2	The League of Nations, which since 1931 set the amount of dangerous drugs to be manufactured worldwide, limits the 1937 level of morphine to 45 tons. . . . In Bandoeng, Java, Dutch East Indies, the League's two-week long Conference of Central Authorities of Far Eastern Countries on the Traffic of Women opens, with the purpose of suppressing prostitution in the area.	The French Chamber approves spending an additional 19 billion francs over four years on defense. British magazine *The Banker* reports that Germany spent 12.6 billion marks on defense in 1936–37. . . . Yugoslav War Minister Maritch presents a defense budget of only $45 million with the caution that it compares poorly with preparations other countries are making for war.	The Grand Mufti of Egypt approves the use of birth control for married Muslims.	The leaders of Cuba's House of Representatives, including Dr. Carlos Marquez Sterling, are forced to resign. . . . Leon Cortes, president of Costa Rica, refuses the pay raise Congress voted him, and turns the money over to charity.	Premier Hayashi assumes office with a Cabinet of eight ministers in Japan. . . . Generals Yang Fu-cheng and Chang Hsueh-liang lose control of their troops, who begin pillaging the Shensi capital of Sian late at night.
Feb. 3		Turkey will increase its arms budget by $25 million this year. . . . The foreign ministers of Italy and Turkey meet in Rome. . . . Spanish planes drop bombs near a British battleship off Gibraltar, mistaking it for one of General Franco's vessels. . . . Fighting erupts near Málaga, with both sides claiming to have suppressed movements by the other.		Cuba's army attempts to arrest Dr. Marquez Sterling, former president of the House of Representatives, but desists when senators and representatives rush to his defense.	The government at Nanking threatens to bomb Sian if order cannot be restored. . . . The 33rd Annual Eucharistic Congress, a gathering of world Catholics, opens in Manila, Philippines. Over 100,000 people crowd into Luneta Park for the ceremonies.
Feb. 4		German Ambassador von Ribbentrop, presenting himself to King George VI of Britain, gives the Nazi salute. . . . The Spanish government issues a decree abolishing the "archaic privileges" of husbands and ensuring equality of women. . . . France's Chamber of Deputies argues over whether Premier Léon Blum should slash social programs in favor of defense expenditures.		Dr. Martinez Fraga is elected to head Cuba's House of Representatives.	General Wang I-cheh of the 67th Manchurian Army is assassinated in his sickbed by mutinous troops in north China. Two other army colonels are murdered as well. . . . Japan's Diet adjourns until February 11.
Feb. 5		The Spanish government will try 60 Augustinian monks who harbored "anti-government tendencies," and indict 1,500 others. Groups of prisoners are executed in reprisal for air attacks on Málaga. . . . A week of international plans for a blockade of Spanish ports, made between Britain, Germany, Italy, and France, is halted by the Soviet Union's demand to participate. . . . Poland's leaders present a billion-zloty defense plan and a second plan to establish a war industries "security triangle" in central Poland, at the cost of a half-million zlotys.	The Iranian parliament allows the U.S. company Seaboard Oil of Delaware and others to develop oil fields in Khorassan, in eastern Iran.		If the Nanking government cannot bring its rebellious "red" forces under control, Japan threatens to intervene to restore order.
Feb. 6		The Soviet Union arrests hundreds in the largest purge in 10 years. Former premier Alexis Rykoff is among those facing trial. . . . Italian Premier Benito Mussolini's oldest son, Vittorio, marries Orsola Buvoli in Rome.		Revolution forces President Tiburcio Carias Andino of Honduras to flee his palace at Tegucigalpa. . . . Peru and Argentina sign a two-year trade treaty.	
Feb. 7	In Geneva, the League of Nations convenes an international conference to establish legal status for German expatriates and refugees.	Insurgents close on the port of Málaga, Spain, from several directions, aided by 15,000 recently landed Italian troops. Violence, rapes, and massacres are reported. . . . Columnist Otto Tolischus outlines the plight of Jews in Poland and Europe in a series of articles for *The New York Times*.		Senator David Ayala of Mexico claims that land reform is a failure, that banks and local leaders take profits and commit murder. Many peons have left the communal farms, and those that remain are often treated as slaves.	A radio message from Pope Pius is heard by 600,000 Catholics, closing the 33rd Eucharistic Congress in Manila, Philippines. . . . While six Japanese warships arrive in Shanghai's harbor, General Ku Chu-tung moves toward Lintung in Shensi to establish order. Communist armies desert or retreat into the mountains.
	A Includes developments that affect more than one world region, international organizations, and important meetings of world leaders.	**B** Includes all domestic and regional developments in Europe, including the Soviet Union.	**C** Includes all domestic and regional developments in Africa and the Middle East.	**D** Includes all domestic and regional developments in Latin America, the Caribbean, and Canada.	**E** Includes all domestic and regional developments in Asian and Pacific nations (and colonies).

U.S. Politics & Social Issues	U.S. Foreign Policy & Defense	Economics & Great Depression	Science, Technology & Nature	Culture, Leisure & Lifestyle	
		General Motors asks for an injunction to force sit-down strikers out of its plants in Flint, Mich. . . . The sit-down strike spreads to Chevrolet Plant No. 4, where strikers enter and break windows. Police or company thugs try to move them out. Pickets include members of the Women's Emergency Brigade, organized by Genora Johnson, and they become involved in the violence. The National Guard surrounds the GM buildings with fixed bayonets and orders that no food be passed to strikers.		President Franklin Roosevelt asks Congress to accept Andrew Mellon's art and money for a National Gallery.	Feb. 1
		Judge Paul Gadola orders the strikers out of the Fisher Body Plant and Chevrolet Plant No. 4 by 3 p.m. on February 3. . . . Although martial law has not been declared, 3,500 National Guard troops assemble near Flint, Mich., to help evacuate the strikers. . . . Governor Frank Murphy invites CIO chair John Lewis and General Motors Vice President William Knudsen to meetings, at the secret request of President Roosevelt and Labor Secretary Perkins. . . . A sit-down strike begins at the Kelvinator plant in Detroit.	The walls protecting Cairo, Ill., from flood are holding. In Cincinnati, where floodwaters recede, stores open briefly.	*The Good Earth* opens in New York (it had premiered in Los Angeles three days earlier), and eventually wins star Luise Rainer her second Oscar.	Feb. 2
In a special message to Congress, President Franklin Roosevelt proposes six-year programs of public works. Irrigation and flood control would comprise 24 percent of the programs, and streets and highways 25 percent.	By order of the President, gifts from other countries intended for flood victims may enter the United States duty-free.	Anticipating more rioting, the National Guardsmen surround thousands of strikers and supporters in the Fisher Body Plant and wait. The governor refuses to order the troops into the plant, and continues to meet with CIO Chair John Lewis and GM Vice President William Knudsen.	Federal Relief Administrator Harry Hopkins visits Cairo, Ill., and promises "no red tape" in clean-up and relief operations. The river crests at just under 60 feet and is expected to stay that high for a few days. . . . A flight recorder is presented at a conference on air safety in Washington. The instrument, a barometric altimeter with drum and pens, will be required on commercial airliners in the future.		Feb. 3
	The extension of the Reciprocal Trade Agreements Act is debated in Congress.	Union and company representatives return to sit with the governor and negotiate, spurred on by a phone call from President Franklin Roosevelt asking them to reach a settlement. . . . Congress rejects a move to investigate General Motors, calling such an action too one-sided. . . . Maritime workers in the west, 40,000 strong, vote approval of a new contract and end their strike.	Floodwaters of the Mississippi begin to fall, sparing Cairo, Ill., and other communities.	New York's share of the cost of the upcoming 1939 World's Fair has risen to $8 million.	Feb. 4
President Franklin Roosevelt submits a plan to enlarge the Supreme Court, surprising Congress and the nation. Republicans voice criticism and the stock market falls in reaction, but overall, reception of the plan is favorable in Washington. The plan increases the Supreme Court to a maximum of 15 judges, and declares 70 the retirement age.		Shipworkers on the West Coast return to work, ending a 98-day walkout. . . . In Flint, Mich., warrants are issued for sit-down strikers, but Sheriff T. Woolcott holds off making arrests while labor negotiations continue.	An estimated 120,000 workers fight to keep levees whole as the Ohio River falls a few inches every 24 hours. The Mississippi rises only one-third of an inch daily.	Lou Andreas-Salomé, author, intellectual, and friend of Nietzsche and Rilke, dies of uremia in Göttingen, Germany. The Gestapo burns her library after she dies. . . . A one-man show of Georgia O'Keefe's latest work, most painted in 1936, opens in New York.	Feb. 5
					Feb. 6
		The dispute that shut down a Goodyear plant in Akron, Ohio, is resolved and 5,000 workers will return to their jobs. . . . In New York, building service employees vote to strike citywide. Sporadic, temporary strikes have hit various buildings over the past week.	The year's first dust storm hits parts of Texas, Oklahoma, and western New Mexico, reducing visibility to zero. . . . Landing a plane with a single, small front wheel added to the front of the aircraft was demonstrated over Washington, and is expected to revolutionize planes and piloting.	Nobel Peace Prize recipient Elihu Root dies. He had served in the Senate and two presidential Cabinets, and helped form international organizations devoted to peace. . . . Gags and jokes, overheard during the filming of movies starring the Marx Brothers and other comedians, are being stolen and sold to radio shows.	Feb. 7

F	G	H	I	J
Includes elections, federal-state relations, civil rights and liberties, crime, the judiciary, education, healthcare, poverty, urban affairs, and population.	*Includes formation and debate of U.S. foreign and defense policies, veterans affairs, and defense spending. (Relations with specific foreign countries are usually found under the region concerned.)*	*Includes business, labor, agriculture, taxation, transportation, consumer affairs, monetary and fiscal policy, natural resources, pollution, and accidents.*	*Includes worldwide scientific, medical, and technological developments, natural phenomena, U.S. weather, and natural disasters.*	*Includes the arts, religion, scholarship, communications media, sports, entertainment, fashions, fads, and social life.*

	World Affairs	Europe	Africa & The Middle East	The Americas	Asia & The Pacific
Feb. 8		General Franco's forces enter Málaga in the early morning, and arrest 5,000 during the day. Some reports state that 20,000 Italian recruits were the first to take the city. An estimated 15,000 loyalists hide in the mountains. . . . While continuing to buy machinery from Germany, Russia is withholding the raw materials it committed to ship in a 1936 trade accord.		In Orizaba, Veracruz, Mexico, a young girl is killed and 70 Catholics arrested as police raid a private church service. Following the ouster of the Archbishop of Chiapas last week, the incident indicates that government-church relations are not settled.	Premier Hayashi of Japan promises "no radical changes." . . . Government troops take control of Sian, and civil war has been averted.
Feb. 9	A cut wire prevents Leon Trotsky from speaking via telephone from Mexico to 6,500 people assembled in New York.	Led by a Nazi majority, Danzig's ruling body changes electoral laws to make removal of opposition forces easier. . . . Following a night of violence in which 22 were injured, students at the university in Vilna, Poland, declare "a day without Jews," picketing and barring Jews from classes.		Between 5,000 and 15,000 people storm and reopen churches in Orizaba, Veracruz, that had been closed by the government months ago. President Lázaro Cárdenas of Mexico orders an investigation into the killing of the 14-year-old girl by police in that city. . . . Governor Winship of Puerto Rico asks the legislature for more funding for education, and recommends that sterilization be considered to improve the race.	
Feb. 10		Arnold Bernstein, a Jew and operator of Arnold Bernstein and Red Star Lines, is charged in Hamburg, Germany, of violating exchange laws. A government trustee will run his shipping lines until the trial is completed. . . . Insurgents in Spain capture the city of Motril, 45 miles from Málaga. . . . Roman newspapers acknowledge that 16,000 Italian troops secured the insurgent victory at Málaga.		Mexico's Interior Minister says the legislature of Veracruz has repealed a law prohibiting religious ceremonies . . . A group of 45 members of the House of Representatives in Cuba organizes to oppose the military clique headed by Col. Fulgensia Batista.	
Feb. 11		British Chancellor of the Exchequer Neville Chamberlain announces a forthcoming bill to spend £400 million over five years on defense. . . . Anti-Semitic riots break out in universities in Warsaw and Vilna, Poland.		In spite of yesterday's announcement of a repeal of the law against religious celebrations, the governor of Veracruz attempts to close all churches—leading to a rush by at least 20,000 persons to reopen them. Citizens post guards to ensure the churches remain open.	The Japanese Cabinet assents to a general budget reduction with large cuts to rural relief, and the Emperor extends the Diet's "vacation" until February 14.
Feb. 12		Poland reveals its long-anticipated government reorganization, becoming a one-party state. . . . Informal talks begin between Belgium and Germany, aimed at getting the Reich's acknowledgment of Belgium's neutrality. . . . By law, Germany's railroads and the Reichsbank today are no longer independent corporations, but government entities.		The Chilean President is authorized to spend 10 million pesos to purchase planes for the military.	In Sian, Shensi, bankers gather to discuss a financial crisis. As his forces evacuated the city, General Yang Fu-cheng withdrew $9 million, and other monies are unaccounted for.
Feb. 13		Fighting is now worse at the Valencia Highway, leading from Madrid to the sea. Bombs fall on Arganda, 15 miles from Madrid, and the coastal city Almeira through the night, and the dead have not been counted. . . . All members of the Protestant Board in Germany resign after 18 months of attempting to compromise with the Nazi government. Suppression of church activities by the secret police is a major factor in their decision to disband.		Conflicting reports from Honduras fuel rumors of revolution, and the Carias government has arrested 1,000 persons.	Almost 700 people, many of them women and children, die in a theater fire in Antung, Manchukuo. The movie theater was packed with 1,500 people celebrating the New Year. Japanese troops patrol the area and aid in relief.

A	B	C	D	E
Includes developments that affect more than one world region, international organizations, and important meetings of world leaders.	*Includes all domestic and regional developments in Europe, including the Soviet Union.*	*Includes all domestic and regional developments in Africa and the Middle East.*	*Includes all domestic and regional developments in Latin America, the Caribbean, and Canada.*	*Includes all domestic and regional developments in Asian and Pacific nations (and colonies).*

U.S. Politics & Social Issues	U.S. Foreign Policy & Defense	Economics & Great Depression	Science, Technology & Nature	Culture, Leisure & Lifestyle	
A compromise involving the retirement of two Supreme Court judges is discussed on Capital Hill, while the Court hears arguments in a dispute between the Virginia Railway and an AFL bargaining unit.		Despite constant press reports that negotiations are "near collapse" or blocked, Governor Frank Murphy continues to meet with GM and union representatives and keeps both sides talking. . . . Secretary of Agriculture Henry Wallace, with the President's approval, proposes a revival of the AAA, previously invalidated by the Supreme Court.	As the crest of the Mississippi River passes Memphis, the worst of the flood danger seems to be over. WPA chief and administrator Harry Hopkins presents a recovery plan to President Franklin Roosevelt and the nation to restore refugees to their homes and rebuild cities.		Feb. 8
The Supreme Court hears arguments over the constitutionality of the Wagner Labor Relations Act, brought by the Associated Press, which was forced, under the act, to reinstate a fired employee. . . . The La Follette Senate subcommittee hears testimony about labor espionage from the Pinkerton Detective Agency. The witness reveals that surveillance had been conducted on the Assistant Secretary of Labor when he conciliated a strike at Chrysler in 1935.	In a demonstration of nonstop flight over the sea, nine bombers flew from Panama to Miami Beach, landing safely. The first leg of the trip, from Miami Beach to Panama, was completed in less than eight hours.	Chrysler Corporation gives a pay raise averaging 10 percent to all its employees, which will cost the company between $13 and $14 million. . . . President Franklin Roosevelt signs the Deficiency Appropriations Bill, which includes $790 million for WPA funding.	As floodwaters subside, the Red Cross will use railroad box cars and tents to house refugees in Cincinnati and other Ohio cities.		Feb. 9
To implement the President's restructuring of the Supreme Court, House leaders introduce a bill to force mandatory retirement at age 70 on the judges. . . . With unusual speed, the Supreme Court hears arguments on three cases testing the Wagner Act.		The President asks Congress to work with other agencies to formulate a plan of land, resource, and technology use to end droughts and dust storms on the plains. . . . Building service employees strike in 23 New York apartment buildings, turning off radiators and elevators. In all but one building, service resumes as building owners sign contracts with the union.	In the wake of another commercial plane crash, the Bureau of Air Commerce recommends 10 safety measures, including the use of radio compasses and flight recorders. The recommendations result from last week's Air Safety Conference in Washington.		Feb. 10
President Franklin Roosevelt meets with key Congressmen to push forward his Supreme Court reorganization and head off attempts to block his agenda.		At 2:45 a.m., Governor Frank Murphy announces an end to the 44-day-long sit-down strike at General Motors. After an agreement is signed at noon, workers evacuate the plants. GM agrees to recognize the United Auto Workers as the bargaining agent and drops all charges and court actions against the strikers. Employees agree to return to work while their union conducts negotiations. GM also announces a five cents per hour wage increase for all employees, costing the company $25 million per year. . . . Steel and auto stocks soar at the news of the settlement.	Amelia Earhart announces her intention of flying round the globe within the next month, starting from Oakland, Calif. Her navigator on the California-Australia part of the trip will be Capt. Harry Manning.	A court dismisses complaints of obscenity brought against the novel *A World I Never Made*, by James T. Farrell. . . . Baseball manager and team owner Connie Mack is interviewed in a demonstration of television, sponsored by Philco.	Feb. 11
Before the La Follette subcommittee, Robert Pinkerton, owner of the Pinkerton Detective Agency, twice refuses to give names of agents who gathered information in the recent GM strike. He says to reveal the agents' names puts their lives at risk, and he risks a contempt charge for his recalcitrance.	The construction of six destroyers and three submarines is delayed due to a steel shortage. Suppliers will not bid on the contracts for the ships because of the Walsh-Healey Law, which holds government suppliers to standards such as a 40-hour work week.	General Motors plants gear up and place orders with parts suppliers, and 100,000 employees will return to work by February 16. Ongoing labor issues at six non-GM plants may slow production. . . . The report of the President's committee on farm tenancy is published. It recommends protection of civil rights of tenants. . . . Rubber plants in Akron, Ohio, employing more than 35,000, announce pay increases of five to eight cents per hour.			Feb. 12
		Martial law is declared in Anderson, Ind., when a non-union worker is chased into a tavern. Authorities claim carloads of union agitators from Flint incited riots where 10 were injured; others claim police caused the problems. . . . The Kelvinator strike continues; the union abandons its attempt to starve a dozen guards and allows food to be delivered.		James L. Johnson, Jr., the first African American in 62 years admitted to the Naval Academy, is forced to resign.	Feb. 13

F	G	H	I	J
Includes elections, federal-state relations, civil rights and liberties, crime, the judiciary, education, healthcare, poverty, urban affairs, and population.	Includes formation and debate of U.S. foreign and defense policies, veterans affairs, and defense spending. (Relations with specific foreign countries are usually found under the region concerned.)	Includes business, labor, agriculture, taxation, transportation, consumer affairs, monetary and fiscal policy, natural resources, pollution, and accidents.	Includes worldwide scientific, medical, and technological developments, natural phenomena, U.S. weather, and natural disasters.	Includes the arts, religion, scholarship, communications media, sports, entertainment, fashions, fads, and social life.

	World Affairs	Europe	Africa & The Middle East	The Americas	Asia & The Pacific
Feb. 14	Worldwide, $11 billion was spent on arms in 1936, double what was spent in 1934. . . . Germany contracts to build two naval battleships for Venezuela.	Pope Pius walks for the first time in 72 days. . . . The city of Valencia is shelled during the night. . . . Yugoslavia is owed 360 million dinars by Germany, a country that has purchased raw materials and now rejects all efforts to collect payment. . . . In his sermon, Munich's Cardinal criticizes the Reich for repeatedly violating the concordat it signed with the Vatican in 1933.		Using a constitutional loophole to avoid elections, Gen. Jorge Ubico begins a second term as president of Guatemala. . . . Catholic and Protestant churches open to worshippers in Veracruz, Mexico, for the first time in years. Masses were banned by order of Governor Aleman.	
Feb. 15		Chancellor Adolf Hitler orders the election of a new General Synod of the German Evangelical Church. . . . After demonstrations by anti-Semitic, fascist groups throughout Romania, Premier George Tatarescu tenders his resignation to King Carol, though it has not been accepted. The King is unhappy with his government's response to the rising power of the fascist Iron Guard. . . . As fighting continues south of Madrid, leftist forces claim that over 1,000 insurgents have been killed in the last two days. . . . The premiers of Greece and Yugoslavia and the foreign ministers of Romania and Turkey meet in Athens as the Balkan Entente, set up by the League of Nations to respond to German rearmament.		Canadian Prime Minister MacKenzie King assures his country that no ties or promises with Great Britain will pull Canada into a war.	Premier Hayashi addresses the Japanese Diet, stressing his desire for harmonious relations with China and the Soviet Union. The Cabinet comes under immediate criticism because none of the parties in the Diet are represented in the Ministry. . . . In China, the Nationalist Party, or Kuomintang, holds its plenary session.
Feb. 16	King Carol of Romania demands the recall of envoys who joined in the fascist Iron Guard march February 13. Italy and Germany have complied; Japan, Portugal, and the former Spanish minister have yet to respond.	Beginning its five-year defense buildup, Britain sets a schedule for completing 12 naval ships, two tank battalions, and multiple air force facilities. . . . Led by Britain, European nations set February 21 as the deadline for banning volunteers to Spain, and (with Portugal dissenting) March 6 as the date for a naval cordon around Spanish ports to prevent intervention. . . . Premier Kyosti Kallio has been elected to a six-year term as president of Finland, unseating the popular incumbent.		Fast-moving forest fires, some deliberately set to clear land, threaten towns in southern Chile.	Chinese Communist armies drop their socialist principles and conform to Nanking's expectations, forming a united front against the Japanese.
Feb. 17		Dr. Norman Bethune of Montreal reports that 150,000 women and children fled Málaga, desperate and near starvation. Some reached Almeira, where German and Italian planes dropped bombs last week.	After five days of heavy rains, the Komati and Umbulusi rivers of Mozambique flood. Up to 2,000 people drown.		In Japan, former minister and liberal politician Yukio Ozaki voices support for a nonaggression pact with Russia, and criticizes the military influence and power.
Feb. 18	The Hague approves a 10 percent increase in defense spending for the Netherland East Indies. The increase includes a purchase of 13 bombers from U.S. manufacturers.			Mexican President Lázaro Cárdenas and Governor Aleman of Veracruz confer. Observers expect that officials will limit the number of priests allowed in certain areas. . . . Former Colombian president and ambassador to the Holy See, Dr. Enrique Olaya Herrera, dies in a Rome clinic. He was expected to become Colombian president again this spring.	Gen. Chang Hsueh-liang, who kidnapped Chiang Kai-shek last year, maintains his military position and is now forgiven by the Nanking government. . . . En route to Washington for a state visit, President Quezon of the Philippines says that Japan is not a threat to his nation.
Feb. 19	According to Japanese newspapers, Japan perceives the U.S. endorsement of Britain's buildup of its navy as a threat to Japanese dominance in the Pacific. . . . Cuba and Great Britain sign a commercial treaty granting Britain tariff concessions and exemptions.	Meetings conclude between Czechoslovakia and the German Activist Party, aimed at mutual understanding of German minorities in that country . . . Fighting around Madrid intensifies as insurgents and loyalists battle for the Valencia Road and Jarama River areas. . . . Pastor Wiesler, a respected churchman who was part Jewish, is found hanging at Sachsenhausen concentration camp in Germany. His death is ruled a suicide; the charges that led to his detainment are never proved.	In Tiberias, Palestine, 30 Jews, 30 Arabs, and British police are injured in a melee that starts with youths throwing oranges.	Cuba begins to deport foreign workers as it threatened, sending 450 Haitians to Port au Prince. Two camps are built to house workers while they await deportation. The goal is to preserve jobs for Cubans. . . . Riots over food and prices break out in Guadalajara, Mexico.	Japan will partially lift its five-year embargo on gold and begin exporting the metal. . . . India's Congress party, which favors separation from Britain, wins control of Bihar and Orissa, and is expected to win in the central provinces, Berar, and Madras. Muslims may share power in three other provinces. . . . At the Kuomintang, offers of compromise and peace are extended to the Chinese Communist forces. Communist leader Chou En-lai indicates compromise will be accepted.

A	B	C	D	E
Includes developments that affect more than one world region, international organizations, and important meetings of world leaders.	Includes all domestic and regional developments in Europe, including the Soviet Union.	Includes all domestic and regional developments in Africa and the Middle East.	Includes all domestic and regional developments in Latin America, the Caribbean, and Canada.	Includes all domestic and regional developments in Asian and Pacific nations (and colonies).

U.S. Politics & Social Issues	U.S. Foreign Policy & Defense	Economics & Great Depression	Science, Technology & Nature	Culture, Leisure & Lifestyle	
		A wage increase of 12 percent benefits 135,000 workers and will cost the textile industry $30 million annually. The three-year contract is won by the Amalgamated Clothing Workers of America. . . . As police block the largest New York hotels to avert the sporadic strikes of building employees, the unions discuss an all-out strike.			Feb. 14
The fate of President Franklin Roosevelt's proposal to change the Supreme Court rests with 34 undecided Senators, most of them Democrats. The House is expected to approve the plan.		In Flint, Mich., 26,500 General Motors employees return to their jobs, and 36,000 more will report in this week. Overall, 70,000 GM workers return to work today. . . . Goodyear and Firestone companies announce pay increases for their employees.	Dust storms spread over four southwestern states.	Sonja Henie performs for a sold-out crowd at Madison Square Garden.	Feb. 15
The Sumners Bill, allowing Supreme Court judges to retire at 70 as President Franklin Roosevelt has proposed, comes to the full Senate. . . . By executive order of the President, all employees of the federal prison system become part of the Civil Service.		President Franklin Roosevelt addresses farm tenancy, asking Congress to work with state and local agencies to correct the poverty and loss of farmers. . . . Packard raises pay by five cents per hour for 12,500 employees in Detroit, and gives a $10 per month increase to salaried workers. . . . In Detroit, the Kelvinator strike ends with a pay increase for employees.	Dr. Wallace H. Carothers, working for Du Pont, receives a patent for nylon, a synthetic fabric.	President Franklin Roosevelt intervenes in the case of James L. Johnson, Jr., who was forced to resign from the Naval Academy, ordering an investigation. . . . Actor John Barrymore files for bankruptcy.	Feb. 16
Two proposals for constitutional amendments changing the Supreme Court are introduced in the Senate. . . . Ten men working on the Golden Gate Bridge in San Francisco, Calif., fall to their deaths as scaffolding collapses.		The United Mine Workers union, representing 400,000, begins negotiations with companies for a new contract. Workers ask for $6 per hour and a 30-hour work week; soft-coal companies offer no increase and a 40-hour week.		In Portland Ore., J. Smutz, formerly May Yohe, recovers after violent hallucinations cause her to try to jump from a moving bus. Smutz was once married to Lord Francis Hope, owner of the Hope diamond, and wore the jewel. She scoffs at the idea of a curse affecting her.	Feb. 17
	During war games on San Clemente Island off California, an exploding shell on the battleship *Wyoming* kills six marines and injures 10 others. . . . President Franklin Roosevelt asks Assistant Secretary of the Navy Charles Edison to investigate the steel shortages holding up construction of navy ships.	The President suggests that Congress legislate crop insurance for farmers, starting in 1938.		Representatives of King Gustav V of Sweden bring the Nobel Prize for Literature to playwright Eugene O'Neill, who is hospitalized in California. . . . The selection of a site in Washington and the design by John Russell Pope for the $3 million Jefferson Memorial is announced.	Feb. 18
		In Anderson, Ind., 19 union members are indicted by a grand jury for their actions in the riot a week ago. . . . In Detroit, five factories are occupied by sit-down strikers, mostly women. . . . In North Chicago, tear gas is thrown during a two-hour battle between police and sit-downers, with little result other than minor injuries. . . . Norman Redwood, a leader in a subway workers' strike, is shot to death in front of his home; police detain other union leaders. A building contractor affected by the strike is later arrested for the murder.			Feb. 19

F	**G**	**H**	**I**	**J**
Includes elections, federal-state relations, civil rights and liberties, crime, the judiciary, education, healthcare, poverty, urban affairs, and population.	Includes formation and debate of U.S. foreign and defense policies, veterans affairs, and defense spending. (Relations with specific foreign countries are usually found under the region concerned.)	Includes business, labor, agriculture, taxation, transportation, consumer affairs, monetary and fiscal policy, natural resources, pollution, and accidents.	Includes worldwide scientific, medical, and technological developments, natural phenomena, U.S. weather, and natural disasters.	Includes the arts, religion, scholarship, communications media, sports, entertainment, fashions, fads, and social life.

	World Affairs	Europe	Africa & The Middle East	The Americas	Asia & The Pacific
Feb. 20	Five hand grenades wound Italian Viceroy Graziani in Addis Ababa, Ethiopia. General Liotta of the East African air forces loses an eye; Coptic prelate Kyrillos and several Ethiopian chieftains are also injured or killed. Initial reports claim the perpetrators escape; later informants say that 40 men are arrested on the spot. . . . The Paraguayan government announces its withdrawal from the League of Nations.			A proposed law in Mexico will create an oil company under the control of the government, and oust foreign oil companies. Stockholders of Petro-Mex have been told that a meeting on March 1 will liquidate that company, of which 49 percent is publicly held. . . . Religious unrest in Mexico spreads north; in Coahuila and Chihuahua Catholics demonstrate over the killing of a priest who was beaten by police. . . . The Cabinet of Colombia's President Lopez Pumarejo resigns in response to the political turmoil caused by the death of Dr. Olaya Herrera, a candidate for the presidency.	Generalissimo Chiang Kai-shek tries to resign from the many offices he holds, but for the second time, his resignations are not accepted by the government.
Feb. 21	The ban on volunteers joining either side in the Spanish civil war is now in effect. Britain, France, Germany, Italy, Sweden, Greece, Portugal, Belgium, and Czechoslovakia have taken action to ensure compliance; the Soviets accept the plan, as do 17 other nations. Current international volunteers are estimated at 60,000 with the insurgents and 35,000 with loyalist troops. . . . Mussolini orders 30,000 Italian troops into Addis Ababa, and arrests 2,000 Ethiopians in response to yesterday's violence. . . . Rioting between Italians and Ethiopians is reported in French Somaliland.	Col. Adam Koc forms the new, one-party government in Poland and invites all Poles to join. The 1935 Constitution, the army, and the Catholic Church will maintain their positions. . . . Spanish insurgents open a new offensive in Oviedo, while continuing to push at Madrid and fight along the Valencia Road. . . . Premier Léon Blum repeats France's need of "breathing space" before the country can tackle social problems with renewed energy.		Rumors of revolution in Honduras are confirmed, and in a three-hour battle near Progreso, 60 are killed. Gen. Justo Umana claims to command 1,000 rebels.	The Japanese Cabinet will try economic and cultural approaches to China, and postpone political moves until relations improve. A truce exists between the Diet and Cabinet. . . . Voting ends in India; 33 million cast ballots.
Feb. 22	Germany declines the League of Nations' invitation to discuss the distribution of raw materials among nations. . . . Premier Benito Mussolini orders death for those who threw the grenades in Ethiopia and death for any chieftains who oppose Italian troops—even those in unoccupied areas of the country. General Liotta's leg has been amputated.	The price of metals jumps as much as 10 percent on European markets. . . . German Foreign Minister Neurath arrives for a visit with Austria's Chancellor Schuschnigg and is met by rioting in Vienna, as between 8,000 and 15,000 Nazis chant slogans. Two hundred Nazis are jailed.		In Brazil, Gen. Miguel Costa and 480 other prisoners appear before a tribunal for their part in a 1935 uprising. . . . The entire Venezuelan Cabinet resigns. Observers say the ministers objected to President Lopez Contreras's methods in stopping leftist demonstrations among students.	Japan arms itself principally in response to Soviet expansion, War Minister General Sugiyama says.
Feb. 23	Former Governor Zoli of Eritrea reveals in Roman newspapers that the grenades thrown in Addis Ababa were intended to kill the viceroy and allow an army of 3,000 to storm Addis Ababa. Most of the rebel troops, two days away from the city, are surrounded and killed by Italian forces. Ras Desta Demtu, a son-in-law of Haile Selassie and one of the rebel leaders, escapes with a few men. In Addis Ababa, all Ethiopians found with guns are executed.	Another insurgent drive begins in Spain, this one in Viver, 34 miles from Valencia—a city subjected to air raids today. Madrid was shelled this afternoon. . . . The government of Germany reveals another 500 million mark public loan. . . . The Romanian Ministers of Justice and the Interior resign. Premier Tatarescu takes over the Interior ministry himself.		Catholics march and demonstrate in Veracruz, demanding the keys to local churches. . . . Canada and Great Britain sign a three-year trade pact allowing Canada free entry for $250 million of goods to Britain.	
Feb. 24	Former Emperor Haile Selassie of Ethiopia accepts an invitation and will send a representative to attend the coronation of King George VI of Britain. The Italian press is outraged. . . . Ras Desta Demtu, who would have been the representative at the coronation, is captured by troops under Italian leadership in Ethiopia and executed. . . . Emilio Darder, mayor of Palma; Alejandro Jaume, envoy of Uruguay; former mayor Antonio Mateo of Inca; and Antonia Ques, a politician, are executed before a jeering crowd in Majorca, Spain. The killings, and many others, are kept secret for weeks.	In another day of intense fighting near Madrid and Oviedo, both sides claim casualties in the thousands. . . . In France and Germany, major rivers flood lowlands, stop ships, and threaten Paris, Cologne, and other cities. . . . Anti-Semitic demonstrations at two Hungarian universities drive Jewish students from schools.		Eduardo Santos is the choice of Colombian liberals to replace presidential candidate Dr. Olaya Herrera.	Fisticuffs break out between two members of Japan's Diet. . . . The Congress Party has taken most of the seats in Madras, Bombay, and the central provinces.
Feb. 25	Three members of the American Joint Distribution Committee return from Poland and report that a third of that country's 3.5 million Jews are in desperate circumstances, facing starvation.	En route from Africa to London, a British liner hits a Spanish sub-sea mine which blows a 15-foot hole in the hull. Tugs pull the ship and its 300 passengers to Marseilles. . . . In Madrid, loyalists set off mines beneath a theater housing insurgents, killing them. . . . The French Senate defeats a bill giving the government power to adjust tariffs.		Accusations of graft against War Minister Niero of Colombia are raised in the House of Representatives.	The Japanese press sees the hundreds of recent military promotions and transfers issued by Japan as a rebuilding of army unity and a consolidation of the army's power.

A	B	C	D	E
Includes developments that affect more than one world region, international organizations, and important meetings of world leaders.	*Includes all domestic and regional developments in Europe, including the Soviet Union.*	*Includes all domestic and regional developments in Africa and the Middle East.*	*Includes all domestic and regional developments in Latin America, the Caribbean, and Canada.*	*Includes all domestic and regional developments in Asian and Pacific nations (and colonies).*

U.S. Politics & Social Issues	U.S. Foreign Policy & Defense	Economics & Great Depression	Science, Technology & Nature	Culture, Leisure & Lifestyle	
	At the request of the Labor Department, Carnegie-Illinois Steel and its affiliate U.S. Steel will set up two plants to comply with standards in the Walsh-Healey Law. The steel companies will sign contracts to supply both the Navy and TVA.	The President signs a bill extending the FHA for another two years.		This week, President Franklin Roosevelt meets with William Andrew Johnson, a 79-year-old former slave who had once been owned by President Andrew Johnson. A Knoxville salesman is trying to secure a pension for Johnson. . . . Harvard anthropologist Earnst Hooton speaks to a Kansas City audience about human evolution, emphasizing the need for sterilization of the unfit to purge our society of imbeciles and morons.	Feb. 20
In his radio address, Rev. Coughlin argues against President Franklin Roosevelt's Supreme Court proposals.		For the third time, Fansteel president R. J. Aitchison refuses an invitation from Governor Henry Horner of Illinois to meet with him and negotiate an end to the sit-down strike in North Chicago. As in Flint, Mich., a court order to remove strikers has not been implemented.	Two flying cars, designed by Walter Waterman, fly from California to Ohio. The Arrowbiles featured detachable wings and a Studebaker engine.		Feb. 21
Congressional hearings on the proposed changes to the judiciary will begin March 9.			The Black Rapids glacier in Alaska sets speed records at 220 feet a day.		Feb. 22
		A Chicago meeting of 16 railroad unions representing 800,000 employees (about 50 percent of the country's rail workers) asks for a 20 cent per hour raise for all. . . . Governor Henry Horner meets separately with CIO men and Fansteel head Aitchison but does not seem hopeful about a settlement. . . . A Douglas aircraft plant in Santa Monica, Calif., is shut down by sit-downers. . . . National Guard troops have been dismissed from duty in Anderson, Ind.			Feb. 23
	The possibility of opening a World War I-era West Virginia factory to supply steel for the U.S. Navy is being studied.		The President urges Congress to create a provisional authority to operate the Bonneville hydroelectric project.	Max Baer, former world heavyweight champ, leaves the State Athletic Commission without a renewal of his license to fight, but with sharp words for the behavior of the commissioners. . . . Yankees owner Colonel Ruppert says Lou Gehrig is offered $31,000—or nothing. Gehrig has yet to sign with the team.	Feb. 24
An anti-lynching bill sponsored by Senators Van Nuys and Wagner is introduced in Congress.	Congress passes a resolution extending until 1940 the President's power to make foreign trade agreements.	Fansteel head Aitchison refuses to recognize the union as talks break down. . . . In California, 350 police, armed with machine guns and indictments, surround 343 strikers in the Douglas plant. The sit-downers submit to arrest, ending their strike. . . . Steel producers begin raising wholesale prices; speculation is that pay increases for employees will follow in order to stave off demands for "closed shop" unions.		*Of Mice and Men*, by John Steinbeck, is published.	Feb. 25
F Includes elections, federal-state relations, civil rights and liberties, crime, the judiciary, education, healthcare, poverty, urban affairs, and population.	**G** Includes formation and debate of U.S. foreign and defense policies, veterans affairs, and defense spending. (Relations with specific foreign countries are usually found under the region concerned.)	**H** Includes business, labor, agriculture, taxation, transportation, consumer affairs, monetary and fiscal policy, natural resources, pollution, and accidents.	**I** Includes worldwide scientific, medical, and technological developments, natural phenomena, U.S. weather, and natural disasters.	**J** Includes the arts, religion, scholarship, communications media, sports, entertainment, fashions, fads, and social life.	

	World Affairs	Europe	Africa & The Middle East	The Americas	Asia & The Pacific
Feb. 26	Japan will press for free markets and access to raw materials for all colonial territories at the next League of Nations conference.	After verbal battles over financial policies in the Chamber of Deputies, French Premier Léon Blum survives a vote of confidence. . . .The success of German Foreign Minister Neurath's visit to Austria is debated; Chancellor Schuschnigg insists that the restoration of the Hapsburg monarchy, which Germany opposes, is an internal question for Austrians to decide. . . . Former President Schultess of the Swiss Federal Council received Chancellor Hitler's promise to respect Swiss neutrality, according to current President Motta.. . . Insurgent Gen. Quiepo de Llano fires on and seizes a Netherlands ship, claiming it is carrying war material to loyalists.	A curfew is imposed on Latakia, Syria, after clashes between French troops and the Iron Shirts (Syrian fascists) kill 11 and injure more than 40.	Colonel Batista of the Cuban army declines presidential candidacy but calls for a new constitution in his country. . . . Mexican Catholics from Veracruz try to petition the president and others to turn over church keys, but without success.	In Osaka, Japan, 300 geishas retreat to a mountainside temple in what the press terms a sit-down strike.
Feb. 27	Ernest Hemingway embarks for Spain as a journalist. . . . Italian officials claim the numbers reported killed in Ethiopia are pure speculation, and that such information is not in the public domain, nor is it anyone else's business. Reports circulate that as many as 6,000 Ethiopians were killed.	The buying and selling of foreign securities is forbidden in Germany, unless the securities are sold to the government-controlled Reichsbank. . . . German churches are urged by the government to voluntarily share their lands with the landless, or be forced to do so in the future. . . . Premier Hodza says Czechoslovakia will cooperate with the German Sudeten Party to improve the employment of the German minority, who make up 22 percent of the population. . . . Both Madrid and Valencia face food shortages and shelling by insurgents.		In Colombia, Eduardo Santos severs ties with the newspaper *Tiempo*, freeing himself for presidential candidacy. President Lopez Pumarejo fills the vacancies in his Cabinet. . . . As Catholics arm themselves, Veracruz officials impose censorship over the press. . . . Mexican President Lázaro Cárdenas budgets $14 million for education over six years, half of the funds dedicated to improving American Indian education. . . . The Supreme Court in Mexico voids leases held by a Mexican subsidiary of Royal Dutch Shell Oil.	Japan's Diet is informed of a defensive first-strike plan for use against enemy air bases, developed by the army and navy. . . . Mohandas Gandhi walks seven miles to attend a Congress Party meeting. This is his first involvement in politics since 1934.
Feb. 28	The eldest son of Haile Selassie will journey from Jerusalem to represent his father at the coronation of George VI.	Democrats interrupt a Nazi party meeting in Belgrade, Yugoslavia; the resulting melee leaves 11 injured. . . . In Aussig, Nazi leader Konrad Henlein denounces official tolerance of Bolsheviks and demands full autonomy for Germans in Czechoslovakia. . . . Soviet authorities order the transfer of 2.25 million acres from state farms into farming collectives by April. . . . A French cargo ship hits a mine off the Catalan coast. Despite damage, the ship gets to a Spanish harbor; no injuries are reported.		Buses carry anti-Catholic demonstrators to a gathering of 5,000 before a Cordoba, Veracruz, church, where Catholics barricade themselves inside to pray. . . . Gambling is now legal in Panama. Bids for casino concessions are due March 8.	A law ensuring male succession is passed in Manchukuo, where Henry Pi Yu, or Kang Teh, the former emperor of China, is now Emperor. . . . Hundreds of Japanese soldiers arrive at Peiping in north China as replacements, authorities say, for troops that will return home.
Mar. 1	The Soviet news agency TASS publishes evidence that Japan spied on Russia and links it to Trotsky.	Three members of the Iron Guard, a fascist group, stab and beat Prof. Trajan Ratu, rector of Jassy University in Romania. . . . The U.S. Consulate in Málaga opens after a five-month closure. . . . Lloyd's of London raises its rates to insure cargo on ships traveling in the mined waters near Spanish ports. . . . The new Polish government party assumes the name Camp of National Unity. Col. Adam Koc invites all Poles to join, but not Jews. . . . President Kallio, a farmer, is inaugurated in Finland.		Mexico nationalizes its oil production after stockholders of Petro-Mex vote to dissolve the company. President Lázaro Cárdenas signs a decree setting up the new company under full government ownership.	
Mar. 2	While allowing the registration of German bonds for U.S. investors, the SEC warns that Germany has undisclosed debts of up to 5 billion reichsmarks. . . . The League of Nations reports that four democracies—the United States, Britain, the Netherlands, and France—hold 60 percent of the world's raw materials.	Universities in Romania close and the government is torn over the fascist attack yesterday. . . . The Fascist Grand Council of Italy approves five years of military increases, including the total militarization of males between 18 and 55. . . . Britain's navy announces specifics for its defense spending: 70 cruisers and 5,300 aircraft by 1939, 25 capital ships by 1942. . . . Foreign Minister Anthony Eden reiterates Britain's determination to not give any territory to satisfy Germany's demands for the return of its colonies.		By executive decree, President Lázaro Cárdenas creates a new oil administration in Mexico, able to regulate exports and prices. As foreign leases expire, the president may turn them over to National Petroleum; all new resources are also within his power to assign.	The Congress Party, under the leadership of Pandit Nehru, now controls six of 11 provinces in India and continues to work against the constitution.

A	B	C	D	E
Includes developments that affect more than one world region, international organizations, and important meetings of world leaders.	*Includes all domestic and regional developments in Europe, including the Soviet Union.*	*Includes all domestic and regional developments in Africa and the Middle East.*	*Includes all domestic and regional developments in Latin America, the Caribbean, and Canada.*	*Includes all domestic and regional developments in Asian and Pacific nations (and colonies).*

U.S. Politics & Social Issues	U.S. Foreign Policy & Defense	Economics & Great Depression	Science, Technology & Nature	Culture, Leisure & Lifestyle	
		Gas canisters fly into the North Chicago Fansteel plant in the early morning. Strikers fight police for an hour, but are ultimately forced from the plant. . . . In Detroit, where 22 plants are affected by sit-down strikes, Governor Frank Murphy sends a state labor commissioner to open a local office and offer mediation services where needed.		Boxer Max Baer gets his license to fight from a unanimous athletic commission.	Feb. 26
President Franklin Roosevelt sends all governors a "model soil law" aimed at imposing standards on farmers to conserve soil. . . . Six movie theaters, all under the same management, are targets of tear and mustard gas bombs that drive patrons out into the night. Labor problems are suspected. . . . General Motors President Alfred Sloan unveils his nonprofit foundation, which will underwrite economic research.				Baseball's new Negro American League announces the schedule of its inaugural season.	Feb. 27
		Meyer Adelman, a leader in the Fansteel strike, is arrested in Wisconsin on charges of conspiracy and contempt.	Howard Hughes wins the Harmon Trophy in Paris, awarded by the International League of Aviators for outstanding achievement.	Ninety-eight American writers publish a declaration against the killing of civilians in Spain, and urge Americans to take a moral stand. Carl Sandburg, Langston Hughes, Thornton Wilder, Upton Sinclair, and Dorothy Parker are some of the signatories.	Feb. 28
The Supreme Court favors the New Deal in a split decision on currency vs. gold payments, affirming Congress' power over the monetary system. . . . The President signs the Sumners Bill.	The Senate hears arguments on the Pittman Neutrality Bill.	Philip Murray of the Steel Workers Organizing Committee and Benjamin Fairless, chairman of Carnegie-Illinois Steel, conduct contract negotiations. The meeting is a surprise to the public. . . . The courts limit pickets at the Fansteel plant and forbid mass meetings of strikers in the county. . . . Hosiery mills in Pennsylvania shut down as thousands of workers there begin a strike.			Mar. 1
	Leading steel companies adopt a 40-hour workweek and will bid on naval needs for 25 million pounds of steel.	The President sends a report on the old NRA to Congress, hoping that ways can be found to rewrite the act and avoid past pitfalls. . . . Carnegie Illinois Steel agreed to an eight-hour workday, 40-hour week, a wage increase, and overtime pay to apply to all employees, not just union members. . . . Douglas Aircraft in Santa Monica gives a five-cent per hour raise to employees. . . . The hosiery strike spreads.	Howard Hughes receives the Harmon Trophy for aviation from President Franklin Roosevelt in the Oval Office.	The film *Lost Horizon* premiers in San Francisco.	Mar. 2

F	G	H	I	J
Includes elections, federal-state relations, civil rights and liberties, crime, the judiciary, education, healthcare, poverty, urban affairs, and population.	Includes formation and debate of U.S. foreign and defense policies, veterans affairs, and defense spending. (Relations with specific foreign countries are usually found under the region concerned.)	Includes business, labor, agriculture, taxation, transportation, consumer affairs, monetary and fiscal policy, natural resources, pollution, and accidents.	Includes worldwide scientific, medical, and technological developments, natural phenomena, U.S. weather, and natural disasters.	Includes the arts, religion, scholarship, communications media, sports, entertainment, fashions, fads, and social life.

	World Affairs	Europe	Africa & The Middle East	The Americas	Asia & The Pacific
Mar. 3		Premier Colijn of the Netherlands opens an international conference on trade barriers and economic cooperation among the members of the Oslo Confederation: Belgium, Luxemburg, Denmark, Sweden, Finland, and Norway. . . . Toledo is the focus of fighting in Spain, as loyalists try to retake the city. . . . Austrian Chancellor Schuschnigg cancels a trip to Rome due to Italy's resistance toward restoring the Hapsburgs to power. . . . Negotiations for a trade pact between France and Germany open in Berlin.		Eight men are hospitalized and 66 jailed after labor violence erupts in a Sarnia, Ontario, metal foundry. Non-union workers drive sit-down strikers out in a two-hour battle.	President Quezon of the Philippines begins trade talks in Washington with U.S. officials, in anticipation of his country's 1946 independence.
Mar. 4	Germany protests remarks made by Mayor Fiorello LaGuardia of New York, insulting Adolf Hitler. The mayor's comments were made at a fundraiser to combat Nazism.	To increase Italy's population, the government orders that favoritism for parents of large families in employment, pay, loans, and other areas be legislated. . . . A report on Jews in Germany shows that of 409,000 still there, 14 percent are without work, 20 percent live in poverty, and most would like to leave the country, but cannot. . . . A Greek vessel hits a mine off the Spanish coast; 21 sailors die in the explosion.		A revolt over water use near a rural Mexican town results in the murder of seven soldiers, the execution of five rebel leaders, and the jailing of 100 of the 800 citizens of Xalatiaco.	
Mar. 5	Secretary of State Cordell Hull apologizes to Germany for Mayor LaGuardia's remarks.	After much debate, France passes financial measures to shore up confidence in trade, reduce unemployment, and stabilize the franc. A defense loan will be made soon and may be paid in gold. . . . Government leaders in Hungary are warned that a German minority, bolstered by foreign support, plans a pro-Nazi takeover.		Premier MacKenzie King of Canada visits Washington, spending the night at the White House.	
Mar. 6	Treasury Secretary Henry Morgenthau denies a request to appoint a New York bank to act as an agent for France's new $1 billion defense loan. . . . The third day of riots between European and native employees leads to several deaths at mines in the French colony of Tunisia. French troops are being rushed to trouble spots.	French maritime workers call a strike and bring the port of Bordeaux to a halt, allowing only foreign vessels to leave. . . . An insurgent cruiser attacks a Spanish-owned passenger ship, killing several women and children. The 180 passengers are refugees returning home to Bilbao.	Authorities hope a curfew curbs the random violent acts perpetrated by Arabs and Jews in Palestine. . . . Egypt formally asks for admission to the League of Nations.	Bowing to criticism from the Senate, President Laredo Bru of Cuba asks for ratification of a trade treaty made with Britain last month. . . . Catholics in Veracruz begin a campaign of passive resistance and boycotts, hoping to persuade the government to reopen churches.	The geisha strike ends in Osaka. Police help negotiate a settlement that includes recognition of their union. . . . Japan agrees to allow $3 million worth of seized properties in Japan to revert to foreign ownership in 1942.
Mar. 7		Ships of Norwegian and British registry are stopped by insurgent ships near Spain, who demand they go to Ceuta, in Spanish Morocco. Most refuse. . . . Dock workers in Bordeaux return to work after favorable negotiations.		Elections take place in Chile after six months of political uncertainty. Right-wing majorities win seats in the Chamber of Deputies and Senate.	Rumors report famine and uprisings in the Szechwan province of China.
Mar. 8	The United States joins 14 other nations at a League of Nations conference in Geneva, Switzerland, to discuss the distribution of sources of raw materials. . . . The wife of Rabbi Stephen S. Wise of New York writes to Secretary of State Cordell Hull, protesting the insults hurled at Mayor Fiorello LaGuardia and the women of New York in the German press. She asks him to take action. . . . The German newspaper *Angriff* prints a long quote deriding Jews, attributing it (falsely) to Benjamin Franklin.	Insurgents in Spain, with 250 tanks and 70 planes, launch a surprise attack on Gaudalajara, northeast of Madrid. . . . An insurgent ship attacks an arms-laden vessel that sailed out of New York two months ago, headed for Spain. Passengers and crew are rescued after the shelling in the Bay of Biscay. . . . Italian newspapers suggest that Italy used diplomatic channels to thwart a plot to restore the Hapsburg monarchy in Austria. . . . Germany denies as "libel" the charge that it supported a planned coup in Hungary. . . . Turkey's budget for 1937–38 is revealed, with $80 million marked for defense projects. . . . In a speech at a Swedish university, Danish Premier Stauning rejects a pan-Scandinavian defense responsibility, saying that Denmark is not "a watchdog or guardian for Scandinavia." . . . Two hundred professors in Romania threaten to strike over a new law forcing them to teach "political education" in conformance with government policy.		President Getulio Vargas of Brazil intervenes in Matto Grosso, an area troubled for two months by often violent conflict between the governor and assembly of the area.	Japan's new Foreign Minister Sato promises to treat China as an equal and correct past mistakes.

A	B	C	D	E
Includes developments that affect more than one world region, international organizations, and important meetings of world leaders.	*Includes all domestic and regional developments in Europe, including the Soviet Union.*	*Includes all domestic and regional developments in Africa and the Middle East.*	*Includes all domestic and regional developments in Latin America, the Caribbean, and Canada.*	*Includes all domestic and regional developments in Asian and Pacific nations (and colonies).*

U.S. Politics & Social Issues	U.S. Foreign Policy & Defense	Economics & Great Depression	Science, Technology & Nature	Culture, Leisure & Lifestyle	
	The Neutrality Act (Pittman Bill) passes the Senate, replacing neutrality acts passed in 1935–36, and giving the President power to restrict trade and travel to belligerents in foreign wars (or civil wars). The House will debate the Bill March 9. . . . The State Department announces a ban on travel to Spain for all Americans—ambulance workers included.	Steel stocks advance by up to seven points because of the labor settlement of Carnegie-Illinois. . . . A truck is torched on the second day of a truck-drivers' strike in Rhode Island involving 2,000 men.	The General Wildlife Federation, with J.N. Darling as its head, is formed during a St. Louis meeting of 1,000 people concerned about conservation of land and water resources.	Albert Einstein becomes honorary chairman of the American Committee Appeal for the Jews in Poland, a group hoping to raise $1 million for its cause in 1937.	Mar. 3
Citing the problems confronting the nation, and the Supreme Court's stance against solving them, President Franklin Roosevelt frames his judicial restructuring along party lines, and demands action from Democrats.		U.S. Steel Corp. says steel prices will rise from $3 to $8 per ton on April 1. . . . With a half-million steel workers in the labor organizations affiliated with John L. Lewis and the CIO (Committee on Industrial Organization), William Green demands that unions affiliated with his AFL (American Federation of Labor), as well as state and local labor boards, not support the CIO.		Luise Rainer, Paul Muni, and *The Great Ziegfeld* win Academy Awards.	Mar. 4
	The House passes a half-billion dollar Naval Appropriations Bill, which goes to the Senate next. . . . The U.S. Embassy in Addis Ababa, Ethiopia, will close on March 31, and its officials are recalled.	After a nine-hour meeting between unions, companies, and the governor of Rhode Island, the truckers' strike ends peacefully. . . . The United Auto Workers union serves an ultimatum to Chrysler, demanding to represent its 67,000 workers. . . . In Chicago, 6,000 cab drivers are on strike.		*Life* magazine announces that its circulation has passed one million.	Mar. 5
		Firestone Rubber closes its plants and 10,000 are out of work. Strikers demand recognition of their union as sole bargaining agent. . . . Six governors of heavily industrialized states meet with President Franklin Roosevelt, airing concerns about cuts in WPA relief that their states cannot afford. . . . A three-hour sit-down strike against Chevrolet in Flint, Mich., ends when all parties agree to negotiate on March 8.			Mar. 6
		Strikers at Bethlehem Steel in Lebanon, Penn., demand a minimum daily wage of $5 and want the CIO as their union.		The body of expatriate Russian journalist and adventurer Serge Zolotoohin is found in the sea near his empty yacht. His wife, missing, is believed drowned as well.	Mar. 7
		Forced to answer "yes" or "no," Chrysler rejects the demand of workers to be exclusively represented by the United Auto Workers. Sit-down strikes spread through all its plants. . . . Twelve of the 24 hosiery mills in Reading, Penn., are occupied by sit-down strikers. . . . A strike against Chevrolet plants (part of General Motors) recommences, then breaks up once more as negotiations continue. An estimated 13,200 employees are affected. . . . In St. Louis, Mo., electrical workers walk off their jobs. . . . Garment workers, printers, coffin makers, and laborers in many industries and locations call strikes for better wages and working conditions and union representation.	An earthquake hits the Great Lakes area just before midnight and is felt south to Tennessee and Kentucky. Centered in Anna, Ohio, it is the second shaker in one week. It probably measures 5.4, the largest quake to ever hit Ohio.	An amendment allowing divorce in 30 days is introduced in Nevada, because Idaho recently reduced its residency requirement to six weeks, providing some competition for divorces. . . . Yale University starts a Roosevelt-for-King club, which spreads to other universities. Plans for Franklin I's coronation are under way.	Mar. 8

F	G	H	I	J
Includes elections, federal-state relations, civil rights and liberties, crime, the judiciary, education, healthcare, poverty, urban affairs, and population.	*Includes formation and debate of U.S. foreign and defense policies, veterans affairs, and defense spending. (Relations with specific foreign countries are usually found under the region concerned.)*	*Includes business, labor, agriculture, taxation, transportation, consumer affairs, monetary and fiscal policy, natural resources, pollution, and accidents.*	*Includes worldwide scientific, medical, and technological developments, natural phenomena, U.S. weather, and natural disasters.*	*Includes the arts, religion, scholarship, communications media, sports, entertainment, fashions, fads, and social life.*

	World Affairs	Europe	Africa & The Middle East	The Americas	Asia & The Pacific
Mar. 9	British troops battle rebels led by the Islamic "holy man of Ipi" in Waziristan, a province of northwest India. . . . European miners in Tunis threaten to strike if the native miners unionize. Tunisian miners agree to submit grievances to an "umpire."	The Romanian government drops last month's demands that German and Italian envoys be recalled. . . . Italian soldiers, 14,000–16,000 strong, are deployed in the new insurgent offensive, 28 miles north of Guadalajara. . . . Germany adopts a measure allowing the seizure of foreigners and their possessions as retaliation, in case foreign countries take measures against Reich citizens or property.		President Anastasio Somoza of Nicaragua fixes the exchange rate at two cordobas per dollar, to speed shipments of coffee and halt speculation. . . . Chile's Finance Minister Gustavo Ross resigns, shocking his right-wing constituents. It is believed he resigned because the government now includes elected socialists and fascists.	
Mar. 10	Italian Premier Benito Mussolini cruises to Tobruk in North Africa, the first stop on a tour of Italian colonies. . . . The U.S. Ambassador in Berlin is instructed to protest the often-obscene comments about New York's Mayor Fiorello LaGuardia in the German press.	Insurgent forces push 12 miles closer to Guadalajara. . . . Reich Church Minister Hans Kerrl has lost Hitler's confidence and is unofficially stripped of authority . . . Premier Daranyi of Hungary claims talk of outside influence threatening his country's sovereignty is hysterical and unfounded.			President Quezon says he plans programs for agricultural and industrial growth in the Philippines, and urges the United States to grant full independence soon.
Mar. 11	Marshall Balbo, governor of Libya, welcomes Premier Mussolini to Tobruk.	France opens subscriptions for a loan of 5 billion francs, the first installment of a 10.5 billion franc total. Ninety percent of the loan is for defense. . . . Germany announces that shops will be labeled as German or Jewish, and that Germans will be forbidden to buy from or consort with Jewish merchants. . . . Fistfights break out in the Belgian Senate between Rexists and liberals. Order is restored in an hour, and apologies tendered.		Brazil's Senate votes to extend the state of war (martial law) for 90 days.	Former Japanese minister Ozaki asks publicly why Japan is rearming. . . . Japan's Premier Hayashi moves into a new "assassination-proof" home. . . . Two million Chinese in the Honan province suffer from a famine.
Mar. 12	U.S. Ambassador Dodd meets with German Foreign Minister Neurath and delivers a rebuke over obscene and vicious remarks in the German press. . . . In Derna, Libya, Premier of Italy Benito Mussolini dedicates the 1,250-mile coastal highway. . . . The League of Nations conference on raw materials adjourns until June 21, unwilling to discuss the transfer of colonial territories, "from whence raw materials are drawn."	Germany suggests to Britain a non-aggression pact between Germany, France, and Belgium, overseen by Britain and Italy, without League of Nations involvement. . . . Former prime minister David Lloyd George scolds Britain for neglecting the "food front" in its defense plans, pointing out the danger of food shortages during a war. . . . Rebel forces in Spain, six miles from Guadalajara, are stopped by loyalists using 70 Russian tanks. . . . Bolstering Spanish claims that Italy is waging an undeclared war in Spain, captured Italian prisoners confirm that 40,000 to 50,000 Italians serve with Franco's insurgents. . . . Splitting the German church into two bodies, one Christian and one Nationalistic, is suggested in a proclamation from the combined Lutheran Bishops and Confessional Synods.		Roberto Garcia, mayor of Matamoros, Mexico, is assassinated and a political rival is arrested for the crime.	
Mar. 13	Rude jokes about New York and its mayor cease, but no apology is received from Germany.	The French government takes over the Creusot Steel Works, a large private arms factory, through use of the Nationalization Law. . . . Czech Premier Hodza promises protections to Jewish schools and groups in his country. . . . Danish Premier Stauning retreats from his remarks of March 8, saying he would discuss defense with other northern rulers.		A three-day rail strike in Colombia ends with President Lopez's promise to arbitrate the disputes with the Railways Council. . . . Cuba and Chile sign a trade treaty, as storms destroy crops in southern Chile. . . . President Lázaro Cárdenas of Mexico inaugurates an archaeological site in Oaxaca, where Dr. Alfonso Caso found three Mixteca tombs earlier in the week. . . . Venezuela exiles 48 Communists.	A drought in the Szechwan province of China has killed 3,000 since January 1, while famine in Honan kills thousands as well.
Mar. 14		Germany protests Yugoslavia's cutting of export to Germany by 50 percent, due to an unpaid 8 million marks.	Two Jewish shepherds are killed by Arab raiders.	President Lázaro Cárdenas of Mexico announced that citizens have "complete liberty" to attend church. He remains opposed to priests interfering in politics. . . . Dead birds and fish line Peru's coast, as happened in 1925. A phenomenon known as the El Niño current, bringing water from the Equator, may be responsible.	Japan's Premier Hayashi endorses the suggestion that the military tend its own business and not interfere in financial and administrative matters. . . . Japan's military appears to be withdrawing from parts of the Chahar province in China.

A	B	C	D	E
Includes developments that affect more than one world region, international organizations, and important meetings of world leaders.	*Includes all domestic and regional developments in Europe, including the Soviet Union.*	*Includes all domestic and regional developments in Africa and the Middle East.*	*Includes all domestic and regional developments in Latin America, the Caribbean, and Canada.*	*Includes all domestic and regional developments in Asian and Pacific nations (and colonies).*

U.S. Politics & Social Issues	U.S. Foreign Policy & Defense	Economics & Great Depression	Science, Technology & Nature	Culture, Leisure & Lifestyle	
In a "fireside chat," President Franklin Roosevelt points out how the Supreme Court has hampered economic and social recovery, and urges the nation to trust him to reinvigorate the judiciary.		Governor of Michigan Frank Murphy cuts short a Florida vacation to negotiate a settlement between Chrysler and striking employees. The dispute has now idled 69,000 workers. . . . The CIO will begin drives to enroll 2.25 million workers in the oil and textile industries, and will organize itself into state and local bodies, as the AFL does. . . . Gunfire erupts in the Chicago taxi strike, leading to arrests but no injuries. . . . The service employees of ten New York apartment buildings strike for six hours. . . . Chicago's meat packing houses announce a pay increase of nine cents per hour for 200,000 employees nationwide.	Manila, capital of the Philippines, is rattled by a sharp earthquake.	Paul Elmer More, American educator, essayist, and leader of New Humanism, dies.	Mar. 9
A disagreement over whether New York or Montreal will be the terminal for transatlantic flights is all that holds up a deal between Pan American and Imperial Airways of Great Britain for air service between the two countries.		In court, Chrysler charges the CIO, UAWA, their heads, and the strikers with conspiracy in refusing to vacate Chrysler property. . . . Further strikes erupt in major cities; in Detroit, the 12-story Crowley Milner & Co. department store is forced to close when employees walk out at noon.		Due to nervous exhaustion, Noel Coward closes his successful New York show, *Tonight at Eight-thirty*. At least $24,000 in ticket refunds will be made.	Mar. 10
		Negotiations stall as General Motors accuses the union of permitting 18 sit-down strikes since the February 11 agreement that ended the Flint strike. The United Auto Workers of America Union claims its members are discriminated against by GM. . . . Labor Secretary Frances Perkins publicly invites James Rand, president of Remington Rand Corp., to meet her and attempt to resolve the 10-month-long strike at his company. . . . Firestone Tire employees call a strike, having been out of work since March 6.			Mar. 11
		Michigan Governor Frank Murphy returns from vacation to mediate in labor disputes, but General Motors and its employees have settled their strike. The contract between union and GM bans future sit-down strikes. . . . The Western Electric Company in Chicago raises pay for 12,000 employees by 10 cents per hour. Several Illinois area factories and plants raise wages as well: Bendix, Caterpillar, Fairbanks, Morse & Co., and others. Thirteen labor disputes idling 9,000 workers are ongoing in Chicago alone. . . . Chrysler says that as its offices and records are held by strikers, it cannot make its payroll.		Charles-Marie Widor, French composer, dies. . . . Joe DiMaggio signs with the Yankees for his second year as a major-league player for an undisclosed amount. Rumors say he doubled his salary of last year, $8,500.	Mar. 12
Senator Wheeler of Montana and Indian Affairs Commissioner John Collier clash over whether the government should pay to maintain communities on tribal lands, or push for the integration of American Indians into urban areas.	The State Department will issue passports to Spain to physicians, nurses, and healthcare workers.	Chrysler argues for the removal of sit-down strikers in court while pickets parade outside. The hearing will continue on Monday.		Elihu Thomson, scientist, friend of Thomas Edison, and holder of 800 patents, dies.	Mar. 13
For the third time, a New York temple is defaced with swastikas. Such vandalism occurs sporadically throughout the city.		Union delegates sign an accord after 13 hours of discussion, ending the strife between auto workers and General Motors. . . . The National Labor Relations Board rules that Remington Rand Corp. resorted to bribery and lies, acting ruthlessly and illegally in trying to break the strike against it. The NLRB orders the company to reemploy up to 4,000 workers, and to bargain with an AFL-chartered union.			Mar. 14

F	G	H	I	J
Includes elections, federal-state relations, civil rights and liberties, crime, the judiciary, education, healthcare, poverty, urban affairs, and population.	*Includes formation and debate of U.S. foreign and defense policies, veterans affairs, and defense spending. (Relations with specific foreign countries are usually found under the region concerned.)*	*Includes business, labor, agriculture, taxation, transportation, consumer affairs, monetary and fiscal policy, natural resources, pollution, and accidents.*	*Includes worldwide scientific, medical, and technological developments, natural phenomena, U.S. weather, and natural disasters.*	*Includes the arts, religion, scholarship, communications media, sports, entertainment, fashions, fads, and social life.*

	World Affairs	Europe	Africa & The Middle East	The Americas	Asia & The Pacific
Mar. 15		In the worst of winter weather, fresh loyalist troops join the front in Guadalajara. Constant shelling of Madrid continues. General Franco announces that the city is doomed to fall. . . . Twelve Jewish students from Warsaw University are attacked by Nazi students and hospitalized. . . . Chancellor Adolf Hitler meets with Denmark's King Christian; speculation is that they discuss a nonaggression pact. . . . Marie, the queen mother of Romania, recovers from illness amid rumors of poison.	Tensions in Palestine increase as Arab raiders shoot and kill three Jewish travelers. Other attacks, including bombs, are reported—all aimed at Jews.	Peasants protest the seizure of communally held land for redistribution in Ixtlahuaca, Mexico. Twelve are killed in rioting.	
Mar. 16	Premier Benito Mussolini of Italy, cheered by 100,000 people, enters Tripoli on a white charger, in a display of pageantry and triumph.	A film showing and counterdemonstration between fascist and socialist groups in Clichy, France, becomes a riot. Police fire on the crowd, killing five and injuring 150. . . . Stockholders of the Reichsbank meet; a secret debt of 20 billion marks is disclosed. . . . Insurgent air strikes kill seven in Barcelona, but Guadalajara is the scene of the most intense fighting. Loyalists claim to have dropped 760 bombs on Brihuega, a town occupied by insurgents since last week.		After 18 months of legal wrangling, the government of Bolivia accuses Standard Oil of fraud by evading royalty payments, cancels its leases, and seizes its wells and property.	
Mar. 17	The February 24 public execution in Majorca, Spain, of an Uruguayan diplomat and other prominent men is revealed. The men were shot by rebels before a jeering crowd of 3,000 in a cemetery. Other political prisoners are still held in the prison, and it is feared that thousands may have been executed there. . . . Secret negotiations continue in Paris aimed at ending the strife between Arabs and Zionists in Palestine. . . . In Tripoli before 100,000, Premier of Italy Benito Mussolini emotionally pledges peace, confirms rearmament, promises protection and prosperity to Muslims under the Italian flag, and accuses the League of Nations of attempting to "throttle" Italy. Later in the day he promises protection to the Jews of Libya as well.	Britain begins investigation of charges that Italy landed troops in Cadiz on March 5, violating the nonintervention pact of February 20. The investigation will be turned over to the League of Nations.			Japan will not obey a London pact of 1936 limiting guns on naval ships to 14 inches.
Mar. 18	Haile Selassie asks the League of Nations to conduct an inquiry and record the horrors of last month's massacres in Ethiopia. . . . The Pope issues an encyclical condemning communism. . . . Loyalist forces retake the Spanish colony of Rio de Oro in Africa. . . . At Bu Grara, Libya, Premier Benito Mussolini of Italy receives a gem-studded sword from Muslims and again pledges protection to them.	Loyalist forces retake the town of Brihuega, north of Madrid. Millions of rounds of ammunition, mortars, grenades, and machine guns are abandoned on the road by retreating insurgents. Italian losses are 650 lives and nearly 2,000 injuries. . . . A half-day strike of 1 million workers is held in Paris to protest fascism and the deaths during a riot two days ago.		In Brazil, 40 prisoners held in connection with the 1935 revolt are freed for lack of evidence.	President Manuel Quezon of the Philippines, clarifying remarks made earlier, gives 1939 as a target date for Philippine independence. . . . The All-India Congress in Delhi authorizes elected Congressmen to accept their offices, cooperating with other parties in spite of their desire for complete independence.
Mar. 19		Italy will boycott the upcoming coronation of George VI due to the invitation extended to Haile Selassie of Ethiopia. . . . Propaganda Minister Joseph Goebbels is behind the ownership change of UFA, Germany's largest and last remaining independent film production company. . . . Loyalist General Miaja announces a 10-mile gain of land beyond Guadalajara, while insurgents claim to take a strategic hill near the Jarama Valley. . . . France's rearmament plans are unveiled; they exceed present funding.			

A	B	C	D	E
Includes developments that affect more than one world region, international organizations, and important meetings of world leaders.	Includes all domestic and regional developments in Europe, including the Soviet Union.	Includes all domestic and regional developments in Africa and the Middle East.	Includes all domestic and regional developments in Latin America, the Caribbean, and Canada.	Includes all domestic and regional developments in Asian and Pacific nations (and colonies).

U.S. Politics & Social Issues	U.S. Foreign Policy & Defense	Economics & Great Depression	Science, Technology & Nature	Culture, Leisure & Lifestyle	
The Supreme Court outlaws special taxes imposed on a government official, but the case raises many questions. The Court recesses for two weeks without ruling on the Wagner Act.		A sit-down strike at the Brooklyn Jewish Hospital ends as police, with a court order charging organizers with endangering patients, use operating tables and axes to break down doors and remove strikers. . . . A Michigan judge orders strikers out of Chrysler plants by 9:20 a.m. on March 17. . . . In defiance of the NLRB order to reinstate employees, Remington Rand says it will take the NLRB to court. . . . General Electric sits with CIO and union representatives to discuss company-wide benefits and wages.		Writer H. P. Lovecraft dies of cancer in Rhode Island at age 46. . . . Congress passes a bill allowing acceptance of the art and money gifted by Andrew Mellon.	Mar. 15
		Department store clerks of H.L. Green strike and bar customers from five New York stores. . . . The nation's railroads and 21 unions agree on pensions for 1.5 million employees, to be legislated by Congress. . . . While Michigan Governor Frank Murphy conducts all-day talks, Chrysler sit-down strikers arm themselves with tools and vow not to be evicted. . . . New Jersey is hit with several sit-down strikes, in spite of the governor's boasts last month that such actions would not be tolerated.		Sir Austen Chamberlin, a Nobel Peace Prize winner for his work in crafting the Locarno Pact, dies.	Mar. 16
Sit-down strikes are denounced in the Senate during debates.		Two hundred cab drivers riot in Chicago's loop, battling police and scabs and wrecking cabs. Their strike is in its 12th day and idles 5,500 drivers. The riot was touched off by the hiring of strikebreakers to drive cabs in the Loop at $7 per day. . . . In Detroit, 30,000 pickets support 6,000 sit-down strikers in Chrysler plants. Governor Frank Murphy threatens to use force to ensure public safety. . . . A second strike at Brooklyn Jewish Hospital results in 39 arrests and 66 firings. . . . The NLRB asks a federal court to enforce its orders to Remington Rand Corp.	After extensive tests and preparations, Amelia Earhart embarks on her 27,000-mile world flight from Oakland, traveling toward Hawaii. . . . At 30,000 watts, the world's most powerful television station is planned for France's World's Fair. Its antenna will sit atop the Eiffel Tower.		Mar. 17
The New London School in Texas explodes when a spark from an electric tool ignites gas. Between 298 to 319 are killed, many of them children. Rescuers dig through the night, fearing that as many as 600 are lost. One of the reporters covering the story is a rookie named Walter Cronkite.		Secretary of Labor Frances Perkins brokers a tentative agreement between the Remington Rand Corp. and the AFL's William Green, representing striking workers. . . . The CIO kicks off an effort to unionize 1.25 million textile workers. . . . Numerous strikes in varied industries continue nationwide.	Amelia Earhart lands her $80,000 "flying laboratory" in Honolulu and spends the night, waiting for good weather.	A source close to David O. Selznick reveals that Miriam Hopkins will play Scarlett O'Hara, and Janet Gaynor will portray Melanie in Gone with the Wind. Male leads will be Clark Gable and Leslie Howard. . . . Lou Gehrig signs with the Yankees for $36,000 plus a $750 signing bonus.	Mar. 18
		A Detroit court orders the arrest of 6,000 Chrysler sit-down strikers on contempt charges, but Sheriff Thomas Wilcox does not have the manpower to enforce the order. . . . Police end seven sit-down strikes in food plants and shoe stores. A drug store chain, hotels, and a trucking company settle their strikes with pay increases, while a new strike is called in a creamery—all in Detroit. Other large cities have similar situations.	During a Philadelphia symposium on early man, Father Teilhard de Chardin describes, through interpreters, Peking Man, found in a Chinese cave.		Mar. 19

F	G	H	I	J
Includes elections, federal-state relations, civil rights and liberties, crime, the judiciary, education, healthcare, poverty, urban affairs, and population.	Includes formation and debate of U.S. foreign and defense policies, veterans affairs, and defense spending. (Relations with specific foreign countries are usually found under the region concerned.)	Includes business, labor, agriculture, taxation, transportation, consumer affairs, monetary and fiscal policy, natural resources, pollution, and accidents.	Includes worldwide scientific, medical, and technological developments, natural phenomena, U.S. weather, and natural disasters.	Includes the arts, religion, scholarship, communications media, sports, entertainment, fashions, fads, and social life.

	World Affairs	Europe	Africa & The Middle East	The Americas	Asia & The Pacific
Mar. 20	Loyalist Spain contracts with Mexico for 1.7 million pesos' worth of munitions.	Spanish insurgents attack Pozoblanco in an effort to seize mercury mines in the area. . . . Although it is kept secret, the French plug gaps in the Maginot Line with mines, upended rails, and other obstacles meant to stop tanks.		The Ontario legislature in Canada passes a minimum wage and labor standards bill. . . . *El Tiempo* reports that Venezuela teeters between dictatorship and Bolshevism, and that the country is beset by looting, riots, and the burning of hundreds of homes and businesses.	
Mar. 21	Six days of war games involving land, sea, and air forces in Hong Kong conclude; the British find their defenses "adequate." . . . Following the conviction of a clerk for espionage, Moscow informs Japan that shipping company personnel are expelled. Japan claims the clerk was framed to allow the Soviets to take over Japanese business.	In a Palm Sunday encyclical read in Berlin and elsewhere, Pope Pius XI harshly criticizes Nazi dogma and its practitioners. . . . A decree from Joseph Stalin and Premier Molotoff annulling grain debts of farmers to the government is read as an admission of the failure of last year's crops, due to drought. . . . France takes possession of two aircraft plants as nationalization of defense industries continues.		A demonstration calling for independence in Ponce, Puerto Rico, becomes a riot and 19 men, both police and civilians, are killed.	Hundreds die daily due to the drought and famine in Szechwan province, China.
Mar. 22		Insurgents rally to face loyalist troops 20 miles north of Guadalajara. . . . Catholics in Germany feel the Pope's message comes too late to help a weakened and powerless church. . . . Yugoslavia's Premier Stoyadinovitch is buffeted by criticism within his own country as he prepares for a visit from Italy's foreign minister.			A Japanese trade mission to Shanghai meets little success. China balks at trade until Japan's policies in north China change.
Mar. 23		Belgium's King Leopold III visits London and takes diplomatic steps toward ensuring Belgium's neutrality. . . . German farmers who fail to meet government demands for output might have their land seized and rented to others, Commissar Hermann Goering announces. Grants, loans, and subsidies for farm improvements will be increased. . . . Unwilling to battle Catholics and Protestants simultaneously, Nazi Minister for Church Affairs Hans Kerrl rolls back Protestant church governments to their status of February 15. . . . Premier Benito Mussolini of Italy rails against criticism in the British press, and his envoy in London states that Italian troops will stay in Spain until the war ends.			
Mar. 24		France's Foreign Minister Yvon Delbos warns other diplomats that his country's patience with Italy's interference in Spain wears thin. . . . Insurgents shell Guadalajara and fight for the mines at Almaden. The loyalist drive north has been halted.		Justice Minister LaPointe of Canada declares that sit-down strikes are illegal in that country.	Japan and Burma agree to trade raw and finished cotton. . . Japan denies rumors, fueled by its refusal to accept limitations on guns on ships, that it plans to build extralarge battleships. . . . Soldiers fire guns into a mob of 800 starving farmers who try to seize rice from ships in Yungchwan. Other stories of food riots and thefts in the Szechwan province abound.
Mar. 25	In Tangier, 50 Italian sailors vandalize offices of a Spanish newspaper that offended them. The paper's manager shoots at the vandals, wounding three.	Yugoslavia and Italy sign a political and trade pact, guaranteeing their borders for five years. . . The Spanish government protests the interference of other countries on its seas and in its commerce. . . . Saying that he would rather have Italy's anger than Italy's contempt, David Lloyd George urges Britons to stand up to Mussolini. . . . In Spain, fighting is fierce around Pozoblanco, near the Almaden mercury mines. Madrid suffers heavy shelling as well. . . . Dr. Joseph Goebbels unveils a rating system for German films, ranking their conformance with Nazi values.			
	A *Includes developments that affect more than one world region, international organizations, and important meetings of world leaders.*	**B** *Includes all domestic and regional developments in Europe, including the Soviet Union.*	**C** *Includes all domestic and regional developments in Africa and the Middle East.*	**D** *Includes all domestic and regional developments in Latin America, the Caribbean, and Canada.*	**E** *Includes all domestic and regional developments in Asian and Pacific nations (and colonies).*

U.S. Politics & Social Issues	U.S. Foreign Policy & Defense	Economics & Great Depression	Science, Technology & Nature	Culture, Leisure & Lifestyle	
Hundreds of funerals take place throughout Rusk County, Texas, for the children and teachers killed at the New London School. . . . Dr. F. Frazier, speaking at a seminar, warns that racial pride and intolerance could result in economic discrimination against Negroes.		Mounted police, swinging nightsticks, roughly remove female sit-down strikers from a Detroit cigar factory. . . . Homer Martin of the UAWA threatens a general strike of all auto workers except General Motors if Michigan Governor Frank Murphy sends the National Guard to remove Chrysler sit-down strikers. . . . After a meeting with the CIO ended in deadlock, managers of 12 outlet stores in Rhode Island close to prevent a sit-down strike, forcing 5,000 employees out. . . . The judge hearing arguments over strikers in hosiery plants orders a cooling-down period, delaying arguments.	With a blown-out tire on takeoff from Hawaii, quick maneuvering on Amelia Earhart's part prevents tragedy. She and her crew sail back to California, and the round-the-world trip is postponed.	In the biggest deal of the Negro leagues so far, the Homestead Grays get future Hall of Fame players Judy Johnson and Josh Gibson for $2,500 and two journeyman players.	**Mar. 20**
		The CIO votes for a general strike of stores in Providence, R.I., affecting at least 10,000 employees.			**Mar. 21**
A letter from Chief Justice Charles Evans Hughes is read in Congress. He writes that changes to the Supreme Court are unnecessary and would impair its efficiency.	The Senate passes a Navy appropriations bill of $500 million.	A clerks' strike in Providence affects 90 stores. . . . Railway workers ask for a 20 percent pay raise effective May 1. The raise would add $120 million to the payroll. . . . In Detroit, union leaders present evidence that Chrysler violated the Wagner Act and kept a blacklist of union men. They charge that the Chrysler records were withheld from the La Follette Senate hearings on labor espionage.	The *Hindenburg* arrives in Rio de Janiero, opening its 1937 season.		**Mar. 22**
		After a one-day strike, 12,000 store employees in Rhode Island will return to work, receiving 5–10 percent more in pay. . . . An estimated 60,000 auto workers rally at Cadillac Square in Detroit. . . . Governor Frank Murphy of Michigan summons CIO head John L. Lewis and chairman Walter Chrysler to meet at his office the next day. . . . Over two days, Chicago's police methodically remove or evict all sit-down strikers in the city.			**Mar. 23**
		President Franklin Roosevelt will meet next week with Congressional leaders to discuss sit-down strikes. . . . Governor of Michigan Frank Murphy announces a partial agreement to end the auto workers' strike. . . . A labor attorney who helped negotiate an end to the Chicago taxi drivers' strike apparently changed the terms of the settlement in the contract. That strike is resumed.	Dust storms and tornadoes plague the Midwest. Oklahoma schools close for two days due to zero visibility, and twisters in Alabama and Kentucky take at least two lives.	The 1937 payroll for major league baseball is $3.2 million—the highest ever.	**Mar. 24**
		Homer Martin and other union officials visit sit-down strikers at Detroit area auto plants from 2 a.m. on, with news that Chrysler agrees to allow collective bargaining. All plants are vacated without incident. . . . Mayor Fiorello LaGuardia brokers an agreement with New York retail clerks who have been on strike since March 13. The employees get some raises, a minimum wage, and the right to bargain through a union.	Southern California rocks with a 6.0 earthquake centered 60 miles northeast of San Diego.	President Franklin Roosevelt signs the bill accepting Andrew Mellon's gifts to the country, valued at $65 million. . . . Arturo Toscanini celebrates his 70th birthday in Vienna.	**Mar. 25**

F	G	H	I	J
Includes elections, federal-state relations, civil rights and liberties, crime, the judiciary, education, healthcare, poverty, urban affairs, and population.	*Includes formation and debate of U.S. foreign and defense policies, veterans affairs, and defense spending. (Relations with specific foreign countries are usually found under the region concerned.)*	*Includes business, labor, agriculture, taxation, transportation, consumer affairs, monetary and fiscal policy, natural resources, pollution, and accidents.*	*Includes worldwide scientific, medical, and technological developments, natural phenomena, U.S. weather, and natural disasters.*	*Includes the arts, religion, scholarship, communications media, sports, entertainment, fashions, fads, and social life.*

	World Affairs	Europe	Africa & The Middle East	The Americas	Asia & The Pacific
Mar. 26	A mission from the Vatican, under a Papal Nuncio, embarks for Ethiopia. All other missions in the country, some who have served there for decades, are ordered out by Italian authorities.	Loyalists claim to have pushed insurgents back, not just from Pozoblanco, but out of Málaga as well. . . . The Cabinet of Catalan Premier Tarradellas resigns . . . The Italian public is indignant and angry over the words of Lloyd George and others in the British House of Commons. . . . Widespread strikes in Poland involving 100,000 workers have led to boycotts, and now attacks against Jewish-owned businesses, including bombings. . . . Yugoslavia's order to cut exports to Germany by 50 percent was never enforced due to diplomatic pressures, and new efforts are under way to reduce the German debt.		Eight hundred students at a charity school ask for self-government, and 60,000 students leave classes all over Mexico to demonstrate in support of their cause.	Indian provinces are hamstrung by Congress Party majorities that cannot act without violating the constitution. Mohandas Gandhi is traveling to Madras to address the issues.
Mar. 27	A Spanish freighter, loaded with munitions, is rearmed in Mexico and will attempt to run the blockade around Spain. . . . Japan formally tells Britain that it does not accept limitations on the caliber of guns installed on ships. . . . Doubling prices on Russian iron cause heavy losses for Japanese manufacturers.	Unofficially, Italy assures Britain and France that no more troops will be sent to Spain. . . . Loyalist planes from Cartagena bomb Motril and Málaga, which are still held by insurgents, as well as Melilla in Spanish Morocco. Fighting and shelling continue. . . . A British steamer is targeted by insurgent ships, who fire six shells before allowing it to proceed.		Fearing pro-independence demonstrations on Easter Sunday, the National Guard and Army troops have been put on alert in Puerto Rico. . . . Students in Mexico refuse to return to class. . . . The National Labor Federation supports President Lázaro Cárdenas' plan that Mexican farmworkers and laborers will be represented in the next congress, to be elected in June.	Japanese business leaders assess the potential for economic ties with China and announce that politics and past militarism stand in the way. . . . In Bombay, India, the leader of the Congress Party refuses to form a government unless the British governor promises not to use some of his constitutional powers.
Mar. 28		Elections in Bulgaria are preceded by the arrests of hundreds of potential "agitators." Elections two weeks ago are deemed false.		Cuba hosts a regional radio conference, and will follow with an Inter-American Radio Conference November 26. Sharing bandwidth without interference is the goal.	The Congress Party refuses to form ministries in Madras and the Central provinces, as well as in Bombay. . . . Fifty or more lepers are shot and buried in a pit in Yeongkong, in the Kwangtung province, China. The news is spread by missionaries and reaches the United States in a week.
Mar. 29		France and England agree to act together on any violations reported of the Spanish Non-Intervention Treaty. . . . Loyalist forces announce the bombardment of insurgent bases in the Balearics. . . . Strikes and the sharply rising cost of living cause unrest in Britain.		Six thousand students fill Havana University, open for the first time in four years. . . . Drought and famine cause 18,000 to leave their homes in Ceara, in Brazil's interior, and to plead for government aid. . . . Earthquakes rattle Costa Rica and Panama. . . . To prevent violence, Colombia has barred political meetings and broadcasts until after elections on April 4. . . . Canada's 117,000 rail workers have pay restored and end their strike threat.	Six Indian provinces now decline to form governments, leaving the country in deadlock. What will happen when the new constitution becomes effective April 1 is unknown. Processions and demonstrations have been banned for that day. . . . The government in Manchukuo announces that 200 men from Antung province have been executed or imprisoned for plotting against the Japanese. The conspiracy was uncovered in August.
Mar. 30	Mexico instructs its delegate in Geneva to ask the League of Nations to back the loyalist government of Spain and end the civil war there.	Spanish insurgents purge their own ranks of a conspiracy. Reports claim that 200 loyalist prisoners are executed in Malaga; in Olveida, 150 rebels are shot; in Asturias and Algeciras, 50. Loyalists again claim to take Pozoblanco. . . . General Franco's press claims that 62,000 were killed by the government in Madrid, and that 12,000 have been killed in Valencia. . . . Britain reminds General Franco that attacks on British ships would be considered acts of piracy.			Mohandas Gandhi accuses the government of flouting the will of the majority in India.
Mar. 31	Soviet gold totaling £38 million sails to the United States via London, and may be used to pay for metals and rubber purchased by the Soviet Union.	The High Commissioner in Spanish Morocco denies reports of a rebellion within Franco's forces, which informants say took place at the Tetuan Airdrome. . . . Insurgents under General Mola push on Madrid once more, dropping 14 bombs. Air raids by Franco's forces on Durango and other nonmilitary targets kill 300. . . . Germany is building planes and will have 500 by June, doubling its first-line forces.		For encouraging parents to keep their children out of Mexico's socialist schools, Father Francisco Flores is sentenced to a year in prison as an example to others.	Japan's Diet dissolves; the announcement shocks media and political circles. . . . At midnight, Burma and Aden become British colonies independent of India.

A	B	C	D	E
Includes developments that affect more than one world region, international organizations, and important meetings of world leaders.	Includes all domestic and regional developments in Europe, including the Soviet Union.	Includes all domestic and regional developments in Africa and the Middle East.	Includes all domestic and regional developments in Latin America, the Caribbean, and Canada.	Includes all domestic and regional developments in Asian and Pacific nations (and colonies).

U.S. Politics & Social Issues	U.S. Foreign Policy & Defense	Economics & Great Depression	Science, Technology & Nature	Culture, Leisure & Lifestyle	
William Henry Hastie is the first African American to be appointed a judge. He will serve in the Virgin Islands. . . . In New York, seven are found guilty of conspiracy and extortion in a restaurant racketeering trial prosecuted by Thomas Dewey.		Governor of Michigan Frank Murphy, John Lewis, and Walter Chrysler sit in conference for 11 hours and are close to an agreement. . . . An agreement ending the taxi strike in Chicago is signed. . . . A three-week-long strike at Bethlehem Steel is settled. . . . In Queens, New York, police stand by as six "bouncers" physically remove 19 sit-down strikers from an etched products plant.		Frederick I. Maytag dies at 80 in Los Angeles. He manufactured washing machines since 1907.	Mar. 26
President Franklin Roosevelt, after meeting with Senate majority leader Joseph Robinson and others, reiterates his "hands-off" policy regarding sit-down strikes.		Some produce handlers in Buffalo walk out, but others sign accords with merchants. . . . The United Auto Workers of America seeks an injunction against Chrysler Corp. under the Wagner Act. If current negotiations fail, the union will press charges stemming from years of labor espionage on the company's part. Negotiations between Governor of Michigan Frank Murphy, Walter Chrysler, and CIO head John Lewis continue through Easter Sunday.			Mar. 27
		CIO head John Lewis leaves Detroit to join the United Mine Workers talks; the governor and Chrysler chief will continue talks. . . . AFL president Green disavows sit-down strikes and labels them illegal.		Polish composer Karol Szymanowski dies of tuberculosis in Switzerland.	Mar. 28
The Supreme Court upholds the Frazier Lemke Act, granting bankruptcy protections to farmers. It also reverses a 10-month-old decision and upholds the concept of a minimum wage for women. The Court rules as well that railroads have to allow collective bargaining.		Firestone executives hold fast to their refusal to talk to the CIO or grant sole bargaining rights.		Robert Frost is given the Mark Twain Society Gold Medal.	Mar. 29
The speeches on the radio, in legislatures, and before civic audiences by politicians and legal scholars about President Franklin Roosevelt's proposed reorganization of the Supreme Court are growing increasingly vitriolic, and charges of lies are made by both sides.			The Pan American Clipper lands in New Zealand after a 7,000-mile, 13-day trip. The plane pioneers a commercial route from California to "Australasia."		Mar. 30
		Though negotiations continue, 400,000 soft coal miners reject a tentative agreement and prepare to strike tomorrow. . . . The House strikes a favored section of the Farm Tenancy Bill that would have funded ownership of rented farms. It's a blow to the President, but others considered the section socialistic.		Mary Harlan Lincoln, the wife of Abraham Lincoln's oldest son, dies in Washington at age 90.	Mar. 31

F	G	H	I	J
Includes elections, federal-state relations, civil rights and liberties, crime, the judiciary, education, healthcare, poverty, urban affairs, and population.	*Includes formation and debate of U.S. foreign and defense policies, veterans affairs, and defense spending. (Relations with specific foreign countries are usually found under the region concerned.)*	*Includes business, labor, agriculture, taxation, transportation, consumer affairs, monetary and fiscal policy, natural resources, pollution, and accidents.*	*Includes worldwide scientific, medical, and technological developments, natural phenomena, U.S. weather, and natural disasters.*	*Includes the arts, religion, scholarship, communications media, sports, entertainment, fashions, fads, and social life.*

	World Affairs	Europe	Africa & The Middle East	The Americas	Asia & The Pacific
Apr. 1		Madrid enjoys a respite from fighting, but loyalists advance in other areas: north toward Burgos and south as far as Ceuta in Spanish Morocco. The insurgents attack near Bilbao, and drop bombs on Jaen, in Cordoba. . . . Today is the deadline set for each home in Switzerland, a neutral country, to be prepared for air attacks. . . . The Little Entente meets in Belgrade: Foreign Ministers of Czechoslovakia and Romania talk with the Yugoslav Premier.	Isset Pasha, interim Grand Vizier and Premier of the Ottoman Empire, dies in Istanbul.	Mexico assures the United States that it will respect the Neutrality Law, and not ship any U.S.-made munitions to Spain. . . . General Motors employees at two plants in Ontario, Canada, threaten to strike. Ontario's Minister of Labor calls a meeting for April 2.	Elections in Japan for new representatives will be held April 30. . . . The Congress Party of India successfully calls for general strikes as the new constitution goes into effect.
Apr. 2	The Tri-Partite Preparatory Textile Conference opens in Washington, D.C., with delegates from 23 countries.	Spanish insurgents capture peaks in Bilbao, the Basque capital. Bilbao's defenses are called an Iron Ring and include trenches and tunnels circling the city, defended by artillery. Loyalists claim to gain more territory in Cordoba. Fifteen fast Russian bombers used by loyalists kill 50 in the workers' section of the city, the government claims. According to insurgents, a hospital was hit. . . . The Little Entente meeting ends with expressions of solidarity and an agreement that any pact with Hungary must involve all three nations. Yugoslavia's pact with Italy is privately criticized in the meeting.		Union officials and General Motors executives begin talks with Ontario Minister David Croll.	Because of rising prices and shortages, the Japanese Cabinet issues decrees lifting tariffs on iron and steel.
Apr. 3	A recent law banning the Nazi party angers German settlers in South West Africa, a former German colony, and they lodge a protest with the League of Nations.	In Germany, four pastors are arrested for allowing two visiting Swiss pastors to speak at their church. . . . Insurgents drop as many as 4,000 bombs on nonmilitary targets such as Durango and a nearby asylum. Jaen is shelled in reprisal for the bombing of a hospital in Cordoba. Rebels also set fire to forests and bridges in the Cordoba province. . . . Russia's Commissar of Communication Yagoda is dismissed for criminal actions stemming from the recent Trotskyite trials. He once headed the secret police.			Pu Chieh, the brother and heir of Emperor Kang Teh of Manchukuo, marries Hiroko Saga, a Japanese commoner.
Apr. 4	Moulay Hafid, Sultan of Morocco forced to abdicate in 1912, dies in France at age 61.	Loyalists bomb Avila and claim to outflank Franco's troops near Cordoba. Rumors spread of anti-Franco demonstrations in Ceuta and Tetuan in Spanish Morocco. . . . The Finnish Labor Party approves the idea of a Scandinavian defense plan.		Elections are held in Colombia, but conservatives boycott them. Eduardo Santos wins a majority. . . . In Mexico, women vote for the first time in primaries, but will not be allowed to vote in the general election in July.	The geishas of Osaka who went on strike a month ago have now formed a joint stock company, Osaka Geisha.
Apr. 5	The League of Nations holds a sugar conference in London, hoping to ensure international cooperation in production. The conference is attended by 23 nations. . . . The German government agrees to pay $22.5 million to U.S. companies in war debts arising from explosions. While not admitting blame, Germany agreed to the figure in negotiations last year. . . . Germany protests the recent proclamation banning Nazi activities in South West Africa.	Insurgents destroy Ochandiano, a Basque town six miles from Durango. Loyalists take the town of La Guanjuela in Cordoba. A loyalist warship bombs Ceuta.. . . . The use of 80 Russian pursuit planes, noted for speed, is behind recent loyalist victories. The planes are called Chatos, or 1-15s and 1-16s. . . . President Benes of Czechoslovakia arrives in Belgrade for a state visit to Yugoslavia. . . . Reports emerge about demonstrations in Greece against the Metaxas dictatorship.		Brazil's Supreme Court weighs the legality of the election of governor in Sao Paulo.	Japan adopts a conciliatory policy toward China as it heads into elections.
Apr. 6	Japan's 57-hour workweek and low wages are criticized at the Textile Conference.	Chato planes fly in the Basque region, where heavy fighting continues. The town of Durango begins to evacuate. . . . Insurgent planes drop bombs near British ships. . . . The Lutheran Council and Confessional Synods ignore government decrees in Germany and appoint their own leadership.		President Lázaro Cárdenas bans the sale of liquor on Fridays, Saturdays, and Sundays in Mexico. In Indian areas, liquor cannot be manufactured or sold.	

A	B	C	D	E
Includes developments that affect more than one world region, international organizations, and important meetings of world leaders.	*Includes all domestic and regional developments in Europe, including the Soviet Union.*	*Includes all domestic and regional developments in Africa and the Middle East.*	*Includes all domestic and regional developments in Latin America, the Caribbean, and Canada.*	*Includes all domestic and regional developments in Asian and Pacific nations (and colonies).*

U.S. Politics & Social Issues	U.S. Foreign Policy & Defense	Economics & Great Depression	Science, Technology & Nature	Culture, Leisure & Lifestyle	
		Unauthorized strikes close Chevrolet plants in Michigan, idling 30,000. Chevrolet is a division of GM.... An estimated 11,500 WPA workers in California join up to 3,000 East Coast WPA strikers, protesting "starvation wages." ... Also striking are 400,000 soft coal miners in 12 states. . . . During a discussion of the Guffey-Vinson Bill regulating commerce of soft coal in the Senate, an amendment is proposed banning sit-down strikes.			Apr. 1
		In order to curb sharp price rises in steel and other materials, the President announces a cutback in the purchase of durable goods. Federal spending will focus on consumer goods instead.... Ford Motor Company is hit by sit-down strikers in Kansas City after distributing layoff notices to 300 employees. . . . After 24 hours, union leaders convince Chevrolet employees to end their strike. Plants will reopen April 5. . . . Miners end their strike, winning a two-year contract covering 300,000 workers in eight Appalachian states. The remaining miners will get similar contracts, and soft coal prices will rise by 25 cents per ton. . . . Governor Benson of Minnesota is outraged at the actions of deputy sheriffs, who used tear gas to break up a strike, stormed union offices, and arrested 54 machinists. Enraged workers then damaged the plant. The governor freed the 54 men, restoring order.		Dizzy Dean, backed up by many of his Cardinals teammates, scuffles with reporters in Tampa and gives one a black eye.	Apr. 2
		Ford settles its strike quickly, agreeing to discuss wage increases in future talks. . . . Homer Martin, head of the auto union, cautions GM workers that unauthorized strikes hurts them. Talks to end the Chrysler strike continue. . . . A committee representing 33 unions calls a general strike in Wilmington, Del., in support of truck drivers who have been on strike for 20 days. The strike ends after eight hours, when the governor and mayor call a conference with truckers.			Apr. 3
		Both sides in the Chrysler strike meet all day. . . . Thousands parade through Akron, Ohio, in support of Firestone Tire workers still on strike.	The Glenn Martin Aircraft Company unveils a design for planes capable of carrying 40 passengers on transatlantic trips lasting 19–21 hours. . . . A.L. Durkee of Bell Telephone Laboratories announces that scientists can now predict radio and magnetic interference six years ahead. Studies of 200 years of sun spot activity makes this possible.		Apr. 4
Secretary of State Cordell Hull accepts a medal from the Woodrow Wilson Foundation, and warns against an arms race that would lead to either economic collapse or a military explosion.		After days of debate, the U.S. Senate votes against an amendment that would ban sit-down strikes and passes a bill regulating coal commerce.			Apr. 5
		An agreement ending the month-long Chrysler strike is signed just before midnight. CIO head Lewis will present the new contract to auto workers tomorrow. . . . Three General Motors plants in Michigan close due to sit-down strikes. One is simply a bad joke: the workers pretended to strike just before quitting time.			Apr. 6

F	G	H	I	J
Includes elections, federal-state relations, civil rights and liberties, crime, the judiciary, education, healthcare, poverty, urban affairs, and population.	Includes formation and debate of U.S. foreign and defense policies, veterans affairs, and defense spending. (Relations with specific foreign countries are usually found under the region concerned.)	Includes business, labor, agriculture, taxation, transportation, consumer affairs, monetary and fiscal policy, natural resources, pollution, and accidents.	Includes worldwide scientific, medical, and technological developments, natural phenomena, U.S. weather, and natural disasters.	Includes the arts, religion, scholarship, communications media, sports, entertainment, fashions, fads, and social life.

	World Affairs	Europe	Africa & The Middle East	The Americas	Asia & The Pacific
Apr. 7	Turkey complains about raids across the borders of Turkey and Syria, blamed on bandits from Alexandretta. . . . Delegates to the London conference on sugar are pessimistic that nationalist conflicts can be settled.	An Italian newspaper accuses France of violating the nonintervention pact to aid the loyalist regime, providing weapons, planes, and officers. . . . In Germany, the treason trial of seven men begins, three of them priests accused of participating in a Catholic-Communist conspiracy to undermine the government. . . . As Pomerze week ends in Poland, the German Foreign Office warns Poland about maintaining the accord between their countries. Pomerze week was organized to push for Polish rights. . . . Czech President Benes receives assurance from Prince Paul that no Yugoslav-Hungarian pact is planned. . . . Both sides in Spain describe fierce fighting in the Basque region. Loyalists claim gains in Madrid, Cordoba, and Avila.			One and a half square miles of the Tondo section of Manila, Philippines, is destroyed by fire, leaving 25,000 homeless.
Apr. 8	Chinese delegates to the textile conference discuss the problem of smuggling, abetted by foreign powers in their country. . . . The World Jewish Congress in Geneva learns that Danzig is considering anti-Semitic legislation similar to Germany's.	A soccer match between France and Italy is cancelled as tensions rise between the two countries, both accusing the other of violating the nonintervention pact. . . . Poland dissolves certain commercial cartels it holds responsible for price rises and passes other economic measures, warning that those who defy the new rules will go to concentration camps.		As 3,700 General Motors employees in Canada walk out, Ontario's Premier Hepburn warns the CIO that chaos and foreign agitation will not be tolerated in his country. . . . President Anastasio Somoza of Nicaragua nationalizes the Pacific Railroad. . . . Ambassador Fraga of Cuba invites U.S. bondholders, collectively owed $84 million, to a meeting in Cuba. The bonds, in default since 1933, were issued for public works during the Machado administration. . . . Rival unions clash in a textile factory in the state of Puebla, Mexico. Eight people are killed.	Through speeches in England, Mohandas Gandhi is asked to meet with the British Viceroy of India.
Apr. 9	The French franc and the British pound fall in value, possibly due to rumors that the buying price of gold would be lowered in the United States. Once President Franklin Roosevelt denies the rumors, the currencies rally. . . . Delegates at the Textile Conference debate the concept of a world cotton cartel to regulate prices. . . . Japanese pilot Masaaki Iinuma lands his Kamikaze plane in London after an elapsed flying time of 94 hours, 18 minutes from Tokyo, shattering previous records.	General Miaja and loyalists attempt to lift the siege of Madrid with an early morning attack from the south and west, at Garabitas and Casa de Campo. Insurgents bomb villages in the Basque region as they move closer to Bilbao. . . . King Carol of Romania exiles his brother Nicholas, who has ties to fascist groups. The reason given is Nicholas's marriage to a divorcée. . . . In a radio address, Austria accuses Germany of using its press to launch political attacks on Austria.			Stories circulate that lepers and the blind are being rounded up and shot by civil authorities in Kwangtung province, China.
Apr. 10	The commission led by Dr. John Dewey investigating Leon Trotsky's alleged attempts to overthrow the Soviet government begins in the home of Diego Rivera in Mexico. . . . Italy grants Libya partial self-government in a system of prefects overseeing provinces, much like Italy's. . . . The League of Nations ends its fourth session on slavery, but as all such sessions are secret, no data or decisions are released. . . . The world's first film treaty is made in Germany with Italy. Separate agreements with Japan guarantee distribution of German films in that country.	After four ships carrying food to Spain are turned away by insurgent ships enforcing their own blockade, a British battleship sails for Bilbao from Gibralter. A Norwegian destroyer and two German submarines are also en route. . . . A Belgian Cardinal instructs Catholics to vote against Rexists in tomorrow's election, virtually guaranteeing results. . . . The Berlin Jewish School is forced to close for two months; no explanation given. Jewish sport clubs have also been closed.		The Nazi movement in Chile is deemed a threat to public order. Nazi meetings are forbidden, and the symbols and uniforms are banned. . . . Negotiations similar to those conducted with Michigan's Governor Frank Murphy are not possible in Canada, where Premier Hepburn refuses to allow talks with any "foreign" union officials in the GM strike there.	Denouncing Britain's imperialistic attitude in India, Mohandas Gandhi suggests a three-person panel to decide whether governors can promise noninterference with the elected Congress Party representatives of their provinces.
Apr. 11		After a Cabinet meeting, the British Prime Minister orders more battleships to the Bay of Biscay. They will remain outside Spain's territorial waters. . . . Loyalist forces blow up a Madrid bridge to isolate insurgent troops. Insurgents begin steady, daily shellings of the capital. . . . Premier van Zeeland receives 76 percent of the votes cast as Belgians reject fascist candidate Degrelle. . . . King Boris of Bavaria postpones rebuilding his government, and his popularity lags. . . . Turkish Premier Inonu and his Foreign Minister arrive in Yugoslavia for a week-long visit.		Five thousand striking auto workers rally in Canada and call for United Auto Workers organizer Hugh Thomson to represent them. Premier Hepburn refuses to recognize Thomson or his union. . . . Republican leaders in Cuba publicly call the present military dictatorship a failure, implying that President Laredo Bru is no more than a figurehead. . . . A two-day-long general strike in Mexicali, Baja California, protesting the rates charged for electricity, is settled.	

A	B	C	D	E
Includes developments that affect more than one world region, international organizations, and important meetings of world leaders.	*Includes all domestic and regional developments in Europe, including the Soviet Union.*	*Includes all domestic and regional developments in Africa and the Middle East.*	*Includes all domestic and regional developments in Latin America, the Caribbean, and Canada.*	*Includes all domestic and regional developments in Asian and Pacific nations (and colonies).*

U.S. Politics & Social Issues	U.S. Foreign Policy & Defense	Economics & Great Depression	Science, Technology & Nature	Culture, Leisure & Lifestyle	
In New York, Jane Bolin becomes the first African-American woman appointed Assistant Corporation Council, in the Court of Domestic Relations.		CIO head John L. Lewis tells a cheering crowd of 25,000 Chrysler workers about their new contract. The strike costs Chrysler an estimated $87 million. . . . Henry Ford declares that his company will never recognize any union, as he confirms that a second, brief, sit-down strike occurred at his plant in St. Louis, Mo. . . . At least 3,000 dairy farmers, angry over the loss of business caused by a strike at the Hershey plant in Pennsylvania, break into the factory, beat and drag out the strikers, forcing them to run a gauntlet. . . . Congress votes 75–3 to condemn sit-down strikes, labor espionage, and any refusal of the right to bargain collectively. The resolution is passed on to the House.		Wisconsin Rep. Raymond Cannon asks the Department of Justice to investigate baseball for anti-trust violations, since it is a monopoly that coerces players to sign with the same team or be barred from playing.	Apr. 7
	U.S. legations close their embassies in Tripoli, Libya, and Addis Ababa, Ethiopia.	Hershey shuts down its plant, unable to guarantee the safety of its workers. . . . Caterpillar Tractor Co. settles its labor dispute with 11,500 employees, who will return to work tomorrow. . . . A New York strike at Etched Products, now in its third week, erupts into a riot as strikers attack non-striking female workers, as well as the guards escorting them to the plant.			Apr. 8
		An AFL official involved in the original break between the AFL and CIO head John L. Lewis claims to get a death threat. Most feel a final split between the two labor groups is near. . . . Half of Hershey's labor force reports for work; the other half goes to the picket lines. . . . Blind workers are in the fifth day of their sit-down strike at a charity workshop in New York, asking for a $15 per week wage. A sympathy strike at a second workshop continues.			Apr. 9
Lyndon Johnson, a proponent of President Franklin Roosevelt's court restructuring, wins a Congressional seat held for 24 years by Texan James Buchanan. His victory over seven other candidates is the first electoral test for the President's judiciary plan, but he spends voting day in the hospital with appendicitis.		The CIO begins a drive to bring 270,000 telephone company employees into a CIO-affiliated union. . . . In Hershey, Penn., company officials meet with government mediators and all will talk with the CIO tomorrow.			Apr. 10
Eight men and a 15-year-old boy are shot in front of a CIO union in Galena, Kans., after a demonstration by a rival mining union that drew 4,000 men. Beatings are reported in neighboring towns.				Ralph Ince, actor and director, brother of Thomas Ince, dies in a London auto accident.	Apr. 11

F	G	H	I	J
Includes elections, federal-state relations, civil rights and liberties, crime, the judiciary, education, healthcare, poverty, urban affairs, and population.	*Includes formation and debate of U.S. foreign and defense policies, veterans affairs, and defense spending. (Relations with specific foreign countries are usually found under the region concerned.)*	*Includes business, labor, agriculture, taxation, transportation, consumer affairs, monetary and fiscal policy, natural resources, pollution, and accidents.*	*Includes worldwide scientific, medical, and technological developments, natural phenomena, U.S. weather, and natural disasters.*	*Includes the arts, religion, scholarship, communications media, sports, entertainment, fashions, fads, and social life.*

	World Affairs	Europe	Africa & The Middle East	The Americas	Asia & The Pacific
Apr. 12	The League of Nations meets in Montreux to discuss Egyptian autonomy. Egypt submits two proposals asking for the cessation of foreign privileges ("capitulations") and proposing a transitional system. . . . Nazi leader Josef Riedel dies hours after being shot by two men in Buenos Aires, Argentina. The killers escape. Police suspect burglary.	Rather than provoke an incident, Britain backs away defending ships carrying food to Bilbao, and instructs ships to avoid Spanish waters. . . . Insurgents claim France has trained 200 loyalist pilots; Russia is also accused of providing planes and training. . . . An unspecified number of Soviet workers who tried to sabotage subway construction are "liquidated," according to a government newspaper. . . . Representatives from the Scandinavian countries visit Belgium for talks.			Government troops in the Philippines, fighting Muslims on Mindanao Island, announce that they have taken the last Moro stronghold.
Apr. 13	Leon Trotsky defends himself against treason by re-creating his travels in Europe, proving he could not have met with his accusers, but his records are incomplete. . . . Greece announces plans to create a state-owned oil monopoly; British and U.S. companies protest.	Germany's Economic Minister Dr. Schacht arrives in Belgium for two days of talks on trade and raw materials. . . . Due to refugees, Bilbao's population is near 400,000 and food shortages force rationing. . . . Except for synagogues, all Jewish gatherings in Germany are prohibited for 60 days. . . . Saying that it will not tolerate interference in internal affairs, Germany protests the Papal Encyclical of March 21.	South Africa averts a Cabinet crisis by tabling a bill that would outlaw the employment of white women by "Asiatics," understood to mean Indians. Instead, a gentleman's agreement discouraging such employment resolves the issue.	Demanding complete loyalty or resignations from his Cabinet, Premier Hepburn of Ontario bolsters his police force, determined to break the strike at General Motors.	
Apr. 14	Italian newspapers accuse France of sending Algerian troops, as well as ammunition and trucks, to help loyalist forces in Spain. . . . All League of Nations delegates favor ending the capitulations in Egypt, but disagree on the details. . . . The Spanish government, after months of delays, allows 1,400 refugees at the Chilean Embassy in Madrid to begin to depart in small groups.	A pro-Czech paper supporting Premier Schuschnigg's views is confiscated in Austria—after it had been available for several days. German pressure is suspected, as one article urges a Czech-Austrian pact to guard against danger from Germany.		Two members of Premier Hepburn's Cabinet resign after his ultimatum the previous day. The Premier rejects help or advice from Dominion officials. The pro-union mayor of Oshawa, Canada, informs Homer Martin, the head of the UAWA, that unless a general strike of GM is called in the United States, he will advise Canadian strikers to give up. . . . After a radio address celebrating Pan American Day, President Franklin Roosevelt privately assures statesmen of his continuing policies of peace, trust, and—in Cuba's case—of noninterference.	
Apr. 15		Italy reverses its refusal to withdraw troops from Spain, and discusses recall with Britain. . . . After a week of fighting in the Casa de Campo section of Madrid, insurgents attack south, along the Valencia Road. The daily bombing of the city continues. . . . Ex-prince Nicholas of Romania, supported by the Iron Guard, refuses to leave his country. He repudiates any association with the fascist group. . . . In a quest for scrap iron, Germany buys four ships with a total tonnage of 26,283 within a few days.	Sporadic violence in Palestine continues with the murder of an Arab police official by Arab terrorists.	In Montreal, 5,000 dressmakers, members of the CIO-affiliated ILGWU, strike for higher wages. Longshoreman groups in Ontario also walk off their jobs. . . . In Detroit, the auto workers' union agrees to settle its Canadian strike without demanding recognition of the CIO as an international bargaining unit.	In Japan, an imperial decree exempts iron imports from tariffs for one year.
Apr. 16	The World Textile Conference exhorts all nations to reduce trade barriers and set up national boards to regulate working conditions and wages. A statement about reducing hours is voted out of the summary. . . . Outraged Germans accuse Communists in the death of Josef Riedel in Argentina, terming the crime a political assassination. . . . Wheat prices collapse in world markets.	Loyalists open a new front, 150 miles north of Madrid near Teruel City, which is held by insurgents. Bombs fall in parts of Madrid, Algeciras, and the small town of Culera, near the French border.		A general strike in Medellin, Colombia, shuts down power, water, and traffic. Workers say their requests for better pay are being ignored.	
Apr. 17	In a letter to Chair John Dewey, Carleton Beals resigns from the commission investigating the charges against Leon Trotsky.	Basque defenders halt insurgents at Eibar, a city of 25,000, with machine guns and air support. In Madrid, monks and women are arrested and charged with plotting against the government.		Negotiations between local unions and General Motors seem to end the strike in Oshawa, but the talks break down when Premier Hepburn orders local union representatives out of his office. Homer Martin holds that GM violated the agreements ending the U.S. strike, and threatens a general walkout of all 110,000 employees. . . . The first shipment of Virgin Islands rum, a PWA project, heads for New York. Seven thousand cases made from cane juice and carrying the name Government House Rum, will arrive April 27.	

A	B	C	D	E
Includes developments that affect more than one world region, international organizations, and important meetings of world leaders.	Includes all domestic and regional developments in Europe, including the Soviet Union.	Includes all domestic and regional developments in Africa and the Middle East.	Includes all domestic and regional developments in Latin America, the Caribbean, and Canada.	Includes all domestic and regional developments in Asian and Pacific nations (and colonies).

U.S. Politics & Social Issues	U.S. Foreign Policy & Defense	Economics & Great Depression	Science, Technology & Nature	Culture, Leisure & Lifestyle	
		The Supreme Court hands down five surprisingly broad rulings supporting the Wagner National Labor Relations Act. Their decisions place national companies under the regulatory powers of Congress and affirm labor's right to organize. . . . A federal grand jury indicts James Rand and Pearl Bergoff for bringing strikebreakers across state lines to the Remington Rand Corp. plant.	In Rugby, England, Sir Frank Whittle tests his invention, the first jet engine, at the British Thomson-Houston factory. . . . Drs. Claude Hudson and Ernest Jackson present landmark work in carbohydrate chemistry to the American Chemical Society.	Abdülhak Hamid, Turkish playwright, often called the Shakespeare of the Ottomans, dies at age 86.	Apr. 12
During its debate on the Gavagan Anti-Lynching Bill, the House receives news of two lynchings in Duck Hill, Miss., involving torture and burning.		Due to a growing deficit, President Franklin Roosevelt asks all government department heads to cut expenditures through June. . . . In New York, 40 blind workers march on City Hall, asking help in securing better wages.	In an air speed test arranged around having breakfast in Connecticut, lunch in Miami, and dinner in New York, Lt. Com. Frank Hawks misses dinner—but is otherwise unhurt—when his plane crashes at Newark Airport.		Apr. 13
Chairman Sumners of the House Judiciary Committee is against a federal anti-lynching bill as an infringement of states' sovereignty. He calls Mississippi Governor White, who in turn asks the local district attorney to investigate yesterday's lynchings, which all decry as barbarous.	President Franklin Roosevelt appoints the Joint Preparatory Commission on Philippine Affairs, aimed at easing the economics of independence. . . . The 1937 *Aircraft Year Book* lists the United States as sixth in military air strength, behind Britain, France, Russia, Italy, and Germany.	Detroit police use tear gas to end a month-old strike at Yale and Towne Manufacturing. Most of the 150 sit-down strikers were women.		Attorney General Homer Cummings refuses to investigate major-league baseball for anti-trust violations.	Apr. 14
Prompted by the atrocity in Duck Hill, Miss., the House passes the Gavagan Anti-Lynching Bill.		Secretary Henry Morgenthau announces "new money" loans of $50 million in treasury bills per week to keep the government operating. . . . Two strikes, one of radio workers, keep ocean liners in port.		The discovery of the rich 6,300-year-old tomb of Ti, a landowner buried at Saqqara, is announced in Cairo.	Apr. 15
Violence, including bombings, against union organizers in the coal industry is the subject of testimony before the La Follette subcommittee. . . . William Redmond, an African-American student turned away from the University of Tennessee's School of Pharmacy, loses his court case asking admission. He is told that the Board of Education or the legislature, not the courts, should decide the issue.	Six weeks of war games "defending" Hawaii start, with the participation of 152 vessels sailing from California and 474 aircraft.	The first intervention of the NLRB since its "legalization" by the Supreme Court results in a settlement of the ship workers' strike. . . . Homer Martin, head of the United Auto Workers of America, announces he will file charges against Henry Ford under the Wagner Act. . . . The seven-week-long hosiery workers' strike ends with agreements for collective bargaining and a 40-hour week.			Apr. 16
The Senate Judiciary Committee extends its hearings on the Court Reorganization Bill another ten days.		The International Seamen's Union challenges the NRLB settlement with ship workers, because the request for NRLB intervention came from the employer, rather than the workers.	Organ Pipe Cactus National Monument in Arizona is set aside as a government preserve.	Tex Avery and Bob Clampett direct a cartoon called *Porky's Duck Hunt*, introducing the character Daffy Duck. Mel Blanc provides the voice.	Apr. 17

F	**G**	**H**	**I**	**J**
Includes elections, federal-state relations, civil rights and liberties, crime, the judiciary, education, healthcare, poverty, urban affairs, and population.	Includes formation and debate of U.S. foreign and defense policies, veterans affairs, and defense spending. (Relations with specific foreign countries are usually found under the region concerned.)	Includes business, labor, agriculture, taxation, transportation, consumer affairs, monetary and fiscal policy, natural resources, pollution, and accidents.	Includes worldwide scientific, medical, and technological developments, natural phenomena, U.S. weather, and natural disasters.	Includes the arts, religion, scholarship, communications media, sports, entertainment, fashions, fads, and social life.

	World Affairs	Europe	Africa & The Middle East	The Americas	Asia & The Pacific
Apr. 18	Soviet papers announce the defection of entire detachments, with their officers, from Manchukuo to Soviet territory.	Poor weather holds General Franco's troops from taking Bilbao, but he announces that the fall of that city is imminent.... The National Council of the Socialist Party meets at Puteaux and debates the future of France. The extremist bloc dissolves in support of Premier Léon Blum.... Hungarian Premier Daranyl says his country will negotiate with other Danube states only if Hungarian minorities in those states are guaranteed equality.		Half of Montreal's dressmaking firms accept the CIO as their bargaining agent, and their employees will return to work tomorrow.	China unveils a national defense council consisting of Chiang Kai-shek as Chair, with Generals Feng Yu-hsiang, Ho Ying-chin, and Pai Chung-hsi. These men, who were at cross purposes and near civil war last summer, work now to stop Japan's domination.
Apr. 19		To isolate Spain and its civil war, 60 ships—from Britain, France, Germany, and Italy—begin their patrols. The blockade is supported by 27 nations including Portugal. The Spanish government terms it unjust and promises to protect its own ships.... With the Decree of Unification, General Franco merges his support into one party, a coalition of fascist and Catholic groups.... Destruction of Spain's largest arms factory, near Toledo, is reported. Franco claims he has 500 artillery guns prepared to shell Bilbao. ... The Gestapo raids and closes all B'nai B'rith lodges in Germany, seizing property and arresting over 60 of the now-defunct organization's leaders and holding them overnight.		The Venezuelan Congress opens. Elected members comprise one-third of the members; appointees of the late dictator make up the balance.... The mayor of Oshawa presents a settlement before 3,000 striking GM workers, who loudly reject it. The mayor's proposals exclude union recognition. Premier Hepburn says he might accept AFL participation, but not the CIO.	The Joint Preparatory Committee on Philippine Affairs holds it first meeting.
Apr. 20	In response to Japan's fortifications on the southern tip of Formosa, Britain begins strengthening the defenses of Hong Kong.... Juan Trippe and his company, Pan American Airways, receive formal permission from several countries to use their air space when transatlantic flights begin in two months.	One British ship breaks through the blockade to deliver food to Bilbao, where, with clear weather, insurgents have renewed attacks. While they capture two nearby towns, loyalists take several towns near Teruel. ... British Chancellor of the Exchequer Neville Chamberlain announces a business tax as high as 33.3 percent, and income tax rates of 25 percent.... Germany's Protestant church poll will not take place until autumn.... Paris suffers labor unrest; a cinema workers' strike ends, but hotel and restaurant workers threaten to walk out.	Charges are announced against two Iraqi officials who used their high positions to profit from selling arms to both Spanish insurgents and loyalists.	Ontario Premier Hepburn guarantees protection to General Motors workers who wish to return to work.	
Apr. 21	Transpacific air service begins as the China Clipper leaves California for Manila, with connecting flights to Macao and Hong Kong.	The shelling of Madrid by insurgents worsens, as 30 people are killed in one morning.... Premier Benito Mussolini of Italy rejects arms reduction in an interview and predicts the death of the League of Nations.... Director Lyadoff of the Mali Theatre in Moscow is dismissed and arrested. The accusations against him include wrecking the theatre, corrupting the cast, and squandering money on the unproduced (as yet) *Boris Gudonoff*.... French Defense Minister Édouard Daladier arrives in London for talks.... The Chair of Poland's political party, which excludes Jews, explains that Poland has too many Jews and must worry about jobs for Poles.		Thousands of Integralistas, or fascists, march in Rio De Janeiro; they claim 800,000 members.	
Apr. 22	Argentina and the Netherlands sign a trade pact.... The Chilean Ambassador, A. Nunez Morgado, is searched and his luggage seized as he tries to leave Spain. A protest is filed; he remains in Valencia until his belongings are restored.	Premiers Mussolini of Italy and Schuschnigg of Austria meet in Venice with their foreign ministers. Mussolini makes clear his opposition to Hapsburg restoration and points out that Nazis within Austria are equally opposed to it. He advises Schuschnigg to abandon plans for restoration lest he provoke an uprising in his own country and invite German intervention. He also advises Austria to form no close ties to Czechoslovakia.... In Finland, the conference between Finland, Sweden, Denmark, and Norway ends with pledges of cooperation and support for the Oslo convention.... Polish Foreign Minister Józef Beck arrives in Romania to reinforce mutual respect and interests.... Col. Hermann Wilhelm Goering and his wife come to Rome for talks.		General Motors officials and local union heads meet in Premier Hepburn's office and negotiate terms, kept secret until all employees vote on them.	The Canberra Conference of Protection of Aborigines in Australia recommends absorbing the growing numbers of "half-castes" into white society through education and service employment.

A	B	C	D	E
Includes developments that affect more than one world region, international organizations, and important meetings of world leaders.	*Includes all domestic and regional developments in Europe, including the Soviet Union.*	*Includes all domestic and regional developments in Africa and the Middle East.*	*Includes all domestic and regional developments in Latin America, the Caribbean, and Canada.*	*Includes all domestic and regional developments in Asian and Pacific nations (and colonies).*

U.S. Politics & Social Issues	U.S. Foreign Policy & Defense	Economics & Great Depression	Science, Technology & Nature	Culture, Leisure & Lifestyle	
			Wright Aircraft releases information about its Super Clippers, developed in secret for Pan American Airways and the military, which can carry up to 72 passengers.		Apr. 18
		Remington Rand Corp. takes steps to rehire the last 700 employees left out of work due to the strike.	U.S. Officials worry that 160 of the nation's airports are obsolete, unable to accommodate the large planes being built, or to meet safety standards.		Apr. 19
Popular preacher Father Divine hides from process servers and police after fleeing Harlem. He is charged with fraud by a former devotee, and his followers are charged with felonious assault after stabbing the process server with an ice pick.		President Franklin Roosevelt announces a relief budget of $1.5 billion for 1938, and promises no tax increases until the next session of Congress. The deficit for 1937 is $2.56 billion. . . . The first of three labor conferences hosted by Secretary of Labor Frances Perkins results in pledges to uphold the Wagner Act. Those attending include the presidents of the AFL and Standard Oil, and the heads of many unions, government agencies, and companies.		On Opening Day, Gee Walker of the Detroit Tigers hits (in order) a home run, a triple, a double, and a single. The Tigers win over Cleveland, 4–3. . . . The original A Star is Born, starring Janet Gaynor and Fredric March, written by Dorothy Parker, premieres in Los Angeles.	Apr. 20
		In Auburn and Lewiston, Maine, marching strikers pelt police with rocks one day after their four-week strike is declared illegal. Police deploy tear gas, the National Guard is called in, and the CIO claims, on behalf of the shoe factory workers, violation of the Wagner Act.		William Davidson dies. With his two brothers and friend William Harley, he helped build the first motorcycle in 1903, and was vice president of Harley-Davidson Motor Company.	Apr. 21
Student Peace Day is celebrated nationwide, as thousands of high school and college students vow, "I refuse to support the Government of the United States in any war it may conduct."		The AFL calls for a conference of all its affiliated unions in one month, and attacks the CIO as illegal and irresponsible.	Dr. Wendell Stanley reports on new research that "isolates" viruses that cause diseases, including certain cancers, arthritis, and infantile paralysis. Dr. Stanley will receive the Nobel Prize for Chemistry in 1946.	Satchel Paige and 19 other players leave the Negro League to play for the Dominican Republic League, and are banned for life from the Negro League.	Apr. 22

F	G	H	I	J
Includes elections, federal-state relations, civil rights and liberties, crime, the judiciary, education, healthcare, poverty, urban affairs, and population.	Includes formation and debate of U.S. foreign and defense policies, veterans affairs, and defense spending. (Relations with specific foreign countries are usually found under the region concerned.)	Includes business, labor, agriculture, taxation, transportation, consumer affairs, monetary and fiscal policy, natural resources, pollution, and accidents.	Includes worldwide scientific, medical, and technological developments, natural phenomena, U.S. weather, and natural disasters.	Includes the arts, religion, scholarship, communications media, sports, entertainment, fashions, fads, and social life.

	World Affairs	Europe	Africa & The Middle East	The Americas	Asia & The Pacific
Apr. 23		Three ships loaded with food, protected by British battleships, run the blockade to arrive in Bilbao. . . . Insurgents begin a second day of heavy bombardment of Bilbao, capturing hill positions and dropping bombs up to 500 pounds. Shelling of Madrid continues as well. General Franco sets up a 20-man junta to help him rule. . . . The show trial of three priests and four laymen in Germany ends. . . . Italian-Austrian talks end without a pledge from Italy to safeguard Austrian independence. . . . The Soviet newspaper *Pravda* discloses arrests and liquidations of foreign spies since August.		A mass meeting of GM employees ratifies the new contract in Ontario. . . . To end the often violent union strife in Mexico, President Lázaro Cárdenas announces he will amend labor laws to eliminate minority union group rights. . . . The Petorca volcano in Chile erupts, with earth tremors and columns of smoke and ash.	
Apr. 24	Argentine police arrest a 25-year-old burglar who confesses to the shooting of Nazi Josef Riedel during a robbery.	The official ceremony guaranteeing Belgium's neutrality but releasing the country from the Locarno Pact, takes place in Brussels with ambassadors from France and Britain. . . . Last week, 1,000 Protestants in Darmstadt, Germany, demonstrated in defiance of Nazi rules. . . . After 12 days of shelling, Madrid is quiet for a day. Loyalists appoint a council of 33 anti-fascists to administer the city, freeing General Miaja to concentrate on military matters. . . . Austrian Premier Schuschnigg, responding to reports in Italian papers, denies any intention of bargaining with Nazis.			In India, 33,000 British troops march through Waziristan, meeting little resistance from forces of the Holy Man of Ipi.
Apr. 25	The Chilean Ambassador leaves Spain for France.	The mountain peaks of the Enchortas, which foiled Napoleon, fall to Franco's forces as insurgents push closer to Bilbao. The shelling of Madrid resumes. . . . Germany's secret preparations for a Dusseldorf fair to rival Paris's in May are revealed.			
Apr. 26	In a House of Commons speech, Britain promises India and Mohandas Gandhi that its governors will not interfere in provincial policy. . . . Investigating alleged industrial sabotage by foreigners, the Soviet Union arrests Soviet bank officials as "enemies of the people." Their dealings with Japanese and German Trotskyites are examined. . . . Chile and the Netherlands negotiate a trade treaty.	Air strikes begin against Guernica, a historic Basque city of 5,000, in late afternoon as market day is coming to a close. Three hours of air raids are carried out by the Condor Legion, made up of German planes. Civilians are strafed with machine gun fire on the road. Casualties are estimated at over 1,650; at least 3,000 bombs drop, some up to 1,000 pounds. Incendiary bombs fall at the end, to create the appearance that the fleeing Basques burned their own city. . . . Minister Hermann Wilhelm Goering spends an hour with Premier Benito Mussolini in Rome, but no report of their talks is given. . . . The first quarter of Britain's defense loan, £100 million, is floated. . . . The Soviet Vice Commissar of Defense announces that U.S. mass-production techniques will be used to speed airplane manufacture.		As the Thames River in Ontario rises, police evacuate 6,000 in the communities around London. . . . Premier Patullo of British Columbia announces annexation of the Yukon Territory, subject to approval of the BC legislature. . . . House leaders of the Democrat and Republican parties in Cuba challenge each other to a duel, to be fought this week.	
Apr. 27		Durango and Marquina are occupied by General Mola, leading the insurgent forces. Eibar is in ruins; its arms factories exploded and fires may have been set by Basque defenders as they fled. . . . Scandinavian countries protest illegal seizure of their ships and goods by insurgent ships. . . . Romania sentences eight Iron Guards to life in prison for a 1936 killing. . . . By using holidays and the upcoming fair to delay votes, French Premier Léon Blum extends his "breathing spell" for several months. . . . The Pope suffers a mild heart attack.		After the Integralista manifesto is read in Brazil's Congress Hall on April 24, Integralista chief Barboza Lima is arrested in Congress as an agitator.	

A	B	C	D	E
Includes developments that affect more than one world region, international organizations, and important meetings of world leaders.	Includes all domestic and regional developments in Europe, including the Soviet Union.	Includes all domestic and regional developments in Africa and the Middle East.	Includes all domestic and regional developments in Latin America, the Caribbean, and Canada.	Includes all domestic and regional developments in Asian and Pacific nations (and colonies).

U.S. Politics & Social Issues	U.S. Foreign Policy & Defense	Economics & Great Depression	Science, Technology & Nature	Culture, Leisure & Lifestyle	
Father Divine is found in Connecticut and arrested for felonious assault. . . . After 44 days, the Senate Judiciary Committee ends hearings on the Court Reorganization Bill.		Rioting breaks out again as striking shoe workers confront National Guardsmen after a rally. Twelve people are detained, then released by the heavily armed troops . . . The Aluminum Company of America, owned by Andrew Mellon, is sued under anti-trust laws, and its dissolution is sought. . . . In Stockton, Calif., 63 men are injured, 12 seriously, when police fire shotguns and use gas to break up a cannery strike. The melee starts when strikers stop a spinach truck entering a cannery. . . . Hershey employees, back at work, vote out the CIO as their union. . . . Near San Francisco, 1,200 Ford employees strike due to claims of discrimination toward union members. They weld the gates shut, but union officials negotiate a truce around midnight.		Violet Wells Norton is found guilty of misusing the mail, but not of more serious charges, in her attempts to collect money from Clark Gable. She claims he fathered her daughter, born in England; he presented evidence of living in the Pacific Northwest when their supposed affair took place.	Apr. 23
		The Independent Automobile Employees Association is formed in Flint, Mich. Six thousand men sign up to show their antipathy toward the CIO. . . . Frantic negotiations involving the National Mediation Board continue through the weekend to avert a rail strike by 25,000 workers that would paralyze New York and New Jersey transport.		Amelia Earhart appears at Gimbels in New York, selling collector envelopes to go with her on her round-the-world trip.	Apr. 24
		California's State Federation of Labor forms a new union for striking cannery workers. The new union will negotiate, and the old leaders are pushed out of power. . . . In Maine, shoe workers rally before City Hall and promise to keep their food depots open. A judge had ordered them closed. Five companies of National Guard troops stand by.	Yale unveils the work of Prof. Ernest Pollard, measuring the nucleus of an atom. In 10 years, Prof. Pollard will also be recognized as one of the developers of radar.		Apr. 25
The Supreme Court frees Angelo Herndon, imprisoned in Georgia under a law that forbids forceful resistance to U.S. authority. The decision leaves doubt as to whether the law is questioned, or simply its application to Herndon, an African American and a Communist. . . . The President surprises the House, asking it to put aside labor legislation until it votes on his Court Reorganization Bill.		New York and New Jersey avoid a transit strike. Using his authority under the Railway Labor Act, the President mandates a 60-day truce and appoints an emergency board to examine the disputes. . . . Owing to recent Supreme Court decisions, companies such as Carnegie-Illinois Steel are ending their "company representative" plans, withdrawing support and facilities. . . . In Maine, the Supreme Court allows the food depots to stay open. Company and union officials meet for the first time since the shoe workers' strike began. . . . Pearl Bergoff and Remington Rand president James Rand are charged with violating federal law in their strikebreaking activities. Trial is set for May 17.	Floodwaters from the Allegheny and Monongahela rivers threaten Pittsburgh. The Potomac and Tidewater regions also flood, sporadically inundating airports, rail lines, and a power plant.		Apr. 26
		Rep. Cannon introduces a bill impounding 15 percent of all expenditures for fiscal year 1938, with a few exceptions. The President would be empowered to restore any part of the impounded funds. . . . Progress is made in all-day talks to end the Maine shoe strike, but disagreement remains over rehiring all strikers. . . . A CIO-affiliated union signs a contract with Firestone Tire and Rubber, ending a two-month-long strike by 10,000 employees.	A rivet forged of California gold, intended as the last rivet to go into the $35 million Golden Gate Bridge, shatters at the dedication ceremony. A steel rivet is found; the bridge is completed.		Apr. 27

F	G	H	I	J
Includes elections, federal-state relations, civil rights and liberties, crime, the judiciary, education, healthcare, poverty, urban affairs, and population.	Includes formation and debate of U.S. foreign and defense policies, veterans affairs, and defense spending. (Relations with specific foreign countries are usually found under the region concerned.)	Includes business, labor, agriculture, taxation, transportation, consumer affairs, monetary and fiscal policy, natural resources, pollution, and accidents.	Includes worldwide scientific, medical, and technological developments, natural phenomena, U.S. weather, and natural disasters.	Includes the arts, religion, scholarship, communications media, sports, entertainment, fashions, fads, and social life.

	World Affairs	Europe	Africa & The Middle East	The Americas	Asia & The Pacific
Apr. 28	The working committee of the All-India Congress Party desires more of an assurance on nonuse of British governors' privileges than was provided in the speech two days ago. The speech is interpreted as misleading and discourteous. . . . Princeton and Yale join England's Oxford University in declining invitations to send delegations to the bicentennial of Germany's Goettingen University. Harvard tentatively accepts.	Insurgents deny bombing Guernica as reports from many eyewitnesses reach the press about the destruction of the city. In Bilbao, 30,000 Basque troops dig in to repel an insurgent siege. . . . Britain and France are asked to help evacuate Basque residents of Bilbao by sea as Franco's troops press closer. . . . Father Roussaint, the first of the seven men tried last week in a German People's Court, is sentenced to 11 years in prison for "preparation for high treason." Other sentences range from 18 months to five years; three men are acquitted of charges. . . . The Reich forms a New York corporation to acquire raw materials from United States, paying in kind rather than cash. . . . The French government proposes taking over railroads and raising fares to get the railroads out of debt. . . . Two academies in Warsaw close due to anti-Semitic riots and attacks.		In Chile, high prices and low stocks of agricultural goods—including staples such as wheat—cause alarm and some restrictions, as politicians try to fix the situation.	
Apr. 29		A "diplomatic source" in Paris blames Col. Hermann Wilhelm Goering for planning the attack on Guernica and providing the craft and pilots to carry it out. . . . One thousand Catholic monks—or one of every 13 serving in Germany—are arrested, accused of immorality by the Reich courts. A newspaper campaign exposing homosexuality and more lurid crimes supports the charges. Seizure of monastery records over a year ago, to investigate financial transfers, is the source of some charges.		President Lázaro Cárdenas plans to divide land among peasants in Mexicali, Baja California. The land, seized under the Agrarian Code, belonged to the Colorado River Company, which had invested $10 million in it. The United States backs the company's protests to Mexico. . . . Strict censorship cuts off news from Brazil for a day. A tense political situation between the president, governor, and military leaves doubt as to who is in control.	
Apr. 30	The last foreign privileges in Egypt will end in 1949, the League of Nations announces.	General Franco's only battleship sinks after either striking a mine or being hit with bombs dropped by loyalist planes. Fishing boats and an insurgent destroyer pick up surviving crew. . . . President Eamon de Valera presents a new constitution to the free state of Ireland. Pending voter approval, Eire will elect a president who will appoint ministers and a judiciary. . . . Water from the Volga River flows into a new, 80-mile canal to Moscow. . . . Two of the largest Jewish-owned companies in Germany are now in Aryan hands: M. Kempinsky's well-known restaurants, and the Loeser and Wolff cigar plant and stores. The Aryanization of smaller firms is a daily occurrence.		The Yukon Council opposes annexation to British Columbia and proposes a vote. . . . Quebec's Premier Duplessis orders the arrest of Bernard Shane of the ILGWU and labor leader Raoul Trepannier on conspiracy charges stemming from the recent dressmakers' strike.	Japan votes for new representatives, but observers report the populace is disinterested. . . . General Yang Hu-chen, who led a coup attempt last year, resigns as a commissioner of Shensi province to travel in Europe.
May 1	Britain keeps the United States apprised of talks between them and Japan about China. Japan seeks to arrange a loan for China and promises to respect territorial integrity. China watches the attempt at rapprochement with skepticism.	Insurgents bombard Madrid. Near Jaen, loyalists capture a mountain sanctuary where 250 civil guards and their families have been barricaded since the start of the war. As Bilbao's Iron Ring of defense is tested, a British destroyer picks up the Ambassador and his staff. No refugees are allowed to board the ship. . . . On the eve of the coronation, 25,000 London busmen walk off their jobs, to be joined by 125,000 off-duty workers. . . . In Poland, bombs are thrown by fascists at Jewish and socialist May Day parades. . . . Adolf Hitler, addressing a crowd of 1.5 million, rails against churches, warning them not to interfere in his state.		A 100-year-old border dispute between Peru and Ecuador remains unresolved as talks break down after six months. . . . The governor of Puerto Rico signs a law allowing the dissemination of birth control information. . . . President Vargas of Brazil still controls his country, but has declared martial law and removed a governor from office.	Early election returns in Japan show candidates in opposition to the Cabinet are winning victories. . . . In a plebiscite, women in the Philippines regain the right to vote.
May 2		Plans to evacuate children from Bilbao rely on loyalist and British ships getting to a port frequently shelled by insurgent planes. . . . A Polish court sentences 44 members of Unakor, the Ukrainian National Cossacks, to hard labor. With aid from German and Russian collaborators, they stockpiled weapons and planned an uprising.	King Ibn Saud of Saudi Arabia rails against Western ways, saying he would kill any of his subjects who adopted them.	Former Cuban president General Menocal splits from the Democratic Party, posing a new threat to the army-supported regime of President Laredo Bru.	The supporters of Premier Hayashi win only 11 seats of the 466-seat Diet. The Premier faces the worst defeat in Japan's history.

A	B	C	D	E
Includes developments that affect more than one world region, international organizations, and important meetings of world leaders.	Includes all domestic and regional developments in Europe, including the Soviet Union.	Includes all domestic and regional developments in Africa and the Middle East.	Includes all domestic and regional developments in Latin America, the Caribbean, and Canada.	Includes all domestic and regional developments in Asian and Pacific nations (and colonies).

U.S. Politics & Social Issues	U.S. Foreign Policy & Defense	Economics & Great Depression	Science, Technology & Nature	Culture, Leisure & Lifestyle	
The La Follette subcommittee continues to hear riveting testimony about violence and threats in the mines of Harlan County, Ky. . . . In Los Angeles, four of Father Divine's followers are indicted for transporting an underage African-American female across state lines for immoral purposes. New York prosecutors promise a grand jury investigation into the preacher's activities.		A negotiator from the NLRB works for a settlement with the blind sit-down strikers in New York. . . . Stock prices in the United States and Europe drop sharply due to President Franklin Roosevelt's caution against rising prices and other news.		Official birthdate of Saddam Hussein, ruler of Iraq.	Apr. 28
	Congress puts all other business aside to vote on the Neutrality Bill. It will be rushed to President Franklin Roosevelt, who is en route to a fishing trip in Texas. The previous Neutrality Act expires at the end of this month.	A federal court halts the anti-trust case against Aluminum Company of America. A similar case had been tried in 1912, and the company already complies with a consent decree issued then.	Harvard physicists J. C. Street and Edward C. Stevenson reveal the discovery of previously unknown positive and negative particles in cosmic rays, which will eventually be called muons.	Actor and playwright William Gillette dies in Hartford, Conn.	Apr. 29
			At the meeting of the American Physical Society, Prof. Hans Bethe of Cornell (a future Nobel laureate) explains the heat released by bombarding atoms with deuterons.		Apr. 30
	The Neutrality Act becomes effective.	The sit-down strike of blind workers in New York ends with terms consistent with the Wagner Act. . . . In San Francisco, 3,500 workers belonging to six different unions strike 15 leading hotels at 5 p.m. . . . Three thousand movie technicians strike and picket Hollywood studios.			May 1
		The 5,600 members of the Screen Actors Guild (SAG) will learn on May 5 whether they support the movie technicians' strike, which affects nine studios. . . . Telephones, elevators, maids, bellboys, and even heat are nonoperational in the San Francisco hotels where service workers continue their strike. . . . The 243,000-member ILGWU (International Ladies' Garment Workers Union) snubs the AFL by not inviting them to their 23rd convention, and condemning their "rule or ruin" tactics in dealing with the CIO.			May 2

F	G	H	I	J
Includes elections, federal-state relations, civil rights and liberties, crime, the judiciary, education, healthcare, poverty, urban affairs, and population.	Includes formation and debate of U.S. foreign and defense policies, veterans affairs, and defense spending. (Relations with specific foreign countries are usually found under the region concerned.)	Includes business, labor, agriculture, taxation, transportation, consumer affairs, monetary and fiscal policy, natural resources, pollution, and accidents.	Includes worldwide scientific, medical, and technological developments, natural phenomena, U.S. weather, and natural disasters.	Includes the arts, religion, scholarship, communications media, sports, entertainment, fashions, fads, and social life.

	World Affairs	Europe	Africa & The Middle East	The Americas	Asia & The Pacific
May 3	The Permanent Court of International Justice begins its 40th session. . . . Britain delays decisions about Japan, awaiting political developments. . . . The divorce of Wallis Warfield Simpson, fiancée of the Duke of Windsor, is declared absolute by a British court.	The family of Basque President Aguirre flees to France with foreign diplomats. General Franco will not allow a sea evacuation of noncombatants, suggesting instead a safety zone north of the city. France and Britain defy him and send ships. . . . Gunfights between anarchists and police erupt in Barcelona, and the central telephone office is stormed. Violence spreads through the city as radio broadcasts attempt to restore order. Reports blame an anarchist uprising and Catalan President Lluís Companys sends for troops. . . . King George VI asks his ministers to try and end the bus strike in London before his coronation. . . . Germany's Foreign Minister Neurath arrives in Rome for talks; Premier Kurt Schuschnigg of Austria goes to Hungary.		Mexican newspapers announce that 1.7 million Mexicans have received communal lands from the government, which implies that 45 percent of the population lives on their own land. . . . Besides Mount Petorca, two other volcanoes in Chile, Mounts Planchon and Quizapu, have become active. . . . The Quebec Parliament debates the ongoing dressmakers' strike.	Japanese Premier Hayashi speaks to the Emperor, then announces that he will stay in office due to a political "emergency" and will seek compromise with the new Diet.
May 4	When London's Non-Intervention Committee suggests banning aerial bombings of undefended towns (such as Guernica), Germany's Ambassador von Ribbentrop protests that such events are inevitable in war.	Gunfights continue in Barcelona, where a general strike is called. Factions labeled Trotskyist, anarchist, socialist, workers, and communist fight for control. . . . The few buildings to survive Guernica's initial bombing, such as the cathedral, are shelled and damaged as fighting rages through the Basque region. . . . Vatican diplomats approach Hitler, insisting that the Catholic Church and schools be left alone. . . . Hungary shows off its troops and weaponry in its first military parade, before Austrian leaders.	Police in Palestine believe they have uncovered an international arms ring. They charge arms dealer Rueben Schenzvit in last month's murder of Jacob Zwanger, a Russian Jew, though Schenzvit's Arab henchman has confessed to the crime.	In a power shift, Brazil's Congress elects Pedro Alexio as Speaker and (by default) vice president of the country.	
May 5	German Ambassador von Ribbentrop reverses himself and agrees that air attacks against civilians should be banned.	A new coalition of several factions governs Barcelona under President Lluís Companys. . . . British warships stand ready to escort two Spanish ships carrying 5,000 refugees from Bilbao. . . . Talks between Italy and Germany develop plans for close communication to exchange political, industrial, and economic information. Both countries agree to ignore the League of Nations. . . . In Germany, trials of Catholic monks proceed apace, with sentences for immorality ranging from one to five years. Judges in Coblenz sentence seven today, 11 on May 3. These public trials occur only after long, private inquiries have elicited guilty verdicts. . . . The Nazi majority of the Danzig Senate votes to extend its emergency powers for four more years.		The Supreme Court of Mexico strikes down a Chihuahua law mandating only one priest per state.	
May 6	A five-year pact between 22 nations is signed at the World Sugar Conference in London. Production, export quotas, and marketing will be regulated by an international council. . . . The Paraguayan Embassy in Madrid is raided, and a radio transmitter seized. Four hundred women and children refugees are removed from the building.	Anarchists briefly gain control of Barcelona and demand the withdrawal of assault troops. Death squads kill several prominent anarchists in their own homes. Four hundred die and 1,500 are injured in the few days of fighting. . . . Bulgaria shows off tanks and new weaponry in a military parade; like Hungary and Austria, the country has been arming itself beyond the limits imposed by peace treaties.			
May 7	Although flags fly at half-staff in Germany, Graf Zeppelin intends to go ahead with its transatlantic flight schedules and reports few cancellations. Rumors of sabotage to the Hindenburg are discounted. . . . Harvard reconsiders and joins Yale, Dartmouth, the University of Pennsylvania, and other schools in declining the invitation to attend Goettingen University's bicentennial.	Barcelona is quiet, and Premier Caballero visits. Anarchists hold the cities of Gerona and Figueras, near the French border. Saragossa is heavily bombed by loyalist forces, while insurgent planes continue to bomb Basque villages. . . . French Premier Léon Blum secures the cooperation of unions and labor for the next few months. . . . The Little Entente meets in Yugoslavia, affirming unity, while Czech President Benes tours the German areas of his country, pressing for pro-German cooperation.		Mexican newspapers report that the Supreme Court pledges support for the administration and its policies. Since President Lázaro Cárdenas reduced the justices' terms from life to six years, they have not ruled against him and will probably uphold his decisions regarding foreign policies and investments. . . . The heavily guarded trial of 35 men accused of leading the 1935 revolt begins in Rio de Janeiro, Brazil.	

A	B	C	D	E
Includes developments that affect more than one world region, international organizations, and important meetings of world leaders.	Includes all domestic and regional developments in Europe, including the Soviet Union.	Includes all domestic and regional developments in Africa and the Middle East.	Includes all domestic and regional developments in Latin America, the Caribbean, and Canada.	Includes all domestic and regional developments in Asian and Pacific nations (and colonies).

U.S. Politics & Social Issues	U.S. Foreign Policy & Defense	Economics & Great Depression	Science, Technology & Nature	Culture, Leisure & Lifestyle	
A Florida claims court awards Seminole Indians $11,000 for breach of an 1856 treaty, reducing their 1935 award to one percent of the original amount.		At the start of a workweek, the Hollywood strike expands to 6,000 employees. Studios are charged with hiring strikebreakers. . . . Alfred P. Sloan becomes chair of General Motors and William Knudsen president in a company reorganization. A dividend of $1 per share of common stock for the first quarter is also announced.	The zeppelin *Hindenburg* leaves Germany for New York on its first trip of the season. A delay of 48 hours for its next flight, due in New York May 13, is announced so that coronation newsreels can be transported.	Margaret Mitchell, author of *Gone With the Wind*, is the first woman to win a major Pulitzer Prize.	May 3
	President Franklin Roosevelt dislikes changes recommended by the House to his sugar bill, and may scrap it.	Shoe strikers in Maine vote to return to work, and in 15 days, vote on a bargaining unit under the Wagner Act. . . . In Hollywood, a gang breaks into a nonstriking film workers' union hall. Six men are hospitalized. Producers meet with heads of the SAG, which is not on strike. . . . Labor Secretary Frances Perkins appeals publicly for more conferences and fewer strikes and lockouts.		With bases loaded in the 11th inning, the Washington Senators pull off a triple steal to win the game. Cleveland is the loser.	May 4
The La Folette Senate subcommittee investigating labor espionage adjourns so that perjury charges can be studied.		General Motors in St. Louis, Mo., sees another sit-down strike over the firing of 37 workers, as 3,700 walk off their jobs.			May 5
		Philadelphia's largest nonunion hosiery mill is stormed by 300 workers who then stage a sit-down strike. The action follows a week of lesser demonstrations. One hundred police and thousands of CIO sympathizers stand by. . . . In Maine, six CIO leaders are sentenced to six months in jail for violating injunctions barring their strike.	The *Hindenburg* burns over Lakehurst, N.Y. Thirty-six are killed or mortally injured as the airship burns in 34 seconds, the fire fed by hydrogen cells. Amazingly, 62 people on the ship survive. Many journalists are present, and the event is caught on newsreels. . . . The $10 million Mellon Institute of Industrial Research in Pittsburgh is dedicated.		May 6
		The St. Louis strike against GM is settled, and 4,000 will return to work on May 10. The settlement gives seniority to temporary workers. . . . The CIO protests the jailing of six shoe workers in Maine and writes to the La Follette subcommittee of the Senate for support. . . . Union leaders in Hollywood accept picketing help from the CIO, longshoremen, and other unions. They plan to picket theaters nationwide.	Herbert Morrison's description of the *Hindenburg* crash, recorded for Chicago station WLS, is broadcast containing the words, "Oh, the humanity." . . . Five sets of newsreel footage capturing the crash are rushed to theaters. . . . Captain Lehmann dies of his burns from the *Hindenburg* crash.		May 7

F	G	H	I	J
Includes elections, federal-state relations, civil rights and liberties, crime, the judiciary, education, healthcare, poverty, urban affairs, and population.	Includes formation and debate of U.S. foreign and defense policies, veterans affairs, and defense spending. (Relations with specific foreign countries are usually found under the region concerned.)	Includes business, labor, agriculture, taxation, transportation, consumer affairs, monetary and fiscal policy, natural resources, pollution, and accidents.	Includes worldwide scientific, medical, and technological developments, natural phenomena, U.S. weather, and natural disasters.	Includes the arts, religion, scholarship, communications media, sports, entertainment, fashions, fads, and social life.

	World Affairs	Europe	Africa & The Middle East	The Americas	Asia & The Pacific
May 8	In a speech, John Dewey charges Soviet Ambassador Troyanovsky with trying to sabotage the investigation into Leon Trotsky's actions.	Thousands of government assault troops arrive from Valencia to restore order in Barcelona. The horribly mutilated bodies of 12 young men arrested a few days before in Barcelona are found. The corpse of the arrested Prof. Berneri and two of his friends are also found. . . . The Italian press withdraws from Britain, angry with the criticism of Italy's policies toward Ethiopia and Spain. Reporters are recalled from London, and most British papers will be banned in Italy. . . . New rules in Germany force all girls between 17 and 21 to wear the uniform and participate in the activities of the Hitler Youth. . . . In Düsseldorf, Commissar Hermann Goering opens Germany's exposition of national products.		Brazil sentences the 35 on trial for their roles in the November 1935 revolt. Six are released for time served, and others receive terms of up to 27 years. New charges are leveled against the governor of Pernambuco.	
May 9		Mounts Solluve and Jata are captured by the insurgents under General Mosa from Basque defenders. Thousands of refugees from Bilbao have been carried to France by Spanish, British, and French ships. . . . Celebrating the first anniversary of its African conquest, Italy stages a military parade, with 25,000 fascist troops and 10,000 African troops marching. The general wage of Italian workers increases by 10–12 percent. . . . As Minister of Aviation, General Hermann Goering orders a halt to *Graf Zeppelin* service until the investigation into the crash is complete.			
May 10		Insurgent planes bomb a monastery and villages near Bilbao, attempting to cut off that city's water. . . . In London, 300,000 visitors crowd to see George VI's coronation ceremonies. It is expected that over a million Brits from outside the city will visit as well. The busmen's strike continues, and other groups of workers also threaten a general strike.			
May 11	Dignitaries and mourners gather at the Hamburg-American Pier at West 46th Street in New York for funeral services for 28 people killed in the *Hindenburg* crash.	The coronation of King George VI takes place in London. Over a million spectators line the six-mile route from Buckingham Palace to Westminster Abbey. . . . Due to the Italian boycott of British news, the Vatican newspaper *Osservatore* is the only available source of coronation news in Rome. . . . Debate on a new Irish constitution proposed by President de Valera opens in the Dail Eireann. A concurrent demonstration in Dublin against the British monarchy by extremists confronts police and is eventually dispersed.	Arabs declare themselves in mourning over a British decision to allow 770 Jewish immigrants into Palestine before the end of July.	Governor Yocupicio of Sonora reopens the cathedral in Hermosillo after a three-year closure brought about by a former governor who closed all churches and expelled all priests. . . . The former, impeached president of Cuba, Dr. Miguel Mariano Gomez, asks his country's Supreme Court to reinstate him.	
May 12		Over 3,000 Spanish government troops have been killed in recent attacks on Toledo, according to rebel sources. In Bilbao, 7,400 have been evacuated but 300,000 people are still under siege in the city.		Tensions ease in Brazil as President Vargas transfers military power from Governor Flores de Cuna to a military commander. The power struggle between the two men has a long history.	

A	B	C	D	E
Includes developments that affect more than one world region, international organizations, and important meetings of world leaders.	*Includes all domestic and regional developments in Europe, including the Soviet Union.*	*Includes all domestic and regional developments in Africa and the Middle East.*	*Includes all domestic and regional developments in Latin America, the Caribbean, and Canada.*	*Includes all domestic and regional developments in Asian and Pacific nations (and colonies).*

U.S. Politics & Social Issues	U.S. Foreign Policy & Defense	Economics & Great Depression	Science, Technology & Nature	Culture, Leisure & Lifestyle	
	Two naval airmen die as their plane crashes into the Pacific during war games.	The SAG elects to support the nine-day strikes of technical and craft employees, and top stars will begin walking picket lines on May 10.	The U.S. Navy appoints its own board to investigate the *Hindenburg* crash, simultaneously with a commission appointed by the Commerce Department.	War Admiral, the favorite, wins the Kentucky Derby.	**May 8**
		Most major studios agree to meet strikers' demands. The SAG will picket independent studios who do not, and picket theaters nationwide until a full settlement is reached. . . . The settlement with Packard, a division of General Motors, is the first to guarantee a union (the UAWA) exclusive bargaining rights, effective for one year.			**May 9**
The only African-American Congressman, Arthur Mitchell, files a $50,000 lawsuit against the Pullman Company and the Illinois Central and Rock Island Railroads. He was ejected from his car as the train entered Arkansas, threatened, and forced to sit in a substandard car.		Federal arbitrator Frank Laughlin gives 50,000 Manhattan workers a raise and a week of paid vacation. The settlement is between the Realty Advisory Board on Labor Relations and the Building Service Employees Union. . . . The Friedman-Harry Marks Clothing Company, whose labor dispute was decided by the Supreme Court, signs a contract with Amalgamated Clothing Workers, giving its 900 workers a 36-hour week.	A three-person panel begins investigation of the *Hindenburg* crash for the United States. A five-man committee of zeppelin experts from Germany is en route to New York.		**May 10**
The New York City Bar Association votes to admit women.		The House slashes President Franklin Roosevelt's proposed 1938 relief allocation by one-third, and votes against making the CCC a permanent agency—although it extends the CCC for another two years.		*Captains Courageous*, with Spencer Tracy (in an Oscar-winning role) and Freddie Bartholomew, opens in New York. . . . Maurice Evans, starring in *Richard II* in New York, is presented the Delia Austrian Medal of the Drama League for the most distinguished performance of the year.	**May 11**
		John L. Lewis of the CIO tells the ILGWU meeting in Atlantic City that U.S. workers have lost confidence in the AFL, and that he will not make peace with that organization. . . . A CIO strike closes the Jones-Laughlin Steel Plant in Pittsburgh, idling 27,000 workers. . . . Two short strikes over raises by 25 workers shut down a General Motors plant once again; work will resume tomorrow while the matter is negotiated.			**May 12**

F	G	H	I	J
Includes elections, federal-state relations, civil rights and liberties, crime, the judiciary, education, healthcare, poverty, urban affairs, and population.	*Includes formation and debate of U.S. foreign and defense policies, veterans affairs, and defense spending. (Relations with specific foreign countries are usually found under the region concerned.)*	*Includes business, labor, agriculture, taxation, transportation, consumer affairs, monetary and fiscal policy, natural resources, pollution, and accidents.*	*Includes worldwide scientific, medical, and technological developments, natural phenomena, U.S. weather, and natural disasters.*	*Includes the arts, religion, scholarship, communications media, sports, entertainment, fashions, fads, and social life.*

	World Affairs	Europe	Africa & The Middle East	The Americas	Asia & The Pacific
May 13		The British destroyer *Hunter* strikes a mine off the coast of Spain that kills eight and injures 20. . . . A German pilot, shot down by Basques, admits to dropping bombs on Guernica. Insurgent leaders and their allies have denied the raid, claiming the city was destroyed with fire set by its own citizens. . . . Germans reveal that a seaplane and submarine harbor and fortifications are under construction on the Baltic Sea, north of Hamburg. . . . Germany imposes a 100 percent tax on imported rubber, previously duty-free, to finance efforts to manufacture artificial rubber. . . . A bomb destroys a statue of George II in Dublin. The act is seen as the "anti-coronation" statement of Irish extremists. . . . In Brest-Litovsk, Poland, the son of a Jewish butcher kills a policeman. Jews make up half the population of 50,000 in the city, and for 18 hours they are the targets of looting, burning, stoning, and other violence. Police do nothing.		Mexico will tax as profit 35 percent of the gross on all sales of foreign companies. Most U.S. salesmen protest and will reduce their business there. . . . The Cuban Supreme Court hears arguments against a recent presidential decree that forces companies to hire women at a rate of 50 percent. They claim the law, which may put 20,000 men out of work, is unconstitutional.	
May 14	The Empire Conference of free nations within the British Commonwealth—Great Britain, Canada, New Zealand, Australia, and South Africa—begins in London.	Three thousand insurgents in Madrid, besieged for weeks in the University City section, split into factions and exchange gunfire, reportedly divided over whether or not to surrender. . . . Anti-Jewish rioting in Poland enters a second day and spreads to other cities.		An investigative committee sponsored by the ACLU leaves for Puerto Rico to inquire into the riots of March 21 in Ponce.	
May 15		While insurgent planes bomb Valencia and kill 38 people, Spanish Prime Minister Caballero asks for his ministers' resignations. . . . In Albania, former Cabinet Minister Toto and the army launch a rebellion, sparked by a new law prohibiting the veiling of women. . . . Christian X, King of Denmark and Iceland, celebrates his 25th anniversary on the throne. . . . Nazi police close a Catholic seminary in Heiligenstadt, citing "wretched moral conditions" among the students. One Catholic order, Maristen Schulbruder, has moved to Hungary, after eight of its schools were closed. Trials of monks and laymen, many prompted by morals charges, continue. . . . Anti-Jewish rioting in Poland spreads to Warsaw, where a bomb is set off, and to other towns. In Brest-Litovsk, the records, inventories, and the homes of up to 1,200 Jewish businessmen have been destroyed.	A hunger strike among Arabs held in Acre prison along with a general strike in Haifa result in the release of 100 prisoners. All were held because of involvement in uprisings.	Armando Salles de Oliveira of the Constitutionalista Party launches his campaign for the presidency of Brazil, with the support of leaders allied with the Vargas revolution of 1930. . . . Mexico's Secretary of War, General Camacho, orders the disarming of landowners and merchants—but not of peasants.	Japan's premier, supported by the military, circumvents the results of recent elections by appointing advisory bureaus, who will draft legislation and guide financial policy. . . . High Commissioner McNutt informs envoys in Manila that all correspondence with the Philippine Commonwealth must be sent to him.
May 16		Premier Caballeros of Spain is forced to resign. . . . All members of the secretariat of Soviet trade unions, except for its head, are fired and called "enemies of the people." Four men are arrested and charged with malfeasance. . . . In Yugoslavia, fighting between police and peasants in Gospic results in six deaths and the burning of buildings.		After weeks of controversy, the Colombian government has not intervened to protect the interests of the Colombia Tobacco Company from newcomer British American Tobacco Company.	

A	B	C	D	E
Includes developments that affect more than one world region, international organizations, and important meetings of world leaders.	Includes all domestic and regional developments in Europe, including the Soviet Union.	Includes all domestic and regional developments in Africa and the Middle East.	Includes all domestic and regional developments in Latin America, the Caribbean, and Canada.	Includes all domestic and regional developments in Asian and Pacific nations (and colonies).

U.S. Politics & Social Issues	U.S. Foreign Policy & Defense	Economics & Great Depression	Science, Technology & Nature	Culture, Leisure & Lifestyle	
		Nearly 6,000 employees strike at the Pittsburgh Steel Company. Union leaders forecast a nationwide strike of 178,000 steel workers at four independent companies that have not signed with unions: Bethlehem, Crucible, Youngstown, and Republic.			May 13
Charges are dropped against Father Divine and his followers when witnesses, including the victim, cannot identify those who stabbed a process server last month. Approximately 1,500 people, mostly African Americans, were present when the crime occurred; all the witnesses called by the court are white.		The December 14 injunction against the TVA is dissolved, freeing the agency to complete construction on some projects while it awaits a lower court decision on the constitutionality of the TVA Act. . . . Steel workers of Pittsburgh and Jones-Laughlin return to work. Their employers agree to recognize the Steel Workers Organization Committee and hold consent elections within two weeks. . . . The federal board negotiating with New York transit workers and railways announces that a settlement is reached, granting some raises and ensuring further negotiations with the longshoremen's union.	Henry T. "Dick" Merrill completes the first commercial round-trip flight between Europe and the United States, crossing the North Atlantic in 24 hours—a new record.		May 14
		Two thousand maids, bellboys, cooks, and other service employees walk out of eight St. Louis hotels. . . . The AFL suspends three Los Angeles unions, including a branch of the ILGWU covering 10,000 workers, for long-time affiliations with the CIO.		Phillip Snowden, Viscount of Ickornshaw, British politician, and the Labor/Socialist party's first Chancellor of the Exchequer, dies. . . . War Admiral, a race horse, wins the Preakness.	May 15
		The SAG negotiates a 10-year-long contract. Two of the film craft unions on strike will return to work, but the other nine unions are holding out for a closed shop. . . . The one-day strike of hotel workers in St. Louis, Mo., is settled with an agreement for a closed shop.			May 16

F	G	H	I	J
Includes elections, federal-state relations, civil rights and liberties, crime, the judiciary, education, healthcare, poverty, urban affairs, and population.	*Includes formation and debate of U.S. foreign and defense policies, veterans affairs, and defense spending. (Relations with specific foreign countries are usually found under the region concerned.)*	*Includes business, labor, agriculture, taxation, transportation, consumer affairs, monetary and fiscal policy, natural resources, pollution, and accidents.*	*Includes worldwide scientific, medical, and technological developments, natural phenomena, U.S. weather, and natural disasters.*	*Includes the arts, religion, scholarship, communications media, sports, entertainment, fashions, fads, and social life.*

	World Affairs	Europe	Africa & The Middle East	The Americas	Asia & The Pacific
May 17		Juan Negrín becomes the new Premier of Spain and forms a Cabinet, excluding syndicalists. . . . Fierce fighting by both sides for the past week results in a stalemate in the Basque region. The steamer *Habana* delivers nearly 4,000 refugees to France, half of them children. . . . In its quest to root out sabotage, the Kremlin establishes military councils requiring all commands to be countersigned by Communist Party members. . . . Austria's Foreign Minister Schmidt visits France; observers speculate about a defense pact between the two nations and Britain.		In a bid to avert a strike in 10 days, Mexico's oil workers are given a pay raise. . . . To keep bread prices down, Ecuador's government builds and will operate a large bakery.	A boiler explosion on a small launch near Hong Kong kills 30 people.
May 18		Insurgents enter Amorebieto, nine miles from Bilbao, after machine guns and incendiary bombs render it harmless. . . . Although the government of Albania says a localized revolt was crushed, reports of sporadic fighting continue.		Governor Manero of Tabasco says he will not persecute Catholics in the Mexican state, but points out that priests must be married to conduct ceremonies—it is in the constitution. . . . Exiles from Honduras report that 130 prominent persons are being held by President Andina, along with 700 other political prisoners.	Japan's two leading political parties announce their goal of bringing down Premier Hayashi's government.
May 19	Spain asks the League of Nations to reconsider intervention in its civil war.	The Basque towns of Munguai, Maruri, and Plencia are bombed into submission by insurgent planes, who also strafe those who try to escape. . . . Germany demands that the Vatican rebuke Archbishop Mundelein of Chicago for his sharp criticism of the recent show trials of monks and laymen in Germany.			
May 20		Contrary to earlier reports, Basque forces hold Munguai still, and claim that German planes dropped incendiary bombs on it this morning. . . . News is revealed that the Soviet Union shot 44 citizens in Siberia. Their crime was spying for Japan; at least one of those executed was a woman. . . . Dr. Guido Schmidt, Austria's foreign minister, affirms Austria's ties with the Reich, Italy, and Hungary, rebuffing advice from France to join the Little Entente.			
May 21	A Soviet team lands at the North Pole to establish a permanent scientific station and a base for flights between Russia and America.	Heavy shelling of Madrid by insurgents resumes. In Bilbao, captured German pilots are tried and condemned for their roles in bombing towns and strafing roads with machine guns. The ship *Habana* leaves Bilbao for Britain with 3,800 children. . . . A television transmitter is placed on the Eiffel Tower. . . . The German secret police seek those who gave information to Archbishop Mundelein in Chicago. Those convicted of treason could be beheaded. . . . Nikolai Bukharin, once a top Bolshevist and economic adviser, is removed as head of the Institute of Sciences. . . . Czech police arrest 109 Nazis at a rally, attended by 14,000, for using the forbidden Hitler salute.			
May 22	The Soviet Union claims the North Pole as its own territory. The United States disputes this since there is no land there, but only international water and ice. All hail the Soviet achievement, however.	French sources estimate that 300,000 have died in the 10 months of the Spanish civil war. . . . Soviets execute at least 20 more people accused of plotting to overthrow the state in Tiflis, Georgia. . . . The Reich has seized and closed 18 Catholic print shops and presses, according to the *Osservatore Romano*. . . . Over the past week, the Gestapo arrests six Protestant pastors for attacking the state at church assemblies. In addition, 30 have been forbidden to preach. . . . Sporadic outbreaks of looting and violence against Jews continue in Poland. The government, after nine days of silence, dismisses two city administrators in Brest-Litovsk, but a socialist paper is the only media condemning the attacks.		Deputy Filhu of Brazil warns his country against Nazi propaganda, pointing out the increased trade with Germany and that country's desire for raw resources.	

A	B	C	D	E
Includes developments that affect more than one world region, international organizations, and important meetings of world leaders.	*Includes all domestic and regional developments in Europe, including the Soviet Union.*	*Includes all domestic and regional developments in Africa and the Middle East.*	*Includes all domestic and regional developments in Latin America, the Caribbean, and Canada.*	*Includes all domestic and regional developments in Asian and Pacific nations (and colonies).*

U.S. Politics & Social Issues	U.S. Foreign Policy & Defense	Economics & Great Depression	Science, Technology & Nature	Culture, Leisure & Lifestyle	
Senate subcommittee efforts to compromise on the Court Reorganization Bill collapse. It will be presented to the full Senate with an adverse report.		Two of the targeted steel companies, Republic and Youngstown, announce that if a strike occurs they will shut down their plants and wait it out.... Pickets overturn a car filled with returning workers near Columbia Studios in Hollywood. Police break up fights; 5,000 film workers are still on strike. . . . A new Agricultural Adjustment Act is introduced in Congress.			May 17
Conservative Justice W. Van Devanter, age 78, announces his retirement from the Supreme Court.		A Kearny, N.J., shipyard with naval construction contracts shuts down after a demonstration turns into a strike, triggered by the suspension of one employee who participated in a previous sit-down.			May 18
President Franklin Roosevelt vetoes a bill authorizing $5 million for the 1939 New York World's Fair. . . . Based on testimony received by the La Follette subcommittee, the Justice Department sends federal agents to investigate civil rights abuses in Harlan, Ky.		Governor Frank Murphy of Michigan successfully demands the end to a strike of Consumers Power Company employees that darkened the Saginaw Valley for several hours. . . . Up to 1,000 Bethlehem Steel employees stage a 24-hour strike for higher wages, then agree to return to work for one week before further action is taken. . . . Coal miners in Illinois stage a sit-down strike in a mine.		Pitcher Dizzy Dean starts a brawl that empties all the benches in a game between the New York Giants and St. Louis Cardinals.	May 19
		Governor Frank Murphy opens negotiations between workers and power company officials by warning that the state will not tolerate breaks in electrical service. . . . Employees of the Jones and Laughlin Steel Corp. vote throughout the night on whether a CIO-affiliated union should represent them. . . . The Senate votes to make the CCC a permanent organization, and will ask the House for a conference.	The volcano of Santa Ana in El Salvador shows activity, worrying a nearby city of 75,000 people.	Dizzy Dean and Jim Ripple are fined $50 each for instigating the sixth-inning brawl in St. Louis.	May 20
	Secretary of State Cordell Hull reorganizes the State Department, folding the Mexican Division into a new Division of American Republics.	Workers at Jones and Laughlin choose the CIO Steel Workers Organizing Committee by almost 70 percent. . . . Yale and Towne Manufacturing in Detroit, whose workers have been on strike since March 9, closes its Detroit plant permanently. It was the site of a violent clash with police on April 14. . . . Actors complain that pickets vandalize their cars at studios.	Amelia Earhart's rebuilt airplane suffers an engine fire as she lands in Tucson, Ariz., after a test flight.		May 21
	In a Foreign Trade Week speech, Secretary of State Cordell Hull says that self-sufficiency is not a sound policy for any nation.	The SAG protests harassment of actors by striking film workers while the 80,000-strong Theatrical Stage Employees union threatens a strike. . . . Superior Mine and union representatives visit striking miners underground to secure permission to bargain for them in Illinois. . . . Workers will return to the shipyard in Kearny, N.J., on May 24 with a new union and pay schedule.		Hank Greenberg hits the longest home run ever in Fenway Park, to the right of the flagpole.	May 22

F	G	H	I	J
Includes elections, federal-state relations, civil rights and liberties, crime, the judiciary, education, healthcare, poverty, urban affairs, and population.	Includes formation and debate of U.S. foreign and defense policies, veterans affairs, and defense spending. (Relations with specific foreign countries are usually found under the region concerned.)	Includes business, labor, agriculture, taxation, transportation, consumer affairs, monetary and fiscal policy, natural resources, pollution, and accidents.	Includes worldwide scientific, medical, and technological developments, natural phenomena, U.S. weather, and natural disasters.	Includes the arts, religion, scholarship, communications media, sports, entertainment, fashions, fads, and social life.

	World Affairs	Europe	Africa & The Middle East	The Americas	Asia & The Pacific
May 23		Insurgents press closer to Bilbao, and loyalists take seven towns near Guadalajara. . . . All Catholic dioceses in Germany receive instructions: on June 5, they are to coordinate efforts to recruit members into Catholic youth groups. . . . Admiral Cavagnari, Italy's Undersecretary of the Navy, causes concern when he declares that Italy is now a world power and has outgrown the Mediterranean Sea.			High Commissioner McNutt's actions and pronouncements confuse Filipinos. . . . In skirmishes between British soldiers and the troops of the Fakir of Ipi, several men as well as noncombatant villagers have died.
May 24	The League of Nations begins its 97th session in Geneva with speeches about withdrawing foreign troops from Spain. . . . The Empire Conference begins its discussions of defense.	With construction only 80 percent complete, French Premier Léon Blum and President Albert Lebrun open the International Exposition of Art and Technology in Paris, on the centenary of the Arc de Triomphe. The Exposition will be seen by 34 million people during its five-month run. . . . A two-hour "strike" and demonstration by Poland's 3 million Jews closes business nationwide in protest over the recent pogroms of Brest-Litovsk. The Polish press ignores the strike. . . . Germany presents a written protest over Archbishop Mundelein to the Vatican.		The Cabinet of President Lopez of Colombia resigns en masse.	
May 25	Admiral Kobayashi of Japan and 300 of his men are cheered as they march through Berlin on a state visit. . . . Haile Selassie notifies the League of Nations that he will not be present to vote tomorrow, resolving a delicate diplomatic situation as he is a deposed emperor.	Spanish anarchists, formerly allied with the loyalist government, stage an uprising in Barbastro. One hundred are reported killed; troops are deployed to contain the fighting. . . . Through his newspaper, Premier Benito Mussolini tells Italian Jews to support fascism wholeheartedly, oppose Zionism, and accept Nazi principles—or leave Italy. . . . The Gestapo arrests all five members of a Confessional Synod governing board. . . . Europe's rate of armament increases: 29 nations employ 6 million in their armed forces, with 28 million reservists. Direct military expenses exceed $10 billion this fiscal year.		President Alfonso Lopez of Colombia resigns, fulfilling his promise to do so when Congress manifests distrust in him as leader. . . . Leading foreign petroleum companies in Mexico have formed a union to deal with employees, a Sindicator. . . . José Americo de Almeida is nominated for the presidency of Brazil, joining two other candidates: Armando Salles de Oliveira and Plinio Salgado. Elections are January 3. . . . A hurricane hits Acapulco, Mexico, knocking out communications.	
May 26	Egypt is admitted to the League of Nations as its 59th member.	Insurgents shoot down a French commercial plane with four passengers who incur minor injuries. General Franco calls the plane an aerial blockade runner. . . . Netherlands election results support Premier Colign and are seen as a loss for the National Socialist Party. . . . London's busmen end their strike with a provisional agreement.		Bolivia and Paraguay resume diplomatic relations.	
May 27	Spain presents a "White Book" to the League of Nations documenting Italy's aggressive involvement in the Spanish civil war.	Premier of Spain Juan Négrin prohibits the newspaper La Batalla, published by a Trotskyist group. . . . German government employees are told that they can be fired if they do not protest when Nazis are insulted in church. The administration is thought to be incensed over the Vatican's attitude.		At 5 a.m., torrential rains send 3 million pounds of gold tailings and mud from the Dos Estrellas Mine into Tlalpujahua, Michoacan, Mexico. Parts of the town are buried under 90 feet of debris. An estimated 168 people die. . . . A nationwide strike of 17,000 oil workers in Mexico paralyzes the country. . . . In Nogales, Sonora, Mexico, 5,000 Catholics march through the streets to the cathedral, where they force open the doors. One hundred Catholics occupy the church throughout the night. . . . Governor Winship of Puerto Rico flies to Washington after gathering data to discount the ACLU report that is critical of him.	

A	B	C	D	E
Includes developments that affect more than one world region, international organizations, and important meetings of world leaders.	*Includes all domestic and regional developments in Europe, including the Soviet Union.*	*Includes all domestic and regional developments in Africa and the Middle East.*	*Includes all domestic and regional developments in Latin America, the Caribbean, and Canada.*	*Includes all domestic and regional developments in Asian and Pacific nations (and colonies).*

U.S. Politics & Social Issues	U.S. Foreign Policy & Defense	Economics & Great Depression	Science, Technology & Nature	Culture, Leisure & Lifestyle	
		The executive council of the AFL asks its membership to declare a war to the finish with the CIO.		John D. Rockefeller, founder of Standard Oil, dies at age 97.	May 23
The Supreme Court issues three decisions upholding the constitutionality of Social Security's old age pensions and unemployment insurance.		Following President Franklin Roosevelt's recommendation, Congress receives bills establishing wage and hour standards and abolishing child labor. . . . AFL speakers address the 300 delegates at their conference in Cincinnati, Ohio, blaming the CIO for the rift and charging them with having Communist ties. . . . WPA writers, worried that proposed funding means a 25 percent cut in their ranks, begin a strike. . . . Crucible Steel signs an agreement, averting a walkout by its 18,000 employees.		The Woodrow Wilson Peace Medal is presented to Ambassador Norman H. Davis.	May 24
With Social Security approved by the courts, 29 amendments previously held will see action in Congress, giving coverage to more groups. . . . New trials are ordered for the Scottsboro defendants, to begin July 6.		Steel workers affiliated with the CIO start a spontaneous strike against Republic Steel in Ohio. . . . The United Automobile Workers opens its campaign to unionize Ford Motor Company, holding a six-hour day and $8 daily wage as a goal. Two offices are opened by the union, whose slogan is "Unionism, not Fordism."		Detroit Tigers manager Mickey Cochrane suffers a fractured skull, hit by a ball pitched by Yankee Bump Hadley.	May 25
	President Franklin Roosevelt submits eight agreements made during the Inter-American Conference in December dealing with the maintenance of peace, cultural exchange, and other issues.	Strikes against Youngstown, Republic, and Inland Steel companies begin tonight, idling between 75,000 and 80,000 workers. . . . Ford workers harass and eventually injure union organizers—some of them women—who try to hand out information at Ford gates. In Richmond, Calif., pickets close the Ford plant.		Samuel Goldwyn and Alexander Korda negotiate to buy United Artists from founders Mary Pickford, Charlie Chaplin, and Douglas Fairbanks.	May 26
		Ohio Governor Martin L. Davey asks union leaders and officials from Youngstown and Republic Steel to meet with him. In Niles, parents of Republic Steel workers, worried that their daughters are being held prisoners, storm the mill. With the help of a lawyer, they are allowed in and some daughters return home. Others stay at the mill. . . . The management of Ford accuses unions and media of staging disturbances outside the plant; however, local authorities are investigating the involvement of Ford private police. . . . Between 7,500 and 14,500 WPA workers in New York strike for one day, asking that more funds be available in 1938 to continue their programs.	Signaled by a foghorn, pedestrians cross the two-mile span of the Golden Gate Bridge for the first time, starting at 6 a.m. By mid-afternoon, 100,000 people have crossed.		May 27

F	G	H	I	J
Includes elections, federal-state relations, civil rights and liberties, crime, the judiciary, education, healthcare, poverty, urban affairs, and population.	Includes formation and debate of U.S. foreign and defense policies, veterans affairs, and defense spending. (Relations with specific foreign countries are usually found under the region concerned.)	Includes business, labor, agriculture, taxation, transportation, consumer affairs, monetary and fiscal policy, natural resources, pollution, and accidents.	Includes worldwide scientific, medical, and technological developments, natural phenomena, U.S. weather, and natural disasters.	Includes the arts, religion, scholarship, communications media, sports, entertainment, fashions, fads, and social life.

	World Affairs	Europe	Africa & The Middle East	The Americas	Asia & The Pacific
May 28	The Empire Conference in London reaches agreements on defense, but finds roadblocks in discussions on trade with America.	With very little pomp, Neville Chamberlain becomes Britain's Prime Minister. . . . Insurgent planes drop 90 bombs on Valencia, causing 200 deaths. Seven are killed at the Paraguayan consulate, and the Red Cross shelter is hit. Loyalist planes shell Italian and British ships, killing seven crew members. Loyalists also attack an insurgent air base, destroying dozens of planes. . . . French diplomats arrange an exchange of four captured German and Swiss pilots, held by Basques, for four prisoners in insurgent hands. . . . Minister of Propaganda Joseph Goebbels speaks before a crowd of 20,000 for two hours, excoriating churches worldwide and in Germany for their immorality and interference. . . . Norway, Denmark, Finland, Sweden, Belgium, the Netherlands, and Luxemburg sign the one-year Trade Pact of Oslo.		The "sit-down" occupation of the Nogales Cathedral spreads to other parts of Sonora, Mexico. The Bishop of Sonora appoints a pastor to the cathedral, and workmen repair the long-padlocked building. . . . Secret sessions of Cuba's House and Senate are held to resolve difficulties with President Laredo Bru.	Japan's two largest political parties ask the Cabinet to resign, saying that the body hurts national unity and hinders policy.
May 29	The League of Nations resolves its discussion of Italian and other foreign soldiers in the Spanish civil war by endorsing London's Non-Intervention Committee's right to work on it. . . . The League develops a Fundamental Law for the Sanjak of Alexandretta, demilitarizing the city and giving it greater autonomy.	The German battleship *Deutschland* is bombed by Spanish loyalist and Russian planes near the island Ibiza, killing 23 crewmen and injuring 83. Spain claims the planes were fired upon first. . . . Seven insurgent planes drop bombs on Barcelona and its suburbs before 4 a.m., and many are killed as their apartments collapse and bury them.		Other unions join Mexico's oil workers in a general strike. Before the strike began, oil companies had reached an agreement with unions led by Lombardo Toledano, but the Mexican Labor Board interfered with the settlement. The general strike is seen as a face-off between Toledano and President Lázaro Cárdenas.	
May 30	The Empire Conference debates control of gold, but decides that as results depend on Russia's cooperation, gold should be discussed in other venues.	The National Confessional Synod in Germany instructs pastors to protest attacks against churches, pointing out that the Nazis have subsumed the role of church in peoples' lives. . . . After a late Cabinet meeting, Germany warns it will take action over the bombing of the *Deutschland*, and demands to know what the Non-Intervention Committee will do. . . . A Spanish passenger liner sinks after being hit by a bomb; 60 drown and 100 survivors are rescued by fishing boats and others.		Companies declare that the 34 demands of oil workers in Mexico are impossible, but the Labor Board finds the strike began legally. . . . After 12 hours of often secret debate, Cuba's House passes a bill granting amnesty for all crimes—save gangsterism and terrorism—committed through May 20, 1937. The bill goes to the Senate.	
May 31		The Catalan government blames a torpedo from an Italian submarine for sinking the Spanish passenger ship. . . . German battleships pound the loyalist-held city of Almeria with 200 shells for one hour. . . . Italy and Germany withdraw from participation in the Non-Intervention Committee until ships' safety from bombs can be assured. . . . Chancellor Adolf Hitler grants the Reich's highest honor to a foreigner to Premier of Italy Benito Mussolini and Minister Galeazzo Ciano. . . . Marshal Ian Gamarnik, Assistant Commissar of War in the Soviet Union, commits suicide.		The House and Senate of Cuba meets in hurried, secret sessions to produce a motion denouncing any attempt to dissolve Congress and establish a corporate system of government. . . . President Lázaro Cárdenas of Mexico refuses to meet with foreign oil companies over the strike. . . . Catholics in Nogales are told that the government will return the cathedral to them, and so they end their occupation. . . . For the second time, President Alfonso Lopez of Colombia gives his resignation to the Senate and they refuse it with a vote of confidence in him.	After 118 days in office, Premier Hayashi gives his resignation and that of his Cabinet to Emperor Hirohito of Japan.
Jun. 1		Loyalists resolve factional fighting and renew unity in the wake of the German bombardment of Almeria. . . . Italian warships speed to Spain to take up patrol positions vacated by Germany. Although both have withdrawn from the Non-Intervention patrols, Italy fears that Russian war materiel is being shipped. . . . Prime Minister Neville Chamberlain withdraws his business profits tax plan.		Sixteen parishes in Sonora take possession of their churches and hear Mass for the first time in three years. . . . President Laredo Bru of Cuba announces that new taxes, on exports and on each person, will be necessary to cover next year's budget. . . . Elections in British Columbia endorse the liberal policies of Premier Pattullo.	Nobleman Prince Fumimaro Konoe accepts the office of Premier in Japan.

A	B	C	D	E
Includes developments that affect more than one world region, international organizations, and important meetings of world leaders.	*Includes all domestic and regional developments in Europe, including the Soviet Union.*	*Includes all domestic and regional developments in Africa and the Middle East.*	*Includes all domestic and regional developments in Latin America, the Caribbean, and Canada.*	*Includes all domestic and regional developments in Asian and Pacific nations (and colonies).*

U.S. Politics & Social Issues	U.S. Foreign Policy & Defense	Economics & Great Depression	Science, Technology & Nature	Culture, Leisure & Lifestyle	
President Franklin Roosevelt asks for an investigation into tax evasion by the wealthy.		Thirty police block a column of 1,000 demonstrators outside a Republic Steel mill in Chicago. Twenty-six are injured in the resulting melee. . . . CIO pickets interfere with shipping in New York, demanding that ships use their members to man radios, rather than the AFL men already aboard.	President Franklin Roosevelt opens the Golden Gate Bridge to vehicles by pressing a button in Washington.		May 28
		Pickets in Youngstown, Ohio, arm themselves with clubs and block delivery trucks at both Youngstown and Republic Steel. . . . The AFL and CIO clash on ships again. An AFL group of 25 storms onto the mail ship *Oriente* in New York Harbor and seizes its radio room. The ship cancels its trip; the AFL counts this as a victory.			May 29
		Another march of 1,000 strikers on Republic Steel in Chicago turns violent. Police stop their demonstration with tear gas and claim that some of the strikers fired on them before they fired back. Strikers contend that police opened fire from behind the crowd. Ten men die or are mortally wounded; 90 are hospitalized, 29 with gunshot wounds. Among the hospitalized are 26 police. Orlando Lippert of Paramount Newsreels captures parts of the riot on film. . . . Three AFL radio men holding the ship *Oriente* are forced by hunger to surrender to authorities; the CIO claims victory.		In Pittsburgh, golfer Denny Shute wins the PGA (he also placed first in November 1936).	May 30
		While steel workers cry for murder charges to be filed against police, Illinois Governor Henry Horner meets with a Republic Steel manager, officials from the union, the State and Federal Departments of Labor, and the U.S. Attorney General. Paramount Newsreel decides to suppress Lippert's film. To avoid pickets, airplanes drop bundled food into Republic's plants in Niles, Ohio, where 300 employees continue to work.		Before almost 62,000 fans at the Polo Grounds in New York, the Dodgers end Giant Carl Hubbell's 24-game winning streak.	May 31
	Expressing grave concern, Secretary of State Cordell Hull appeals to Spain and Germany to peacefully settle their problems.	In a message to Congress, President Franklin Roosevelt asks that tax loopholes be plugged and lists specific tricks that the wealthy use to evade paying taxes. . . . Working late into the night, the House passes a $1.5 billion 1938 relief bill asked for by the President. . . . The motion picture strike ends with the absorption of the Painters Union into another group, with a 10 percent wage increase.	With navigator Fred Noonan, Amelia Earhart flies from Miami to Puerto Rico in 7.5 hours, on the first leg of her west-to-east world trip.		Jun. 1

F	G	H	I	J
Includes elections, federal-state relations, civil rights and liberties, crime, the judiciary, education, healthcare, poverty, urban affairs, and population.	Includes formation and debate of U.S. foreign and defense policies, veterans affairs, and defense spending. (Relations with specific foreign countries are usually found under the region concerned.)	Includes business, labor, agriculture, taxation, transportation, consumer affairs, monetary and fiscal policy, natural resources, pollution, and accidents.	Includes worldwide scientific, medical, and technological developments, natural phenomena, U.S. weather, and natural disasters.	Includes the arts, religion, scholarship, communications media, sports, entertainment, fashions, fads, and social life.

	World Affairs	Europe	Africa & The Middle East	The Americas	Asia & The Pacific
Jun. 2	The Empire Conference in London discusses trade in the Pacific, with Australia's Prime Minister pressing for a treaty between Pacific powers. The proposal is not well-received.	Germany's War Minister visits Italy and confers with Premier Benito Mussolini, Foreign Minister Galeazzo Ciano, and King Victor Emmanuel. . . . Germany reveals that 915 cases against Catholic monks are ongoing; a cadre of prosecutors has been investigating since autumn 1935; more men are arrested daily; and that the trials could continue for years.		Mexico's President Lázaro Cárdenas threatens government intervention if striking oil workers and the 17 companies that employ them do not settle by June 3.	An anti-Japanese mob burns four buildings on a 400-acre farm jointly run by both Chinese and Japanese interests. Japan lodges a protest with the Hopei-Chahar Council. . . . After five hours of talks, Prince Konoe is unable to persuade Kenji Kodama to become Finance Minister. A second choice, Okinoya Kaya, does not inspire the same confidence.
Jun. 3	The International Labor Organization opens its 23rd session in Geneva with 51 nations participating. . . . At the League of Nations Opium Advisory Committee, Egypt charges Japan with being responsible for 90 percent of the world's illicit narcotics problem. Japan denies this, but acknowledges being overwhelmed by the narcotics production in China.	Britain submits a new plan for naval patrols enforcing the Non-Intervention Pact, involving "safety zones" respected by Spanish combatants. They hope to bring back Italian and German participation. . . . General Emilio Mola, leader of insurgent troops in the Bilbao area, dies with four others as their airplane crashes into a mountain. General Franco asks General Fidel Dávila to take command of forces in northern Spain. . . . The Soviet Union finds saboteurs and "enemies of the people" in the Osoaviakhim, the agency that trains youth for the army, as well as in many military units. Spies are discovered in education and industry. For example, the man responsible for drilling oil wells that never produced is executed. . . . The Duke of Windsor (the former Edward VIII of England) and Wallis Warfield Simpson marry in Monts, France.		Carlos de Macedo Soares is inducted as Minister of Justice and the Interior in Brazil. His office will oversee the upcoming presidential election. . . . Premier Hepburn accuses Prime Minister King of Ontario of being too liberal and vacillating on the CIO's intrusion into Dominion labor. His tirade is viewed as a bid to take control of his party.	In Japan, Prince Konoe forms his Cabinet.
Jun. 4	Ignoring last-minute pleas for clemency from the United States, Germany executes 21-year-old Helmuth Hirsch. Declared a U.S. citizen through his father's citizenship, the Jewish man had been secretly tried on mysterious charges.	Madrid endures a night and day of heavy shelling, targeting both the central area and working-class neighborhoods. . . . Berlin's confrontational Rev. Niemoeller of the Confessional Protestant Church lectures against giving in to the demands of Nazis. . . . War Minister Werner von Blomberg of Germany spends a second day viewing new Italian machine guns, planes, and artillery. . . . Secretary-General Dimitroff of Comintern (Communist International) asks the proletariat worldwide to take action in defense of Spain's government.		Mexico's President guarantees that railroads will run in spite of the oil workers' strike, and uses the resources of his new state-owned oil company to alleviate shortages. . . . Members of Cuba's House of Representatives report that they have been threatened with bodily harm for their anti-army stance.	In a well-received, brief radio address, Premier Konoe asks for unity while he works to heal divisions. . . . Nanking increases its control while Szechwan Governor Liu Hsiang loses prestige and power.
Jun. 5	Rioting between Turks and Arabs at Antioch and Alexandretta leaves more than 30 injured. Martial law is declared.	Italy accepts Britain's new plan for patrolling Spain, with reservations: Italy does not want to "consult" before taking actions against an attack. . . . Marshal Gamarnik, who killed himself May 31, is accused of espionage by *Pravda*, the Soviet newspaper. . . . In Munich, a popular priest who is a veteran and amputee is arrested.		Mexico's President Lázaro Cárdenas announces he will end the oil workers' strike, presumably by dictating a settlement.	
Jun. 6		The Condor Legion, known for its attack on Guernica, shoots down the last Basque airplanes. Poor weather does not stop the ground fighting and shelling of Basque ridges and hills, as insurgents fight with defenders for each position. . . . A call to youth to join Catholic groups is issued and priests in Germany read a prepared statement at Sunday Mass. Hitler Youth interrupt services at churches in Munich, resulting in fights. Ten priests are arrested. . . . Soviet production in most industries lags; the blame is laid on Trotskyists and saboteurs who spread confusion. A third Five-Year Plan is announced to start in 1938, with a stated goal of surpassing the United States.		Mexican oil workers continue their strike, in defiance of President Lázaro Cárdenas's declaration that the strike would end. . . . Puerto Rico's Supreme Court recently finds unconstitutional a 1919 law setting the minimum wage at $1 per day. In response, needle manufacturers shut their plants, putting up to 100,000 out of work until the wage issue is settled.	Several wealthy sugar plantation owners in the Philippines argue against independence, saying the country is not ready for it.
	A *Includes developments that affect more than one world region, international organizations, and important meetings of world leaders.*	**B** *Includes all domestic and regional developments in Europe, including the Soviet Union.*	**C** *Includes all domestic and regional developments in Africa and the Middle East.*	**D** *Includes all domestic and regional developments in Latin America, the Caribbean, and Canada.*	**E** *Includes all domestic and regional developments in Asian and Pacific nations (and colonies).*

U.S. Politics & Social Issues	U.S. Foreign Policy & Defense	Economics & Great Depression	Science, Technology & Nature	Culture, Leisure & Lifestyle	
		Two planes dropping food for Republic Steel workers in Warren, Ohio, crash. Bullets are blamed; snipers shoot at planes in Niles as well. . . . A grand jury investigates the beating of 18 people handing out union information at the gates of a Ford plant last week. Ford challenges the jurisdiction. . . . Members of the Painters Union reject the settlement announced yesterday, and the film strike is still on. . . . AFL boards expel unions affiliated with the CIO; in New York City, 46 unions representing up to 300,000 members are ejected.	Amelia Earhart lands in Venezuela. She plans to fly to Dutch Guiana tomorrow, and Brazil the following day.	Dizzy Dean gets a suspension for statements made two weeks ago.	Jun. 2
		President Franklin Roosevelt asks Congress to set up seven TVA-style regional power agencies that would tackle problems of flooding, erosion, and drought in the country. . . . The Steel Workers Organizing Committee (SWOC) announces it will work with other unions to stop or delay iron ore deliveries to Republic and other steel companies. . . . Seven thousand mourners attend the mass funeral in Chicago for seven of those killed when Sunday's demonstration turned violent.	Drs. Percy Bridgman (Nobel Laureate, 1946) and Ernest Lawrence (Nobel Laureate, 1939) receive $2,500 awards from the Research Corp. of New York. Dr. Lawrence invented the cyclotron.	Refusing to sign a repudiation of words he claims he never said, Dizzy Dean threatens to sue President Frick of baseball's National League for depriving him of making a living.	Jun. 3
Members of the La Follette Senate subcommittee, which investigates civil liberties and labor espionage, visit Youngstown, Ohio.		Strikers prevent rail cars and trucks from delivering food and mail to Republic Steel plants. . . . A riot between strikers from other companies and workers at the Newberry Lumber Mill in Michigan leaves one dead. The Sheriff sends for the National Guard. . . . The Furriers Joint Council calls for a strike of 13,000 fur workers in New York.		Baseball lifts Dizzy Dean's suspension.	Jun. 4
Alabama's Supreme Court acquits Sheriff Corbitt of Henry County of impeachment charges in the February 1 lynching of Wes Jordan. . . . The National Women's Conference opens its conference in Atlantic City with an address by Dr. Edith Hooker, pointing out that 10 million working women earn 40–60 percent less than men simply because of their gender. Speakers call for an equal rights amendment.		Sheriff Elser and 45 deputies break through the picket line outside Republic Steel in Youngstown, Ohio, to deliver a rail car full of food to the plant. Immediately after, pickets tear up the rail tracks with acetylene torches. . . . The mayor of Chicago orders Republic Steel to cease housing its employees in its plants. The company orders Pullman rail cars brought in to house employees. . . . In Detroit, the Ford Brotherhood of America (FBA) signs up 7,000 members in two days. Founders say Ford employees want nothing to do with national unions.		War Admiral becomes a triple-crown-winning horse after placing first in the Belmont Stakes.	Jun. 5
		Although a vote of all Ford employees in Richmond, Calif., was 2 to 1 against a settlement, a vote today of UAWA members favors the same settlement 5 to 1. Workers are expected to return to Ford tomorrow. . . . Representatives of 80 unions in Illinois ask President Franklin Roosevelt to intervene in the Republic Steel strike; he does not respond. Railroads in the area appeal to the governor, threatening layoffs if nothing is done.	Soviet scientists leave four men and a dog to carry on studies for one year at the North Pole, while the rest leave in planes. . . . The 88th annual meeting of the American Medical Association hears of "psycho-surgery"—lobotomies—for the "soul sick." The surgeries, performed on 20 mental patients, are based on the work of Dr. Moniz of Portugal, described in journals last year.		Jun. 6

F	G	H	I	J
Includes elections, federal-state relations, civil rights and liberties, crime, the judiciary, education, healthcare, poverty, urban affairs, and population.	*Includes formation and debate of U.S. foreign and defense policies, veterans affairs, and defense spending. (Relations with specific foreign countries are usually found under the region concerned.)*	*Includes business, labor, agriculture, taxation, transportation, consumer affairs, monetary and fiscal policy, natural resources, pollution, and accidents.*	*Includes worldwide scientific, medical, and technological developments, natural phenomena, U.S. weather, and natural disasters.*	*Includes the arts, religion, scholarship, communications media, sports, entertainment, fashions, fads, and social life.*

	World Affairs	Europe	Africa & The Middle East	The Americas	Asia & The Pacific
Jun. 7		An estimated 4,200 refugees reach France on the ship *Habana*. Bombs fall on Madrid, Bilbao's suburbs, Granada, and Palamos. . . . In Germany, the Superior Prussian Court decides that not even churches have legal protection from police action. The police "act in the interest of state security," and may interpret that mandate as they please.		Mexican oil workers have two demands: a promised raise and an audit of their employers to determine their ability to pay. President Lázaro Cárdenas intervenes to grant this and get them back to work. . . . Brazil's Minister of Justice Soares arranges the release of 108 political prisoners, with another 200 to follow tomorrow. Many are suspected Communists with no formal charges against them.	
Jun. 8		Insurgents launch new attacks in Cordoba, anxious to control its mercury mines. . . . In spite of concessions made to labor, which were expected to result in economic improvements, the French government finds itself deeper in debt. . . . Sporadic anti-Nazi demonstrations throughout Yugoslavia mark the visit of German Foreign Minister Neurath.		While oil employees are ordered back to their jobs, the oil companies withdraw their previously offered raises. A loophole in Mexican law supports them. . . . Several men shoot at Judge Robert A. Cooper of Puerto Rico, less than a day after several Nationalists he had convicted are sent to serve prison sentences in the United States. . . . Peru accuses Ecuador of sending troops into a disputed area, which Ecuador denies.	
Jun. 9	Britain's Royal Commission considers partitioning Palestine into two parts: Trans-Jordan, with an Arab population, and a Jewish state, both to remain under British authority. Arabs and Jews alike are against the plan.	The commands of five military districts in the Soviet Union are changed, indicating purges of army officers. . . . Germany orders the Baha'i cult dissolved. . . . France's credit is at its lowest point since the franc crashed in 1926.		Mexico's oil strike ends at noon, with employers withholding the pledged raises. An audit of the oil companies will proceed. . . . As tensions over disputed territory flare again, Bolivia and Paraguay break diplomatic relations, restored only last month.	North China offers to cooperate with Japan in the building of a railway if Japan restores Hopei province to Chinese rule. The offer is seen as a refusal of Japanese aid, since giving up the province is unlikely.
Jun. 10	British, French, and U.S. delegates at the International Labor Conference in Geneva warn about defense and armament buildups that tax citizens and put economic recovery efforts at risk.	Spanish loyalists launch a surprise attack on Guadalajara, capturing prisoners and munitions. Insurgents pound the Iron Ring around Bilbao. Bad weather kept them from attacking by air over the past days. . . . Basque clergy present complaints to the Vatican about the bombing of Guernica and other civilian targets, including churches.			
Jun. 11		Hungarian General Lukacs (real name Matei Zalka) suffers a mortal head wound when a shell hits his car as he reviews loyalist troops in Huesca. . . . Eight Soviet army leaders are tried behind closed doors. . . . Prof. Carlo Roselli and his brother Nello, both anti-fascist refugees living in France, are murdered. . . . Premier Léon Blum's bill for a 40-hour week for hotel and restaurant workers is defeated by a revolt in the Senate, a telling loss for his party.			Japanese officials confirm rumors of unrest in Chahar province, China, that have persisted for months, but dismiss the reported rebellion of Manchukuoan and Mongolian troops as minor disturbances.
Jun. 12		Insurgent troops breach Bilbao's Iron Ring with artillery and air strikes. . . . The Ambassadors of Germany, Italy, and France agree with Britain to patrol and enforce the Non-Intervention Pact, but Spanish cooperation is still sought. . . . Eight Soviet generals, including Michael Tukhachevsky, are executed after being found guilty of collaborating with German and Japanese agents to overthrow the government. . . . German Foreign Minister Neurath visits Hungary, advising that country to make no agreements with Czechoslovakia.		Paraguay's army mutinies against President Rafeal Franco on the second anniversary of the Chaco peace settlement. The revolt began when the army refused to give up possession of a road ceded to Bolivia in the accord.	

A	B	C	D	E
Includes developments that affect more than one world region, international organizations, and important meetings of world leaders.	*Includes all domestic and regional developments in Europe, including the Soviet Union.*	*Includes all domestic and regional developments in Africa and the Middle East.*	*Includes all domestic and regional developments in Latin America, the Caribbean, and Canada.*	*Includes all domestic and regional developments in Asian and Pacific nations (and colonies).*

U.S. Politics & Social Issues	U.S. Foreign Policy & Defense	Economics & Great Depression	Science, Technology & Nature	Culture, Leisure & Lifestyle	
Subpoenas are issued by the La Follette Senate subcommittee for newsreel footage and private films shot on May 30 of the Chicago steel riot.		Police arrest eight people for picketing, taking them from their homes in the early morning. The mother of three young children is among those arrested. Outraged, thousands of UAWA supporters march into Lansing, Michigan's business district and blockade streets. The UAWA is affiliated with the CIO. Governor Frank Murphy intervenes, and the crowd disperses when the pickets are released. . . . Eight men and one woman are sentenced to six months in jail for conspiracy in the Maine shoe workers' strike. Three are acquitted.	Amelia Earhart leaves Brazil for French Senegal in Africa.	Actor Jean Harlow, age 26, dies of uremic poisoning and kidney failure.	Jun. 7
Birth control is officially recognized by the American Medical Association. Doctors may investigate practices and advise patients on the topic.	President Franklin Roosevelt asks Congress to mark $160 million for rebuilding the merchant marine.	The mayor of Monroe, Mich., calls for armed citizen volunteers to bolster the police as a Republic Steel plant is reopened on June 10. . . . The AFL calls on all its associated unions to walk off their jobs in Lansing, the site of yesterday's CIO action.	The longest total eclipse of the sun in 1,200 years occurs; best viewing is in Peru.		Jun. 8
		The CIO shuts down power plants, cutting service to half a million customers in Michigan and Wisconsin. CIO leaders fly in to stop the strike, and workers settle for the same pay raise and concessions offered yesterday. . . . The Associated Press reports that 123,000 workers in 18 states are on strike.			Jun. 9
	Representatives of 400 Jewish organizations ask the State Department to conduct investigations of the pogroms and violence directed at Jews in Poland, through its embassy.	Rioting flares at Republic Steel in Youngstown, Ohio, where 14 pickets are arrested, two police beaten, and one man slightly wounded by a bullet. Two hundred tear gas bombs restore order. Union heads accuse the sheriff of inciting the riot. Youngstown's mayor swears in 100 volunteer deputies, asks for special powers, and orders additional munitions.	Amelia Earhart lands at Gao, along the Niger River in French West Africa, less than eight hours after leaving Dakar, French Senegal. She will depart for Western Anglo-Egyptian Sudan tomorrow morning.	Robert Laird Borden, prime minister of Canada from 1911–20, dies in Ottawa.	Jun. 10
The Senate votes to investigate interference in the mail, stemming from the steel workers' strike. Post office employees are said to have refused parcels of food addressed to steel plants.		Tear gas and other fumes drive away pickets in Monroe, Mich., allowing 500 steel workers to return to their jobs. Worried about CIO retaliation against the town, vigilantes with baseball bats patrol the streets. The mayor asks Governor Frank Murphy to declare martial law. . . . In Saginaw, a strike of 5,000 workers at a Chevrolet plant may idle as many as 14,000. The cause is management's discipline of a union representative.		R.J. Mitchell, who designed the Supermarine S6B and Spitfire aircraft, dies of cancer.	Jun. 11
		Workers at Bethlehem Steel in Johnstown, Penn., join the three-week-old strike. . . . Governor Martin Davey of Ohio holds an 11-hour meeting with SWOC and steel company officials that adjourns in a deadlock until June 15. . . . On Sunday, June 13, a "labor holiday" is threatened for Youngstown, Ohio. Governor Frank Murphy of Michigan receives pledges of a Sabbath truce at the mass CIO meeting in Monroe. . . . The NLRB orders secret elections to settle CIO vs. AFL disputes on ships.			Jun. 12

F	G	H	I	J
Includes elections, federal-state relations, civil rights and liberties, crime, the judiciary, education, healthcare, poverty, urban affairs, and population.	Includes formation and debate of U.S. foreign and defense policies, veterans affairs, and defense spending. (Relations with specific foreign countries are usually found under the region concerned.)	Includes business, labor, agriculture, taxation, transportation, consumer affairs, monetary and fiscal policy, natural resources, pollution, and accidents.	Includes worldwide scientific, medical, and technological developments, natural phenomena, U.S. weather, and natural disasters.	Includes the arts, religion, scholarship, communications media, sports, entertainment, fashions, fads, and social life.

	World Affairs	Europe	Africa & The Middle East	The Americas	Asia & The Pacific
Jun. 13		Basque tanks and desperate defenders battle insurgents as Bilbao's Iron Ring is overcome. Basque police stop the insurgents from killing the prison's loyalist inmates. . . . In Huesca and Saragossa, 63 loyalist planes bomb insurgent positions. . . . Leaders of Soviet auto, tractor, and combine industries—including two American Communists living in Russia—are ordered to reorganize for greater efficiency within 10 days, or face trials.	Shots are fired at the commander of the Palestine police in Jerusalem. A chauffeur is struck and the assailants escape.		
Jun. 14	Due to strong opposition, Britain drops its proposal to divide Palestine in two.	Insurgents circle Bilbao, but defenders hold on to positions in mountains and hills. Ships land 5,300 refugee children in France, while foreign embassies and more children and women flee Bilbao. . . . After passing the new constitution, Ireland's government is dissolved and July elections are called. . . . At Svobodnie, the same place as the May 20 executions, the Soviets shoot to death 28 employees of the Trans-Siberian Railway for sabotage and spying.		The second Conference on Canadian-American Affairs opens in Ontario. . . . Two members of Cuba's House of Representatives, Narcisco Moran and Manuel Penabaz, exchange blows and draw guns in the capitol building of Havana. One gun jams and shots go wild, then other Representatives intervene.	
Jun. 15	To maintain calm relations with Italy, Switzerland recognizes the conquest of Ethiopia. . . . Finland makes its war debt payment to the United States, but 12 nations default on $1.5 billion owed in payments and arrears. . . . The Empire Conference in London ends, with little progress made.	In Germany, 48 pastors are under arrest and more are detained for questioning about their attitudes toward the state. . . . In Poland, the trial opens for the youth who killed a policeman in a fit of despair, kicking off 18 hours of anti-Jewish rioting in Brest-Litovsk. The trial is quick and results in a death sentence. Anti-Semitic demonstrations are not allowed. . . . The German-Polish convention dividing Upper Silesia between the two nations expires July 14 and Poland will not renew it.			Japan's Foreign Minister Hirota asks the Cabinet to adopt fiscal policies to control the budget, centering on balancing foreign accounts, expanding production, and forecasting supply and demand. The Cabinet agrees, and announces a five-year plan for production in both Japan and Manchukuo.
Jun. 16		The Iron Ring of defenses is shattered in a 12-hour bombardment, but Basque soldiers continue to fight. Twelve-inch shells fall in Bilbao, burying residents in their homes. . . . Also in Spain, the POUM (an extreme Communist party) is outlawed and 200 of its members are arrested in Madrid and Barcelona, accused of using radio transmitters to pass information to Franco's troops. Andres Nin, POUM's leader, escapes . . . . Falange leader Manuel Hedilla, who opposed Franco's policies even while allied with him, is court-martialed and condemned. . . . Italy and Germany rejoin patrols of the Non-Intervention Committee around Spain. . . . President Cherviakoff of White Russia (Belarus) commits suicide as 45 of his colleagues are arrested and charged with treason and conspiracy. A party meeting last week termed the collectives in Belarus "hotbeds" of Polish espionage.		Charges of conspiracy against the government are made involving two generals in Brazil, where a state of martial law is just lifting.	
Jun. 17	The Palais de Tokyo opens at the Paris Exposition—the building will house the Musée National and the Museum of the City of Paris in the future. . . . A committee of the International Labor Conference in Geneva endorses a 40-hour week for the textile industry, but doubts that the upcoming plenary session will approve it.	Thousands of bombs fall on Bilbao. The Basque government evacuates and a defense junta holds the city. . . . In Cartagena, the Spanish battleship *Jaime I* is bombed, sinks, and 300 men are killed. . . . Andres Nin, head of POUM, is found in Barcelona, arrested in secret, and tortured for information by Alexander Orlov, a Russian NKVD agent. . . . Loyalist forces show they can bomb a town out of existence too, by destroying Chimillas, near Huesca. . . . German police raid offices of the Prussian Synod, and half its pastors may have been arrested. The rest are in hiding. Those who contribute to the churches are also subject to arrest.		Full constitutional guarantees are restored in Brazil after 19 months of martial law. . . . President Laredo Bru of Cuba drops the new taxes he proposed on June 1.	Moro Islamic leaders on the island of Mindanao in the Philippines retreat to fortified positions in the hills and announce revolt against the government.

A	B	C	D	E
Includes developments that affect more than one world region, international organizations, and important meetings of world leaders.	*Includes all domestic and regional developments in Europe, including the Soviet Union.*	*Includes all domestic and regional developments in Africa and the Middle East.*	*Includes all domestic and regional developments in Latin America, the Caribbean, and Canada.*	*Includes all domestic and regional developments in Asian and Pacific nations (and colonies).*

U.S. Politics & Social Issues	U.S. Foreign Policy & Defense	Economics & Great Depression	Science, Technology & Nature	Culture, Leisure & Lifestyle	
		Ten thousand CIO supporters gather in a park outside Monroe, Mich., to deride Republic Steel and Monroe's mayor, and disperse peaceably after. . . . In Johnstown, a riot at the Cambria Works of Bethlehem Steel between pickets and departing workers injures 15. . . . Nine non-union men in a crowd of 200 are hit by buckshot as they gather outside a UAWA office in Anderson, Ind. The shots come from inside the building and six union members are arrested.	After an hour and 14 minutes in Khartoum, Amelia Earhart continues her trip, en route to Arabia.	In a parody of the maps illustrating the Spanish civil war battlefronts, *The New York Times* prints a map of the Great Lakes region, showing strikes, marches, and movements on the different fronts.	Jun. 13
The Senate Judiciary Committee passes final judgment on the Court Reorganization Bill, calling it "needless, futile, and utterly dangerous." . . . Alabama's Supreme Court affirms the 75-year sentence imposed on Heyward Patterson, one of the Scottsboro defendants. The other eight defendants will be retried in July; Patterson will appeal to the Supreme Court.		Confrontations between picketers and non-striking workers at Republic's Cambria Works in Johnstown, Penn., start late in the day and continue through the night. . . . Responding to a call from John L. Lewis and the CIO, 9,500 coal miners in West Virginia and Pennsylvania strike to support steel workers. . . . Four thousand shipyard workers in New York and New Jersey join an ongoing strike for higher wages and a closed shop, doubling the total number of strikers.			Jun. 14
Senator Robert Wagner accuses steel companies of acting in bad faith, and President Franklin Roosevelt, in a press conference, wishes the companies would commit to writing what they agree to orally.		An early morning riot at the Cambria Works injures 10, two critically. Governor George Earle orders state police to Johnstown, and the mayor swears in 350 special police. . . . Before a closed steel plant in Ambridge, Penn., 500 men and women fight in a CIO vs. AFL melee; at least 20 are injured. . . . Strikers blow up train tracks near the Republic plant in Warren, Ohio. . . . Governor Martin Davey's attempt to settle the steel strike fails when representatives of Republic and Youngstown Steel leave talks, refusing to sign with any union.			Jun. 15
The La Follette Senate subcommittee travels to Chicago to view more films made of the deadly Memorial Day riots in Chicago.		Near New York, five of the largest shipyards hit by a strike shut down. . . . In Pennsylvania, Johnstown's mayor asks President Franklin Roosevelt to remove the CIO and its "murderous elements" as violence continues near the Bethlehem Steel plant. Stabbings, kidnappings, and small bombs are used. The company again refuses to allow a consent vote among its 80,000 employees. Leaders of the Republic and Youngstown companies refuse to continue talks with Governor Martin Davey of Ohio.	Imperial Airlines starts regular service between New York and Bermuda.	Six hundred people gather to see the Federal Theater Project's, *The Cradle Will Rock*, directed by Orson Welles. Told that the play would not be shown, all walk to another theater in New York, where playwright Marc Blitzstein performs his score on the piano, and WPA cast members sing their parts from seats in the audience. The play is about a steel strike.	Jun. 16
SWOC head Philip Murray gives testimony to the La Follette subcommittee about the Memorial Day shootings in Chicago. Senators express shock over the unprovoked attacks by police shown on film.		President Franklin Roosevelt instructs the Labor Secretary to appoint a mediation board to find resolution in the steel strike. . . . Workers return to the Cambria Works in Johnstown, Penn., as peace is restored with strikers and pickets. . . . The NLRB intervenes in the shipworkers' strike in New York, where 12,000 are now idled.	Amelia Earhart flies from Karachi, India, for Calcutta. . . . A Soviet plane leaves Moscow, attempting to fly over the North Pole and on to Oakland, Calif.	The 54th Street home of the late John D. Rockefeller as well as that of John D. Rockefeller, Jr., will be the site of the future modern art museum. . . . Over 18,000 seats were sold for the WPA production of *The Cradle Will Rock* through July, and people are beginning to ask for refunds. Most feel the musical's controversial topic is being censored.	Jun. 17

F	G	H	I	J
Includes elections, federal-state relations, civil rights and liberties, crime, the judiciary, education, healthcare, poverty, urban affairs, and population.	Includes formation and debate of U.S. foreign and defense policies, veterans affairs, and defense spending. (Relations with specific foreign countries are usually found under the region concerned.)	Includes business, labor, agriculture, taxation, transportation, consumer affairs, monetary and fiscal policy, natural resources, pollution, and accidents.	Includes worldwide scientific, medical, and technological developments, natural phenomena, U.S. weather, and natural disasters.	Includes the arts, religion, scholarship, communications media, sports, entertainment, fashions, fads, and social life.

	World Affairs	Europe	Africa & The Middle East	The Americas	Asia & The Pacific
Jun. 18	Through diplomatic channels, Japan says "no" to a U.S. request to restrict gun caliber on ships to 14 inches. . . . Turkey's Foreign Minister Aras leaves for Iran and Iraq, where he will attempt to negotiate a treaty between all three nations and Afghanistan.	The Bilbao government (or what remains of it) is ordered by Spain to destroy factories that could be used by insurgents, and refuses. . . . All members of the *Fascisti* party in Italy must subscribe to *Popolo d'Italia*, the paper Mussolini founded. . . . Purges continue in the Soviet Union. Seven railroad officials in Turkestan are condemned as Trotskyists for putting rail cars out of commission.		Brazil releases 345 political prisoners, doubling the number freed since June 3. . . . The Conference on Canadian-American Affairs closes with assurances of mutual aid in case of war.	
Jun. 19		Militia surrender Bilbao to insurgents, who walk into the city without a shot fired. . . . Germany says loyalist submarines fired torpedoes twice at its cruiser *Leipzig* last week, and hints at reprisals. . . . The French Senate votes down Premier Léon Blum's fiscal bill, but the Chamber of Deputies votes for it once again. Another Senate vote comes tomorrow. . . . Germany announces land redistribution; small farms will be combined into collectives. . . . Germany, indignant over the alleged torture of a German national in Prague, prints veiled threats about Czechoslovakia's geographic situation.		Brazil's former president charges the European company Itadira Iron with attempting to take over and monopolize Brazil's iron mining industry.	
Jun. 20		Insurgents ship food to Bilbao, which was under heavy siege for nine days. Italian papers credit Italian troops in the Black Arrow brigade for the taking of the city. . . . Nearly 1,000 Catholic schools in Bavaria, which is 70 percent Catholic, are ordered closed by the Nazi government. . . . The execution of 36 more spies near the Trans-Siberian railroad is reported.			
Jun. 21		POUM head Andres Nin is killed by Soviet agents. . . . Germany and Britain are at odds over the *Leipzig* incident: the Reich wants action and is offended that Britain wants information. . . . The French Senate again blocks his legislation for more financial powers, so Premier Léon Blum and his Cabinet resign. The Popular Front ends. Senator Camille Chautemps, a Radical Socialist, is asked to form a Cabinet. . . . All Catholic schools in Bavaria will be secularized. Upcoming trials of Catholic priests and pastors on immorality charges will justify the drastic action, Nazi officials announce. In Berlin at a neo-pagan solstice festival, a crowd of 130,000 cheer as Minister Joseph Goebbels mocks and attacks the Catholic Church.		Near Tampico, 150 Mexican oil workers riot and attack a company attorney; troops are called to restore order. . . . A wave of strikes and violence close oil refineries in Trinidad. In two separate incidents, police open fire on crowds of demonstrators. Six are killed, at least 34 injured, and businesses, including sugar refineries and docks, close down.	
Jun. 22	The report of the Royal Commission on Palestine is signed. While initially kept secret, the report recommends separate Jewish and Arab states, maintaining its Mandate only in a corridor around Jerusalem.	Britain and France reject calls for immediate retaliation against loyalist Spain over the alleged attacks on the *Leipzig*; Germany and Italy settle for a verbal warning to Spain. . . . The Cabinet of new French Premier Camille Chautemps is formed, with Yvon Delbos retained as Foreign Minister, and Léon Blum serving as Vice President. . . . Soviets reveal the command of the Osoaviakhim, a huge defense agency, has been discharged because of criminal disorganization and misuse of funding.		British marines land to restore order in Trinidad, but four oil workers die in continuing riots. Rail and communications lines are cut.	

A	B	C	D	E
Includes developments that affect more than one world region, international organizations, and important meetings of world leaders.	Includes all domestic and regional developments in Europe, including the Soviet Union.	Includes all domestic and regional developments in Africa and the Middle East.	Includes all domestic and regional developments in Latin America, the Caribbean, and Canada.	Includes all domestic and regional developments in Asian and Pacific nations (and colonies).

U.S. Politics & Social Issues	U.S. Foreign Policy & Defense	Economics & Great Depression	Science, Technology & Nature	Culture, Leisure & Lifestyle	
A grand jury in New York begins investigating the business of Father Divine, prompted by a two-hour fight at one of his "heavens" at which people were injured.		The new Federal Mediation Board, headed by Charles P. Taft II, meets in Cleveland. . . . The SWOC files charges with the NRLB against Republic Steel. . . . Republic and other companies hint they may open plants soon to put men back to work; strikers claim the companies act in defiance of government attempts to settle the strike. . . . The UAWA asks local unions to discipline members who start unauthorized strikes.	After a night spent in Calcutta, Amelia Earhart leaves for her next stop: Bangkok, Siam.	Gaston Doumergue, who served two terms as prime minister and one term as president of France, dies. . . . Producer John Houseman delivers a commercial production of *The Cradle Will Rock*, with all performers taking a short leave of absence from the WPA.	Jun. 18
		In preparation for an expected 40,000 marchers, Governor George Earle asks Bethlehem Steel to shut its Cambria Works, and late at night sends state troops to Johnstown, Penn. . . . Violence erupts in Youngstown, Ohio, when police fire tear gas into a crowd of pickets that refuses to disperse. The crowd runs at police, guns fire, and seven policemen are shot, two seriously. Two men are killed, and 12 men and six women injured. The CIO asks for state troops, saying local police fired on a peaceful demonstration.	A monsoon forces Amelia Earhart into an unscheduled layover in Burma.	J.M. Barrie, the Scottish playwright best known for *Peter Pan*, dies.	Jun. 19
		The CIO calls off its march in Johnstown, Penn., and pickets leave after Bethlehem Steel is forced to close by state police in the early morning. The area is now under "modified martial law." . . . In Cleveland, the appointed mediation board meets with union leaders.	After 63 hours of flying from Moscow over the North Pole, a Soviet plane lands in Vancouver, Wash., forced down by rain before reaching California.		Jun. 20
A Federal Appeals Court in Philadelphia issues the first ruling on sit-down strikes in the Apex Hosiery case: they are an "unlawful and criminal" seizure of property.		Top management from all four steel companies involved in the strike meet with the Federal Mediation Board, but will not meet with union representatives. Republic Steel chair Tom Girdler refuses any agreements, written or oral, with the CIO. . . . President Franklin Roosevelt sends telegrams to the chairs of Republic and Youngstown steel companies, asking them to keep their plants closed. . . . Pickets defy a court order and assemble before a Republic Steel plant in Warren, Ohio, at night, after hearing it will open tomorrow. . . . John L. Lewis, CIO head, announces a drive to unionize 800,000 civilian government workers.	Amelia Earhart's plane is overhauled while she rests in Java, before leaving for Australia.	Walt Disney reveals that F. Salten has purchased the rights to *Bambi*, which will be made into a full-length animated film. Disney showed *Snow White and the Seven Dwarfs*, a picture now in production, to RKO executives last week. He will start work on *Bambi* as soon as his 500 technicians finish *Snow White*.	Jun. 21
President Franklin Roosevelt and Governors Martin Davey and George Earle are attacked in both houses of Congress for their actions in the steel strike. Earle is accused of positioning himself for a presidential run in 1940. . . . The Senate passes the 1938 Relief Bill for $1.5 billion, as President Franklin Roosevelt had asked.		Learning that managers intend to ignore President Franklin Roosevelt's appeal, Governor Martin Davey declares martial law in Ohio to prevent the scheduled reopening of the Republic Steel plants. Thousands of armed pickets in Youngstown stand outside the gates as three companies of National Guardsmen arrive. No violence occurs, although 150 armed men traveling to the area are arrested and dynamite is confiscated. Charles P. Taft II and his mediation board also visit Youngstown to meet with company officials. . . . Unions representing 300,000 rail workers vote in Chicago to strike for higher pay, but no date is set. . . . Labor cuts and terminations of WPA projects in the arts result in sit-down strikes, as thousands in New York and elsewhere receive pink slips.		In Chicago's Comiskey Park, 60,000 fans watch the Brown Bomber of Detroit, Joe Louis, knock out James Braddock in the eighth round to win the world heavyweight title.	Jun. 22

F	G	H	I	J
Includes elections, federal-state relations, civil rights and liberties, crime, the judiciary, education, healthcare, poverty, urban affairs, and population.	Includes formation and debate of U.S. foreign and defense policies, veterans affairs, and defense spending. (Relations with specific foreign countries are usually found under the region concerned.)	Includes business, labor, agriculture, taxation, transportation, consumer affairs, monetary and fiscal policy, natural resources, pollution, and accidents.	Includes worldwide scientific, medical, and technological developments, natural phenomena, U.S. weather, and natural disasters.	Includes the arts, religion, scholarship, communications media, sports, entertainment, fashions, fads, and social life.

	World Affairs	Europe	Africa & The Middle East	The Americas	Asia & The Pacific
Jun. 23	The International Labor Conference in Geneva adjourns with a plea for worldwide acceptance of a 40-hour week in all industries.	The Basque government and many refugees flee to Santander, and insurgent troops push west to that city as well. . . . Germany and Italy withdraw from patrols of the Non-Intervention Committee; 18 German warships gather near Spain. . . . German police arrest eight leaders of the Prussian Synod at night; only Reverend Niemoeller is missed. . . . Correspondents from Russia relate that thousands are denounced or expelled daily in Stalin's greatest purge. Most government officials of Uzbekistan are ousted as another plot is discovered.		President Lázaro Cárdenas announces the nationalization of 13,000 miles of railways in Mexico, promising to reimburse foreign owners for their investments. . . . On a ranch in Tabasco, Mexico, nine die in a gun battle, including a sheriff, when authorities try to stop a religious service in a private home.	
Jun. 24		German police arrest seven more ministers, some leaders of the Confessional Synods.			Japanese newspapers publish the government's six-year plan for increased production and armaments, requiring 600 million yen worth of equipment.
Jun. 25	Goettingen University celebrates its 200th birthday, but most major U.S. institutions do not attend.	Italy, having withdrawn from patrols but not from the Non-Intervention Committee (regarding Spain), wants to approve any changes in patrols. The situation between European nations is tense. . . . Based on personal letters sent to the Vatican and some American friends, the German Bishop of Speyer is accused of treason by Nazis.		Mexico's farms are decreed under state control by President Lázaro Cárdenas. Prices, imports, exports, and all facets of production may now be regulated by the state. . . . The United States will provide technical assistance to Brazil's navy as it designs and builds three destroyers. . . . British planes drop leaflets on Trinidad, printed with the governor's plea to workers to return to work.	Tungans, the Muslims of Chinese Turkestan, join with Islamic tribes to revolt. The government of Chinese Turkestan is more closely linked to the Soviets than to faraway Nanking.
Jun. 26		Loyalist Spain refuses to guarantee safety for ships of the Non-Intervention Committee. Italy promises long-term support of Franco's army in the Spanish civil war. A loyalist ship is sunk by a torpedo shot from a submarine, the first indication that Germany and Italy have formed a submarine blockade of loyalist ports. . . . At a party honoring a Soviet scientist back from the North Pole, the absence of several officials—including the chief of the Soviet Air Force—leads to speculation of further arrests.			
Jun. 27		Germany withdraws many of its warships from Spanish waters. . . . Over three years, all government funding to Bavaria's churches will be eliminated. The churches' hostile attitude toward the state is blamed, the government announces.		Premier Hepburn of Ontario, Canada, claims that CIO head John L. Lewis made a $500,000 campaign contribution to President Franklin Roosevelt, which has corrupted and biased his government. . . . Crom, Mexico's Labor Federation, denounces fascism and Communism in response to the Nationalization of farms and railroads, a move interpreted as socialist.	

A	B	C	D	E
Includes developments that affect more than one world region, international organizations, and important meetings of world leaders.	*Includes all domestic and regional developments in Europe, including the Soviet Union.*	*Includes all domestic and regional developments in Africa and the Middle East.*	*Includes all domestic and regional developments in Latin America, the Caribbean, and Canada.*	*Includes all domestic and regional developments in Asian and Pacific nations (and colonies).*

U.S. Politics & Social Issues	U.S. Foreign Policy & Defense	Economics & Great Depression	Science, Technology & Nature	Culture, Leisure & Lifestyle	
Governor George Earle announces his support for President Franklin Roosevelt for a third term. . . . After much criticism and investigation, six arrest warrants are issued for those who interfered with mail deliveries to Republic Steel in Ohio. . . . The Senate considers a proposed Equal Rights for Women Amendment.		The CIO calls a "labor holiday" sympathy strike in Niles and Warren, Ohio, and 10,000 workers walk off WPA and other jobs. . . . A strike of mail room employees at Pittsburgh's newspapers stops production for a third day.			Jun. 23
		The CIO cancels its labor holiday after a deal is made between the SWOC and law enforcement in Warren and Niles. Passes will allow the same number of men to enter and leave steel mills, maintaining a status quo. . . . Tom Girdler of Republic Steel, speaking before the Senate Post Office Committee, says the only way he will sign a contract with the CIO is if the U.S. Supreme Court forces him. . . . The Federal Mediation Board in Cleveland makes no progress. . . . Pittsburgh newspapers' mail clerks reject a compromise negotiated by a union, making their strike illegal. They then learn that outside union workers could be called in to replace them, so they revote and return to work.			Jun. 24
		Governor Martin Davey admits defeat in his attempts to end the steel strike through negotiations. He instructs the 4,500 National Guard called up in Youngstown, Warren, and Niles, Ohio, to safeguard those returning to work. Four small bombs are thrown in separate drive-bys. The CIO angrily accuses Davey of strike-breaking. . . . Martial law ends in Johnstown, Penn., but law enforcement stands by as thousands of coal miners pour into the city to show support for strikers.		Actor Colin Clive, best known for playing Dr. Frankenstein in the movies, dies of tuberculosis.	Jun. 25
		The Federal Mediation Board admits defeat in the steel strike. . . . Governor Martin Davey of Ohio says Labor Secretary Frances Perkins told him to use all his power to force Republic's chair, Tom Girdler, to sign an agreement. Perkins denies this. . . . Over 18,000 steel workers return to their jobs in Youngstown as the National Guard stands by. Mills open in other Ohio locations and in Johnstown, Penn. . . . The NLRB charges Ford Motors with assaulting UAWA organizations and sets a hearing for July 6. . . . Six hundred striking WPA workers hold Harold Stein, head of the Federal Arts Project, in his New York office for 15 hours until he agrees to their demand for a review board. Almost 12,000 WPA workers in New York have received pink slips.	Testing is complete on a new amphibian plane made by Grumman Company. Ten of the twin-engine planes have been sold already, rewarding Grumman's first foray into the commercial market.	Mary Pickford marries Buddy Rogers in Los Angeles, and will put Pickfair, the mansion built with former husband Douglas Fairbanks, on the market for $500,000.	Jun. 26
President Franklin Roosevelt asks a panel of teachers and representatives of labor, business, and government to conduct a six-month investigation. They are to study the relation of federal aid and policies to education on the state and local level.		Ohio CIO chief accuses Governor Martin Davey of waging "a campaign of terror against the workers" by refusing to remove troops protecting nonstriking workers. Davey repeats that the Labor Secretary asked him to use his subpoena power to force steel company heads to the bargaining table. He says he will not, nor will he allow their property to be seized by strikers. . . . In Johnstown, Penn., strikers begin 24-hour a day picketing, and nonstrikers' cars are vandalized. . . . Indiana's governor refuses state troops to guard the reopening of steel mills tomorrow, saying he expects settlement of the strike within 24 hours.	Amelia Earhart lands on Timor Island in the Dutch East Indies, then departs for Australia.		Jun. 27

F	G	H	I	J
Includes elections, federal-state relations, civil rights and liberties, crime, the judiciary, education, healthcare, poverty, urban affairs, and population.	Includes formation and debate of U.S. foreign and defense policies, veterans affairs, and defense spending. (Relations with specific foreign countries are usually found under the region concerned.)	Includes business, labor, agriculture, taxation, transportation, consumer affairs, monetary and fiscal policy, natural resources, pollution, and accidents.	Includes worldwide scientific, medical, and technological developments, natural phenomena, U.S. weather, and natural disasters.	Includes the arts, religion, scholarship, communications media, sports, entertainment, fashions, fads, and social life.

	World Affairs	Europe	Africa & The Middle East	The Americas	Asia & The Pacific
Jun. 28	The 10th Session of the International Studies Conference, focused on science and sponsored by the League of Nations, begins. . . . In Berlin, Adolf Hitler opens an international trade and economic conference with 1,800 delegates. Russia does not participate.	Santander, the only city left in Basque hands, floods with hundreds of thousands of refugees. Franco's troops are now 20 miles from the city.		Former senator Luis Muñoz Marín, recently expelled from the Liberal Party, claims the presidency of a new party in Arecibo, Puerto Rico. The head of the Liberal Party finds the news of little importance, since the new party, the ASI, is unrecognized.	
Jun. 29	The Soviet Union promises Japan to withdraw troops from disputed islands in the Amur River, between Siberia and Manchukuo. . . . France warns the United States that the current economic crisis may force it to withdraw from the tripartite monetary agreement of last September.	The 27 member nations of the Non-Intervention Committee meet over guarding Spain's coast. Italy and Germany will not patrol, but object to France and Britain being the only nations with ships. . . . As Georges Bonnet takes office as France's new Finance Minister, he acts to close the Bourse indefinitely and suspend commercial payments in gold. Premier Camille Chautemps asks the Senate to give him the powers they denied Léon Blum to handle the financial crisis. . . . France nationalizes another arms plant in Le Havre. . . . Rumors circulate of an army shakeup in Albania, including the removal of General Aranitas for his mishandling of the recent Toto revolt.			
Jun. 30		In the early morning hours, France's Chamber of Deputies votes fiscal power to Premier Camille Chautemps's Cabinet. The Senate does likewise. The franc is cut loose from gold and allowed to drop in value. . . . As Belgium's Premier van Zeeland returns from a visit to the United States, his Csabinet splits over pro-German amnesty laws. . . . Germany's Minister for Church Affairs Hans Kerrl sets up governmental finance boards to run the fiscal affairs of all churches, synods, and offices.		Now that Mexico's government controls cotton production, brokers learn that half their international sales profits will go to the government.	
Jul. 1	Japan claims that Soviet gunboats fired on Japanese soldiers swimming in the Amur River near Manchukuo (Manchuria). Soviets say Japanese cutters shelled their ships. Ambassadors of both countries meet for hours and agree on mutual troop withdrawals and further talks. . . . In South Africa, a new law bars German residents from participating in local politics, unless they become naturalized British subjects. . . . Thomas J. Watson, president of IBM and incoming president of the International Chamber of Commerce, is the first American decorated by Adolf Hitler for contributions that are "deserving of the German Reich."	Germany and Italy offer a counterproposal for patrols of the Non-Intervention Committee: control of the Spanish coast should be left to Spain's warring sides, and both those sides be accorded "belligerent" rights. Most committee members vote against the plan. . . . Nazis arrest Reverend Niemoeller for his bold attacks on government practices. . . . An estimated 1.5 million men and women vote in the Irish Free State. Early returns indicate a victory for Eamon de Valera and his new constitution, but the election ends in a stalemate. . . . Hungary's Regent for 17 years, Admiral Horthy, is voted royal prerogatives by the Chamber of Deputies, with the Socialist deputies abstaining. Hungary is a kingdom, rather than a republic, but its throne is vacant. . . . Britain begins using the phone number "999" for emergencies.			
Jul. 2	The Ninth Congress of the International Chamber of Commerce closes in Berlin. Due to France's monetary crisis and the political situation, little is accomplished.	Bulgaria arrests 140 fascists at the Black Sea resort of Varna, holding them responsible for six bombings. . . . The "liquidation" of two groups of spies is revealed by Soviet authorities. Seventy farmers, workers, and army personnel near Leningrad (St. Petersburg) purportedly set up a radio station to pass coded information to Estonia. Another 50–70 people in White Russia (Belarus) were said to be part of a Polish espionage ring.		Mexico imposes further royalties on foreign oil companies, overturning their original leases and contracts.	

A	B	C	D	E
Includes developments that affect more than one world region, international organizations, and important meetings of world leaders.	*Includes all domestic and regional developments in Europe, including the Soviet Union.*	*Includes all domestic and regional developments in Africa and the Middle East.*	*Includes all domestic and regional developments in Latin America, the Caribbean, and Canada.*	*Includes all domestic and regional developments in Asian and Pacific nations (and colonies).*

U.S. Politics & Social Issues	U.S. Foreign Policy & Defense	Economics & Great Depression	Science, Technology & Nature	Culture, Leisure & Lifestyle	
A Senate Committee ends its investigation of the Post Office's refusals to deliver food in the steel strike, referring further action to the La Follette subcommittee on civil liberties.		Michigan's legislature passes a Labor Relations Act, confirming the right of workers to bargain, establishing limits to picketing, and setting up mediation boards. . . . Three CIO members are arrested for bombings in Warren, Ohio. . . . Although pickets march and tension and racial violence outside the plant still occur, Bethlehem Steel is declaring the strike against its Cambria Works over, and claims production is back to normal. . . . President Franklin Roosevelt signs a bill continuing the CCC through 1940.		Copper millionaire Solomon Guggenheim unveils a foundation promoting abstract and non-objective art and art education.	Jun. 28
		Charles P. Taft II, head of the failed Mediation Board, confers separately with President Franklin Roosevelt and Secretary of Labor Frances Perkins. . . . Water mains in Johnstown, Penn., leading to the Cambria Works, are blown up with dynamite. The mayor informs union leaders and President Franklin Roosevelt that he will no longer be responsible for the safety of strikers and CIO agitators. . . . New York police eject 126 WPA strikers from offices, and 500 pickets fight to stop the ejections, as funding cuts and project terminations force more WPA employees out of work.	Amelia Earhart leaves Australia for Lea, New Guinea, beginning the most difficult part of her round-the-world trip.		Jun. 29
Confronted by pictures of the Memorial Day Massacre, Chicago police officials admit to the La Follette subcommittee that seven of the men killed were shot in the back.		Indiana's steel mills reopen as Governor Maurice Townsend negotiates a truce between the CIO and Inland and Youngstown Steel: the companies will accept the SWOC as bargaining unit pending a decision by the NLRB. . . . In Johnstown, Penn., union leader James Mark, who had been warned of his safety by the mayor, plans a mass meeting of miners for July 4. . . . Three Republic mills in Canton, Ohio, reopen, but 75 pickets are arrested and eight men injured in a rock-throwing incident with National Guard troops.	Amelia Earhart takes off for tiny Howland Island as several U.S. ships stand on alert to assist her. No flyer has attempted the 2,570-mile trip before.	Franklin D. Roosevelt, Jr., third son of the President, marries industrial heiress Ethel DuPont.	Jun. 30
		The Mediation Board's report on the steel strike negotiations becomes public and faults the independent steel companies for their refusal to meet with union leaders. . . . Youngstown Company president Purnell denies coming to any agreement with the CIO in Indiana. He keeps his mills closed, but over 9,000 return to work at Inland plants. . . . The CIO argues in court that deployment of state troops in Ohio was a violation of the Wagner Act, interfering with the collective bargaining process. . . . WPA battles in New York continue: crowds of up to 300 people, mostly women, unsuccessfully try to break into offices in two locations. Fifteen are injured, including three handicapped workers, and five arrested.		Northwest Passage by Kenneth Roberts is published.	Jul. 1
A compromise bill for court reorganization is submitted to Congress, replacing the controversial measure under debate for nearly six months. It allows for one additional judge each year to be added to the Supreme Court for each judge who reaches age 75 and does not retire.		Upset with CIO attempts to woo its unions away, the AFL calls a holiday for 25,000 truckers, bringing business in Philadelphia to a halt, snarling traffic, and leaving food and milk to spoil in warehouses. . . . Paramount Newsreel releases the six-minute film of Chicago's Memorial Day riots. Chicago's Police Movie Censor Bureau bans the newsreel in that city.	Amelia Earhart does not arrive at Howland Island; Coast Guard and Navy ships begin a search.	For the first time in its history, the U.S. Amateur Athletic Union declines an invitation to compete in track and field events in Germany, citing the Nazi repressions of freedom. . . . American Donald Budge takes the singles championship at Wimbledon.	Jul. 2

F	**G**	**H**	**I**	**J**
Includes elections, federal-state relations, civil rights and liberties, crime, the judiciary, education, healthcare, poverty, urban affairs, and population.	*Includes formation and debate of U.S. foreign and defense policies, veterans affairs, and defense spending. (Relations with specific foreign countries are usually found under the region concerned.)*	*Includes business, labor, agriculture, taxation, transportation, consumer affairs, monetary and fiscal policy, natural resources, pollution, and accidents.*	*Includes worldwide scientific, medical, and technological developments, natural phenomena, U.S. weather, and natural disasters.*	*Includes the arts, religion, scholarship, communications media, sports, entertainment, fashions, fads, and social life.*

	World Affairs	Europe	Africa & The Middle East	The Americas	Asia & The Pacific
Jul. 3	The Soviet withdrawal of troops from the Amur Islands, after 37 Soviet soldiers are confirmed killed, is viewed by Japan as proof that recent purges have weakened the Soviet Union.	Insurgent planes bomb Santander, the last holdout of the Basques, and drop shells near a British patrol ship. Loyalists send 20 planes against insurgent headquarters in Salamanca. . . . The chief of the Soviet secret police in Leningrad accuses Catholic priests of using the secret confessional to manipulate parishioners into spying for Poland and Japan. Newspapers disclose other espionage rings involving clergy, especially in Vladivostok, where members of many congregations are arrested. . . . The leaders of Germany and Italy sign accords on socio-political issues, furthered by the exchange of workers between their countries. . . . Germany announces that its anti-Jewish laws will spread to Upper Silesia. Jewish officials, for example, must retire by the end of August.		Brazil's Minister of Justice Soares promises a sweeping modernization of the police and penal systems. . . . Six thousand Catholics arrive in Mexico City from the state of Queretaro to plead for the opening of five churches. One-third of the pilgrims made the 200-mile journey on foot. They are told that such decisions take time.	
Jul. 4	With the help of students from the Sorbonne who work all night, the U.S. pavilion opens at the Paris International Exposition.	The car of Portugal's Premier, Dr. Antonio de Oliveira Salazar, blows up seconds after he and two others leave it to attend Mass. . . . A soccer match between Austria and a team from Genoa erupts into a free-for-all, ending the game in a tie. . . . A Soviet newspaper announces the executions of 64 people in the Trans-Siberian rail town of Svobodnie. All were convicted of spying for Japan.		Exploded bombs are found under two bridges leading into San Juan, Puerto Rico. No doubt intended to disrupt traffic, they did little damage.	
Jul. 5	The League of Nations second General Conference of National Commissions for Intellectual Cooperation starts in Paris. The subject is intellectual property rights. . . . Rumors that the Peel Commission recommends splitting Palestine causes unrest. All available troops are rushed to Palestine, and Britain is ready to declare martial law at the first sign of trouble.	The roof of the famous Bridge of Sighs in Venice, Italy, made of two tons of lead, has been stolen. It was built in 1595; the theft was discovered as rain leaked through the ceiling.		With Governor Fletcher's assurance that their grievances have been heard, Trinidad's oil workers return to their jobs, ending a month of strikes and random violence. . . . A decree in Mexico grants workers the right to collective bargaining and strikes.	
Jul. 6	Japan charges that Soviet troops attacked twice on the Manchukuo-Siberia border and were beaten back. Soviet reports claim heavy casualties on both sides.	Heavy censorship by the Spanish government stifles the news from Spain; General Miaja releases nothing that may help Franco's troops. The International Brigades (IBs)—made up mostly of Soviet men and arms—launch attacks on Brunete, west of Madrid. The goal is to pull insurgent troops away from the Basque region. . . . Final voting results in the Irish Free State show the new constitution approved, but Eamon de Valera without a clear majority of delegates. . . . Germany allows the use of "transfer marks" for Jews wishing to emigrate, but who have been unable to transfer their funds. . . . Italy announces that 60 new military airports are under construction.			
Jul. 7	Britain makes public the Peel Commission report, which, as expected, recommends a division of Palestine based on "irreconcilable" differences between Arabs and Zionists. The report describes separate Jewish and Arab states, with Britain retaining control in a third area, comprised of Jerusalem, Bethlehem, and a corridor to the sea. Authorities in London hail the report and promise quick action.	Jacob Doletsky, director of TASS, the Soviet news agency, is arrested along with other "Trotsky bandits." The arrests may have occurred weeks ago; the news is just now coming out.			Japanese troops conduct night maneuvers on the Lugou Bridge near Peiping (Beijing). As Peiping is surrounded on three sides by Japanese-held lands, this is the only road into the city held by the Chinese. The Japanese demand entry into the city, threatening to open fire if they are refused. . . . After three months, the elected members of the All-India Party vote to take office without any assurances from British governors about the use of their "special powers."

A	B	C	D	E
Includes developments that affect more than one world region, international organizations, and important meetings of world leaders.	Includes all domestic and regional developments in Europe, including the Soviet Union.	Includes all domestic and regional developments in Africa and the Middle East.	Includes all domestic and regional developments in Latin America, the Caribbean, and Canada.	Includes all domestic and regional developments in Asian and Pacific nations (and colonies).

U.S. Politics & Social Issues	U.S. Foreign Policy & Defense	Economics & Great Depression	Science, Technology & Nature	Culture, Leisure & Lifestyle	
		At the request of Cleveland's mayor and sheriff, Governor Martin Davey agrees to call in National Guard troops when Republic Steel opens its Cleveland plants on July 6. . . . After a night of negotiations, Mayor Wilson announces the end of the AFL holiday in Philadelphia at dawn. Elections allowing employees of two companies to choose between AFL and CIO unions will be held. . . . Dynamite is found on railroad tracks near the Cambria Works in Johnstown, Penn., and a fired Bethlehem employee is arrested. Johnstown expects up to 40,000 CIO supporters at a rally tomorrow.	Storms interfere with the search for Amelia Earhart and Fred Noonan. Radio operators in California are certain they recognize her voice in a 7 a.m. SOS call. . . . Pan American Airways, in conjunction with England's Imperial Airways, starts regular, scheduled service between New York and London.		Jul. 3
		Governor George Earle addresses a Johnstown, Penn., crowd of under 15,000, proclaiming that he is a friend of labor. Smaller crowds gather in Youngstown and Warren, Ohio. Rain and thunderstorms keep attendance low, but the CIO image suffers.	The aircraft carrier Lexington and 98 planes leave California to aid in the search for Amelia Earhart. Radio operators report hearing her state her position as near a reef.		Jul. 4
		The American Newspaper Guild continues to picket the Seattle Star, shut down since July 3. . . . National Guard troops arrive in Cleveland for the reopening of four Republic Steel facilities tomorrow. . . . The 1,150 drivers of two bakeries in Philadelphia vote for representation by the AFL, forcing the CIO to withdraw. Overall, 14,000 bakery workers are affected by the vote.			Jul. 5
Majority Leader Joseph Robinson introduces the new, compromise court reorganization bill in the Senate. . . . Eight of the Scottsboro defendants are arraigned once more in Alabama for rapes allegedly committed in 1931. Individual trial dates are set as the men plead innocent.	The War Department awards a $4.1 million contract to Curtiss Wright Aircraft for 210 pursuit planes, capable of a speed of 300 miles per hour.	President Franklin Roosevelt discloses that last month he asked all executive branch agency and department heads to cut expenses by 10 percent. His goal is to cut $400 million from the federal budget through June 1938. . . . Felony warrants are issued naming the Ford Company and 14 employees (including six "John Does") in the May 26 beating of a union representative. . . . A grand jury indicts 200 men in Youngstown, Ohio, for actions last month connected with the steel strike, such as rioting and carrying concealed weapons. . . . A man in Menominee, Mich., dies as he falls off a car and is dragged beneath it. The car was trying to get through picket lines surrounding a furniture plant; the victim was picketing and jumped onto the car. . . . In Brooklyn, police arrest 10 when strikers pelt nonstriking workers with rocks. The union and strikers mass before the police station and 58 more men and women are arrested.	The highest recorded temperature ever recorded in Canada (114°F) is reached in Yellow Grass, Saskatchewan. . . . A Pan American clipper airship completes the nearly 2,000-mile Atlantic crossing and lands in Ireland, where President Eamon de Valera welcomes the crew. The Imperial Airways plane lands in Newfoundland.	The WPA officially drops any plans to support The Cradle Will Rock, the musical about a steel strike. . . . Lord Baden-Powell uses radio to address the 28,000 Boy Scouts assembled in Washington, D.C., for a Jamboree. President Franklin Roosevelt will visit the Scouts tomorrow.	Jul. 6
		The Aluminum Company of America in Alcoa, Tenn., is the site of a riot where one striker and one policeman are shot to death, and 28 others are injured. State troops with machine guns now guard the plant, which had just reopened after an unsettled seven-week strike. . . . A branch of the ILGWU in New York calls a strike of 35,000 cloakmakers, who walk out of 1,500 businesses.	As the hunt for Amelia Earhart continues, 104,000 square miles have been searched.	During the All-Star game, a hit by Earl Averill fractures Dizzy Dean's toe. Forced to change his pitching style, his arm will suffer and cut short his career.	Jul. 7

F	G	H	I	J
Includes elections, federal-state relations, civil rights and liberties, crime, the judiciary, education, healthcare, poverty, urban affairs, and population.	Includes formation and debate of U.S. foreign and defense policies, veterans affairs, and defense spending. (Relations with specific foreign countries are usually found under the region concerned.)	Includes business, labor, agriculture, taxation, transportation, consumer affairs, monetary and fiscal policy, natural resources, pollution, and accidents.	Includes worldwide scientific, medical, and technological developments, natural phenomena, U.S. weather, and natural disasters.	Includes the arts, religion, scholarship, communications media, sports, entertainment, fashions, fads, and social life.

	World Affairs	Europe	Africa & The Middle East	The Americas	Asia & The Pacific
Jul. 8		Franco sends troops and the Condor Legion to defend Brunete. . . . French Finance Minister Georges Bonnet's plan for economic stability calls for sharp increases in income and sales taxes, with 2.5 billion francs in rail taxes for passengers and freight. Fees on tobacco, oil, telephone, and postage will all go up. . . . Newspapers report that Prince Mdivani of Georgia and seven others were executed by the Soviet Union as spies.			At midnight, Japanese forces open fire on Peiping with artillery and machine guns. Tanks roll along the Lugou Bridge. Initial reports blame the incident on "night maneuvers" by the Japanese, who had not informed the Chinese about their activities.
Jul. 9	Turkey, Iran, Iraq, and Afghanistan meet in Tehran to sign a non-aggression pact: the Oriente Entente.	Spanish loyalists and the IBs take Quijorna, a town close to Brunete. The Abraham Lincoln Brigade of American volunteers loses several men, and at least 40 are wounded. . . . The Non-Intervention Committee meets and cannot resolve the question of naval patrols around Spain. The Earl of Plymouth is asked to conduct private negotiations. . . . The Pavilion of Peace opens at the Paris Exposition. . . . Italy bars the entry of the Austrian soccer team. The match of July 4 was to be replayed in Genoa. The Austrian team appeals to Il Duce, who orders them to leave Italy within 24 hours.		Catholics open churches by force in Chiapas, Mexico, and police arrest eight people.	After Chinese troops recapture the 850-foot-long Lugou Bridge, both Japan and China agree to withdraw troops and respect a truce. Japan sends its Ambassador from Peiping to Nanking (Nanjing), indicating that Japan considers the incident of national, rather than local, importance. Japan also demands punishment for Chinese instigators and wants guarantees of future safety.
Jul. 10	The Arab world voices opposition to the division of Palestine. The Mufti of Jerusalem, the King of Iraq, the Arab High Committee, and the Sheik of Koweit (Kuwait) all protest in writing.	Although loyalists claim success in the fight for Brunete, insurgents say they have killed 3,000 government soldiers and wounded 6,000 more. Franco's troops use 150 bombers and 150 pursuit planes to drive back the loyalists. . . . A long-threatened strike by Paris's hotel and restaurant workers starts. Workers ask enforcement of the 40-hour workweek law; employers say it is impossible. Many workers ignore the strike order.			Japanese forces storm two Chinese villages as a truce evaporates. The Japanese claim they were attacked and provoked; the Chinese claim Japan simply stalled for time while reinforcements arrived.
Jul. 11		The Non-Intervention Committee remains deadlocked, but France threatens to suspend patrols rather than be the only nation subjected to searches on the seas. . . . As more workers join the strike in Paris, small melees break out in the Montmartre area resulting in 20 arrests. . . . In their Sunday sermons, the Lutheran churches of Germany announce an official appeal for peaceful relations with the Nazi government.	As Arab opposition mounts to the division of Palestine, rioting breaks out in north Syria. Up to 20 people are killed, including the District Governor.		Through diplomatic channels, China warns Japan that it will stand up to any further aggression. Both sides rush more troops to Peiping, and both sides have presented ultimatums to the other, including demands for apologies.
Jul. 12	Muslim religious leaders vow to excommunicate Arabs who support the partitioning of Palestine. The Jewish Labor Party also rejects it.	Fed up with the ineffectiveness of the Non-Intervention Pact, France announces it will not submit to international control along its border with Spain in the Pyrenees, though French patrols of the border will continue to operate. . . . A German priest is sentence to three months in prison for "abetting racial defilement." He performed a marriage between a Jew and non-Jew.			Up to 10,000 Japanese troops from Manchukuo arrive near Peiping, and a new Chinese army joins resident troops as fighting breaks out once more. General Sung Cheh-yuan (Song Zheyuan) of the 29th Army arrives in Tientsin (Tianjin).

A	B	C	D	E
Includes developments that affect more than one world region, international organizations, and important meetings of world leaders.	*Includes all domestic and regional developments in Europe, including the Soviet Union.*	*Includes all domestic and regional developments in Africa and the Middle East.*	*Includes all domestic and regional developments in Latin America, the Caribbean, and Canada.*	*Includes all domestic and regional developments in Asian and Pacific nations (and colonies).*

U.S. Politics & Social Issues	U.S. Foreign Policy & Defense	Economics & Great Depression	Science, Technology & Nature	Culture, Leisure & Lifestyle	
Two hours of shouting occupies the Senate as they try to agree on rules limiting filibusters over the revised court bill.		William Green, head of the AFL, blames John L. Lewis and the CIO for the failure of the steel strikes, saying that CIO tactics have alienated the public. . . . Eight men are indicted in Warren, Ohio, for setting bombs during the strike. . . . Journalists who witnessed the May 26 attacks on union men refer to Ford employees as "typical hoodlums" before the trial examiner. . . . Negotiations to end the aluminum workers' strike in Tennessee collapse. . . . Two shipyards of the 20 shut by strikes in New York and New Jersey try to reopen and defy the CIO-affiliated strikers. At one location, thousands of strikers gather to harass the "scabs" and throw rocks and bricks. Police cars escort the 600 workers away.			Jul. 8
	At the close of a state visit by China's Foreign Minster Kung, Treasury Secretary Henry Morgenthau reveals a plan allowing China to exchange silver currency for gold in the United States, enabling greater purchases of military supplies.	Harold Robertson of the Gospel Army reports that 70,000 people in the San Joaquin Valley in California are homeless, and some are starving. A conference of local, state, and federal officials is needed. . . . Police remove pickets and the *Seattle Star* resumes publication. The strike against it, triggered by a teamster dispute, is not supported by other unions. . . . Men and women injured in the May riot at Ford Company's River Rouge facility testify before the NLRB, telling of beatings and abuse.		Oliver Law, fighting with the Abraham Lincoln Brigade near Brunete, Spain, is killed leading a charge. Law was a Communist, labor organizer, and the first African American to command white troops.	Jul. 9
	The two new battleships built for the Navy this year will have 16-inch guns installed. In April, the United States had pushed for an international limit of 14 inches, but Japan would not agree.	The NLRB will investigate charges made against the Aluminum Company of America in Alcoa, Tenn.		Seabiscuit wins the Butler Handicap in Empire City. The horse has won $82,025 this year and is the champion handicap star in training. . . . President Franklin Roosevelt signs a bill promising $3 million for New York's upcoming World Fair.	Jul. 10
		The union hall in Massillon, Ohio, is the site of late-night fighting between police and striking Republic Steel workers. Three men die, others are struck by bullets, and 141 are arrested. . . . On the advice of AFL chief William Green, employees of the Aluminum Company of Alcoa, Tenn., vote to end their strike. The head of the local union resigns.	Directors of the search for Amelia Earhart put their chances at "one in a million," though planes from the *Lexington* will join the effort tomorrow.	Composer George Gershwin, who brought jazz and modern music to the concert hall and opera stage, dies while working in Hollywood. Gershwin was 38 years old and suffered from a brain tumor. . . . Elroy Robinson sets a new world record for running the half-mile: 01.49.6.	Jul. 11
President Franklin Roosevelt asks Congress to take action on farm legislation and ensure crop stability before another crisis emerges.		State troops now patrol Massillon, Ohio. CIO offices are closed and pickets prohibited in the wake of last night's violence. Witnesses claim Republic Steel employees fired into the union crowd. . . . The cloakmakers' strike ends after several days of negotiations. They win a 10 percent wage increase and, in 1939, a 32.5-hour week. . . . The CIO announces a new drive to unionize 2 million state and local government workers, acknowledging civil service rules against striking. . . . At the NLRB hearing, union organizers, former employees, and journalists tell of intimidations, beatings, and chases committed against them by Ford Company thugs.			Jul. 12

F	G	H	I	J
Includes elections, federal-state relations, civil rights and liberties, crime, the judiciary, education, healthcare, poverty, urban affairs, and population.	Includes formation and debate of U.S. foreign and defense policies, veterans affairs, and defense spending. (Relations with specific foreign countries are usually found under the region concerned.)	Includes business, labor, agriculture, taxation, transportation, consumer affairs, monetary and fiscal policy, natural resources, pollution, and accidents.	Includes worldwide scientific, medical, and technological developments, natural phenomena, U.S. weather, and natural disasters.	Includes the arts, religion, scholarship, communications media, sports, entertainment, fashions, fads, and social life.

	World Affairs	Europe	Africa & The Middle East	The Americas	Asia & The Pacific
Jul. 13		Loyalists claim they have shot down 25 insurgent planes in two days in the Brunete area, and say the bodies of 1,000 insurgents still lie unburied in Quijorna. . . . Although publicly denying that the border is open, France allows passage of weapons to the insurgent armies. . . . Hermann Goering unveils new measures for Germany's four-year plan, tightening domestic distribution of goods and promoting foreign trade. . . . King Leopold of Belgium rejects the resignation of Premier van Zeeland and asks him to form a new Cabinet. . . . On the eve of Bastille Day, 1,500 French Communists fight with a right-wing party in a Paris suburb.		Bolivian President Toro resigns 13 months after the coup that put him in power; Army Col. German Busch takes over. Busch is said to be supported by both the military and the general public.	
Jul. 14		General Franco tells journalists that his forces brought down 57 loyalist planes in eight days of fighting around Brunete and that he lost only five planes. He claims the loyalist push met success for a few days, but that the battle is over now. . . . Britain presents a compromise plan for non-intervention to the House of Commons; it grants belligerent rights to both sides in Spain if foreign volunteer troops are withdrawn. . . . A two-day Congress of European National Minorities begins in London.			A three-hour gun battle continues into the early morning hours south of Peiping. Japan's Cabinet supports the military action and will send reinforcements as needed.
Jul. 15		Over 100 planes battle and drop bombs over Madrid in the afternoon. . . . The Polish-German Convention in Upper Silesia expires. Nothing replaces the League of Nations agreement, and minority Poles and Germans in different areas worry about their treatment.			Lofa is the site of a battle between 700 Japanese troops and Chinese; the Japanese claim they were ambushed. Refugees from the town and farms rush to Nanyuan. In Tokyo, reports indicate that diplomatic negotiations are restoring order. Japanese civilians evacuate from China. General Sung meets with Lt. Gen. Katsuki in Tientsin.
Jul. 16		Government troops attack Ciempozuelos in a surprise move 20 miles south of Madrid; they also bomb five airfields used by the insurgents. A ship carrying 800 wounded Italian volunteers arrives home.			Japan's War Office deploys troops from Japan to north China. Authorities warn the people of Japan that war is imminent. Japan continues to fortify its positions south of Peiping, while China appeals to other nations under the Nine-Powers Treaty, the Kellogg Act, and the League of Nations.
Jul. 17	Abandoning diplomacy, Pope Pius XI praises Cardinal Mundelein of Chicago for his sermon and stand against Hitler. . . . Chile fears a mob attack on its Madrid Embassy, where 200 or more refugees live. Chile asks for diplomatic assistance from many countries, including the United States.	Loyalists announce the killing of 600 Moorish troops who were spotted crawling through the darkness to new positions 15 miles south of Madrid. . . . General Franco rejects the new British compromise on non-intervention, but the other nations agree to accept it as a basis for further talks. . . . The Anglo-Russian and Anglo-German Naval Agreements are signed. Allowing the two countries to build 10,000-ton cruisers will bring naval capabilities into balance, it is hoped.			In India, cars of the Delhi-Calcutta Express train jump their rails, plunging over an embankment and killing 107 people.
Jul. 18	U.S. businesses in Tientsin, which control 60 percent of the imports and exports, expect heavy losses if war comes.	The first anniversary of the Spanish civil war is celebrated by heavy fighting near Brunete. More planes are shot down, tanks are deployed, and grenades are thrown. . . . British industry reveals it must find alternate sources of iron ore. The mines in Spain's Basque region, a major supplier to Britain in the past, are now in insurgent hands. . . . Chancellor Adolf Hitler announces that art works must be understandable to the average man or they will be suppressed as "artistic Bolshevism." . . . A large bomb intended to kill Col. Adam Koc, head of Poland's political party, explodes early, killing the would-be assassin at the gate of Koc's home.		Riots and gunshots interrupt a march of 20,000 Integralistas in São Paulo, Brazil. Three people die, 18 are hospitalized, and many more injured; some are trampled. . . . President Carias of Honduras claims that his country enjoys pledges of mutual protection with Guatemala and El Salvador against political enemies.	Japan demands the withdrawal of China's 37th and 29th armies and all other troops in Peiping, threatening to shell the city if they do not leave. General Sung says China will not abandon Peiping. . . . A Japanese paper reports the death of 110 girls due to an explosion in a munitions factory in Chungking. . . . Japan's army in China announces that General Sung has apologized and withdrawn the 29th Army from Peiping. The War Office in Japan, however, considers the apology a meaningless gesture, and the presence of the 29th Army an invasion.

A	B	C	D	E
Includes developments that affect more than one world region, international organizations, and important meetings of world leaders.	Includes all domestic and regional developments in Europe, including the Soviet Union.	Includes all domestic and regional developments in Africa and the Middle East.	Includes all domestic and regional developments in Latin America, the Caribbean, and Canada.	Includes all domestic and regional developments in Asian and Pacific nations (and colonies).

U.S. Politics & Social Issues	U.S. Foreign Policy & Defense	Economics & Great Depression	Science, Technology & Nature	Culture, Leisure & Lifestyle	
As debate continues on the revised court bill, head counts show that it lacks support for passage.... At the new rape trial of Clarence Norris, testimony from the first Scottsboro trial is read, refuting the testimony of one accuser. The other accuser has since recanted.		The Youngstown mill in East Chicago reopens after 46 days. Total cost in wages for the steel strike is estimated at $4.5 million.... In Ohio, court testimony is given in the CIO's attempt to prevent the use of state troops against strikers.... Two shipyards in Brooklyn reopen with no violence, but very few workers show up.	Dr. Morris Fishbein, editor of the *Journal of the American Medical Association*, predicts that a substance injected into women's veins will someday prevent conception for 2–3 years at a time.	Ernest Dalton, last surviving member of Kansas's infamous Dalton Gang, dies in Los Angeles.	Jul. 13
Senator Joseph Robinson of Arkansas, a key figure in the Court Reorganization Bill, dies at home of a heart attack.		In Ohio, a grand jury indicts nine CIO strikers for interfering with mail.	In a second flight over the North Pole from Moscow, Soviet pilots set a new distance record: 6,262 miles. They try to reach San Diego, but fog forces them to land in a cow pasture in Riverside, Calif., where they hold up English signs asking for baths, food, and sleep.		Jul. 14
In spite of recanted testimony, Clarence Norris is condemned to death for the third time.... Although urged by many to withdraw the Court Reorganization Bill, President Franklin Roosevelt will continue to fight for its passage.... Twenty miners are burned and crushed to death in an explosion at the Baker Mine in Indiana.		Citizen groups from 12 states send delegates to Johnstown, Penn., for a preliminary meeting to make the Right to Work anti-strike movement into a national organization. The movement started with the steel strike.... Charges against the *Seattle Star* are filed with the NLRB; the strike against the newspaper continues.			Jul. 15
The Appellate Court upholds the conviction of Lucky Luciano.... Three oil tankers explode in Atlantic City, injuring 175 people—most are sprayed with burning oil.	Responding to China's appeals, Secretary of State Cordell Hull asks for restraint, a lowering of barriers, abstinence from the use of force, and respect and observance of all international agreements—all without mentioning any country by name.	For defying the injunction against picketing in the month-old shipyard strike, a union leader is sentenced to 30 days in prison. Later, strikers throw rocks at workers leaving the Robins Drydocks under police protection. Eight men are injured and nine strikers arrested.... The NLRB tells Republic Steel to appear in court on July 21 and defend itself against charges of threatening employees and beating union organizers.			Jul. 16
		Shipyard workers in New York and New Jersey continue to picket, defying court orders.			Jul. 17
	Bell Aircraft of Buffalo, N.Y., is building a twin-engine fighter plane to carry a crew of five for the Army Air Corps. The XMF-1 is currently undergoing testing.	William Green of the AFL takes on Heywood Broun, president of the American Newspaper Guild—a union affiliated with the CIO. Green calls Broun a Communist stooge and claims he has sold his constituents down the river.	The search for Amelia Earhart and Fred Noonan is called off by the Navy. The search is said to cost $4 million (the President denies this), but no trace of the plane or aviators is found.		Jul. 18

F	G	H	I	J
Includes elections, federal-state relations, civil rights and liberties, crime, the judiciary, education, healthcare, poverty, urban affairs, and population.	*Includes formation and debate of U.S. foreign and defense policies, veterans affairs, and defense spending. (Relations with specific foreign countries are usually found under the region concerned.)*	*Includes business, labor, agriculture, taxation, transportation, consumer affairs, monetary and fiscal policy, natural resources, pollution, and accidents.*	*Includes worldwide scientific, medical, and technological developments, natural phenomena, U.S. weather, and natural disasters.*	*Includes the arts, religion, scholarship, communications media, sports, entertainment, fashions, fads, and social life.*

	World Affairs	Europe	Africa & The Middle East	The Americas	Asia & The Pacific
Jul. 19		Heavy losses force loyalist troops to abandon their assault on Brunete. The Condor Legion planes and ground forces use machine guns to mow down retreating troops. Franco is said to have 42,000 troops deployed, with 84,000 in reserve. In Barcelona, more POUM leaders are arrested. . . . Germany completes the negotiation of trade treaties with Spanish insurgents. . . . Armed police break up a religious procession of 5,000 in Belgrade, Yugoslavia. Conflict between the Catholic and Serbian Orthodox churches led to the violence; priests are arrested, a Bishop is among the seriously injured, and religious banners are shredded. The government claims the demonstration was by Communists.			Chiang Kai-shek says China will fight rather than be subjugated to Japanese demands, and claims that the Lugou Bridge incident was not a chance occurrence. Chinese troops are still in Peiping; General Sung denies any intention of withdrawing them. According to Japan, China has agreed in writing to cease all anti-Japanese activities.
Jul. 20	The League of Nations opens an eight-day Conference on Higher Education in Paris.	Loyalists report that their forces, using machine guns, inflicted terrible casualties on insurgents, up to 10,000. . . . Paris waiters accept a six-day, 40-hour workweek, approved by the government, and end the café strike. . . . Minister Georges Bonnet convinces the French Cabinet to approve further financial cuts, but allow an increase of 6 billion francs for defense. . . . The Soviet Union's execution of another 24 Trotskyists and spies on the Trans-Siberian railroad is announced. . . . Belgrade police fire into a crowd of Orthodox Serbs who chant anti-government slogans, then charge the crowd with fixed bayonets, injuring many. Public protests are spreading throughout Yugoslavia.			Japan's army begins shelling Wanping and the Lugou Bridge. Wanping's barracks and arsenal burn. The port of Tangku, near Tientsin, is captured.
Jul. 21		Claiming that resistance is crushed, loyalists in Spain push their line forward a kilometer or two. . . . Eamon de Valera is reelected President of the Executive Council of the Irish Free State. . . . Clashes of Orthodox Serbs and police continue, with brutal treatment doled out by the police. The approval of a Concordat with the Vatican is blamed for much of the agitation.		Charging that oil companies are not complying with contracts, workers in three Mexican districts resume a strike.	General Sung's 37th Army, which was rumored to be withdrawing, stands fast and fights in Peiping. . . . Troops and munitions continue to arrive by rail, reinforcing both Chinese and Japanese positions.
Jul. 22	Britain's House of Commons refuses to approve or block the division of Palestine, leaving the issue in the hands of the League of Nations.	After nearly two weeks' peace, Madrid is heavily shelled again.			A train with soldiers form China's 37th Army leaves Peiping for the south, and is replaced by 600 men from the 132nd, under Gen. Zhou Dengru. . . . Reinforcements depart for Peiping from the Shensi (Shaanxi) province as well.
Jul. 23		Spanish insurgents advance in Tereul, while other battlefronts seem stalemated. . . . A Soviet report reveals that eight officials of the Young Communist Association have been removed and accused of corrupting the young and being enemies of the people. . . . Yugoslavia votes to ratify the Vatican Concordat hours before the ailing Orthodox Patriarch dies. Heavy police presence prevents mob violence.			Tokyo papers report the withdrawal of both Chinese and Japanese troops in Peiping and Tientsin. The Chinese government in Nanking denies any acceptance of Japan's demands.
Jul. 24		Insurgents recapture Brunete in a day-long battle, driving loyalists out. The fighting is said by some to be the worst of the war. . . . Mourning for the Serbian Patriarch takes on political overtones: the governments offer of a state funeral is refused; Ministers who voted for the Concordat with the Vatican are excommunicated.			Journalists report that the situation around Peiping has cooled off.

A	B	C	D	E
Includes developments that affect more than one world region, international organizations, and important meetings of world leaders.	Includes all domestic and regional developments in Europe, including the Soviet Union.	Includes all domestic and regional developments in Africa and the Middle East.	Includes all domestic and regional developments in Latin America, the Caribbean, and Canada.	Includes all domestic and regional developments in Asian and Pacific nations (and colonies).

U.S. Politics & Social Issues	U.S. Foreign Policy & Defense	Economics & Great Depression	Science, Technology & Nature	Culture, Leisure & Lifestyle	
Alabama unexpectedly waives the death penalty in the trial of Scottsboro defendant Andy Wright.		Heywood Broun calls AFL president William Green "the greatest single obstacle in the path of the labor movement." . . . A few men picket in the shipyard strike while the NLRB investigates labor practices of Robins Drydock and others.			Jul. 19
In Tallahassee, Fla., two African-American men accused of stabbing a policeman are lynched. Masked men take them from jail at 3 a.m.; they are shot 15–20 times and left outside town. The House has already passed an anti-lynching bill; the Senate has had one on its calendar for a month, with no action taken. . . . Rumors circulate that President Franklin Roosevelt is about to shelve his unpopular Court Reorganization Bill.		The Jones Farm Bill, which some call a substitute AAA, is introduced in the House. . . . A judge orders the Ford Motor Company and eight men to stand trial for assaults at the River Rouge factory in May.		Guglielmo Marconi, Nobel Laureate and inventor of the wireless, dies of a heart attack at age 62 in Rome.	Jul. 20
Senator Alben Barkley of Kentucky is elected new Senate Majority Leader, the post held by the late Joseph Robinson. . . . Andy Wright is sentenced to 99 years in prison for rape. Clarence Norris's execution is set for September 24, but an appeal is immediately filed.		The police chief of Massillon, Ohio—which has only 18 officers—tells the NLRB that he was instructed by the National Guard to hire extra men from a list. The list, submitted by Republic Steel employees, included Republic Steel employees. . . . In Detroit, a Ford spokesman rails that the NLRB is an irresponsible "traveling court of inquisitors." . . . Mayor Fiorello LaGuardia of New York orders an investigation of possible police brutality at Robins Drydock. A crowd of 1,000 gathered at the drydock, throwing stones and bricks at police.	After hearings, the Department of Commerce issues its report blaming the *Hindenburg* disaster on St. Elmo's Fire: electro-luminescent corona discharge.	The manager of baseball's St. Louis Browns, Roger Hornsby, is fired for betting on horse racing.	Jul. 21
The Senate votes to send the Court Reorganization Bill back to the Judiciary Committee, in effect killing the bill. The Senate also overrides the President's veto on the Farm Loan Bill. . . . Victoria Price repeats her story of rape in the one-day-long retrial of Scottsboro defendant Charlie Weems.		The La Follette Senate subcommittee issues a report blaming and censuring the Chicago police for their actions in the Memorial Day riots outside Republic Steel.	A strong earthquake jolts Fairbanks, Alaska. Estimates put it at 7.3.		Jul. 22
Before Charlie Weems's case goes to the jury, the defense attorney for all Scottsboro defendants, Samuel Liebowitz, calls the proceedings a frame-up and "sanctimonious hypocrisy," and the idea of justice for African Americans "poppycock."		The United Mine Workers and the Steel Workers Organizing Committee (SWOC), both CIO unions, accuse the Roosevelt administration of indifference to workers' rights and company-sponsored violence. . . . Strike-breaking dock workers report being stoned on their way to work, miles from New York shipyards.		*Saratoga*, Jean Harlow's last film, with Clark Gable and Hattie McDaniel, is released.	Jul. 23
Charlie Weems is sentenced to 75 years in prison. Four of the Scottsboro defendants are released; state police escort them to the state line before the court announces that charges against them are dropped. Rape charges are also dropped against a fifth man, in prison for assaulting a guard.		After studying 200 decisions rendered in two years by the NLRB, the U.S. Chamber of Commerce finds the Board inconsistent in interpreting employer rights, bargaining units, and elections. . . . A striker at a Brooklyn shipyard is beaten; men are arrested for carrying concealed weapons. . . . Four men are injured and 18 arrested in vandalism of wagons and offices, resulting from a strike of the Great Atlantic and Pacific Tea Company (A&P) in Philadelphia.		Seabiscuit sets a track record to win the Yonkers Handicap.	Jul. 24

F	G	H	I	J
Includes elections, federal-state relations, civil rights and liberties, crime, the judiciary, education, healthcare, poverty, urban affairs, and population.	Includes formation and debate of U.S. foreign and defense policies, veterans affairs, and defense spending. (Relations with specific foreign countries are usually found under the region concerned.)	Includes business, labor, agriculture, taxation, transportation, consumer affairs, monetary and fiscal policy, natural resources, pollution, and accidents.	Includes worldwide scientific, medical, and technological developments, natural phenomena, U.S. weather, and natural disasters.	Includes the arts, religion, scholarship, communications media, sports, entertainment, fashions, fads, and social life.

	World Affairs	Europe	Africa & The Middle East	The Americas	Asia & The Pacific
Jul. 25		Loyalists lost 20,000 troops and insurgents lost 17,000 in the fight for Brunete. General Franco decrees this day—the feast day of St. James, or Santiago—a national holiday once again. A dawn air raid on Barcelona drops bombs and strafes citizens with machine guns for an hour . . . *Pravda*, the Communist Party paper, declares a "merciless" purge of enemies and Trotskyists at newspapers, magazines, and publishers. . . . The Gestapo arrests the younger brother of Reverend Niemoeller, also a pastor, but holds him only one day. . . . Tom Barry, leader of the Irish Republican Army, who has been in hiding for a year, is arrested in the Irish Free State. . . . The Orthodox Church in Yugoslavia excommunicates every government member who worked for ratification of the Vatican Concordat, forcing Prince Paul to leave most of his guards, ministers, and secretaries behind when he went to church.		President Batista of Cuba announces a three-year economic plan to stabilize sugar and mining, reorganize agricultural schools, and redistribute land.	Vice Chief of General Staff Hsiung Pin visits General Sung and other Chinese military leaders, angering the Japanese authorities, who now demand that the 37th Army be withdrawn. Three troop transports arrive from Japan at Tangku, delivering munitions.
Jul. 26		In a spectacular night battle over Madrid, five insurgent planes are shot down. . . . After hours of debate, the Non-Intervention Committee remains deadlocked over what to do. . . . Prince Paul of Yugoslavia leaves Belgrade and will not attend the Patriarch's funeral. The Orthodox Church's excommunications invalidate the oaths of office of public officials, and—because of constitutional rules—may render them unable to hold their positions. . . . The Soviet Union enjoys a record grain crop, but harvesting efforts and transportation are not keeping up.		A Catholic church in Nogales, Sonora, Mexico, reopened June 4 by the governor, is scheduled to be closed by federal officials. Parishioners hold a "kneel-down" strike and refuse to vacate the church.	Japan launches air strikes, targeting Chinese troop barracks in Langfang, between Peiping and Tientsin. Fighting breaks out at the southwest gates of Peiping as well, as Chinese troops throw grenades at Japanese soldiers forcing their way in. . . . In Tokyo, Emperor Hirohito meets with Premier Konoe and other leaders. The Premier calls his Cabinet together; the Diet is already in an emergency two-week session.
Jul. 27		In a push north from Brunete, General Franco claims to have destroyed two loyalist brigades, leaving only 10 percent of the 3,000 soldiers alive. . . . The German government requisitions all wheat and rye crops this year to safeguard the Reich's bread supply. . . . In Upper Silesia, where agreements have expired, arguments begin over the language used in courts: German or Polish.			Japan's General Matsui delivers a note at midnight to General Sung's representatives, warning clearly that the action at the southwest gates would not be forgiven. Japan captures Nanyuan Town before noon and inflicts heavy casualties on the 37th and 132nd armies. An attack on Peiping begins before midnight. In Tungchow (Tongzhou) at the eastern edge of Peiping, the 39th Brigade, consisting of 400–500 Chinese soldiers armed with swords and rifles, is annihilated by Japanese airplanes and shells. The American Jefferson Academy is also bombed.
Jul. 28		The insurgent push near Tereul has been steady, and Franco's forces hold 12 more towns and 1,000 square kilometers of territory. . . . Bombs explode in Northern Ireland during a state visit by King George VI; the nearest blasts a hole in the sidewalk half a mile from the King. . . . On the eve of the Patriarch's funeral, opposition parties—Serbians, even Communists and fascists—stand against Premier Stoyandinovitch of Yugoslavia. . . . Reverend Niemoeller will stand trial on four charges, the Reich announces: seditious activity, abuse of the pulpit, inciting disobedience, and actions contrary to a specific ministerial law.		Argentina proposes a multilateral treaty recognizing political asylum as a principle of international law.	Chinese peasants dig traps and holes in the muddy road to stop Japan's convoys from reaching Tientsin and Peiping. Japan shells the defenses outside the walled city of Peiping and fleeing Chinese troops rush inside.

A	B	C	D	E
Includes developments that affect more than one world region, international organizations, and important meetings of world leaders.	*Includes all domestic and regional developments in Europe, including the Soviet Union.*	*Includes all domestic and regional developments in Africa and the Middle East.*	*Includes all domestic and regional developments in Latin America, the Caribbean, and Canada.*	*Includes all domestic and regional developments in Asian and Pacific nations (and colonies).*

U.S. Politics & Social Issues	U.S. Foreign Policy & Defense	Economics & Great Depression	Science, Technology & Nature	Culture, Leisure & Lifestyle	
			A 7.3 earthquake causes death and destruction in Mexico. The epicenter is 114 miles southeast of Mexico City.	In a double-header, Mel Almada of the Washington Senators hits five home runs in the first game, and four in the second, an 18-inning record.	Jul. 25
Anti-lynching legislation is attached as a rider to a Senate bill and is defeated.		After an 87-day strike, hotel workers in San Francisco approve a compromise offer, but may stay out of work until all unions have settled with hotels. . . . Police charge a line of 2,000 pickets blocking access to the Corrigan-McKinney plant of Republic Steel in Cleveland, and eight are injured. A striker is run down and killed by a car, and the violence escalates and continues all day. One thousand workers march on City Hall. The SWOC hall is trashed, at least 40 are injured, and Safety Director Eliot Ness reports over 100 cars damaged. Police use tear gas to control the crowd, and Republic employees, armed with clubs and pick handles and wearing white armbands, attack pickets throughout the day. At 11 p.m., 500 employees leave the plant and attack the pickets.	Farnsworth Television signs a licensing agreement with AT&T, hoping to clarify patents so that television and other communications can be developed.		Jul. 26
		Fighting in Cleveland between strikers and Republic Steel workers continues through the morning. Eliot Ness issues a proclamation banning assemblies within 500 yards of Republic plant gates.		After 10 years, the United States wins back the Davis Cup in tennis. The champions are Donald Budge and Frankie Parker.	Jul. 27
		Five trucks are burned in garages of the A&P in Philadelphia, as a truckers' strike against the company continues.			Jul. 28

F	G	H	I	J
Includes elections, federal-state relations, civil rights and liberties, crime, the judiciary, education, healthcare, poverty, urban affairs, and population.	Includes formation and debate of U.S. foreign and defense policies, veterans affairs, and defense spending. (Relations with specific foreign countries are usually found under the region concerned.)	Includes business, labor, agriculture, taxation, transportation, consumer affairs, monetary and fiscal policy, natural resources, pollution, and accidents.	Includes worldwide scientific, medical, and technological developments, natural phenomena, U.S. weather, and natural disasters.	Includes the arts, religion, scholarship, communications media, sports, entertainment, fashions, fads, and social life.

	World Affairs	Europe	Africa & The Middle East	The Americas	Asia & The Pacific
Jul. 29		The Republican (loyalist) government in Spain reports submarine attacks on five of its ships, including one carrying refugees. . . . A late-night train derailment near Paris kills 30 people. . . . Rail service stops many from attending the Serbian Orthodox Patriarch's funeral, so the violence is less than expected. At memorial services in Sarajevo, one woman dies and 50 are injured. . . . Local newspapers say the Soviet Union has purged the Premier and other leaders of Tadjikastan (Tajikistan).	Before both houses of Parliament in Cairo, Farouk is invested as King of Egypt—the first independent King since the days of the Pharaohs. Next February 11—his 18th birthday by Western reckoning—a coronation will take place.		Fighting in Tientsin starts at 2 a.m. at a rail station. Throughout the day, Japan drops bombs on the large city, killing thousands and destroying offices, warehouses, rail stations, administration buildings, and Nankei University. Tientsin's defending troops, armed with rifles and machine guns, are quickly overwhelmed. The port of Taku is destroyed by shells from Japanese warships. In the evening, Premier Chiang Kai-shek says this is only the opening of a war Japan has long sought, and declares China will not compromise or surrender.
Jul. 30	The League of Nations Mandates Commission begins consideration of the division of Palestine.	The insurgent air force destroys the village of Las Rozas, Spain. . . . France approves a limit (17 billion francs) on next year's expenses for the first time in its history. . . . *Pravda* reminds Soviets that protecting the state is a duty of all citizens, and urges them to betray friends to authorities for any illegal or suspicious activity.			In Tungchow, Chinese "Peace Preservation Corps" hear rumors of victories by their own armies. Their leader Yin Ju-keng disappears, but the corps mutiny against Japanese administration, set up 19 months ago, and kill up to 300 Japanese and Koreans. . . . Using tanks and artillery, Japan takes control of the Lugou Bridge and Changsintien rail terminal, cutting access of the Chinese army to Peiping. Although vastly outnumbered, Japan's modern weaponry proves decisive and they hold the Tientsin area. Troops have not entered Peiping, but Japanese authorities pick new administrators to govern the city. Japan reports that 50,000 Chinese troops approach from the south.
Jul. 31		Loyalist towns evacuate as the insurgents push their gains in eastern Spain further. . . . Prime Minister Neville Chamberlain sends a personal note to Premier Benito Mussolini in order to rebuild relations between Britain and Italy. . . . A bomb in Belfast explodes 50 yards from a police barracks. . . . Newspapers of the Karelian Soviet report a Trotskyist plot in paper and timber mills, purged last year with seven executions.		The new Bolivian regime reinstates the 1880 Constitution, ending the Socialist state of deposed President Toro.	Japan's planes bomb 20 trains bringing Chinese troops north. They also shell Paoting, 80 miles from Peiping, where the trains originated. . . . Han Fu-chu, ruler of Shantung (Shandong)—which borders Hopei (Hebei)—consults with General Chiang Kai-shek.
Aug. 1	The Soviet Union charges that its Tientsin Embassy was raided and wrecked by "White Russians" (Belarusians), with the collusion of a Japanese intelligence officer.	Through secretly distributed handbills, the Berlin Confessional Synod accuses the Nazi Church Ministry of trying to put the church under a dictatorship. Sixty church leaders are currently in custody. . . . A Soviet paper reports the trial (but no date or outcome) of 30 religious practitioners, including a bishop and several priests. They stand accused of counter-revolutionary activity in Orel, near Moscow. . . . In Yugoslavia, Josip Broz Tito reads a manifesto to Communists in the woods near Zagreb.			Japan moves against pockets of resistance in the Tientsin (Tianjin) area, where the dead bodies are becoming a health hazard. . . . Japanese reinforcements smash the Gung-ho (Tongzhou) mutiny; the subsequent shelling of the city is termed punitive by most observers.
Aug. 2	The League of Nations studies why the British Mandate of Palestine has become unworkable, before deciding whether the territory should be divided. . . . The World Zionist Council favors the plan, though it wants certain changes favoring Jewish settlers.	Insurgents capture 350 square miles near Teruel, but it is largely a wild area with no strategic value. General Franco commutes the death sentence of insurgent leader Manuel Hedilla, imprisoned in Las Palmas. . . . Premier Benito Mussolini sends a personal note to the British Prime Minister, inviting British reporters back to Italy and ending the Italian press's three-month boycott of Britain. . . . The Gestapo arrests Dr. Otto Dibelius, an associate of Reverend Niemoeller, who insists Jesus was Jewish.		Mass is celebrated at Jalapa, the capital of Veracruz, Mexico. New regulations will allow 14 priests in the state, rather than the one allowed for the past six years.	China mobilizes for large-scale war: troops head toward Hopei (Hebei) province. . . . Japan's trade reaches a record deficit, and new taxes are pending approval by the Diet.

A	B	C	D	E
Includes developments that affect more than one world region, international organizations, and important meetings of world leaders.	*Includes all domestic and regional developments in Europe, including the Soviet Union.*	*Includes all domestic and regional developments in Africa and the Middle East.*	*Includes all domestic and regional developments in Latin America, the Caribbean, and Canada.*	*Includes all domestic and regional developments in Asian and Pacific nations (and colonies).*

U.S. Politics & Social Issues	U.S. Foreign Policy & Defense	Economics & Great Depression	Science, Technology & Nature	Culture, Leisure & Lifestyle	
At the Hippodrome in New York, defense attorney Samuel Leibowitz reveals the agreement that freed four Scottsboro defendants. The late Attorney General of Alabama promised them freedom in exchange for an admission of assault unrelated to rape. The judge in the latest trials blocked the deal until the new Attorney General used his influence. The four defendants still in prison will be freed within two years—including Clarence Norris, sentenced to death.		Protesting the arrest of several strikers at Robins Drydock, 2,000 shipyard workers, with spouses and children, sit on trolley tracks near the Brooklyn police station. . . . The NLRB ends its hearing of Ford and the UAWA, but allows 10 days for either side to submit rebuttal testimony.		Economist and Nobel Laureate Daniel McFadden is born in Raleigh, N.C.	Jul. 29
					Jul. 30
Southern Senators rail against the Wages and Hours Bill, saying it could economically crush their states, but the bill passes.		The CIO pledges $100,000 to support the shipyards' striking workers in New York and New Jersey. . . . The NLRB asks that five Dearborn police be disciplined for their inaction during the Ford riot on May 26. . . . While negotiators settle the bakery drivers' strike in Philadelphia, labor action against the A&P injures six company guards. . . . The NLRB serves a complaint against Weirton Steel of West Virginia, charging that bribes, threats, terrorism, and espionage were used against workers.		Charles Hires, who built a beverage empire and sold most of it to Nestle in 1917, dies at age 86. He was chairman of the board of Hires Root Beer.	Jul. 31
					Aug. 1
		A CIO-affiliated union asks Robin Drydock to negotiate and end the two-month strike; the company refuses. In response, the union calls for a large demonstration.			Aug. 2

F	G	H	I	J
Includes elections, federal-state relations, civil rights and liberties, crime, the judiciary, education, healthcare, poverty, urban affairs, and population.	*Includes formation and debate of U.S. foreign and defense policies, veterans affairs, and defense spending. (Relations with specific foreign countries are usually found under the region concerned.)*	*Includes business, labor, agriculture, taxation, transportation, consumer affairs, monetary and fiscal policy, natural resources, pollution, and accidents.*	*Includes worldwide scientific, medical, and technological developments, natural phenomena, U.S. weather, and natural disasters.*	*Includes the arts, religion, scholarship, communications media, sports, entertainment, fashions, fads, and social life.*

	World Affairs	Europe	Africa & The Middle East	The Americas	Asia & The Pacific
Aug. 3	A League of Nations Council on Rural Hygiene in Far Eastern Countries commences in the Dutch East Indies (Indonesia).	The outlawed Marxist-Trotskyist party POUM holds a mass meeting in Barcelona. The Spanish government arrests 400 members. . . . Chancellor Hermann Goering orders museums, even those privately owned, to get rid of "un-German" art. Surrealism, impressionism, cubism, and modern art must be removed.		The national assembly of the Liberal Party of Cuba, which supports policies of the previous ruler, dissolves a day after President Fulgencio Batista warns them against any political moves. . . . The Mexican committee appointed in June to audit foreign-owned oil companies recommends a pay raise totaling $7 million for 18,000 employees. . . . Guatemalan soldiers shoot two Honduran opposition leaders who took refuge in Guatemala. Official reports claim the men were trying to escape, but the accord between Central American countries protecting leaders from opposition is well known.	Japanese planes bomb the northward-bound Chinese troops near the border of Hopeh and Shantung (Shantong) provinces. Japanese infantry, with artillery and tanks, move south to engage China's fresh troops as well as those of the 29th Army, now reforming. Troop ships arrive from Japan, and reinforcements come from Manchukuo (Manchuria); Japan's troop strength is estimated at 20,000. China's central government sends troops into Chahar (part of Inner Mongolia) province in the north to bolster it against a Japanese takeover.
Aug. 4		Loyalist General Miaja claims his Brunete offensive of last month killed 20,000 insurgent troops and broke the morale of Franco's army. . . . The Vatican accepts an official insurgent diplomatic representative from Spain. . . . A new teachers' handbook in Germany titled *The Jewish Question in Teaching* advises injecting anti-Semitism into every subject. . . . A Siberian newspaper reveals that 72 more people were shot for spying and sabotage on the Trans-Siberian Railroad. All of the executions, totaling 310, are connected to a train wreck that derailed 48 cars months ago near the city of Irkutsk.		Twenty-six trade and culture agreements go to the parliaments of Chile and Bolivia for approval. . . . British and U.S. oil interests in Mexico term the recommended raise to employees "grossly unfair."	While civilians flee the capital city of Nanking (Nanjing), Chiang Kai-shek brings together generals Pai Chung-hsi, Li Tsung-jen, and Shih Ching-ling; former mayor of Peiping, Chin Teh-chun (Qin Dechun); and many other top military and political leaders. . . . A typhoon disrupts rail traffic between north China and Hopeh. Hundreds of trains have supplied Japan's forces over the last week, but none can travel now due to flooding in Korea and Manchukuo. The Japanese media keeps the destruction out of the news. . . . Mohandas Gandhi meets with Viceroy Linlithgow in Delhi, India.
Aug. 5		Shortages of food in Santander, the last large Basque city in Spain, now swollen with refugees, approaches famine conditions.			Journalists point out that almost all news from the battlefront in China is controlled by the Japanese. . . . Wang Ching-wei (Wang Jingwei), chair of the Central Political Council, calls for peace in a widely reported radio address.
Aug. 6		Unidentified planes drop bombs near British, Greek, and French ships, and hit an Italian ship 30 miles from Algiers. The captain of the Italian ship, the *Mongioia*, dies of his injuries. . . . General Franco's constitution is approved, creating a single political party. . . . Dr. Otto Dibelius is acquitted in Germany, and Church Minister Hans Kerrl loses some prestige.			Japan officially states that it may expand its undeclared war as far north as the Yellow River. . . . Thousands of Japanese leave the Peiping area, and many evacuate Nanking, a city of 1 million. . . . In an agreement with Mayor Wu, Japan pulls all its citizens and six battleships out of Hankow, its concession in the central province of Hubei. Japanese authorities consider the town indefensible if attacked, and worry over the anti-Japanese sentiment there. . . . General Chang Tze-chung (Zhang Zizhong) resigns as head of the Hopeh-Chahar Political Council, pleading ill health.
Aug. 7	Thirty-seven nations register formal agreement with Secretary of State Cordell Hull's declaration of July 16 calling for peace and respect of treaties. Bulgaria, Hungary, and South American nations, however, denounce some treaties as unfair and imposed by force.	Britain accuses insurgent forces of the bombings of vessels near Algiers, but General Franco denies the attacks. . . . French papers reveal that Andres Nin, the Catalan POUM leader arrested in mid-June, was taken from prison nearly a month ago, and his dead body was dumped outside Madrid. . . . The Spanish government authorizes private Catholic worship. . . . Britain expels three German journalists without explanation.		President Lázaro Cárdenas of Mexico begins land reform in the Yucatan, breaking up henequen estates and giving parcels of land to the peasants that work it.	Ambassador Kawagoe arrives in Shanghai to speak with Chinese officials and try to negotiate a peace settlement. . . . Japanese citizens leave several areas: Canton (Guangzhou), Yunnan, and Wuhu in Anhwei (Anhui). Kiukiang (Jiujiang) and other ports are being evacuated as well.
Aug. 8		Spanish insurgents report that Barcelona is plagued by street fighting between loyalist, Communist, and Catalan factions. . . . The Ministry of Justice in Madrid claims to be searching for Andres Nin, who disappeared a month ago. . . . Several hundred people march through Dahlem, Germany, in support of Reverend Niemoeller after their prayer meeting is prohibited. Of the 115 that are arrested, only 48 are held for a day. . . . A decree is read in Belgrade Orthodox Churches, denying rites to the Yugoslav Premier, his ministers, and many members of parliament.			Major General Kawabe leads 3,000 Japanese troops into Peiping, taking possession of the city while Japanese planes drop leaflets into the streets. . . . National hero General Tsai Ting-kai and other leaders arrive in Nanking. All put personal enmity and past factional fighting behind to unite and fight Japan's invasion. . . . In Tientsin, telegraph lines are cut after French officials refuse to allow Japanese censorship.

A	B	C	D	E
Includes developments that affect more than one world region, international organizations, and important meetings of world leaders.	Includes all domestic and regional developments in Europe, including the Soviet Union.	Includes all domestic and regional developments in Africa and the Middle East.	Includes all domestic and regional developments in Latin America, the Caribbean, and Canada.	Includes all domestic and regional developments in Asian and Pacific nations (and colonies).

U.S. Politics & Social Issues	U.S. Foreign Policy & Defense	Economics & Great Depression	Science, Technology & Nature	Culture, Leisure & Lifestyle	
The National Republican Club says in a resolution that President Franklin Roosevelt's New Deal is Marxist and works against the Constitution, inspiring class warfare. . . . Police in Boston raid and close offices of the Birth Control League.		At Robins Drydock, a confrontation between 3,000 union supporters and 500 police results in three arrests. In spite of rock-throwing and firecrackers, no one is injured. . . . An "AFL-CIO" union is suggested in Lowell, Mass., by eight railroad brotherhoods. The idea is 18 years ahead of its time. . . . The Teamsters in Philadelphia stage the second sympathy strike in a month, paralyzing city deliveries for a day. An estimated 5,000 men participate; nonstrikers are beaten and vehicles vandalized and turned over.		Lou Gehrig plays in his 1,900th consecutive baseball game.	Aug. 3
		Five hours after declaring Philadelphia was in a state of emergency, the mayor announces on the radio that the Teamsters' strike is settled. Teamsters reject his settlement, demanding a closed shop at A&P, and mob confrontations and vandalism ensue. Police arrest dozens, and the mayor announces they will be held in jail for a week as "professional thugs." . . . On the East Coast, 65,000 silk workers threaten to strike on August 9. . . . Chrysler employees belonging to two unions vying for control come to blows in Detroit, where 10 are injured and the plant is forced to close, idling 21,000.	After killing several people and leaving thousands homeless in Burma and the Philippines, a typhoon hits China's east coast.		Aug. 4
The Senate receives a bill listing ways to block 47 tax evasion tricks.		Random violence continues in Philadelphia, but the sympathy strike ends with the imprisonment of 60 "outlaw strikers." . . . Rock-throwing at nonstriking workers escorted by 300 police at the Robins Drydock leads to more arrests.		For the second year, the American yacht Ranger wins the America's Cup. . . . Stella Dallas premiers; Barbara Stanwyck gets an Oscar nomination for this film.	Aug. 5
The House passes the Sugar Bill, setting limitations on imports from Hawaii, Puerto Rico, and the Virgin Islands, in spite of a threatened veto. . . . The Senate passes the Warren-Steagall Housing Bill.	The United States signs a trade agreement with the Soviet Union, extending lower tariffs in return for a pledge of $40 million in purchases over a year. . . . Most Americans in China who were south of the Yellow River are evacuating the area.	A truce with Philadelphia's taxi drivers is declared at 2 a.m., forestalling a threatened strike. . . . Six police are cited for neglect of duty by the Dearborn Safety Commission in relation to the NLRB Ford hearings. . . . Four Republic Steel Workers in Cleveland stab a striker at CIO headquarters; arrests follow. . . . One New York shipyard signs a settlement with the AFL, but the strike continues.			Aug. 6
The Senate approves the compromise court bill when Vice President John Nance Garner unexpectedly pushes it through during a break, with less than 20 Senators in the chamber.	Secretary of State Cordell Hull, acting at the President's request, asks Congress to lease old, unused naval ships to Brazil and other South American countries to help them protect their interests.	AFL and CIO representatives meet with workers of almost every union in Philadelphia and agree to work jointly for labor gains. . . . Chrysler's Plymouth plant in Detroit remains closed as negotiators meet all day and craft a settlement. . . . The mayor of Philadelphia lifts the "state of emergency" and releases 51 men held in jail without bail. The truck strike is ongoing.		At Suffolk Downs, Seabiscuit sets a track record of 1:45 for a mile and an eighth.	Aug. 7
		Chrysler employees ratify a settlement and will return to work tomorrow.			Aug. 8

	World Affairs	Europe	Africa & The Middle East	The Americas	Asia & The Pacific
Aug. 9		Anarchists in Spain rally around former premier Largo Caballero. The recent claims that Andres Nin simply disappeared with his guards anger the anarchists and turn them against Premier Juan Negrín. . . . In retaliation for Britain's expulsion, the Reich expels a *London Times* reporter. . . . The trial of Reverend Niemoeller is delayed so that more evidence can be gathered. It was to start on August 10. . . . Reports eke out that many Orthodox priests are under arrest in Yugoslavia.		A week-old textile strike of 10,000 workers in Quebec, Montreal, turns violent. After an announcement that talks were deadlocked, hundreds of strikers began throwing bricks and rocks at delivery trucks. They threw some bales of material into a canal and set fire to another bale. . . . In Venezuela, more than 60 die when a holiday excursion boat founders on Lake Maracaibo.	A Japanese naval officer and his chauffeur are killed at an airport near Shanghai by Chinese Peace Preservation guards. A guard dies and a civilian is killed by a stray bullet. The surviving guard claims the Japanese officer fired first. Panic spreads through the region. . . . Japan's ports and hotels are clogged with refugees returning home from China.
Aug. 10	El Salvador resigns from the League of Nations for economic reasons. It is the seventh Latin American country to do so.	POUM member and journalist José Escudera awaits trial in Valencia after his arrest with Andres Nin and others. The controversies and stories about POUM members display the rifts in loyalist ranks. Premier Juan Negrín dissolves the Council of Aragon and arrests many of the anarchist leaders.	Kurds attack Amouda in Syria, pillaging stores owned by Christians. Violent clashes in northeast Syria have gone on for a month.	Ecuador opens a Constitutional Convention in Quito. . . . In Peterborough, Ontario, 150 female textile strikers—many of them teenagers—charge police with rotten eggs and tomatoes. Men join in; police use tear gas and arrest 15 people. . . . U.S. and British oil firms in Mexico tell the government they may choose to close rather than pay wage increases that they say will cost $18 million annually.	A team of Chinese and Japanese investigators study the airport killing. Both sides agree that diplomatic means will be used to diffuse a tense situation. There are 12 Japanese warships at Shanghai.
Aug. 11	The World Zionist Council in Geneva votes 2 to 1 for the partition of Palestine and creation of a Jewish state. . . . French planes and infantry attack Kurds in Syria, suppressing rebellion and violence.	Asturian miners near Oveido battle with insurgent troops, rushing out of mines to throw grenades, but are mowed down by machine guns. An insurgent air strike drops 30 bombs on Santander, the Basque city. . . . A loyalist captain claims the Italian ship *Saetta* torpedoed and sank his tanker, killing 12 men. . . . In Upper Silesia, Poland expels three German pastors. . . . The French government raises taxi fares, and 8,000 Paris cabbies—95 percent—strike in protest. . . . Germany becomes the first nation to conquer its unemployment problems caused by the Great Depression; the Reich suffers a labor shortage.	General Bakr Sidqi, dictator of Iraq since the coup last October, is assassinated by a soldier in Mosul. The commander of the air force is slain with him. The assassin, a Kurd, is related to a minister murdered during Sidqi's ascent to power.	The Refugee Economic Corporation in New York reveals the purchase 50,000 acres of land in Costa Rica, to be used as homes for Jews leaving Nazi Germany.	The U.S. Consul and other diplomats attend secret talks aimed at a settlement in Shanghai. Japan presents demands, which include removal of Peace Preservation troops and city defenses. The mayor of Shanghai refuses. . . . Japanese air and ground forces attack Nankow, a mountain pass north of Peiping, where the Chinese army's 89th Division is digging in. The rail station there is destroyed. . . . In Peiping, the Japanese take over telegraph and postal offices and media outlets. Anti-Japanese literature is removed from schools and bookstores.
Aug. 12	A proposal to settle 200,000 Jews in Palestine at a cost of $175 million is presented to the World Zionist Congress in Geneva. . . . French troops patrol Antioch and have ejected Kurd vandals from several villages in the Jerizah district of northeast Syria.	In Barcelona, loyalists take over the police and defense functions, as well as border control, from the Catalan government, ending Catalonian independence.			Thirty-two Japanese warships now mass at Shanghai, bringing 4,000 fresh troops. An aircraft carrier and other ships are at the mouth of the Yangtze River. Shanghai is home to 3.5 million people. . . . China's Finance Minister Kung arranges loans with several European banks.
Aug. 13		Insurgent planes sink a Danish ship; the crew is rescued. Reports of submarine attacks over the last few days circulate. The International Brigades (IBs) begin an attack on insurgent positions near Cordoba. Insurgents begin their final push on Santander, the last Basque capital.		Mexico changes its agrarian code, facilitating the seizure and redistribution of land by the government.	After a three-hour meeting, Premier Konoe's Cabinet declares they will negotiate with China for an end to hostilities, ironically on the day when fighting begins in earnest. . . . The Chapei and Hongkew (Kongkew) areas of Shanghai are shelled, and the forts at Woosung come under artillery fire from warships. Japanese bombs burn the Jukong wharf and tall buildings in the city. Rain from a typhoon quenches the fire overnight. . . . An estimated 4,000 Chinese troops hold the Nankow pass against Japanese artillery for a third day, as Japan receives reinforcements from its Kwantong (Guandong) Army.
Aug. 14				After three weeks of violence by workers and unions, martial law is imposed, and troops watch over the Poza Rica oil fields in Mexico.	Bombardment of Shanghai begins at 4 a.m., but Chinese guns in the mountains fire on Japanese ships before then. Over 1,000 are killed—many by bombs dropped on the city, most from Chinese planes, hitting hotels and main roads and a refugee center packed with Chinese citizens. Others are killed by the anti-aircraft fire of the Japanese. . . . Sian (Xi'an), recently in rebellion against Nanking's rule, now pledges all available troops to fight the Japanese.

A	B	C	D	E
Includes developments that affect more than one world region, international organizations, and important meetings of world leaders.	*Includes all domestic and regional developments in Europe, including the Soviet Union.*	*Includes all domestic and regional developments in Africa and the Middle East.*	*Includes all domestic and regional developments in Latin America, the Caribbean, and Canada.*	*Includes all domestic and regional developments in Asian and Pacific nations (and colonies).*

U.S. Politics & Social Issues	U.S. Foreign Policy & Defense	Economics & Great Depression	Science, Technology & Nature	Culture, Leisure & Lifestyle	
		The largest U.S. cotton crop in six years has senators from cotton-producing states asking for price protections. . . . Thirty thousand silk workers—more than half the 58,000 employed—heed the CIO call to strike. . . . Philadelphia's threatened taxi strike is averted with a settlement of increased commissions and a closed shop for drivers. . . . A record-breaking 2,512 strikes were begun in the first six months of 1937.			Aug. 9
Joseph Kennedy, Chair of the Maritime Commission, announces a comprehensive survey of the merchant marine and the shipping industry. . . . Senator Gerald P. Nye attacks the export of scrap iron to Japan, which currently accounts for 50 percent of sales.		Eight CIO members are indicted for assault and intimidation against non-striking shipworkers in New York. . . . The silk strikers number 40,000, but violence mars a meeting of nonstrikers in Hazleton, Pa. A melee breaks out when a speaker criticizes John L. Lewis and the CIO; dozens of people suffer minor injuries. . . . President Franklin Roosevelt announces that he wants farm crop controls passed or he may withhold approval on commodity loans.			Aug. 10
The Senate, hoping to adjourn by August 21, is tied up with debates on the anti-lynching bill and other legislation.		An agreement raising wages and improving hours and working conditions ends the strike of A&P drivers in Philadelphia. . . . A settlement in Pennsylvania mills will send 8,000 of the 30,000 striking silk workers back to work. . . . The United Auto Workers of America (UAWA) distributes pamphlets outside the Ford plant in River Rouge, without incident. . . . The ACLU demands Brooklyn police discipline officers who beat two Robins Drydock strikers in the police station on July 16.		Pulitzer Prize-winning novelist Edith Wharton dies in France. . . . Ernest Hemingway slaps Max Eastman in the face with a book after the two authors trade insults and compare their manly chest hair. Eastman claims he then threw Hemingway over the desk; Hemingway denies this. . . . *The Life of Emile Zola* premiers. The movie will be nominated for many Oscars, winning for Best Film, Best Writing, and Best Supporting Actor (Joseph Schildkraut).	Aug. 11
Senator Hugo Black of Alabama is the surprise nominee to the Supreme Court. . . . The anti-lynching bill is set aside until the 1938 session.	Argentina protests the use of older U.S. ships by Brazil as a violation of U.S. neutrality.				Aug. 12
The Senate passes the sugar bill with compromises to avoid a presidential veto.	Secretary of State Cordell Hull announces that the plan to lease old naval ships to other countries is on hold. . . . The Navy flight-tests a new super plane, the Sikorsky XPBS-I.	Secretary of Labor Frances Perkins appoints a federal mediator to reach a settlement in the silk workers' strike.	On a flight crossing the North Pole from Moscow to the United States, a Soviet plane piloted by Sigizmund Levanevsky goes down with six men between Alaska and the North Pole.		Aug. 13
		Sixty factories sign agreements with silk workers, ensuring that 6,000–8,000 will return to work by August 18. . . . The CIO offers to send New York and New Jersey shipworkers back to their jobs if all employees are reinstated without discrimination, and if the shipyards agree to abide by NLRB rulings.	A radio message is received from Soviet pilot Sigizmund Levanevsky and search planes depart from Fairbanks, Alaska. The plane and crew are never found.		Aug. 14

F	G	H	I	J
Includes elections, federal-state relations, civil rights and liberties, crime, the judiciary, education, healthcare, poverty, urban affairs, and population.	Includes formation and debate of U.S. foreign and defense policies, veterans affairs, and defense spending. (Relations with specific foreign countries are usually found under the region concerned.)	Includes business, labor, agriculture, taxation, transportation, consumer affairs, monetary and fiscal policy, natural resources, pollution, and accidents.	Includes worldwide scientific, medical, and technological developments, natural phenomena, U.S. weather, and natural disasters.	Includes the arts, religion, scholarship, communications media, sports, entertainment, fashions, fads, and social life.

	World Affairs	Europe	Africa & The Middle East	The Americas	Asia & The Pacific
Aug. 15		The Spanish government creates its own secret police (Soviets were performing this task). Political meetings in Barcelona are prohibited. Insurgents push toward Santander in two columns, moving quickly and capturing many towns. . . . Many anti-Stoyadinovitch quasi-religious demonstrations take place in Yugoslavia. Three people are killed when police fire on a crowd of 2,000 in Mladenovac. . . . An estimated 3 million people enjoy parades and pageantry in Berlin's 700th birthday celebration. . . . A Catholic pilgrimage at Speier-on-the-Rhine is canceled when 150,000 Nazis show up for a counter-demonstration. . . . In Minsk, White Russia, six Trotsky spies are condemned to death for poisoning army troops.		A military coup launched two days ago in Paraguay is completed with the removal of President Franco. . . . Prime Minister Mackenzie King of Canada appoints the Rowell Commission to examine the British North America Act. . . . Steel and textile strikes in Quebec bring more violence. Several riots break out and attempts are made to burn the homes or cars of both steel company owners and union heads. . . . In Campos, Brazil, gunfire erupts in a melee between Integralistas and anti-fascists. Sixteen men and women die; 100 are wounded. . . . The President of Mexico, Lázaro Cárdenas, announces he will cut officials' salaries—including his own—to give teachers better pay next year.	In spite of the typhoon, Japanese planes shell Shanghai, Nanking, Hangchow (Hangzhou), and Nanchang in the Kiangsi (Jiangxi) province, as well as Chinese air bases in provinces far to the south. . . . China estimates that 1,500 men have died in the ongoing battle for Nankow Pass.
Aug. 16		Insurgents capture munitions factories at Reinosa as their two columns press north through the Cantabrian Mountains. . . . The Soviet Union ousts two Commissars: Gregory Grinko and A. Grishmanoff, and two Vice Commissars.	The Iraqi Cabinet resigns amid rumors of disorder in the army.	General Cedillo, a conservative, resigns from President Lázaro Cárdenas's Cabinet in Mexico. . . . After a week of demonstrations, 200 shots are fired into buildings during a confrontation between Catholic and socialist students at the University of Mexico. No one is injured. . . . Paraguay will restore its 1870 Constitution, says its provisional president, Dr. Felix Paiva.	Airplanes battle over Shanghai by night and day, dropping more bombs, most aimed at Japanese targets including warships. Japanese planes bomb airports. Over 30,000 Chinese troops occupy the industrial area of Pootung (Pudong), across the river from Shanghai.
Aug. 17		After three days of pushing toward Santander, insurgents have taken 20 villages, including Las Arenas. . . . By order of the Spanish government, the Socialist and Communist parties form a pact. . . . The vice president and 10 other department heads have been removed from the Soviet State Planning Commission, which administers the Five-Year Plans. A list of the charges against these "enemies of the people" is published in *Izvestia*.	Premier Eamil Midfai of Iraq forms a new Cabinet and restores some stability to the country.	Nicaraguan troops tracking rebel forces engage in a gun battle that kills seven. The leader, General Altamirano, escapes.	Japan closes all its Embassies and Consulates throughout China. . . . U.S. and British citizens are allowed to leave Shanghai safely. The city is flooded with up to a million refugees, many homeless. Sixty-four refugee camps exist; cash is rare, and looting for food is common.
Aug. 18	The League of Nations completes its discussion of the Palestinian mandate and will publish a report next month. International Jewish groups continue to meet and debate the issue in Geneva.	Loyalists move artillery and troops closer to Santander. Insurgents claim government resistance has collapsed and take full advantage, moving ahead quickly. . . . Berlin parks now include "ghetto" benches for Jews; they may not sit in other areas.			Japan holds the Hongkew and Yangtzepoo sections of Shanghai, formerly home to 1 million people, now deserted. At night, Japanese planes and ships inflict heavy shelling on both sides of the Whangpoo (Huangpu) River, while Chinese artillery shoots back. . . . Japan's Diet will convene on September 3 to organize the country's economy for war. The Cabinet will prepare the plans.
Aug. 19		A Spanish ship is torpedoed and beached in the Aegean Sea. This is the second such attack; a Spanish ship sank in the same area on August 15. . . . Portugal severs diplomatic relations with Czechoslovakia over its refusal to sell arms to Portugal. . . . The large Wetheim department store in Berlin, like many other businesses, is Aryanized by the removal of its Jewish owners from management.		Mexico's President Lázaro Cárdenas continues to alarm conservatives by proclaiming that the country will become a "democracy of workers," while defending land redistribution. . . . Rioting on Great Inagua, Bahamas, takes one life. The commissioner, a landowner, and 12 others escape the island on a boat and contact authorities. Buildings and the telegraph station are burned. The damage is later determined to be the work of a small gang led by two men.	Japan claims its troops have broken through the Nankow Pass. After two weeks, they have advanced only a few miles; the pass is 15 miles long. The Great Wall is damaged by shelling. . . . Eight Japanese planes bomb suburbs of Nanking. . . . Japan calls so many men to military service that the Tokyo police must look for 500 new officers to replace those entering the military.
Aug. 20	Americans are evacuated from Santander, Spain. . . . Premier of Italy Benito Mussolini wishes to make peace with Britain and France, he says, and no longer insists on League of Nations recognition of his African conquests. He only asks that Haile Selassie be excluded from League activities. . . . Stepan Dybetz, head of the Soviet Union's tractor industry and a former American, is denounced as a "lying adventurer" for not improving production problems after a warning in June.	France orders planes and warships to protect shipping, Turkey reroutes ships, and London's underwriters quadruple risk factors on ships in the eastern Mediterranean. . . . Eight men are convicted and shot in Leningrad (St. Petersburg) for sabotage and terrorism. A Soviet paper also announces the trial and executions in Irkutsk of 32 more Trotskyist rail employees—including a woman whose job was to boil water to serve to passengers. She was killed for poisoning those passengers.			Chinese troops fight for ground in the International Settlement of Shanghai, hoping to extend their territory to the Whangpoo River and stop Japanese ships from landing. Japan attempts the same strategy from Pootung on the opposite side of the river; one-quarter of the city burns. . . . Hong Kong, receiving 10,000 refugees daily, reports that over 200 people have died of cholera. Vaccine is being shipped to the city.

A	B	C	D	E
Includes developments that affect more than one world region, international organizations, and important meetings of world leaders.	*Includes all domestic and regional developments in Europe, including the Soviet Union.*	*Includes all domestic and regional developments in Africa and the Middle East.*	*Includes all domestic and regional developments in Latin America, the Caribbean, and Canada.*	*Includes all domestic and regional developments in Asian and Pacific nations (and colonies).*

U.S. Politics & Social Issues	U.S. Foreign Policy & Defense	Economics & Great Depression	Science, Technology & Nature	Culture, Leisure & Lifestyle	
		A State Mediation Board in New York summons representatives of companies and labor together to end the nine-week old shipworkers' strike.			Aug. 15
	The United States calls for an emergency evacuation of American women and children from Shanghai.	Todd Shipyards, the owner of Robins Drydock, and United Shipyards do not attend the meeting arranged by the State Mediation Board. Their presidents will be subpoenaed and another meeting is scheduled. A striker at Robins Drydock is attacked and beaten. . . . Eddie Cantor will head the new American Federation of Radio Artists, an AFL union. . . . The NLRB hearing on Weirton Steel of West Virginia begins.			Aug. 16
In spite of uninvestigated allegations that he was once in the Ku Klux Klan, Hugo Black wins Senate approval as the Supreme Court nominee. . . . The south's seventh lynching this year occurs in Covington, Tex., where a man is dragged from custody by a gang, hanged from a bridge, and shot with 30 bullets.	Secretary of State Cordell Hull outlines a foreign policy toward China and Japan focused on removing Americans from China and avoidance of invoking the Neutrality Act. The United States will send 1,200 marines to support the 1,100 troops already in Shanghai.	Eight union printers working at the Seattle Star fight with 10 pickets who try to block them from the paper's offices. Police arrest five pickets, and the Star files charges with the NLRB. . . . Twelve silk mills with 13,500 employees form an anti-CIO association, saying their workers do not want union representation. . . . Todd Shipyards and Robins Drydock take their subpoenas to a State Supreme Court judge, who orders the mediation board to show cause.			Aug. 17
Alabama's Governor David Bibb Graves selects his own wife, Dixie, to take Hugo Black's Senate seat.		President Franklin Roosevelt signs the Tydings-Miller bill, which may change interpretation of anti-trust laws and affect the ongoing case against the Aluminum Company of America. . . . Former workers at Weirton Steel tell the NLRB of its "hatchet gang," which terrorized union sympathizers.			Aug. 18
	The United States announces that Brazil will lease old destroyers for training purposes.	Shipyard workers vote to end their nine-week strike and return to work. Robins Drydock employees voted against the settlement and may continue to picket. Later in the day, they accept the settlement. . . . The NLRB investigation into Weirton Steel hears testimony of severe beatings, death threats, and firings.		Topper, with Cary Grant and Constance Bennett, opens in New York.	Aug. 19
John L Lewis, William Green, and other labor leaders attack Democrats for shelving the Wages and Hours Bill so that Congress can break early.		Fifteen thousand textile workers in Pennsylvania will return to work; companies agree to allow collective bargaining. Only 12,000 silk workers remain on strike.			Aug. 20

F	G	H	I	J
Includes elections, federal-state relations, civil rights and liberties, crime, the judiciary, education, healthcare, poverty, urban affairs, and population.	Includes formation and debate of U.S. foreign and defense policies, veterans affairs, and defense spending. (Relations with specific foreign countries are usually found under the region concerned.)	Includes business, labor, agriculture, taxation, transportation, consumer affairs, monetary and fiscal policy, natural resources, pollution, and accidents.	Includes worldwide scientific, medical, and technological developments, natural phenomena, U.S. weather, and natural disasters.	Includes the arts, religion, scholarship, communications media, sports, entertainment, fashions, fads, and social life.

	World Affairs	Europe	Africa & The Middle East	The Americas	Asia & The Pacific
Aug. 21	A shell hits the U.S. cruiser *Augusta* in the Whangpoo River, killing one sailor and injuring 18 others. . . . Loyalist Spain protests to the League of Nations over Italy's "flagrant aggression," and accuses Italy of sinking four Spanish ships. . . . Russia and China sign a five-year non-aggression pact.	Only 25 miles of road lie between insurgents and Santander. Loyalists launch an all-day assault on Huesca in the northeast, but air attacks force them to retreat. . . . The state-ordered killing of an unknown number of peasants who stole grain in 1932 is termed a mistake of Trotskyists who perverted and mis-applied the law, according to A. Vishinsky, the Chief Prosecutor of the Soviet Union. . . . A nationwide farmers' strike in Poland leads to rioting. At least 17 peasants are killed in several incidents.			Japan's Premier Konoe says the country is prepared for a long war, and will settle it without foreign intervention. . . . After an evening bomb attack by the Japanese, a third of the International Settlement of Shanghai is on fire. . . . A battle rages on the railroad 30 miles southwest of Peiping; each side has 30,000 troops involved. Torrential rain and mud grounds planes.
Aug. 22		Insurgents smash through defenses around Santander, occupying parts of the surrounding hill towns. . . . A crowd of 5,000 Serbs pelts the Yugoslav Minister of Forests and Mines with tomatoes, rotten eggs, and rocks as he tries to give a speech. Anti-government parades and demonstrations occur throughout the country. . . . The Soviet Mongolian War Minister, Marshal Demid, dies of poisoning.			Five hundred inmates of the Ward Road Jail are freed, but over 6,000 remain imprisoned as separate fires surround the facility. Japanese authorities refuse to allow them to leave. . . . Japan claims to land 50,000 more troops (China claims it is 15,000) 12 miles from Shanghai. Three divisions use artillery cover to invade the Chwansa, Shihtzelin Forts, and Paoshan Creek areas from the heavily damaged Woosung Forts.
Aug. 23	The summary report published by the League of Nations accepts the Peel Commission and its recommended division of Palestine, but recommends the British mandate continue until the Arab and Jewish sectors are ready for statehood.	The Italian Black Arrow troops, a large part of the insurgent columns pushing toward Santander, takes Castro-Urdiales, the former head-quarters of the Basque army. . . . Polish peasants continue their strike, blocking roads and fighting with police; some are killed. The strikers want the return of former premier Wincenty Witos, exiled in Czechoslovakia. . . . A Soviet paper announces the executions of nine more traitors in Leningrad.			A heavy shell hits a large store in the International Settlement of Shanghai at 1 p.m., killing over 200 people, possibly as many as 400. Investigators will attribute the attack to a Chinese plane. . . . Kalgan (Zhangjiakou) in the north is bombed by Japanese planes.
Aug. 24		Torrelavega, the only point of retreat besides the sea for Santander's defenders, is taken by insurgents without resistance. Loyalists and IBs launch attacks on Quinto, Belchite, and other rail towns in the north. . . . Rioting continues in Poland. Two are killed and 20 wounded when police fire into a crowd, aiming low and hitting legs. Sixty Jews in the area are beaten as well.		Police arrive in Great Inagua, Bahamas, and find the rioting ended. In Cuba, 14 American and British men are arrested for bringing arms into the country. They claim to have escaped the rioting in Great Inagua by boat, and say their craft drifted for four days while they went without food and water. Cuba holds the men for investigation for one week.	New fires blaze in the Pootung industrial area of Shanghai. . . . Japanese troops claim to hold Kalgan, a gateway to Mongolia, and to have broken through the Nankow Pass in a day and a half of hand-to-hand fighting. Reporters will refute this with eyewitness accounts as the fighting continues and shelling goes on for days in those regions. . . . Stock prices in Tokyo have fallen 10–30 percent in the last month.
Aug. 25	France, Britain, and the United States are among many nations sending delegates to the Nazi Party Convention in Nuremburg this September, at the invitation of Chancellor Adolf Hitler.	Santander comes under machine-gun fire from a few positions; insurgent planes shell them. Basque President Aguirre and Commander Gamir escape to France by boat. . . . Industrial workers stage a 24-hour strike in Krakow. . . . The Gestapo in Upper Silesia has arrested over 40 Polish notables and refuses to let children attend Polish schools, forcing them into German schools. . . . The trial begins for seven agricultural officials in Ostrov, near Leningrad, charged with trying to destroy collective farms.			Vice Admiral Hasegawa proclaims a blockade along an 800-mile stretch of China's coast, from north of Shanghai almost to Hong Kong. Chinese ships will be stopped; Japan may stop foreign ships as well. . . . Dozens of bodies of Chinese soldiers float on the Whangpoo River. Their hands are bound and they were clearly killed after being taken prisoner.
Aug. 26	The British Ambassador is gravely injured when Japanese fliers shell his car and strafe it with machine gun fire. He was traveling from Nanking to Shanghai in a car displaying his diplomatic emblems. . . . Chile studies bids from Japan and Italy for warships.	Loyalists say they have overcome 1,500 defending troops to occupy Quinto and surround Belchite. They claim to be within four miles of Saragossa. . . . Even as Britain delivers a stern warning to General Franco that attacks on ships will not be tolerated, insurgent planes attack another British tanker. . . . Jewish-owned cafés in Upper Silesia are ordered closed.	In Mombasa, Kenya, a clash between Arab and Luo tribes causes nine Arab deaths. Such skirmishes are frequent and involve thousands, with both sides armed with swords and knives. The few police in the area are now authorized to use guns on such crowds.	A 19-year-old student confesses to the June 8 attempt on Judge Robert Cooper's life in Puerto Rico. He and nine other Nationalists, including Cooper's driver, planted dynamite and shot at Cooper, who was not hurt.	Japan announces that it will fire on buildings flying foreign flags when necessary, as its enemies may fly foreign flags to trick them. . . . China accuses Japan of using gas bombs at the Nankow Pass.

A	B	C	D	E
Includes developments that affect more than one world region, international organizations, and important meetings of world leaders.	*Includes all domestic and regional developments in Europe, including the Soviet Union.*	*Includes all domestic and regional developments in Africa and the Middle East.*	*Includes all domestic and regional developments in Latin America, the Caribbean, and Canada.*	*Includes all domestic and regional developments in Asian and Pacific nations (and colonies).*

U.S. Politics & Social Issues	U.S. Foreign Policy & Defense	Economics & Great Depression	Science, Technology & Nature	Culture, Leisure & Lifestyle	
Congress adjourns, leaving much undone and many rancorous feelings.			A 7.5 earthquake rocks Manila, Philippines, where hundreds of refugees from China rest.		Aug. 21
					Aug. 22
		The UAWA opens second annual convention in Milwaukee, representing 400,000 workers. . . . Thirteen men are injured in rioting near Pittsburgh's Heppenstall Steel Company, closed since July. The plant's vice president attempted to enter and a riot broke out.			Aug. 23
		A crowd of 1,000 gathers before the Heppenstall Steel plant, told that there were nonstriking workers inside. . . . William Green of the AFL charges that many Communists are on the payroll of the CIO.		*Dead End*, based on a Broadway play by Lillian Hellman, premiers in New York. Nominated for four Oscars, it becomes the first in a series starring the "Dead End Kids"—later the Bowery Boys.	Aug. 24
President Franklin Roosevelt signs the revised Court Reorganization Bill, modifying lower courts.	Governor Joseph B. Poindexter of Hawaii says the island is "impregnable." The army is building the world's largest air field there: Hickam Field.	Rail workers, 250,000 strong, demand a 20 percent raise and are refused. The Railroad Labor Act provides for mediation and mandates a 30-day notice before any strike action can be taken.			Aug. 25
		The Federal Reserve Bank lowers its rediscount rate to 1 percent—the lowest of any central bank ever.	Dr. John Northrop (Nobel Laureate, 1946) publishes research on the bacteriophage, a protein, extracted from bacteria, that destroys germs.	Andrew Mellon, financier, philanthropist, and Secretary of the Treasury under three presidents, dies at age 82.	Aug. 26

F	G	H	I	J
Includes elections, federal-state relations, civil rights and liberties, crime, the judiciary, education, healthcare, poverty, urban affairs, and population.	Includes formation and debate of U.S. foreign and defense policies, veterans affairs, and defense spending. (Relations with specific foreign countries are usually found under the region concerned.)	Includes business, labor, agriculture, taxation, transportation, consumer affairs, monetary and fiscal policy, natural resources, pollution, and accidents.	Includes worldwide scientific, medical, and technological developments, natural phenomena, U.S. weather, and natural disasters.	Includes the arts, religion, scholarship, communications media, sports, entertainment, fashions, fads, and social life.

	World Affairs	Europe	Africa & The Middle East	The Americas	Asia & The Pacific
Aug. 27	Britain says it will take "appropriate action with the Japanese government" when it receives further information on the attack on its Ambassador.	Franco sends troops north to defend Saragossa. . . . Communists and anti-communists clash in the loyalist strongholds of Valencia and Barcelona, and possible uprisings are rumored. . . . Insurgent planes drop bombs on four British steamers near Gijon. . . . Pope Pius XI gives "de facto" recognition to Franco's insurgents as the government of Spain. . . . A roundup of Soviet trials gleaned from local papers include 13 veterinary workers accused of poisoning cattle, 11 top party leaders in Georgia plotting to overthrow the local government, and 11 minor officials, also in Georgia, charged with disrupting agriculture.		Quebec's Prime Minister announces that the textile strike is settled after roundtable discussions. . . . President Lázaro Cárdenas promises Mexican women that he will give them the right to vote soon.	Chinese troops withdraw from Shanghai and its surrounding areas. More Japanese troops disembark near the Woosung battlefields, where many villages are reduced to rubble. . . . Chinese and Japanese forces fight at Lotien, 12 miles north of Shanghai, and report thousands of casualties. . . . In Japan, the four-year-old automobile division of the Toyoda Automatic Loom Works is set up as a separate company: Toyota Motor Company.
Aug. 28		France claims it has taken in over 80,000 Spanish refugees and is sending many people from Santander back to Spain. Barcelona suffers food shortages and cannot take more people. Insurgent forces say up to 65,000 have surrendered to them in the Santander area. . . . Poland's 3.5 million Jews declare this a day of fast and prayer, and invite Jews in other countries to do likewise. . . . Soviets fire and denounce officials of its Civil Aviation Administration in the latest search for Trotskyists. . . . Government ministers are again met with rotten food and jeering crowds at several sites in Yugoslavia. At the Serb town of Valjevo, 20 people are shot when police fire into the crowd.		The informant in the assassination plot against Judge Robert Cooper is found dead of a gunshot wound to the head after being released from prison. His death is ruled a suicide.	At least 200 Chinese civilians die and hundreds more are injured when 16 Japanese planes drop incendiary bombs on the Shanghai suburb of Nantao. The city has no military targets and the rail stations were not hit. . . . Japan claims to hold Lotien, as well as the Nankow Pass and Kalgan (again).
Aug. 29	China and the Soviet Union sign a nonaggression pact. . . . For the attack on its Ambassador, Britain presents three demands to Japan: an apology, punishment for the perpetrators, and assurance of no recurrence.	Fighting is heavy around Saragossa, from Belchite to Huesca, with insurgents claiming the edge. Insurgent planes shell Valencia in a surprise attack. . . . Two women are shot for poisoning children's food in Leningrad. . . . The Yugoslav government closes an Orthodox church printing office for turning out anti-government pamphlets.			Hundreds more Chinese civilians are killed and injured in air attacks on Nanking, Shanghai, and Nanchang (in the Kiangsi province).
Aug. 30	The British government will build a refugee camp for 1,000 Ethiopians in Isiolo, Kenya. . . . China complains to the League of Nations that Japan is exploiting the Lugou Bridge incident to conquer more territory and force China into war.	Loyalist forces focus their strength on Belchite, trying to take the town from insurgents. . . . Parliament passes bills to redesign and reorganize the British army. . . . The Little Entente meets; one item discussed is the rearmament of Romania. . . . The Polish government protests that German police are taking children by force to German schools in Danzig.	The morning murder of a bus passenger on the road to Tel Aviv sets off more violence. Gunshots are fired in Jaffa and a bomb is thrown in Tel Aviv, causing injuries. The victims are all Jewish.		In the face of international criticism, Japan promises not to bomb civilians "at the present time." . . . A Chinese pilot mistakes the U.S. liner President Hoover for a Japanese troop ship and drops bombs, killing a crewman and injuring others. Chinese authorities apologize and offer reparations. The United States orders passenger ships out of the Shanghai area and will use military ships for evacuation.
Aug. 31	Generalissimo Chiang Kai-shek appeals to the world's nations to intervene in the undeclared war, saying that Japanese aggression threatens the trade and safety of all.	A submarine torpedoes and sinks a Russian steamer off the coast of Algiers; all aboard escape. . . . Premier van Zeeland calls Belgium's parliament to a special session to answer Rexist charges that he received bonuses and a salary from the National Bank long after becoming premier. . . . The French Cabinet sets up a National Railway, fusing six lines into one state-run company as of next January.	Two Jewish workers are killed in Samaria and an Arab is shot to death in Jerusalem. Two Arabs die from gunshots in other cities. Newspapers and authorities plead for an end to violence. At the same time, arms are being smuggled through Damascus, Syria, with some knowledge by the Arab High Committee.		Both sides fortify and reinforce positions along a wedge pushing north from Shanghai into Chinese-held territory. To the south, Japanese planes approach Canton and shell nearby airports. The International Settlement in Shanghai sees its quietest day in weeks. The first cases of cholera are reported.

A	B	C	D	E
Includes developments that affect more than one world region, international organizations, and important meetings of world leaders.	Includes all domestic and regional developments in Europe, including the Soviet Union.	Includes all domestic and regional developments in Africa and the Middle East.	Includes all domestic and regional developments in Latin America, the Caribbean, and Canada.	Includes all domestic and regional developments in Asian and Pacific nations (and colonies).

U.S. Politics & Social Issues	U.S. Foreign Policy & Defense	Economics & Great Depression	Science, Technology & Nature	Culture, Leisure & Lifestyle	
	Secretary of State Cordell Hull ends his "watch and wait" position with diplomatic messages to Japan, warning against interfering with U.S. vessels. He tells both China and Japan that the United States will hold the countries responsible for damage to American lives and property. . . . A New York Congressman adds his plea to others, asking Secretary Hull to reconsider his acceptance of an invitation to the Nazi Congress Party fête in Nuremburg.	The UAWA votes $1 per member, or $400,000, for a war chest used to unionize Ford workers.			Aug. 27
Judge Callahan of Alabama denies a request for new trials for three imprisoned Scottsboro defendants. Attorney Samuel Leibowitz will appeal to the Supreme Court for the third time.		Representatives of five railway unions and major rail companies meet with federal mediator Dr. William Leiserson in Chicago. . . . Based on CIO charges, Bethlehem Steel is ordered to an NLRB hearing in Johnstown, Pa., in September. . . . The NLRB will hear testimony this week from Goodyear Tire and Rubber of Alabama, and union members who claim they were beaten and abused. . . . Weirton Steel attorneys threaten to call thousands of witnesses to their NLRB hearings.		The Dodgers suspend star baseball player Van Lingle Mungo indefinitely for refusing the Dodger trainer's program to keep in shape. . . . An ocean liner disembarks 993 passengers in New York without revealing that 29 crew members were ill with typhoid.	Aug. 28
					Aug. 29
				Welsh fighter Tommy Farr goes all 15 rounds with Joe Louis in Yankee Stadium, but Louis wins the decision.	Aug. 30
				Rookie Rudy York, playing for the Detroit Tigers, beats Babe Ruth's record for the most home runs in one month; he hits 18. . . . Actors Tallulah Bankhead and John Emery marry. The bride's father, the nation's Speaker of the House William Bankhead, gives her away.	Aug. 31

F	G	H	I	J
Includes elections, federal-state relations, civil rights and liberties, crime, the judiciary, education, healthcare, poverty, urban affairs, and population.	Includes formation and debate of U.S. foreign and defense policies, veterans affairs, and defense spending. (Relations with specific foreign countries are usually found under the region concerned.)	Includes business, labor, agriculture, taxation, transportation, consumer affairs, monetary and fiscal policy, natural resources, pollution, and accidents.	Includes worldwide scientific, medical, and technological developments, natural phenomena, U.S. weather, and natural disasters.	Includes the arts, religion, scholarship, communications media, sports, entertainment, fashions, fads, and social life.

	World Affairs	Europe	Africa & The Middle East	The Americas	Asia & The Pacific
Sept. 1		A torpedo from a submarine sinks the British steamer *Woodford*. One man is killed, six injured. Later, torpedoes narrowly miss a British destroyer off Spain's coast. The destroyer drops depth charges. . . . The Soviet paper *Izvestia* purges itself, firing a writer for distorting facts and doing political harm. In the Caucasus region, seven traitors are executed. . . . Hungary's Premier Daranyi informs the German Ambassador that Hungary will no longer allow Nazi pamphlets promoting dictatorship to be circulated. . . . In Poland, this is Anti-Jewish Month. Poles are urged to boycott all Jewish businesses, and pickets stand outside shops to taunt and sing. In the countryside, anti-Jewish agitators grow more brutal as the authorities do nothing to stop them.	Four Arabs are murdered near two different Jewish settlements.		More Japanese troops land in Yangtzepoo, and heavy fighting is reported in Woosung. In Hong Kong, British authorities protect 1,300 Japanese from angry Chinese rioters. Aerial strikes become a daily occurrence in Canton (Guangzhou), Shanghai, Nankow, Tientsin (Tianjin), Peiping (Beijing), the inland city of Hankow (Hankou), and the coastal provinces in between: Fukien (Fujian), Chekiang (Zhejiang), and Kiangsu (Jiangsu). . . . China's ambassador in Tokyo offers a non-aggression pact with Japan.
Sept. 2	General Hermann Goering issues a threat at the Congress of Germans Abroad: if Jews outside the Reich engineer a boycott of German goods, German Jews will pay.	The insurgents begin to move into the Asturian state. Loyalist forces have been pushed back from their assault on the Saragossa region in the past days and assemble their forces around Belchite. . . . Britain seconds France's call for a conference on piracy, to be attended by Mediterranean nations. . . . Former Polish Premier Paderewski publishes a manifesto (which authorities seize) calling for elections, the return of former leader Witos, and the end of concentration camps. . . . Moscow's paper *Pravda* announces that Ukrainian Premier Liubchenko has killed himself because of anti-Soviet activities.	In Meknes, French Morocco (Morocco), thousands gather before the courthouse where leaders of recent demonstrations are on trial. The previous demonstrations were over water rationing. The crowd turns violent as punishments are handed down. Shots fired from rooftops and by troops kill between 10 and 15 men, and over 40 are injured.		Incendiary bombs are dropped on the Hongkew area of Shanghai. Chinese planes from Soochow (Suzhou) damage the Japanese airfield and positions along the Yangtze River. Japanese planes shell Liuho, a city north of Lotien, and Japanese ships offload more troops between Liuho and Woosung. . . . In the south, a severe typhoon with winds up to 160 miles per hour lashes Hong Kong. At least 300 are killed in the storm.
Sept. 3		While loyalists enter Belchite, insurgents take the town of Potes, 15 miles from Santander. . . . Britain sends four ships to patrol the Mediterranean as east European nations rue the loss of products and revenue due to ship attacks. The Soviet Union openly blames Italy for the sinking of its ship. . . . Germany's Nuremburg Laws are enforced in Upper Silesia, forcing many Jews out of their official positions.			Shanghai warehouses, shipyards, ships, and the Japanese Consulate are damaged by bombs and machine gun fire through the day. Forced to halt troop deployment, Admiral Hasegawa threatens immediate punitive retaliation by his Third Fleet. . . . Chinese troops fight to retake portions of Lotien. . . . Far to the south in Amoy, Japanese planes and three ships fire on military targets.
Sept. 4	Since no part of Shanghai or the International Settlement is safe, the envoys of the United States, Britain, and France ask China and Japan to move their undeclared war to the south and east.	Insurgent troops cross the Deva River and invade the loyalist stronghold of Asturias from the east. Franco's rebels and government troops engage in hand-to-hand fighting in Belchite's streets. . . . The submarine activities in the Mediterranean keep Russian munitions from reaching the Spanish government.	Random violence in Palestine continues: a Jewish youth throws a bomb onto a bus, killing two Arab women; and an Arab broker who sold land to Jews is shot in Haifa.	A Nicaraguan stamp with a map of the country that shows part of Honduras as being part of Nicaragua becomes an international incident. The area questioned on the stamp has been in dispute for years; Nicaragua will not withdraw the stamp.	Eight Japanese warships are forced away from Shanghai by Chinese artillery strikes. Japanese planes drop 50 bombs on the city of Ningpo (Ningbo), just south of Shanghai. . . . Japan, in control of Kalgan (Zhangjiakou), capital of the Chahar (Inner Mongolia) province, installs a government of 100 notables, independent of China. The nominal head is Prince Teh or Demchugdongrub. . . . In Japan, the Diet opens with an unprecedented short speech by the Emperor. He blames the hostilities on China's provocative attitude and misconstruction of Japanese intent.
Sept. 5		Insurgents capture the coastal city of Llanes. To encircle the port of Gijón, a brigade begins to traverse the mountains and gorges of the Picos de Europa, and the pass of El Mazuco. . . . Protestant Confessional Churches in Germany tell parishioners to resist the state's attempt to dominate the church. . . . A quarter million people in 13 tent cities await the opening of the Nuremberg Party Congress tomorrow. . . . France and Britain invite 10 nations to a conference on piracy. . . . Among 10 people executed by firing squad today in Leningrad are three cooks, condemned for serving spoiled meat.		Argentina votes delegates to elect a new president, Dr. Roberto Ortiz, from the same party as retiring leader Agustin Justo. Violence mars the elections in and around Buenos Aires, where three policemen die trying to control separate demonstrations.	Japanese planes continue to drop bombs on civilian areas of Shanghai, killing at least 200 noncombatants. . . . Japan extends its blockade to cover the entire coast of China, excepting certain cities with access required by foreign treaties: 2,700 miles.

A	B	C	D	E
Includes developments that affect more than one world region, international organizations, and important meetings of world leaders.	*Includes all domestic and regional developments in Europe, including the Soviet Union.*	*Includes all domestic and regional developments in Africa and the Middle East.*	*Includes all domestic and regional developments in Latin America, the Caribbean, and Canada.*	*Includes all domestic and regional developments in Asian and Pacific nations (and colonies).*

U.S. Politics & Social Issues	U.S. Foreign Policy & Defense	Economics & Great Depression	Science, Technology & Nature	Culture, Leisure & Lifestyle	
President Franklin Roosevelt signs the Wallace-Steagall Bill for low-cost housing and slum clearance.		President Franklin Roosevelt signs the Sugar Bill with reluctance, objecting to the limits on Hawaiian, Cuban, and Puerto Rican imports.			Sept. 1
	Merchant ships will be used to evacuate U.S. citizens from China, but they will have military escorts. As U.S. property is destroyed, such as the jointly owned Chenju radio station, businesses ask government about compensation from Japan.	A strike of 15,000 New York painters enters its second week, and over 100 painters are arrested for picketing and blocking traffic.		Pierre De Coubertin, a French historian who started the modern Olympic Games, dies in Geneva, Switzerland.	Sept. 2
		In a Labor Day radio talk, CIO head John L. Lewis warns politicians that the labor vote may reconsider its support if elected representatives duck their responsibility to workers. . . . Seven hundred employees of Indiana's Morgan Packing walked off their jobs late yesterday, striking for higher wages. Three hundred farmers organize overnight to chase off the pickets and reopen the plant so that their 125 truckloads of tomatoes and corn could be processed.	A 7.2 earthquake rocks Alaska.		Sept. 3
	William Dodd, the U.S. Ambassador to Germany, considers resignation after his recommendation to Secretary of State Cordell Hull that the United States not accept Germany's invitation to Nuremburg is revealed.	Bethlehem Steel replies to the National Labor Relations Board (NLRB), saying that the Board's demand for documentation and appearances with five days' notice is unreasonable. It adds that the charges against Bethlehem are vague and need clarification. . . . The NLRB will hear charges against Ford's Somerville plant based on United Auto Workers of America (UAWA) charges.			Sept. 4
	The United States reminds Mexico of the 1928 Morrow-Calles Agreement protecting U.S. rights in Mexico. U.S. oil companies have at least $200 million invested there. . . . President Franklin Roosevelt says any U.S. citizens who remain in China do so at their own risk.		Dr. Harold Clayton Urey, who won the 1934 Nobel Prize in Chemistry, announces he has found a way to produce heavy nitrogen isotopes for research.		Sept. 5

F	G	H	I	J
Includes elections, federal-state relations, civil rights and liberties, crime, the judiciary, education, healthcare, poverty, urban affairs, and population.	Includes formation and debate of U.S. foreign and defense policies, veterans affairs, and defense spending. (Relations with specific foreign countries are usually found under the region concerned.)	Includes business, labor, agriculture, taxation, transportation, consumer affairs, monetary and fiscal policy, natural resources, pollution, and accidents.	Includes worldwide scientific, medical, and technological developments, natural phenomena, U.S. weather, and natural disasters.	Includes the arts, religion, scholarship, communications media, sports, entertainment, fashions, fads, and social life.

	World Affairs	Europe	Africa & The Middle East	The Americas	Asia & The Pacific
Sept. 6	After eight days, Japan replies to Britain's demand for an apology for the attack on its Ambassador in China. Claiming the investigation is ongoing, Japan issues no apology.	In Asturias, the Battle of El Mazuco begins. A ground attack is unsuccessful. The Condor Legion carpet-bombs the loyalist positions. . . . After days of desperate fighting, the 600 insurgent soldiers barricaded in Belchite's cathedral surrender. . . . The Soviet Union officially charges Italian submarines of sinking two Soviet ships and demands reparation; Italy denies responsibility. . . . Six officials of Tashkent, capital of the Soviet state of Uzbek, are removed for spending city funds on women and liquor.			Japan's air and sea forces batter Woosung with shells and attack air and rail stations west of Shanghai. Far to the south, Sanmei, a town near Hong Kong, is shelled. . . . News is revealed that Japan has conducted air raids in the north for several weeks. Chinese troops mass near important rail stations, such as divisions of the Peiping-Hankow Railway.
Sept. 7		Insurgents launch a new attack to retake Belchite. Three loyalist battalions—less than 5,000 men—under Commander Carrocera arrive in El Mazuco. . . . The insurgent cruiser *Baleares* meets a loyalist convoy which, worried about air attacks, flees. Two loyalist cruisers engage the *Baleares*, hitting it twice in the afternoon. . . . The Soviet Union will attend the European conference on piracy, now set to begin in three days in Nyon, Switzerland. . . . Chancellor Adolf Hitler opens his party's Congress by reaffirming Germany's ties with Italy and Japan.		A coup d'etat starts, using radio and media, in Asuncion, Paraguay. Coup leaders want deposed president Rafael Franco to return to power. Street fighting rages through the day, with the army making no decisive move.	China takes the offensive, driving Japanese forces away from Woosung and the Paoshun areas, near the Yangtze River. Japanese forces make gains in Kiangwan, and guns blaze all night in that area. Fighting in Lotien, northwest of Shanghai, claims hundreds of casualties. . . . Missionaries in China bring word that hospitals and schools are being deliberately targeted and bombed. Japanese authorities claim that the buildings were used by Chinese snipers.
Sept. 8		Heavy fog in El Mazuco leads to hand-to-hand fighting; the insurgents advance a mile. . . . After a second, stronger accusation from the Soviets about submarine attacks, Italy announces it will not attend the Nyon conference and Germany does likewise.	The Pan Arab Conference begins in Bludan, Syria. Four hundred attend, but no Arab country sends official representatives.	Order is restored in Paraguay. Former president Rafael Franco, flying in from Argentina, turns his plane around and returns to exile. . . . A military tribunal in Brazil hears appeals from 35 men convicted in the 1935 Leftist uprising.	Many businesses in Shanghai burn or suffer damage from bombs. Japanese fliers shell a train carrying refugees away from the city, killing 300 and injuring 400. The Chinese government announces it will commence air strikes against Japanese ships. . . . The Diet of Japan approves a $600 million war budget.
Sept. 9	The League of Nations issues a gloomy economic report, seeing little progress made toward goals. . . . After receiving a letter and picture from the glamorous wife of Harold Dahl, General Franco agrees to exchange the American pilot for a prisoner held by the Valencia government. Dahl, flying for the loyalists, had been captured and condemned to death.	Insurgents fire on Asturian defenses (the "Covadonga line"). Their strategy is to surround Gijón. An insurgent brigade continues to pound at the pass of El Mazuco, using artillery and incendiary bombs, but machine gun fire keeps them back.		Paraguayan President Paiva suspends the Constitution and declares martial law for two months.	Japan announces that all rails and transportation channels, as well as all communication centers, are military targets and will be bombed. Refugee groups wishing to use trains must make arrangements through diplomatic sources. . . . The southern ports of Amoy and Swatow (Shantou) suffer bombardments by Japanese planes. In the north, China constructs barriers in the Yangtze River made of debris and sunken ships filled with concrete to keep Japanese warships away from Nanking (Nanjing).
Sept. 10	The League of Nations Council session convenes in Geneva. The separation of the League's covenant from the Treaty of Versailles is slated for discussion. . . . Japan insists on the right to fish in Siberian waters up to the three-mile limit, angering the Soviet Union, which has seized 28 boats recently.	Crowds of demonstrators in Gijón demand early surrender to Franco's forces. Insurgents take the hill of Biforca in Asturias. . . . The Nyon Conference convenes to discuss piracy and the Spanish war. The Soviets threaten reprisals against pirate ships and submarines. Nonattendees Italy and Germany sneer at the conference, but from the start it takes decisive action. . . . Berlin's entire diplomatic corps turns out at the Nuremberg Rally, with four exceptions: the Soviet, Vatican, Peruvian, and Norwegian envoys are absent.	The Arab Congress ends with a list of demands centering on opposition to the division of Palestine and the exclusion of Jews as anything but a powerless minority there. The demands will be submitted to the League of Nations.	By decree of President Lázaro Cárdenas, the Bank of Mexico may act without the hindrance of most regulations until August 31, 1938. . . . Two uniformed observers in the Chaco neutral zone are arrested and held for hours by Paraguayan police. In the interest of peace, the incident is kept secret until newspapers reveal it on September 14.	Fighting and shelling continues in the same areas of China. Shanghai reports 200 cases of cholera. The disease spreads through the Yangtze River Valley, as far as Nanking. . . . Japan opens an offensive on Machang, an area 35 miles south of Tientsin, with aerial raids and artillery fire. . . . Communist General Mao Tsetung (Mao Zedong) leads huge armies east toward Shansi (Shanxi) province to block Japanese troops.
Sept. 11		In Santander, an estimated 50,000 prisoners in concentration camps await trial by insurgent courts. . . . A bomb at an employers' hall kills two policemen in Paris; a second bomb at a trade association building caused damage, but no deaths. . . . The Nyon conferees agree that each nation shall patrol their own waters, the Soviet Union and nations near the Black Sea will share patrol duties for that sector, and Britain and France will patrol much of the Mediterranean with 60 destroyers.			Japan claims capture of Machang after heavy fighting through the night.

A	B	C	D	E
Includes developments that affect more than one world region, international organizations, and important meetings of world leaders.	*Includes all domestic and regional developments in Europe, including the Soviet Union.*	*Includes all domestic and regional developments in Africa and the Middle East.*	*Includes all domestic and regional developments in Latin America, the Caribbean, and Canada.*	*Includes all domestic and regional developments in Asian and Pacific nations (and colonies).*

U.S. Politics & Social Issues	U.S. Foreign Policy & Defense	Economics & Great Depression	Science, Technology & Nature	Culture, Leisure & Lifestyle	
		In San Francisco, where the CIO and AFL battle over Teamsters and warehouse and dock workers, the AFL declines to march in the Labor Day parade because the CIO will be there.			Sept. 6
		Stock market prices fall 2–10 points, partly due to overseas news of war, triggering large sell-offs. . . . Douglas Aircraft in Los Angeles, Calif, closes its subsidiary, Northrop, saying that it "no longer exists as an industrial entity." Both companies have suffered from strikes led by the CIO.			Sept. 7
	Secretary of State Cordell Hull and Joseph Kennedy, Chair of the Marine Commission, issue a warning to U.S. ships in the Mediterranean about attacks from unidentified ships and submarines.	Denying a request for postponement, the NLRB opens hearings with Bethlehem Steel in Johnstown, Pa. . . . In San Francisco, the Teamsters, an AFL union, complete a blockade of the ports begun at the end of August, thus idling CIO longshoremen. The fight is over who—AFL or CIO—gets to organize warehouse workers.			Sept. 8
		In San Francisco, the AFL Teamsters reject a settlement offer by the CIO that would have brought the NLRB in to negotiate. The next move in organizing warehousemen is unclear.			Sept. 9
		Another drop of 2–10 points on leading stocks—worse than last Tuesday's—triggers a selling wave. . . . The NLRB meeting in Johnstown, Pa., hears evidence on Bethlehem Steel's relations with both labor and the Citizens Committees, which were against strikes because they interfered with employees' "right to work."	The $37 million Wheeler Dam in Alabama is dedicated.	Author and playwright Sergei Tretyakov is either executed or kills himself in Soviet prison; he was arrested July 27 for espionage.	Sept. 10
					Sept. 11

F	G	H	I	J
Includes elections, federal-state relations, civil rights and liberties, crime, the judiciary, education, healthcare, poverty, urban affairs, and population.	*Includes formation and debate of U.S. foreign and defense policies, veterans affairs, and defense spending. (Relations with specific foreign countries are usually found under the region concerned.)*	*Includes business, labor, agriculture, taxation, transportation, consumer affairs, monetary and fiscal policy, natural resources, pollution, and accidents.*	*Includes worldwide scientific, medical, and technological developments, natural phenomena, U.S. weather, and natural disasters.*	*Includes the arts, religion, scholarship, communications media, sports, entertainment, fashions, fads, and social life.*

	World Affairs	Europe	Africa & The Middle East	The Americas	Asia & The Pacific
Sept. 12	In Ethiopia, Italy severs the Coptic church from the Patriarch in Alexandria, Egypt, and puts it under state control.	Unable to advance through the valley leading to El Mazuco, insurgents climb the Sierra ridge, with peaks up to 7,500 feet, carrying their own equipment. Government forces abandon munitions as they give up their positions.		An eight-week old strike against the Mexican Eagle Oil Company in Poza Rica results in fuel shortages affecting industry, impacting U.S. investors. President Lázaro Cárdenas asks the workers for cooperation.	A typhoon whips southern Japan, killing 70, knocking out communication and rail lines in places, and devastating rice crops. . . . Journalists estimate that 400,000 Chinese troops mass in the north while another 400,000 are in the Shanghai and coastal provinces. Japan has 180,000 and 100,000 troops in those areas, respectively. An estimated 1.5 million refugees swell the population of Shanghai.
Sept. 13	The 18th League of Nations Assembly session opens, and China files an appeal against Japan's invasion. . . . The Soviet Union asks Japan to close its embassies in Odessa and Novosibirsk, Siberia. Six Japanese embassies remain open in Soviet states, and Japan hosts six Soviet embassies.	Franco's press reports that an anarchist faction rules Gijón and has executed the government officials who lost Basque strongholds in the past months. The loyalist defenders weaken in El Mazuco. . . . Seyyid Riza, Kurdish leader of the springtime uprising in the Darsim area of Turkey, surrendered to authorities, it is revealed. . . . The Danzig (Gdansk) Gestapo censors Polish mail and arrests Polish postmen who deliver it. . . . In Germany, Heinrich Himmler decrees that Jews can be released from detention if they emigrate. Many arrested on Kristellnacht take advantage of this offer.		Mexico reveals that its armed peasant reservists now form an army as big as the regular army. The 47,439 peasant troops are organized into 98 regiments. . . . Brazil's Supreme Military Tribunal overturns the sedition conviction of the former mayor of Rio de Janeiro, Pedro Ernesto Baptista, stemming from the 1935 uprising.	Japan captures the city of Tatung (Datong), an important railway hub in Shansi province, and claims that all Chinese armies have been driven out of the Chahar province. . . . In a speech boycotted by both the Congress and Congress Nationalist parties, the Viceroy of India lauds the new constitution and urges the princes of India to move forward.
Sept. 14		Insurgents push the loyalists from the commanding Sierra Llabres. To the south, loyalists defend Turbina with hand grenades, fighting in heavy fog. . . . Italy, absent from the Nyon Conference, refuses to participate in Mediterranean patrols unless it has a role equal to France's and Britain's. . . . A Soviet decree speeds up the trial process for "wreckers." Trials may commence within 24 hours after charges are made, and death sentences may be carried out immediately. . . . The first Czech president and national hero, Thomas Masaryk, dies at age 87.		Talks to settle the Poza Rica strike cease, in defiance of the president's call for cooperation. Mexico's oil production is down by 60 percent.	China confirms estimates of 35,000 casualties in the month of fighting in Shanghai. Japan claims to occupy more towns in the north. . . . Five days of air raid drills begin in Tokyo, involving 40,000 volunteers.
Sept. 15	British insurance underwriters abolish standards on shipments of oil or arms to China; this is expected to affect shipping. . . . Japan proclaims that it will ignore any decisions by the League of Nations about China. . . . Sometime in mid-September, Ethiopians at Adowa kill 200 Italian troops, prompting the Italian Viceroy to cancel a trip. This follows a late-August ambush on a convoy, during which Ethiopians burned 200 trucks.	Insurgents capture the pass at El Mazuco. With winter and snow approaching, the columns moving toward Gijón prepare to join and attack. . . . The French franc falls to a new low without government attempts to stabilize it. . . . The Polish government protests to the Danzig Senate over the Gestapo's interference with mail from Poland. . . . Croats and Serbs ally in Yugoslavia, forming a single voting block to change the government and force Premier Stoyadinovitch to hold elections.		President Lázaro Cárdenas intervenes to end the oil strike in the Poza Rica fields of Veracruz, Mexico. The British-owned oil company will pay workers 75 percent of their wages for the strike period. . . . Paraguayan officials offer excuses in the detention of two neutral observers last week and assurances that it will not happen again.	Japan's forces push Chinese troops south from Peiping and Tientsin, and away from strategic rail lines. Twenty thousand mounted cavalry troops are key in this push, with Japanese planes shelling Chinese positions in advance of ground attacks. A naval and air battle takes place near Canton, where both sides claim to sink each other's ships.
Sept. 16	The League of Nations refers China's complaint to its Far Eastern Advisory Committee.	In Spain, the peak of Turbina falls to the insurgents. The loyalists still hold the three peaks of Peñas Blancas. Insurgents attack with 16 battalions, but are kept from the summit by rain and fierce fighting. Madrid is shelled after two weeks of relative peace; Portbou, near the French border, is bombed and its railways are ripped apart; close to 20 people are killed as bombs fall on Valencia and its port. . . . French police uncover a secret society, Les Cagoulards, who stockpile weapons and plot to return the monarchy to France.		Catholics in Coatepec, Veracruz, Mexico, march, demonstrate, and break open churches after being allowed to hold Mass last night. The demonstrators set up guards so that the government cannot close the churches again.	Over 650 cases of cholera are reported in the International Sector of Shanghai. In the north, Japan shells Taiyuan, capital of the Shansi province. Poor weather keeps planes from flying in many areas.
Sept. 17		British patrol ships near Malta sight two submarines flying the insurgent flag and escorted by Italian and German destroyers. A torpedo narrowly misses a British aircraft carrier nearby. France and Britain withdraw from patrolling Spain's coast for the Non-Intervention Committee and move their ships to the Mediterranean Sea.		In Ponce, Puerto Rico, 11 men stand trial for the Palm Sunday killing of a policeman during a riot.	Retreating from Shanghai, Chinese forces stand at the Lotien-Shuangtsaoten section of the North Shanghai Railway. Japanese sources say 50,000 Chinese troops are caught south of Peiping between rivers and rail lines.

A	B	C	D	E
Includes developments that affect more than one world region, international organizations, and important meetings of world leaders.	Includes all domestic and regional developments in Europe, including the Soviet Union.	Includes all domestic and regional developments in Africa and the Middle East.	Includes all domestic and regional developments in Latin America, the Caribbean, and Canada.	Includes all domestic and regional developments in Asian and Pacific nations (and colonies).

U.S. Politics & Social Issues	U.S. Foreign Policy & Defense	Economics & Great Depression	Science, Technology & Nature	Culture, Leisure & Lifestyle	
Stink bombs and tear gas are set off in 21 New York movie theaters, all within 30 minutes. No one takes credit for the attack.		Since the U.S. Treasury began "sterilizing" gold last December and moving it to an inactive account, nearly $1.4 billion has accumulated; $300 million is transferred to Federal Reserve Banks to insure availability of credit and cash. . . . The AFL severs ties with the American Newspaper Guild after it switches its affiliation to the CIO.			Sept. 12
The Pittsburgh *Post-Gazette* publishes a series of articles accusing Justice Hugo Black of maintaining his membership in the Ku Klux Klan. While the controversy rages, Justice Black vacations in Europe without comment.		Mayor Shields of Johnstown, Pa., ignores the subpoena issued by the NLRB investigating labor practices of Bethlehem Steel. He implies he may fight the subpoena in court. . . . Stocks drop again, and over 2.5 million are traded.			Sept. 13
	President Franklin Roosevelt bans the transmission of arms to China or Japan on government-owned ships, but he does not invoke the Neutrality Act.	The stock market rebounds with gains averaging 2 to 5 points. . . . The Farm Administration presents a new program focused on maximum acreage for cash crops to farm leaders and AAA representatives. Compliance will be rewarded with financial incentives.		Puerto Rico prepares an official protest over a mural painted by Rockwell Kent in Washington D.C.'s new Post Office building, The mural portrays all the Puerto Ricans as Negroid.	Sept. 14
Farmers in Warren County, Ga., hold African-American workers at gunpoint, refusing to let them accept higher pay in neighboring counties to pick cotton.	Spain's government negotiates to pay $30 million in preexisting debt to Americans, and will send a commission to the United States to discuss property losses due to the civil war.	President Franklin Roosevelt and John L. Lewis of the CIO talk at the White House. . . . At the NLRB hearings, Bethlehem Steel demands the names of employees who belong to the union to prove that they do not discriminate against them. Rebuffed, the company threatens to call all 15,000 employees to testify as to their membership.			Sept. 15
					Sept. 16
In a speech marking the 150th anniversary of the Constitution, President Franklin Roosevelt recommits to his program of social reform, including the reorganization of the Supreme Court.	China protests that the U.S. partial embargo of war material favors Japan over China.			The third image on Mt. Rushmore in South Dakota is unveiled. Abraham Lincoln's 66-foot-tall face rests next to those of George Washington and Thomas Jefferson.	Sept. 17

F	G	H	I	J
Includes elections, federal-state relations, civil rights and liberties, crime, the judiciary, education, healthcare, poverty, urban affairs, and population.	*Includes formation and debate of U.S. foreign and defense policies, veterans affairs, and defense spending. (Relations with specific foreign countries are usually found under the region concerned.)*	*Includes business, labor, agriculture, taxation, transportation, consumer affairs, monetary and fiscal policy, natural resources, pollution, and accidents.*	*Includes worldwide scientific, medical, and technological developments, natural phenomena, U.S. weather, and natural disasters.*	*Includes the arts, religion, scholarship, communications media, sports, entertainment, fashions, fads, and social life.*

	World Affairs	Europe	Africa & The Middle East	The Americas	Asia & The Pacific
Sept. 18	Egypt's Foreign Minister tells the League of Nations that the proposed division of Palestine ignores Arabs' rights. His is the first dissenting voice heard in Geneva.	Insurgents take Mt. Pajares. A break in fog and rain allows their planes to strafe loyalist positions on Peñas Blancas, but loyalists hold on with grenades and machine guns. . . . A plane drops bombs near a British destroyer, then flies toward Gijón, a city still held by loyalists. . . . Berlin and many parts of Germany will participate in "Black Week," simulating air raids and blackouts and testing alarms and responses.			Six air raids by Chinese pilots over Shanghai result in fires and death in Yangtzepoo and the International Settlement.
Sept. 19		In Brest, France, Spanish insurgents try unsuccessfully to steal a submarine under repair. French police later arrest the insurgent governor of Irun, Spain, for the attempt. . . . The Sella River is the scene of new fighting, while insurgents continue to pound Peñas Blancas with artillery. The German head of the Condor Legion secures permission to bomb the Asturian coast from insurgent General Dávila. . . . Local newspapers of the Soviet Union continue to report executions. In the Black Sea province, six die for mismanaging farms and preparing for revolt. A paper reveals that 20 "wreckers" were shot in Siberia for spying for Japan.		The Supreme Court of Mexico strikes at land seizures, ruling that expropriations must be paid for with real, and not "illusory," funds. Americans, with an estimated $2 billion invested in Mexico, favor the ruling, though it indicates a fracturing of the court's previous loyalty to President Lázaro Cárdenas.	In the largest air raid so far, 43 Japanese planes attack Nanking in the morning, and another 23 attack in the afternoon. To the north, using the recently captured Tatung as a base, Japanese troops push farther into Shansi province, and Chinese soldiers gather to stop them at the Yenmen Pass (Yenmenguan).
Sept. 20	The Permanent Court for International Justice opens its 41st session in The Hague.	Madrid is wracked by bombs all day, and loyalist shells destroy the last remaining school in the University City sector, the Agronomy Engineering School. . . . Jewish senators in Warsaw complain to Polish authorities of increasing attacks and beatings of Jews on the streets.			After a warning to foreign embassies and neutral ships, 50 Japanese planes drop bombs on Nanking for three hours. Canton suffers a 90-minute air raid. Japan warns of further attacks on Nanking, calling it the base of military opposition. . . . In Shanghai, where there are over 1,000 cases of cholera, 120 deaths are attributed to the disease. In Hsinking, Manchukuo (Changchun, Manchuria), 198 cases of bubonic plague are reported.
Sept. 21	Separately, the United States and Britain appeal to Japan through diplomatic channels to not carry out threatened air raids on civilians in Nanking.	The loyalist troops of Spain strike unexpectedly in the south, destroying three insurgent-held towns 50 miles northwest of Córdoba. . . . Italy, France, and Britain will meet to discuss Italy's inclusion in Mediterranean patrols. . . . A crowd of 2 million stands along the funeral route of Thomas Masaryk through Prague. . . . In Warsaw, police claim to be overwhelmed by organized youth gangs who attack Jews throughout the city. At night, Jewish shops are smashed and vandalized.			Although noon was set as a deadline by Japanese authorities, no attack is made on Nanking today. Many people leave the city, and several embassies board gunboats. . . . Chinese troops dig in 10 miles north of Paoting, ready for an assault on their 100-mile line of fortifications by the Japanese.
Sept. 22	London newspapers publish a letter from Japan expressing regret over the injury to Britain's Ambassador in China and pledging to exercise great care toward safeguarding noncombatants in the future. That the letter appears as Japan drops bombs on Nanking, causing 200 civilian casualties, is an irony not lost on most.	Insurgents take Peñas Blancas, ending the battle of El Mazuco and setting the stage for the invasion of Gijón. In the south, both sides fight for towns in Córdoba and Badajoz. . . . Eight high county officials in Moscow province are shot for graft and maladministration. . . . President Ataturk of Turkey removes Ismet Inonu as prime minister because of ill health, and names Jelal Bayar as temporary head of the Cabinet. Most believe that the president is unhappy with Inonu's decisions regarding the Soviet Union, the League of Nations, and the Nyon agreement.		The foreman of the jury that indicted Nationalist Party officials for sedition in Puerto Rico is assassinated.	After further warnings, 50 Japanese planes bomb Nanking for 90 minutes in the morning. A second raid in the afternoon involves 14 planes. The Kuomintang (Communist Party) headquarters is hit five times. Train and ferry stations are also targeted. Nearly all of the 200 casualties fall in the Hsiakwan slum area, near a rail station. . . . In other areas: Chinese planes shoot down Japanese planes during four air raids over Canton. A Japanese column enters Suiyuan (Inner Mongolia), and Chinese defenses around Paoting weaken. . . . Japanese submarines sink 11 Chinese fishing boats in a fleet, killing 300 men, women, and children. The survivors in a 12th boat drift at sea for five days before being picked up by a German ship. . . . Philippines President Manuel Quezon denounces a court decision that denied compensation to a worker killed while following orders. He orders government contracts withheld from the company.
Sept. 23		Snow falls as insurgent columns begin to circle Gijón. . . . Italy promises to send no more troops to Spain. No pledges are made about those already in Spain, rumored to number 150,000.			Fighting continues in Shanghai, and bombs are dropped on Kiangyin (Jiangyin) and other towns on the Yangtze River, as well as on railroad towns in the Shantung (Shandong) province. Air raids on Canton have taken 2,000 lives.

A	**B**	**C**	**D**	**E**
Includes developments that affect more than one world region, international organizations, and important meetings of world leaders.	*Includes all domestic and regional developments in Europe, including the Soviet Union.*	*Includes all domestic and regional developments in Africa and the Middle East.*	*Includes all domestic and regional developments in Latin America, the Caribbean, and Canada.*	*Includes all domestic and regional developments in Asian and Pacific nations (and colonies).*

U.S. Politics & Social Issues	U.S. Foreign Policy & Defense	Economics & Great Depression	Science, Technology & Nature	Culture, Leisure & Lifestyle	
		Employees of cigar manufacturer H. Anton Bock & Co. end their sit-down strike after 149 days—the longest on record.		Paul Waner of the Pittsburgh Pirates makes 200 hits for the eighth year in a row.	Sept. 18
	Secretary of the Treasury Henry Morgenthau appoints Harold Graves to overhaul the Internal Revenue Bureau and eliminate red tape.				Sept. 19
Stink bombs and tear gas are set off in seven New York theaters just before 9 p.m. As all theaters are part of the Springer-Cocalis chain, which is being picketed by the CIO, the labor dispute may be behind the bombs.	The U.S. Ambassador to China and part of his staff leave Nanking, a move criticized by the Chinese. Most countries' envoys stay there. . . . Secretary of the Treasury Henry Morgenthau begins economic and financial conferences with Britain.	By executive order of the President, the National Emergency Council will dissolve on December 31.		Another mural, this one in the office of the Postmaster General, stirs controversy. In "The Dangers of the Mail," Colorado artist Frank Mechau depicts American Indians scalping a bevy of nude women.	Sept. 20
		The AFL begins a council of west coast port unions, designed as much to exclude the CIO as to recruit AFL members.		J.R.R. Tolkien's The Hobbit, or There and Back Again, with illustrations by the author, is published in London: 1,500 copies go on sale.	Sept. 21
The President embarks on a trip to the northwest United States.	The United States delivers a strongly worded protest to Japan's Foreign Office over the bombing in Nanking.	Secretary of Agriculture Henry Wallace announces a shift in policy, abandoning "parity pricing" for farm products. The department will focus instead on increasing farmers' purchasing power to pre-war levels.			Sept. 22
					Sept. 23

F	**G**	**H**	**I**	**J**
Includes elections, federal-state relations, civil rights and liberties, crime, the judiciary, education, healthcare, poverty, urban affairs, and population.	Includes formation and debate of U.S. foreign and defense policies, veterans affairs, and defense spending. (Relations with specific foreign countries are usually found under the region concerned.)	Includes business, labor, agriculture, taxation, transportation, consumer affairs, monetary and fiscal policy, natural resources, pollution, and accidents.	Includes worldwide scientific, medical, and technological developments, natural phenomena, U.S. weather, and natural disasters.	Includes the arts, religion, scholarship, communications media, sports, entertainment, fashions, fads, and social life.

	World Affairs	Europe	Africa & The Middle East	The Americas	Asia & The Pacific
Sept. 24	Generalissimo Chiang Kai-shek accuses signatories of the Nine-Power Treaty, including the United States, of abrogating their responsibilities by taking no action to stop Japan's invasion. Delegates from both England and France ask China not to invoke the League's Article 17, which could force them into imposing sanctions against Japan.	The Spanish government arrests 108 anarchists for plotting a coup. They claim 7,500 conspirators were organized, ready to attack public buildings in Madrid and military targets as Franco's army moved into the city. Employees at Chilean and Argentinean embassies were involved. . . . A Siberian paper reports that 26 executions took place on September 18, and another 19 occur today in Vladivostok. All of the condemned were accused of espionage, Trotskyism, and plots.	Two wealthy Arabs are murdered in their homes, one near Nazareth, the other near Acre.		After firing shells at the city walls for days, the Japanese conquer Paoting. Japan's records say 25,800 people were killed taking the city. Thirty thousand Japanese soldiers will rampage and rape for a week. They burn all the schoolbooks, library books, and years of records kept by the Agricultural Institute. . . . One thousand die when the slum district of Hankow, part of the Wuhan area, is bombed and strafed with machine gun fire. . . . In the International Settlement of Shanghai, cholera cases rise to 1,600, and at least 200 Japanese soldiers die of the disease.
Sept. 25	The Italian government in Eritrea executes four Italian men for robbing and killing five Ethiopians. . . . Japan declines an invitation from the League of Nations to sit on its Far East Advisory Council, meeting on September 27.	Loyalists claim to blast into oblivion men and munitions in hundreds of trucks near Huesca. . . . Premier of Italy Benito Mussolini and Chancellor Adolf Hitler meet in Munich for three days of fêtes and talks in Germany. . . . Premier van Zeeland of Belgium withdraws his proffered resignation and agrees to continue at the head of the government rather than leave it in crisis. . . . The Soviet grain harvest is greater than any in 50 years, up to 15 million tons higher than any other year.	In Alexandria, a crowd of 80,000 pushes forward to see Egypt's King Farouk. Twenty-two people are trampled or suffocated to death, most of them children.		Chinese forces kill 1,000 Japanese soldiers and capture 100 trucks filled with supplies at the Battle of Pinghsingkwan (Pingxingguan), a narrow pass in Shansi province. Meanwhile, five waves of planes bomb Nanking for seven hours, destroying a $1 million electric plant and killing 600 people. The Wuhan cities, Nanchang, Kiangyin, and Canton, are shelled again. . . . President Manuel Quezon of the Philippines invites critics to impeach him. He has been outspoken about justice for workers, often denied in his country's courts.
Sept. 26	The Soviet Union delivers a strong warning to Japan not to bomb its Embassy in Nanking. . . . In the face of worldwide condemnation, Japan's Admiral Tadao Honda denies that bombs are used on noncombatants.	Many fronts in Spain—Madrid, Toledo, Jaca (near Huesca), Fuentes de Ebro (near Saragossa), and the Sella River in Asturia—see action. . . . Executions of "wreckers" in the Soviet Union are reported almost daily in local newspapers.	British Commissioner of Galilee L. Yelland Andrews is assassinated while leaving an Anglican Church in Nazareth. His bodyguard is killed as well. Three assassins escape.		Japan launches an attack along a 40-mile line from Lotien to Kiangwan, but Chinese forces, strongly entrenched, hold the line. Poor weather keeps planes from flying over Nanking. Journalists point out that neither side is taking any prisoners in this conflict.
Sept. 27	Britain's Ambassador in Tokyo delivers another protest to the Japanese government. . . . Soviet and Japanese troops mass on both sides of the Siberian border. . . . In Geneva, the International Labor Organization holds a conference to standardize the collection of labor statistics.	Insurgents, moving up the Sella River, capture a key town 30 miles from Gijón. . . . Over a million people line Berlin's streets to cheer Premier of Italy Benito Mussolini and Chancellor Adolf Hitler. Observers think a rapprochement with Britain is the next step to reviving a Four-Powers Pact. . . . Anti-Jewish gangs in Warsaw, Poland break into a Jewish-Socialist political office, set fires, shoot and wound four people, and bomb the door as well. A bomb is found and disarmed at a Jewish publisher, but another explodes on a crowded street, injuring 18 people.	In connection with the assassination of Commissioner L. Yelland Andrews, 106 Arabs are arrested.		Thirty Japanese planes bomb the Canton-Hankow Railway and neighboring towns; air raids kill over 100 civilians in Shanghai. A $20 million chemical plant near Nanking, built with U.S. help two years ago, is targeted, but poor weather keeps most planes on the ground.
Sept. 28	The League of Nations Assembly endorses a resolution by its Committee on the Far East, condemning the Japanese air attacks on towns and civilians. The League deadlocks on any decisions on Spain. . . . The Soviet Ambassador in Nanking departs by air suddenly. . . . Argentina denies Spain's allegations that any embassy employees were involved in a plot in Madrid and suggests that the accusation might be a way to stop evacuations.	Spanish loyalists control the Usera suburb of Madrid after seven hours of hand-to-hand fighting around an area called the "trench of death." Retreating insurgents destroy the trench with mines as they abandon it. Ten days of fighting continue in the Córdoba region over control of mines near Penarroyo. . . . Before a crowd of 1 million and with radio broadcasts connecting 20 countries, leaders Adolf Hitler and Benito Mussolini predict that fascism will bring world peace. . . . The Soviet Union condemns 31 people in several provinces for spoiling grain, adding weevils to grain, and mismanaging farms. . . . Soviet army and navy war games involving the city of Vladivostok conclude.			Japan rejects as "fabricated propaganda" stories that submarines fired on Chinese fishing boats. Army spokesmen express Japan's frustration with China's refusal to withdraw from Shanghai. Chiang Kai-shek may have forced his army into a fight to the death, hoping to inspire foreign intervention. . . . Fighting still rages at Yenmen Pass. Chinese troops under Communist General Chu Teh (Zhu De) are said to number 100,000. Japanese forces scale mountains to the east of the pass, hoping to outflank the defenders.

A	B	C	D	E
Includes developments that affect more than one world region, international organizations, and important meetings of world leaders.	*Includes all domestic and regional developments in Europe, including the Soviet Union.*	*Includes all domestic and regional developments in Africa and the Middle East.*	*Includes all domestic and regional developments in Latin America, the Caribbean, and Canada.*	*Includes all domestic and regional developments in Asian and Pacific nations (and colonies).*

U.S. Politics & Social Issues	U.S. Foreign Policy & Defense	Economics & Great Depression	Science, Technology & Nature	Culture, Leisure & Lifestyle	
		Stocks, bonds, and commodities fall amid heavy trading. . . . Twelve thousand truckers in upstate New York walk off their jobs after six weeks of wage talks stall.	In England, the Chain Home Station—the first air defense system using radar—becomes fully operational.		Sept. 24
		CIO longshoremen in San Francisco break through AFL picket lines, and AFL Teamsters form wedges to force themselves through the CIO lines. . . . The upstate New York truckers' strike ends when companies agree to a 3.5 cents per mile hauling fee.			Sept. 25
				Blues singer Bessie Smith dies in a hospital following a car accident in Mississippi. Rumors persist that a "white" hospital refused to treat her, but are untrue. . . . Zora Neale Hurston's *Their Eyes Were Watching God* is published.	Sept. 26
		In a Denver meeting of metal trades unions representing 700,000 workers, the AFL is urged to cut all remaining ties with the CIO. The AFL convention will be held in Denver next week.			Sept. 27
		In a radio speech given at the new Bonneville Dam in Oregon, President Franklin Roosevelt promises a balanced budget in 1939 and asks Congress to act to create planning and power agencies throughout the country. . . . In Port Huron, Mich., 400 AFL workers form a wedge to break through CIO picket lines at the Mueller Brass works, where they work. Fifteen are injured; state police armed with tear gas keep order. The CIO called the strike, though most of the employees are with AFL unions.			Sept. 28

F	G	H	I	J
Includes elections, federal-state relations, civil rights and liberties, crime, the judiciary, education, healthcare, poverty, urban affairs, and population.	*Includes formation and debate of U.S. foreign and defense policies, veterans affairs, and defense spending. (Relations with specific foreign countries are usually found under the region concerned.)*	*Includes business, labor, agriculture, taxation, transportation, consumer affairs, monetary and fiscal policy, natural resources, pollution, and accidents.*	*Includes worldwide scientific, medical, and technological developments, natural phenomena, U.S. weather, and natural disasters.*	*Includes the arts, religion, scholarship, communications media, sports, entertainment, fashions, fads, and social life.*

	World Affairs	Europe	Africa & The Middle East	The Americas	Asia & The Pacific
Sept. 29	The 99th League of Nations Council meets.	Neither side is winning in the battle for Jaca, Aragon, in northeast Spain. . . . Pope Pius XI warns that Communism, neo-paganism, and atheism threaten Christian civilization, and advises Catholics to say the Rosary. . . . *Pravda* announces the execution of 10 "terrorists" who caused a shutdown at the power plant where they worked on September 19. In Leningrad, a military court condemns 16 officials of a chemical plant for plotting with German agents.		In Brazil, General Dutra uncovers the "Cohen Plan," a documented plot for a Communist takeover. The Cohen Plan turns out to be a fraud, but Dutra and President Getulio Vargas use it to assume dictatorial powers over the next few months.	The Chapei (Zhabei) and Pootung districts of Shanghai are heavily bombed through the morning, but ground troops are unable to move into Chapei. Chinese troops, trained by Germany and under the command of Chang Fa-Kwei, hold the area with machine guns. Canton and Nanking are shelled, with the Japanese pilots and gunners focusing exclusively on military targets. . . . Cholera has now reached Tangku, near Nanking. In the International and French sections of Shanghai, there are 1,965 cases and 17 deaths from bubonic plague. . . . An epidemic disease, probably a form of dysentery, strikes over 5,200 people in Fukuoka, Japan, killing 280 in a few days.
Sept. 30	Britain approves the sale of fighter planes to China. . . . The League of Nations adopts a resolution endorsing nonintervention and demanding the withdrawal of foreign troops in Spain.	Former Spanish premier Largo Caballero is ousted as head of the Socialist Deputies, on the eve of the first meeting of Spain's Cortes (Parliament) since February. . . . France announces that 55,000 refugees in France will be returned to Spain before winter, starting immediately. . . . To resolve problems in Upper Silesia, Germany and Poland agree on a pact guaranteeing the rights of Poles in Germany and Germans in Poland. . . . British, French, and Italian governments will review and approve a plan to share Mediterranean patrol duties outlined in the Nyon agreement.			Tsingyuen, a town near Canton, is bombed, as are airfields at Ningpo, Soochow, Hangchow (Hangzhou), and Chinhai.
Oct. 1		Spanish insurgent planes drop shells on a school in Barcelona, killing at least 15 children and injuring 70 more. Thirty-five buildings are destroyed in the city as insurgents start a campaign of heavy shelling. On the north coast, Covadonga falls to the insurgents.	Britain deports members of the Arab High Committee in Palestine. Its president, the Mufti of Jerusalem, will not leave the Mosque el Omar, but he is stripped of his offices and income. Other leaders are taken by ship to the Seychelles. Press censorship is enforced and communications are cut.		After a night of artillery fire, groups of Japanese soldiers continue hand-to-hand fighting in the Chapei (Zhabei) district of Shanghai, but defenders do not let them advance. The German-trained 88th Division of China's National Army entrenches. . . . Two thousand cases of cholera and over 500 deaths are reported in the International Settlement of Shanghai.
Oct. 2	The League of Nations Assembly votes to end nonintervention toward Spain, but as it is not unanimous, the vote is not binding.	Britain and France demand that Italy pull its "volunteers" out of Spain. . . . The Soviets state that nonintervention ended when Britain and France ceased patrols. The Soviets want to ship arms to the Spanish government. . . . French police arrest an Italian anarchist for the September 11 bombings in Paris. . . . The Soviets reveal that the president, premier, and three commissars of the Tajik Soviet Republic (Tajikistan) have been removed from office for spying.		Brazil's Congress approves a 90-day "state of siege" (martial law) at the request of President Getulio Vargas, based on evidence of a plot to overthrow the government.	Japanese forces cross into Shantung (Shandong) province from the more northern province of Hopeh (Hebei). In Shansi (Shanxi) province, just below the Yenmen Pass, the walled city of Teichow, located near coal and iron mines, falls to Japan. Communication is cut between Shansi's two armies: the Eighth Route Army of Communist troops and that of Governor Yen Hsi-shan.
Oct. 3		Insurgent warships shell Barcelona and their planes bomb Valencia, hitting theaters and markets and killing over 100 people. . . . Thirty Londoners are hospitalized and 111 arrested after mobs of anti-fascists stop the scheduled march of a 2,000-strong fascist group along the Thames. . . . The executions of the president, vice president, and six high officials of Soviet Adjaria (part of Georgia) for treason are reported. Nine former officials are on trial in Moscow, but a new decree may spare many lives by allowing prison sentences of 25 years instead of death.	Arabs in many Palestinian cities close their shops in protest over the government's recent acts. . . . In Egypt, the meeting of a new political party breaks into small fights when Blueshirts—supporters of Premier Nahas Pasha—interrupt the meeting with demonstrations.		The Chapei district is bombarded again from warships, ground troops, and tanks, but Chinese soldiers hold their ground. To the north of Shanghai, however, Japanese troops gain a mile of ground covering 36 small villages near Liuhang. The buildings in the area are ruined by shelling but are still occupied, as the rice crop needs harvesting if the farmers are to eat over the winter.

A	B	C	D	E
Includes developments that affect more than one world region, international organizations, and important meetings of world leaders.	*Includes all domestic and regional developments in Europe, including the Soviet Union.*	*Includes all domestic and regional developments in Africa and the Middle East.*	*Includes all domestic and regional developments in Latin America, the Caribbean, and Canada.*	*Includes all domestic and regional developments in Asian and Pacific nations (and colonies).*

U.S. Politics & Social Issues	U.S. Foreign Policy & Defense	Economics & Great Depression	Science, Technology & Nature	Culture, Leisure & Lifestyle	
		George Rutledge, a banker in Johnstown, Pa., turns over to the NLRB records of the Citizens Committee formed during the steel strike. The records support his testimony that Bethlehem Steel contributed up to $30,000 to the anti-strike group. . . . AFL Teamsters go back to work, allowing hundreds of trucks to enter terminals in San Francisco and Oakland. The Teamsters ended their embargo after officials said that farmers stood to lose $100 million in produce if it continued.		Track and field athlete Ray Ewry, who won eight Gold Medals in the 1900 and 1904 Olympics, dies at age 62.	Sept. 29
	In a brief note, Japan responds to the U.S. protest of September 22 regarding the bombing of Nanking, announcing that there will be no change in their policy.	UAWA head Homer Martin says he has received threats since dismissing some top union organizers. At a Detroit hotel, he displays a gun when a group of 40 men demand to speak to him in his hotel room. Martin and the men later meet for three hours at a union hall. . . . Due to the high price of wholesale meat, 5,000 butcher shops belonging to the Confederation of Kosher Butchers threaten to strike tomorrow and not reopen after the Sabbath.			Sept. 30
New Supreme Court Justice Hugo Black addresses the nation by radio and admits he once joined the Ku Klux Klan, but quit before becoming a Senator and says his record speaks for itself. The speech and his decision to remain a justice are heavily criticized. . . . A Texas grand jury admits failure in attempts to identify the six men who lynched a man in Covington in mid-August.		Five hundred employees of Apex Hosiery in Philadelphia visit the mayor to ask for protection from the CIO. The employees, mostly women, claim the CIO promotes violence and intimidation. Apex, with its own company union, is the only company still being picketed; other hosiery mills settled with the union in July.			Oct. 1
President Franklin Roosevelt visits and speaks at the construction site of the Grand Coulee Dam in Washington state.		Kosher butchers strike in New York by refusing to open their shops at sunset. Isolated fights with rival butchers lead to 20 arrests. . . . The CIO offers to admit Apex Hosiery's company union to its ranks and end the picketing. . . . U.S. shoe makers, represented by civic and trade groups, publicize their objections to Secretary of State Cordell Hull's reciprocal trade agreement with Czechoslovakia. They feel lower tariffs will destroy their industry and cost American jobs. Secretary Hull dismisses this as "propaganda."	All sections of New Orleans experience street flooding, ranging from a couple of inches to four feet deep. Over 13 inches of rain falls in 22 hours; the flooding is the worst since 1927.		Oct. 2
		Railroad companies and unions avert a strike and agree on a pay increase of 44 cents per day, adding $35 million a year to payrolls.	The American Viscose Company completes the first factory devoted to rayon production in Nitro, W.Va., with an expected output of 20 million tons per year.		Oct. 3

	World Affairs	Europe	Africa & The Middle East	The Americas	Asia & The Pacific
Oct. 4	In Geneva, Britain proposes invoking the Nine-Power Treaty, which guarantees an Open China, to the League of Nations.	A torpedo narrowly misses a British destroyer near Spain, and depth charges are dropped. After days of speculation, British authorities announce that the torpedo attack never happened. . . . The Yugoslav Cabinet changes slightly, but observers feel the only purpose was to show Serb and Croat reformers that Premier Stoyadinovitch is still in control. . . . News of executions continues to appear in Soviet newspapers. In the last two weeks, 114 people have been executed for crimes such as espionage, hooliganism, and spoiling grain. The head of the Moscow zoo and several animal keepers are removed and tried for scaring and poisoning the animals.		In Brazil, former army officer Triffino Correa is arrested. He is suspected of involvement in the recently revealed plot to overthrow the government and is accused of being one of 35 leaders of the 1935 leftist conspiracy.	Japan's Foreign Office releases a report detailing the reasons for attacks upon 20 Chinese fishing boats. According to the report, some were transporting arms or soldiers and others fired upon Japanese ships first. . . . In Shantung, the city of Tehchow (Dezhou) is reported captured by the Japanese, though fighting continues for two days before the Chinese confirm this. . . . The Japanese are accused of using poisoned gas during a two-day attack on the Lotien-Liuhang areas.
Oct. 5	Prompted by U.S. President Franklin Roosevelt's speech, the League of Nations Far Eastern Advisory Committee condemns Japan as an invader and expresses moral support to China.	Spanish government troops in Madrid have been isolating insurgents near the Usera suburb for two weeks; tonight there is close fighting with bayonets and hand grenades. . . . Premier Benito Mussolini's 20-year-old son Bruno flies airplanes for Spain's rebels, leading a squadron of 23 Italian pilots. . . . Polish universities set aside "ghetto seats" in classrooms for Jewish students. The Nationalist press hails this as the next step in eliminating Jewish students altogether. In some schools, Jewish students stand rather than accept such seats.	South African police use rifles, bayonets, and tear gas to stop the fighting in gold mines among 2,000 native workers. Authorities state that rivalry between Pondo and Basuto tribesmen is to blame for two days of violence.		Aerial dogfights take place over Nanking (Nanjing) and the capital of Shansi, Taiyuan. The former city is bombed and its airfield heavily damaged. This makes the 50th air attack on Nanking.
Oct. 6	The League of Nations unanimously adopts the resolution of its committee, paving the way for discussions by the Nine-Power signatories.	Rebel advances in Asturia, Spain, are hampered by days of fog and snow and by snipers. Spain's National Defense Minister strips the army of all political authority. . . . Britain and France give Italy 24 hours to respond to their demand to discuss removing troops from Spain. . . . The Serb-Croat alliance begets the Agrarian-Democratic Party in Yugoslavia, demanding an end to dictatorship. . . . Turkey will build an air force and is placing orders for 1,000 planes with European and U.S. companies.		Premier Mitchell Hepburn is reelected in Ontario, Canada, with a large majority. . . . Torrential rains damage the Matagalpa region of Nicaragua.	Warships shell Chapei in preparation for another assault, but Japanese troops are beaten back once again. In the south, Canton (Guangzhou) reports air strikes after three days of peace. Fishing villages and boats in the province of Kwangtung (Guangdong) are shelled; hundreds are reported killed. Military targets and airfields in Nanking are shelled in three raids, and other northern cities are bombed as well.
Oct. 7		Spanish insurgent planes drop bombs and leaflets demanding surrender on Cangas de Onis, near Gijón, in Asturias. . . . German music teachers are forbidden to instruct Jewish students by a new decree. . . . Workers in Poland threaten a general strike over the suspension of the board of a teachers' union. The strike is averted when Premier Skladkowski meets with the Labor Federation.		President Getulio Vargas gives power to state governors and to a committee headed by Minister de Macedo Soares during Brazil's "state of war." Strict censorship of the mail and press is imposed. The political prisoners released in June are rearrested.	Observers of Japan say the country cannot back down from its stand in China without showing weakness and that Japan is truly surprised by other nations' condemnations. . . . Fighting renews near Paoting (Baoding), the captured capital of Hopeh. During the night, Japanese gunships on the Whangpoo (Huangpu) River fire a heavy barrage on Chapei, Pootung, and Hongkew in Shanghai.
Oct. 8	In answer to criticisms about its actions in China, Japan's Foreign Office states that the League of Nations and the United States lack understanding of the true circumstances. Japan blames China for the initial incident, the spread of violence, and the threat to peace, which Japan endeavors to resolve.	In southern Spain, insurgents bomb Reus and Alicante, and loyalists bomb Majorca. . . . Britain threatens to allow France to open its border with Spain (which is unofficially open), and still waits on an answer about discussing troop withdrawals. Meanwhile, Italian planes and troops are delivered to insurgent forces, and Italy's Libyan garrison is reinforced. . . . A German appeals court rules there is no justification for incarcerating Reverend Niemoeller, but he is not released. . . . Jewish students in Poland stage a three-day strike against "ghetto seating."	In Egypt, a Muslim student demonstration and march against Britain's policies toward Palestine is broken up by authorities.		Warships again shell Shanghai. In the drive toward Taiyuan along the rail lines, Japan claims to capture Chengting. Chinese troops mass and fortify positions along the south bank of the Yellow River in Shantung. Twenty Japanese bombers attack Taian (Tai'an), also in Shantung. . . . Once more, Japan is accused of using poison gas in China.

A	B	C	D	E
Includes developments that affect more than one world region, international organizations, and important meetings of world leaders.	*Includes all domestic and regional developments in Europe, including the Soviet Union.*	*Includes all domestic and regional developments in Africa and the Middle East.*	*Includes all domestic and regional developments in Latin America, the Caribbean, and Canada.*	*Includes all domestic and regional developments in Asian and Pacific nations (and colonies).*

U.S. Politics & Social Issues	U.S. Foreign Policy & Defense	Economics & Great Depression	Science, Technology & Nature	Culture, Leisure & Lifestyle	
In spite of vitriolic protests, Hugo Black takes his seat on the Supreme Court for the first time. . . . The year's eighth lynching takes place in Florida, when five hooded men stop a sheriff transporting an African-American prisoner at midnight. The prisoner, J.C. Evans, is shot to death.		A trial commences in Madison, Wisc., on price-fixing charges for 46 oil company executives, 23 oil companies, and 3 trade publishers. . . . At the AFL convention in Denver, Colo., William Green attacks the CIO and declares he will drive it out of existence.			Oct. 4
	President Franklin Roosevelt declares that "America hates war," and will work for peace, implying that certain aggressive countries should be quarantined as if they were diseased. He warns that isolation and neutrality will not help the United States evade the instability in the world.	New York Mayor Fiorello LaGuardia meets with a committee from the Federation of Kosher Butchers in an attempt to end the strike. . . . Forty-four Pennsylvania coalminers refuse to leave Shaft #7, staging a strike 1,350 feet below ground. The miners have been battling for weeks over different pay methods at the Lehigh Navigation Coal Company.			Oct. 5
	The State Department declares Japan an aggressor and violator of treaties, citing the Nine-Power Treaty and the Kellogg-Briand Pact. Many see this as abandoning U.S. neutrality.	A ruling by the National Labor Relations Board (NLRB) allows smaller, "craft" unions to coexist with plantwide industrial unions. This angers the CIO because the smaller unions are AFL-affiliated. . . . Four of the "stay-down" coalminers leave the strike due to illness.		The Yankees and the Giants meet once again for the World Series baseball championship; all games will be played in New York. . . . Planning for next season, the Brooklyn Dodgers acquire shortstop Leo Durocher from St. Louis, trading away four other players.	Oct. 6
	The United States accepts an invitation to a Nine-Power summit in Belgium on October 30.	Business continues to produce and sell at high levels in spite of cuts in many federal funds, such as veterans' bonuses and relief, the Treasury announces. . . . The Federation of Kosher Butchers yields to rabbinical and civic pressure and will reopen shops on October 9. . . . The AFL, which is boycotting German goods as long as Nazis are in power, suggests a boycott on Japanese products.	Polish judge, politician, and activist Maria Szyszkowska is born in Warsaw.		Oct. 7
Alabama's Attorney General files protests with the Supreme Court over the efforts of Heywood Patterson, a Scottsboro defendant, to have his conviction overturned.	The CIO announces a drive to unionize defense, munitions, and naval shipyard workers. . . . Britain's Prime Minister Neville Chamberlain hails the speech by U.S. President Franklin Roosevelt and calls the United States "the most powerful country in the world."	CIO officials urge the end of the "stay-down" strike over concerns for the miners' health. However, 7,000 coalminers walk away from their work in support, defying the CIO, John L. Lewis, and their employer, Lehigh Navigation Coal Company. . . . At Mayor Fiorello LaGuardia's request, federal and state officials meet with representatives of the Kosher butchers at New York's City Hall.			Oct. 8

F	G	H	I	J
Includes elections, federal-state relations, civil rights and liberties, crime, the judiciary, education, healthcare, poverty, urban affairs, and population.	Includes formation and debate of U.S. foreign and defense policies, veterans affairs, and defense spending. (Relations with specific foreign countries are usually found under the region concerned.)	Includes business, labor, agriculture, taxation, transportation, consumer affairs, monetary and fiscal policy, natural resources, pollution, and accidents.	Includes worldwide scientific, medical, and technological developments, natural phenomena, U.S. weather, and natural disasters.	Includes the arts, religion, scholarship, communications media, sports, entertainment, fashions, fads, and social life.

	World Affairs	Europe	Africa & The Middle East	The Americas	Asia & The Pacific
Oct. 9	Italy offers its diplomatic support to Japan.	Insurgents renew their drive on Cangas de Onis, on the main road to Gijón, with heavy air strikes. . . . Italy refuses to participate in discussions of troop withdrawal in Spain. . . . Yugoslavia's Premier announces that the Vatican Concordat—which has caused riots and new political coalitions—will not be submitted to the Senate for approval. . . . In Romania, some socialist unions declare they will not take jobs that belonged to racial minorities who were forced out. The union members are deemed "anti-patriots."		Swarms of locusts destroy half the crops in Nicaragua, and automobiles must use snow chains to get through the piles of dead bugs on the roads.	Japanese forces launch a 90-mile offense along the Peiping-Hankow Railroad and east to Shengtze. Twenty Chinese divisions engage them at Shihkiachwang. Towns in Shansi and Hunan provinces, as well as Shanghai, are bombed by Japanese fliers. . . . In a radio address, Generalissimo Chiang Kai-shek warns China not to depend on outside help and prepares them for a long war.
Oct. 10		An anti-fascist mob of 10,000 attacks a rally and injures speaker Sir Oswald Mosley in London. . . . Berlin's Catholic Bishop von Preysing describes a slow, systematic de-Christianizing of Germany in a widely published letter. . . . The head of the Danzig (Gdansk) Nazi party announces a new drive against Jews, starting with a boycott of shops. . . . Heinrich Rutha and 13 other members of the Czech Nazi party are arrested for practicing homosexuality.		In Veracruz, Mexico, the military commander kills the state's Attorney General, then is shot and killed himself by an aide. The aide then commits suicide.	Japan's General Terauchi captures Shihkiachwang by outflanking troops along the Huto River. . . . Nanking hospitals treat soldiers suffering from burns and blisters from mustard gas attacks.
Oct. 11	In a show of support for Japan, Italy and Germany recall officers and experts in China who had helped that country build up its air force.	Insurgents capture Cangas de Onis after incendiary bombs reduce the town to ruins. Rumors tell of severe food shortages in Gijón, now crowded with refugees. Madrid suffers its worse bombing of the war: at least 1,500 shells in 70 minutes (Ernest Hemingway helps to count). . . . The Agrarian-Democratic Party joins with the Legitimists (the pro-monarchy party) to form a large coalition in Hungary. . . . The Premier of Azerbaidjan is removed from office. In the last few months, leaders of all Soviet republics have been replaced.		General Cedillo, formerly with President Lázaro Cárdenas's Cabinet, has armed the largest private army in Mexico, in San Luis Potosi. He is now beset by federal troops with orders to divide his estates among communal groups of peons.	Warships on the Whangpoo shell Shanghai; the Canton-Hankow Railroad and several airfields are also bombed and damaged.
Oct. 12	Three Japanese planes fire machine guns at three cars carrying British envoys on a major highway outside Shanghai. No one is hurt.	The Spanish government announces that all ministries will move to Barcelona from Valencia. . . . France and Yugoslavia renew a pact of friendship for five years. . . . Poland arrests 70 fascists for anti-Jewish rioting; the purpose is to eliminate particular far-right groups, rather than to protect the rights of Jews. . . . *Pravda* and *Izvestia* announce Soviet congressional elections on December 12, when up to 100 million may vote. . . . In the Buryat-Mongolian Soviet Republic (Buryat Republic, Russia), 54 people are shot for espionage.		For a reason never clarified, President Rafael Trujillo of the Dominican Republic orders all Haitians in his country killed. The military murders thousands with clubs and machetes. Over 20,000 may have died; the news is suppressed.	Japanese forces report capturing more towns as they push south through Hopeh toward the Shansi province. . . . Japanese authorities deny using gas in any attack.
Oct. 13		Fearing an attack on Minorca, British and French ships patrol the sea near the Spanish islands. . . . To appease Italy, Britain agrees to take the issue of removing volunteers from Spain back to the Non-Intervention Committee. . . . While recent elections in France support the current government, run-offs today indicate a split with socialist factions. . . . Germany pledges in writing to respect Belgium's territorial integrity and neutrality.		The U.S. State Department is told that Mexico's foreign policy is based on eliminating foreign investors and holding Mexico for Mexicans.	Japanese planes bomb towns along railroads in several provinces in nine separate raids. The Japanese capture of Kweisui (Hohhot), capital of the far-eastern province of Suiyuan (Inner Mongolia), is confirmed. . . . Foreigners report army desertions and a collapse of Japanese authority in outlying areas of Manchukuo (Manchuria).
Oct. 14	Italy makes public that 102 Italian troops died combating uprisings in the Shoa (Shewa) district of Ethiopia during September. Many Ethiopians were killed as well, and rebel leaders were executed. . . . China accuses Japan of gas attacks before the League of Nations.	Insurgent and loyalist artillery pound each other across eight miles of the 150-mile-long Aragon front. The main attack is at Fuentas de Ebro. At least 180,000 men on both sides have entrenched. . . . In Poland, 1,000 Jewish students strike a second time against "ghetto seats" in universities.	In Palestine, an Arab is killed by his own bomb as he attacks a bus and 11 Jews are injured. A second bus attack results in another Arab death and five Jews hurt. Six more are injured when a train traveling to Haifa is dynamited. Sabotage derails a train engine and three men, all Arab, attempt to attack passengers. Two of the three are shot and killed; the third is wounded.		Japanese spokesmen estimate that 200,000 Chinese soldiers have died in the ongoing struggle for Shanghai. In the Chapei district, Chinese troops take the offensive and pound Japanese positions through the night.

A	B	C	D	E
Includes developments that affect more than one world region, international organizations, and important meetings of world leaders.	Includes all domestic and regional developments in Europe, including the Soviet Union.	Includes all domestic and regional developments in Africa and the Middle East.	Includes all domestic and regional developments in Latin America, the Caribbean, and Canada.	Includes all domestic and regional developments in Asian and Pacific nations (and colonies).

U.S. Politics & Social Issues	U.S. Foreign Policy & Defense	Economics & Great Depression	Science, Technology & Nature	Culture, Leisure & Lifestyle	
Father Charles Coughlin announces he will quit his radio show after Archbishop Edward Mooney withholds approval of an article.	State Department officials meet with all U.S. Consuls in Mexico to exchange information and consider changes in policy.	Five thousand Kosher butchers open their shops upon promises of inquiries into high prices. Meat is 2 to 5 cents per pound cheaper than last week. . . . Employers tell "stay-down" strikers that their wage demands will be met when they leave the mine; strikers insist on seeing the offer in writing or they will stay in the mine until they die.			Oct. 9
Prof. Albert Einstein writes to the YMCA on its Founders' Day fête, and urges all to reject compromise with tyranny and oppression.		Governor George Earle of Pennsylvania obtains an agreement from management of the Lehigh Navigation Coal Company and personally carries it down to Shaft #7. Ten thousand people cheer as the governor and stay-downers emerge from their mine, ending their strike.		The New York Yankees win the World Series in five games.	Oct. 10
The Supreme Court rejects a request from Boston attorneys to remove Justice Hugo Black from the bench.		In an effort to unionize interstate truckers, the AFL calls on the 61,000 union drivers in Pennsylvania to picket. . . . At its annual convention, the AFL votes to expel CIO-affiliated unions.		Ogden Mills, secretary of the treasury under President Herbert Hoover, dies at age 53. . . . Former Army chief of staff Maj. Gen. Douglas MacArthur announces his retirement at the end of this year. . . . A young Isaac Stern plays his first New York City concert in Town Hall.	Oct.11
President Franklin Roosevelt calls a special session of Congress for November 15 to discuss social legislation such as crop controls, minimum wages, and regional planning.	The U.S. Consul General in Syria, J. Theodore Marriner, is shot to death by an Armenian man who was denied a visa.	The CIO asks for a conference with 100 men each from the AFL and CIO to work for common goals.		Seabiscuit, a racehorse, wins the Continental Handicap by five lengths.	Oct. 12
		At its convention, the AFL attacks the practices of the NLRB as well as the Wages and Hours Bill before Congress. The CIO, holding its conference in Atlantic City, also criticizes the NLRB.			Oct. 13
		The AFL sends a message to the CIO, suggesting a smaller body than the 200 proposed to attend the discussion. The meeting is scheduled for October 25.	Television pictures are broadcast from the Empire State Building in New York to a 3 by 4-foot screen at Radio City—a distance of 15 blocks.		Oct. 14

F	G	H	I	J
Includes elections, federal-state relations, civil rights and liberties, crime, the judiciary, education, healthcare, poverty, urban affairs, and population.	Includes formation and debate of U.S. foreign and defense policies, veterans affairs, and defense spending. (Relations with specific foreign countries are usually found under the region concerned.)	Includes business, labor, agriculture, taxation, transportation, consumer affairs, monetary and fiscal policy, natural resources, pollution, and accidents.	Includes worldwide scientific, medical, and technological developments, natural phenomena, U.S. weather, and natural disasters.	Includes the arts, religion, scholarship, communications media, sports, entertainment, fashions, fads, and social life.

	World Affairs	Europe	Africa & The Middle East	The Americas	Asia & The Pacific
Oct. 15	Italy and Yemen agree to extend their 1926 treaty for 25 years.	The governor, judges, and officials of Asturias arrive in France, having fled Gijón.	Two British constables are ambushed and killed in Palestine. . . . The capitulatory system ends in Egypt, and a 12-year transition period to independence begins.		A unit of China's Eighth Route Army recaptures towns in northern Shansi, including the mountain passes at Yenmen and Pinghsingkwan (Pingxingguan). Japanese planes damage rail stations at Hangchow in Chekiang (Zhejiang) province. In Shanghai, the Pootung industrial area is shelled again.
Oct. 16		Spanish loyalists strike at Saragossa with planes and tanks. Up to 400,000 troops are involved. . . . As the Non-Intervention Committee meets, Italy offers to withdraw some troops from Spain if foreign troops are withdrawn from loyalist forces. . . . A Nazi party is formed from three groups in Hungary in support of the Horthy administration.	The Grand Mufti of Jerusalem escapes from his sanctuary in the Mosque of Omar into Damascus, Syria. . . . Terrorists burn the Lydda airport of Palestine that is under construction. In retaliation, British troops occupy Lydda, fining it £5,000. They arrest 150 Arabs and blow up two houses where terrorists live.	Reserves in the Bank of Mexico fall to 52.2 percent.	Japanese planes bomb the coastal cities of Shantung province, as well as Hangchow and towns as far south as the Kiangsi (Guangxi) province. . . . Japanese officers assemble reporters in Shanghai and announce that China is using poison gas, not Japan.
Oct. 17		Asturians begin to evacuate, burning towns as the insurgents approach. . . . Czech police suppress a Sudeten Deutsch Party (Nazi) demonstration. The Party earned about 15 percent of the vote in the last elections.	Several attacks against Jews throughout Palestine, including the shooting death of a 10-year-old boy, bring reactions from authorities. Eighteen houses are dynamited by police, and armed guards will ride on trains.	In Brazil, Governor Flores de Cunha resigns with his Cabinet over the requisition of troops from his state, Rio Grande do Sul. Citing dangers from Communists in the state, President Getulio Vargas puts a military officer in charge instead of appointing a new governor.	In Shansi, 50,000 Japanese soldiers are trapped and cut off from supply lines as Chinese troops now hold important mountain passes, pinning them in. Paotow (Baotou), a major city in Suiyuan, falls to Japan's Manchukuoan troops. Chinese planes raid Yangtzepoo and Hongkew in Shanghai through the night.
Oct. 18		General Franco reinforces his Aragon front using many Italian troops; the four Navarese Brigades in Asturia press closer around Gijón, capturing all towns in the area. . . . Italy claims only 40,000 of its troops serve with Franco, implying that Britain and France are manipulating the truth. . . . German papers accuse Czech police of beating the Nazi party members who demonstrated yesterday, and urges intervention by Germany in Czech affairs. In a letter to President Benes, Konrad Henlein, leader of the Sudeten Deutsch, demands autonomy for the Sudentenland.	Notable among several violent incidents in Palestine is an armed band of 20 Arabs that attacks a police station, disarms the police, and drives them away.	A Supreme Court ruling in Cuba forces the country into unplanned elections before April 1938.	Fierce fighting rages in Shansi province. In Shantung, refugees run from the capital city Tsinan (Jinan) as battle comes within 30 miles. In Shanghai, 1,400 Chinese troops and 3,000 Japanese die in an all-out attack, in addition to hundreds of noncombatants. . . . British authorities in Hong Kong begin an investigation into the attacks on fishing junks. . . . President Manuel Quezon of the Philippines asks for independence in 1939 before his National Assembly.
Oct. 19		The Non-Intervention Committee meets but makes no progress. . . . Italy attacks its deficit and funds its arms buildup by raising taxes. Stock companies must pay a 10 percent levy on capital. . . . Jewish factories, shops, and offices close in protest of "ghetto seats" in Poland's universities.	Bombs are thrown in Jewish settlements and at transportation lines, and shots are fired in Palestine.		Japanese planes make several raids over Nanking and drop 500-pound bombs close to U.S. ships. In Shanghai, Japanese spokesmen warn that all railroads, warehouses, and stations are legitimate military targets. . . . Japan's Cabinet approves a nearly $60 million cut from its budget to meet war costs.
Oct. 20		Suburbs of Gijón see hand-to-hand fighting, and parts of the city burn. . . . Italy breaks the Non-Intervention Committee deadlock, proposing that belligerent rights be given to both sides in Spain after a token amount of foreign volunteers are withdrawn. Britain and France agree. . . . Czechoslovakia protests the "aggressive and menacing" attacks by the German press. Foreign Minister Neurath replies that grave, unwarranted Czech attacks on Germans in Sudeten are the cause. . . . In five months, Soviet papers have reported 527 executions for sabotage or espionage. The actual total is rumored to be twice that amount.	Defying League of Nations principles, the Palestinian government restricts Jewish immigration. Random violence continues; 39 have died since July 7, when the division of Palestine was proposed. Of those who died, 33 were Arab.		The Eighth Route Army of China is active in Shansi province, although Japan denies losing control of the Yenmen Pass. In Nanking, administration buildings and airfields are damaged by 500-pound bombs dropped from Japanese planes. China claims to drive Japanese troops from north Shantung province. Chinese planes shell targets in seven night raids over Shanghai. Rather than fire anti-aircraft guns, the Japanese send their own planes aloft to chase away the enemy. At the Kiangsi capital, Nanchang, bombs damage factories, barracks, and an engineering school.
Oct. 21		Spanish insurgents capture Gijón and loyalists abandon their siege of Oveido. In Gijón, rapes, murders, and looting go on for days, amid parades and victory celebrations. . . . Danzig has dissolved the Catholic Center Party, allowing the National Socialist Party complete control. Minority Poles have no representation. . . . In Irkutsk, Siberia, 45 more executions are reported. The perceived threat of Japanese aggression is reflected in many of the charges of espionage. . . . While papers expose the existence of "Sudeten Brigades" in Germany, the Czech Cabinet votes to postpone municipal elections. It also bans all political gatherings.	A Jewish policeman, bus passengers, and a university professor are all shot and injured in different attacks in Palestine. The professor later dies.	The United States, Costa Rica, and Venezuela officially offer to mediate in the boundary dispute between Nicaragua and Honduras.	Chinese and Japanese troops battle for Tachang, six miles north of Shanghai. Several districts of Shanghai are shelled during the night. Air fields and arsenals in Nanking are bombed. In Shansi, Japanese troops try to repair rails and engines to reestablish a link with forces fighting China's Eighth Route Army.

A	B	C	D	E
Includes developments that affect more than one world region, international organizations, and important meetings of world leaders.	*Includes all domestic and regional developments in Europe, including the Soviet Union.*	*Includes all domestic and regional developments in Africa and the Middle East.*	*Includes all domestic and regional developments in Latin America, the Caribbean, and Canada.*	*Includes all domestic and regional developments in Asian and Pacific nations (and colonies).*

U.S. Politics & Social Issues	U.S. Foreign Policy & Defense	Economics & Great Depression	Science, Technology & Nature	Culture, Leisure & Lifestyle	
		The International Longshoremen's Association, an AFL affiliate, calls a strike along the south Atlantic and Gulf coasts. In Tampa, Fla., 1,200 longshoremen walk off the job. The issues are higher wages, overtime, and shorter hours.		U.S. telegraph companies stop charging for punctuation in telegrams. . . . To Have and Have Not by Ernest Hemingway is published. . . . Shirley Temple's Heidi is released.	Oct. 15
A coal gas explosion in Mulga, Ala., kills 34 miners. . . . The Supreme Court agrees to review the case brought in April against the Aluminum Company of America.		From Tampa, Fla., up to Wilmington, N.C., 8,000 longshoremen strike. The majority of the men are African American.		Seabiscuit ends the Laurel Stakes horserace in a dead heat with Heelfly.	Oct. 16
		In Ardmore, Okla., 60 stripper wells of the Jones Oil Company are closed when employees strike over the firing of 12 union employees. Another strike that began for similar reasons, against independent oil companies on land owned by former U.S. senator William B. Pine, has gone on for four days.		Donald Duck's nephews, Huey, Dewey, and Louie, make their first appearance in a comic strip. . . . J. Bruce Ismay, once head of the White Star Line and a survivor of the Titanic, dies in London at age 74.	Oct. 17
		The stock and bond market suffers its worst decline in six years, as steel stocks lead the way down. . . . President Franklin Roosevelt now predicts a federal budget deficit of nearly $700 million. He orders the Public Works Administration (PWA) and the Reconstruction Finance Corporation (RFC) to make no further commitments for the fiscal year.			Oct. 18
		After another morning of selling, the stock market rallies. The heaviest day of trading since 1933 ends with 745 stocks down and 189 up.		Nuclear physicist and Nobel Laureate Lord Ernest Rutherford dies in England.	Oct. 19
		Yesterday's late rally continues, and 871 stocks close at higher values. Bonds and commodities also rise. The market in London is cautious. . . . The Northrup plant of Douglas Aircraft in California, closed by a strike since late August, will reopen and offers preferential hiring to former employees. . . . Oklahoma's governor meets with company and CIO officials over the oil strike. State troops guard the oil fields.			Oct. 20
		The CIO and Jones Oil Company agree to allow maintenance on idle pumps in Oklahoma, and half the state troopers are sent home.			Oct. 21

F	G	H	I	J
Includes elections, federal-state relations, civil rights and liberties, crime, the judiciary, education, healthcare, poverty, urban affairs, and population.	Includes formation and debate of U.S. foreign and defense policies, veterans affairs, and defense spending. (Relations with specific foreign countries are usually found under the region concerned.)	Includes business, labor, agriculture, taxation, transportation, consumer affairs, monetary and fiscal policy, natural resources, pollution, and accidents.	Includes worldwide scientific, medical, and technological developments, natural phenomena, U.S. weather, and natural disasters.	Includes the arts, religion, scholarship, communications media, sports, entertainment, fashions, fads, and social life.

	World Affairs	Europe	Africa & The Middle East	The Americas	Asia & The Pacific
Oct. 22		In rebel-controlled Spain, a decree sets up the Fascist National Council, with General Franco at its head. He becomes a dictator with the right to name his successor. . . . The Non-Intervention Committee hits snags as members try to agree on the details and timetables of the October 20 compromise. . . . In Danzig markets, Jewish traders are beaten and forced away.	Fighting erupts in the Khemisset region of French Morocco. Incited by nationalist speeches, 1,000 Arabs attack government buildings. French colonial troops suppress the rioting quickly, and within a day most leaders are tried and sent to prison.	President Frederico Paez of Ecuador resigns suddenly and without explanation. His War Minister, General Alberto Enriquez, is appointed "Supreme Chief."	A mass meeting in Kweisui, capital of Suiyuan province, leads to a declaration of independence from China, according to Japanese sources. Suiyuan changes its name to Mongolia and will be governed in a style like Manchukuo, answering to Japan.
Oct. 23		Barcelona's chief of police uncovers a widespread espionage ring operating in many military branches, which sends information to insurgents through a base in France. . . . Italy warns that it will make no more concessions and blames the Soviet Union if Non-Intervention talks fail. . . . Jewish shop windows are smashed and businesses vandalized in Danzig; the police do nothing.	Capping weeks of agitation, 1,000 anti-government rioters in Cairo, Egypt, are controlled by two police battalions, and 60 are hurt. Later, pro-government blueshirts riot and break windows.	To bring its arms program up to date, Nicaragua announces that all public employees will donate one month's salary toward rearmament. . . . In Brazil's Rio Grande do Sul state, two former military leaders are arrested for urging their troops to attack federal forces.	Not for the first time, a Japanese incendiary bomb falls on an American sector of Shanghai, injuring several and prompting diplomatic exchanges. Officials explain that a small gas tank exploded and fell from the plane. American experts do not accept this.
Oct. 24		French freighter *Oued Mella* sinks 50 miles from Barcelona after being bombed by an unidentified plane. The crew is rescued.	Anti-government students stage a sit-in at Giza University in Cairo. When 400 police arrive to dislodge them, they throw stones; six are injured in the melee.	Puerto Rico's police are criticized in a report by Earle K. James on the March 21 riots in Ponce, where 19 died. . . . Fifteen thousand Mexican Jews organize to ask President Lázaro Cárdenas for legal protection, pointing to anti-Jewish articles in the press, and legislation before Congress that would force many Jews out of business.	Fighting spreads to Honan (Henan) province. In the International Sector of Shanghai, a Japanese plane repeatedly machine-guns a party of 20 Europeans on horseback, as well as other civilians. Five men die and several are wounded. One of the dead is a British soldier.
Oct. 25	The Nine-Power Conference in Brussels will be postponed until November due to the upheaval in Belgium's government.	An aircraft marked with a Maltese cross bombs and destroys a French ship near Minorca. . . . Premier Paul van Zeeland of Belgium and his Cabinet resign amid allegations of improper payments at the National Bank. . . . Croat party leader Vladimir Matchek announces a fight to the finish with Yugoslav Premier Stoyadinovitch.	Authorities arrest four leaders of the Nationalist movement in French Morocco. Among documents seized in their homes, authorities find evidence of a vast Arab plot to reestablish a Muslim empire, engineered from Syria and Egypt.	Ministers of Haiti and the Dominican Republic deny the mid-month killing spree of Haitians. They declare that no border dispute exists and the rumors of 1,700 people killed are an exaggeration. . . . Exiled former governor Flores de Cunha of Brazil is accused of buying and importing $500,000 in arms from Germany.	Japanese troops and equipment crowd onto trains for Manchukuo, where they are needed to put down rebellions. At the same time, Japan opens a two-pronged drive on Taiyuan in Shansi province. . . . Observers say that a hundred villages near Shanghai are frequently bombed and strafed by Japanese planes, killing many noncombatants.
Oct. 26	Japan apologizes to Britain for the death of a British soldier in Shanghai.	Fifty thousand insurgent troops leave Asturias to join assaults on Madrid, and the city prepares its 56 air raid shelters. . . . Dr. Schacht announces he is no longer Germany's Economic Minister, but still heads the Reichsbank.	Arab terrorists ambush six buses traveling to Jerusalem. One passenger is killed and an Arab guard injured as local police fight off the terrorists until nightfall. Several other incidents, aimed mainly at Jewish settlements, are reported.		Japanese forces capture Tachang, north of Shanghai.
Oct. 27	Although Japan signed the original treaty, its Cabinet declines an invitation to the Nine-Power meeting, rescheduled for November 3 in Belgium. . . . The Japanese government apologizes to the United States for the attack on American citizens in Shanghai on October 24.	Unfounded rumors that Madrid surrendered to General Franco affect European stock markets. . . . Throughout Poland, the "ghetto seating" in schools causes controversies as students refuse to sit in them and some professors forbid the seats in their classrooms. This in turn provokes anti-Jewish gangs to heckle students and picket Jewish shops.	Nationalists and police clash again in French Morocco. Four Muslim men die, and nine others—including six police—are injured in Port Lyautey. Sixty rioters are arrested. Meanwhile, the first squadron of French planes arrives for air maneuvers in North Africa next month.	The Mexican state of Sonora, under Governor Yocupicio, has resisted land reform for months, but now capitulates to President Lázaro Cárdenas's policy. Rich farmland in Sonora's Yaqui Valley, much of it American-owned, will be redistributed to peons. . . . In line with President Cárdenas's wishes, U.S. and British oil companies sign an agreement with unions to abolish strikes. . . . In Cuba, the governor of Havana province is jailed in connection with the public murder of the president of a provincial council last week.	Chinese soldiers of the 88th Division finally abandon the Chapei section of Shanghai, setting off bombs and fires. Japanese planes drop 25- and 50-pound bombs on the retreating troops. . . . A Japanese plane dive-bombs and machine-guns a known British outpost in Shanghai five times. . . . Near the Hopeh-Shansi border, Japanese troops seize a pass and finally break the stalemate between armies. They begin their advance on Taiyuan. . . . In Fukien (Fujien) province, the island of Quemoy is occupied by Japan.
Oct. 28		Flooding in northeastern Spain disrupts military operations. Insurgents announce a blockade of the government's east coast. . . . Premier Benito Mussolini pledges Italy's support for Germany's claims to former colonies. . . . In Belgium, socialist Henri de Man will form a Cabinet as the new Premier.	At least a thousand die, probably several thousands, as a hundred villages are washed away by floods in Syria. . . . In French Morocco, police arrest hundreds of followers of Nationalist leader Moulay Allal el-Fassi.	To combat price increases forced by the bakers' union, Argentina prohibits the export of wheat and flour. Army and penitentiary bakeries have been alerted that they may have to work at full capacity to prevent bread shortages. . . . Defying government orders, Mexico's oil workers strike and close down a pumping station in the Poza Rica fields.	Confounding the Japanese expectations, Chinese troops hold fast and continue to shell Japanese positions and ships. One battalion remains in Chapei, under the command of Hsieh Chin-yuan (Xie Jinyuan). Their fight will be remembered as that of "The 800 Heroes." A 12-foot-wide Chinese flag is brought in to them by a female guide, Yang Huimin, who swims across the Soochow (Suzhou) River to deliver it. The flag is hung above the Sihang Warehouse.

A	B	C	D	E
Includes developments that affect more than one world region, international organizations, and important meetings of world leaders.	Includes all domestic and regional developments in Europe, including the Soviet Union.	Includes all domestic and regional developments in Africa and the Middle East.	Includes all domestic and regional developments in Latin America, the Caribbean, and Canada.	Includes all domestic and regional developments in Asian and Pacific nations (and colonies).

U.S. Politics & Social Issues	U.S. Foreign Policy & Defense	Economics & Great Depression	Science, Technology & Nature	Culture, Leisure & Lifestyle	
First Lady Eleanor Roosevelt speaks at Mother A.M.E. Zion Church in Harlem. New York Mayor Fiorello LaGuardia also talks.					Oct. 22
		Another day of falling stocks follows two days of gains. The market is down for the week. . . . An agreement is reached between longshoremen and shipping companies in Savannah, Ga.			Oct. 23
			Jean Batten of New Zealand sets a new record for flying from Australia to England: 5 days, 18 hours, 15 minutes.	In Long Island, N.Y., songwriter Cole Porter suffers compound fractures in both legs when his horse bucks and falls on him.	Oct. 24
The Supreme Court, with Justice Hugo Black recused, declines to hear the case of Scottsboro defendant Haywood Patterson, serving a 75-year sentence.		A three-man committee from the AFL and 10 representatives of the CIO meet in Washington for a peace parley. . . . Stock prices soar, and demand for Chrysler is so strong that trading is halted on that stock for an hour. . . . New Orleans shipowners agree to a pay raise for dock workers, ending the longshoremen's strike in that port and a 15-year dispute between northern and southern ports.		A Toledo businessman buys controlling interest in *Social Justice*, the publication of Father Coughlin. . . . Casey Stengel is named manager of the Boston Bees (Braves) baseball team. He formerly handled the Brooklyn Dodgers.	Oct. 25
		The CIO lays out terms before the AFL, asking jurisdiction over all industrial workers. The AFL finds this unacceptable.	A French seaplane, the *Lieutenant de Vaisseau Paris*, flies from French Morocco to Maceio, Brazil, and sets a new distance record of 3,435.3 miles in 34 hours, 28 minutes.		Oct. 26
	U.S. ships and troops in Shanghai announce they will fire on any aircraft attacking Americans. . . . Secretary of State Cordell Hull upholds reciprocal trade treaties as best for U.S. farmers, insisting that the tariffs of Smoot-Hawley hurt U.S. farmers more than any other group.	Shipping companies offer a new contract ending the strike against Atlantic ports. . . . The Federal Reserve Board lowers margin requirements from 55 to 40 percent, effective November 1. . . . While agreeing to meet again, the AFL rejects CIO proposals.			Oct. 27
		William Knudsen, the head of General Motors, speaks against further taxes on profits.	Rivers flood lowlands in Pennsylvania, Maryland, and West Virginia, forcing many from their homes. . . . Hungarian scientist Albert von Szent-Gyorgyi wins the Nobel Medal for Medicine for his work in isolating vitamins A and C.		Oct. 28

F	G	H	I	J
Includes elections, federal-state relations, civil rights and liberties, crime, the judiciary, education, healthcare, poverty, urban affairs, and population.	*Includes formation and debate of U.S. foreign and defense policies, veterans affairs, and defense spending. (Relations with specific foreign countries are usually found under the region concerned.)*	*Includes business, labor, agriculture, taxation, transportation, consumer affairs, monetary and fiscal policy, natural resources, pollution, and accidents.*	*Includes worldwide scientific, medical, and technological developments, natural phenomena, U.S. weather, and natural disasters.*	*Includes the arts, religion, scholarship, communications media, sports, entertainment, fashions, fads, and social life.*

	World Affairs	Europe	Africa & The Middle East	The Americas	Asia & The Pacific
Oct. 29		Insurgent General Quiepo de Llano claims several peaks in the contested mining area near Penarroyo in Córdoba, Spain. . . . At the Non-Intervention Committee meeting, the Soviet representative refuses to agree to grant belligerent rights. German Ambassador von Ribbentrop insists that decisions be unanimous, thus preventing a move without Soviet approval. . . . Mikhail Chernoff, the Soviet Commissar of Agriculture, is removed from office. In the last two months under his rule, 246 people have been executed for mismanaging corporate farms and 189 for damaging grain. A newspaper in Soviet Georgia reports the trial of 47 plotters who made two attempts on Josef Stalin's life, in 1933 and 1935. Thirteen of the accused were high-ranking officials in Abkhazia, an independent region of Georgia. The late Abkhaz president, Nestor Lakoba, was the ringleader. . . . Leon Trotsky's youngest son, Sergei Sedoff, an engineer arrested in a purge, is reported to die on this day as well, though the circumstances remain mysterious.	French and Senegalese troops impose tight curfews on several Moroccan cities as a plot to overthrow Sultan Siddi Mohammed, as well as French authorities, is suppressed. Borders are watched closely and tribunals operate through the night, convicting 255 agitators. . . . Shots fired at crowds in several areas of Palestine kill one Jewish man in Jerusalem and wound several others, including an Arab policeman.	By government order, the Poza Rica strike ends at 11:30 p.m. Mexico City's oil supply is already affected. At midnight, the pumping station at Palmosola is shut down by a new strike.	Chinese forces announce their retreat from Shanghai has stopped and their defenses along a north-south line are holding. . . . Japan claims to have lost less than 10,000 troops in China, but says China has lost 425,000.
Oct. 30	The Soviet-Manchukuoan border is the scene of minor skirmishes and major troop buildups, as both sides expect military aggression from the other.	President Manuel Azana of Spain signs the decree moving his government to Barcelona. . . . A rebel plane bombs and sinks a British freighter off the Catalan coast; no one is hurt. . . . Italy recalls its Ambassador to France because the French Ambassador in Rome has not presented credentials properly. . . . Dimitri Gitscheff, once a Cabinet minister, is sentenced to a year in jail for violating a Bulgarian law dissolving political parties. He is the leader of the Peasants Party.		A new Cabinet is appointed and sworn in by General Ernesto Montagne, premier of Peru, replacing the old Cabinet that resigned last night.	Fifteen shells fall in the International Settlement of Shanghai in the night and early morning, all from Japanese planes. Three Britons die and 40 are injured; Chinese noncombatants are killed as well. . . . Japan gives a one-day ultimatum to the last Chinese battalion in Chapei. Receiving orders from General Chiang Kai-shek, the surviving 358 soldiers withdraw, escaping to the International Settlement while nine wounded men stay in Chapei and provide cover. British troops disarm and intern them. Twenty-six are wounded in the escape; 200 dead are left in Chapei.
Oct. 31			French General Nogues discovers and crushes another anti-government plot in Fez, French Morocco. . . . An Arab band makes a second attack (the first was on October 18) on a police station in Daharieh, Palestine. Villagers rush to the station to prove they were not part of the attacking band.	El Salvador refuses to extradite General Encarnacion Arita to Honduras where he is charged with murder. The General participated in a failed Honduran uprising earlier this year and lives as a political refugee.	Three British soldiers are wounded in Shanghai when a Japanese shell aimed at new Chinese positions crashes into their hut. . . . The Nantao region of Shanghai is targeted by Japan; half of its 600,000 residents have fled. Japan claims that 20,000 Chinese troops hide there. . . . West of the International Settlement, Japanese troops cross the Soochow River through the night on temporary bridges.
Nov. 1	The League of Nations Conference on Terrorism begins in Geneva.	Loyalist Madrid begins a week of celebration in honor of the 20th anniversary of the Russian Revolution. . . . Municipal elections in England strengthen the Labor Party and fascist candidates are rejected. . . . Yugoslav police shoot into a crowd to break up a meeting of the Peasant Party in Novi Gradic, Croatia; four people die.	French authorities order the Mufti of Jerusalem to leave Syria. . . . More flooding in Syria leaves 60,000 homeless in Jebel Druze and Latakia (Al Ladhiqiyah), recently ceded to Syria by France. At least 2,000 die. Palestine is also affected, with 10 people missing.	The Inter-American Radio Conference opens in Havana. Its goal is to develop a unified policy for airwave use in advance of an international conference in Cairo in February. . . . Mexico's government nationalizes "sub-soil" rights, including oil. U.S. and British oil companies are ordered to increase wages by a third.	The Eighth Route Army of China, along with other Communist forces, is being reorganized into the Fourth Army under General Yeh Ting. Operating in the eight southern provinces, the Fourth Army will become official on December 25, 1937.
Nov. 2		Insurgents bomb the Catalan city Lerida (Lleida), far from any battlefront, in mid-afternoon. Over 50 children are among the 225 dead. . . . Spanish Defense Minister Prieto proclaims that deserters trying to reach France will be shot to death.		An army revolt engineered by former president Rafael Franco fails, and martial law is imposed in Paraguay. . . . Mexican courts refuse to hear cases from landowners whose property was seized for redistribution by the federal government.	Chinese troops claim to drive the Japanese back east and north across the Soochow (Suzhou) River. Japanese armies in Honan (Hunan) province march toward Changteh (Changde).
Nov. 3	The Nine-Power Far Eastern Conference opens in Brussels, Belgium. Fourteen nations attend, with more to join in a few days. Japan is absent.	Barbastro, 30 miles from Lerida, is bombed by insurgents and between 70 and 80 people die. . . . Britain decides to exchange envoys with Franco's rebel government in Spain. . . . Police in Danzig (Gdansk) seize the bank deposits of Jewish merchants. . . . Police arrest 40 students at Zagreb University in Yugoslavia for anti-government demonstrations sparked by the shootings in Croatia.	The trial of nationalist Messali Hadj, leader of the Party for Algerian People, begins.	A Bahamian court sentences brothers George and Willis Duvalier to death for their parts in the August riots on Great Inagua.	Hungjao in Shanghai is the latest district to see heavy fighting and shelling. . . . In Shansi (Shanxi) province, Japanese troops claim to capture Sinhsien. They say the fight for that city cost China 30,000 casualties.

A	B	C	D	E
Includes developments that affect more than one world region, international organizations, and important meetings of world leaders.	Includes all domestic and regional developments in Europe, including the Soviet Union.	Includes all domestic and regional developments in Africa and the Middle East.	Includes all domestic and regional developments in Latin America, the Caribbean, and Canada.	Includes all domestic and regional developments in Asian and Pacific nations (and colonies).

U.S. Politics & Social Issues	U.S. Foreign Policy & Defense	Economics & Great Depression	Science, Technology & Nature	Culture, Leisure & Lifestyle	
		The CIO opens a drive to build an industrial union of furniture and bedding workers; the AFL sees this as a "warlike gesture," bound to hurt the ongoing peace talks.	As the ocean liner *Britannic* cruises from London to Ireland, six experts watch a television set in a stateroom. "Telephotograms" are sent twice a day through October 31 from the BBC studios.		Oct. 29
					Oct. 30
					Oct. 31
		President Franklin Roosevelt announces financing of $85 million in loans to corn farmers through the Commodity Credit Corporation, with Reconstruction Finance Corporation (RFC) funding.		Groucho and Chico Marx (but not Harpo) are fined $1,000 each for using material on a radio show owned by other comedy writers.	Nov. 1
	The United States declines Cuba's invitation to join with American states in mediating Spain's civil war.				Nov. 2
Rep. Arthur Mitchell, an African American, testifies before the Interstate Commerce Committee about being forced into a second-class rail car during a trip through the south in April.				War Admiral wins his eighth consecutive horserace, the Pimlico Special. His total winnings of $166,500 is the highest in 1937.	Nov. 3

F	G	H	I	J
Includes elections, federal-state relations, civil rights and liberties, crime, the judiciary, education, healthcare, poverty, urban affairs, and population.	*Includes formation and debate of U.S. foreign and defense policies, veterans affairs, and defense spending. (Relations with specific foreign countries are usually found under the region concerned.)*	*Includes business, labor, agriculture, taxation, transportation, consumer affairs, monetary and fiscal policy, natural resources, pollution, and accidents.*	*Includes worldwide scientific, medical, and technological developments, natural phenomena, U.S. weather, and natural disasters.*	*Includes the arts, religion, scholarship, communications media, sports, entertainment, fashions, fads, and social life.*

	World Affairs	Europe	Africa & The Middle East	The Americas	Asia & The Pacific
Nov. 4		The French freighter *La Corse* escapes an air attack by insurgent planes off the coast of Spain near Barcelona. . . . Germany executes two Communist labor leaders, ignoring a request for clemency from William Green of the AFL sent months ago. . . . Heinrich Rutha hangs himself in his cell. The former official of the Sudeten Nazi Party was awaiting trial on immorality charges in Czechoslovakia. Other leaders of a Nazi youth group were arrested with him.	Arab terrorists in Palestine shoot and wound bus passengers and make attacks on a police station, a pipeline, and private homes.	Mexico cancels treaties and nationalizes 2 million acres of land, including 350,000 acres leased by Standard Oil in Tabasco and Chiapas. A French company loses 500,000 acres.	The fighting in Shanghai centers on the Soochow River. Japanese forces hold their position on the south side in the face of a Chinese onslaught that tries to force them back to the north.
Nov. 5	Japan's strongest force is massing along the Manchukuoan-Soviet (Manchuria-Russia) border, giving rise to fears that Japan will try to capture Vladivostok. . . . Germany's Ambassador to China, Oskar Trautman, transmits Japan's demands to China. General Chiang Kai-shek finds them unacceptable.	Spanish government planes bomb Saragossa and score a hit on a munitions dump. . . . In a secret meeting, Chancellor Adolf Hitler lays out a detailed plan of war preparations needed to ensure that Germany gets its needed "living space." . . . A new German-Polish pact governs treatment of minorities (Germans in Poland, and Poles in Germany), and may lay the groundwork for Poland's inclusion in an anti-Communist agreement. . . . Austrian Foreign Minister Guido Schmidt visits Berlin. Germany has cut its imports from Austria by 40 percent and owes the country $11 million.	In Lebanon, the assassin of U.S. Consul James Marriner is condemned to death by hanging. . . . Two British soldiers are shot and killed by Arab terrorists outside Jerusalem's Old City.		Japanese troops reach Taiyuan, capital of Shansi, and wait for reinforcements outside the city. The large railway city of Changteh in Honan province is variously reported as being in Japanese or Chinese hands.
Nov. 6	The Nine-Power conferees send a note to Japan asking the country to exchange views with a small group, in accordance with the Treaty. . . . Japan signs the Anti-Communism Pact with Germany and Italy. Italy then recognizes Japan's conquest of Manchukuo.	Heavy fighting resumes in Aragon as the weather clears.	Uprisings and terrorist acts occur regularly in Trans-Jordan (Jordan), but the news is suppressed by the government. On this day, Arab extremists bomb several buildings, cut telephone lines, attack a police station, and indulge in a two-hour gun battle with police. . . . Shootings in Palestine leave two Arabs dead, killed by police.	Minister Pastoriza of the Dominican Republic cables *The New York Times*, claiming the rumors of 1,000 Haitians dead in a border dispute is "absolutely ridiculous."	Japan lands new forces at Hangchow (Hangzhou) Bay, 110 miles south of Shanghai. As Japanese ships shell the shore through the fog, columns of men push inland; 40 planes bomb villages in advance of the marching shock troops, who travel through Chekiang (Zhejiang) province.
Nov. 7		Madrid celebrates the anniversary of standing fast against Franco's forces, which began their assault on the Spanish capital one year ago. . . . Celebrating the 20th anniversary of the Bolshevik Revolution, 1.5 million people parade in Moscow's Red Square. . . . Police in Hungary raid homes at 5 a.m. and drag over 500 Jewish men and women to jail. The goal, authorities say, is to find Polish Jews who have been sneaking into the country illegally. . . . In Germany, 95 Protestant pastors and lay leaders are imprisoned. Police have expelled 37 from their pulpits and 36 from their communities.		Mexico's congress passes laws aimed at Jews, including a request for a list of all Jews in Mexico and their property.	The Japanese forces landed at Hangchow Bay are reportedly within 25 miles of Shanghai. In Shanghai, Japanese troops have built bridges across the Soochow River. . . . Outside of Taiyuan's 35-foot-tall walls, Japan demands the city's surrender. Chinese troops defend the city with artillery and machine guns.
Nov. 8		The Soviet Ambassador to Italy asks for clarification of Italy's signature on the Anti-Communism Pact, and how it affects an agreement of friendship between Italy and the Soviet Union. . . . An anti-Semitic exhibit titled "The Eternal Jew" opens in Nuremberg. Anti-Semitic postal cards are issued to mark the occasion. . . . Belgium's new Premier Paul Spaak announces his new Cabinet, with Henri de Man as Finance Minister. . . . The Paris International Exposition is extended through 1938.		Brazil's Minister of Justice de Macedo Soares resigns without public explanation. Jose Campos, author of a new constitution, is appointed in his place. . . . Paraguay lifts martial law and releases many recently arrested prisoners. . . . New rumors hint that as many as 2,700 Haitians have died in the Dominican Republic since October 5. . . . Locusts, having destroyed half the crops of Nicaragua, are now being eaten by millions of seagulls.	At least 40 ships continue to shell the coast near Hangchow as more Japanese troops are landed; 25,000 of the troops landed earlier approach Sungkiang (Songjiang). Chinese troops evacuate Pootung to rush to Sungkiang's defense. Three days of bad weather clear, so Japanese airplanes shell Chinese troops as they retreat from Pootung and other Shanghai districts. . . . In Taiyuan, Japanese artillery pounds the city walls. Japan claims to hold one-third of the city. . . . In Kiangsu (Jiangsu) province, rail coaches are shelled and up to 200 civilians killed.
Nov. 9	Military planes leave France for maneuvers in Tunisia, Syria, French Morocco, Madagascar, and French Indo-China (Vietnam).	Heavy fighting on Spain's Aragon front centers around the Gallego River and valley. General Franco gives notice that he has mined and will blockade the coast of loyalist Spain. . . . Anti-Jewish riots break out in a few Polish universities where "ghetto seats" are still unused or not permitted. Several people are injured, and Jews who took part in earlier demonstrations are fined. . . . Reports of more Soviet trials and executions of high officials in both Abkhazia and Azerbaijan, near the Caucasus, reach Moscow.	In Palestine, five young men are shot to death while working on a road outside a Jewish colony. From this point on, Jewish groups take retaliatory action. Police use search dogs to track the killers back to the Arab village of Yalou and arrest 16 men.	Using new, anti-Communism laws, Quebec's Prime Minister Duplessis shuts down a Communist newspaper and a print shop, beginning a "red" purge in his province. . . . Both the Dominican Republic and Haiti censor news heavily, but travelers in Cuba report a mobilization of Dominican troops and up to 5,000 Haitian deaths. Some say attacks on unarmed Haitian laborers continue.	Chinese troops abandon Shanghai, leaving their outposts as late as dawn and setting fire to some buildings. Twelve thousand troops stay in the Nantao district, where they are shelled and machine-gunned. At least 6,000 civilians are trapped with them, unable to escape. Tens of thousands rush from Nantao and Pootung to European-held areas for refuge. An estimated 4 million Chinese, one-fourth of them refugees, live in Shanghai, along with thousands of foreigners. . . . After days of shelling and heavy street fighting, Japan claims capture of the Shansi capital, Taiyuan. No Chinese soldiers surrender.
	A *Includes developments that affect more than one world region, international organizations, and important meetings of world leaders.*	**B** *Includes all domestic and regional developments in Europe, including the Soviet Union.*	**C** *Includes all domestic and regional developments in Africa and the Middle East.*	**D** *Includes all domestic and regional developments in Latin America, the Caribbean, and Canada.*	**E** *Includes all domestic and regional developments in Asian and Pacific nations (and colonies).*

U.S. Politics & Social Issues	U.S. Foreign Policy & Defense	Economics & Great Depression	Science, Technology & Nature	Culture, Leisure & Lifestyle	
		While no commitments are made, the AFL and CIO talks are on friendly terms. Telegrams and messages indicate that most workers would like to see the two groups reconcile.			Nov. 4
The Duke and Duchess of Windsor cancel a much-publicized trip to the United States when union organizers threaten demonstrations against their host, Charles Bedaux. Bedaux's timing system of labor measurement has caused strikes and protests in many areas.		AFL and CIO officials discuss the place of labor and unions in industrial plants and mass production. . . . Secretary of Agriculture Henry Wallace suggests that cotton farmers reduce plantings to stabilize the market. . . . An advisory board of industry and labor representatives meets to discuss expanding Social Security to cover an additional 13 million people. The program covers 35 million already.		Seabiscuit sets a track record at Pimlico while winning the Riggs Handicap, and also takes the lead moneymaker title from War Admiral. Seabiscuit has now won $167,142 for the year. . . . Leopold Stokowski celebrates his 25th anniversary as conductor of the Philadelphia Orchestra.	Nov. 5
	The State Department, hearing rumors of the murder of Haitians in the Dominican Republic last month, orders U. S. Minister R.H. Norweb back to the Dominican Republic. He had been attending the Inter-American Radio Conference in Havana.	The Agricultural Adjustment Administration (AAA) will pay farmers $1.5 million to feed excess potatoes to livestock and keep them off the market.			Nov. 6
An old 80-room mansion in Kingston, N.Y., one of Father Divine's "heavens," burns down. It is the second huge fire in a year to take the preacher's property.					Nov. 7
					Nov. 8
Joseph Kennedy, Chair of the Maritime Commission, releases a comprehensive report on the dismal state of the U.S. shipping industry. He suggests a subsidy of $25 million a year, training for seamen, mediation boards for labor, and other amendments to the Merchant Marine Act.		President Franklin Roosevelt offers government cooperation and construction loans to utilities if they change their pricing methods. . . . Testimony that James Rand of Remington Rand paid to suppress evidence in his ongoing trial is given in a Connecticut court. Rand is charged with strikebreaking activities across state lines.		The first Labor Party prime minister of England, James Ramsay MacDonald, dies en route to South America. He suffered a heart attack while taking a doctor-ordered vacation.	Nov. 9

F	G	H	I	J
Includes elections, federal-state relations, civil rights and liberties, crime, the judiciary, education, healthcare, poverty, urban affairs, and population.	Includes formation and debate of U.S. foreign and defense policies, veterans affairs, and defense spending. (Relations with specific foreign countries are usually found under the region concerned.)	Includes business, labor, agriculture, taxation, transportation, consumer affairs, monetary and fiscal policy, natural resources, pollution, and accidents.	Includes worldwide scientific, medical, and technological developments, natural phenomena, U.S. weather, and natural disasters.	Includes the arts, religion, scholarship, communications media, sports, entertainment, fashions, fads, and social life.

	World Affairs	Europe	Africa & The Middle East	The Americas	Asia & The Pacific
Nov. 10		General Franco sends the loyalist government of Spain an ultimatum, demanding surrender by December 5. . . . The Danzig Senate publishes decrees prohibiting all political parties. There is little reaction as the decree was expected. . . . A conflict with Col. Gen. Hermann Goering over speeding up the Four-Year Plan is given as the reason for the recent resignation of Germany's Economics Minister.	Britain announces new rules to quell terrorism in Palestine. As of November 18, carrying arms or bombs can earn the death penalty. Military courts will deal with offenders.	Brazil's President Getulio Vargas unveils a new constitution, giving himself the power to rule by decree. Congress and most state and municipal bodies are dissolved. The president addresses the country by radio, explaining his reasons and asking the army to stay aloof from politics. . . . British and U.S. oil companies reject President Lázaro Cárdenas's salary demands for Mexican oil workers.	Japanese shock troops, tanks, and machine guns assault the last Chinese-held positions in Shanghai. Shells fly over the International Settlement into Nantao, prompting protests from European and U.S. officials. Japan's ships try to land troops during the night but are driven off by Chinese machine guns.
Nov. 11		Catalan and loyalist forces continue to skirmish with insurgents in northeastern Spain. . . . Britain passes the Coal Bill: effective in 1942, all coal will be owned by the government and managed by an appointed commission. . . . The Soviet Union arrests its ambassadors to Germany, Poland, and Turkey, as well as the heads of Soviet tourism and agriculture and an aircraft designer. . . . Extremists set off a large bomb at dawn on Armistice Day in Dublin, Ireland. Buildings are damaged, but no one is injured.	In spite of curfews and new rules, bombings and shootings continue in Palestine. Today the victims were Arabs.	Brazilian President Getulio Vargas's Cabinet resigns, along with two governors who have been replaced with military commanders. No violence is reported.	Japan lands 40,000 new troops in Hangchow Bay, where 34 warships now assemble. The latest recruits head for Yuyao, on the way to the city of Hangchow. . . . Under orders, Chinese troops in Nantao evacuate and turn themselves and their weapons over to authorities in the French Concession of Shanghai. . . . Up to a thousand may be dead in Tsumakoi, a mining village in Japan. A landslide clogs two of four shafts leading to the mine, causing gas to build and explode.
Nov. 12	Japan declines another invitation to attend meetings of the Nine-Power Far Eastern Conference.	Britain's Viscount Halifax, former Viceroy of India, will meet with Chancellor Adolf Hitler next week. . . . For the second time in five months, the leadership of White Russia (Belarus) changes. Premier Grad and Vice Premier Yuravloff are removed from office. . . . France's President Albert LeBrun inaugurates Le Bourget Airport. The site of Charles Lindbergh's landing, it has been rebuilt into the largest airport in Europe.		Eagle Oil, a subsidiary of Royal Dutch-Shell Oil, is promised concessions in the rich Poza Rican oil fields by Mexico's President Lázaro Cárdenas. . . . Brazil's Fascist Party is dissolved by its leader, who says the new constitution renders political parties unnecessary. Brazil's Supreme Court ratifies the new constitution.	Ten miles west of Shanghai, Japanese troops capture Nansiang. . . . Japanese planes bomb an Episcopalian mission, hospital, and church 95 miles from Nanking (Nanjing). The compound is being evacuated.
Nov. 13		President Azaña of Spain addresses his country via radio, defending the republic. . . . A report from Leningrad (St. Petersburg) reveals that prominent authors, professors, and diplomats have been purged in Finland and Estonia. . . . Romania's King Carol asks Ion Mihalache, leader of the National Peasant Party, to form a Cabinet and work with former premier Voivod, who is pro-Nazi. The current premier, Gheorghe Tatarescu, has not resigned.	Prisoners riot in Isiolo, Kenya, East Africa, at a camp holding 500 unarmed Ethiopians accused of deserting the Italian army. Guards fire into the crowd, killing nine and wounding 27—including 10 guards.	In a press conference, Brazil's President Getulio Vargas says his government is not fascist and will not enter into pacts with European nations. . . . Haiti asks the United States, Cuba, and Mexico to help settle the problems between Haiti and the Dominican Republic which led to the deaths of thousands last month.	Traveling west from Shanghai, the Japanese army has formed six columns to strike at different positions in China's defenses. Observers suspect a drive on Nanking by Japanese troops is planned. Fighting is reported in Kiating, Liuho, Taitsang, and nearby cities on the Yangtze River, Kunshan and Soochow.
Nov. 14		Moscow and Leningrad restrict the sale of liquor near schools and factories. . . . Ion Mihalache declines the offer of King Carol, so Premier Gheorghe Tatarescu is asked to form a coalition Cabinet in Romania.	Violence escalates in Palestine. After six men—five Arabs and one Jew—are killed and many other people injured in bus attacks, random shootings, and gang fights, police arrest the Jewish Revisionist Party leader and many of his followers.		By Japan's estimate, tens of thousands of Chinese soldiers die fleeing from air attacks near Soochow, Taitsang, and Kunshan. . . . After weeks of relative calm, Japanese troops renew a drive on Tsinan (Jinan), capital of Shantung (Shandong), moving along the Tientsin-Pukow Railway. . . Fresh Japanese troops, landed at Hangchow Bay, capture Sungkiang (Songjiang), Tsingpu, and—using motorized sampans—Pingwang.
Nov. 15	Fifteen of the 19 countries at the Nine-Power Conference vote for a referendum describing Japan's actions toward China as "out of step." Italy vote against the mild criticism, and three countries abstain.	A trial begins in Hamburg, Germany, for Arnold Bernstein and several directors of his Red Star Shipping Line, which has been run by trustees since February. They are accused of violating foreign exchange laws and could get the death penalty for "economic treason." . . . Seyyid Riza, his son, and five others die by hanging for their parts in the Kurdish uprising in Turkey last spring.	In Palestine, 45 Jews are arrested for the recent violence and 24 are sentenced to three months in a concentration camp near Acre.	Mexico's agreement with Eagle Oil is published. It overturns the guarantees to foreign investors in the 1928 Morrow-Calles Agreement, imposing royalties of up to 35 percent where none existed before. The implication is that Standard Oil and others could regain their oil fields if they agree to the new royalties.	Japan captures Kunshan, and the cities of Soochow and Wusih undergo intense shelling. . . . General Han Fu-chu, governor of Shantung, leads resistance to Japan but his loyalty to Nanking is questionable. He acts independently and has rejected the help of General Li Tsung-jen of Kwangsi (Guangxi) province.
Nov. 16	France bars the movement of men or munitions through Indo-China. Within days it is revealed that Japan has threatened France with reprisals should Indo-China be used to supply Chinese troops.	A wealthy contractor in France is arrested and found to be a member of the Cagoulards, an anti-fascist, anti-Communist group advocating violence and assassination. French police, who have secretly infiltrated the group, suspect there may be 30,000 members. More arrests and seizures of munitions stockpiles follow. . . . Efforts to form a coalition government in Romania fail; former premier Gheorghe Tatarescu will put together a functional Cabinet, mostly from his own party.		Cuban police arrest two young men and uncover a plot to assassinate Chief of Staff Batista.	The Japanese march toward Tsinan pushes south across the Yellow River. Hundreds of Japanese planes bomb Kiangsu province. Soochow and the walled city of Changshu are heavily shelled as well. . . . The Red Cross estimates China has suffered 800,000 casualties and thinks that 175,000 Chinese died at Shanghai and 250,000 died in north China.

A	B	C	D	E
Includes developments that affect more than one world region, international organizations, and important meetings of world leaders.	*Includes all domestic and regional developments in Europe, including the Soviet Union.*	*Includes all domestic and regional developments in Africa and the Middle East.*	*Includes all domestic and regional developments in Latin America, the Caribbean, and Canada.*	*Includes all domestic and regional developments in Asian and Pacific nations (and colonies).*

U.S. Politics & Social Issues	U.S. Foreign Policy & Defense	Economics & Great Depression	Science, Technology & Nature	Culture, Leisure & Lifestyle	
		President Franklin Roosevelt meets with business leaders and economic advisers, formulating ways to stimulate housing construction. . . . The NLRB orders Consolidated Edison of New York to break its contracts with an AFL union, saying that the union was forced on 30,000 employees and discriminates against a CIO union. The AFL and the company vow a court fight with the NLRB.	The Nobel Prize for Physics goes to Clinton Davisson of New York and George P. Thomson of London for their discovery of electron diffraction. The Nobel Chemistry Prize is awarded to Walter Haworth of England and Paul Karrer of Switzerland for work in carbohydrates, flavins, and vitamins.	The Nobel Prize for Literature is given to Frenchman Roger Martin du Gard.	Nov. 10
	The United States prepares to reopen its Consulate in Bilbao, Spain, an area now in rebel hands.		German pilot Wurster flies a Messerschmitt at just over 379 miles per hour, beating the speed record of 352.3 set by Howard Hughes in 1935. . . . A typhoon hits seven provinces of the Philippines, killing 33 people and leaving more than 40,000 homeless.		Nov. 11
					Nov. 12
		General Motors offers a new contract to employees that excludes almost everything asked for by the United Auto Workers of America (UAWA): wage increases, annual vacations, a 35-hour week, and shop steward program. The contract is rejected. . . . AFL's International Brotherhood of Electrical Workers takes out newspaper ads to list charges against the NLRB.			Nov. 13
	The United States agrees to join with Cuba and Mexico in negotiating for peace between Haiti and the Dominican Republic.			Ernest Hemingway announces he has written The Fifth Column, a play, in Madrid.	Nov. 14
Congress reconvenes in an extraordinary session called by the President. In a written message, President Franklin Roosevelt draws attention to an industrial recession and economic uncertainties, and mentions four areas needing immediate attention: agriculture, labor, executive reorganization, and planning for natural resources.		The CIO asks the NLRB to hold a consent election at Consolidated Edison for union representation. . . . Pickets at the Presto Lock Company in Brooklyn throw bricks and vandalize a car and the building. Police arrest 16 for rioting. The plant has been closed for a month by a strike, and rumors that it was to reopen led to the melee.			Nov. 15
A filibuster over an anti-lynching bill slows the Senate, and the House of Representatives finds its plans for action in disorder due to rebel Republicans.		Post offices deliver 85 million cards for the census of the unemployed; 72 percent return the card within a few days, giving the government a count of 10.8 million unemployed.			Nov. 16

F	G	H	I	J
Includes elections, federal-state relations, civil rights and liberties, crime, the judiciary, education, healthcare, poverty, urban affairs, and population.	Includes formation and debate of U.S. foreign and defense policies, veterans affairs, and defense spending. (Relations with specific foreign countries are usually found under the region concerned.)	Includes business, labor, agriculture, taxation, transportation, consumer affairs, monetary and fiscal policy, natural resources, pollution, and accidents.	Includes worldwide scientific, medical, and technological developments, natural phenomena, U.S. weather, and natural disasters.	Includes the arts, religion, scholarship, communications media, sports, entertainment, fashions, fads, and social life.

	World Affairs	Europe	Africa & The Middle East	The Americas	Asia & The Pacific
Nov. 17		British Cabinet Minister Lord Halifax travels to Germany, the first official step of Neville Chamberlain's appeasement policy. . . . Clergy may no longer join the Nazi party in Germany. . . . Poland's foreign office declares that Poland will not interfere in Danzig's internal affairs. . . . After six months of talks, Czechoslovakia and Hungary sign a commercial agreement. . . . Nursery school teachers in Leningrad are tried for plotting to distort education and abuse children.		Mexico's Chamber of Deputies studies the expropriation of all flour mills in the country.	Soochow, Wusih, and Wukiang, cities on the path between Shanghai and Nanking, are shelled once more. Chinese troops hold back Japanese advances at Kashing (Jiaxing). . . . The Chinese government sends several ministries to relocate in Hangkow (Hankou, part of Wuhan), and several councils to Chungking (Chongqing), in anticipation of a Japanese attack.
Nov. 18		Reinforcing loyalist Spain's desire to separate politics from the military, former foreign minister Alvarez del Vayo resigns as Commissar General of land forces. Small skirmishes and troop movements along the Aragon front continue as all wait to see where and when the insurgent push will come.	Since August, well-armed native groups in Ethiopia have been raiding Italian outposts. There have been 113 airplanes used to bring supplies and munitions to the outposts, and the planes have also bombed and strafed the Ethiopians.		Rain and mud restrict Japanese movements on the ground and in the air. Thousands of Chinese and foreigners flee Nanking, leaving behind boarded shops and abandoned homes. . . . Japan announces that 80,000 of its soldiers have been lost since August 23 and nearly 30,000 wounded. . . . In India, in response to a plea by Mohandas Gandhi, 1,100 political prisoners are freed in Bengal.
Nov. 19		Spanish insurgent planes drop bombs on two cities near the Aragon front. . . . The huge armament stores and mystery of the Cagoulards contributes to a vote of confidence for French Premier Camille Chautemps in the Chamber of Deputies. . . . A typhoid epidemic flares in a London suburb, and a member of Parliament is among the 114 cases reported in two weeks. Before the epidemic ends, it will claim 43 lives. A laborer working on a well is the cause.		In a formal agreement, Argentina gives Bolivia cross-country access so that Bolivia's oil can be shipped.	Japan claims to capture Kashing and to be within seven miles of both Soochow and Changshu. . . . A trade pact signed between Japan and India in 1934 is extended until 1940.
Nov. 20	Italy's King Victor Emmanuel III appoints a prince, the Duke of Aosta, as new Viceroy of Ethiopia, and Premier Benito Mussolini puts himself in charge of the Ministry of Italian Africa.	Thirty-five loyalist planes bomb Saragossa in retaliation for yesterday's bombings. . . . In Romania, the parliament dissolves and elections are scheduled for the week before Christmas. The head of the National Peasant Party resigns, to be replaced by the party's former leader, Dr. Iulius Maniu.	Reports emerge that Arab unrest in Palestine is caused by a few Syrian mercenaries, who in turn are supported by Italy.	President Anastasio Somoza of Nicaragua accepts the brokered peace terms to settle a border conflict with Honduras.	Japan's General Matsui reports that Soochow is captured and occupied without a shot being fired. The mutiny of Manchurian troops is later revealed to be the cause. . . . Chiang Kai-shek's government formally announces the move from Nanking to Chungking. . . . Japan establishes a China Sea Fleet to blockade China's coast against Chinese shipping.
Nov. 21		A train collision near Seville, Spain, kills 49. In war news, insurgents bomb the cities of Alicante and Monzon. . . . The Soviet Commissariat of Education is accused of harboring wreckers who kept hundreds of thousands of children out of schools. . . . Swiss authorities detain the Count of Paris. The Count and 700 of his followers entered Switzerland for a secret meeting that may be connected to the Cagoulards. A manifesto from the Duke of Guise, the Count's father and pretender to the throne of France, is distributed.	In Beirut, 800 Lebanese nationalists fight with French troops. Fifty are injured, and one Senegalese soldier dies. Hundreds are arrested.		Japan announces capture of the Fushan (Foshan) forts, 30 miles northeast of Soochow. Japanese troops capture many strategic points, approaching Nanking from several directions. . . . Sporadic fighting in the Waziristan province of India (now part of Pakistan) continues; three British soldiers have been killed in the last week.
Nov. 22	A conference of the directors of Europe's medical schools begins under League of Nations auspices. . . . Over the past two weeks, 50–100 Soviet planes have been flown to China for use in defense against Japan.	The Non-Intervention Committee communicates with both sides in Spain about withdrawing 3,000 foreign volunteers each, in return for belligerent status. . . . *Izvestia* publishes news that seven bishops and many other clergy have been arrested throughout the Soviet Union, charged with plotting and espionage. . . . Viscount Halifax returns to London without any positive results from his talks with Chancellor Adolf Hitler.	Palestinian police surround the village of Mazar and arrest Sheik Farhan al-Sadi, an aged rebel leader believed to be behind many terrorist attacks.		The Japanese Embassy announces that as a conqueror, it will take control of all Shanghai, including the International Settlement and French Concession. . . . The city of Wusih, 100 miles from Nanking, is captured. Chinese troops try to reform on lines west of Wusih and are heavily bombed. Bombs fall in other cities and on troops between Fushan and Kiangyin, along the Yangtze.
Nov. 23	Chinese diplomats call on U.S. and British delegates to the Nine-Power Conference, trying desperately to get stronger language into the final resolution. They are unsuccessful. The resolution is signed on November 24.	Austria, Hungary, and Italy renew the Danubian Pact through June 1938. . . . Although his trial has not finished, the Reich takes over Arnold Bernstein's Red Star Lines and settles debts with his creditors.		Richmond Petroleum, a subsidiary of Standard Oil, files seven suits in Mexico City courts asking injunctions against the nationalization of 350,000 acres.	As Chinese troops dig trenches and fortify positions in and around Nanking, Japanese planes drop messages demanding surrender. Also over that city, Soviet airplanes engage in dogfights with Japanese pilots.

A	B	C	D	E
Includes developments that affect more than one world region, international organizations, and important meetings of world leaders.	*Includes all domestic and regional developments in Europe, including the Soviet Union.*	*Includes all domestic and regional developments in Africa and the Middle East.*	*Includes all domestic and regional developments in Latin America, the Caribbean, and Canada.*	*Includes all domestic and regional developments in Asian and Pacific nations (and colonies).*

U.S. Politics & Social Issues	U.S. Foreign Policy & Defense	Economics & Great Depression	Science, Technology & Nature	Culture, Leisure & Lifestyle	
		For the third time in three days, General Motors employees in Michigan stage a brief sit-down strike. The latest is in Pontiac's Fisher Body plant.			Nov. 17
The Senate filibuster against the anti-lynching bill continues for a third day.	The United States and United Kingdom announce that formal negotiations for a most-favored-nation reciprocal trade treaty between them will begin, and a reciprocal treaty with Canada will be sought also.	James Rand of Remington Rand Corp. is found not guilty of strike-breaking activities across state lines. . . . Union leader Patrick Corcoran is shot to death in Minneapolis, Minn., after threats are phoned to several union heads. . . . Consolidated Edison asks the appellate court to review the NLRB decision of November 10.		The Nobel Peace Prize is awarded to Britain's Viscount Cecil of Chelwood for his work with the League of Nations. The Viscount was awarded an honorary degree at Columbia University 10 minutes after learning of the Nobel Prize award.	Nov. 18
		The latest strike in Pontiac, Mich., idles nearly 15,000 GM workers and is carried out in defiance of union heads, who ask strikers to desist. . . . Layoffs prompt sit-down strikes against three Goodyear Tire and Rubber plants in Akron, Ohio, keeping 12,000 employees from work. Company spokesmen say the plants will reopen on November 22, no matter what, and the union threatens picket lines. Police stand by. . . . President Franklin Roosevelt asks the Federal Trade Commission to investigate possible monopolistic practices by businesses that contributed to the rise in the cost of living this year.	Another typhoon hits the Philippines, killing at least 247, mostly on Leyte and Cebu islands, and causing $4 million in damage. An estimated 147,000 are left homeless. . . . At the Bonneville Salt Flats, Captain Eyston of England sets a new land speed record of 311.42 miles per hour.		Nov. 19
		Sit-down strikers leave the Goodyear Tire and Rubber plants as Ohio's Governor Martin Davey readies 2,000 state troopers. The union calls for a formal strike vote.		A Vatican delegate states support for the Archbishop that corrected Father Coughlin last month. The priest has not returned to his radio shows since.	Nov. 20
The Senate Agriculture Committee agrees on a Farm Bill providing both voluntary and imposed controls on major crops. It ignores the President's desired spending cap of $500 million.		UAWA officials meet with local union heads and hear the grievances that led to the unauthorized strike against General Motors. . . . Goodyear and union officials craft a proposal promising recognition of seniority and no more layoffs in 1937. The agreement is accepted after a five-hour meeting involving 3,000 union members.			Nov. 21
		Homer Martin, president of the UAWA, addresses the 200 remaining sit-down strikers in Pontiac, Mich., for 90 minutes, convincing them to give up their strike and follow him out of the plant.		Father Coughlin asks his followers to stop sending letters asking his return to the airwaves.	Nov. 22
The six-day-long filibuster against the anti-lynching legislation before the Senate ends as discussion moves to the Farm Bill.		The Securities and Exchange Committee warns stock exchanges to reform themselves to better "serve the public interest."		Poet W.H. Auden is awarded the King's Gold Medal, the first given by George VI.	Nov. 23

F	G	H	I	J
Includes elections, federal-state relations, civil rights and liberties, crime, the judiciary, education, healthcare, poverty, urban affairs, and population.	Includes formation and debate of U.S. foreign and defense policies, veterans affairs, and defense spending. (Relations with specific foreign countries are usually found under the region concerned.)	Includes business, labor, agriculture, taxation, transportation, consumer affairs, monetary and fiscal policy, natural resources, pollution, and accidents.	Includes worldwide scientific, medical, and technological developments, natural phenomena, U.S. weather, and natural disasters.	Includes the arts, religion, scholarship, communications media, sports, entertainment, fashions, fads, and social life.

	World Affairs	Europe	Africa & The Middle East	The Americas	Asia & The Pacific
Nov. 24	Privately, Chiang Kai-shek agrees to accept Germany as a negotiator with Japan.	Viscount Halifax tells the British Parliament that Chancellor Adolf Hitler actually meant what he wrote in *Mein Kampf*. . . . French Interior Minister Marx Dormoy unveils some details of the Cagoulards after raiding a Paris bank that fronted and funded their plots. Armed overthrow of the government was their aim, and recruitment had spread to Algeria. . . . Paul Janson takes office as the new Premier of Belgium.	Under new anti-terrorism laws, 75-year-old Sheik Farhan is quickly tried and condemned to death in Palestine. Ironically, he is convicted in the murder of an Arab, Radi Abboushi, whom he had killed as an informer.	In Cuba's Senate galleries, 600 students demonstrate over delays in an amnesty bill.	General Chu Teh (Zhu De) is leading guerilla bands in Shansi, and Mao Tze-tung (Mao Zedong) prepares his Communist troops to battle the Japanese in Shensi (Shaanxi) province. . . . Japan appoints its own customs officers in Shanghai, replacing European officers. . . . Incendiary bombs dropped by Japanese pilots strike homes in Canton, killing over 60 people.
Nov. 25		Heavy shelling in Madrid by insurgents begins before midnight: the first bombardment in 40 days. Later in the morning, 120 bombs fall on Guadalajara. . . . In Romania, National Peasant Party leader Dr. Iulius Maniu causes controversy by forming electoral pacts with the Iron Hand and other fascist groups. . . . Paris's International Exposition closes until next May. . . . French police arrest Eugene Delonde, thought to be the leader of the Cagoulards. . . . Walther Funk, known to be loyal to Col. Gen. Hermann Goering, is named as Germany's Economic Minister.	All businesses and schools in Beirut shut in a strike against the government.	Mexico's president asks the National Railroad Workers Syndicate to operate the rails and pay the government $3.78 million per year. . . . Heavy rains over the past few days cause flooding that kills 70 people in Jamaica and 10 in Cuba.	With the fall of Huchow, Japanese troops are in position for a three-sided attack on Nanking. Chinese and foreign residents in historic Hangchow plead for it to be named a safety zone, and thus spared from bombing. . . . Shanghai is swollen with 2 million refugees and food supplies are short.
Nov. 26		Lwow (Lviv) University in Poland declares this to be a "Week Without Jews." Nazi pickets hold back any Jewish students who try to attend classes. Several people are injured. . . . In London, 12 deaths are blamed on three days of some of the heaviest fog ever. Drownings, ship collisions, and an airplane crash are all blamed on the low visibility.		Cuba's former president, Gerardo Machado, wanted on murder and embezzlement charges, enters the United States from Canada for surgery. He is put under arrest in a hospital.	Most non-military Chinese government officials leave Nanking. West of Wusih, shelling is continuous and heavy. Canton is bombed again.
Nov. 27	The United States, Great Britain, France, and other countries make diplomatic "representations" (not protests) over Japan's takeover of customs in Shanghai. Millions of dollars in outstanding bonds and loans are affected.	General Franco's surrender demand of November 10 is publicized. This may explain why he has not attacked in full strength. . . . Chancellor Adolf Hitler declares he will make Berlin an "eternal capital" with an expensive beautification and building program. . . . In Sofia, Bulgaria, 200 people are arrested in demonstrations, which the government banned, celebrating the Trianon Treaty. . . . Julius Streicher and a panel of race experts visit Danzig to teach civic authorities how to enforce the Nuremberg Laws and solve their "Jewish problem." . . . In Austria, 30 socialist leaders are arrested in early morning raids. The news is kept secret for 10 days.	The hanging of Sheik Farhan causes Arab demonstrations and strikes throughout Palestine, Syria, and Iraq.	Three priests are arrested in Veracruz, Mexico, for performing religious ceremonies.	By the end of this month, China will have placed another boom to block the Yangtze River 16 miles from Nanking. . . . Japan shells cities along the Yangtze in Anwhei (Anhui) province and in Liyang, southwest of Nanking. Japanese columns also advance on Hangchow, far to the south.
Nov. 28		General Franco blockades the coast of Spain, using the island of Majorca as his base. He ignores designations of the Non-Intervention Committee, stating that all ships attempting to enter Spanish government-controlled ports will be stopped. . . . The village of Colmenar Viejo, near Madrid, is bombed by insurgents and 50 are killed—49 of the victims are women and children.	Four shots are fired at the car of Egyptian Premier Nahas Pasha, but no one is hurt. The shooter is caught. Throughout the day and night, demonstrating bands chant slogans and break windows in Cairo. . . . In Palestine, terrorists surround a bus full of Jewish laborers and open fire; one man is injured. Police arrive to help and are fired at as well; one policeman dies.		Japanese troops capture Ihing, located on the main road to Nanking from Lake Tai. . . . Fighting between Moros and the Philippine government continues, and one soldier is killed in Lanao province.
Nov. 29	Italy formally recognizes Manchukuo as an independent state. . . . This is the first day of independence for Alexandretta. The Syrian flag is removed, but controversy erupts over keeping the French flag raised. Demonstrators throw a bomb into a Syrian school that does not join in the celebrations for Alexandretta. Arabs and Armenians demonstrate against independence.	Britain denies that insurgent Spain has the right to blockade ports. . . . Provincial papers in the Soviet Union report 154 executions for treason and espionage in November. Observers note that several important officials are missing, such as the Ukrainian Premier and the former Consul General in New York. . . . After 16 months of exile due to death threats, Nicolas Titulescu returns to Romania. National Peasant Party leader Dr. Iulius Maniu's recent pacts with the Iron Hand guarantee his safety.	Cairo police try to restore order and arrest the leader of Egypt's extreme nationalist party, called the Green Shirts, for attempted murder. The accused, Izzedine Abdul Kader, is the 25-year-old grandson of Urabi Pasha, leader of the 1879 Urabi Revolt. . . . More shootings take place in Palestine.	The trial of 11 nationalists in Ponce, Puerto Rico, which has gone on for over 10 weeks, may terminate because of the illness of jurors.	Japan surrounds the Kiangyin Forts after many days of battle and claims to conquer it, then takes Wutsin, an important railroad city. Over 100 bombs are dropped on Chinkiang (Zhenjiang), 40 miles from Nanking. Nanking is also shelled. . . . Communication with Shanghai is cut because Chinese telegraph operators refuse to cooperate with Japanese military authorities.

A	B	C	D	E
Includes developments that affect more than one world region, international organizations, and important meetings of world leaders.	*Includes all domestic and regional developments in Europe, including the Soviet Union.*	*Includes all domestic and regional developments in Africa and the Middle East.*	*Includes all domestic and regional developments in Latin America, the Caribbean, and Canada.*	*Includes all domestic and regional developments in Asian and Pacific nations (and colonies).*

U.S. Politics & Social Issues	U.S. Foreign Policy & Defense	Economics & Great Depression	Science, Technology & Nature	Culture, Leisure & Lifestyle	
		Over 500 Ford Company employees in St. Louis, Mo., cross lines of up to 1,000 UAWA pickets. The union called the strike, and Ford has filed for an injunction to halt it. . . . Charges of assault made against Ford Company and its employees for actions on May 26 are dropped due to lack of evidence. . . . Harkening to President Franklin Roosevelt's speech on November 9, the head of Consolidated Edison announces that over $100 million will be spent on expanding services over the next two years.			Nov. 24
		A Thanksgiving strike of Greyhound bus drivers in 16 northeastern states begins one minute after midnight, with 1,300 drivers demanding increased wages and a closed shop. Routes between New York and Philadelphia are most heavily affected. A bus leaving Boston is stopped and vandalized.			Nov. 25
		In Maryland, 11 men are arrested for stopping a Greyhound bus and beating the driver. Other isolated incidents of bus damage are reported.			Nov. 26
President Franklin Roosevelt threatens to veto bills calling for increased spending if funding sources are not provided, leaving the new Farm Bill in doubt.		The Ford Company's request for an injunction against picketers in St. Louis, claiming it fears violence, is delayed for a week. . . . Greyhound affiliates file lawsuits asking $6.3 million in damages for the disruptions to their service. A federal negotiator meets with union heads representing Greyhound drivers in Cleveland. . . . The NLRB charges the Associated Press (AP) with dismissing nine employees for union activities. . . . A 1931 contract between Remington Rand and IBM is voided by the courts as monopolistic. The contract controlled the manufacture of most tabulating and sorting machines in the United States.			Nov. 27
	The United States demands to be consulted by Japan when customs organization in China is decided.	Seven burials are postponed when 350 gravediggers go on strike at Greenwood Cemetery in Brooklyn, N.Y. A layoff of 85 men is the reason.		Pianist Josef Hoffman marks his golden jubilee at New York's Metropolitan Opera House. He made his debut there at age 11 on November 29, 1887.	Nov. 28
		President Franklin Roosevelt outlines changes to the National Housing Act and announces a five-year program dependent on private industry spending up to $16 billion on new and affordable housing. . . . Although all agree that talks between union and company are going well, Greyhound sends letters to its drivers demanding they report to work December 1, or face firing. . . . In their ongoing talks, the CIO asks the AFL to put in writing its assurances about industrial union organization; the AFL refuses. . . . Mediation fails in the Brooklyn cemetery strike, and Mayor Fiorello LaGuardia threatens to call an emergency under the sanitation and health laws and have city workers bury the dead.			Nov. 29

F	G	H	I	J
Includes elections, federal-state relations, civil rights and liberties, crime, the judiciary, education, healthcare, poverty, urban affairs, and population.	*Includes formation and debate of U.S. foreign and defense policies, veterans affairs, and defense spending. (Relations with specific foreign countries are usually found under the region concerned.)*	*Includes business, labor, agriculture, taxation, transportation, consumer affairs, monetary and fiscal policy, natural resources, pollution, and accidents.*	*Includes worldwide scientific, medical, and technological developments, natural phenomena, U.S. weather, and natural disasters.*	*Includes the arts, religion, scholarship, communications media, sports, entertainment, fashions, fads, and social life.*

	World Affairs	Europe	Africa & The Middle East	The Americas	Asia & The Pacific
Nov. 30		Insurgents bomb Madrid and Guadalajara. . . . France's Premier Camille Chautemps and Foreign Minister Yvon Delbos end their visit to London. As a result of their talks with counterparts Neville Chamberlain and Anthony Eden, a long-term discussion of appeasing Germany with the return of colonies is expected.		Demonstrations and strikes in Haiti express the public's unhappiness with President Stenio Vincent's passive attitude toward the Dominican Republic.	A huge ammunition dump 20 miles from Nanking explodes. Under the leadership of General Tang Shenzhi, Nanking prepares for attack: sandbag barricades and barbed wire guard some of the city's gates, and seven rings of trenches and gunnery nests surround the city as well. Precious artwork is being removed to safer environs. Diplomats ask for a safety zone around the University of Nanking, enclosing $2 million of U.S. property that could hold 200,000 refugees. The Japanese have not responded to this request but foreigners and Chinese officials are going ahead with the plan.
Dec. 1	Japan recognizes General Franco's rebel regime in Spain. . . . China protests Italy's recognition of Manchukuo. . . . General Chiang Kai-shek meets with Ambassador Trautman of Germany to reconsider Japan's terms, which he rejected November 5. Chiang then meets with his military advisors. . . . France sends a division of cruisers to China's coast to fight any Japanese attempts to control the French Concession.	Spanish government dispatches report five failed attacks by insurgents near Toledo. . . . Yvon Delbos, France's foreign minister, embarks on a tour of eastern Europe, visiting heads of state. . . . German Church Affairs Minister Hans Kerrl says 8,000 Catholic monks and brothers, or 50 percent of Germany's total, have been charged with criminal acts since the Nazi ascent to power.			Chinese troops defend the Kiangyin Forts. Travelers report that Japan has taken over Chikkai and Taikam Islands, off the Kwangtung (Guangdong) province coast.
Dec. 2	The Spanish insurgent government recognizes Manchukuo.	Insurgent planes bomb and strafe eight villages in loyalist Spain. . . . The 12 Nazi Party youth workers arrested with Heinz Rutha, who killed himself, begin their trials in Czechoslovakia.			Chinese reinforcements from Szechwan (Sichuan) drive the Japanese back from cities in eastern Anwhei (Anhui) province. A Japanese air raid 12 miles from the capital of Chekiang (Zhejiang) province leaves 1,000 dead.
Dec. 3		Madrid is heavily shelled by insurgents. . . . Soviet diplomat Alexandre Barmine, envoy to Greece, refuses his recall order, flees, and resigns. In a published letter, he names others who have disappeared after being recalled who were condemned on false accusations. . . . In France, 13 billion francs are approved for Minister Edouard Daladier's defense budget. . . . French Foreign Minister Yvon Delbos confers with his Berlin counterpart, then travels on to Poland. . . . News comes that wealthy merchant, benefactor, and art patron Alfred Toepfer of Hamburg has been imprisoned by the Reich.		A wave of articles in Mexican newspapers reflects growing anti-Semitism, especially in the Nationalist Party. In 1937, 22 percent of all "undesirables" deported by Mexico have been Jewish. . . . By decree, Brazil's President dissolves all political parties.	A grenade is thrown during a Japanese victory parade through Shanghai's International Settlement. Four soldiers are injured; the man who threw the bomb is shot dead. Later, Japanese troops block streets and string barbed wire in the American-held part of the International Settlement in Shanghai. U.S. Marines demand that they leave. They do, and an incident is averted. . . . While not formally recognizing a safety zone in Nanking, Japanese authorities say they will try to avoid it.
Dec. 4		Insurgents bomb Terencon, 40 miles from Madrid, for the third time in a week. Two hospitals are destroyed. Loyalists bomb Almudevar.	Reports emerge that Syrian agitators, using religion as a recruitment tool, are entering northern Palestine to start a holy war.	Cuba asks for extradition of its former president, Gerardo Machado, listing 10 counts of murder against him.	Japan announces capture of towns near Shanghai and along railways leading to Nanking. In the north, Chinese troops stop the Japanese with intense guerilla fighting in many provinces. Americans still in Nanking are ready to board the U.S. gunboat *Panay* when necessary.
Dec. 5		Spanish loyalists start a new defensive at Teruel, a small city in southern Aragon that Franco's forces hold. . . . Catholic Bishop von Preysing of Berlin denounces Church Minister Hans Kerrl's statements from the pulpit and lists his actions against churches.			Near the Wuhu Forts, Japan bombs three British ships. Two captains are injured and at least 200 Chinese are killed. . . . Japan takes control of the Kiangyin Forts and gains a stockpile of munitions there. The boom blocking the Yangtze River remains in place, blocking ships from access to Nanking. Chinese troops try to reform a line of defense. East of Nanking, 300,000 Chinese troops assemble. . . . Tokyo papers and officials admit to a quandary: achieving most military objectives in China has not brought Chinese submission.
Dec. 6		Yugoslavia's Premier Milan Stoyadinovitch visits with Premier Benito Mussolini and Italy's top officials; Foreign Ministers Yvon Delbos of France and Josef Beck of Poland talk.			Japan tells Britain its bombers at Wuhu were aiming at ships on the river known to be holding Chinese soldiers. . . . Advances continue; the boom at Kiangyin is broken; and Japanese troops capture cities on the way to Nanking, reaching the city's gates by sunset. Most escape routes are blocked; Japanese planes bomb Pukow, across the Yangtze. . . . Su Hsi-wan is named mayor of Shanghai and environs by the Japanese.
	A Includes developments that affect more than one world region, international organizations, and important meetings of world leaders.	**B** Includes all domestic and regional developments in Europe, including the Soviet Union.	**C** Includes all domestic and regional developments in Africa and the Middle East.	**D** Includes all domestic and regional developments in Latin America, the Caribbean, and Canada.	**E** Includes all domestic and regional developments in Asian and Pacific nations (and colonies).

U.S. Politics & Social Issues	U.S. Foreign Policy & Defense	Economics & Great Depression	Science, Technology & Nature	Culture, Leisure & Lifestyle	
President Franklin Roosevelt, in another message to Congress, asks for drastic spending cuts in highway funding. The Congress is angry and resentful over this interference.		The cemetery strike is settled after the company and union meet. Mayor Fiorello LaGuardia promises a fact-finding commission, and some workers will go on part-time shifts to give work to those previously laid off. . . . Arrests are made in Boston and several people are hurt in Rhode Island when random violence spreads in the Greyhound bus strike. . . . Wendell Willkie, president of Commonwealth & Southern Corp., proposes new utility pricing and policies consistent with President Franklin Roosevelt's New Deal goals.			Nov. 30
The U.S. Attorney General files antitrust suits against Western Union, Postal Telegraph, and subsidiaries. . . . A federal court in Pennsylvania rules that schools cannot expel students for not saluting the flag.		The Greyhound drivers' strike ends but no closed shop. . . . The National Labor Relations Board (NLRB) asks Ford Motor Company to answer charges of unfair labor practices on December 16.			Dec. 1
		William Green of the American Federation of Labor (AFL) and John L. Lewis of the Committee for Industrial Organization (CIO) meet for the first time in months for talks.			Dec. 2
		After a two-hour second meeting, peace talks between leaders of the AFL and CIO fail. John L. Lewis insists the AFL admit back CIO unions before proceeding on other points, and the AFL refuses, feeling this would lead to infighting.		*Dandy*, which in 1999 became the world's longest-running children's comic, is first published in London.	Dec. 3
Not waiting for the AFL recommendations that will be submitted next week, Representatives are pushing the Wages and Hours Bill into Congressional debate.	The U.S. Consul to Spain, unable to take up his post in Bilbao without acknowledging Franco's insurgents as a governing body, is called home.		Another typhoon hits the central Philippines, isolating the island Samar. Outbreaks of dysentery following previous storms take more lives. . . . The Canal Zone (Panama) experiences heavy flooding from rains.		Dec. 4
					Dec. 5
	Undersecretary of State Sumner Welles says that division of U.S.-owned estates in Latin America is acceptable if fair payment is made.	The Supreme Court allows New York to go ahead with its anti-trust case against Aluminum Company of America. . . . Police use tear gas to end a demonstration outside a Ford Motor Company plant in Kansas City.		Yehudi Menuhin, age 21, performs the U.S. premiere of Schumann's Violin Concerto at Carnegie Hall. . . . Father Coughlin announces he will resume his radio shows in the new year.	Dec. 6

F	G	H	I	J
Includes elections, federal-state relations, civil rights and liberties, crime, the judiciary, education, healthcare, poverty, urban affairs, and population.	Includes formation and debate of U.S. foreign and defense policies, veterans affairs, and defense spending. (Relations with specific foreign countries are usually found under the region concerned.)	Includes business, labor, agriculture, taxation, transportation, consumer affairs, monetary and fiscal policy, natural resources, pollution, and accidents.	Includes worldwide scientific, medical, and technological developments, natural phenomena, U.S. weather, and natural disasters.	Includes the arts, religion, scholarship, communications media, sports, entertainment, fashions, fads, and social life.

	World Affairs	Europe	Africa & The Middle East	The Americas	Asia & The Pacific
Dec. 7	Turkey informs France that it denounces its nonaggression treaty with Syria.	An insurgent air raid over Barcelona kills at least 50 people. Loyalist planes shell Majorca, the insurgents' major air base. . . . With replies from both Spanish loyalist and insurgent authorities, the Non-Intervention Committee discusses details of withdrawing "volunteers" from each side. . . . With much dissent, Britain's House of Commons passes an air raid precautions bill. . . . Two men are killed in Lugo, Romania in a clash between Iron Guard fascists and liberals.		The Ponce, Puerto Rico, trial of 10 nationalists accused in a June 8 assassination attempt ends as three jurors are ill. A new trial will begin January 10.	At daybreak, General Chiang Kai-shek, his wife, and top advisers leave Nanking in separate planes. When the city does not open to them in the morning, Japanese generals send 90 planes to bombard Nanking. Huge fires result. Generals Pai Chung-hsi, a Communist leader and advocate of guerilla warfare, and Chang Fah-kwei command Chinese troops inside the city walls.
Dec. 8		Madrid is shelled by insurgents, and a push at the loyalist town of Quijorna, 15 miles from Madrid, is begun. . . . Romania bars political speeches critical of King Carol. Politicians can be arrested for voicing attacks on his Cabinet as well. The King meets with Minister Yvon Delbos of France. . . . Valery Mezhlauk, former chair of the Soviet Planning Commission and known to many Americans, joins the list of missing Soviet officials.	Palestinian newspapers report a compromise peace agreement between Jewish and Muslim leaders, including the exiled Mufti of Jerusalem. Minimum land ownership for Arabs and a population cap of 35 percent for Palestine's Jews are part of the truce. *The New York Times* warns this story may be false.	President Stenio Vincent of Haiti says 8,000 Haitians have been killed in the Dominican Republic since October and denies that "border clashes" describe the crimes—he calls them "mass murder."	Three columns of Japanese troops begin the assault on Nanking. In one gruesome battle near Nanking, 300 Chinese soldiers are trapped and forced to the top of a hill by set fires, where they are machine-gunned. . . . Delegates of South Hopeh (Hebeh) province, under Japan's guidance, secede from China.
Dec. 9	The League of Nations Economic Committee concludes a brief 47th session with a report on raw materials.	In Czechoslovakia, suspended sentences are given to 14 young men arrested with Heinrich Rutha on homosexuality charges. . . . In Romania, a coalition of the National Peasant Party, Iron Guard, and other groups accuse the government of wrongdoing in the current electoral campaign. They promise punishment if any of the coalition comes to power.		Mexico asks U.S. oil companies to pay royalties if they wish to continue operating in the country. Company executives head to Mexico for discussions. . . . In Veracruz, President Lázaro Cárdenas orders the closure of a church that was the site of arrests two weeks ago and says it will be made into a library.	Nanking is circled by 100,000 Japanese troops, who engage in heavy fighting at the gates and near Sun Yat-sen's tomb on Purple Mountain. From Shanghai, General Matsui demands surrender by noon on December 10. Japan announces capture of two major cities on the Yangtze: Chinkiang (Zhenjiang), capital of Kiangsu (Jiangsu) province, and Wuhu. Bombing in the south continues.
Dec. 10		After nine days of heavy rain, sunshine brings an air battle between insurgents and loyalists. Between 100 and 250 planes fight 50 miles east of Saragossa, Spain. In a different area, insurgents report 200 dead in fighting around Brunete. . . . The Austrian government restores the estates of the Hapsburg family. . . . A train wreck during a snowstorm in Scotland kills 34 people.	In Haifa, Palestine, Arabs kill a Jewish boy and an Arab man in separate incidents. A Jewish policeman is seriously wounded.	Nicaragua and Honduras sign a Pact of Reciprocal Agreements. It does not set a disputed boundary but provides peaceful arbitration methods. . . . In the Mexican state of Tampico, 5,000 oil workers walk off their jobs for a 24-hour strike, defying President Lázaro Cárdenas. . . . A 30-day stay in deportation hearings for former president Gerardo Machado of Cuba is granted.	Japanese forces break through the Kungwha (Zhonghua) Gate in the evening, assisted by Chinese spies. Chinese troops fight back. Foreigners in the city plead for a three-day truce so that noncombatants can leave; no authorities respond. . . . The Japanese Cabinet declares that only complete capitulation from China will be accepted.
Dec. 11	Italy withdraws from the League of Nations. Premier Benito Mussolini calls the League a "tottering temple" that paves the way for war.	Church Minister Hans Kerrl of Germany decrees Dr. Friedrich Werner, an attorney, is in charge of the Protestant Church.			Japanese soldiers manage to scale walls during the night and mount machine guns there. Chinese troops hold them off, however. Aerial bombardment of Nanking begins again in the morning, and some shells fall in the designated safety zone. Fires destroy much of Pukow's waterfront docks across the river.
Dec. 12	Japanese planes attack U.S. and British ships on the Yangtze River, sinking the U.S.S. *Panay*. Three men die and 48 are injured, including the commander. Four British gunboats and several unarmed ships are also attacked. Although Japan claims the attack was unintentional, Japanese pilots had been ordered to fire upon any and all ships on the Yangtze. Witnesses report machine gun fire from Japanese ships preceded the bombing. . . . The board headed by Dr. John Dewey says that Leon Trotsky is not guilty of the charges leveled by the Soviet Union. Their investigation began in April.	Elections are held in the Soviet Union. Ninety million people, or 96.5 percent of those eligible, vote for Josef Stalin and other officers of the Supreme Soviet, who mostly run unopposed. . . . Mounted Yugoslav police charge crowds of demonstrators in Belgrade, injuring several people, as France's Minister Yvon Delbos visits the capital.			In addition to multiple raids over Nanking and the Nanchang airfield, the northern city of Sian (Xi'an) in Shensi (Shaanxi) province is bombed. In Fukien (Fujian) province, papers report the execution of 140 Formosans for espionage against Japan. Formosa (Taiwan) is a Japanese colony.
Dec. 13	Japanese Foreign Minister Hirota expresses profound apologies to the United States over the *Panay's* sinking. . . . The League of Nations publishes its yearbook, noting the growth in military spending. In 1937, $4.5 billion was spent on armaments in Europe; $2.6 billion elsewhere.	Rumors of the execution of Valery Mezhlauk and other former Soviet high officials and diplomats reach the West. . . . France and Yugoslavia sign a trade pact.	Daily incidents of violence occur in Palestine; a bus is bombed today.		Nanking's Chansung Gate falls to Japan before dawn, and troops advance about 100 yards into the city. At least 6,000 Chinese soldiers are killed at the gate. Throughout the day the Japanese push farther into the city. Although China denies it, at nightfall Japan announces that Nanking has fallen.

A	B	C	D	E
Includes developments that affect more than one world region, international organizations, and important meetings of world leaders.	*Includes all domestic and regional developments in Europe, including the Soviet Union.*	*Includes all domestic and regional developments in Africa and the Middle East.*	*Includes all domestic and regional developments in Latin America, the Caribbean, and Canada.*	*Includes all domestic and regional developments in Asian and Pacific nations (and colonies).*

U.S. Politics & Social Issues	U.S. Foreign Policy & Defense	Economics & Great Depression	Science, Technology & Nature	Culture, Leisure & Lifestyle	
		In Minneapolis, Minn., union leader Miles Dunne is ambushed by three men but escapes. Dunne is the successor of Patrick Corcoran, who was ambushed and murdered November 17. One of three men under investigation for the murder is rearrested.		Baseball's National League will permit night games, but the American League will not.	Dec. 7
The National Association of Manufacturers adopts an eight-point Platform for American Industry and asks government to help create more wealth, rather than simply redistribute it.	Joseph Kennedy, currently head of the Maritime Commission, is asked to be Ambassador to England. His nomination will be placed before the Senate in January. Current Ambassador Bingham is hospitalized and will only live a few more days.	Police arrest 60 members of United Auto Workers of America (UAWA) for obstructing traffic in Dearborn, Mich. The union members were distributing leaflets near the gates of a Ford plant.			Dec. 8
		Works Progress Administration (WPA) head Harry Hopkins announces that 1,575,000 are employed on WPA projects, and another 350,000 will get jobs within a few weeks. . . . In Minneapolis, Minn., a strike of drivers closes 12 warehouses. The union involved had been led by the murdered Patrick Corcoran.		Nils Gustaf Dalén, Nobel Prize for Physics winner and inventor of the sun valve, dies. A gas explosion blinded him just before winning the prize in 1912.	Dec. 9
The Farm Bill—also called the Crop Control Bill for its provisions—passes the House.		The UAWA calls a strike of Ford Company's Kansas City plant. Police arrest all 49 pickets.			Dec. 10
		The CIO sends layoff notices to 200 of its 652 employees.			Dec. 11
			Floods in northern California may have peaked; 5,000 are homeless and thousands of farmland acres are under water. Levees broke along the Sacramento and Feather rivers.	The Washington Redskins defeat the Chicago Bears to become the National Football League champions. . . . Mae West and Don Ameche perform a skit called "Adam and Eve" on NBC radio. Mae West, as Eve, makes gasping noises as the snake in the Garden of Eden pushes its way through a picket fence. She ends by saying, "There…there… now you're through!" She also tells dummy Charlie McCarthy, "You're all wood and a yard long." NBC spends most of the following week apologizing, and Mae West is banned from radio for nearly a decade.	Dec. 12
The Wages and Hours Bill is hotly debated in the House.	Secretary of State Cordell Hull demands full apologies and compensation for the Panay sinking, and asks that President Franklin Roosevelt's feelings be communicated directly to the Emperor. While Britain expresses outrage as well, the two governments do not act jointly.	In a New Deal victory, the Supreme Court upholds the Treasury Department's power to call liberty bonds for redemption without paying further interest. . . . Nineteen thousand men of the National Maritime Union, created in May in opposition to the International Seamen's Union, vote to join the CIO.		German heavyweight boxer Max Schmeling knocks out Harry Thomas in the eighth round at Madison Square Garden. In Berlin, the fight is heard over loudspeakers in restaurants and nightclubs.	Dec. 13

F	G	H	I	J
Includes elections, federal-state relations, civil rights and liberties, crime, the judiciary, education, healthcare, poverty, urban affairs, and population.	Includes formation and debate of U.S. foreign and defense policies, veterans affairs, and defense spending. (Relations with specific foreign countries are usually found under the region concerned.)	Includes business, labor, agriculture, taxation, transportation, consumer affairs, monetary and fiscal policy, natural resources, pollution, and accidents.	Includes worldwide scientific, medical, and technological developments, natural phenomena, U.S. weather, and natural disasters.	Includes the arts, religion, scholarship, communications media, sports, entertainment, fashions, fads, and social life.

	World Affairs	Europe	Africa & The Middle East	The Americas	Asia & The Pacific
Dec. 14	President Eamon de Valera of the Irish Free State recognizes Italy's conquest of Ethiopia.		King Farouk of Egypt and his Cabinet are in conflict; he refuses to sign bills sent to him. The Cabinet threatens to resubmit the bills to the legislature; if approved, they will become law without his signature.	President Stenio Vincent of Haiti invokes the 1923 Gondra Treaty and asks an international convention to adjudicate the killings of Haitians by the Dominican Republic.	Japan forms a provisional government in Peiping (Beijing), and renames the city Peking.... Eight to nine thousand people are executed in front of the Shangyuan Gate of Nanking. Other massacres of up to 10,000 at a time occur; witnesses tell of crowds dowsed with kerosene and burned, or of people forced into pits, their hands bound and buried alive.... Refugees from Nanking—some having fled Shanghai as well—rush east toward Hankow (Wuhan).... Provincial elections in the Philippines are marred by sporadic riots and violence.
Dec. 15		Spanish government forces strike back at the insurgents near Teruel; the insurgents claim flooding, not enemy attacks, has damaged their communications.... France and Germany agree on a pact governing currency, pasturage, and rights of passage on their common borders.... Nazis in Austria, irate over a window smashed by a Jewish merchant, retaliate with the slogan that 1,000 windows of Jewish shops will pay. Over the next weeks, bricks and rocks are thrown from cars and streets through windows of Jewish businesses.			Japanese Embassy officials claim to have no news of Nanking, other than the fighting is ended and fires rage. In fact, they are trying to impose order on troops rampaging through the city. Nanking has 300,000 civilians. A reporter leaving the city describes mass executions and "four days of hell."
Dec. 16	Italy withdraws from the International Labor Organization (ILO).... France and Syria sign an agreement.	Loyalist forces take 200 prisoners in Teruel as they continue their offensive. Insurgents insist that this is all part of a plan, and the attackers of Teruel will be caught in a trap.... France is beset by strikes of bakers, food sellers, and tire makers. A strike of department store clerks was just settled.... The chief of the Soviet Astronomical Council is removed and the Council is dissolved, accused of inactivity and procrastination. In a related purge, German Jewish doctors that immigrated to the Soviet Union are said to be under arrest.		The strike leader blamed for riots in Trinidad on June 21 is sentenced to two years of hard labor.	Rear Admiral Mitsuzawa of Japan is relieved of duties over the *Panay* sinking. Japan promises military honors and full restitution, as well as apologies. . . . In a radio address, General Chiang Kai-shek exhorts his country to fight on, acknowledging 300,000 casualties so far. . . . Journalists report widespread looting by soldiers of both sides in Nanking. Civilians are killed, including children and the aged; bodies are left in every street. Rape is also widespread. Over 100,000 people seek refuge in the Safety Zone, but Chinese soldiers are dragged from there en masse and executed. Five thousand civilians are taken from the Overseas Chinese Center to the Xiaguan Station, where they are killed and dumped into the river. An eyewitness later tells of the machine-gunning of tens of thousands of refugees at Straw Sandals Gorge and Swallow Cliff.
Dec. 17		As the trial ends for Arnold Bernstein in Germany, the trustee of his shipping lines prepares to sell it to Aryans. Most of the sale price will go to the government to pay fines and charges.			Near Nanking, three columns of Japanese troops march to attack the new line of 30 Chinese divisions, over 200 miles in length.
Dec. 18		Loyalist forces encircle Teruel, cutting off the insurgents that occupy the area. Snow is over two feet deep and temperatures are near zero. Ten rebel prisoners are sent into the city with a demand for surrender. When the demand is refused, an air attack follows.... Reports from France hint at a link or munitions sale between Spanish insurgents and the secret society recently uncovered.	King Farouk of Egypt threatens to dismiss Premier Nahas Pasha.	U.S. oil companies in Mexico are ordered to increase wages by one-third. . . . Dominican Republic President Rafael Trujillo accepts the Gondra Treaty terms and invites the United States, Cuba, and Mexico to be conciliators.	Most American journalists left Nanking on December 12 or 13, but other witnesses to the "shocking misconduct" of Japanese soldiers continue to tell their stories.
Dec. 19		Loyalists claim Teruel, but insurgents say they hold only a corridor of the city.... Eight former Soviet officials are executed for high treason. An ambassador and a friend of Stalin are among those killed. . . . The Soviet Union announces completion of a new railway in Siberia, 1,800 miles long.	After a Jewish policeman is kidnapped and killed, army, police, and air force officers search villages throughout northern Palestine. Anyone with guns or ammunition is arrested.	Sixteen U.S. and British oil companies issue a joint statement claiming the wage increases ordered by Mexico violate labor laws.	Two U.S. warships arrive at Tsingtao (Qingdao) to evacuate 300 Americans in case of a Japanese attack. In that northern city, nine Japanese-owned cotton mills that employ 24,000 have been destroyed by Chinese troops.

A	B	C	D	E
Includes developments that affect more than one world region, international organizations, and important meetings of world leaders.	Includes all domestic and regional developments in Europe, including the Soviet Union.	Includes all domestic and regional developments in Africa and the Middle East.	Includes all domestic and regional developments in Latin America, the Caribbean, and Canada.	Includes all domestic and regional developments in Asian and Pacific nations (and colonies).

U.S. Politics & Social Issues	U.S. Foreign Policy & Defense	Economics & Great Depression	Science, Technology & Nature	Culture, Leisure & Lifestyle	
The Senate defeats an amendment to restore the President's desired $500 million cap to the Farm Bill.				Walt Disney's company announces that *Pinocchio*, rather than *Bambi*, will be its next animated color release.	Dec. 14
Over several days, a New York State Commission on Conditions of Urban Negroes hears testimony of rent-gouging and discrimination in employment and union membership.		A strike of Automat employees now in its fifth month results in the arrest of 37 pickets in Times Square in New York City for disorderly conduct. . . . At the Ford plant in Kansas City, police arrest 161 men and women, some with their children, who are picketing. This follows arrests of 91 on December 14, and 49 the day before that. Police and Ford officials insist that there is no strike.			Dec. 15
		Strikes of shipworkers leave passengers stranded in New York, while crewmen in Baltimore who held a sit-down strike on a ship in September are convicted of mutiny. . . . Police in Dearborn, Mich., arrest 208 union members for "obstructing traffic" as they distribute brochures near Ford plants. . . . In a speech before the Steel Workers' convention, John L. Lewis announces that the AFL must take back all 4 million CIO members or none at all.			Dec. 16
The Senate passes the Farm Bill, but not in the form asked by the administration. The House sends the Wages and Hours Bill to its Labor Committee, which means it will not be considered until the regular congressional session.	A temporary trade pact is signed between the United States and Italy. An 1871 agreement expired before negotiations on a new treaty were completed.	Two officers and a bystander get shotgun pellet wounds in Kansas City as police escort Ford workers from the plant in a motorcade. In at least 20 separate fights, 104 are arrested. Tear gas is deployed, bricks are thrown, and a dozen men are beaten.	The Tiber River floods parts of Rome as it reaches its highest stage in 67 years.	The Legion of Decency demands an inquiry into radio suggestiveness, and preachers and Congressmen call Mae West and her brand of humor "filthy."	Dec. 17
The House passes amendments to the National Housing Act.		The 36 defendants in Illinois of the mine bombings are found guilty. The bombings took place in 1932–35.		The FCC demands complete information from NBC on its December 12 broadcast with Mae West.	Dec. 18
				The installation of a painting by José Maria Sert fills the spot in Rockefeller Center's RCA Building that once held an uncompleted mural by Diego Rivera. Rivera's work, featuring Lenin, was found offensive and halted in 1933.	Dec. 19

F	G	H	I	J
Includes elections, federal-state relations, civil rights and liberties, crime, the judiciary, education, healthcare, poverty, urban affairs, and population.	*Includes formation and debate of U.S. foreign and defense policies, veterans affairs, and defense spending. (Relations with specific foreign countries are usually found under the region concerned.)*	*Includes business, labor, agriculture, taxation, transportation, consumer affairs, monetary and fiscal policy, natural resources, pollution, and accidents.*	*Includes worldwide scientific, medical, and technological developments, natural phenomena, U.S. weather, and natural disasters.*	*Includes the arts, religion, scholarship, communications media, sports, entertainment, fashions, fads, and social life.*

	World Affairs	Europe	Africa & The Middle East	The Americas	Asia & The Pacific
Dec. 20	Foreign Secretary Anthony Eden of Britain indicates no action will be taken against Japan in south China unless an actual invasion of Hong Kong occurs.	Loyalists send three columns into the center of Teruel to engage in hand-to-hand fighting for control of the city. Insurgents claim they are recapturing towns in the Teruel area. . . . The Soviet Union celebrates the 20th anniversary of its political police, now called NKVD. . . . Hungary's Regent, Admiral Horthy, rejects any talk of his assuming the throne. (The king remains in exile.) . . . Romania votes for deputies, and four die and 300 are arrested in violent incidents. Senate elections will be on December 22.	The Coptic Church in Egypt excommunicates the bishop that Italy named Prelate to Ethiopia. Italy's designation split the Coptic Church for the first time since the fourth century.	Haiti raises the death toll from October's massacre in the Dominican Republic to over 12,000. . . . The Cuban Senate passes an amnesty bill freeing all political prisoners. Charges against former president Gerardo Machado, currently in a New York hospital, will be dropped as a result.	
Dec. 21	Three hundred American and British evacuees from Hankow are stopped by a boom in the Yangtze River and must return. . . . Britain's rhetoric shifts from "peace at any price," as Prime Minister Neville Chamberlain says the Empire will look after its own interests and is losing patience. . . . Minister Yvon Delbos of France says his country will look after its own interests in Asia, as well as sustain "white prestige" in the area. . . . The Soviet Union announces a one-year extension of its current agreement with Japan, allowing fishing in its Pacific waters.	The Spanish government announces the capture of Teruel (again). Bayonets are used against the last insurgents, who—loyalist dispatches say—make their stand in a bull ring.	Egypt's King Farouk threatens to dissolve the government if his demands are not met by the Cabinet. He wishes to appoint a third of the Senate and eliminate the blueshirt youth organizations of the Wafd Party, among other things.	A coup d'etat is attempted in Paraguay by Major Estigarribia, who is killed when he leads his followers against army troops in Asuncion.	Japan continues a military push north from Nanking, through Pukow and toward Hangchow (Hangzhou), the capital of Chekiang province. . . . In Wakayama, Japan, 48 children are killed in a fire at a movie theatre.
Dec. 22		Victorious government troops in Spain claim to move west from Teruel to Albarracin. Heavy fighting is still reported in Teruel, however. . . . Three more Soviet envoys serving in Europe disappear. . . . In Romanian elections, Premier Gheorghe Tatarescu's government is voted out and the Liberal Party suffers unexpected losses. The National Peasant Party receives less than 20 percent of the vote, only a little more than the Iron Guard (fascists), with 16 percent.	The executive committee of the Wafd, or Nationalist Party, of Egypt agrees to withdraw from politics, hoping to ease a tense political crisis.		Japan claims to take the mountain resort of Mokanshan as its forces drive toward Hangchow. Air attacks damage Nanchang airport. A Japanese force heading north passes through Chuhsien and leaves 1,000 dead. . . . Letters from missionaries and others in Nanking tell of the slaughter of civilians and other horrors. Hospitals were looted, and doctors and nurses robbed.
Dec. 23		Loyalist sources say that 400 well-armed insurgents are making a desperate stand in Teruel, Spain, preventing a complete takeover. In fact, thousands of rebels are fighting in several areas of the city. . . . After eight days of a strike, police try to remove sit-down strikers at Goodrich Rubber in France. A pre-arranged signal brings telephone and aviation workers to link arms and defy police. . . . Romania shifts its vote tally. Instead of district representation, the country's votes are counted as a whole, giving Premier Gheorghe Tatarescu's party more seats. . . . University professors in Poland sign a manifesto against ghetto seating.	Palestinian police chase an Arab gang from the scene of a bus attack in Haifa to a spot west of Tiberias. One hundred Arabs fight with police troops until surrounded; 11 men die. . . . In military courts in Palestine, five Arab men are sentenced to death.		Cities and rail stations fall to Japanese troops on the way to Hangchow. An army spokesman says Chinese troops will be given a chance to simply retreat from the historic and beautiful city, thereby preserving it from attack. Foreigners are advised to leave. In the night, Chinese forces withdraw, blowing up newer buildings as they leave, including a power plant. . . . In the south, thousands flee inland from Canton (Guangdong), believing a Japanese attack is imminent.
Dec. 24		Spanish insurgents claim to hold onto the high ground in Teruel, while reinforcements gather to circle and take back the city. The seminary is occupied by rebels as well, who fight throughout the night. Other strongholds are the Civil Guard headquarters and a Bank of Spain building. . . . One hundred French army vehicles deliver food to Paris's central markets, as truckers strike in sympathy with warehouse employees. Steel workers, bakers, and even movie studio hands are on strike. . . . Pope Pius XI decries the persecution of the Catholic Church in Germany in a speech to the College of Cardinals.			Japan captures the city of Hangchow. Commanders proclaim a three-day holiday for troops, who loot wine and food shops, break into homes, rape, and run wild. Chinese women flee to foreign-controlled refugee centers for protection. . . . Other Japanese troops cross the Yellow River to circle Tsinan (Jinan), the capital of Shantung (Shandong) province, and begin a siege.

A	B	C	D	E
Includes developments that affect more than one world region, international organizations, and important meetings of world leaders.	Includes all domestic and regional developments in Europe, including the Soviet Union.	Includes all domestic and regional developments in Africa and the Middle East.	Includes all domestic and regional developments in Latin America, the Caribbean, and Canada.	Includes all domestic and regional developments in Asian and Pacific nations (and colonies).

U.S. Politics & Social Issues	U.S. Foreign Policy & Defense	Economics & Great Depression	Science, Technology & Nature	Culture, Leisure & Lifestyle	
A nine-year-old decision is reversed when the Supreme Court says that evidence obtained through wiretaps may not be used in criminal prosecutions. . . . Senators Wheeler and Truman attack the railroads, saying they speculate with stockholders' money, lie to government agencies, and falsify balance sheets.	Japan's Foreign Office retracts earlier denials and admits that the *Panay* was fired upon. General Harada then claims that the *Panay* fired first, but retracts this within 24 hours.	In New York, AFL and CIO representatives agree to work against the current trend to curtail picketing. . . . In Kansas City, Mo., sheriffs stop and search a motorcade of Ford employees on their way to work and arrest 25 for having concealed guns and blackjacks. . . . The trial ends for 63 arrested in Chicago's Memorial Day riot. Charges are reduced to unlawful assembly for 57 men and women, and a $1 fine collected. The six men accused of being leaders are fined $10.		After a long illness, German General Erich von Ludendorff, hero of World War I, dies.	Dec. 20
The special session of Congress ends with little accomplished and no major legislation passed. . . . The summary by the Senate's subcommittee on labor espionage is released. Three further reports will follow. Headed by Senator La Follette, the summary warns that industrial espionage threatens the country and all its businesses, and must be stopped.	The Navy sets up a no-fly zone along California's coast south of San Diego, expanding along the border with Mexico as far east as Arizona. The Navy claims the area is for testing; others speculate that a secret military base will be built. . . . President Franklin Roosevelt warns that peace cannot be won through blind isolation.	In their last attempt at peace talks, committees of the AFL and CIO part ways, unable to find common ground or compromise.	Governors Lehman and Hoffman of New York and New Jersey open the Lincoln Tunnel.	Walt Disney's feature-length cartoon, *Snow White and the Seven Dwarfs*, premiers in Los Angeles, Calif. . . . Frank B. Kellogg, Nobel Peace Prize recipient and former senator, ambassador, and Secretary of State, dies in St. Paul, Minn.	Dec. 21
In a letter, President Franklin Roosevelt insists that Congress take responsibility for a balanced budget.	Japan's Foreign Office, in an interim report, denies that the *Panay* was targeted by Japanese guns; it claims a Chinese ship fired on the *Panay*.	In New Jersey, where a bus line strike has been going on for three months, a bomb is tossed into a garage and rips part of its roof off.	The Lincoln Tunnel opens to traffic in New York City.	Chicago votes to license pari-mutuel brokers, allowing legal off-track betting on horse races. Once the mayor signs the bill, it will be effective for January 6 track openings.	Dec. 22
	In Tokyo, U.S. Ambassador Joseph Grew and U.S. military representatives meet with Japan's army and navy leaders for three hours as they explain the events that led up to the *Panay* sinking.	The NLRB finds Ford Motor Company in violation of the Wagner Act, and orders it to reinstate 29 employees fired for union activities and give them back pay. Ford says it will appeal the ruling all the way to the Supreme Court, if need be. . . . Chrysler lays off 55,000 employees and cuts workweeks to 32 hours.	A large earthquake hits Mexico, centered in the Guerrero state.		Dec. 23
	Japan's official apology is delivered, and the United States studies it carefully for assurances against future attacks.	Homer Martin, head of the UAWA, tries to arrange a conference with Ford Motor Company but is rebuffed.		The name of Mae West is banned in every NBC studio in the country, due to her December 12 show.	Dec. 24

F	G	H	I	J
Includes elections, federal-state relations, civil rights and liberties, crime, the judiciary, education, healthcare, poverty, urban affairs, and population.	Includes formation and debate of U.S. foreign and defense policies, veterans affairs, and defense spending. (Relations with specific foreign countries are usually found under the region concerned.)	Includes business, labor, agriculture, taxation, transportation, consumer affairs, monetary and fiscal policy, natural resources, pollution, and accidents.	Includes worldwide scientific, medical, and technological developments, natural phenomena, U.S. weather, and natural disasters.	Includes the arts, religion, scholarship, communications media, sports, entertainment, fashions, fads, and social life.

	World Affairs	Europe	Africa & The Middle East	The Americas	Asia & The Pacific
Dec. 25		Most of France's strikes are settled: bakers will return to work tomorrow and Goodrich workers agree to a truce through January 3.... Germany releases over 50 pastors from prison for the Christmas holidays, but they must return to jail in a few days. Rev. Neimoeller and 50 others are kept incarcerated. In addition, 120 ministers will be released tomorrow, and all charges against them dropped. ... The Soviet Union announces 16 death sentences for crimes ranging from improper storage of store dummies and stocking unpopular merchandise, up to murder.	Near Tiberias in Palestine, 43 Arabs have been killed in the past two days and 20 more injured. Planes aid in the search for Arabs who hide in the hills of Galilee. Four thousand police guard visitors to Bethlehem at the Church of the Nativity.... An arms factory is found and shut down in Lebanon; it was supplying Palestinian terrorists.		Japan announces that punitive actions will be taken in Tsingtao against those who destroyed Japanese property there. Refugees arriving in Shanghai report that trenches and fortifications line the city's beaches and that 240 looters were executed by the Chinese defenders. . . . Chinese authorities report that outbreaks of either revolt or guerilla violence south of Tsinan have wiped out a Japanese battalion. ...At about this date, China's casualties pass one million.
Dec. 26	German Ambassador to China Oskar Trautman brings new, stiffer terms for China's surrender from Japan to General Chiang Kai-shek.	The BBC announces it will soon broadcast messages in several languages to refute the anti-British propaganda of Italy.... Romania abandons reconfiguring the votes as unconstitutional. Premier Gheorghe Tatarescu and his Cabinet resign.... At a Requiem Mass, the Iron Legion, the military arm of the Austrian Legitimists, appears in uniform for the first time. Representatives of the government and the Hapsburgs are also present.		The leaders of Haiti and the Dominican Republic exchange pledges not to wage war. At the same time, the Dominican Minister dismisses the charges and casualty figures as misleading and untrue.	Japan moves seven ships into position and blockades Tsingtao, but says foreign ships will not be affected.
Dec. 27		The Soviets denounce six top officials of the Transport Commissariat as treasonable wreckers, removing them from office.... The family of 67-year-old Prince Michael Radziwill of Poland is trying to have him declared incompetent, thereby preventing his marriage to a Jewish woman. The aristocratic Radziwills are active in Polish politics.	Over 90 percent of the Arab terrorists—including those who have engaged the British forces in Galilee for four days—are Syrian immigrants who come to Palestine with arms and funding, according to authorities.	President Lázaro Cárdenas of Mexico is personally responsible for a move to force Jews to leave the country, according to an editorial in El Nacional.	Chinese troops burn many buildings in Tsinan as they retreat and the city surrenders to Japan. Fighting continues in some sections. Chinese soldiers also blow up bridges, cutting transportation between Tsinan and Tsingtao.... Vice Admiral Hasegawa proclaims the reopening of Shanghai districts, but lists 10 offenses against military authority punishable by death including espionage, injuring Japanese troops, or harboring those who commit such injuries. This decree prevents foreign embassies from coming back to the city.
Dec. 28	Deposed Ethiopian leader Haile Selassie sends telegrams to all member nations of the Oslo Convention, asking that they not recognize the Italian conquest of his country. The Netherlands proposed such recognition.	Loyalists partially overcome the Spanish insurgent force in a Teruel seminary. However, the rebels escape to a nearby convent and continue to fight. . . . The Soviet Minister to Norway refuses a recall from his government and worries that his two grown sons will be held as hostages in Moscow, waiting his return.... At midnight, the Irish Free State will become Ireland.... Octavian Goga of the anti-Semitic German National Christian Party is asked by King Carol to form a new government in Romania. The choice is not popular; Goga's party received less than 10 percent of the vote in recent elections.		Mexico stops the movement of over 100 empty tank cars owned by U.S. companies headed for the oil fields. Since the U.S. companies have so far refused to pay strike wages, the government, by law, can seize property to pay those wages. . . . Mexico expropriates the unused racetrack at Agua Caliente. The racetrack closed due to President Lázaro Cárdenas's prohibition of gambling. The ownership is 85 percent American.	Japanese troops shell and occupy an island near Macao claimed by Portugal.
Dec. 29		Insurgent generals Aranda, Mujica, and Varela launch a counterattack for Teruel, leading three columns. Armies must fight in fog, snow, and ice.... France's former premier Pierre-Etienne Flandin brings troubling word that Germany's territorial demands are increasing. Since Germany has been ignored, it now wants Alsace returned. Germany later denies that this was said.... French subway, gas, electrical, and waterworks employees in Paris go on strike. Bus drivers, street cleaners, and garbage collectors join in.... Premier Octavian Goga's new government replaces all Romania's prefects with anti-Semitic members of his own party. New laws also suppress newspapers and create a nationwide army to stifle protest.	Egyptian soldiers return to duty in Khartoum in Anglo-Egyptian Sudan. Britain took full control of the country and expelled them in 1924, after the assassination of Sir Lee Stack.	U.S. and British oil companies ask Mexico's Supreme Court for an injunction stopping the seizure of their property to pay wages. They list 19 violations of the country's labor code committed by the government.	Unless China ceases its "anti-Japanese tactics," Japanese armies may have to push their attack 1,000 miles inland, says General Matsui, commander in the Yangtze region.... Retreating armies in Tsinan took most of the city's food with them, say authorities, so a crisis exists there. The countryside in many provinces is filled with hungry, destitute refugees.

A	B	C	D	E
Includes developments that affect more than one world region, international organizations, and important meetings of world leaders.	Includes all domestic and regional developments in Europe, including the Soviet Union.	Includes all domestic and regional developments in Africa and the Middle East.	Includes all domestic and regional developments in Latin America, the Caribbean, and Canada.	Includes all domestic and regional developments in Asian and Pacific nations (and colonies).

U.S. Politics & Social Issues	U.S. Foreign Policy & Defense	Economics & Great Depression	Science, Technology & Nature	Culture, Leisure & Lifestyle	
	Secretary of State Cordell Hull accepts Japan's apology for the *Panay's* sinking. The only condition is the continued respect for U.S. rights in China.			Arturo Toscanini conducts the first of 10 radio concerts for NBC Radio from New York, with the governor and other dignitaries present. The NBC Symphony Orchestra is hand-picked for this series. Tickets are requested by 23,000; less than 1,500 per concert get in.	Dec. 25
	The State Department asks Mexico to slow its drive on industrialization and seizure of properties, using the U.S. purchase of silver as leverage. Thirteen percent of Mexico's government income comes from U.S. silver purchases.				Dec. 26
The Tuskegee Institute announces that there were eight lynchings in 1937, the same as 1936. All victims were African Americans, and all lynchings happened in the south.			A major earthquake and several aftershocks kill four people near the border of Guatemala and El Salvador.		Dec. 27
		General Motors announces a layoff of 30,000 employees. The 205,000 remaining workers will be put on a 24-hour workweek. . . . In Springfield, Ill., 36 men are sentenced to four years in prison and given $20,000 fines. All were found to have participated in dynamiting and other acts of terrorism in the coal fields during five years of inter-union fighting.	Pan American Airways inaugurates the Samoan Clipper, flying between Hawaii and New Zealand, connecting with British Imperial Airways flights to Australia and other Pan Am flights to California.	Composer Maurice Ravel dies in Paris at age 62. He had been ill since an auto accident and recently underwent neurosurgery.	Dec. 28
	In Los Angeles, 22 sit-down strikers at Douglas Aircraft receive fines of up to $600 in court. The strike took place in February in Santa Monica.				Dec. 29

F	G	H	I	J
Includes elections, federal-state relations, civil rights and liberties, crime, the judiciary, education, healthcare, poverty, urban affairs, and population.	Includes formation and debate of U.S. foreign and defense policies, veterans affairs, and defense spending. (Relations with specific foreign countries are usually found under the region concerned.)	Includes business, labor, agriculture, taxation, transportation, consumer affairs, monetary and fiscal policy, natural resources, pollution, and accidents.	Includes worldwide scientific, medical, and technological developments, natural phenomena, U.S. weather, and natural disasters.	Includes the arts, religion, scholarship, communications media, sports, enter-tainment, fashions, fads, and social life.

	World Affairs	Europe	Africa & The Middle East	The Americas	Asia & The Pacific
Dec. 30	Japan formally apologizes to Britain for the bombing of its ships on December 12.	The Bank of Spain building where insurgents in Teruel held out is blown up. . . . Three reporters are killed in Caudete, Spain, a Teruel suburb, when a bomb hits their car. Bradish Johnson, age 26, of *Newsweek* is killed immediately. British reporter Richard Sheepshanks dies later, and AP correspondent Edward J. Neil lives for three days. Hal Philby, a fourth journalist, is not seriously injured. . . . France's utility workers' strike is settled with a compromise wage offer. . . . Germany uses secret messages to foreign correspondents to reveal news of an anti-Nazi meeting in Berlin. The press is skeptical. . . . New laws in Romania expropriate lands owned by Jews.	King Farouk of Egypt reprimands and dismisses Nahas Pasha as Premier and appoints Mohammad Mahmud Pasha in his place. The Wafd is out, and the Liberal Constitution Party is in.	Sixteen U.S. and British oil companies in Mexico refuse to pay the wage increase demanded by the government. . . . President Getulio Vargas extends for another three months the moratorium on liquidating mortgages, pleasing coffee plantation owners.	Chinese troops wreck Tsingtao, burning or blasting every Japanese-owned business, as well as communication and rail infrastructure. Most of Tsingtao's 600,000 residents flee.
Dec. 31		Battling through a snowstorm, three columns of Spanish insurgents force their way toward Teruel. One column rescues rebels trapped in isolated buildings (this is later disputed). Up to 200,000 men battle, according to some reports. . . . The French Senate refuses to approve funds to reopen the International Exposition in Paris next year, leaving its fate in doubt. . . . The second Soviet Five-Year-Plan ends. A new one starts tomorrow, but no schedule has been published. . . . More new laws in Romania: Jews cannot be in the liquor business. Jews cannot live in villages. Minorities may not work in newspapers or manage theaters. Foreign experts must, in most cases, leave the country. . . . Poland increases its guard along its border with Romania, anticipating crowds of Jewish immigrants—including many holding Polish citizenship.			All authorities leave Tsingtao, putting the city in the hands of foreigners. . . . Up to 200,000 Chinese soldiers in Shantung province may be trapped between two Japanese armies, one moving north from Pukow and the other south from Tsinan. . . . An American mission school, now emptied, is damaged when Canton is heavily shelled for an hour.

A	B	C	D	E
Includes developments that affect more than one world region, international organizations, and important meetings of world leaders.	Includes all domestic and regional developments in Europe, including the Soviet Union.	Includes all domestic and regional developments in Africa and the Middle East.	Includes all domestic and regional developments in Latin America, the Caribbean, and Canada.	Includes all domestic and regional developments in Asian and Pacific nations (and colonies).

U.S. Politics & Social Issues	U.S. Foreign Policy & Defense	Economics & Great Depression	Science, Technology & Nature	Culture, Leisure & Lifestyle	
		Interior Secretary Harold Ickes speaks out against big business, defending his antitrust program and accusing 200 corporations of trying to enslave America. President Franklin Roosevelt wants to use trust-busting laws to push private companies into lowering new housing costs.		Newsreel footage of the December 12 *Panay* bombing reaches U.S. movie theaters.	Dec. 30
		President Franklin Roosevelt lowers the price for domestically mined silver by about 13 cents, to 64.64 per ounce. . . . The Federal Trade Commission (FTC) officially orders all building supply trade groups to stop illegal business practices that suppress competition. . . . Edsel Ford and the Ford Company in Buffalo, N.Y., are charged with three violations of the Wagner Act by the NLRB. . . . There were 4,394 strikes in the first 11 months of 1937, according to the Labor Department.			Dec. 31

F
Includes elections, federal-state relations, civil rights and liberties, crime, the judiciary, education, healthcare, poverty, urban affairs, and population.

G
Includes formation and debate of U.S. foreign and defense policies, veterans affairs, and defense spending. (Relations with specific foreign countries are usually found under the region concerned.)

H
Includes business, labor, agriculture, taxation, transportation, consumer affairs, monetary and fiscal policy, natural resources, pollution, and accidents.

I
Includes worldwide scientific, medical, and technological developments, natural phenomena, U.S. weather, and natural disasters.

J
Includes the arts, religion, scholarship, communications media, sports, entertainment, fashions, fads, and social life.

1938

Adolf Hitler (left of center) accepts the ovation of the Reichstag after announcing the "peaceful" acquisition of Austria. Berlin, March 1938.

	World Affairs	Europe	Africa & The Middle East	The Americas	Asia & The Pacific
Jan.		The Italian government announces the expansion of its Naval Construction Program of 1937.... In Budapest, representatives of Hungarian, Italian, and Austrian governments confirm the protocols between the three countries. ... The Supreme Soviet, the new legislative body created under the country's Constitution of 1936, gathers for the first time.	The British government appoints a new commission under Sir John Woodhead, postponing the Peel Commission partition plan for Palestine. ... The wedding of King Farouk I of Egypt and Queen Farida Zulficar takes place in Cairo.	The Mexican government raises tariff rates from 100 to 200 percent on imported goods, damaging imports from the United States. ... The Dominican Republic and Haiti sign an immigration agreement.	The Japanese army gains control of the strategic port of Qingdao in the Sino-Japanese conflict.
Feb.	The League of Nations holds a third conference on German refugees.	The Hungarian government arrests many leaders of the National Socialist Party. ... German National Socialists take direct control of the military and diplomatic corps. ... The Unionists' victory in the Northern Ireland elections ends hope for a merger with Eire. ... King Carol of Romania takes on dictatorial powers.			Japan refuses to give Britain and the United States any data on its naval fleet. ... Three hundred swimmers are dragged out to sea by three waves. All except five are saved.
Mar.		In response to the Austrian government's call for a national referendum on independence, German troops seize control of the country. ... Nicolai Bukharin and other Old Guard Bolsheviks are tried for treason. They are found guilty and executed. ... Chancellor Hitler conducts an official state visit to Rome, where he gets an impressive state reception.	Sir Harold MacMichael is appointed British High Commissioner for Palestine. ... Oil is discovered in Saudi Arabia.	Mexican courts support the government's decision to force oil companies to increase wages for workers. ... The Mexican government announces that the property of American and British oil companies operating in Mexico will be nationalized.	Japanese forces reach the Yellow River region but suffer attacks from Chinese guerillas, who have better control of rural areas. A puppet government is established in Nanking. ... The Japanese government passes the National Mobilization Bill, which gives the state absolute control in the Japanese economy.
Apr.	The foreign ministers of Denmark, Finland, Norway, and Sweden meet to discuss a common defense policy for the region. ... The Permanent Court of International Justice holds its first session of the 1938 judicial year in The Hague.	The Anglo-Irish Treaty establishes closer links between Britain and Eire.... A national plebiscite in Austria approves the union with Germany. ... Edouard Daladier forms a new government in France.			
May	The Council of the League of Nations accepts the Swiss appeal for unconditional neutrality. ... The Vatican recognizes Francisco Franco's Spanish government. ... A four-day conference at Utrecht approves a provisional constitution for the World Council of Churches.	The Bulgarian government dissolves the National Socialist Party. ... Adolf Hitler again visits Premier Benito Mussolini in Rome. ... Douglas Hyde, a Protestant, becomes the first president of Eire.	Work begins on Tel Aviv Harbor.	The Brazilian government suppresses an uprising of the *Integralista* organization which has strong links to the German government.	The Japanese army conducts a series of military campaigns that extend its control of China.
Jun.	The International Labor Organization holds its 24th session in Geneva.	German anti-Jewish laws are extended to Austria as a result of the *Anschluss*. ... Eamon De Valera wins an overwhelming mandate in the Irish elections, becoming prime minister under the new constitution.	British authorities execute the Jewish terrorist Solomon ben Yosef.	Troops from Ecuador and Peru clash over a border dispute between the two countries. ... Chile announces its intention to withdraw from the League of Nations.	
Jul.	The Oslo Agreement promoting trade between Belgium, the Netherlands, Luxembourg, Denmark, Norway, and Sweden is terminated.	A German government decree makes all citizens liable to short-term labor service in the event of a national emergency. ... The French and Turkish governments sign an agreement regarding the future of the Alexandretta province. ... King George VI and Queen Elizabeth conduct an official state visit to Paris.	During the summer, terrorist groups organize attacks in Palestine that reflect the tensions between Jews and Arabs.	The Venezuelan government announces its withdrawal from the League of Nations. ... The Bolivian and Paraguayan governments sign the final peace treaty that officially ends the Chaco War.	Japanese and Soviet armies clash at Changkufeng Hill, on the border of Siberia, Korea, and Manchukuo. A truce follows, but relations between the countries remain tense.
Aug.	The League of Nations hosts a conference in Bandoeng in the Dutch East Indies to promote rural health in the Far East.	The Hungarian regent, Admiral Nicolas Horthy, conducts a state visit to Germany. ... The British and French governments support Bulgaria's rearmament program with a $10 million loan. ... The Italian government announces a new racial program that will discriminate against Jews.		The citizens of Bolivia and Paraguay vote to approve the Chaco Peace Treaty.	
Sept.	The League of Nations hosts a conference in Mexico City on rural health in Latin America. ... The League of Nations declares that Japan is the aggressor in the Sino-Japanese War.	In the Sanjak of Alexandretta elections, Turkish candidates win the absolute majority of the Assembly. Turkey assumes control of the region with the proclamation of the Republic of Hatay. ... Hitler demands self-determination for the Sudeten Germans and issues an ultimatum to Czechoslovakia. At the Munich Conference, Hitler obtains the cession of Sudetenland to Germany.		The Mexican government signs barter agreements with Germany, Japan, and other countries exchanging the oil expropriated from U.S. companies with goods.... A coup by rebels linked to the German government fails in Chile.	The Japanese government creates the United Council of China in Peiping as the first step to setting up a protectorate and overthrowing Chiang Kai-shek's Nationalist Chinese government.

A	B	C	D	E
Includes developments that affect more than one world region, international organizations, and important meetings of world leaders.	*Includes all domestic and regional developments in Europe, including the Soviet Union.*	*Includes all domestic and regional developments in Africa and the Middle East.*	*Includes all domestic and regional developments in Latin America, the Caribbean, and Canada.*	*Includes all domestic and regional developments in Asian and Pacific nations (and colonies).*

U.S. Politics & Social Issues	U.S. Foreign Policy & Defense	Economics & Great Depression	Science, Technology & Nature	Culture, Leisure & Lifestyle	
President Roosevelt establishes the March of Dimes, an organization to fight poliomyelitis.	Congress does not approve Rep. Louis Ludlow's constitutional amendment that would require a national referendum to confirm a declaration of war passed by Congress. . . . President Roosevelt proposes to British Prime Minister Neville Chamberlain a world conference on disarmament. Chamberlain refuses.		General Motors begins mass production of diesel engines.	Thornton Wilder's play *Our Town* is first performed publicly in Princeton, N.J.	Jan.
		The U.S. Federal Crop Insurance program is authorized.	The first Baird color TV is demonstrated at the Dominion Theatre in London. . . . A toothbrush becomes the first commercial product to be made from nylon yarn.	Thornton Wilder's play *Our Town* opens on Broadway. . . . Joan Tozzer and Robin Lee win the U.S. female and male figure skating championships, respectively.	Feb.
	Secretary of State Cordell Hull recognizes Mexico's right to nationalize foreign property but demands fair compensation.		Two hundred people die in the Los Angeles area due to floods and landslides.	Glenn Cunningham sets a new world record for the indoor mile run.	Mar.
The Supreme Court adopts Erie Railroad Co. v. Tompkins, which overturns a century of federal civil-procedure law.	The Roosevelt administration suspends its policy of buying Mexican silver above world prices.		Roy Plunkett discovers the polymer polytetrafluoroethylene, later known as teflon.		Apr.
The House Committee on Un-American Activities begins its work.	The joint American-Philippines Committee issues a report that recommends the gradual repeal of U.S. tariffs on Philippine goods over a period of 22 years. . . . Congress passes the Vinson Naval Act.		Sandoz Laboratories manufactures LSD.	Thornton Wilder is awarded the Pulitzer Prize for Literature.	May
The Civil Aeronautics Authority is established.		Congress creates the Federal Housing Administration to insure construction loans.	The Olympian Flyer express train crashes in Montana killing 47 people. . . . A 500-ton meteor lands in an empty field near Pittsburgh.	Action Comics features the first *Superman* issue. . . . Babe Ruth is signed as the Dodgers' coach for the rest of the season. . . . Italy wins the 1938 football World Cup.	Jun.
	The U.S. government asks for arbitration on the Mexican decision to confiscate the property of U.S. multinationals. The Mexican government rejects the arbitration.		Nestle starts the production of instant coffee after years of research.	Howard Hughes sets a new around-the-world flying record in 3 days, 19 hours, and 17 minutes. . . . Owen Wister, novelist and author of *The Virginian*, dies.	Jul.
Blues guitarist Robert Johnson dies after ingesting poisoned whiskey. . . . President Roosevelt dedicates the Thousand Islands Bridge connecting the United States and Canada.			A synthetic vitamin K is first produced.		Aug.
	In spite of pressure from oil companies, the Roosevelt administration maintains its Good Neighbor Policy toward Mexico. . . . President Roosevelt appeals to Hitler and Mussolini to find a peaceful solution for the Sudeten crisis.		A hurricane hits New York and New England killing 600 people.	The site of the 1940 Olympics changes from Tokyo, Japan, to Helsinki, Finland ,because of the Sino-Japanese War.	Sept.

F	G	H	I	J
Includes elections, federal-state relations, civil rights and liberties, crime, the judiciary, education, healthcare, poverty, urban affairs, and population.	*Includes formation and debate of U.S. foreign and defense policies, veterans affairs, and defense spending. (Relations with specific foreign countries are usually found under the region concerned.)*	*Includes business, labor, agriculture, taxation, transportation, consumer affairs, monetary and fiscal policy, natural resources, pollution, and accidents.*	*Includes worldwide scientific, medical, and technological developments, natural phenomena, U.S. weather, and natural disasters.*	*Includes the arts, religion, scholarship, communications media, sports, entertainment, fashions, fads, and social life.*

	World Affairs	Europe	Africa & The Middle East	The Americas	Asia & The Pacific
Oct.	The League of Nations tries to preserve international security by separating the Covenant of the League from the World War I peace treaties.	French Communists and socialists withdraw their support to the Daladier government because they disapprove of the Munich Agreement. German troops march into Sudetenland. . . . Czech President Eduard Benes resigns and leaves the country. . . . The Fascist Grand Council abolishes the Chamber of Deputies, eliminating the last remnant of democracy in Germany.	Arab extremists kill 20 Jews in Tiberias and capture a number of towns in Palestine. The British army regains control of most cities by the end of the month. . . . Libya is declared an integral part of Italy.	The arbitration by six presidents of American republics assigns most of the Chaco region to Paraguay and provides Bolivia with an outlet to the Pacific. . . . Ecuador asks for international arbitration of its border dispute with Peru.	The Japanese launch a major offensive in southern China, taking several major cities from the Chinese. . . . The British government appoints the Duke of Kent as the new Governor-General of Australia.
Nov.	The British, Canadian, and American governments signed a major trade agreement.	After a German diplomat is assassinated in Paris by a Jew, a series of organized attacks on synagogues and Jewish property multiply across Germany. . . . Cornliu Cordeanu, together with 13 leaders of the Romanian Iron Guard, are shot by guards during a transfer between prisons. . . . Turkish President Kemal Ataturk dies.	The Woodhead Commission concludes that all the plans designed so far for Palestine are impractical. New negotiations begin between Arabs and Jews. . . . The Egyptian government starts a major armament program.		The Japanese government officially rejects the Open Door policy stated in the Nine-Power Treaty on China.
Dec.		Tensions rise between France and Italy over respective colonies. Italy invalidates the Franco-Italian Treaty of 1935. . . . Following the Munich Agreement, the British government takes important steps to modernize its army and introduces the "national registry" for war service.	The Iranian government breaks diplomatic relations with France.	The eighth Pan-American Conference takes place in Lima, Peru. The Declaration of Lima reaffirms pan-American solidarity.	

A	B	C	D	E
Includes developments that affect more than one world region, international organizations, and important meetings of world leaders.	Includes all domestic and regional developments in Europe, including the Soviet Union.	Includes all domestic and regional developments in Africa and the Middle East.	Includes all domestic and regional developments in Latin America, the Caribbean, and Canada.	Includes all domestic and regional developments in Asian and Pacific nations (and colonies).

U.S. Politics & Social Issues	U.S. Foreign Policy & Defense	Economics & Great Depression	Science, Technology & Nature	Culture, Leisure & Lifestyle	
Oberlin College in Oberlin, Ohio, admits four female students and becomes the first institution of higher learning to offer the same college programs to men and women.		The Fair Labor Standards Act becomes law, establishing the 40-hour workweek and forbidding child labor in factories. . . . The federal hourly minimum wage is set at $0.25 an hour.	Chester Carlson and Otto Kornei perform the first successful test of their photocopier in New York.	Orson Welles performs a dramatic radio adaptation of H.G. Wells's *War of the Worlds* on CBS. Millions of Americans are thrown into a panic from what they believe is a real threat.	Oct.
Crystal Bird Fauset becomes the first African-American woman to be elected to a state legislature. . . . John C. Lewis is the first president of the Congress of Industrial Organizations.	U.S. Secretary of State Cordell Hull officially complains against the Japanese violation of Chinese integrity emphasizing the U.S. support for the Nine-Power Treaty.			Pearl Buck receives the Nobel Prize for Literature. . . . Kate Smith sings Irving Berlin's "God Bless America" on the radio for the first time.	Nov.
The State of California starts executions in gas chambers. . . . Daniel Roper resigns as Secretary of Commerce, a position he has held since President Roosevelt's inauguration in 1933.	The Department of State refuses to recognize the new Japanese policy in the Far East.		An electronic television system is patented by V.K. Zworykin.		Dec.

F	G	H	I	J
Includes elections, federal-state relations, civil rights and liberties, crime, the judiciary, education, healthcare, poverty, urban affairs, and population.	Includes formation and debate of U.S. foreign and defense policies, veterans affairs, and defense spending. (Relations with specific foreign countries are usually found under the region concerned.)	Includes business, labor, agriculture, taxation, transportation, consumer affairs, monetary and fiscal policy, natural resources, pollution, and accidents.	Includes worldwide scientific, medical, and technological developments, natural phenomena, U.S. weather, and natural disasters.	Includes the arts, religion, scholarship, communications media, sports, entertainment, fashions, fads, and social life.

	World Affairs	Europe	Africa & The Middle East	The Americas	Asia & The Pacific
Jan. 1	Britain dispatches anti-aircraft equipment and up to 1,000 troops to Alexandria, Egypt. . . . Alexander Gelver, a 24-year-old American, is shot for spying. Gelver was brought to the Soviet Union by immigrating parents while a minor.	French Defense Minister Daladier stops the issuance of licenses to export goods to Romania and Yugoslavia. This stops arms shipments to those countries, because of their growing ties to Italy. The move is later denied. . . . In Germany, Jewish doctors and dentists are barred from panel practice—which effectively keeps them from working.	A report on Palestine shows that, although a depression exists, new capital increased by 200 percent. Nineteen new Jewish settlements and 151 Jewish cooperatives were built. Sixty new Arab cooperatives were built.	Mexico suspends the increased wage demands made on U.S. and British oil companies, until the country's Supreme Court renders its decision. However, President Lázaro Cárdenas of Mexico sets aside the Morrow-Calles Agreement and announces that foreign oil companies must pay royalties to continue business in Mexico.	Chinese troops have left the coastal city of Tsingtao and Japanese troops have not yet arrived. The areas of Suchow and Taishan in the Shantung province are heavily bombed and damaged by Japanese planes.
Jan. 2	Germany's Ambassador to China, Oskar Trautman, conveys Japan's demands for surrender to Gen. Chiang Kai-shek. They are rejected.	Romania's former foreign minister, Nicolae Titulescu, living in Switzerland, now joins the National Peasant Party and pledges to its leader, Dr. Maniu, to work with him to defeat fascism.		Longshoremen in Puerto Rico walk away from their jobs, and no ships can be unloaded.	Two homemade bombs are thrown at Japanese officials in Shanghai; no one is hurt. . . . Chinese troops withdraw from the plains of Shantung, as Japanese forces capture the city of Taian.
Jan. 3		The Romanian stock market is in disarray, and a newspaper claims that Jews are withdrawing all their funds, preparing to leave the country. . . . Eight of the highest officials in Soviet Armenia's agricultural agencies have been executed for treason. Another seven await trial, while one more has committed suicide.	Former premier Nahas Pasha interrupts Egypt's Chamber of Deputies, reading a statement of "no confidence" in the Cabinet. He then leads a walkout of his followers, splitting the Wafdist Party. King Farouk tries to suspend Parliament; his speaker is shouted down. Later, Nahas Pasha calls for the government to resign.	U.S. and British oil facilities in Tampico, Mexico, close ostensibly for repairs—but operators announce they will not open until current issues with the government are resolved.	Gen. Chiang Kai-shek resigns as China's Premier to focus his energies on the war. Gen. Pai Chung-hsi is Vice-Commander. Dr. H.H. Kung becomes Premier. . . . Chinese planes now raid Nanking, dropping bombs on airfields and on Japanese warships on the Yangtze River.
Jan. 4		Loyalist forces in Teruel, Spain, claim they've held off four onslaughts by insurgents, who are renewing their efforts to retake the city. . . . Romania decrees that no Jew may employ a non-Jewish servant under age 40, in order to circumvent traffic in white slavery.	Exports in Ethiopia have come to a standstill, as coffee plantations are left untended. Most citizens use passive resistance to defy Italy. . . . A new commission under Sir John Woodhead will study the division of Palestine, delaying the actual partition for months.	President Getulio Vargas of Brazil decrees that cultural societies may not discuss or engage in politics.	Chinese sources claim that the Japanese have been driven from Hangchow. . . . Japanese planes drop over 100 bombs on Hangchow's airfield.
Jan. 5		The Spanish government orders the civilians of Madrid not involved in the war effort to evacuate the city. . . . Romania's anti-Semitic policies are mildly protested by France and Britain. The countries fear a strong outcry would push Romania closer to Germany.	Britain fortifies the Suez Canal area against air attacks, and will build a military base at Geneffa.	To cope with its economic problems, Nicaragua doubles the salaries of all government employees. . . . Cane cutters in Jamaica strike; 1,400 stage a demonstration that causes the plantation owner to flee. . . . Reports of an uprising by the army against President Ubico of Guatemala are categorically denied by the government.	Reports from Hangchow say the city has suffered continuous violence, rapes, and looting since its occupation on December 24. The Japanese military claims to have its soldiers under control now.
Jan. 6		Both insurgent and loyalist artillery pound Teruel from opposite sides, but neither gains ground. Americans in the International Brigade are deployed in this action. . . . Spanish Socialist leaders call for an end to the bombing of cities not on battlefronts, but are ignored.		President Lázaro Cárdenas will allocate 2 million pesos to establish a National Polytechnic Institute in Mexico.	Japan's war in China will double its military expenditures and raise next year's budget by 50 percent. . . . Japanese planes bombard airfields in Hangchow; the Chinese use smoke-screens to protect the airfields with some success.
Jan. 7	Japanese soldiers accost two British policemen in the International Settlement of Shanghai.	Spain's military governor in Teruel brokers the surrender of insurgent troops, which end up numbering 2,700. An additional 3,000 civilians surrender as well. The commander who surrenders is denounced as a traitor by Franco's followers.		Pursuing an anti-Communist policy, Quebec's Prime Minister Duplessis authorizes a raid on a Jewish cultural association and the seizure of 800 Yiddish books.	Sixty thousand Japanese troops launch a push against the Lung-Hai railroad, the main route to the new capital Hangchow.
Jan. 8		The Moscow theater of controversial producer Y. Meyerhold is dissolved, and his future left in doubt. He is accused of misusing funds on bad productions, but his work is known throughout the world.	The government of Tunisia expels anti-French agitator Hassan Nouri. A general strike and parade ensues in Bizerte. Police fire on the crowd, killing six and wounding 37.	The United States will buy 35 million ounces of Mexican silver, and the U.S. stabilization fund is maintaining the peso's exchange rate, enabling the continuance of President Lázaro Cárdenas's social reforms.	
Jan. 9	A French priest is killed and another wounded when Japanese planes bomb a Catholic church at Nanning in the Kwangsi province.	The Budapest Conference starts, with the foreign ministers of Italy, Austria, and Hungary meeting. . . . On a hill outside Budapest, a group of about 50 Nazi skiers attacks a smaller group of Jewish skiers, and 25 are injured. Police arrest 14 Nazis.		As the longshoremen's strike enters its second week, the threat of a food shortage hangs over Puerto Rico. Other workers face layoffs as no exports can be made.	Japanese troops along the Lung-Hai railway may trap the 100,000 Chinese troops under the command of Gen. Li Tsung-jen. Reinforcements are on their way.
Jan. 10		The Soviet press denounces 21 Bishops of the Orthodox Church as saboteurs and terrorists. . . . Four members of the Cagoulards are held in the Paris bombings of September 11.	Archaeologist James Leslie Starkey, traveling from his excavation site at Lachish, is killed by armed Arabs. His chauffeur is allowed to drive away.	The second trial of eight Puerto Rican Nationalists accused of shooting at a judge begins and ends quickly. The defense will not cooperate in picking jurors or questioning witnesses, so the judge declares all guilty and imposes five year prison terms on them.	The city of Tsingtao is taken when 12 Japanese warships offload troops at its port. Chinese defenders left days ago, so there is no fighting.

A	B	C	D	E
Includes developments that affect more than one world region, international organizations, and important meetings of world leaders.	Includes all domestic and regional developments in Europe, including the Soviet Union.	Includes all domestic and regional developments in Africa and the Middle East.	Includes all domestic and regional developments in Latin America, the Caribbean, and Canada.	Includes all domestic and regional developments in Asian and Pacific nations (and colonies).

U.S. Politics & Social Issues	U.S. Foreign Policy & Defense	Economics & Great Depression	Science, Technology & Nature	Culture, Leisure & Lifestyle	
		A partial report on November's unemployment census shows 10.8 million Americans out of work. Almost 2 million are women. . . . Thirty six million people are now paying into Social Security.	There are 43 million motor vehicles in the world, and almost 82 percent are in the United States.	The University of Alabama's Crimson Tide suffers its first Rose Bowl defeat, at the hands of California's Golden Bears (UC Berkeley). In the second Cotton Bowl, Rice beats Colorado.	Jan. 1
					Jan. 2
Congress reconvenes; the "Big Navy" Bill is their first priority—a response to last month's bombing of the *Panay*.		The Supreme Court upholds the Public Works Administration's power and utility programs. The Administration is free to loan funds to municipal utilities—a victory for the New Deal.			Jan. 3
		Chairman Eccles of the Federal Reserve Board tells Senators that only government intervention can stop the sharp drop in consumer purchasing power.			Jan. 4
George Sutherland announces his retirement from the Supreme Court on January 18.	For defense spending in fiscal year 1939, President Franklin Roosevelt asks Congress for $1 billion.	The President submits a budget asking $7 billion in spending, creating a deficit of $950 million. . . . Seattle's 1,500 longshoremen walk off their jobs in a strike. . . . New York's automat workers settle their five-month strike with little gain.			Jan. 5
The House tackles appropriations and spending.		William Knudsen, president of General Motors, appears before a Senate subcommittee on relief, and says that he expects sales to rebound in the spring. Business was down 50 percent in December.			Jan. 6
Southern Senators filibuster the Anti-Lynching Bill. Senator William Borah says such a bill goes against the principles of democracy.					Jan. 7
	U.S. diplomats in Hangchow get reports on the looting of American homes and businesses in Nanking.				Jan. 8
		The Maritime Commission approves subsidies for seven companies to begin construction of 20 ships.		Father Coughlin returns to the airways, urging the American Federation of Labor (AFL) and the Committee for Industrial Organization (CIO) to end their quarrel.	Jan. 9
Governor Hoffman of New Jersey decides 110 persons will share a $25,000 award. New Jersey offered the reward for the arrest and conviction of the killer of Charles Lindbergh's child. One hundred of the claimants are bank tellers who helped identify ransom payment bills; they will get $25 each.	The House defeats the Ludlow Bill after the President sends a letter arguing against it. The bill would have required a national referendum before war was declared—unless the country was attacked.	This week, Chrysler reemploys 55,000 workers laid off December 23.			Jan. 10

F	G	H	I	J
Includes elections, federal-state relations, civil rights and liberties, crime, the judiciary, education, healthcare, poverty, urban affairs, and population.	Includes formation and debate of U.S. foreign and defense policies, veterans affairs, and defense spending. (Relations with specific foreign countries are usually found under the region concerned.)	Includes business, labor, agriculture, taxation, transportation, consumer affairs, monetary and fiscal policy, natural resources, pollution, and accidents.	Includes worldwide scientific, medical, and technological developments, natural phenomena, U.S. weather, and natural disasters.	Includes the arts, religion, scholarship, communications media, sports, entertainment, fashions, fads, and social life.

	World Affairs	Europe	Africa & The Middle East	The Americas	Asia & The Pacific
Jan. 11	The French issue an "energetic protest" to Japan over the January 9 incident. As the message is delivered in Tokyo, Nanning suffers another air attack.	The Dutch freighter *Hannah* is torpedoed near Cape San Antonio, Spain; all aboard are rescued. . . . Soviet purges are leveled at managers and scientists in the Academy of Agriculture.		Brazil suspends orders that would deport up to 1,000 Jews. All are in Brazil illegally from European countries. Brazil's move is seen as both humane and anti-fascist.	Japan's Imperial Council meets for the first time in 24 years to hear Foreign Minister Hirota speak, and decide on conditions for future relations with China.
Jan. 12		As the Budapest Conference ends, Hungary and Austria agree to recognize Franco's Spain. Italy was not able to persuade them to leave the League of Nations. . . . The newly elected Supreme Soviet meets for the first time.			China's experienced Eighth Army troops organize and train guerilla units near Hangchow and Suchow, and Chinese planes continue to shell warships on the Yangtze River.
Jan. 13		Spanish insurgents bomb a train which they say was transporting loyalist troops. Loyalists claim the train carried wounded men and was clearly marked with a red cross. . . . Poland's Lwow University opens—with ghetto seating for Jewish students—after a two-month closure in protest. The president of the University resigned yesterday. . . . A new law in Germany bars Jews from entering the medical or dental fields.			Confusing reports over broken communication lines indicate that Chinese troops staged a surprise attack and drove Japan's forces away from Tsining. . . . Yingtak, 85 miles north of Canton, is shelled three times a week, because of the railroad station there.
Jan. 14		Behind closed doors, after an all-night session of the Chamber of Deputies, the government of French Premier Camille Chautemps collapses, and he resigns. Georges Bonnet, Finance Minister, is asked to form a new Cabinet. Socialists and Communists refuse to support Bonnet.		Talks fail in the Puerto Rico longshoremen's strike. Governor Winship is in a hospital with broken ribs and unable to intervene. Food for the island is imported through the Dominican Republic.	Mongolian troops, with Soviet support, reinforce their border with Suiyuan province, which is under Japanese control.
Jan. 15	Agents of Japan attempt to establish $50 million in credit to purchase machinery from the United States for use in Manchukuo.	The Soviet Union stops all commercial payments to Italy, principally over fuel oil shipped to Italy that is not being paid for as promised. . . . A law prohibiting Romanians from working as servants for Jews sparks demonstrations and window-smashing.	A manifesto by the outlawed Palestine Arab High Committee, now operating in Syria, criticizes Britain's proposed partition of Palestine.	A church said to date back to the time of Cortéz is burned by a mob in Veracruz while police and firemen stand by.	Japanese troops control Tsining again, but by nightfall China is claiming the city. Chinese sources say Tsining has changed hands several times in the past week.
Jan. 16		Barcelona suffers through five insurgent air raids in two days. . . . Leon Blum, former prime minister, is asked by France's President to form a government after Georges Bonnet fails. The Rightists refuse to support Blum. . . . A terrible review of the Soviet film *Treasure Island* leads to news that the head of the Soviet movie industry and several people involved in the production have been removed as "enemies of the people."			Prime Minister Konoe of Japan refuses to negotiate with Chiang Kai-shek any longer, a declaration which becomes policy. . . . Journalists say the area between Shanghai and Nanking, once populated with hundreds of thousands, is now a wasteland. Homes and villages are burnt and shelled, and crops rot in the fields. . . . Sugar workers in Pampanga province, Philippines, strike when 129 workers in a nearby quarry are arrested for their strike.
Jan. 17	Italy sends its first colonists to Ethiopia to begin cultivation of their newly awarded lands. Italy plans to have 800 colonists in Africa by the end of 1938, and settle 15,000 families within three years. . . . The *Nantucket Chief* is captured by Spanish insurgent ships, who claim the U.S. tanker was delivering Russian oil to the port of Barcelona. The tanker is escorted to Majorca.	A battalion of American and Canadian troops, fighting for the loyalist cause at Teruel, stop an insurgent cavalry attack with heavy machine gun fire. . . . In London, Britain and Ireland begin talks on political and economic issues. Irish Prime Minister Eamon de Valera insists Ireland be reunited with Ulster in the north, and that Catholic minorities there be treated fairly.		A factional fight between labor unions results in a one-day general strike in Orizaba, Veracruz, Mexico. Violence erupts and eight men die, while 25 are injured in street fighting. President Lázaro Cárdenas arrives and vows not to leave until the labor strife is settled.	Chinese troops use Russian planes to shell airfields used by Japanese pilots. . . . Three thousand Chinese troops fight in the Pootung area of Shanghai, interfering with the food supply entering the city.
Jan. 18		The Soviet Union's Central Committee, led by Josef Stalin, announces an end to the purges, and orders offices and commissariats to reinstate purged members.		The government of Ecuador orders the expulsion of alien Jews not working in agriculture. . . . In St. Hyacinthe, Quebec, 46 people die in a fire at a Catholic boarding school for boys.	Reinforcements are rushed to Japanese-held Hangchow as China counter-attacks.
Jan. 19	British troops at the International Settlement in Shanghai clash with Japanese officers who demand that Chinese people in the Settlement be turned over.	Spanish insurgents stage bombing raids between Valencia and Barcelona, killing hundreds. . . . Premier Goga of Romania says he will ask the League of Nations to decide the fate of half a million "foreign" Jews that he intends to expel.		By presidential decree, Mexico increases tariffs from 100 percent to 200 percent on goods from the United States. President Lázaro Cárdenas's goal is to reduce imports, except for machinery.	Winter storms slow fighting in Shantung province. Chinese sources claim that their troops are in position to attack Wuhu, on the Yangtze River, and move closer to Hangchow.

A	B	C	D	E
Includes developments that affect more than one world region, international organizations, and important meetings of world leaders.	*Includes all domestic and regional developments in Europe, including the Soviet Union.*	*Includes all domestic and regional developments in Africa and the Middle East.*	*Includes all domestic and regional developments in Latin America, the Caribbean, and Canada.*	*Includes all domestic and regional developments in Asian and Pacific nations (and colonies).*

U.S. Politics & Social Issues	U.S. Foreign Policy & Defense	Economics & Great Depression	Science, Technology & Nature	Culture, Leisure & Lifestyle	
As the filibuster against the Anti-Lynching Bill continues for a fifth day, Democrats worry that their party will split along north-south lines.	Trade treaty negotiations with Italy halt. Although all aspects of the treaty are mutually agreeable, Premier Benito Mussolini insists that the United States recognize King Victor Emanuel as Emperor of Ethiopia. The United States refuses.	Secretary Henry Wallace tells Congress that U.S. farms are experiencing bumper crops, accompanied by a slump in prices, leading to a greater need for rural relief funds.	The Samoan Clipper is lost in the Pacific near Pago Pago. The clipper carried mail, freight, and seven crewmen; it had not begun transporting passengers.		Jan. 11
			A severe earthquake, said to last 20 minutes, hits Japan. . . . A typhoon reaches Luzon, the main island of the Philippines.		Jan. 12
		After a three-year strike, a federal court orders mining unions in Freeburg, Ill., to pay $117,000 in damages to the United Electric Coal Company.			Jan. 13
As the filibuster on the Anti-Lynching Bill persists, Louisiana's Senator Ellender proposes amendments to outlaw marriage between different races.		In a press conference, the President speaks against holding companies, saying he finds them unnecessary and would like to eliminate them.		The Federal Communications Commission issues a rebuke to NBC and 59 affiliates for the December 12 broadcast featuring Mae West. The FCC found the script vulgar and indecent.	Jan. 14
The President nominates former U.S. Solicitor General Stanley Reed to the Supreme Court. Reed has never served as a judge but is a popular choice.		Responding to the President's comments, Wendell Willkie, head of Commonwealth and Southern Corporation, offers to sell its subsidiary utilities in the Tennessee Valley to the government, thereby breaking up its holding company.			Jan. 15
		Workers at Crucible Steel in Harrison, N.J., stage a sit-down strike over contract violations. When the police tell them no picketing will be allowed, employees walk out, just before midnight. . . . Between mid-October and January 15, 2.8 million nonagricultural jobs were lost.		Benny Goodman plays to a lively crowd at Carnegie Hall; the concert is recorded.	Jan. 16
	The United States delivers a note of protest to Japan over the illegal seizure of American property in Nanking and Hangchow. The protest is not made public for 10 days, and the outrages continue.	Governor Earle of Pennsylvania asks the President to investigate monopolistic practices by coal companies. . . . Ford Motor Company makes an offer to its St. Louis employees, who've been on strike since late November. Ford will grant some concessions if the union withdraws its charges.		The nationwide campaign for the National Foundation for Infantile Paralysis begins.	Jan. 17
		The strike at Crucible Steel ends with negotiations.			Jan. 18
	Eighteen Navy planes land at Pearl Harbor, Hawaii, after flying 2,570 miles from San Diego in 20 hours, 12 minutes—a record for a mass flight. The Navy has now transferred 42 planes to the Pearl Harbor base.	The President addresses the 49 members of his Business Advisory Council, asking for ways to reconcile businesses large and small with labor, suppliers, transportation, and customers.		In Buffalo, N.Y., a man is convicted of driving drunk based on the evidence of his own blood, analyzed by a chemistry professor at the University of Buffalo Medical School.	Jan. 19

F	G	H	I	J
Includes elections, federal-state relations, civil rights and liberties, crime, the judiciary, education, healthcare, poverty, urban affairs, and population.	Includes formation and debate of U.S. foreign and defense policies, veterans affairs, and defense spending. (Relations with specific foreign countries are usually found under the region concerned.)	Includes business, labor, agriculture, taxation, transportation, consumer affairs, monetary and fiscal policy, natural resources, pollution, and accidents.	Includes worldwide scientific, medical, and technological developments, natural phenomena, U.S. weather, and natural disasters.	Includes the arts, religion, scholarship, communications media, sports, entertainment, fashions, fads, and social life.

	World Affairs	Europe	Africa & The Middle East	The Americas	Asia & The Pacific
Jan. 20		At least 100 people die in further shelling from insurgent planes in Barcelona, Valencia, and Tarragona, Spain. Fighting continues in the Teruel area as well, on the ground and in the air. Loyalists bomb the barracks of the Condor Legion in Salamanca, and 225 are killed.	King Farouk of Egypt, 17, weds 16-year-old Farida Zulfikar.		Nanking faces food and medicine shortages. International relief workers claim Japanese authorities are blocking their requests for needed supplies in refugee camps. In response, Japanese officials take over the relief operations, claiming that among the quarter million refugees are 1,500 armed Chinese troops.
Jan. 21	Sun Ke (son of Sun Yat-sen) arrives in Moscow to plead for Soviet military action on behalf of China. Over the next few weeks, he meets with Josef Stalin and Foreign Minister Litvinoff, but his mission is a failure.	Witnesses in Teruel, Spain, tell government investigators that during the insurgent occupation between 3,000 and 4,000 people were executed for leftist sympathies. . . . In Bucharest, Romania, Jewish lawyers are beaten when they try to enter the courts. Kosher slaughter is forbidden, and Jewish-owned shops are ordered to stay open on the Sabbath.			Japan continues to bar foreigners (except diplomats) from entering Nanking due to lawless and dangerous conditions. In Shanghai, Japanese authorities say they will censor cables, rather than embarrass the army by passing along descriptions of their conduct in Nanking.
Jan. 22	Doctors and medical units funded by the League of Nations begin arriving in China with vaccines. The anti-epidemic work will be headquartered in Hangchow, with mobile units in other parts of the country.	Romania's newest law demands that 1 million Jews present paperwork proving citizenship. In some areas, documents must date to 1918.		In an effort to lower prices on food and clothing, Nicaragua's Congress legislates that merchants' profits must be kept under 20 percent.	Japan's Foreign Minister Hirota explains the undeclared war in China by saying that China was invited to join Japan's anti-Communist bloc, and rejected the opportunity. Japan has since done what was necessary to gain cooperation from China.
Jan. 23		Spanish government planes bomb Seville, and Barcelona is shelled by insurgents. Insurgents also kill 30 near the French border as they bomb Puigcerda. . . . Romania's economy is not doing well. The price of coal and other commodities drops as Jewish middlemen stop buying.		A delegation of Puerto Rican business leaders will appeal to President Franklin Roosevelt, asking him to act to stop the longshoremen's strike. Over 75,000 workers are idled by the strike.	Japan says they have expelled the 1,000 Chinese troops fighting in the Pootung area near Shanghai. . . . The Soviet Embassy in Hangchow burns in an accidental fire.
Jan. 24	A squadron led by Bruno Mussolini, son of Italy's Prime Minister, flies 2,500 miles from Rome to Dakar in French West Africa, the first leg of a trip to Brazil.	Insurgents claim that Teruel has been evacuated and that loyalists hold only the northern part of the city. . . . The Bulgarian Cabinet resigns and will be rebuilt by Premier Kiosseivanoff.			In Shantung province, former governor Gen. Han Fu-chu is executed for disobeying orders and abusing his position. . . . Addressing the Commonwealth Assembly, Philippine President Quezon says he wants to tax the wealthy based on their ability to pay. He has already eliminated poll taxes.
Jan. 25	Bruno Mussolini makes the 3,200-mile Atlantic crossing in under 14 hours, landing at Rio de Janeiro. The purpose of his trip is to promote goodwill and trade.	In Paris, the labor problems that caused the general strike in December are settled. Municipal workers will get the same wage as government workers. . . . In Greece, opposition leaders, including former Premier Sophoulis, are arrested and exiled for speaking against Gen. Metaxas's regime.		Governor Winship of Puerto Rico, just out of the hospital, gives longshoremen and shipping companies 48 hours to settle their strike or face government intervention.	
Jan. 26	An Ethiopian legation in London says 6,000 Italians have died in battle over the last two months, trying to hold onto their new colony. Italy dismisses this claim as "fantastic."	In a Paris suburb, 14 men are killed when thousands of hand grenades explode in a police laboratory. The grenades were seized by police from the *Cagoulards*. . . . German Catholics learn they may not go to the upcoming Eucharistic Congress in Hungary, which 25,000 had been expected to attend in the summer.			Guerilla tactics prove effective against Japan's armies, stopping the Japanese from closing in on Suchow for weeks. Three Chinese planes are shot down as they shell an airfield in Nanking, but pilots claim to destroy a fuel depot and ruin 30 enemy planes.
Jan. 27	The League of Nations Council begins its 100th session. . . . Paul van Zeeland, Belgium's former premier, presents a long-awaited report recommending an international economic pact headed by Britain, France, Germany, Italy, and the United States.	Austria rounds up 65 Nazi leaders for questioning, and releases most of them. . . . Bulgaria arrests 300 for Communist activities.			Japanese planes shell Hangchow and Nanchang, destroying six planes on the ground.
Jan. 28	Britain, France, the Soviet Union, and China draft a resolution in Geneva asking the League of Nations to take a stronger stand in China.	In a long talk with his Romanian counterpart, Britain's Foreign Secretary tries to influence Romania's policy toward Jews. . . . Greek authorities arrest 15 for plotting to kill Gen. Metaxas, and say the men will be detained for one year.			
Jan. 29		Soviet Minister of Justice Nikolai Krylenko is arrested, eleven days after being removed from his post. . . . King Carol assures Britain and France of Romania's friendship and says there will be no violence toward Jews in his country. . . . News reports claim 1,000 Communists have been arrested in Bulgaria.	Thousands of copies of manifestoes, printed in Syria, reach Palestine, Iraq, Hedjaz, and other Arab communities. The pamphlets list alleged British atrocities, such as tearing up the Koran.	Although Governor Winship of Puerto Rico has made proposals in the longshoremen's strike that the union is considering, shipping company representatives on the island respond that they have no authority to accept his offers.	Japanese authorities restrict access to certain areas of Shanghai from foreigners.
	A Includes developments that affect more than one world region, international organizations, and important meetings of world leaders.	**B** Includes all domestic and regional developments in Europe, including the Soviet Union.	**C** Includes all domestic and regional developments in Africa and the Middle East.	**D** Includes all domestic and regional developments in Latin America, the Caribbean, and Canada.	**E** Includes all domestic and regional developments in Asian and Pacific nations (and colonies).

U.S. Politics & Social Issues	U.S. Foreign Policy & Defense	Economics & Great Depression	Science, Technology & Nature	Culture, Leisure & Lifestyle	
Senator Ellender completes 27 hours and 45 minutes of filibustering against the Anti-Lynching Bill. He spoke for six days, with interruptions and quorum calls from his own party.		A five-day strike that shut down three newspapers in Oregon ends with pay raises and a new contract.			Jan. 20
		The President meets with officials of auto makers and loan companies at the White House, expressing his concern about extreme overselling techniques and consumer credit. . . . A Federal Court upholds the Tennessee Valley Authority's (TVA's) right to compete with private utilities.		James Braddock is judged the winner in a heavyweight fight with Great Britain's champion Tommy Farr. After the decision, Farr throws a photographer halfway across his dressing room. . . . Austrian conductor Erich Leinsdorf, age 25, makes his U.S. debut at New York's Metropolitan Opera House.	Jan. 21
In Madison, Wisc., a three and a half month trial of 16 oil companies and 30 executives ends in convictions for all on gasoline price-fixing charges. . . . Southern Senators agree to continue their 14-day filibuster of the Anti-Lynching Bill.		Spokesmen for the iron and steel industry, like many others to appear before the Senate Committee on Unemployment, expect an upturn and increased business in 1938.	A major earthquake of over 6.7 hits Hawaii, causing minor landslides, broken windows, and panic.		Jan. 22
				Entertainer Eddie Cantor develops a spin for the fundraising drive for the National Foundation for Infantile Paralysis. He begins a radio campaign asking for everyone to send a dime to the White House, in a "March of Dimes."	Jan. 23
Trying to end the filibuster over the Anti-Lynching Bill, Majority Leader Barkley starts holding the Senate in session until late night.		The SEC imposes strict rules to curtail short sales on the stock market, effective February 8.			Jan. 24
Stanley Reed is confirmed as an Associate Justice on the Supreme Court.		Asked if he agrees with the head of a major steel company that prices cannot be lowered without cutting wages, President Franklin Roosevelt says cutting wages would be "moral bankruptcy." . . . The TVA begins negotiations to buy smaller utilities.		An exhibition at New York's Museum of Modern Art features 20 photographs of a new, cantilevered house being completed at Bear Run, Pennsylvania. It is the public's introduction to Fallingwater, designed by Frank Lloyd Wright.	Jan. 25
The Senate invokes the cloture rule to end the filibuster.		John L. Lewis of the CIO announces that either the CIO or the AFL should become part of the other organization on February 1, and work out the details in subsequent meetings. The AFL declines. . . . Jersey City's Mayor Hague considers the CIO a Communist group and says he will not allow them in his city.			Jan. 26
Vice President John Garner interrupts the Senate for a vote on cloture of the filibuster, but fails to get the necessary votes.	News of America's January 17 protest to Japan is released; it is revealed that a U.S. envoy was slapped in the face by Japanese soldiers as he questioned the soldiers' occupation of American-owned property.		The Falls View International Bridge, which sat for years a quarter-mile below Niagara Falls, plunges into the Niagara River gorge. An ice jam had pounded the bridge for two days.	John Dos Passos's 1,500 page trilogy, U.S.A., is published.	Jan. 27
	In a message to Congress, the President asks for large increases in national defense. His Army and Navy expenditures will cost $800 million. He points to the arms build-ups of other nations as a threat to U.S. safety.	John L. Lewis of the CIO charges AFL head William Green of misrepresenting and betraying his own union, the United Mine Workers.		Over 30,000 dimes are received in the morning delivery of White House mail.	Jan. 28
				After a month's preparation and publicity, the National Foundation for Infantile Paralysis is officially launched by President Franklin Roosevelt on the eve of his 56th birthday. Fifteen thousand fundraising dances are held.	Jan. 29

F	G	H	I	J
Includes elections, federal-state relations, civil rights and liberties, crime, the judiciary, education, healthcare, poverty, urban affairs, and population.	Includes formation and debate of U.S. foreign and defense policies, veterans affairs, and defense spending. (Relations with specific foreign countries are usually found under the region concerned.)	Includes business, labor, agriculture, taxation, transportation, consumer affairs, monetary and fiscal policy, natural resources, pollution, and accidents.	Includes worldwide scientific, medical, and technological developments, natural phenomena, U.S. weather, and natural disasters.	Includes the arts, religion, scholarship, communications media, sports, entertainment, fashions, fads, and social life.

	World Affairs	Europe	Africa & The Middle East	The Americas	Asia & The Pacific
Jan. 30	Britain's Foreign Secretary Anthony Eden warns Romania that he will ask for a special session of the League of Nations if Romania continues to pursue anti-Semitic programs.	Insurgent planes bomb Barcelona in two morning raids, leaving over 400 dead. A children's home is hit, and 158 children die. Insurgents also launch a surprise attack on the front, starting in Penarroyo and continuing northwest.			Chinese forces claim the victory in fighting at Mengyin in Shantung province.
Jan. 31		The Endymion, a British steamship, is sunk near Cartagena, Spain. Eleven are killed. . . . Due to the Barcelona bombings, Spain's Parliament moves its opening session to a mountaintop monastery.	A day after a band of 40 Arabs opened fire on a police patrol in northern Palestine, troops surround all villages in the Jenin area. Eleven Arabs and two British soldiers die in fighting.	Haiti and the Dominican Republic sign an Immigrant Agreement, and the Dominican Republic agrees to set up an indemnity fund of $750,000 for the deaths of Haitians in October.	Japanese sources say 3,000 Chinese soldiers have died in the last two days in battles in Shantung and Anhwei provinces.
Feb. 1	The International Convention of Telecommunications opens in Egypt, with 62 nations and hundreds of private companies in attendance. The meeting, called to revise telegraph, telephone, and radio regulations, will last until April 4.	Britain deploys eight destroyers to hunt the submarine that torpedoed the Endymion. The Spanish government insists that Franco's forces could only have gotten submarines from Italy, even though Italy is one of the countries patrolling for pirate submarines. . . . Premier Chautemps of France begins conferences aimed at ending air bombardments of civilians.	In Palestine, British Royal Air Force planes bomb an Arab band hiding in a wooded area near Haifa, and kill 15 men.		Japanese authorities claim to reunite the Hopeh and East Hopeh provinces, which were split by the invasion, under a provisional government. . . . Battle rages around a key railroad junction at Mingkwang, 100 miles from Suchow (Xuzhou). Up to half a million troops are engaged.
Feb. 2	The League of Nations adjourns after voting on a resolution that "deplores" the Far East situation. Dr. Koo, China's delegate, calls the resolution "inadequate," but reserves the right to ask the League for more positive measures later.	Britain's Foreign Secretary Anthony Eden asks Italy and France to sink any submarine found in patrol areas, and announces that Britain's patrol ships will increase in number. . . . Foreign Minister Istrate Micescu claims victory over the Jews in a suit presented to the League of Nations. However, rather than take immediate action on the suit, the League decides to treat petitions brought against Romania by Jews as "not urgent."	King Farouk of Egypt issues a decree dissolving his Chamber of Deputies.		After being held back by Chinese forces for a month, the Japanese army in Anhwei captures Pengpu, a strategically important railway town.
Feb. 3		France orders its patrol ships to fire on any submarines in its patrol areas. . . . The Spanish government pledges no air strikes on civilians while talks are conducted to end such attacks. Gen. Franco of the insurgents does not reply, but his planes bomb Madrid and the border town of Figueras.			In Shantung province, the Japanese army captures Chefoo. . . . Japan's War Minister says 20,000 Japanese soldiers have died in the last seven months. . . . . A plot to overthrow Canton's government by assassination is discovered, and martial law is imposed by authorities.
Feb. 4		In Germany, Foreign Minister Konstantin von Neurath resigns and Ambassador Joachim von Ribbentrop takes his place. Chancellor Adolf Hitler takes over the War Ministry himself and appoints army commander Walther von Brauchitsch head of the Wehrmacht. . . . The British freighter Alcira sinks after an attack by two Spanish rebel planes.			Japan continues to bomb areas between captured Pengpu and Japan's next target, Suchow.
Feb. 5	The United States, France, and Britain all officially demand that Japan reveal, by February 20, the size and numbers of naval ships being built.	Seeing fewer moderates in the new hierarchy of the Reich, other nations speculate that a "putsch" against Austria is planned. . . . In Austria, violence against Jews erupts.	A gun battle over local elections in the town of Nazlet Khalaf, Egypt, leaves 10 dead and 48 injured.	Governor Winship negotiates a settlement in the longshoremen's strike in Puerto Rico. Union members will accept or reject it on February 7.	Kwangtung province in southern China is heavily bombed by Japanese planes.
Feb. 6		Two Iron Guard fascists die in clashes with Romanian troops, and party officials demand a state funeral for them. Premier Goga refuses, and a rift develops between government and the fascist group.			China receives arms shipments from Czechoslovakia and other nations visited by H.H. Kung last year. Kung, now the Premier, toured Europe as governor of the Central Bank of China.
Feb. 7	The League of Nations convenes a conference to provide legal assistance to German refugees.	Spanish insurgents regain 400 square miles of territory north of Teruel. . . . Foreign Secretary Anthony Eden of Britain warns that his country will act against Spanish rebel attacks in the future, rather than simply protest.			After a memorial service, Gen. Iwane Matsui of Japan admits serious "indiscipline" among the troops stationed at Nanking. He reports that efforts to stop excesses and force respect for Chinese people and property are under way.
Feb. 8		Blaming worn machinery, espionage, and other factors, the Soviet Union lowers production quotas in several heavy industries, including coal and steel.		Puerto Rican longshoremen approve the settlement of their strike. The ship owners must next decide on acceptance.	Japanese planes bomb Hankow and two other cities on the Yangtze River. Military barracks, airfields, steel foundries, and communications facilities are targeted.

A	B	C	D	E
Includes developments that affect more than one world region, international organizations, and important meetings of world leaders.	Includes all domestic and regional developments in Europe, including the Soviet Union.	Includes all domestic and regional developments in Africa and the Middle East.	Includes all domestic and regional developments in Latin America, the Caribbean, and Canada.	Includes all domestic and regional developments in Asian and Pacific nations (and colonies).

U.S. Politics & Social Issues	U.S. Foreign Policy & Defense	Economics & Great Depression	Science, Technology & Nature	Culture, Leisure & Lifestyle	
		The labor rift grow deeper as William Green of the AFL denounces the Non-Partisan League—which has always been Socialist—as a "ventriloquist's dummy" for the CIO.		Before a crowd of 21,000 in Hamburg, Germany, Max Schmeling defeats South African heavyweight Ben Foord in a decision.	Jan. 30
Senator Robert Wagner, author of the Anti-Lynching Bill, sets it aside so other legislation can be considered.	The State Department accepts Japan's regrets over the slapping of its envoy in Nanking. Japan promises courts-martial of 20 soldiers and their commanding officer.	Strikers at Crucible Steel in New Jersey accept a settlement that grants most of their demands—better hours, rehiring of laid-off employees, and a seniority system.		Future Queen Beatrix of the Netherlands is born to Crown Princess Juliana and her husband, Prince Bernard.	Jan. 31
		The CIO votes to strike from its constitution all references to the AFL. . . . U.S. Steel borrows $50 million to expand its operations, following up on a statement that it planned to spend $80 million in 1938. . . . The President meets with a delegation of the United Auto Workers of America.	An 8.5-magnitude earthquake on the Banda Sea floor near Indonesia generates a tsunami, damaging the Kai Islands.		Feb. 1
	Diplomatic efforts secure a promise to release the *Nantucket Chief* and its American crew from insurgent Spain. The ship was carrying Russian oil consigned to loyalist Spain when it was seized last month, 80 miles from the coast of Spain.	Employees of Crucible Steel in Jersey City, N.J., return to work. Their strike began January 26. . . . While the United Mine Workers decide to ban Communists from their ranks, the CIO says it will not bar anyone based on politics.	Soviet icebreakers leave Murmansk to rescue scientists trapped on an Arctic ice floe that split during a storm yesterday. The men and most of their equipment are on a block of ice approximately 200 yards by 300 yards.		Feb. 2
	In night maneuvers near San Diego, Calif., two Navy bombers collide in midair, killing 11 men. It is the worst air disaster ever for the U.S. Navy.	Homer Martin, head of the CIO-affiliated UAWA, calls for the expulsion of Communists from American labor. . . . President Franklin Roosevelt signs a Housing Bill, insuring home mortgages up to 90 percent of their maximum value.			Feb. 3
The Senate defeats another attempt to end the filibuster over its Anti-Lynching Bill.		A demonstration of over 80,000 auto workers fills Cadillac Square in Michigan, protesting layoffs and demanding more government help. . . . A National Labor Relations Board report finds that Ford Motor Company coerced employees in its Somerville plant.	John Baird successfully transmits a color television picture from the Dominion Theatre in London.	Thornton Wilder's play *Our Town* premiers at the Henry Miller Theater in New York.	Feb. 4
		A strike of retail clerks begun in mid-December ends. Employees of 57 Whelan Drug Stores in New York will return to work over the next three months—without raises, a closed shop, or other benefits.		British censors impose an age limit of 16 for viewers of *Snow White and the Seven Dwarfs*, fearing the film will cause nightmares in children.	Feb. 5
	Secretary of State Cordell Hull says his offers of reciprocal trade treaties promote peace and fair treatment to all nations. His speech, broadcast over the radio, claims that the belief that nations can exist without international cooperation is a "fallacy."		A Soviet dirigible preparing to rescue the stranded scientists in the Arctic crashes, killing 13. Icebreakers attempting to reach the scientists, whose camp has drifted over 1,100 miles since March 1937, battle storms.		Feb. 6
With very little warning, the Senate Judiciary Committee opens hearings on an Equal Rights Amendment, originally introduced in 1923. Many women's groups like the National League of Women Voters are opposed to the Amendment, feeling it would eliminate social protections for women.		Responding to the United Mine Workers' changes in their constitution, the AFL revokes the charter of it and two other major unions. AFL head William Green resigns his 48-year membership in the mining union.		Harvey Firestone, founder of Firestone Tire and Rubber, dies at age 60.	Feb. 7
Al Capone is under observation in Alcatraz hospital, possibly suffering from dementia due to untreated syphilis.	Secretary of State Hull reassures the Senate Foreign Relations Committee in writing that America has no agreements with any other countries to pursue joint policies toward war.	A day before the U.S. Steel Corporation renews a contract with the workers' union, independent steel companies act to cut prices, destabilizing the wage and price structure.			Feb. 8

F	G	H	I	J
Includes elections, federal-state relations, civil rights and liberties, crime, the judiciary, education, healthcare, poverty, urban affairs, and population.	Includes formation and debate of U.S. foreign and defense policies, veterans affairs, and defense spending. (Relations with specific foreign countries are usually found under the region concerned.)	Includes business, labor, agriculture, taxation, transportation, consumer affairs, monetary and fiscal policy, natural resources, pollution, and accidents.	Includes worldwide scientific, medical, and technological developments, natural phenomena, U.S. weather, and natural disasters.	Includes the arts, religion, scholarship, communications media, sports, entertainment, fashions, fads, and social life.

	World Affairs	Europe	Africa & The Middle East	The Americas	Asia & The Pacific
Feb. 9	In Moscow, Chinese envoy Sun Ke is told by Soviet Foreign Minister Litvinoff that the Soviets will not act alone to aid China, and that China's best tactic would be to get the United States involved in its defense.	Sporadic clashes mark elections in Northern Ireland. The voters decide to remain in the United Kingdom, and not ally with Ireland. . . . Romania's Juridical Committee strikes down last month's decree, which questioned Jewish citizenship, as unconstitutional. . . . Soviet Envoy Feodor Butenko, who disappeared from his post in Romania on the 6th, is still missing. The Soviets charge that a political crime was committed.			Two columns of Japanese troops move toward positions west of Suchow that would cut off up to 400,000 Chinese soldiers from the interior, though such an action is not completed. . . . Chiang Kai-shek appoints Chou En-lai Vice Minister in charge of mass training, the highest position given to a Communist leader in the coalition government.
Feb. 10	Seven countries sign the League of Nations' pact on German refugees, which outlines rights to travel documents, travel, residence, and other issues.	King Carol of Romania dismisses Parliament and dissolves the fascist government of Premier Goga. Many anti-Semitic laws are invalidated, and strict press censorship is enforced. Patriarch Cristea, known to be anti-Semitic, is appointed Premier.		Shipping resumes in Puerto Rico as all parties accept a settlement. Returning workers get 40 cents an hour with further increases to be negotiated later; the previous hourly wage was 32 cents.	An official Chinese relief agency reports that 10 million people have fled their homes, and half of them are destitute and near starvation.
Feb. 11	The U.S. tanker *Nantucket Chief* arrives at Gibraltar, the first leg on its trip home after being released by Spanish rebels. Its captain tells of daily beatings at the hands of insurgents.	Spanish insurgents continue the random bombing of towns far behind most battle lines. . . . Nazi sources confirm "difficulties" in conservative branches of the German army, but deny rumors of mutiny.	Celebrations in Egypt mark the 18th birthday of King Farouk.	A Mexican Constituent Assembly scheduled for March 31 in Mexico City will be weighted in favor of the army, giving them 101 seats, compared to labor's 100.	
Feb. 12	Japan refuses to reveal its naval building plans to the United States, France, and Britain, opening the door to an arms race. . . . Japan apologizes in writing for attacks on Americans and American property in Nanking, offering explanations and listing efforts to stop such actions.	Austria's Premier Schuschnigg is suddenly summoned to meet Chancellor Hitler. He is told to include Nazis in his government and give Austria's Nazis greater freedom, or risk military invasion. . . . King Carol of Romania announces that a new Constitution will be written, and that foreigners who settled in Romania without official permission (i.e., Jewish refugees) must leave.		Mexico's cooperative farms suffer increasingly from unemployment and unrest. In Tlalhualipan, Hidalgo, violence breaks out when Mexican police oust 60 protesting agrarians from a building, and fire on them. Thirteen die, including a woman and her baby.	
Feb. 13	Unaware of Adolf Hitler's demands of the Austrian Premier, American and European observers see the talks between Germany and Austria as a move toward accord which can encompass Britain and France as well.			After a second trial, eleven Puerto Rican Nationalists are acquitted in the death of a policeman during a riot on Palm Sunday last year. . . . Mexico's Interior Ministry orders an investigation of all foreigners, aimed at ousting Jews.	
Feb. 14	Great Britain opens its new naval base in Singapore.	Reports emerge that Premier Schuschnigg was given several ultimatums on his visit to Germany on February 12. . . . Josef Stalin says that the Soviet Union should organize workers in other countries, to provide help in case of an attack.			Bombing weakens the Chinese troops defending the area around Chengchou. Hundreds are killed and more than 500 buildings wrecked. The Baptist Hospital, crowded with refugees, is hit by three bombs.
Feb. 15	French Commander Charles Huntzinger meets with Turkish authorities to discuss the Sanjak of Alexandretta. He makes a secret commitment that in case of a European or international war, Turkey may occupy the Sanjak. Turkey agrees to remain neutral and allow safe passage through the Dardenelles for French ships.	A new defensive drive by loyalists is attempted at Teruel, Spain, surprising the rebel fighters. The Washington and Lincoln Battalions of American volunteers capture over 100 insurgent prisoners with minimal casualties.		A mob of 800 storms and sets fire to a Tijuana jail, police station, and federal building in northern Mexico, seeking to lynch the murderer-molester of an eight-year-old girl. Six people were shot and six others trampled as police restored order. The law provides no death penalty for such crimes.	Chinese defenders succeed in halting the Japanese push toward Suchow. . . . Soviet and American volunteer fliers join in attacks on Japanese positions at Sinsiang, Changteh, and Chihsien, where munitions and planes are destroyed.
Feb. 16		Premier Schuschnigg names pro-Nazi Dr. Artur Seyss-Inquart as Austria's Interior Minister, and puts Dr. Guido Schmidt in charge of Foreign Affairs, fulfilling Hitler's demands. Other ministers are appointed, all known to be favorable to Germany. . . . Missing Soviet envoy Butenko surfaces in Rome, claiming he fled Romania for his life, and that the Soviet secret police had been sent to kill him. . . . In Paris, Leon Sedoff, son of Leon Trotsky, dies after a brief illness. He was likely poisoned.		The Mexican Supreme Court is asked to decide whether the country's Labor Board can force foreign oil companies to pay higher wages. . . . The state of Rio Grande do Sul in Brazil reveals that all Nazi and fascist organizations have been shut down on orders of President Vargas.	Attempts by the Congress Party to work with India's new Constitution suffer setbacks. In the United Provinces and Bihar, Provincial Premiers resign in protest as the British Governors there invoke special powers to veto the release of political prisoners. . . . Several American women missionaries are injured by Japanese bombers in an attack on Kaifeng.
Feb. 17		Spanish insurgent Gen. Juan Yagüe leads Moroccan troops to Teruel, crossing the Alfambra River. They will prove to be the decisive factor in the battle for Teruel. . . . In Czechoslovakia, Nazis provoke a riot near the border by breaking into a political meeting.		In Tijuana, Mexico, soldiers place the confessed killer of an eight-year-old girl before a firing squad, declaring that the man—a soldier himself—has been court-martialed. His execution eases tension in the town.	

A	B	C	D	E
Includes developments that affect more than one world region, international organizations, and important meetings of world leaders.	*Includes all domestic and regional developments in Europe, including the Soviet Union.*	*Includes all domestic and regional developments in Africa and the Middle East.*	*Includes all domestic and regional developments in Latin America, the Caribbean, and Canada.*	*Includes all domestic and regional developments in Asian and Pacific nations (and colonies).*

U.S. Politics & Social Issues	U.S. Foreign Policy & Defense	Economics & Great Depression	Science, Technology & Nature	Culture, Leisure & Lifestyle	
		U.S. Steel renews its contract with 240,000 employees. . . . Before the U.S. Congress, President Joseph Ryan of the International Longshoremen charges that the National Maritime Union, a CIO affiliate, is a Communist-run organization.	The Golden Gate Bridge in San Francisco bends over 12 feet during a hurricane, but does not break. Fifteen days of rain in California's Central Valley causes flooding and six deaths.		Feb. 9
The President asks Congress for an additional $250 million in relief funds.		The Senate states, for the record, that it does not believe Joseph Curran, head of the National Maritime Union, is a Communist.	Fifteen die in a storm in Rio de Janeiro, Brazil, that rips up homes and floods streets. . . . Snow falls in Palestine, tying up shipping.		Feb. 10
		Faced with union demands they consider excessive, furriers lock out 4,000 workers in New York. . . . Ford Motor Company denies charges of unfair labor practices in an NLRB hearing in Kansas City.	African countries south of the equator attempt to vaccinate cattle as a rinderpest plague sweeps through their stock.	In London, BBC Television presents the first Sci-Fi TV show: a 35-minute adaptation of the play *RUR (Rossum's Universal Robots)* by Karel Capek.	Feb. 11
			In Central California, 16 have died and 2,000 are homeless as floodwaters break the Pajaro levee. A snowslide in the Sierras kills two more people.		Feb. 12
					Feb. 13
After days of hearings about an Equal Rights Amendment for women, the Senate Judiciary Committee ties in a vote, and will reconsider the issue.		An Appellate Court orders Remington Rand Corporation to negotiate with the AFL, which will represent its employees.	The National Association of Broadcasters begins a three-day meeting to organize and regulate the radio industry.	The "Singing Valentine" is introduced and becomes an instant hit. The 10 girls originally hired to sing out Valentine's Day lyrics are soon supplemented by others, and the fad spreads from New York to at least 50 other cities.	Feb. 14
	The President reiterates for the press the necessity of building a navy capable of defending both coasts.	The AFL's vice president Matthew Woll responds to remarks of Josef Stalin about the world's workers supporting the Soviet Union. Woll says that Stalin deserves no more support from American labor than Hitler or Mussolini.	Robert Williams receives the Willard Gibbs Medal of the American Chemical Society for his work on vitamins.		Feb. 15
The Senate filibuster of the Anti-Lynching Bill continues as another vote on cloture fails.		Prompted by New York's mayor, Fiorello LaGuardia, fur companies and their unions submit to a State Mediation Board. . . . In his role as outgoing Maritime Commission Chairman, Joseph Kennedy tells Congress that mediation laws are badly needed in the shipping industry. . . . The President signs the Agricultural Adjustment Act, which permits the administration to set price and yield controls on rice, cotton, wheat, corn, and tobacco.	A rescue plane reaches the four Soviet scientists marooned on an ice floe near Greenland. Ivan Papanin and his men are left with supplies as an icebreaker makes its way toward them. The pilot, Genady Vlasov, flies off to rescue two other searchers from the icebreaker who were stranded.	Arturo Toscanini withdraws from the Salzburg Festival because of developments in Austria, where it is held. . . . Author Antoine de Saint-Exupéry and his pilot are injured in a plane crash in Guatemala.	Feb. 16
			A tornado devastates Rodessa, Louisiana, leaving 21 dead.		Feb. 17

F	G	H	I	J
Includes elections, federal-state relations, civil rights and liberties, crime, the judiciary, education, healthcare, poverty, urban affairs, and population.	*Includes formation and debate of U.S. foreign and defense policies, veterans affairs, and defense spending. (Relations with specific foreign countries are usually found under the region concerned.)*	*Includes business, labor, agriculture, taxation, transportation, consumer affairs, monetary and fiscal policy, natural resources, pollution, and accidents.*	*Includes worldwide scientific, medical, and technological developments, natural phenomena, U.S. weather, and natural disasters.*	*Includes the arts, religion, scholarship, communications media, sports, entertainment, fashions, fads, and social life.*

	World Affairs	Europe	Africa & The Middle East	The Americas	Asia & The Pacific
Feb. 18		Insurgents push loyalists from their mountain positions northeast of Teruel. Volunteers of the International Brigade, including at lease seven Canadians, die in the fighting. . . . The Netherlands rushes through a bill that more than triples its defense budget.	In Palestine, Arabs fire on a taxi, killing a Royal Air Force officer and wounding another man and a woman.	The estate of Mexico's former president Plutarco Calles is distributed among the peasants of La Magdalena.	
Feb. 19	France and Japan sign a trade treaty.	Premier Schuschnigg assures a delegation of Jewish businessmen that they have nothing to worry about under Austria's new administration. . . . A three-hour Cabinet session clarifies the differing opinions of British Foreign Minister Eden and Prime Minister Chamberlain over Germany and Italy. Eden may resign, but both sides—and most of the world—wait to hear the speech from the Reichstag on February 20.			Chinese troops dynamite the longest steel bridge in China, spanning the Yellow River, to block the Japanese. . . . In India, Congress Party leaders debate which methods to use to gain independence from Britain. . . . Foreign missionaries, including 100 Americans, have been denied passes by Japanese military officials to return to their facilities in areas between Shanghai and Nanking.
Feb. 20	Chancellor Adolf Hitler announces in his speech that Germany recognizes Japan's government in Manchukuo.	In his speech before the Reichstag, Chancellor Adolf Hitler promises to protect all Germans in Europe, claiming that the 10 million Germans in Austria and Czechoslovakia have the right to self-determination. . . . Britain's Foreign Minister Eden resigns, as he cannot support the current policy of the Prime Minister toward Italy. Viscount Halifax, known to be friendly toward the Reich, will replace Eden.	Hundreds of armed Arabs enter Jenin, Palestine, where they fire on government buildings and shoot at street lights and windows. Police drive them off with machine guns.	Roberto Ortiz becomes Argentina's 21st president.	
Feb. 21		Loyalist troops blow up their munitions inside Teruel before fleeing the area for Valencia. . . . Britain's Prime Minister leads the debate in the House of Commons over relations with fascist nations. In spite of opposition led by former Minister Eden, the majority is clearly with the Prime Minister.	Troops assemble in Jenin, Palestine, then fan south, searching without success for the terrorists that raged through the city on February 20 .		Gen. Iwane Matsui, who planned and commanded the capture of Nanking, leaves China for Tokyo and retirement. He is replaced by Gen. Shunroku Hata.
Feb. 22		Britain's Winston Churchill and David Lloyd George join the attack on England's current foreign policy, Churchill warning against submitting to totalitarian states for the sake of peace. . . . Hungarian police arrest 73 Nazis, including party leader Ferenc Szálasi, suspected of a plotting a coup.			A Japanese column drives south from Sinsieng toward the Yellow River as planes bomb the Chinese defenders along the river.
Feb. 23		Rebel warships shell towns on the Catalan coast of Spain. . . . Talks between Ireland and Britain resume in London, with Premier Eamon de Valera meeting with Prime Minister Neville Chamberlain.			Chinese planes drop bombs on Formosa, a Japanese possession since 1895. This first attack on Japanese territory kills eight, and causes panic in Japan, where papers report that Chinese bombers are approaching Kyushu. . . . Reports of the burning of villages along rail lines and the Hwai River by Japanese troops, and of abuse of civilians, fuel terror in central China.
Feb. 24		Premier Schuschnigg of Austria vows to defend his country's independence and says Austria has gone "thus far and no further." Germany sees the speech as defiant. Nazi demonstrations continue in spite of bans. . . . Romanians vote for their new constitution, which gives the King absolute veto power. The Congress is reduced in size and the King will appoint half of all Senators.		Speaking before a congress of Mexican labor, President Lázaro Cárdenas asks for support in difficult economic times, and blames many problems on foreign oil companies and world aggression.	Airfields along China's southern coast are shelled by Japanese planes. The Japanese are determined to stop further attacks on Formosa by destroying planes and airfields. . . . Malaria spreads among troops and civilians along the Yangtze River. The disease is rare in the north, and people there have less resistance to it.
Feb. 25		The Balkan Entente countries (Greece, Turkey, Romania, and Yugoslavia) meet in Angora.			In Tokyo, Japan's Diet debates the National Mobilization Bill. The bill would allow the administration to suspend or override the Japanese Constitution. . . . Japanese troops capture Lingshih Pass in the Shansi province, but fighting continues as the strategic point changes hands several times.

A	B	C	D	E
Includes developments that affect more than one world region, international organizations, and important meetings of world leaders.	*Includes all domestic and regional developments in Europe, including the Soviet Union.*	*Includes all domestic and regional developments in Africa and the Middle East.*	*Includes all domestic and regional developments in Latin America, the Caribbean, and Canada.*	*Includes all domestic and regional developments in Asian and Pacific nations (and colonies).*

U.S. Politics & Social Issues	U.S. Foreign Policy & Defense	Economics & Great Depression	Science, Technology & Nature	Culture, Leisure & Lifestyle	
	Joseph Kennedy is sworn in as Ambassador to Britain.	The President removes restrictions on the Reconstruction Finance Corporation (RFC), and presses for loans that will increase employment.	The German Auto Show opens in Berlin and will run through March 6. A popular display is a model of a new automobile factory which will be the largest in the world, and a town to house workers. The town becomes Wolfsburg, where the Volkswagen is built.	The madcap comedy film *Bringing Up Baby*, starring Katharine Hepburn and Cary Grant, debuts.	Feb. 18
	In an address to farmers, Secretary of State Cordell Hull maintains that his policy of using trade pacts contributes to "economic well-being and peace."	Bartenders and chefs on the offshore gambling ships in Southern California picket against unfair labor practices at the docks where customers catch "water taxis" to take them to the gambling ships.	The Soviet icebreakers *Taimyr* and *Murman* rescue scientists and remove their equipment from the ice floe. The men spent eight months in the Arctic. . . . Avalanches bury fishing villages on Saghalien Island in Japan, killing 77 people.		Feb. 19
The Senate votes to end its month-long filibuster of the Anti-Lynching Bill and take up urgent legislation, but does not invoke cloture.		The CIO and the General Electric Company announce a national agreement for union representation of 27,000 employees in five plants. If employees in 15 other plants vote for the CIO-affiliated union, 60,000 workers could be represented.			Feb. 20
			Astronomer George Ellery Hale, who helped found the Yerkes, Mt. Palomar, and Mt. Wilson observatories, dies.		Feb. 21
					Feb. 22
The President passes on to Congress an advisory committee report, requesting funds to address inequalities in schools across the nation, starting with $70 million in 1939.		The Bituminous Coal Board revokes its minimum prices, and will conduct hearings to set new prices.	As levees along Arkansas' Red River fail, thousands of acres flood, and several people are killed. The Red Cross estimates more than 22,000 will become refugees. This winter sees high-water records for several rivers in the state.	Before a crowd of 20,000 at Madison Square Garden in New York, Joe Louis knocks out Nathan Mann in the third round of a heavyweight title fight. . . . Dizzy Dean signs to play baseball for another year with the Cardinals for about a third less than his salary for last year, $27,000.	Feb. 23
			The first nylon-bristle toothbrush is produced by DuPont in Arlington, N.J. Previous toothbrushes had animal-hair bristles.	Judy Garland is cast as Dorothy in *The Wizard of Oz*. . . . Professor Raymond Pearl of Johns Hopkins University presents charts on longevity, showing that tobacco use measurably shortens people's lifespans.	Feb. 24
	Through diplomatic channels, the United States warns that Japan will be held responsible for injuries or damage to American interests in China.	General Motors announces pay cuts starting at 10 percent for 50,000 employees. Union members are protected from such cuts.			Feb. 25

F	G	H	I	J
Includes elections, federal-state relations, civil rights and liberties, crime, the judiciary, education, healthcare, poverty, urban affairs, and population.	*Includes formation and debate of U.S. foreign and defense policies, veterans affairs, and defense spending. (Relations with specific foreign countries are usually found under the region concerned.)*	*Includes business, labor, agriculture, taxation, transportation, consumer affairs, monetary and fiscal policy, natural resources, pollution, and accidents.*	*Includes worldwide scientific, medical, and technological developments, natural phenomena, U.S. weather, and natural disasters.*	*Includes the arts, religion, scholarship, communications media, sports, entertainment, fashions, fads, and social life.*

	World Affairs	Europe	Africa & The Middle East	The Americas	Asia & The Pacific
Feb. 26	Prompted by foreign propaganda on the radio, President Franklin Roosevelt appoints a committee to study international broadcasting. The emphasis will be on Pan-American broadcasts.	France's Chamber of Deputies votes overwhelmingly for rearmament and in favor of the government's support of the League of Nations, the Franco-Soviet Pact, and the independence of Austria and Czechoslovakia. . . . Reports surface that Alexander Yegorov, the Soviet's highest ranking military officer and member of the Communist Central Committee, has been arrested in a purge.		Brazil's President Getúlio Vargas announces plans for infrastructure development to be funded, he hopes, by the voluntary contributions of the nation's wealthy.	Chinese guerilla fighters strike behind Japanese lines north of Nanking, in Chanpaling, where they manage to cut off Nanking from three columns of troops. The Japanese columns are forced to give up recent gains north of the Hwai River, where fighting continues.
Feb. 27		A showdown develops in Graz, Austria, as heavily armed government troops and police are deployed to stop a march of 60,000 Nazis. The Nazi group cancels the march, but swastikas and Nazi symbols are evident throughout the city.		For the second time in six months, Nicaragua is plagued by locusts. This swarm extends 24 miles.	Madame Chiang Kai-shek steps down as head of China's air force, after two years. Her brother, T.V. Soong, will be appointed to replace her. . . . Chinese planes break up Japanese encampments along the north bank of the Yellow River.
Feb. 28	The International Labor Organization in Geneva holds a conference to help colonial migrants. . . . After many weeks' delay, Britain appoints a commission to study the partition of Palestine.	Poland's Populist party, representing 20 million peasants, meets to discuss possible strikes and other actions to effect change in the government.	Arab terrorists kill a Jewish guide and teacher near Abou Sousa in Palestine. In another incident, an Arab band attacks a Jewish settlement in the Beisan Valley, battling with watchmen.		Gen. Li Tsung-Jen coordinates the mobilization of Shansi and Anwhei provinces' civilians against the Japanese occupation. . . . The debate continues in Tokyo over the National Mobilization Bill, which detractors say is illegal and unclear.
Mar. 1		In Graz, Austria, 16,000 participate in a Nazi parade, overwhelming the police who try to stop them. . . . On the third anniversary of the German air force founding, Air Minister Goering threatens terrible havoc should Germany be attacked.		Mexico's Supreme Court upholds wage increases for oil workers, demanded by the country's Labor Board. British and American oil companies respond that financially they cannot accept the decision.	
Mar. 2		The "Trial of the 21" begins in Moscow. Those accused include highly placed administrators, commissars of industry, prominent doctors, Izvestia editor Nicolai Bukharin, and former premier Alexei Rykoff. . . . France's Defense Minister Daladier promises a bill asking 4 billion francs for armaments. . . . Britain revises its defense expenses for this year, raising the total to over £343 million.			Japanese troops claim great gains throughout the southern part of Shansi province, and intend to cross the Yellow River into Shensi province, a Communist stronghold.
Mar. 3		The Reich informs the Soviet Union that Germany's two remaining embassies in that country will close by May 15, and asks that the Soviets close their embassies in Germany by the same date. . . . A compromise reached by Austria's pro-Nazi Minister Seyss-Inquart in Graz yesterday is repudiated by the government—which says it will enforce a ban on swastikas and the "Heil, Hitler" greeting.	After five years of exploration by Standard Oil, oil is found in Dhahran, Saudi Arabia.		Japanese forces capture Linfen, once the Chinese headquarters of Shansi province, as well as towns along the Yellow River, bordering Shensi province. . . . A Labor Party leader in Japan is beaten, and Japan's Home Minister is blamed for not taking precautions against extremist political groups.
Mar. 4		Czech Prime Minister Hodza says that in spite of Adolf Hitler's pledge to protect German minorities, his country will "defend, defend, defend herself!" against foreign aggression. . . . Nikolai Krestinsky confesses, and tells listeners at his Soviet trial about an intricate plot to assassinate Josef Stalin and take over the Kremlin.	The arrival of a new British High Commissioner in Palestine sparks riots. One thousand British troops battle armed Arabs in Jenin. . . . Student strikes in Baghdad, Iraq, reflect agitation over a treaty to share the Basra harbor with Iran, due to be ratified on March 6.		
Mar. 5	From Mexico, Leon Trotsky denies that he took $1 million from the Soviet government, an accusation that was raised during the current trial in Moscow.	Britain sends "amity terms" to Italy with an envoy. At least 5,000 Italian troops have landed at Cadiz, Spain, recently to join the insurgent forces. . . . In a speech praised by Germany, Hungarian Premier Daranyi promises rearmament, and calls for a reduction of Jews in the economic and business sphere. . . . An orderly demonstration of up to 15,000 Nazis greets Interior Minister Seyss-Inquart in Linz, Austria.		Cuba holds Congressional elections, in which all candidates support Col. Batista.	Chinese troops stop the advance of Japan's forces near Linfen. The "model governor" of Shansi for the last 25 years, Yen Hsi-shan, recently forced out, now directs his army from Shensi province.

A	B	C	D	E
Includes developments that affect more than one world region, international organizations, and important meetings of world leaders.	Includes all domestic and regional developments in Europe, including the Soviet Union.	Includes all domestic and regional developments in Africa and the Middle East.	Includes all domestic and regional developments in Latin America, the Caribbean, and Canada.	Includes all domestic and regional developments in Asian and Pacific nations (and colonies).

U.S. Politics & Social Issues	U.S. Foreign Policy & Defense	Economics & Great Depression	Science, Technology & Nature	Culture, Leisure & Lifestyle	
	The FBI arrests two men and a German woman in connection with a European spy ring. The FBI paints them as inept, but hopes to discover other agents.				Feb. 26
		Farmers participating with the programs of the Agricultural Adjustment Act are guaranteed 12 cents per bushel of wheat.	Through the purchase of private plants, the U.S. government is now the only producer of helium in the world. A contract with the German Zeppelin Corporation is expected.		Feb. 27
		In defiance of their own union, 15,000 hosiery workers in Philadelphia walk off their jobs in 65 different mills. The strike is prompted by an arbitration board's decision to allow bonus pay reductions that amount to a 6–7 percent pay loss.			Feb. 28
	The House Naval Affairs Committee allocates $3 million for an experimental dirigible, much to the President's displeasure. . . . Since its inception in fall of 1935, the National Labor Relations Board (NLRB) has handled cases involving 3.2 million workers; 9,150 of its 12,485 cases have been settled, half by mutual agreement.			Gabriele D'Annunzio, Italian poet, author, war hero, and friend of Mussolini, dies of a stroke and is given a state funeral. . . . Out of Africa, by Isak Dinesen, is published and the U.S. edition of J.R.R. Tolkien's The Hobbit also appears in bookstores. . . . William Randolph Hearst begins to sell and give away part of his fabulous art and antiquity collection, valued at $15 million.	Mar. 1
			Five days of heavy rains in Southern California cause landslides and damage. A wooden bridge in Long Beach is washed away, water overflows a dam in Santa Ana, and avalanches crush homes in the San Fernando Valley.		Mar. 2
	The House passes the Pittman Neutrality Act, which would circumscribe the President's actions in case of war.				Mar. 3
	U.S. Marines in Shanghai stop a patrol of 75 Japanese soldiers from entering the International Settlement's American zone.	Three taxis are burned, and another vandalized in two separate strikes in New York.	Diplomats of the United States and Brazil speak during the initial Pan-American radio broadcast from Washington, D.C.		Mar. 4
	The United States formally claims two uninhabited islands in the central Pacific, Canton and Enderbury, which may be suitable for air bases. Lands in Antarctica are also claimed. The UK may dispute this, and negotiations are anticipated.	Director Lilienthal of the Tennessee Valley Authority (TVA) proposes municipalities buy private power plants in the Tennessee River basin. . . . Major cab companies in New York lock out 6,000 drivers because of the vandalism by striking workers.			Mar. 5

F	G	H	I	J
Includes elections, federal-state relations, civil rights and liberties, crime, the judiciary, education, healthcare, poverty, urban affairs, and population.	Includes formation and debate of U.S. foreign and defense policies, veterans affairs, and defense spending. (Relations with specific foreign countries are usually found under the region concerned.)	Includes business, labor, agriculture, taxation, transportation, consumer affairs, monetary and fiscal policy, natural resources, pollution, and accidents.	Includes worldwide scientific, medical, and technological developments, natural phenomena, U.S. weather, and natural disasters.	Includes the arts, religion, scholarship, communications media, sports, entertainment, fashions, fads, and social life.

	World Affairs	**Europe**	**Africa & The Middle East**	**The Americas**	**Asia & The Pacific**
Mar. 6	The Italian Viceroy of Ethiopia presents the gold, jewel-encrusted crown of Haile Selassie to new "Emperor" Benito Mussolini in Rome.	Near Cartagena, Spain, loyalist and insurgent ships meet by chance and fire on each other in the night. Hours later, loyalists sink the rebel cruiser *Baleares* at Cape Palos. . . . Voting begins for a new Parliament in Bulgaria. Government candidates are defeated by older, left-wing party representatives.			From positions on the south shore of the Yellow River, Japanese forces shell Chinese river boats and artillery stores in Kunghsien on the north bank, in preparation for a crossing. An attempted crossing further east yesterday was repulsed.
Mar. 7		Spanish insurgents launch five air raids on Cartagena in retaliation for the sinking of the *Baleares*. . . . Austrian labor delegates, previously opposed to Premier Schuschnigg's government, now support him over Nazism.	An American citizen in Palestine, George Katimi, is arraigned for throwing a bomb from a car, near a Jewish labor commissary in Jerusalem in January. He is acquitted within a week.	As Mexico's deadline for payment of wage increases to oil workers passes, the government embargoes the bank accounts of foreign oil companies who are now in default. . . . The Cuban military uncovers a revolutionary group plotting a coup, and kills four men in a raid. Many prominent politicians, including party leaders and a former mayor of Havana, are implicated and arrested.	Japanese authorities report the capture of key towns in Shansi province, saying they have virtual control of all rail lines and communications there. . . . Prince Ta, the pro-Japanese ruler of Suiyuan province in Mongolia, is arrested. In his absence, Muslim and Mongol troops unite against Japan under Manchurian leader Ma Chanshan.
Mar. 8	Former president Herbert Hoover meets with Chancellor Adolf Hitler in Germany and tells him that his principles are intolerable to most Americans.	Former head of the Soviet Union's secret police Genrikh Yagoda confesses to poisoning Maxim Gorky and Gorky's son, along with several others, during his Moscow trial. . . . Moscow's secret police arrest a Soviet woman who had been taking notes at the Trial of the 21 for *New York Times* journalists—with the permission of authorities.			The Japanese shell the Lung-hai railroad north of the Yellow River, belying their claim that they control the rails in Shansi province.
Mar. 9		Austria's Premier Schuschnigg, defying the Reich, calls for a vote on independence on Sunday, March 13. Only "yes" ballots will be supplied; those opposing independence must bring their own "no" ballots.			Furious fighting rages at Szeshui, on the south bank of the Yellow River in Honan province. Japan calls for reinforcements to hold the town as Chinese troops cut dikes to flood the area, so that tanks cannot be used.
Mar. 10		Nazis demonstrate throughout Austria against Sunday's vote, and labor organizations stage counter-demonstrations. . . . Spanish insurgent troops under General Yagüe capture Belchite and other towns in Aragon. American volunteers in the International Brigades are among the defenders. . . . Premier Camille Chautemps resigns, saying that France needs a stronger government to enact new financial policies.	British troops kill 32 Arab men in another large fight in northern Galilee, Palestine. Meanwhile, death sentences are handed out to terrorists involved in the battle of last week.		
Mar. 11		German troops mass on the Austrian border. Nazi mobs take over Vienna. Premier Schuschnigg is forced to resign under threat of an armed invasion. President Miklas at first refuses to put Dr. Seyss-Inquart in charge, but does so when it is clear that German troops are entering the country. Italy refuses assistance and France's government is still forming; although nations protest the takeover, none act. Most of Austria's neighbors shut their borders to refugees.	British troops fight with 300 Arabs in the area of Palestine now called the "bloody triangle," between Jenin, Nablus, and Tul Karm.	Brazilian authorities begin arresting Integralistas after infiltrating a group that plans to overthrow the Vargas government, led by Plínio Salgado. The plot involves both civilian and military members. Salgado manages to evade capture.	Japanese forces say they still hold Szeshui, and from there have cut through the Lung-hai railway. Hoku, a city leading into Shensi province, is in Japanese hands.
Mar. 12		The Wehrmacht's Eighth Army enters Austria, and Adolf Hitler crosses the border at his birthplace, Braunau. . . . Of the 21 defendants in Moscow, 18 are sentenced to die as soon as the trial ends. . . . Three columns of Spanish insurgents push between 30 and 50 miles in four days along the Aragon front.			Chinese troops claim to recapture Hoku, but the Japanese occupy the city again within a few days, and are able to make forays across the Yellow River from it. . . . Chinese newspapers report that Manchurian troops are defecting to fight on behalf of China.
Mar. 13		President Miklas is ousted, and Austria becomes part of the Reich through proclamation. A plebiscite will be held April 10 to ratify the union, or *Anschluss*. To ensure the vote, 70,000 people will be arrested in Austria over the next week. Violence against Jews is frequent and public, and supporters of the old regime are arrested. . . . Nikolai Bukharin, Soviet author and politician, is executed, the first to die of the 18 condemned men.			

A	B	C	D	E
Includes developments that affect more than one world region, international organizations, and important meetings of world leaders.	*Includes all domestic and regional developments in Europe, including the Soviet Union.*	*Includes all domestic and regional developments in Africa and the Middle East.*	*Includes all domestic and regional developments in Latin America, the Caribbean, and Canada.*	*Includes all domestic and regional developments in Asian and Pacific nations (and colonies).*

U.S. Politics & Social Issues	U.S. Foreign Policy & Defense	Economics & Great Depression	Science, Technology & Nature	Culture, Leisure & Lifestyle	
					Mar. 6
	A trade treaty drastically reducing tariffs on Czech imports is signed. American glass and shoe producers had protested the treaty earlier, but now accept it.				Mar. 7
		The Interstate Commerce Commission (ICC) allows a compromise increase in rail freight rates, which many feel is insufficient. . . . Noted Wall Street firm Richard Whitney and Company is suspended by the New York Stock Exchange (NYSE) for insolvency.			Mar. 8
		In Hatboro, Pa., a five-week-long strike sponsored by the CIO turns violent. Hundreds of nonstrikers, most members of the AFL, attack 150 sit-downers at the Roberts and Mander Foundry with bricks and tear gas. The strikers turn on fire hoses, but are forced from the building as police restore order.			Mar. 9
The President sends a $2 billion, six-year plan for water control and infrastructure projects to Congress.		Union spokesmen in Hatboro accuse the Roberts and Mander Foundry of supplying the teargas and weapons to strikebreakers, and demand an investigation. . . . Richard Whitney, once president of the NYSE, is indicted for stealing $105,000 in securities.		Luise Rainer, an Austrian and a Jew, wins the Best Actress Oscar for the second year running. Spencer Tracy is Best Actor, and *Zola* Best Film of 1937. . . . *Jezebel*, a movie which will win Bette Davis an Oscar next year, is released.	Mar. 10
		President Franklin Roosevelt meets with TVA directors in the White House. TVA Chair Arthur E. Morgan refuses to present evidence backing his accusations of dishonesty and mismanagement against Directors Harcourt Morgan and David Lilienthal.	The American Chemical Society awards Dr. Phoebus Levene a medal for excellence. Dr. Levene identified the components of DNA, but the real significance of his work is not realized for decades.		Mar. 11
Senators on the Civil Liberties Commission question the mayor of Johnstown, Pa., about accusations that he and others were given thousands of dollars by Bethlehem Steel during the strike last year.		Most of the world's currencies fall due to the Austrian crisis, and investors put their money into dollars. . . . Company officials end the strike at Roberts and Mander Foundry in Hatboro by acknowledging a CIO union as sole bargaining agent for its employees.		Lou Gehrig signs a $39,000 contract with the Yankees.	Mar. 12
				Attorney Clarence Darrow, who defended Loeb and Leopold, Big Bill Heywood, and John Scopes, dies at age 80.	Mar. 13

F	G	H	I	J
Includes elections, federal-state relations, civil rights and liberties, crime, the judiciary, education, healthcare, poverty, urban affairs, and population.	Includes formation and debate of U.S. foreign and defense policies, veterans affairs, and defense spending. (Relations with specific foreign countries are usually found under the region concerned.)	Includes business, labor, agriculture, taxation, transportation, consumer affairs, monetary and fiscal policy, natural resources, pollution, and accidents.	Includes worldwide scientific, medical, and technological developments, natural phenomena, U.S. weather, and natural disasters.	Includes the arts, religion, scholarship, communications media, sports, entertainment, fashions, fads, and social life.

	World Affairs	Europe	Africa & The Middle East	The Americas	Asia & The Pacific
Mar. 14		As the "Nazification" of Austria continues, a crowd of 200,000 cheers wildly when Chancellor Adolf Hitler enters Vienna. . . . France assures Czechoslovakia of its support. . . . Stirred by Germany's takeover of Austria, Britain's Home Secretary asks the public for a million volunteers for air raid defense. The actual number needed is 46,000. After three weeks, less than 8,000 have enrolled, and the drive is judged an embarrassing failure.	For the period of April through September, Britain's Colonial Secretary sets a quota of 2,000 for Jewish immigrants to Palestine who are of independent means. In addition, 200 hardship cases may be admitted. Jewish laborers will not be admitted.	The Labor Board of Mexico delivers an ultimatum to the 17 American and British oil companies in default on wages: pay by 3:35 p.m. tomorrow. The companies claim they cannot comply.	The Chinese government in Hankow imposes foreign exchange restrictions that throw Shanghai financial firms into a panic. The aim is to stop capital from leaving the country.
Mar. 15		Spain's loyalists are in full retreat before the insurgent columns that push toward the Mediterranean coast. Premier Negrín flies to Paris to ask for help and is refused. . . . The men condemned in the Trial of the 21 are executed in Moscow. . . . The head of the Sudeten German Party warns the Czech Chamber of Deputies that they should bow to German demands.			President Quezon of the Philippines says a "reexamination" of Philippine independence is called for.
Mar. 16		Emil Fey, once Austrian Vice Chancellor, kills his wife and son before committing suicide, apparently in fear of Nazi arrest. . . . In Austria, all women's organizations and Masonic lodges are dissolved. The Catholic Bishop of Graz and clerics of many denominations are arrested, as are Socialists. Jews are humiliated in streets, their property seized, and Germans replace Jews in orchestras and cultural groups.			Both Chinese and Japanese fliers shell enemy airfields. A Japanese column in southern Shantung province takes Tangshan.
Mar. 17	Soviet Foreign Minister Litvinoff asks for an immediate international conference (excluding Germany, Italy, and Japan) to discuss recent aggression in Europe.	Up to 80,000 Polish troops mass at the border as Poland issues an ultimatum to Lithuania, demanding normal diplomatic relations and a settlement of the Vilnius region. . . . As German troop convoys continue to pour across Austria, observers worry that their goal is the border with Czechoslovakia. . . . The Soviet Union promises to defend the Czechs if they are attacked.			Using ships and artillery, the Japanese pound four concentrations of Chinese troops within 75 miles of Shanghai. The surprise attack forces a retreat of the Chinese.
Mar. 18		Soviet newspapers report that the Metropolitan Bishop of Gorky and other clergy have been executed for spying. . . . Chancellor Adolf Hitler addresses the Reichstag, claiming his actions spared Austria a civil war.		Mexico nationalizes all foreign-owned oil; American and British investors lose a total $450 million. Control is technically given to the 18,000 oil workers. . . . Quebec printers, dissatisfied with their wages and hours, walk out and halt the district's five newspapers.	Major fighting in China centers around Tenghsien in Shantung province. The Japanese objective is nearby Suchow, 70 miles south. Chinese guerilla actions have destroyed bridges and rail lines in the area, impeding Japanese troop movements.
Mar. 19		Lithuania accedes to Poland's demands, averting war. Diplomatic relations between the countries will begin by March 31. . . . The Reich demands that Czechoslovakia break its alliance with the Soviet Union. The demand is refused, but Czech leaders make concessions to German districts, allowing them to elect German leaders.			Japan takes Tenghsien after heavy street fighting. China says that all defenders died in the battle, and the city walls were leveled by shelling.
Mar. 20		Insurgent planes bomb Spanish coastal towns, which has become a regular occurrence. Eight people die and 35 are injured today.		Quebec's printers agree to arbitration and return to work.	An army under Gen. Terauchi sits less than 20 miles north of Suchow, while a second force under Gen. Hata is stalled 86 miles to the south, according to Japanese dispatches from China.
Mar. 21		Pope Pius XI again urges Gen. Franco to stop the bombing of Spanish cities. A previous appeal was made in February. . . . Barcelona's loyalist government estimates that Gen. Franco has 60,000 Italian troops at his disposal.		Claiming their lives were threatened, dozens of American and British oil company employees flee the states of Veracruz and Tamaulipas, and the Isthmus of Tehuantepec, Mexico.	Communist forces mobilize an army of half a million peasants in Hopeh province, sandwiched between Japanese-held territories.
Mar. 22		As outrage in Britain over the *Anschluss* subsides, a British pledge to support Czechoslovakia appears unlikely. A motion to relax immigration quotas and allow more Austrian refugees into the country is defeated.			Chinese forces drive the closest Japanese troops to Suchow 10 miles farther north. The Japanese have taken much of the local railway on the Grand Canal but Chinese troops hold the terminus at Taierhchuang.

A	B	C	D	E
Includes developments that affect more than one world region, international organizations, and important meetings of world leaders.	Includes all domestic and regional developments in Europe, including the Soviet Union.	Includes all domestic and regional developments in Africa and the Middle East.	Includes all domestic and regional developments in Latin America, the Caribbean, and Canada.	Includes all domestic and regional developments in Asian and Pacific nations (and colonies).

U.S. Politics & Social Issues	U.S. Foreign Policy & Defense	Economics & Great Depression	Science, Technology & Nature	Culture, Leisure & Lifestyle	
The President sends Congress a message about the "alarming" state of America's forests and suggests an inquiry.	Germany's Ambassador notifies Secretary of State Cordell Hull that Austria no longer exists. The United States is faced with a policy dilemma of whether or not to recognize Germany's new state, and what to do about treaties with Austria.	Richard Whitney pleads guilty to theft, and to other uncharged, similar thefts.			Mar. 14
		Representatives of railroad management and labor meet with the President to discuss the financially weak industry.	Tornadoes strike seven states from Alabama to Illinois, killing 24 people.		Mar. 15
	The U.S. Army and Navy conduct war games in the Pacific. One goal is to test Hawaii's strength as the westernmost defensive point, with a sea and air attack on Pearl Harbor—the second such exercise in the past year.		President Franklin Roosevelt presents the Harmon trophy to Henry "Dick" Merrill, as the year's outstanding aviator.		Mar. 16
The President appoints a three-man committee to examine and make recommendation about the nations' railroads.				Recently-divorced conductor Leopold Stokowski and movie star Greta Garbo meet reporters in Italy, where they have been sharing a villa for three weeks, and announce they will not marry. "I only want to be let alone," Garbo declares.	Mar. 17
		After a second, unproductive meeting with TVA Chair Morgan, the President demands evidence of Morgan's accusations by March 21.		Shirley Temple's *Rebecca of Sunnybrook Farm* is released.	Mar. 18
	The annexation of Austria is accepted as fact by the United States, but Germany's methods are condemned in a statement by Secretary Cordell Hull.			The Metropolitan Opera House tells George Balanchine that his contract will not be renewed. When Balanchine leaves, his American Ballet Ensemble, which he founded, goes with him.	Mar. 19
The Labor Department makes public a study on women's pay, which is typically 60–70 percent lower than men's. The Department blames the discrepancy on lack of unions and the traditional belief that women's work has little cash value.					Mar. 20
	The House passes a billion-dollar naval construction bill and sends it on to the Senate. . . . The United States declines a request from Canada to negotiate the diversion of water to fuel an Ontario power plant, saying that an overall policy of resource development would be better for both countries.	Defying the President, TVA Chair Morgan will not substantiate his claims that others are guilty of malfeasance, and refuses to resign his post.			Mar. 21
Charles Weems, one of the Scottsboro defendants still imprisoned, is slashed across the face and chest by a guard who claims Weems held weapons.	The United States presents a $2.2 million bill to Japan for damages to the ship *Panay*, bombed in December. . . . American oil companies ask the U.S. State Department for diplomatic action against Mexico.	President Franklin Roosevelt dismisses Arthur E. Morgan as Chair of the TVA.	Spokesmen for Pan-American Airways and its rival, American Export Lines, testify before the House Merchant Marine Commission over jurisdiction of routes.	Shirley Temple wins a $10,000 libel suit against a recently-defunct London paper *Night and Day*, and the author Graham Greene. Greene wrote of 9-year-old Temple's "dubious coquetry" and her "well-shaped and desirable little body."	Mar. 22
F Includes elections, federal-state relations, civil rights and liberties, crime, the judiciary, education, healthcare, poverty, urban affairs, and population.	**G** Includes formation and debate of U.S. foreign and defense policies, veterans affairs, and defense spending. (Relations with specific foreign countries are usually found under the region concerned.)	**H** Includes business, labor, agriculture, taxation, transportation, consumer affairs, monetary and fiscal policy, natural resources, pollution, and accidents.	**I** Includes worldwide scientific, medical, and technological developments, natural phenomena, U.S. weather, and natural disasters.	**J** Includes the arts, religion, scholarship, communications media, sports, entertainment, fashions, fads, and social life.	

	World Affairs	Europe	Africa & The Middle East	The Americas	Asia & The Pacific
Mar. 23		Spanish insurgents break through the government forces surrounding Huesca at the extreme north of their Aragon front, and take the city. . . . Chancellor Adolf Hitler orders that a new navy of warships be built for the Danube River. . . . Stormtroopers in Vienna force passing Jews to spend the afternoon scrubbing sidewalks on their hands and knees, to the delight of assembled crowds.		An estimated 200,000 workers parade before Mexican President Lázaro Cárdenas in the capital, in a demonstration against imperialism.	With fierce fighting at Fengkiu, Chinese troops keep Japan from crossing the Yellow River to Kaifeng. . . . After being held for four months, 300 Chinese prisoners attempt to break out of a concentration camp in Shanghai's French Concession.
Mar. 24		The French government faces another crisis as the Senate votes against Premier Blum's financial proposals. . . . Lithuania's Cabinet resigns in anger over the capitulation to Poland, and President Antanas Smetona asks Rev. Vladas Mironas to form a new government. . . . With new support from the German Christian Social Party, the Sudeten German Party is now the largest party in Czechoslovakia.		Oil production at the newly-seized facilities in Mexico is cut to 50 percent because of lack of storage facilities and poor rail transportation. However, many foreign markets have stopped buying, and some plants are closing down.	Australia announces a three-year, $43 million budget for defense and rearmament.
Mar. 25	A party led by British volunteers leaves Lanchow in Kansu province in northwest China for Shanghai, with supplies from the Soviet Union. Lanchow, with five airfields, is an important distribution center for war materiel.	In a campaign speech for the upcoming Austrian vote, Chancellor Adolf Hitler threatens that Germany will watch over all Germans in Europe and protect them. . . . Poland passes a law depriving Jews of citizenship if they live abroad, fail to serve in the army, or engage in anti-Polish activities.			The Japanese capture Changyuan in Honan province, another point on the Yellow River where a crossing could be made. Also in Honan, fighting continues at Fengkiu. As in most places in Shantung and Shansi, neither side has made gains, but casualties are high.
Mar. 26		Speaking in Vienna, Minister Hermann Goering warns all Jews to leave Austria. . . . In their charge east, two Spanish insurgent columns trap between 10,000 and 20,000 loyalist troops in the Alcubierre Mountains, 25 miles from Saragossa.			Prime Minister Konoe keeps Japan's Diet in session an extra day, so that it will pass the National Mobilization Bill. The bill allows the government to assume dictatorial powers over the economy if warranted. The Prime Minister promises it will not be invoked during the military action in China.
Mar. 27	German and Austrian citizens in other countries are allowed to vote 10 days before or five days after the April 10 plebiscite. In Costa Rica, Panama, Argentina, and other countries, German ships will ferry voters beyond the three-mile limit so they can vote. Certain Brazilian states forbid this, and U.S. maritime laws prohibit such practices.	Spanish loyalists burn their headquarters in Barbastro and dynamite its bridges before fleeing in advance of a rebel occupying force. . . . The Sudeten German Party demands elections in Czechoslovakia. . . . Priests in Austria's Catholic churches read a decree from their Bishops, praising the Nazis and advising parishioners to vote for them next month.		Because of the nationalization of oil facilities, the United States announces it will halt its monthly purchases of Mexican silver. The value of the peso falls even further on the news. . . . Gen. Alfredo Baldomir is elected president of Uruguay.	Chinese forces claim to recapture two rail towns on the Yellow River, and Taokow, as well as Lincheng in Shansi. . . . Witnesses attest to the deliberate burning of hundreds of farms in Hopeh province by Japanese troops.
Mar. 28		Premier Negrín of Spain asks for 100,000 volunteers to fight within 10 days, and another 40,000 to help build fortifications. . . . German Sudeten Party leader Konrad Henlein meets with Adolf Hitler, and is instructed to make unreasonable demands of the Czech government.	Near Haifa, Palestine, terrorists kill four Jews from the same family; one is 12 years old. Two Jewish brothers from Germany are shot on Mount Scopus.		Parades and a new national anthem mark the beginning of Japan's new puppet regime in Nanking, with posts held by Chinese officials. The "Reformed Government of the Republic of China" will administer the Japanese-controlled areas of central China, but Peiping's provisional government holds wider authority.
Mar. 29	Diplomatic protests are made by the Soviet Union to Japan over Manchukuo's failure to pay installments on the Chinese Eastern Railway, which the Soviets sold in 1935. . . . In letters to several nations, China accuses Japan of dropping typhoid germs over Communist headquarters in Yenan, Shensi province. China claims information that more such biological warfare is planned.	In Vienna, Austria, an arrest warrant is issued for Archduke Otto, the claimant to the Hapsburg throne. He is charged with treason. . . . The Soviet office that directs flights and scientific expeditions in the Arctic—recently viewed as heroic endeavors—is now criticized and marked for a purge. . . . German authorities refuse a passport to Sigmund Freud, who wishes to leave Austria for the Netherlands. Dr. Freud is in his 80s.			China's conservative ruling party, the Kuomintang, announces the opening of its annual meeting in Chungking. The 400 delegates actually meet for five days in Hankow, a location kept secret to avoid Japanese raids.
Mar. 30		In Austria, Nobel Prize recipient Erwin Schroedinger stands to lose his post at the university for his "unfriendly" emigration from Germany in 1933. In a moment of weakness, he recants his opposition to Nazism, a move he will always regret. . . . Archduke Josef Ferdinand of the Hapsburg family is sent to a concentration camp. . . . Prince Franz I of Liechtenstein, age 84, abdicates in favor of his grandnephew, Prince Franz Joseph. The new ruler immediately places Nazis in Cabinet positions.			Japanese forces near Taierhchwang now number 5,000. Fighting goes on as the Japanese dig in and try to expand their holdings in Shantung along rail tracks and the canal. Fifty thousand Chinese troops try to hold Taierhchwang against Japanese attacks and air raids.

A	B	C	D	E
Includes developments that affect more than one world region, international organizations, and important meetings of world leaders.	Includes all domestic and regional developments in Europe, including the Soviet Union.	Includes all domestic and regional developments in Africa and the Middle East.	Includes all domestic and regional developments in Latin America, the Caribbean, and Canada.	Includes all domestic and regional developments in Asian and Pacific nations (and colonies).

U.S. Politics & Social Issues	U.S. Foreign Policy & Defense	Economics & Great Depression	Science, Technology & Nature	Culture, Leisure & Lifestyle	
					Mar. 23
	The United States asks 29 nations in Europe and the Americas to help Austrian and German political refugees by cooperating in emigration policies, with funding from private organizations.				Mar. 24
From Warm Springs, Ga., the President conducts a telephone campaign to push passage of his Reorganization Bill, which has been hotly debated in the Senate.	After a year of negotiations, Japan agrees to cease salmon fishing in Alaskan waters.			Battleship, a son of champion Man O'War, wins England's 100th Grand National steeplechase—the first American-bred horse to do so.	Mar. 25
			A 24,000-mile round-trip flight between London and New Zealand ends, with 10 flight records broken for time and speed between various points. RAF-trained New Zealander Arthur Clouston flew with his friend, journalist Victor Ricketts.		Mar. 26
					Mar. 27
The Supreme Court rules that utility holding companies must register with the Securities and Exchange Commission. Other decisions uphold rulings by the NLRB, and bar racial discrimination in enforcing labor rights. . . . The Senate passes the Reorganization Bill; it now goes to the House of Representatives.					Mar. 28
	The United States insists that Mexico reconsider its seizure of oil company property on the grounds that the country cannot make adequate financial compensation.	In Belvedere, Ill., six persons—including the mayor—are hurt in a melee outside the National Sewing Machine Company. Six men tried to return to work in a plant closed by 800 strikers. . . . In Detroit, 20 nonstriking workers need police escorts to enter the Federal Screw Works after violence injures seven. . . . Police use tear gas to control pickets at Connor Lumber and Land in Laona, Wisc., when a disputed union election causes violence between CIO and AFL members.	The Fansworth Company announces testing of a new type of television projector, developed by Harry Bamford, which gives a continuous, clear picture. . . . A Queens County Court allows the use of a lie detector test administered by Father Sumners of Fordham University, on a man accused of theft. The machine says he is innocent, and the man is acquitted after nine hours of deliberation.	The Jefferson Memorial Commission unveils both the design and location for a new $3 million memorial in Washington, D.C.	Mar. 29
	Secretary of State Cordell Hull demands compensation for property seized from U.S. companies. As he acknowledges Mexico's right to expropriate the property to begin with, negotiations proceed on a friendly basis.	Another riot at the Federal Screw Works in Detroit injures 35 strikers and five police officers. The violence began as 150 police and 15 mounted officers escorted nonstriking workers from the plant, and were pelted with rocks and sticks.	Twenty-six tornadoes strike Illinois, Kansas, Missouri, and Arkansas, causing 40 deaths.		Mar. 30

F	G	H	I	J
Includes elections, federal-state relations, civil rights and liberties, crime, the judiciary, education, healthcare, poverty, urban affairs, and population.	Includes formation and debate of U.S. foreign and defense policies, veterans affairs, and defense spending. (Relations with specific foreign countries are usually found under the region concerned.)	Includes business, labor, agriculture, taxation, transportation, consumer affairs, monetary and fiscal policy, natural resources, pollution, and accidents.	Includes worldwide scientific, medical, and technological developments, natural phenomena, U.S. weather, and natural disasters.	Includes the arts, religion, scholarship, communications media, sports, entertainment, fashions, fads, and social life.

	World Affairs	Europe	Africa & The Middle East	The Americas	Asia & The Pacific
Mar. 31	The United States, Britain, and France announce that they will not observe the ship-building restrictions of the London Treaty, because of Japan's refusal to reveal ship plans. . . . At least 14 nations have accepted Secretary of State Cordell Hull's proposal of one week ago to assist political refugees from Germany and Austria.	Six thousand loyalist troops—half a division—followed by civilian refugees hike 60 miles across the snow-covered Pyrenees from Spain into France, seeking asylum. . . . German planes continue a daily shelling of Spain's coastal towns as insurgent infantry from the west approach the towns by land.	Six are killed and 30 injured in clashes between political parties, as parliamentary elections take place in Upper Egypt. The Cairo area (Lower Egypt) will vote on April 2. . . . At least 2,700 Jews emigrate to Palestine in March, many from Austria.	President Lázaro Cárdenas of Mexico negotiates for the sale of oil at bargain prices to undisclosed buyers. High profile businessmen F.W. Rickett and Bernard Smith from the United States and Britain participate; Mexico hopes the sale will enable it to make payments on the oil properties expropriated two weeks ago. . . . In a note to the U.S. Ambassador in Mexico, Cárdenas promises to honor its obligations—presumably, to pay for the property expropriated on March 18.	
Apr. 1	Britain and the United States cite the Escalator Provision of the 1936 London Naval Treaty as rationale to increase the size and guns of new battleships. Also cited is the belief that Japan is installing larger guns on its new ships.	The Vatican rebukes Austria's Cardinal Innitzer and his Bishops for their statement approving of Nazis on March 27. There can be no compromise with Nazism, the Holy See warns. . . . In Switzerland, the Nestlé Company tries out a new product it has been working on for seven years: Nescafé instant coffee.	American missionaries are ordered by the Italian government to leave Ethiopia within 24 hours.	Negotiator F.W. Rickett works on a deal to sell 25 million barrels of Mexican oil to a secret buyer. If completed, the sale will fund Mexico's initial payment to the United States for expropriated land and wells.	
Apr. 2	The Soviet Union accuses Japan's envoy in Kabul, Afghanistan, of trying to recruit the Soviet Minister to Afghanistan as a spy. The Soviets ask Japan to close three of its remaining six embassies in the Soviet Union by the end of this month.	France, Britain, and Czechoslovakia officially recognize that Austria is now part of Germany. Italy, Japan, Poland, Turkey, and insurgent Spain have already done so. . . . An estimated 8,000 Spanish refugees have entered France at Bagnères de Luchon, directly north of Lerida. Most are soldiers.	Parliamentary elections in Lower Egypt overwhelmingly support the government against the Wafdist party. Five people are killed in election-related violence in rural areas.		China's Kuomintang conservative party gives Chiang Kai-shek the new title "Tsung Tsai," translated as Director-General, with increased authority. He becomes the permanent chair of the party with veto powers over all legislation.
Apr. 3		A 90-minute shelling of Madrid by insurgents is the worst the capital has endured so far. . . . In his first radio speech, Hungarian Regent Miklós Horthy declares he will uphold peace and order, and reminds his followers that Germany is a friend to their nation.	Voting in the Minia province of Egypt results in a tie, forcing another election. Six people die in clashes, including two brothers, both prominent men campaigning for their nephew, Sultan Saadi.		Although Japan claimed to take Hanchwang yesterday, Chinese troops say they are in control of the city again.
Apr. 4	Japan's Ambassador complains to the Soviet Union that Soviet volunteers are flying for China. Soviet Foreign Secretary Litvinoff denies this, but asserts his country's right to deploy men and materiel in China if it chooses. . . . Ecuador and Germany sign a barter treaty in which Germany is granted "most favored nation" status.	The value of the French franc rises on rumors of Premier Blum's financial program, to be presented to the Chamber of Deputies soon. . . . Britain sends its battleship Hood to Barcelona to help with evacuations, and asks Gen. Franco to stop bombing five British ships in the harbor.		The trial begins of 10 military men in Cuba, who are charged with conspiracy. The men were arrested after a planned coup was uncovered last month.	Japan claims that over 100,000 Chinese forces in Shantung flee south in a disorganized retreat. Chinese reports acknowledge that most of a division of troops was sacrificed to fight off a flanking maneuver by Japan, southeast of Taierhchwang.
Apr. 5	Responding to a Japanese charge that the Soviets are aiding China, and that constitutes a belligerent action, Foreign Minister Litvinoff says that as Japan denies that a state of war exists, there can be no belligerency.	As the insurgent army nears the coast of Spain, power stations are damaged by shells and sporadic blackouts occur. Loyalists dynamite bridges as they retreat. . . . Spreading strikes among auto workers and taxi drivers in Paris bode ill for Premier Blum's economic proposals.		The Bishop of Guadalajara, Mexico, suggests that oil workers give up a day of pay each month to help the government pay its debt for the seized oil fields. . . . Trinidad's sugar workers strike for higher wages, forcing the four largest factories to close.	Trains crowded with refugees collide in Yencheng, killing 80 people. . . . Chinese guerilla bands strike at Japanese troops and convoys within 15 miles of Shanghai, at Sungkiang.
Apr. 6		Austria's Cardinal Innitzer is summoned to Rome and speaks to the Pope. He retracts his advice to parishioners to vote for the Nazis, but the Austrian press will not print the retraction. . . . The Scandinavian Defense Conference concludes. As Denmark will not challenge Germany, the other countries—Finland, Norway, and Sweden—decide to see to their own defenses.		The Mexican government orders that 20 percent of proceeds from oil exports be put into a fund to pay for the expropriation of oil fields and facilities.	The Chinese capture Taierhchwang. The victory has far-reaching implications, infusing the Chinese with hope, destroying the myth of Japanese infallibility in war, and convincing many American military advisers that China can win a war with Japan.
Apr. 7		Spanish insurgents capture Tremp, site of the Catalan district's largest hydroelectric power plant. Troops under General Solchaga seize the plant in the early morning before retreating loyalists can destroy or sabotage it. . . . Despite the shaky position of the government, French Foreign Minister Paul-Bancour queries European allies about defending Czech independence.	Terrorists ambush and kill two young men working in a Jewish commune in northern Palestine, one Canadian and one American.	Quebec passes a third bill opposed by labor, incorporating trade unions. The first two bills exempted government employees from wage laws and bargaining, and made union membership strictly voluntary.	Over a million people in Hankow celebrate the victory at Taierhchwang, the first sure defeat of the Japanese in an open battle. The Chinese suffered an estimated 7,500 casualties, out of the 46,000 troops involved in the attack.

A	B	C	D	E
Includes developments that affect more than one world region, international organizations, and important meetings of world leaders.	Includes all domestic and regional developments in Europe, including the Soviet Union.	Includes all domestic and regional developments in Africa and the Middle East.	Includes all domestic and regional developments in Latin America, the Caribbean, and Canada.	Includes all domestic and regional developments in Asian and Pacific nations (and colonies).

U.S. Politics & Social Issues	U.S. Foreign Policy & Defense	Economics & Great Depression	Science, Technology & Nature	Culture, Leisure & Lifestyle	
The House debates the Reorganization Bill and barely averts a filibuster attempt.	Returning from his tour and study of Europe, former president Herbert Hoover warns against commitments to the democracies there, lest the United States be drawn into war. He sees Communism as dying, but fascism as a major threat.	B.F. Goodrich, Goodyear, and Firestone Tire Companies announce pay cuts of 10 to 20 percent for salaried employees. . . . Wage reductions result in a walkout of 700 employees at a linoleum plant in Trenton, N. J. . . . General Electric signs a union contract covering 30,000 employees in six different cities, giving them the "prevailing wage" in their locations.			Mar. 31
Reporting on a three-year investigation into AT&T, Paul Walker of the FCC says rates could be cut 25 percent without affecting net earnings. Other recommendations from the $5 million study include lowering excessive temporary rates, and giving the FCC approval authority over AT&T policies. . . . Rebelling against House leadership, Representatives refuse to vote on the Reorganization Bill.	The United States stops its purchases of Mexican silver, as announced last month. However, the United States continues to buy "spot" silver from Mexico.	When talks between the CIO and the Consumers Power Company collapse after seven weeks, utility workers in the Saginaw Valley of Michigan take control of 13 plants and go on strike. . . . A fur dealer in New York is beaten in violence connected with an ongoing strike. Random beatings and vandalism occur daily as up to 15,000 fur workers remain idle after two months. . . . Seventy-three unions, both AFL and CIO, in three states establish a board to study labor and industrial espionage.		*The Yearling* by Marjorie Kinnan Rawlings is published. The novel will win the Pulitzer Prize next year. . . . Joe Louis knocks out Harry Thomas in the fifth round to retain his world heavyweight championship.	Apr. 1
			Scientists at the Massachusetts Institute of Technology report they can now predict thunderstorms up to 36 hours in advance, thanks to "flow patterns" charted by airplane and balloon data.		Apr. 2
	The U.S. Consulate in Barcelona moves to San Vincente de Llevaneras.	Two million people depend on the power plants held by strikers in Michigan; so far, there have been no blackouts.	Ten spectators are killed and scores injured when a race car skids into a crowd at the *Mille Miglia* race in northern Italy. Premier Benito Mussolini cancels the annual race next year, but it will resume at a 100-km track in Brescia, starting in 1940.	The Guggenheim Foundation hands out 58 grants totaling $135,000. Recipients include Mexican composer and conductor Carlos Chavez, who takes over the NBC Orchestra from Arturo Toscanini, and anti-Nazi German painter George Grosz.	Apr. 3
		The President approves a Congressional investigation of the Tennessee Valley Authority (TVA). . . . Governor Murphy of Michigan meets with utility workers, who agree to release the power plants they hold.			Apr. 4
	Japan asks for an itemization of the bill presented by the United States for the sinking of the *Panay*.	The President publicly expresses his dislike for a proposed railroad subsidy, saying that other industries might demand federal subsidies to avoid layoffs as well.			Apr. 5
	The United States acknowledges the Reich's takeover of Austria, and asks Germany to pay Austria's debt to the U.S.: $38.5 million in bonds, and $26 million in war debt.		At DuPont Chemical's Jackson Laboratory in New Jersey, Dr. Roy Plunkett accidentally discovers Teflon while experimenting with Freon.	Jewish entertainers fete Albert Einstein at a New York theater. Dr. Einstein then asks for international support for Palestine as a haven for refugees.	Apr. 6
			A tornado near Aliceville, Ala., kills 11 people and destroys a four-block area of homes. Accompanying storms and flash floods kill 13 more; 20,000 are homeless in Alabama and Georgia. Further west, a blizzard hits the Texas panhandle.		Apr. 7

F	G	H	I	J
Includes elections, federal-state relations, civil rights and liberties, crime, the judiciary, education, healthcare, poverty, urban affairs, and population.	Includes formation and debate of U.S. foreign and defense policies, veterans affairs, and defense spending. (Relations with specific foreign countries are usually found under the region concerned.)	Includes business, labor, agriculture, taxation, transportation, consumer affairs, monetary and fiscal policy, natural resources, pollution, and accidents.	Includes worldwide scientific, medical, and technological developments, natural phenomena, U.S. weather, and natural disasters.	Includes the arts, religion, scholarship, communications media, sports, entertainment, fashions, fads, and social life.

	World Affairs	Europe	Africa & The Middle East	The Americas	Asia & The Pacific
Apr. 8	The British government demands that Mexico return its expropriated properties.	Premier Léon Blum of France resigns. Socialist Eduoard Daladier is asked to form a government.	In Jerusalem, the government orders the closure of the Church of the Holy Sepulchre.		
Apr. 9			Riots between nationalists and French police in Tunis leave 13 dead. Buses are burned and 60 are arrested as martial law is declared. France rushes reinforcements to the city. . . . Arturo Toscanini arrives in Palestine to conduct a series of concerts in Tel Aviv.		Inspired by the victory at Taierhchwang, two battalions of Chinese police rebel against the puppet government installed by the Japanese in Tsinan, capital of Shantung province.
Apr. 10		Fifty million Germans and Austrians vote, and over 99 percent of them approve the union of Germany and Austria. The ballots are not secret, however. . . . The Socialist Party in France decides not to participate in Premier Daladier's Cabinet, but will decide later whether or not to support his fiscal policies.		Mexico postpones a strike by power workers in six major cities for twenty days, while negotiations continue.	In Lanao province, Philippines, 12 are killed in clashes with Moro tribesmen.
Apr. 11	The Soviet Union protests that Japanese planes are flying over Siberia. Japan worries that the Soviets are mobilizing for war.	French workers plow and shovel snow in the Pyrenees, clearing a path for the thousands of Spanish refugees fleeing to France. . . . Austrian officials report that General Zehner, Secretary of State before the *Anschluss*, committed suicide while in custody; 168 political prisoners, including former ministers, government officials, and journalists, are sent to Dachau concentration camp.	The first (and only) passenger alights from a ship in Tel Aviv Harbor in Palestine. The harbor was officially opened in late February, but because of quarantines, delays, and misinformation, passengers have disembarked at Haifa instead.	Brazil hosts diplomats and ministers from the United States, Argentina, Peru, and Chile, all gathered to discuss the Chaco dispute, disarmament, and refugee immigration.	Japanese authorities still deny any loss of ground at Taierhchwang, but American witnesses have seen the city and back the Chinese version of events.
Apr. 12	Mexico tells Britain it will not return seized properties, and will compensate oil companies directly, without government interference. F.W. Rickett announces that his negotiations for the sale of Mexican oil have failed, largely because of Britain's demand.	Eyewitnesses report that convoys carrying supplies—including tanks and planes—for loyalist Spain are passing through the French border daily. . . . Spanish insurgents commandeer a British-owned hotel in Algeciras, a Spanish city near Gibraltar. German flight instructors and experts will be quartered there.			Five thousand Japanese troops and artillery pour into Shantung province and push south toward Lini. Japan fears a threat to Tsinan, the capital. . . . Japanese industrialists are informed that government control of defense industries will be permanent.
Apr. 13	Britain announces a plan to purchase aircraft from the United States and Canada.	Working through the night, Premier Daladier obtains from Parliament a vote of confidence and six weeks to implement his fiscal policies unhindered. Striking Paris workers, 150,000 strong, are his first challenge. . . . Danish Nazis interrupt Parliament, firing blanks at a minister and raining pamphlets over the assemblage.		Bolivia rejects the proposed settlement of the Chaco dispute, crafted by the five nations meeting in Brazil. . . . President Enriquez of Ecuador appoints a new Cabinet of army officers, with only one civilian serving as Foreign Minister.	General and governor Yen Hsi-shan, driven out of Shansi last month, regroups his troops and reenters the province, holding towns near the Yellow River. . . . Chinese troops, aware that Japanese reinforcements are en route, fight to encircle the enemy in Yihsien.
Apr. 14		Planes of the Spanish insurgency bomb a hospital train, killing 10 people and injuring many others, including six Americans.			Although Japan continues to deny the Taierhchwang defeat, a Cabinet crisis brews over it in Tokyo. With rigid censorship, the Japanese public is not aware of the defeat. . . . China announces the execution of eight generals, for corruption, rape, or cowardice.
Apr. 15		A strike of aviation workers in France ends, but auto and metal plants are still idle.		Canadian seamen leave ships when called to strike by their union. Seven hundred men walked off 25 ships in Toronto harbor.	In Tokyo, Premier Konoe is said to be ready to resign rather than invoke the National Mobilization Act. When it was passed, he promised not to use it during the Chinese hostilities.
Apr. 16		The British-Italian Agreement is signed, recognizing Italy's conquest of Ethiopia, and Britain's right to its protectorate in Arabia. Italy promises a complete withdrawal from Spain at the end of the civil war. . . . Sixty thousand auto workers in France agree to end their 10-day strike. The hope is that others strikers—up to 100,000 strong—will also return to work. . . . Czech President Benes announces amnesty for political prisoners.	France dissolves the Neo-Destour Nationalist organization in Tunisia, and raids its headquarters in several cities near the port of Susa. . . . In a gun battle in the hills near Nablus, Palestine, 16 Arabs are killed by the military authorities. In a separate incident, a car of six Jewish men is fired on near El Bassa, and three men are killed.	Colombian oil workers return to work with the promise that the government will investigate their wage request. . . . In Ontario, Canada, 40 lake steamships are now idle because of the seamen's strike. . . . Mexico announces that a national sugar cooperative will regulate prices and production in the industry.	Japanese troops in Yihsien, fighting in the hills and the city, are said to be starving. Reinforcements are still 75 miles away. Japan imposes strict censorship on all news from Shantung. . . . In Hopeh, Chinese Communist troops encircle the Japanese at Paoting, having blown up most bridges and escape routes in the area.

A	B	C	D	E
Includes developments that affect more than one world region, international organizations, and important meetings of world leaders.	Includes all domestic and regional developments in Europe, including the Soviet Union.	Includes all domestic and regional developments in Africa and the Middle East.	Includes all domestic and regional developments in Latin America, the Caribbean, and Canada.	Includes all domestic and regional developments in Asian and Pacific nations (and colonies).

U.S. Politics & Social Issues	U.S. Foreign Policy & Defense	Economics & Great Depression	Science, Technology & Nature	Culture, Leisure & Lifestyle	
Joining House Republicans to vote against the Reorganization Bill are 108 Democrats, a blow to the President. The stand is seen as notification that Congress feels slighted by demands for more Presidential powers.		The International Shoe Plant in Missouri will cut pay for 30,000 employees by 10 percent next month.	Scattered cities from New England to Arizona, and the entire state of Pennsylvania, ban this week's issue of *Life* magazine, which features four pages of photographs showing the birth of a baby.		Apr. 8
	The Army Air Corps contracts to buy 37 C-33 airplanes, a modified version of the DC-2, from Douglas Aircraft.	The NLRB finds that Republic Steel violated the Wagner Act when it suppressed union activities and manipulated groups such as the Massillon Law and Order League. The NLRB also holds the steel company responsible for three deaths during the Massillon riots of July 1937.			Apr. 9
New York makes syphilis testing mandatory for those seeking marriage licenses; it is the ninth state to do so.					Apr. 10
President Franklin Roosevelt asks Congress for unspecified legislation to aid the nation's railroads. . . . The Supreme Court rules that excluding Negroes from a jury denied a Kentucky defendant a fair trial.		Congressmen and administration leaders meet with the President to reassess recovery legislation. . . . Thirteen thousand Detroit auto workers stage a "slow-down" that closes Plymouth and Mack plants for a day.	France is installing underground cables to bring television to Limoges, Toulouse, and Bordeaux.	Jackie Coogan, 23 years old and recently married to Betty Grable, files a lawsuit against his mother and stepfather. He asks an accounting for $4 million in earnings for his work in movies like *The Kid*.	Apr. 11
		Animal trainers and riggers strike for higher wages from the Ringling Brothers and Barnum and Bailey Circus. The strike is settled in one day. . . . After broker Richard Whitney is sentenced to prison, the Securities and Exchange Commission begins an investigation into his affairs.	Frank Larsen, publisher of *Life*, is arrested in the Bronx for the "obscene" pictures of birth that he published. Trial is set for April 19.	Feodor Chaliapin, considered the greatest bass singer of the 20th century, dies of leukemia in Paris at age 65.	Apr. 12
	The President meets with Cabinet members and religious leaders to discuss emigration of political refugees in Europe.	The President signs a bill allowing the Reconstruction Finance Corporation (RFC) to make loans to businesses. . . . The Department of Commerce reports that the decline in U.S. production has slowed, though production is still below 1937 figures. . . . Leaders of 38 CIO-affiliated unions vote to form a permanent organization, rivaling the AFL.			Apr. 13
		In a fireside chat, President Roosevelt presents a $5 billion program to end the business recession—$3 billion is to be spent over the next few months; nearly a third will be repayable loans; $1.4 billion in funding will come from the gold reserves.			Apr. 14
		Rail companies ask for a conference to discuss voluntary wage reductions. Unions representing a million employees say "no."			Apr. 15
		Twelve hundred truck drivers in Rochester, N.Y., strike for higher wages, as do bus and taxi drivers in Columbus, Ohio. Retail clerks refuse to cross the picket lines of warehouse workers at four Philadelphia department stores. Auto workers at Buick and Chevrolet plants in Michigan vote to strike on May 1 if threatened pay cuts are implemented. UAWA workers strike at a California Ford plant.		The St. Louis Cardinals trade Dizzy Dean to the Chicago Cubs. . . . With Orville Wright standing by, Henry Ford dedicates the original Wright Cycle Shop, transplanted from Dayton to Ford's Greenfield Village in Dearborn, Mich.	Apr. 16

F	G	H	I	J
Includes elections, federal-state relations, civil rights and liberties, crime, the judiciary, education, healthcare, poverty, urban affairs, and population.	Includes formation and debate of U.S. foreign and defense policies, veterans affairs, and defense spending. (Relations with specific foreign countries are usually found under the region concerned.)	Includes business, labor, agriculture, taxation, transportation, consumer affairs, monetary and fiscal policy, natural resources, pollution, and accidents.	Includes worldwide scientific, medical, and technological developments, natural phenomena, U.S. weather, and natural disasters.	Includes the arts, religion, scholarship, communications media, sports, entertainment, fashions, fads, and social life.

	World Affairs	Europe	Africa & The Middle East	The Americas	Asia & The Pacific
Apr. 17		Romania uncovers an anti-government plot by the fascist party Iron Guard, as well as stockpiles of guns and ammunition held by party leaders. One hundred are arrested. . . . Reporting increased production for the first quarter of 1938, the Soviet press credits the influx of young Stalinists in management.	A bomb thrown from a car into an Arab cafe in Haifa, Palestine, kills one man and injures seven others, both Jew and Arab.		Rioting in Bombay, India, between Hindus and Muslims kills four people and injures 68 others.
Apr. 18		The Pope sends an apostolic blessing to Gen. Franco. . . . On orders from the Gestapo in Berlin, at least 3,000 Austrian Jews in the Burgenland province (along the border with Czechoslovakia) are stripped of their belongings and driven to the Jewish sector of Vienna.	Twelve Tunisians and four Italians get prison sentences of up to one year for their roles in the April 9 riots.	Ships' clerks and other employees go on strike again in San Juan, Puerto Rico.	Chinese troops say they have recaptured many cities in north and west Shansi, and now besiege Tatung. The charge of using poison gas is again leveled at Japan.
Apr. 19		Protestant clergymen in the Reich must take a civil oath of obedience to Hitler. . . . France begins talks toward a treaty with Italy, similar to England's. . . . In a radio speech, Gen. Franco tells Spain, "We have won the war." The Barcelona government sentences 39 men and women to death for treason.		Cuba doles out prison sentences of two to three years for military men convicted of plotting against the government. Three are acquitted. . . . Brazil bans all foreign propaganda.	Chinese troops capture a 20-mile section of the Grand Canal between Hanchwang and Taierhchwang. In Lini, however, Japanese troops breach the walls and enter the city.
Apr. 20		The Soviet Union forbids and denounces purges in collective farms. . . . Spanish insurgents push north, capturing mountain passes in the Pyrenees near the French border.	French authorities arrest 16 nationalists in Djerba, Tunisia. . . . In northern Palestine, a four-hour gun battle between Arab attackers and guards at a Jewish settlement leaves five Arabs dead. British troops kill five others in a separate band, who are believed to have killed an Arab policeman on April 19.	In the Mexican states of Toluca and Guanajuato, 11 people are killed and dozens injured in three separate fights over the distribution of land.	Helped by newly arrived reinforcements, Japan captures Lini. Chinese troops there withdraw to Yihsien, 30 miles away. The city of Hanchwang is also abandoned.
Apr. 21	Britain again protests to Mexico over the seizure of oil company properties. . . . In secret, Mexico ships oil from seized properties via an Italian tanker to buyers in Italy and Germany.	With all attention focused on the east, insurgents stage a surprise attack on Madrid. Insurgent planes also bomb sites near the French border, killing a dozen people. . . . Retired scholar Douglas Hyde is chosen to be Ireland's first president. . . . Poland's Camp of National Unity, the only political party, expels anti-Semitic and fascist extremists.	Two British soldiers are killed in a gun battle near a well in Palestine; stray bullets kill a man and woman standing by. Other random attacks leave two Arab men dead.	Ship employees return to work, obeying an order of a Governor's board in Puerto Rico. Shipping companies agree to arbitration.	Japanese troops, now on the offensive, move toward Yihsien, where 5,000 troops are holding the city. A reported 100,000 Japanese troops are now in the area, against 200,000 Chinese soldiers. . . . Premier Konoe of Japan, claiming he has been ill for three weeks, returns to his duties and says that action in China is going according to plan.
Apr. 22		Spanish insurgents capture troops from the International Brigade, including 70 Americans.			Chinese troops mass in the hills around Lini and launch a drive to retake the city. The Japanese troops once trapped in Yihsien join the larger force defending Lini. . . . Chinese pilots, rushed through training by Russian volunteers, are taking over most missions.
Apr. 23		Austria begins a purge of "non-Aryan" books at its National Library. Paul Heigl, the newly appointed Nazi director, also embarks on a campaign of adding to the library's collections by looting Jewish art and book collections. . . . The French franc plummets on rumors of dissension in the Daladier Cabinet.	In Beirut, seven die in clashes between Muslims and Christians. The French-appointed Premier is Muslim. . . . Authorities arrest another 135 nationalists in Tunis, and set up a concentration camp to hold the more than 500 detainees.	Landslides and floods damage crops, kill livestock, and isolate towns in Colombia.	Japanese planes bomb and sink two passenger ships between Macao and Kowloon, killing over 100 people. . . . A cholera epidemic breaks out in Hardiwar, the United Provinces of India. Tens of thousands of pilgrims were in the city for the Khumba Mela religious festival, and the disease claims 100 lives a day.
Apr. 24		During a two-day congress, Konrad Henlein tells Czechoslovakia's Sudeten Germans that the current situation is intolerable, and his party demands complete autonomy. These demands are called the Carlsbad Decrees. . . . The Soviet Union announces mass arrests of religious leaders for treason and other charges, naming 25 of them. . . . Estonia elects its first President, Konstantin Päts.	Egypt's Premier resigns in a disagreement with the King over Cabinet appointments. King Farouk does not accept the resignation, but the Cabinet is reorganized. . . . Guiga Bahri Ben Hamoda, a Tunisian nationalist leader, is arrested in Paris.		Japan reports victories in Kiangsu province, bringing them closer to control over the Lung-hai railroad. The Japanese push is now toward Pihsien in Kiangsu, about 15 miles southeast of Taierhchwang.

A	B	C	D	E
Includes developments that affect more than one world region, international organizations, and important meetings of world leaders.	*Includes all domestic and regional developments in Europe, including the Soviet Union.*	*Includes all domestic and regional developments in Africa and the Middle East.*	*Includes all domestic and regional developments in Latin America, the Caribbean, and Canada.*	*Includes all domestic and regional developments in Asian and Pacific nations (and colonies).*

U.S. Politics & Social Issues	U.S. Foreign Policy & Defense	Economics & Great Depression	Science, Technology & Nature	Culture, Leisure & Lifestyle	
		California's Newspaper Guild settles the strike in San Francisco that stopped publication of five papers.			Apr. 17
		Crucible Steel reopens three plants in New Jersey and 2,250 employees return to work after a five-week strike over the lockout of 70 workers. . . . UAWA members force the closure of General Motors Fisher Body Works and a Buick plant in Flint, locking out 5,000 employees. . . . In San Francisco, 1,000 longshoremen battle the pickets of a sailors' union, and 20 men are injured.			Apr. 18
The defense for Roy Larsen, publisher of *Life* magazine, calls 21 doctors and other experts who deny the magazine's pictures of birth are obscene. The trial is continued.	The President remains undecided about selling helium to Germany for use in dirigibles. The U.S. government has a monopoly on helium, and fears Germany could use it for military purposes.	For a second day, UAWA pickets refuse to allow anyone into the Buick or Fisher plants who cannot prove their union dues are paid. . . . Produce merchants in Rochester agree to trucker's terms, but other companies have not settled and 90 percent of the drivers remain on strike.	NBC begins five hours a week of scheduled television broadcasting from the top of the Empire State Building. . . . The Anatolian region of Turkey is rocked by 13 earthquakes, killing hundreds of people.		Apr. 19
				Joe DiMaggio accepts a $25,000 contract with the New York Yankees. He had reportedly wanted $40,000.	Apr. 20
		The UAWA in Detroit closes eight plants with dues-collecting tactics that keep employees from entering. Also in Detroit, pickets block seven Bohn Aluminum facilities over seniority rights, and strike at four other companies over wage cuts.	Dr. Alexis Carrel (Nobel Prize winner) and Charles Lindbergh describe the "Lindbergh pump" that can keep organs alive for 11 years—the forerunner of the artificial heart.	Jacqueline Cochrane receives the Bendix Trophy as Best Aviatrix of 1937. . . . The U.S. Mint picks a design by Felix Schlag for the new Jefferson nickel.	Apr. 21
An explosion in a Keen Mountain, Va., coal mine kills 54 men instantly.	Japan hands over a check for payment in full of damages to the *Panay* and its crew.		Astronomer Robert McMath shows pictures of a solar storm, with plumes of hydrogen flaming upward 150,000 miles.	A California judge, citing Jackie Coogan's case, says he will not approve contracts for underage performers until guardians agree to deposit half of the child's salary in a trust fund.	Apr. 22
		The U.S. Chamber of Commerce joins Congressmen and others in attacking the President's $5 billion recovery program as the wrong approach to the nation's woes. . . . The UAWA membership votes for a strike against Chevrolet and Buick, but Homer Martin, UAWA chief, promises to follow the grievance procedures.			Apr. 23
				Sculptor George Grey Barnard dies of a heart attack in New York. Famous for his Lincoln statues, his last, incomplete work was of Abel, betrayed by his brother Cain.	Apr. 24

F	G	H	I	J
Includes elections, federal-state relations, civil rights and liberties, crime, the judiciary, education, healthcare, poverty, urban affairs, and population.	Includes formation and debate of U.S. foreign and defense policies, veterans affairs, and defense spending. (Relations with specific foreign countries are usually found under the region concerned.)	Includes business, labor, agriculture, taxation, transportation, consumer affairs, monetary and fiscal policy, natural resources, pollution, and accidents.	Includes worldwide scientific, medical, and technological developments, natural phenomena, U.S. weather, and natural disasters.	Includes the arts, religion, scholarship, communications media, sports, entertainment, fashions, fads, and social life.

	World Affairs	Europe	Africa & The Middle East	The Americas	Asia & The Pacific
Apr. 25		Britain and Ireland sign an accord; Ireland pays £10 million and Britain relinquishes Irish ports. . . . Field Marshal Goering signs a decree ordering all Jews who own more than 5,000 marks to register their property. The decree allows the Reich to "utilize" the property. . . . Czechoslovakia calls Henlein's demands "unacceptable." . . . German Nazi politician Joseph Buerckel is named ruler of Austria, answerable only to Chancellor Adolf Hitler.			In India, state troops are dispatched to prevent hostilities between the ruling families of Sikar and Jaipur, over a personal matter. The British governor claims to settle the matter in a few days. . . . In the Mysore state of India, police fire into a crowd of nationalist demonstrators, killing 32 people.
Apr. 26	As U.S. universities and libraries offer to buy books from Austria's National Library, authorities publish assurances that there will be no book burnings or sales. Non-Aryan books will be put in storage.	Largely due to armaments spending, Britain raises its income tax to an unprecedented 27.5 percent. . . . Emperor Zog of Albania, a Muslim, marries a Catholic Hungarian Countess in a civil ceremony. . . . German newspapers, known to speak for the government, demand that all Jews leave Vienna by 1942.			India announces that 21 people have died in Hindu-Muslim violence this week; 2,171 were arrested. . . . In Shantung, Japanese troops capture two fortified hilltop positions that overlook the Lung-hai railroad near Pihsien.
Apr. 27	After three weeks of talks, Japan and the Soviet Union are deadlocked on issues involving prisoners and seized boats, fishing rights, and building projects in Siberia.	Premier Daladier of France arrives in London for a three-day conference with Britain over mutual defense issues. . . . Greece and Turkey sign a Friendship Treaty. . . . Newspapers report that an estimated 18,000 have been arrested in Vienna in the last three weeks, and that 30,000 to 40,000 were arrested in the city before April 6. The actual number is much higher.	Britain's commission to study the partition of Palestine arrives in Jerusalem.		To stop the flow of war materiel from the Soviet Union, Japan launches a campaign in northwest China, and captures cities in Suiyuan province. . . . In Pihsien, Chinese sources admit that a regiment from the Yunnan province in the south was wiped out in a battle with Japanese troops.
Apr. 28		Britain and France agree on a unified command structure in case of war, and will begin immediately to combine supplies and munition stockpiles. . . . Germany decrees that Jews of all nationalities must declare their property.			The Japanese advance toward the Lung-hai railroad is slowed, but not stopped, by Chinese infantry and artillery.
Apr. 29		Britain and France end their parley with an agreement to work to keep Germany from attacking Czechoslovakia. . . . Nazis in Sofia, Bulgaria, smash windows and riot in anti-Jewish demonstrations.	Plans are published in newspapers for a 50-mile barbed wire fence that will keep Syrian brigands from crossing into Palestine.	President Getulio Vargas of Brazil decrees that all oil refineries will be operated by Brazilian companies. Only one facility, still under construction, is affected.	Between 40 and 50 Japanese planes engage a Chinese force half the size over Hankow. China claims to shoot down 20 planes and lose 12. Japan claims its pilots shot down 50 Chinese planes, out of 80 that flew, and lost only two.
Apr. 30	The League of Nations publishes Switzerland's request to have its neutrality recognized.	Bulgaria disbands its Nazi party. . . . Pope Pius XI leaves Rome for Castel Gandalfo, evading Chancellor Hitler who will visit in three days. . . . Omission of the names of military leaders from the lists of May Day honorees in the Soviet Union indicates that the purges continue. . . . A crowd of 5,000 watches in Salzburg, Austria, as books by Jews and former Premier Schuschnigg are burned.	In Cairo, speeches call for boycotts of both Jews and the British, who plan to divide Palestine. . . . In Palestine, six Arab policemen are killed by Arabs.	Voters in Colombia elect Liberal Eduardo Santos as president. Conservatives and Communists refuse to participate in the election.	Chinese guerillas blow up the only railway bridge between Peiping and Japanese positions in southern Hopeh. . . . A new and more aggressive Vice Admiral, Koshiro Oikawa, takes command of the Japanese fleet in south China.
May 1		Spanish Premier Negrín asks for peace, but Gen. Franco demands unconditional surrender. . . . May Day processions in Poland are marred: a bomb is thrown at a Jewish Socialist parade, and a Nationalist fires a gun on a parade in Kielce. . . . Police arrest 14 Nazis in Hungary for anti-Semitic acts. . . . All journalists in Austria with Jewish blood are fired, and many are sent to concentration camps.		The ownership of Mexican railroads passes to the workers, by decree.	Chinese and Japanese forces battle over Tancheng in southern Shantung. . . . Japanese planes bomb the Lung-hai rail corridor, the Yangtze River valley, and railroads leading from Hankow.
May 2		By decree, Prime Minister Daladier of France raises all taxes by 8 percent. . . . Although the House of Commons approves Britain's new treaty with Italy by a 3 to 1 vote, Labor party leaders criticize the "scandalous" treatment of Ethiopia. . . . Britain's Foreign Minister, Viscount Halifax, urges Czechoslovakia to make concessions to Germany to preserve peace.		In Jamaica, a strike of 1,000 sugar workers, begun yesterday at the Tate and Lyle estate, turns violent. Police fire into the crowd and kill six after rioters burn a car. The workers are demanding better pay and housing.	Chinese troops circle Tancheng while waiting for reinforcements.

A	B	C	D	E
Includes developments that affect more than one world region, international organizations, and important meetings of world leaders.	Includes all domestic and regional developments in Europe, including the Soviet Union.	Includes all domestic and regional developments in Africa and the Middle East.	Includes all domestic and regional developments in Latin America, the Caribbean, and Canada.	Includes all domestic and regional developments in Asian and Pacific nations (and colonies).

U.S. Politics & Social Issues	U.S. Foreign Policy & Defense	Economics & Great Depression	Science, Technology & Nature	Culture, Leisure & Lifestyle	
The President asks Congress for specific "short and simple statutes" on taxes.		The UAWA calls two sit-down strikes over wage cuts, closing Gar-Wood factories in Detroit. . . . The Supreme Court issues a decision upholding New Deal policies on municipal bankruptcies, It decides against the government in the "Stockyards Case," saying that companies are entitled to "fair and open hearings" in "quasi-judicial proceedings."	Dr. Herbert Ives of Bell Laboratories describes an "atomic clock" using hydrogen atoms in a vacuum tube. The first atomic clock, built in 1955, will use cesium atoms in a microwave cavity.	*The Adventures of Robin Hood*, starring Errol Flynn and Olivia de Havilland, premieres.	Apr. 25
A Bronx jury acquits the publisher of *Life* magazine of indecency charges.	Germany withdraws from New York's 1939 World's Fair. The move may be connected to the delay in procuring helium, or antipathy toward New York's Mayor LaGuardia, a critic of Hitler. . . . Congress approves the Navy Appropriations Act, calling for over $546 million in expenditures.	Sixteen of the nation's business and industrial leaders pledge to the President their cooperation in bringing about economic recovery. . . . UAWA members attack pickets belonging to an independent union in Indiana.	Tornadoes level Oshkosh, Nebr., killing six people.		Apr. 26
		Henry Ford meets with President Franklin Roosevelt, who cannot change Ford's mind that "government [sh]ould get out of business." . . . The Gar-Wood strike ends as the company announces a profit-sharing plan. . . . Overproduction is blamed for the shutdown of Fisher and Chevrolet plants in upstate New York.			Apr. 27
Governor Phil LaFollette of Wisconsin and his brother, Senator Robert LaFollette, found the National Progressives of America Party. It stands against fascism, socialism, and relief to the able-bodied.					Apr. 28
	The President asks Congress to allocate funds for two more battleships, which would put six under construction.	Claiming that their financial situation is desperate, 100 railroad executives meet in Chicago where they vote to ask their 925,000 unionized railroad employees to take a 15 percent wage cut on July 1.			Apr. 29
	The President names Myron Taylor as the delegate to the international efforts to assist German and Austrian refugees. . . . The military reveals that an army and naval base will be built on Midway Island, at a cost of $2 million. A similar facility may be built on Wake Island.	The NLRB may reconsider rulings against Republic Steel, Ford, and other companies, due to the Supreme Court decision on Kansas City Stockyards on April 25. . . . The 12-day strike at seven Bohn Aluminum plants in Detroit is settled. . . . April's unemployment total is just over 10 million—including nearly three million people with WPA and CCC jobs.		Bugs Bunny makes his debut in the eight-minute long *Porky's Hare Hunt*.	Apr. 30
					May 1
		Four textile mills in Lowell, Mass., cut employee pay.		Thornton Wilder's play *Our Town* wins the Pulitzer Prize for Drama. *The Late George Apley*, by John P. Marquand, wins the Pulitzer for Best Novel.	May. 2

F	G	H	I	J
Includes elections, federal-state relations, civil rights and liberties, crime, the judiciary, education, healthcare, poverty, urban affairs, and population.	*Includes formation and debate of U.S. foreign and defense policies, veterans affairs, and defense spending. (Relations with specific foreign countries are usually found under the region concerned.)*	*Includes business, labor, agriculture, taxation, transportation, consumer affairs, monetary and fiscal policy, natural resources, pollution, and accidents.*	*Includes worldwide scientific, medical, and technological developments, natural phenomena, U.S. weather, and natural disasters.*	*Includes the arts, religion, scholarship, communications media, sports, entertainment, fashions, fads, and social life.*

	World Affairs	Europe	Africa & The Middle East	The Americas	Asia & The Pacific
May 3	Japan asserts that the Soviets have supplied 500 planes and 200 pilots to China.	Floodlights, pageantry, and a crowd of 300,000 greet Chancellor Hitler as he arrives in Rome for a state visit. . . . Approximately 600 shells fall in two afternoon insurgent raids on Madrid, Spain, killing 50 people. . . . Official Nazi newspapers in Germany warn Jews plainly to flee the country, saying that Jews are the enemy and are not wanted.		Jamaica's sugar strike spreads to another plantation, and at least three people die as police again fire into a crowd. Fifty are injured, and 90 arrested.	Japan remains silent on military actions in southern Shantung, leading all to believe that China has the upper hand. . . . Chiang Kai-shek sends Sun Ke back to Moscow to ask for Soviet help. Specifically, he will ask for more loans, and for Soviet troops along the border.
May 4		Douglas Hyde is elected the first Protestant President of Eire (Ireland). . . . From Castel Gandolfo, Pope Pius XI decries the swastikas on display in Rome. . . . The "Little Entente," meeting in Sinaia, Romania, with Czech and Yugoslav ministers, discusses their minority problems and possible aggression against Czechoslovakia.		Col. Batista of Cuba suspends his own Three-Year Plan until a new constitution can be written, saying this is for the good of the country.	China claims the Japanese armies retreat in Shantung, and that major casualties were inflicted on them in hand-to-hand fighting at Tancheng.
May 5	Complaints continue between Japan, the Soviet Union, and Korea, all claiming that their borders are not respected.	France agrees to close its border with Spain as soon as foreign volunteers in the civil war begin to depart. . . . The castle of Max Reinhardt, Austrian theatrical director and founder of the Salzburg Festival, is seized by Nazis. Reinhardt is Jewish.			Although admitting high casualties, Chinese sources report significant gains along the Lung-hai rail front. The Japanese have been pushed several miles north from Pihsien, out of Kiangsu province.
May 6		France and Britain jointly press the Czech government to make concessions to Germany, and ask Minister Goering to ease Germany's demands on Czechoslovakia. . . . Britain's War Minister Hore-Belisha meets with women leaders to discuss recruiting and training women in certain army tasks.	Arab leader Issa Battat is killed near Hebron, Palestine, by police. He was suspected in the death of archaeologist Leslie Starkey on January 10.		
May 7		Leaders Hitler and Mussolini express undying friendship between their countries at a state banquet in Rome.			Peiping is under attack by thousands of Chinese soldiers who rely on local fighters to aid them. Battles are also reported in Japanese-held territory north of Tsinan in Shantung. Also in Shantung, a French priest is shot dead and seven women, three of whom were nuns and two novitiates, are killed.
May 8	A shipment of 20,000 pounds of U.S.-made aerial bombs departs from Philadelphia on the *Frankenwald*, bound for Germany. Three previous shipments, all to unnamed American buyers with State Department approval, have already arrived.	Nazis and Sudeten Germans taunt police and riot as Czechoslovakia lifts its ban on political demonstrations. . . . Spanish insurgent ships try to seize the refurbished *Nantucket Chief*, which had been captured in January, then released. The ship, now under the British flag and renamed the *Refast*, is defended by a British destroyer.			Yingtak, a rail town near the city of Canton, is said to be the most bombed town in China. Since the beginning of this month, Japan has attempted landings at several islands in southern provinces of Canton and Fukien. The Fukien government moves from the coast to 100 miles inland.
May 9	The 101st session of the League of Nations opens to discuss recognition of the conquest of Ethiopia, Jewish refugees, and the undeclared war in China. China charges the use of poison gas by Japan. A three-hour closed-door discussion over Ethiopia ends with no decision. . . . The World Bank issues a report stating that "spendthrift nationalism," even as it's practiced in a democracy, cannot end the worldwide depression.	After 16 years, the Soviet Union catches up with P. Storozhev, last follower of the anti-Communist Antonov band of rebels, and executes him. A Soviet court also condemns to death the captains of two ships that collided in the Caspian Sea, for terrorism. . . . Fine restaurants in Madrid and Barcelona must reduce prices from 50 to 10 pesetas, to provide meals for all classes, the government declares.	No Arab group cooperates with the British commission studying the partition of Palestine. Arab leaders ask instead that Britain end its mandate and that Jews live in Palestine as a minority group.	Workers at the Ford assembly plant in Mexico strike for collective bargaining, with the government's approval. Ranch workers on six Mexican estates owned by William Randolph Hearst also strike for higher wages. . . . In the midst of a drought, Bermuda must import fresh water from New York.	The southern Chinese provinces of Yunnan and Kweichow, home to 20 million people, mobilize for war. . . . Japan's Foreign Minister Hirota reiterates the policy stated in January, that Japan will not negotiate with the government of Chiang Kai-shek.
May 10	Romania threatens to withdraw from the League of Nations if forced to testify about its treatment of Jews. . . . While delegate Dr. Wellington Koo pleads China's case before the League of Nations, Sun Ke meets with Josef Stalin and other Soviet officials, who agree to supply arms to China, accepting payment in tin, wood, and other resources.	Chancellor Adolf Hitler returns to Berlin after a visit to Rome that cements the Rome-Berlin Axis. . . . The Soviet Union arrests twelve more clergymen in Leningrad for espionage, debauchery, and treason.			Japan lands soldiers on Amoy in Fukien province after a long day of fighting. Twelve battleships and 20 planes assist in capturing the island.

A	B	C	D	E
Includes developments that affect more than one world region, international organizations, and important meetings of world leaders.	*Includes all domestic and regional developments in Europe, including the Soviet Union.*	*Includes all domestic and regional developments in Africa and the Middle East.*	*Includes all domestic and regional developments in Latin America, the Caribbean, and Canada.*	*Includes all domestic and regional developments in Asian and Pacific nations (and colonies).*

U.S. Politics & Social Issues	U.S. Foreign Policy & Defense	Economics & Great Depression	Science, Technology & Nature	Culture, Leisure & Lifestyle	
		Republic Steel gets a court order restraining the National Labor Relations Board from taking action against them. . . . An unauthorized strike against General Motors puts 1,200 auto workers in Bay City, Mich., out of work.			May 3
	With Presidential approval, Senator Nye of North Dakota introduces a bill to lift arms embargoes against Spain. This would allow the United States to be neutral or not according to international law—not neutrality legislation.	Inland Steel again appeals the April 5 NLRB ruling against it. In light of the April 25 Supreme Court decision, Inland claims that it was not treated fairly.		German pacifist Carl von Ossietsky dies of tuberculosis at age 48. Chancellor Adolf Hitler considered him an enemy of the state, and kept him in a concentration camp for years before Ossietsky won the 1935 Nobel Peace Prize.	May 4
Six officials of a Nazi youth summer camp in Yaphank, N.Y., are arrested. An investigation by a veterans' group found violations of law. Such camps and German organizations are common in the United States.		The U.S. Chamber of Commerce demands a repeal of the Wagner Act (which drives the NLRB) and asks investigation of all New Deal recovery legislation of the past eight years.			May 5
	The Munitions Control Board reports that China bought $2.5 million worth of military hardware, including airplane parts. Much of this is paid for by Secretary Morgenthau's purchase, from China, of 50 million ounces of silver through March and April.	The NLRB will investigate a three-month long strike and work stoppage of fur workers in New York. The union claims 3,000 employees are locked out by 260 manufacturers and sue for back pay. Companies claim they were forced to close after a month of strikes by 15,000 employees.	Zeppelin designer Dr. Hugo Eckener arrives from Germany to plead for helium. Secretary of the Interior Ickes worries that airships might be used for military purposes.		May 6
		Director Hopkins of the Works Progress Administration (WPA) tells the House that approximately 20 million people, or 6 million families, are receiving public assistance. The nation's Acting Budget Director predicts a $3.7 billion deficit for fiscal 1939.		Octavian Goga, for 53 days Romania's anti-Semitic prime minister, dies following a stroke at his Transylvanian estate. Goga was also a poet and playwright. . . . The College of William and Mary confers an honorary Doctorate of Fine Arts on Georgia O'Keefe.	May 7
	Secretary of State Cordell Hull speaks on the first radio broadcast to South America. CBS carries the program, the first in a series, from the Pan-American Union in New York City.			S.E. Morison and his *Tercentennial History of Harvard* wins the Loubat Prize, awarded every five years, for the best work in North American history. . . . Marian Anderson gives her final recital of the season at New York's Carnegie Hall.	May 8
	The United States formally and emphatically protests the application to Americans of Germany's policy, which requires all Jews to register their property in Germany.	A group representing 200 fur companies demands government action against what it calls a reign of terror by a union it claims is led by Communists.			May 9
	A U.S. cruiser is dispatched from Manila, Philippines, to safeguard American interests in southern coastal China. The gunboat *Asheville* is already in the area. . . . The President begins talks with his advisors about the sale of helium to Germany.	After four weeks, a strike of warehouse workers in Philadelphia department stores ends with an undisclosed agreement. Drivers and clerks had refused to cross picket lines. . . . The executive board of the United Auto Workers (UAW) says it will punish wildcat strikers with suspension or firing.			May 10

F	G	H	I	J
Includes elections, federal-state relations, civil rights and liberties, crime, the judiciary, education, healthcare, poverty, urban affairs, and population.	Includes formation and debate of U.S. foreign and defense policies, veterans affairs, and defense spending. (Relations with specific foreign countries are usually found under the region concerned.)	Includes business, labor, agriculture, taxation, transportation, consumer affairs, monetary and fiscal policy, natural resources, pollution, and accidents.	Includes worldwide scientific, medical, and technological developments, natural phenomena, U.S. weather, and natural disasters.	Includes the arts, religion, scholarship, communications media, sports, entertainment, fashions, fads, and social life.

	World Affairs	Europe	Africa & The Middle East	The Americas	Asia & The Pacific
May 11	Spain's Foreign Minister del Vayo asks the League of Nations to cease non-intervention policies, because they allow the insurgents to get supplies, but not the elected government.... Based on President Roosevelt's suggestion, an international conference on refugees will be held in July in Evian, France.	A three-day meeting of the Oslo powers—the Scandinavian countries, with Luxemburg, the Netherlands, and Belgium—ends with the decision not to extend the 1937 trade agreement... Four and a half million Ukrainians in Poland demand autonomy, claiming the "normalization" program of three years ago has failed.		In Brazil, Integralistas (fascists) attack the residence of President Getulio Vargas. Lt. Julio Nascimento, part of the conspiracy, lets them in. He had earlier ordered guards to their barracks and locked up ammunition. Vargas's family take up arms and defend themselves until the army arrives and overpowers the Integralistas. Twelve die and more are injured. Martial law is declared.	Japan delivers a prolonged air raid to Suchow; China claims 300 civilian deaths. The American Presbyterian Mission is hit but no deaths are reported there.
May 12	Before the League of Nations, Haile Selassie and Lord Halifax of Britain debate the recognition of Italy as conqueror of Ethiopia. In the end, the League makes no decision but leaves recognition to individual nations.... The German government recognizes Manchukuo and sets up consular relations.	Robert Eikhe, Soviet Commissar of Agriculture, becomes the fourth commissar to be removed from his post in six weeks.... France begins a major ship building program.... The devaluation of the French franc causes fiscal problems in Belgium, where two ministers resign.	In Iraq, the Prophet Muhammad's birthday is celebrated by a general strike and a week of protests over the proposed division of Palestine.	One hundred Integralistas are arrested in Brazil, including five employees of a German bank. German arms, found on many of the Integralistas, arouse suspicions that Nazis were involved.... Colombian students demonstrate in several locations. Demonstrators stone police and wreck buildings in Bogotá, where 120 are arrested.	In Tokyo, the fighting along the Lung-hai railroad is presented as China's last, great struggle in a losing war.... Evacuation of Suchow begins, with Chinese troops moving out to the west.... Japan reports gains in southern Shantung, in the city of Yungcheng.
May 13	Nine abstentions mark a roll-call vote at the League of Nations, with Britain and three allies winning dismissal of Spain's plea to end nonintervention.... Mexico breaks off diplomatic relations with Britain and recalls its ambassador.	Romania's government falls, and Regent Horthy asks Bela Imrédy to be Premier. Imrédy is expected to impose restrictions on Nazi activities.... The Belgian Cabinet resigns, and Socialist Paul Spaak is asked to form a new government.... The news emerges that Spanish insurgent Gen. Yagüe has been removed from command and imprisoned. He had made a speech in Burgos mildly critical of Gen. Franco.		Fights between liberals and conservatives kill four and injure others as buildings are burned the state of North Santander, Colombia.	The Japanese continue to capture towns in Shantung, while the Chinese take back cities in Shansi. Battles in Anwhei, Honan, and Kiangsu provinces continue to be fought with neither side gaining. Japanese planes bomb Chengchow, killing hundreds. An American Southern Baptist Mission suffers a direct hit.
May 14	The League of Nations acknowledges Swiss neutrality, which excludes Switzerland from economic sanctions imposed on other nations.... Chile announces it will withdraw from the League.... As the League ends its session, it urges its members to seriously consider requests for aid from China.	Germany's tennis star Baron von Cramm is sentenced to a year in prison for homosexuality. Von Cramm confessed to a relationship with a Jewish man several years ago, before such conduct was declared illegal.... England's worst drought since 1785 ends in a downpour.	In Palestine, British troops are ambushed while they confiscate weapons in the Acre district. Planes with machine guns are called in to defend the troops; 23 Arabs and one Briton die.	More than 800 arrests in Brazil are connected to the failed Integralista coup.... Colombia bans all public gatherings and imposes censorship on radio and newspapers to stop the violence.	Japan begins secret and massive troop movements, from Manchukuo into north China. Over 75 trains are counted in 18 hours.
May 15		Fighting in Spain centers on the Teruel-Albocacer Road, where loyalists hold back insurgent troops pushing east to the sea.... In Budapest, fascists throw bombs at a parade of Hungarian veterans, but none explode.	A plot to overthrow the Lebanese government of Syria is discovered, and 20 conspirators arrested.	Mexico announces it will ship only oil from nonexpropriated fields. The U.S. Consuls say they cannot confirm where oil comes from and cannot cooperate with this plan.... The state of San Luis Potosí, Mexico, controlled by Gen. Saturnino Cedillo and his private army, protests President Cárdenas' oil policies.	While both sides argue over who holds Tangshan, clearly the road east of that city—which leads to Suchow—is full of Japanese troops and tanks. Japanese columns also advance on Suchow from the west. To the north of Suchow, Chinese troops hold Suhsien and Hanchwang, though both cities are under attack.
May 16		The Vatican exchanges envoys with Gen. Franco's government, officially granting it recognition as the legitimate government.... Only hours after France opens a subscription drive for a five billion franc loan for defense, the issue is oversubscribed. France orders 100 planes from the United States.	Alarmed over the level of anti-Jewish propaganda in Egypt, the government warns its Palestinian refugees and students that they will be deported if they participate in political activities.... Under heavy guard, the British Commission commences to hear testimony on the division of Palestine.		Japan sends two tank battalions to the west of Suchow, to cut off the Chinese armies' only escape route. China now has 600,000 soldiers in Kiangsu to defend the city; Japan brings eight divisions, 240,000, soldiers to the fight.
May 17	The German Ambassador to Brazil calls on the Foreign Minister in Rio de Janeiro. Nine Germans were arrested, and six are still held in connection with the failed coup of May 11.	The Reich declares a canal between the Danube and Rhine rivers, running along the Main, will be finished by 1945.... The Czech press accuses the Social Democrat Party of forcing candidates of other parties out of elections by threatening them with unemployment.		The Dominican Republic elects President Trujillo's hand-picked successor, Dr. Jacinto Penardo, as president.	Moving faster than anyone expected, Japanese troops begin their attack on Suchow. Civilians flee as artillery is fired from Mount Pawang.... Income taxes in Japan have increased by 10 percent recently, to help pay war expenses.
May 18		Talks between France and Italy falter over Soviet pressure to keep supplying arms to Spain through France, which Italy opposes. Another problem is Italy's desire for an Italian protectorate in Tunisia, now under French rule.		Mexico's President Cárdenas leads troops to formally charge Gen. Cedillo with rebellion. The general is allowed to remain at his estate in San Luis Potosí. Cárdenas stays in the area to see that the general's private army of 15,000 soldiers is disarmed or absorbed into the Federal Army.	China denies that Suchow is being shelled, and claims to be holding Japan's troops at bay along the Lung-hai railroad, driving some divisions back several miles, to Tanshan and other sites.
May 19		German troops mass near the border with Czechoslovakia. Germany insists the troop movements are simply routine.... Spanish insurgents bomb the coastal capital of Castellon; one bomb hits a hospital and children are killed.		Most of Gen. Cedillo's men slip quietly into the hills, with their arms.	Japan claims to hold all of Suchow, excluding the southern area. Two munitions depots burn in the city.

A	B	C	D	E
Includes developments that affect more than one world region, international organizations, and important meetings of world leaders.	*Includes all domestic and regional developments in Europe, including the Soviet Union.*	*Includes all domestic and regional developments in Africa and the Middle East.*	*Includes all domestic and regional developments in Latin America, the Caribbean, and Canada.*	*Includes all domestic and regional developments in Asian and Pacific nations (and colonies).*

U.S. Politics & Social Issues	U.S. Foreign Policy & Defense	Economics & Great Depression	Science, Technology & Nature	Culture, Leisure & Lifestyle	
	The sale of helium to Germany is halted; only an act of Congress changing existing law could enable a sale.	The 1938 Revenue Bill, designed to raise $5.3 billion in taxes, goes to the President for signature. . . . When the Bigelow-Sanford Carpet Company cuts wages by 10 percent, 6,000 workers in two states go on strike. . . . A crowd of 10,000 demonstrates against fur companies in New York. That strike is in its 14th week.			May 11
		After much debate, the House passes the $3 billion Relief Recovery Bill. . . . Secretary of Agriculture Wallace writes to Chief Justice Hughes, accusing the court of shifting positions on the NLRB from 1936 to 1938. . . . Four lawsuits are filed against Republic Steel over deaths and injuries in the 1937 Memorial Day riots.	LSD—d-Lysergic Acid Diethylamide—is synthesized for the first time in Sandoz Laboratories, Basel, Switzerland. Its psychedelic effects will not be discovered for five years.		May 12
	All attempts to modify neutrality laws are postponed until the next Congressional session.	The Supreme Court is asked to intervene in conflicting decisions regarding the NLRB and Republic Steel.		Charles Guillaume, French physicist and Nobel Prize recipient for his work in nickel alloys, dies.	May 13
	The President signs a bill making Armistice Day, November 11, a national holiday. . . . Recent war games highlight weaknesses in the Army Air Corps, according to generals.				May 14
			French pilot Elizabeth Lion breaks the nonstop record for women, set by Amelia Earhart in 1932, by flying 2,666 miles. . . . In Tokyo, pilots Fujita and Takahashi break another 1932 record for speed and time flown over a closed course. They fly 10,000 kilometers in 62 hours, 23 minutes.		May 15
		In London, Ky., the trial begins of 69 defendants from 22 coal mining companies accused of murder, arson, and violations of the Wagner Act. . . . The Supreme Court upholds the NLRB's actions in the Mackay Radio case: that Mackay must rehire workers engaged in a legal strike. The Court also rules that Mackay had the right to hire replacement workers.		Joseph Baermann Strauss, designer of the Golden Gate Bridge and 500 others, dies in Los Angeles, Calif., at age 68.	May 16
	The President signs the Vinson Naval Expansion Act, allocating $1.2 billion for the U.S. Navy.		The radio quiz show *Information Please!* debuts on NBC's Blue Network and airs until 1952.		May 17
After contentious elections and allegations, the Department of Justice begins an investigation into the tactics of Mayor Frank "Boss" Hague of Jersey City, N.J.		Chairman Madden of the NLRB defends his agency on CBS Radio.			May 18
	Dr. Ignatz Griebl, once leader of the American Nazi party, escapes to Germany. He is wanted by Federal agents who have questioned him in connection with a spy ring uncovered February 26.	The Railway Labor Executives Association says rail employees will strike if companies cut wages by 15 percent as threatened.	Andre Dupeyron sets a new distance record for women, flying 2,703 miles. . . . Students at New York University watch the world's first televised lecture.	Walt Disney purchases the film rights to *Alice in Wonderland*, by Lewis Carroll—including the rights to illustrations by Tenniel.	May 19

F	G	H	I	J
Includes elections, federal-state relations, civil rights and liberties, crime, the judiciary, education, healthcare, poverty, urban affairs, and population.	Includes formation and debate of U.S. foreign and defense policies, veterans affairs, and defense spending. (Relations with specific foreign countries are usually found under the region concerned.)	Includes business, labor, agriculture, taxation, transportation, consumer affairs, monetary and fiscal policy, natural resources, pollution, and accidents.	Includes worldwide scientific, medical, and technological developments, natural phenomena, U.S. weather, and natural disasters.	Includes the arts, religion, scholarship, communications media, sports, entertainment, fashions, fads, and social life.

	World Affairs	Europe	Africa & The Middle East	The Americas	Asia & The Pacific
May 20	The Joint America-Philippine Committee Report, reducing U.S. tariffs between 1946, when independence will be granted, until 1960, is signed.	Hungary passes a bill limiting Jews to 20 percent of any trade or profession. . . . Konrad Henlein, leader of the Sudeten Germans, again leaves Czechoslovakia.	Britain will redistribute its troops and "replant the Union Jack" in an attempt to restore order in Palestine.	Skirmishes with bands of Gen. Cedillo's "army" results in several deaths and arrests in Mexico. The bands seem to be operating independently.	Japan's news agency announces a triumphal entry into Suchow. While casualties are high, most Chinese troops escape. . . . Six Chinese planes drop leaflets on the Japanese island of Kyushu in a "goodwill raid."
May 21	Contracts are signed between China and Germany; Germany provides military advisers and pilot training.	Czechoslovakia mobilizes 400,000 troops along its borders. This event triggers a German decision to expand the Luftwaffe. Soon, 500,000 workers are building airplanes round the clock. . . . France reassures its Czech envoy of its support in case of unprovoked attack, while Britain uses all diplomatic channels to urge the Czech government toward appeasing Germany. . . . Turkey passes an emergency defense bill to reinforce its coastline and harbors, and enlarge its navy and air force.		An unidentified plane drops four bombs on an airfield in San Luis Potosí. The "uprising" of Gen. Cedillo, while colorful, is not a serious threat. . . . A Nazi Congressman fires a gun during Chilean President Allesandri's speech to the Congress, and a bomb explodes outside the building. No one is seriously injured in the melee, and the President, who will step down in December, finishes his speech.	China admits that Suchow was evacuated on May 19, and that Japanese troops hold the city. Chinese forces are now concentrated in south Shantung, Anwhei, and Honan provinces.
May 22	Italy begins war games in Libya, simulating an attack on French Tunisia. . . . The League of Nations hosts an International Dialogue of Students in Luxemburg.	Much of Europe spends this Sunday waiting for war, but Germany begins to withdraw its troops from the border as local elections proceed in Czechoslovakia. France joins Britain in urging appeasement. . . . The Spanish government uncovers evidence that officers have conducted between 20 and 30 executions of rebel sympathizers, without trial. . . . King Boris III of Bulgaria opens Parliament for the first time in four years.		Amid rumors of attempted attacks on the presidential palace, more troops in Mexico are mobilized to confront the army of Gen. Cedillo.	
May 23		Konrad Henlein returns from Germany to confer with Premier Hodza of Czechoslovakia. . . . Britain assures France it will act to defend France—but will not risk war over Czechoslovakia. . . . In the Netherlands, Soviet secret police plant a bomb to kill a Ukrainian nationalist.		The government of Mexico issues a statement confirming the solidarity of all governors, and portraying Gen. Cedillo as the victim of hostile manipulators. . . . A general strike in Jamaica leads to violence as shots are fired and police attack crowds at several locations.	Japan claims to have trapped a quarter million Chinese soldiers in the area south of the Lung-hai railroad between Tangshan and Suchow, extending south into Anwhei province.
May 24		Insurgent planes drop bombs on Valencia, Barcelona, and Portbou, near the Spanish-French border. . . . France votes to spend 11 billion francs on public works over three years.	Several violent incidents in Palestine occur: Jewish bands shoot at Arabs, stones are thrown at Jewish workers, two bombs explode, and a bus is fired upon. Twenty-seven people are injured, and three die: an Arab, a Jew, and a Russian nun.	A mother and two sons, standing on the sidelines, are killed in Jamaica when police open fire on a crowd. About 400 police try to maintain order, supplemented by local militia.	China admits retreating from Taierhchwang and much of southern Shantung.
May 25	The Soviet Ambassador to the United States says his country will defend Czechoslovakia and France against aggression.	Germany presents a list of border violations by the Czech military, along with an official protest.	More violence, promulgated by both Jews and Arabs, takes lives in Palestine. Vandals cut an oil pipeline as well.	Government troops kill 30 as the insurgency of Gen. Cedillo spreads to the state of Guanajuato. . . . More people are wounded as strikes continue in Jamaica. Besides better wages, the strikers demand the release of Alexander Bustamante, a labor leader jailed for sedition.	Journalists are flown over areas in Shantung where fighting has stopped, seeing hundreds of burned and abandoned villages. In addition, areas west of the Tientsin-Pukow railroad remain under water as dikes were cut last year by Chinese troops.
May 26	At the 34th annual Eucharistic Congress of the Catholic Church in Budapest, Hungary, 2 million Catholics watch a six-mile procession of the Eucharist down the Danube River.	The Non-Intervention Committee meets, and Britain, France, Italy, and Germany agree to a withdrawal plan for volunteers fighting in Spain. Only the Soviet envoy dissents. . . . Responding to Germany's charges, Czechoslovakia claims that 34 German planes have flown over Czech air space. . . . Marshal Pétain, hero of the Great War, warns France against idealism, pointing out the reality of a strong Germany that has torn up its peace treaties.	British police kill six of seven Arabs who were making bombs near Herzila, Palestine, and a constable dies as well.	Troops loyal to Gen. Cedillo in Guanajuato cut rail tracks and derail the Sunshine Express, which runs between Mexico City to Laredo, Texas. . . . Mexico's Ambassador to the United States presents a plan to pay $150 million for oil property expropriated from U.S. owners. . . . Ecuador claims that its border outpost was attacked by Peruvian troops and gunboats. Peru says Ecuadorian troops invaded plantations on Peru's side of the Napo River, then retreated.	Prince Konoe reforms the Japanese Cabinet, putting six ministries into the hands of military men.
May 27	The League of Nations hosts the 11th Session of the International Studies Conference in Prague.	In Romania, Corneliu Codreanu, leader of the Iron Guard, is sentenced to prison and hard labor for ten years. . . . Irish Prime Minister de Valera dissolves Parliament and calls for elections in June. . . . French Prime Minister Daladier announces that anti-aircraft guns and other defenses will be installed along France's border with Spain.	Arab bands kill Arab village leaders in southern Palestine.	Longshoremen in Puerto Rico get a large pay raise, the result of negotiations since their six-week strike earlier this year.	

A	B	C	D	E
Includes developments that affect more than one world region, international organizations, and important meetings of world leaders.	*Includes all domestic and regional developments in Europe, including the Soviet Union.*	*Includes all domestic and regional developments in Africa and the Middle East.*	*Includes all domestic and regional developments in Latin America, the Caribbean, and Canada.*	*Includes all domestic and regional developments in Asian and Pacific nations (and colonies).*

U.S. Politics & Social Issues	U.S. Foreign Policy & Defense	Economics & Great Depression	Science, Technology & Nature	Culture, Leisure & Lifestyle	
		The U.S. Solicitor General asks the Supreme Court to reconsider the Stockyards decision of April 25, as it conflicts with a 1936 decision.			May 20
		John L. Lewis of the CIO pledges $50,000 to aid the 15,000 fur workers out of jobs.			May 21
Wisconsin's Farm-Labor-Progressive coalition snubs the LaFollettes and their new National Progressives of America Party at a nominating convention.				The Dodgers announce that night lighting will be installed at Ebbets Field in Brooklyn.	May 22
Two Supreme Court decisions expand the Federal government's ability to tax state salaries and activities.		Police in Duluth, Minn., use tear gas to break up a picket line at newspaper offices, and the governor readies the National Guard. The strike is starting its eighth week. Union officials say the crowd of 500 was peaceful when attacked by police.	The Douglas DC-4, designed to carry 42 passengers for United Airlines, is tested in Santa Monica, Calif.	Kurt Schuschnigg's autobiography, *My Austria* (smuggled out of the country), is published.	May 23
Interior Secretary Harold Ickes takes a quick trip to Ireland to marry the 25-year-old daughter of the U.S. Minister there.	France's Ambassador to the United States asks for American support to prevent a German-Czech war.	The President expresses dissatisfaction with a $212 million provision in the Recovery Bill, for parity payments on certain products. . . . In a trial of mining companies, one—Black Mountain Coal—turns on the other defendants, testifying that the companies did indeed unite to fight unions.		Buddy, the first seeing-eye dog in service, dies at the Morristown, N.J., training facility. Her owner was with her.	May 24
		The Duluth, Minn., newspaper strike ends with a 40-hour, 5-day workweek and a compromise agreement allowing some departments to stay out of the guild.			May 25
The House Committee on Un-American Activities (also called the Dies Committee) begins, investigating activities of the Ku Klux Klan and German-American Nazism. . . . The Joint Congressional Committee investigating the Tennessee Valley Authority (TVA) hears charges of sabotage and lying from the current directors. The previous Chair spoke yesterday.		Workers at American Brass in Detroit, on strike since April 19, riot when a policeman "accidentally" discharges tear gas. Fifty-five are injured; some are beaten by police for not moving when ordered. The police were escorting groups of nonstriking workers through a crowd when the problems began. . . . The 15-week-old strike of fur workers in New York ends with a three-year contract guaranteeing eight months of continuous employment per year, at better wages.			May 26
In a radio speech, the President says the new tax bill will become law without his signature, citing loopholes and changes he wants fixed next year. . . . The U.S. Communist Party announces an 87 percent gain in membership over two years. It now has 75,000 members.	A Nazi officer and three other men are arrested for spying and taken from the German ship *Bremen*. The investigation dates back to February and may involve many others.	Police use tear gas and clubs to clear 4,000 CIO-union rubber workers from the gates of Goodyear Tire in Akron, Ohio. A strike was called in the early morning after negotiations failed. . . . Ford, General Motors, and Chrysler are indicted by a federal grand jury for conspiracy to commit anti-trust violations.			May 27

F	G	H	I	J
Includes elections, federal-state relations, civil rights and liberties, crime, the judiciary, education, healthcare, poverty, urban affairs, and population.	Includes formation and debate of U.S. foreign and defense policies, veterans affairs, and defense spending. (Relations with specific foreign countries are usually found under the region concerned.)	Includes business, labor, agriculture, taxation, transportation, consumer affairs, monetary and fiscal policy, natural resources, pollution, and accidents.	Includes worldwide scientific, medical, and technological developments, natural phenomena, U.S. weather, and natural disasters.	Includes the arts, religion, scholarship, communications media, sports, entertainment, fashions, fads, and social life.

	World Affairs	Europe	Africa & The Middle East	The Americas	Asia & The Pacific
May 28	Oil from expropriated facilities in the Mexican state of Tampico is secretly loaded on an Italian tanker, bound for Italy and Germany.	Representatives of Sudeten Germans meet with the Czech Premier. In municipal elections, Nazis gain offices in German areas. . . . Former Austrian Chancellor Schuschnigg is taken from his home under guard, to the headquarters of the secret police in Vienna.		Federal troops chase Gen. Cedillo into the hills; he is believed to be on foot.	Japanese troops capture Kweiteh in the early morning, At Lanfeng, 7,000 troops with Gen. Doihara are forced out of the city. Chinese forces recapture Menghsien on the Yellow River.
May 29		Gen. Juan Yagüe returns to the front in Spain, denying that he was ever arrested. The insurgent government blames loyalist planes for recent attacks on French towns.			Japanese troops speed from the north and west to Lanfeng. Chinese forces at that city are being resupplied through Kaifeng. Both these cities stand between Japan's armies and Hankow, the temporary capital.
May 30	The League of Nations' International Institute of Intellectual Cooperation hosts a Conference of New Theories in Modern Physics, in Warsaw. Scientists such as Neils Bohr and Arthur Eddington discuss applications of quantum theory. Germany does not permit Dr. Werner Heisenberg to attend.	The Czech government orders its population to participate in defense work. Children over age six must take military or first aid training; adults age 30 to 60 will provide first aid or civil defense service. . . . Chancellor Hitler signs a secret order calling for war in Czechoslovakia by October.		Although Gen. Cedillo is still loose, most of his followers have either surrendered or been captured, and President Cárdenas pronounces the rebellion over.	Two unidentified planes over Kyushu in Japan cause panic and blackouts.
May 31		German planes, flying for the Spanish rebels, bomb the city of Grenollers, 16 miles from Barcelona. An estimated 200 people die, mostly women. . . . Police raid Berlin cafés, looking for criminals. They arrest 350 people—all but 20 of them Jewish. . . . In Austria, the property of composer Erich Korngold is seized. Mr. Korngold is abroad.		Six people are killed in the Mexican state of Tabasco, as they parade for the right to build a church. Churches in the area had been razed under a previous administration. . . . Strikes break out in different cities in Jamaica, and looting becomes common.	Cholera epidemics force Shanghai officials to restrict passage into the city to foreigners with inoculation certificates. . . . The government in Hankow begins to remove records and certain offices to other cities.
Jun. 1	Chinese envoys in the United States, Europe, and the League of Nations ask aid in halting the bombing of civilian centers by Japan, for humanitarian reasons.	Austria's former premier Schuschnigg marries his fiancée by proxy, with his brother saying the vows for him. . . . In a speech in Parliament, Hungary's Foreign Minister praises most neighbors but criticizes the Czech government for treating its Hungarian minority poorly.		Peru claims that Ecuadorian troops attacked Peruvian plantations on the Napo River for the second time. In the ensuing fight, one soldier is killed. Ecuador says Peru is the invader.	
Jun. 2	The 24th International Labor Conference opens in Geneva, Switzerland. . . . Chile officially withdraws from the League of Nations.	The Soviets assent to plans by the Non-Intervention Committee for removing volunteer troops from Spain and halting arms shipments. . . . Nazi leader Szalasi is sent to prison in Hungary. New Premier Imrédy says he's against "Aryan propaganda." . . . The Nazis announces the end of mass arrests in Austria, sending a last group of 200 beggars and street musicians to work on a canal in Bremen.	Turkish troops mass on the border of the Sanjak of Alexandretta. Turkish Minister Davaz presents France with a list of complaints about the Sanjak's treatment of Turks as an election approaches.	Ecuador's former president and dictator Federico Paez escapes into Colombia rather than face charges about missing money.	Chinese troops fight to retake Hofei in Anwhei province. After four days of bombing, Canton erects bamboo barricades around buildings, and large hideouts in the hills.
Jun. 3		Chancellor Adolf Hitler decrees that all degenerate art must be taken from galleries and museums in Germany without compensation. He will decide what is to be done with it. . . . France sends a convoy of food over the Pyrenees to the "lost" division of loyalist troops, who hold 10 mountain passes near the border.	Two young men, members of the Jewish Revisionist group, are condemned to death in Palestine for shooting at a bus. One sentence is later commuted because the man is 19 years old. . . . French authorities declare martial law in Alexandretta, deploying foreign legionnaires and Moroccan troops to keep order.	Ecuador's Cabinet, composed of military men, resigns to fight Peru. . . . Catholics in Tabasco receive a letter from Mexcio's Interior Department, dated May 12, barring persecutions of Catholics in that state. . . . Six months of drought in the Bahamas ends with torrential rainstorms. . . . Rioting spreads in Jamaica, where four people die and 50 are injured in clashes with police.	General Doihara's division north of Lanfeng receives reinforcements from across the Yellow River. More troops are moving west to help Doihara, who is encircled by Chinese divisions.
Jun. 4	John Winant, first head of the Social Security Administration, is named next Director of the International Labor Office.	Dr. Sigmund Freud, age 82, is allowed to leave Austria for France with his daughter Anna. They will then settle in England. . . . Both sides in eastern Spain remain stalled in most places. Insurgent Spain announces to any who would mediate that "unconditional surrender of the enemy" is the only way to end the war.			Reinforced Japanese troops attack Lanfeng. Japan's divisions throughout Anwhei and Honan provinces are supplemented with fresh troops. . . . Japanese gunboats on the Yangtze River bombard Tatung and Kweichih. . . . Canton suffers through a two-hour bombardment that kills at least 600 people.
Jun. 5		Nine planes stray 15 miles from the Spanish border into French territory and drop bombs. . . . Seventy thousand march in Bratislava, demanding Slovak autonomy from the Czech government. In Prague, 120,000 march in support of the government.			Canton is bombed again and 300 people die. The Wongsha and Taishatou stations are hardest hit. Thousands flee the city. . . . Japanese warships move west along the Yangtze, supporting ground forces in Anwhei province. . . . China evacuates Kaifeng as Japanese forces move closer.
	A Includes developments that affect more than one world region, international organizations, and important meetings of world leaders.	**B** Includes all domestic and regional developments in Europe, including the Soviet Union.	**C** Includes all domestic and regional developments in Africa and the Middle East.	**D** Includes all domestic and regional developments in Latin America, the Caribbean, and Canada.	**E** Includes all domestic and regional developments in Asian and Pacific nations (and colonies).

U.S. Politics & Social Issues	U.S. Foreign Policy & Defense	Economics & Great Depression	Science, Technology & Nature	Culture, Leisure & Lifestyle	
	An arrest warrant is issued for Dr. Griebl, now in Germany, and for others who testified before a grand jury about espionage and then fled the country.	CIO unions in Detroit threaten a one-day general strike in retaliation for police attacks on May 26. . . . Negotiations begin in Akron, Ohio, to settle the strike against Goodyear Tire, while 2,000 union members march to City Hall. . . . Baton Rouge police in Louisiana arrest 36 strikers who storm the Consolidated Chemical plant.			May 28
Anti-Nazi German-American groups demonstrate before California Hall in San Francisco, as German-American Nazis hold their convention.		Akron Mayor Schroy accuses the CIO of rebellion, and will mobilize all city police when the Goodyear plant opens tomorrow. Union heads call the mayor "morally bankrupt" and claim he foments class hatred.			May 29
		Five hours of negotiations in Akron result in an agreement acceptable to company and union. The Goodyear plant will reopen tomorrow, the strike will end, and negotiations on some issues will continue.		Yankee Stadium in New York hosts baseball's biggest crowd: 83,533 people. 6,000 additional fans are turned away at the gate.	May 30
The Democratic leadership in Congress announces that no Reorganization Bill will be submitted this session.		The Supreme Court upholds the NLRB's right to reopen its case against Republic Steel. The Court refuses a request received May 20 to reconsider the Stockyards case, calling the charge that the Court had reversed itself "unwarranted."		Lou Gehrig plays his 2,000th consecutive game.	May 31
A Massachusetts commission reports that Communists control the CIO National Maritime Union on the east coast.	The United States asks Japan to remove obstacles keeping Americans away from their property in the Shanghai area. Japan takes immediate action in China and Tokyo. . . . The U.S. Treasury announces that under four separate agreements, it has been buying silver from China. Between 1936 and next July, 250 million ounces will have been purchased. What is not announced is that China purchases munitions with the proceeds.	The President writes the Senate, asking it to make pending Recovery legislation as flexible as possible, to do the most good. . . . Six thousand members of a Remington Rand employee association walk off their jobs for one hour to protest the Supreme Court's refusal to overturn a 1936 case with the National Labor Relations Board.		*Action Comics* debut with Superman, a character created by Jerry Siegel and Joe Shuster.	Jun. 1
		The Securities and Exchange Commission opens hearings into abuse and looting by financiers of investment trusts. . . . The National Maritime Union stages a one-day strike over tactics of a rival union affiliated with the AFL.		Opera star Lily Pons and conductor André Kostelanetz marry.	Jun. 2
	The United States condemns the bombing of civilians in Spain and China.	The Senate passes a $3.7 billion Relief and Recovery Bill. Assured of future funding, the Works Progress Administration uses its current cash to create 300,000 jobs per week this month.	The Mayon volcano in the Philippines begins to erupt for the first time in 11 years.		Jun. 3
			Douglas Aircraft's DC-4, being built for United Airways, takes its first test flight.	John Flanagan, Olympic gold medalist in the 1900, 1904, and 1908 Olympics for the hammer throw, dies in Ireland. He had competed for the United States.	Jun. 4
					Jun. 5

F	G	H	I	J
Includes elections, federal-state relations, civil rights and liberties, crime, the judiciary, education, healthcare, poverty, urban affairs, and population.	Includes formation and debate of U.S. foreign and defense policies, veterans affairs, and defense spending. (Relations with specific foreign countries are usually found under the region concerned.)	Includes business, labor, agriculture, taxation, transportation, consumer affairs, monetary and fiscal policy, natural resources, pollution, and accidents.	Includes worldwide scientific, medical, and technological developments, natural phenomena, U.S. weather, and natural disasters.	Includes the arts, religion, scholarship, communications media, sports, entertainment, fashions, fads, and social life.

	World Affairs	Europe	Africa & The Middle East	The Americas	Asia & The Pacific
Jun. 6	Theodore Roosevelt, Jr., heading a relief organization, warns that 60 million people are refugees in China, and epidemics such as cholera and typhoid are bound to occur.	Anti-aircraft guns drive off more planes that invade French air space from Spain. . . . Bratislava is again the site of a huge demonstration, this one celebrating Czechoslovakia's 20th year as a nation. . . . At least 84 people die in air raids over coastal cities in Spain.	Voting registration starts again in Alexandretta, Turkey. It was halted last week after 100 people died in political fights and rioting. . . . A land mine kills a British soldier in Palestine.	Jamaican police fire on a crowd and wound two people. Six others are hurt in different clashes.	On the direct orders of Gen. Chiang Kai-shek, Chinese defenders dynamite levees on the Yellow River north of Kaifeng to slow the Japanese advance. The resulting flood, one of the worst in history, will kill over half a million people in the next few weeks.
Jun. 7	American citizen Arthur Talent, who came to the Soviet Union as a seven-year-old child in 1924, is executed for spying. Many Soviet citizens, who immigrated with their American parents years ago, are caught up in the purges. . . . The League of Nations reveals that it cashed a dues check from Haile Selassie as ruler of Ethiopia—in spite of refusing to support him on May 12.	German planes shell Valencia and Alicante on the coast. 50 die in Alicante, and three British ships are hit. The British ship *Maryat*, struck by shells on June 4, still burns. . . . The German Sudeten party under Konrad Henlein delivers a declaration to the government of 14 points, calling for division of Czechoslovakia into autonomous states. The declaration is kept secret.		Jamaican police again fire into a crowd, this time in Trelawny, where one striker is killed. . . . Ecuador charges that Peruvian troops hold prisoners and occupy land seized on June 1, and that gunboats and planes are lined up at the border. Peru says Ecuadorian troops invaded its territory.	Japan's Rear Admiral Nomura says bombing in China will continue until China ceases its resistance, and points out that Canton, a port that receives munitions, is a legitimate target. . . . Although the city has been evacuated, intense street fighting is reported as Japanese troops under Gen. Doihara move into Kaifeng.
Jun. 8		Spanish insurgent planes shell the British-owned port of Gandia, which is on Spain's Mediterranean coast. In Figueras, near the border with France, 40 are killed in an air raid. . . . Arrests, mostly of Jews, and deportation to Dachau or public work sites like Styria, continue in Austria, in spite of the June 2 claim that mass arrests were finished.		Two more Jamaicans are wounded as police shoot into a crowd. Employees of the local power company agree to arbitration and return to work; Jamaica has been without electrical power since their strike began.	For the 12th consecutive day, Canton is bombed by Japanese planes. After a night raid, the official estimate of casualties since May 28 is 3,000 dead and 5,000 injured. . . . In Shansi province, 8,000 Japanese have been pushed southeast to Houma by troops led by Gen. Wei Li-huang.
Jun. 9	Britain's Royal Air Force contracts to buy 400 planes from Lockheed Corporation. . . . Mexico reveals that oil from expropriated facilities is being sold and transported to Italy and Germany. Eighteen tankers will leave Mexico this month.	Two more British ships are bombed in Spanish ports, and several men are killed. . . . Sudeten German leaders meet with Czech Premier Hodza again after presenting their demands to the government.		Rains bring an end to six months of drought in Puerto Rico.	Japanese troops are within 30 miles of Chengchow, and await reinforcements. . . . A Japanese advance through Anwhei province, deadlocked for weeks, is now moving forward.
Jun. 10	A settlement is reached for American claims of property damage from 1910 to 1920, the time of Mexico's revolution; $219 million in claims were filed, but only $9 million of those were found to have merit. Of these, Mexico will pay $5.4 million.	A Czech army major boasts on the radio that the border is fortified with machine gun nests. . . . Spanish insurgent bombers sink two British and one French ship, all three damaged in earlier raids in separate ports. . . . Richard Schmitz, former mayor of Vienna, dies at Dachau. He was taken there following an operation for cancer.	A nine-foot-tall barbed wire fence is being erected to protect Palestine from foreign terrorists. Due to be completed in August, sections are already being torn down and carried away by Arab bands.	The Chaco Peace Conference is breaking down after three years. Both countries who warred and agreed to the armistice in 1935, Bolivia and Paraguay, have since overthrown their governments. Both lay claim to the region, neither wants to compromise.	Chinese troops blow up and burn buildings and terminals, as they abandon Chengchow to the Japanese. . . . Chinese fliers claim to sink two Japanese warships on the Yangtze River. . . . Waterworks and electrical plants in Canton's suburbs are bombed, cutting services to parts of the city.
Jun. 11		By the end of this month, all Jews in Germany, and their spouses and children, are required to register possessions with values exceeding $2,000, or 5,000 marks.		A general strike is called in the state of Puebla, Mexico, in sympathy with a textile workers' strike.	Japan's commander in chief warns all foreign ships and embassies to stay away from the Yangtze River between Wuhu in Anwhei and Hukow in Kiangsi province. Japanese troops dynamite bridges between Chengchow and Hankow to block Chinese troops.
Jun. 12	France and Turkey negotiate over the Sanjak of Alexandretta. Turkey wishes to station troops there and France does not object. The Armenians and other minority citizens of the Sanjak, though, fear for their treatment and rights under Turkish authority.	In the last third of a series of municipal elections in Czechoslovakia, German districts vote for the Sudeten German party, but Social Democrats still hold a majority of seats in the country. . . . In Munich, the principle synagogue is demolished to make room for a parking lot. The city's Jewish community was given a 24-hour ultimatum and offered 15 percent of the building's assessed value, which they refused.			Flooding, caused by the destruction of levees along the Yellow River, hampers Japanese troops and keeps them from Chengchow. . . . Rumors of a rift between Chinese Communists and the ruling Kuomintang party emerge in Hankow, Sian, and other key cities.
Jun. 13	Soviet Gen. Lushkoff defects, crossing the border into Manchukuo. He was chief of the secret police in the Far East, but fears he will be killed in a purge. . . . An Arab village in the Sanjak of Alexandretta is burned, reportedly by a band of Turks.	After heavy street fighting, insurgents capture Castellón de la Plana and its port, Grao. . . . Munich announces that its largest Protestant church will be torn down by July 10 due to subway construction.	A bomb is thrown at Syrian Premier Mardam's car by two youths who elude capture.	A four-hour battle in the Mexican state of Puebla results in the death of two brothers, one a general, both aides of Gen. Cedilla.	Villages in north Honan province are submerged in rising floodwaters, which has forced many Japanese troops back east to Kaifeng.
Jun. 14	Gen. Chiang Kai-shek asks Soviet Ambassador Orelski directly for support, but the Soviet Union will not be drawn into the war.	Chancellor Adolf Hitler lays the cornerstone to start a rebuilding project in Berlin. The work is expected to last 25 years and cost 25 billion marks. . . . British Prime Minister Chamberlain says the country can do nothing about the bombing and sinking of British ships in Spanish ports. . . . France announces plans to maintain a standing army of one million by 1940.		Mexico reveals that 76 rebel soldiers were killed in the last 12 days in Guanajuato. Other bands have surrendered to federal authorities.	Missionaries say 30 million Chinese are fleeing west to escape the Japanese invaders.
	A *Includes developments that affect more than one world region, international organizations, and important meetings of world leaders.*	**B** *Includes all domestic and regional developments in Europe, including the Soviet Union.*	**C** *Includes all domestic and regional developments in Africa and the Middle East.*	**D** *Includes all domestic and regional developments in Latin America, the Caribbean, and Canada.*	**E** *Includes all domestic and regional developments in Asian and Pacific nations (and colonies).*

U.S. Politics & Social Issues	U.S. Foreign Policy & Defense	Economics & Great Depression	Science, Technology & Nature	Culture, Leisure & Lifestyle	
				Ogden Nash's *I'm A Stranger Here Myself* is published.	Jun. 6
			The new Boeing Clipper 314 is flown for the first time near Seattle. The "flying boat" is being built for Pan American Airways. . . . The DC-4 continues its test runs as well, flying over Los Angeles, Calif.		Jun. 7
		To comply with NLRB orders, Remington Rand Corporation announces it will furlough 800 employees hired since a 1936 strike. That will make room for the mandated rehiring of strikers.	Anthropologist Robert Broom buys a bone fragment and traces it back to a cave in southern Africa, discovering the new species *Australopithecus robustus*, which lived two million years ago.		Jun. 8
	The United States reveals secret provisions in the 1917 Lansing-Ishii agreements: Japan agreed not to interfere with other nations in China. . . . The U.S. Ambassador to Germany delivers a note demanding payment for Austria's loan, due June 1.	Forty-five bakeries in Seattle, Wash., close as bakers strike for higher wages.			Jun. 9
Alabama's Supreme Court upholds the prison sentence of Charles Weems and Andy Wright (75 and 99 years).	Secretary of State Cordell Hull urges U.S. manufacturers not to sell planes to Japan, saying that the U.S. condemns Japan's attacks on civilians and should not materially encourage them.	To avoid a threatened filibuster by southern Senators, the Senate compromises on the Wage and Hours Bill (technically, the Fair Labor Standards Act). Twenty-five cents per hour will be the minimum wage, rising to 30 cents in a year. No further guarantees of raises are made, disappointing those who sought to bring it to 40 cents. The bill also outlaws child labor.	A tornado kills 14 people, derails a train, and destroys 21 homes in Clyde, Texas.		Jun. 10
			An earthquake is felt in London and Paris, and most strongly in Belgium. . . . England, France and northern Italy suffer the effects of a spring drought—the worst in 150 years— and late frosts, affecting wheat crops, vineyards, and dairy pastureland.		Jun. 11
					Jun. 12
CIO head John L. Lewis visits House Speaker Bankhead and Majority Leader Rayburn to push for passage of the Walsh-Healey Bill—also called the Blacklist Bill. It would bar companies that run afoul of the NLRB from winning government contracts.		Homer Martin suspends five officers from the United Auto Workers for factionalism. The men are suspected of Communist ties.			Jun. 13
The WPA will buy $10 million of surplus clothes from manufacturers, for distribution to the needy. . . . Congress stays in session until midnight to finish work on bills on wages and hours, flood control, relief, and other matters, so that they can adjourn tomorrow. The Blacklist Bill is tabled.		Mayor Frank Hague of Jersey City testifies in a suit brought against him by the CIO and American Civil Liberties Union, for tactics used in suppressing strikes. On the stand, Hague—who is also Vice Chair of the National Democratic Party—says he would like to build a concentration camp in Alaska and put all the nation's Communists there.		*The White Stag* by Kate Seredy wins the John Newbery Medal for children's books. The first Caldecott Medal goes to Dorothy Lathrop's *Animals of the Bible*.	Jun. 14

F	G	H	I	J
Includes elections, federal-state relations, civil rights and liberties, crime, the judiciary, education, healthcare, poverty, urban affairs, and population.	*Includes formation and debate of U.S. foreign and defense policies, veterans affairs, and defense spending. (Relations with specific foreign countries are usually found under the region concerned.)*	*Includes business, labor, agriculture, taxation, transportation, consumer affairs, monetary and fiscal policy, natural resources, pollution, and accidents.*	*Includes worldwide scientific, medical, and technological developments, natural phenomena, U.S. weather, and natural disasters.*	*Includes the arts, religion, scholarship, communications media, sports, entertainment, fashions, fads, and social life.*

	World Affairs	Europe	Africa & The Middle East	The Americas	Asia & The Pacific
Jun. 15	Mexico agrees to ship 10 million barrels of oil to Germany over the next six months. Germany will pay in goods and machinery.	In northeastern Spain, rebel planes and a lack of food in the Bielsa Valley force loyalist soldiers across the French border. Insurgents bomb, then capture, Blazquez in the Cordoba province. French and British ships are also shelled. . . . In Germany, Georg and Anna Schwitzer are beheaded for spying. . . . The Reich calls its mass arrests of Jews "Operation June." Jews are picked up for minor reasons and deported to concentration camps.		In the state of Veracruz, Mexican police find and slay 12 bandits who robbed an army payroll carrier and murdered several guards. Federal police also disarmed the police of Las Casas, Chiapas, over local election violence. . . . An attempt to try Jamaican labor leaders for sedition fails when the charges are dropped for lack of evidence.	More than 12,000 have died in a cholera epidemic in the United Provinces of India. The outbreak started in late April. . . . In Shanghai, 123 people are hospitalized with cholera. Japan is requiring inoculation certificates for those who leave the area for Japan. . . . More breaks in the Yellow River levees inundate crops. The widespread view among Chinese is that anything that will stop the Japanese is worth the sacrifice.
Jun. 16		Theaters and public markets are barred to Germany's 400,000 remaining Jews. No one in the military may rent from a Jew. New rules for businesses owned or funded by Jews are published. . . . All British women between 17 and 65 are asked to join in civilian defense as air raid wardens, drivers, and nurses.		Britain deploys 100 policemen from Bermuda to Jamaica, to restore order. Police reinforcements are also called into British Guiana.	The Yellow River flood spreads over 500 square miles. More rain could break other levees and add to the destruction.
Jun. 17		Claiming that a bank failure in 1931 requires compensation, the Nazi government of Austria demands $10 million for the release of Baron Louis Rothschild. His property in Austria has already been seized. . . . A Czech plane flies over Bavaria; Germany protests the "constant provocation" and threatens action.		Peru and Ecuador agree to release prisoners and withdraw troops from their borders. . . . Banditry increases in Mexico; In Oaxaca 18 people are killed and 32 held for ransom.	
Jun. 18		Jews throughout Germany besiege embassies, looking for protection. Under the new rules, many cannot buy food or clothes—non-Jewish stores will not sell to them. Up to 65 army buses a night carry Jews from Berlin to Buchenwald concentration camp.	Five Arabs, including one woman, are slain in Palestine in two separate incidents.	In the three months since Mexico seized foreign-owned oil fields, salaries for oil workers have been cut 65 percent.	Swatow in Canton province reports that cholera is spreading there.
Jun. 19		The Soviet newspaper *Pravda* names 10 prominent Communists of the Ukraine now under arrest. The new purge in the area is conducted by a rising star in the Soviet, Nikita Krushchev. . . . Pastors of Germany's churches are reluctant to recite a required loyalty oath to Chancellor Adolf Hitler.	Five Arabs and two Jews die in Palestinian violence.	Gen. Alfredo Baldomir is inaugurated as President of Uruguay. The previous president ruled as a dictator; Baldomir promises to restore constitutional democracy.	
Jun. 20	Soviet Gen. Lushkoff, former Chief of Secret Police, arrives in Tokyo to begin his exile and collaboration with Japan.	A Soviet army paper, the *Red Star*, says an ongoing purge over the last four months has rid the military of Bolshevists.			Chinese forces intensify guerilla and sniper activities north of the Yellow River.
Jun. 21		The Non-Intervention Committee meets in London and accepts Britain's plan to first count, then remove, volunteers from Spain. France unofficially closes the border with Spain. . . . Gen. Franco defends his bombing of ships in Spanish harbors, saying that hundreds of British ships deliver contraband to the loyalist government. . . . Germany and Italy acknowledge Switzerland's neutrality.	A bomb is thrown at a movie theatre in Tel Aviv, the first act of terrorism in that city. In other incidents in Palestine, Arabs fired into stores and near police stations, killing one person. British troops fire on a band tearing down the new electrified fence, killing two men.	Slaughterhouse workers in Jamaica join the ongoing strike.	Japanese planes bomb Hainan Island east of the Gulf of Tonkin, for a third consecutive day. An American oil company in Kwangsi is also shelled. . . . Japan issues a map of China and advises foreigners to evacuate marked areas, from Hainan Island north to lands already occupied by Japan, and from the coast to several hundred miles inland.
Jun. 22	The ILO conference closes its session with the decision to work with individual governments toward a 40-hour workweek, and to address the issue again in June 1939.	Two British ships, *Sunion* and *Thorpeness*, are bombed and sunk near Spain; one sailor is killed. Other ships are attacked. Britain protests the action.		Operators of Mexico's silk and rayon factories offer the keys to those factories to the Labor Board. They claim they cannot stay in business unless they're allowed to cut hours drastically. Otherwise, the employees can have the factories.	German newspapers quote China's Foreign Minister Wang Chung-hui as desiring peace and mediation by a third party. Japan rebuffs the comments and reiterates that it will not negotiate with Gen. Chiang or the Kuomintang.
Jun. 23	The Turkey-Afghan friendship accord of 1928 is renewed. . . . The League of Nations Opium Advisory Committee adopts a resolution saying that the area of China under Japanese control has become a world menace. The committee shied from a stronger statement for fear of offending Japan.	Minister Goering issues a decree that conscripts all Germans, male and female, Jew and Aryan, for short-term labor projects. The law, effective July 1, guarantees pay commensurate with people's usual jobs. . . . German police head Himmler announces that all Catholic student and alumni organizations are dissolved, and German Jews are banned from all universities.	In two separate incidents in Jaffa, Palestine, an Arab proprietor and a Jewish customer are shot to death as they conduct business. Many others are injured; some by police who use clubs to break up crowds.		Japan will implement its National Mobilization Act on July 15. The law was passed March 26. . . . The U.S. gunboat *Asheville* anchors near Swatow to protect Americans there. Two hundred people have died of cholera in Swatow, and Chinese troops mobilize for defense. . . . As floodwaters recede, Japanese troops and ships continue up the Yangtze River.

A	B	C	D	E
Includes developments that affect more than one world region, international organizations, and important meetings of world leaders.	*Includes all domestic and regional developments in Europe, including the Soviet Union.*	*Includes all domestic and regional developments in Africa and the Middle East.*	*Includes all domestic and regional developments in Latin America, the Caribbean, and Canada.*	*Includes all domestic and regional developments in Asian and Pacific nations (and colonies).*

U.S. Politics & Social Issues	U.S. Foreign Policy & Defense	Economics & Great Depression	Science, Technology & Nature	Culture, Leisure & Lifestyle	
CIO head John L. Lewis visits Speaker Bankhead again to plead labor's case for the Walsh-Healey Bill, but is unsuccessful. . . . The President signs 52 bills from Congress, and vetoes one (the Emergency Farm Credit Interest Bill), knowing Congress will override the veto.	Once again, Finland is the only country to pay its war debts to the United States.			Forty thousand fans watch the first night baseball game at Ebbets Field. The Dodgers lose to the Cincinnati Reds as Reds pitcher Johnny Vander Meer throws his second consecutive no-hitter. . . . German expressionist painter Ernst Ludwig Kirchner commits suicide in Davos, Switzerland. His art is labeled "degenerate" by the Reich.	Jun. 15
Congress adjourns after approving $12 billion in spending for fiscal year 1939, the largest peacetime outlay ever.	Germany's Economic Minister Funk repudiates responsibility to pay Austria's loans, which the United States asked for formally on April 6 and June 9. He indicates that Germany, for practical purposes, will negotiate to satisfy the U.S. demands.				Jun. 16
The Alabama Supreme Court upholds the death sentence for Clarence Norris in the Scottsboro rape case.	The United States rejects Minister Funk's claims, and demands payment on Austria's loans.	The judge in the Harlan County trial of coal companies acquits four defendants, but declares the other 58 must take their chances with the jury. For five weeks, witnesses have testified about the tactics used by police and coal companies to suppress unions.			Jun. 17
				Babe Ruth signs on as a coach with the Brooklyn Dodgers at $15,000 a year. . . . In Minnesota, Louis Zamperini breaks the record for running a mile in collegiate meets, and leads the USC Trojan team to a fourth national championship in track and field.	Jun. 18
			A bridge span collapses under a train near Miles City, Mont. Forty-seven die in the wreck.		Jun. 19
Away from the White House for his son's wedding, the President signs 37 bills.	A Federal Grand Jury indicts 18 people for espionage, saying they worked for the German War Ministry. Fourteen of those indicted have already left the country.	On the fifth day of a strike at Eagle Pencil in New York, 150 strikers battle police, throwing eggs and rocks; 11 are arrested.	Dr. Florence Siebert is awarded the Trudeau Medal for isolating and purifying the tubercle bacillus—which is being used to develop the tuberculosis test.		Jun. 20
		The President signs the $3.7 billion Relief and Recovery Bill.			Jun. 21
		Ending a long dispute with the AFL, the NLRB gives the CIO jurisdiction over longshoremen in all Pacific Coast ports. . . . Two striking teamsters are shot in New Orleans. . . . A strike over a 25 percent pay cut strands the Ringling Brothers and Barnum and Bailey Circus in Scranton, Pa.		At Yankee Stadium, before a crowd of 80,000, Joe Louis knocks out Max Schmeling in the first round, retaining his heavyweight championship.	Jun. 22
The President signs more bills— including the McCarran Civil Air Authority Act, establishing the Civil Aeronautics Authority.	The army makes plans, with $23 million from the War Department Supply Bill, to upgrade coastal defenses. . . . In the wake of mass arrests and deportation in Austria, Jews line up at the U.S. Embassy in Vienna, but are told that monthly visa quotas have already been met.	As a first step toward ending a strike, a three-person arbitration committee will decide whether Eagle Pencil will elect a union for collective bargaining. Employees currently act with an independent union.	The "Oceanarium" Marine Studios (later Marineland) open in Florida.		Jun. 23

F	G	H	I	J
Includes elections, federal-state relations, civil rights and liberties, crime, the judiciary, education, healthcare, poverty, urban affairs, and population.	Includes formation and debate of U.S. foreign and defense policies, veterans affairs, and defense spending. (Relations with specific foreign countries are usually found under the region concerned.)	Includes business, labor, agriculture, taxation, transportation, consumer affairs, monetary and fiscal policy, natural resources, pollution, and accidents.	Includes worldwide scientific, medical, and technological developments, natural phenomena, U.S. weather, and natural disasters.	Includes the arts, religion, scholarship, communications media, sports, entertainment, fashions, fads, and social life.

	World Affairs	Europe	Africa & The Middle East	The Americas	Asia & The Pacific
Jun. 24	Protocols for the International Agreement for the Regulation of Whaling are signed in London. . . . An ongoing battle between British troops and the tribes of Waziristan in India has revealed a planned overthrow of Afghanistan's government. The plot leader is a Syrian who has been building up a private army.	The Non-Intervention Committee is stumped on where to get the $2.25 million needed to count and house volunteers in Spain while they are removed from the fighting. . . . Reports of typhoid fever and foot and mouth disease in northern Catalonia cause France to set guards at its border.	A Jewish man is stabbed to death, an Italian priest is kidnapped and killed, and bombs injure several Arabs in incidents in Jaffa and Tel Aviv. British authorities close off the cities and impose curfews.	The Mexican press blames Jews for problems of the textile industry and asks for their expulsion, as a new wave of anti-Semitism grips Mexico. Over the next three days, 25 Jewish-owned small textile firms will be forced to close.	Six men in Shanghai are gunned down, one fatally. All were Chinese, working with the Japanese in various positions.
Jun. 25	German economic projects in Iran worry the Soviet Union. Germany is building an airport at Teheran, and a shipbuilding facility on the Caspian Sea—close enough to attack the Soviet Union.	Responding to remarks made on June 20, Italy declares that it will go to war with Spain if attacks are made upon Italian cities. . . . Ireland inaugurates its first president, Douglas Hyde.	Terrorists kill an Arab in a Haifa hospital in Palestine, even though he was not the man they sought.		Japanese planes bomb Swatow and Hainan Island. Further north, an American Lutheran mission in Shantung province is bombed.
Jun. 26		Elections to the Supreme Soviet take place throughout the Soviet Union. The victory of Stalin's candidates is a foregone conclusion. . . . A plot by Sudeten Germans in Czechoslovakia to kidnap prominent Social Democrats is uncovered.	Reprisal killings between Jews and Arabs occur in the area of Jaffa and Tel Aviv.		In the United Provinces of India, 35,000 cholera cases have been reported, half of them fatal. . . . Thousands are inoculated against cholera in Shanghai, where cholera is also reported.
Jun. 27	Britain and France warn Japan that they will act if the island of Hainan, in south China, is invaded. Hainan is between Hong Kong and French Indo-China. . . . Germany summons its Ambassador to China, Dr. Trautmann, to Berlin and asks China to invalidate contracts with German advisers signed over a month ago.	Gen. Franco, leader of Spain's insurgency, suggests to journalists that there be one port, far from war fronts, for nonmilitary commerce. Administered by neutral nations, it would be off-limits for air raids. . . . Two more British ships are shelled in Alicante's harbor, with four casualties. The port of Gandia is bombed as well. A British destroyer there does not attempt to fire on the planes.	In Tel Aviv and other Jewish cities in Palestine, marches, prayers, and shop closures mark a spirit of mourning for Solomon ben Yosef, sentenced to die for throwing a bomb at a bus. . . . Tulkarem, an Arab city, holds a general strike to protest Turkish designs on Alexandretta. British authorities impose martial law and a curfew.		
Jun. 28	France sends troops to the largest of the Paracel Islands, south of Hainan Island, between Indo-China and the Philippines.	A ship in Memel, Lithuania, turns its firehoses on a crowd of 7,000 pro-Nazis, mostly German. A riot ensues and many are seriously injured. Police restore order by closing the streets. . . . Britain's Ambassador in Rome asks Italy to halt the bombing of ships in Spain's harbors. . . . Britain, France, Germany, and Italy agree to split the Soviet Union's portion of the cost of removing volunteers from Spain. Although part of the Non-Intervention Committee, the Soviet Union refuses to pay.	British courts refuse clemency for Solomon ben Yosef, condemned for a bus bombing in which there were no casualties. Demonstrations are stopped by club-wielding police.	Jamaica's legislators draft bills to raise wages, but announce that taxes must go up to cover the higher pay for government workers.	China admits to 10,000 casualties near Matang, and charges Japan with using poison gas.
Jun. 29		Italy and Gen. Franco respond to British complaints by promising that British ships will not be attacked outside Spanish waters, and will be avoided if possible in ports. Also, neutral ports will be established. . . . Czech Premier Hodza broadens his talks with minorities to include Hungarians and Poles, as well as Germans, but no progress is made. . . . France decrees it will no longer send prisoners to its penal colonies in French Guiana.	Solomon ben Yosef is hanged at Acre Prison, Palestine; demonstrations in Tel Aviv are quickly suppressed. In Tiberias, a bomb thrown at a Jewish wedding celebration injures seven.		In Tokyo, Japan issues decrees prohibiting the private sales of cotton and iron. These items can only be used for military purposes now. . . . Another political murder of a Chinese official known to collaborate with Japan occurs in Shanghai. Two bystanders are killed as well.
Jun. 30	Turkey and France agree that equal numbers of French and Turkish troops will maintain order in the Sanjak of Alexandretta. Under the agreement, Turkey abandons all territorial claims. Syria, speaking for many Syrians living in the Sanjak, threatens noncooperation.	Reich Commissioner Joseph Buerckel announces that former Austrian Chancellor Schuschnigg will stand trial for high treason. . . . In Vienna, 30,000 Jewish employees are dismissed from jobs, even as Nazi officials claim that no such order was given.			Japan claims that levees on the Yellow River will be repaired within a month. China claims that most farms and villages in flood's path were evacuated safely. Neither claim is valid.

A	B	C	D	E
Includes developments that affect more than one world region, international organizations, and important meetings of world leaders.	*Includes all domestic and regional developments in Europe, including the Soviet Union.*	*Includes all domestic and regional developments in Africa and the Middle East.*	*Includes all domestic and regional developments in Latin America, the Caribbean, and Canada.*	*Includes all domestic and regional developments in Asian and Pacific nations (and colonies).*

U.S. Politics & Social Issues	U.S. Foreign Policy & Defense	Economics & Great Depression	Science, Technology & Nature	Culture, Leisure & Lifestyle	
President Franklin Roosevelt talks to the nation by radio about the coming primaries. He urges Americans not to vote for defeatists.	Germany answers the U.S. note of May 9, exempting American citizens who live abroad from registering their property in Germany.	U.S. Steel subsidiaries cut prices by 6 to 17 percent, but promise there will be no cut in wages. After the President mentions this in his radio chat, the steel companies deny that the promise was made. Stock prices on steel rise with the denial. . . . The mayor of Scranton, after failed negotiations, tells the Ringling Brothers and Barnum and Bailey Circus that they present a health hazard and must leave.	On receiving permission from France to land at Le Bourget Airport, Howard Hughes announces his plans to fly around the world.		Jun. 24
Back at the White House, President Roosevelt signs 121 bills passed by Congress, including an act modernizing food and drug regulation, funding appropriations, and civil service expansions. He vetoes 30 bills, including the Walsh-Healy Act.	For the second time in four days, a diplomatic protest is made to Japan over the slapping of an American woman by a Japanese soldier. In both incidents—one in Nanking and one in Tsingtao, the women were slapped when they did not respond to questions in Japanese.	Fifteen hundred circus workers vote to return to winter camp in Florida rather than take a pay cut. Many workers disagree and blame the union, saying they would take the cut to continue the tour. A $15,000 payroll will be made as soon as banks open. . . . The WPA uses funding for a new "buy and give" program, purchasing surplus stocks to distribute to the needy. American business is critical of the program.		A Tisket, A Tasket by Ella Fitzgerald is the top selling record in the country.	Jun. 25
Columbia University publishes a pamphlet labeling the American Legion "fascist and unpatriotic," and deploring its effect on education and politics. Legion leadership responds that higher education is a "hotbed of Communism."		At the President's request, the WPA raises its wages in 13 southern states, so that no one earns less than $1 a day. In New York, the highest WPA wage is $98 a month. . . . Banking rules nationwide will be liberalized July 1, affecting commercial loans and investments.		James Weldon Johnson, author and poet of the Harlem Renaissance and civil rights activist, is killed when his car is hit by a train.	Jun. 26
The Decatur Daily of Alabama publishes an ad asking the governor for pardons for the five Scottsboro defendants still in jail.		In pouring rain that has drenched their tents, the Ringling Brothers and Barnum and Bailey Circus packs up, hoping to leave Scranton by midnight and return to Florida.			Jun. 27
Based on the President's last radio talk, a blacklist is rumored to exist of uncooperative Congressional Democrats slated to be "purged" in the next elections. . . . The President signs a bill creating the Olympic National Park in Washington.		The CIO asks federal intervention in New Orleans, where they say union officials are being arrested, beaten, and thrown out of the state by police. . . . Seamen who staged a sit-down strike on an American vessel are charged with mutiny and fined in Philadelphia. . . . New York's Supreme Court Justice Cotillo issues an injunction permanently barring union pickets in the labor strikes against Busch Jewelry Company.			Jun. 28
Earl Browder, head of the U.S. Communist Party, admits under oath before Congress that his group is part of the Communist International, with links to Moscow.		Judge Cotillo's ban on pickets is immediately defied, and 20 warrants are issued against union members.	Twelve inches of rain falls on Japan in less than 20 hours, causing landslides in many areas. An earthquake adds to the destruction, and 100 people die.		Jun. 29
	The United States, France, and Britain sign an accord raising naval ship size limits to 45,000 tons.			On the eve of the 75th anniversary of the Battle of Gettysburg, 1,600 veterans of the Civil War converge at the site. The oldest is 106; most are in their 90s.	Jun. 30

F	G	H	I	J
Includes elections, federal-state relations, civil rights and liberties, crime, the judiciary, education, healthcare, poverty, urban affairs, and population.	Includes formation and debate of U.S. foreign and defense policies, veterans affairs, and defense spending. (Relations with specific foreign countries are usually found under the region concerned.)	Includes business, labor, agriculture, taxation, transportation, consumer affairs, monetary and fiscal policy, natural resources, pollution, and accidents.	Includes worldwide scientific, medical, and technological developments, natural phenomena, U.S. weather, and natural disasters.	Includes the arts, religion, scholarship, communications media, sports, entertainment, fashions, fads, and social life.

	World Affairs	Europe	Africa & The Middle East	The Americas	Asia & The Pacific
Jul. 1	Soviet Gen. Lushkoff's diary is published in Tokyo newspapers.	The Reich and Britian sign a new agreement regulating payment of Austria's debt to Britain. . . . Italy forbids the translation or public display of books by Jewish authors. . . . Battlefield tours of Spain start. The nine-day package, costing 400 pesetas, begins in Irun and ends in Guernica. . . . To challenge abortion laws in England, Dr. Alec Bourne turns himself in to police, after performing an abortion on a 15-year-old rape victim.		Mexico announces a 12 percent tax on all exports.	Chinese planes attack Japanese ships and soldiers near Matang. Japanese planes raid Hukow and Wuhsueh. the next cities up the Yangtze. They also bomb Swatow, killing an estimated 300, including 200 schoolchildren.
Jul. 2		Italy's Foreign Minister Ciano tells Britain that Gen. Franco agrees to stop bombing British ships, while a plan is developed for neutral ports. . . . The Czech government rejects demands from German Sudeten party as unreasonable.		Reports that Paraguay is buying dozens of war planes from Italy fuels fear that the Chaco War may flare up again.	Japanese planes bomb cities in Shansi province, as well as Swatow in the south. . . . Cholera breaks out near Kaifeng.
Jul. 3	A Franco-Turkish pact of friendship is signed in Angora, Turkey, while a military agreement governing the Sanjak of Alexandretta is signed by representatives of France, Turkey, and Syria. However, negotiations for a treaty of friendship between Turkey and Syria are broken off over disagreements on Turkish troops in the Sanjak.	Nazi decrees give thousands of Jewish tenants two weeks to vacate their homes in Vienna's suburbs. Jews are also expelled from government-owned houses and apartments.		The goal of the May 11 Integralista uprising in Brazil was the assassination of President Vargas, according to an official report. Thirty men have been indicted, and 143 are held in the attempted takeover of the Navy Ministry.	Shanghai reports 15 new cases of cholera daily. Nearly a million inoculations have been given, and 41 people have died. . . . Heavy rains pour down on the Yangtze. Japanese pilots report that levees west of Matang have been cut. Chinese pilots claim to sink a Japanese aircraft carrier near Anking.
Jul. 4		Almeria in southern Spain is proposed by Gen. Franco as a neutral port site. . . . Alicante and the Barcelona suburb of Gava are bombed in Spain.	Violence in Jerusalem and the area between Jaffa and Tel Aviv kills six men and injures others. The clashes, between Jews and Arabs, result in curfews and closed streets.	Bolivia rejects a final mediation effort by neutral countries to settle the Chaco dispute in Argentina.	Gen. Doihara, who led the fighting at Lanfeng and Kaifeng, returns to Tokyo. . . . A few thousand cholera cases over a widening area in central China alerts health officials that a major epidemic is coming. . . . A series of air raids on the western city of Loyang kills 94 persons, many of them prisoners.
Jul. 5	Martial law is lifted as the first of 2,500 Turkish troops arrive in the Sanjak of Alexandretta, to assume their police duties. They will serve with French troops from France, Senegal, Morocco, and Tunisia. . . . Twenty-eight German military advisers and their General leave China. This ends a nine-year relationship on orders from the Reich, presumably because closer ties with Japan are sought.	All 26 nations in the Non-Intervention Committee accept the plan to remove 20,000 foreign volunteers from Spain. The Spanish government and rebels must now approve it. . . . Spanish insurgents under Gen. Aranda push down the coast, while another brigade comes east. Both are within 20 miles of Sagunto and Nules, cities that have been bombed heavily for weeks. German Junkers shell Badalona for two days. Italian-made planes bomb Madrid and several coastal cities. . . . Osservatore Romano, the Vatican newspaper, says that anti-Jewish propaganda and its results are "anti-Christian" and "inhuman."	Five people, both Jew and Arab, are killed and others injured in four separate attacks in Palestine. . . . Seven hundred Suez Canal workers stage a sit-down strike for higher wages.	Cuba's government approves a new amnesty bill. A previous measure was vetoed by the president, but Congress feels amnesty is a prerequisite for elections.	Japan claims capture of Hukow, along with munitions left by fleeing Chinese. The city is being evacuated, but whether it's in Chinese or Japanese hands remains in doubt for several days.
Jul. 6	Thirty-two nations assemble in Evian, France, for the Conference on Jewish Refugees. . . . Tokyo newspapers report that 10 former associates of Gen. Lushkoff, all in the secret police, have been executed in the Soviet Union. . . . China claims ownership of the Paracel Islands, which France fortified late last month. . . . W.R. Davis & Company of New York contracts to buy $10 million of Mexican oil, intended for European fascist countries.	A Hungarian court sentences Nazi and fascist leader Szalasi to three years in prison for "incitement." . . . Paris administrators order 1.75 million gas masks to be distributed to citizens, free of charge.	Riots in Haifa erupt after two bombs are thrown into an Arab marketplace. Twenty-seven die and 103 are injured, some as a result of police gunfire. Police arrest the leader of local Jewish Revisionists and his followers. In other areas of Palestine a bomb thrown from a train kills a girl; other incidents cause 10 deaths. Six Arabs have been sentenced to death in two days.		Mao Tse-tung leads the Communist contingent of the new People's Political Council in Hankow. The 200-member body is chaired by Wang Chung-hui of the Kuomintang, and represents the Socialist and Youth parties as well. . . . Chinese sources claim the Japanese troops in southern Shansi province are retreating after three days of battle.
Jul. 7	U.S. Delegate Myron Taylor is named President of the Refugee Conference. Statements on immigration policy from all nations present are read. Golda Meir is in Evian as part of a Palestinian delegation, but they are not allowed to sit in on the conference.		On the anniversary of the Royal Commission Report, 600 Arabs cross into Palestine from Trans-Jordan and battle British police. Five die and more are injured. Other clashes take lives in different parts of Palestine. Authorities believe that Arab tribes mass along the Syrian border, where an electrified fence has been completed. Two battalions of British troops are en route from Egypt to keep order.	A strike at copper mines in Rancagua, Chile, idles 10,000 workers. Employers want higher pay and walk out when miners are dismissed to cut costs.	On the one-year anniversary of the undeclared war in China, Gen. Chiang Kai-shek asks the people of Japan to rise up against their leaders' militarism. . . . In Shanghai, both Japanese and Chinese civilians are killed in shootings and bombings. Japanese soldiers take up posts in French Concession and International Settlement, searching foreigners and making arrests. Diplomatic protests are registered.
Jul. 8	A delivery of 200 planes from the Soviet Union is made to the Chinese. The planes are tested and flown from Turkestan through Mongolia. Chinese pilots bring them to Hankow.	Spanish insurgents capture the town of Nules after hand-to-hand fighting. . . . Austria, now a part of the Reich, allows divorce for the first time.	A 12-year-old girl and three older companions, all Jewish, are arrested after throwing a bomb that kills several Arabs in Jerusalem, Palestine. Arabs close their businesses and strike in several towns.		The last few civilians and foreigners leave Hankow, but the Chinese still hold the city. . . . Using oxygen tanks to achieve greater altitude, Chinese bombers make five raids along the Yangtze, hitting the Anking airfield and Japanese planes on the ground.
	A *Includes developments that affect more than one world region, international organizations, and important meetings of world leaders.*	**B** *Includes all domestic and regional developments in Europe, including the Soviet Union.*	**C** *Includes all domestic and regional developments in Africa and the Middle East.*	**D** *Includes all domestic and regional developments in Latin America, the Caribbean, and Canada.*	**E** *Includes all domestic and regional developments in Asian and Pacific nations (and colonies).*

U.S. Politics & Social Issues	U.S. Foreign Policy & Defense	Economics & Great Depression	Science, Technology & Nature	Culture, Leisure & Lifestyle	
The Census Bureau puts the U.S. population at 130,215,000. . . . New York becomes the ninth state to require a syphilis test before marriage.	The War Department awards $14.4 million in contracts for new planes and equipment—the largest peacetime order.	The nation's fiscal year starts with a $3 billion deficit and a debt between $37 and 40 billion. The deficit for fiscal 1938 was $1.46 billion. . . . The trial of 14 picketers who defied Judge Cotillo's injunction begins, and charges are dismissed. The union agrees not to picket until an Appeals Court reviews the case.		American Don Budge wins the men's singles event at Wimbledon for the second year. . . . For ladies this summer, "toy" hats perched on the head at a jaunty angle are the latest fad.	Jul. 1
	More American ships rush to Swatow, China, to evacuate U.S. citizens.			American Helen Wills Moody takes her eighth Wimbledon title.	Jul. 2
At sunset on the 75th anniversary of the Battle of Gettysburg, President Roosevelt addresses 1,600 veterans and 150,000 visitors, and lights the "eternal flame" on a peace memorial on Oak Hill.			A steam locomotive in Britain pulling seven cars sets a speed record of 203 kilometers (126 miles) per hour.		Jul. 3
Vice President Garner says he will not run for a third term; speculation about President Franklin Roosevelt's intention is rife.		Barred by court injunction from picketing, union members pass out circulars to holiday beachgoers and hire an airplane to pull a banner, drawing attention to their strike against Busch Jewelry in New York.		Suzanne Lenglen, "La Divine," dies at age 39 of pernicious anemia at her home in France. One of the top tennis players of all time, she won 25 Grand Slam titles.	Jul. 4
Governor Bibb Graves of Alabama commutes the death sentence of Clarence Norris, one of the Scottsboro defendants, to life in prison. . . . The Federal Communications Commission issues rules governing radio broadcasts of political speeches. Most notable: any station allowing a candidate to speak must allow equal time to other qualified candidates.		The President declares the South "the nation's number one economic problem."	In Japan, 600 people die in the flood and mudslides of the Great Hanshin Flood. Most of the business district of Kobe is under 12 feet of water. Japan minimizes the disaster in its newspapers.		Jul. 5
The trial of six directors of a summer camp in Yaphank, N.Y., begins, with testimony of required Nazi salutes and Hitler oaths.	Japan responds to the U.S. note of May 31, that asked the return of American property in Shanghai, by pointing out that much of the area is still a dangerous war zone. Military necessity, Japan says, guides its actions. The response is not made public for 10 days.	Former Tennessee Valley Authority Chair Arthur Morgan sues for reinstatement with back pay, claiming the President had no right to fire him. . . . Thirty labor lawyers meet to plot strategy and challenge Judge Cotillo's injunction against picketing.			Jul. 6
		A National Labor Relations Board examiner asks Ford Motor Company in St. Louis, Mo., to reinstate 192 employees involved in a labor dispute last November, and accept collective bargaining. The company asks to present oral arguments to the full board. . . . The Red River Lumber mill in Westwood, Calif., closes after a strike is called because of a 17.5 percent pay cut.			Jul. 7
The President campaigns for Democratic candidates in Ohio and Kentucky, and will give speeches for Oklahoma and Arkansas candidates tomorrow.					Jul. 8

F	G	H	I	J
Includes elections, federal-state relations, civil rights and liberties, crime, the judiciary, education, healthcare, poverty, urban affairs, and population.	Includes formation and debate of U.S. foreign and defense policies, veterans affairs, and defense spending. (Relations with specific foreign countries are usually found under the region concerned.)	Includes business, labor, agriculture, taxation, transportation, consumer affairs, monetary and fiscal policy, natural resources, pollution, and accidents.	Includes worldwide scientific, medical, and technological developments, natural phenomena, U.S. weather, and natural disasters.	Includes the arts, religion, scholarship, communications media, sports, entertainment, fashions, fads, and social life.

	World Affairs	Europe	Africa & The Middle East	The Americas	Asia & The Pacific
Jul. 9		The Reich publishes a timetable for the exclusion of Jews from certain jobs, for example, from the beginning of 1939 they may not trade or broker real estate, or loans and contracts, or manage homes or land.	As casualties mount in Palestine, Britain calls in an armored car regiment from Egypt.	Bolivia and Paraguay agree to submit their remaining differences over the Gran Chaco to a third party for arbitration. . . . Mexico agrees to legalize Jewish refugees who have come to the country in the last five years.	Japanese troops besiege Kiukiang, 30 miles upriver from Hankow. American and British ships anchor nearby. Japan warns all ships away, and says 20,000 reinforcements are being rushed to this stretch of the Yangtze River. More troops also head to southern Shansi.
Jul. 10		Spanish insurgent forces split into four columns to push south: two along the coast toward Sagunto, and two several miles inland toward Segorbe. . . . Bombers flying from Majorca attack British ships at Valencia's wharves three times. . . . In France, Reims Cathedral, rebuilt largely with donations from the Rockefellers after being damaged in the Great War, is rededicated.	In Haifa, Palestine, four bombs are thrown: two into Jewish-owned buses where they cause many casualties. Three bombing incidents in Jerusalem injure both Arabs and Jews. Shootings and gang violence kill more people.	Two villages in Oaxaca, Mexico, fight over land; seven people are killed in the violence.	With hot weather, cholera cases rise; in Shanghai, there are up to 70 new cases per day. . . . Japanese forces try to cross Lake Poyang to approach Kiukiang, and are driven back. U.S. and British gunboats attempt to leave the area, but are stopped by mines in the river. Chinese planes continue to bomb and strafe Japanese ships on the Yangtze.
Jul. 11	American, British, and French delegates at Evian propose a permanent body to discuss problems of all refugees.	Spain's government charges Italy with preparing two battalions for service with Gen. Franco, even as it pretends to cooperate with the Non-Intervention Committee plans. Italy continues to ship planes and munitions to rebel ports. . . . Germany says it can now produce rugs from human hair and viscose; squads will sweep barbershops regularly to collect hair.	Twelve more people are killed in Palestinian violence. Haifa, Tiberias, Tul Karm, and a settlement on the Plain of Sharon are scenes of attacks. Newspapers are suspended, strict curfews imposed, and Jewish leaders call for calm.	Mexico reveals that five U.S.-owned mines in Jalisco, Sonora, Durango, and Chihuahua have been taken over by the government and given to the employees. Mines once owned by Britain, France, and Mexico itself have also been turned over to employee cooperatives.	Chinese troops dynamite buildings and bridges in Kiukiang, as evacuations continue. Fighting goes on at Hankow as well.
Jul. 12	Germany terminates all trade with Brazil. Relations between the countries have not been good since German involvement was suspected in the May Integralista uprising. . . . Venezuela resigns from the League of Nations.	The Spanish government accepts the plan of the Non-Intervention Committee.	Freshly-landed British troops rush to Haifa and other trouble spots in Palestine. Since July 5, 95 have died and over 250 have been injured, the majority Arabs. Eight Arabs die in a shootout with police as they attempt to sabotage the Iraq Petroleum pipeline. The Imam of the El Aqsa Mosque, Sheik Ali Nur el Khatib, is assassinated by Arabs.	The United States will be one of six neutral nations to arbitrate the final peace settlement between Bolivia and Paraguay, which involves the exact position of a border through the Gran Chaco.	Canton's Wongsha station is bombed, and sampans in the area are sunk by Japanese planes. The day's heaviest air raid is on Wuchang, across the Yangtze from Hankow. Six hundred casualties result, and 50 bombs fall on American mission buildings.
Jul. 13	Responding to a plea from China and the Red Cross, the United States arranges, in conjunction with the Philippines, to provide 3 million cholera vaccinations to China—half of what is asked for. The League of Nations sends out a plea, and Romania, Egypt, and Yugoslavia pledge a total of 1.6 million doses.	Barcelona and towns along the northern Catalan coast are bombed by insurgents.	Two Jews are stoned to death in separate attacks in Haifa. A general strike by Arabs enters its seventh day.		In Shansi province, Japanese troops approach Yuanchu. Chinese forces have surrounded garrisons in Yuncheng, Wensi, and Hotsin for a month, forcing Japanese planes to drop food and arms to their troops. Japan claims that reinforcements have arrived to turn the Chinese away. . . . China reports that Japanese bombers struck a concentration camp at Tsengcheng in the south, killing 240 people.
Jul. 14	Japan announces the suspension of the 1940 Olympic Games, which were to have been held in Tokyo. Immediately, several other cities make bids for the summer games. Winter events, originally given to Sapporo, Japan, will be planned in Oslo, Norway, though Canada has also volunteered. . . . In Evian, the Intergovernmental Committee on Refugees votes to make itself permanent and will meet again in August. Little else is decided, giving the correct impression that nothing will be done about Jewish refugees fleeing the Reich.	Italy publishes its new racial policy: the Italian race has remained "pure" and Aryan for 1,000 years and must remain free from contamination through intermarriage.			Canton is bombed for the third day in a row. Casualties are heavy in a slum area, crowded with refugees. . . . Chinese authorities claim that 25 Japanese ships have been sunk on the Yangtze since July 1, and 19 others disabled. Japan denies that any ships have sunk. . . . Japanese pilots bomb Canton, Nanchang, and Hankow, as well as villages around Lake Poyang.
Jul. 15	Japan demands that the Soviet Union remove its troops in the hills west of Lake Khasan, near Vladivostok. Japan claims the area as its territory. The Soviet Union refuses; Japan calls the Soviet presence an invasion of their Korean border.	The proposed Nationalities Statute of Czechoslovakia will give provincial governments to German and Hungarian regions, increase representation in public office, and make the use of their language official in their provinces. . . . W.R. Davis, who negotiated the $10 million Mexican oil deal, is sued in London courts by Danish plaintiffs over oil deals he made in 1932 through 1935. . . . While Parliament debates the wisdom of armament purchases, Britain's Air Secretary reveals a new order for 1,000 aircraft.	Two Jewish girls are held and accused of throwing a bomb into an Arab market in Jerusalem, killing 10 and injuring 29—many of them women and children. A riot in the city of Safed pits Jews against Arabs until police restore order. Other killings and attacks bring curfews and armored patrols.	Four thousand Jamaican workers form an island wide organization for better wages and working conditions. . . . Chilean President Alessandri invites mining union representatives to his office and asks them to return to work while negotiations continue.	Japanese planes attack towns around Lake Poyang but the invaders' drive west is stalled before Kiukiang. . . . Chinese troops claim the recapture of Namoa Island.
	A Includes developments that affect more than one world region, international organizations, and important meetings of world leaders.	**B** Includes all domestic and regional developments in Europe, including the Soviet Union.	**C** Includes all domestic and regional developments in Africa and the Middle East.	**D** Includes all domestic and regional developments in Latin America, the Caribbean, and Canada.	**E** Includes all domestic and regional developments in Asian and Pacific nations (and colonies).

U.S. Politics & Social Issues	U.S. Foreign Policy & Defense	Economics & Great Depression	Science, Technology & Nature	Culture, Leisure & Lifestyle	
A mob in Cordele, Ga., lynches John Dukes, a 60-year-old black man, burning him alive. Dukes had shot the local sheriff, who shot back. He was hit and probably dying himself when seized.		To comply with the recent Supreme Court ruling, the NLRB reopens its case against Republic Steel, reissues its findings as a preliminary report, and gives the company 10 days to ask to present oral arguments. . . . A sixth CIO officer is arrested and charged with syndicalism in connection with a two-month-old strike against Maytag Corporation in Ohio. The strike of 1,500 was called over a 10 percent pay cut; the plant has shut down.		Supreme Court Justice Benjamin Cardozo dies of a heart attack.	Jul. 9
			Howard Hughes and four companions depart New York for Paris, in a modified Lockheed 14 plane named *The New York World's Fair 1939.*		Jul. 10
			Howard Hughes lands at Paris, making the flight in 16 hours, 35 minutes. After refueling, he heads for Moscow, confirming speculation that he intends to go around the world.		Jul. 11
After stumping in Texas, the President arrives in Colorado. . . . Six directors of a Nazi-leaning German camp in Yaphank, N.Y., are found guilty of violating the state's civil rights laws. Their total fines are $13,000; only the camp president receives jail time. "Camp Siegfried" continues to operate.		The NLRB's hearings on Weirton Steel, in their 11th month, move from Ohio to Pittsburgh because of threatened violence. The NLRB has barred one of Weirton's attorneys, angering workers belonging to the company union. The NLRB allows the attorney a hearing next week, to defend or explain his "contemptuous" behavior.	Hughes lands in Moscow after less than eight hours' flying time.		Jul. 12
		An early-morning riot at the Red River Lumber sawmill in Westwood, Calif., results in gunfire and beatings. By dawn, 800 "deputized" men rouse CIO members from their beds and evict them; 500-1,000 men are thrown out of town. The riot started when the company tried to reopen the mill with "company union" men. . . . Homer Martin purges Communist elements in the United Auto Workers, firing union officials. Those ousted claim that Martin is consolidating his own power.	Hughes leaves Omsk, Siberia, heading toward Yakutsk. He is one day ahead of Wiley Post's record time set in 1933.		Jul. 13
The President, speaking in San Francisco, expresses hope for world disarmament. . . . Two nights of race riots begin in Pittsburgh's North Side, involving thousands of people.	Over the past weeks, Treasury Secretary Morgenthau and Agriculture Secretary Wallace crafted a proposed loan to China in to be paid with cotton and food products, but Secretary of State Cordell Hull would not approve the deal. Morgenthau announces instead that the United States will continue buying silver from China.	The expelled CIO men and their families are allowed to collect their belongings in Westwood, Calif., but are otherwise kept out of town.	Hughes lands in Fairbanks, Alaska, after a 12-hour, 17-minute flight, refuels, and leaves for New York. He lands at Bennett Field in the afternoon and a crowd of 20,000 greets him. His official time for going around the world is 3 days, 19 hours, 17 minutes.		Jul. 14
The Senate begins inquiries into abuse of pension and old age funds in political campaigns in Kentucky, Pennsylvania, and Tennessee.	The United States challenges the takeover of one of five mines in Mexico, using diplomatic channels.	A New York Supreme Court judge limits picketing at Eagle Pencil, and disallows any interference with non-striking workers.			Jul. 15

F	G	H	I	J
Includes elections, federal-state relations, civil rights and liberties, crime, the judiciary, education, healthcare, poverty, urban affairs, and population.	Includes formation and debate of U.S. foreign and defense policies, veterans affairs, and defense spending. (Relations with specific foreign countries are usually found under the region concerned.)	Includes business, labor, agriculture, taxation, transportation, consumer affairs, monetary and fiscal policy, natural resources, pollution, and accidents.	Includes worldwide scientific, medical, and technological developments, natural phenomena, U.S. weather, and natural disasters.	Includes the arts, religion, scholarship, communications media, sports, entertainment, fashions, fads, and social life.

	World Affairs	Europe	Africa & The Middle East	The Americas	Asia & The Pacific
Jul. 16	Finland is awarded the 1940 Olympic Games.	Spanish insurgents under Gen. Varelos capture key towns as they force their way east along the main road between Teruel and Sagunto. . . . The Soviet newspaper *Izvestia* writes that Britain's policy of appeasement and compromise is the greatest danger to world peace.		Mexico's President Lázaro Cárdenas turns the oil field operations over to workers by decree.	China's Peoples Political Council closes its first session with pledges of unity against Japan. . . . Planes bomb Nanchang airfield, destroying 17 Chinese planes. Chinese positions at Kiukiang are also shelled, as they have been for the last week. . . . Rain is washing out roads in Honan, cutting supply lines to Kaifeng and Lanfeng. Yellow River levees are breached in some places, though the cities themselves are expected to be safe.
Jul. 17		A bullfight and festival in Saragossa mark "Africa Day," a celebration in honor of Moroccan troops who started Spain's civil war two years ago. . . . A special emissary from Germany visits Britain's Foreign Minister Halifax, with overtures of friendship.	Three Jews and three Arabs are killed near Acre and Tel Aviv, Palestine. A general strike by Arabs is held in Trans-Jordan.	Bolivia and Paraguay accept the peace terms initialed on July 9.	Chinese pilots claim to sink four more Japanese vessels on the Yangtze. . . . A British surgeon confirms by autopsies that mustard and chlorine gas were used on Chinese soldiers. . . . In the south, Canton and its Wongsha station, the Canton-Hankow railway, and Yingtak are shelled.
Jul. 18	Japan warns Soviet forces near the border with Korea to evacuate. . . . The Netherlands seizes a ship carrying Mexican oil. Since Royal Dutch Shell was never paid for expropriated oil and property, it claims the cargo belongs to the company.	German stocks dive in their worst day since the Nazis came to power. Declining foreign trade and tension over Czechoslovakia are blamed. . . . Chancellor Hitler decrees that all German citizens must deliver service or goods for military ends whenever required. . . . Soviet playwright Vladimir Kirshon is executed. . . . In Britain, the King's physician testifies on behalf of Dr. Bourne, on trial for performing an abortion on a rape victim.	An Arab band of 50 attacks a Jewish settlement in Trans-Jordan, but is beaten away, with one death on each side.		Japan claims air victories in China, shooting down eight planes and destroying others on the ground at Nanchang.
Jul. 19	Japan and its Manchukuoan protectorate again protest the "invasion" by the Soviet Union. Newspapers in Tokyo demand war.	King George VI of England pays a state visit to France. . . . Insurgent planes bomb a British ship in Valencia's harbor. Barcelona's 14th century cathedral is struck as well, and the area around Segorbe suffers continual bombardment all day. . . . In Britain, Dr. Bourne is freed by a jury, opening the door to changes in abortion laws.			
Jul. 20	Japan's War Minister Itagaki calls an emergency meeting to discuss the border situation with the Soviet Union. . . . Trade between Brazil and Germany, suspended July 12, resumes.	Chancellor Hitler sends greetings to King George, following up on his emissary's visit on July 17. . . . Three heavy bombardments by insurgent planes flying over Valencia, Spain, result in damage to the wharves, and the U.S. Embassy in Madrid is hit by four shells. . . . Viennese observers say that humiliations of Jews have started again in Austria. Raids by Nazis on cafés now confront Czechs as well as Jews, often breaking dishes and windows.			China announces plans to move most ministries, including the Foreign Ministry under Wang Chung-hui, from Hankow to Chungking by the end of this month; Gen. Chiang Kai-shek and military offices will remain in Hankow. The province just south of Chungking, Kweichow, is suffering from floods; thousands are missing. . . . Up to 300 are injured in the Indian state of Punjab, as a group of Sikhs, demonstrating against taxes, are charged by police.
Jul. 21	Japan's Ambassador argues with Soviet Foreign Minister Litvinoff, refusing to accept his maps showing the disputed area as being in Soviet territory. Tokyo papers allege that a Japanese soldier was killed by a Soviet. Later reports accuse the Soviets of launching boats across the Amur River and invading with 160 men, who were quickly beaten back.	Pope Pius XI condemns the racism and "exaggerated nationalism" of fascist states as contrary to Catholic teaching. . . . Reich administrators are overwhelmed with the task of Aryanizing Jewish property in Austria. Only one-third of it has been confiscated and examined so far.	An Arab band of up to 100 men stab and kill two Jewish families and set fire to their homes in northern Palestine. In all, nine Jews die.	Paraguay and Bolivia sign a treaty of friendship, ending the Chaco dispute.	Seasonal rains swell the Yungting, threatening Peiping and Tsinan. The Yellow River and the Grand Canal are at flood stage as well. Japanese troops cut embankments on the Lung-hai rail line to divert floodwaters away from Kaifeng. The Yangtze River is far above its normal stage for this time of year.
Jul. 22	Japan's spokespersons tone down the border situation with the Soviet Union, denying that threats have been made.	Germany proposes that Britain chair an arbitration group of four nations to settle the German Sudeten situation. Britain refuses because Czechoslovakia is excluded. . . . In Spain, two insurgent columns in the Valencia province join to shell and attack the walled city of Viver.	Eleven people are killed in Palestine; eight by police. The eight are members of the gang that killed families yesterday.		Japan receives reinforcements at Hankow, where fighting has been going on for over three weeks. Chinese planes shell ships on the Yangtze; Japanese planes bomb Changsha and the airfield at Hankow.
Jul. 23	The World Conference for Action on the Bombardment of Open Towns and the Restoration of Peace convenes in Paris. Its figures say that 16,532 noncombatants were killed by Japanese planes in China from July 1937 through June 1938; 21,752 were wounded.	Britain urges Czechoslovakia to concede some issues to SdP (German nationalist party) to appease the Reich. . . . The seven nations of the Oslo Accords meet in Copenhagen, Denmark. . . . The Nazis hold their first Salzburg Festival, opening with a performance of *Die Meistersinger* by Wagner.		The mining strike in Chile ends, with help from President Alessandri. The company will take back 250 discharged workers and promises a slight pay raise.	Japanese forces continue to pound Kiukiang, dropping 200 bombs on Chinese positions. By evening, the docks are in flames. . . . A power plant two miles from Canton is raided by 18 Japanese planes. Changsha, capital of Hunan, is also bombed.

A	B	C	D	E
Includes developments that affect more than one world region, international organizations, and important meetings of world leaders.	*Includes all domestic and regional developments in Europe, including the Soviet Union.*	*Includes all domestic and regional developments in Africa and the Middle East.*	*Includes all domestic and regional developments in Latin America, the Caribbean, and Canada.*	*Includes all domestic and regional developments in Asian and Pacific nations (and colonies).*

U.S. Politics & Social Issues	U.S. Foreign Policy & Defense	Economics & Great Depression	Science, Technology & Nature	Culture, Leisure & Lifestyle	
	American Jews now living in Palestine ask for help from the United States, desiring more security in their settlements.				Jul. 16
			Douglas Corrigan takes off from New York in a nine-year-old plane with no radio. He has repeatedly been denied permission to cross the Atlantic by the Bureau of Air Commerce.		Jul. 17
	Secretary of State Cordell Hull says the United States is not satisfied with Japan's recent note.	Former TVA Chair Dr. Arthur Morgan testifies before a Senate subcommittee that the other directors and President Roosevelt were responsible for any failures. . . . Railroad company and union representatives remain deadlocked in talks on wage cuts that will affect 900,000 workers. . . . At the Maytag plant in Newton, Iowa, 450 employees break with the CIO-affiliated union, accept the 10 percent pay cut, and return to work.	Over 28 hours after leaving New York, "Wrong-Way" Corrigan lands in Ireland, claiming his compass got stuck.	*Scoop*, by Evelyn Waugh, is published.	Jul. 18
A public pool in Elizabeth, N.J., is closed after racial rows between bathers. Similar fights five years ago led to an unofficial "whites only" policy. African-American children began to use the pool 10 days ago. . . . A Federal judge in Wisconsin sets aside 29 convictions of individuals and oil companies convicted of raising and setting gas prices in 1935 and 1936. The guilt of five men and 12 companies, decided in January, is affirmed.	President Cárdenas of Mexico says the United States has made no demands about expropriated oil, but has only asked questions.	Iowa's National Guard is summoned to keep order in the 10-week-old strike against the Maytag Company. Strikers have cut telephone lines and halted company trucks. . . . In Chicago, police and sheriff use tear gas against 300 pickets who try to stop 150 strikebreakers from returning to work at a hardware foundry. This strike also was called over a 10 percent wage cut, seven weeks ago.	The Bureau of Air Commerce suspends Douglas Corrigan's experimental license and aircraft certificate. New York prepares for a ticker-tape parade, like the one that honored Howard Hughes. Steamship companies offer him free passage and Corrigan societies form throughout the country. He has contracts to tour and speak on behalf of American and United Airlines.	Joan Crawford and Franchot Tone announce their separation.	Jul. 19
Eight movie companies are named in an anti-trust suit brought by the state of New York. This case will last until 1948 and result in the rearrangement of the movie industry.		Street fights involving 500 people near the Maytag plant in Newton, Iowa, are quickly suppressed by the National Guard. Two men are jailed. . . . Company correspondence advocating the use of "pressure" on journalists is introduced at the NLRB hearing against Republic Steel.		Lupe Velez files for divorce from Johnny Weissmuller for the third time.	Jul. 20
	Secretary of State Cordell Hull tells Mexico in no uncertain terms that arbitration is demanded in the expropriation cases, and that fairness is required if the two countries are to continue as good neighbors.	The Works Progress Administration adds 200,000 new jobs in the 11 states of the south. . . . Amid charges of incompetence on all sides, the Congressional committee investigating the TVA impounds all minutes of TVA board meetings since 1933.		Author Owen Wister (*The Virginian*) dies, age 78. Bernard Henry Kroger, founder of the retail store chain, dies at 78. . . . Warner Brothers' London office tries to negotiate to bring Dr. Sigmund Freud to Hollywood to consult on Bette Davis' new movie, *Dark Victory*. . . . *My Sister Eileen*, by Ruth McKenney, is published.	Jul. 21
		An Appeals Court overturns an NLRB ruling against Fansteel. The NLRB had ordered the company to hire back fired employees who participated in a strike.		*Love Finds Andy Hardy*, starring Mickey Rooney and Judy Garland, and Shirley Temple's *Little Miss Broadway* are released.	Jul. 22
		In Harlan County, Ky., the trial of coal companies accused of violating the Wagner Act winds down. The FBI begins an investigation into efforts at jury-tampering. . . . The Maytag plant in Iowa remains closed as state police with machine guns watch the streets.			Jul. 23

F	G	H	I	J
Includes elections, federal-state relations, civil rights and liberties, crime, the judiciary, education, healthcare, poverty, urban affairs, and population.	Includes formation and debate of U.S. foreign and defense policies, veterans affairs, and defense spending. (Relations with specific foreign countries are usually found under the region concerned.)	Includes business, labor, agriculture, taxation, transportation, consumer affairs, monetary and fiscal policy, natural resources, pollution, and accidents.	Includes worldwide scientific, medical, and technological developments, natural phenomena, U.S. weather, and natural disasters.	Includes the arts, religion, scholarship, communications media, sports, entertainment, fashions, fads, and social life.

	World Affairs	Europe	Africa & The Middle East	The Americas	Asia & The Pacific
Jul. 24		The countries of the Oslo Accords, determined to stay out of conflicts between the great powers, reject the League of Nations' rule about imposing sanctions. The will ask the League to remove Article XVI.	A Jewish committee to organize defenses against Arab terrorists meets in Tel Aviv. It levies a tax to fund the defenses and calls for volunteers.	A stunt plane at an air show in Bogotá, Colombia, crashes into a crowd of 50,000. Fifty-three people are killed and 150 injured—many sprayed by burning gasoline.	Fighting is intense along seven miles toward Kiukiang. Japanese planes bomb Chinese positions along the lake, and Kiukiang, Hukow, and Changsha's airfield. . . . Chinese sources say Japanese troops are withdrawing from Shansi.
Jul. 25		British Prime Minister Chamberlain asks Viscount Runciman to go to Prague and urge the Czech government to make more concessions to the SdP (German nationalist party). As the French endorse the effort, the Czech government agrees to Runciman's mediation. . . . Spanish government forces take the offensive, crossing the Ebro River to engage insurgents. . . . The Secretary General of Italy's Fascist Party announces that vigorous anti-Semitic policy will be followed from now on.	Sixty-five people are killed when a buried bomb goes off early in the morning at a Haifa market in Palestine. Seven more die in the rioting that follows. Jewish-owned houses are burned in retaliation; most of the bombing victims are Arab.	An officer is killed during an assassination attempt on Governor Winship of Puerto Rico. Fifteen shots are fired as the governor reviews a parade. Police shoot and kill one man and arrest two nationalists for murder.	With clear weather, Japan presses toward Kiukiang and enters the city by nightfall. Chinese officers ask all foreigners to leave Kuling, a resort area 4,000 feet above the Yangtze, 10 miles from Kiukiang. . . . Japanese planes bomb the cement works in the Saichuen section of Canton.
Jul. 26		Spanish loyalists take 10 towns on their drive south and west of the Ebro. They hope to force insurgents to break off their drive on Valencia and send troops north. . . . A draft copy of the Czech government's Nationalities Statute is made public and, as expected, is heavily criticized by Henlein's followers.	A Jewish father and son near Mishmar Hayardin are murdered. Bombs are found and removed near a Jewish playground and at an Arab market that was bombed two weeks ago. Other retaliatory clashes claim more victims throughout Palestine. . . . In French Morocco, 17 are injured in rioting between Algerians and Moroccans.	In Brazil, the leader of the Integralista plot of May 11 is sentenced to 10 years hard labor. Lt. Nascimento, who helped the attackers from the inside, also gets 10 years. Twenty-three others receive prison sentences, and trials for an additional 143 defendants will be held in the future. . . . In Ponce, Puerto Rico, a total of 13 men are arrested for the attempted assassination of the governor.	Japanese troops fully control Kiukiang; cholera is reported among the refugees who fled the town. . . . The 52 Americans at Kuling cannot leave the city by any road. Chinese officials work to find them a safe haven. . . . In Rangoon, Burma, thousands of Buddhists demonstrate to express outrage over published excerpts from an insulting book. This becomes the Than Tun race riot, continuing for three days. Brutal violence by police exacerbates the crowds' anger.
Jul. 27	Britain warns Japan that it will protect its interests in China with action, if need be, and hints at possible assistance to China.	Though heavily shelled by enemy planes, loyalist forces reach Gandesa, an insurgent base since April, 15 miles from the Ebro River. There they are stopped, unable to take the city. On the coast, rebel pilots in Junkers drop bombs, some incendiary, on Tarragona. In Gandia harbor, the British ship *Dellwyn* is bombed for the third night, and sinks with two British warships standing by. . . . Berlin police issue instructions for Aryans on how to acquire Jewish property.	Sheik Hamid, Imam of a mosque in Acre, is assassinated—reportedly by an Arab. Snipers and stone-throwers render main roads unsafe in Palestine. A delegation of Arab women demands that all Jews be disarmed.	Mexico's Supreme Court rules that the expropriation of American and British oil properties is legal, and that the government may take up to 10 years to pay for them.	Japanese gunboats shell Chinese defenses on the Yangtze at Tienkaichen. . . . The city of Teian, directly south of Kiukiang, is bombed.
Jul. 28		Soviet newspapers describe a "great purge" in the far east over the last few months, connected with Japanese espionage. . . . Warships and planes shell cities along Spain's coast. Insurgent planes bomb the *Kellwyn*, sister ship of the *Dellwyn*, killing an observer for the Non-Intervention Committee. . . . In Germany, men may not marry until their civic and army service is completed. . . . Dr. Leo Baeck, Jewish leader in Berlin, calls for international help for Germany's remaining 300,000 Jews.	British troops stage preemptive raids to stop Arab bands from congregating in the hills of Palestine.	Plinio Salgado, leader of Brazil's Integralistas, and Gen. Flores de Cunha, a former governor now living in Uruguay, are charged with abetting the May 11 coup attempt. Both men remain at large.	Three days of rioting in Rangoon between Burmese Buddhists and Muslims, mostly Indians, leaves 360 dead, including women and children. Newspapers are shut down and strict curfews imposed, but outbreaks of racial and religious violence continue. . . . Japanese planes bomb Teian and supply positions along several railways north and south, as well as the new Chinese positions along the Yangtze.
Jul. 29	Japanese detachments try to seize land on Chengkufeng Hill, overlooking Lake Khasan. Soviet troops force them to withdraw. Both sides claim casualties.	Britain's House of Commons recesses after Labor members criticize the lack of response to the *Dellwyn's* sinking. . . . Insurgent planes bomb the small town of Falset on the Ebro, destroying much of it and killing 40 people. . . . The Pope continues to attack Italy's new racist policies, stressing the universal nature of the Church and of humanity. . . . Nikolai Krylenko, former Soviet Commissar of Justice, is tried, publicly confesses, and is immediately executed. . . . An anti-fascist uprising against the Greek government on Crete is suppressed and censored within four hours.			Chinese troops fight south of Kiukiang and west of Kuling. Communication with Kuling has been cut for several days. Japanese planes continue to shell Nanchang, Teian, and rail lines, while Chinese planes concentrate on Hukow. Refuges in the Lu Mountains are also being shelled and strafed by Japan, say Chinese sources; Japan denies this.

A	B	C	D	E
Includes developments that affect more than one world region, international organizations, and important meetings of world leaders.	Includes all domestic and regional developments in Europe, including the Soviet Union.	Includes all domestic and regional developments in Africa and the Middle East.	Includes all domestic and regional developments in Latin America, the Caribbean, and Canada.	Includes all domestic and regional developments in Asian and Pacific nations (and colonies).

U.S. Politics & Social Issues	U.S. Foreign Policy & Defense	Economics & Great Depression	Science, Technology & Nature	Culture, Leisure & Lifestyle	
				Television audiences in London see a broadcast of Shakespeare's *Julius Caesar*.	Jul. 24
					Jul. 25
The county sheriff seizes the German "Camp Siegfried" in Yaphank, as the fines imposed on six officers on July 12 have not been paid.		Governor Kraschel of Iowa refuses a demand by Maytag Company to remove National Guard troops and lift martial law. The company wants to reopen its plant and let non-striking workers work. The governor is accused of courting labor for their votes.			Jul. 26
					Jul. 27
	Charging that Japanese troops have flagrantly violated agreements about bringing troops and supplies through the American sector of Shanghai, U.S. Marines set up checkpoints to stop the traffic.	Police arrest 13 union members on charges of intimidating workers at Eagle Pencil.		*The Horse and Buggy Doctor*, by Arthur Hertzler, is published.	Jul. 28
		State troopers seize the list of "back-to-work" employees at the Maytag Company in Iowa, keeping them out of union hands. They already hold the company's payroll records under lock and key. The governor keeps the factory closed.			Jul. 29

F	G	H	I	J
Includes elections, federal-state relations, civil rights and liberties, crime, the judiciary, education, healthcare, poverty, urban affairs, and population.	Includes formation and debate of U.S. foreign and defense policies, veterans affairs, and defense spending. (Relations with specific foreign countries are usually found under the region concerned.)	Includes business, labor, agriculture, taxation, transportation, consumer affairs, monetary and fiscal policy, natural resources, pollution, and accidents.	Includes worldwide scientific, medical, and technological developments, natural phenomena, U.S. weather, and natural disasters.	Includes the arts, religion, scholarship, communications media, sports, entertainment, fashions, fads, and social life.

		World Affairs	Europe	Africa & The Middle East	The Americas	Asia & The Pacific
Jul. 30		Chinese Premier Dr. Kung tells the Soviet envoy in China that the Soviets are the real targets of Japan's aggression, and presses for action.	In defiance of the Pope, Premier Mussolini declares that Italy "will go straight ahead" with its new race policy.... Germany proclaims its western border (with the Netherlands, Belgium, France, and Switzerland) a closed area, much as its border with Poland was closed months ago. The border is now lined with cement and steel fortifications. . . . Greek ruler Metaxas is named "premier for life."	Both Northern and Southern Rhodesia, British colonies, protest the suggestion made by Britain that 500 European Jews be settled there. They are not, they point out, "an annex of Palestine."		While Rangoon remains quiet, rioting erupts in Mandalay, Burma. . . . Evacuation of Nanchang, capital of Kiangsi, begins, although many civilians have already left. . . . The Yellow River in Shansi is rising quickly, endangering north Honan and Anwhei provinces.
Jul. 31		Japan "reclaims" territory from the Soviets in a night battle at Changkufeng and other hills. Both sides claim the other was the invader and aggressor, and both claim to be in possession of the disputed area.	Bulgaria gains the right to rearm by signing the Salonika Pact and promising nonaggression toward other signers. This accord, with the Balkan Entente (Greece, Yugoslavia, Turkey, and Romania), lifts military and border restrictions imposed by treaties.	Five bombs explode in Haifa, Palestine, and kill a young woman. That and the deaths of eight Arabs shot by troops, brings the death toll for July alone to 201. Late at night, six more Arabs are killed in a gun battle with British troops.	Allegations of plotting against President Cárdenas by high officials in the government are voiced by left-wing senators in Mexico.	Observers note that in most areas of China, Japan holds only rail lines and selected cities. The countryside is far beyond their control, and guerilla forces operate freely. . . . Chinese anti-aircraft guns shoot down a plane near Anking carrying Japan's Admiral Kato and other officers; all are killed.
Aug. 1		Japan claims to shoot down five planes while repulsing a Soviet tank attack at Changkufeng (Zaozernaya to the Soviets), in the contested border area between Siberia and Korea.	Spanish Gen. Miaja tries another diversion, capturing the bluff of Camarena, near Teruel, in an effort to draw insurgent troops to the area and away from Valencia. . . . Germany rolls out a plan to finance the new Volkswagen plant: citizens can pay five marks a month in advance for their car, taking delivery in 1946. Queues form quickly. By tomorrow night, the Strength Through Joy offices handling the finance plans run out of applications.	Dissatisfied with British justice and high fees, Arabs in Palestine set up their own courts in villages. Using Islamic Law to guide judgments, these courts decide small and large disputes, and can impose death sentences. . . . Road mines, bombs in Haifa, and shootings in Palestine continue the violence.	Jamaica celebrates the 100th anniversary of emancipation.	Japan claims that reinforcements are approaching Kiukiang. Chinese sources acknowledge that Japanese captured Hwangmei, 30 miles away on the Hupeh-Anwhei border. China points out that all bridges and usable infrastructure were destroyed before Japan's advance. . . . In Hilo, Hawaii, police fire buckshot into a crowd of strikers and sympathizers, injuring 36 people.
Aug. 2		In an early morning battle, the Soviet Union deploys six army divisions and 30 tanks at Shachofeng Hill. Japan says the Soviet troops at that site, much fewer in number, are defeated in hand-to-hand combat.	The Czech parliament announces it will adjourn without voting on the Nationalities Statute. German Sudetens are gleeful and hail Lord Runciman's upcoming visit as a victory for their side. . . . Twelve thousand children from the Basque region in Spain have yet to be returned to their families.			Chinese troops cut a serious breach into Yangtze River levees 10 miles west of Kiukiang, 125 southeast of Hankow. . . . Japan acknowledges serious attacks of guerilla troops in the Shanghai area. . . . A British captain and two Chinese crewmembers are killed when their customs ship is gunned and bombed by Japanese planes on the Yangtze River.
Aug. 3		The now-permanent Refugee Committee of 27 countries meets in London, to work on a proposal asking the Reich's cooperation in allowing Jews to emigrate with their money and property. . . . The League of Nations sponsors a Rural Health Conference for Far Eastern Countries in Bandoeng, Dutch East Indies.	Barcelona is heavily shelled at night, but only two people die. Shelling along the coast continues daily. . . . Germany announces that non-Aryan doctors will be barred from practice at the end of September. Italy says no foreign Jews may attend its schools. . . . Hungary's two largest Nazi groups unite.			In an air battle near Hankow, Japan claims to shoot down 32 of 54 Chinese planes; China says it lost six. China claims to down 12 enemy planes; Japan says only two were lost. In addition, China says that the Japanese bombs were intended to destroy a dam protecting Hankow from floodwaters. . . . Twenty-five die in two separate riots between Muslims and Buddhists in Burma.
Aug. 4		Japan initiates peace talks on the border conflict, while Korea and eastern Japan order a blackout, for fear of Soviet attack. Foreign Commissar Litvinoff agrees to talks but warns the Soviet will dictate terms.	Romania passes a Minorities Statute granting language rights and separate schools for the seven ethnic groups making up a third of the country. . . . In the Pyrenees, Spanish loyalists set a 19-mile fire near Sort to force the rebels to evacuate. . . . France will loan Bulgaria 1 billion levas to finance its rearmament.	Ten die in Palestine, all Jewish, because of land mines and shootings.	By decree, Mexico seizes 1,800 acres of land in Jalisco from its U.S. owners.	Chinese guerillas say they've inflicted heavy casualties on Japanese troops leaving China for Manchukuo by train. . . . Chinese troops bomb the air base at Anking. . . . Japanese gunboats approach Lungping on the Yangtze. Fighting rages on both sides of the river.
Aug. 5		Neither Japan nor the Soviets will cede the disputed territory, which was made part of Siberia in the 1886 Hunchin Treaty, negotiated with China. A four-hour artillery fight on the border takes many casualties.	Spanish insurgents drop hundreds of bombs on Sort at dawn. . . . Italy insists it will not persecute its 44,000 Jewish citizens: its stated goal is to prevent a "subrace of half-breeds."	As four more people die in Palestine, the British Commission has a new idea: reducing the proposed Jewish part of Palestine's division down to 400 square miles of the Sharon Valley. The Arab portion of the state, under the new plan, would remain under British rule. Every side hates the idea.		As Japanese troops leave north China for Manchukuo or Korea, and flooding halts most tanks and trucks, Chinese guerillas become more active, especially around Peiping, Tsientsin, and in Hopeh and Shansi provinces.
Aug. 6		Arriving at China's new capital of Chungking, Premier Kung cables Ambassador Koo in France. France has been assisting in Soviet negotiations for several days. Koo is instructed to stop France from helping make peace for the Soviets. China wants the Soviets to go to war, and diplomat Sun Ke is on his way to Moscow. . . . Russian planes bomb a Korean rail station.	After 11 days of fighting on the Ebro front, most of it without gain for either side, Spanish insurgents push forward with massive artillery bombardments followed by tanks and infantry. The rebels report 2,000 prisoners taken, and 6,000 casualties for the loyalists. They claim at least 5,000 government troops now hide in forests and hills, unable to rejoin their regiments. Loyalists deny this.			Flooding north of the Yangtze worsens, isolating cities and destroying farms and villages. . . . Twenty-seven Japanese bombers with 36 pursuit planes deal heavy damage to Hankow's airfield.

A	B	C	D	E
Includes developments that affect more than one world region, international organizations, and important meetings of world leaders.	Includes all domestic and regional developments in Europe, including the Soviet Union.	Includes all domestic and regional developments in Africa and the Middle East.	Includes all domestic and regional developments in Latin America, the Caribbean, and Canada.	Includes all domestic and regional developments in Asian and Pacific nations (and colonies).

U.S. Politics & Social Issues	U.S. Foreign Policy & Defense	Economics & Great Depression	Science, Technology & Nature	Culture, Leisure & Lifestyle	
A mustard gas bomb explodes at a Boston movie theater; no one is seriously hurt.		Governor Kraschel of Iowa orders the National Guard to stop the NLRB hearing of charges against the Maytag Company, because it might destroy the peace by "stirring people up."		On his 75th birthday, Henry Ford is awarded Germany's Grand Cross of the German Eagle, the first American to be so honored. Chancellor Adolf Hitler has long been an admirer of Ford.	Jul. 30
Sufi Abdul Hamid, who brought the "Don't Buy Where You Can't Work" campaign from Chicago and was sometimes called the Harlem Hitler, dies in a plane crash in view of hundreds of Sunday motorists in New York.					Jul. 31
		After nearly three months, the Harlan, Ky., trial of coal companies, with 55 defendants, ends in a mistrial. A decision on retrial will be made in September. . . . The National Labor Relations Board postpones its hearing against Maytag for 48 hours, avoiding a confrontation with Iowa's governor and National Guard.			Aug. 1
	The $2 million University of Shanghai, owned by the American Baptist Church, is still in Japanese hands and efforts to reclaim it have been futile.	Unions representing 914,000 rail workers formally reject the 15 percent wage cut proposed by railroad operators. The issues goes to the National Mediation Board in Washington, D.C.			Aug. 2
Agents reveal the purchase of a 50-room mansion on Madison Avenue in New York by Father Divine, for use as his residence.	Mexico refuses arbitration and argues that indemnities for seized land do not have to be—and cannot be—paid all at once. Mexico asks the United States to accept payment based on its ability and circumstances.			Entertainer Eddie Cantor, at a lunch honoring him for raising $500,000 for Jewish refugees, calls Henry Ford "a damned fool" for accepting a medal from Nazis.	Aug. 3
The Senate Civil Liberties Committee takes testimony in the steel strikes of last summer. Law enforcement and company officials admit to arming strikebreakers and company men.		Governor Kraschel of Iowa backs down, allowing both the NLRB hearing and the Maytag plant to reopen. The Committee for Industrial Organization union votes to reject a contract, but accept the 15 percent wage cut, and everyone returns to work.	Dr. Niels Bohr, addressing a body of anthropologists in Denmark, warns against racism and prejudice.	Warner Brothers negotiates with Selznick International to take over the production of Gone With the Wind. Norma Shearer has withdrawn, and Bette Davis is being considered for the role of Scarlett. . . . Pearl White dies in Paris at age 49 of cirrhosis of the liver. Injuries from her Perils of Pauline movie days left her dependent on drugs and alcohol for a relief from pain.	Aug. 4
		Harry Hopkins, head of the Works Progress Administration, promises off-season WPA jobs for the agricultural south.		A million people cheer "Wrong-Way" Douglas Corrigan during his ticker-tape parade in New York City.	Aug. 5
	A trade pact with the Soviet Union is renewed for a year, with a Soviet promise to purchase $40 million worth of goods from the United States in that time.			Twenty-year-old Bobby Riggs wins the Southampton Invitational for the second time, and will play in the Davis Cup tennis match.	Aug. 6

F	G	H	I	J
Includes elections, federal-state relations, civil rights and liberties, crime, the judiciary, education, healthcare, poverty, urban affairs, and population.	Includes formation and debate of U.S. foreign and defense policies, veterans affairs, and defense spending. (Relations with specific foreign countries are usually found under the region concerned.)	Includes business, labor, agriculture, taxation, transportation, consumer affairs, monetary and fiscal policy, natural resources, pollution, and accidents.	Includes worldwide scientific, medical, and technological developments, natural phenomena, U.S. weather, and natural disasters.	Includes the arts, religion, scholarship, communications media, sports, entertainment, fashions, fads, and social life.

	World Affairs	Europe	Africa & The Middle East	The Americas	Asia & The Pacific
Aug. 7	Soviet troops drive a wedge north of Changkufeng, trapping a Japanese force on a hill. Both sides claim to out-flank the other in the mountains.	A British freighter is sunk in a Spanish harbor after being bombed by insurgents in three separate raids. . . . The Soviet Union offers a home to 600 German and Italian soldiers in loyalist Spain's International Brigades. . . . The Soviets uncover a plot to form a separate republic in Azerbaijan, and indict 14 people. Industrial purges in the Soviet Union continue. Vice Commissar of Foreign Affairs Stomoniakoff, an expert in far eastern affairs, is removed from office; no reason given.	A 13-year-old Jewish girl, with a 17-year-old accomplice, throws a bomb at a bus, killing four Arabs and injuring 36.		Japanese and Chinese forces fight for the road at Susung as the Yangtze rises, flooding the area. It remains in Chinese hands.
Aug. 8	Japan's Ambassador again asks for a peaceful settlement. Commissar Litvinoff demands an end to Japanese attacks, and implies punitive reprisals may follow.	The Spanish insurgent Defense Ministry calls up 18-year-olds for service, confirming speculation that the rebels are short on manpower. . . . Reichsführer-SS Himmler sends prisoners from Dachau concentration camp to a small town near Linz, Austria, to begin work on Mauthausen concentration camp.	Britain's Colonial Secretary Mac-Donald pays a quick visit to Palestine before continuing on to Malta. His trip was kept secret.		A separatist plot in South China, led by Chen Chung-fu, is uncovered. It would have put the country under Japanese control without a fight. . . . After several days, Japanese troops retreat from attempts to take Shahochen near Poyang Lake. . . . In Canton, more than 100 people, many of them children, are killed as the cathedral is bombed. Leaflets from the Japanese promise 10 days of continuous bombing.
Aug. 9	Intense shelling along four miles of disputed border continues day and night, between Soviet and Japanese forces. . . . China again reports to the League of Nations, backed by evidence (autopsy reports), that the Japanese Army is using poison gas in China.	Spanish loyalists open a new offensive, crossing the Segre River between Lerida and Balaguer to invade insurgent territory. Rebels push for new territory in the Almaden region.	Islamic leaders in Iraq issue a fatwa to prepare for jihad in Palestine. Thousands of young men volunteer for the cause in Baghdad.		Canton's waterfront is shelled; 600 are killed in two days of bombing. . . . Near Poyang Lake, Japanese troops gain some territory south of Shahochen.
Aug. 10	After another day of heavy fighting and casualties, a truce is negotiated between the Soviets and Japan.	Spanish insurgents open floodgates above the Segre, halting further river crossings by loyalists. They push their own advance in Almaden 15 miles forward. . . . The synagogue in Nuremburg is destroyed.	Two cars driven by Palestinian Arabs are stopped in Syria. Police find dynamite, cartridge belts, and other munitions packed in them.	Mexico's 12 percent export tax goes into effect, with exceptions for industries like mining, that cannot stay competitive under the tax. . . . Costa Rica's government approves the proposed expropriation of and payment for an American power company. . . . Citizens of Bolivia and Paraguay vote to approve the Chaco Peace Treaty.	Twenty thousand Japanese reinforcements from Anwhei are ordered to Kiukiang, from where a drive on Hankow will begin. . . . Clouds cover Canton, sparing it from an air raid.
Aug. 11	A cease-fire goes into effect on the Siberian-Korean border. The casualties are never known. Japan claims that 1,200 Russians were killed, and 526 Japanese; the Soviets claim they lost 236 soldiers, and the Japanese 600.	Gen. Franco and his advisers are still studying the plan of the Non-Intervention Committee. All other parties have accepted the plan, which calls for a 45-day waiting period before volunteer soldiers are removed from Spain.			A raid of 27 Japanese planes on the Wuhan cities of Wuchang and Hanyang causes 400 casualties. Far south, in spite of cloud cover, bombs fall on Canton but few people are hurt. . . . Shahochen, 70 miles north of Nanchang, sees fierce fighting as a Japanese force tries to drive south.
Aug. 12		Germany speeds up the building of fortifications on its borders, calls up 750,000 reservists, and requisitions trucks and autos, all for "autumn maneuvers." Other countries are concerned.	Ten Arabs die in clashes between British troops and armed bands in northern Palestine. A member of the Jewish volunteers, acting as watchmen for small settlements, is fatally wounded.		Over 350 bombs are dropped on the same areas of the Wuhan cities by 72 Japanese planes. Casualties are estimated at 124 deaths, and 680 injuries. Wuchow in Kwangsi province, 120 miles west of Canton, is bombed by 20 planes.
Aug. 13		Finland admits 55 Austrian Jews, all destitute, after a Cabinet meeting on their fate. Their passports are invalid but a Jewish community in Helsingfors assumes responsibility for them. . . . Spanish insurgents capture Cabeza de Buey, 15 miles west of Almaden.	French authorities in Tunis lift martial law after several weeks. . . . In Palestine, a British officer and a Jewish couple are shot and killed; others are wounded in several incidents.		With reinforcements from Anking, Japanese troops advance to within 100 miles of Hankow, but are stopped in the hills near Juichang.
Aug. 14	Although both sides have retreated, the Soviets accuse Japan of advancing on Changkufeng Hill. The settlement between the countries has not been signed, as Japan is waiting for instructions from its government.	Barcelona suffers through four air raids since last night. Two Spanish insurgent columns converge on the Almaden region with its mercury mines. Further north, on the Ebro River, government forces claim to shoot down 18 rebel planes: Fiats, Heinkels, and Messerschmitts. . . . A French steamer traveling from Marseilles to Morocco strikes a mine and sinks but all aboard are rescued.	A band of 200 Arabs surrounds a Jewish settlement near Nahalal, but are forced away by police. Other bands in different areas burn three packing houses, uproot a grove of 400 trees, and fire guns. . . . Reactionary Jewish groups spread fear that Britain will sign a truce with Arabs, cutting off Jewish immigration to Palestine.		

A	B	C	D	E
Includes developments that affect more than one world region, international organizations, and important meetings of world leaders.	Includes all domestic and regional developments in Europe, including the Soviet Union.	Includes all domestic and regional developments in Africa and the Middle East.	Includes all domestic and regional developments in Latin America, the Caribbean, and Canada.	Includes all domestic and regional developments in Asian and Pacific nations (and colonies).

U.S. Politics & Social Issues	U.S. Foreign Policy & Defense	Economics & Great Depression	Science, Technology & Nature	Culture, Leisure & Lifestyle	
The Uptown Chamber of Commerce in New York agrees that a third of all retail jobs in Harlem will go to African Americans.		In California, four large unions withdraw from the CIO Industrial Union Council, denouncing its leader, Harry Bridges, as a Communist. The four unions are the International Ladies Garment Workers, United Auto Workers, United Rubber Workers, and United Shoe Workers.		Dramatist and teacher Constantine Stanislavsky dies in Moscow at age 75.	Aug. 7
		Eagle Pencil's strike ends with a contract. Dismissed workers will be rehired and all will get a 40-hour week.			Aug. 8
Father Divine brings 2,500 "angels" from Harlem to spend the day on his new estate on the Hudson River. . . . Senator Pope of Idaho, a New Deal supporter, is defeated for reelection, though Democrats do well in other primaries.		The ILGWU refuses to join a state labor coalition in New York, fueling rumors that it will withdraw from the CIO. . . . The NLRB certifies the Screen Writers Guild to bargain with movie producers.			Aug. 9
The President endorses a challenger in the U.S. Senate race in Georgia, rather than the Democratic incumbent.	Ecuador becomes the 18th nation to sign a reciprocal trade agreement with the United States . . . The United States and Britain agree to joint use of Canton and Enderbury Islands in the Pacific for communication and air travel stations.	The U.S. Attorney General's office investigates New York's fur industry and the Communist-led, CIO-affiliated fur workers' union, for anti-trust law violations. Contractors complain that the new labor contract is designed to cut them out of the fur business.			Aug. 10
The Congressional Committee on Un-American Activities meets for the first time, chaired by Texas Rep. Martin Dies.			A 3,985-mile flight ends in New York after 24 hours and 58 minutes. The *Brandenburg*, a Lufthansa airplane, is the first to cross the Atlantic from Berlin, westward, without stopping.		Aug. 11
Up to 500,000 Americans are in Nazi organizations or are sympathetic to them, the Dies Committee hears. Fritz Kuhn, head of the German American Bund, is suspected of being its ringleader, and of setting up espionage networks in the United States for the Reich.		The National Emergency Council's report on the south is made public. It states that 4 million, or half the families, live in inadequate housing. The average income is $314, compared to $604 in the north. The report is expected to generate new programs and legislation.			Aug. 12
Before the Dies Committee, John Frey, vice president of the American Federation of Labor, names 284 CIO members who are Communists, and claims 60 of the CIO's officers are or have been affiliated with the Communists. He promises more names, up to 500.		The Public Works Administration says it has approved 1 billion jobs in 40 days—all non-Federal projects.		Blues guitarist Robert Johnson is poisoned by a bartender at a roadhouse near Greenwood, Miss., and lingers for a few days before dying.	Aug. 13
			The return trip of the *Brandenburg* airplane sets another record from New York to Berlin: 19 hours and 54 minutes. . . . Snow falls in Yorkshire, England.		Aug. 14

F	G	H	I	J
Includes elections, federal-state relations, civil rights and liberties, crime, the judiciary, education, healthcare, poverty, urban affairs, and population.	Includes formation and debate of U.S. foreign and defense policies, veterans affairs, and defense spending. (Relations with specific foreign countries are usually found under the region concerned.)	Includes business, labor, agriculture, taxation, transportation, consumer affairs, monetary and fiscal policy, natural resources, pollution, and accidents.	Includes worldwide scientific, medical, and technological developments, natural phenomena, U.S. weather, and natural disasters.	Includes the arts, religion, scholarship, communications media, sports, entertainment, fashions, fads, and social life.

	World Affairs	Europe	Africa & The Middle East	The Americas	Asia & The Pacific
Aug. 15	All Japanese troops withdraw from Changkufeng while negotiators work.	Germany's "autumn maneuvers" begin. . . . Both sides in Spain's civil war agree to an exchange of prisoners, refugees, and political leaders, brokered by Britain. . . . The British-owned port of Gandia in Spain is shelled again.	In Palestine, nine Jews, some of them police, are killed in an ambush near Haifa. British troops arrive to battle the ambushers, killing seven of them. In other areas, bombs and sniper attacks injure several people. . . . The Woodhouse Commission meets in London to discuss the partition of Palestine.	Cuba's President Laredo Bru vetoes the Congress' Amnesty Bill, again.	Chinese troops retake Shahochen, along with supplies that the Japanese abandoned when they fell back to Kiukiang. Both sides still battle for Juichang. In this area, affected by the flooding of the Yangtze, up to 60 percent of the soldiers are ill with malaria, dysentery, or cholera.
Aug. 16		Belgium begins war games along its border with Germany and the Netherlands. . . . Near Almaden, Spain, 100 insurgent troops are caught by their enemies in a rail tunnel. They refuse to surrender and are killed by grenades thrown into the tunnel. . . . The Boerse, Germany's stock market, slumps.	Two executions take place in Palestine in two days, one of an Arab and one of a Jew. A bomb kills a British lieutenant and wounds other soldiers.	Mexico seizes three U.S.-owned estates, totaling 5,000 acres.	Communications are restored with Kuling. Hwangmei, 20 miles north of the Yangtze, has changed hands several times in the last week. . . . Chinese troops assault Japanese near Hangchow, capital of Chekiang, in Japanese hands for eight months. . . . Shanghai's International Settlement complains to the Japanese government about the behavior of local troops.
Aug. 17		In a 15-page report, Sudeten German Party representatives reject the Nationalities Statute of the Czech government. . . . A dock strike in Marseilles leads to spoilage of thousands of loads of food. The French government threatens to impose martial law. . . . Finland will allow no further Jewish immigrants; it has 100 and turns away 40 more who are about to sail from Germany. Switzerland lets 1,000 illegal immigrants stay, but warns it will close its borders if the trend continues. . . . Starting in 1939, all Jews in Germany must have Jewish names. Those that do not will add the monikers Israel or Sarah to their names.	An Arab gang attacks a prison camp and kidnaps the family of a Jewish inspector. Elsewhere in Palestine, two British officers are killed by a land mine. Snipers, bombs, beatings, and more land mines claim other casualties.		Both Japan and China reinforce their armies on the Yangtze; the Japanese in preparation for an attack on Hankow, the Chinese to block them. Japanese ships and planes bomb Chinese positions along the river, including Shahochen. . . . Changsha, capital of Hunan, is bombed, and suffers heavy casualties.
Aug. 18		Premier Negrín of Spain and a diplomat representing the insurgents are both in Zurich, Switzerland. . . . Viscount Runciman meets with Konrad Henlein, head of the SdP (German nationalist party). . . . Two Poles are beaten unconscious in Danzig for failing to salute a Nazi banner. Guns and ammunition are being smuggled into Danzig—enough, Polish sources claim, to arm a force of 25,000.	Arabs ambush a British military column near Acre, Palestine. Thirty-seven Arabs die, most in machine gun fire from airplanes, and two British soldiers die. . . . A bus leaving Lydda is stopped, its guard killed, and all passengers kidnapped. This and other fatal bombings, one involving a child, lead to a raid on Nablus by British troops, in which all homes and people are searched, and many are taken by authorities. Several Arabs and a British soldier die in clashes there.	To combat economic problems, Cuba starts a $6 million public works program, cuts government spending (including salaries) by 10 percent, commences price controls and promises to punish profiteers, and expels 50,000 West Indian workers.	All Japanese men between 24 and 34 without military training are ordered to "stand by" by the War Office. . . . The Hengyang airbase in Hunan, as well as Canton railways, are bombed. . . . 400 Japanese troops disembark on Amoy, near Tungan, where they are fought by Chinese defenders. Three Japanese ships with further reinforcements are near the coast.
Aug. 19		Swiss authorities send back hundreds of Austrian and German Jews who cross the border at night. They will admit no Jews without visas. . . . In Czechoslovakia, the Runciman mission informs citizens that ethnic Germans will be appointed to political offices in several districts, within two weeks. . . . Barcelona is hit with its heaviest air raid since March; over 150 people die there and in towns just to the south.	Hundreds of Arabs attack Hebron, Palestine, at night, taking control of a few government buildings and cutting phone lines. Troops from Jerusalem are sent into the fight. Other large fights start near Acre and the Plain of Sharon.		As reinforcements arrive, 1,000 Japanese troops push from Hwangmei toward Hankow, avoiding the main road and reaching Lungtou. Flooding in the area impedes their movements.
Aug. 20	Soviets protest to Japan that the crew of a Russian ship was tortured after being captured on May 31.	Finland sends 60 Jews, including those granted refuge on the 13th, back to Germany. . . . In Danzig, Nazis throw a Polish railroad officer from a speeding train. The man loses a hand and both feet.	In Palestine a curfew and added security is imposed on Jerusalem, due to rumors of an imminent Arab attack. Hebron, after a night of fighting, is under military rule. The children kidnapped on the 17th are released unharmed, but their parents are still held by Abu Durra, an Arab leader.		Japanese troops, many freshly arrived, mass along the Hupeh-Anwhei border for an assault on Hankow as floodwaters subside. Chinese forces claim to route Japanese troops landed from warships near Kiukiang. . . . Japanese authorities deny any losses to Chinese guerillas near Peiping, but daily reports tell of skirmishes outside city gates, and throughout the north.

A	B	C	D	E
Includes developments that affect more than one world region, international organizations, and important meetings of world leaders.	Includes all domestic and regional developments in Europe, including the Soviet Union.	Includes all domestic and regional developments in Africa and the Middle East.	Includes all domestic and regional developments in Latin America, the Caribbean, and Canada.	Includes all domestic and regional developments in Asian and Pacific nations (and colonies).

U.S. Politics & Social Issues	U.S. Foreign Policy & Defense	Economics & Great Depression	Science, Technology & Nature	Culture, Leisure & Lifestyle	
		The AFL challenges the NLRB decision of June 22, aligning Pacific Coast longshoremen with the CIO. If the NLRB does not reverse its decision, the AFL threatens to go to court. . . . The Ford Company files 573 objections to the NLRB's preliminary report on its labor practices in St. Louis. . . . As production increases, Ford calls 24,000 men back to work at the River Rouge plant, and 1,700 back in New Jersey.			Aug. 15
Defense attorneys request pardons for the five imprisoned Scottsboro defendants, but Alabama's Attorney General will only consider two cases. Time limits for appeals for the other three men have not expired yet. He promises a decision in 48 hours.	Secretary of State Cordell Hull proposes all nations adhere to seven points for international order and law. Economic reconstruction, adherence to treaties and international law, and disarmament are some of his points.	The Interstate Commerce Commission sets minimum trucking rates for the first time, in the New England and central states. . . . As of July 1, the PWA has approved over 4,000 projects for the year 1938, at an estimated cost exceeding $1 billion.		Robert Johnson dies. A collection of his recordings is released in 1961, leading to his reputation as the greatest blues guitarist of all time.	Aug. 16
Pardons for the Scottsboro defendants are unanimously denied by the state of Alabama. . . . Rep. Mason of the Dies Committee on Un-American Activities charges eight federal officials of being members of a Communist front organization. . . . The President urges defeat of Democratic incumbents in upcoming primaries in New York and Maryland, as they are against his New Deal. Roosevelt's interference is seen as instrumental in the defeat last month of Kentucky's governor. South Carolina's Senator Ellison Smith has been in office 30 years, but Roosevelt wants him purged as well.				Henry Armstrong bests Lou Ambers in a 15-round fight to be the first man to hold three boxing titles: featherweight, welterweight, and lightweight champion.	Aug. 17
	On a state visit to Canada, President Franklin Roosevelt assures the Dominion that the United States would defend its neighbor against any invasion. . . . Japan apologizes for incidents in Shanghai last week.				Aug. 18
At Philadelphia County Prison, 650 of 1,481 prisoners start a hunger strike over the poor food served.		The National Guard troops in Iowa are ordered home; the Maytag strike has been over for two weeks.	At the British Association for the Advancement of Science annual gathering, an inquest is conducted on the remains of 250,000-year-old Swanscombe Man (which in the 21st century, is thought to be Woman), discovered by a dentist three years ago.		Aug. 19
The American League for Peace and Democracy, which has 4 million members, is accused of being a Communist front organization before the Dies Committee.			Howard Hughes flies from Glendale, Calif., to New York in 10 hours, 32 minutes—a new record.	Lou Gehrig hits his 23rd career grand slam—a record that's never been matched. . . . Racehorse War Admiral surpasses the earnings record of his sire, Man O' War. War Admiral's earnings are $251,700.	Aug. 20

F	G	H	I	J
Includes elections, federal-state relations, civil rights and liberties, crime, the judiciary, education, healthcare, poverty, urban affairs, and population.	Includes formation and debate of U.S. foreign and defense policies, veterans affairs, and defense spending. (Relations with specific foreign countries are usually found under the region concerned.)	Includes business, labor, agriculture, taxation, transportation, consumer affairs, monetary and fiscal policy, natural resources, pollution, and accidents.	Includes worldwide scientific, medical, and technological developments, natural phenomena, U.S. weather, and natural disasters.	Includes the arts, religion, scholarship, communications media, sports, entertainment, fashions, fads, and social life.

	World Affairs	Europe	Africa & The Middle East	The Americas	Asia & The Pacific
Aug. 21	Japan protests to the Soviet Union that seven Soviet bombers flew over Korea yesterday. . . . In secret, Germany purchases two tanker-loads of Mexico's oil per month in exchange for newsprint. The first shipment leaves from a formerly British refinery in Tampico for Hamburg.	Gen. Franco, leader of the Spanish insurgency, rejects the plan to withdraw volunteers, put forward by the Non-Intervention Committee. This act also puts the Anglo-Italian treaty on hold till the Spanish civil war ends. . . . Admiral Horthy, Regent of Hungary, pays a state visit to the Reich. . . . In Polish cities, 15,000 demonstrate about the treatment of Poles in Danzig, following up on a diplomatic protest. . . . The Pope speaks out against "exaggerated nationalism."			Floods in northern Korea kill at least 363 people; 350 more are missing. The floods follow weeks of rain and have destroyed most communication and power lines. . . . Japan keeps the Yangtze River closed to international ships between Shanghai and Wuhu due to "military necessity." . . . Chinese guerillas attack Japanese outposts near Shanghai, including the Hungjao airport. A British citizen in the area is killed.
Aug. 22	The Mandates Commission of the League of Nations publishes a report criticizing Britain for the situation in Palestine. The report mentions restrictions on Jewish immigration, and concern over the unforeseen violence. . . . Reporters investigating the floods near Yuki, Korea, see evidence of shelling and machine gunning from the recent border dispute between Japan and the Soviet Union.	The German government in Austria unveils justifications for holding criminal trials of former leaders in Vienna. Evidence will show the corruption and cruelty of the former regime, it is claimed.			Japan renews an attack south of the Yangtze. Towns around Poyang Lake are attacked. After intense fighting at Juichang, China claims that Japan uses poison gas to disable defenders and take the city. . . . Chinese guerillas open fire on Japanese positions on the western edge of Shanghai with machine guns, but are driven off. Shanghai's International Settlement sees three more assassinations of Chinese collaborators.
Aug. 23	Courts in the Netherlands say that the origin of the oil on freighters from Mexico has not been proved, and so it will not hold the ships. Oil companies, who lost property in Mexico's expropriations, will appeal.	In Germany, Jews or men married to Jews can no longer access their safe deposit boxes, unless accompanied by police. License plates will identify cars owned by Jews. . . . The Little Entente (Yugoslavia, Romania, and Czechoslovakia) meets in Bled, Yugoslavia. They agree on mutual nonaggression with Hungary, even while Hungary's leader is visiting Germany. . . . Italy begins its census of Jews in that country, putting their number at 57,425.	British police in Palestine confront an Arab band near Cana. Fourteen Arabs are killed, and munitions seized.		Gen. Chen Cheng in Hankow orders the dissolution of all Communist student and worker organizations. . . . Japan moves its army headquarters in China from Shanghai to Nanking. . . . Japanese troops enter Juichang, west of Kiukiang on the Yangtze River.
Aug. 24		German papers deny that Hungary has made any deal with the Little Entente, but says instead that Germany will guarantee Hungary's borders against aggression. . . . Ten former officials in Azerbaijan are sentenced to death by the Soviets. . . . The Spanish government arrests four men on an American ship as spies. Insurgents claim to make progress against the loyalists near the Ebro River, but the fighting is costly for both sides. Loyalists claim to have shot down more than 30 insurgent planes of Italian and German manufacture in two days.	A band of Arabs takes a cache of weapons from the police station in Lydda, Palestine. . . . A British Commissioner is shot by Arabs and later dies in Jenin. A 22-hour curfew is imposed on Jenin, and police search the town.		Japanese planes shoot down a passenger plane 30 minutes after it leaves Hong Kong. The plane is machine-gunned repeatedly and forced into water, where it sinks. Only three men, including the American pilot, make it to land. The 14 others, including women and children, are shot or drown. . . . The loss of freight and munitions from Canton, destroyed by 13 days of bombing, is having an effect on troops in central China.
Aug. 25	The 12th European Minority Congress meets in Stockholm. Jews do not attend. One delegate mocks the League of Nations, saying that minorities were worse off for its sabotage.	Britain instructs Lord Runciman to advise the Czech government to give complete autonomy to the German Sudetens. . . . French Premier Daladier tells his party that the Reich's mobilization of two million men faces them with a situation unknown since 1914, necessitating longer workweeks. . . . Gen. Franco says that his planes will bomb any convoys carrying gasoline from France into Spain. On average, 100 such trucks carry fuel each day.	While sniping and sabotage incidents go on, Arab terrorists make it known that they intend to ruin the orange crop and continue their violence through the winter.		Japan will not guarantee the safety of civilian aircraft flying over China, but will not target foreign-owned airlines. The aircraft shot down yesterday had a 51 percent Chinese ownership. . . . Flooding in northern Korea has claimed 943 lives and destroyed at least 4,463 houses.
Aug. 26	Japan holds the crew of 13 from a Soviet ship that ran aground near Hokkaida.	Spanish government troops continue to hold back insurgents, both at the Ebro River and near Almaden, where the rebels are stuck at Cabeza del Buey. . . . SdP (German nationalist party) head Henlein inflames Germans in Czechoslovakia, demanding rights of self-defense. Clashes between Germans and Czechs are set off through the weekend.	In Jaffa, Palestine, 23 Arabs, including two children, die and 70 are wounded in a bombing at a market. A riot ensues; police stations and Jewish-owned businesses are vandalized. Several people are struck by bullets before order is restored. Tanks and armored cars patrol the streets, and machine-gun nests guard the area between Tel Aviv and Jaffa.		Japanese authorities censor news of the high rates of disease plaguing their troops, but malaria, dysentery, and cholera are epidemic. In central China, the temperatures approach 100°F, and dead bodies and waste lie all around. . . . Out of Shansi, the report comes that 40 walled towns and 800 villages, or 650,000 homes, have been burned, leaving two million people homeless. Seventy thousand have been executed by the Japanese.

A	B	C	D	E
Includes developments that affect more than one world region, international organizations, and important meetings of world leaders.	*Includes all domestic and regional developments in Europe, including the Soviet Union.*	*Includes all domestic and regional developments in Africa and the Middle East.*	*Includes all domestic and regional developments in Latin America, the Caribbean, and Canada.*	*Includes all domestic and regional developments in Asian and Pacific nations (and colonies).*

U.S. Politics & Social Issues	U.S. Foreign Policy & Defense	Economics & Great Depression	Science, Technology & Nature	Culture, Leisure & Lifestyle	
					Aug. 21
Four ringleaders of the Philadelphia County Prison hunger strike, placed in an isolation area called Klondike, are found dead. Investigators claim they died by violence, and probably killed each other. Coroners are skeptical. Twenty-one other strikers were also in isolation cells.	Secretary of State Cordell Hull sends a new note to Mexico about property seizures without compensation, calling them "unadulterated confiscation." He demands that Mexico pay for the $10 million in farm and ranch-land recently taken.	Although there has been no boycott, the Commerce Department says U.S. imports from Japan are down 47 percent for the first half of 1938. . . . Acting on an April complaint against the Ford Company in Long Beach, Calif., the NLRB recommends rehiring of 450 UAW members, with back wages.			**Aug. 22**
Investigators declare that stifling steam heat killed four prisoners in Philadelphia County Prison, and left others of the 21 survivors near death. Two guards are arrested. Police imply that up to eight more may face arrest.			The British Association for the Advancement of Science discusses Dr. Broom's discovery in June of a new skeleton: *Australopithecus (Paranthropus) robustus.* Sir Arthur Keith, a leader in the field, says the discovery has destroyed what scientists thought they knew about "drawing the line between anthropoid and man."		**Aug. 23**
		In California, a freight car loaded by nonunion workers is being hauled from city to city in the San Francisco area. For 10 days, picket lines form wherever it appears. Workers refuse to cross the CIO picket lines, are discharged, and their warehouse shuts down.			**Aug. 24**
		Seventy-nine warehouses in the San Francisco area shut down. Businesses that rely on them also close. Two thousand of the 8,000 warehouse workers are laid off. . . . CIO head John L. Lewis tries to make peace in the UAW, where many officers have been ousted.	A hurricane hits the Yucatan, and all communication with Cozumel Island is lost.	MGM will distribute *Gone With the Wind,* and will loan Clark Gable to David Selznick for the picture. . . . Author Aleksandr Kuprin dies in Moscow.	**Aug. 25**
	In Tokyo, the U.S. Ambassador delivers a note of "emphatic objection" over the attack on a passenger airplane in China.	Twenty-one more warehouses close in San Francisco—fully 50 percent of all warehouses there. The closures aggravate a threatened strike by retail clerks; the Retailers Council refuses to negotiate. . . . Secretary of Agriculture Henry Wallace announces that the government will start buying surplus wheat, both for export and relief.		Nobel Prize-winning physicist Erwin Schrödinger is fired from the University of Graz in Austria for political reasons.	**Aug. 26**

F	G	H	I	J
Includes elections, federal-state relations, civil rights and liberties, crime, the judiciary, education, healthcare, poverty, urban affairs, and population.	Includes formation and debate of U.S. foreign and defense policies, veterans affairs, and defense spending. (Relations with specific foreign countries are usually found under the region concerned.)	Includes business, labor, agriculture, taxation, transportation, consumer affairs, monetary and fiscal policy, natural resources, pollution, and accidents.	Includes worldwide scientific, medical, and technological developments, natural phenomena, U.S. weather, and natural disasters.	Includes the arts, religion, scholarship, communications media, sports, entertainment, fashions, fads, and social life.

	World Affairs	Europe	Africa & The Middle East	The Americas	Asia & The Pacific
Aug. 27		Sir John Simon, speaking for the British government, says war in Czechoslovakia could quickly spread to the rest of Europe, and Britain could be involved. . . . Insurgent ships fire on a Spanish warship for two hours in the Strait of Gibraltar. A direct hit kills 32 men—24 of them rebel prisoners. The disabled vessel makes it to port. . . . The French Premier receives the support he needs to override the 40-hour law, although the law itself will not be changed.	Under heavy guard, two new colonies are founded in Palestine for Jews from the Third Reich. . . . In Jaffa, Tul Karm, Nablus, Gaza, and other areas, isolated violence results in death for youths, police, British troops, Arabs, and Jews. Property is burned and looted. Newspapers hint at the possible involvement of Nazi Germany in Arab unrest and funding.		Japanese planes bomb Chinese positions near Kiukiang and Poyang Lake all day. Forces in the area have been fighting with little gain for over a month; the Japanese want to move tanks and infantry south for an assault on Nanchang.
Aug. 28		Former Minister Prieto of Spain says the entire world betrayed and abandoned the elected government. . . . A letter from the College of Bishops is read in Catholic churches throughout Germany. It demands the end of attacks on Christianity by the Nazis. . . . SdP (German nationalist party) leader Henlein cancels his speeches at Lord Runciman's request. The two meet; Runciman tells Henlein to cease his rhetoric calling for self-defense. . . . France moves troops to its borders with Germany and Italy for maneuvers.	Two Greek monks, kidnapped a week ago, are found dead near Tul Karm. Arab bands attack Arab and Jewish villages, and burn rail stations. The violence is moving southward from northern Palestine.	Mexican newspaper *El Universal* reveals that once, when President Lázaro Cárdenas ordered the expropriation of land for farmers, the owner was reimbursed 100,000 gold pesos. The owner was the head of the Federal Agriculture Department.	The death of the Regent of Tibet and a subsequent army revolt—which failed—is reported by missionaries. . . . Japanese troops are not able to overcome the Chinese, and their drives, both north and south, stall five miles from Juichang.
Aug. 29		Uniformed Nazis raid and vandalize a Danzig synagogue, while police refuse to intervene. . . . Britain announces Royal Navy maneuvers, starting September 5.	Most violence today is caused by Arab gangs, attacking or sniping at both Jewish and Arab villages or buses. Fatalities and injuries result. Troops find dynamite and ammunition loaded in a taxi near Nablus.		Chinese guerillas raid Hungjao, a Shanghai suburb, and burn bridges near the golf club where the Japanese Ambassador and his guests are playing.
Aug. 30		After long debate, Britain empowers its Ambassador to warn Germany against starting a war. . . . France reaffirms its decision to defend Czechoslovakia. . . . European currencies tumble on war fears. . . . Barbed wire is strung by Switzerland along its border with Austria, to stop the illegal night crossings of Jews. . . . Luxemburg closes its border to Jews.			Japan claims great advances, not just in its push from Juichang but in Anwhei, capturing many towns in a drive west to Honan. Subsequent reports cast doubt on these claims. . . . Chinese bombs hit the American ship *President Hoover*, killing one man and injuring others.
Aug. 31		A group of Austrian Jews, living on a barge on the Danube for months and refused entry to other countries, is told the mooring ropes will be cut in six days if they don't leave Hungarian waters. . . . Greece allows passage of a train carrying 760 visa-less Jews bound for Palestine. . . . Members of the International Brigades in Spain, offered furloughs by the government, leave for France. . . . Hungary announces it will not sign the accord with the Little Entente, announced on the 23rd until Czechoslovakia has resolved its military problems.	Snipers continue to take lives, both Jew and Arab, in Palestine.		Chinese troops celebrate the containment of Japanese assaults, saying that the Japanese lost 3,000 troops in their attempt to break through defenses near Juichang. . . . An air raid on Fungshun in Canton province kills at least 200 noncombatants.
Sept. 1	This month, over 1,000 Koreans die in flooding in the area fought over by Japan and the Soviet Union last month.	France begins training new draftees; within four days it expects to have 825,000 in its army. . . . All Jews in Italy, even citizens, who entered the country since 1919 must leave within six months. An estimated 20,000 people are affected. . . . Religious and private schools in Germany must close down by September 19. . . . A British commission studies 46 air attacks on Alicante, Spain, by insurgents, and judges that five targeted civilians exclusively.		President Lázaro Cárdenas responds to Secretary Hull's note as he opens Mexico's Congress, saying the U.S. demand would force the weak to obey the will of the strong. Cárdenas says that land seizures will continue, and payment will be made in accordance with Mexico's laws.	British and French residents of Tsientsin are ordered to leave in two weeks by Japanese authorities. The order is rescinded within two days, then completely denied.
Sept. 2	As stipulated in the treaty between France and Turkey, the Sanjak of Alexandretta becomes the autonomous Republic of Hatay.	Italy bars all Jewish teachers and students from Italian schools. . . . Spanish coastal cities are bombarded almost every day by insurgent planes or ships.	In Jaffa and in Jerusalem, Palestine, bullets and bombs are used against Jews and Arabs, but the perpetrators are Arab. A mosque is set ablaze.		Japanese pilots bomb Wuchow in Kwangsi province, targeting the university as they did last week.
Sept. 3	The International Communist League founds a new organization, the Fourth International, in France, backed by Leon Trotsky's followers who were disappointed in Stalin's domination of the Third International.	Anti-Jewish rioting and expulsion of Jews have been occurring for weeks or more in the Soviet Union, in White Russia, the Ukraine, and Kiev.		Brazil tries 175 Integralistas for their parts in the May attempt to take over the government. Sixteen men are acquitted, and 159 get prison terms of up to 10 years.	

A	B	C	D	E
Includes developments that affect more than one world region, international organizations, and important meetings of world leaders.	*Includes all domestic and regional developments in Europe, including the Soviet Union.*	*Includes all domestic and regional developments in Africa and the Middle East.*	*Includes all domestic and regional developments in Latin America, the Caribbean, and Canada.*	*Includes all domestic and regional developments in Asian and Pacific nations (and colonies).*

U.S. Politics & Social Issues	U.S. Foreign Policy & Defense	Economics & Great Depression	Science, Technology & Nature	Culture, Leisure & Lifestyle	
	On the 10th anniversary of the Kellogg-Briand Pact, Secretary of State Cordell Hull reminds the United States that war's cost is high, even for victors. Others point out an unintended consequence of the Pact: undeclared wars in China and Spain. Since the Pact was signed, 2.5 million have died in war.	AFL president William Green invites "disillusioned" CIO affiliates to rejoin the AFL. . . . The United Mine Workers sign a contract with the Harlan County Coal Operators Association in Kentucky, setting wages and hours. The NLRB drops charges against 16 companies as part of the agreement. The Department of Justice, though, will not drop its charges. . . . The WPA rolls hit 3,066,953 this week—a new record.	Britain's Capt. George Eyston breaks the land speed record again, driving a car 345.49 miles per hour at the Bonneviille Salt Flats in Utah. . . . As northeast Mexico faces a tropical storm, a tornado hits Rhode Island, ripping off roofs.		Aug. 27
	Every day, 100 emigrants from the Reich enter the United States as political refugees. The embassy in Berlin accepts no more applications from Jews, as the quota for the next two years is filled.	UAW members in Wisconsin, Minnesota, and north Illinois—46,000 strong—separate from the CIO. . . . In San Francisco, union leaders accuse warehouse owners of conspiracy in trying to crush the CIO union.			Aug. 28
		John L. Lewis of the CIO is asked to stop interfering in the UAW by its members.	Major de Seversky sets a new east-to-west record, crossing the United States in 10 hours and 3 minutes. . . . Moons number 10 and 11 are discovered orbiting Jupiter.		Aug. 29
"Cotton Ed" Smith of South Carolina keeps his Senate seat of 30 years.		A truce is struck in San Francisco by the Council of 43, a group of business leaders, with CIO West Coast leader Harry Bridges. Thirty-one hundred workers are idled by the warehouse closures.		Max Factor dies in Beverly Hills, Calif., at age 61.	Aug. 30
	Japan repudiates responsibility in the shooting down of a Chinese passenger plane, saying the United States is an uninvolved third party.	Attempts to mediate a wage dispute between railway workers and employers collapse as unions reject the compromise solution.			Aug. 31
The inquest into four prisoner deaths at Philadelphia County Prison in Holmesburg, Pa., reveals that turning on steam heat in the isolation block was standard treatment.		Three hundred members of the Workers Alliance riot before a relief agency in Brooklyn, demanding more adequate funds.	Tokyo is hit by its worst typhoon since 1905, leaving 175 dead and many missing; the initial damage estimate is $28 million. . . . Mayor LaGuardia of New York City announces that United, TWA, Pan American, and other airlines will begin service at a North Beach airport now being built with Works Progress Administration (WPA) funds.	Frank Capra's You Can't Take It with You is released in theaters.	Sept. 1
A coroner's jury holds 12 guards and two prison administrators responsible for the Holmesburg prisoner deaths, due to criminal negligence. The case goes to a grand jury.					Sept. 2
			Jacqueline Cochrane beats nine men to win the Bendix trophy in an air race from Los Angeles to Cleveland, Ohio, and on to Bendix, N.J.		Sept. 3

F	G	H	I	J
Includes elections, federal-state relations, civil rights and liberties, crime, the judiciary, education, healthcare, poverty, urban affairs, and population.	Includes formation and debate of U.S. foreign and defense policies, veterans affairs, and defense spending. (Relations with specific foreign countries are usually found under the region concerned.)	Includes business, labor, agriculture, taxation, transportation, consumer affairs, monetary and fiscal policy, natural resources, pollution, and accidents.	Includes worldwide scientific, medical, and technological developments, natural phenomena, U.S. weather, and natural disasters.	Includes the arts, religion, scholarship, communications media, sports, entertainment, fashions, fads, and social life.

	World Affairs	Europe	Africa & The Middle East	The Americas	Asia & The Pacific
Sept. 4		Hungary's Premier Imrédy announces new programs for rearmament, compulsory military training, anti-Semitic laws, labor camps, and more. . . . Jewish doctors will be barred from practice in Danzig as of October 1. . . . Ten people die and many more are injured when a Royal Air Force plane crashes into homes in a London suburb.	A university student is held in Cairo after a shot is fired in a crowd, near Egypt's King Farouk.	Mexico delivers a formal diplomatic note to the United States, affirming that land seizures may continue without immediate payment. . . . Between 10,000 and 20,000 Nazis parade in Santiago, Chile, supporting their presidential candidate.	A Japanese troop train in Shansi province is blown up by Chinese guerillas, killing scores of men. . . . Riots between Muslims and Buddhists erupt again in Rangoon, Burma. Ten people die and 40 are injured.
Sept. 5	Sir Neill Malcolm, the League of Nations' High Commissioner for Refugees from Germany, publishes a report, stressing the large numbers of Jews, Catholics, and non-Aryans who will be forced to leave Germany, and the inadequate response of nations so far.	The Czech Parliament drafts a last offer to the Sudeten Party, to be delivered tomorrow. . . . France cancels all military leave and masses soldiers along the Maginot Line. . . . German troops conduct practice maneuvers on their side of the Rhine. Alarmed, the Belgian Cabinet asks King Leopold to return early from his vacation in Italy.	In Palestine, an Arab Sheikh is shot and killed, as well as a Jewish railroad foreman and a clerk. The killers of all are presumed to be Arab snipers.	In Santiago, Chile, an armed fascist group takes over several office buildings near the presidential palace. After four hours of artillery and machine gun fire, the rebels, mostly Nazis, surrender. At least 100 bodies are removed from the buildings; over 50 are wounded.	Japanese planes again attack a passenger airplane, this one near the western border of Kuangtung. The plane lands safely with 10 bullet holes in the fuselage. Japan estimates that 10,000 Chinese troops have died during the last week of fighting near the Yangtze River, most at Poyang Lake.
Sept. 6		The British fleet begins maneuvers in the North Sea. . . . After striking dockworkers reject a final offer, France puts the port of Marseilles under military control. . . . The Sudeten Party makes no response to the latest Czech government offer, and seems to be stalling.	Six Arabs are killed in confrontations with British troops in Palestine. Three others die as victims of snipers, and six Jews die as well. Arrests, vandalism, and injuries occur throughout the country.	Chilean police raid Nazi headquarters, confiscate explosives, and arrest hundreds of Nazis in the country.	
Sept. 7		Czech Sudeten Party leader Henlein confers with Adolf Hitler, then leaves Nuremburg abruptly. . . . France's General Confederation of Labor, representing five million workers, pledges to work for national defense.	The aunt of King Farouk of Egypt, who owns the Khan al-Khalili bazaar in Cairo, serves a 30-day notice to shopowners. Modern buildings are planned to replace the 600-year-old market, though this never happens. . . . South Africa announces defense plans that will cost $6 million over three years.		
Sept. 8		Finland approaches Sweden for aid in bolstering defenses in the Åland Islands. . . . Greece forbids all preaching, except on behalf of the Orthodox religion. Violators, including missionaries, can be fined, imprisoned, or expelled.			
Sept. 9	The League of Nations starts its 102nd Council session. . . . Britain and France file protests over China's refusal to set up a "safety zone" in Hankow. . . . Charles Lindbergh meets with French Air Minister La Chambre and tells him of German air strength. His words are taken to the Prime Minister.	At Nuremburg, Chancellor Adolf Hitler declares that Germany will "capitulate to no one." This is interpreted as a response to Britain's stated willingness to go to war if Czechoslovakia is attacked.	In spite of rigid curfews, Arab bands nightly attack police stations to steal arms, barricade roads, and cut communication lines in Palestine. Jewish settlements are also attacked nightly, but local guards are usually able to drive off the terrorists.		Japanese troops advance on Hwangchwan. . . . Demonstrations in Chinese cities demand action from the League of Nations. . . . Twenty thousand women are ordered to leave Hankow for safety.
Sept. 10		Sudeten Party leaders and Czech Premier Hodza meet to reopen negotiations, but little is accomplished. Disorder is reported in most cities. President Benes gives a radio address, urging cooperation and calm.			Two columns of Japanese troops far north of Hankow, in Honan province, push west and intend to converge on the city from the north.
Sept. 11		Sudeten Party members demonstrate and cry "Sieg Heil!" and other Nazi slogans in cities throughout Czechoslovakia. Minor incidents of violence occur. . . . Britain makes its position clear to Germany: a war with Czechoslovakia will not be quick, and France and Britain may enter the fight.	Six Jewish constables are killed in an ambush by an Arab band.		Japanese troops fight a 24-hour battle south of Kiukiang, with heavy artillery, air raids, and—the Chinese claim—gas attacks, but the Chinese defenses hold. . . . Fresh Japanese troops are moved into the areas north of Hankow.
Sept. 12	The League of Nations Assembly meets for the 19th time.	Chancellor Hitler's closing speech at the Nuremburg Rally says democracies oppress minorities, as in Czechoslovakia. He calls President Benes a liar and demands self-determination for the Sudeten Germans. . . . Mobs in Czechoslovakia bomb schools, ransack buildings and loot Jewish- and Czech-owned businesses. . . . Switzerland mines the bridges and tunnels near its borders to guard against invaders.		As the number of arrested Nazis and confiscated arms grow, the Chilean Cabinet resigns. Congress approves the declaration of a "state of siege" giving President Alessandri special powers.	

A	B	C	D	E
Includes developments that affect more than one world region, international organizations, and important meetings of world leaders.	Includes all domestic and regional developments in Europe, including the Soviet Union.	Includes all domestic and regional developments in Africa and the Middle East.	Includes all domestic and regional developments in Latin America, the Caribbean, and Canada.	Includes all domestic and regional developments in Asian and Pacific nations (and colonies).

U.S. Politics & Social Issues	U.S. Foreign Policy & Defense	Economics & Great Depression	Science, Technology & Nature	Culture, Leisure & Lifestyle	
			Anthony LeVier of California wins the Greve Trophy and sets a new air speed record of 250.88 miles per hour.		Sept. 4
			A second typhoon hits Japan's Shikoku Island, where casualties are light. . . . American Roscoe Turner wins the 300-mile Thompson Trophy air race and sets a speed record of 283.419 miles per hour.	Donald Budge clinches the Davis Cup for the United States, playing against Australian Adrian Quist.	Sept. 5
	Agents for foreign clients who promote, publicize, or engage in political activities or public relations have 30 days to register with the State Department, under a new law.	The National Labor Relations Board tells the Ford Motor Company to bargain with the CIO and reinstate 129 employees in Richmond, Calif. Ford has 10 days to comply.			Sept. 6
		Police keep order as mass picketing begins in San Francisco. Six thousand retail clerks, mostly women, strike 27 department stores.	A synthetic version of vitamin E is announced by Swiss scientists at the American Chemical Society meeting. They beat a Minnesota team working on the same problem by three days.	W.C. Fields is offered $150,000 to play the Wizard of Oz in the movie, according to the papers.	Sept. 7
The President ignores a request for more clerks, investigators, and attorneys to help the Dies Committee on Un-American Activities.		Small fights break out and a store executive is beaten in San Francisco's retail clerks strike. . . . General Motors calls back 24,000 workers to plants in Flint, Mich., gearing up production.		Boys Town with Spencer Tracy is released.	Sept. 8
	While not giving specifics on foreign policy, the President says the idea that the United States simply allies with Great Britain on current issues against Germany is completely wrong.	Railroads announce that a 15 percent wage cut will take place October 1; but they expect the President to appoint a commission that will delay the action.		Lou Gehrig plays his 2,100th consecutive game, and hits the ball four times. . . . A Sister's Memoir, by Asia Booth Clark, sister of John Wilkes Booth, is published 64 years after being written.	Sept. 9
A Republican rally that promised a free meal in Pittsburgh, Pa., is mobbed and overrun by 55,000 people.					Sept. 10
		Bomb blasts at seven New York City fur shops reopen labor disputes.			Sept. 11
		In Long Beach, Calif., Ford Company answers an NLRB decision by claiming it was denied a full and fair hearing. Ford also says that former employees could not be reinstated as the plant closed (temporarily) on September 4. . . . San Francisco retailers issue an ultimatum to salespersons, demanding they accept a new contract. They refuse, and will not cross the retail clerks' picket lines.			Sept. 12

F	G	H	I	J
Includes elections, federal-state relations, civil rights and liberties, crime, the judiciary, education, healthcare, poverty, urban affairs, and population.	Includes formation and debate of U.S. foreign and defense policies, veterans affairs, and defense spending. (Relations with specific foreign countries are usually found under the region concerned.)	Includes business, labor, agriculture, taxation, transportation, consumer affairs, monetary and fiscal policy, natural resources, pollution, and accidents.	Includes worldwide scientific, medical, and technological developments, natural phenomena, U.S. weather, and natural disasters.	Includes the arts, religion, scholarship, communications media, sports, entertainment, fashions, fads, and social life.

	World Affairs	Europe	Africa & The Middle East	The Americas	Asia & The Pacific
Sept. 13		France consults with Britain, and admits to being unprepared for war. . . . Martial law is declared in the German Sudeten districts in Czechoslovakia. The Sudeten Party demands it be lifted in six hours. . . . France and Britain urge President Benes to hold an election as the Sudeten Party demands.			
Sept. 14	Japan declares it will support its ally, Germany, in case of hostilities. Foreigners and businesses in the international areas of Chinese cities are alarmed. . . . German and Italian funds support the Arab terrorists in Palestine, journalists report. Funding from Arabs in Iran, Iraq, and Syria is minimal.	In the last two days, 13 Czechs—10 of them police—and 10 ethnic Germans die in clashes, which are termed riots by some and attempts at revolution by others. At Sudeten Party offices, stockpiles of ammunition are found. . . . British Prime Minister Chamberlain announces he will fly to Germany, an unprecedented move that surprises all.	In Palestine, snipers kill and wound several Jews, including doctors and police. Others are killed by mines, or are beaten to death. Ten Arabs die when their bus hits a land mine; more die or are wounded by bullets in different towns.	Four thousand copper miners strike in Sonora, Mexico. In the state of Coahuila, 4,500 coal miners have been on strike for two weeks.	Japanese forces announce the capture of Matowchen, on the Yangtze River.
Sept. 15		Prime Minister Chamberlain meets with Chancellor Hitler at Berchtesgaden. He learns that Germany is willing to start a world war to annex Czechoslovakia. . . . Thousands of armed Sudeten Germans riot in Schwaderbach and other border cities; many are killed and injured. . . . Konrad Henlein and other Sudeten Party leaders escape across the border to Germany. The Czech government issues an arrest warrant for Henlein as a traitor.	At Tetuan, Spanish Morocco, 35 people die in rioting between anti-government insurgents and Moroccans, and over 400 are arrested. . . . Britain moves 8,000 troops to Palestine, many from India.	Chilean President Alessandri refuses to accept the resignations of his Cabinet members, saying that the country needs a working government to get through the current crisis. All but three ministers withdraw their resignations.	Journalists in China are shown containers of four different gases, captured from Japanese troops. A little gas is released from one, to demonstrate its effectiveness; reporters cough and have sore throats for an hour.
Sept. 16	In the midst of the Czech crisis, Britain asks the League of Nations to make military and economic sanctions optional to members. The sanctions will be invoked automatically in case of aggression. . . . China's delegate asks the League to employ Article XVII, embargo arms, and force Japan to stop the use of gas and of bombing civilian targets.	Czechoslovakia outlaws the Sudeten Party and prepares for war. By nightfall, newspapers report 23,000 "persecuted" Sudeten Germans cross the border into Germany. . . . Insurgent planes bomb Barcelona and its harbor, killing more than 30 and damaging four British ships. . . . The Red Cross will distribute flour for bread throughout Spain, starting in October.	A two-day battle in the hills near El Ghassania, Palestine, where two Arab bands were celebrating an accord, leaves three dead and several wounded. British troops attack with planes and artillery.	Chile's government investigates a second Nazi plot, without revealing details. Nazi operatives are still in hiding.	A delegate to the League of Nations says 1 million Chinese have died in the undeclared war, and 30 million have been wounded or made homeless.
Sept. 17		Czech leaders—who have been excluded from deals and discussions about their country's fate—reject the plebiscite proposed by Lord Runciman, saying it would lead to civil war. Martial law is imposed on the entire country and relative calm is restored. . . . Germany's media reports that 37,000 have fled across Czech borders with tales of atrocities.	Arab bands take over Bethlehem; Arab police join the invaders and the small British force withdraws.		
Sept. 18		French Prime Minister Daladier and Foreign Minister Bonnet meet with their British counterparts in London. They decide to advise the Czech government to accept Germany's demand, give up all territories with a majority of Germans, and nullify all current treaties and alliances. . . . Chancellor Hitler calls the Czech situation a tumor that poisons all Europe, and is impatient to act.			
Sept. 19	Spain's Foreign Minister del Vayo excoriates the League of Nations for their inaction, not just toward Spain but China, Austria, and now Czechoslovakia. . . . The Seventh International Management Conference meets in Washington, D.C., with 2,000 delegates from 21 countries.	Czechoslovakia's people express incredulity and betrayal as the advice offered by France and Britain is made public. The government asks France if it will stand by its defense commitment, if Czechoslovakia rejects the Anglo-France plan. . . . A strike of 75,000 building trade workers begins in Paris, but defense workers remain on their jobs.			South of the Yangtze, the Japanese advance is stalled 10 miles west of Juichang. Pilots drop glass containers of gas on Chinese positions.
Sept. 20	The League of Nations debates on Palestine, and the bombing of civilians by air. Japan is invited to participate in the League's discussions about Article XVII.	Premier Hodza rejects the plan of Britain and France, requesting arbitration under the Locarno Treaty. Britain and France find this unacceptable. . . . The Hungarian Premier and the Polish Ambassador visit Chancellor Hitler, staking their claims to Czech provinces with large minorities. . . . German officials hint that the Fuhrer may raise his demands.			

A	B	C	D	E
Includes developments that affect more than one world region, international organizations, and important meetings of world leaders.	Includes all domestic and regional developments in Europe, including the Soviet Union.	Includes all domestic and regional developments in Africa and the Middle East.	Includes all domestic and regional developments in Latin America, the Caribbean, and Canada.	Includes all domestic and regional developments in Asian and Pacific nations (and colonies).

U.S. Politics & Social Issues	U.S. Foreign Policy & Defense	Economics & Great Depression	Science, Technology & Nature	Culture, Leisure & Lifestyle	
		The Sudeten Party ultimatum in Europe sends the stock market down several points, as heavy selling closes the day. . . . San Francisco Mayor Rossi works on compromises to end the retail clerks strike.			Sept. 13
A visit by the Ku Klux Klan, complete with cross burnings, fails to keep African Americans from voting in Starke, Bradford County, Fla.	Unofficially, U.S. Consulates in Europe advise American travelers to return home.	The selling wave continues on the stock market. . . . The CIO longshoremen's union in northern California breaks off negotiations with ship owners. The CIO Warehousemen's Union files suit against warehouse owners for wages lost due to the lockout begun last month.	In Germany, the new *Graf Zeppelin II* takes its first flight—with hydrogen gas, as the United States will not sell helium to the company. The zeppelin travels 575 miles in Germany. . . . NBC television conducts its first "man on the street" interviews in New York City.		Sept. 14
The Dies Committee is told that 40 percent of the writers working for the WPA in the Federal Writers Project are Communists. . . . In 13 primaries and conventions this week, eight of the Democrats who opposed the President's Reorganization Bill are renominated—including three whom President Franklin Roosevelt actively campaigned against.		European money is exchanged for U.S. dollars in record amounts. . . . The Ford Company files an appeal in the case against its St. Louis plant, charging the NLRB examiner with misconduct.	John Cobb of England sets a new land speed record, 350.2 miles per hour, at the Bonneville Salt Flats in Utah.	Novelist Thomas Wolfe dies at age 37 in Seattle, three days after unsuccessful surgery for tuberculosis of the brain. . . . Former Premier of Spain Manuel Garcia Prieto dies at age 77. . . . After paying $50,000 for the film rights to *Rebecca*, by Daphne du Maurier, David Selznick hires Alfred Hitchcock to direct.	Sept. 15
	A Jewish newspaper in Germany appeals to President Franklin Roosevelt for refuge, asking the United States to amend immigration laws temporarily and allow more Jews to leave Germany at once.	The CIO and the UAW make peace, agreeing to let a panel arbitrate the fate of four men ousted by UAW president Homer Martin.	George Eyston reclaims the land speed record with a run of 357.5 miles per hour at the Bonneville Salt Flats in Utah.	*Dynasty of Death*, by Taylor Caldwell, is published, as well as Edith Wharton's last novel *The Buccaneers*.	Sept. 16
In Snow Hill, Md., a race riot erupts. The police chief claims he was forced to fire on African Americans as they insulted the police, and one man dies. Twenty-one are arrested. The police chief is exonerated.	China presents a check to the United States through its ambassador, paying for damages to the *President Hoover* and indemnities toward the death and injury of its crew. . . . Dr. Hu Shi, who once supported the peace movement of Wang Ching-wei, is appointed China's Ambassador to the United States.	A five-month old strike in Toledo, Ohio, turns violent. The Federal Creosoting Company plant reopened yesterday with nonstrikers. Two hundred strikers and sympathizers approach the guards, who open fire with shotguns. Thirteen are injured. . . . Pacific Coast shipping and warehouse companies accept union president Harry Bridges' invitation to restart negotiations.			Sept. 17
					Sept. 18
The mayor of Snow Hill, Md., warns all "unemployed Negroes" to get out of town. The police will conduct a "census" and African Americans without jobs in the city will be jailed for vagrancy.					Sept. 19
The Superintendent of the Philadelphia County Prison in Holmesburg, as well as the Deputy Warden and eight guards, are indicted for manslaughter or second degree murder. Four prisoners on a hunger strike died when steam heat was turned on in their cells last month.			Meteorologists watch a hurricane that veers away from Florida, and misses the Bahamas as well.		Sept. 20

F	G	H	I	J
Includes elections, federal-state relations, civil rights and liberties, crime, the judiciary, education, healthcare, poverty, urban affairs, and population.	Includes formation and debate of U.S. foreign and defense policies, veterans affairs, and defense spending. (Relations with specific foreign countries are usually found under the region concerned.)	Includes business, labor, agriculture, taxation, transportation, consumer affairs, monetary and fiscal policy, natural resources, pollution, and accidents.	Includes worldwide scientific, medical, and technological developments, natural phenomena, U.S. weather, and natural disasters.	Includes the arts, religion, scholarship, communications media, sports, entertainment, fashions, fads, and social life.

	World Affairs	Europe	Africa & The Middle East	The Americas	Asia & The Pacific
Sept. 21	At the League of Nations meeting, Premier Negrín of Spain surprises everyone by announcing the immediate withdrawal of all foreign volunteers from combat, whether or not the insurgents follow suit.	Britain and France warn Czechoslovakia that it faces invasion. Realizing the truth of this, Czechoslovakia agrees to give the Sudeten provinces to Germany. . . . Britain's Prime Minister faces opposition to his policy, led by Anthony Eden and Winston Churchill. France's leaders, as well, are divided. . . . The Soviet Union says it intends to stand by its promise to defend Czechoslovakia if attacked.		Belmiro Valdeverde, the chief of the May 11 Integralista uprising in Brazil, escaped from prison a few days ago, the authorities announce.	In fierce fighting, Chinese troops hold off Japanese forces assaulting Tienchiachen. Chinese forces claim to retake nearby Sungshankow.
Sept. 22	Japan sends its official refusal to participate to the League of Nations. . . . Ambassador Joseph Kennedy asks Charles Lindbergh, who is visiting Britain, to write a summary of Germany's air strength and capabilities for the British, which he delivers.	Britain's Prime Minister Chamberlain visits Chancellor Adolf Hitler at Godesburg, Germany. To Chamberlain's horror, Hitler expands his demands. . . . Czech Premier Hodza resigns; General Syrovy is appointed Premier and builds a new Cabinet. . . . Britain begins fitting Londoners for gas masks and calls for more air raid volunteers.			Japan creates the United Council of China at Peiping, declaring that China is a protectorate.
Sept. 23	The Spanish government, through the League of Nations, asks for help feeding three million refugees in Spain.	Czech President Benes mobilizes the army; his order is read over the radio in five different languages. Czech citizens cheer, and recruiting stations are full of volunteers. . . . France's Prime Minister says the country will go to Czechoslovakia's defense if it is attacked.			Journalists are again shown evidence of the Japanese use of gas, which Chinese sources claim is used daily in the Yangtze battles.
Sept. 24		Prime Minister Chamberlain returns to Britain. He tells the Czech Ambassador that Hitler demands annexation of the Sudeten provinces, consideration of Poland and Romania's demand for territory, and demobilization of the army. . . . France orders a mobilization of up to 500,000 additional troops and advises Parisians to get out of the city, in case of air raids.	Rail service to and from Jerusalem halts indefinitely, and trains and the mail to other Palestinian stations are disrupted by sabotage. Authorities abandon some towns as terrorists take over police stations or other offices.		
Sept. 25		Acknowledging that Germany's demands are unacceptable, the British and French do not advise the Czech President to accept them. Instead, the Cabinets of Britain and France craft compromises while Czechoslovakia prepares for war. Germany has set October 1 as the deadline for submission.		Over the last week, Mexico strengthens diplomatic ties with Cuba and Colombia, receives visitors from Chile, and continues trade with Europe—all actions supportive of President Cárdenas's policy of avoiding American imperialism.	Constant rain for two days slows the Japanese advances both north and south of the Yangtze River.
Sept. 26		Britain, France, and the Soviet Union affirm that they will go to war if Czechoslovakia is attacked. Support from Romania, Bulgaria, and Yugoslavia is also expected. . . . All Germans are ordered to listen to Chancellor Hitler's radio address on the Czech situation. He says they must have the Sudeten territories, but insists this will be the "last territorial demand."			Canton is bombed by Japanese planes; 50 people die near the waterfront. Wuchow, Liuchow, and rail lines are also shelled.
Sept. 27		As expected, Czechoslovakia rejects Germany's demands. . . . Chancellor Hitler rejects suggestions brought by Britain's envoy, and mobilizes his armies for war. . . . Italy and Belgium call up army reservists. . . . Britain has printed 50 million ration cards, and has plans ready for war mobilization—including the protection of stained glass windows and national treasures.			Japanese planes bomb Hankow's airport, and continue a week-long campaign of bombing towns in the vicinity of the capital. A heavy air attack on waterworks near Canton cuts off that city's water supply.
Sept. 28	For the first time, the League of Nations invokes Article XVI, recommending sanctions against Japan as an aggressor state and asking members to support China.	Chancellor Hitler relents and invites the leaders of Italy, France, and Britain to meet him in Munich tomorrow. The Four-Power Conference will decide peace or war over Czechoslovakia—a country not invited to the parley. . . . Britain mobilizes its navy, calling up 60,000 reservists. . . . Germany calls all ships home, throwing international shipping into turmoil. . . . France removes the stained glass windows from Chartres Cathedral.			The Chinese defense of Tienchiachen is weakening after 10 days of bombardment and costly battles. . . . In Yunnan province, far south, the capital Yunnanfu is bombed for the first time. Its airfield and university are damaged and at least 80 people die.

A	B	C	D	E
Includes developments that affect more than one world region, international organizations, and important meetings of world leaders.	Includes all domestic and regional developments in Europe, including the Soviet Union.	Includes all domestic and regional developments in Africa and the Middle East.	Includes all domestic and regional developments in Latin America, the Caribbean, and Canada.	Includes all domestic and regional developments in Asian and Pacific nations (and colonies).

U.S. Politics & Social Issues	U.S. Foreign Policy & Defense	Economics & Great Depression	Science, Technology & Nature	Culture, Leisure & Lifestyle	
Governor La Follette, who founded the new Progressive Party, gets the most votes in the Wisconsin primary.	The head of the Army Air Corps, Maj. Gen. Westover, and a crewman are killed in a plane crash near Los Angeles, Calif.		The "Long Island Express," a hurricane with sustained winds up to 160 miles per hour, hits New York and New England; 63,000 people become homeless and between 500 and 700 die—half of them in Rhode Island, where tidal waves sweep victims out to sea.	Room Service, a Marx Brothers comedy with Lucille Ball, is released.	Sept. 21
			Rivers in New England rise, threatening the area with more flooding.	Rebecca, by Daphne du Maurier, is released. Already a bestseller in England, Rebecca goes into a fourth printing by the time it hits U.S. bookshelves. . . . Hellzapoppin premiers on Broadway in New York, and becomes the longest-running show to date. Its last performance will be in December 1941.	Sept. 22
	In Czechoslovakia, 5,100 Americans are warned to leave by the U.S. envoy there.	U.S. stock prices fall on fears of war.	Between 100,000 and 150,000 relief workers—from the Red Cross, the U.S. Army, and other agencies—are deployed throughout New York, New Jersey, Rhode Island, and the New England states, battling floods and hurricane damage.	A time capsule with 1,100 feet of microfilm is buried at the grounds of the 1939 New York World's Fair.	Sept. 23
		Harry Hopkins removes Fred Healy, the WPA administrator in New Mexico, for allowing political interference in his program. . . . The longshoremen, warehouse workers, and employers of San Francisco agree to renew contracts, with minor compromises, and return to work.		J. Donald Budge wins the first Grand Slam in tennis, taking titles at Wimbledon, and the French, Australian, and U.S. Open finals.	Sept. 24
	President Roosevelt appeals directly to Chancellor Hitler and President Benes to negotiate further, in the interest of peace.	Railroad workers vote to strike rather than accept a 15 percent pay cut. Per the Railroad Labor Act, 60 days notice must be given, so the 930,000 workers will not strike until December 1.			Sept. 25
				Columbia Pictures announces that Frank Capra will direct Mr. Deeds Goes to Town, with Gary Cooper in the title role.	Sept. 26
	The President sends a telegram to Chancellor Hitler, asking, for the sake of humanity, that he continue negotiations over Czechoslovakia. NBC and CBS translate his message into five languages and broadcast it in Europe and the Americas.	U.S. stock markets, which have declined with war worries, creep back up in response to Chancellor Hitler's latest, less warlike speech. . . . Talks deadlock in a week-old strike of 15,000 truck drivers in New York. Mayor LaGuardia assigns city workers to drive Sanitation Department vehicles to keep important supplies—medicines and food—moving.	In Glasgow, Scotland, Queen Elizabeth, with Princesses Elizabeth and Margaret, christens the liner Queen Elizabeth.	If I Were King, with Ronald Colman and Basil Rathbone, premiers in New York City.	Sept. 27
The tax collector on Long Island, N.Y., says property owners who lost their homes in the hurricane must still pay taxes on them. Bodies are still being recovered.	The United States asks Japan and the Soviet Union to communicate with Germany and Czechoslovakia, urging further negotiations.	The stock market rises on the hope of peace.			Sept. 28

F	G	H	I	J
Includes elections, federal-state relations, civil rights and liberties, crime, the judiciary, education, healthcare, poverty, urban affairs, and population.	Includes formation and debate of U.S. foreign and defense policies, veterans affairs, and defense spending. (Relations with specific foreign countries are usually found under the region concerned.)	Includes business, labor, agriculture, taxation, transportation, consumer affairs, monetary and fiscal policy, natural resources, pollution, and accidents.	Includes worldwide scientific, medical, and technological developments, natural phenomena, U.S. weather, and natural disasters.	Includes the arts, religion, scholarship, communications media, sports, entertainment, fashions, fads, and social life.

	World Affairs	Europe	Africa & The Middle East	The Americas	Asia & The Pacific
Sept. 29	Soviet Foreign Minister Litvinoff scolds the League of Nations for failing to act against Germany and Italy's intervention in Spain, and failing to uphold the elected government there.	Britain, France, Germany, and Italy sign the Munich Pact, giving Chancellor Hitler about 50 percent of the territories he demanded at Godesburg outright—with farms, industries, and cities intact. Ownership of the other 50 percent of the Sudeten areas will be decided in a plebiscite. All Czechs who do not want to become citizens of the Reich, and all military personnel, have only a few days to evacuate.			Japan's Foreign Minister Gen. Ugaki resigns from the Cabinet. . . . Japan reports that Tienchiachen is finally captured, though casualties are high. China says the Japanese lost 6,000 men in the fighting. Chinese defenders retreat to Kirchun. . . . News of Japanese advances causes a panic, and roads leading from Hankow and the Wuhan cities are clogged with refugees, both civilians and government workers.
Sept. 30	Countries throughout the world are relieved that war is averted, but all continue their preparations for war. . . . The League of Nations recommends sanctions against Japan—but the recommendation is non-binding on members.	British Prime Minister Chamberlain and Chancellor Hitler make a non-aggression declaration. Czechoslovakia learns that if the proposal is refused, neither France nor Britain will give military aid when Germany invades. "Under protest to the world," Czechoslovakia accepts the annexation. . . . Poland demands that Czechoslovakia surrender the Teschen district by noon, October 1. . . . The licenses of all Jewish traveling sales agents in Germany expire.		Chile's crops are being ruined by a prolonged drought.	In Shanghai, the first Premier of the Chinese Republic is assassinated. Three men break into his home to kill 78-year-old Tang Shao-yi with hatchets. . . . Chinese troops report victories south of the Yangtze, claiming to drive a Japanese force back to the borders of Hupeh province. Another battle near Teian lasts two days and results in a loss to Japan.
Oct. 1	China's leader Chiang Kai-shek asks the Soviet Union to carry out sanctions against Japan.	German troops enter Czechoslovakia. Jews, gypsies, Czech army troops, and those who do not wish to live under the Reich flee to Czechoslovakia's interior, taking only what they can carry. . . . While most of Britain cheers Prime Minister Chamberlain as a hero, First Lord Admiral Duff Cooper resigns in protest over the Czechoslovakia settlement. . . . France dismisses its reservists. . . . The Munich Accord dissolves the Little Entente. Alliances between France, Poland, and the Soviet Union crumble, and much of Europe is unsettled, though relieved.	In two different battles between British authorities and Arab bands, 52 Arabs die. One fight takes place in Ramallah, where British troops use planes to scatter and defeat the rebels.		Defying his government, Wang Ching-wei publicly urges peace talks. . . . With Tienchiachen captured, Japan focuses efforts on Panpishan, a mountain city directly across the Yangtze. . . . Japanese planes drop leaflets over Chengchow, warning foreign missionaries to leave the city. Chengchow has been bombed several times in the past few weeks.
Oct. 2		Polish troops take Teschen from Czechoslovakia, with its coal mines and steel mills. . . . Czechoslovakia agrees to negotiate with Hungary, over southern territories with a majority of ethnic Hungarians in the population. . . . Czechoslovakia tries to stop the flood of refugees from the Sudeten, saying people will be returned to their home towns.	Arab terrorists attack families at night and burn homes in the Jewish quarter of Tiberias, Palestine, killing 20—including 11 children. The synagogue is burned and other buildings damaged. Phone lines were cut in advance. Six Arabs die in the attack. In Jaffa, six Arabs, including a child, die when a bomb they are constructing explodes.		Japan claims to capture towns along the Fu River, which is surrounded by swamps, south of the Yangtze. . . . Communist leader Chou En-lai returns to Hankow, to help in the defense of the city.
Oct. 3	Japan's Foreign Office says it will be difficult to cooperate with the League of Nations in the future, due to their actions of September 30.	Chancellor Hitler, along with German Sudeten Party leader Henlein, enters triumphantly into the Sudetenland. . . . Britain's Parliament authorizes a loan of $10 million to Czechoslovakia. . . . On the anniversary of Gen. Franco's accession to power, planes drop 178,000 loaves of bread on Madrid.			
Oct. 4		Through newspapers, the Soviet Union tells France they are no longer allies, because of France's abandonment of Czechoslovakia. . . . France restores diplomatic relations with Italy. . . . Czech President Benes works to keep Slovaks from seceding and joining Hungary.		Two years of negotiations in Washington, D.C., between Peru and Ecuador over borders, break up without resolution.	Australia increases its militia and arms manufacturing. . . . Twenty Japanese troop transport ships reach the sea near Formosa (Taiwan).
Oct. 5		Czechoslovakia's President Eduard Benes resigns due to German pressure. . . . The Reich prepares a bill for reparations owed by the Czechs, for injustices toward the Germans since 1918. . . . Hungarian troops invade Czech territory at two points, but quickly withdraw when they meet opposition. . . . In France, the Popular Front of Socialist and Communist parties loses all influence in Premier Daladier's government.	Near Mount Tabor and Safed in Palestine, British troops use planes and machine guns to kill approximately 50 Arabs, part of the group that attacked Tiberias three days ago. . . . Acknowledging the deteriorating situation in Palestine, Britain's Colonial Office calls a conference to discuss policy changes.		

A	B	C	D	E
Includes developments that affect more than one world region, international organizations, and important meetings of world leaders.	Includes all domestic and regional developments in Europe, including the Soviet Union.	Includes all domestic and regional developments in Africa and the Middle East.	Includes all domestic and regional developments in Latin America, the Caribbean, and Canada.	Includes all domestic and regional developments in Asian and Pacific nations (and colonies).

U.S. Politics & Social Issues	U.S. Foreign Policy & Defense	Economics & Great Depression	Science, Technology & Nature	Culture, Leisure & Lifestyle	
		Silent pickets reappear at 12 Busch Jewelry stores, three months after Judge Cotillo's controversial injunction against picketing. A company attorney promises that contempt charges will be filed against the pickets as they are arrested. Employees have been on strike since mid-May. . . . A sit-down strike of 300 workers is started in Sioux City, Iowa, at the Swift Packing House.	A tornado in Charleston, S.C., kills 32 people.	Walt Disney Enterprises, Disney Film Recording Company, and Liled Realty and Investment Company are absorbed into Walt Disney Productions.	Sept. 29
	President Franklin Roosevelt, through the State Department, asks Poland to refrain from force against Czechoslovakia.	As meat spoils at the Swift Packing House, police get warrants to arrest 125 strikers. The men, all members of a CIO union, flee.		*While England Slept*, by Winston Churchill, is published. . . . In Hollywood, comedian Fanny Brice files for divorce from producer Billy Rose. . . . Actors Ronald Colman and Benita Hume marry at San Ysidro Ranch in California.	Sept. 30
		The Swift plant in Sioux City shuts down, with 100 employees continuing to work as guards and clean-up crew inside. Iowa courts forbid the strikers to molest these workers.			Oct. 1
American Nazi leader Fritz Kuhn is forced to abandon his speech and flee a crowd of 5,000 veterans, who break into a hall in New Jersey. Later the same day, Kuhn speaks before 4,000 supporters in Andover, and at sites in New York without major incidents.		The annual report of the American Federation of Labor condemns an "unholy alliance" between the Committee for Industrial Organization and the National Labor Relations Board.	The Research Council on the Problem of Alcohol is formed, the first scientific effort to track and document the issues of drinking. Many prestigious scientists and institutions are involved.	Marshal Alexandru Averescu, wartime general, then premier of Romania, dies at age 75.	Oct. 2
				Abe Lincoln in Illinois, a play by Robert Sherwood, is premiered in Washington, D.C.	Oct. 3
		President Franklin Roosevelt sends a message to the AFL convention, asking that labor factions make peace. . . . The United Auto Workers reinstate leaders ousted by president Homer Martin months ago, on the recommendation of CIO peacemakers.			Oct. 4
		The United States asks Italy to exempt the 200 American Jewish residents of Italy from new restrictions and decrees.			Oct. 5

F	G	H	I	J
Includes elections, federal-state relations, civil rights and liberties, crime, the judiciary, education, healthcare, poverty, urban affairs, and population.	*Includes formation and debate of U.S. foreign and defense policies, veterans affairs, and defense spending. (Relations with specific foreign countries are usually found under the region concerned.)*	*Includes business, labor, agriculture, taxation, transportation, consumer affairs, monetary and fiscal policy, natural resources, pollution, and accidents.*	*Includes worldwide scientific, medical, and technological developments, natural phenomena, U.S. weather, and natural disasters.*	*Includes the arts, religion, scholarship, communications media, sports, entertainment, fashions, fads, and social life.*

	World Affairs	Europe	Africa & The Middle East	The Americas	Asia & The Pacific
Oct. 6		Britain's House of Commons approves the Prime Minister's actions regarding Czechoslovakia by 366 to 144, and adjourns for the month. . . . Italy bans marriages between Italians and Aryan foreigners, unless special permits are obtained. Marriages to non-Aryans are forbidden with no exceptions. . . . Insurgent planes drop bread on Alicante. Civilians, fearing poison, will not eat it.		A Mexican envoy returns from the United States with State Department suggestions regarding payment for seized land.	
Oct. 7		Newspapers report purges in Siberia, where 14 men were shot recently at Novosibirsk. . . . Germany gives Turkey 150 million marks trade credit for military and industrial purposes. . . . The passports of all German Jews are invalidated for foreign travel, and require special signatures. . . . Ten planes drop 100 bombs on Tarragona, Spain, a city with no military targets. Seven people die, and 30 homes and a hospital are destroyed.	Britain, working with Middle Eastern leaders, crafts an Arab-Jew armistice proposal for Palestine.		A coal mine explosion on Hokkaido, Japan, kills 151 workers. . . . Japan reveals long-range plans for China. After what has happened in Europe in the last fortnight, Japan is certain that England and France's involvement in Chinese affairs will diminish. . . . Japan claims it has encircled Teian and cut the Teian-Nanchang railway 16 miles from the city.
Oct. 8		A mob attacks St. Stephen's Cathedral in Vienna, Austria. Cardinal Innitzer, a supporter of the *Anschluss*, is injured as stained glass windows are smashed and the church and rectory are vandalized. . . . Gen. Franco announces he will send home Italian troops fighting for the Spanish insurgents. . . . Italy abolishes the Chamber of Deputies.	Diplomats discuss a proposal by Iraq's Foreign Minister: equal rights and representation for Jews in Palestine, but an end to Jewish immigration, making them a permanent minority. At the Arab Congress in Cairo, Egypt, Syria proposes a similar plan, annexing Palestine and the Trans-Jordan to Syria. Zionists protest, citing the Balfour Declaration.	The Supreme Court of Mexico dismisses the expropriation cases brought by British and U.S. oil companies, on a technicality. . . . Mexico denies admission to political exiles, even if they travel as tourists. The country expels 200 Austrian Jews who entered as tourists.	Kichun, 505 miles west of the sea on the Yangtze, is captured. Japanese ships move further west along the river, shelling Chinese positions. The Chinese dynamite a hill to block the river.
Oct. 9	Soviet Foreign Minister Litvinoff decides that no sanctions will be invoked against Japan. No other country imposes sanctions.	Hitler Youth groups demonstrate, bang drums, and call for Cardinal Innitzer's deportation to Dachau while Mass is celebrated in Vienna's cathedral. . . . The Reich dismisses its reservists. . . . Spanish insurgent pilots shell Aguilas, a city near Cartagena, and hit a British ship in Barcelona's harbor.	Britain will ship more troops and artillery to Palestine over the next two weeks. . . . The Arab Inter-Parliamentary Congress, meeting in Egypt, declares the Balfour Declaration null, void, and illegal. . . . In Cairo, former premier and Wafdist party head Nahas Pasha is slightly injured when a mob rushes his car.		
Oct. 10	As Charles Lindbergh flies to Berlin, Soviet newspapers criticize him for insulting their air force and planes.	German troops complete their takeover of Sudeten territories. Germany claims all private property, including livestock, in the occupied zones. . . . Hungary begins its negotiations for territory; Czech leaders call their initial demands "outrageous." . . . A Macedonian terrorist kills Bulgaria's army chief of staff. The assassin commits suicide after confessing to a plot, authorities say.	British troops reoccupy Bethlehem. In Beisan Valley, with planes and infantry, British forces kill 11 Arabs and capture munitions.	Arbitrators set the border of the Chaco zone between Paraguay and Bolivia. Recognizing the military victories of the Chaco War, Paraguay gets most of the area.	
Oct. 11		Cardinal Innitzer of Austria publishes a pamphlet of advice to Catholic parents that angers Nazis. The mayor of Vienna rebukes him. . . . Italy halts the issuance of business licenses to Jews, outlawing the transfer of existing licenses as well. . . . Hungary deports hundreds of Jews to concentration camps.	The Arab Inter-Parliamentary Congress in Egypt issues demands, including an end to Jewish immigration, nullification of the Balfour doctrine, and amnesty for all Arab political prisoners.	Dr. Felix Paiva is elected President of Paraguay.	
Oct. 12	The British Ambassador in Japan registers concern over British interests in Hong Kong and is reassured that Japan has no designs on them. Some observers believe that Britain's reluctance to take military action in Europe encouraged Japan's attack in the south.	Czechoslovakia asks Chancellor Hitler to mediate in talks with Hungary. Sections of Czechoslovakia are under martial law due to border crossings by Hungarian and Polish terrorists. . . . As German governments are set up in the Sudeten territories, Jews and Communists are subjected to the same laws as in the Reich. . . . The Soviets deforest, depopulate, and fortify a belt 100 miles wide along the Ukrainian border as a defense against Germany.	Arabs shoot or stab Arabs in Jenin, Haifa, and Jaffa. Battles between Arab groups and British troops claim casualties in Nablus, and on the Hebron-Jerusalem road.		
Oct. 13	Japan warns foreigners in south China not to allow Chinese troops to build defense works or travel near foreign-owned property.	Austrian Nazi Commissioner Buerckel announces punitive measures against Catholics: all seminaries will remain closed, and amnesty for religious prisoners is canceled. . . . Hungary abandons talks with Czechoslovakia and submits its demands to Berlin. . . . The Four Powers decide that no plebiscites are necessary in Czech areas with German majorities and give those areas to Germany.			China bars journalists from the front, but claims significant victories near Yangsin, south of the Yangtze. Chinese troops claim to recapture Yikow, and several towns near Sinyang, in the north.
	A Includes developments that affect more than one world region, international organizations, and important meetings of world leaders.	**B** Includes all domestic and regional developments in Europe, including the Soviet Union.	**C** Includes all domestic and regional developments in Africa and the Middle East.	**D** Includes all domestic and regional developments in Latin America, the Caribbean, and Canada.	**E** Includes all domestic and regional developments in Asian and Pacific nations (and colonies).

U.S. Politics & Social Issues	U.S. Foreign Policy & Defense	Economics & Great Depression	Science, Technology & Nature	Culture, Leisure & Lifestyle	
	The United States demands that Japan stop interfering with American rights in China.	The President's Railroad Fact-Finding Board begins to hear testimony.			Oct. 6
The National Women's Party opens their convention with a fundraiser. They hope to raise $1 million to finance efforts to pass the Equal Rights Amendment.		Two Plymouth and Chrysler plants in Detroit, employing 15,000 people, shut down when the UAW members refuse to come to work. The union wants a share-the-work plan with a 32-hour week, which it claims is in its contract.			Oct. 7
The census of the unemployed, presented to the President, notes an unanticipated "problem" contributing to (male) unemployment: higher numbers of women in the workforce since 1930. In November 1937, about 40 million men and 15 million women were employed.		Truck drivers on WPA projects in Ohio threaten to strike, and administrators insist that WPA workers cannot strike. . . . UAW and company representatives in Detroit confer on the 32-hour week, delaying a strike vote by workers.			Oct. 8
			The first radio altimeter, developed by Bell Labs for United Airlines, is demonstrated in flight over New York.	The New York Yankees take their third World Series in a row, beating the Chicago Cubs in four straight games.	Oct. 9
		The AFL declares it will not make peace with the CIO as long as John L. Lewis heads it, and Communists are allowed in it. . . . Union chairs from 60 General Motors plants join in asking for a 32-hour workweek until all laid-off employees are rehired.			Oct. 10
Pleas for three Scottsboro defendants are rejected by the Alabama Board of Pardons.		In Ohio, a truck blockade keeps supplies from WPA projects, idling 6,000 workers.	Twelve hundred scientific luminaries gather at Rutgers University in New Jersey to dedicate the Squibb Institute for Medical Research.	Gale Sondegaard withdraws from playing the Witch in *The Wizard of Oz*; Margaret Hamilton is cast.	Oct. 11
	Ecuador formally asks President Franklin Roosevelt to intervene it its border dispute with Peru. Argentina, Brazil, Chile, and Uruguay have made similar requests.			Filming starts on *The Wizard of Oz*. . . . Shortstop Leo Durocher signs a one-year contract to manage the Brooklyn Dodgers. Babe Ruth leaves his coaching job with the team.	Oct. 12
A 19-year-old African American is lynched in Ruston, La.		Railroad unions present the President's fact-finding board with a plan to resolve the railroads' fiscal problems without cutting wages.		Elzie Crisler Segar, creator of the Popeye cartoon, dies in California at age 44. . . . *Listen! The Wind* by Anne Morrow Lindbergh is published. Within days, a third printing will be required to keep up with the demand.	Oct. 13

F	**G**	**H**	**I**	**J**
Includes elections, federal-state relations, civil rights and liberties, crime, the judiciary, education, healthcare, poverty, urban affairs, and population.	*Includes formation and debate of U.S. foreign and defense policies, veterans affairs, and defense spending. (Relations with specific foreign countries are usually found under the region concerned.)*	*Includes business, labor, agriculture, taxation, transportation, consumer affairs, monetary and fiscal policy, natural resources, pollution, and accidents.*	*Includes worldwide scientific, medical, and technological developments, natural phenomena, U.S. weather, and natural disasters.*	*Includes the arts, religion, scholarship, communications media, sports, entertainment, fashions, fads, and social life.*

	World Affairs	Europe	Africa & The Middle East	The Americas	Asia & The Pacific
Oct. 14	A League of Nations commission assembles in France to verify the withdrawal of foreign volunteers in Spain.	Germany asks Britain to limit its number of planes to 35 percent of Germany's total. Refusal may result in the scrapping of the 1936 Naval Treaty. . . . Hungary mobilizes more troops, while German Chancellor Hitler agrees to mediate the territorial dispute between Czechoslovakia and Hungary. . . . Premier Negrín broadcasts a message denying that Spain will ever be partitioned between factions. Both sides say that only unconditional surrender will end the civil war.	The rash of Arab deaths in Palestine is directed by terrorists in Syria and Lebanon, who are eliminating political opponents, newspapers report. . . . Communication lines are cut this evening, isolating all of Palestine for 19 hours.	Brazil captures Integralista leader Belmire Valdeverde, who escaped from prison last month. He returns to prison and hard labor.	Seventy-five miles from Canton, Japanese troops advance on Tamshui. Chinese forces slow them down, but suffer heavy casualties. Waichow, subjected to constant bombing, is in flames. . . . An American mission at Hsuchang, near Hankow, is bombed by Japanese pilots and many are killed.
Oct. 15	Brazil and Germany recall their ambassadors and break off diplomatic relations with each other.	Germany releases tennis star Baron von Cramm from prison on good behavior, six months early. . . . Germany announces that at the end of the year, Jews may no longer practice law.	A bomb is thrown at Jerusalem's Damascus Gate, and the city is put under heavy curfew, with armed troops patrolling all streets. British troops in Palestine now number over 18,000. . . . The Arab Women's Congress for Palestine, with 500 delegates, begins in Cairo. All speeches are anti-Zionist, affirming that Palestine is an Arab country.	A Nazi propaganda campaign opens in Mexico with two-page newspaper ads promoting Germany and German goods.	Communications and some roads are cut, isolating Hong Kong as Japanese troops advance on Canton. Tamshui falls to the Japanese, as does Waichow. Both cities are in ruins. . . . The Labor Party wins in New Zealand's parliamentary elections.
Oct. 16	British tabloids criticize Charles Lindbergh for his trips to Germany and praise of the Luftwaffe. In fact, Lindbergh used his trips to keep the United States and Britain informed about Germany's air capability. . . . Winston Churchill, in a radio speech to the United States, calls for rearmament and a united front against totalitarian rulers.	Italy claims to uncover an anti-fascist plot and arrests Jews throughout the country. . . . A new wave of violence and vandalism directed against Vienna's remaining 220,000 Jews breaks out, along with anti-Catholic attacks. . . . American and other foreign troops parade in Barcelona before leaving Spain.	In Palestine, the old quarter of Jerusalem is the site of much violence for two days. Arab shops are closed, and bombs are thrown at patrolling British troops. Snipers are active also. Arabs in Jenin and Nablus announce strikes in protest of Britain's military tactics. The Iraq Petroleum pipeline is set on fire.	A long-simmering conflict in the Mexican state of Sonora erupts. Governor Yucupicio's forces exchange gunfire with union leaders.	Japan lands more troops in south China, but Japanese authorities insist that the invasion of Kwangtung province will speed up, and not detract from, the capture of Hankow. . . . A typhoon kills over 45 people in Japan, striking Kyushu Island.
Oct. 17		Germany promises Czech territory to Hungary, if Hungary will guarantee the rights of German minorities there. . . . In Teschen, Polish authorities close Czech schools and tell Czechs to leave. . . . Kemal Ataturk, President of Turkey for 15 years, is seriously ill with cirrhosis of the liver.	Shootings, explosions, and arson continue in the old quarter of Jerusalem, but murders of Jews and Arabs also occur outside the city, at work sites and Lake Huleh, Gaza, and other places.		In Kwangtung, an estimated 60,000 Japanese soldiers have landed in the past week. The Chinese defense is disorganized and composed mostly of provincial troops. All bridges are dynamited as the Chinese soldiers retreat.
Oct. 18	New Zealand announces its willingness to take in Czech refugees. . . . Charles Lindbergh again tours Germany's aircraft factories, seeing the latest developments.	Conservative leader Anthony Eden says Britain's economy must be overhauled, and a nonpartisan effort toward defense begun. . . . Germany extends a trade credit of 60 million marks to Poland.	From Syria, the exiled Mufti of Jerusalem demands an independent Palestine for Arabs alone, and an end to Jewish immigration. . . . In Jerusalem, Arab snipers fire at troops and civilians. The city is under martial law. Britain has a plan in place and enough troops to crush the rebellion, authorities say.		There are 750,000 people remaining in the Wuhan cities, and the Japanese army moves in from three directions. Yangsin is captured. . . . In the south, Japanese troops enter Sheklung, 35 miles east of Canton. Refugees flood inland; the roads and rail lines to Hong Kong are cut.
Oct. 19	Poland recognizes Manchukuo. . . . At a dinner given by the U.S. Ambassador in Berlin, Aviation Minister Goering gives Charles Lindbergh the Service Cross of the Order of the German Eagle with Star. Goering then tells Lindbergh about the new Junker JU-88 aircraft, still very secret. Lindbergh and his wife Anne Morrow Lindbergh house-hunt in Berlin for several days, intending to winter there.	Poland's Foreign Minister Beck visits King Carol of Romania, asking his help to get Czech territory for Hungary. Slovak ministers go to Germany for help. . . . The German press begins a new campaign, claiming the Lithuanian government oppresses Germans in the port city of Memel. . . . Kosher slaughter is outlawed in Italy. . . . Nazis expel Jews from Sudeten territories, but Czechs will not let them enter Czechoslovakia. Hundreds of Jews live in ditches and fields, penniless and homeless.	Going in with great force, Britain occupies the old quarter of Jerusalem within two hours. Eight Arab men and a woman die. The Mosque of Omar (the Dome of the Rock) remains in Arab hands.		In Canton, explosives are planted in buildings and factories to be destroyed rather than occupied by the Japanese. . . . In east Honan and Kwangsi provinces, ground assaults go on 24 hours a day as the Japanese push toward Hankow. Air raids occur daily. One column is within 50 miles of the city.
Oct. 20		Lithuania announces a new effort to better relations with Poland and Germany. Minority rights will be granted to ethnic Poles, and extremist demands to restore Wilna, the former capital now in Polish hands, will be suppressed. . . . Germany warns Hungary and Poland against forming a new border between them out of Czech territory. . . . Czechoslovakia outlaws the Communist Party.	British troops in Jerusalem kill six Arabs and wound 11 more who try to escape over the city's walls. Authorities say Gen. Haj Mohammed, trained in the Imperial German Army, began commanding and organizing the Arab terrorists six months ago.		Japanese troops are now 20 miles north of Canton, having avoided major Chinese defenses at Tsungfa. Japanese columns also approach from the east. French forces defend Canton's international sector in Shameem. Between 50,000 and 100,000 people are still in the city.

A	B	C	D	E
Includes developments that affect more than one world region, international organizations, and important meetings of world leaders.	*Includes all domestic and regional developments in Europe, including the Soviet Union.*	*Includes all domestic and regional developments in Africa and the Middle East.*	*Includes all domestic and regional developments in Latin America, the Caribbean, and Canada.*	*Includes all domestic and regional developments in Asian and Pacific nations (and colonies).*

U.S. Politics & Social Issues	U.S. Foreign Policy & Defense	Economics & Great Depression	Science, Technology & Nature	Culture, Leisure & Lifestyle	
The trial begins for a woman and two men charged with spying for Nazi Germany. A third man pleads guilty, and 14 others indicted have fled the country.	The President reveals that a study of U.S. defenses has been ongoing for months, and that a plan will be set before Congress and the people on January 3. The plan will increase spending on new and existing facilities, and may include recommendations for mass production of armaments. . . . Responding to letters and telegrams, Secretary Hull says the State Department will communicate with Britain about Palestine.				Oct. 14
		Labor Secretary Frances Perkins proposes a 13-member board to mediate the rift between the AFL and CIO.		*Abe Lincoln in Illinois* makes its New York debut with excellent reviews.	Oct. 15
A group of 150 anti-Nazis carry an American flag into a meeting of 1,000 Nazis in Chicago, setting off a riot. Police arrest 13.				Aaron Copland's ballet *Billy the Kid*, composed for the American Ballet Caravan, opens in Chicago.	Oct. 16
Near Smyrna, Ga., a school for African Americans is burned, and several African Americans are stoned and beaten, after a black man reportedly confesses to the murder of a white farmer and his adult daughter. Nineteen white men will get prison and fines for their parts in the rioting.	The United States agrees to mediate, with other nations, between Ecuador and Peru.			Former Czech president Eduard Benes accepts an invitation to lecture at the University of Chicago.	Oct. 17
		Over the next two weeks, General Motors will call back 35,000 workers and rescind pay cuts made in February. The stock market rises sharply on the news. . . . Strikers and sympathizers, 1,000 strong, attack the Swift Packing House in Sioux City, Iowa, with bricks and stones, threatening the workers inside. Police use tear gas and batons to break up the mob.		Hairdressers' associations adopt a joint resolution criticizing Greta Garbo for wearing her hair down and straight. It hurts their business.	Oct. 18
	The Untied States asks Germany again to take responsibility for Austria's war debts.	The NLRB orders Republic Steel to rehire 5,000 employees terminated during the strike of May 1937, and to cease interfering with labor organizing. . . . National Guard troops arrive in Sioux City to reopen the Swift Packing House.		*Knickerbocker Holiday*, a musical by Maxwell Anderson and Kurt Weill, opens in New York City. Walter Huston sings *September Song* in the production.	Oct. 19
	Italy responds to the U.S. concerns about the 200 American Jews in Italy, saying exceptions to laws are made for foreign Jews.	A grand jury indicts 73 people for corruption involving WPA programs in New Mexico. Relatives of Senator Chavez and state and federal officials are among those indicted. . . . Police arrest five women and 15 men at the Aerovox Corporation in Brooklyn, N.Y. A strike, called nine weeks ago over a 15 percent pay cut, turns into a melee when police try to escort nonstriking workers into the building.	Anticipating a "billion dollar enterprise," the Radio Manufacturers Association announces it will gear up production of televisions for home use this spring, with pictures approximately 7 by 9 inches.		Oct. 20

F	G	H	I	J
Includes elections, federal-state relations, civil rights and liberties, crime, the judiciary, education, healthcare, poverty, urban affairs, and population.	Includes formation and debate of U.S. foreign and defense policies, veterans affairs, and defense spending. (Relations with specific foreign countries are usually found under the region concerned.)	Includes business, labor, agriculture, taxation, transportation, consumer affairs, monetary and fiscal policy, natural resources, pollution, and accidents.	Includes worldwide scientific, medical, and technological developments, natural phenomena, U.S. weather, and natural disasters.	Includes the arts, religion, scholarship, communications media, sports, entertainment, fashions, fads, and social life.

	World Affairs	Europe	Africa & The Middle East	The Americas	Asia & The Pacific
Oct. 21	From Paris, the International Chamber of Commerce urges a return to the gold standard and an end to "cheap money." . . . In Germany, Charles Lindbergh tours the Dornier airplane works and sees the new Zeppelin.	Barcelona suffers through nine air raids and 500 bombs in 27 hours. . . . Hitler Youth groups attack Catholic churches and offices in Vienna with bats and stones. . . . The Czech War Ministry and Red Cross bring food and supplies to Jews living in fields, but refuse to allow them entry to Czechoslovakia. . . . Czechoslovakia voids its mutual assistance pact with the Soviet Union.	A British soldier is killed by a sniper in Jerusalem, prompting authorities to cancel passes that would allow Muslim men to visit mosques. In other parts of Palestine, murders, sabotage, and bombings occur. Near Nablus, troops call in air support as they battle a band that ambushed a convoy of trucks.		Led by tanks, Japanese troops enter Canton and encounter almost no resistance. All bridges, including the $8 million bridge over the Pearl River, are destroyed by retreating Chinese, as are many public buildings. Most of the business district is on fire.
Oct. 22	Japan warns foreign ships to leave waters near Hankow and Canton so they are not accidentally shelled. American ships decide to stay. . . . Germany halts the emigration of Jews to South-West Africa, as it is a former German colony.	Czechoslovakia sends a new proposal to Hungary. Meanwhile, Czech troops in the disputed area have killed and captured several Hungarian terrorists. . . . French Aviation Minister Guy La Chambre plans to increase production of planes to 200 per month by the end of 1939.		Mexican President Cárdenas invites U.S. and British oil companies to present their claims to Mexican courts for settlement, rather than going through diplomatic channels. . . . A coup d'état is foiled in Peru.	Japan implements an economic blockade against Chinese forces—largely Communist—in Shansi and eastern Hopeh provinces.
Oct. 23			Thirty-nine Arabs die in the four-day sweep of old Jerusalem. Britain begins to withdraw troops from the city.		Six Japanese planes attack a British ship near Changsha. There are no casualties. A Chinese troop ship, likewise bombed on the Yangtze, suffers 1,000 casualties. . . . Japanese planes bomb Hankow, beginning at dawn and continuing all day. . . . A refugee ship is bombed and sunk; 2,000 die.
Oct. 24	Czechoslovakia informs the League of Nations that Hungarian planes drop bombs, and troops cross the border to commit acts of terrorism. . . . The League's Mandate Commission meets; the Japanese delegate is absent.	With advice from Germany, Italy, and Poland, Hungary offers a final compromise to the Czechs, asking 30 percent less than previously. . . . In the last six months Germany's profits from its escape tax is nearly 112 million marks. The escape tax is the 25 percent tax on possessions of émigrés—usually Jews.		Mexico finalizes the expropriation of five American-owned properties this week, totaling 43,237 acres.	Martial law is declared in Hankow as Japanese troops come within 20 miles of the city. For maximum speed, invading troops continue to skirt, rather than confront, Chinese forces en route. Planes drop bombs and strafe the city and roads all day.
Oct. 25	Japan expresses "deep regret" for the accidental bombing of a British ship. . . . In spite of a decision to close the penal colony, France decides to ship 1,000 "habitual" criminals to Devil's Island in French Guiana, starting next month. . . . Italy declares that Libya is now a part of Italy.	A report on French arms manufacturers criticizes slow production. Another report says little has been done in defense preparations for months, in spite of available funds. . . . The latest Reich loan is oversubscribed and is raised from 1.5 to 1.85 billion marks. . . . Yugoslavia signs a trade pact with Germany.	Egypt plans to build 36 naval vessels. . . . As the citrus harvesting season begins in Palestine, all wonder what effect it will have on Arab terrorism. Most workers in the orchards are Arabs.	Chile elects a new president, Pedro Aguirre Cerda, of the Popular Front. . . . The seizure of 4,307 acres belonging to Congressman William Lemke is finalized in Mexico.	In Hankow, defenders blow up barracks, airfields, rail stations, and even bridges, cutting off their own escape from the Japanese, who enter Hankow at nightfall. . . . Britain appoints the Duke of Kent as Governor General of Australia.
Oct. 26		Both Czech and German guards forbid the delivery of food or water to the Jewish outcasts in the land between countries. . . . Czechoslovakia agrees to let Germany and Italy arbitrate a settlement with Hungary. . . . Germany begins to arrest and deport approximately 17,000 Polish-born Jews. Poland protests.	Palestine reduces its immigration quota from 6,100 to 4,870 for the next six months. . . . British troops fan over the hills near Haifa to root out terrorists.		Japan denies fiscal responsibility for damages to neutral property during hostilities. . . . The city of Teian, far east of Hankow, is finally taken by the Japanese.
Oct. 27	The Netherlands demands payment from Mexico for Royal Dutch Shell properties seized in March. This is the fourth communication; previous efforts were not made public.	French Premier Daladier starts talks aimed at accords with Italy and Germany. . . . The Spanish government charges that Italy, while removing 10,000 volunteers from the rebel army, sent 4,549 troops with arms on 16 different ships to resupply the insurgents. . . . Yugoslav police arrest 30 members of the Nazi party, including its chief, over literature attacking the regency.	Terrorists murder the mayor of Tiberias, a Jew. In the hills of northern Palestine, British troops erect makeshift camps bordered with barbed wire to hold hundreds of Arabs for questioning.	President Cárdenas of Mexico promises to stop land seizures while negotiations with the United States are ongoing over payment for expropriated land.	Kuomintang leaders urge Gen. Chiang Kai-shek to deal with Wang Ching-wei and his peace faction. Chiang announces that his government will not surrender nor accept mediation.
Oct. 28	Japan protests French shipments of arms to China and threatens "consequences." France denies that such shipments took place.	Germany sends a fraction of the arrested Polish Jews directly to concentration camps. Most, though, are loaded onto cattle trains bound for the Polish border, which they are forced to cross at gunpoint. Poland threatens to expel Germans in retaliation.			Gen. Chiang Kai-shek issues a proclamation to his country, saying that China will fight on. . . . Japanese troops encounter resistance in towns north of Canton.
Oct. 29	Fourteen ships carrying 18,000 colonists leave Italy for Libya.	Germany stops its arrests of Polish Jews. By this time, 1,500 Polish Jews are left at Chojnice, Poland, near Danzig. Others are dropped at Radzionka, including children from an orphanage and 28 rabbis. . . . Nazi Gen. von Epp, leader of the German Colonial League, demands the return of Germany's colonies.	British troops drive 300 cars to Gaza at night for a raid at dawn. Eight thousand Arabs are searched and questioned, and several hundred disarmed and detained.		Up to 100,000 Chinese refugees huddle in the British Concession of Hankow. . . . Japanese planes drop propaganda leaflets saying Wang Ching-wei is heading a new Chinese government.

A	B	C	D	E
Includes developments that affect more than one world region, international organizations, and important meetings of world leaders.	Includes all domestic and regional developments in Europe, including the Soviet Union.	Includes all domestic and regional developments in Africa and the Middle East.	Includes all domestic and regional developments in Latin America, the Caribbean, and Canada.	Includes all domestic and regional developments in Asian and Pacific nations (and colonies).

U.S. Politics & Social Issues	U.S. Foreign Policy & Defense	Economics & Great Depression	Science, Technology & Nature	Culture, Leisure & Lifestyle	
The Dies Committee on Un-American Activities listens to judges and officials describe the 1937 sit-down strike in Flint, Mich. The judge accuses Governor Murphy (who is presently campaigning for reelection) with treason for his handling of the strike, and all witnesses charge interference by Communists.		Four lumber companies in Arkansas and Mississippi blame the new Fair Labor Standards Act for their closures, claiming they cannot meet expenses under its rules.	A typhoon hits Tokyo, leaving thousands homeless. At least 226 die, and another 250 are missing.		Oct. 21
	The War Department completes a survey on the war capabilities of American industries, marking 10,000 plants as the backbone of war production.	Warehouse workers in San Francisco accept a new contract and end their work stoppage, which lasted 105 days.	Chester Carlson and Otto Kornei conduct the first successful test of the photocopier in Queens, N.Y. Six years pass before the men can interest investors in their device, however.	Vaudeville star May Irwin dies in New York City.	Oct. 22
			Up to 100 men from Romania are missing in a storm on the Black Sea.		Oct. 23
		The Fair Labor Standards Act goes into effect, setting 25 cents as the minimum wage and banning child labor. Some businesses shut down within hours, putting 80,000 people out of work.	Ford previews its 1939 models, including the new Mercury.		Oct. 24
President Roosevelt sets down in writing his concern that the Dies Committee "permitted itself to be used in a flagrantly unfair and un-American attempt to influence an election." He writes specifically of the "lurid" charge of treason leveled at Governor Murphy.	Trade talks between Britain and the United States resume.	Judge Cotillo finds another 11 CIO pickets and their attorney guilty of contempt of court. Two picketers get the maximum sentence, but appeal the ruling.			Oct. 25
	Citing the state of the world and policies of certain countries, the President says arming for national defense is necessary.				Oct. 26
		A federal court tells Mayor Hague of Newark, N.J., and other officials that they may not stop people from speaking, passing out pamphlets, or moving around the city. The suit stems from the mayor's actions against CIO members.	E.I. DuPont de Nemours and Company announce that the late Wallace Carothers and his team invented the first completely synthetic fiber: nylon. The company says it will name and patent each new weave construction.		Oct. 27
In Dayton, Ohio, 34,000 students and 1,300 teachers are sent home until January 1. The state has run out of money to run the public schools.					Oct. 28
In a 26-page letter, Rep. Dies accuses Labor Secretary Perkins of deceiving the Justice Department to aid labor leader Harry Bridges, a Communist.		The President's Railroad Fact-Finding Board recommends that companies drop the proposed 15 percent wage cut for employees.			Oct. 29

F	G	H	I	J
Includes elections, federal-state relations, civil rights and liberties, crime, the judiciary, education, healthcare, poverty, urban affairs, and population.	Includes formation and debate of U.S. foreign and defense policies, veterans affairs, and defense spending. (Relations with specific foreign countries are usually found under the region concerned.)	Includes business, labor, agriculture, taxation, transportation, consumer affairs, monetary and fiscal policy, natural resources, pollution, and accidents.	Includes worldwide scientific, medical, and technological developments, natural phenomena, U.S. weather, and natural disasters.	Includes the arts, religion, scholarship, communications media, sports, entertainment, fashions, fads, and social life.

	World Affairs	Europe	Africa & The Middle East	The Americas	Asia & The Pacific
Oct. 30		Relief workers from Warsaw arrive at Zbaszyn, a Polish border town, to help Jewish refugees set up a makeshift camp. A few hundred of the injured and young children are taken to Warsaw. Within a few days, approximately 10,000 Polish Jews expelled from Germany gather at Zbaszyn, most staying until August 1939, when they are taken to concentration camps.			A new press campaign in Tokyo says Japan pursues its interests alone, and attacks other nations who would interfere. . . . Hankow's slums and shacks, as well as buildings used by snipers, are set aflame by Japanese troops. Amid the looting and pillaging, Hankow's golf course reopens, and Americans and Europeans resume play.
Oct. 31		France refuses entry to over 200 foreign volunteers wounded in the Spanish civil war, saying France cannot pay for their hospitalization. . . . Insurgents bomb the Spanish coast, killing at least 70 people. Many casualties result when a train is shelled 20 miles south of Valencia.	British troops take over Jaffa, imposing a 24-hour curfew and conducting house-to-house searches. . . . All Jews in Palestine halt work at 2 p.m. and assemble at synagogues, to hear a manifesto on internal defense, and to start a fundraising drive.		South of Hankow, and north of Canton, Japanese columns take control of other cities and rail lines. Heavy fighting goes on north of the Yangtze River as well.
Nov. 1		Britain's Parliament reconvenes and Prime Minister Chamberlain stresses appeasement and defense as top aims. . . . Insurgent air raids in Barcelona, Spain, damage a British ship. . . . The Polish government sends tents and medical supplies to thousands of Jewish refugees at Zbaszyn, but will not allow them to enter the country. . . . Poland and Czechoslovakia conclude negotiations; Poland gets two Slovak territories in addition to the Teschen.	Arabs in Palestine begin a three-day strike, protesting a new law that forces all males over 16 to get permits to travel in cars. In Haifa 75 Arabs are held by the military, who conduct searches there and in other cities.	A drought ruins the sugar cane crop in Puerto Rico, in turn hurting the rum industry. . . . Twenty-one German Jewish refugees are returned to Germany from Mexico. Arriving on the ship *Orinoco* on October 16, they were never allowed to enter the country. All have tourist visas, but Mexico says they are immigrants, not tourists.	Witnesses report looting and rape by Japanese soldiers throughout the Wuhan cities. Slum areas deemed too difficult for police are burned. . . . Japanese troops land from 30 ships in the southern province of Fukien.
Nov. 2	Japan severs all ties with the League of Nations.	Germany and Italy meet in Vienna and decide that Hungary gets 4,800 square miles of Czech territory, with a population of 860,000. The occupation may proceed on November 5. Delegates from the countries sign the agreement, written in Italian and German only. . . . A ship under contract to Britain is sunk by a Spanish insurgent plane, 10 miles from Norfolk in the North Sea.	Arabs in Beirut, Lebanon, riot on the 21st anniversary of the Balfour Declaration; 15 are injured.	In spite of its pledge on October 27, Mexico expropriates 100 acres from American Charles Miller.	Japan bombs Shekki, ahead of their advance on the West River. More Japanese troops are landed at Amoy in Fukien. . . . Fighting continues around Poyang Lake, and Japanese troops capture towns as they move south from Hankow.
Nov. 3		Insurgents slowly gain ground in Spain's Ebro River region. . . . Over 200 bombs fall in Madrid, one hitting the U.S. Embassy building, abandoned for over a year. . . . Thousands of Jews, Slovaks, and Czechs flee their villages before the Hungarian troops move in.			Japan issues a declaration of its war aims: total "mutual aid and coordination"—economically, politically, and culturally—between Japan, China, and Manchukuo. Japan hopes that other nations will "adapt their attitudes" to the new conditions. Japan also scolds western democracies over their possession of colonies on other continents.
Nov. 4	Japan declares the 1922 Nine-Powers Treaty obsolete.	Autonomous Slovakia allows German citizens to wear the swastika. Slovaks in Bratislava wreck Jewish shops and torment Jews in the streets. Czechs, Slovaks, and Hungarians all accuse the Jews of siding with their enemies. . . . An anti-Ukrainian mob in Lwow, Poland, wrecks a hotel and vandalizes a newspaper office.		Cuba allows the 21 Jews on the *Orinoco* to disembark while it considers their cases.	Gen. S. Hata makes Hankow his base for the Japanese army in the Yangtze Basin. Countries engaged in shipping in China are warned to avoid Changsha, 200 miles south of Hankow, and Shasi, 120 miles west on the Yangtze. Heavy fighting is anticipated. Tungshan, east of Hankow, is captured by the Japanese after two days of fighting.
Nov. 5		Hungarian troops advance peacefully into their newly-acquired territories. . . . Italy announces that only 3,522 Jewish families, of 15,000 in Italy, will be exempt from new restrictions placed on Jews. The exemptions are due to military or fascist service, and are subject to review. . . . Observers estimate that up to half a million people from the Sudeten and Teschen areas are now refugees; 20,000 are Jewish.		Mexico decides that immigrants who've "lost nationality" (i.e., Jews) may enter the country only if they agree to "raise Mestizo families."	Japanese Gen. Doihara says retired warlord Wu Pei-fu will lead a new Chinese government answerable to Japan. . . . A British doctor in Canton confirms the use of chlorine and mustard gases by the Japanese. . . . Disgruntled Japanese workers in Tauyuan, Shansi province, explode a munitions stockpile, killing 300 Japanese soldiers.
Nov. 6		Chancellor Hitler denounces "war agitators" such as Britain, calling the words of Winston Churchill "complete stupidity." . . . Soviet Premier Molotoff says that a second world war has begun, and accuses Germany of being behind the Japanese "invasion" of Siberia last summer.	Defying the British police who search the city, Arab bands rob a Haifa post office, shoot at army trucks, and set fire to a warehouse holding government goods.		Tokyo newspapers imply that retaliation may follow if the United States takes economic measures to enforce the Nine-Powers treaty. . . . Japanese troops capture Tsungyang, a major step en route to Changsha. . . . President Quezon puts the provinces of Cebu and Bulacan under military rule due to pre-election political riots in the Philippines.

A	B	C	D	E
Includes developments that affect more than one world region, international organizations, and important meetings of world leaders.	*Includes all domestic and regional developments in Europe, including the Soviet Union.*	*Includes all domestic and regional developments in Africa and the Middle East.*	*Includes all domestic and regional developments in Latin America, the Caribbean, and Canada.*	*Includes all domestic and regional developments in Asian and Pacific nations (and colonies).*

U.S. Politics & Social Issues	U.S. Foreign Policy & Defense	Economics & Great Depression	Science, Technology & Nature	Culture, Leisure & Lifestyle	
				Orson Welles' version of H.G. Wells' *War of the Worlds* is broadcast. Although well-advertised as a play, thousands of people panic and flee their homes, believing that Mars is invading.	Oct. 30
Representative Dies charges the White House with using its prestige to crush his committee's efforts.	Thirty governors and half the members of Congress sign a petition to the President, asking him to urge Britain to keep Palestine open as a homeland for Jews.	The President asks railroad owners to accept the recommendations of his Board and drop their proposed wage cut. . . . The Securities and Exchange Commission adopts new rules to protect customer money from mishandling by brokers. Most were prompted by the Richard Whitney investigation of last April. . . . Nearly a quarter million workers returned to jobs in October, the Labor Department reports.		The Federal Communications Commission requests and studies the script of *War of the Worlds* but is uncertain what to do; no rules were broken. . . . Young violinist Yehudi Menuhin is barred from performing with the Los Angeles Symphony because he will not join a musicians' guild.	Oct. 31
			The Owens-Corning Fiberglas Corporation separates from parent companies Owens-Illinois and Corning Glassworks.	The "Race of the Century" between War Admiral and Seabiscuit takes place at Pimlico. Seabiscuit wins by three lengths.	Nov. 1
Teachers in Dayton, Ohio, are asked to work for three to five weeks without pay until state funds arrive.	The U.S. Navy will open bids on designing and building a dirigible for under $3 million.	In Ohio, 577 tobacco workers at the P. Lorillard plant call off a month-long strike as 500 National Guardsmen assemble. The governor called the troops due to a riot last week, charging a CIO "invasion" of his state.			Nov. 2
				Man's Hope, a novel about the Spanish civil war by Andre Malraux, is published.	Nov. 3
The July convictions of American Nazis running a camp in New York are overturned by an appellate court. . . . An estimated 30,000 to 50,000 workers, mostly in the south, have been laid off due to the Fair Labor Standards Act.		Railroads withdraw their threatened 15 percent pay cut, averting a possible strike by over 900,000 workers.		Jack Haley replaces Buddy Ebsen as the Tin Man in *The Wizard of Oz*. The aluminum dust used for makeup put Ebsen in the hospital; makeup for Haley is changed to an aluminum paste. . . . *The Great Waltz*, with Luise Rainer and Maliza Korjus, is released.	Nov. 4
	The President works on a new budget, expected to triple the number of airplanes for the Army.	The Public Contracts Board and Labor Secretary Perkins recommend pay raises in the steel industry, affecting the lowest-paid workers. Ninety-five percent of steel companies, most of whom hold government contracts, would be affected.		Arturo Toscanini and the NBC Symphony Orchestra premier the *Adagio for Strings* by 28-year-old Samuel Barber.	Nov. 5
	The United States protests violations of the Open Door policy to Japan.				Nov. 6

F	G	H	I	J
Includes elections, federal-state relations, civil rights and liberties, crime, the judiciary, education, healthcare, poverty, urban affairs, and population.	Includes formation and debate of U.S. foreign and defense policies, veterans affairs, and defense spending. (Relations with specific foreign countries are usually found under the region concerned.)	Includes business, labor, agriculture, taxation, transportation, consumer affairs, monetary and fiscal policy, natural resources, pollution, and accidents.	Includes worldwide scientific, medical, and technological developments, natural phenomena, U.S. weather, and natural disasters.	Includes the arts, religion, scholarship, communications media, sports, entertainment, fashions, fads, and social life.

	World Affairs	Europe	Africa & The Middle East	The Americas	Asia & The Pacific
Nov. 7		Herschel Grynszpan, a 17-year-old Polish Jew, shoots a German Embassy official in Paris. Grynszpan's family is among those recently deported from Germany to Poland. His victim, Ernst vom Rath, lingers for two days, then dies. . . . Spanish insurgents capture Mora de Ebro. The port of Tarragona, 40 miles away, is bombed nine times through the night and morning.			Japan forms and capitalizes the North China Development Company to rebuild China. The United States sees this as a rebuke to its October 6 protest. . . . Japan files a protest, saying a British ship opened fire with machine guns on Japanese troops who were fighting guerillas. The incident occurred last month, on the Yangtze River.
Nov. 8		A local official allows 51 Jews, including the elderly and children, to enter Czech territory. . . . Germany's newspapers call for reprisals for the shooting of an embassy official in Paris.			Japan extends its war zone, warning foreigners away from Yunnan, bordering Burma and Indo-China, north to Kansu, adjacent to Mongolia. Szechwan province suffers its first air raid at Chengtu airfield.
Nov. 9		"Kristallnacht"—the night of broken glass—erupts throughout Germany on the news of Ernst vom Rath's death. The two-day, government-orchestrated attack on Jews results in the destruction of up to 500 synagogues, 7,000 shops, and 29 department stores. . . . Marshal Vasily Blyukher, Soviet military commander during the Changkufeng Hill crisis, is tortured and dies in prison. . . . France recognizes Italy's conquest of Ethiopia.	Britain's Cabinet decides that partitioning Palestine is not possible, and proposes a conference with Arabs and Jews.		Japanese bombers flying north from Kwangtung province bomb cities in Hunan, killing 200 people.
Nov. 10	Chile and Germany extend their trade agreement for another six months.	As Kristallnacht continues, 50,000 Jewish males are arrested and many are sent to concentration camps; at least 35 and possibly 200 are killed, mostly by public beatings. Jewish children hide in the woods as their orphanage burns in Dinslaken; many end up in the Netherlands. At least 15,000 Jews are arrested in Austria; mobs in the Sudeten drive Jews out of the area. Six million marks will be paid out by insurance companies for the damages of this rampage, which the Reich seizes. . . . Kemal Ataturk, founder and president of Turkey for 15 years, dies.	Arabs groups declare they will not attend a conference unless the Balfour Declaration is first rejected.	On the same day that negotiations conclude between Mexican and U.S. diplomats over payment for seized agrarian land, nine American and British oil companies file suit in Mexico's courts. They ask the return of their properties.	Severe fighting is reported at Yochow, 80 miles north of Changsha, in Hunan.
Nov. 11	The Permanent Court of International Justice opens its third 1938 session.	Turkey's National Assembly elects Gen. Ismet Inonu President. . . . Nazi leaders defend the anti-Jewish rioting of the last two days, saying that Germans were following their "healthy instincts." The United States and many European countries condemn their actions; Propaganda Minister Goebbels warns that Germany's Jews will pay for exaggerations in the foreign press.			Japanese troops capture hillsides around Yochow, and by moonlight enter the city, scaling its walls and fighting hand-to-hand.
Nov. 12		Hermann Goering meets privately with Nazi leaders to plan the elimination of Jews from the German economy. . . . A fine of 1 billion marks is levied against Jews collectively, and they must pay to repair their wrecked homes and businesses. New restrictions bar them from any business work after January 1. . . . France's government revalues gold and takes other steps to revive its economy. . . . France turns away Jewish refugees at the border, unless they have visas.		More expropriation, both of oil fields and mines owned by American companies, are threatened in Mexico to resolve labor problems.	Fires still burn in Hankow, and cholera breaks out. . . . Civilians begin to evacuate Changsha. Foreign residents take shelter at Yale-in-China University or in an oil company-owned compound on the Siang River. Chinese army troops head west or south.
Nov. 13	Over the next week, politicians and civic and religious leaders in Britain, the United States, and other countries express disgust with Germany's recent actions toward Jews.	Third Reich extremism accelerates. To help pay the billion-mark fine, assessments of up to 150,000 marks are made on wealthy Jews, which must be paid tomorrow. All businesses will be Aryanized. Salzburg announces it has cleared out all Jews. . . . The Netherlands doubles its border guards as German Jews congregate and beg for entry.	British pilots and infantry free Jericho in Palestine from the Arab terrorists who have held it several days. During their "occupation," police stations, post offices, and other government buildings were burned.	Anti-Semitism in the cities of Colombia is fueled by recent immigration. The government prepares a bill to bar Jews and other minorities from certain industries, and to halt issuance of visas to Jews.	Chinese forces claim to recapture several cities near Tsungfa, including Tsungfa. Chinese merchants refuse to return to Canton, delaying Japanese plans to organize the city.
	A *Includes developments that affect more than one world region, international organizations, and important meetings of world leaders.*	**B** *Includes all domestic and regional developments in Europe, including the Soviet Union.*	**C** *Includes all domestic and regional developments in Africa and the Middle East.*	**D** *Includes all domestic and regional developments in Latin America, the Caribbean, and Canada.*	**E** *Includes all domestic and regional developments in Asian and Pacific nations (and colonies).*

U.S. Politics & Social Issues	U.S. Foreign Policy & Defense	Economics & Great Depression	Science, Technology & Nature	Culture, Leisure & Lifestyle	
Two California politicians sue Harper Knowles for libel because of statements he made before the Dies Committee on Un-American Activities, claiming they were influenced by the Communist Party.		A federal judge permanently enjoins Mayor "Boss" Hague of Jersey City from forbidding the CIO or ACLU to meet in his city. . . . Ford and Chrysler Motor Companies promise specific reforms in their financing policies, in return for consent decrees dropping anti-trust suits against them.	Two Royal Air Force bombers fly from Egypt to Australia, setting a new distance record of 7,162 miles. . . . Japan suffers a series of earthquakes, two estimated in the 7.6 range, starting on the evening of November 5 through today.		Nov. 7
Elections in 47 states give Republicans 89 seats in Congress, as well as 11 governorships. The LaFollettes' new Progressive Party in Wisconsin makes a poor showing. Californians vote against the "Ham and Eggs" pension plan, a plan offering $30 in scrip every Thursday to nonworking residents over 50. In Pennsylvania, Crystal Bird Fauset becomes the first African American woman elected to a state legislature.					Nov. 8
		Over 3 million shares—a record—are traded as stocks go up on the election news.			Nov. 9
			An 8.2-magnitude earthquake rocks the Shumagin Islands in Alaska, setting off a small tidal wave that hits Hawaii, but does little damage.	Pearl S. Buck wins the Nobel Prize for Literature.	Nov. 10
Alabama Governor Bibb Graves, who promised to pardon the remaining Scottsboro defendants on November 14, conducts interviews with the five inmates. He finds them rude and sullen, and says two sounded coached.		The 250,000-strong members of the International Ladies Garment Workers Union split from the CIO. The union decides on independence from both the CIO and the AFL.	Professor Enrico Fermi of Rome wins the Nobel Prize in Physics.	Kate Smith sings *God Bless America* for the first time, during a radio broadcast celebrating Armistice Day. . . . Mary Mallon, the original "Typhoid Mary," dies of a stroke. She had lived in isolation for over 20 years, after outbreaks of typhoid were traced to her cooking four times over 10 years. . . . Charles Lindbergh and his family cancel plans to winter in Berlin because of the anti-Semitic riots.	Nov. 11
	The United States and Mexico agree to a plan on payment for agricultural land expropriated since 1927, to begin with a $1 million payment in May 1939. Annual indemnity payments will follow.	Telegraph companies—including Western Union—are denied their requested exemption from the new minimum wage, and must pay their messengers 25 cents per hour.			Nov. 12
		The National Labor Relations Board reaffirms its April decision that Inland Steel must bargain collectively with its employees and put its agreement in writing. The decision stems from a strike in summer 1937.		Mother Frances Xavier Cabrini is the first American citizen beatified by the Roman Catholic Church.	Nov. 13

F	G	H	I	J
Includes elections, federal-state relations, civil rights and liberties, crime, the judiciary, education, healthcare, poverty, urban affairs, and population.	Includes formation and debate of U.S. foreign and defense policies, veterans affairs, and defense spending. (Relations with specific foreign countries are usually found under the region concerned.)	Includes business, labor, agriculture, taxation, transportation, consumer affairs, monetary and fiscal policy, natural resources, pollution, and accidents.	Includes worldwide scientific, medical, and technological developments, natural phenomena, U.S. weather, and natural disasters.	Includes the arts, religion, scholarship, communications media, sports, entertainment, fashions, fads, and social life.

	World Affairs	Europe	Africa & The Middle East	The Americas	Asia & The Pacific
Nov. 14		In Germany, all Jews are expelled from high schools and universities. Jews may no longer trade stocks; all brokers are to refuse their orders. . . . Due to bad weather, Czech authorities allow some Sudeten Jews to enter and receive shelter for 48 hours. They will then be taken back to the no-man's-land between borders. . . . The Vatican reveals that protests from the Pope regarding Italy's new "Aryan-only" marriage laws have been ignored by Premier Mussolini and King Victor Emmanuel.			Hunan province, south of Hankow, becomes the new battleground as Chinese forces entrench near Siangtan, south of the capital, Changsha. All of Changsha is burning, though Japanese troops are still over 80 miles away. The fire will rage for five days and take 2,000 lives. Large areas of Hankow are still in flames. . . . Japan refuses to open the Yangtze River to shipping, in spite of protests from the Untied States and European countries.
Nov. 15		The Netherlands sets up two camps for Jewish refugees from Germany and asks other European nations to do the same. Belgium refuses; other countries do not respond. . . . France and Germany reach a preliminary agreement guaranteeing France's eastern border and giving Germany free reign in eastern Europe.	Fakhri Nashashibi submits a memo to the British Commissioner denouncing terrorism as coming solely from the Mufti of Jerusalem. The Mufti, Nashashibi says, does not speak for all Arabs.	Argentina agrees to accept Jewish refugees from Germany who are farmers. Nearly 250 Polish Jews arrive by ship, with visas and farming implements. . . . Since the Fair Labor Standards Act went into effect, Puerto Rico has laid off 21,343 people, out of 27,457 employed before. Over 18,000 of those laid off were tobacco workers; the rest worked in needlepoint.	Japanese planes attack Chinese rail stations, military posts and trains, and gunboats. Other air targets are widespread: Ichang in Hupeh, Changteh in Hunan, Kingshan, 75 miles from Hankow, southern Kwangtung, eastern Chekiang, and Lanchow, capital of Kansu.
Nov. 16		Britain acknowledges Italy as the conqueror of Ethiopia. . . . Germany builds pontoon bridges over the Danube and announces it will take control of four more Slovak towns. . . . Germany has collected over 9 million marks from Jews in Berlin alone to pay for repairs to their property—which will then be Aryanized. . . . Insurgents enter Ribbaroja, ending Spain's Battle of the Ebro. The three months of fighting cost 100,000 combined casualties.	The Arab High Committee, which has fled Palestine, tells Britain it refuses to negotiate with Jews.		Chinese troops retreat from Hunan province but continue to fight as guerilla forces. They claim to recapture towns from the Japanese, most notably Taierhchwang. . . . Japanese planes raid Sian, capital of Shensi province, and inflict heavy damage, cutting rail lines.
Nov. 17		Winston Churchill fails to muster the necessary votes to force industries to make armaments for Britain. . . . Prime Minister Chamberlain says governors in colonies have been queried as to how many Jewish refugees they can absorb. . . . Danzig's Nazis say that all synagogues are destroyed and most Jews arrested or driven off. They warn that Catholic churches and convents will be next.	Two British platoons and a detachment of guards are ambushed at dusk after clearing an Arab town of rebels. They suffer seven casualties but drive off the Arab attackers. . . . The leader of a faction of Arabs opposing the Mufti of Jerusalem's group is shot down in Jerusalem; his assassin escapes. Other violence, which has become routine, continues.		Two people are killed and 150 arrested in a strike at a jute mill near Calcutta, India. The dispute involves 30,000 workers. . . . Tokyo confirms that within a month, Gen. Wu Pei-fu will head a collaborative government in central China. Wu has already been given a large fund to begin his organization. . . . Towns in west Kiangsi (Jiangxi) province are being burned by the Chinese as they are deserted, say Japanese pilots.
Nov. 18		An explosion at a munitions plant near Barcelona kills 400 workers, who suffocate or burn. No news of the blast is published in Spain. . . . King Carol of Romania ends a state visit to Britain without the economic help and trade concessions he hoped to achieve. . . . After consulting with the Netherlands, Belgium's Foreign Minister says his country will no longer turn away Jewish refugees at its border.		Col. Batista, military leader of Cuba visiting in New York, says his country will provide a haven for refugees from Nazi Germany, and urges other countries to do the same.	Japan explains that all goods transported on the Yangtze River are for its armies, and not commercial purposes. Other nations have complained that their ships are not allowed to use the Yangtze. . . . Chinese planes attack Japanese positions 40 miles from Changsha. Japanese planes bomb an airfield in Kiangsi, and shell downtown Sian, in spite of a snowstorm.
Nov. 19	Germany rejects attempts to negotiate with the Inter-Governmental Refugee Committee that was set up after the Evian Conference. Germany insists that Jewish refugees depart the Reich with nothing. The country's two justifications are that Jews stole or extorted their wealth from Germans, and that the Refugee Committee plan is a politically-motivated attack against Germany.	Polish or Hungarian terrorist clashes kill six in the Ruthenian area of Czechoslovakia. Hungary claims 39 Hungarian gendarmes were killed in the revolt while trying to restore order. . . . Germany denies press reports that 200 Jews were executed at Buchenwald concentration camp. . . . 15,000 Jews have lost jobs in Italy since November 10. . . . Ukrainians complain of punitive mistreatment in Poland, due to conflicts in east Galicia.	The mayor and a councilman of Lydda, Palestine, both members of a party in opposition to the Mufti of Jerusalem, are assassinated. . . . Egypt's King Farouk commits the country to expanded defense. New bills for mandatory army service and increased funding are before Parliament.	A strike of electrical workers in five Mexican states is settled after nine days, with the help of compromises asked by President Lázaro Cárdenas.	Japanese authorities say that 200,000 guerilas are active in the triangle between Nanking, Hangchow, and Shanghai, and the Yangtze River will remain closed to commercial shipping to prevent trade with them. . . . The Burma Road, connecting Yunnan with Szechwan, will be opened next month.
Nov. 20	Today is declared a Day of Prayer for the Oppressed.	The Netherlands processes 300 entry permits per day for Jewish refugees at the border. Officials say they would admit more if other nations commit to sheltering the immigrants. The Netherlands and Switzerland take children without delays or paperwork. . . . In Germany, the Gestapo searches foreigners' homes for Jews. . . . German troops continue to occupy Czech towns, often expelling dozens of Jews across the Czech border—where they are denied entry.		A crowd of 10,000 assembles in Santiago, Chile, demanding that Nazi-run schools be closed, and that Chile allow refugee immigration.	Three Chinese officials are executed for setting the fires that destroyed most of Changsha. They apparently panicked, believing the Japanese were close, and acted before orderly evacuations had begun. Currently, the Japanese are fighting 40 miles from Changsha. . . . Japan closes more rivers in China to foreign navigation. In many areas Japanese goods enjoy a monopoly and high profits result. . . . A huge munitions depot in Mukden, Manchukuo, is destroyed mysteriously; 200 men die. Chinese guerillas take credit.
	A Includes developments that affect more than one world region, international organizations, and important meetings of world leaders.	**B** Includes all domestic and regional developments in Europe, including the Soviet Union.	**C** Includes all domestic and regional developments in Africa and the Middle East.	**D** Includes all domestic and regional developments in Latin America, the Caribbean, and Canada.	**E** Includes all domestic and regional developments in Asian and Pacific nations (and colonies).

U.S. Politics & Social Issues	U.S. Foreign Policy & Defense	Economics & Great Depression	Science, Technology & Nature	Culture, Leisure & Lifestyle	
	The United States recalls its Ambassador from Germany. . . . The president confers with WPA Administrator Hopkins, Secretary Morgenthau, and military leaders about shifting manpower from relief jobs to defense work.	General Motors announces new plans to stabilize employment through slow periods, guaranteeing employees with over two years' seniority a percentage of income all year. . . . As the CIO's annual convention opens, President Franklin Roosevelt sends a note asking the warring factions to try to get along.			Nov. 14
The five imprisoned Scottsboro defendants are denied pardon. . . . The Dies Committee on Un-American Activities considers investigating the LaFollette Senate Committee on Civil Liberties, to determine if it was influenced by Communists.	President Franklin Roosevelt, in a press conference, says making the American continent impregnable from air attack is a goal.		Television cameras capture and broadcast live pictures of a fire in New York that are "amazingly clear."		Nov. 15
Americans own 37.7 million radios, according to research by NBC. . . . The New York police squad assigned to protect the German Embassy and officials has been reformed, and is composed entirely of Jewish officers.		Inland Steel announces it will not comply with the NLRB ruling, but will take the matter to an appellate court.			Nov. 16
	The United States signs reciprocal trade agreements with Canada, the United Kingdom, and all its colonies, lowering or abolishing duties on many items. . . . The administration, discussing the Jewish refugee problem, points out that Congress would have to change immigration laws to permit entry of more refugees. The quota from Germany and Austria is filled for the next 14 months.	The CIO threatens a boycott of Ford products if the company refuses to bargain collectively.		The Nobel Peace Price is given to the Nansen International Office for Refugees in Switzerland.	Nov. 17
	Japan replies to the U.S. note of October 6, denying that Japan intends to discriminate against the United States, but affirming that a "new order" is being built in China. The United States takes this as a dismissal of the Open Door policy. . . . The President tells Labor Secretary Perkins to extend the visitors' visas of up to 15,000 political refugees from Germany for six months, and to continue extending them each six months.	John L. Lewis is unanimously elected as head of the new Congress of Industrial Organizations, a new group replacing the old CIO. . . . In a radio speech, AFL president William Green calls for a boycott of German goods.			Nov. 18
	The Navy Department will spend $33.4 million to increase its own facilities and modernize those of contractors, to support an enlarged shipbuilding program. Eighty ships will be under construction by the end of the year.	The United Auto Workers Executive Board, supporting President Homer Martin, votes to expel the Detroit District Council, which it says is Communist-dominated. . . . Police in Jersey City take signs from picketers, violating the court order of November 7.			Nov. 19
				In his radio show, Father Coughlin quotes Nazi statistics to prove that Jews support Communism, and lists unsubstantiated atrocities committed by Jewish-backed Communists. The radio station says the preacher uttered "mistakes of fact." The station corrected his "facts" prior to broadcast, with citations, but the priest read the original speech. . . . Jazz singer Ethel Waters plays in Carnegie Hall.	Nov. 20

F	G	H	I	J
Includes elections, federal-state relations, civil rights and liberties, crime, the judiciary, education, healthcare, poverty, urban affairs, and population.	*Includes formation and debate of U.S. foreign and defense policies, veterans affairs, and defense spending. (Relations with specific foreign countries are usually found under the region concerned.)*	*Includes business, labor, agriculture, taxation, transportation, consumer affairs, monetary and fiscal policy, natural resources, pollution, and accidents.*	*Includes worldwide scientific, medical, and technological developments, natural phenomena, U.S. weather, and natural disasters.*	*Includes the arts, religion, scholarship, communications media, sports, entertainment, fashions, fads, and social life.*

	World Affairs	Europe	Africa & The Middle East	The Americas	Asia & The Pacific
Nov. 21	Britain announces its plan to help the Jewish refugees from Nazi Germany: immigration to the uplands of British Guiana in South America or Tanganyika, a former German colony in east Africa. Smaller African properties may be available for settlement in Southern Rhodesia, Kenya, and Nyasaland. Britain's Prime Minister expects that private funding will pay for resettlement. . . . Japan and the Reich sign a cultural pact, recognizing their racial principles.	A wave of strikes stops industries in France. New decrees prohibit strikes; observers see a showdown between capitalist and socialist ideas. . . . Journalists in Spain get documentation of Italian troops who entered the country in October, along with supplies of munitions and new planes. . . . Fighting at the Segre River in Spain results in few gains for either side.	British troops take over Beersheba in Palestine, occupied by Arab forces for six weeks. At least three Arab leaders opposed to the Mufti of Jerusalem have been shot in the last four days.		Chinese troops claim to have beaten back Japanese forces to within three miles of Canton. Japan reports taking back towns near Hankow. . . . Japanese planes shell Pootung and suburbs of Shanghai, where Chinese guerillas are positioned.
Nov. 22		Italy and Germany inform Poland and Hungary that they must accept current borders with Czechoslovakia. . . . Strikes spread in France; each time police pull sit-downers from a plant, employees in another factory sit down. . . . France is hopeful over Chancellor Hitler's statement that he would like to be good neighbors. . . . A Gestapo newspaper warns democracies that unless they take Jews from Germany, Germany will starve and exterminate them. . . . Finland dissolves its fascist organization, the Patriotic National Movement.			
Nov. 23		France and Germany agree on a non-aggression pact, to be signed next month. . . . In Valenciennes, France, 26,000 workers in 40 factories strike. . . . Hungary's Premier Imrédy and his Cabinet resign, having lost support of Parliament. . . . Italy and Germany sign a pact regulating cultural relations. . . . A citizenship law for the Sudeten and Czech lands is passed, giving Germany the right to expel non-Germans, and the Czechs the right to expel Germans.			Japanese planes bomb Sian, and the headquarters of China's Eighth Route Army. . . . In the south, Japan lands 2,000 troops on the east bank of the Pearl River.
Nov. 24		Angered over decrees lengthening the 40-hour workweek, French workers expand strikes from the northeast to Paris. Police use tear gas to remove 12,000 workers in a Renault plant. . . . Britain's Prime Minister and Foreign Minister meet in Paris with their French counterparts, discussing defense, the Reich, and the Spanish civil war. . . . Multiple air strikes on Barcelona by Spanish insurgents continue night and day. Loyalist troops abandon the Segre battle after 16 days, saying it was never more than a diversion.	Anti-Semitic rioting injures 38 Jewish men and women in Johannesburg, South Africa. The violence started after fascists broke up an anti-fascist demonstration.	Mexico reveals seizure of 2 million acres (3,100 square miles) in the northeast, an extension of the west Texas oil field, from U.S. owners.	Japanese troops are still stalled in their drive south to Changsha. . . . Fighting comes within 20 miles of Hong Kong. . . . Guerilla troops in Honan and southern Shansi attack and burn Japanese-held rail stations and tracks.
Nov. 25	Secretary Hull sails with the U.S. delegation for Lima, Peru, to attend the eighth Pan-American Conference in December.	Polish troops cross the Czech border a week ahead of the scheduled occupation date, leading to violence. . . . The French General Confederation of Labor calls a general strike of 5 million workers on November 30. . . . Germany demands that all Jewish students repay loans within two weeks. All Jewish retail stores and mail order businesses must cease and liquidate immediately, but salaries must be paid out through January 1. . . . Ireland prepares to take 20 Jewish refugee families. Britain and France announce that 10,000 refugees each will be taken in by their colonies.		Bolivia declares martial law and fights a leftist revolt, arresting 20 leaders.	An attempt to assassinate the mayor of Shanghai is foiled, and the assassin is killed by police. . . . Japanese troops capture a village four miles from Hong Kong.
Nov. 26		In north France, 50,000 striking workers are ordered into the military by Prime Minister Daladier. . . . Poland and the Soviet Union renew their non-aggression pact. . . . Firefighters use hoses to disperse a crowd of 20,000 in Sofia, Bulgaria, who demand the return of territory lost 19 years ago. One person dies; 360 are arrested. Martial law and press censorship are imposed. . . . Nazis ban swing music in Germany. . . . Anti-Semitic riots in Hungary result in 35 arrests.	British infantry and pilots wipe out a band of 15 Arab terrorists in Lower Galilee.	Bolivia and Paraguay resume full diplomatic relations, exchanging ambassadors.	Japanese troops fight Chinese army "remnants" to within a half mile of Kowloon, which is British territory. At least 1,000 Chinese soldiers cross the border and are interned by the British. In a few instances, Japanese troops cross into Kowloon but quickly withdraw. . . . An area near Samshui, 30 miles from Canton, is heavily bombed by 50 planes to remove 12,000 Chinese troops. . . . A munitions dump near Taiyuan in Shansi explodes, killing 300; Chinese guerillas take credit.

A	B	C	D	E
Includes developments that affect more than one world region, international organizations, and important meetings of world leaders.	*Includes all domestic and regional developments in Europe, including the Soviet Union.*	*Includes all domestic and regional developments in Africa and the Middle East.*	*Includes all domestic and regional developments in Latin America, the Caribbean, and Canada.*	*Includes all domestic and regional developments in Asian and Pacific nations (and colonies).*

U.S. Politics & Social Issues	U.S. Foreign Policy & Defense	Economics & Great Depression	Science, Technology & Nature	Culture, Leisure & Lifestyle	
The sixth lynching this year occurs in Wiggins, Miss., as a mob of 200 hangs Wilder McGowan. An aged, socially prominent white woman had been attacked the night before, but could not name her assailant.		A strike by the CIO-affiliated Livestock Handlers' Union shuts down Chicago's stockyards. The union agrees to a truce tomorrow, so that animals can be cleared from the yards before the strike resumes. . . . Iowa's Governor Kraschel dismisses the 225 National Guard troops still in Sioux City. A force of 600 was sent a month ago to keep order at the Swift Packing Plant during a strike. The strike is ongoing.	Two landslides in St. Lucia, West Indies, kill at least 60 people—mostly workers clearing a road of previous slide debris.	Mary Lincoln Isham, a granddaughter of the 16th president, dies and leaves a portrait of Abraham Lincoln, painted by George P.A. Healy, to the White House.	Nov. 21
	The United States asks Germany for assurances that American citizens who are Jewish will not be subjected to the same discriminatory rules as German Jews. . . . Secretary of State Cordell Hull says Japan's recent reply is unsatisfactory.	Informally, the President says Georgia will get no more WPA funding until the state legislature cooperates with the federal government and establishes a public works authority.			Nov. 22
Interior Secretary Harold Ickes criticizes Rep. Dies and his committee at a press conference.		Another landslide in St. Lucia leaves hundreds missing. The final death total is never known but may be as high as 340. . . . Firefighters and Civilian Conservation Corps workers battle wildfires in the hills and canyons of Southern California, from San Diego north to Santa Barbara counties.	A Rodgers and Hart musical based on Shakespeare's *Comedy of Errors*, *The Boys from Syracuse*, opens in New York.		Nov. 23
Rep. Dies says that Secretary of the Interior Harold Ickes and Secretary of Labor Frances Perkins should resign.				*Angels with Dirty Faces*, starring Jimmy Cagney, Humphrey Bogart, Pat O'Brien, and the Dead End Kids, premiers. Cagney is chosen "Best Actor" by the New York Film Critics Circle, and is nominated for an Oscar.	Nov. 24
	The State Department tells its Embassy in Berlin (which is still open) to prod Germany over the debt owed on behalf of Austria.	As the fifth day of the Chicago stockyards strike ends, AFL spokesmen say their workers, who have respected the CIO-sponsored strike, will return to work on November 28.			Nov. 25
	Germany announces its Ambassador to the United States, en route to Germany, will not return.			Father Coughlin refuses to comply with radio network WMCA's new rule that he submit his speeches 48 hours before broadcast. The radio station lowers the deadline to four hours.	Nov. 26

F	G	H	I	J
Includes elections, federal-state relations, civil rights and liberties, crime, the judiciary, education, healthcare, poverty, urban affairs, and population.	Includes formation and debate of U.S. foreign and defense policies, veterans affairs, and defense spending. (Relations with specific foreign countries are usually found under the region concerned.)	Includes business, labor, agriculture, taxation, transportation, consumer affairs, monetary and fiscal policy, natural resources, pollution, and accidents.	Includes worldwide scientific, medical, and technological developments, natural phenomena, U.S. weather, and natural disasters.	Includes the arts, religion, scholarship, communications media, sports, entertainment, fashions, fads, and social life.

	World Affairs	Europe	Africa & The Middle East	The Americas	Asia & The Pacific
Nov. 27		Prime Minister Daladier orders the military to take over all French railroads to prevent a strike by rail employees. . . . Hungarian Regent Horthy refuses the resignation of Premier Imrédy and asks him to form a new government. . . . Poland completes its occupation of Czech lands. The Czechs evacuate early to stop border skirmishes, but lethal violence still occurred. . . . Anti-Semitic rioting leads to a bomb blast in the Banat region of Romania, killing three and injuring 40. . . . Poland agrees to admit Jewish refugees over 65 years old.	British troops in Palestine now concentrate on clearing terrorists and seizing arms from small Arab villages rather than the large cities. The only reported violence is the continued Arab shootings of Arab opponents of the Mufti of Jerusalem, al-Husseini.		Thirty thousand Chinese workers begin work to convert marshy land near Shanghai into a large air field for Japan. Construction has also started on a large military base for the Japanese at the mouth of the Whangpoo River, near Shanghai. Foreigners are banned from the site, but barracks for 20,000, an airfield, and gun emplacements are being built. . . . Japan stages three air attacks on Hengyang in Hunan, and one on Ichang, and on Chuki in Chekiang province. Japan claims ground victories near the Shansi-Hopeh border.
Nov. 28		Northern Catalan towns in Spain are shelled, and two British ships are damaged by insurgent-dropped bombs. . . . Four new corps are added to Germany's army, bringing it to 1 million strong. . . . Premier Daladier addresses France by radio, asking citizens to support the government.	British troops surround an Arab band south of Haifa, with air support. Eleven Arabs die, and four British soldiers are wounded. A bomb injures several Jewish men in Haifa, and two Arab men are killed in a sniping incident. Overall, authorities claim violence has been significantly reduced.		Gen. Eiki Tojo, Vice Minister of War, tells Japan's munitions manufacturers that the country must be able to fight wars on two fronts: China and the Soviet Union. . . . Still 40 miles from Changsha, the Japanese force is said to be digging in for the winter. Other divisions are arrayed from Taien to Hankow, and north to Yochow.
Nov. 29	Germany demands the arrest of Mexico's top labor organizer, because he made disparaging comments about Adolf Hitler.	Belgium withdraws from the Non-Intervention Committee, and recognizes Gen. Franco's government as legitimate. . . . French troops are called out to stand ready near ports and large cities. . . . Synagogues and Jewish-owned factories are set afire and 101 suspected fascists are arrested in Cluj, Romania. . . . The aunt and uncle of Herschel Grynszpan are sentenced to four months in prison and fined 100 francs for sheltering the 17-year-old after he was denied residency in France. No interpreter was available for their trial. . . . An explosion near Donegal kills two members of the Irish Republican Army; more explosives are found nearby.	In Umm Azzinatt, a battle between Arabs and British troops kills 43 Arabs and two British soldiers.	Mexico refuses entry to 14 Jews and returns them to Germany, without letting them disembark.	Following British protests, Japan apologizes for border incursions near Hong Kong, and moves operations from the area.
Nov. 30	The League of Nations' Conference for Intellectual Cooperation opens in Paris.	France's one-day general strike fails, as the Prime Minister requisitions all public service employees to work for the government. Laborers in Paris choose to ignore the strike call, giving a clear signal to Daladier to proceed with his economic plan. . . . Italy's Chamber of Deputies calls for the appropriation of territories belonging to France: Tunisia, Corsica, Nice, and Savoy. . . . Germany's police pass curfews prohibiting Jews from appearing in public at certain hours: the first concrete steps toward creating a ghetto. . . . Germany's foreign trade declines by a sudden 8 percent this month.		About 7,230 acres of grazing land near Texas is expropriated by Mexico from an owner in the United States. Mexico announces the land will be divided among 59 descendents of slaves who emigrated in the 1860s.	Prince Teh, of Japanese-controlled Inner Mongolia, says he wishes to unite all Mongolian people and revive their language and culture. . . . Japanese pilots drop incendiary bombs on Kweilin in Kwangsi province. Seventy-two die and hundreds are injured.
Dec. 1		In France, the Secretary of the General Confederation of Labor and union leaders lose government and private positions after their failed strike. Up to 80,000 workers are fired for not working. . . . France asks Italy the meaning of yesterday's demonstration over territory. . . . Five insurgent planes drop 75 bombs on Barcelona and its harbor. . . . Britain asks citizens to sign up voluntarily for a "war registry," putting their individual skills to use.	The Iraqi Senate and King approve the oil concession to British-owned Basrah Petroleum. . . . A group headed by Fakhri Nashashibi claiming to represent 70,000 Arabs meets with British authorities. They are opposed to the Mufti of Jerusalem's terrorist policies.	Ecuadorian President Borrero resigns after a stormy and factionalized administration of 110 days.	Japan's new budget is its highest ever, though the military expenses in China are presented separately. The amount funding immigration to Manchukuo is doubled. . . . Japan reopens the Yangtze River to limited commercial shipping. . . . Interior Minister John McEwen announces that Australia will accept 15,000 refugee immigrants over three years.
Dec. 2	As the Inter-Governmental Committee on Refugees meets, France and the Netherlands say they can place 10,000 refugees each in their colonies.	France's Prime Minister asks companies to rehire employees who followed their union's orders to strike. Throughout France, 20,000 workers remain on strike. . . . Brigades of the Young Communist League "raid" Moscow stores, searching for reasons for shortages. The raiders find evidence of poor distribution, hoarding, and "speculation" in unofficial markets.	An ambush kills three Jewish officers and leads to a British attack on the Arab band responsible. Daily violence and assassinations show that order has not been imposed in Palestine.	Dr. Mosquera Narvaez, a Liberal, is the new President of Ecuador.	Chinese troops are forced to pull out of Tsungfa, which they recaptured November 13. . . . A Chinese force attacking Tungshan, 65 miles south of Hankow, is beaten back and a third of the 2,000 soldiers are killed. . . . Japanese planes bomb Yiyang, Hunan, in the middle of a snowstorm, setting several warehouses on fire.

A	B	C	D	E
Includes developments that affect more than one world region, international organizations, and important meetings of world leaders.	Includes all domestic and regional developments in Europe, including the Soviet Union.	Includes all domestic and regional developments in Africa and the Middle East.	Includes all domestic and regional developments in Latin America, the Caribbean, and Canada.	Includes all domestic and regional developments in Asian and Pacific nations (and colonies).

U.S. Politics & Social Issues	U.S. Foreign Policy & Defense	Economics & Great Depression	Science, Technology & Nature	Culture, Leisure & Lifestyle	
	The President confers with returned U.S. Ambassadors from Italy and Germany. The Ambassador to Germany will be reassigned by the State Department.			WMCA and two other stations refuse to broadcast Father Coughlin's radio show, but many stations carry it. The priest rebroadcasts his previous address, relying on it to defend himself against exaggerated charges.	Nov. 27
		None of the men promised by the AFL show up for work at the Chicago stockyards. Negotiations with the CIO continue.		German immigrant artist George Groz becomes an American citizen.	Nov. 28
	A 74-point program of cooperation with other countries in the Americas is made public by the President, and will be presented to Congress. . . . The United States will cut its tariff on sugar from Cuba, and Cuba likewise cuts tariffs on certain U.S. food imports.			Harvard University announces 20 new scholarships of $500 each for refugee students from Germany.	Nov. 29
		Henry Ford urges the United States to take in Jewish refugees, saying there will be jobs and opportunities for all.			Nov. 30
The Congressional Temporary National Economic Committee opens a two-year investigation into American business and the influence of monopolies. . . . The Dies House Committee on Un-American Activities questions Homer Martin, president of the United Auto Workers.		Blocks away from the Chicago stockyards, gunmen attack union leader Herbert March, who escapes. The 11-day old strike is over a closed shop, written contract, and union dues collection.	In the nation's worst auto accident, a school bus stalls on train tracks during a snowstorm in Utah, and is hit by a freight train. The driver and 25 of the 32 students die.	Moscow audiences see the film *Alexander Neivsky* for the first time, and director Sergei Eisenstein is restored to favor in the Soviet Union.	Dec. 1
The President relaxes his ban on letting Georgia have WPA funds, saying the state has made efforts to cooperate with the federal program over the past two weeks.		General Motors shuts down two plants in Flint, Mich., when a UAW walkout idles 10,000 workers. GM says the strike is in violation of its contract with workers.	Robert Lee Cannon and Albert Kessel become the first people to die in California's gas chamber. . . . Torrential rains leave 9,000 homeless and wipes out crops in the Philippines. In southeast Turkey, flooding kills 72 people and thousands of head of cattle.		Dec. 2

F	G	H	I	J
Includes elections, federal-state relations, civil rights and liberties, crime, the judiciary, education, healthcare, poverty, urban affairs, and population.	*Includes formation and debate of U.S. foreign and defense policies, veterans affairs, and defense spending. (Relations with specific foreign countries are usually found under the region concerned.)*	*Includes business, labor, agriculture, taxation, transportation, consumer affairs, monetary and fiscal policy, natural resources, pollution, and accidents.*	*Includes worldwide scientific, medical, and technological developments, natural phenomena, U.S. weather, and natural disasters.*	*Includes the arts, religion, scholarship, communications media, sports, entertainment, fashions, fads, and social life.*

	World Affairs	Europe	Africa & The Middle East	The Americas	Asia & The Pacific
Dec. 3		Hundreds of French ship and dock workers walk off jobs at Le Havre. Over 300 American volunteer soldiers from Spain are among passengers stranded by the strike. . . . Jews in Germany are warned to stay indoors as Germans celebrate National Solidarity Day. New laws restrict Jews from driving, and they are advised to move to the northern part of the city as other areas will be barred to them. . . . Anti-aircraft guns repel insurgent planes in Barcelona, but other cities in northeast Spain are bombed and at least 55 people die.			Japanese plans are balked by Gen. Wu Pei-fu's refusal to lead a collaborative government. The aging general says he will be glad to take over if every Japanese soldier leaves China—but not before. . . . Winter storms stall military actions in north and central China. Japanese gains are held to conquered cities and rail lines. Troops still mass 50 miles north of Changsha, and within 50 miles of Kiukiang. In the north, Japan's troops stay south of the Yellow River, with a large force in Paoting.
Dec. 4		About 1,300 seamen are fired for striking in Le Havre, France. The union sends a delegation to the General Confederation of Labor in Paris. . . . A pro-French demonstration of 30,000 is held outside the Italian Embassy in Corsica. . . . 800 refugee children enter France from Germany. . . . Iron Guard fascists attempt another assassination in Romania. Over 2,000 fascists are jailed and police search for more. . . . Two thousand Jewish servants lose their jobs in Italy due to new laws.	In Tunis, a pro-French crowd of 500 vandalizes Italian-owned businesses, and 15 are arrested. . . . Arabs submit to the British rule requiring identification permits for all traveling males. Transporting citrus fruit to market necessitates the change; for weeks no Arab has been legally able to drive.		After bombs destroy a half-mile square section of Kweilin in Kwangsi province, pilots drop leaflets saying the city is being punished because of its loyalty to Gen. Chiang Kai-shek.
Dec. 5		French naval officers and crews stand ready to man ocean liners in Le Havre. . . . France's Finance Committee approves a 1939 defense budget of over 18 billion francs. . . . Six hundred Jewish children leave Vienna for new homes in Britain, and possibly the United States. The Scottish home of Earl Balfour, who wrote the Balfour Declaration, will house 200 refugee children. . . . New decrees in Germany give local authorities the right to strip Jews of valuables and property. Jews are forbidden to buy or hold real estate. All assets must be put in state-controlled banks within a few weeks.	Ambushes kill four men in Palestine, both Jew and Arab.	Swastikas line the streets of Lima, Peru. German and Italian "observers" lobby with delegates arriving for the Pan-American Conference.	The U.S. gunboat *Luzon* is the first warship permitted to sail down the Yangtze River from Hankow to Shanghai. . . . Japanese ships in the Gulf of Tonkin shell areas 70 miles from French Indo-China, in Kwangsi. . . . Electricity to much of Hankow is cut to conserve dwindling coal resources.
Dec. 6		In Paris, Germany's Foreign Minister Ribbentrop signs a nonaggression pact with France. . . . Romania files a protest with the German Embassy over savage reporting in German papers about King Carol's personal life. . . . Insurgent pilots have bombed 30 towns and their fields in loyalist Spain since December 2, killing over 300 people. . . . Memel, Lithuania, will hold elections on December 11, and Nazi violence and clashes occur. An American journalist is beaten for refusing to give the Nazi salute.			From Canton, Japanese forces move southwest to capture Kongmoon. Pakhoi, 70 miles from Indo-China, fights off an attempt to land troops. . . . The *Luzon* stops near Kiukiang to pick up Americans trapped for months at Kuling, but Chinese troops refuse to allow foreigners to leave the mountain resort.
Dec. 7		Fascists in Naples, Italy, demonstrate for the "return" of Tunisia. . . . Media in Berlin continue their stories on Romania, predicting a revolution, accusing the government of murdering fascists, and implying that King Carol's mistress, Madame Lupescu—who is Jewish—orchestrates the killings. . . . The governor of Memel, Lithuania, resigns. . . . Jews working at construction sites in Vienna must wear a yellow star armband.		Workers walk out of the world's largest silver mine, the Real del Monte, in Pachuco, Mexico, demanding higher wages. The United States Smelting Company, the mine owner, says it cannot pay their price.	Wang Ming, representing the Communist Party of China, says the Japanese are trying to drive a wedge between Communists and the party of Chiang Kai-shek, the Kuomintang.
Dec. 8	Mexico and Germany sign a deal trading oil from expropriated fields for a $17 million credit in machinery and products.	Britain protests that Germany's new laws of December 5 do not exempt foreigners, and violate a 1923 treaty. . . . Students from the Sorbonne stage a mock demonstration in Paris, demanding "Venice for the French!"	Italian slogans and threats start riots and disorders in Tunis, quelled only when troops from Algiers arrive. . . . Anti-French demonstrations are held in Libya. . . . British soldiers arrest 35 members of an Arab band in Tul Karm, Palestine, as well as local magistrates participating in an illegal trial.		
Dec. 9	Japan tells Ambassadors from the United States and Britain that the Nine-Powers Treaty is invalid, and that China, Japan, and Manchukuo will look out for their interests, engaging in foreign trade when appropriate.	In Corsica, students stone the Italian Embassy. . . . Ethnic clashes continue in areas of Czechoslovakia and its former territory, in some cases whipped up by radio broadcasts.		The Eighth Pan-American Conference begins in Lima, Peru. Press censorship is strict, and delegates find that their offices are searched and correspondence opened.	China claims victory after a three-hour battle at Yungsui, 30 miles north of Nanchang. In the south, Tsungfa is again the scene of fighting, and Japanese warships shell the coast.
	A *Includes developments that affect more than one world region, international organizations, and important meetings of world leaders.*	**B** *Includes all domestic and regional developments in Europe, including the Soviet Union.*	**C** *Includes all domestic and regional developments in Africa and the Middle East.*	**D** *Includes all domestic and regional developments in Latin America, the Caribbean, and Canada.*	**E** *Includes all domestic and regional developments in Asian and Pacific nations (and colonies).*

U.S. Politics & Social Issues	U.S. Foreign Policy & Defense	Economics & Great Depression	Science, Technology & Nature	Culture, Leisure & Lifestyle	
	The United States and Iraq sign their first trade treaty, granting most-favored-nation status.	The UAW and GM reach agreement: all plants will reopen on December 5, negotiations will begin, and those who called the unauthorized strike will be disciplined by the union.			Dec. 3
		With Chicago's Mayor Kelly mediating, stockyards owners agree to collective bargaining with the CIO and written contracts. After 13 days, the strike ends.		Father Coughlin claims Henry Ford's November 30 statement was written by Detroit's Rabbi Franklin and published by "controlled newspapers." . . . Philanthropist Dr. Godfrey Lowell Cabot establishes the Maria Moors Cabot Awards, in memory of his wife. The prizes, the first in international journalism, will be awarded by Columbia University.	Dec. 4
In a speech broadcast over the radio, the President reaffirms his dedication to the New Deal and points out that much of the world looks to the United States for leadership.	Cuba's Ambassador says a $50 million loan to his country will be made by the United States through the Export-Import Bank in Washington, D.C.	The Supreme Court decides that the National Labor Relations Board has jurisdiction over the Edison Company, but limits its authority over aspects of Edison's labor contracts.	A typhoon kills 305 people, ruins crops, and leaves thousands homeless in the central Philippines. Rain mixes with ash from the slopes of the Mayon volcano to slide down and bury the village of Camalig, known to be home to more than 20,000 people.		Dec. 5
			The United States files charges against the whaling ship *Frango* and accompanying ships, for defying Coast Guard warnings and international treaties. The crew slaughtered at least 900 whales with explosive harpoons; 90 of the whales were young and under the legal size.	Davey O'Brien, a 150-pound quarterback, wins the Heisman Trophy.	Dec. 6
The President writes to Alabama Governor Bibb Graves, asking him to pardon the Scottsboro defendants. . . . Rep. Thomas of the Dies Committee says he will start impeachment proceedings against Labor Secretary Perkins, because she has not taken steps to deport Harry Bridges, a Communist and West Coast labor leader.	The United States asks Germany for assurance that American Jews' rights and property in Germany will be respected.				Dec. 7
	The President calls the U.S. Ambassador to China home for a consultation.	The NLRB reissues a decision against Douglas Aircraft in Santa Monica, Calif. The company is ordered to reinstate 32 workers with back pay, and to allow the UAW to represent workers. Owner Donald Douglas calls the ruling "absurd." . . . In San Francisco, businesses and industries unite in an employers' council, to bargain collectively.		The movie version of George Bernard Shaw's *Pygmalion* premiers. Mr. Shaw will share an Oscar for screenwriting with other contributors to the film.	Dec. 8
	The President says all intelligence agencies will coordinate efforts to stop foreign espionage. . . . Britain's former Foreign Minister Anthony Eden visits the United States.				Dec. 9

F	**G**	**H**	**I**	**J**
Includes elections, federal-state relations, civil rights and liberties, crime, the judiciary, education, healthcare, poverty, urban affairs, and population.	*Includes formation and debate of U.S. foreign and defense policies, veterans affairs, and defense spending. (Relations with specific foreign countries are usually found under the region concerned.)*	*Includes business, labor, agriculture, taxation, transportation, consumer affairs, monetary and fiscal policy, natural resources, pollution, and accidents.*	*Includes worldwide scientific, medical, and technological developments, natural phenomena, U.S. weather, and natural disasters.*	*Includes the arts, religion, scholarship, communications media, sports, entertainment, fashions, fads, and social life.*

	World Affairs	Europe	Africa & The Middle East	The Americas	Asia & The Pacific
Dec. 10		France's Chamber of Deputies votes in favor of Prime Minister Daladier and his policies. Communists and Socialists voted as a block against him. . . . French ship workers in Le Havre end their strike. . . . While not officially sanctioned, anti-Semitic activities in Czechoslovakia involve firing of Jewish workers, and exclusion of Jewish artists in exhibitions and societies.	French planes, ships, and troops arrive to reinforce Tunis, Tunisia, where anti-Italian demonstrations continue.	Brazil promises asylum to any refugee, legal or illegal, who files an application by December 21.	Thirty-two foreigners isolated at Kuling brave storms to descend the mountain and board a Japanese ship bound for Shanghai. Over 150 people remain at Kuling.
Dec. 11		Nazis win a clear victory in Memel, Lithuania's elections for new Diet members. . . . Yugoslav elections reaffirm Premier Stoyadinovitch's party with a small majority, although the government claims no returns are received from Croatia and Dalmatia. Violent clashes and several deaths occur at polling places, and charges of fraud are raised. . . . A bill asking for Ukrainian autonomy is rejected by the Polish Parliament.	Land mines and snipers take more lives in Palestine.		Wang Ching-wei, leader of the Kuomintang, says that the Nine-Powers Treaty is not obsolete simply because Japan violated it. . . . Chinese guerilla forces report inflicting thousands of casualties on Japanese soldiers in Shansi province.
Dec. 12		Britain and France ask Germany to respect the autonomy of Memel, Lithuania. . . . Bulgaria accepts several hundred Jewish refugees, hoping they will move on to Palestine.			Japanese forces claim that 10,000 guerillas surrendered to them near Shanghai, but admit that six times that number still raid from positions in the Yangtze delta.
Dec. 13		Foes of President Smetona of Lithuania are arrested. . . . Near Hamburg, Germany, 100 prisoners from the Sachsenhausen detention facility begin work on the Neuengamme concentration camp.		After several clashes, Ecuador's President Mosquera Narvaez dissolves the Assembly and orders elections. Several Socialist Assembly members are arrested.	Chinese authorities claim more gains in several provinces, by both guerilla troops and regular army forces, including the capture of Waichow.
Dec. 14	France complains that Japan has cut off food supplies and water to the French Concession in Shanghai. France says Japan is angered over French refusal to turn over anti-Japanese agents seeking asylum. . . . The Bank for International Settlements in Switzerland says it is ready to cooperate with nations in transferring property or otherwise aiding Jews who emigrate.	Foreign Minister Bonnet reiterates that France will not yield one inch of territory to Italy. . . . Italy sets it budget for 1939–40, allowing a 4.75 billion lire deficit. . . . Romania's Cabinet draws up a 10-year plan to "reduce the influence" of Jews. The plan emphasizes emigration and cooperation with other nations. . . . Czechoslovakia passes a bill allowing the constitution to be easily changed when desired, enabling authoritarian government.	Jews and Arabs die in several days of violence in northern Palestine. British troops arrest over 40 Arabs in small villages near Haifa.		Gen. Chiang Kai-shek calls a conference to announce policy changes and purge his government of "defeatist elements," such as the peace faction led by Wang Ching-wei.
Dec. 15	Reichsbank president Dr. Schacht meets with Refugee Committee members to present a plan for Jewish emigration. The German plan demands a ransom for each Jew released. While unsavory, the plan opens the door to negotiations with Germany.	In Germany, the first installment of the one billion mark fine is due from Jews. Those with over 5,000 marks must pay 5 percent of their owned wealth. . . . Prime Minister Chamberlain reminds the leaders of Germany that Britain has greater cash resources and might outlast other nations in a war. . . . By decree, Gen. Franco of the Spanish insurgency restores citizenship to deposed King Alfonso. . . . The Spanish government reveals that members of a spy ring have been tried, with 200 death sentences and 200 prison terms meted out.	In two separate incidents in Palestine, a British soldier and a prominent Arab are shot to death. The Arab was an enemy of the Mufti of Jerusalem.	Ecuador's President is forced to accept a compromise by the army, which supports Congress. Elections will be held January 15, and Congress will meet February 1 to elect a new President. President Mosquera Narvaez will step down at that point.	Gen. Chiang Kai-shek flies to Sian in Shensi province to inspect defenses. Japanese artillery is active daily in Shensi. . . . Japanese troops report limited success against guerila bands near Shanghai, Chekiang province, and north of Nanking. They claim to inflict casualties and drive the bands away. . . . Former governor James Fugate is killed on the Philippine island of Mindanao. An American educator, Fugate lived in the Philippines for over 35 years. . . . Military hero Pibul Songgram becomes Prime Minister of Siam. There have been two attempts on his life—by gunshots, and poison—in the past six weeks.
Dec. 16		German servants working in other countries are asked to return home by May 1939. . . . Poland warns the Czech government that Ukrainian revolutionary groups are active in Czechoslovakia.	Arab taxis and buses begin operation for the first time this month in Palestine.	The Pan-American Conference adopts the liberal trade policies proposed by Secretary Hull, but not his policy on defense. Argentina, Chile, and Brazil—who benefit most by trade with Europe—lead the opposition to Hull's mutual defense agreement.	Gen. Pai Chung-hsi is vice-commander of all China's armies. . . . The Yellow River floods, breaking through dikes in Honan and Kiangsu provinces.

A	B	C	D	E
Includes developments that affect more than one world region, international organizations, and important meetings of world leaders.	Includes all domestic and regional developments in Europe, including the Soviet Union.	Includes all domestic and regional developments in Africa and the Middle East.	Includes all domestic and regional developments in Latin America, the Caribbean, and Canada.	Includes all domestic and regional developments in Asian and Pacific nations (and colonies).

U.S. Politics & Social Issues	U.S. Foreign Policy & Defense	Economics & Great Depression	Science, Technology & Nature	Culture, Leisure & Lifestyle	
The President announces that all papers connected with his presidency will be kept in an archive at his Hyde Park estate, which in turn will be given to the government on his death.		Cotton farmers vote to continue crop market quotas through 1939; tobacco farmers vote against such quotas.	In Sydney, Australia, 75 mile-per-hour winds fan brush fires, knock out communication lines, and beach boats in the harbor.	The Trapp Family Choir performs in New York for the first time, at the Town Hall. . . . The burning of Atlanta is filmed for *Gone With the Wind*. David O. Selznick meets Vivien Leigh for the first time; he's been considering her for the role of Scarlett for months.	Dec. 10
	America's Ambassador to China meets with Gen. Chiang Kai-shek, who asks for economic support. Otherwise, Chiang says, the United States will lose its Far East investments to Japan, and China will seek help from the Soviet Union.		Based on research gathered near the North Pole, Soviet scientists claim that the global climate is slowly warming.	Christain Lous Lange, the Norwegian pacifist awarded the 1921 Nobel Peace Prize and former premier of Sweden, dies at age 69. . . . Cardinal Mundelein of Chicago, in a radio address, says that Father Coughlin does not speak for the Catholic Church.	Dec. 11
The Supreme Court rules that the University of Missouri Law School must admit qualified African-American student Lloyd Gaines, or a law school must be established at Lincoln University, Missouri, for black students. Gaines will disappear in March 1939, never getting the education he fought for.	The U.S. Maritime Commission begins an investigation into two Japanese shipping lines, accused of unfair practices in the Americas.	The Board of Directors of pharmaceutical company McKesson and Robbins demands the resignation of top officers. An $18 million fraud is revealed, hidden by nonexistent warehouses and drugs. . . . Republic Steel asks an appeals court to order the NLRB to reopen its case and allow the company to present more testimony.		Comedian George Burns pleads guilty to jewelry smuggling, having bought bracelets from those who smuggled them into the United States. . . . "Wrong-Way" Douglas Corrigan has earned $75,000 in the last 90 days.	Dec. 12
		The President increases funding for the Federal Housing Authority from $2 billion to $3 billion, to insure home mortgages.			Dec. 13
	Germany's reply to the U.S. note of December 7 is vague and ambivalent.	Arrest warrants are issued for three officers of the McKesson and Robbins Company—including president F. Donald Coster, who bought the company in 1926 and worked with family members to steal money for years. Accountants Price Waterhouse never suspected that whole inventories were fictitious; the scandal leads to a major overhaul of accounting practices. . . . The Securities and Exchange Commission lists nine charges of fraud against Fidelity Investments. The West Virginia company is insolvent; its liquidation will go to the Supreme Court.	Hans Bethe of Cornell University (a future Nobel Laureate) wins the Morrison Prize for his theories identifying the elements of solar energy production.		Dec. 14
Commerce Department Secretary Daniel C. Roper resigns. . . . At the Dies Committee's last public hearing, Bishop Leonard of the Methodist Episcopal Church testifies. He says Labor Secretary Frances Perkins should be replaced by a man and that aliens on relief rolls should be deported. He also suggests that publications of the government printing office be closely examined.	The United States sends a fourth note to Germany, demanding that American citizens not be subject to anti-Semitic laws. . . . The United States extends a $25 million credit to China through the Export-Import Bank.	Fingerprints reveal that McKesson and Robbins head F. Donald Coster is actually Philip Musica, a lifelong swindler.		Ground is broken in Washington, D.C., for the new Jefferson Memorial.	Dec. 15
	Japan is surprised and indignant over the U.S. loan to China, seeing it as prolonging the undeclared war.	F. Donald Coster/Philip Musica commits suicide; the other company officers under arrest are his brothers.			Dec. 16

F	G	H	I	J
Includes elections, federal-state relations, civil rights and liberties, crime, the judiciary, education, healthcare, poverty, urban affairs, and population.	*Includes formation and debate of U.S. foreign and defense policies, veterans affairs, and defense spending. (Relations with specific foreign countries are usually found under the region concerned.)*	*Includes business, labor, agriculture, taxation, transportation, consumer affairs, monetary and fiscal policy, natural resources, pollution, and accidents.*	*Includes worldwide scientific, medical, and technological developments, natural phenomena, U.S. weather, and natural disasters.*	*Includes the arts, religion, scholarship, communications media, sports, entertainment, fashions, fads, and social life.*

	World Affairs	Europe	Africa & The Middle East	The Americas	Asia & The Pacific
Dec. 17	Britain makes a £450,000 credit available to China to build roads from Burma. This will be charged against a £10 million credit from the British Board of Trade, which now awaits Parliament approval.	Italy informs France that their 1935 agreement defining territories is null because ratifications were not exchanged. . . . For 10 days, Spanish loyalists have anticipated a large insurgent offensive. Because of poor weather, the only activity has been air bombardment of towns in loyalist territory. . . . Britain tells Czech negotiators that any loans to Czechoslovakia hinge upon provisions for emigration of refugees.		Chile, Argentina, and Mexico block Secretary Hull's efforts for a policy on diplomatic options for land expropriations, deferring the issue for the next Pan-American Conference in five years.	Three days of air and naval bombardments by Japan begin, focused on Chinese guerilla positions. Among the targets are Pakhoi, a port in southern Kwangsi, sites along the Pearl River, and areas south of Chefoo in Shantung.
Dec. 18	The Soviet Union sets midnight as the deadline for a response from Japan on fishing rights in Siberian waters. Japan wants the old treaty renewed without change; the Soviet Union wants to withdraw 40 areas from the treaty.	Poland demands that Czechoslovakia stop its anti-Polish activities, including the encouragement of Ukrainians in their plots against Poland. . . . Hungary aligns itself with the fascist axis, against Bolshevism. . . . Organized Hungarian terrorists slip across the Czech border at night.	Fakhri Nashashibi leads a pro-British demonstration of 2,000 Arabs near Hebron. . . . Sheikh Said al-Khatib is shot dead in Jerusalem, the second Arab associated with the Mosque of Omar (Dome of the Rock) to be killed in two days.		Five Japanese divisions of troops are transported from Shantung, Hopeh, and Shansi provinces to Manchukuo to fight both the Communist Chinese Eighth Route Army and the threat of Soviet invasion.
Dec. 19		Hungarian terrorists seize the Slovak city of Slanic and surrounding villages. Four detachments of Slovak troops are dispatched. Hungary says the dispute was between city residents, and no force invaded. . . . Romania negotiates with France and Britain for 150,000 visas to relocate Jews to colonies. . . . Nazi leaders in the free city of Danzig announce that all Jews must leave by April 1, 1939. All property will be confiscated. . . . Espionage documents are found in the luggage of a British Vice Consul in Spain, who is soon cleared of blame. A British porter with access to the luggage commits suicide.		Eighty-two bodies are recovered from the wreckage of a passenger train near Barbecena, Minas Gerais, Brazil. The train, pulling wooden coaches, collided with a freight train, derailed, and burned. It was carrying Boy Scouts as well as laborers.	
Dec. 20	Germany invites George Ruplee, director of the Inter-Governmental Committee on Refugees, to Berlin for conferences. . . . France continues to enforce its ban on goods traveling to China through Indo-China. In return, Hainan Island is left alone by the Japanese. Shipments to China now come through Burma to Yunnan province.	At least 25 people have died from cold in Britain. In Paris, the temperature is 10 degrees at night. Jewish refugees are still living in tents, stables, and fields in regions just beyond the Reich's borders. . . . New purges in Soviet Ukraine result in the dismissal of five executives of the Young Communists Organization.			Japan installs the "Kwangtung Provincial Government" in Canton, with collaborator Pang Tung-yen as Chair. . . . Burma begins a program of civil disobedience against imperialism. In Rangoon, hundreds are injured when British troops rush sit-down demonstrations in the streets by students and children.
Dec. 21	Japan reviles Britain and the United States in newspapers, painting the United States as a tool of Britain.	Britain will spend £20 million to reinforce private homes to withstand air raids. . . . Poland's Parliament asks for a speedy emigration of all Jews. . . . Hoping to stop terrorism, Slovakia's Cabinet plans a plebiscite in areas ceded to Hungary. . . . Eight towns in Catalonia, Spain, are bombed by insurgents, leaving 26 dead.		A broken wheel throws 14 rail cars off the tracks 45 miles from Mexico City, killing 40 people. Most were government employees heading to Veracruz on holiday.	Windows are smashed and motorists attacked in Burma.
Dec. 22		Czechoslovakia suspends all Jewish teachers and professors from German, but not Czech, schools. All Jewish government officials are dismissed. . . . Police arrest 34 IRA members in early morning raids in Northern Ireland, for plotting to overthrow the government with multiple assassinations. . . . Nine hundred men, most from Vienna, are released from Dachau. They join the 7,000 let out of German concentration camps over the last fortnight. Many suffer from pneumonia and have lost limbs because of frostbite.		Brazil's new immigration law takes effect, requiring registration of 3 million immigrants and restriction of future immigrants to 2 percent of the nationality's entry over 50 years.	A state of emergency is declared in Burma, where nearly 100 have been arrested. Three men, one a member of the House of Representatives, are fined and imprisoned, to the acclaim of demonstrators. . . . Tokyo announces its terms for peace in China. They include freedom for Japan to trade, live, deploy troops, and exploit resources anywhere in China, but no territory is demanded. . . . A smallpox epidemic is reported in Shanghai. . . . The Joint Commission of the Peiping and Nanking governments meets and discusses reprisals against nations that aid China's Kuomintang.

A	B	C	D	E
Includes developments that affect more than one world region, international organizations, and important meetings of world leaders.	Includes all domestic and regional developments in Europe, including the Soviet Union.	Includes all domestic and regional developments in Africa and the Middle East.	Includes all domestic and regional developments in Latin America, the Caribbean, and Canada.	Includes all domestic and regional developments in Asian and Pacific nations (and colonies).

U.S. Politics & Social Issues	U.S. Foreign Policy & Defense	Economics & Great Depression	Science, Technology & Nature	Culture, Leisure & Lifestyle	
		The FBI begins to interview family members and sort through the fraudulent dealings of the Musica brothers, including bootlegging and arms smuggling. The McKesson and Robbins Company survives as McKesson Corporation. . . . Picket lines of 1,000 concerned citizens—women, children, Chinese, and Caucasian—picket a Greek ship in San Francisco. Longshoremen will not cross the lines to load the ship; its cargo is scrap iron for Japan.	Locusts destroy Nicaragua's bean crop, but leave the rice alone.		Dec. 17
At a Zionist association dinner, Interior Secretary Ickes condemns Nazis as "brutal dictators" who commit "crimes against humanity," and says Henry Ford, Charles Lindbergh, and any Americans who have accepted medals from them have foresworn their birthright.	The United States and Turkey complete a trade agreement granting most-favored-nation status. . . . Italy promises that the rights of American citizens in Italy will not be affected by new restrictions on Jews.	The Advisory Council on Social Security publicizes recommendations to expand the program to cover domestic and farm employees.		Two thousand picketers parade before New York station WMCA, over its refusal to broadcast Father Coughlin's radio show.	Dec. 18
	Treasury Secretary Morgenthau announces continuing credit to China against its gold reserves, a rebuff to the Japanese. Japan's Foreign Minister Arito terms the loan a "regrettable act" and "dangerous."	The AFL and CIO join in demanding that Oregon be cut off from Social Security funding because of its new anti-labor law, affecting unemployment insurance for workers involved in labor disputes.		With time off for good behavior, Al Capone could be released from Alcatraz to serve a one-year sentence in Cook County Jail. However he is dangerous and delusional due to medical problems. A conference with prison officials and Capone's family will decide his fate.	Dec. 19
A Washington, D.C., grand jury indicts the American Medical Association, three other groups, and 21 leading physicians and surgeons under the Sherman Anti-Trust Act, for "restraint of trade." The charge claims that organized medicine unfairly suppresses medical groups and cooperatives.	Jewish organizations ask the United States to relax its rules and grant, in advance, the 56,000 visas it would allow for 1939 and 1940 to immigrants from the Reich. . . . Germany tells the United States that legacies and inheritances of American Jews will be respected, and that exchange in full will be provided.	Bethlehem Steel and other, smaller companies contend that the minimum wage proposed on November 5 by Secretary Perkins and the Labor Board would hurt their industry, and thus hurt defense. They claim Secretary Perkins exceeds her authority by proposing such a change.	An 11,000-mile commercial phone and radio link opens for the first time between Washington, D.C., and Australia.	Paulette Goddard and Vivien Leigh take technicolor screen tests for Gone With the Wind—the only actresses to do so.	Dec. 20
	The United States agrees to sell 500,000 bushels of wheat per month, for six months, to the Red Cross for distribution in Spain. . . . Germany tries to deliver a protest over Secretary Ickes' speech of December 18, calling it "coarse and insulting." Acting Secretary of State Welles rejects the protest. He says that Germany has shocked the American people, and points out the insults that German newspapers print against U.S. leaders.				Dec. 21
	The investigation of Japanese shipping begun on December 12 ends as the two shipping companies agree to change their unfair practices and pricing immediately. . . . Senator Pittman, chair of the Foreign Relations Committee, comments that the American people do not like the governments of Japan or Germany, and the people have the right to enforce morality in their treaties.				Dec. 22

F	G	H	I	J
Includes elections, federal-state relations, civil rights and liberties, crime, the judiciary, education, healthcare, poverty, urban affairs, and population.	Includes formation and debate of U.S. foreign and defense policies, veterans affairs, and defense spending. (Relations with specific foreign countries are usually found under the region concerned.)	Includes business, labor, agriculture, taxation, transportation, consumer affairs, monetary and fiscal policy, natural resources, pollution, and accidents.	Includes worldwide scientific, medical, and technological developments, natural phenomena, U.S. weather, and natural disasters.	Includes the arts, religion, scholarship, communications media, sports, entertainment, fashions, fads, and social life.

	World Affairs	Europe	Africa & The Middle East	The Americas	Asia & The Pacific
Dec. 23	The German press has a field day with the fact that President Roosevelt is given the American Hebrew Award, for promoting understanding between Christians and Jews. Reich newspapers attack Secretary Ickes, Senator Pittman, and the influence of Jews in the United States with sarcastic and colorful words.	Insurgents launch three separate offensives on the Segre River, from Seros north to Tremp, in Catalonia, Spain. . . . Germany's newest decree bars Jews from serving as managers in business or industrial offices. . . . Hungary's Parliament debates anti-Jewish laws. . . . Poland deports 100 Czechs from Teschen in retaliation for border terrorism incidents. . . . . In France, the aunt and uncle of Herschel Grynszpan are released from prison. His murder trial is ongoing; his attorneys urge him to say that vom Rath, the German Embassy official killed, had seduced him. Grynszpan refuses.			
Dec. 24		Pope Pius XI reveals that fascists have attacked the offices of Catholic Action in several Italian cities lately—news that has been suppressed by the Italian press.		Twenty-one nations attending the Pan-American Conference sign the Declar-ation of Lima, affirming solidarity against foreign aggression—military, economic, cultural, or political. . . . President Pedro Aguirre Cerda is inaugurated in Chile.	
Dec. 25		A collision of two passenger trains near Etulia, Bessarabia, Romania, kills 93 and injures 340. . . . Spanish insurgents make gains of up to five miles on the southern end of their new front.			Japanese pilots bomb major cities in three provinces: Wuchow and Kweilin in Kwangsi, Sian in Shensi, and Changteh in Hunan. . . . China's Foreign Minister Wang Ching-wei leaves Chungking for Hong Kong, either due to illness, or to negotiate a truce with the Japanese.
Dec. 26	Italians broadcast rumors into French Somaliland, inciting the population against the French. Italian troops have manned posts on the border with Eritrea since January, stirring up trouble.	France tells Italy that if the 1935 treaty is null, new talks between their two countries alone should be initiated. . . . Fighting is heavy near Borjas Blancas, Spain, 16 miles east of Lerida, after heavy shelling. . . . Spanish insurgents announce the arrest of 50 for espionage, including British and French subjects. . . . Pravda editor Mikhail Kolzoff has been arrested, Soviet papers reveal.	Violence in Palestine increases: a deputy of Fakhri Nashashibi is killed, and a cousin's home is bombed; a Jewish carpenter is killed by a sniper and two Arab police are wounded by a bomb. A British banker is believed kidnapped.		The Japanese Diet opens; its only task is to obey the Emperor by passing the 8 billion yen budget. . . . Wang Ching-wei disappears. . . . An attempt to bomb Chungking is driven off by Chinese planes. . . . Japan opens an offensive in Shansi, 75 miles from Linfen, and bombs Chinese positions there.
Dec. 27	France claims Italian troops have crossed Somaliland borders to occupy unfortified oases.	Spanish towns east of Balaguer, Spain—the midpoint of the 100-mile front—are heavily shelled. The British ship Stanhope sinks in Barcelona's harbor. The Italian press boasts of the accomplishments of its brigades in Spain. . . . A new German decree segregates Jews from Aryans on trains. The German papers point to America's Jim Crow laws as an example of a working system. . . . Crowds gather in Surany, a city ceded to Hungary, where demonstrations began on December 24. Hungarian police fire into a crowd, killing two Slovak men. Police beat at least 200 others.		At the Pan-American Conference in Peru, the eight-point peace plan brought by Secretary Hull becomes the Declaration of American Principles, stressing mutual cooperation and respect for laws.	Gen. Chiang Kai-shek reiterates his belief that Wang Ching-wei, head of the Kuomintang, is receiving medical treatment for illness.
Dec. 28	France deploys a second battleship to the port of Jibuti in French Somaliland. In addition, 1,000 Senegalese troops will depart from Marseilles on December 31, to join the 1,500 troops already in French Somaliland.	A rebel tank assault near Balaguer in Spain follows the bombing yesterday. Fighting and bombing continues at Borgas Blanca, as well as points north and south. . . . After exposing past abuses, Soviet officials tighten labor regulations. Maternity leave is cut; vacation and disability insurance is tied to length of employment. . . . Romania begins separate negotiations with its German and Hungarian minorities. At issue are language, schools, religion, and civil rights. . . . A protest is lodged and Hungary apologizes for the violence at Surany, promising that all responsible will be punished.	Five deported Palestinian Arab leaders, released from the Seychelle Islands, are refused entry to Lebanon and Syria by French authorities.		Fighting goes on in Shansi province, with Japanese columns and planes attacking Chinese positions along the Fen River and rail lines. Severe fighting is also reported in Chekiang, southwest of Shanghai, and in Soochow.

A	B	C	D	E
Includes developments that affect more than one world region, international organizations, and important meetings of world leaders.	*Includes all domestic and regional developments in Europe, including the Soviet Union.*	*Includes all domestic and regional developments in Africa and the Middle East.*	*Includes all domestic and regional developments in Latin America, the Caribbean, and Canada.*	*Includes all domestic and regional developments in Asian and Pacific nations (and colonies).*

U.S. Politics & Social Issues	U.S. Foreign Policy & Defense	Economics & Great Depression	Science, Technology & Nature	Culture, Leisure & Lifestyle	
Harry Hopkins, head of the WPA, is named new Secretary of Commerce.	Responding to a perceived threat in Europe, the Navy Department makes permanent the U.S. Atlantic Squadron. Under Admiral William Leahy, the squadron had been temporary.	The President's committee of experts on the railroad delivers recommendations. Among them: establish national policy and a Transportation Board, and centralize regulations nationwide under the Interstate Commerce Commission. . . . An Appeals Court in New York upholds Judge Cotillo's right to enjoin all pickets, based on his decision that the right to picket was abused.		Margaret Hamilton's Wicked Witch costume catches fire during the filming of *The Wizard of Oz*, forcing her to take a six week hiatus to recover from burns.	Dec. 23
Harry Hopkins is sworn in at the White House as Secretary of Commerce. . . . Rev. Allan Knight Chalmers releases correspondence proving that Alabama Governor Bibb Graves broke his word to pardon the Scottsboro defendants.				German Architect Bruno Taut dies. . . . Melvyn Douglas brings movie stars and entertainers, including Gene Autry and Eddie Cantor, to a Christmas party for "Dust Bowl" children now living in the San Joaquin Valley in California.	Dec. 24
				Czech author Karel Capek dies at age 48 of double pneumonia. Reportedly, he refused to eat after the German invasion of his homeland.	Dec. 25
	Ambassador John Grew in Tokyo registers protests over bombing of American property in China on 10 separate occasions.				Dec. 26
	The President announces a plan for training 20,000 pilots annually, which he hopes to have installed in colleges nationwide by the next school year.		The 103rd National Parliament of Science opens in Richmond, Virginia, and research about mental health is a major focus.	Russian poet Osip Mandelstam dies in a Soviet labor camp. . . . More arrests are made in the McKesson and Robbins investigation, this time for blackmail against the late Philip Musica/Coster.	Dec. 27
Frank Murphy, outgoing governor of Michigan, will be appointed U.S. Attorney General. . . . Congressmen hint at their plans for the coming session; all expect a new reorganization bill, and Senator Van Nuys will try again for an anti-lynching bill. Speculation about new defense spending fuels the most talk.		Bethlehem Steel says it will contest the NLRB report. The company says it follows the spirit of the Labor Act and that the NLRB findings are counterproductive.	The scientists gathered in Virginia hear about the newly discovered role of histamines in allergies and asthma, and Dr. S.A. Korff discusses his latest research on cosmic rays.		Dec. 28

F	G	H	I	J
Includes elections, federal-state relations, civil rights and liberties, crime, the judiciary, education, healthcare, poverty, urban affairs, and population.	*Includes formation and debate of U.S. foreign and defense policies, veterans affairs, and defense spending. (Relations with specific foreign countries are usually found under the region concerned.)*	*Includes business, labor, agriculture, taxation, transportation, consumer affairs, monetary and fiscal policy, natural resources, pollution, and accidents.*	*Includes worldwide scientific, medical, and technological developments, natural phenomena, U.S. weather, and natural disasters.*	*Includes the arts, religion, scholarship, communications media, sports, entertainment, fashions, fads, and social life.*

	World Affairs	Europe	Africa & The Middle East	The Americas	Asia & The Pacific
Dec. 29	Iran cuts off diplomatic relations with France, offended over newspaper articles that they feel mock the Shah.	In France, police arrest the head of Pathé-Natan Film Company and three friends who, through at least 33 dummy companies, are accused of defrauding stockholders of 140 million francs. . . . More than 1,500 German refugee children are now in Britain and arrangements are complete to bring 600 more from the Polish border area of Zbaszyn. . . . Greek police arrest several prominent citizens, and charge them with trying to arrange a coup d'état. Police say a foreign power was involved in the plot, and promised territory for its help. . . . British representatives arrive in Berlin for talks with the Reich on amending naval treaties.	Learning that France will not honor a promise for full independence in 1939, Syria's Independent Nationalist Party demands that the Syrian Premier ask for independence immediately.		Chinese positions are shelled in Shansi, especially where the Fen joins the Yellow River. . . . Service on north-south lines of the Peiping-Hankow Railway is suspended to allow Japanese troop transport. . . . A devastating air raid on Kweilin burns and blasts large parts of the city. The American Baptist Hospital is destroyed by incendiary bombs.
Dec. 30		The Spanish loyalist destroyer *Diez* is shelled and run aground as it tries to slip by insurgent warships outside Gibraltar's port. Several men die. . . . Hungary's Premier Imrédy affirms his adherence to the Rome-Berlin Axis, including its racial policies. . . . As Danzig threatens to expel Polish Jews, Poland warns the city that it will expel Danzig citizens in retaliation.			A contradictory proposal for peace from Wang Ching-wei suggests complete cooperation with Japan, economically and militarily. The published statement leaves no doubt that Wang has parted ways with Gen. Chiang Kai-shek.
Dec. 31	Approximately 320 Jewish refugees from Germany land in Shanghai.	British naval delegates return from Germany after talks, with no concessions made by Germany on the size or armaments of new ships. . . . Spanish insurgents continue to push east, in some areas gaining up to 20 miles in the last week. . . . Hlinka guardsmen throughout Slovakia demonstrate against Hungarian violence. . . . At least 2,000 Jews committed suicide in the Third Reich in 1938.	The Syrian Parliament refuses to meet with a French Senatorial delegation; instead, it urges the government to rebel. . . . Sir Charles Tegart, an adviser to the police in Palestine, is ambushed and narrowly escapes being shot. His assistant is killed. . . . In Palestine in 1938, death totals from terrorism are: 450 Jews, 1,925 Arabs, and 125 Britons.		

A	B	C	D	E
Includes developments that affect more than one world region, international organizations, and important meetings of world leaders.	Includes all domestic and regional developments in Europe, including the Soviet Union.	Includes all domestic and regional developments in Africa and the Middle East.	Includes all domestic and regional developments in Latin America, the Caribbean, and Canada.	Includes all domestic and regional developments in Asian and Pacific nations (and colonies).

U.S. Politics & Social Issues	U.S. Foreign Policy & Defense	Economics & Great Depression	Science, Technology & Nature	Culture, Leisure & Lifestyle	
	The U.S. Chargé d'Affaires in Germany delivers a note asking if U.S. citizens are included in the December 23 decree, barring Jews from management.	Judge Cotillo's injunction against picketing expires at midnight, so pickets from two CIO unions appear at 12 stores owned by Busch Jewelry. . . . Brokerage head Joseph Sisto is expelled from the New York Stock Exchange for inflating and profiting from his own stock.	Pictures of gas molecules and the smallpox virus, taken through an ultramicroscope—or electron microscope—are shown to scientists in Virginia by Dr. Vladimir Zworykin of RCA, one of the inventors of television. The electron microscope was completed in April at the University of Toronto. . . . At the Parliament of Science, 280 anthropologists unanimously approve a resolution stating that there is no scientific basis for theories of racial superiority.		Dec. 29
	Germany states that as long as America panders to Jewish interests at the expense of German ones, relations between the United States and the Reich cannot improve.				Dec. 30
	Through its Ambassador in Tokyo, the United States refuses to recognize Japan's "New Order" in China. A new note delivered to Japan demands that American rights in China be respected.	According to Dun and Bradstreet, business failures in 1938 rose 41 percent from 1937. . . . Automobile sales this year are down 47 percent from 1937's total. However, car and truck sales rose dramatically in November and December.			Dec. 31

F	G	H	I	J
Includes elections, federal-state relations, civil rights and liberties, crime, the judiciary, education, healthcare, poverty, urban affairs, and population.	*Includes formation and debate of U.S. foreign and defense policies, veterans affairs, and defense spending. (Relations with specific foreign countries are usually found under the region concerned.)*	*Includes business, labor, agriculture, taxation, transportation, consumer affairs, monetary and fiscal policy, natural resources, pollution, and accidents.*	*Includes worldwide scientific, medical, and technological developments, natural phenomena, U.S. weather, and natural disasters.*	*Includes the arts, religion, scholarship, communications media, sports, entertainment, fashions, fads, and social life.*

1939

Visitors at the New York 1939 World Fair stroll down the ramp leading from the Trylon next to the Perisphere, parts of the World of Tomorrow.

	World Affairs	Europe	Africa & The Middle East	The Americas	Asia & The Pacific
Jan.	The League of Nations hosts an international conference in Santiago on American intellectual cooperation.	Prime Minister Neville Chamberlain and Foreign Secretary Lord Halifax conduct an official visit to Rome to confer with Premier Benito Mussolini. The visit has few results. . . . Following Italian claims on Tunisia and Corsica, Premier Edouard Daladier of France makes official visits to the two colonies.		A violent earthquake kills almost 30,000 people in Chile.	More than 70 people die in Victoria, Australia, in a large bushfire.
Feb.	Pope Pius XI dies.	Spanish Nationalists gain control of Barcelona and the region of Catalonia. . . . Hungarian Premier Bela Imredy resigns from power after conducting an aggressive anti-Semitic policy when it becomes known that his great-grandfather was Jewish. . . . France and Britain recognize Franco's government in Spain.	The Palestine Conference in London ends with the rejection from both Arabs and Jews of British plans for the region.		Japanese forces occupy the island of Hainan, a strategic point to control the southern Chinese coast.
Mar.	Eugenio Pacelli is elected as the new Pope Pius XII.	Due to German expansion, French Premier Edouard Daladier receives from parliament the power to govern by decree. He speeds up the rearmament program and the mobilization of reserves. . . . Slovakia, Bohemia, and Moravia become a German protectorate.			Gandhi starts another fast to force the ruler of the small state of Rajkot to implement political reforms.
Apr.		The Belgian Fascist Party loses all its seats but four in the national election. . . . The Italian army seizes control of the kingdom of Albania. . . . The British and French governments sign the Mutual Aid Agreement with Poland, Greece, and Romania, promising military aid in case of invasion.	King Ghazi of Iraq dies in an automobile accident in Baghdad.	Peru announces it will withdraw from the League of Nations.	R.G. Menzies is the new Australian prime minister. . . . Subhas Chandra Bose resigns as president of the Congress Party in light of the party's rejection of his radical independence plan for India.
May		The Hungarian government introduces new harsher anti-Semitic laws. . . . Spain withdraws from the League of Nations. . . . The German government offers nonaggression pacts with Scandinavian and Baltic states. . . . Germany and Italy announce their military alliance known as the "Pact of Steel."	The British government announces a new plan for Palestine that entails the region's independence within 10 years. Both Arabs and Jews criticize the proposal.	King George VI and Queen Elizabeth go on an official visit to Canada.	Serious fighting between Manchukuo and Mongolian military forces breaks out on the Mongolian frontier, increasing Russo-Japanese tensions.
Jun.	The International Labor Organization holds its 25th session in Geneva.	Hitler guarantees the inviolability of Yugoslav borders. . . . George VI and Queen Elizabeth are the first reigning monarchs to visit the United States. Their visit is designed to strengthen Anglo-Saxon relations in response to European tensions. . . . Scandinavian countries reject Hitler's nonaggression offer.			Fifty native Indian states reject a British plan to establish India as a federation. . . . The Japanese establish a blockade on the Chinese port of Tianjin (Tientsin), a British treaty port. The action represents a violation of international conventions.
Jul.		The Nazis successfully continue their campaign of closing down Jewish businesses.			
Aug.		A number of border incidents between Germany and Poland precipitate the Danzig-Polish crisis. Chancellor Hitler orders the invasion of Poland in spite of international appeals. . . . The German and Soviet governments announce their non-aggression pact.	Chaim Weizmann informs England that Palestine Jews would fight in a possible world conflict.		General Zhukov heads the Russian offensive against the Japanese invasion of Mongolia. . . . Isoroku Yamamoto is appointed supreme commander of the Japanese fleet.
Sept.		The German army, air, and naval forces launch a joint attack against Poland. Britain and France declare war against Germany. . . . Soviet forces invade eastern Poland. . . . Members of the Iron Guard, a Romanian fascist organization, murder Premier Armand Calinescu.	The South African parliament rejects neutrality in the European war and declares war on Germany.	The Pan-American Conference adopts the General Declaration of Neutrality for American republics.	The Soviet and Japanese governments sign an armistice, ending the fighting on the Mongolian-Manchukuo frontier.

A	B	C	D	E
Includes developments that affect more than one world region, international organizations, and important meetings of world leaders.	Includes all domestic and regional developments in Europe, including the Soviet Union.	Includes all domestic and regional developments in Africa and the Middle East.	Includes all domestic and regional developments in Latin America, the Caribbean, and Canada.	Includes all domestic and regional developments in Asian and Pacific nations (and colonies).

U.S. Politics & Social Issues	U.S. Foreign Policy & Defense	Economics & Great Depression	Science, Technology & Nature	Culture, Leisure & Lifestyle	
Union leader Tom Mooney, jailed since 1916, is freed.	U.S. President Franklin Roosevelt asks Congress for $552 million in defense expenditures to prepare the country for war.	President Roosevelt asks for an extension of the Social Security Act to cover more women and children.	The Hewlett-Packard partnership is formed in Palo Alto, Calif. . . . The uranium atom is first split in an experiment at Columbia University.		Jan.
The Supreme Court outlaws sit-down strikes. . . . The Daughters of the American Revolution forbid African-American contralto Marian Anderson to sing at Constitution Hall because of her race. First Lady Eleanor Roosevelt resigns her membership.				Lillian Hellman's *Little Foxes* premieres in New York.	Feb.
President Roosevelt names William O. Douglas to the Supreme Court. . . . Georgia and Massachusetts finally ratify the Bill of Rights.	The Roosevelt administration signs a series of agreements with Brazil ensuring financial aid. . . . The U.S. Ambassador in Berlin is recalled in protest of the annexation of Bohemia and Moravia. . . . Laurence Steinhardt is named as the U.S. Ambassador to the Soviet Union.			Clark Gable marries Carole Lombard in Arizona while filming *Gone With the Wind*. . . . *The Philadelphia Story*, starring Katharine Hepburn, opens in New York.	Mar.
Connecticut ratifies the Bill of Rights.	President Roosevelt recognizes Franco's Nationalist government in Spain. . . . President Roosevelt sends diplomatic notes to Chancellor Adolf Hitler of Germany and Premier Benito Mussolini of Italy, requesting assurances that they would not attack European or Middle Eastern countries for a period of 10 years.			Secretary of the Interior Harold L. Ickes invites Marian Anderson to sing a triumphant outdoor concert at the Lincoln Memorial before a crowd of 75,000 and a radio audience of millions. . . . John Steinbeck's *The Grapes of Wrath* is first published. . . . New York's World Fair, also called "The World of Tomorrow," opens.	Apr.
	The U.S. submarine *Squalus* sinks off the coast of New Hampshire. Due to efficient rescue operations, 33 people survive.		Regular transatlantic air service begins as a Pan-Am plane takes off from Fort Washington to Marseilles.	Lou Gehrig's consecutive series of 2,130 games in major league baseball comes to an end.	May
	The SS *St. Louis*, carrying more than 900 Jewish refugees, is denied permission to dock in Florida. The ship returns to Europe in what becomes known as the "Voyage of the Damned."			Frank Sinatra makes his first appearance with the Harry James band.	Jun.
Howard Long is hanged at the New Hampshire State Prison for the killing of 10-year-old Mark Neville Jensen.	The Senate ratifies the Panama Treaty of 1936, which gives commercial rights of the canal to the Panama government. . . . The Roosevelt administration withdraws from the trade pact of 1911 with Japan.		Edwin H. Armstrong, U.S. radio engineer, starts the first FM radio station in Alpine, N.J.	Lou Gehrig is honored by more than 60,000 fans during a special event at New York City's Yankee Stadium for his farewell to baseball due to amyotrophic lateral sclerosis.	Jul.
Moses Annenberg, owner of the *Philadelphia Inquirer*, is indicted by a federal jury in Chicago for evading $3.2 million in taxes.	President Roosevelt proposes arbitration for the Polish-Danzig crisis. Germany refuses.			The MGM musical *The Wizard of Oz* premieres in Hollywood.	Aug.
President Roosevelt proclaims a limited national emergency.	The United States announces its neutrality in the war in Europe. President Roosevelt calls for a special session of Congress to pass legislation to allow the sale of arms to France and Britain.		Igor Sikorsky tests the first helicopter. . . . Paul Hermann Muller, a Swiss pesticide researcher, first synthesizes DDT.		Sept.

F
Includes elections, federal-state relations, civil rights and liberties, crime, the judiciary, education, healthcare, poverty, urban affairs, and population.

G
Includes formation and debate of U.S. foreign and defense policies, veterans affairs, and defense spending. (Relations with specific foreign countries are usually found under the region concerned.)

H
Includes business, labor, agriculture, taxation, transportation, consumer affairs, monetary and fiscal policy, natural resources, pollution, and accidents.

I
Includes worldwide scientific, medical, and technological developments, natural phenomena, U.S. weather, and natural disasters.

J
Includes the arts, religion, scholarship, communications media, sports, entertainment, fashions, fads, and social life.

	World Affairs	Europe	Africa & The Middle East	The Americas	Asia & The Pacific
Oct.		The Soviet government signs military agreements with Lithuania and Latvia, gaining the right to have military bases in both countries. . . . The British and French governments sign a Treaty of Mutual Assistance with Turkey. . . . The German *U-47*, led by Gunther Prien, sinks the British battleship HMS *Royal Oak* in Scotland, killing 833.			
Nov.	The Permanent Court of International Justice holds its third session of the 1939 judicial year in The Hague.	The British government declares a blockade on German imports and exports. . . . The Red Army invades Finland after the Finnish government rejects a series of Soviet demands for access to military bases. . . . Hungarian revolutionary Bela Kun dies. . . . Hitler escapes an assassination attempt in Berlin.			Japanese forces make important progress in southern China, isolating the region from contacts with French Indo-China.
Dec.	The League of Nations Assembly holds its 20th session in Geneva. . . . The League of Nations formally expels the Soviet Union from the organization for its aggression against Finland.	Three British cruisers attack the German pocket battleship *Graf Spee* and force the German warship into Uruguayan waters.	A series of violent earthquakes in Turkey kill more than 30,000 people.		

A	B	C	D	E
Includes developments that affect more than one world region, international organizations, and important meetings of world leaders.	*Includes all domestic and regional developments in Europe, including the Soviet Union.*	*Includes all domestic and regional developments in Africa and the Middle East.*	*Includes all domestic and regional developments in Latin America, the Caribbean, and Canada.*	*Includes all domestic and regional developments in Asian and Pacific nations (and colonies).*

U.S. Politics & Social Issues	U.S. Foreign Policy & Defense	Economics & Great Depression	Science, Technology & Nature	Culture, Leisure & Lifestyle	
New York Municipal Airport, later renamed LaGuardia Airport, is dedicated.	President Roosevelt bans war submarines from U.S. ports and waters.	The federal hourly minimum wage is set at $0.30 an hour.	President Roosevelt meets with Albert Einstein and other scientists to confer about the development of a nuclear bomb.	*Mr. Smith Goes to Washington* by Frank Capra opens in Washington. . . . American Western writer Zane Grey dies.	Oct.
President Roosevelt lays the cornerstone of the Jefferson Memorial in Washington, D.C. . . . Al Capone is freed from prison.	The United States amends the Neutrality Act of 1937 so that selling weapons to France and Britain becomes possible.	President Roosevelt declares that Thanksgiving will take place a week earlier in an effort to encourage more holiday shopping.	Ernest O. Lawrence is awarded the Nobel Prize for Physics for his work on the cyclotron.	*Ninotchka,* starring Greta Garbo, premieres.	Nov.
	The Roosevelt administration sends a diplomatic note protesting the British policy of seizing German goods on U.S. ships.			Lou Gehrig is elected to the Baseball Hall of Fame. . . . Actor Douglas Fairbanks dies. . . . *Gone With the Wind* opens in Atlanta. . . . Ma Rainey, an American blues singer and composer known as the "Mother of the Blues," dies.	Dec.

F	G	H	I	J
Includes elections, federal-state relations, civil rights and liberties, crime, the judiciary, education, healthcare, poverty, urban affairs, and population.	*Includes formation and debate of U.S. foreign and defense policies, veterans affairs, and defense spending. (Relations with specific foreign countries are usually found under the region concerned.)*	*Includes business, labor, agriculture, taxation, transportation, consumer affairs, monetary and fiscal policy, natural resources, pollution, and accidents.*	*Includes worldwide scientific, medical, and technological developments, natural phenomena, U.S. weather, and natural disasters.*	*Includes the arts, religion, scholarship, communications media, sports, entertainment, fashions, fads, and social life.*

	World Affairs	Europe	Africa & The Middle East	The Americas	Asia & The Pacific
Jan. 1	An arms factory sells controlling interest to the Czechoslovakian government for $10.3 million; the country will manufacture arms for Germany. . . . Britain attempts to find homes for refugee German and Polish children; Germany wishes to remove 150,000 young Jews from the country. . . . The International Peace Conference of Women Leaders postpones its conference for one year. . . . Adolf Hitler's territory acquisition adds 10 million people to his regime. . . . Propaganda Minister Joseph Goebbels calls 1938 the year of the "Great German Reich."	The greatest battle of the Spanish civil war rages. . . . Britain intends to terminate trade pact with Russia. . . . There are over 1.8 million unemployed in Britain. . . . New German laws ostracizing Jews are effective today.		The eighth Pan-American Conference sets goals: solidarity against aggression, peace, and reduced trade barriers.	Military experts note Japanese "achievement" and China's "seeming ineptitude" in a review of Sino-Japanese hostilities. . . . Experts see great improvement in Japanese bombing abilities.
Jan. 2	Former Polish premier Wladislas Sikorski predicts that Western democracies will not remain neutral if Germany attacks Russia. . . . Joseph Goebbels states that world pressure will not change the German attitude toward Jews.	Gen. Francisco Franco announces that all Spanish citizens will be trained to "take up arms." . . . German industry is operating at capacity, but the stock market is depressed. . . . Thousands dance at Britain's Piccadilly Square on New Year; some carry black coffins with the lettering: He did not get winter relief. . . . Czechoslovakian statesmen share a "bloodless revolution" plan.			Reconstruction of seized north China will cost Japan billions of yen.
Jan. 3	The Ruthenian government adopts the name of Carpatho-Ukraine through a German initiative. . . . Adolf Hitler and Benito Mussolini exchange New Year messages and renew close cooperation.	Forty thousand Corsicans who died in World War I defense of France are remembered. . . . The French protest against Italian Premier Benito Mussolini, preferring "death to servitude." . . . Germany permits Quakers to provide relief to "non-Aryans." . . . Youth in Greece are required to join Greek National Youth, modeled on Germany's program. . . . Soviets convict five secret police who obtained false confessions; the death penalty is anticipated. . . . Spanish insurgents arrest the British consul and his wife.	An Irish parliament member attempts to relocate one million German Jews to Palestine.		Punishment is promised for Chinese who assist the Japanese government.
Jan. 4	Only two American nations—Mexico and Guatemala—exchange New Year's greetings with Adolf Hitler. . . . European nations spend a significant part of their budgets on arms; France and Britain make their arms budgets public, while Germany, Italy, and Russia do not.	An estimated 85 percent of British sympathize with Russia rather than Germany, citing the unpopularity of Hitler and poor treatment of Jews as reasons. . . . The Polish foreign minister is to meet with Adolf Hitler about Polish-German relations. . . . Franco's insurgent army lays claim to a Spanish loyalist center, Artesa de Segre. . . . A high treason trial against ex-Nazi Ernest Niekisch starts in Berlin.			Prince Fumimaro Konoe resigns as Japan's Premier, following a disagreement over China policy.
Jan. 5	President Franklin Roosevelt hints at support for economic sanctions for aggressors; Japan may be the first target. . . . The Polish government is courting diplomatic relationships with Germany and Italy. . . . Palestine, Canada, and South American countries are to receive 10,000 non-Aryan refugees; funds come, in part, from Britain.	An attempt is made to create an "all party" system in Britain, with the main goal of peace and unity. . . . French Premier Edouard Daladier reviews the defense line along the North African border of French territories. . . . Sweden and Finland attempt to fortify the Aland islands against German or Russian invasion. . . . Spanish loyalists claim to still hold key territory.	The King of Saudi Arabia sees no Middle East peace until Arabs obtain rights; he blames Jewish propaganda for the U.S. perception of the situation.	Congress grants the former president of Chile the right to leave the country, despite protests of the Chilean Nazi party. . . . Chile is at social, political, and economic crossroads, attempting to modernize and industrialize. . . . The term of El Salvador's presidency is extended six years with the support of the Nazi and fascist regimes.	Baron Kiichiro Hiranuma is confirmed as the new Premier of Japan; the Cabinet remains much the same. . . . Fighting between China and Japan resumes. . . . Chinese advances are made in railway and highway construction. . . . The new Japanese Premier is called the "Hitler of Japan."
Jan. 6	Germany is disturbed by hints of economic sanctions by the United States; France and Britain are expected to follow the U.S. lead. . . . Italian Premier Benito Mussolini rejects a U.S. proposal to send Jewish refugees to Ethiopia; he suggests Russia, Brazil, or the United States.	Polish-German diplomacy talks last three hours. . . . Borjas Blancas falls to Franco's Spanish insurgency. . . . British Prime Minister Neville Chamberlain applauds Roosevelt's State of the Union speech. . . . Hungary is considering a move to one political party.		The Lima Consul General denies spying on U.S. news reporters at the Pan-American Conference.	The Japanese Premier is considering the abolishment of the inner Cabinet, but states this is not a move toward a one-party political system.
Jan. 7	British-French talks are scheduled before Prime Minister Neville Chamberlain meets with Premier Benito Mussolini. Chamberlain is expected to request Mussolini's aid in persuading Hitler to allow the evacuation of Jews.	A bloody clash occurs at the Czechoslovakia and Carpatho-Ukraine border. One dozen die and Germany is seen as a potential instigator. . . . The Italian press accuses President Franklin Roosevelt of manufacturing a sense of danger to keep Latin American countries in line and to appease Jewish capitalists.		Mexico criticizes President Franklin Roosevelt's desire to repeal the Neutrality Act, while Brazil praises the speech.	Japan attributes increased tension between Japan and the United States to President Roosevelt's speech about aggressors.

A	B	C	D	E
Includes developments that affect more than one world region, international organizations, and important meetings of world leaders.	*Includes all domestic and regional developments in Europe, including the Soviet Union.*	*Includes all domestic and regional developments in Africa and the Middle East.*	*Includes all domestic and regional developments in Latin America, the Caribbean, and Canada.*	*Includes all domestic and regional developments in Asian and Pacific nations (and colonies).*

U.S. Politics & Social Issues	U.S. Foreign Policy & Defense	Economics & Great Depression	Science, Technology & Nature	Culture, Leisure & Lifestyle	
Lt. Gov. T. Frank Hayes is indicted for defrauding Waterbury, Conn., of $1 million. . . . First Lady Eleanor Roosevelt asks the nation to heed the voice of youth. . . . Congress considers broadening Social Security; making lynching a federal crime; and increasing veteran pensions.	The U.S. Army cancels its participation in a war games exercise in Puerto Rico and the Caribbean, citing cost and time factors. . . . The Department of Commerce tests a new fuel-efficient diesel aircraft engine.	Nearly half of federal funds are spent on job recovery; still 11 million people are unemployed. . . . The American Institute of Architects predicts an increase in building. . . . Congress is to review criticism of New Deal farming programs. . . . Political leaders request a reduction in WPA funding. . . . A man denied a higher pension spends his last 21 cents to buy rope to hang himself. . . . President Franklin Roosevelt and the new Congress must negotiate a revival of the fourth New Deal.	The largest mass flight of "flivver" planes is set to begin. . . . Record lows are noted in infant mortality and deaths of mothers in childbirth.	Newsreel editors set a self-regulatory code to avoid offensive material. . . . A Brooklyn museum exhibit features Hans Holbein and Pablo Picasso.	Jan. 1
		An overall review of the Works Progress Administration programs is being conducted by Harry L. Hopkins. Curtailing of the WPA may allow more direct relief needs to be met. . . . New Deal crop plans are under review. . . . The National Cooperative Milk Products Federation is dissatisfied with the British and Canadian trade pact, calling Uncle Sam "out-traded."	Hormone extraction is hoped to help premature babies survive. . . . Scientists state that brain waves are as individual as fingerprints.	*Rebecca* by Daphne du Maurier tops best-seller lists. . . . The American Chess Federation championship ends in deadlock. . . . Two American publishers announce plans to release an unabridged edition of Adolf Hitler's *Mein Kampf*. . . . The champion racehorse Seabiscuit is back in training.	Jan. 2
New Attorney General Frank Murphy is sworn into office on his mother's Bible. . . . A House committee urges pure water legislation.		Diggers of the Panama Canal pressure the government for pensions. . . . President Roosevelt is expected to address the need for a defense budget, unemployment relief funds, and railroad rehabilitation. . . . The Supreme Court may rule on the constitutionality of the Tennessee Valley Authority power program. . . . The cigarette industry is very strong, with 163 billion cigarettes produced in 1938. . . . The oil industry is down by 50 percent.	The tuberculosis death rate decreases 9 percent. . . . Sulphur shows promise in medicine and sanitation; it is a potential tool in fighting pneumonia. . . . Pure oxygen is shown to combat seasickness. . . . An x-ray unit small enough for hospital installation is invented that weighs only 4,000 pounds.	The 2,000th anniversary of the Roman emperor Augustus's birth is honored by the Metropolitan Museum of Art. . . . Tennessee beats Oklahoma, 17–0, in the Orange Bowl. . . . New York film critics name *The Citadel* best movie. . . . Television is expected to become a "prominent industry."	Jan. 3
The Dies Committee charges in writing that Communist and Nazi sympathizers are infiltrating the federal government. . . . President Roosevelt and his wife give an annual dinner honoring the diplomatic corps. . . . Rumors circulate that Felix Frankfurter will be appointed to the Supreme Court; Roosevelt says that no decision has yet been made. . . . William B. Bankhead is reelected as Speaker of the House. . . . William S. King is named clerk of the Senate, Oswald D. Heck as Speaker.	The Navy recommends establishing 41 defense bases, 15 of them immediately.	Senator Barbour demands liquidation of the WPA to return relief programs to state control. . . . A special committee is formed to recommend legislation designed to reduce political connections to the WPA. . . . Eleven thousand taxi drivers strike in New York. . . . A report reveals that WPA funds are used for political purposes in three states.	Lincoln Ellsworth lands on an unexplored Antarctic island and collects specimens. . . . The British will refuel a plane in the air over the Atlantic Ocean.	Actor Jackie Coogan and his actress wife Betty Grable are living apart; conflicting messages about a possible divorce are given. . . . A two-year study indicates that informal educational programs work better for slow or maladjusted students. . . . Italy loans $20 million of art for the San Francisco World Fair, including works by Raphael, Michelangelo, and Botticelli.	Jan. 4
The former secretary of commerce, Daniel Roper, denies using a government boat for pleasure. . . . Al Capone pays fines in hope of a timely release from Alcatraz Prison. . . . Congress sharply divides along party lines in response to President Roosevelt's State of the Union speech. . . . Republican presidential candidate Thomas Dewey calls 1940 the Year of the Republican. . . . The New York governor urges a wire-tapping ban.	President Franklin Roosevelt reports the Navy needs an additional $36.5 million for ships and ordnance. . . . Roosevelt wishes to see Neutrality Act legislation revoked.	President Franklin Roosevelt warns Congress about slashing the budget, citing the importance of national defense and reduction of unemployment. . . . Concern rises over drought in the Wheat Belt. . . . The administrator of veterans' affairs reports that veterans need jobs and hospital care, not pensions.			Jan. 5
Felix Frankfurter is nominated as Supreme Court Justice; the move is called one of President Roosevelt's "most popular appointments." . . . Aviator Amelia Earhart is legally declared dead after being missing for 17 months. . . . President Roosevelt nominates Harry Hopkins as Secretary of Commerce.	It is anticipated that President Franklin Roosevelt will present a $1.3 billion defense budget, the largest ever in peacetime. . . . Naval cooperation between the United States and Britain is seen as a key to peace.	President Franklin Roosevelt suggests new taxes to cover a $9 billion budget. . . . The national debt reaches nearly $45 billion. . . . Sixty-one percent of Americans polled say the New Deal is costing too much.	Bad weather delays further exploration of the Antarctic interior.	Pitcher Dizzy Dean signs a contract with the Chicago Cubs. . . . A commemorative service is held to honor Theodore Roosevelt on the 20th anniversary of his death tomorrow.	Jan. 6
The Department of Justice is to investigate alleged criminal violations by Communist and fascist groups in the country.	One hundred U.S. ships are to pass through the heavily guarded Panama Canal on their way to maneuvers in the Atlantic. . . . Col. Charles Lindbergh gives government officials a confidential report about German air strength.	New York taxi drivers end their strike.	The National Association of Evangelists disagrees with Darwinism being taught in public schools.	President Franklin Roosevelt's grandson is christened in the White House. . . . Singer Marion Anderson performs at Carnegie Hall.	Jan. 7

F	G	H	I	J
Includes elections, federal-state relations, civil rights and liberties, crime, the judiciary, education, healthcare, poverty, urban affairs, and population.	*Includes formation and debate of U.S. foreign and defense policies, veterans affairs, and defense spending. (Relations with specific foreign countries are usually found under the region concerned.)*	*Includes business, labor, agriculture, taxation, transportation, consumer affairs, monetary and fiscal policy, natural resources, pollution, and accidents.*	*Includes worldwide scientific, medical, and technological developments, natural phenomena, U.S. weather, and natural disasters.*	*Includes the arts, religion, scholarship, communications media, sports, entertainment, fashions, fads, and social life.*

	World Affairs	Europe	Africa & The Middle East	The Americas	Asia & The Pacific
Jan. 8		British Prime Minister Neville Chamberlain is to visit France and Italy. He denies he will serve as a mediator between the two countries.	Residents of Tunisia say they are accustomed to foreign rulers fighting over their land; France and Italy are just the current situation.	Congress reviews the expansion of the Panama Canal through Nicaragua.	The Chinese army makes a surprise attack on Hangchow, a city long held by the Japanese.
Jan. 9	Although British Prime Minister Neville Chamberlain and Italian Premier Benito Mussolini deny the rumor, it is believed that the main purpose of their meeting is to discuss French-Italian issues.	Both sides in the Spanish civil war report gains. . . . Hungarians renew the fight with Czechs on the frontier. . . . Italian Premier Benito Mussolini summons the Fascist Grand Council to meet on February 4 to set Italy's course for 1939. . . . Pay cuts are ordered for Soviet plant workers, with dismissal required for those who are 20 minutes late to work. . . . Two French warships arrive at Djibouti, a territory of contention between France and Italy.	Arab delegates are expected to demand national rule at the upcoming London conference. . . . The Council of Jewish Organizations requests help in colonizing Jewish refugees in Palestine.	The new Chilean government offers justification and explanation for sweeping changes in official positions.	Chinese forces report they reclaim Wencheng.
Jan. 10		Britain publishes proposed evacuation areas for children if war strikes. . . . Adolf Hitler dedicates the new chancellery of the Reich, which took 8,000 men nine months to complete. . . . A plot to assassinate King Carol of Romania is foiled.			Japan eases its hold on Shanghai to appease critics. . . . The Chinese military builds a 1,400-mile road for munitions and supplies.
Jan. 11	Chile and Britain renew their trade pact for another six months. . . . The Chairman of the Inter-Governmental Committee of Refugees negotiates better trade arrangements with Germany in exchange for help in emigrating Jews from the country. . . . Japan threatens retaliation if the United States and Britain exert economic pressure because of China.	The Czech Cabinet is split on anti-Semitic legislation. . . . Hungary threatens a counter-attack if Czechoslovakian troops invade their territory. . . . Princess Mafalda of Italy is critically ill. . . . Talks between British Prime Minister Neville Chamberlain and Italian Premier Benito Mussolini begin today, focusing on French-Italian issues.		At the Conference of Intellectual Cooperation in Chile, Mexico's proposal to allow unlimited access and entry of all books is defeated . . . A Pan-American Highway Conference begins in Chile. . . . Gen. Saturnino Cedillo, who led a revolt against the Mexican government last May, dies in a skirmish with Federal troops.	Telephone and mail service is restored in major Chinese cities. . . . The Nanking regime of China makes a plea for peace.
Jan. 12	Italian Premier Benito Mussolini reassures the Japanese government of their mutual friendship. . . . International negotiations are underway to help Jewish people leave Germany. . . . A world conference on wheat is planned, with exports being a main topic. . . . The foreign minister of the Japanese-dominated Chinese government of Nanking protests the British move to close a police station in international territory.	Admittance to the Academy of Sciences of the Soviet Union is to depend, in part, on the candidate's adherence to Marxist beliefs. . . . The British protest after Franco's fighters cross into territorial waters of Britain. . . . British Prime Minister Neville Chamberlain and Italian Premier Benito Mussolini meet and pledge peace. . . . The wedding of Italian Princess Maria is postponed because of the illness of Maria's sister, Mafalda.		Chile's new government pushes for reforms to lower the cost of living and to achieve socialist objectives.	
Jan. 13	French politicians commend President Franklin Roosevelt on his commitment to liberty as the 150th anniversary of French liberty is commemorated.	British Prime Minister Neville Chamberlain watches a two-hour demo of how Italy's youth keep fit— a combination of gymnastic and rifle drills. . . . Chamberlain sees a "good-sized gap" between British and Italian viewpoints on French issues.			A brushfire in Australia's Victoria province kills 71 people.

A	B	C	D	E
Includes developments that affect more than one world region, international organizations, and important meetings of world leaders.	Includes all domestic and regional developments in Europe, including the Soviet Union.	Includes all domestic and regional developments in Africa and the Middle East.	Includes all domestic and regional developments in Latin America, the Caribbean, and Canada.	Includes all domestic and regional developments in Asian and Pacific nations (and colonies).

U.S. Politics & Social Issues	U.S. Foreign Policy & Defense	Economics & Great Depression	Science, Technology & Nature	Culture, Leisure & Lifestyle	
Al Capone, suffering from paresis, moves to Terminal Island Prison from Alcatraz. . . . The Dies Committee, charged with investigating "un-American activities" is called "un-American" for its methods used to investigate. . . . The North Carolina College for Negroes will start a graduate program with funding from the WPA. . . . Radical socialist Thomas Mooney receives a pardon after 22 years in prison for a bombing conviction.	President Franklin Roosevelt's critics in Congress intend to back increased spending for defense, while refusing to back social and unemployment programs.	Proposed legislation will ask that household workers be limited to 60-hour workweeks. . . . President Roosevelt is agreeable to the new economic program, but asks that Congress not put changes into effect before July 1, fearing that rapid changes would be harmful.	A micro-camera and polarized light are used successfully to detect postage stamp fraud.	Judy Garland and other stars join the first Screen Guild Radio Show to raise money for the Motion Picture Relief Fund. The show will run until 1952.	Jan. 8
The American Bar Association is asked to approve a resolution censuring Nazis. . . . Calls are made for the abolishment of the Dies Committee and the formation of a Department of Justice committee that genuinely investigates "un-American activities."	Gen. William Haskell states that American industry is not prepared for war, nor does the United States have a sufficient supply of raw materials. . . . The Navy completes design of two 45,000-ton battleships; said to be the most powerful ever designed. . . . Jewish War Veterans of the United States vow to continue the fight against Communism.	The American Federation of Labor demands nine changes in labor amendments. . . . The steel industry rebounded to 52 percent capacity in December.	Motorists breathe into a balloon-like "drunk-o-meter" to test alcohol consumption. . . . Cornell University develops an improved atom-smashing gun.	Owners revive the American Professional Football League; play is set to begin in the fall.	Jan. 9
Religious leaders urge President Franklin Roosevelt to aid refugee German children. . . . The American Bar Association approves a ban on sit-down strikes. . . . Buggsy Goldstein and bodyguard Seymour Magoon, notorious Brooklyn gangsters, are exonerated on conspiracy charges. . . . For the first time in U.S. Congressional history, a woman is given chairmanship of a committee: Rhoda Fox Graves assumes leadership of the Agricultural Committee.	The Budget Bureau receives a bill for the establishment of a "great chain of air, submarine, destroyer, and mine bases." . . . A moral ban on sale of munitions to Japan is revealed.	Striking truckers agree to move perishable foods to a Boston market. . . . France is buying more from the United States, especially fruits and petroleum. . . . House Republicans attack New Deal spending.			Jan. 10
A therapeutic pool for sufferers of infantile paralysis opens in the Bronx. . . . The American Bar Association seeks a ban on divorces requested by mail. . . . Comedian Jack Benny is indicted on a jewelry smuggling count; comedian George Burns pleads guilty.	Ambassadors Joseph Kennedy and William Bullitt tell Congress that war is imminent in spring as Italian Premier Benito Mussolini imitates Adolf Hitler's land acquisition. . . . A former Herbert Hoover Cabinet member warns that President Franklin Roosevelt may provoke war by acting as judge of the world.	The American Farm Bureau Federation asks President Franklin Roosevelt to make private jobs more attractive than relief jobs. . . . The House of Representatives slashes President Roosevelt's relief budget by $150 million.		Col. Jacob Ruppert, owner of the New York Yankees, is in failing health. . . . Cowboy actor Max Baer wants a rematch with heavyweight boxer Joe Louis. . . . A widow exhumes her husband's body in search of a winning lottery ticket. The ticket is found in his suit pocket. . . . Ford Frick, president of the National League, commemorates the 100th anniversary of baseball.	Jan. 11
President Franklin Roosevelt is criticized for his nomination of Frank Murphy as Attorney General. . . . The editor of New Republic magazine denies Communist ties during a Dies hearing. . . . Eleanor Roosevelt asks every American to donate a dime toward finding a cure for infantile paralysis and says this "March of Dimes" must be spearheaded by women. . . . Felix Frankfurter, Supreme Court nominee, appears before a Senate subcommittee to answer questions about accusations of radicalism. . . . Prison warden Frank Craven is convicted of involuntary manslaughter after four prisoners die of heat stroke in Holmesburg, Pa.	Congress debates the Neutrality Act and how it affects national defense. . . . Military leaders appeal to the government for increased research and standardization of equipment for national defense and emergency purposes.	The House Civil Service Chairman pushes to separate politics and the WPA. . . . The seven-day trucker strike ends in Boston after the governor personally meets with truckers. . . . Harry Hopkins, Secretary of Commerce nominee, concedes error in making political speeches while working with WPA programs. . . . A bill is introduced to establish a minimum wage for domestic workers. . . . House Representatives fight to restore the slashed $150,000 to the relief budget.		Harvard University appoints its first dean, George Chase. . . . Interest in Adolf Hitler's book, Mein Kampf, increases at libraries. . . . The Foundation of the Blind brings "talking books" to blind children in schools.	Jan. 12
The American College of Dentists outlines an insurance plan to aid lower-income families. . . . The National Labor Relations Board argues that employers should not be allowed to fire staff who participate in sit-down strikes over unfair labor practices. . . . Congressman Ben Cravens dies of pneumonia soon after his seventh term begins.	Roosevelt requests a quick appropriation of $552 million for planes needed for national defense.	The Security and Exchange Commission will inquire about a potential monopoly of the insurance industry.	An 8 by 10-inch photo is sent by wire from Chicago to New York in just five minutes.	A $1 million offer for racing thoroughbred Man 'O War is refused. . . . The hat industry, concerned that the average man does not own 12 hats—the number needed, they say, to be a well-dressed man—publishes a list of best-hatted men. . . . Son of Frankenstein is released.	Jan. 13

F	G	H	I	J
Includes elections, federal-state relations, civil rights and liberties, crime, the judiciary, education, healthcare, poverty, urban affairs, and population.	Includes formation and debate of U.S. foreign and defense policies, veterans affairs, and defense spending. (Relations with specific foreign countries are usually found under the region concerned.)	Includes business, labor, agriculture, taxation, transportation, consumer affairs, monetary and fiscal policy, natural resources, pollution, and accidents.	Includes worldwide scientific, medical, and technological developments, natural phenomena, U.S. weather, and natural disasters.	Includes the arts, religion, scholarship, communications media, sports, entertainment, fashions, fads, and social life.

	World Affairs	Europe	Africa & The Middle East	The Americas	Asia & The Pacific
Jan. 14	The Reich assures the United States that American citizens in Germany will be treated well. . . . Britain sends a strongly worded note to Japan, demanding an open door in China.	The Pope holds an audience with British Prime Minister Neville Chamberlain. . . . Adolf Hitler reportedly tells Italian Premier Benito Mussolini to avoid war in 1939. . . . Hungary signs an anti-Communist document and is anticipated to withdraw from the League of Nations. According to French reports, Spanish rebels are changing their capital from Barcelona to Valencia.	An Arab revolt against British control of Palestine disbands as two Arab chiefs flee.		The new Japanese Premier Hiranuma denies a unitary party system is planned. . . . Japanese forces repair a railroad damaged by Chinese guerillas. . . . The Japanese Empress dons a maternity girdle to commemorate the beginning of her 9th month of expectancy.
Jan. 15		Lines of people in Moscow wait to see Lenin's body—15 years after his death. . . . Spanish insurgents take Terragona and Reus in Catalonia.	The United Palestine Appeal closes its Washington conference and asks for entrance to Palestine for 100,000 Jewish refugees.	A congressional election is held in Ecuador. Women were granted the right to vote two days ago.	Japan claims victory in the Hangchow area of China. . . . Two hundred are killed after Japan bombs the Chinese capital of Chungking. The American girls' school is hit, but there are no casualties.
Jan. 16	The United States and Britain jointly protest Japan's plan to dominate China and subordinate third-world countries.	Italian Premier Benito Mussolini states that French-Italian issues cannot be considered until after the Spanish civil war ends. . . . Britain and France may give free port privileges in Djibouti to Italy. . . . Spanish rebels increase bombing efforts. . . . The German foreign minister visits Poland to celebrate the fifth anniversary of the nonaggression pact between the two countries.		The Chilean leadership determines to help the poor, even at the expense of other classes of citizens. . . . A new constitution is being formed in El Salvador.	
Jan. 17	Germany pushes to become the primary supplier to Chile. Britain would be hurt more by the move than the United States. . . . The Japanese government is suspicious of the proposed U.S. fortification of Guam, and threatens to smash whoever attempts a foothold in China. . . . The Worldwide Jewish Congress refuses to accept a Jewish relocation plan that rewards Germany economically.	The Irish Republican Army is blamed after bomb blasts hit Britain. . . . Approximately 80,000–100,000 unemployed Czechs are to be sent to Germany. . . . The Duke of Alba suggests the Spanish monarchy may be restored after the civil war ends.			Japanese and Chinese are buying more U.S. products.
Jan. 18	The Italian foreign minister attempts to establish a Rome-Budapest-Belgrade triangle as newspapers warn of war in the spring. . . . The first of Britain's 200 Lockheed bombers leaves the United States for delivery.	A convention of Arab delegates meets in England. The Egyptian premier stays home because of the unsettled outlook in the Mediterranean. . . . Britain is on high alert after nine bombings. The Irish Republican Army is suspected. . . . France launches a new 35,000-ton battle cruiser. . . . Nearly 80 French vessels practice war maneuvers in the Strait of Gibraltar. . . . Census work begins in Russia. No questions are asked about religion or social class. . . . The Reich requires medical students to take a class on race science.			China asks the League of Nations for economic sanctions against Japan for its military aggression.
Jan. 19	A Mexican envoy to Germany denies any secret purpose to the trip. . . . Talks are delayed on Jewish refugees in Germany. Hitler is not available to discuss concessions.	Rumors suggest that German Propaganda Minister Joseph Goebbels may receive the new post as chief Nazi district leader. . . . Italians are accused of bombings in Spain. The League of Nations receives a request for civilian aid. . . . Spanish rebels enter Pons, on the road to France.		The Chilean Nazi party changes its name to the Popular Socialist Vanguard. They shun Hitlerism. . . . Half of Canada's government is expected to resign if the suggestion is made to send troops abroad.	The U.S. ambassador to China sees no end in sight to the Sino-Japanese war.
Jan. 20	Birth control advocate Margaret Sanger declares peace will exist only after countries match their birth rate with available resources. . . . France grants the U.S. a six-month permit for trans-Atlantic flights, expected to commence in June. . . . The League of Nations passes feeble resolutions about the Spanish civil war and the Sino-Japanese war.	Financial genius Dr. Hjalmar Schacht is ousted as head of Germany's Reichsbank. Newspapers report that he retired.		El Salvador seizes many rebels; executions are rumored.	Japan considers stricter film censorship.

A	B	C	D	E
Includes developments that affect more than one world region, international organizations, and important meetings of world leaders.	Includes all domestic and regional developments in Europe, including the Soviet Union.	Includes all domestic and regional developments in Africa and the Middle East.	Includes all domestic and regional developments in Latin America, the Caribbean, and Canada.	Includes all domestic and regional developments in Asian and Pacific nations (and colonies).

U.S. Politics & Social Issues	U.S. Foreign Policy & Defense	Economics & Great Depression	Science, Technology & Nature	Culture, Leisure & Lifestyle	
Five convicts that escaped their Alcatraz prison cells are caught attempting a desperate swim to freedom. . . . House Representatives pass a $725 million relief bill, though the funds are restricted and the decision is not unanimous.	Roosevelt anticipates a bottleneck of plane production due to the shortage of skilled workers. . . . Col. Sylvain Raynal, hero of World War I, dies from the long-term effects of gassing. . . . A U.S. fighting fleet passes through the Panama Canal under heavy guard. Training exercises are scheduled in the Atlantic.		Explorer Lincoln Ellsworth reports that the Antarctic ice cap is receding.	New York City is likely to legalize smoking in all theaters. . . . The French pavilion of the New York World Fair is dedicated. . . . A snowstorm covers New York City in eight inches of powder and causes a severe traffic jam. . . . Col. Jacob Ruppert, owner of the New York Yankees, dies of phlebitis. . . . Vivien Leigh is to play opposite Clark Gable in *Gone With The Wind*.	Jan. 14
Congress is expected to review farming legislation, with wheat, corn, and cotton crops at the forefront of the discussion.	President Franklin Roosevelt invites the Brazilian foreign minister to visit Washington. . . . The United States considers the fortification of the island of Guam. An angry reaction is anticipated from Japan. . . . A new antibomber plane is off the ground and out of sight in 90 seconds.		Insulin crystals, which benefit those with diabetes, are patented.	The Federal Communications Commission grants permission to create four experimental tele-stations.	Jan. 15
The Chief of Army Engineers requests $350 million for flood control. . . . Polls indicate 73 percent of women and 62 percent of men approve of Eleanor Roosevelt's active role in U.S. politics.	The American Aeronautics Association proposes air-training courses for boys before they attend college.		The assistant of explorer Lincoln Ellsworth crushes his knee and nearly drowns during the Antarctic exploration. . . . Use of frozen gasoline is found to curb plane peril.	An estimated 33 million hope to attend the nation's World Fair. . . . Henry Fonda is to play the lead role in *Young Mr. Lincoln*.	Jan. 16
The Senate Judiciary Committee approves Felix Frankfurter for Supreme Court Justice and Frank Murphy as Attorney General. . . . The CIO attempts to mend a rift among auto union factions. . . . Eleanor Roosevelt defends the press, saying that the public is right to fear a government with too much influence.	The Army air chief states that the United States ranks fifth or sixth in current air defense power.	Theater employees use sit-down strike tactics to protest WPA budget cuts. . . . An integrated system of relief—federal, state, and local—is urged. . . . President Franklin Roosevelt requests an extension of the Social Security Act to benefit children and the elderly.		J.P. Morgan quits the board of the American Museum of Natural History after 30 years. . . . Boxer Joe Louis begins intense training for his heavyweight bout against John Henry Lewis. . . . Church leaders urge closing of the World Fair on Sundays. . . . About 14,000 spectators welcome Olympic gold medallist Sonja Henie at an ice skating program held at Madison Square Garden.	Jan. 17
Legislators consider a shorter wait period between a marriage application and the date of the wedding. . . . Felix Frankfurter is unanimously confirmed as Supreme Court Justice. Frank Murphy is confirmed as Attorney General, 78–7.	The House and Senate voice no objections over President Franklin Roosevelt's wish to speed up defense programs. . . . President Franklin Roosevelt says he knows of no request for funds to fortify Guam as a naval base.	Actors' groups support the radio strike. Strikers refuse to accept that advertising firms, rather than agencies, hire them. . . . The establishment of a bipartisan board for WPA relief programs is backed. . . . Farmers protest the current milk pact with dealers and producers. . . . President Roosevelt seeks to end tax immunity through legislation.	A new drug, Sulfapyridine, is hailed as the cure for pneumonia.	Edward G. Barrow is selected as the new president of the New York Yankees. . . . *Barber of Seville* is performed at the Metropolitan Opera House. . . . Baseball star Mel Ott breaks his finger in a home mishap.	Jan. 18
The Federal Communications Commission bans "super power" broadcasting. . . . Two groups merge to form the Birth Control Federation of America. . . . Felix Frankfurter is sworn in as Supreme Court justice. . . . The Senate is expected to debate the nomination of Harry Hopkins as Secretary of Commerce.	The House authorizes 3,000 new Army airplanes. . . . President Franklin Roosevelt backs a fortification plan for Guam.	Throughout this week, Actors Equity and other unions representing movie stars, musicians, and stage performers meet and vote to support a strike against radio sponsors.		The National Institute of Arts and Letters presents an award to poet Robert Frost.	Jan. 19
Thomas Dewey bans a move on nominating him for the presidency. . . . The American Federation of Radio Artists votes to strike over pay issues. . . . Senate foes of Harry Hopkins question him for five hours about his inability to stamp out partisan actions in the WPA program.	Aviation training for youth is favored by 87 percent of those polled. . . . The Naval Board requests $65 million from the Senate for bases on Guam. . . . U.S. companies are now in consensus on banning airplane exports to Japan.	The Senate considers keeping relief funding intact during cold winter months. . . . The President of the American Tariff League declares reciprocal pacts a failure and an invitation to foreign industry.			Jan. 20

F	G	H	I	J
Includes elections, federal-state relations, civil rights and liberties, crime, the judiciary, education, healthcare, poverty, urban affairs, and population.	Includes formation and debate of U.S. foreign and defense policies, veterans affairs, and defense spending. (Relations with specific foreign countries are usually found under the region concerned.)	Includes business, labor, agriculture, taxation, transportation, consumer affairs, monetary and fiscal policy, natural resources, pollution, and accidents.	Includes worldwide scientific, medical, and technological developments, natural phenomena, U.S. weather, and natural disasters.	Includes the arts, religion, scholarship, communications media, sports, entertainment, fashions, fads, and social life.

	World Affairs	Europe	Africa & The Middle East	The Americas	Asia & The Pacific
Jan. 21	Finland prepares to host the 1940 Olympics, budgeting $7.5 million. . . . Mexican oil goes to fuel Italian ships after the oil is refined in Houston, Tex., duty free.	Britain sees the dismissal of the Reichsbank president as a bad portent. . . . Newspapers indicate that Joseph Goebbels may go in front of a Nazi tribunal to answer scandalous personal questions and may need to resign. . . . A Soviet Labor Discipline Line Law sends executives who fail to discharge truant workers to jail. . . . German bonds are weak in the market after Schacht's ouster as Reichsbank president.		Brazil announces its five-year plan: $30 million will be spent annually on public works and defense.	Gen. Chaing Kai-shek is appointed chairman of the People's Political Council, replacing the ousted Wang Ching-wei. . . . The Japanese War Minister Gen. Iragaki tells his government that China still puts up "formidable resistance."
Jan. 22	The moderate influence of the Reichsbank president is praised; his removal causes concern worldwide. . . . Approximately 110 Jews freed from concentration camps arrive in Vienna. . . . The League of Nations will transport 200 paintings in danger of harm from the Spanish civil war.	Barcelona is the target of air raids. . . . The French deputy protests the British "invasion" of Minquiers Islands. . . . London hears that Italian planes are bulletproof. . . . The "lax and lazy" continue to be punished under strict Soviet labor laws. . . . Russia observes the 15th anniversary of Lenin's death.			Dr. Sun Fo, Son of Sun Yat-sen, predicts China's victory over Japan by the end of 1939.
Jan. 23		Barcelona residents are asked to stop work for a week and aid in defense of the city. . . . France reinforces guards at the Spanish border as anxiety increases. . . . The Nazi party converts the army from a nonpolitical independent party into the political arm of the National Socialist regime.		Chile names a female envoy to Central America. Gabriela Mistral is the first female to hold such a position.	Over one million cases of malaria have been reported in Fukien province, China.
Jan. 24	The Arab Defense Party will not have a delegate at the London conference. . . . Communists in Spain urge the United States to lift the arms embargo. . . . Germany boycotts U.S. films.	Germany pressures Czechoslovakia to renounce treaties with Russia and France. . . . Barcelona is placed under martial law as Franco's forces close in; leaders flee. . . . Prime Minister Neville Chamberlain urges the British to fill civilian defense unit vacancies. . . . France will receive Spanish refugees and expects 100,000–500,000 along the Catalan border. . . . Princess Maria of Italy marries Prince Louis of Bourbon-Parma.		An earthquake estimated at 8.3 hits Concepción, Chile. Between twenty-eight and thirty thousand people die. Five cities, including Chillán, and many towns are destroyed.	An estimated 30,000 civilians per day flee Chungking as Japanese forces continue bombing raids.
Jan. 25	The Soviet government believes it is nearly to a stage where it no longer needs to buy from or sell to democracies.	Britain begins enrollment in war aid help, printing 20 million booklets describing jobs available. . . . Barcelona is hit by 47 air bombing raids. The government flees the city. . . . An American ship arrives in the Barcelona area to pick up American refugees. Diplomats are told to stay.			The Japanese premier shares a plan to handle a potential embargo by Britain and the United States. . . . Attacks on Shanghai are likely as the seventh anniversary of the Japanese attack on Chapei approaches.
Jan. 26	Japan denies it plans to attack Russia, but threatens to destroy Soviet troops if they start aggression. . . . Germany and Poland hail an accord. Poles refuse to support schemes against Western powers.	Barcelona falls to insurgents. Refugees from the city turn back, as shells make roads to the north impassable. . . . Sir Stafford Cripps, the British Labor Party's "ablest lawyer" is removed from the party after he makes verbal attacks on Prime Minister Neville Chamberlain. . . . Nazi Propaganda Minister Joseph Goeb-bels is shorn of some powers. . . . Insurgents bomb a Spanish port as Americans are leaving.	Turkey gets a new Cabinet. Refik Saydam replaces Jelal Bayar as Prime Minister.	The Canadian government plans nearly $64 million in expenditures for defense. . . . Brazilian police arrest Plinio Salgado, the chief of the banned fascist *Integralista* party, who has been in hiding.	
Jan. 27	France rejects the Japanese nominee for ambassador, an action seen as a political snub.	Americans leaving Spain reach France safely. . . . Britain is invincible, states the British Home Secretary. . . . French Premier Edouard Daladier announces that the hour of peril nears. . . . Franco's troops enter Barcelona. . . . Italian Premier Benito Mussolini sees foes "biting dust" and projects a "new Europe." . . . Industrial towns Badalona and Sabadell fall to Spanish rebels without a fight. . . . The Reich hails Barcelona's fall.		Secretary of State Cordell Hull asserts actions are being taken to improve the relationship with Mexico. . . . U.S. aid is rushed to Chilean earthquake victims.	

A	B	C	D	E
Includes developments that affect more than one world region, international organizations, and important meetings of world leaders.	Includes all domestic and regional developments in Europe, including the Soviet Union.	Includes all domestic and regional developments in Africa and the Middle East.	Includes all domestic and regional developments in Latin America, the Caribbean, and Canada.	Includes all domestic and regional developments in Asian and Pacific nations (and colonies).

U.S. Politics & Social Issues	U.S. Foreign Policy & Defense	Economics & Great Depression	Science, Technology & Nature	Culture, Leisure & Lifestyle	
A court acquits Prohibition-era gangster George "Bugs" Moran on counterfeiting charges. . . . The anticipated impeachment of UAW head Homer Martin takes a twist when Martin locks himself in his office and suspends 15 members of the board.	A new method of building planes, using plastic, will make the process 20–30 times faster.	The Undersecretary of the Treasury says the administration is changing from relief focus to economic recovery.		Paramount Studios cancels its contract with actor George Raft after nearly seven years when he refuses a role. . . . One-third of the estate of the late New York Yankees owner Col. Jacob Ruppert goes to a former actress Helen Winthrope Weyant who appears shocked at bequest. She inherits $300,000.	Jan. 21
			The atom nucleus is seen as a boon to cancer treatments, as radiation is expected to complement x-rays in cancer care, according to British doctor C.D. Ellis.	A plea is made to allow professional tennis players to participate in the Wimbledon tournament. . . . Gate receipts for Sonja Henie's ice skating shows total $1 million.	Jan. 22
President Franklin Roosevelt supports modified anti-lynching legislation. . . . Roosevelt is expected to introduce long-term health improvement legislation. . . . The second James Hines trial begins. Hines is accused of using Tammany influence to protect gangsters. . . . Fistfights disrupt a UAW meeting as president Homer Martin's future is discussed.		The Bituminous Coal Commission warns Congress to cut coal losses by establishing minimum prices for soft coal; $37 million is lost annually.	Astronomers trace Crab Nebula to the explosion of a powerful star. . . . Physicians believe that the rare but fatal Cushing's Disease is caused by too many hormones.	The United Daughters of the Confederacy end their protest over the selection of Englishwoman Vivien Leigh as Scarlett O'Hara in Gone With the Wind.	Jan. 23
The Senate confirms Harry Hopkins as Secretary of Commerce by a 58–27 vote. . . . President Franklin Roosevelt introduces a national health care plan to Congress. Federal and state cooperation is needed, Roosevelt says, and the cost will be $850 million over 10 years. . . . Men are encroaching upon women's jobs, says the director of the Women's Bureau of the Department of Labor.	Legislators introduce many bills on the Neutrality Act, increasing pressure on President Franklin Roosevelt. . . . Delegates of the Cause and Cure of War committee are expected to pressure Congress and President Roosevelt to ban war materials exports to Japan. First Lady Eleanor Roosevelt questions the ethics of hiding behind the Neutrality Act.		Permatron, a magnetically controlled, gas-filled industrial tube, is introduced at an exhibition by Raytheon Products. Scientists expect many practical uses for the tube.	The movie Gunga Din premieres in Los Angeles. Cary Grant, Victor McLaglen, and Douglas Fairbanks star. . . . George Sisler, Eddie Collins, and "Wee" Willie Keeler are chosen for the Baseball Hall of Fame.	Jan. 24
District Attorney Thomas Dewey is the most popular potential Republican candidate for president. . . . Martin Dies, chairman of the House Committee Investigating Un-American Activities, is found to owe back taxes. . . . President Roosevelt seeks major reform of the Federal Communications Commission. . . . Seventy percent of Americans oppose a six-year term for the presidency.	About 250 clergy ask President Franklin Roosevelt to lift the Spanish arms embargo, fearing Franco's success.		Seventeen million cases of trichinosis are believed to exist in the United States, but are difficult to diagnose.	Joe Louis successfully defends his heavyweight title for the fifth time. He knocked out John Henry Lewis in the first round.	Jan. 25
Jury selection is complete in the trial of James Hines.	The Conference on Cause and Cure of War recommends changes in the Neutrality Act, 296–5.	Homer Martin resigns from the executive board of the CIO.	The Institute of Aeronautical Sciences meets. U.S. air science lags as compared to Europe.	Seven hundred events are listed for the World Fair. . . . Lou Gehrig accepts a $4,000 pay cut in his contract with the New York Yankees.	Jan. 26
Motion picture financer Jules Brulatour claims to have accidentally shot himself in the neck. Police are attempting to confirm the likelihood of the scenario. . . . The CIO suspends Homer Martin as president of the UAW. . . . The Euthanasia Society drafts mercy killing legislation for consideration in New York.	A big base located on Guam would be a "safeguard," Rear Admiral Hepburn tells the Naval committee. . . . President Roosevelt announces approval of the sale of battle planes to France.	The Senate votes on WPA cuts.		The World Fair will boast 50 penguins from the south polar regions. . . . John Henry Lewis requests a rematch with Joe Louis. . . . Jimmy Foxx signs a contract with the Red Sox. The salary estimate is $30,000. His goal is to become the highest-paid player in baseball.	Jan. 27

F	G	H	I	J
Includes elections, federal-state relations, civil rights and liberties, crime, the judiciary, education, healthcare, poverty, urban affairs, and population.	Includes formation and debate of U.S. foreign and defense policies, veterans affairs, and defense spending. (Relations with specific foreign countries are usually found under the region concerned.)	Includes business, labor, agriculture, taxation, transportation, consumer affairs, monetary and fiscal policy, natural resources, pollution, and accidents.	Includes worldwide scientific, medical, and technological developments, natural phenomena, U.S. weather, and natural disasters.	Includes the arts, religion, scholarship, communications media, sports, entertainment, fashions, fads, and social life.

	World Affairs	Europe	Africa & The Middle East	The Americas	Asia & The Pacific
Jan. 28	Germany asserts it is strong enough to make more claims on the world, even at the expense of war. . . . A German newspaper asks the United States to set a good example and accept 100,000 Jewish refugees. . . . The League of Nations will help 2,000 Spanish children move to France.	The exiled King and Queen of Spain attend a church service in Rome to celebrate the fall of Barcelona. . . . Lord Chatfield will be named Britain's Minister for the Coordination of Defense. . . . Food lines in Barcelona are one mile long. . . . Josef Stalin announces the first Russian Congress since 1934.		Chileans feel new earthquake tremors.	Chinese Marshal Wu Pei-Fu accepts a "puppet post" that aims to unite Japanese governments in conquered Nanking and Peiping. . . . Japan resumes bombing of the Lung-hai railway.
Jan. 29	Britain predicts world crisis, but no war. . . . Arab delegates reach London for a conference on Palestine.	Austrian offices close, and its ministries are distributed throughout the Reich. . . . Soviet workers who are fired for tardiness are eligible for work at other companies.	Egypt plans to tear down current Cairo bazaars and rebuild.		A pacification plan for Japanese-occupied areas of China is set. . . . Subhas Chandra Bose is elected president of India's Congress Party.
Jan. 30		Sir Stafford Cripps appeals his ouster from the British Labor Party. . . . France reinforces its border to prevent an influx of Spanish deserters. . . . Barcelona returns to normal after its fall in the Spanish Civil War and public services are restored. . . . In a major speech before the Reichstag, Adolf Hitler justifies Germany's aggression and warns other nations against "meddling."		Aftershocks terrify people in Chile, even as American aid arrives.	According to War Minister Itagaki, Japan's army plans a long stay in China.
Jan. 31	Adolf Hitler proclaims his determination to regain Germany's colonies and for Germany, Italy, and Japan to receive entitled riches.	The Soviet government outlines the third five-year plan. Heavy industry is emphasized. . . . France shuts the Spanish border and thousands are turned back. . . . In a temporary capital, Figueras, the Spanish government tries to reorganize its defenses.			Fifty Siam army officers retire without pension after attempting to replace the 13-year-old King Ananda Majidol with his uncle. . . . General Chen Chien of China's army denies reports that Gen. Wu Pei-fu has agreed to head a puppet government.
Feb. 1		Prime Minister Neville Chamberlain provides a guarded response to Hitler's speech, saying peaceful actions must accompany words. . . . Spanish refugees in France are fed free rice or beans and meat. . . . Italy hails Germany's war pledge. Premier Benito Mussolini is expected to deliver a speech to the nation today, but does not do so.		Volcano activity joins earthquakes in Chile.	Reports emerge of heavy fighting as the Japanese army moves up the Yangtze towards Ichang in four columns.
Feb. 2	Soviets accuse Japanese soldiers of a Siberian raid.	The Romanian Premier appoints Armand Calinescu as Vice Premier and temporary War Minister. . . . France seeks a Catalonian truce, fearful that retreating Spanish troops will land on French soil. . . . Bowing to Reich pressure, the Czech government will expel the majority of Jews. . . . Hitler is expected to ask France and Britain to peacefully return former German colonies. . . . Hungary joins the Anti-Comintern Pact with Germany, Japan, and Italy. . . . Belgian Premier Spaak is beaten and bloodied by ex-soldiers because he appointed a man convicted of wartime treason to a seat in the Academy of Medicine. Speak's condition is not serious.		President Franklin Roosevelt pleads for aid to Chile. . . . Mexico City faces electrical outages until summer, as the waters that fuel its hydroelectric plants are at their historical lows.	The Japanese Empress awaits the birth of her child; midwives are standing by.
Feb. 3	An estimated 83 percent of Americans and 85 percent of Britons are against France and Britain returning colonies to Germany. . . . The Vatican claims subtle church persecution in Germany. . . . Nazis call President Franklin Roosevelt a dictator. . . . Heavyweight boxer Max Schmeling arrives in the United States. He denies he was punished by Germany for criticizing Joseph Goebbels.	Executions are expected as Spanish Republican officers are captured. . . . Prime Minister Neville Chamberlain shuns a one-party system in Britain. . . . Twelve dictators will rule Britain in war; each is responsible for a self-contained region. The government is said to order 1.2 million baby gas masks. . . . The Soviet government cuts direct ties with Hungary because of Hungary's relationship with Germany, Italy, and Japan. . . . France cancels executions today when the executioner does not show for work; the executioner had died in a subway station.			Chungking police pay Chinese residents two cents for each rat killed. Cats and terriers are not enough to control the rat population. . . . The Japanese military seizes control of 15 industries.

A	B	C	D	E
Includes developments that affect more than one world region, international organizations, and important meetings of world leaders.	Includes all domestic and regional developments in Europe, including the Soviet Union.	Includes all domestic and regional developments in Africa and the Middle East.	Includes all domestic and regional developments in Latin America, the Caribbean, and Canada.	Includes all domestic and regional developments in Asian and Pacific nations (and colonies).

U.S. Politics & Social Issues	U.S. Foreign Policy & Defense	Economics & Great Depression	Science, Technology & Nature	Culture, Leisure & Lifestyle	
Two receive the death penalty under a new, stricter kidnapping law. . . . On the eve of their strike, radio performers agree to negotiate.	Rear Admiral Arthur B. Cook says that Pearl Harbor is inadequate as the sole Pacific base.	The Senate upholds WPA cuts, 47–46. President Roosevelt is stunned by the defeat.	The American Institute of Electrical Engineers discusses a new type of turbine engine that may save companies millions of dollars annually.	The dean of Cornell University asserts that football has a disquieting influence on students. . . . Boxer Joe Louis considers exhibition tours. . . . The famous Irish poet and Nobel prize winner W.B. Yeats dies after a short illness.	Jan. 28
			It is discovered that an atom explosion frees 200 million volts.	Boston University stresses the value of dance as exercise. . . . Glenn Cunningham wins the Boston mile race for the fifth year.	Jan. 29
Congress focuses on defense, plane sales, and issues with France, Mexico, and Guam. . . . Gangster George Weinberg, who was set to testify against Tammany leader James Hines, commits suicide. . . . Felix Frankfurter is sworn in as Supreme Court Justice.			A new type of radio may revolutionize short-wave science and assist in television and aviation. . . . All Hunter College students are to be x-rayed to determine prevalence of tuberculosis.	Writing in the New England Journal of Medicine, A Harvard neurologist Wilfred Bloomberg touts Benzedrine as help for chronic alcoholism, but warns wives against slipping the compound into their husband's coffee.	Jan. 30
Comedian George Burns's plane is grounded. Burns's sentencing for smuggling is delayed. . . . Eight thousand people attend the President's birthday ball, where $25,000 is raised for infantile paralysis, or "polio." . . . The notorious swindler known as Dapper Dan is caught posing as an immigration agent. . . . Harry Hopkins suspends 17 ship operators who may have accepted gratuities.					Jan. 31
President Franklin Roosevelt directs Attorney General Frank Murphy to investigate efforts to influence Federal judges. George Burns is fined nearly $18,000 in a jewelry smuggling conviction. . . . Labor groups and advertisers will fight a proposed ban on billboards. . . . Ousted UAW president Homer Martin is accused of unfair labor practices. . . . The Dies Committee investigating "un-American activity" is accused of unfairness, usurpation of power, and evading duty.	The Army drops the use of Morse code, as radio and tapes supplant the need. . . . President Franklin Roosevelt agrees to help European democracies in all ways short of war.	A grand jury inquires into WPA fraud and graft. . . . Ten thousand elevator operators and service employees stage a strike in New York, asking a 15 percent wage increase.	The New York governor proclaims Social Hygiene Day to focus on curbing venereal diseases.	Humphrey Bogart will appear in the movie Escape From Alcatraz.	Feb. 1
A jury hears testimony in the conspiracy trial of Frank Hayes, the mayor of Waterbury, Conn. . . . Several members of the House denounce the Dies Committee, which is investigating "un-American" activities.	The Assistant Secretary of War calls present defense plans merely a first step. . . . Former president Herbert Hoover accuses President Franklin Roosevelt of expanding foreign policy powers without approval.	A five-year fight between the Tennessee Valley Authority and private utility companies nears resolution.			Feb. 2
The Dewey Bill backs evidence seizure without a warrant, but limits wire tapping. . . . Half of the San Quentin prisoners eat bread only in protest of prison meals. More fruit is requested. . . . Officials admit giving out "hush" money in the conspiracy trial of the mayor of Waterbury, Conn. . . . The United Textile Workers of America will leave the CIO and rejoin the AFL. . . . The House votes to extend the inquiry into the Dies Committee for one year.		Herbert Hoover calls President Franklin Roosevelt's hydroelectric energy program wasteful. . . . New York's two-day long strike of building service employees ends after Mayor LaGuardia negotiates a settlement. 100,000 people were idled by the strike.			Feb. 3

F	G	H	I	J
Includes elections, federal-state relations, civil rights and liberties, crime, the judiciary, education, healthcare, poverty, urban affairs, and population.	Includes formation and debate of U.S. foreign and defense policies, veterans affairs, and defense spending. (Relations with specific foreign countries are usually found under the region concerned.)	Includes business, labor, agriculture, taxation, transportation, consumer affairs, monetary and fiscal policy, natural resources, pollution, and accidents.	Includes worldwide scientific, medical, and technological developments, natural phenomena, U.S. weather, and natural disasters.	Includes the arts, religion, scholarship, communications media, sports, entertainment, fashions, fads, and social life.

	World Affairs	Europe	Africa & The Middle East	The Americas	Asia & The Pacific
Feb. 4	Japan reports four days of continuous fighting with the Russians along Manchukuo's borders.	Britain agrees with the U.S. suggestion to explore British Guinea as a refuge for Jews. . . . Joseph Goebbels ends the careers of five "Aryan" actors who made witticisms at the Reich's expense. . . . Princess Juliana of the Netherlands is expecting her second child.			
Feb. 5	The United States sells more arms to China than to Japan, according to Secretary Hull. . . . A Nazi newspaper asks First Lady Eleanor Roosevelt to cease making political comments.	Girona, Spain, falls to Franco's forces. . . . The new French executioner is 80 years old. Tradition allows him to pardon the first convict he sees, but the convict prefers death. . . . France will wage war against abortion. A higher birth rate is sought to rival population growth in fascist countries. . . . Joseph Goebbels sponsors a joke contest to prove that Nazis have a sense of humor. . . . Hitler continues the Reichsbank purge, and three more directors are dismissed. . . . Spanish Loyalists are said to ask Britain to negotiate peace with Gen. Franco.		Mexican workers march to demonstrate support of Cuba's Col. Batista, who is visiting President Cardenas.	
Feb. 6	Japanese political parties draft stern legislation requesting more aggressive tactics toward Russia. . . . Arab delegates refuse to sit in the same room as Jews in a conference held in London. Prime Minister Neville Chamberlain opens the conference with groups meeting in separate chambers. . . . Japan refuses to cooperate with a treaty even after the United States, Britain, and France request cooperation.	France reopens its border to the fleeing loyalist army. . . . Hungary and Russia end diplomatic ties. . . . Reich clerics report oppression after pleading for peace.			China lists 1,500 new bombing casualties.
Feb. 7	Japan reports its failure to resolve its border dispute with Russia.	The Spanish president arrives in France and has refugee status. . . . Four Spanish Communists are punished for fleeing Barcelona.		El Salvador insists its government is democratic and denies Nazi or fascist influence.	
Feb. 8	Japan says it is not worried about the U.S. fortification of Guam, calling it a U.S. vulnerability. . . . The British are partially successful at removing money from Japanese institutions. . . . Arab delegates are split on the Palestine question at the London conference.	Fleeing Loyalist soldiers bring large quantities of arms to France. . . . The Spanish President, Manuel Azana, will remain in France and live in the Spanish Embassy.			Military experts suggest that Japan needs 500,000 more troops to subdue China. . . . The Japanese delay an attack on a Chinese resort so that an American gunboat can evacuate stranded foreign citizens.
Feb. 9	Australia disputes a claim that Lincoln Ellsworth made that grants 80,000 acres of the Antarctic to the United States. . . . Russia seeks a pact with Black Sea countries that would form an eastern bloc to forestall German efforts. . . . Soviets announce the repulsion of a Japanese attempt to capture "Island #227" in the Argun River. . . . At the London conference on Palestine, Arab leaders demand that the Jewish refugee problem be kept separate from their discussions. The Arabs desire independence and an end to the British Mandate.	Franco pledges the removal of Italian and German soldiers from Spain. Britain will recognize the new government once foreign soldiers are removed. . . . Franco waits for Madrid to surrender. Rebels want France to return ships, gold, and artwork stored there. . . . The Irish support a bill to control bombings. The bill includes punishment for treason. . . . Italy says France violates international law by allowing a Spanish Loyalist Cabinet to operate there.			The last Labor Party disbands in Tokyo.
Feb. 10	Pope Pius XI dies shortly before the 17th anniversary of his papacy. Cardinals move into Vatican cells and will remain there until a new Pope is chosen. The Pope's last words were, "God bless you, my children. Let there be peace." . . . Soviets warn Japan they no longer are weak on the frontier.	France and Britain will accept Franco once the civil war officially ends and no longer insist upon foreign soldiers leaving the country as a condition of acceptance. . . . A high Soviet police official is shot for framing an innocent person.		The American-owned oil company Petrolera is forced to cease operations in Mexico. The Mexican government claims Petrolera owes back wages.	Japan lands forces on Hainan Island, across from the Gulf of Tonkin, in China. France and Britain worry over their interests in Southeast Asia. . . . India's legislature passes a resolution urging withdrawal from the League of Nations.

A	B	C	D	E
Includes developments that affect more than one world region, international organizations, and important meetings of world leaders.	Includes all domestic and regional developments in Europe, including the Soviet Union.	Includes all domestic and regional developments in Africa and the Middle East.	Includes all domestic and regional developments in Latin America, the Caribbean, and Canada.	Includes all domestic and regional developments in Asian and Pacific nations (and colonies).

U.S. Politics & Social Issues	U.S. Foreign Policy & Defense	Economics & Great Depression	Science, Technology & Nature	Culture, Leisure & Lifestyle	
The House considers a financial reorganization bill for railroads. . . . New York City club women honor the wife of Chiang Kai-shek for her peace work and spirit of humanity. . . . The Attorney General creates a civil rights unit to protect individual liberties. . . . A lawyer confesses to perjury in the Waterbury conspiracy case. . . . Some Senators challenge President Roosevelt over his alleged statement that France is America's front-line defense. Roosevelt denies making the statement.			Explorer Lincoln Ellsworth's ship is due at Tasmania today, as his Antarctic expedition comes to a close.	Author James Joyce completes *Finnegans Wake* after 17 years. . . . Recently pardoned labor leader Tom Mooney asks for a divorce from his wife, who spent 22 years trying to free him. His wife refuses.	Feb. 4
An estimated 69 percent of Americans do not favor a third term for President Franklin Roosevelt. . . . Iowa legislators sleep in death row cells for a "thrill." One says the bed was "nice and soft."	Admiral William D. Leahy may stay on as Naval Chief of Operations past his retirement date.			Mervyn LeRoy produces the movie *The Wizard of Oz*. . . . The World Fair will feature an "all gas" exhibition home.	Feb. 5
AFL and CIO relations are improving. . . . Floods leave 30,000 people homeless in Kentucky, West Virginia, Tennessee, and Ohio. . . . The Texas governor gives a 30-day reprieve to a man sentenced to capital punishment to illustrate the cruelty of the death penalty.		A major trade boon is seen as a result of a TVA/private utility company peace deal.	Smoking alone does not cause heart disease, a study shows, although nicotine may be a factor in disease.	Hollywood nominates George Bernard Shaw for an award for *Pygmalion*. . . . Marlene Dietrich signs to perform in *The Image* for a French company.	Feb. 6
A House Representative seeks protection of the bald eagle. . . . Court testimony reveals that James Hines, a Tammany official, demoted police with good records.		The Public Works Administrator recommends a permanent public works department.		The World Fair will employ 1,000 hostesses. . . . Charlie Chaplin completes the script of his next movie, *The Great Dictator*. It includes a speaking part for Chaplin.	Feb. 7
After a third-grader pours her father's wine into her coffee, her father forces her to drink the mixture and then sends her to school. The girl falls and fractures her head. . . . First Lady Eleanor Roosevelt scorns Nazi advice to stop discussing politics and she repeats her views.		A barber who charges a quarter for a haircut is sent to jail for price fixing.		Mothers-in-law form an association to promote marital bliss, and refuse to censure jokes made about them.	Feb. 8
The AFL and CIO jointly sponsor a plan to admit 10,000 refugee children into the United States under a Quaker program. . . . The Securities and Exchange Commission will present evidence that insurance companies forge signatures of policyholders when electing directors as common practice.	The House Military Affairs Committee urges the bolstering of military equipment, which they say is currently woefully inadequate.				Feb. 9
The House votes to tax government workers the same as private individuals.	Republicans support nearly all of President Roosevelt's defense plan, but are uncertain about the importance of fortifying Guam.	The Chairman of the Securities and Exchange Commission says that huge corporations degrade moral values and threaten democracy. . . . Senator James Byrnes files a relief reform bill that combines six different agencies and creates a permanent relief organization. . . . The WPA extends dental service for the most needy.		Olympic officials drop women's gymnastics. . . . The National Football League names Joe Carr as president for a 10-year term. . . . Fighting dogs bite actress Helen Hayes. She has injuries on her chin and arms and is also treated for nervous shock. . . . Ethel Merman and Jimmy Durante perform *Stars in Your Eyes* at the Majestic Theater.	Feb. 10

F	G	H	I	J
Includes elections, federal-state relations, civil rights and liberties, crime, the judiciary, education, healthcare, poverty, urban affairs, and population.	*Includes formation and debate of U.S. foreign and defense policies, veterans affairs, and defense spending. (Relations with specific foreign countries are usually found under the region concerned.)*	*Includes business, labor, agriculture, taxation, transportation, consumer affairs, monetary and fiscal policy, natural resources, pollution, and accidents.*	*Includes worldwide scientific, medical, and technological developments, natural phenomena, U.S. weather, and natural disasters.*	*Includes the arts, religion, scholarship, communications media, sports, entertainment, fashions, fads, and social life.*

	World Affairs	Europe	Africa & The Middle East	The Americas	Asia & The Pacific
Feb. 11	The body of Pope Pius XI lies in state, as world leaders pay homage. Adolf Hitler sends a message that the next Pope should be political, and should understand the laws of the times. . . . The papal conclave is postponed to March 1. . . . India withdraws from the League of Nations, accusing the League of failing to carry out punitive powers and protesting Britain's policy in Palestine. . . . Japan defends its seizure of Hainan. . . . German students in North America are to send back information to the Reich about the political and economic situation there.	The Spanish loyalist government will move its capital to Madrid, and intends to fight to the end against Franco. . . . Spanish rebels complete their conquest of the frontier. . . . The Reich will launch a 35,000-ton battleship, the largest in the history of the German navy.		Oswaldo Aranha, the Brazilian minister of foreign affairs visits Washington D.C., bringing with him experts in trade and banking.	
Feb. 12	All faiths unite in praising the late Pope Pius XI. His body rests in St. Peter's Basilica after a solemn procession. Two of three American Cardinals sail to Rome to participate in the election of the new Pope. . . . Japanese rush the Soviet border and quit the China fronts. "Authorative" sources say 600,000 troops have moved north.	Germany permits Jews to reenter trades until they can emigrate. . . . The Society for the Protection of Ancient Buildings struggles with a bat problem in old British churches. . . . Insurgent Spanish forces halt their victory celebration to mourn the Pope. . . . Premier Augustin Volosin's party wins a large majority in the election in Carpatho-Ukraine.	The Palestine conference makes little headway; the refusal of Arab delegates to meet with Jewish delegates suggests a deadlock.		Rioting between Moslems and Hindus in Delhi, India, claim twenty lives. Five hundred are arrested. . . . In Burma, police fire on a procession of twenty thousand people. Two dozen are killed.
Feb. 13	Five Cardinals lead the Vatican contest. . . . England's only Cardinal leaves for Rome to participate in the conclave. . . . France sees a general European war as loyalists' only chance to hold on to Spain. . . . Tokyo attempts to calm France, while also taking over customs duty on the seized island of Hainan.	Adolf Hitler struggles to absorb Austria. . . . The Irish officially recognize the government of Franco. . . . Papal colors fly throughout Germany. The swastika, which must normally fly next to all other symbols, is not flown in this instance. . . . The Soviet press criticizes Pius XI for defending capitalism.			The Japanese House of Representatives is set to approve the largest budget in the country's history, though at 3.7 million yen it is seen only as a first installment.
Feb. 14	The Vatican prepares to house the conclave, and must create simple accommodations for 400 people.	Adolf Hitler puts a wreath on Otto von Bismarck's tomb. The founder of the second Reich is a personal hero of Hitler's.			Japan's House of Representatives votes approval of armed occupation of Siberian islands and fishing grounds.
Feb. 15	France buys 500 more war planes from the United States, for a total of 615. . . . The world watches the old stove pipe at the Vatican. Its smoke will announce when a new Pope has been named. . . . Workers digging a grave for Pius XI discover that it already contains the body of an archbishop. . . . War with the Soviets would enable Japan to quit the China fight without losing face. . . . British Colonial Secretary Malcolm MacDonald unveils a proposal giving equal political representation to Jews and Arabs in Palestine. No one likes the plan.	The British House of Commons keeps the ban on women in the stock exchange despite argument that females would not get "jitters" in a crisis. . . . British officials can now compel journalists to reveal sources in instances of espionage. . . Madrid orders resistance to the death, if necessary. . . . Romanian Baptists may form churches again. . . . Hitler launches a 35,000-ton battleship named *Bismarck*. . . . The Reich seeks 800,000 to work on farms and forbids laborers from changing assigned jobs. . . . Bela Imredy, the anti-Semitic Hungarian premier is forced to resign. After creating a bill barring those of Jewish descent from holding office, it is announced that the premier himself is of Jewish descent.		Mexican Communists plead for unity and cite the danger of fascism. . . . Mexico reduces the lunch and siesta break for workers from four hours to three.	Japan completes seizure of Hainan. The island is to serve as a stronghold for Japan. . . . China continues its guerilla war in the central provinces.
Feb. 16	Governments attempt to sway the Cardinals' votes in the selection of a new Pope. Even their servants are being courted for favors. . . . Deputies urge a strong Indo-China defense against Japan. Submarines are declared an indispensable tool.	Britons mistrust regional dictators being chosen for wartime posts. . . . Ireland will raise defense outlays, spending £5.5 million on war materials. . . . The Spanish police arrest a *London Daily Herald* newspaper correspondent traveling in France with 45 pieces of diamond jewelry. . . . A Soviet court strips a Red Army officer of his title and sentences him to five years in a labor camp for slander.		Brazilian envoy Aranha indicates he may stay in Washington, D.C., until Roosevelt returns from the Caribbean since he would like to meet with the President again.	The Chinese attack in a wide range of areas. Guerillas are said to be seriously menacing in the central region.

A	B	C	D	E
Includes developments that affect more than one world region, international organizations, and important meetings of world leaders.	*Includes all domestic and regional developments in Europe, including the Soviet Union.*	*Includes all domestic and regional developments in Africa and the Middle East.*	*Includes all domestic and regional developments in Latin America, the Caribbean, and Canada.*	*Includes all domestic and regional developments in Asian and Pacific nations (and colonies).*

U.S. Politics & Social Issues	U.S. Foreign Policy & Defense	Economics & Great Depression	Science, Technology & Nature	Culture, Leisure & Lifestyle	
The Assistant Attorney General of New York sifts through bribery charges against high-level police officers. . . . Film financier Jules Brulatour pays a $500 fine for a weapons charge to avoid 30 days in a workhouse. . . . First Lady Eleanor Roosevelt hails female reporters. She presents four prizes of $100 each. . . . Secretary of the Interior Harold Ickes stands by his statement that the press is not as free as it should be in a democracy. . . . The United States celebrates the 130th birthday of Abraham Lincoln. . . . President Roosevelt's doctor confines him to bed with a 99.6-degree fever.				The ancestral home of Ralph Waldo Emerson, which later became the home of Nathaniel Hawthorne, is slated to become a public shrine. . . . The Federal Trade Commission orders the manufacturer of D. Gosewich's Garlic Tablets to stop claiming the product lowers blood pressure, removes bloodstream impurities, and strengthens intestines, among other claims. . . . Film star Joan Crawford files for divorce against Franchot Tone, accusing him of cruelty. Tone would expect her to socialize on evenings she needed to practice movie lines, the suit claims.	Feb. 11
The Institute of Public Opinion finds growing resistance to President Roosevelt's liberal policies. Conservatives fare better. . . . The New York League of Women Voters prepares materials against an Equal Rights Amendment. . . . A Congressional subcommittee opposes favors for small business. A monopoly study suggests that business size should not affect penalties given. . . . President Roosevelt will not place the traditional Lincoln wreath today because he is ill.	Senator Robert La Follette notes parallels to the current situation and 1917. He urges Congressional participation in foreign policy to keep the United States out of war. . . . Eighteen new destroyer ships are delayed by engineering defects revealed in the turbines.		Aviation experts look to a light beryllium alloy for aircraft construction.	The Postmaster General announces a new stamp to commemorate baseball's centennial. . . . A court decrees that a bar bouncer cannot eject a man who is holding his liquor and is able to pay for drinks until the 4 a.m. closing time. . . . Glenn Cunningham wins a mile race by a two-foot margin. . . . Margaret Fishback publishes the etiquette guide When to Behave—and Why and takes jibes at Emily Post.	Feb. 12
John F. Kennedy, the 21-year-old son of a U.S. Ambassador, will have a six-month trial period as an office boy at the London and Paris embassies. . . . George R. Holmes, the Washington bureau chief of the International News Service, dies of a heart attack. President Roosevelt pays tribute.	Air defense plans will go to House debate this week. Attacks on Roosevelt are expected, but the funds bill is anticipated to pass.			The wife of John D. Rockefeller, Jr., sells two rare pieces of Buddhist art to the Metropolitan Museum of Art. There is no room in her new apartment to display the art.	Feb. 13
Congress halts in homage to Pope Pius XI, the first such tribute to a spiritual leader. . . . First Lady Eleanor Roosevelt displays Goya etchings, a gift from Spain, despite protests. . . . Supreme Court Justice Louis Brandeis retires amid rumors of ill health. . . . New York Mayor Fiorello La Guardia orders police to assist bar owners who wish to close early.	France contracts to buy 500 war planes from American manufacturers.	Herbert Hoover warns that the New Deal will eventually lead to inflation.	Mount Vesuvius rises visibly. . . . Explorer Lincoln Ellsworth believes that the U.S.-Australia dispute over the Antarctic territory is good, since it generates interest in the region.	The championship horse Seabiscuit is lame after a race defeat. The horse has a damaged ligament in his left leg.	Feb. 14
Democrats ask President Franklin Roosevelt to solidify the party for 1940 by working with Congress. . . . The Senate kills a bill that would allow women to serve on juries. A female Senator says that most women do not want more responsibility. . . . A mother of two attempts a holdup with a children's toy pistol. . . . President Roosevelt recovers from a brief illness and is set for a trip to the Caribbean. . . . Speculation exists that William O. Douglas, SEC chairman, may replace the retired Louis Brandeis as Supreme Court Justice.	A poll indicates that 55 percent of Americans think businessmen have better ideas for the economy than the New Deal.			Swiss fashion producers plan to push organdy as a silk substitute, capitalizing on anti-Japanese sentiments. . . . Jack Benny is allowed by the court to complete his film before beginning his smuggling trial. . . . The State Motion Picture Division bans Yes, My Darling Daughter, calling it an affront to morals and worrying it will encourage trial marriages. . . . Victor Fleming replaces George Cukor as director of Gone With the Wind.	Feb. 15
Secretary of Agriculture Henry Wallace exempts 24 foods from new mandatory food labels. The exemption is good for two years. . . . House Democrats plan to sound out voters on real mandates. A national survey will be created. . . . The American Labor Party votes to purge Communists from its membership. . . . A ceremony at the capital honors the memory of Susan B. Anthony, suffragist.	The House votes for 3,000 more planes as war is anticipated, with a vote of 367–15.			The World Fair sets prices: 75 cents for adults, 25 cents for children, with a special dime-day held once a week for youth. . . . Kentucky Derby officials expect a record crowd of 100,000. . . . Tallulah Bankhead appears in Lillian Hellman's play, The Little Foxes. . . . Katharine Hepburn previews The Philadelphia Story in Hartford, Conn.	Feb. 16

F	G	H	I	J
Includes elections, federal-state relations, civil rights and liberties, crime, the judiciary, education, healthcare, poverty, urban affairs, and population.	Includes formation and debate of U.S. foreign and defense policies, veterans affairs, and defense spending. (Relations with specific foreign countries are usually found under the region concerned.)	Includes business, labor, agriculture, taxation, transportation, consumer affairs, monetary and fiscal policy, natural resources, pollution, and accidents.	Includes worldwide scientific, medical, and technological developments, natural phenomena, U.S. weather, and natural disasters.	Includes the arts, religion, scholarship, communications media, sports, entertainment, fashions, fads, and social life.

	World Affairs	Europe	Africa & The Middle East	The Americas	Asia & The Pacific
Feb. 17	Britain submits a secret plan to Arab nations that offers an alternative to an independent state. . . . First Lady Eleanor Roosevelt urges a world role for the United States and predicts trouble ahead. . . . Dr. von Bergen, German envoy, urges Cardinals to choose a Pope that favors fascism. . . . The fund for Pope Pius XI's monument is expected to be 520,000 lire.	The German Law Academy replaces the terms "Aryan," "German-blooded" and "of German and cognate blood" with "Europe-racial." . . . Barcelona judges face rebel courts. The judge who condemned many to death aboard the prison ship *Uruguay* is one of the first to be tried. . . . Germany deplores the British armament plan and finds it an attempt to destroy the spirit of the Munich agreement. . . . The vice president of the Reichsbank suffers a nervous breakdown so severe that he may not return to work. . . . The House of Lords demands deep underground shelters in case of a London raid.		The Brazilian Minister Aranha urges nations of the Americas to repel alien ideologies.	The Japanese plan to land more troops at Hainan and warn foreign ships to avoid the 30-mile area by Taichow Bay. . . . Railway cars full of arms leave Burma for China, traveling on the new, 2,100-mile road.
Feb. 18	Britain outlines its plan for Palestine. Zionists would need to concede on immigration issues but the constitution would prevent Jews from a political minority position. . . . Japan reassures the United States about Hainan island, saying it would not occupy the land beyond military necessity.	British air force training deaths mount. Some say the training is too swift. . . . Belgian police guard the Spanish Consulate in Brussels after nine Spanish insurgent members attempt to seize the building. . . . The Reich's Minister of Education shuts down a Catholic institution for interfering with freedom of academic teaching. . . . The French confiscate Spanish gems worth millions and may use these jewels to pay for refugee care. . . . The French find no mystery in the 1938 death of Leon Trotsky's son, ruling out poisoning.	Hearing a report that Italy has called up 150,000 reservists, France puts troops on the alert in Tunisia and other African possessions, and bolsters defenses there.		In Hopei and Hunan provinces, Chinese guerilla fighting continues as the Japanese claim victory.
Feb. 19	Arms and troop movements add to world tension. The United States and Britain build up defenses while Axis powers maneuver for positions. . . . Experts fear a long papal conclave if results are not announced within two or three days. . . . France fears an Italian attack in African territories and bolsters troops there.	Insurgents shell Madrid and there are many casualties. . . . Italian Premier Benito Mussolini reviews elite bodyguard units on the 18th anniversary of the founding of the group. . . . Goebbels criticizes Germans who have pictures of Kaiser Wilhelm in their homes, but not pictures of Hitler. He calls them "unrefined."		Gen. Antonio Rodriguez, Peru's Minister of Government and Interior escorts President Oscar Benavides to a ship, returns home, and declares himself head of the nation, but is killed in the coup attempt.	
Feb. 20	A Japanese blockade of Chinese ports causes American shippers to redirect vessels. . . . President Roosevelt's war fears mystify Europe. Italy suspects theatricals while Germany believes the United States is spurring the arms market. . . . U.S. Cardinals carry weight in selection of the new Pope.	Poland and the Soviet Union sign a trade treaty. The pact is seen as a sign of the Reich's lessening influence on its neighboring country. . . . In the United States, 10,000 rally for recognition of Franco's government.		Chilean leftists see new threats from rightist groups. The administration will announce a big plan for aid for quake victims. . . . Peru rounds up suspects in the foiled coup, including Gen. Cirilo H. Ortega.	Japan loses 2,000 men in a Chinese counter-attack. . . . The foreign minister in the Nanking regime is slain by gunmen. Japanese planes shell a rail station in Hong Kong, killing one policeman.
Feb. 21	Cardinals intend to continue the policies of Pius XI. The U.S. cardinals agree with his doctrine of full spiritual control.	Britain will finance £580 million in arms with a tax increase. . . . Franco's forces prepare to fight, dropping the idea of a loyalist surrender. . . . Hitler recognizes healing practitioners who do not have medical training or a license. Those with intuitive ability to cure the sick can practice under the title of *heilpraktiker*, or healing practitioner. . . . Premier Mussolini is willing to meet with Hitler and Franco.	Five Muslim nations support an independent Arab state in Palestine: Egypt, Iraq, Saudi Arabia, Trans-Jordan, and the Kingdom of Yemen.		Japan's Parliament demands the army take over Shanghai completely.
Feb. 22	Britain protests Japan's attack of Hong Kong, believing the attack was a test to gauge British reaction. . . . Britain drafts a plan for Palestinian peace. Proposals for both sides should be ready by next week. . . . China's Chiang Kai-shek gives thanks for foreign aid, according to a U.S. missionary. . . . The daughter of an exiled German novelist tells a group in the United States that 37 percent of German youth are flat-footed because of excessive marching. . . . Papal ties with France are a vital issue in selection of the new Pope.	Britain and Germany begin trade talks. Adolf Hitler links the colonies and other political issues with any commerce agreement. . . . Britain launches a 35,000-ton battleship, *George V*. . . . Franco reviews a parade of 80,000. The military display is the greatest since Armada days. . . . France and Britain plan recognition to guide the new Spain. Demands for mercy and a free regime are to be dropped, diplomats say. . . . Hubert Pierlot, Belgian Premier, creates a Cabinet list to present to King Leopold. He stresses this is not a combination of Catholic and Socialist choices, as predicted.		The Mexican Federation adopts a six-year plan calling for government in business, and plans for this to serve as a platform for the Mexican Revolutionary Party.	Both Japanese and Chinese spokesmen report a big victory in an air battle at Lanchow. . . . Japan says the Shanghai seizure was necessary to curb assassins.

A	B	C	D	E
Includes developments that affect more than one world region, international organizations, and important meetings of world leaders.	*Includes all domestic and regional developments in Europe, including the Soviet Union.*	*Includes all domestic and regional developments in Africa and the Middle East.*	*Includes all domestic and regional developments in Latin America, the Caribbean, and Canada.*	*Includes all domestic and regional developments in Asian and Pacific nations (and colonies).*

U.S. Politics & Social Issues	U.S. Foreign Policy & Defense	Economics & Great Depression	Science, Technology & Nature	Culture, Leisure & Lifestyle	
The Montana State Senate bans hangings within 25 miles of a city. . . . The repeal of a law that forbids teaching evolution in Tennessee fails.				The World Fair Corporation president anticipates $3 million in advance ticket sales. . . . Baseball player Joe DiMaggio predicts a "big year" for himself. . . . Katharine Hepburn stars in *The Philadelphia Story*. . . . Seabiscuit's x-ray shows no break.	Feb. 17
The Department of the Treasury projects the deficit for 1939 as $4 billion, and says it has spent more in 7.5 months than it expects to bring in during one year. . . . Rep. Martin Dies undergoes emergency appendix surgery.	The Army plans to mobilize big numbers in the East, the largest amount seen since World War I. . . . In a radio speech, President Franklin Roosevelt warns aggressive nations to stay out of the Americas.	The Chamber of Commerce president warns that the New Deal moves the country toward state capitalism.		John Barrymore will perform with his wife, Elaine Barrie, in *My Dear Children*.	Feb. 18
American passport applications fall by 20 percent. . . . The Child Welfare League of America lists the pros and cons of spanking foster children. . . . President Franklin Roosevelt may cut his trip short after hearing disturbing news of potential aggression against countries friendly with the United States. . . . A Catholic group opposes the movement toward legalizing mercy killing.			Chemists patent a new sleep potion that is less toxic with better results.	Finland looks forward to hosting the Olympics.	Feb. 19
The Prison Association of New York urges a new system for state prisons, citing its need for classifying and placing prisoners. . . . President Franklin Roosevelt stays in touch with Washington by radio as he sails back home. . . . A war ambulance replaces the dragon in a Chinese New Year parade as a symbol of grim reality in China.	The U.S. naval fleet scatters all over the South Atlantic and Caribbean in the largest war maneuvers ever staged in American waters. . . . The Guam debate will be heard in the House. The bill faces attack by those who fear the United States is "inviting trouble" with Japan.			The World Fair crowd visits exhibits. Attendance is close to 138,000.	Feb. 20
A revised anti-lynching bill is introduced in the Senate. . . . A rally of 22,000 Nazis is held in Madison Square Garden. Scuffles occur. . . . The Senate Majority Leader Perley Pitcher dies alone in a hotel. Legislation adjourns for one week. . . . President Franklin Roosevelt visits Guantanamo Bay, Cuba, a strategic site for defense of the Panama Canal.		President Franklin Roosevelt's ban on new taxes puzzles the Treasury.		A jeweled necklace given to Lola Montez by King Ludwig I of Bavaria does not sell at auction. . . . The New York Yankees president predicts the rest of the team will sign contracts by Saturday. . . . Buddy Abbott, Jr., pickets after being fired by his uncle from the Abbott and Costello comedy team. . . . British monarchs plan to visit the World Fair in June. . . . The Golden Gate International Exposition opens in San Fransicso.	Feb. 21
Darryl Zanuck, 20th-century movie chief, buys the contract of a popular radio performer and bans her from the air. Zanuck did the same with Tyrone Power last week. . . . After the death of the Senate Majority Leader, Perley Pitcher, two names rise for consideration: Arthur Wicks and Benjamin Feinberg. . . . A Senate committee warns of danger if the United States opposes alteration of the Philippines Independence Act.	The Naval Affairs Committee says that strong defense is the only answer, urging the fortification of Guam. . . . President Roosevelt widens war fleet games, with defense as the goal. . . . Major Gen. Arnold, the chief of the Army Air Corps warns that Germany could fly to the United States to attack if they establish bases in South America.	First Lady Eleanor Roosevelt says the New Deal is not a permanent solution, but a stop-gap measure that gives the country time to think. . . . President Franklin Roosevelt requests that $150,000 cut out of the New Deal budget be reinstated. He receives the silent treatment from Congress on the issue.	Lord Rothschild, head of the British bank, travels to the United States to consult with scientists about matters that interest him.	The San Francisco fair draws more attendance than the 1933 fair in Chicago. The attendance of the first two days stands at 237,409, as compared to 172,559. . . . Spanish surrealist artist Salvador Dali assures viewers that he does not understand his art, either. . . . Joseph Prance, founder of the Kiwanis group, dies after surgery. . . . Internationally known polo star Pat Roark dies of brain injuries after a fall during a game. . . . *Tarzan* actor Johnny Weissmuller will re-wed after a divorce from Lupe Velez is final. . . . Nadia Boulanger will be the first woman to conduct the Philadelphia Orchestra.	Feb. 22

F	G	H	I	J
Includes elections, federal-state relations, civil rights and liberties, crime, the judiciary, education, healthcare, poverty, urban affairs, and population.	Includes formation and debate of U.S. foreign and defense policies, veterans affairs, and defense spending. (Relations with specific foreign countries are usually found under the region concerned.)	Includes business, labor, agriculture, taxation, transportation, consumer affairs, monetary and fiscal policy, natural resources, pollution, and accidents.	Includes worldwide scientific, medical, and technological developments, natural phenomena, U.S. weather, and natural disasters.	Includes the arts, religion, scholarship, communications media, sports, entertainment, fashions, fads, and social life.

	World Affairs	Europe	Africa & The Middle East	The Americas	Asia & The Pacific
Feb. 23	The idea of a non-Italian Pope wins more favor. The Archbishop of Quebec is the leading non-Italian contender. . . . Arab-Jewish talks may be held in London. Delegates from Egypt and Iraq may attend. . . . The Cardinals' cells for the conclave are near completion. They vary significantly in comfort and appearance. . . . France will resist any threats of force and notes solidarity with the United States. . . . Japan will train 30,000 brides for Japanese men living in Brazil. Grooms will select their bride by photo. . . . An unnamed vessel sends a mystery SOS, announcing an attack by a submarine torpedo.	Prime Minister Neville Chamberlain hints that idle youth will get work building camps for air raid refugees. . . . The Czech foreign minister stresses the importance of amity with Germany. . . . The British parliament considers a flogging amendment for bombers. . . . France fears a new war crisis as Italy mounts troops and Germany increases munitions.	The French study the danger in Tunisia. A clash between French and Italian troops is reported there, but officials deny reports.	A Pan-American highway opens in El Salvador and Guatemala. Both are proud of the modern advancement that taps into primitive areas.	As political assassinations continue, Japan threatens action in Shanghai's International Settlement if the Chinese do not curb terrorism. . . . . . . The former Indian president, Pandit Nehru, quits Congress.
Feb. 24	Arabs still urge an independent Palestine. Discussions with Jews in London fail to find basis for compromise. . . . Japan agrees to compensate Britain for the bomb dropped on Kowloon and to punish the officer involved. . . . The hunt for a torpedoed ship ends in mystery. . . . An Italian's arrest stirs Cardinals. The man is allegedly held for advocating a non-Italian Pope.	Franco asks for aid for feeding the hungry in Madrid. . . . Moscow launches a battleship, though foreign observers doubt the report. . . . The Reich demands that Jews cede valuables.			The Japanese premier agrees that religions contrary to the "Way of the Gods" should not exist, and Christian shrines are neglected.
Feb. 25	Cardinals seek a curb on the new pontiff, and want more independence. . . . The Cardinal from Boston is still under consideration for Pope. . . . The conclave cells closest to the chapel are set for the oldest and most infirm Cardinals. . . . The Japanese press says the decision by the U.S. House of Representatives not to fortify Guam will aid relations between the two countries, but China is disappointed.	The body of the Bishop of Teruel is found among victims of the retreating Spanish Loyalist forces. . . . The French vote on recognition of Franco is stormy, but passes, 323–261. . . . Hungary smashes a Nazi unit, dissolves the National Socialist organization, and arrests many leaders. Hungary also signs an anti-Communist pact. . . . The Reich raises income taxes for bachelors and spinsters. Penalties are also assessed for childless couples.			An estimated 350,000 flee the Chinese capital of Chungking.
Feb. 26	Japan bases its plans on war with the Soviet Union.	Czechs exempt Germans from the army. . . . An exodus of Italians from France begins by order from Rome. The motives include need for manpower in Italy. . . . Polish students smash windows of the German Embassy in protest of Adolf Hitler. . . . One hundred Jews must leave Germany daily.			Twenty gunmen interrupt the Chinese New Year celebration and assassinate the foreign minister of the Reformed Nanking Government. . . . A four-month expedition leads to the discovery of Asia Minor forts from 714 B.C.E. The meeting place of the royal court of the Vannic Kingdom and fine pottery are dug up. . . . The Chinese government will use donkeys, horses, and mules to haul supplies and save fuel.
Feb. 27	London sees an Arab independent state in Palestine. . . . A fast decision in the papal selection is expected as Cardinals are busy with consultations. . . . Supporters of a U.S.-born nun, Mother Elizabeth Seton, seek sainthood for her. . . . Italy bans three Swiss reporters. Political motives are suspected.	Anti-German riots continue in Poland. . . . President Manuel Azana of the Spanish Republic quits his post and leaves France. This act frees the powers to act on recognition of Franco. . . . France and Britain officially recognize Franco's government.			The Japanese renew their claim on Shanghai and expect armed rule. . . . Prince Fumitaka Konoe flunks out of Princeton University and returns to Japan to assume the duties of dean at a Japanese college.
Feb. 28	Cardinals discuss their policy on Jews, one of the most important issues facing Italy. . . . A Nazi ship is said to film war simulations by U.S. ships.	Soviets claim significant growth in their navy. . . . The six-day old Belgian Cabinet already resigns over disagreements about financial measures. . . . Germany and Italy fear a British-French attempt to pull Spain away from the Berlin-Rome axis, and are suspicious of recognition given to the Franco government. . . . Nadejda Konstantinova Krupskaya, widow of Lenin, dies only hours after her 70th birthday. She worked for the communist cause her entire life. . . . President Manual Azana of Spain resigns.	Two bombs explode in a Jerusalem market and 28 Arabs die. . . . Jews reject the Palestine plan, and unanimously rule out the proposed Arab independent state.	Eight persons, most of them German, are arrested in Mexico for spying. One is the brother-in-law of Count von Helldorf, a friend of Adolf Hitler.	Bad weather forces the pioneer China-Burma flight to cancel. . . . Japanese policy continues to promote non-discrimination against Jews.

A	B	C	D	E
Includes developments that affect more than one world region, international organizations, and important meetings of world leaders.	*Includes all domestic and regional developments in Europe, including the Soviet Union.*	*Includes all domestic and regional developments in Africa and the Middle East.*	*Includes all domestic and regional developments in Latin America, the Caribbean, and Canada.*	*Includes all domestic and regional developments in Asian and Pacific nations (and colonies).*

U.S. Politics & Social Issues	U.S. Foreign Policy & Defense	Economics & Great Depression	Science, Technology & Nature	Culture, Leisure & Lifestyle	
James Hines, Tammany leader, does not testify on his own behalf on corruption allegations, and the trial stage ends. . . . The Daughters of the American Revolution refuse to rent Constitution Hall to "noted Negro contralto" Marian Anderson. The American Union for Democracy protests.	A Senate group lifts limits on airplanes. The Military Affairs Committee approves 6,000.		The grandson of Theodore Roosevelt, Quentin, plans an expedition to China to seek rare scrolls and manuscripts.	The Yale University president avows academic freedom for those on campus. . . . Glenn Cunningham wins his 21st consecutive indoor race. . . . Pitcher Bob Feller re-signs with the Cleveland Indians at last year's salary. . . . Searchers unearth an old Richard Wagner score. Some believe this song has never before been played. . . . The average fairgoer to the New York world fair spends $2.40, which compares favorably to the $1.17 spent at the Chicago fair.	Feb. 23
	President Franklin Roosevelt leads a war game survey. He will meet with naval chiefs to devise a plan.			Police watch Sally Rand's fair display. So far, she has not been arrested for scarcity of costume, as occurred in Chicago. . . . Bette Davis and Spencer Tracy win Academy Awards.	Feb. 24
Thomas Dewey urges the conviction of Tammany leader James Hines, saying it will remove a cancer from the heart of government. . . . The third Supreme Court Justice dies within two months. Alonzo McLaughlin succumbs to pneumonia.		The Secretary of Commerce says the new focus is no longer on reform but on private jobs.	Health Services estimates the lifespan of babies born in 1938 to be 62 years.	A revised version of Yes, My Darling Daughter passes censorship. . . . The Puritan is banned for "solicitation on the street, lewd dance halls, indecent acts of prostitutes." . . . Schools will teach arithmetic, algebra, and geometry as one subject as an experiment.	Feb. 25
Thomas Dewey successfully prosecutes James Hines. The court victory is thought to increase Dewey's chances of receiving the Republican nomination for president in 1940.	A House bill asks to add 43 air squadrons.		A double-barreled television "eye" makes cameras more sensitive. . . . Twenty-five percent of homes in urban southern states are without gas or electric heat. . . . Philco Radio and Television Corporation will offer televisions to the public in May. . . . The Pennsylvania College for Women has students formulate vanishing creams as a science project.	Speculation increases about Charlie Chaplin's The Great Dictator.	Feb. 26
A legislative committee reports widespread bias against Negroes. . . . Only one-third of U.S. voters intend to vote for President Franklin Roosevelt if he runs for a third term. About 31 percent expect him to attempt a third term. . . . The Supreme Court outlaws sit-down strikes.					Feb. 27
A man kills his bride after only three hours of marriage. The sentence is 20 years to life. . . . The Senate selects Joe Hanley as Majority Leader, who replaces Perley Pitcher who died last week. . . . Harold Ickes, secretary of the interior, calls for reorganization of the federal government; saying the current system is a peril to democracy. . . . Eleanor Roosevelt resigns from Daughters of the American Revolution after their decision not to rent Constitution Hall to the African American singer Marian Anderson.			Telephone use is up by 11.6 percent from 1932–37, according to a census.	Warner Bros. withdraws the film Devil's Island, featuring a French penal colony, after the French protest. . . . Yankee catcher Bill Dickey signs a contract for the 1939 season. . . . Humphrey Bogart and Bette Davis will appear in Old Maid.	Feb. 28

F	G	H	I	J
Includes elections, federal-state relations, civil rights and liberties, crime, the judiciary, education, healthcare, poverty, urban affairs, and population.	Includes formation and debate of U.S. foreign and defense policies, veterans affairs, and defense spending. (Relations with specific foreign countries are usually found under the region concerned.)	Includes business, labor, agriculture, taxation, transportation, consumer affairs, monetary and fiscal policy, natural resources, pollution, and accidents.	Includes worldwide scientific, medical, and technological developments, natural phenomena, U.S. weather, and natural disasters.	Includes the arts, religion, scholarship, communications media, sports, entertainment, fashions, fads, and social life.

	World Affairs	Europe	Africa & The Middle East	The Americas	Asia & The Pacific
Mar. 1	Cardinals are scheduled to meet in conclave today to begin selection of a new pope.	Experts see London finishing battleships much faster than its rivals. . . . The Reich takes charge of $100 million worth of Catholic Church property in Austria. Some monks and abbots stay, but many leave. . . . The Academy of Medicine urges France to store blood for war injury treatment.	A 24-hour curfew is set up in the Jewish section of Jerusalem. Disorder does not abate.		Japan creates new rules for foreigners visiting the country.
Mar. 2	British Prime Minister Neville Chamberlain will discuss a new offer with Jewish delegates. Political parity in Palestine is the focus. . . . The announcement of the Pope will be made in the traditional way, not through a broadcast at the Sistine Chapel. . . . The Vatican door shuts as the conclave officially begins.	Spanish newspapers call Manuel Azana cowardly for resigning the office of president. . . . Immigration aid is urged for the 500,000 Catholics who face exile from Germany. . . . British Prime Minister Neville Chamberlain attends his first-ever party at the Soviet Embassy. . . . Britain piles up civil defense aids, including sandbags and gas masks. . . . Diego Martinez Barrio assumes presidential duties in Spain. . . . Franco asks Italy to recall its army from Spain. . . . Vienna punishes Jews who did not leave the country, sending them to concentration camps.			Japan adds significant funds to its budget for warfare: 5.27 billion yen to cover warfare expenses against China and arming for a Soviet clash. . . . Japan's Empress gives birth to a daughter. . . . A shifting of forces in China indicates a shortage of Japanese troops. . . . A munitions blast near Osaka wipes out an entire village.
Mar. 3	Cardinals elect Eugenio Cardinal Pacelli to papacy. London sees this choice as favorable to peace. The new Pope selects the name Pius XII. . . . Cardinals support the new pope's decision to counter materialism. . . . Italy quits using radio as a propaganda tool in Latin America. . . . Japan pays Britain $20,000 in compensation of bombing its territory. . . . The Reich expresses reservations over the new pontiff. . . . British groups seek funding for victims of fighting in Palestine, especially children.	Josef Stalin places the ashes of Lenin's widow by her husband's tomb.			The Japanese Emperor will present his new daughter with a sword and skirt. He will name her in seven days. . . . Mohandas Gandhi decides to fast in protest of lack of democratic reforms in India. . . . Shanghai's International Settlement and French Concession will allow Japan to share policing duties, ending the disagreement.
Mar. 4	Franco agrees to hold a prisoner exchange between Spain and the United States. . . . The Italian press interprets the new pontiff's peace views as reproof of democratic pacifism. . . . The friendship of President Franklin Roosevelt and Pius XII gives rise to renewed diplomatic talks.	Britain appoints an envoy to the new Spanish government. . . . Germany expels 500 Jews. Their destination is believed to be Palestine. . . . The Reich agrees to continue with the Jewish emigration program. . . . The Reich plans a drive against alcohol and tobacco, and encourages others to emulate the good habits of Hitler. . . . Colonel Segismundo Casado begins a week-long anti-Communist coup in Madrid, and tries unsuccessfully to negotiate with Gen. Franco.			The Japanese attack Chinese strongholds.
Mar. 5	Gandhi's fast causes political problems for Britain. London is asked to intervene to help resolve the India conflict. . . . An American expert on Japan states that financial collapse is not imminent for Japan.	Germany now pays firms in vouchers, rather than in cash. . . . Hitler's book *Mein Kampf* nets millions in sales.			Japan occupies Lungkow and two other cities in Shantung province.
Mar. 6		Belgium plans an election, as Cabinet formation is at an impasse. . . . Germany drafts Jews for work, but separates them from Aryan workers. . . . The Romanian premier, who led both the country and the Romanian Greek Orthodox Church, dies in France of pneumonia.			Gandhi weakens as his fast continues in Rajkot, India.
Mar. 7	German Cardinals confer with the Pope, and hope to effect an understanding of the church's role in the Reich.	So far 1,842 cases of art that were sent to France for protection during the civil war have been returned to Spain in good condition.		Chilean ex-Nazis support the president of Chile.	Japan plans a navy equal to the strongest modern fleet. Japan is not a Totalitarian state, nor opposed to Britain, France, or the United States, Foreign Minister Hachiro Arita says.

A	B	C	D	E
Includes developments that affect more than one world region, international organizations, and important meetings of world leaders.	*Includes all domestic and regional developments in Europe, including the Soviet Union.*	*Includes all domestic and regional developments in Africa and the Middle East.*	*Includes all domestic and regional developments in Latin America, the Caribbean, and Canada.*	*Includes all domestic and regional developments in Asian and Pacific nations (and colonies).*

U.S. Politics & Social Issues	U.S. Foreign Policy & Defense	Economics & Great Depression	Science, Technology & Nature	Culture, Leisure & Lifestyle	
The Attorney General urges taxation of federal employees. . . . A censorship issue causes an FCC clash. The FCC commissioner insists on preservation of free speech, but is overruled. . . . A refugee expert says Jewish refugees will not displace U.S. workers. . . . Thomas Dewey avoids political factions and declines offers to boost him as the 1940 presidential candidate. . . . The Senate advances an "anti-Red" bill that would ban public jobs for Communists.	The Navy Department signs a contract for $24 million in armor materials for battleships. . . . The Secretary of the Navy says the Army needs protection from work of subversive agents.		Explorer Lincoln Ellsworth plans to spend the winter of 1941 in an Antarctic camp.	Spencer Tracy gives his Academy Award to Father Flanagan, whom he portrays in an award-winning movie, *Boys Town*.	**Mar. 1**
	The Army reorganizes the entire air corps, and anticipates an increase of 5,000–6,000 new fighter planes. . . . The Army plans to increase intelligence in Latin American countries. . . . The Army asks plane manufacturers to move operations away from the coast, and to protect themselves by an interior location.	The president of the General Electric Company urges Congress to balance the budget to restore confidence.		The Chaplin film, *The Great Dictator*, sees delays after the leading lady Paulette Goddard accepts a role with Bob Hope on another movie. . . . A John Wayne movie, *Stagecoach*, directed by John Ford, is released. The film will make Wayne a major star.	**Mar. 2**
	The Navy plans a gun salute to welcome President Franklin Roosevelt back to the United States.		Howard Carter, the Egyptologist who discovered King Tut's tomb, dies.	Actor Bert Lahr asks for an annulment. He says his wife has been insane for the past five years.	**Mar. 3**
Congress celebrates the 150th anniversary of the first Congressional meeting. . . . First Lady Eleanor Roosevelt christens the *Yankee Clipper*, the flagship of transatlantic passenger planes.		President Franklin Roosevelt opens labor peace talks at the White House with representatives of the AFL and CIO.		Joe DiMaggio accepts a salary of $26,500 from the New York Yankees. . . . Conductor Bruno Walter arrives in the United States. He refuses to conduct in Germany under Hitler's rule.	**Mar. 4**
Census takers start the task for 1940. The enumeration of 132 million Americans is the most comprehensive ever. . . . College researchers unearth a letter written by Thomas Jefferson. The letter emphasizes Jefferson's religious liberalism.			General Electric patents an x-ray of one million volts.	Studebaker debuts a car for lower-income families. . . . Dodger pitcher Van Lingle Mungo disappears after talks with baseball commissioner Kenesaw Mountain Landis.	**Mar. 5**
	Senators debate a war referendum.		A returning explorer tells of a jungle utopia—a village in India that knows no anger.		**Mar. 6**
A war objector confesses to tossing a bomb into the audience at the Chicago Grand Opera Company in 1917, and says he is glad no one was hurt. . . . *American Hebrew Magazine* awards President Franklin Roosevelt a medal for promoting religious tolerance. . . . The Homer Martin faction of the UAW bans Communists, Nazis, and fascists.	The Senate votes by almost 2–1 to increase Army Air Corps planes by 6,000. The House had only approved 5,500.		A doctor shares information with the Southeastern Surgical Congress that common boils cause paralysis and, if near the spine, even death.	The Father of the Dionne quintuplets does not understand why the British King and Queen ask the children to travel 180 miles to Toronto, rather than travelling to the United States to see them in their nursery. . . . Clark Gable's wife Rhea obtains a divorce on grounds of desertion. He has announced that he will marry actress Carole Lombard.	**Mar. 7**

F	G	H	I	J
Includes elections, federal-state relations, civil rights and liberties, crime, the judiciary, education, healthcare, poverty, urban affairs, and population.	Includes formation and debate of U.S. foreign and defense policies, veterans affairs, and defense spending. (Relations with specific foreign countries are usually found under the region concerned.)	Includes business, labor, agriculture, taxation, transportation, consumer affairs, monetary and fiscal policy, natural resources, pollution, and accidents.	Includes worldwide scientific, medical, and technological developments, natural phenomena, U.S. weather, and natural disasters.	Includes the arts, religion, scholarship, communications media, sports, entertainment, fashions, fads, and social life.

	World Affairs	Europe	Africa & The Middle East	The Americas	Asia & The Pacific
Mar. 8	The U.S. German Consul states that Hitler's "heir" is already chosen, but no announcement is forthcoming. . . . Pius XII will review pleas that he head a world religious order during crisis. . . . The Vatican bans all reporters after the press reports on a meeting between the Pope and German Cardinals.	Nationalist radio insists that Franco will conquer Madrid as he conquered Barcelona, and no amnesty will be given. . . . The Bible still outsells *Mein Kampf* in Germany. . . . The Czech police patrol the Ukraine area after a change in Carpatho-Ukraine government. . . . Romania will honor the body of the patriarch, Miron Cristea.			China admits the loss of Han River City. . . . Gandhi ends his fast, sipping orange juice after reform concessions are made.
Mar. 9	Britain suspends talks with Arab and Jewish delegates, and intends to draw up and impose its own plan on Palestine. . . . Britain provides the Chinese government with a £5 million credit to bolster China's monetary system. . . . France is pleased with Britain's plan to contribute troops. . . . Pope Pius XII confers with the Reich envoy.	Britain will put 300,000 men in France in case of war. . . . Franco picks the Duke of Alba as the British envoy. . . . A Spanish Communist leader known as "La Pasionaria" refuses to discuss how she escaped from Spain and arrived in France. . . . Madrid smashes Communist forces within the city. . . . Franco blocks all Republican ports, and orders warships to sink all entering craft, regardless of how they are registered.	Iraq seizes 50 officers on charges of conspiracy to overthrow the government.		Tokyo plans military self-sufficiency in three years. . . . Japanese raiders strike at Ichang. Heavy Chinese losses are feared. . . . The infant Japanese Princess is named Takako Suganomiya after an 8th-century poem. She will be called Princess Suga.
Mar. 10	The United States protests the bombing of Ichang. American missions are attacked in spite of the flag waving overhead. . . . Italy reassures Britain that it has no intention to increase troops in Libya. . . . The Vatican rushes coronation plans for Pope Pius XII. A light miter is needed as the pope suffers from severe neuralgia. . . . The Reich attacks the idea of a Pan-American coalition, instead proposing Spanish-U.S. control of South American countries.	Britain warns Italy that ships will resist attempts to sink them at blockades around Spain. . . . France makes 200,000 gas masks available to Paris residents. Those who fail to apply for them will face a fine. . . . Paris asks the Spanish Communist leader La Pasionaria to leave the area. . . . A Communist revolt in Madrid led by Col. Casado ends with surrender by the communists. . . . Soviet Communists are to meet in Moscow for the first party Congress since 1934. Stalin is expected to speak. . . . Franco blocks all Republican ports, and orders warships to sink all entering craft, regardless of how they are registered. . . . Nazis deny a threat to the Dutch and Swiss.			Japanese planes drop fifty bombs on Weinan, a city near Sian, China.
Mar. 11	The British Home Minister Sir Samuel Hoare suggests that Britain, France, and the three dictators meet for talks to preserve peace. He also wants the blessing of the United States. . . . Huge crowds pray at the tomb of Pius XI. . . . The Reich claims to map 135,000 square miles of Antarctic territory. . . . An American ship runs the Franco blockade with no ill consequence.	All non-Italian Jews must leave Italy. . . . Franco's navy frees the British ship that broke the blockade. . . . The Czechoslovakia government ousts the Slovak premier, Joseph Tiso, placing him under house arrest, along with other prominent ministers and members of the Hlinka Guards. Germany will provide aid to the new government. . . . The Madrid battle flares anew.			Japan's Parliament says the war in China cannot end while Britain supports China.
Mar. 12		The commemoration of the 20th anniversary of the American Legion will include an unveiling of a tablet in Paris.			Japanese advance their offensive in Hupeh and report 3,500 Chinese dead in two weeks of fighting.
Mar. 13	A fascist editor claims that Italy is arming African natives. The editor is considered Mussolini's mouthpiece. . . . A vast throng watches Pius XII receive the papal crown.	The Foreign Policy Association suggests that the Reich is economically weak in key areas, including trade balance issues. . . . Bombs explode in the Czech capital of Bratislava after a demonstration. The bombs may have been set to give German troops an excuse to "restore order."			Crime soars in Shanghai.
Mar. 14	The British draft a plan for Palestinian rule. The proposal will be presented to the cabinet tomorrow. . . . Pope Pius XII blesses Irish groups in anticipation of St. Patrick's Day events.	Madrid is calm again as the fighting between Loyalist factions ends. . . . Czechoslovakia, Bohemia, and Moravia are absorbed into the Reich. . . . Czech statesmen agree to a loss of freedom in a three-hour meeting. Autonomy is promised. . . . Hungarians drive across Ruthenia (Carpatho-Ukraine), aiming for the common border with Poland. . . . Romanian troops occupy about 20 villages in Carpatho-Ukraine.		Costa Rica preserves the only true democracy in Central America, a touring correspondent says.	Japan moves toward monopoly in China, as foreign traders are barred from the interior.
Mar. 15	Britain proposes a five-year delay in the formation of a Palestinian state.	Chancellor Adolf Hitler arrives in Prague after inspecting his troops. Citizens were told of their country's takeover by the Reich in a radio broadcast. . . . A raid in Valencia, Spain, kills 12 civilians. There is no military target near where the bombs fell. . . . Prime Minister Chamberlain cancels trade talks between Britain and Germany. . . . The Reich invades Czechoslovakian provinces without opposition.		Argentina finalizes barter deals with Germany and Italy, trading wheat for trucks and equipment.	War brings riches to Chinese banks. . . . India lacks unity for independence from Britain. The congress is unable to speak for Muslims, Sikhs, and other minorities.
	A *Includes developments that affect more than one world region, international organizations, and important meetings of world leaders.*	**B** *Includes all domestic and regional developments in Europe, including the Soviet Union.*	**C** *Includes all domestic and regional developments in Africa and the Middle East.*	**D** *Includes all domestic and regional developments in Latin America, the Caribbean, and Canada.*	**E** *Includes all domestic and regional developments in Asian and Pacific nations (and colonies).*

U.S. Politics & Social Issues	U.S. Foreign Policy & Defense	Economics & Great Depression	Science, Technology & Nature	Culture, Leisure & Lifestyle	
The Women's Prison Association urges psychiatric help for the wayward, saying that many women and girls can be made useful. . . . Ousted UAW president Homer Martin starts an independent union.	Admiral William Leahy, Chief of Naval Operations states that the U.S. fleet is now superior to any in the world. . . . President Franklin Roosevelt openly states opposition to the current neutrality laws.	Officials weigh a food-scrip plan that would give the needy a paper that is redeemable for food in stores. . . . The American Federation of Actors bans all WPA jokes. . . . Congressmen walk through picket lines as hotel and restaurant workers go on strike in the nation's capital.		Actress Marlene Dietrich is set to become an American citizen.	Mar. 8
		The AFL agrees to discuss forming a Congress of American Labor with the CIO.	The daughter of Mme. Curie arrives to lecture on her mother's radium discovery and the role of women in science. . . . A doctor tells of a new surgery that cuts pre-frontal nerves and cures insanity.	Trainer Tom Smith says the racehorse Seabiscuit will not race until 1940. . . . Author Pearl Buck chastises women with education and talent who do not exercise their talents, calling them "wasteful" and comparing them unfavorably to women in China.	Mar. 9
Al Capone aids the United States in the tax evasion case against John Torrio. . . . Martin Dies, chairman of the Special House Committee to Investigate Un-American Activities, proposes an anti-Communist and anti-fascist bill. . . . New York Mayor Fiorello La Guardia warns new policewomen recruits not to gain weight, and gives the same advice to men.		President Franklin Roosevelt sifts through ideas for tax cuts, and supports less spending, if possible. . . . AFL and CIO talks fail to reach an agreement.		Early radio star Ernest Hare dies. His claims to fame include being part of the first on-air comedian team and the first to sing into a tomato soup can as a microphone at an experimental radio station. . . . The Shirley Temple film The Little Princess opens in New York theaters. . . . The oldest living Shaker observes her 104th birthday. Her eyesight is so keen that she still sews.	Mar. 10
The papal coronation ceremony will play on radio all night. . . . A high school principal explains traits that employers expect from girls today, including slimness, a sweet voice, and the ability to "speak pure American." . . . James Hines offers to resign his Tammany post after his conspiracy conviction, but the resolution is tabled after members protest against his resignation.	The Roosevelt administration wishes to allow Latin American countries use of U.S. shipbuilding plants when they are not in use.	Accountants determine the worth of the Pepsi-Cola Company to be $7.9 million. . . . Union musicians, engineers, and firemen threaten to join the four-day old strike in Washington, D.C.		Earl Averill refuses the contract offered to him by the Cleveland Indians.	Mar. 11
The papal rites are heard on the radio by U.S. listeners.	An opinion poll shows U.S. citizens willing to provide food and military supplies to France and Britain, but 83 percent draw the line at sending troops.		Scientists note that excessive cigarette smoking causes nausea.		Mar. 12
Senator Key Pittman of Nevada introduces a bill that would allow the President to sell naval vessels and arms to any American republic.		New York Supreme Court judge Salvatore Cotillo rules that "closed shops" can exist only when a union has a majority of employees. The ruling stems from an eight-month long strike at Busch Jewelry Co.	Prof. Albert Einstein plans a quiet day for his 60th birthday. He should become a U.S. citizen in another year.		Mar. 13
		President Franklin Roosevelt asks congress for relief funding of $150 million to last through June.	Prof. Albert Einstein believes he is close to uncovering the master key to the universe.		Mar. 14
A New York Supreme Court justice upholds the Board of Education's right to ban teachers from holding a second job. . . . Child star Jackie Coogan wins a $150,000 settlement against his mother and stepfather. . . . The end of the Czech state stirs emotion in Washington, D.C. The United States helped form the nation after World War I.		The National Association of Master Plumbers announces that 95 percent of all bathrooms are in the United States.		The former boxing champion Abe Attell remarries.	Mar. 15

F	G	H	I	J
Includes elections, federal-state relations, civil rights and liberties, crime, the judiciary, education, healthcare, poverty, urban affairs, and population.	Includes formation and debate of U.S. foreign and defense policies, veterans affairs, and defense spending. (Relations with specific foreign countries are usually found under the region concerned.)	Includes business, labor, agriculture, taxation, transportation, consumer affairs, monetary and fiscal policy, natural resources, pollution, and accidents.	Includes worldwide scientific, medical, and technological developments, natural phenomena, U.S. weather, and natural disasters.	Includes the arts, religion, scholarship, communications media, sports, entertainment, fashions, fads, and social life.

	World Affairs	Europe	Africa & The Middle East	The Americas	Asia & The Pacific
Mar. 16	Arab and Jewish delegates both refuse Britain's new proposal for Palestine.	Two portions of the former Czech country will retain the names Bohemia and Moravia. . . . Britain seeks the release of Czechoslovakian men and women considered foes of the Nazi party. . . . The British Minister of Coordination of Defense says that the British aim is power sufficient to deter any aggressor. . . . British officials are bitter over Germany's broken promises. . . . Britain's Ambassador Sir Neville Henderson is recalled from his post in Berlin. . . . Hitler's flag flies over Prague's historic citadel. Czechs weep and hurl snowballs at tanks. . . . Hungarian troops march through Carpatho-Ukraine and some reach the Polish border. . . . The Soviet army has doubled over the past five years, now reaching 3 million.	The Egyptian Princess Fawzia weds Iranian heir, Crown Prince Riza Pahlevi, uniting two leading Muslim sects. The newlyweds are both teenagers.		A Chinese offensive is set to begin in April. One-third of the army will be sent behind Japanese lines for guerilla warfare.
Mar. 17	The Czech envoy Vladimir Hurban in the United States refuses to leave unless he receives a letter from the Czech president. . . . Japan sends troops to the Soviet border. . . . Jews unite to bar the British plan for Palestine, saying the proposal is not even a basis for discussion.	Anxiety reigns in eastern Europe after Germany overtakes Czech lands. . . . Three different flags fly over the Carpatho-Ukraine in one day. . . . Hungarian troops storm into and subdue the Carpatho-Ukraine capital city of Huszt. . . . Over 100 appointments are announced in Madrid as Communists are ousted from government. . . . About 450 Sudeten refugees arrive safely in Poland, after leaving Prague three days ago. . . . Russians are cold to world events and believe Germany will turn on Romania next, not Ukraine. . . . Slovakia is now a Hitler "protectorate." London and Paris may recall envoys.			The Chinese claim victory, repulsing the Japanese army by the Han River. . . . The American Baptist Hospital in Chengchow is hit twice by bombs dropped by Japanese planes. Chengchow suffers 400 casualties.
Mar. 18	Dr. Eduard Benes, the former Czech president, sends a protest to the United States, France, Britain, and Russia, asking them to combat crime, saying the Czech people are powerless. . . . Some U.S. Congress members agree to condemn Hitler; others wish to remain out of war concerns. . . . The United States suspends mail going to Czechoslovakia. Letters are held in transit and subject to recall. . . . Discussions on Palestine end in discord. Britain plans to impose a proposal.	The Reich wants Romania to serve as a farm country supplied by German industry. The Bucharest army is kept in readiness. . . . Hitler keeps Italian Premier Benito Mussolini informed of Reich moves by telephone and courier. The fascist press tells the public that Italy's concerns will not be neglected. . . . Prime Minister Neville Chamberlain denounces Hitler. He vows that peace-loving nations will meet threats with solidarity. . . . French Premier Daladier asks for dictatorial powers to move quickly to defend France against the Reich. . . . Former Czech officials bid the country to cooperate with the Reich. Waves of suicides are seen in the takeover. . . . Hitler demands trade control of Romania. . . . Poland worries about the increased influence of Hitler, and expects the Nazis to vote to return the Lithuania area to Germany. . . . Russians are happy as the head of the secret police is removed. They also expect Germany to ask for Soviet business. . . . Germany remains defiant of foreign critics, asserting a sweet revenge for the Czech leader's anti-German stance. . . . Switzerland plans to fight to maintain its independence, the federal councilor says. Hitler pilgrimages are banned.		Chile doubts the danger of an epidemic as nearly 300,000 earthquake victims have been inoculated against typhoid and other diseases since the January 24 earthquake.	
Mar. 19	The British proposal for Palestine suggests an immigration limit for Jews of 75,000 over a five-year period and gradual control to Arabs. Delegates do not approve but Britain will most likely impose this plan. . . . A U.S. legislator plans to ask the House to close the German Embassy and cut all ties with the country. . . . Chiang Kai-shek asks the United States to institute an arms ban on Japan. . . . The former Indian missionary Henry Lunn is dead. The peace champion is remembered for his League of Nations tour to promote worldwide accord. . . . New annexations place 600,000 more Catholics under Reich control.	Britain airs the lightweight boxing championship on television. This is the first public airing of a television program in the country. . . . The Russian army guards Ukraine. Stalin denies any fear of Germany. . . . A fascist newspaper in Italy compares Prime Minister Neville Chamberlain to Winston Churchill, the British statesman whom Italy considers a great foe. . . . Germany denies an economic ultimatum was given to Romania to abandon industry.			

A	B	C	D	E
Includes developments that affect more than one world region, international organizations, and important meetings of world leaders.	Includes all domestic and regional developments in Europe, including the Soviet Union.	Includes all domestic and regional developments in Africa and the Middle East.	Includes all domestic and regional developments in Latin America, the Caribbean, and Canada.	Includes all domestic and regional developments in Asian and Pacific nations (and colonies).

U.S. Politics & Social Issues	U.S. Foreign Policy & Defense	Economics & Great Depression	Science, Technology & Nature	Culture, Leisure & Lifestyle	
	Washington leaders hesitate to make a final decision about the Neutrality Act with so much flux in Europe. . . . President Roosevelt plans to strengthen defense after the chaos in Europe, saying the world has "temporarily gone mad."			Fastball pitcher Walter Johnson signs up to broadcast baseball games by radio. . . . The major who loaned his horse to Gen. George Custer shortly before the Battle of Little Big Horn dies at age 91.	Mar. 16
A representative accuses President Franklin Roosevelt of using "urgency" as a way of keeping power. He lists 39 emergencies discussed by Roosevelt in his speeches.			Physicians try a new test to detect cancer. Initial results are encouraging, they say.		Mar. 17
Sixty thousand Irish march on Green Fifth Avenue, braving biting winds. . . . President Franklin Roosevelt wears a green suit, shamrock, and green carnation on St. Patrick's Day.			Near Alder, Wash., ten men die in a test flight of Boeing Aircraft's Stratoliner, a 33-passenger plane.	Midwives still reportedly deliver 10 percent of babies, according to the U.S. Census Bureau.	Mar. 18
President Franklin Roosevelt declares April as Cancer Control Month and asks states to do likewise. . . . A Congressional group flies to Ciudad Trujillo to witness the opening of Christopher Columbus's tomb. Photographs will be permitted. . . . A survey shows that 67 percent of Americans approve of First Lady Eleanor Roosevelt's decision to resign from the DAR after the group disallows African-American Marian Anderson from singing in Constitution Hall.	Army planes will test a new radio eye device that winks 750 million times per second and aids in blind flying. . . . The Army is ready to order new lighter bomber planes. . . . The Army speeds its drive to build a larger air force. Recruiters visit colleges to distribute flyers. . . . Congressional authorization puts the U.S. first in battleships, destroyers, and submarines.	The Dept. of Agriculture fieldtests a program of using Food Scrip, or stamps, to distribute surplus food to those on relief. The program could increase food purchases by $250 million a year.	The first National Wildlife Week is under way. Proponents seek to curb depletion of the habitat.	Alfred Hitchcock considers a film version of Daphne du Maurier's novel, *Rebecca*.	Mar. 19

F	G	H	I	J
Includes elections, federal-state relations, civil rights and liberties, crime, the judiciary, education, healthcare, poverty, urban affairs, and population.	Includes formation and debate of U.S. foreign and defense policies, veterans affairs, and defense spending. (Relations with specific foreign countries are usually found under the region concerned.)	Includes business, labor, agriculture, taxation, transportation, consumer affairs, monetary and fiscal policy, natural resources, pollution, and accidents.	Includes worldwide scientific, medical, and technological developments, natural phenomena, U.S. weather, and natural disasters.	Includes the arts, religion, scholarship, communications media, sports, entertainment, fashions, fads, and social life.

	World Affairs	Europe	Africa & The Middle East	The Americas	Asia & The Pacific
Mar. 20	The former Czechoslovakian leader compares the Nazi roust to being guillotined. He warns the United States it has major role to play in world events. . . . Turks express shock that Czechs did not fight to keep their homeland and express concern over the Reich.	Romania signs a commercial agreement with Germany but says no ultimatum was issued by the Reich. . . . Britain suggests a bloc to resist the Reich. Soviets respond cautiously. . . . The French senate strongly upholds Premier Edouard Daladier, granting him emergency authority. . . . The Reich parades through silent Prague; Czechs maintain grim self-control. . . . The German press calls Hitler the "Aggrandizer of the Reich," a title given to medieval rulers who expanded empires.		U.S. and Dominican officials stress Pan-American solidarity and lay a wreath on the tomb of Christopher Columbus.	
Mar. 21	Canada pledges support to Britain. . . . Joseph Goebbels criticizes democracies, saying words such as humanitarianism and international rights should be forgotten. . . . Britain rushes to bolster the defense of Hong Kong, sending 15,000 troops to diminish weakness against a Japanese attack. . . . The U.S. Secretary of Commerce believes the Reich is too impoverished for an extended war.	The British Princesses Elizabeth and Margaret are to make their first speeches—in French. . . . Franco praises Hitler's reincorporation of territory, but Italian Premier Benito Mussolini remains silent. . . . Britain and France push for a "Four Powers" declaration against further aggression in Europe. Poland and Russia consider the proposal. . . . The Reich gets oil rights in Romania. . . . Police deny the wave of suicides in Prague.		Chile rushes to aid the homeless, and buildings are being erected as part of the earthquake relief effort.	
Mar. 22	Albert Einstein asks for aid for the persecuted, and urges help to avoid a return to barbarism.	The Fascist Grand Council stresses Italian support of Adolf Hitler. . . . Effective April 1, Germany will ration edible fats in the former Austria. Farmers there are urged to breed silkworms. . . . The last president of Czechoslovakia officially dissolves the Czech parliament. . . . Lithuania yields the Memel Corridor to Germany. . . . Valencia awaits peace, but gets more bombs. . . . Gandhi exhorts the world to disarm.			Millions in China are homeless.
Mar. 23	Four hounded Jews, after persecution in Italy, Germany, and Austria, deliberately end their lives by jumping into the sea. . . . Rumors circulate that the Reich aims to build military bases in Iceland. . . . Moscow sees Britain as yielding to a six-nation parley to deal with worldwide threats.	Nazis hail the return of the Memel Corridor. . . . Frenchman Hubert Lagardelle, a friend of Italian Premier Benito Mussolini visits Paris in hope of changing French policy toward Italy. . . . Hitler sails for Memel as Lithuania signs a surrender treaty. . . . Non-interventionist control around Spanish borders collapses, and troops are sent home.		The International Congress of American Democracies sets up anti-fascist fronts and creates national units for the cause.	Japan and China deem a final accord far away, though both are weary of fighting.
Mar. 24		After entering Memel in triumph, Hitler delivers a speech. The printed speech includes an implied threat, saying that German suffering must end. . . . The German penal code will apply to Czechs. . . . Hitler drives slowly through frenzied crowds at Memel, taking over the city in triumph. . . . A Hungarian earthquake starts a war scare along the borders. . . . Hungarians invade Slovenia. . . . The Italian King gives a speech that suggests a possible accord with France. . . . Slovaks resist a Hungarian takeover.			
Mar. 25	Japan envisions free reign in the East. The United States and Britain will be too engrossed with Hitler, they believe.	Hungarian fliers raid the interior of Slovenia. . . . Anglo-Soviet trade talks begin. . . . Autonomy talks on Romania are held. Autonomy for Hungarian and German minorities in Romania is the subject of discussion. . . . Germany expresses joy over the Romanian pact. It gains control over industry, agriculture, and natural resources. . . . Romania is not enthusiastic over the German trade accord. . . . Italian Crown Prince Humbert agrees to see the French envoy. A sense of relief is noted after the discussion.			
Mar. 26		Prague officials hurry to adopt anti-Jewish laws similar to the Reich's. . . . While Madrid is quiet, the Spanish insurgents opened a new round of fighting near Cordoba. Surrender negotiations break down. Gen. Franco accuses the Loyalist leaders of delaying tactics.			The Japanese extend control to the northern Chinese territory. They must eradicate guerillas before exploiting the country's natural resources.

A	B	C	D	E
Includes developments that affect more than one world region, international organizations, and important meetings of world leaders.	*Includes all domestic and regional developments in Europe, including the Soviet Union.*	*Includes all domestic and regional developments in Africa and the Middle East.*	*Includes all domestic and regional developments in Latin America, the Caribbean, and Canada.*	*Includes all domestic and regional developments in Asian and Pacific nations (and colonies).*

U.S. Politics & Social Issues	U.S. Foreign Policy & Defense	Economics & Great Depression	Science, Technology & Nature	Culture, Leisure & Lifestyle	
The Neutrality Act debate nears in Congress as some urge easing the law. . . . The National Urban League notes a spiritual awakening to the plight of Negro citizens, even in southern states.	A professor of fundamental theology of the Catholic University fears the fusion of Hitler and Stalin based upon their hatred of God.		Professor Pierre Montet of Strasbourg University reveals the discovery of a gold sarcophagus in an Egyptian tomb near ancient Tanis. A silver sarcophagus is found inside the gold, the first known appearance of silver in Egypt.		Mar. 20
Elliot Roosevelt, son of the President, sees Vice President John Garner as the leading candidate for the presidency. . . . Five hundred members of the CIO union bolt to the AFL. . . . A frail 61-year-old widow protects her $1 grocery money from a robber using a broomstick.			The gold and silver sarcophagus found yesterday contains the body of King Sheshonq. It is one of the richest finds ever.	James Stewart will star in *Mr. Smith Goes to Washington*. . . . The author whose book inspires the movie *The Birth of a Nation* remarries; 75-year-old Thomas Dixon marries a literary assistant.	Mar. 21
Thomas Dewey's popularity as a presidential candidate increases sharply after James Hines's corruption conviction. . . . The Senate curbs President Roosevelt's reorganization plan by one vote. Reconsideration is sought.			The Franklin Institute gives a prestigious award to Dr. Edwin Powell Hubble for the study of nebulae outside the galaxy. . . . Medical students at Israel Zion Hospital in Brooklyn watch an operation performed in another building via television.		Mar. 22
The CIO chairman swears that the organization will not dissolve as it makes peace with the AFL. . . . Congress adopts a big defense bill. No opposition is heard. . . . A DAR official insists that she did not receive the resignation of Eleanor Roosevelt.			Albert Einstein baffles an airport public relations officer with complicated math formulas as a joke.	Top dancer Bill Robinson opens in the Broadway show *The Hot Mikado*, an African American version of the operetta *The Mikado*.	Mar. 23
Former Confederates who knew Thomas Stonewall Jackson disapprove of a proposed monument to him at Manassas Battlefield as inaccurate. . . . Tammany leader James Hines receives a sentence of four to eight years for conspiracy. He begins discussing an appeal process with lawyers while in Tombs Prison.		Marriner Eccles, Federal Reserve System Chairman, an advocate of President Roosevelt's spending policies, challenges Congress to slash the budget as a test. The public seems economy minded, he says, and this should be a guide.		Joe DiMaggio delivers two home runs. . . . Finland progresses with Olympic planning. . . . Basil Rathbone appears as Sherlock Holmes in *The Hound of the Baskervilles*, premiered in New York City.	Mar. 24
	Some Senators urge caution over proposed changes to the Neutrality Act. . . . Only 10 of 50 Senators proposing a war levy bill have read the material. Four of them are authors of the bill.	A House Representative sees the lack of jobs, rather than foreign affairs, as the focus of the 1940 presidential campaign.		John Barrymore returns to the stage after a 15-year absence, playing the role of a thrice-married actor in *My Dear Children*.	Mar. 25
The Phi Alpha fraternity prohibits the paddling of freshman initiates.			Liver cancer is less likely in those with a high yeast diet, research suggests. . . . Curing foot ailments may help lower blood pressure, experts say.	Sincere admirers of swing music organize an Anti-Jitterbug Club. . . . A man obtains a divorce at age 94, and dances the night away at a pension meeting.	Mar. 26

F	G	H	I	J
Includes elections, federal-state relations, civil rights and liberties, crime, the judiciary, education, healthcare, poverty, urban affairs, and population.	*Includes formation and debate of U.S. foreign and defense policies, veterans affairs, and defense spending. (Relations with specific foreign countries are usually found under the region concerned.)*	*Includes business, labor, agriculture, taxation, transportation, consumer affairs, monetary and fiscal policy, natural resources, pollution, and accidents.*	*Includes worldwide scientific, medical, and technological developments, natural phenomena, U.S. weather, and natural disasters.*	*Includes the arts, religion, scholarship, communications media, sports, entertainment, fashions, fads, and social life.*

	World Affairs	Europe	Africa & The Middle East	The Americas	Asia & The Pacific
Mar. 27		German troops gather near the Swiss line and are believed to be moving toward assisting Italy. . . . Premier Benito Mussolini sounds mild in a Moscow speech celebrating the 20th anniversary of his party. . . . The Polish rebuff German attempts to negotiate control of the city of Danzig. . . . Romania scorns a trade pact with Germany as equal to surrender and says the country will fight to the limit to protect its independence.		The African mosquito ravages Brazil with 10 percent of the population killed in some areas. A U.S. invasion by the insects is feared.	The Japanese smash their way to Nanchang in the Kiangsi province. The battle line is 100 miles long, but fighting now centers around city gates.
Mar. 28	Danish royalty tour the Panama Canal area. They will also visit the World Fair exhibits in the United States. . . . Gen. Franco's Interior Minister and brother-in-law, Ramon Serrano Suner, announces the fall of Madrid and warns the world's democracies to "keep their hands off Spain."	The former president of Czechoslovakia sees a revolt if the country is provided with aid. He urges U.S. leadership in the endeavor. . . . Clashes continue on the Slovak border. Hungary puts strong pressure on Slovak negotiators to settle all matters before Nazi minister Joseph Goebbels arrives for a visit. . . . Madrid moves civilians as Franco nears. Nationalists report the capital's defenses are crumbling. . . . Portugal realigns itself with Britain. Mistrust of Italy and Germany are the key factors. . . . Rome now favors a deal with Mediterranean territories that favor Italy. . . . The fall of Madrid marks the end of the Spanish Civil War, which lasted 32 months.	British troops shoot an Arab rebel chief in Jerusalem as he attempts to break through a cordon. . . . A Syrian revolt may be developing but no demonstrations greet the new Cabinet.		Japanese invaders find the city of Nanchang empty. Chinese dynamite bridges and set fire to buildings.
Mar. 29	A Franco aid says that the general will not attempt to regain Spanish colonies in the Americas. . . . Spain's Minister of the Interior warns the world's democracies to keep their hands off his country. . . . The Japanese Institute is set up in New York. Its goal is to dispel U.S. misconceptions about the country. . . . The wealthy Maharajah of India marries a U.S. woman who nursed him. He tells subjects his marriage gives him the peace of mind needed to rule.	The British Admiralty asks for a ban on sailor flogging if the punishment is banned for criminals. . . . Bombs damage the historic Thames River bridge, believed to be a retaliation for the sentencing of nine involved in other Irish Republican Army bombings. . . . Spanish war casualties are estimated to total five percent of the population. . . . Prime Minister Neville Chamberlain bars military conscription, not wishing to upset the harmony with labor. . . . Franco's tactics with Madrid earn praise by the French, though coolness still exists in the relationship between the two countries.	The Kut Barrage, a new irrigation dam in Iraq waters the spot known as the traditional site of the "Garden of Eden." The dam opened yesterday in a ceremony presided over by King Ghazi.		
Mar. 30	The Vatican hails Franco, and feels his country will return to the ancient faith of its fathers.	Britain will double its army, though still no conscription is planned. . . . Italians view Premier Edouard Daladier's assertion that France will not cede territory as a bar to future discussions. . . . Slovaks ask the Reich to curb Hungary, and are willing to cede a 650-mile area if a similar amount of land is given back.			The Japanese Premier Hiranuma clarifies that his country is neither democratic nor totalitarian and therefore will not confront either bloc.
Mar. 31	U.S. Cardinals return from the Vatican, happy with the choice of Pope. . . . The United States predicts that Spain will use Franco's victory as a wedge to spread fascism to Latin America.	The Franco regime arrests 100,000 and decrees the death penalty for sedition, sniping, looting, or sabotaging services. . . . Belgians speed fort construction in response to Nazi agitation. . . . The British Cabinet acts to stop the Reich, announcing that Britain and France will fight for Poland, if attacked. . . . Nazi Minister of the Interior Dr. Wilhelm Frick hints that the Polish government abuses minorities. The Reich is displeased with the status of Germans there. . . . Hungarians reject the newest Slovak offer, refusing to accede territory as an exchange. . . . Mussolini insists that Italy cannot remain "suffocated" in the Mediterranean. . . . Spain regains possession of Spanish art held by the League of Nations.		Canada bans the draft for overseas service.	China admits the Nanchang loss but reports other victories. Japanese-sponsored regimes are to disregard the rights of powers sympathetic to China.
Apr. 1	Japan annexes seven French islands; they can be used as air and ship bases. . . . The United States notes the Japanese menace in the Pacific. . . . A Nazi plot to seize Patagonia, Argentina, is aired. Germans charge the plot is based on a forged document, but Argentina begins an investigation.	General Franco announces the end of the civil war. . . . A British newspaper raises Nazi ire by reporting that German troops near Poland. . . . A hushed House of Commons hears Britain's pledge to fight if Germany attacks Poland. Soviet aid is held certain. . . . Slovakia gives up 800 square miles; Hungary concedes two villages.			The Chinese attack the Shanghai area and approach Hangchow.

A	B	C	D	E
Includes developments that affect more than one world region, international organizations, and important meetings of world leaders.	Includes all domestic and regional developments in Europe, including the Soviet Union.	Includes all domestic and regional developments in Africa and the Middle East.	Includes all domestic and regional developments in Latin America, the Caribbean, and Canada.	Includes all domestic and regional developments in Asian and Pacific nations (and colonies).

U.S. Politics & Social Issues	U.S. Foreign Policy & Defense	Economics & Great Depression	Science, Technology & Nature	Culture, Leisure & Lifestyle	
A strike of projection room operators in New York could tie up movie distribution nationwide. The strike begins today.				The American Professional Football League plans to expand to 8 or 10 teams from the current 6.	Mar. 27
Congressmen from urban and rural states battle over funding for agriculture and relief.			A pathologist tells of new ways to grow bone marrow that is helpful in treating blood cancers.	Will H. Hays, the president of the Motion Picture Producers and Distributors of America notes a trend away from boy-meets-girl films to those promoting Americanism. . . . The American Art Association will sell a Raphael painting, *Madonna of the Pinks*. . . . Fair officials provide blind children with Braille information about the events. . . . A man who buys a 65-cent oyster dinner finds 11 pearls. . . . American Adventurer and author Richard Halliburton disappears in a Pacific typhoon.	Mar. 28
New York Mayor Fiorello La Guardia asks for the abolishment of a lunacy board. He recommends that questions of sanity be turned over to city hospitals.	President Franklin Roosevelt speeds the acquisition process for two 45,000-ton battleships. Japan's situation is cited as one reason for these vessels.			A University of Pennsylvania student wins a goldfish derby by eating 25 of them whole. He douses them in ketchup and drinks them down with orange juice—and then eats a steak dinner. . . . A judge refuses to award Joan Crawford a divorce from Franchot Tone by mail, and insists on a court date.	Mar. 29
A husband and wife are to serve on the same jury. The "permissive woman juror law" created this possibility.				Actors protest a raise in hotel rates during the New York World Fair. Many are evicted. . . . Film stars Clark Gable and Carole Lombard wed. . . . The Animal Rescue League plans drastic action if fish swallowing contests continue.	Mar. 30
Penologists urge better education in U.S. prisons, asking for inmates to be classified by educational needs. . . . President Franklin Roosevelt receives news of his 9th grandchild, a boy.	The Non-Sectarian Committee for German Refugee Children plans the placement of 20,000 youth. Quakers in Germany will determine who will come to the United States. . . . A Washington official predicts a strong debate over the Neutrality Act. British Prime Minister Neville Chamberlain's speech about Poland is expected to impact the debate.		The World Fair displays new plastic used in auto windshields.	The World Fair displays noted French art. Paintings, sculptures, and tapestry are loaned to the United States by museums. . . . The U.S. Olympic Committee believes Detroit stands a good chance for 1944.	Mar. 31
Charles Kimble, said to be the oldest living Union soldier, dies at age 101.		The Treasury reports that the debt will surpass the previous record, as the total amount nears $40 billion. . . . Secretary of Commerce Harry Hopkins presents President Roosevelt with a plan to aid small business.		A pathologist and other specialists warn that fish gulpers may suffer from anemia. Boston College promises "drastic punishment" for those who continue with the activity. . . . A rare Edgar Allen Poe book is found. The first printing of *The Murders in the Rue Morgue* surfaces.	Apr. 1

F	G	H	I	J
Includes elections, federal-state relations, civil rights and liberties, crime, the judiciary, education, healthcare, poverty, urban affairs, and population.	*Includes formation and debate of U.S. foreign and defense policies, veterans affairs, and defense spending. (Relations with specific foreign countries are usually found under the region concerned.)*	*Includes business, labor, agriculture, taxation, transportation, consumer affairs, monetary and fiscal policy, natural resources, pollution, and accidents.*	*Includes worldwide scientific, medical, and technological developments, natural phenomena, U.S. weather, and natural disasters.*	*Includes the arts, religion, scholarship, communications media, sports, entertainment, fashions, fads, and social life.*

	World Affairs	Europe	Africa & The Middle East	The Americas	Asia & The Pacific
Apr. 2	The Argentinean government arrests a Nazi chief amid speculation of a plot to seize Patagonia. Authorities are not convinced by the German Embassy's claim that the document detailing the seizure was forged. . . . The Japanese seizure of the Spratly Islands forestalls the French, who planned to claim the islands. . . . The Nazis envision control of the world's resources. . . . Pilgrims journey to Rome. The celebration begins with Mass and will end with Easter blessing.	The Duke of Alba, Spain's Ambassador to London visits with Franco about the political situation. The envoy recently met with Italian Premier Benito Mussolini. . . . Britain maps food control during war. . . . Racial problems in Yugoslavia take a sharper turn since the German drive in Czechoslovakia. . . . Franco's war foes receive the bill for Spain's reconstruction. Prisoners will be put to labor. . . . Hitler dares Britain to start a fight; Chamberlain asks Mussolini to mediate. . . . The Reich offers unquestioning support to Hitler. Those who disapprove hold their tongues.	Egypt pushes the defense of the Nile River. The recognition of its strategic value prompts the decision.	The Brazilian army will begin copying the discipline of the German army.	Chinese troops attack Japanese positions west of Hankow. A battle for the city of Kaoan continues, with Chinese accusations of poison gas use by Japan. . . . Sian is shelled.
Apr. 3	Japan and the Soviet Union sign a fishing pact. . . . Japan broadcasts a goodwill message at the U.S. World Fair and says relations between the two countries are growing closer.	Romania expects an arms pledge by Britain today. . . . Italy warns Poland that ties to Britain are dangerous. . . . Madrid Catholics flock to churches to hear Palm Sunday Mass for the first time since 1936. . . . Yugoslavian and Croat leaders meet for formal negotiations; concessions are likely. . . . Moderates sweep the Belgian elections as pro-Nazis are beaten. . . . France is defiant in the face of war threats. . . . The food shortage eases in Madrid. Nationalists bring in eggs and milk. . . . The Soviets would back collective peace; editorials are increasingly contemptuous toward Britain and France. . . . The former Polish premier Col. Walery Slawek attempts suicide.			Four Chinese forces gain near Hankow.
Apr. 4	Britain offers to assist any land threatened by the Reich.	Poland will meet with Britain. Poland is opposed to a group pact that would include the Soviets. . . . Col. Walery Slawek, former Polish premier, dies after shooting himself. He served as the spiritual father of the Polish constitution. . . . Bulletproof glass surrounds Hitler during his speech. The Reich says the glass is to protect his notes from blowing away and to keep Hitler from catching cold. . . . French President Albert Lebrun consents to seek reelection. . . . War guilt trials start in Spain. In Valencia, 21 are executed. . . . Italy appears ready to take control of Albania; troops are massed at the port. . . . Negotiators agree on new Slovenian-Hungarian borders. Slovenia cedes 386 square miles.	King Ghazi of Iraq dies in a suspicious auto accident. His heir is the three-year-old Emir, Feisal.		
Apr. 5	The U.S. Ambassador to Spain says the bombing of civilian areas to lower resistance failed during the civil war, and hardened resolve instead. . . . France increases its defenses in the Sanjak area of Syria after Turkey announces its desire to annex the 10,000-square mile district. . . . The Vatican studies air raid safety measures. An ancient tower will serve as refuge for the Pope and art. . . . Argentine police raid a Nazi office. The informer admits he sought vengeance against the Gestapo for the death of his wife.	Rival powers seek control over Albania; Italy boasts an advantage over Yugoslavia. . . . Danzig Nazis riot over talks between London and Poland. . . . Nazis close the Protestant Confessional Church seminary after outspoken ministers offend the Reich. . . . Hungary signs a pact on the Slovak border. . . . Poles agree to a British alliance; Albania is threatened. . . . An Albanian prince is born to King Zog and a part-American Queen.	Three-year-old Feisal becomes King Feisal II of Iraq. The British Consul, George Monck-Mason, is slain in Mosul after rumors circulate that the British killed King Ghazi.	An anti-fascist riot occurs in Mexico.	The Japanese seize Kongmoon for the third time this week. There are thousands of Chinese casualties. . . . Chinese papers report that former Premier Wang Ching-wei plotted with Japan to form an anti-Chaing Kaishek government in China.
Apr. 6	Chances for peace are considered slim unless Germany stops its aggression.	The Albanian army takes precautions to maintain independence. . . . Hitler conscripts all German youth, withdrawing adhesion on a voluntary basis. . . . France reelects Albert Lebrun as president over protests from the left. . . . Britain's Princess Elizabeth, 12, appears at her first official diplomatic fête. . . . Albanians believe that Italy aims for occupation of Greece and Turkey. . . . Hitler and Mussolini confer. They intend to combat any military encirclement of the Reich.	The Egyptian chief the of royal cabinet resigns, giving no reason. An anti-British agenda is pushed. . . . The King of Iraq is buried today among throngs of people. The death is ruled accidental.		Anti-guerilla measures by Japanese troops in China are said to include the burning of villages and the killing of males between the ages of 12 and 40 years old.
Apr. 7	Protestants beg for the Pope's aid in stopping Franco's un-Christian actions toward war foes.	Italy announces that the army and navy forces are already heading to Albania. . . . Britain makes a preliminary move toward offering Hungary military protection. . . . Germans belittle the Anglo-Polish pact.			Japan intensifies bombing using the captured Nanchang air field as a base. . . . Joseph Lyons, the Australian prime minister, dies of a heart attack.
	A *Includes developments that affect more than one world region, international organizations, and important meetings of world leaders.*	**B** *Includes all domestic and regional developments in Europe, including the Soviet Union.*	**C** *Includes all domestic and regional developments in Africa and the Middle East.*	**D** *Includes all domestic and regional developments in Latin America, the Caribbean, and Canada.*	**E** *Includes all domestic and regional developments in Asian and Pacific nations (and colonies).*

U.S. Politics & Social Issues	U.S. Foreign Policy & Defense	Economics & Great Depression	Science, Technology & Nature	Culture, Leisure & Lifestyle	
The Federal Trade Commission criticizes anti-trust laws, saying poor wording plus narrow court construction hampers enforcement. . . . Masked men kill a convicted slayer who was given a life sentence instead of the death penalty. . . . A mysterious ban on Hitler's speech causes 400 radio stations to become silent.	The military plans air war games along the New England-New York coast that will include 16 Navy vessels, 100 planes, and Coast Guard ships. . . . The nation's chemists meet tomorrow and will focus on new developments in defense.	The Committee on State and Local Taxation of the U.S. Chamber of Commerce urges states to focus on decreased taxation rather than increased expenditures. Federal, state, and local taxes peak at $14.5 billion in 1938.	A patent owner claims that by adding water to gasoline in a special way power increases by 25–60 percent.	Warner Bros. completes the movie, *Confessions of a Nazi Spy*. . . . Joe DiMaggio's five hits fuel the Yankee's 15–2 win. . . . A survey shows that 60 percent of fathers help with household chores.	Apr. 2
The AFL accuses the CIO of circulating false propaganda about the union. . . . The American Civil Liberties Union defends Nazi propaganda, saying it cannot bar one type of free speech and not another. . . . New York Mayor Fiorello LaGuardia maps out a plan to study lunacy, asserting that a comprehensive understanding is needed.			At the American Chemical Society meeting, Cornell biologist Vincent de Vigneaud describes a new form of synthetic amino acid.		Apr. 3
Addison Johnson, a former warden of Sing Sing, dies. No prisoner escaped during his tenure.		The New Deal maps aid to small businesses, including plans to provide easier financing and better access to research.	Cornell medical men find a new chemical to reveal life's secrets. A new form of amino acid promises the key to bodily processes.	A championship goldfish gulper receives a suspension from college for disrupting the educational process.	Apr. 4
A New York Police lieutenant pleads not guilty to charges of theft of police records. . . . A judge releases James Hines on a bail of $35,000 pending his appeal. . . . An ashamed Jack Benny pays a $10,000 fine for smuggling jewelry into the country for his wife. Two hundred fans listen to the judge scold Benny. . . . The Senate confirms William Douglas as Supreme Court Justice, 62–4.	The Army forms a plan for a military air expansion.	The CIO-approved AFL convention elects Roland Thomas as the new president. Three Communist-backed candidates fail to secure a spot on the executive board. . . . Chicago reelects Mayor Edward Kelly even though the Republican vote is the largest ever for the city.	An atom microscope gains wider use by scientists. . . . The American Physical Society opposes a ban on cooperating with Reich scientists.	The Metropolitan Opera offers a rendition of *Carmen*.	Apr. 5
The United States observes the 22nd anniversary of its entry into World War I. . . . Communist-backed candidates win 13 of 19 executive spots on the CIO-sanctioned UAW board. No claims are made that these men are actually members of the Communist Party.	The U.S. Embassy in Japan delivers its fifth written protest in two weeks, over aerial bombings of American property in China.	A member of Congress charges that the New Deal is one-way ticket that favors northern states. . . . President Roosevelt asks states to end tariffs, which he says are more destructive to the economy than international ones.	Dr. W.F. Petersen, a professor of pathology notes that more males are conceived in cold weather. . . . A new drug checks the growth of tuberculosis bacilli in test tubes.	France bans Warner Bros. films for two months as a rebuke for the anti-France *Devil's Island*. . . . Stanley Cup play begins. The Boston Bruins are the favorites over the Toronto Maple Leafs.	Apr. 6
	The Army reprieves nine elderly Army mules slated for execution.	A battle in the Senate bars quick action on new WPA funding.	Blindness in babies has been reduced by 75 percent over the past 30 years. . . . An automatic phone device gives weather information to all who call.		Apr. 7

F	G	H	I	J
Includes elections, federal-state relations, civil rights and liberties, crime, the judiciary, education, healthcare, poverty, urban affairs, and population.	Includes formation and debate of U.S. foreign and defense policies, veterans affairs, and defense spending. (Relations with specific foreign countries are usually found under the region concerned.)	Includes business, labor, agriculture, taxation, transportation, consumer affairs, monetary and fiscal policy, natural resources, pollution, and accidents.	Includes worldwide scientific, medical, and technological developments, natural phenomena, U.S. weather, and natural disasters.	Includes the arts, religion, scholarship, communications media, sports, entertainment, fashions, fads, and social life.

	World Affairs	Europe	Africa & The Middle East	The Americas	Asia & The Pacific
Apr. 8		Alarm grows in the Balkan states after Italy invades Albania. The conquest of Albania would provide Italy with oil for war needs. . . . Albania lacks enough men for a modern war. Albanians strongly resist attack, and women join the defense forces. . . . Albania's Queen flees with her two-day-old baby to Greece while King Zog remains and offers terms to Italy. . . . Albania protests the attack to the United States and awaits word from President Roosevelt. . . . The Reich hails the Italian action in Albania as strengthening the Axis powers. . . . Russia believes that an attack on Yugoslavia is next.			Chinese troops gain ground near Canton. . . . Australia names Sir Earle Page as the new prime minister, but the news travels slowly as they publish no paper on Good Friday.
Apr. 9		Franco plans to say good-bye to German and Italian troops as they leave Spain in mid-May. . . . Albanian King Zog flees.			
Apr. 10	Pope Pius XII pleads for peace in his Easter message.	Italy holds a firm grip on Albania. . . . Amid rumors that Italy intends to take over the island of Corfu, Britain warns Italy to stop aggression. . . . Germany expects no further dissention over Albania. . . . Italians replace the white flag with the flag of Albania as a peace gesture in the seized country. . . . The Balkan awaits the lead of democracies. A pact is being developed between Britain and Greece, observers believe.			Chinese forces attack and disable three main railways linking Peiping with Paotow, Pachow, and Nanking.
Apr. 11	Albania's royal family may settle in Egypt. Greece does not seem willing to receive them. . . . Argentina reveals Nazi spying. Party members there are subservient to Berlin's orders. . . . Egypt fears Italy's power, worried it is on the list for fascist aggression.	The Albanian Queen Geraldine is said to suffer two hemorrhages during her escape over rocky roads. . . . Italy threatens to impose martial law if Albanians protest the occupation. . . . Italy boasts a military force of 950,000. . . . The Netherlands puts troops on the border. A flank attack on Belgium by the Reich is feared. . . . The British fleet sails after the decision is made to protect Greece. The Greek isle of Corfu has great strategic value as a naval base.			
Apr. 12	Arab states are to receive proposals on Palestine from London. . . . Hungary and Peru notify the League of Nations that they will resign their seats when the term expires.	Albanians will vote on new rule today. The assembly is likely to vote for autonomy with strong ties to Italy. . . . Germany renews verbal attacks on Britain. . . . The British woo Italy by a delay on the Soviet deal. . . . Bulgaria officially dissolves the Fascist Party. . . . The French fleet departs; its goal is not revealed. . . . Italian Premier Benito Mussolini warns a big army is ready, with more than 1 million men. . . . Poland summons army reservists. . . . Yugoslavia seeks a neutral course, wanting to stay out of war. . . . Britain and Greece reach an agreement, believed to be that Britain can use Greek ports in exchange for protection.			Quentin Roosevelt, son of the President, asks permission to visit Tibet. He is presently in Chungking, China. . . . The Japanese report victories in Shansi.
Apr. 13	Nazi Propaganda Minister Joseph Goebbel's newspaper accuses President Roosevelt of war mongering and demands an answer to the charge. . . . An estimated 100,000 French-African Muslims protest the Albanian seizure by Italy. . . . The Reich will defend the Antarctic region.	Greece clings to its neutral stand and does not acknowledge a deal with the British. . . . The Albanian Constituent Assembly offers the crown to Italian monarchs, retaining autonomy except in defense. . . . The British royal family practices air raid drills. . . . The Reich bids Poland to publish the German demands that led to the Polish-Anglo accord, saying the German demands are not unreasonable. . . . A Reich town will financially reward unmarried mothers who announce their intent ahead of time. The goal is to increase the birth rate. . . . Romania charges a Hungarian menace and troops gather at the border. . . . Turkey plans to join the Anglo-French alliance; Greece is still aloof.			The Chinese continue a widespread push and admit the loss of Kaoan. . . . Nine Japanese planes shell the treaty port of Mengtsz, forty miles north of Indo-China.

A	**B**	**C**	**D**	**E**
Includes developments that affect more than one world region, international organizations, and important meetings of world leaders.	Includes all domestic and regional developments in Europe, including the Soviet Union.	Includes all domestic and regional developments in Africa and the Middle East.	Includes all domestic and regional developments in Latin America, the Caribbean, and Canada.	Includes all domestic and regional developments in Asian and Pacific nations (and colonies).

U.S. Politics & Social Issues	U.S. Foreign Policy & Defense	Economics & Great Depression	Science, Technology & Nature	Culture, Leisure & Lifestyle	
Eight thousand crowd in St. Patrick's Cathedral for a Good Friday Three-Hour Agony Service. . . . Debate on the Neutrality Act issue splits the House by party lines.		A group of cotton state and Midwest senators ask $1.3 billion in subsidies and farm aid for next year.	Physicians explain how the front of the brain rules future thoughts, and the back governs thoughts of the past.		Apr. 8
		Illegal aliens add to work problems, the Commissioner of Immigration and Naturalization, Rudolph Reimer, says.		Ninety percent of female college students consider marriage their "greatest ambition."	Apr. 9
Six more states require blood tests before marriage as a measure to combat the spread of venereal disease.			A Yale scientist says humans have been growing larger over the past few generations. Increasing pelvic size is a clue.	The *Spalding Baseball Guide* will italicize rule changes in this year's rules. . . . *Wuthering Heights* is scheduled to appear in theaters.	Apr. 10
President Roosevelt returns from a 10-day vacation to find legislators agitated over the imminence of war in Europe.	A World War I draft dodger agrees to return to the United States to accept punishment. . . . The Foreign Relations Committee of the Senate may ask President Roosevelt for a Japanese embargo and/or other retaliatory measures.			The Citizen Committee on Planned Parenthood urges distribution of birth control information. Abortion rings menace women, Margaret Sanger says. . . . Stan Laurel and Oliver Hardy begin work on a new film.	Apr. 11
A poll shows that 65 percent of U.S. citizens favor a boycott of Germany.	The movement for repeal of the Neutrality Act shows surprising strength at a House Committee meeting.			The fifth conference on marriage says a good family life is a curb against all 'isms.' . . . A judge grants a divorce to Joan Crawford. The actress explains away dinners with her estranged husband by saying they will stay friendly. . . . An Ohio woman wins the American Mother of 1939 award. Her four children hold 31 college and university degrees.	Apr. 12
John Torrio, one-time partner of Al Capone, receives a 2.5-year penitentiary sentence for tax fraud.				*Wuthering Heights*, starring Merle Oberon and Lawrence Olivier, is released. The film will win multiple Oscars, including one for Olivier and for Director William Wyler.	Apr. 13

F	G	H	I	J
Includes elections, federal-state relations, civil rights and liberties, crime, the judiciary, education, healthcare, poverty, urban affairs, and population.	Includes formation and debate of U.S. foreign and defense policies, veterans affairs, and defense spending. (Relations with specific foreign countries are usually found under the region concerned.)	Includes business, labor, agriculture, taxation, transportation, consumer affairs, monetary and fiscal policy, natural resources, pollution, and accidents.	Includes worldwide scientific, medical, and technological developments, natural phenomena, U.S. weather, and natural disasters.	Includes the arts, religion, scholarship, communications media, sports, entertainment, fashions, fads, and social life.

	World Affairs	Europe	Africa & The Middle East	The Americas	Asia & The Pacific
Apr. 14	Japanese bombers raid a "treaty port" along the French-owned railway. . . . Pope Pius XII is not disturbed as air raid tests occur.	Belgians dig trenches and find bodies from World War I. . . . An Italian crowd hails Premier Benito Mussolini after the council praises the offer of Zog's crown. . . . Romania and Greece are wary of French and British pledges, fearing the anger of fascists. . . . The Slovakian Cabinet plans a celebration for Hitler's birthday, April 20. . . . French Premier Edouard Daladier affirms joint aid to Romania and Greece with Britain. Polish bonds are reiterated and Russian and Turkish negotiations are under way. . . . Germany sees Spain as a valuable ally, and advises the country to choose its friends wisely. . . . Germany charges Britain with making a move toward war. Britain is maneuvering smaller countries into forming a circle around Germany, the Reich says. . . . Gibraltar works on its defenses as troops mass nearby.	Arif Abdul Razik, Arab rebel leader, surrenders to French Military authorities in Syria. He was fleeing British troops and will now be exiled.		Chinese guerillas flood coal mines near Tatung, now in the hands of the Japanese.
Apr. 15	Nazis assail President Roosevelt's speech as a "Holy Crusade" against the Reich. . . . Pope Pius XII calls women to social service.	Albania resigns from the League of Nations with a curt telegram notice. . . . Premier Benito Mussolini greets the German Air Minister in Italy. They will seek ways to offset stronger defenses against the Axis. . . . The Reich navy moves near Gibraltar, recalling the old crisis that led to World War I. . . . Poland and Romania pledge to unite in armed resistance to German aggression.	The British seize a cache of arms from Arab rebels.	Latin America marks Pan-American Day.	The Chinese assault three railways.
Apr. 16	The Balkans rejoice over a U.S. peace bid. The individual naming of nations by President Roosevelt impresses them. . . . Because of large European orders of U.S. planes, China cannot buy any. . . . Hitler faces a severe world test; his dictatorial rule meets growing resistance. . . . A small-town U.S. newspaper invites British royalty to visit and eat ham and eggs, fried chicken, and enjoy fresh air.	Albanian resources are useful for Italy. Minerals are seen as the tool toward self-sufficiency in Italy. . . . Gibraltar's boom defenses swing into place. Rumors say Italian and Spanish troops are nearby. . . . Nearing 50, Hitler worries about his ailments: coughing spells, sleeplessness, and his need for glasses. He has six doctors. . . . The Italian King gets the crown of Albania. . . . Britain sends 35 bombers to Greece.	Iran hails the Crown Prince Reza Pahlavi and his new bride.		Maori tribes prepare to celebrate 100 years in New Zealand.
Apr. 17	The Japanese minimize Roosevelt's peace appeal, calling it a "mere circular diplomatic telegram." . . . King Tut's trumpets echo across the world. The soldier playing the trumpets from his tomb is broadcast on radio to the United States and Britain. . . . Pope Pius XII hopes that Spain applies justice to crimes, but offers kindness to those led astray.	Germany expects Hitler to continue expansion by economic tactics, even if he is balked politically. . . . Foreigners living in France may serve in the military, a new decree states. . . . Four French warships arrive at Gibraltar while British speed defenses. Rumors of Spanish troop masses cause feverish activity.			
Apr. 18	Washington determines Italy to be a weak war partner for Germany. The Reich would shoulder the bulk of economic needs and fighting supplies.	The Polish and Romanian foreign ministers, Josef Beck and Grigore Gafencu, discuss the Soviet Union's role as a protector. . . . The Reich church must relinquish taxes, forfeit public rights status, and allow the cathedrals to be used for neo-pagan ceremonies. . . . Germany appoints Franz von Papen as Ambassador to Turkey. He is expected to counteract Britain's attempts to bring Turkey into the alliance with France.			Japan claims part of the China Sea. The strategic area is 300 miles long and touches holdings of France, Britain, and the United States.
Apr. 19	The Italian press makes personal and venomous jibes at U.S. President Franklin Roosevelt.	A 15th-century Albanian relic, the Skanderberg helmet, is missing from a museum. The Italians intended to give it to the new King. . . . Britain pledges help to the Dutch, Swiss, and Danes if they are attacked. . . . Britain names regional commissioners who will have great power during war. . . . Hitler is seen as inciting the Portuguese to revolt and join with Spain, demonstrating that the Reich cannot be encircled. . . . Lithuania transfers a railway to the Reich, yielding 85 miles. . . . Posters tell Parisians how to evacuate the city.			

A	B	C	D	E
Includes developments that affect more than one world region, international organizations, and important meetings of world leaders.	Includes all domestic and regional developments in Europe, including the Soviet Union.	Includes all domestic and regional developments in Africa and the Middle East.	Includes all domestic and regional developments in Latin America, the Caribbean, and Canada.	Includes all domestic and regional developments in Asian and Pacific nations (and colonies).

U.S. Politics & Social Issues	U.S. Foreign Policy & Defense	Economics & Great Depression	Science, Technology & Nature	Culture, Leisure & Lifestyle	
The Dies Committee secretary says its office was broken into, and "snoopers" rifled through desks and committee files. . . . A man gulps a 5.5-inch trout to avoid a $21.47 penalty for keeping fish less than 6 inches long. . . . After a woman dies in a sanitarium, officials find $100,000 in cash and $400,000 in securities hidden on her and in her room. . . . U.S. Lutherans oppose U.S. ties to the Vatican, as the separation of church and state is seen to be violated.		The Great Depression causes delays in marriage, conference experts say. Topics discussed include secret marriages and accepting financial help from parents. . . . The economy group rushes a new relief bill to the Senate.		John Steinbeck publishes a "magnificent" new novel, *The Grapes of Wrath*. . . . Four female bridge players hold perfect hands; the odds are 1 in 158 billion, experts say. . . . Roosevelt agrees to toss out the first pitch at the Washington-Yankees opening baseball game.	Apr. 14
A "human fly" saves a man from a Bronx fire. He scales the side of a building and carries the lawyer to safety. . . . Police guard Col. Charles Lindbergh on his return home, who declines to discuss the specifics of his visit. . . . President Roosevelt extols George Washington and his decision to accept the presidency. Talk of a third term for Roosevelt is revived.	Some Senators charge that President Roosevelt's speech foments revolts and that the President is meddling abroad.			Of 90 baseball writers, 78 pick the Yankees to repeat their win; 10 pick Boston; 2 Cleveland.	Apr. 15
The First Lady agrees to be a foster mother of a 12-year-old boy orphaned by the Spanish civil war.	Roosevelt asks Hitler and Mussolini to pledge 10 years of peace. He promises trade in return. . . . The Army and Navy move to bases for war games. Offenses and defenses are not to be dramatized. . . . The Army wants a song to inspire aviators and offers a prize of $1,000. . . . The Atlantic fleet will remain in East Coast waters. . . . A sudden order for the fleet to leave the Atlantic is not explained.		Chemists at the University of Michigan, led by Dr. Werner Bachmann, announce the synthetic production of a naturally occurring sex hormone, equilenin, an early form of premarin.	The Boston Bruins hope to clinch the Stanley Cup tonight.	Apr. 16
A group may picket the Daughters of the American Revolution's 48th continental congress unless they begin renting their facilities to Negroes. . . . A peace plea takes center stage with Congress.				The Boston Bruins win the Stanley Cup, four games to one, for the first time in 10 years. . . . Marian Anderson wins an ovation at Carnegie Hall. . . . Nelson Eddy and the Philadelphia Orchestra perform at the Metropolitan Opera.	Apr. 17
William O. Douglas begins his Supreme Court duties, following his swearing in today. . . . A Hindu cult buys a residence in New York that will be altered to become its headquarters. . . . President Roosevelt heaps abuse on the current parole system, citing a need to better protect society.		Homer Martin, president of one branch of the UAW, will encourage followers to return to the AFL.			Apr. 18
New York votes to bar criminals from the World Fair. The law is aimed at pickpockets. . . . A DAR representative explains the ban on Negro performers, most recently Marian Anderson. She says that experiences in the past were "unpleasant" and the policy is in conformity with current custom.	The Army calls Charles Lindbergh to duty and assigns him to survey and report on air research facilities.	A new trial food stamp program for the needy is set to debut in Rochester, N.Y. Grocers will cooperate with the plan.	The audience at the New York Museum of Science and Industry hears the beating of a mechanical heart. The device will be on display at the World Fair.	Visitors to the New York World Fair will fly over the United States of 1960. The vision of the future shows no slums and orderly traffic patterns. . . . Fire destroys a Paris ship containing $500,000 of art for the U.S. World Fair. An Italian workman is held as a suspect.	Apr. 19

F	G	H	I	J
Includes elections, federal-state relations, civil rights and liberties, crime, the judiciary, education, healthcare, poverty, urban affairs, and population.	*Includes formation and debate of U.S. foreign and defense policies, veterans affairs, and defense spending. (Relations with specific foreign countries are usually found under the region concerned.)*	*Includes business, labor, agriculture, taxation, transportation, consumer affairs, monetary and fiscal policy, natural resources, pollution, and accidents.*	*Includes worldwide scientific, medical, and technological developments, natural phenomena, U.S. weather, and natural disasters.*	*Includes the arts, religion, scholarship, communications media, sports, entertainment, fashions, fads, and social life.*

	World Affairs	Europe	Africa & The Middle East	The Americas	Asia & The Pacific
Apr. 20		Paris suspects arson in a liner fire as simultaneous flames begin in different parts of the ship. One case of art is destroyed. . . . Britain denies an attempt to encircle Germany. . . . Hitler's birthday fête will set a high mark. It is said to dwarf the Kaiser's celebration of 30 years ago. . . . The former Czech president says Soviets kept faith and were prepared to help the Czechs. . . . Spain celebrates Unification Day.	Jewish agencies in Palestine ask for aid for 263 refugees from central Europe, who have been stuck on a cattleboat for months.	Chile suffers extensive earthquake damage. An observatory fears more seismic disturbances. . . . William Mellon returns to the United States after a scientific expedition. He reports of glaciers in South American jungles.	Chiang Kai-shek says peace is impossible if Japan continues its conquest.
Apr. 21	Pope Pius XII approves a crusade of prayer. He suggests that children spend May praying to Virgin Mary for peace.	Bulgaria pushes territory claims, declares neutrality, and says that no secret deals will be made. . . . German companies will build a Turkish sea base near Ismid. The project is awarded to German firms despite bids put in by Britain and the Netherlands. . . . Italian Premier Benito Mussolini derides U.S. President Franklin Roosevelt's peace plea. . . . Nazis celebrate Hitler's birthday with a parade that lasts four hours.		El Salvador Nazis celebrate Hitler's 50th birthday, holding a rally and flying the swastika. . . . Half of the buildings in an important mining city in Chile must be razed following the earthquake.	
Apr. 22	Two U.S. visitors to Germany say the German people are shocked by their government's treatment of minorities, and that they abhor Nazi terror.	The National Party urges Czech unity and seeks to build up resistance to German aggression. . . . The Queen of England presents her daughter, Princess Elizabeth, with silk stockings on her 13th birthday. . . . Rome celebrates its 2,692nd birthday. . . . Fleet moves indicate a secret British-Turkish pact. Soviets seek a triple accord.			
Apr. 23	Japan sees danger in being linked too closely with the world's dictators. . . . Egyptians are stirred by the recent visit of Nazi Propaganda Minister Joseph Goebbels. Rumors say he discussed war steps with Germans living there. . . . England's King and Queen plan a North American trip. It will take 10 days to pack the Queen's gowns.	Twenty aviators die in three separate French military crashes. Gen. Vuillemin, air minister, orders inquiries. . . . An estimated 100,000 Spanish children are housed in French refugee camps and await adoption. . . . The British attitude toward dictators hardens. Public indignation may force the government's hand. . . . France guards two railway lines after receiving tips that foreigners plan to cause wrecks. . . . The French build a base on the Algerian coast.	The Egyptian King Farouk and Queen Farida both suffer from chickenpox.		
Apr. 24	Chileans resent the attitude of the German farming community in their country. German parents refuse to send their children to Chilean schools. . . . A cardinal dies in Italy, leaving the College of Cardinals with 11 vacancies.	Britain unexpectedly sends Sir Nelson Henderson, its Ambassador, back to Germany. . . . When the British discover that blackout lamps, used for air-raid practice drills, are made in Germany, the drill is called off. . . . Paris expects the London Cabinet to press compulsory military service. France feels that Britain must increase its manpower. . . . The Reich defines how to teach religion, which must stress duty to the state. . . . The night watchman is held on arson charges in connection with the Paris liner fire. The death penalty is possible.	263 Jewish refugees are ordered to leave Palestine's harbor at Haifa on the Greek cattleboat they arrived on. Another 218 illegal immigrants are arrested in Jaffa.	German Canadians oppose aggression.	China lists gains in its vast offensive, saying Kaoan has been taken for the second time this month. . . . The Japanese deny defeats.
Apr. 25	Turkey holds out for a Soviet pledge. The United States says Turkey wants reassurance of Soviet aid before entering the alliance.	Italy focuses its attention on Romania. The Hungarian-Yugoslav pact may be shelved until Romania issues are resolved. . . . The British negotiate to win over Romanians. They will offer markets and credits in a deal for arms and oil. . . . The British Cabinet agrees unanimously on conscription. A truce deal by Hitler may be in the works. . . . Italy expels the second *Chicago Daily News* correspondent. The reporter was giving arbitrary and false news, Italy says.		The Bolivian President, Germán Busch, declares totalitarian rule. As a dictator, he will do away with congress and basic law.	China bans panda hunting to save the dwindling species.

A	B	C	D	E
Includes developments that affect more than one world region, international organizations, and important meetings of world leaders.	*Includes all domestic and regional developments in Europe, including the Soviet Union.*	*Includes all domestic and regional developments in Africa and the Middle East.*	*Includes all domestic and regional developments in Latin America, the Caribbean, and Canada.*	*Includes all domestic and regional developments in Asian and Pacific nations (and colonies).*

U.S. Politics & Social Issues	U.S. Foreign Policy & Defense	Economics & Great Depression	Science, Technology & Nature	Culture, Leisure & Lifestyle	
Marian Anderson's manager offers DAR a choice of 15 dates, asking them to reconsider banning the singer because of her race. . . . President Franklin Roosevelt addresses Young Democrats clubs, saying liberals are the only hope for the Democratic party and tells everyone else to get out.	In just 19 minutes, the Senate passes a Navy air base bill that approves $66.8 million for new or expanded facilities	A drive to ban Communists from WPA activities forms at the Capitol.	Clouds hide a solar eclipse. Professional and amateur astronomers are disappointed.	Universal Pictures negotiates for film rights to Theodore Dreiser's *Sister Carrie*. . . . Treasures worth $100 million arrive from 60 foreign countries for the World Fair held in New York. . . . The movie *Dark Victory* premieres; Bette Davis will earn an Oscar for her performance.	Apr. 20
A speaker at the convention of the American Society of Newspaper Editors says the American press is "most honest" and he urges them to "save heat for Hitler." . . . President Roosevelt seizes upon the war crisis to hide failures, Senator Taft says, and he should focus on ills at home.	Charles Lindbergh urges more plane research, and says Germany is the leader in Europe.				Apr. 21
A judge sentences 44 in a bootlegging plot, including four former federal agents and four suspended police officers. The judge says government workers who violate their oath deserve no mercy. . . . Senator William Borah says true neutrality is impossible for the United States.				Cleveland Indians pitcher Bob Feller strikes out 10 batters. . . . The World Fair displays one of four original copies of the Magna Carta. . . . Orchestra leader Herbie Kay seeks a divorce from actress Dorothy Lamour.	Apr. 22
First Lady Eleanor Roosevelt attends the funeral services of her nephew, who died in a plane crash.	The Army will enlist 370 cadets for air training every six weeks. Cadets must be unmarried U.S. citizens. . . . A poll shows that 73 percent of Americans agree with a peace conference attempt.	Congress weighs a plan for permanent relief.	Soviet scientists discuss preventative measures for grippe. A serum is said to offer immunity for one month. . . . Lake Mead in Las Vegas almost covers up an ancient Indian city. Archaeologists are recovering data.		Apr. 23
		President Franklin Roosevelt asks for $1.5 billion in relief funds for 1940. . . . Republicans offer 12 steps to business recovery, and call for strict neutrality and a ban on reckless spending.		The young actor Tyrone Power marries Anne Charpentier, an actress known as Annabella.	Apr. 24
Senator Bilbo of Mississippi asks for federal aid so that U.S. Negroes can form colonies by Liberia in Africa. . . . Pope Pius XII names a Boston bishop as a new Archbishop. . . . The American Red Cross chairman urges delegates to prepare for world crises.	The House approves a large Army bill. The Senate still needs to approve $508 million.	President Franklin Roosevelt will combine 12 relief groups into three agencies. The name of the WPA will disappear in the reorganization.	The National Academy of Sciences speaker Professor H.S. Burr shares the electrical component of life; he finds constant magnetic fields in organisms, which he says molds individual characteristics until death.		Apr. 25

F	G	H	I	J
Includes elections, federal-state relations, civil rights and liberties, crime, the judiciary, education, healthcare, poverty, urban affairs, and population.	*Includes formation and debate of U.S. foreign and defense policies, veterans affairs, and defense spending. (Relations with specific foreign countries are usually found under the region concerned.)*	*Includes business, labor, agriculture, taxation, transportation, consumer affairs, monetary and fiscal policy, natural resources, pollution, and accidents.*	*Includes worldwide scientific, medical, and technological developments, natural phenomena, U.S. weather, and natural disasters.*	*Includes the arts, religion, scholarship, communications media, sports, entertainment, fashions, fads, and social life.*

	World Affairs	Europe	Africa & The Middle East	The Americas	Asia & The Pacific
Apr. 26	In a speech to the American Red Cross, President Roosevelt warns those who would enslave and dominate others that the United States would provide firm defense. . . . Hitler's speech will air in the United States. A reply to U.S. President Franklin Roosevelt's speech is expected. . . . Japan still avoids war aid to Germany and opposes fighting Britain.	Berlin University rescinds a doctoral degree given to a well-known female Jewish suffragist. . . . The Belgian premier asks for special powers to be granted to the King in times of defense need. . . . Britain's conscription will call up millions. Hitler snubs Britain's ambassador. . . . The French curb the press in racial attacks. Anti-Semitism and defamation based on blood or religion is punishable by fine or prison. . . . Poles expect Hitler to be conciliatory and will not make more concessions. . . . The Reich releases Jews from concentration camps and orders them to leave the country. In two months, those remaining will go back to concentration camps.		The new Bolivian regime lists discipline as its goal. The dictator charges that the struggle of privilege and extremism cause chaos. . . . Venezuela proposes a Latin American League to protect economic interests. . . . The Bolivian regime is neither Fascist nor Nazi, a spokesperson says.	The Chinese are advancing to take Nanchang. . . . A Chinese coolie transport system moves goods at night, thwarting the Japanese.
Apr. 27	Norway's royalty will arrive in the United States today.	Croats and Yugoslavs reach a basic agreement. The details are to be released soon. . . . Britain negotiates for a four-country pact with France, Turkey, and Russia. . . . The Belgian chamber gives the premier special powers. The bill goes to the senate tomorrow. . . . Soviets welcome the British conscription act. . . . The German Protectorate of Bohemia-Moravia gets a government. General Alois Eliash is the new Premier, appointed by President Emil Hacha.			China's arms road faces flooding. The rainy season is expected to cause problems. . . . Australia's new prime minister appeals to the country to take full part in affairs of the area, stressing defense tasks.
Apr. 28	With an Anglo-Soviet pact at hand, Soviets say they will assist Europe against aggression. . . . The Axis alliance presents a problem to Japan. European entanglements give leaders pause as Soviets consider their position. . . . President Franklin Roosevelt suggested a meeting between Hitler and Mussolini months ago, a new report says, but Hitler rejected the idea.	In a speech before the Reichstag, Adolf Hitler denounces the nonaggression treaty with Poland and demands the return of Danzig to Germany. . . . Poland refuses to cede territory and makes defense preparations. . . . Prime Minister Neville Chamberlain hints at a levy on wealth and limits on war profits. . . . Mussolini summons the Minister of War and the Undersecretary and Minister of Finance to his retreat to confer. . . . President Roosevelt plans no response to Hitler's speech.			
Apr. 29	Japan feels relieved by Hitler's address. He made no threat of war and did not mention the Orient. . . . President Roosevelt greets his royal guests, Prince Olav and Princess Martha of Norway. . . . Talks with Germany are not barred, Roosevelt says. Hitler's speech is interpreted as leaving the opportunity for a trade and arms parlay.	Britain does not find solace in Hitler speech, but finds the situation full of danger. . . . Hitler's speech leaves Italians feeling troubled. . . . French see peril in a bond with Poland. . . . Poland is held next on the Reich agenda. Nazis are apparently willing to abide by pacts as long as nations stay subservient.			
Apr. 30	Japan has its hands full with war with China. In the third year of fighting, Japan is unlikely to give aid to Hitler. . . . Hitler derides President Roosevelt in a speech and attacks British policy.	Many suspect a German victory over Poland without a break with Britain is the goal of the Reich. . . . Europe weighs the strength of the Berlin-Rome Axis. It is believed to be powerful only if dictators keep out of war. . . . Italians express dismay over Hitler's speech, alarmed at the prospect of war with Poland. . . . A world movement striving for Czechoslovak freedom has grown under the former president Eduard Benes, who is now a lecturer at the University of Chicago. . . . Poles fail to see a war over Danzig and believe a compromise can be effected.		Bolivia's dictator Gérman Busch is absolute; he abolishes laws and courts.	
May 1	Arabs are ready to sign a Palestine accord. Concession is sought from Britain to save face. . . . The Japanese back the Reich in the "warmonger" issue.	Nazis press Italy for a military tie. Reich army chief Col. Gen. von Brauchitsch is in Rome. . . . Italy will restrict Jewish citizens in their choice of professions. . . . Nazis say the key to peace is in the hands of democracies. They must clarify if they want war. . . . Stalin places new men in power. Purging the country of bureaucrats is thought to be his goal.		President Franklin Roosevelt speaks. He says nations of this hemisphere are united in their wish for peace.	Chinese predict a big Nanchang attack to regain the city.

A	B	C	D	E
Includes developments that affect more than one world region, international organizations, and important meetings of world leaders.	*Includes all domestic and regional developments in Europe, including the Soviet Union.*	*Includes all domestic and regional developments in Africa and the Middle East.*	*Includes all domestic and regional developments in Latin America, the Caribbean, and Canada.*	*Includes all domestic and regional developments in Asian and Pacific nations (and colonies).*

U.S. Politics & Social Issues	U.S. Foreign Policy & Defense	Economics & Great Depression	Science, Technology & Nature	Culture, Leisure & Lifestyle	
Republicans push a budget cut plan despite mounting protests. . . . Publishers dedicate a statue that declares freedom of the press. "Bend no knee to earthly dictators," the president of the American Newspaper Publishers Association says, "but to God, alone."		Congress gives President Franklin Roosevelt's relief reorganization plan a friendly reception, though relief outlay questions are still unresolved. . . . The Senate unanimously votes for four-year terms for State Senators. The 1941 legislature must confirm the decision.	Airlines describe early challenges with food. A three-minute egg takes six minutes to cook at a 5,000-foot altitude and milk curdles almost instantly.	Baseball player Joe DiMaggio announces he will wed actress Dorothy Arnoldine Olsen.	Apr. 26
			Stellar evolution holds the key to the earth's age and our future, a physicist says.	John Barrymore faces a divorce suit from his fourth wife.	Apr. 27
The Ford Motor Company and General Motors Corporation give the Danish royalty free cars. . . . Ulysses S. Grant's new tomb will open on his birthday. The gloomy atmosphere is gone from the refurbished structure.		President Roosevelt asks employers to revamp hiring policies to ensure fairness to those aged 40 and up.	The Federation of American Societies for Experimental Biologists discuss activation of the human ova, and share possibilities of "fatherless" human beings given birth by women who are not their actual mothers.	Victor Fleming withdraws from directing Gone With the Wind. Sam Wood will replace him.	Apr. 28
Congress's reaction to the Hitler speech varies. Some see a glimmer of hope for peace while others confirm pessimism. . . . Hitler's speech seems to have no effect on opinions about the Neutrality Act.	An anonymous critic of President Roosevelt paints "war maker" on the White House gate in red paint. The Secret Service quickly scrub it off.		At the meeting of the American Societies for Experimental Biology, two teams of doctors present evidence that smoking irritation is caused by inhalation, not nicotine.		Apr. 29
The Federal Lighthouse Service celebrates its 150th anniversary. The service aids navigation along 40,000 miles of shoreline.		A survey charts the best paying work. For college graduates, dentistry, forestry, and telephone work are the best options. . . . A big rise in employment is reported by Labor Secretary Perkins in March.		Author Dorothy Parker releases a new collection of short stories, Here Lies. The vignettes make for fascinating reading, a reviewer says. . . . Transportation lines are ready to handle huge fair crowds efficiently. . . . Joe DiMaggio is hurt in a Yankee loss. . . . The New York World Fair officially opens.	Apr. 30
Television is able to record the President's speech for the first time in history.	Congress speeds its response to President Franklin Roosevelt's defense plan. Hitler's speech highlights the need for greater defense.		Prof. Albert Einstein cuts his explanation of the cosmic ray from "volumes" to 700 words.	Joe DiMaggio rests in a hospital after hurting his leg in a loss to the Washington Senators. Crowds are ordered away. . . . Robert E. Sherwood wins the Pulitzer Prize for drama, for his play, Abe Lincoln in Illinois. Marjorie Kinnan Rawlings' novel The Yearling also wins.	May 1

F	G	H	I	J
Includes elections, federal-state relations, civil rights and liberties, crime, the judiciary, education, healthcare, poverty, urban affairs, and population.	Includes formation and debate of U.S. foreign and defense policies, veterans affairs, and defense spending. (Relations with specific foreign countries are usually found under the region concerned.)	Includes business, labor, agriculture, taxation, transportation, consumer affairs, monetary and fiscal policy, natural resources, pollution, and accidents.	Includes worldwide scientific, medical, and technological developments, natural phenomena, U.S. weather, and natural disasters.	Includes the arts, religion, scholarship, communications media, sports, entertainment, fashions, fads, and social life.

	World Affairs	Europe	Africa & The Middle East	The Americas	Asia & The Pacific
May 2	Democracies speak of bigger cruisers, the type banned by the London Naval Treaty of 1936, to meet the Reich threat. Britain approaches the United States and France. . . . Hitler warns that foes are better off by buying German commodities rather than taking refugees who are "most inferior." . . . Nazi minister Joseph Goebbels scorns the culture of the United States, saying the country has contributed nothing of value and that Nazis are far ahead in that regard. . . . In the United States, 5,000 hear Prince Olav of Norway speak. He is gloomy on the outlook for peace. . . . Japan's spokesman agrees with Hitler and decries U.S. and British interference in world affairs.	Bad weather delays the flights of German and Italian officials to Libya. No indication is given for the reason for the proposed meeting. . . . The British draft a bill that conciliates the Irish. The conscription acts omit Ulster and list other modifications. . . . Britain hesitates over a Soviet tie, reluctant to offend Spain, Portugal, or the Vatican. . . . Three explosions damage French power lines near the German border. . . . Juan Negrin, former loyalist premier of Spain, predicts a Franco collapse.		Latin Americans celebrate May Day. Fifty thousand Chileans vow to resist fascism and fight for workers' rights.	The Oga earthquake wrecks 1,000 homes in Japan. An entire village disappears. . . . A crowd of 10,000 in Chungking pledges loyalty to Chiang Kai-shek. War actions cause heavy casualties to invaders, the Chinese say.
May 3		Anti-Germany riots flare in Slovakia. . . . Britain will oust Nazis and spies. . . . Prime Minister Neville Chamberlain asks for the patience of Soviets. He says that the views of many must be considered to form a peace bloc. . . . The French Cabinet debates Premier Edouard Daladier's term. The Cabinet may need to resign May 10. . . . Hitler, a noted teetotaler, now drinks beer with low alcohol content. . . . A showdown is anticipated between Germany and Poland. Warsaw's claim of equality to Germany is called "brazen and insane chauvinism."			The royal family of Japan chooses 24 boys to serve as playmates for the prince. Half will play with him on Wednesdays and half on Saturdays. . . . Japan threatens the neutral Shanghai International Settlement. No reply is received for suppression of anti-Japanese groups.
May 4	Tokyo hears the Axis powers' alliance draft. . . . The United States worries about the resignation of the Soviet Foreign Minister, Maxim Lituinoff a significant development in the face of a European crisis.	Hungary adopts an anti-Jewish law, and 300,000 citizens face exile. . . . Rumors say that Hungary will annex Slovakia. Officials deny the move.	Jews in Palestine open two new settlements.		Japan's Foreign Minister Hachiro Arita pledges not to harass law-abiding Jews. . . . Japanese bombers kill hundreds in a Chungking raid. Planes cause huge damage in China's capital.
May 5	Japan tells the Axis alliance its decision, which is believed to be negative. . . . Russia drops collective security. Foreign countries are puzzled.	German Field Marshall Goering arrives in Italy. Premier Benito Mussolini will attempt to mediate the Polish issue. . . . The son of the Archduke dies in a German concentration camp. He was arrested after smashing an illuminated Nazi sign with his umbrella. . . . Italy aims to unite schools with fascism. Teaching of the classics will only occur with "especially adapted" students. . . . Latvia accepts a pact with the Reich. . . . Poland rejects a Reich demand for Danzig, but keeps the door open. . . . A Reich housing law segregates Jews and can end leases when other housing is available.		Argentina finds the Nazi menace real. Berlin directs the local party, they say, and flouts laws.	The Chungking raids ruin embassies. Germany and Britain suffer.
May 6		The moderation and firmness of the Polish Foreign Minister Josef Beck cheers France and Britain. . . . Croat talks fail in Yugoslavia. . . . German anger at Poland mounts.			Chungking fights vast fires started by Japanese bombing.
May 7	France is strong in Africa and ready to take the offensive for defeat of fascism. . . . Germany and Italy hint at a new move in Africa. Talk of an attack on Egypt is heard from Rome. . . . Spain leaves the League of Nations.	Britain and Turkey agree to a mutual aid pact that aids the Balkans and Near East. The proposal will be sent to Moscow. . . . Bulgarians demand the return of former territories. . . . Europe sets up staple reserves. All countries organize stores for possible war. . . . Gibraltar officials censor all messages. The governor is given the power to see all cables. . . . Moscow's silence on recent events is total. No editorials give hint of the Soviet position.			

A	B	C	D	E
Includes developments that affect more than one world region, international organizations, and important meetings of world leaders.	Includes all domestic and regional developments in Europe, including the Soviet Union.	Includes all domestic and regional developments in Africa and the Middle East.	Includes all domestic and regional developments in Latin America, the Caribbean, and Canada.	Includes all domestic and regional developments in Asian and Pacific nations (and colonies).

U.S. Politics & Social Issues	U.S. Foreign Policy & Defense	Economics & Great Depression	Science, Technology & Nature	Culture, Leisure & Lifestyle	
Crosses blaze in Miami. A motorcade carrying 35 white-robed figures tell Negroes not to vote. African Americans in Miami ignore the threats and vote in record numbers. . . . Advocates of the New Deal assert that President Roosevelt must run again for re-election.	The Army orders all of the Caribbean under unified military command to decrease the possibility of enemy naval lines entering the region. President Franklin Roosevelt sets up a Puerto Rico force to bar enemy bases. . . . The cash-carry portion of the Neutrality Act expires. No attempt is made to extend it. . . . Officers of the Navy fleet get a war warning. They may get called upon to defend the country at any time.	A House committee hears how Communists influenced WPA writers.	Anesthetics vary in their effect on the brain, an American Society for Clinical Investigation speaker says. Inhaled anesthetics cause the highest electrical frequencies. . . . New televisions attract throngs to stores, amazed by the clarity of the picture.	Lou Gehrig voluntarily stops his game-playing streak at 2,130 games. He is not hitting well and asks for a break, his record will stand for 56 years.	May 2
Methodists renew their crusade against alcohol and create a temperance board to promote public morals.	The Army says it needs three months to mobilize a fighting force of one million men. . . . Many Senators oppose the suggestion to delay deciding upon the Neutrality Act until the next session. . . . Congress fights to continue to hold sessions during crisis. The fear is that the United States will become involved in a foreign war.				May 3
A doctor allegedly participates in a poison ring. Poison is used to kill people for insurance money. . . . The Women's Division of the National Amateur Athletic Federation criticizes those who exploit girls and put sex into sports.	The Navy plans to change its enlistment term from four years to six. No one under age 18 will be accepted.		The New York World Fair exhibits make science fun and easy to understand for visitors.	John Barrymore moves to tie up his funds. He says he has never contested a divorce before because of chivalry, but this time is different. . . . Lou Gehrig is puzzled over his batting decline and cries during his first day of inactivity. . . . World Fair attendees participate in a television show.	May 4
Congress resumes its "Red Hunt" with the WPA, and may ask arts project workers if they are Communists. . . . A study reveals that superstitions are still rife, and that adults are often more gullible than children.		The president of the American Bankers Association agrees that the Social Security Act needs to be changed. . . . The U.S. Chamber of Commerce demands that Congress repeal curbs on business, saying the wage-hour law must go.	An 82-inch telescope, second-largest in the world, is dedicated at the McDonald Observatory in Texas.		May 5
The House votes to imprison aliens not accepted in their own country because of crime. Critics compare this idea to a concentration camp. . . . The Federal Housing Administration envisions the end of slums. . . . Police seek an ex-prosecutor's son wanted in two deaths. The son recently wrote a paper on the "perfect crime." . . . Olympic sprinter Jesse Owens files for bankruptcy.			The Italian government announces a rare find of a Neanderthal skull on the coast between Rome and Naples.	A noted physician visits the World Fair and explains the mechanical heart on display. . . . Kentucky Derby officials expect a crowd of 70,000.	May 6
The Speaker blames unemployment for the emotional unrest of youth, saying it causes normal life to be halted. . . . The former mayor and former police chief of Salt Lake City, Utah, are sentenced to one year each in county jail for permitting gambling.		An extensive report shows that there is a chance for economic recovery if the government will aid. Conditions are better than many thought.		Four thousand observe a baseball game in Cooperstown, N.Y., to honor baseball's centennial. . . . World Fair visitors get free chest x-rays.	May 7

F	G	H	I	J
Includes elections, federal-state relations, civil rights and liberties, crime, the judiciary, education, healthcare, poverty, urban affairs, and population.	Includes formation and debate of U.S. foreign and defense policies, veterans affairs, and defense spending. (Relations with specific foreign countries are usually found under the region concerned.)	Includes business, labor, agriculture, taxation, transportation, consumer affairs, monetary and fiscal policy, natural resources, pollution, and accidents.	Includes worldwide scientific, medical, and technological developments, natural phenomena, U.S. weather, and natural disasters.	Includes the arts, religion, scholarship, communications media, sports, entertainment, fashions, fads, and social life.

	World Affairs	Europe	Africa & The Middle East	The Americas	Asia & The Pacific
May 8	Pope Pius XII urges peace to ease anxiety and asks that May be Universal Prayer Month.	Germany scores a blow to encirclement. An alliance with Italy is forming. . . . The King and Queen of England participate in a boat drill, donning life preservers at the sound of a siren. . . . Czechs celebrate their national festival without orders from German overlords. The swastika is absent. . . . Hungary arrests 52 Nazis who practiced party activities after the party was banned. . . . Germany hails the fall of Soviet Foreign Minister Cap. Litvinoff, seeing this as the end of active Russian opposition.			The death toll rises in Chungking. Estimates range from 3,000 to 10,000.
May 9		Hitler wishes to negotiate with Stalin. The Reich wants to neutralize Russia with a non-aggression pact and then focus on Poland. . . . The King of England's ship fights through fog. The royal couple strolls on the deck. . . . Nazis say the Axis tie is unlimited and will provide for unity without compromise.	Italo Balbo, the Italian Governor of Libya travels to Egypt. He receives a chilly welcome by the press.	Chile builds shelters for the 700,000 left homeless after the quake.	Japan rejects protests on its raids, saying it cannot help damaging foreign property near targets. Bombings of Amoy and nearby towns continue.
May 10	Bolivia offers oil to the Reich as barter. It seeks help in exploiting confiscated fields and building pipelines. . . . A Chinese author urges writers to disown dictators. He calls Hitler a distorter of history and "Il Duce," or Mussolini, a second-rate novelist.			U.S. army officials leave for Brazil. The visit is important, the U.S. says, to future relationships. . . . Chile's new envoy, Alberto Cabero, pushes a strong U.S. tie. He assures investors that their government is not extremist.	Japan bars relief to Ningro, and may extend the ban to other cities.
May 11	All Scandinavian countries, except Denmark, are expected to say no to Germany's offer of nonaggression pacts.	A book teaches German soldiers Czech phrases for "Where is money" and "If you lie, you will be shot." . . . The British air minister recruits thousands of pigeons to deliver messages from planes. . . . The Danish senate votes to dissolve; a new parliament forms. . . . Italian fascists are urged to stop drinking coffee to spite nations that "want gold" for it. . . . German experts doubt deaths would increase in the next war as compared to World War I.			A big Japanese victory is unlikely in Shanghai. An estimated 150,000 "trapped" Chinese are expected to escape.
May 12		Italians are told not to drink coffee or to reduce quantities. Other drinks encouraged include wine, herb drinks, lemonade, and orangeade. . . . The Soviet League of Militant Atheists states that 30 million still hold religious beliefs after 21 years of attempting to stamp them out. Five-year plans are being designed to end religion in Russia. . . . London sets up four plants to store blood for war transfusion needs.			Chungking remains China's capital. The population thins because of air raids. . . . Shanghai bars all political activity. The penalty is banishment.
May 13	Britain offers the interior of British Guinea for Jewish settlements. Prime Minister Neville Chamberlain promises the establishment of facilities for a refugee colony.	Austrian Nazis claim control over the Catholic hierarchy. The Church can no longer name priests or other Church officials without approval of the party. . . . French Premier Edouard Daladier's policies win a chamber vote, 375–230. . . . Germany bans free beer and tobacco for minority and female workers in breweries and tobacco factories. . . . Hitler's Elite Guards swoop in and arrest 21 Czech police. Some attempt suicide. . . . Nazis free banker Louis Rothschild after 13 months as a Gestapo prisoner. Friends say Rothschild will sue to regain his confiscated fortune. . . . An estimated 1.5 million Nazi troops are already in the field, aiming to wear down the foe before war begins.			Japan invades an island considered a concession area. The United States protests.

A	B	C	D	E
Includes developments that affect more than one world region, international organizations, and important meetings of world leaders.	Includes all domestic and regional developments in Europe, including the Soviet Union.	Includes all domestic and regional developments in Africa and the Middle East.	Includes all domestic and regional developments in Latin America, the Caribbean, and Canada.	Includes all domestic and regional developments in Asian and Pacific nations (and colonies).

U.S. Politics & Social Issues	U.S. Foreign Policy & Defense	Economics & Great Depression	Science, Technology & Nature	Culture, Leisure & Lifestyle	
		The WPA ends adult education forums as not worth the effort and expense.	Ordinary house mice are found to carry a dangerous brain disease, according to the Public Health Service. How the disease, lymphocytic choriomeningitis, transfers from mice to men is not yet known.	Daphne du Maurier's *Rebecca* and John Steinbeck's *Of Mice and Men* are to be made into movies.	**May 8**
Identifying a "coal emergency," President Roosevelt asks union and company officials to present a plan for resumption of mining.		AFL leaders and the Labor Board meet to discuss changes in the Wagner Act.			**May 9**
A biographer says Woodrow Wilson desired a third term as president to establish the League of Nations, but friends discouraged the idea. . . . President Roosevelt's second reorganization plan dooms or changes scores of agencies. The proposals stir no fight. . . . An Ohio House bill bans women from serving as cocktail waitresses. "Women can't mix a good cocktail," the legislator says.	Methodists back war objectors. . . . Constatine Oumansky is named Soviet Ambassador to the U.S.	Mayors urge a House committee to recommend continuation of the WPA. . . . Roosevelt is aroused by the farm bill request and says he will ask for taxes to cover the increase.	The World Fair exhibit on cancer helps dispel mystery surrounding the disease, and indicates that hope exists with early treatment. . . . The president of the New York Dental Society urges the creation of sub-dentists. They would perform basic services for low-income people.		**May 10**
The Florida Senate passes a bill for the primary with white voters only. The Negro Citizens Service League objects. . . . Although unable to give the President the plan he demanded, John L. Lewis and the United Mine Workers called off their strike in the areas west of the Appalachians, and will return to work.			Sulfanilamide aids smallpox and reduces scars. . . . A National Parks System employee finds three new caves 900 feet below Carlsbad Caverns. The new realm is named Pluto's Palace.	R.L. Ripley leases three floors of a New York City building to create a museum of oddities. . . . The American Social Hygiene Association sets up a fair display to spread sex education and show how to combat venereal diseases. . . . A lost China throne, a $2 million relic from the golden days of emperors, is found in an ordinary shipping crate in Hoboken, N.J. and will be displayed at the World Fair.	**May 11**
The President's son Elliot warns of curbs on radio content. He says it will lead to muzzling of the press. . . . The ex-wife of the Supreme Court Justice who disappeared in 1930 testifies she is convinced of his death. . . . The New York Senate bans race exclusion and passes a bill to deny benefits to unions guilty of discrimination. . . . Widows past 30 attract the bulk of younger mates, a Metropolitan Life Insurance study shows.				John Barrymore's estranged wife files a 12-page suit. She charges the actor with fits of temper and rage. . . . A World Fair display shares the story of childbirth, and presents the development of an embryo to combat prudish attitudes.	**May 12**
Mayor Fiorello LaGuardia rededicates the amusement portion of the World Fair. An electric eel is to provide "juice" for the starting signal. . . . The AFL awaits a peace move by the CIO. Rival chiefs are asked to set aside personal feelings during negotiations. . . . The FBI is ready to aid the poison ring inquiry, and offers technical aides and a laboratory.	President Roosevelt recommends the Chief of Naval Operations, Admiral William Leahy, to serve as Governor of Puerto Rico. The announcement takes the Navy by surprise.		Specialists push a drive to spread news about arthritis.	This month's edition of *Detective Comics* (#27) features a new hero: Batman, by Bob Kane.	**May 13**

F	**G**	**H**	**I**	**J**
Includes elections, federal-state relations, civil rights and liberties, crime, the judiciary, education, healthcare, poverty, urban affairs, and population.	*Includes formation and debate of U.S. foreign and defense policies, veterans affairs, and defense spending. (Relations with specific foreign countries are usually found under the region concerned.)*	*Includes business, labor, agriculture, taxation, transportation, consumer affairs, monetary and fiscal policy, natural resources, pollution, and accidents.*	*Includes worldwide scientific, medical, and technological developments, natural phenomena, U.S. weather, and natural disasters.*	*Includes the arts, religion, scholarship, communications media, sports, entertainment, fashions, fads, and social life.*

	World Affairs	Europe	Africa & The Middle East	The Americas	Asia & The Pacific
May 14	A Zionist leader warns Britain that its Palestine plan would create ghettos for Jews, and thinks bloodshed would be likely. . . . Japan's caution pleases France; more evidence of opposition to the Axis is received.	Prime Minister Neville Chamberlain's position weakens as the House of Commons suspects he still favors appeasement. . . . Czechs must toil faster for Nazis, facing a compulsory labor program in line with German standards. . . . France holds military forces ready on land and sea; tension rises as Hitler is said to be ready to visit frontiers. . . . Germany lays down the Italian war strategy. . . . London completes evacuation plans. . . . Italian Premier Mussolini gives a speech in Turin. He declares war unnecessary. An attack on France is the likely subject.			Chiang Kai-shek's fan mail is as large and as varied as that of movie stars; he receives requests for a pair of his shoes or his wife's pajamas.
May 15		Italian Premier Benito Mussolini's talk heartens the British and international optimism rises. . . . France welcomes Mussolini's moderate tone. It is believed he realizes he could not win the war. . . . The Nazi press ignores Il Duce's peace view speech.			
May 16	Jewish leaders ask British Prime Minister Neville Chamberlain to permit the House of Commons to vote independently on the Palestine issue, and not be bound by a party vote.	Bulgarians raise a cry over Romanians—leaflets demand blood in reprisal for killings near the border. . . . A Finnish thief, sentenced to 12 years hard labor, asks for execution. The judge denies the request as there is no capital punishment in Finland. . . . The French see Italian Premier Benito Mussolini trapped by errors of aggression in Ethiopia, Spain, and Albania. . . . South Tyrol causes strain upon the Axis. Citizens are disappointed that Hitler did not get this territory back from Italy. . . . Soviets find fault with the British security pact and little headway is made on negotiations.		Argentina bans foreign political parties and dissolves the German Nazi party.	
May 17		The House of Commons turns down a bill that would give military conscripted men the right to vote at age 20. The first 40,000 are called up to start training on July 15. . . . France and Britain reportedly agree on aid to the Soviets, said to offer a guarantee if Moscow resists an attack from the west to defend its neighbors. . . . Italian Premier Benito Mussolini visits the frontier defenses. . . . Albanian King Zog asks the League of Nations to restore the independence of his country.	Palestine fears a violent outbreak today. British troops patrol on the eve of publication of the plan for Palestine.	Chile deports more foreigners.	
May 18	Britain plans to make Palestine independent by 1949. The plan would curtail the Jewish population and have Arabs outnumber them 2–1. . . . Japan yields at Amoy; recalling most of its forces after demands from France, Britain, and the United States. . . . The president of the Zionist Organization of America charges Britain with shamelessly reversing its Palestine policy. . . . The Pope participates in a rare church rite, riding through Rome. This has not been conducted in 93 years.	The Czechs plan an Aryan cultural unit. The influence of the Reich is seen. . . . Madrid is ready for Franco's victory parade. Franco may share his foreign policy message. . . . Three nations—Norway, Sweden, and Finland—reject the Reich pact. Denmark accepts a nonaggression accord.		Bolivia adheres to the Axis powers. This is feared as a foothold for fascism and a dangerous precedent for Latin America. . . . The French hail the King and Queen of Britain as they land in Quebec; 50,000 children sing the British anthem.	
May 19	The King of England is hesitant about visiting the U.S. Congress. He wants the visit to stay personal, not political. . . . The average Briton's view of the United States irks Ambassador Joseph Kennedy. He asks the press to expand U.S. news coverage.	Franco is in Madrid for the peace fête. He will receive the highest military honors. . . . Guards watch Hitler carefully as he scans the border regions. . . . The Reich orders the ouster of "stateless" Jews by July 31, or they will enter concentration camps. . . . Slovakia loses the last of its liberty as the Minister of the Interior, who was cool to the Reich, is named as Minster to the Vatican.	There is one dead and 180 hurt as Palestine riots continue over the British plan for the region.		

A	B	C	D	E
Includes developments that affect more than one world region, international organizations, and important meetings of world leaders.	*Includes all domestic and regional developments in Europe, including the Soviet Union.*	*Includes all domestic and regional developments in Africa and the Middle East.*	*Includes all domestic and regional developments in Latin America, the Caribbean, and Canada.*	*Includes all domestic and regional developments in Asian and Pacific nations (and colonies).*

U.S. Politics & Social Issues	U.S. Foreign Policy & Defense	Economics & Great Depression	Science, Technology & Nature	Culture, Leisure & Lifestyle	
Illinois women win the right to jury duty. . . . The American Labor Party discusses purging all Communists from membership.	The Army and Navy plan to spend $30 million to fortify Puerto Rico, planning to create the "Hawaii of the Atlantic."			Veteran manager Connie Mack shares baseball stories with youth at the World Fair.	**May 14**
Yesterday's sermons focus on Mother's Day. Training for mothers is termed vital and those who call parenthood a privilege are praised.		London is puzzled over U.S. economic woes, and feels U.S. business is hindered by a "do nothing" policy. . . . President Roosevelt views tax issues today. . . . Troops gather in Kentucky as coal-union men prepare to picket mines.	A physician reports that potassium salts relieve hives, hay fever, and illness from foods.	Actress Barbara Stanwyck and actor Robert Taylor wed.	**May 15**
American Booksellers Association speakers urge booksellers to reduce prices. Books are as life-giving as food and water, one says, and should therefore be as common. . . . Buggsy Goldstein and bodyguard Seymour Magoon are on trial for conspiracy for the third time. . . . A jury finds Dapper Don guilty of extortion. . . . The Senate will act on the tax bill. President Franklin Roosevelt leaves no doubt that he wants the profits tax policy left in place. . . . Georgia Democrats see a third-term move being made by Roosevelt.		The National Mediation Board chairman urges broad mediation for labor issues. A nationwide conciliation plan is suggested. . . . An investigator says the Ohio WPA project hid excess costs. Ohio relief was used for administrative work.		The American League will turn on lights. A crowd of 38,000 is expected for the first game after dark, held in Philadelphia, Pa. . . . The American Mother of 1939 honoree is mildly critical of New York. She says it is not best place to raise a family.	**May 16**
A lawyer who confessed to racketeering faces a sentence of 640 years. He complains when given a sentence of 20 months, saying that he atoned for his sins. . . . The Ohio legislature kills a bill that would ban female bartenders. . . . The White House chooses a simple menu for the visiting British royalty, including calf's head soup, filet of flounder, and frozen cheese and cress salad.		Doctors dispute WPA medical data. The number of people lacking a doctor is closer to 40,000; not 40 million, as reported. . . . The President refuses a union plea from Kentucky coal mines, warning of strife.		NBC televises the first baseball game, a college game between Columbia and Princeton.	**May 17**
A one-day veteran wins the fight for his job. A court upholds his brief army service and orders him reinstated to his post.	Col. Charles Lindbergh favors swift war planes, and warns the government of the superior Reich military.	Grocers approve a food stamp plan. The government is satisfied with the second day of testing. . . . Bloodshed is feared as Harlan, Ky., coal miners do not sign a CIO pact. Machine guns and bayonets are held ready. . . . Schools feed 119,000 needy daily. The Board of Education and WPA reach a new record in care of children.		Four popular restaurants add services at the World Fair with a seating capacity of 2,000. . . . The American Booksellers Association condones "trash" for children, and says any exciting story will keep them reading.	**May 18**
The FBI captures "Rose of Death." The police call her a "professional widow" and investigate the deaths of several former husbands. . . . Martin Dies asserts his House committee uncovered evidence of an organized anti-Semitism campaign.		Gunfire rattles Harlan, Ky. Snipers fire hundreds of shots and a machine gun is used, but no one is hit as mines reopen.		Myrna Loy and William Powell will make a new *Thin Man* film. . . . A Sears & Roebuck study indicates that women dress to please themselves, not their husbands, although they hope their spouses will like their look.	**May 19**

F	G	H	I	J
Includes elections, federal-state relations, civil rights and liberties, crime, the judiciary, education, healthcare, poverty, urban affairs, and population.	*Includes formation and debate of U.S. foreign and defense policies, veterans affairs, and defense spending. (Relations with specific foreign countries are usually found under the region concerned.)*	*Includes business, labor, agriculture, taxation, transportation, consumer affairs, monetary and fiscal policy, natural resources, pollution, and accidents.*	*Includes worldwide scientific, medical, and technological developments, natural phenomena, U.S. weather, and natural disasters.*	*Includes the arts, religion, scholarship, communications media, sports, entertainment, fashions, fads, and social life.*

	World Affairs	Europe	Africa & The Middle East	The Americas	Asia & The Pacific
May 20	The Bolivian envoy Dr. Luis Fernando Guachalla denies a fascist tie in talks with the United States State Department. He repudiates ties to the totalitarian states of Europe.	Britain works out a new Soviet plan after Prime Minister Neville Chamberlain is assailed for not pushing through an agreement. Chamberlain says concessions cannot lead to new demands. . . . The British claim a device that foils submarines. The new detector is said to make the fleet nearly impregnable. . . . Bulgarian anger at Romania rises; reports of reprisals against families of fugitives adds to indignation. . . . Hitler declares Germany's forts invincible. . . . Franco reviews 150,000 troops.			Gandhi states that his March fast was coercion to achieve goals, and he apologizes.
May 21	The Anglo-Soviet snag is linked to Tokyo. The Japanese threat to form an alliance with the Reich causes delay.	Soviets print millions of copies of the Communist "bible," a guide to communist thought and action. . . . Franco takes up peace tasks. Lassitude and intrigue serve as his two greatest obstacles. . . . Germany now focuses on eastern forts. The new defense system is called a warning to Poles who talk of an attack on the Reich. . . . London-Paris-Moscow treaty talks continue, despite diplomatic difficulties. . . . New ties to the Reich trouble Italians. The military alliance is accepted, but with misgivings.			Chinese envoy Victor Hoo Chi-tsai tells the League of Nations that the Japanese openly encourage the Chinese to use opium.
May 22	Members of the British Peel Commission recommend separate areas in Palestine for Arabs and for Jews. . . . The King and Queen of Britain walk through the World Fair alone. Enthusiastic veterans slap the back of the King and grip the hand of the Queen.	The French Foreign Minister Georges Bonnet says force cannot rule Europe and a spirit of domination is not tolerable. . . . Czechs are the target of a Fascist split. The goal is said to be the removal of remaining autonomy and control of police. . . . Germans discard thoughts of war, saying Hitler will not deliberately involve the Reich. . . . The Italian-German pact is said to demand prompt, unquestioning, mutual aid in war. . . . A Pole kills a German in Danzig disorder. Both sides protest. . . . Reich mothers get awards for offspring to raise the birthrate and symbolically offer their children to Hitler.			
May 23	Japan felicitates Germany and Italy and praises their pact, but holds the previous pact sufficient.	Berlin accuses the Allies of inciting Poles. . . . The Axis powers sign The Pact of Steel, a 10-year agreement to remake Europe. . . . The blatancy of the Axis causes doubts; cynics wonder why unity would require an alliance assurance. . . . Italy sees a sphere set aside by the pact and a free hand in Africa.			
May 24	An air clash occurs on the Manchu border. The Japanese report dogfights started by Soviet Outer Mongolian forces.	Hitler reserves his favorite march, *Badenweiler*, for his use only. The Reich can punish those playing the music without Hitler present. . . . Britain and France praise the League of Nations and seek an end to member desertions. . . . London's Czech gold goes to Germany. . . . The Reich appears chagrined at the quiet response to the German-Italian pact; the press warns democracies of underestimating the weight of the new pact. . . . Italy awaits a response by the non-Axis bloc, holding that the military pact puts the next step in the hands of Britain and France.			
May 25	Soviets subsidize Far East settlers. The motive is held to be creating a self-sustaining area in case of war with Japan.	Vienna police fine American Express for overcharging Jewish ticket users. . . . The British agree to a Soviet pact for mutual aid. The Cabinet approves the pact, which protects these two countries, plus France. . . . France sees an accord with Russia close. . . . Anti-Italian feeling is strong in Greece. Hatred near the Albanian border brings about a state of constant vigilance.			Chinese smash foes in Hupeh. Japanese forces scatter. . . . Japan defends its right to send forces into the International Settlements in China, rejecting British and U.S. opposition.
May 26		Germany warns Jews that a law barring them from Aryan housing will begin soon. . . . German police jail high Czech officers. . . . Italy calls 19,400 home from Spain.		The U.S. will push a trade pact in Latin America according to Commerce Secretary Hopkins.	The Japanese bomb Chungking again. Heavy casualties and panic take a toll. . . . A Japanese spokesperson warns that foreign vessels will be searched up to 100 miles from shore.

A	B	C	D	E
Includes developments that affect more than one world region, international organizations, and important meetings of world leaders.	Includes all domestic and regional developments in Europe, including the Soviet Union.	Includes all domestic and regional developments in Africa and the Middle East.	Includes all domestic and regional developments in Latin America, the Caribbean, and Canada.	Includes all domestic and regional developments in Asian and Pacific nations (and colonies).

U.S. Politics & Social Issues	U.S. Foreign Policy & Defense	Economics & Great Depression	Science, Technology & Nature	Culture, Leisure & Lifestyle	
New York takes elaborate precautions to protect the British royal guests at the World Fair. . . . The American Newspaper Publishers counsel disputes Roosevelt's view on freedom of the press. He denies that government protects that freedom. . . . A grand jury indicts 12 in poison deaths, including the widowed Rose of Death. . . . The Federation of Business and Professional Women's Clubs urge women to scan legislation that restricts interests. Basic rights are denied, they say.		The government sends surplus food, including grapefruit, to idle miners in Harlan County, Ky. . . . Kentucky guards ban Communists headed to the miner strike zone.	Doctors use vitamin K for coagulation. Hemorrhage prevention is noted on jaundiced patients.		May 20
The National Association of Real Estate Boards asks for assistance in the fight on slums, and suggests joint action between realtors and city agencies. . . . Some Washington elite feel slighted over not being invited to the royal garden fête and make their anguish known. . . . The Southern Baptist Church deplores President Roosevelt's overtures to Pope Pius XII. . . . A judge bars fishing as a reason for divorce. Husbands are entitled to enjoy fishing, he says, and wives who object are unreasonable. . . . A mathematics study shows that girls lead boys in test scores.		The U.S. Chamber of Commerce drafts a tax revision plan and asks Congress to avoid punitive and reform levies. . . . President Roosevelt's labor goals include high wages and fair profits. . . . Harlan, Ky., miners get their first contract.	A state report sees hope in insulin treatments as an aid to the insane. . . . A doctor creates a system for clarity in x-rays.	The World Fair building quivers as jitterbugs vie for silver cups. Dance enthusiasts please a noisy audience with modern steps.	May 21
		Federal agents begin an inquiry of civil rights violations in Harlan, Ky. They invite press and have miners testify about National Guard actions.	Scientists plan an expedition to claim Antarctica for the United States. Confident of Congressional approval, Dr. Ernest Gruening, Director of Territorial Affairs, drafts a request for funds.	The Dionne quintuplets leave their home for their first ever trip—going to meet the King and Queen of England in Toronto.	May 22
		Federal scrutiny pacifies Harlan, Ky. Both troops and picketers are quiet.		The Dionne quintuplets kiss the Queen. She hugs all five sisters. . . . War fever is seen as an aid to disease. The cost of two weeks of war would be sufficient to wipe out tuberculosis.	May 23
The New York Archbishop takes his new post in a solemn ceremony at St. Patrick's Cathedral. . . . A judge sentences Thomas Pendergast for insurance fraud. A Missouri paper says the 15-month sentence is a failure to punish gross betrayal.		Negotiations in Harlan, Ky., hold for recess after only one coal company signs a contract with the union. Food distribution continues.		The French pavilion of the World Fair shows varied treasures: art, gems, and perfumes are among the special exhibits seen as exotic.	May 24
Alcatraz Prison adds 100 cells. . . . Silent Bill Perry, a man who refused to speak for 50 years after being jilted at the altar, dies.		The Army provides trucks for Harlan, Ky., employees who wish to work. The fight seems deadlocked.	Engineers picture the car of tomorrow: teardrop shaped with a rounded front and pointed tail.		May 25
		Senators say that the New Deal causes poverty by barring economic revival, adding that the Roosevelt administration is leading the U.S. to economic slavery.			May 26

F	**G**	**H**	**I**	**J**
Includes elections, federal-state relations, civil rights and liberties, crime, the judiciary, education, healthcare, poverty, urban affairs, and population.	Includes formation and debate of U.S. foreign and defense policies, veterans affairs, and defense spending. (Relations with specific foreign countries are usually found under the region concerned.)	Includes business, labor, agriculture, taxation, transportation, consumer affairs, monetary and fiscal policy, natural resources, pollution, and accidents.	Includes worldwide scientific, medical, and technological developments, natural phenomena, U.S. weather, and natural disasters.	Includes the arts, religion, scholarship, communications media, sports, entertainment, fashions, fads, and social life.

	World Affairs	Europe	Africa & The Middle East	The Americas	Asia & The Pacific
May 27	The King and Queen of England visit a camp of Indian tribes in Canada.	A British editor says the North American continent is better informed than Europe. . . . Danzig Nazis open a new press attack. They say Britain and France would not protect Poland from German attack. . . . Franco has executed 688 since March 28. . . . The German pace causes a strain on the country. An economic association sees a labor shortage and stresses the need for raw materials. . . . The British invite Soviets to observe war games.		Chile's Finance Minister Roberto Wachholtz warns U.S. oil companies that a government oil monopoly is planned by September 3.	Japanese at Amoy set minimum terms. Naval officers demand three more on the Settlement's Municipal Council or troops will stay indefinitely.
May 28	The League of Nations closes its 105th Council, and avoids action on a refortification dispute of the Aland Islands. . . . Britain shapes its policy with an eye on Arabs. Cultivating the friendship of independent states would be a potential asset in case of war.	All Reich schools put war training in the curriculum. . . . The Axis will develop a unified air force. Germany and Italy will turn out the same sizes, speeds, and calibers for easy pilot exchange. . . . Europe ponders its birthrate, as the poorest countries are producing the most children. . . . The British Princesses enjoy a whirl of activities while their parents are traveling.			The Japanese confront U.S. missionaries. A new policy orders the missionaries to avoid Chinese politics, or pack up and go home.
May 29	A Reich firm reveals a protest made when Japanese stopped their ship.	Neville Chamberlain ends his second year as premier. He marks the anniversary by fishing for trout. . . . The Axis seeks land shifts. Sweeping territorial revisions are urged on the basis of economic parity for the powers. . . . Germany bans the airing of religious programs on the radio. It is said to also be putting a ban on purchases of the Bible and other religious tracts.			
May 30	League of Nations High Commissioner for Danzig Karl Burckhardt meets with Nazi district leader for Danzig, Albert Foerster. Foerster conveyed words received from Adolf Hitler last week.	French Socialists break with Communists. . . . Hungarian Nazis gain in the election, winning 25 percent of parliamentary seats. They will try to unite all opposition parties into a voting bloc.	Attacks on Arabs disturb Palestine. The headsman of a village says visiting Jews fired shots and killed five.		Japan restricts boarding of ships. . . . Japan reports a new northern border clash and says 42 planes were shot down to repulse the raid.
May 31	France expresses surprise at the isolationist view in the United States. Opposition to revision of the Neutrality Act causes wondering. . . . The English King speaks of aid in Asia during a speech in British Columbia. He urges a greater Canadian role in Far East issues.	British Laborites assent to the draft. . . . Nazis seize the castle of the Reich's Catholic Primate. The Archbishop of Salzburg, Sigismund Waitz, finds his belongings removed and the Elite Guard moving in. . . . Russia is ready to enter the alliance with Britain and France and is told the pact will take place immediately, without League of Nations delay. . . . A Spaniard, 21, confesses to shooting 800 Nationalist prisoners and is sentenced to death by garrote.	Arabs retaliate as a bus is fired upon. Crowds stone Jewish-owned vehicles in Jerusalem.		Disease in China continues to rise. War is creating new epidemics, the League of Nations is told.
Jun. 1	China is skeptical of Outer Mongolia clashes between Soviets and Japanese; they think the Japanese exaggerate minor incidents so that Britain sees weaknesses in the Soviet war machine. . . . Dr. Eduard Benes, the former president of Czechoslovakia praises the courage of Czechs at a World Fair speech. His pledge that "we will not die" is met with applause. . . . Captain Gustav Shroeder of the liner Saint Louis fears mass suicide if 917 German Jews are refused entry into Cuba and must sail back toward Germany. . . . When the Queen of England asks to buy an island in Strait of Georgia, she is told they are already hers.	The Soviet Premier and Foreign Commissar Vyachesiaff Molotoff doubts the aims of Britain and France, and says negotiations will continue. . . . Hungary cautions German meddlers, warning the "irresponsible elements" of the Reich against interference. . . . The Reich hails troops home from Spain. . . . The Soviet premier Molotoff drops a bombshell: he never gave any indication that he was going to reject the French and British pact in his speech.	The Palestinian police seize Jews, en masse, and start a drive to round up suspects in terrorism.		Mahmoud, a Malay Prince of Tregganu is to marry Joyce Blensowe, the daughter of an English tailor, despite the objections of his brother, a Sultan.

A	B	C	D	E
Includes developments that affect more than one world region, international organizations, and important meetings of world leaders.	*Includes all domestic and regional developments in Europe, including the Soviet Union.*	*Includes all domestic and regional developments in Africa and the Middle East.*	*Includes all domestic and regional developments in Latin America, the Caribbean, and Canada.*	*Includes all domestic and regional developments in Asian and Pacific nations (and colonies).*

U.S. Politics & Social Issues	U.S. Foreign Policy & Defense	Economics & Great Depression	Science, Technology & Nature	Culture, Leisure & Lifestyle	
Fiorello LaGuardia's doctor warns the New York mayor that he must get more rest and slow his pace at the World Fair. . . . LaGuardia berates political loafers and pledges a renewed effort to end useless jobs. . . . Women see a threat to their security as bills in 19 states would limit the types of jobs available to them.			Dr. Charles Mayo dies of pneumonia. He made the clinic in Minnesota world famous.		May 27
New York city schools start an honors program that will segregate the brightest students. . . . The Dies Committee investigates claims of Communist and fascist activities.			An inventor plans an airplane that lands upside down. . . . A New York woman leading the fight to preserve wildlife achieves notable results in the conservation of birds and forests.	Heavyweight boxers Max Baer and Lou Nova can expect a crowd of more than 25,000 at their bout. . . . Columbia University releases a collection of previously unpublished letters of Ralph Waldo Emerson. . . . The Dionne quints celebrate their fifth birthday.	May 28
The Roosevelt administration spurs Congress to wrap up its session. This move by the executive speeds up decisions on taxes, neutrality, and Social Security. . . . A.J. Nichols, Civil War captain of a Negro regiment dies at age 100. He headed a newspaper chain. . . . Few indigent are drawn to New York because of the World Fair. The fear of officials that the fair would bring throngs of penniless was unwarranted.	Chief of Naval Operations Admiral William Leahy says the Navy is strong enough to bar any single enemy, and may be strong enough to beat any combination of foes.			Marian Anderson, African American contralto, sings at the World Fair. More than 200 are turned away at her sold-out performance. . . . Two communions worship together as Presbyterians and Episcopalians move closer toward union. . . . A group protests that a figure of a Soviet worker toiling under a red star of communism is taller than the American flag at the World Fair.	May 29
Two more men admit guilt in a counterfeit money scheme. A group of men distributed $200,000 in fake funds. . . . World War I draft dodger Grover Cleveland Bergdoff repents the follies of his youth and issues a public apology from his prison cell. . . . The Supreme Court rules that one's place of birth determines citizenship. A girl born in America who moves to Sweden with her family at age four is still a U.S. citizen. . . . Abortionist Louis Duke says he paid 10 percent to public officials for protection. . . . Veterans of three conflicts join patriotic groups in Memorial Day services, as 75,000 march to honor war dead.	The Dies Committee receives information on the Navy and will inquire into a report that says men were dismissed as Communists. .	The House Committee recommends a broader WPA inquiry by a new subcommittee plus an audit, believing the $250,000 cost associated with the inquiry would be compensated by new measures implemented.		A censor descends upon "sexy" shows at the World Fair. Officials order five shows to erase vulgarity and tone down scenes; nude paintings are removed.	May 30
The Capital Hotel in Washington charges $30 for someone to get a peek of the King and Queen from a hotel window. The hotel is along the parade route. . . . President Roosevelt plans a continental tour to assess sentiment toward his administration. He may go as far as Alaska. . . . The royal visit means stiff shirts for Vice President John Garner. The social shunner is pulled to the front in the visit. . . . A survey shows Senator Robert Taft of Ohio as equal to Roosevelt in the presidential race. Many oppose a third term for the President.	Virginia's Senator Byrd is the first southerner to give a Memorial Day speech at Gettysburg. He hails sectional unity. . . . A memorial service hails the Jewish dead of 1776. Flags are placed on graves.	A relief study gives a picture of misery. Shocking conditions are laid to the government's failure to address problems. Federal grants to states are seen as only a remedy to the situation.		John Barrymore is indisposed after a slight heart attack. The condition halts the actor's appearance in Chicago. . . . The Boston Museum of Fine Arts buys a Rembrandt painting for $85,000. . . . Fictional detective Charlie Chan solves another mystery in a new movie. . . . The U.S. flag tops the Soviet star at the Russian pavilion at the World Fair.	May 31
A special prosecutor ends the bribery case against Judge George Martin. The judge clashes sharply with the court when evidence about debts is limited. . . . Birth certificates will list blood test data about syphilis on the back of the form, keeping embarrassing information off the front. . . . New York Mayor Fiorello LaGuardia lists names of people holding dual jobs in schools, and urges a bill to abolish the practice. . . . Legislators plead for insured small business loans by private banks. The setup would put idle dollars to work.	A Major General proposes use of the Army to drive Communists out of the country. A Jewish-led "Red Revolution" is about to overwhelm the country, he says. . . . President Franklin Roosevelt tightens Pearl Harbor security, closing the waters except to those with special permits. . . . President Roosevelt pushes revision of the Neutrality Act. He will not drop his drive to allow the adjournment of Congress.	Negotiation between unions and coal companies in Harlan, Ky., are suspended. No progress has been made in the negotiations.		A huge Belgian collection of diamonds, worth $20 million, arrives at the World Fair under armed guard.	Jun. 1

F	G	H	I	J
Includes elections, federal-state relations, civil rights and liberties, crime, the judiciary, education, healthcare, poverty, urban affairs, and population.	Includes formation and debate of U.S. foreign and defense policies, veterans affairs, and defense spending. (Relations with specific foreign countries are usually found under the region concerned.)	Includes business, labor, agriculture, taxation, transportation, consumer affairs, monetary and fiscal policy, natural resources, pollution, and accidents.	Includes worldwide scientific, medical, and technological developments, natural phenomena, U.S. weather, and natural disasters.	Includes the arts, religion, scholarship, communications media, sports, entertainment, fashions, fads, and social life.

		World Affairs	Europe	Africa & The Middle East	The Americas	Asia & The Pacific

Jun. 2

World Affairs: A second Briton vanishes in China. The officer was sent to find a colonel held by the Japanese, and fails to report to duty. . . . Cuba orders the Saint Louis liner with 917 German Jewish refugees to go back.

Europe: Britain feels confident about Soviet aid. Russian Premier Molotoff's speech causes concern, but his objections are not thought to be insuperable. . . . The Czech police are patient as Fascists march. A crowd of 1,000 watches 50 marchers. . . . Envoys in Russia see hope of a pact. They expect an alliance with Britain and France. . . . Italians complete their withdrawal from Spain. . . . Italy adopts a bill about Jewish surnames and declares all racist clauses in testaments invalid. . . . The Soviet speech reassures Japan, allaying fears of a Russian-German alliance. . . . Nazis occupy Salzburg palace. The Elite Guard flag is hoisted over church property. . . . The Reich guarantees the Yugoslav border.

Asia & The Pacific: Japanese Ambassador Kensuke Horinouchi gives an open-door pledge, saying the nation has no intention of restricting Far East trade.

Jun. 3

World Affairs: The Chinese representative to the League of Nations says Japan plans to sell $300 million in Chinese dollars in opium annually. . . . Argentina, Paraguay, and Mexico shut their borders to 304 German Jewish refugees. . . . The Soviet Union leads capitalist countries in its population increase rate.

Europe: Britain delays Aland Island fortification plans after the Soviet Union protests. . . . Rome leaves war materials in Spain against a former agreement. Britain ignores Italy's broken promise. . . . The Czechs fear a fresh move by the Reich. Tension about direct annexation abound. . . . Hitler displays his army for the Prince Paul Regent of Yugoslavia.

Africa & The Middle East: Twelve die as terror in Palestine rages. British soldiers and Jewish policemen were shot to death in an ambush in the Sharon Valley. Four bombs exploded in Jaffa, killing five Arabs.

Jun. 4

World Affairs: The Reich obtains a Bolivian air base in an arms exchange. Germany will receive raw materials. . . . All U.S. Senators and spouses will receive an invitation to the garden party with British royalty. . . . The Saint Louis tries to land in Florida and is turned away.

Europe: Nazis seek a Catholic truce. The pressure of foreign affairs is believed to cause a lull in attacks on the Church. . . . The Czech resistance disturbs Germany. . . . Danzig Nazis boycott Polish officials. . . . Soviet pressure on the Aland Island issue perturbs Finns. . . . Austrian Jews seek an exodus. Two hundred leave daily, but 200,000 still remain.

Jun. 5

World Affairs: The Saint Louis refugee ship idles off the Florida coast. German Jews aboard await news.

Europe: The Reich predicts a British-Soviet pact. Berlin hesitates on the agreement until the terms are known. . . . French Premier Edouard Daladier denies the encircling plan, and is hopeful for a Soviet pact. . . . Hitler likens the British goals to 1914 and is defiant about an encirclement policy. . . . The Soviets demand more work and less talk. Conferences during working hours are banned in Moscow.

The Americas: San Juan, Puerto Rico, expects a new air base soon.

Asia & The Pacific: China orders the execution of all poppy growers. A bonfire of confiscated opium celebrates the 100th anniversary of the Opium War.

Jun. 6

World Affairs: Cuba opens its doors to German Jewish refugees, offering them temporary refuge in exchange for a bond of $500 each, and guarantees that the refugees will not become burdens.

Europe: Soviet tactics disturb Finns, who prefer collaboration with Sweden to the Anglo-Russian pledge. . . . The German Minister of the Interior Dr. Wilhelm Frick visits Hungary and hears the troubles of Nazis. . . . A man fires a shot at the Duchess of Kent. The suspect is held and a weapon found. . . . Spaniards tackle post-war tasks, creating labor syndicates. . . . The Suez Canal Company rejects an Italian demand for representation in canal management.

Jun. 7

World Affairs: Cuba recloses its doors to Jewish refugees, citing a 48-hour limit on the offer expires. . . . The head of the Irish Republican Army travels to the United States. He denies the visit was timed to match that of the King and Queen of England, but the United States still detains him in a cell. . . . Pope Pius XII seeks to bar Soviets from a pact, and moves to improve relations between democracies and dictatorships. . . . Eight German Jews take poison in a ship off Egypt after three countries reject them.

Europe: France names Gen. G.M. Gamelin Supreme Commander of defense forces. . . . The Baltic states are firm in barring a pledge, insisting upon neutrality. . . . Hitler hails the efforts of German soldiers in Spain as a lesson to foes and derides encircling enemies.

Africa & The Middle East: Tel Aviv is cut off as 14 Arabs die; Britain takes a 24-hour punitive step against the city.

Asia & The Pacific: China progresses in the areas it rules with better transportation, farms, and industry.

A
Includes developments that affect more than one world region, international organizations, and important meetings of world leaders.

B
Includes all domestic and regional developments in Europe, including the Soviet Union.

C
Includes all domestic and regional developments in Africa and the Middle East.

D
Includes all domestic and regional developments in Latin America, the Caribbean, and Canada.

E
Includes all domestic and regional developments in Asian and Pacific nations (and colonies).

U.S. Politics & Social Issues	U.S. Foreign Policy & Defense	Economics & Great Depression	Science, Technology & Nature	Culture, Leisure & Lifestyle	
Pediatricians call the "baby deficit" alarming, noting the lowest birth rate in the nation's history. . . . A former assemblyman faces bribery charges. The jury is complete for Edward Moran's trial. . . . Indicted judge George Martin denies bribery charges. . . . Major General George Moseley tells the House Committee on un-American Activities that U.S. Jews who identify with "world Jewry" should be forbidden from public office.		Business leaders ask President Franklin Roosevelt his views on private capital and plans for recovery. . . . A House group votes three major wage act changes.		Heavyweight boxer Lou Nova celebrates after knocking out Max Baer. "Bring on Joe Louis" is the victory cry. . . . The Yankees coach says Lou Gehrig is going to the Mayo Clinic as a "sick man," but Gehrig calls that a rumor. . . . The American League chooses Connie Mack as its All-Star manager.	Jun. 2
Rear Admiral Richard Byrd urges the United States to protect rights in Antarctica. . . . The 10th Roosevelt grandchild is born prematurely, and dies. . . . New York Mayor Fiorello LaGuardia acts to end nudity at the World Fair, and orders an inquiry over his jurisdiction.				Danes exhibit a 3,000-year-old trumpet at the World Fair that was used to call to war or rites in the Bronze Age.	Jun. 3
A jury finds Judge Martin innocent of fixing the outcome of an abortion case. . . . A foe of married women with jobs issues a debate challenge to First Lady Eleanor Roosevelt, arguing a duplication of jobs within a family creates a poor economy. . . . The son of President Roosevelt asks the public's opinion of a third term via radio broadcast. . . . Backers of Vice President John Garner assert his name will be introduced as a presidential candidate in 1940, even if Roosevelt seeks a third term.		New York school officials find that 50 percent of high school dropouts leave school to get jobs to help support their family.		Fans discuss a 12th-inning triple play executed by the Dodgers' baseball team. . . . Mayo Clinic doctors examine Lou Gehrig.	Jun. 4
Exiles' woes move the American Writers Congress. The audience stands with bowed heads as the names of 45 writers killed in fascist countries are read. . . . A jury convicts Judge Manton on selling justice. Three thousand cases may be reopened. . . . The Parks Department removes World War I memorials from trees, which impede their growth. . . . Puerto Rico asks for U.S. statehood.					Jun. 5
A special prosecutor may ask the governor to remove the judge acquitted of bribery and conspiracy charges. . . . States may still ratify the Child Labor Law amendment to the Constitution, even though it was proposed 15 years ago. . . . The Supreme Court overrules a ban on CIO meetings as a violation of free speech and free assemblage. . . . Isolationists lose the neutrality debate. A House Committee bars a curb on the President's discretion in finding that war exists abroad.				The World Fair Committee picks a New York Times editor as the Woman of 1939. . . . John Barrymore returns to the stage after his heart attack and gives a lively performance.	Jun. 6
Law enforcement seizes the Binghamton mayor while he is in the hospital. He is indicted on 18 extortion counts. . . . A court fines the head of an escort service. He is guilty of operating without a license. . . . The Supreme Court ruling on the CIO pleases President Roosevelt, who sees civil liberties protection strengthened. . . . President Roosevelt does not comment on running for a third term.		At a House Appropriations Committee inquiry, former Communists charge that "Reds" are stirring unrest among the jobless. One testifies that Soviets taught him "street fighting."		Young men from five continents light YMCA Friendship Fires at the World Fair. . . . Fair police accuse a showman of deliberately losing his python as a publicity stunt.	Jun. 7

F
Includes elections, federal-state relations, civil rights and liberties, crime, the judiciary, education, healthcare, poverty, urban affairs, and population.

G
Includes formation and debate of U.S. foreign and defense policies, veterans affairs, and defense spending. (Relations with specific foreign countries are usually found under the region concerned.)

H
Includes business, labor, agriculture, taxation, transportation, consumer affairs, monetary and fiscal policy, natural resources, pollution, and accidents.

I
Includes worldwide scientific, medical, and technological developments, natural phenomena, U.S. weather, and natural disasters.

J
Includes the arts, religion, scholarship, communications media, sports, entertainment, fashions, fads, and social life.

	World Affairs	Europe	Africa & The Middle East	The Americas	Asia & The Pacific
Jun. 8	The British press is agog at the King's U.S. visit. Staff is kept overtime to handle dispatches about the trip. . . . A Japanese flier derides the Soviet air force, saying fights are "one-sided." . . . British royalty help lay the cornerstone of the new Niagara bridge. An electric beam senses their car and releases balloons. . . . Japan predicts the quick participation of the United States in war. . . . Japan threatens neutrals in China, Foreigners are warned after a Briton is killed. . . . U.S. House members may refuse to greet the King and Queen unless the IRA head Sean Russell is released from jail.	Estonia and Latvia sign nonaggression pacts with Germany. . . . Germany deports more Polish Jews.		Mexican students riot outside the U.S. Embassy over the death of aviator Francisco Sarabia, who crashed near Washington yesterday.	India's leader Mohandas Gandhi expresses surprise that his favorite drink contains alcohol. A teetotaler, he will have the drink, Nira, tested.
Jun. 9	The Roosevelts and the British royalty make a historic drive to the White House. Negro spirituals and cowboy songs are part of the program.	Nazis close schools and theaters and impose curfews in the Prague area after a German police officer is slain. . . . The Reich shows guns to Spanish guests. Franco's troops are being trained on the German model. . . . Britain's Foreign Secretary Halifax says Germany can gain living space through negotiations rather than by attacks on neighbors.			In Nanking, poisoned wine at the Japanese Consulate causes two deaths. Eighteen others are sickened. Two Chinese cooks have disappeared.
Jun. 10	The U.S. welcome of the royalty amazes the British. Joseph Kennedy calls the handshake between the King and President Roosevelt the most important of modern times. . . . Queen Elizabeth sees the U.S. press, including women, as setting a precedent. . . . The Reich press scoffs at the British royalty's U.S. visit.	German police jail 1,000 Czechs as further punishment for the slaying of a Nazi police officer, and a fine of 500,000 crowns is imposed on the Kladno district. . . . Jews ordered out of Germany seek aid. . . . Small bombs in British mail hurt postal workers. Irish terrorists are suspected.	Police arrest a Jerusalem bomber. A Jewish woman is seized after placing an explosive among Arabs.		
Jun. 11	The Reich press pictures the King and Queen of England enduring bad manners and painful music in the United States.	Prime Minister Neville Chamberlain perseveres in his attempt to bring Soviets in line with the Stop-Hitler powers. Common danger makes the British-Soviet alliance likely. . . . Germans slay Czech police in a new incident. The local version describes an unprovoked attack. . . . Finland is anxious, fearing a Soviet attempt to end its independence. . . . Hitler sounds a note of deepening impasse. Germans cling to the hope that he will not risk war. . . . Many Jews stay in Germany. Although anxious to leave, they have no hope of finding haven.		As Francisco Sarabia's body is flown to Mexico, 200,000 mourners gather at the airfield.	An air raid kills 500 people in Chengtu, when 27 Japanese planes drop bombs. The West China Union University, an Anglo-American-supported school, was hit and students were killed. . . . Chungking, the capital city, was also bombed heavily. A 1,000-pound bomb hit the German Embassy. . . . Japanese keep their mainland armies. The chief forces are to be kept on the continent, not at home.
Jun. 12	The Roosevelt administration calls the British royal visit a world lesson, and hints to aggressors that peace is best. . . . The King of England tries a hot dog at the U.S. World Fair and asks for more. He also drinks beer. . . . Pope Pius XII sees the rescue of Christian ideas by Franco's troops, saying they fought to defend faith and gave him immense consolation. . . . A Reich editor gibes President Roosevelt on the royal visit, saying the trip was scheduled before Hitler wrecked his leadership. . . . The Spanish press opposes U.S. adoptions of Spanish refugee children, calling it kidnapping.	Czech policy causes a Nazi rift, reports say. . . . Jewish refugees who are refused by Cuba ask British Prime Minister Neville Chamberlain for refuge. . . . Soviet jockeying over a pact has Germany on edge. . . . Hungary's Parliament meets, and the Nazis present a program of anti-Jewish laws and land redistribution.	Archaeologists unearth an ancient factory town called Ezion-geber. The smelting and refining facility is believed to have been built by the Biblical King Solomon. . . . Military and police search Jewish homes in Jerusalem. They hunt for firearms and clues to the latest outrage.		Japanese forces capture cities in Shansi province.
Jun. 13	The German press reports that Jewish reporters in the United States are pleased with the British royal visit. Britain has mixed feelings about the visit, Germany says. . . . The British envoy in China, Ambassador Sir Archibald Clark Kerr, receives a death threat. Troops guard him in Shanghai.	Hungary plans to take Jewish land. The expropriation of 500,000 acres will be given to peasants for farmland. . . . The Reich will draft all girls under age 25 for farm labor. . . . Spain is held to be the center of peril in Europe. . . . Czechs irritate Nazi officials by using radios to aid passive resistance.	A Jewish girl gets a life sentence in Palestine. She is convicted of placing a bomb in a prison.		The Chinese War Minister Ho Ying-chin says Japan has lost 864,500 men to war. Invaders can no longer gain, he says, adding the Japanese have a "helpless" feeling.

A	B	C	D	E
Includes developments that affect more than one world region, international organizations, and important meetings of world leaders.	*Includes all domestic and regional developments in Europe, including the Soviet Union.*	*Includes all domestic and regional developments in Africa and the Middle East.*	*Includes all domestic and regional developments in Latin America, the Caribbean, and Canada.*	*Includes all domestic and regional developments in Asian and Pacific nations (and colonies).*

U.S. Politics & Social Issues	U.S. Foreign Policy & Defense	Economics & Great Depression	Science, Technology & Nature	Culture, Leisure & Lifestyle	
Attorney General Frank Murphy calls Alcatraz a "place of horror," and says the prison exercises vicious psychology on inmates. . . . A court acquits a wealthy bookmaker. New York Mayor Fiorello LaGuardia, enraged, orders him seized, calling him "no good" and a "punk." . . . An authors' agent receives a Sing Sing jail sentence for $30,000 in thefts from clients. . . . Quakers issue refugee facts and seek to dispel fears. A low German immigration total and high Christian percentage are stressed. . . . Witnesses tell the Senate that labor uses new forms of spying.	The House Foreign Affairs Committee halts a neutrality move.	An investigator tells a House Committee that the WPA runs a "unionism school." . . . A survey urges an immigration curb during economic downturns.		Foreign nations express bitterness over labor rows at the World Fair. Fifty-eight say they will not return next year unless the problems are fixed. . . . The baseball commissioner says first basemen violated the rule about glove size. . . . Switzerland refuses to stage the 1940 Winter Olympics unless the full ski program is reinstated. A new site may be needed and Germany is the likely choice.	Jun. 8
New York Mayor Fiorello LaGuardia signs a bill forbidding teachers from holding more than one job.				Actress Katharine Hepburn awakens to find a burglar with her gems. She chases him out of the house. . . . The Swiss must agree to International Olympic Committee rules by noon tomorrow or lose their hosting opportunity.	Jun. 9
The American Association of the Blind provides funds for 260 young blind German Jews to come to the United States. . . . A crowd at the Capitol greets British royalty. The British King places a wreath on the U.S. Tomb of the Unknown Soldier. . . . A Federal Circuit Court of Appeals rules that Hitler has rights to *Mein Kampf*.				German-born Marlene Dietrich becomes a U.S. citizen. . . . London receives the 1944 Olympics hosting honor. . . . Switzerland rejects the 1940 Winter Olympics, which are moved to Germany.	Jun. 10
A psychologist says that shaming children is the weakest tactic in improving behavior. Clear thinking and explaining work much better. . . . Hollywood prepares for the worst as the Attorney General says that six or seven of the biggest men in film face indictment for income tax fraud. . . . The Ku Klux Klan names a former veterinarian as its new chief.	The U.S.S. *Hammann*, the newest destroyer, meets its Navy test, responding perfectly.	Food surpluses spur the food stamps experiment. Overproduction plagues agriculture while the government searches for a solution.		Actor Henry Fonda is in a Panama hospital with a high fever.	Jun. 11
Catholics fight against anti-Semitism, forming a committee to press Christian teachings against racial bigotry. . . . A Yale University professor calls hatred the foe of democracy. Anti movements are deplored as a blow to Americanism.	A chaplain calls 456 new West Point Army officers to dedicate their lives to commission and to defend the nation in times of crisis. . . . The Harvard University president says the United States should identify which islands are so important to national security that the nation will fight to defend them. . . . The neutrality issue is first on the Congressional list.	Union leader Max Zristcky asks President Roosevelt to make another attempt to negotiate peace between the AFL and CIO.		Ten thousand attend the dedication of the Baseball Hall of Fame in Cooperstown, N.Y.	Jun. 12
The U.S. Secretary of the Interior Harold Ickes warns 3,000 foreign-born residents to beware of native "lunatics" who want dictatorship for their country, calling them parlor brutalitarians.		The chairman of the Social Security Board Arthur Altmeyer asks for funds distribution to the states to be based on wealth. He says the present system has caused wide differences among states.	A proposed American Museum of Health would continue to showcase health-related World Fair exhibits.	The Baseball Hall of Fame inducts new members.	Jun. 13

F	**G**	**H**	**I**	**J**
Includes elections, federal-state relations, civil rights and liberties, crime, the judiciary, education, healthcare, poverty, urban affairs, and population.	*Includes formation and debate of U.S. foreign and defense policies, veterans affairs, and defense spending. (Relations with specific foreign countries are usually found under the region concerned.)*	*Includes business, labor, agriculture, taxation, transportation, consumer affairs, monetary and fiscal policy, natural resources, pollution, and accidents.*	*Includes worldwide scientific, medical, and technological developments, natural phenomena, U.S. weather, and natural disasters.*	*Includes the arts, religion, scholarship, communications media, sports, entertainment, fashions, fads, and social life.*

	World Affairs	Europe	Africa & The Middle East	The Americas	Asia & The Pacific
Jun. 14		The Gestapo chief Heinrich Himmler arrives in Prague. The visit is linked to the deaths of two policemen. Unrest continues. . . . Franco will visit Italy in September. The plans give rise to talk that the tie with the Axis will be signed. . . . Franco arrests 247; 26 are women. . . . The German parish of Rev. Martin Niemoeller, defies Nazis. Two thousand gather to reject the new pastor and charge persecution. . . . Belgium, France, Britain, and the Netherlands assure temporary refuge for 907 German Jewish refugees on a ship.	Seven bombs shake Tel Aviv. Five Arab villagers are slain by gunmen.		Japan starts an economic blockade of Tientsin today. Japan warns Britain it must change policy and cooperate wholeheartedly.
Jun. 15	Britain considers reprisals for the Japanese blockade, and weighs closing its ports to Japan. France would aid but Germany is feared. . . . The Japanese tighten the Tientsin cordon and warn Britain that the blockade will increase until it cooperates. . . . The Japanese army is ready to move if Britain retaliates. The clash increases the belief in Japan that Britain is the ultimate enemy, barring the way to victory in China. . . . The Reich releases a U.S. youth imprisoned after writing a short verse mocking the National Socialist Party. He is escorted out of the country.	A British genealogist says Queen Elizabeth is related to George Washington and Robert E Lee. . . . Czechs fear that Nazis will take over Slovakia. They believe Germans may take over the police and jail key figures. . . . Germany vigorously denies plans to seize Slovakia.	Palestine will admit 7,850 Jews by October 1. The schedule "deducts" those who entered illegally.		Japan threatens a rift in Szechwan. Pamphlets are dropped warning people not to help Chiang Kai-shek or else face more raids.
Jun. 16	An international tribunal judges Germany guilty of fraud, sabotage, and collusion in the Black Tom and Kingsland disasters of 1916 and 1917. The decision is believed to be the first in history by which a major power is convicted of fraud by an international justice. Germany has already announced that it will ignore the decision. . . . Britain demands an end to the blockade of Tientsin. Japan tightens the quarantine. . . . The U.S. public favors a Japanese boycott. Sympathy to China rises. . . . The United States may mediate the blockade issue among Japan, Britain, and France.	British Prime Minister Neville Chamberlain forms a Department of Foreign Office to spread news. . . . Hitler takes over the Reichsbank. Under a new reorganization, foreigners are barred from holding shares. . . . Spain will "purify" its press. Journalists must report what they wrote for the Republican cause in the civil war.			
Jun. 17	Rights of U.S. citizens stand in the Tientsin blockade region. The Japanese are wary, but trade is permitted. . . . The Reich rejects the international Black Tom ruling. Germany is not bound by the decision, they say. . . . Italy backs Japan on the blockade issue. . . . Tientsin suffers a food shortage. British warships are said to have been ordered to rush food. . . . The United States defers taking a stand on the blockade, sympathetic to Britain and France but undecided on the course of action.	German Nazis set a goal of four children per family, minimum, saying some mothers may be too lazy, but they owe this responsibility to the nation. . . . The last public execution takes place in France. Eugen Weidmann is guillotined for murder.			
Jun. 18	U.S. Admiral Harry Yarnell travels to Tientsin. . . . The British hold off the Japanese in a Shanghai clash.	Britain combats Germany's encirclement cry. Extensive propaganda is planned. . . . Czechs and Slovaks are deeply stirred. Bitterness and contempt mark their attitude toward Germany. . . . A Danzig shift is inevitable, Nazi minister Joseph Goebbels says. No power can bar the inevitable union with Germany. . . . France guards against Spain, fearing a possible attack by Franco's men.		A fascist influence is seen in the Mexican fracas. The Salvation Party is charged with stirring people up against democracies.	
Jun. 19	Britain believes Japan has second thoughts on pushing a showdown. . . . The wife of Chiang Kai-shek warns the United States on China's woes, calling on the United States to take a stand against aggression. . . . Tientsin and Danzig stop British-Soviet pact talks.	A Danzig fête draws disguised visitors. Nazis and Poles gather in the city. Nazi minister Joseph Goebbels reiterates that the territory is German. . . . An Italian naval ship is set to cruise to the Orient. Britain's isolation is seen. . . . Reich troop movements continue in Slovakia. Soldiers are sent to secret camps on the Polish border.			Chiang Kai-shek has the remains of Genghis Khan taken to China to protect from Japanese seizure.

A	B	C	D	E
Includes developments that affect more than one world region, international organizations, and important meetings of world leaders.	Includes all domestic and regional developments in Europe, including the Soviet Union.	Includes all domestic and regional developments in Africa and the Middle East.	Includes all domestic and regional developments in Latin America, the Caribbean, and Canada.	Includes all domestic and regional developments in Asian and Pacific nations (and colonies).

U.S. Politics & Social Issues	U.S. Foreign Policy & Defense	Economics & Great Depression	Science, Technology & Nature	Culture, Leisure & Lifestyle	
A jury convicts an "immigration consultant" of fraud, who supposedly helps deportables get citizenship. . . . A judge reveals that several witnesses and defendants in a garment racket case have been murdered. Many others have disappeared. . . . Authorities find the body of a man burned alive. They believe he may have been a witness for a racket investigation.	The House gets the Neutrality Bill that Roosevelt favors. Citizens would be barred from belligerents' ships and from helping to finance war.	Reports reach Congress that Roosevelt will demand tax revenue to cover the farm bill outlay, which is $400 million over budget. . . . Mass fistfights break out at a strike of General Motors in Flint, Mich. Two are seriously hurt as CIO men go through AFL picket lines. . . . Importers attempt to amend customs "reign of terror" processes. The agents' efficiency is judged by the fine collected, they say.		The Dominican Republic will exhibit a bust of Christopher Columbus at the World Fair that was discovered in a garage. . . . The scope of television is very limited, radio makers say. Many problems are unsolved, so they advise against false hopes.	Jun. 14
The New York governor approves an end of the lunacy board. He vetoes a bill that would allow judges at will to commit suspects as insane.		Herbert Hoover asserts that jobs can be found for all, once Roosevelt's policies are stopped.		Charlie Chaplin directs that receipts from his film *The Great Dictator* should aid refugees.	Jun. 15
A Father Divine "Angel" buys an exclusive mansion in New Rochelle, N.Y. The white woman follower of the African-American preacher gains title to the property. Neighbors are aghast as carloads of disciples arrive.	Twenty-one Senators sign a declaration opposing President Roosevelt's stand on neutrality.	A CIO union asks for an AFL injunction, charging a boycott on CIO-made products. . . . First Lady Eleanor Roosevelt pleads for the country's youth, declaring their difficulty in finding jobs a government problem.			Jun. 16
A court fight looms over Father Divine's Angel. Neighbors to her new property plan action to oust the "Negro Cult." . . . The FDA seizes 40,000 lipsticks said to contain poisonous or deleterious substances.		The House votes on the 1940 relief bill with drastic WPA control, 373–21. The bill cuts a federally funded theater. . . . President Roosevelt favors a broader tax base. He says a levy on smaller incomes would not balance the budget, but would help citizenship.		An apparition of the Virgin Mary draws a big crowd, though it disappears when a priest changes the street light. . . . Japan sends a dog as a gift to Helen Keller. The author visited Japan two years ago to discuss how blindness is not punishment from gods.	Jun. 17
Marriage is not losing popularity, despite social changes. Although divorce is up, the majority stay wed. . . . Congressional adjournment is questionable without agreement about neutrality. . . . The New York governor assails Republican bills, charging manipulation. . . . Justices clear Buggsy Goldstein and Seymour Magoon of conspiracy and coercion charges.			An inventor patents the "traffic-scope" to prevent head-on crashes. The device allows the driver to see over hills via a prism. . . . Scientists can now clock the speed of lightning and analyze its spectacular habits.	Sigmund Freud publishes a book on Jewish religion, *Moses and Monotheism*. . . . Lou Gehrig leaves for a cruise. The Mayo Clinic refuses to discuss his test results. . . . Blind and deaf, Helen Keller asks a pilot if their altitude is 8,000 feet. She is exactly right.	Jun. 18
					Jun. 19

F	**G**	**H**	**I**	**J**
Includes elections, federal-state relations, civil rights and liberties, crime, the judiciary, education, healthcare, poverty, urban affairs, and population.	*Includes formation and debate of U.S. foreign and defense policies, veterans affairs, and defense spending. (Relations with specific foreign countries are usually found under the region concerned.)*	*Includes business, labor, agriculture, taxation, transportation, consumer affairs, monetary and fiscal policy, natural resources, pollution, and accidents.*	*Includes worldwide scientific, medical, and technological developments, natural phenomena, U.S. weather, and natural disasters.*	*Includes the arts, religion, scholarship, communications media, sports, entertainment, fashions, fads, and social life.*

	World Affairs	Europe	Africa & The Middle East	The Americas	Asia & The Pacific
Jun. 20	Britain withholds retaliatory acts and hopes that Tokyo will curb its army. . . . Tokyo is reluctant to state its claims. The foreign office is apparently waiting for an offer of cooperation with China.	The Italian chief of staff is in Albania, set to push military plans aimed at the Balkans. . . . Five hundred of the German Jewish refugees stranded on a ship are on their way to temporary homes in England and France.			
Jun. 21	The Axis backs Arabs in their freedom quest. The German foreign office announces its determination to support Near East peoples. . . . The Chinese envoy to the United States sees bluffing by the Japanese in the blockade and stresses that Britain has great interests to protect in China. . . . Japan stays firm on Tientsin curbs. The British Ambassador is rebuffed when he talks of the suffering of women and children.	France and Spain move toward an accord. The envoys of both nations say no Axis pact has been made. . . . Hungarian Nazis say they were forced to sign suicide notes in case they are "liquidated" after betraying secrets. . . . A Parisian sells a collection of Napoleon's letters to her sister, bringing in 513,200 francs.			
Jun. 22	Japan orders all foreign warships, including British and U.S. destroyers, to leave the Tientsin port. . . . British troops run the Japanese blockade and get food into Tientsin. France also helps. . . . The Japanese pursue an Italian ship into British waters and fire shots. . . . The former Czech minister to Britain stresses peril to U.S. librarians, urging them to safeguard free choice.	The British and French meet at Singapore. . . . Winston Churchill pledges aid to Prime Minister Chamberlain. The powerful critic of the Cabinet announces his full support of the new foreign policy. . . . The Reich curbs Czech Jews in trade. The Prague government is taken by surprise and tries to keep holdings from Germany. . . . Romania jails killers. Iron Guards receive sentences.		Canadians ask the United States to lead the world, saying that great power brings about great responsibility.	
Jun. 23	The Danish Prince seeks a divorce from an Italian Countess to marry the granddaughter of the U.S. railroad king, Jay Gould. . . . British in Tientsin report indignities. The Japanese force them to strip in public, they say, for examination. . . . The U.S. envoy says Greece is quietly building defenses. . . . Tokyo reports bringing down 49 Soviet planes, while losing five.	Nazi minister Joseph Goebbels reiterates his warning to Britain that central and southeast Europe is the territory of the Reich. . . . France and Italy dispute the Tunisia convention of 1896. . . . Nazis claim power to draft Czechs, and says that they can take direct control of industry in emergencies.		Canadians differ on participation in the Pan-American Union. This may hurt their friendship with the United States, some fear.	
Jun. 24	The German press calls the United States "agitators" after a U.S. admiral refuses to remove ships from Japan's blockaded area. . . . Japan continues insults in Tientsin. A New Zealand official is stripped and slapped. . . . The British King lauds the people of the North American continent upon his return home.	Danzig Nazis plan a military group. . . . France exceeds its plans for planes, now six months ahead of schedule. . . . France signs a pact giving Turkey the Hatay Republic. Signatories stress that days of conquest are over. . . . The British Foreign Minister Lord Halifax says if Germany wants war, they can have war. . . . Italy decrees the death sentence for money smugglers in an attempt to halt the currency flow abroad. . . . Madrid officials list 33 executed and say only 118 are sentenced to death. . . . The Soviet secret police arrest a stage director at his home at night. . . . Ireland outlaws the Republican Army. The ban names the group for the first time.			Japanese reactionaries with scant influence ask the Emperor to assert belligerent rights in China.
Jun. 25	Japanese tighten the Tientsin blockade. The French in the area suffer a food shortage. . . . Brazil will admit German refugees. Three thousand Catholics of Jewish descent will be given prompt entry. . . . Britain presses Japan for a reply to its Tientsin demands. . . . The Nazi press gloats at Britain's plight as more officials are forced to strip at Tientsin.	Four blasts in London terrify the crowd. Irish extremists are blamed as some are slightly injured by glass. . . . The British lay evacuation plans, including means for mass migration. . . . The Finnish envoy stresses neutrality, saying the country will not become a battlefield or springboard. . . . The French ban German propaganda at the border. . . . Italy hastens to utilize Albanian resources. . . . More "last Italians" will leave Spain soon. . . . Reich farmers receive electrical equipment. Power plants are assessed 35 million marks annually. . . . Slovaks end co-education and ask girls to marry rather than pursue careers.	The Syrian press whips the public into a fury over France signing the Hatay Republic to Turkey.		The Japanese navy closes Ningpo; an important Chinese port is lost.

A	B	C	D	E
Includes developments that affect more than one world region, international organizations, and important meetings of world leaders.	Includes all domestic and regional developments in Europe, including the Soviet Union.	Includes all domestic and regional developments in Africa and the Middle East.	Includes all domestic and regional developments in Latin America, the Caribbean, and Canada.	Includes all domestic and regional developments in Asian and Pacific nations (and colonies).

U.S. Politics & Social Issues	U.S. Foreign Policy & Defense	Economics & Great Depression	Science, Technology & Nature	Culture, Leisure & Lifestyle	
A woman who killed her husband with a hammer escapes the reformatory to have a "last good time." She leaves a three-page note to the reformatory head, telling of her aim. . . . A Kiwanis International speaker urges suppression of un-Americanism, favoring deportation of subversive aliens.	President Roosevelt insists on a Neutrality Bill. He demands a vote on the amendments before Congress adjourns.			Police arrest two Fair performers on nudity charges.	Jun. 20
A former Federal Circuit judge receives a two-year sentence after a futile plea. He also receives a $10,000 fine for selling justice. . . . A reporter asks President Roosevelt about a third term. The President tells him to stand in a corner, a slight variation from last year when he recommended a dunce cap for those asking the question. . . . The American Association of University Women hears a proposal of home training for women.	President Roosevelt warns of a neutrality snag. Congress can act more freely in peace, he says, than in wartime.	Actress Tallulah Bankhead asks the Senate Appropriations Committee for WPA aid for the stage. Her father, House Speaker William Bankhead, also a congressman, backs her but her uncle is in doubt. . . . The Citizens' Conference on Government Management contrasts a Mormon relief plan with that of the federal government. The Mormon church frowns on government subsidies.	Large-scale animal feeding experiments give scientists clues to diseases.	The Mayo Clinic diagnoses Lou Gehrig as having infantile paralysis. He will be forced to quit baseball, leaving fans shocked. He takes the verdict philosophically and remains as captain of the team.	Jun. 21
District Attorney Thomas Dewey investigates the finances of the actors' union, the American Federation of Actors, headed by Sophie Tucker. The accountant's report of relief funds is subpoenaed.			Seismograph records show that Bermuda tilts. . . . An archaeologist finds an Iroquois burial site said to be 500 years old. . . . Girls are 16 percent healthier than in 1904, a study shows.	The Dionne quints' doctor says the girls are never spanked. Instead they to go a quiet room to reflect on their sins.	Jun. 22
The high court backs the ill teacher rule. The school board keeps the right to refuse a license based on a teacher's health. . . . The Attorney General Frank Murphy endorses converting Alcatraz to a park. The rock is suitable for almost anything except a jail, he says. . . . The Attorney General is not seeking the vice presidency and says it is too early to comment on a third term for Roosevelt. . . . Franklin Roosevelt and Thomas Dewey are close in the presidential running, a survey indicates.		The AFL heads a move to save the auto union. They fear a return to the CIO. . . . The Senate passes a tax relief bill.		Messages pour in from fans to Lou Gehrig. He is amazed and cheered, but stays in the dugout to avoid demonstration.	Jun. 23
The U.S. birthrate raises for the second time in 20 years. The census bureau thinks the decline is now checked.	Democrats are split on the Neutrality Bill. Leaders expect defections to be offset by Republican support. . . . The Army changes the number of cadence steps from 128 to 120.	The director of Friends of Democracy says labor advocate Tom Mooney uses Communist statements in his post-prison sentence handouts.	Rear Admiral Richard Byrd persists in his Antarctica plan and will seek backing for a third exploration, if necessary.	The author of a book telling women how to be happy and single weds the head of a department store chain.	Jun. 24
Coca-Cola sues Nehi, Inc., asking them to stop calling Royal Crown a "cola." . . . A Dies Committee member asks for curbs on Communists and fascists, saying all "-isms" need to be exposed. . . . Administrative agencies rule increasing amounts of the nation's life and are called the fourth branch of government.		World Fair officials attack labor union practices. Excesses are attributed to the lack of sound business principles. . . . Psychologists propose better working conditions for household servants.	Sharp earthquakes rock the West Coast of the United States.		Jun. 25

F	G	H	I	J
Includes elections, federal-state relations, civil rights and liberties, crime, the judiciary, education, healthcare, poverty, urban affairs, and population.	*Includes formation and debate of U.S. foreign and defense policies, veterans affairs, and defense spending. (Relations with specific foreign countries are usually found under the region concerned.)*	*Includes business, labor, agriculture, taxation, transportation, consumer affairs, monetary and fiscal policy, natural resources, pollution, and accidents.*	*Includes worldwide scientific, medical, and technological developments, natural phenomena, U.S. weather, and natural disasters.*	*Includes the arts, religion, scholarship, communications media, sports, entertainment, fashions, fads, and social life.*

	World Affairs	Europe	Africa & The Middle East	The Americas	Asia & The Pacific
Jun. 26	The Japanese strip a married couple at Tientsin. British ire increases.	France hears the Reich army will attack Poland to stem unrest at home. Nazi acts are seen as a prelude to war. . . . The Reich opens a drive of "rights or war," taunting Britain. Citing Axis unity, Hitler says the future belongs to them. . . . Russia reports a big Mongol battle in which 120 planes are said to clash on the border.			
Jun. 27	Parlays to break the Tientsin deadlock begin in Tokyo. . . . Planes fight again on the Mongol border.	The president of Italy's Fascist Chamber dies of a heart attack. He was at one time believed to be Mussolini's successor. . . . Britain advances navy maneuvers to August to match Europe's danger period. . . . Finnish youth voluntarily build a stone wall on the Soviet border. . . . Germany discounts British war steps, saying conscripts require long training. . . . Italians hasten a road in Albania. They are ordered to finish a highway to the Balkans by August 31. . . . Hungary limits Jewish participation in schools, saying Jews cannot exceed 6 percent of total students.			The remains of Genghis Khan arrive at Sian for safety. A colorful cavalcade brings in the remains of the great conqueror.
Jun. 28	Germany issues an army call in the United States and says Germans aiming for naturalization might be seized if they go to Consulates. . . . Japan consents to a Tokyo parlay on the Tientsin issue. Both sides are anxious to end a dispute that threatens to lead to war.	French Premier Edouard Daladier fears a summer crisis. The situation is the worst in 20 years, he tells parliament. . . . Leaders proclaim Italy's war strength. The nation would win by lightning-fast strikes by valorous forces, military chiefs say. . . . The Nazi press is defiant 20 years after war. "Never again Versailles" is their slogan. . . . Poles shoot down a German plane near Danzig. A pilot who failed to heed a warning is saved by a Reich warship. . . . A Quaker denies Franco aides took food intended for refugee children, saying a few shipments were taken in confusion.	Six Arabs are hurt in a blast. A bomb is placed in an orphanage wall.		The Chinese retake Yuanku.
Jun. 29	Connoisseurs gather in Switzerland to bid on art banned by the Reich. . . . Earthquakes rumble in the Netherlands, Argentina, and Peru. . . . An open door in China is a world need, Chinese ambassadors say. Tokyo would use resources as a weapon of conquest. . . . Outer Mongolia is a Soviet guard. An estimated 250,000 well-trained men in the Republic bar the drive to isolate east Siberia.	Winston Churchill appeals to Hitler to pause. A rash move may undo the work of lifetimes, he warns. . . . Mussolini and Hitler meet, and air war plans are complete. . . . Nazis pour into Danzig to join the army. Young Poles are also active. . . . A Soviet prosecutor warns investigators that too many innocent people are arrested.	An attack on an Arab brings the closing of "Jew shops." A 48-hour closing in Jewish quarters is ordered for abetting terrorism.		
Jun. 30	Italy provides three submarines to Brazil in exchange for coffee and other products. . . . A Japanese officer minimizes results from the Tientsin parlay. He hints at a tighter blockade, but the situation is improving.	The Italian press ignores the situation in Danzig, only printing what the German press is saying. . . . Paris is alarmed that the Reich call for 600,000 men. Some reservists are said to be replacing those sent to Danzig. . . . Poland must keep its sea corridor and Danzig, the Polish president declares. . . . Britain is ready for war, Germany is warned. Poles would resist a coup. . . . Today is the deadline set by the Reich for emigration of all Jews in Berlin. Those remaining in Germany face concentration camps.	Leaders in Palestine deplore terror as 13 Arabs are slain. Two hundred moderates sign an appeal for the end of violence.	The Nicaraguan president Anastasio Somoza Garcia promises a Nicaraguan Canal.	
Jul. 1	The Reich asks the world to admit Danzig belongs to Germany. . . . A Soviet satirist ridicules the Japanese claim of huge Mongol air victories.	Britain sees no immediate German coup in Poland. The Cabinet will determine Polish aid to resist a "peaceful" Danzig seizure. . . . The Reich will hold Czech teachers responsible for anti-German acts of students. . . . The Reichsbank president Walther Funk warns the Reich against gloom; the war of nerves is telling in German businessmen. . . . Germans gibe at the British warning, saying London will not protect Danzig. . . . Spain reports a serious uprising. Civil guards are unable to pacify rebels.	Jewish cafes in Jerusalem are under curfew. One Arab is killed, and 11 injured by a bomb.		The Japanese destroy an American school, which was bombed in an offensive to capture a port.

A	B	C	D	E
Includes developments that affect more than one world region, international organizations, and important meetings of world leaders.	*Includes all domestic and regional developments in Europe, including the Soviet Union.*	*Includes all domestic and regional developments in Africa and the Middle East.*	*Includes all domestic and regional developments in Latin America, the Caribbean, and Canada.*	*Includes all domestic and regional developments in Asian and Pacific nations (and colonies).*

U.S. Politics & Social Issues	U.S. Foreign Policy & Defense	Economics & Great Depression	Science, Technology & Nature	Culture, Leisure & Lifestyle	
The American Bar Association criticizes prisons and judges; sentences are too often based on hunches, they say. . . . The National Woman's Party holds that bars to married women's employment are a step toward fascism. . . . Youth tar and feather a society columnist for the *Washington Times Herald*.	An Army enlisting drive sets a goal of 112,500.	Many on relief are not employable. One-third of households have no one who can work.	Lou Gehrig's case spurs medical research into his baffling disease. The hardening of his spinal cord is not really a form of infantile paralysis, as originally diagnosed.		Jun. 26
A third term boom for President Roosevelt is growing.	The Army begins building a base on Puerto Rico.	President Roosevelt's control of the dollar is voided. The Senate votes to remove the President's authority to further devalue the gold content of the dollar.	Soviet scientists revive plants after 20,000 years of deep freeze.		Jun. 27
				The Yankees show little enthusiasm for baseball under the lights. The ball seems to travel faster at night, they say.	Jun. 28
An elevator operator slaps a boisterous child who falls to the ground and dies. Murder charges are dropped when doctors say the youth died of a cerebral hemorrhage. . . . A married teacher loses a state plea in New York. The board of education backs the demand for information on her spouse's salary, termed reasonable if the husband and wife are both public employees.			The sun influences cosmic rays, scientists discover, providing a clue to magnetic storms.	The Yankees hoist the 1927 championship flag in honor of Gehrig. . . . Silent screen comedian Bobby Vernon dies of a heart attack at age 40. . . . Tony Galento provides exciting moments before losing a heavyweight bout to Joe Louis.	Jun. 29
A Bellevue worker says puppets are used as a psychiatric aid for children. They are an excellent safety valve for problem or maladjusted youth. . . . New York schools reopen their discussion of sex education. Unsolicited opinions indicate most favor instruction. . . . Tammany marks its 153rd birthday.	The Coast Guard takes over supervision of lighthouses, absorbing a 150-year-old service in a governmental reorganization.		Cosmic bullets make dust of atoms, experts say. They are the most destructive particles yet discovered.	Former heavyweight boxing champion Jack Dempsey undergoes a rush appendectomy. . . . Helen Keller "sees" the World Fair through her aide's eyes. Charmed, she promises to visit again. . . . Joe Louis leads praise for Tony Galento's boxing performance. . . . Rotary Clubs celebrate International Day. . . . Minors are still getting into nude shows at the World Fair, an official says.	Jun. 30
The Senate Immigration Committee reports on a proposed bill to shut out aliens for five years. Twenty thousand Reich children are to be admitted if care can be arranged. . . . The NAACP secretary says President Roosevelt has support from African Americans for a third term. . . . The new budget drops all psychiatric care at Sing Sing prison.		Cigarette sales soar on the eve of a new tax. Stores make special arrangements to handle crowds. Some lines are one block long. . . . President Roosevelt signs the relief bill, but condemns it as a hardship.	Scientists seek to harness radiation giants. A test will determine cosmic forces within atom nuclei.	Boxer Jack Dempsey fights post-surgery infection.	Jul. 1

F	G	H	I	J
Includes elections, federal-state relations, civil rights and liberties, crime, the judiciary, education, healthcare, poverty, urban affairs, and population.	Includes formation and debate of U.S. foreign and defense policies, veterans affairs, and defense spending. (Relations with specific foreign countries are usually found under the region concerned.)	Includes business, labor, agriculture, taxation, transportation, consumer affairs, monetary and fiscal policy, natural resources, pollution, and accidents.	Includes worldwide scientific, medical, and technological developments, natural phenomena, U.S. weather, and natural disasters.	Includes the arts, religion, scholarship, communications media, sports, entertainment, fashions, fads, and social life.

	World Affairs	Europe	Africa & The Middle East	The Americas	Asia & The Pacific
Jul. 2	France discounts war aid from the United States. . . . The Japanese tighten the Tientsin blockage and close an international bridge. . . . Princess Irene of Greece and Denmark marries a Duke. Italian Premier Benito Mussolini is a wedding no-show.	The Czechs try to see Hitler and persist in their efforts to submit grievances despite his rebuff. . . . Germans indicate their tactic in Danzig. The old slogan of "self-determination" will be invoked in the free city. . . . Nazis warn employers to hire older women, saying youthful charms do not guarantee the highest efficiency. . . . The Balkan states favor democracies, but feel pressure from the Axis.	Palestine deaths mount with 643 killed in the past six months. Bus lines close.	The U.S. Army creates a defense post in Puerto Rico.	The Chinese rely wholly on guerilla tactics. Burmese and Russian arms allow them to keep up the war. . . . The Japanese abandon a federal Chinese plan. Two regimes will exist.
Jul. 3	The Australian Prime Minister Robert Menzies vows to stand by Britain to its last man and last shilling, even if that means war. . . . A guard in Tientsin renews stripping. . . . The Japanese army claims the capture of Soviet tanks and arms in a land clash on the Mongol frontier.	An army of civilians parades in Britain. Twenty thousand march past the King and Queen in a display of auxiliary defense forces. . . . Nazis bid France to be neighborly and term Britain an inciter.			
Jul. 4	The Tokyo army sets a wide parley scope, saying Britain's entire China policy must change. . . . Brazil receives an apology. Spain regrets the attempt on the life of a retired ambassador. . . . Sixteen countries show gains in employment. The United States has more jobless than last year, and Britain sets a new low. . . . Japan reports that a force of invaders is surrounded and will be annihilated. Four thousand Mongols are said to be trapped. . . . Pope Pius XII shifts peace tactics and sees envoys of small nations.	The Reich derides a possible coup in Poland. Germany has no designs on Warsaw's integrity, they say. . . . The Reich censors dancing and also frowns upon vocals in foreign tongue. . . . The Soviet Union gives a reply to the new pact plan. The nature of the response is not revealed, but more talks with Britain and France are slated.			
Jul. 5	Britain rejects one Tokyo demand as it will not stop backing Chinese currency. . . . China's premier assails Japan as a world menace, linking its enemy to international gangsterism.	Armed forces at 10,000 in Danzig. The free city stays calm. . . . Britons urge a position for Winston Churchill. He is expected to become First Lord of Admiralty. . . . Italy holds aloof over the Danzig dispute. Premier Benito Mussolini may be pressuring Hitler not to drag him into war. . . . Reich commissioners will rule Czech towns. . . . The Reich resumes large war games. . . . The Soviets talk with Britain and France and hit as snag as The Soviets balk at aid to small states in the west. . . . The Tyrolese in Italy go to the Reich. An agreement with Germany is made to control movement from the ex-Austrian area. . . . Nazis assault the Archbishop of Vienna. He is attacked with eggs and epitaphs and struck on the head with a stick.			
Jul. 6	Germany ridicules President Roosevelt's stand on the arms embargo. They accuse him of intending to line up the United States in the encirclement front. . . . Japanese renew the threat at Tientsin. . . . Wounded Japanese jam hospitals. Soviets say 45 planes were felled.	The British deny pleas for aid for refugees and refuse to ease entry rules or provide public funds for Jewish settlements. . . . The Italian Foreign Minister Count Ciano will visit Franco. He is expected to bring up economic and military questions, provided they contribute to check Communism, the professed aim of the Axis. . . . Danzig trucking is heavy at night. Visitors are barred from some areas. . . . Hitler shortens his title to *Der Fuhrer.* He deletes *Reichskanzler* because it implies a politician, rather than a beloved leader. . . . In the Reich, the last remaining Jewish businesses must close.			The former Chinese premier Wang Ching-wei seeks to form a new political party. The foe of Chiang Kai-shek is said to be planning to head a puppet regime in Nanking.
Jul. 7	The AFL warns the International Federation of Trade Unions of a Soviet labor link. This may cause the U.S. organization to withdraw. . . . Japan assails Britain as an enemy. People mark the second anniversary of war in China with a smokeless, meatless, and drinkless day. . . . Moscow describes a big border victory. The Soviet press reports the repulse of the Japanese. . . . Chiang Kai-shek asks for a boycott of Japan. . . . The Rome press turns fire on President Roosevelt. His remarks are held to be Jewish inspired.	Britain extends credits to allies for arms. Poland is likely to get the lion's share. . . . A new British law will extend powers to curb Irish extremists. . . . Germany condemns British credit aid as a cold-blooded attempt to get European gains. . . . Poland asks the press to stay calm. The Danzig mobilization crisis is declared over. . . . The Reich makes Jews sign up for self care. All are placed in one organization, with speedier migration as the aim.	Syrian President Hashim Al-Arassi resigns.		Japan bombs Chungking again. An American hospital is struck, but patients escape. Most civilians are safely in dugouts.

A	B	C	D	E
Includes developments that affect more than one world region, international organizations, and important meetings of world leaders.	*Includes all domestic and regional developments in Europe, including the Soviet Union.*	*Includes all domestic and regional developments in Africa and the Middle East.*	*Includes all domestic and regional developments in Latin America, the Caribbean, and Canada.*	*Includes all domestic and regional developments in Asian and Pacific nations (and colonies).*

U.S. Politics & Social Issues	U.S. Foreign Policy & Defense	Economics & Great Depression	Science, Technology & Nature	Culture, Leisure & Lifestyle	
Father Divine's movement expands as followers buy up Hudson real estate in New York.		Congress opens the fight to take back powers. The New Deal seems to enter a new phase with the revival of contest with the executive. . . . Farm distress continues, and the conditions of the south's sharecroppers and plain states-families are cited. . . . The nation's jobless is under 10 million in May. . . . The New Deal will keep up the fight on money and neutrality.		His doctor says baseball manager Connie Mack is seriously ill. . . . The Negro National Baseball League honors its stars.	Jul. 2
First Lady Eleanor Roosevelt prasies contralto Marian Anderson, saying her gift transcends race.	Roosevelt signs the final Army bill. Over $223 million will be spent for planes and other defense needs.	The AFL opens the drive to unionize stores and contests CIO jurisdiction. . . . A strike move is near at General Motors. The CIO union and the company end negotiations.	A geneticist insists the chromosome, not the gene, holds heredity.	Gary Cooper will star in a film about the life of Judge Roy Bean.	Jul. 3
The American Youth Congress votes down an "anti-Red" resolution. . . . A judge rules that berating one's wife in private is not punishable. . . . Chinese in New York dedicate Callahan's Saloon on Bowery to the Chinese deity of mercy. The old thieves' den is now in the hands of gods. . . . A safer independence day is planned as the city curbs din. Fireworks are generally scarce.	President Roosevelt asserts the U.S. arms embargo increases war peril. He believes it encourages Hitler to use force in pressing demands.			At Yankee Stadium, Lou Gehrig announces his retirement from baseball.	Jul. 4
Fireworks injuries increase. . . . Boys playing leapfrog break Revolutionary War tombstones.	Engineers prepare short-wave radio to challenge the Axis for the airwaves. An increase in the power of German broadcasts had blanketed American efforts. . . . President Roosevelt urges the Senate to reverse the arms embargo.		Soviet scientists create a disease meter. The electrical apparatus aids in diagnosing cancer and tuberculosis. . . . World famous authorities link plant cells to human health and stress the need for vitamins in the human diet.		Jul. 5
		Coal producers seek to steady prices. They will meet to find ways to end demoralization in their markets. . . . Thousands are on a WPA strike over more work but less pay. Those staying out five days will lose their jobs.	Hospitals yield to the machine age. Horse-drawn ambulances are replaced by cars. . . . Life expectancy rises to a record 61.94 years.		Jul. 6
Congress studies the possibility of an Antarctic colony. Aviation bases are one aim. . . . U.S. Secretary of the Navy, Claude Swanson, dies.		The U.S. government adds seven more surplus commodities to the food stamp program. . . . An auto strike shuts four more plants. . . . The AFL orders the strike of 30,000 WPA men in defiance of Congress.		Nine thousand hear Lily Pons sing with the Philadelphia Orchestra. Thousands are turned away.	Jul. 7

F	G	H	I	J
Includes elections, federal-state relations, civil rights and liberties, crime, the judiciary, education, healthcare, poverty, urban affairs, and population.	Includes formation and debate of U.S. foreign and defense policies, veterans affairs, and defense spending. (Relations with specific foreign countries are usually found under the region concerned.)	Includes business, labor, agriculture, taxation, transportation, consumer affairs, monetary and fiscal policy, natural resources, pollution, and accidents.	Includes worldwide scientific, medical, and technological developments, natural phenomena, U.S. weather, and natural disasters.	Includes the arts, religion, scholarship, communications media, sports, entertainment, fashions, fads, and social life.

	World Affairs	Europe	Africa & The Middle East	The Americas	Asia & The Pacific
Jul. 8	Japanese air strikes bomb a British warship. . . . Chinese in the United States hail two years of resistance. . . . U.S. banks safeguard European funds. Individuals and concerns seek haven in case of war. . . . Japan pushes Mongolians back.	German Jews face a crushing task. The one-fourth with property or jobs must care for all, pending emigration. . . . The Reich closes three theological schools. A German magazine calls the study of theology useless.		Argentina opens a Nazi probe and will challenge subversive actions.	Chiang Kai-shek foresees victory in one year, saying the invaders' strength is waning.
Jul. 9	Brazil expels the Japanese. A court upholds a decree permitting the punishment of foreigners. . . . The International Federation of Trade Unions votes for a Russian ban, rejecting the British proposal for Soviet reentry. . . . Japan apologizes for bombing a British ship. Naval staff receive regrets for damage caused in a raid. . . . Tokyo claims a new Mongol rout. Land forces are said to be driven back.	A Czech bastion is secured. Germans take strong measures to hold the country in any future clash. . . . France will rule Syria by council. The constitution is suspended as the Presien'ts resignation terminates the local regime. . . . Eight thousand Germans go from Italy to the Reich. Italians of German descent may choose whether to leave Tyrol.		Chilean volcanoes erupt.	
Jul. 10	Mongolians face a suicide corps. The Japanese are poised for attack against a strong artillery.	Nazis oust Catholic nurses from hospitals. . . . Count Ciano, the Italian Foreign Minister leaves for Spain. A closer tie is expected. . . . A Nazi leader takes charge of Prague University. . . . London feels relief as war threat recedes. The stock market, dominated by world news, recovers on news of Danzig. . . . A Nazi leader hurls defiance in Danzig, telling mass meetings that Hitler will "liberate" the free city.	In Syria, Bahij-al-Khatib is appointed chairman of the Council of Commissioners, replacing the office of President.	An anthropologist reports that women of cults dominate the Brazilian jungle, and that priestesses rule 400,000.	
Jul. 11	Bolivia seeks the friendship of all, asking no special privileges. . . . The United States protests the Chungking raid and tells the Japanese envoy of its disapproval of bombing that menaced Americans.	Prime Minister Neville Chamberlain bars any coup in Danzig. His pledge is sweeping and loopholes are closed. . . . Festive Spain welcomes the Italian Foreign Minister, Count Ciano. The press denies that the visit presages a military pact with the Axis powers. . . . France and Britain unite their programs to meet the Axis threat to colonies. . . . Italy expels Tyrol foreigners. Those in the German-speaking area are told to leave within 48 hours.		An army leftist rebellion fails in Ecuador. . . . Chile foils a coup as troops swear allegiance.	Former Chinese premier Wang Ching-wei will lead a new political party. The Japanese herald the move.
Jul. 12	The Irish army orders munitions from the United States. The total value is put at $10 million. . . . Italy checks the Reich in resisting Pope Pius XII. The Axis nations pull in different directions with Vatican peace efforts. . . . The Japanese besiege Mongolian forces. Thousands attack 200 in a border attack. . . . Japan threatens a Shanghai cordon. The blockade of British industry is said to be part of its plan.	One hundred British bombers fly far over France and back without a hitch. . . . Strife occurs in Franco's ranks. Spaniards reach France with news of clashes. . . . Germany orders threshing machines sealed in Bohemia. Farmers are to take their harvest to supervision centers. . . . Troop moves are seen in Italy's ousting of aliens in Tyrol.		Brazilians discover diamonds in river beds dried up by drought.	
Jul. 13	The Japanese increase their threat to the British. Japanese warn that three more ports will be blockaded after Saturday. . . . The United States suspects the Tyrol oustings by Italy are an anti-spy move. Anxiety mounts as orders for expulsions are given by the secret police. . . . The Vatican extends papal indulgence by radio. Distant listeners can share equally with those present to receive benediction.	Franco and Italian Foreign Minister Count Ciano hold their first meeting, conversing for two hours at the Spanish palace. . . . Nazis resent the idea of Polish flight. They say neutral countries would hold the view of British assistance as a serious provocation. . . . The Reich orders all drivers to report the condition of their vehicles. Violations are punishable by imprisonment. . . . Newspapers hint that the Reich backs a new Balkan bloc. Plans for a virtual alliance of Bulgaria and Yugoslavia are reportedly taking shape.	Immigration of Jews to Palestine is stopped. No quota will be issued for six months starting October 1.		The Japanese birthrate is down because of war, with 304,319 fewer babies born.

A	B	C	D	E
Includes developments that affect more than one world region, international organizations, and important meetings of world leaders.	Includes all domestic and regional developments in Europe, including the Soviet Union.	Includes all domestic and regional developments in Africa and the Middle East.	Includes all domestic and regional developments in Latin America, the Caribbean, and Canada.	Includes all domestic and regional developments in Asian and Pacific nations (and colonies).

U.S. Politics & Social Issues	U.S. Foreign Policy & Defense	Economics & Great Depression	Science, Technology & Nature	Culture, Leisure & Lifestyle	
Thomas Dewey maps his 1940 presidential strategy, with quiet emphasis on publicity and vote-getting strength in interviews. . . . President Franklin Roosevelt orders speed on an Antarctic trip. Germany's move there spurs action to claim territory.			A Russian scientist unearths a Neanderthal skeleton. It is the first ever found in the region.	World Fair officials bar "adults only" signs at shows and forbid barkers to say children are excluded.	Jul. 8
	Cabinet officials urge Senators to repeal the arms embargo.		An explorer returns from the Guiana wilds and brings back a collection of rare animals.	The staff of 140,000 is ready to start its most ambitious inventory, the 1946 U.S. Census.	Jul. 9
The Solicitor General Robert H. Jackson warns the American Bar Association that the United States may cut the fees of lawyers. . . . The National Federation of Business and Professional Women's Clubs surveys new vistas in life for women and finds that prejudices are strong.					Jul. 10
The president of the American Bar Association tells a group that the Supreme Court is shifting. . . . Sophie Tucker, president of the American Federation of Actors, walks out of a courtroom. Testimony about the misuse of relief funds by union leaders continues.	A Senator asks for an open debate over neutrality and calls for an old-fashioned battle on the Senate floor.	The AFL assails Congress for ending the prevailing wage law. . . . The House and Senate receive new bills to undo WPA cuts. Equalized pay is studied. . . . . A jobless man insists that his wife quit work as a domestic. When she refuses, he shoots her, then commits suicide. . . . Many striking WPA workers face ouster. The first dismissals for five-day absences are due tonight. . . . Auto strikers win full picket terms.		Havelock Ellis, noted author, dies. The work of this pioneer of sex study was a target for censure early in his career.	Jul. 11
A broadcasting code cuts controversy. Time will not be sold for debatable issues, a national organization decides.	A Senate committee votes for delay on the neutrality issue.	President Franklin Roosevelt orders enforcement of the WPA act and the strike is extended. Roosevelt makes no move to encourage Congress to take steps to rescind cuts. . . . Women in business fight job curbs. The national federation favors a concerted move to oppose a ban on married workers.		A great-grandmother wins the grandmothers' bathing beauty contest at the World Fair.	Jul. 12
The Senate votes for a federal increase in pension share. The Social Security Act is revised so that the federal government pays on a 2:1 basis with states. . . . The Virginia Institute of Public Affairs urges propaganda and assails censorship, asserting the suppression of ideas leads to dictatorship.	United Spanish War Veterans ask for a new name. They wish for the insertion of "American" to distinguish themselves from veterans of Spain's civil war.	The AFL plans a fight over the WPA. The group urges the prevailing wage principle on Congress and the President. . . . A graphic arts group asks for a boycott of Nazi typefaces. . . . Coal picketers and National Guardsmen clash again in Kentucky. One miner dies.		Admission to the World Fair is cut for big groups. The rate is reduced from 75 cents per person to 50 cents for groups of 500. . . . The Ripley Odditorium opens in New York. The collection of curiosities can be seen by the public. . . . Baseball manager Connie Mack, still hospitalized, feels confident about an American League win in the All-Star game.	Jul. 13

F	G	H	I	J
Includes elections, federal-state relations, civil rights and liberties, crime, the judiciary, education, healthcare, poverty, urban affairs, and population.	Includes formation and debate of U.S. foreign and defense policies, veterans affairs, and defense spending. (Relations with specific foreign countries are usually found under the region concerned.)	Includes business, labor, agriculture, taxation, transportation, consumer affairs, monetary and fiscal policy, natural resources, pollution, and accidents.	Includes worldwide scientific, medical, and technological developments, natural phenomena, U.S. weather, and natural disasters.	Includes the arts, religion, scholarship, communications media, sports, entertainment, fashions, fads, and social life.

	World Affairs	Europe	Africa & The Middle East	The Americas	Asia & The Pacific
Jul. 14	Soviets list tolls in border battles with Japan. Both sides claim victory. . . . The Swiss hear that Germany will lease the port of Trieste from Italy for 10 years.	Czechs cut the telephone wires of the German army. The Reich issues a warning that further tampering will be severely punished. . . . Franco inspects defense lines on the coast near France. . . . Hungary lifts its press ban. The suspended Nazi party organ reappears with new editors. . . . Italy protests the French cession of Hatay to Turkey. . . . Italy marks its first year of racial policy. A paper holds that Jewish influence was purged without incident. . . . The Reich accuses the British Foreign Secretary Viscount Halifax of urging Germans to rise up against the government.	The immigration curb stirs Palestine and the press condemns the action.		
Jul. 15	A Japanese mob menaces the British Embassy in Tokyo. The Japanese press asks Britain to change its policy and cooperate with Japan in east Asia.	Britain announces broad preparations for civilian casualties, including hospitals and special huts. . . . Franco says Spain aims to remain neutral. . . . Rome denies leasing the Trieste port to Germany. . . . Nazis say Hitler is firm on Danzig and his determination to regain the free city is strengthened. . . . Prague jails its first couple in a "mixed marriage" case. A Jewish and non-Jewish pair are convicted on a race-shame charge. . . . Reich troops hold Czech iron works. Military police take control of industries vital to German armament.	Arabs praise the immigration ban on Jewish settlers.	Chile fights typhus. The health minister asks for public cooperation.	
Jul. 16	The Federation of Polish Jews in America buys a colony in Palestine. Five hundred Jewish families are to settle there.	All Tyrol Germans are to leave the province, which is to become 100 percent Italian per an agreement. . . . The Italian Foreign Minister Count Ciano is pleased with his visit to Spain. Thousands line the streets of Madrid. . . . French Premier Edouard Daladier cautions the press on spy news, warning against making political capital of government inquiry. . . . Italy faces a loss in the Tyrol move. Foreigners are leaving at the beginning of the tourist season.			
Jul. 17	Japan threatens a raid into Siberia.	Winston Churchill gains support in London. The Sunday press advocates his inclusion in government. . . . Police suspend Czech papers for three days. An article about speaking Czech is seen as a slight to Germany. . . . A British fascist urges ties to Nazis, saying Hitler would aid world disarmament in exchange for an Eastern Europe pact similar to the Monroe Doctrine.			
Jul. 18	U.S. food demand from Europe is forecast to rise. Military expansion is expected to increase the call for American products. . . . Orthodox Russians in the United States say Poles are razing their churches and charge them with the destruction of 400 edifices. . . . Lebanon admits refugee Jews after an epidemic breaks out on their ship. . . . The Tokyo press sees British submission and shows satisfaction over the first Tientsin talk.	Germany orders Czechs to despoil forests. Germany demands timber at a 150 percent rate of regrowth. . . . The Reich lists overeating as treason. The drain on food is a menace to independence, a public official says. . . . The Tyrolese fight evictions and 26 are reported killed.		Canadians celebrate their 75th year as a nation.	
Jul. 19		In Moscow, 35,000 athletes parade. Boys and girls in shorts and helmets demonstrate military fitness. . . . The British and Polish wrangle over terms of a loan that threatens to affect the alliance. . . . Two thousand Nazi guards arrive at Danzig. . . . Italy denies killings in Tyrol.	A Jewish strike in Palestine proceeds quietly. Guards are ready but no major disorders mark the gesture over the immigration ban.		The Japanese engage in a fierce drive to crush guerillas with 120,000 men attempting to subdue the Chinese.
Jul. 20	British take 50 lepers to a colony near Hong Kong.	The British try to curb Irish terrorism. The government asks for power to treat empire subjects as undesirable aliens. . . . Danzig seizes 20 men for a Marxist plot of anti-Nazi acts. The men face a treason trial. . . . Ruthenians resist the Hungarian regime. A guard detachment is ambushed and martial law is tightened. . . . Albanian King Zog says the fight goes on. He lives in exile in Sweden.			

A	B	C	D	E
Includes developments that affect more than one world region, international organizations, and important meetings of world leaders.	Includes all domestic and regional developments in Europe, including the Soviet Union.	Includes all domestic and regional developments in Africa and the Middle East.	Includes all domestic and regional developments in Latin America, the Caribbean, and Canada.	Includes all domestic and regional developments in Asian and Pacific nations (and colonies).

U.S. Politics & Social Issues	U.S. Foreign Policy & Defense	Economics & Great Depression	Science, Technology & Nature	Culture, Leisure & Lifestyle	
The Ameican Federation of Actors, headed by Sophie Tucker, denies the charge of misuse of relief funds.		Attorney General Frank Murphy sends men to watch the Harlan, Ky., coal picketers.			Jul. 14
Actress Fanny Brice asks for $750,000 and a ban on the further showing of *Rose of Washington Square*. She says the film defames her. . . . Senator Tracey C. Stagg commits suicide. Friends say he was worried about his health. . . . The American Federation of Actors loses its AFL charter when it is found guilty of misusing relief funds. Eddie Cantor will lead the new union.				The World Fair celebrates the birth of the French Republic. Pledges of liberty mark Bastille Day. . . . Iraq offers a world lesson in peace. Four Subeans, followers of John the Baptist who belong to a sect that has been warless for 1,500 years, show silver-making techniques at the World Fair.	Jul. 15
Congressional adjournment promises respite in Washington. The pre-election contest will continue, but with less heat and strain. . . . Trans-atlantic flying is now commonplace. Taking passengers by air to Europe has changed from a dream to a regular occurrence. . . . The court bans a dime edition of *Mein Kampf*, pending a copyright suit.			An early diagnosis of cancer is promised with a new antigen injection test.	English actress Vivien Leigh says she was sometimes told she sounded too Southern when filming *Gone With the Wind*. . . . The parents of six sets of twins plus another child arrive at the World Fair. One set of twins is named Franklin and Eleanor.	Jul. 16
Five hundred actors enroll in the new American Guild of Variety Artists. Sophie Tucker will contest the loss of her group's AFL charter. . . . A 60-year-old man marries a 16-year-old girl as police check a riot. The crowd chases the man into the church and the priest intervenes.		Labor hopes for $1 billion dollars for public works as WPA hopes fade. . . . The Harlan, Ky., coal battle takes its second life. A wounded miner dies despite a blood transfusion.			Jul. 17
First Lady Eleanor Roosevelt declines to participate in a debate over women's jobs. Her challenger states that married women should not be allowed to hold government positions. . . . The Michigan governor aims to reinstate Prohibition. . . . Baseball player Dizzy Dean says he scraped his arm reaching for the phone, denying a domestic squabble. . . . Police arrest a man who stole more than 1,000 items from the World Fair.		The WPA issues 2,000 pink slips to striking workers under police guard; thereafter, 2,500 are to be issued daily.	Dr. Cecilia Gaposchkin, an American scientist finds the brilliance of a supernova related to velocity.	The Chicago White Sox owner is critically ill. . . . Corset producers expect an increase in sales of 10–25 percent. Narrow waistlines are in style. . . . The Prince of India arrives in the United States for a World Fair tour. The absolute ruler is accompanied by many relatives and servants.	Jul. 18
				The owner of the Chicago White Sox dies of heart disease and pneumonia. . . . The Japanese dislike American hurry, says a Japanese member of the World Fair orchestra. He also says that jazz puzzles him.	Jul. 19
A Massachusetts group criticizes the First Lady, condemning her stand of supporting working women.		An agreement ends strife in Harlan, Ky. Miners and operators come to terms, each making concessions.	Herman Casler, the inventor of the biograph, an early moving pictures machine, dies. He exhibited the machine in 1896.	Edmund Heller, naturalist, dies. He is the joint author with Theodore Roosevelt on their Africa expedition.	Jul. 20

F	G	H	I	J
Includes elections, federal-state relations, civil rights and liberties, crime, the judiciary, education, healthcare, poverty, urban affairs, and population.	Includes formation and debate of U.S. foreign and defense policies, veterans affairs, and defense spending. (Relations with specific foreign countries are usually found under the region concerned.)	Includes business, labor, agriculture, taxation, transportation, consumer affairs, monetary and fiscal policy, natural resources, pollution, and accidents.	Includes worldwide scientific, medical, and technological developments, natural phenomena, U.S. weather, and natural disasters.	Includes the arts, religion, scholarship, communications media, sports, entertainment, fashions, fads, and social life.

	World Affairs	Europe	Africa & The Middle East	The Americas	Asia & The Pacific
Jul. 21	The American School headmaster leaves Berlin to enjoy liberty in the United States, seeking to avoid the Gestapo. . . . The Japanese press indicates the country's willingness to negotiate the border dispute with Russia. . . . The Japanese demand that the British surrender. The Tokyo parley reopens with threats to close it unless key points are met.	Hungary's attacks surprise Romania. Increasing tension is noted and the mayor is slain. . . . Italy breaks up Sicilian estates. The land will be irrigated; homes, roads, and villages built to host a larger population. . . . An estimated 100,000 Jews have quit Austria since German annexation. . . . A customs officer kills a Polish guard in the Danzig conflict. Tension increases and versions of the killing vary widely.			
Jul. 22	An American who was jailed in Germany returns to the United States after his arrest for writing doggerel in a beer hall. . . . The Chinese are indifferent to U.S. neutrality laws, believing that the old law was not followed and so the new one would not be, either. . . . Britain agrees to Japan's demand and the parley continues. . . . The Japanese navy threatens the Soviets. A fleet is assembled in northern waters, ready for action.	Germany expects the return of Danzig by peaceful measures, insisting that the free city be restored unconditionally. . . . Hungary seizes a book that predicts the German defeat in war. . . . Italy gives the rights of Trieste to the Reich. The invitation to use transshipping facilities is extended. . . . A Reich pastor dies in a prison camp. He is the first to be punished for fighting Nazi curbs on the church. . . . The Soviet Union constructs a submarine fleet.			
Jul. 23	Birthrates show a worldwide decline. Population increases are due to lower mortality rates. In every country, women live longer. . . . The Chinese worry about the direction of Japanese-British talks, and await a fuller report. . . . Britain agrees to recognize the need for the Japanese army in China. A formula is signed for the parley. . . . Nazis assail the British over China concessions.	It is reported from talks that former Spanish King Alfonso wishes to regain his throne. . . . Ambroise Vollard of Paris dies. He was an early patron of Cezanne, Degas, Renoir, and Rousseau. . . . Czechs may aid the Reich, the state President Emir Hacha says. The announcement causes a stir in predicting war loyalties, and the popular view is different. . . . Germany derides the British offer; overtures for economic appeasement draw raucous laughter. . . . Hungarian Slovaks will be "hostages." The treatment of minorities will be determined by the Budapest acts. . . . Italy again denies disorder in Tyrol. Independent investigation is impossible as the region is closed.			
Jul. 24	Hungary has a plan for the "Jewish problem." It will send them to the United States in exchange for Aryans. . . . Japanese soldiers beat a U.S. Navy man at Hankow. . . . Japan makes six demands on Britain; currency cooperation in China is among them.	The British Commons hears the Tokyo plan; little opposition is expected. . . . A Czech newspaper is banned from publishing for eight days. It criticized the new street names given by Germans. . . . Franco returns one-third of food seized from a refugee commission. . . . Prince Alexander is dead in Bohemia. He was a great friend of the Czechs and beloved by the poor. . . . The Reich admits a materials shortage that is sometimes so acute it threatens a standstill in production. . . . Turks mark the return of Hatay, and troops take over barracks.		In one ceremony 105 couples wed. A chorus of responses echoes in Montreal.	
Jul. 25	Argentina claims Antarctic land in the conflict with Britain and the United States. . . . Britain concedes to Japan the right to security in China, denying its belligerent status. . . . Japan is suspicious of the British course of action. . . . The Pope retires to his summer home, but will return to Rome if needed.	Nazis seize all property of Johann Strauss's family. The Waltz King's relics go into a museum. . . . Reich loan talks are not official, Prime Minister Chamberlain says. . . . Trieste expects new life as a Reich port. . . . Italy seizes the property of Albania's former King Zog and accuses him of pillage, theft, and outrages. . . . At a secret meeting in Warsaw, Poland agrees to give reconstructed "Enigma" code machines to Britain and France, along with data about deciphering the cryptograms sent by Germany.			
Jul. 26	Chiang Kai-shek doubts British betrayal. The Chinese leader stresses that a shift to aid Japan is unthinkable. . . . A band of Palestinian Arabs frees a kidnapped U.S. pastor for $2,500. . . . Italians proclaim a British surrender to Japan. . . . Japan blocks trade to Britain by closing a river. . . . No U.S. policy changes in China, the Secretary of State Hull says. Japan is responsible for any Americans hurt.	The Soviets keep their big fleet in the Near East and claim a submarine lead. . . . Britain considers Soviet army talks and will make an alliance gesture. . . . The Reich press hails its submarine fleet.		Mexican disorder grows in gravity. Federal troops fight rebels and other revolts are brewing.	The Japanese resume night raids in China.

A	**B**	**C**	**D**	**E**
Includes developments that affect more than one world region, international organizations, and important meetings of world leaders.	*Includes all domestic and regional developments in Europe, including the Soviet Union.*	*Includes all domestic and regional developments in Africa and the Middle East.*	*Includes all domestic and regional developments in Latin America, the Caribbean, and Canada.*	*Includes all domestic and regional developments in Asian and Pacific nations (and colonies).*

U.S. Politics & Social Issues	U.S. Foreign Policy & Defense	Economics & Great Depression	Science, Technology & Nature	Culture, Leisure & Lifestyle	
	President Franklin Roosevelt shelves the neutrality plan. Silence on the issue until January is forecast. Only the outbreak of war would revive the issue.	The Senate revolts over the spending bill. Republicans want more time for discussion of the measure. . . . Stores widen the use of multiple prices, finding that offers of two or more items at a reduction spur sales.	Scientists find clues to influenza in the hog virus. They report tracing a swine parasite to earthworms in disease research and deduce a human link. . . . An American astronomer announces evidence of plant life on planet Mars.	English actress Greer Garson makes her Hollywood debut with Robert Taylor.	Jul. 21
School hecklers now study music. A teacher arranges a class for children of the streets after they taunt her.		Crops wither in the widespread drought. Forest fire hazards increase with no rain in sight.		Children's World, the most popular concession at the World Fair, will become Carnivaland to attract adults. A dance floor will be added.	Jul. 22
The American Council on Education urges aid for rural youth. Many are without guidance, the report says. . . . Atlanta welcomes the world's Baptists. Sixty countries send 12,000 for the sixth Congress of Baptist Alliance. . . . New York Mayor Fiorello La Guardia summons Attorney Jane Bolin to his office and swears her in as the first Negro female justice of the Domestic Relations Court.		The bipartisan majority checks the New Deal. A Republication coalition and a big section of Democrats are having their way in the dying Congress.			Jul. 23
AFL stage unions face a serious rift. The AFL refuses to say if the unit led by Sophie Tucker is still in the federation. . . . A cornerstone is laid for a church at a prison, the first in the United States. . . . New York Mayor Fiorello LaGuardia is said to consider joining the race for Chief Judge of the Court of Appeals. Friends say he will run as an independent. . . . The FBI combats the rise in espionage. Cases have increased from 250 to 1,651.				The World Fair sees a very successful weekend with the trial of new low admission rates.	Jul. 24
Politicians doubt New York Mayor Fiorello LaGuardia's court candidacy.				A film studio seeks Humphrey Bogart for a role in Of Mice and Men.	Jul. 25
		Democrats sign a party caucus and ask for the end of raids on the New Deal. They act to bring recalcitrant members into line for the administration. . . . Heat of 90 degrees adds to the huge food loss caused by drought. Fruit ripens prematurely on trees.	New York police chiefs discuss how science can aid crime detection.		Jul. 26

F	G	H	I	J
Includes elections, federal-state relations, civil rights and liberties, crime, the judiciary, education, healthcare, poverty, urban affairs, and population.	Includes formation and debate of U.S. foreign and defense policies, veterans affairs, and defense spending. (Relations with specific foreign countries are usually found under the region concerned.)	Includes business, labor, agriculture, taxation, transportation, consumer affairs, monetary and fiscal policy, natural resources, pollution, and accidents.	Includes worldwide scientific, medical, and technological developments, natural phenomena, U.S. weather, and natural disasters.	Includes the arts, religion, scholarship, communications media, sports, entertainment, fashions, fads, and social life.

	World Affairs	Europe	Africa & The Middle East	The Americas	Asia & The Pacific
Jul. 27	Japan and Britain come to an agreement on the first items regarding China. Britain is seen to have given in on vital matters at the expense of defenders. . . . China is angry over Britain's stand and the pact with Japan is condemned. . . . U.S. exporters express concern that Japan may cancel orders.	Germany gives women free courses on beauty, showing them how to look beautiful on two marks monthly, two minutes daily. . . . Germany lays plans to push television. One station is ready to function and others are being built. . . . The French court convicts two of anti-Semitism, jailing them under an incitement law. . . . Two London bombings kill one and injure 18. Blame is put on the Irish Republican Army. . . . Slovakia increases strictures on Jews. . . . Spain sees Franco yielding on having his brother-in-law serve as premier.			
Jul. 28	The timing of the U.S. pact announcement worries Britain, fearing it will embarrass Tokyo negotiations but hoping for benevolent effect. . . . The Chinese are jubilant over the U.S. pact move. . . . German officials are silent on the U.S. step. . . . The treaty action stuns Japan, and they hint reprisals. U.S. secrecy on the matter irks London.	The Bohemian prelate flees to Poland. The Gestapo searches houses, and jails several railway workers accused of aiding the priest. . . . Britain holds five as bomb suspects. . . . Prime Minister Neville Chamberlain bars extending the parliamentary session, guarding against a coup. . . . Nazis criticize Britain as a colonial power, saying millions lack necessities.		An assassin slays a Mexican general who was a close friend of Mexico's president, Cardenas.	
Jul. 29	Canadians are ready for a curb on Japan and are held certain to terminate trade ties with Tokyo if Britain abrogates the treaty. . . . Italy sees closer ties with Japan. The press is certain that the U.S. blow is intended toward Axis powers. . . . The Pope favors a Reich-Danzig link, reports say. Dominion status for the free city under German authority is reported in the new plan. . . . The Reich and Japan finish their trade pact. . . . Spaniards set up a bank in Mexico.	Britain denies censorship plans. The press creates a committee to deal with censors. . . . France prolongs its chamber by two years. Premier Daladier believes an election at this time is undesirable. . . . Many Irish leave London to avoid a terrorist roundup. . . . A Paris court frees a Communist editor. Applause greets the acquittal in the freedom of press test case.	Excavators uncover an ancient Israeli city in Palestine dating from the 2nd to 13th century.		China claims a big victory in Shansi. The city seized by Japanese is said to be retaken.
Jul. 30	Arms costs for 1939 are totaled at $20 billion, $2 billion above 1938. Britain and France are mainly responsible for the increase. . . . The Japanese set up a Shanghai barrier meant for Britain.	France jails another journalist for anti-Semitism. . . . Czechs resist Germanization. . . . Hitler inspects forts. . . . Italian Premier Benito Mussolini marks his 56th birthday. The paper mentions the celebration, but not his age. . . . The Netherlands royalty anticipates the second birth by the Prince and Princess.		Mexican scientists evolve a way to get more spotted fever vaccine from rats and mice.	A research scholar predicts gains in Chinese culture and recounts gains despite the invasion.
Jul. 31	Many British must flee China. They are warned their lives are not safe. . . . The Prince of India sees the Pope, bringing a retinue of 50 people. . . . More Reich troops are seen in Libya. The Axis plan is said to include an attack on Egypt for the Suez Canal.	Franco decrees that all able-bodied men in Spain aged 18–50 must work 15 days per year without pay. . . . Crews raise a German warship sunk 20 years ago. . . . Hungary charges an attack. Romanian frontier guards are said to have attacked a customs house. . . . The Reich admits a jam in its work program. . . . The Reich, impressed by the British, changes its war plan. They would use detached bands of raiders against Britain.		The Mexican regime attacks a presidential candidate as not revolutionary.	Japan suffers a revolt of Chinese. Four thousand mercenaries are said to have killed officers and joined defense forces. . . . The Japanese destroy an American hospital in China. It is bombed in a plane raid.
Aug. 1	Britain and Japan agree on Tientsin policing. Britain will give up four Chinese prisoners and help curb terrorism. . . . Nazis are said to be holding an American woman. U.S. officials ask German secret police to investigate.	Czechs defy the Reich on the language law, as officials refuse to sponsor the use of German. . . . Italian fascists put a curb on Catholic activities: the Fascist Party wins the right to limit Italian Catholic Action to religious activities only. . . . Poles will try Nazis by court-martial as strong measures are decreed to halt activities among pro-Hitler minorities.			Drunkenness ushers in Bombay's new dry law; natives have their last fling as bars are shut down.

A	B	C	D	E
Includes developments that affect more than one world region, international organizations, and important meetings of world leaders.	Includes all domestic and regional developments in Europe, including the Soviet Union.	Includes all domestic and regional developments in Africa and the Middle East.	Includes all domestic and regional developments in Latin America, the Caribbean, and Canada.	Includes all domestic and regional developments in Asian and Pacific nations (and colonies).

U.S. Politics & Social Issues	U.S. Foreign Policy & Defense	Economics & Great Depression	Science, Technology & Nature	Culture, Leisure & Lifestyle	
A judge bars the racial issue in a hearing against a Communist. He strikes testimony that the accused had white girls dance with Negroes. . . . Customs agents seize 2,000 pieces of Japanese art from a Fifth Avenue store worth $75,000 to $100,000.	The United States gives formal notice of denunciation of the 1911 commercial treaty with Japan, expressing displeasure over treatment of China. The action is unique in U.S. history since the French Revolution. Japan says the U.S. denunciation move is "unthinkable." Britain is gratified by the action.	The CIO vice president opposes labor law changes. He says the amendment would cause industry strife. . . . A grand jury indicts 104 in Harlan, Ky., mine wars. They ask $535,000 in bail bond.			Jul. 27
		General Motors triples its income.	Dr. William Mayo, co-founder of the Mayo Clinic, dies.		Jul. 28
Thomas Dewey plans to offer $25,000 for racketeer Lepke Buchalter, dead or alive. He asks for the reward to end the war of extermination in the garment industry. . . . A poll indicates that 69 percent of Michigan residents disagree with the governor about becoming a dry state.		AFL chiefs map a war on the CIO. The heads of 15 unions confer on strategy.			Jul. 29
A grand jury indicts three big Ohio tire companies—Goodyear, Goodrich, and Firestone—for misleading consumers. . . . The FBI seizes an ex-banker in a wide bond plot. The former vice president is linked to $250,000 in thefts.		A Senate move saves 650,000 WPA jobs.		At age 50, Charlie Chaplin begins to talk on screen. . . . Finland plans for the 1940 summer Olympics, increasing tourist interest.	Jul. 30
		Compulsory unions lose favor, as seen from polls taken of the general public and plant workers.		World Fair officials reduce ticket prices to 50 cents today as rain cuts throngs. . . . The recovery of boxer Jack Dempsey is celebrated by 75 at a dinner fête.	Jul. 31
Clark Gable catches an intruder who uses the actor's own antique pistol to attempt burglary. . . . The Senate votes a lending bill of $1.6 billion, slashing President Roosevelt's plan in half. . . . A tipsy soldier leaps off the Brooklyn Bridge, swims to shore, and heads to a saloon. His only injury is a minor leg laceration.				Film stars Norma Shearer, Charles Boyer, and George Raft visit the World Fair in New York. . . . Dance masters agree that the jitterbug is dying out. They open a convention with the old steps in swifter tempo.	Aug. 1

F	G	H	I	J
Includes elections, federal-state relations, civil rights and liberties, crime, the judiciary, education, healthcare, poverty, urban affairs, and population.	Includes formation and debate of U.S. foreign and defense policies, veterans affairs, and defense spending. (Relations with specific foreign countries are usually found under the region concerned.)	Includes business, labor, agriculture, taxation, transportation, consumer affairs, monetary and fiscal policy, natural resources, pollution, and accidents.	Includes worldwide scientific, medical, and technological developments, natural phenomena, U.S. weather, and natural disasters.	Includes the arts, religion, scholarship, communications media, sports, entertainment, fashions, fads, and social life.

	World Affairs	Europe	Africa & The Middle East	The Americas	Asia & The Pacific
Aug. 2	A German newspaper charges British-U.S. unity in Far East issues.	Britain orders more naval ships as a check to the Reich. . . . The British ration fuel for war use. Substitutes for gasoline are sought for cars. . . . Danzig Nazis say Poles cripple the city's trade; Nazis threaten to end customs at the East Prussian border as food is barred. . . . Franco's press says Gibraltar belongs to Spain. The demand for the return of the rock is expected on the 235th anniversary of its loss. . . . Jews defy a Nazi order, returning to a Prague pool after troopers order them out. . . . Nazis seize a monastery because it aided Tyrolese. . . . Soviets still see a loophole in the British pact proposal. They hold that the British view on indirect aggression fails to meet Moscow's perspective.		Chile attempts to cut the cost of living by barring aliens as retailers.	In Bombay's dry law riots, 43 people are hurt. Muslims clash with Hindus, and liquor dealers resent the new curb. The premier says India will show the United States how to make the program work.
Aug. 3	The United States protests assaults in China. . . . The British warn Japan again, strongly protesting its continuing actions in China.	The British Commons votes for a holiday. The two-month recess is voted by a reduced majority following attacks on Prime Minister Neville Chamberlain. . . . The Czechs conscript workers for farms. Men between 15 and 60 are called up for three months of duty. . . . Danzig expels nuns and seizes the Good Shepherd School for Nazis. . . . Nazis purge the Czech police force. . . . Italy publishes new curbs on Jews. Exceptions are made for war volunteers and early fascists.			
Aug. 4	Japan adds the United States to the list of foes of Asiatics in districts under Japanese rule; this anti-foreign move is fostered in China. . . . The Japanese discuss closer Axis ties.	Italian fascists forbid classics as they purge books. Members of the party also absorb a Catholic aid association. . . . The Reich is considered safe from a sea invasion, as war games are said to back the claim. . . . Spanish families must give the government their budgets. They are ordered to list income and classify expenditures with the "greatest honesty."			
Aug. 5	Americans are ready to flee China's cities as Japan conducts an anti-foreigners campaign. The British Office is pillaged. . . . Britain begins flights to the United States. . . . Prime Minister Neville Chamberlain says Britain may send its fleet to the Far East. He says Japanese insults to the British in China "make his blood boil.". . . The Reich is skeptical of a Japanese alliance, while Italians are happy to have a potential new ally. Tokyo feels forced into an Axis alliance, as a Japanese official accuses the United States and Britain of joint pressure.	A British negotiator leaves Moscow without a political accord. . . . German Bishops deny a Nazi ban; the Vatican reveals that prelates will meet, as usual. . . . An estimated 150 are hurt in London's gas-main blast; buildings and windows crash. . . . Poles offer to end the Danzig trade war. Their note also demands respect for all agreements and warns of consequences. . . . A Princess is born in the Netherlands. The country prepares to celebrate. . . . The Reich gets control of all idle Czechs. A transfer of skilled workers to Germany is feared. . . . Reich plants recall married women for part-time work to help relieve the severe labor shortage.			Japanese bombs damage German and French consulates, killing 10 Chinese.
Aug. 6	Tensions are again dividing Europe as before World War I. Western allies fear that Hitler will try desperate measures to get Danzig. Germans see parallels to 1914, and put the blame on Britain, then and now.	The Austrian Catholic church faces a new blow. Nazis will bar any instruction except by lay teachers. Monks and nuns are forced into emigration by secularization and property seizures. . . . Prime Minister Neville Chamberlain shows strain, yet expresses confidence of voter support. . . . The Czech unity front defies the Nazi drive. Germans are split on appeasement. . . . Poland is likely to demand the end of Reich military moves in Danzig.		Bolivia's dictator German Bush justifies his policies and disavows any foreign ideology. He will use the military service requirement of university students to supply teachers for rural areas.	A Japanese night raid in China badly damages the Belgian Embassy.
Aug. 7	The population of Europe's armies rises to 8 million for periods of crisis. . . . The French drop plans for a Syrian king. The issue will not be raised again until war clouds pass. . . . Moscow derides Japanese prowess, saying that Japan's air force is badly deficient. . . . The Japanese destroy two British ships in a raid.	A Czech boycott irks the Nazi leader. Further resistance to the Reich is revealed as two signs written in both Czech and German are torn down. . . . Spain executes 53 as plotters after the killing of a guard major. . . . Italy stresses its new race policies, and an anti-Semitism report is prepared for Premier Benito Mussolini. . . . The French arrest more in a spy inquiry.			Floods imperil Shansi invaders. Three Japanese columns are cut off without food as roads are bogged.

A	B	C	D	E
Includes developments that affect more than one world region, international organizations, and important meetings of world leaders.	Includes all domestic and regional developments in Europe, including the Soviet Union.	Includes all domestic and regional developments in Africa and the Middle East.	Includes all domestic and regional developments in Latin America, the Caribbean, and Canada.	Includes all domestic and regional developments in Asian and Pacific nations (and colonies).

U.S. Politics & Social Issues	U.S. Foreign Policy & Defense	Economics & Great Depression	Science, Technology & Nature	Culture, Leisure & Lifestyle	
	Albert Einstein writes to President Franklin Roosevelt about using uranium to make an atomic bomb.	President Roosevelt's housing bill fails to pass, and an $800 million companion bill also faces rejection.			Aug. 2
President Franklin Roosevelt signs a "gag" bill limiting the pernicious political activities of federal workers. . . . A crime drive covers the nation: a grand jury will get evidence on criminals and all those who aid them.		Peace following an auto workers' strike seems near in Detroit. . . . A labor leader admits in court that he has accepted Communist help for the union, but denies being part of the party.		A dance instructor creates new steps, teaching "rock and roll" to a dancing masters' class. . . . A Beau Geste remake with Gary Cooper premieres.	Aug. 3
A man breaks his jaw and loses consciousness as he attempts to catch a ball dropped from a blimp. . . . An indicted labor leader asserts that class warfare is in existence. . . . The Attorney General declares an eight-city crime war. New York, Chicago, Boston, and New Orleans are among those specified. . . . Ohio Senator Robert Taft is the first to declare his candidacy in the presidential race for the Republican Party.		Government officials add lard to the list of approved food stamp products. Vegetable shortening is also put on the surplus program.			Aug. 4
Support for Thomas Dewey's presidential candidacy grows. Friends deny he has formed a "brain trust," but he does have a "research bureau." . . . Congress adjourns today. . . . The first smallpox case since 1932 shows up in New York. Many are ordered to be vaccinated. . . . New tactics await delinquent pupils; interesting work and personal help are to be tried as a means of adjusting "bad boys."		President Roosevelt predicts a rise in taxes. He says the defeat of his housing bill will increase the need for relief. . . . Social Security gridlock ends. The House passes a bill to save $1 billion in taxes and widen the scope of the act.	A doctor tests the theory that tick bites spread disease.	World Fair officials stage a theft of rare art. Although the thief is thwarted, the demonstration shows how easily theft could happen.	Aug. 5
Screen and stage star Katharine Hepburn takes sides in the performer's union dispute, speaking out for the AFL-affiliated American Guild of Variety Artist's . . . Officials assail the suggestion that the voting age be cut from 21 to 18.		Congressional debates appear kinder to the public on tax measures, as the implied burden is now on private enterprise, particularly bankers.		Car vacations are expected to reach new highs this year.	Aug. 6
The University of Chicago apologizes to Herbert Hoover, regretting a comment made about buying delegates. . . . Federal agents deny gang leader Louis Lepke is already in custody.		Hollywood unions threaten a strike.		Babe Ruth wins an amateur golf contest.	Aug. 7

F	G	H	I	J
Includes elections, federal-state relations, civil rights and liberties, crime, the judiciary, education, healthcare, poverty, urban affairs, and population.	Includes formation and debate of U.S. foreign and defense policies, veterans affairs, and defense spending. (Relations with specific foreign countries are usually found under the region concerned.)	Includes business, labor, agriculture, taxation, transportation, consumer affairs, monetary and fiscal policy, natural resources, pollution, and accidents.	Includes worldwide scientific, medical, and technological developments, natural phenomena, U.S. weather, and natural disasters.	Includes the arts, religion, scholarship, communications media, sports, entertainment, fashions, fads, and social life.

	World Affairs	Europe	Africa & The Middle East	The Americas	Asia & The Pacific
Aug. 8	The British hold a big stake in Japanese trade, as they supply many products vital to Japan. The Empire's sale of raw materials is a factor in treaty discussions. . . . The British see intent in the Ichang bombing. A naval report says the Japanese also tried to hit a gunboat, and the French are also menaced. . . . The Japanese Emperor opposes any war attempt with Britain. . . . Japanese leaders weigh an Axis tie.	Danzig proposes talks with Poland over the customs dispute. The Nazi Senate's overture is said to evoke positive reaction in Warsaw. . . . Netherlands royalty names the new Princess Irene Emma Elizabeth. Irene means "peace." . . . Italy's war games end abruptly. Premier Benito Mussolini is strangely absent. . . . Loyal Tyrolese may stay in Italy; those who embrace fascism will not be ousted. . . . Salzburg's Catholic center is seized, and more nuns are ousted. . . . A Serb-Croat agreement is said to be signed.			
Aug. 9		An angry Reich press menaces Poland, threatening to wipe the country off the map if criminal agitation continues. . . . Winston Churchill sees war as depending upon Hitler; he scoffs at Axis "liberations" mentioned in a radio address. . . . Italians plan a big parade with 50,000 troops; Premier Benito Mussolini will not attend. . . . Paris sees a storm brewing in Europe. Germany's tone toward Poland and the Danzig Nazi chief's visit to Hitler are cited.			The Chinese have foes in Shansi trapped. They declare the Japanese troops face annihilation.
Aug. 10	Argentina curbs an Italian airline. The company is being investigated for furthering fascist penetration. . . . The Japanese Cabinet shuns an Axis tie. The war minister will present his views to the Emperor today, but a deep rift is reported. . . . The Japanese military threatens Britain on parlay delays, warning of more acts that will make Prime Minister Chamberlain's "blood boil" if terms are not met. . . . The Italian press censors a papal letter, omitting a reference to the inadequacy of fascist tenets.	Yugoslavia's premier flies to Italy to reject Axis demands. Italo-Reich proposals include taking over railroads and the nation's foodstuffs. . . . Members of all Hungarian parties in parliament denounce the Nazis. . . . Slovaks arrest 27 Jews; the group is accused of attacking Germans. . . . Yugoslavia bars the Axis plan to use its materials in case of war.			Wang Ching-wei, former Chinese premier, urges south China to revolt. He asserts the Japanese are ready to make peace.
Aug. 11	Germany resumes gibes against U.S. President Franklin Roosevelt. The press says his failures stir him to incite Poland. . . . Tokyo sees the British as awaiting word from the United States. The delay in the parley is attributed to discussions between Washington and London. . . . U.S. experts aid in the reconstruction of the Chinese transportation system.	The Polish foreign minister says peace is still possible. . . . Czechs flee a Reich train. They break windows and escape to Poland despite guards. . . . Italy, concerned, does not want Budapest to become totally under Reich rule and pushes prudence on Danzig. . . . A Nazi general asks labor to remain calm, stressing the fraternity of worker and soldier and assuring them that Hitler would not lead them into war lightly, only as last resort. . . . Quakers help Spaniards in France find housing. . . . The Reich's aim to control Hungary is now seen; Britain believes Germany will seek to "coordinate" the nation for strategic purposes.			
Aug. 12	Three thousand British troops from India reinforce Singapore.	Austria's prelates meet with the Reich's. . . . Yugoslavia calls up four army units; maneuvers are seen as a response to pressure from Germany and Italy. . . . Italy girds its army and calls up officers. A marshal says the defenses along the French border are strong enough to bar an invasion. . . . Britain and the Soviets begin negotiations focussed on their military powers.			Japanese veil the fate of Americans in Kaifeng. The efforts of U.S. diplomats fail and detention is reported. . . . Part of Shanghai will now exclude Jews. The Japanese-ruled section of the international settlement will bar refugees.
Aug. 13	China condemns the Tientsin accord. . . . Pope Pius XII acts to save the Austrian accord; the treaty has been violated by the Nazis.	Foreign crisis speeds the Croat accord. Yugoslavs show sympathy with the democracies, despite the need for trade with the Axis powers. . . . Germans and Poles argue the Danzig case. The former bases claims on race and self-determination, the latter on fundamental economic need. . . . Hitler continues talks with Italian Foreign Minister Ciano for a third day. . . . Nazi propaganda is going full blast. The press and radio vaunt Axis prowess and belittle all life in democracies.			People in Chungking are accustomed to air raids. Shelter tunnels are hewed out of rock and lanes cut to prevent the spread of fire. . . . A bomb hits the Japanese shipping office in China. Eleven are seriously injured on the anniversary of the start of war. . . . Americans are safe, Japan reports: there has been no attack on missionaries in Kaifeng. Direct word is still sought and Chinese church workers pray for the missing 36.

A	B	C	D	E
Includes developments that affect more than one world region, international organizations, and important meetings of world leaders.	Includes all domestic and regional developments in Europe, including the Soviet Union.	Includes all domestic and regional developments in Africa and the Middle East.	Includes all domestic and regional developments in Latin America, the Caribbean, and Canada.	Includes all domestic and regional developments in Asian and Pacific nations (and colonies).

U.S. Politics & Social Issues	U.S. Foreign Policy & Defense	Economics & Great Depression	Science, Technology & Nature	Culture, Leisure & Lifestyle	
President Franklin Roosevelt signs 100 bills. Patent laws are among the policies altered. . . . A judge rejects a Connecticut ban on birth control. He clears two doctors and a nurse in the test case of the statute. . . . President Roosevelt claims victory on courts despite Congress; he says his "liberal ideas" prevail in the Supreme Court.	The U.S. Army renews the title of lieutenant general.	The WPA cuts rolls but a labor shortage is seen. Some say work projects will be undermanned for a short time only.		New York's Museum of Modern Art acquires banned Reich art; five noted works that are labeled as "degenerate" are on view.	Aug. 8
A Senator speaks out against a third term for President Roosevelt, insisting that a change will best serve the needs of the country. . . . President Roosevelt depicts his foes in Congress in gambler roles; they risk world peace and national well-being to defeat his programs, he says.				The World Fair's only Maori glares at visitors from a pedestal. Disappointed fair-goers want real "savages," not a figure.	Aug. 9
	The Army and Navy choose six civilians as a group to advise the munitions board and help mobilize for war.	President Franklin Roosevelt orders a drive to cut costs. All government agencies are to survey operations for possible economies.			Aug. 10
A judge paroles a 16-year-old burglar to his 13-year-old sister, telling her to report back to him. . . . A New Jersey court upholds the right of the school board to discriminate against married women when giving out pay raises. . . . President Roosevelt warns the Democratic Party not to name a conservative for the 1940 election.		Actors threaten to bolt the AFL. Arbiters are named and a move to the CIO is suggested.	George Vanderbilt catches a rare octopus off the waters of Hawaii. A deep-water creature, it cannot withstand the pressure change and bursts in half when brought into the air.		Aug. 11
	President Roosevelt is ready to call Congress if war threatens. If a world crisis occurs, he will convene a special session.	President Roosevelt assails federalizing aid. He says that proposals to drop dollar-matching with states are a wedge for nationalization. . . . First Lady Eleanor Roosevelt upholds wives' jobs, but decries a family bureaucracy where more than one family member has a government job. Cases of rare need are the exception.		Silent movie star Norma Talmadge divorces comedian George Jessel.	Aug. 12
A member of the Dies Committee says their work will kill off Communism in the United States. . . . A Civil War veteran dies at age 100; he was known as "Hollerin' Johnny" for his yells in battle.			Mayo Clinic doctors reduce hangover headaches by the use of histamine. . . . An expert traces the iron used in horseshoes to 333 B.C.E.		Aug. 13

F	G	H	I	J
Includes elections, federal-state relations, civil rights and liberties, crime, the judiciary, education, healthcare, poverty, urban affairs, and population.	Includes formation and debate of U.S. foreign and defense policies, veterans affairs, and defense spending. (Relations with specific foreign countries are usually found under the region concerned.)	Includes business, labor, agriculture, taxation, transportation, consumer affairs, monetary and fiscal policy, natural resources, pollution, and accidents.	Includes worldwide scientific, medical, and technological developments, natural phenomena, U.S. weather, and natural disasters.	Includes the arts, religion, scholarship, communications media, sports, entertainment, fashions, fads, and social life.

	World Affairs	Europe	Africa & The Middle East	The Americas	Asia & The Pacific
Aug. 14	Walter Funk, Germany's economics minister says the United States has hampered trade for political reasons. He hails the Reich's common sense approach to economics. . . . Japan warns Britons in China; serious outbreaks are seen because of insincerity in negotiations.	Italy wins a delay on Danzig from Germany. . . . Berlin reports a 100 percent agreement between Germany and Italy, but the Italian press has no knowledge of an agreement. . . . The question of Poland is raised during Anglo-Soviet talks.	Egypt's King Farouk accepts the resignation of Premier Muhammad Mahmud and his Cabinet. The Premier gave ill health as his reason for resigning.		
Aug. 15	Anti-British mobs are violent in the Shanghai port. The Consulate is attacked and homes are stoned. . . . The Shanghai settlement bars more refugees. The 500 already on their way from Europe are unaffected by the order.	German police ban Helen Keller's book; no reason is given. . . . Police arrest four IRA leaders in Dublin. England deports five more. . . . The Reich reports on Poles, saying 197 soldiers have deserted to the Reich, mostly out of fear. . . . Slovakia claims Polish territory. . . . Spaniards arrest a Briton, saying his wife did not give a proper salute.			
Aug. 16	The United States blames the Japanese in a slapping case of an American widow by a sentry, calling the incident an affront. . . . Tokyo drafts a plan for its Axis policy. Germany is said to want Japan to commit to military action. . . . The United States wins the release of 20 held in Spain.	The Axis warns that Danzig issues must be resolved promptly. A showdown is foreseen. . . . Britain girds for a violent crisis. Berlin asserts that London lacks the hardness of will to halt a totalitarian expansion. . . . Germany closes its border that faces the Polish frontier. . . . Romania will not cede land. King Carol says he would rather risk world war than yield.		Panama and the United States celebrate the 25th anniversary of the Panama Canal. The first ship to travel the waterway repeats its passage.	
Aug. 17	Eight Latin American nations rally in support of the right of diplomatic asylum. They back Chile in its rift with Spain.	A Danzig guard kills Polish soldiers. Versions of the incident differ. . . . Denmark suspects sabotage following an air crash. Baggage is searched for explosives or flammable material. . . . Germany reveals its demands on Poland: it wants Danzig and the Polish Corridor. . . . Italian newspapers warn Poland not to fight the Reich; Britain and France are too far away to send aid, the press says. . . . The Reich army is ready on the Polish border, prepared to enforce Hitler's claims.		Dominicans mark Independence Day; officials of 76-year-old Republic reaffirm their faith in Pan-Americanism.	The Japanese occupy the Hong Kong border. They drive the Chinese 13 miles from the border of the British territory.
Aug. 18	Britain presses its plans for Palestine, confident of success in the League of Nations Council. The committee finds Britain's policy contrary to the original commitment. . . . China accuses the German Embassy of unreasonable interference after it protests the showing of a Soviet film. The Embassy says the movie has anti-German sentiments. . . . The Japanese rebuff Britain, refusing responsibility for destroying two ships in air raids.	Britain rules out a four-power parley on Danzig, and holds that Poland's interests must remain foremost. . . . Nephews of England's King are in trouble after disclosing a military secret in a typed newsletter given to classmates. . . . Poles deny tales of atrocities, but admit to some arrests of Germans along the border for espionage. . . . The Reich feels a Polish rebuff in ignoring its terms, calling for action in a matter of days.	Egypt's new Premier Aly Maher Pasha forms a Cabinet.	Peru decides not to compete in the 1940 Olympics.	China's harvest is bountiful; granaries are so full that they cannot hold the surplus.
Aug. 19	An American lawyer defends four Chinese in Tientsin. The lawyer visits them in jail and will file a new petition. . . . Britain rules out economic talks with Japan. The Tokyo press is angry and the break-up of the parley is anticipated. . . . A Japanese guard who slapped an American woman will not be punished.	Germany and Slovenia sign an arms pact. Nazis are to command an army of 30,000 with reserves of 300,000. Berlin is expected to send a military ruler. . . . Hungarian Premier Pal Teleki angers the Reich. Said to be anti-German, he may be forced to quit. . . . London sees a German coup and calls Slovakia the Reich's third protectorate. . . . Poles charge Reich atrocities, saying Germany is expelling border families. . . . Stalin gives a speech, saying war betwwen the Western powers is needed for the world revolution to proceed.			South China chiefs denounce separating south China from the north.
Aug. 20	Japan apologizes for a guard that slapped an American woman.	The Italian Foreign Minister Ciano is in Albania. His motive is puzzling; some think he is avoiding the British and French envoys who want to see him. . . . The Czech language is barred in German talks; German must be spoken in all foreign negotiations. . . . Germany is adamant on the Polish question; the time for words is past, officials reiterate.			

A	B	C	D	E
Includes developments that affect more than one world region, international organizations, and important meetings of world leaders.	*Includes all domestic and regional developments in Europe, including the Soviet Union.*	*Includes all domestic and regional developments in Africa and the Middle East.*	*Includes all domestic and regional developments in Latin America, the Caribbean, and Canada.*	*Includes all domestic and regional developments in Asian and Pacific nations (and colonies).*

U.S. Politics & Social Issues	U.S. Foreign Policy & Defense	Economics & Great Depression	Science, Technology & Nature	Culture, Leisure & Lifestyle	
A minister calls self-improvement books "stupid," saying they are popular only because the Bible is not read.					Aug. 14
Film leaders face federal inquiries on racket, tax, and trust charges. . . . A hospital hints that poison is the cause of death of a police officer who testified in an abortion frame-up case against a doctor.			Inventors exhibit boons to mankind at the World Fair in New York. These include a wingless airship, doughnuts with handles, a tearless onion peeler, and a vacuum machine for removing dandruff.		Aug. 15
President Roosevelt suggests changing the Thanksgiving celebration date. A sarcastic senator says he would rather have him abolish winter. . . . The Department of the Interior advises Washington to develop Alaska. The territory can furnish products currently imported from Europe and Asia. . . . The Dies Committee resumes its activities. Hearings are to continue delving into Communist and fascist activities. . . . New York Mayor Fiorello LaGuardia asks for equality for Negro doctors, saying germs don't follow Jim Crow laws.		More states follow Texas's lead and close their oil wells. Others are expected to act soon in an attempt to bolster the falling prices of crude oil.	NBC and Bell Laboratories test static-free radios. Even disruptions from thunder are controlled.		Aug. 16
	Isolationist Senators assail President Roosevelt, saying the President would find another foreign war desirable.			Lupe Velez divorces Johnny Weissmuller, *Tarzan* actor. She had filed three times for divorce before following through. . . . The Technicolor movie *The Wizard of Oz* premieres with Judy Garland and Mickey Rooney in attendance.	Aug. 17
Secretary of the Interior Harold Ickes suggests using Alaska as a refuge. He favors admitting those oppressed abroad to the territory, citing the need to populate the area.					Aug. 18
The American Bar Association is chastised for its color barrier. A borough president says the group has brought disgrace upon itself and pleads for Negro rights.		The AFL suspends the printers' union, taking action for its failure to pay a levy in the campaign against the CIO. . . . Armour & Company and its union near agreement. The union yields to demands to discuss each plant individually.			Aug. 19
New England says no to a proposed Thanksgiving date change. They say the day is as immovable as Plymouth Rock.					Aug. 20

F	**G**	**H**	**I**	**J**
Includes elections, federal-state relations, civil rights and liberties, crime, the judiciary, education, healthcare, poverty, urban affairs, and population.	*Includes formation and debate of U.S. foreign and defense policies, veterans affairs, and defense spending. (Relations with specific foreign countries are usually found under the region concerned.)*	*Includes business, labor, agriculture, taxation, transportation, consumer affairs, monetary and fiscal policy, natural resources, pollution, and accidents.*	*Includes worldwide scientific, medical, and technological developments, natural phenomena, U.S. weather, and natural disasters.*	*Includes the arts, religion, scholarship, communications media, sports, entertainment, fashions, fads, and social life.*

	World Affairs	Europe	Africa & The Middle East	The Americas	Asia & The Pacific
Aug. 21	Three thousand Chinese in the United States pledge war aid, and cheer as the Chinese government leader predicts the nation's spirit will repel the Japanese. . . . A Tientsin flood lifts the blockade; refugees crowd the French and British zones. . . . Tokyo reports a move against the United States. A shift in policy is likely to put pressure on Americans in China. . . . Peace hopes wane; the outlook is the darkest it has been since 1914.	The Polish east border is free. The Soviet frontier is the only one not manned as Warsaw sends reinforcements. . . . Four Reich submarines may be en route to attacking Martinique. The daring German war plan is said to provide the establishment of a Caribbean base. . . . Police arrest 21 Hungarian Nazis; the youth group leaders are charged with secret military acts. . . . Italo-Reich parleys may determine peace or war. Talks are stormy and Premier Mussolini assures King Vittorio Emmanuel III that no steps will be taken without his approval. . . . The Reich and Soviet Union enter a seven-year treaty. The pact is a blow to France and Britain, and Germany will get needed materials.			
Aug. 22	Belgium summons a neutrals' parley. Seven small nations are to discuss security; a mediation idea is denied. . . . The Japanese present new Shanghai demands: they want indemnity for killing two Chinese policemen, punishment for a Briton involved, and an apology. . . . The Japanese list Mongol air defeats, saying 40 planes were shot down Saturday.	The Reich foreign minister denies pressure on Hungary and asserts its independence is essential for balance in Europe. . . . Germany and Russia agree to a nonaggression pact. Germans are elated as fears are lifted. . . . Envoys in Moscow are shocked by the new ties to Germany. The British and French military are expected to leave after failing to achieve an alliance. . . . London staggers under the blow of a Nazi-Soviet pact. The British face a crisis of Reich domination in Europe. . . . Paris is skeptical of the Russian treaty. France is in a nonaggression pact with Germany, but it would not bar aid to Poles. . . . Reich troops jam the roads to Poland. The border bristles with guns and ambulances ready for action.			The Tientsin flood continues to rise. It may reach its crest, but observers note interior rains. . . . Japan bombs and burns a city in western China without any military objective. The United States calls the incident terrorism.
Aug. 23	Americans in Europe start to rush home. . . . Greece is considered sure to support Britain. Despite its anti-democratic rule, Greece fears Italy and cites London's naval strength and France's power. . . . Hong Kong lists its British women, calling on them to register children in case of need for emergency evacuation. . . . The Japanese discern greater dangers; leaders confer on the situation caused by the Nazi-Soviet pact. . . . Rome claims the end of encirclement, believing the Soviet-Reich pact gives the preponderance of power to the Axis and doubting Britain and France will follow up on pledges of aid.	Hitler and Stalin agree to the Nazi-Soviet Pact, formally called a treaty of Nonaggression. Foreign Ministers von Ribbentrop and Molotoff sign the treaty in Moscow. The pact gives Finland and the Baltic States to the U.S.S.R.; Poland is divided between Germany and the Soviets. . . . Britain and France stand by their pledge to the Poles. They rush plans for war and Poland stays calm. . . . The British Cabinet asks the Commons for wartime powers. More troops mobilize. . . . The Czechs decry the British on the Nazi-Soviet pact, blaming them for this new turn of relations. . . . The German press heaps ridicule on Paris and London for supposedly groveling in front of the Kremlin.		Bolivian dictator German Busch dies of a gunshot wound, assumed to be a suicide. Carlos Quintanilla assumes the office of president.	
Aug. 24	Reports suggest that Germans may use Martinique as a base to attack U.S. shipping. . . . Some Chinese hail the Nazi-Soviet pact.	Britons are unmoved by the Nazi-Soviet pact; some believe a secret accord lies behind the nonaggression agreement. . . . Czech leaders urge calmness and no attempt to "fight Britain's war by obstruction." . . . France is mobilized and expects war. The people are confident of their strength to meet the aggressor as peace hopes dim. . . . No military moves are apparent in Italy. . . . Turkey reaffirms its pledges to the Allies.			Hong Kong severs its bridges to China as Japanese troops look on.
Aug. 25	Canada is set to aid the British. The Cabinet is unanimous in its policy; only the extent of aid remains to be decided. . . . Egyptians remain calm; Germans and Italians flee from the country. . . . Britain warns families to leave Hong Kong; the harbor entrance is partially mined and heavy guns are moved to the frontier.	Danzig soldiers march to the border. Secret service men guard bridges and the frontier is partly closed. . . . Frenchmen pour to the front lines; more reservists are called up. . . . Hitler acts to take Danzig and orders the army to be ready. . . . Hitler lays plans with close associates for the partition of Poland; Danzig is the first step. . . . Poland accepts President Roosevelt's offer and will attempt direct talks with the Reich. . . . Reich troops mass on the west border. Switzerland and Belgium note the heavy concentration. . . . Spain looks to Italy as a leader in crisis. . . . A bomb kills five in Coventry, England. The Irish Republican Army is responsible.			A Cabinet shake-up is likely in Japan. A new policy of isolation also brings in a clean slate of domestic administration.

A	B	C	D	E
Includes developments that affect more than one world region, international organizations, and important meetings of world leaders.	Includes all domestic and regional developments in Europe, including the Soviet Union.	Includes all domestic and regional developments in Africa and the Middle East.	Includes all domestic and regional developments in Latin America, the Caribbean, and Canada.	Includes all domestic and regional developments in Asian and Pacific nations (and colonies).

U.S. Politics & Social Issues	U.S. Foreign Policy & Defense	Economics & Great Depression	Science, Technology & Nature	Culture, Leisure & Lifestyle	
				Lou Gehrig visits the Mayo Clinic; a routine check-up on his condition is planned.	Aug. 21
The United States declares peace with honor as its aim.					Aug. 22
				Lou Gehrig receives an encouraging report at the Mayo Clinic.	Aug. 23
U.S. officials frown on overseas travel for citizens.			In Germany, the first turbo-jet aircraft flies. The *Heinkle-178* is piloted by Capt. Erich Warsitz. . . . A Swedish doctor finds a genetic link to anemia and epilepsy.		Aug. 24
Racketeer Louis Lepke surrenders; he never left New York. . . . Actors Equity votes to oust president Sophie Tucker.	U.S. President Franklin Roosevelt sends the Italian King Vittorio Emmanuel III an appeal for peace after he hears a report that the monarch warned Premier Benito Mussolini against war. . . . Elliot Roosevelt urges a political truce. He says his father, the president, would die in defense of his country.				Aug. 25

F	G	H	I	J
Includes elections, federal-state relations, civil rights and liberties, crime, the judiciary, education, healthcare, poverty, urban affairs, and population.	Includes formation and debate of U.S. foreign and defense policies, veterans affairs, and defense spending. (Relations with specific foreign countries are usually found under the region concerned.)	Includes business, labor, agriculture, taxation, transportation, consumer affairs, monetary and fiscal policy, natural resources, pollution, and accidents.	Includes worldwide scientific, medical, and technological developments, natural phenomena, U.S. weather, and natural disasters.	Includes the arts, religion, scholarship, communications media, sports, entertainment, fashions, fads, and social life.

	World Affairs	Europe	Africa & The Middle East	The Americas	Asia & The Pacific
Aug. 26	Americans abroad rush for bookings home. Canceled ship sailings are leaving many stranded. . . . China is not jubilant over the Nazi-Soviet pact. Officials think it may create a clash disastrous for the East. . . . The Nazi-Soviet pact is seen as weakening the Reich as the reaction of the Allies causes a pause. The defection of Italy along with the loss of Japan and Spain are believed possible in the interval needed to review the diplomatic situation.	Nazis feel that general European war is averted. Their demands now include the Polish corridor, Danzig, and parts of Posen. . . . Italy calls up 500,000 for military duty. . . . French engineers cut Rhine bridges by the German border. . . . Premier Edouard Daladier rallies the nation; the French are resolved to see Hitler's "bluff" through. . . . Hitler is reportedly willing to ease his demands on Poland; Britain gets the terms today. . . . The Nazi force is near Denmark. . . . The Nazi-Soviet pact stuns Parisian Communists. They call a meeting to affirm their loyalty to France. . . . The Polish charge raids on the border; Nazi gangs are said to cross over and attack.		Canada summons militia to duty. The Cabinet hears that hope of peace is almost abandoned. . . . Chile suppresses a military revolt. A rising against the popular front is crushed without firing a single shot.	
Aug. 27	All Americans are safe in the Tientsin flood. . . . Canada appeals to three rulers: Premier William MacKenzie urges Germany and Poland to calm their dispute and asks for the Italian premier's help. . . . Japan, deserted, vows to carry on. The Nazi-Soviet pact—between its enemy and ally— does not change national policy.	Winston Churchill declares the situation very grave, saying it is too late for appeasement. . . . France is adamant, holding the Hitlerite system must go to end periodical crises. . . . Hitler demands Britain drop its alliance with the Polish. . . . Hungary rejects the Romanian accord. . . . Italy is optimistic, feeling Poland and the Allies will surrender to Hitler's demands. . . . Nazis block the Rhine to its own nationals.		Chile arrests 65 after a revolt fails. Martial law and new powers for the popular front are proclaimed. . . . Latin America cements its bonds; shunning ties to Europe, the republics enter a new era of neighborliness.	
Aug. 28	German secret police trap a foe of Nazis in Colombia. . . . Italy still lags on war preparedness. Following a mediation request, Premier Benito Mussolini promises Canada every effort for lasting and just peace. . . . Washington is alert for moves abroad.	Germany reassures the Baltic states that the pact with the Soviets is not aimed at them. . . . Croats are jubilant over the new accord. The press sees a new era in the country with an increase of democracy. . . . Hungarian police end a Nazi demonstration, seizing 66. Scores are hurt in fighting. . . . The London Cabinet rules out any retreat but sees hope in playing for time. A note to Hitler is expected to propose a six-month period to precede negotiations. . . . The pact with the Soviets spurs Reich trade.			The Japanese Cabinet quits en masse as a policy shift ends the regime. Troops quit Hong Kong; Germans leave Tientsin.
Aug. 29	Americans are unable to leave Italy; 450 are waiting as two liners drop sailings. . . . The U.S. ambassador to Germany and the Assistant Secretary of War say that the U.S. arms ban breeds war and that it favors the Reich and spurs Hitler. . . . U.S. ships cancel sailings to the Reich.	Britain lays down rules for citizens. The government assumes sweeping control of life, property, and communications. The mere possession of defense data is forbidden. . . . The British admiralty bans ships in the Mediterranean. It orders shipping to shun the "lifeline" route. . . . Danzigers anticipate a big event. Anti-aircraft guns are moved by the Polish border and stores are closed. . . . The British envoy sees Hitler. . . . France closes its borders with the Reich. Rigid censorship is declared as Hitler's decision on war or peace is calmly awaited. . . . London hangs identity labels on 650,000 children as part of an evacuation rehearsal. . . . The Soviet Union fails to act on its pact with the Reich. It waits to see the lineup of Europe before ratifying the agreement.			
Aug. 30	Brazil curbs Germans. New restrictions are put on the children of aliens. . . . A survey shows that 82 percent of the U.S. population would cut off arms shipments to Japan. . . . Gandhi prays for peace. He wishes that Hitler would listen to President Roosevelt's appeal. . . . London Americans hear a safety plan. Four zones are set aside for U.S. citizens.	Autonomous Croats induct a governor. . . . Two Balkan states seek a tie to Hungary: Romania and Yugoslavia press for a nonaggression pact. . . . A diplomatic front engages Premier Mussolini. Britain is said to ask his influence for peace. . . . The French now think Hitler is worried. They feel Germans are under the greatest strain in the present phase of "war of nerves." . . . Germans occupy the Slovak capital. The army marches in "with invitation," but most resent the Nazis. . . . Russians mass soldiers in the west. The fear of an Anglo-German move against Lithuania is held as the cause.			

A	B	C	D	E
Includes developments that affect more than one world region, international organizations, and important meetings of world leaders.	Includes all domestic and regional developments in Europe, including the Soviet Union.	Includes all domestic and regional developments in Africa and the Middle East.	Includes all domestic and regional developments in Latin America, the Caribbean, and Canada.	Includes all domestic and regional developments in Asian and Pacific nations (and colonies).

U.S. Politics & Social Issues	U.S. Foreign Policy & Defense	Economics & Great Depression	Science, Technology & Nature	Culture, Leisure & Lifestyle	
	President Franklin Roosevelt works on war measures.			The first televised professional baseball game is played at Ebbet's Field in Brooklyn, between the Dodgers and the Cincinnati Reds.	Aug. 26
A poll of the public indicates praise of Congress, considered to be doing a good job overall. Republicans fare best.					Aug. 27
Pastor Walter Dworecki of New Jersey's Camden Polish Baptist Church confesses to paying a man $100 to murder his 18-year-old daughter on August 7. Dworecki had taken out a $5,600 insurance policy on the girl in March.		The Resource Committee asks for regulation of energy sources, asserting a federal policy would aid in defense and the economy.			Aug. 28
	While the German liner Bremen is searched in New York, President Roosevelt asserts the U.S.' right to search ships of potential belligerents for arming capabilities.				Aug. 29
N.J. Pastor Dworecki and his accomplice face a death penalty trial.					Aug. 30

F	**G**	**H**	**I**	**J**
Includes elections, federal-state relations, civil rights and liberties, crime, the judiciary, education, healthcare, poverty, urban affairs, and population.	Includes formation and debate of U.S. foreign and defense policies, veterans affairs, and defense spending. (Relations with specific foreign countries are usually found under the region concerned.)	Includes business, labor, agriculture, taxation, transportation, consumer affairs, monetary and fiscal policy, natural resources, pollution, and accidents.	Includes worldwide scientific, medical, and technological developments, natural phenomena, U.S. weather, and natural disasters.	Includes the arts, religion, scholarship, communications media, sports, entertainment, fashions, fads, and social life.

	World Affairs	Europe	Africa & The Middle East	The Americas	Asia & The Pacific
Aug. 31	Washington hears that Hitler is yielding; Italy's king helps with negotiations. . . . Japan fears a war with Russia. . . . The war crisis closes Romania's stand at the U.S. World Fair. Thirty-eight employees are recalled to Romania for fear of being stranded.	Danzig traffic is cut except to Germany. . . . Italy demands an end to the Versailles Treaty. . . . The French say Germans are deserting over the Rhine. Troops flee by swimming and then ask to join the foreign legion. . . . Germans prepare against blockade. . . . The Hungarian border worries Slovakia. While German troops cross the Polish border, fighting with Magyars continues. . . . A London note to Berlin bluntly refuses to discuss the demand for territory and insists on talks. . . . Poles mobilize an army of 2.5 million; all men between ages 21 and 40 are liable to military duty.			A Chinese editor is slain on a Shanghai bridge. He was a close friend of Chiang Kai-shek. . . . Japan will renew its drive against China, saying it will "inflexibly oppose those who obstruct our mission" in East Asia.
Sept. 1	A blow to U.S. "Reds" is seen. The Nazi-Soviet pact is held to be the doom of Communism. . . . Pope Pius XII urges a peace conference. . . . The premier says Japan will keep its ties to the Reich. He indicates he expects U.S. relations to worsen. . . . Tokyo doubts the Soviet Union can be a German ally in war, holding that Russia will benefit only if it stays out of battle.	Britain and France issue ultimatums; Germany attacks Poland on four fronts. . . . Germans seize the free city, and Danzig is made part of the Reich. . . . Britain mobilizes: food buying is limited, censorship is established, telephone service is stopped, and the stock market is closed. . . . Britain hears of bombing in Poland. The French confirm the beginning of war. . . . The conscription age is set at 17 in Russia. . . . Premier Edouard Daladier summons the French Cabinet to confer. News of the attack on Poland spurs immediate reaction; a military response is likely. . . . Italy prepares and divides its forces. The Crown Prince commands one army. . . . Soviet aid to the Reich is limited, but Soviets ratify the nonaggression pact with the Reich.	Egypt hides the treasures of King Tutankhamen.	Canada seeks talks with the United States on defense. . . . Quebec bans the movie screen airing of *Beau Geste*, at the French Consul General's request . . . All exportable Mexican oil has already been sold, government officials say.	
Sept. 2	The Soviet premier's words indicate neutrality. The Reich wants a nonaggression pact between Russia and Japan. . . . The start of strife brings a quick response from President Roosevelt about noncombatants. He pleads for restraint in bombing and asks for a pledge to protect civilians.	British censorship slows dispatches. . . . A cheering Commons backs Prime Minister Neville Chamberlain, united in the ultimatum to Nazis. . . . France mobilizes; 8 million are on call. A state of martial law is declared. . . . The Swiss order full mobilization. . . . Nazi efforts center on keeping the conflict from spreading in Europe. . . . In Paris, evacuation begins in earnest. . . . The Reich closes in on Poland. Success is seen in invasions and control of airspace. . . . Danzig is annexed to the Reich.		The Canadian premier asks parliament to ratify war action. The sending of a volunteer army is hinted. . . . Canada's commissioner expresses pleasure over how his country is portrayed as a vacation land in its World Fair exhibit.	
Sept. 3	Two thousand Americans sail from Britain. . . . Japan believes that the European war will create closer ties between Tokyo and the United States. . . . Hitler promises limited bombing. He responds to President Roosevelt that he will spare open cities if foes do likewise. . . . Japan seeks a way to end the China war. The deadlock strangles industry at a time when Europe needs their goods. . . . Australia declares war on Germany.	Berlin is calm under war curbs. Hitler amnesties jailed army members. . . . Italian neutrality raises a big question: can Mussolini serve as a supply agent for Germany and immobilize French forces. . . . Britain and France declare war. Hitler will not halt the attack on Poland, and Prime Minister Chamberlain calls on the Empire to fight. . . . Twenty-one civilians die in the raid on Warsaw. . . . Hitler's tactics stiffen the British, who are tired of his recklessness. . . . Paris declares an authorization for war.		A Nova Scotia official bans an effigy of Mrs. Franklin D. Roosevelt in a puppet show. . . . Canadians express confidence on the British course of action in the war. . . . The United States plans to push trade agreements with Latin American countries.	
Sept. 4	Canada declares automatic entry into war. . . . The first war forces are relatively small. Reserves of battling nations may bring the total to 40 million men engaged. . . . Britain interns Hong Kong Germans and places them in a Catholic school.	The Allied navies are powerful; they outnumber Germany, 6–1. . . . Berlin is sober over the situation, quieted by the news of Britain's war declaration. . . . The British navy acts, cutting off entrances to the Baltic, North, and Mediterranean Seas. . . . Churchill heads the British Admiralty, performing simple but important war tasks. . . . Premier Edouard Daladier rallies France to fight. . . . Franco asks foes to localize the war. . . . Italy fails to act as its ally fights.		Canada affirms that United States citizens will not need a passport to enter their country during the war.	

A	B	C	D	E
Includes developments that affect more than one world region, international organizations, and important meetings of world leaders.	*Includes all domestic and regional developments in Europe, including the Soviet Union.*	*Includes all domestic and regional developments in Africa and the Middle East.*	*Includes all domestic and regional developments in Latin America, the Caribbean, and Canada.*	*Includes all domestic and regional developments in Asian and Pacific nations (and colonies).*

U.S. Politics & Social Issues	U.S. Foreign Policy & Defense	Economics & Great Depression	Science, Technology & Nature	Culture, Leisure & Lifestyle	
		The WPA drops 25,000 more employees due to funding cuts. This completes the laying off of 70,000 during an 18-month period.		The newest Charlie Chan movie premieres today.	Aug. 31
	The Army widens the rule that bans the married. The new regulation excludes all applications for enlistment by those who have dependents. . . . The Navy will build bases in Alaska. . . . U.S. aviation rules for war are ready.	Chain stores have cut cigarette prices from 17 cents to 16 cents a pack, after taking a "licking" after raising prices. . . . Milk distributors are hurt by the Dairy Farmers Union strike. . . . 21,000 people take the Municipal Civil Service Commission typing test, with 16 high schools needed to accommodate everyone. . . . Shortage of labor halts 20 WPA construction projects, after 25,000 workers were laid off in one day.	A captain warns of vast icebergs. The open summer on Greenland's east coast is sending down a menace to shipping. . . . Surgeons successfully place intestines inside a baby who was born with the organs outside his body.	Miss Alice Marble, the "undisputed world's queen of tennis," defeats Nina Brown of England. . . . City dwellers are setting a new record for Labor Day holiday travel, heading to beaches and mountains. . . . A muntjac baby deer was born at the Bronx Zoo, the first of its species to be born in captivity. . . . The former president of Czechoslovakia, Eduard Benes, publishes a book, *Democracy Today and Tomorrow*. . . . Drastic changes are seen in hat styles, with ribbons, snoods, or draped fullness seen in the back. . . . Richard Barthelmess will return to the screen in *Underground*, after an absence of five years. . . . Basil Rathbone stars in *The Adventures of Sherlock Holmes*.	Sept. 1
	President Franklin Roosevelt promises to keep the United States out of war.	Grain prices soar, with its value increasing by about $300,000,000. . . . A Brooklyn employer is indicted on a wage charge, accused of paying employees three cents an hour, rather than the minimum wage of 25 cents per hour. . . . The grand jury indicts alleged gambling collector on tax evasion charges, claiming that he owes over $210,000. . . . Montgomery Ward doubles its profits, with sales increases of 14 percent. . . . Speculation grips some commodities, as goods anticipated to become scarce are withdrawn from the market.		Australians are predicted to beat the United States team in tennis's Davis Cup. Robert Riggs is to open play for the American side. . . . The observance of Puerto Rico Night opens Labor Day weekend festivities at Atlantic Beach. . . . Alice Marble enters tennis tournament finals. . . . President Roosevelt favors a second year for the World Fair, seeing it as a forum to stress global peace. . . . The National Puzzlers League will meet in Cleveland, with convention proceeds going to aid hospitals.	Sept. 2
The National Safety Council calls the bathroom the site of the fewest home accidents. . . . Convicted Mayor T. Frank Hayes resigns from his Waterbury, Conn. position, citing a "torrent of abuse" that prevents him from doing his job. . . . Michigan's governor criticizes modern dance, saying that it "bewitches and controls" participants and viewers. . . . San Antonio groups demand the recall of their mayor after he allows a Communist group to meet. . . . The nation's interest in art increases, according to the Art Guidance Council.	National interest centers on when Roosevelt will call upon Congress to discuss the possibility of U.S. participation in the war.	The city college in New York is setting up training courses to teach men to become firemen and policemen. . . . Howard Johnson plans to open its 130th ice cream shop and restaurant. . . . Manufacturers hint at a 25–30 percent increase in consumer goods prices. . . . Sign painters convene to discuss regulation of outdoor advertising.	Researchers discover lightweight helium in air. . . . The American Chemical Society arranges a symposium about educational opportunities for women in the field. . . . An inventor receives a patent for his device that scans and maps out sea beds. . . . Charles Lindbergh widens his aid to science, developing a heart-like pump that permits the study of tissue interaction. . . . A New York resident patents a device that guides planes through a system of radio flashes.	From Bull Run to Appomattox, roads through historic Virginia lead tourists to well-preserved sites of famous battles. . . . Elgin Groseclose publishes *Arafat*, a "powerful story of the Near East. . . ." Babe Ruth helps direct a field day for 500 boys at the World Fair. . . . City folk renew ties with the soil at hundreds of rural expositions and county fairs. . . . The World Fair will run in 1940, despite war peril. . . . Alice Marble wins tennis's Essex Bowl. . . . Robert Riggs earns an easy Davis Cup tennis victory.	Sept. 3
New York Mayor LaGuardia bans mass demonstrations during wartime and police disperse crowds. . . . The National Labor Relations Board notes a decline in strikes, from 228 a month in 1937 to 98 monthly in 1939.	President Franklin Roosevelt asks the nation to observe true neutrality.	Air plants speed up their work on war planes, with $25,000,000 worth of orders still unfilled. . . . Steel orders remain up, with August orders exceeding those of July. . . . The revised Social Security Act widens benefits to children, the Society Security Board reports. . . . The public spends more on liquor, post-Prohibition, than it does on government relief, according to the National Women's Christian Temperance Union.	Over 1,000 scientists are expected to attend the third annual International Congress for Microbiology, held in New York. . . . Scientists gather at Harvard University to discuss the effects of the war on science.	Australians capture Davis Cup doubles. . . . Bob Hope is expected to come home from Europe today. . . . Cleveland Indians pitcher strikes out ten batters. . . . Fair throngs exceed 500,000, breaking previous attendance records by a wide margin. . . . Nine out of 11 Broadway shows will host a special matinee in honor of Labor Day. . . . The Hammer Galleries in New York will display the jewels of the last czar of Russia.	Sept. 4

F	**G**	**H**	**I**	**J**
Includes elections, federal-state relations, civil rights and liberties, crime, the judiciary, education, healthcare, poverty, urban affairs, and population.	*Includes formation and debate of U.S. foreign and defense policies, veterans affairs, and defense spending. (Relations with specific foreign countries are usually found under the region concerned.)*	*Includes business, labor, agriculture, taxation, transportation, consumer affairs, monetary and fiscal policy, natural resources, pollution, and accidents.*	*Includes worldwide scientific, medical, and technological developments, natural phenomena, U.S. weather, and natural disasters.*	*Includes the arts, religion, scholarship, communications media, sports, entertainment, fashions, fads, and social life.*

	World Affairs	Europe	Africa & The Middle East	The Americas	Asia & The Pacific
Sept. 5	Japan remains neutral in the European war. . . . About 50 U.S. citizens remain in the Reich to protect interests. American firms are open. . . . Stress on Britain is relieved in the Orient. Japan's irritation at the Reich and desire to pick the winner have modified policy.	Bombs drop on neutral Denmark. The raid is held as unintentional. . . . Britain's war entry beglooms Vienna. The news comes as a surprise and shock to Austrians. . . . Nazi bombers terrorize Warsaw. Many are slain, and damage is heavy. . . . The French and British attack Germans on wide fronts. . . . Germans cut off the Polish corridor. Warsaw concedes the loss of two cities there. . . . A German ship is sunk by a British cruiser. . . . Three Balkan states voice neutrality: the Yugoslav, Romanian, and Bulgarian governments make the declaration.		Canada prepares for Nazi air raids. . . . Canadians pledge a steady newsprint supply and to avoid war profiteering.	
Sept. 6	Gandhi reveals he made a personal plea to Hitler. . . . Fifty thousand in Palestine volunteer for war. Jews and Arabs are ready to assist Britain. . . . The Japanese switch a truck order from the Reich to the United States that totals $10 million. . . . Zionists support Britain; both Arabs and Jews offer support.	Berlin taxes radio sets to keep control of the air. . . . Britain continues leaflet bombing; an anti-Hitler note is dropped. . . . Britain and the Reich lose ships at sea. . . . Germans report control of Silesia and tell of capturing key industrial cities with works intact. . . . London and Paris set curbs on imports. . . . Hitler puts the army in charge of 15 out of 18 districts in Germany. . . . The Reich reports its bureau is flooded by recruits. . . . French radio reports serious disorder in the Reich.	Egypt is now on full war footing. Four military districts are set up	Argentines discard sympathy for the Reich. The press and public are now almost belligerently anti-Hitler.	
Sept. 7	Iraq severs its relationship with Germany. . . . Japan is seen as joining the anti-German bloc. A Chinese supporter suggests that Tokyo and Rome may help Britain and France. . . . Paris expects U.S. policy to evolve, viewing the neutrality arms embargo as only a present policy. . . . U.S. Communists predict Hitler's downfall.	Germans drop bombs in Lithuania along the Polish border. . . . The first Nazi planes approach Britain. Scout ships turn back without battle; pursuers are fired upon with their own artillery. . . . German industries are put on a war basis. A long list of regulations is issued daily. . . . The Nazi army's speed is a surprise. In less than a week, the German forces reach the Polish capital. . . . A new peace effort by Italy is expected.			
Sept. 8	The Japanese suggest the powers quit China, and offers to protect the interests of belligerents in Europe if they withdraw forces. . . . Spain turns to the United States as a supply source and makes inquiries on machinery.	Czechs and Slovaks form legions. . . . French civic life runs smoothly. Mail, railroad services, and markets return to normal. . . . Germans rush troops west to meet France. The Polish army, still intact, defends Warsaw. . . . Germany extends its list of crimes. Violations of new decrees are punishable by long prison terms or even death. . . . Italy sees Germany acting in the Balkans. A Polish collapse would leave the Nazis free to expand in other areas. . . . Jewish emigration from Germany ceases. . . . Polish tactics vex the Nazis. Defenders are accused of arming civilians for guerilla acts. . . . The British raid on a Nazi battleship is called a big victory. . . . . Reich submarines raid allies' ships.			The Japanese occupy the Tientsin YMCA.
Sept. 9	Messages from around the world cheer Britain. . . . Japan is perplexed by the war's inactivity and asks whether the Reich and foes intend to press hostilities. . . . New Zealand enlists 6,600 men for service anywhere in the world.	An official French bulletin says that retreating Germans are blowing up bridges. . . . Berlin envisions deadlock in the west and counts on a quick capture of Warsaw to checkmate Britain and France. . . . Britain prepares the rationing of food but says the move does not indicate a shortage. . . . Britain proclaims a virtual blockade and orders a system of contraband control in retaliation for Reich submarine warfare. . . . The Gestapo arrests many former socialists. Czech leaders are also held. . . . Italy presses for a Balkan bloc. Britain is interested in rapid neutrality moves to bar new alignments. . . . Nazis charge Polish atrocities; 25 mutilated bodies are said to be German.		Canada will defend its own territory and send munitions and airmen to Britain.	
Sept. 10	Argentina fights contraband rules and protests Britain attempting to use the country's food and materials for war. . . . The Japanese premier still holds hope for peace. He thinks Britain and France may withdraw when the Reich settles with Poles. . . . Canada declares war on Germany.	The British proclaim mastery at sea. The Reich is cut off from supplies except from the Baltic, London asserts. . . . Belgian fliers capture two British planes over their airspace. London speeds an apology. . . . German gains in Poland add to the tasks of Allies; the speed of Nazi forces upsets their strategy.		Brazil feels the effect of war on sea trade as few ships arrive.	

A	B	C	D	E
Includes developments that affect more than one world region, international organizations, and important meetings of world leaders.	*Includes all domestic and regional developments in Europe, including the Soviet Union.*	*Includes all domestic and regional developments in Africa and the Middle East.*	*Includes all domestic and regional developments in Latin America, the Caribbean, and Canada.*	*Includes all domestic and regional developments in Asian and Pacific nations (and colonies).*

U.S. Politics & Social Issues	U.S. Foreign Policy & Defense	Economics & Great Depression	Science, Technology & Nature	Culture, Leisure & Lifestyle	
	U.S. neutrality is declared.	Automobile output spurts as 1940 models go into production.	Sulfanilamide is found to check tuberculosis in guinea pigs. . . . Two New York doctors say that psychologists can gauge peoples' emotions by the temperature of their fingers.	Finland halts work on the Olympics and considers canceling the 1940 events. . . . Five thousand participants and spectators gather at the Scottish games held in New Jersey. . . . A meeting of the Cabinet keeps Harold Ickes, Secretary of the Interior, from going to the hospital while his wife gives birth to their son. . . . Millions visit the World Fair over the holiday weekend. . . . Broadway's picture houses were crowded over the holidays.	Sept. 5
	Elliot Roosevelt urges a propaganda curb for radio. He asks the head of broadcasters to put the matter before the FCC. . . . The United States decides to use World War I ships to enforce neutrality. . . . Veterans of the Civil War inspect a modern day fighting unit.	Sharp increases in wholesale food prices are expected to be slow in reaching consumers. . . . The New York Superintendent of Schools urges pay cuts, appealing to all those who make $5,000 or more per year to accept voluntary reductions. . . . 90% of New York's milk distributors have signed pacts that will end the recent strike. . . . Orders for steel pour into America from a flood of foreign companies.	A British doctor isolates the germ responsible for a child-killer disease, rheumatic fever. . . . A new camera takes the fastest pictures ever, with 120,000 possible impressions a minute.	Sam Goldwyn is set to begin production of Blackout Over Europe, starring Gary Cooper. . . . New York actress Rose Keane Shumlin obtains a divorce from Herman Shumlin, producer of the successful Broadway show, The Little Foxes, shocking friends who didn't suspect trouble.	Sept. 6
President Roosevelt asks the nation's law enforcement to help fight espionage and sabotage. Reports are to be given to the FBI. . . . Roosevelt bars censorship, saying he will ask for no curb on press or radio during peace.	President Roosevelt sees a need for fast revision in the ban of arms sales. . . . The Army takes over a Puerto Rico site. . . . The war stimulates U.S. airline travel, as the end of foreign competition brings a heavy demand upon our own industry.	A Representative calls the New Deal a Communist front. A colleague accuses him of making a "cheap speech." . . . August iron production rose nearly 13 percent over July and was 78 percent over 1938 production rates.	Scientists turn the rabies virus into an antidote for the disease.	American designs lead a fashion show, with a black and cerise evening ensemble being favored over French imports. . . . The New York Giants, champions of the National Football League, will challenge collegiate stars to an All-Star game. . . . An international array of stars are prepared to play in the U.S. title tennis tournament. . . . Lavish new fashion designs stress modesty, with high necks and long sleeves.	Sept. 7
The Society of Friends asks for a ban on the sale of "Old Quaker" whiskey in Pennsylvania.	The Army and Navy speed recruitment to enforce neutrality.	Washington sees no new tax need. Assuming neutrality, war should increase revenues. . . . Buick plans to reduce prices on nine automobile models and to add additional features on new cars at no extra cost. . . . New York pays 25 percent of the country's income tax. . . . May Department Stores triples its income over 1938.	Chicago doctors hail freezing cancers as an effective tool in fighting the disease. . . . Princeton researchers trace the luminescence of fireflies and the sea bacteria to two chemicals, stating that their lights are 97 percent effective compared to a 12 percent effective rate of a light bulb.	A College Art Conference speaker discusses finding a life-sized sculpture of Jesus Christ from the 1400s in Florence, Italy. Found in a "dingy little place," Dello Delli is credited as the sculptor . . . Spalding's Official Football Guide for 1939 includes four rule changes of note. . . . The New York Giants beat a team of college All-Stars for the seventh year in a row, keeping their unblemished record. . . . Lupe Velez is set to star in Hot Tamale.	Sept. 8
A former U.S. Communist says that Stalin seized control of the party in 1929. He testifies that the Soviet chief still dictates to American Communists. . . . NBC wins a slander case the centered on remarks made by Al Jolson on a radio program. . . . The president of Notre Dame University seeks better relations with Latin American countries. . . . Railroad officials will cut rates by 25 percent to aid travel to the World Fair.	The Army seeks 17,000 to enlist. The move will make a total of 227,000 under President Roosevelt's new proclamation.	President Franklin Roosevelt insists that food is plentiful, and assures people that prices will not skyrocket as in 1917–18. . . . A manufacturer of nurses' uniforms offers to hold prices steady for the next ninety days, despite the rise in price of cotton. . . . Gains in telephone service is seen as Southern California and Michigan Bell add stations.	A Rockefeller scientist discusses a the discovery of a powerful germ killer that causes pneumonia to yield.	The New York Giants team may be the best professional football team ever assembled, some experts predict. . . . For the third time, a parachute at the amusement zone of the World Fair fails to open, and two women remain 230 feet in the air for 30 minutes. . . . Warner Bros. plans to add eight movies to its 1939–40 schedule to meet American demand and they will also ban all anti-Nazi films. . . . The Roxy theater shows their version of Louis Bromfield's novel, The Rains Came.	Sept. 9
U.S. life expectancy grows by twelve years since the turn of the century.	The United States mobilizes. President Roosevelt takes the first steps to protect the open seaboard and keep peace in the hemisphere.	Building loans rose 28 percent in July, with two thirds of this volume used to start families on their way to home ownership. . . . A builder earns 10 percent on his 500 properties located in the slums of Philadelphia. . . . The president of a Philadelphia bank warns against too low mortgage rates, saying that funds will dry up.	An archaeological expert unlocks the key to the ancestry and history of remote Mexican tribes. . . . Columbia University creates a masters of engineering degree that allows students to obtain a broad, rather than specialized, education. . . . A new resin fiber is made out of salt, coal, air and lime, and will rival silk.	Simon & Schuster publishes A Treasury of American Prints, including more than 2,500 prints. . . . Anna Reiner publishes Five Destinies, a moving novel about children's lives. . . . Ancient relics, including doors of Flemish design and Dutch coins, were discovered in a New Jersey residence.	Sept. 10

F	G	H	I	J
Includes elections, federal-state relations, civil rights and liberties, crime, the judiciary, education, healthcare, poverty, urban affairs, and population.	Includes formation and debate of U.S. foreign and defense policies, veterans affairs, and defense spending. (Relations with specific foreign countries are usually found under the region concerned.)	Includes business, labor, agriculture, taxation, transportation, consumer affairs, monetary and fiscal policy, natural resources, pollution, and accidents.	Includes worldwide scientific, medical, and technological developments, natural phenomena, U.S. weather, and natural disasters.	Includes the arts, religion, scholarship, communications media, sports, entertainment, fashions, fads, and social life.

	World Affairs	Europe	Africa & The Middle East	The Americas	Asia & The Pacific
Sept. 11	Canada proclaims war on Germany. It is the first war declaration in the history of the Dominion. Parliament rushes financing.	Germany batters Warsaw, subjecting it to all-day shelling and continuous air raids. Foes fight in the streets as women and girls dig trenches. . . . The French rush men to the Italian border. A large concentration of men and supplies is seen. . . . Germans warn the Czechs that enlistment in any foreign army is treason. . . . Hitler flies over the eastern front and follows the retreat of Polish troops. . . . Irish sympathies lie with Britain. Germany is not as popular as in 1914. . . . The Reich's economy is on a full war basis. Wages, prices, costs, and supplies are now controlled by official decree. . . . Soviets prepare for a threat in the west. . . . Submarines sink seven ships in two days. Britain confirms the losses.		President Roosevelt bans arms sales to Canada. The Neutrality Act extends to the Dominion after they declare war.	Japanese airplanes devastate the city of Luchow. The bombing leaves the city without medical supplies, the Chinese say.
Sept. 12	The Japanese bar reporters at a Mongol border base. . . . Tokyo now forecasts a long European war, changing its prediction about a quick pace. . . . War shelves the British plan for a federal India.	Berlin announces a counter-blockade. British measures bring prompt notice of retaliation in respect to commerce. . . . A man throws hard rubber balls into a London crowd as a peace protest. The crowd thinks they are bombs and panics. The man receives four weeks of hard labor. . . . Britain bars peace until Hitler goes, saying it will only deal with a trustworthy government. . . . Germans evacuate a base on the island of Sylt. . . . Germany bars Jews on streets at night. . . . Romanian troops move to the frontier.		Bermuda lifts a ban on autos during wartime only.	
Sept. 13	Airlines abroad quit flying to Latin America. The war leaves the United States alone in flights there. . . . A German envoy denies the Reich desires world rule, asserting that Poland is not being invaded for supremacy, but for sentimental objectives. . . . Japan asks for amity with the Soviet Union.	The British withhold pressure on Italy. They believe the time is not right to ask for neutrality rather than non-intervention. . . . The British guard the transfer of men. An expeditionary force of men to France is kept secret until completed. . . . French assaults along the border force Germans into permanent forts. . . . German engineers arrive in Russia to help build up industry, it is said. . . . The Reich appoints Heinrich Himmler, head of the Gestapo, as an official deputy. . . . Nazi air defenses are appalling, the British say. A leaflet raid shows the weaknesses of detectors, searchlights, and batteries. . . . Nazis hint at the purge of Jews in Poland. . . . Germans sink the 16th British ship.		President Roosevelt renews the pledge to Canada. Invasion of the Dominion in war will be resisted by the United States under the Monroe Doctrine.	
Sept. 14	Britain warns that the Reich may try to build submarine and air bases in Latin America. . . . Survivors of a sunken British liner arrive in Canada in oil-stained scraps of clothing; some saw the submarine. . . . A new defense plan is in view in Shanghai. The Japanese military is silent on the withdrawal of French and British troops. . . . The YMCA sets up posts in France as in World War I.	The premier asks for peace for Hungary and declares its policies have not changed. . . . The House of Commons attacks censorship. The lack of information to the public aids the Reich, they say. . . . Prime Minister Chamberlain bars peace with Hitler, telling the Commons that France agrees the menace needs to be destroyed, which would also free the Czechs. . . . Germans bomb open towns; Britain threatens to retaliate. . . . No change in policy is held likely in Italy until Poland reaches a decisive stage. . . . The Reich curtails school. Less important subjects are cut due to the teacher shortage.			
Sept. 15	The British Consul denies his country wants to drag the United States into war. . . . The British seize a U.S. cargo ship. A curb on the Reich's imports for war is held as the only objective. . . . Latin America worries Berlin; an editorial appeals to their self-interest in neutrality. . . . Pope Pius XII begs belligerents to humanize war and save the civilian population from gas and other horrors. . . . The Reich says President Roosevelt is unfair in his policy: Canada can attack, but not be attacked. . . . The United States may aid in a war stalemate. The situation is likened to 1917.	The French push Nazis back into forts. The thrust widens as artillery fire indicates a big Allied offensive is near. . . . Germans rout their foe. France admits there is no front as Poles withdraw and 60,000 prisoners are taken. . . . Poland requests more British aid, particularly by air. . . . Turkey and Romania assure the Reich of non-participation. . . . Russia threatens Poland as her defenses crumble. . . . Hitler makes vast concessions in a pact with Stalin.			

A	B	C	D	E
Includes developments that affect more than one world region, international organizations, and important meetings of world leaders.	*Includes all domestic and regional developments in Europe, including the Soviet Union.*	*Includes all domestic and regional developments in Africa and the Middle East.*	*Includes all domestic and regional developments in Latin America, the Caribbean, and Canada.*	*Includes all domestic and regional developments in Asian and Pacific nations (and colonies).*

U.S. Politics & Social Issues	U.S. Foreign Policy & Defense	Economics & Great Depression	Science, Technology & Nature	Culture, Leisure & Lifestyle	
American typists beat Canadians by a slim margin in a two-week long international typing marathon. . . . Children's Court extends its jurisdiction to a 15-year-old female seeking a divorce from her 20-year-old husband. . . . July birthrates nears a record low.	The Roosevelt administration proposes voluntary military training for the Civilian Conservation Corps. Providing separate units and barring compulsion is expected to allay opposition. . . . President Roosevelt plans a call to Congress before the week ends. The threat of filibuster against the repeal of the arms embargo is not expected to halt him.	Cotton prices go up 89 points in one week. . . . Rising sugar prices lift the feeling of gloom in Puerto Rico, as the island looks forward to a new era of prosperity. . . . A shortage of the wheat supply seems unlikely, with 985,000,000 bushels available for the season and domestic usage predicated at 700,000,000.	Radio waves are being used in a revolutionary new method of drying tobacco. . . . Scientists gather to study America, as delegates from 39 learned societies and universities focus on the background of the New World.	The Metropolitan Museum of Art opens an exhibition of Turkish embroideries, velvets, and brocaded silks from the Ottoman period. . . . Coiffures revive the "cascade" of 1880, revealing the backs of necks in individual styles. . . . More than 100 delegates will attend the first-ever International Congress of the American Musicological Society. . . . Twentieth-Century Fox adds *Jesse James*, starring Henry Fonda, to its schedule. . . . After a $10 million outlay, Finland suspends work on the 1940 Olympic Games for three months.	Sept. 11
	Mayor Fiorello LaGuardia warns public officials to watch their words. Speeches are analyzed abroad, he says, and conclusions drawn.	Shoppers cease panicky buying and hoarding of food. Stocks are replenished and big price upswings are expected. . . . 1939 is a big year for the film industry, with Universal earning nearly $1 million in 39 weeks, compared to a $753,000 loss in 1938. . . . A bumper tobacco crop yields nearly 1.7 billion pounds.	Adages are scrapped in the care of new babies, as the obstetrical college is told that bathing at once and shaking for cries should end. . . . A Chicago chemist warns against cheap cosmetics, charging that manufacturers cater to the penny-pinching element of society but fail to educate the public about risks. . . . Chemists cut hemorrhage peril finding methods to produce ample amounts of vitamin K. . . . A toxin found in the blood of animals with cancer is found to kill off those cells.	Coney Island opens its Mardi Gras week, with 250,000 attending its police safety night. . . . Lucille Ball will star in *Cross Country Romance*. . . . Pearl Buck's first drama, *Flight into China*, appears at the Paper Mill Playhouse. . . . Filmarte Theatre opens its season with a French film, *The End of a Day*. . . . The Whitney Museum of American Art reopens.	Sept. 12
Customers take lax beauty shops to task, complaining about noisy hair dryers and preferring male barbers.			The study of cancer cells is aided by the ancient drug colchicine, making the disease more susceptible to radium and X-rays. . . . Scientists report gains in treating colds, combining adrenalin, ephedrine, and benzedrine with vitamin C. . . . A new treatment for anemia is found, using the extract of embryonic chickens to clot their blood.	Pocket Books announces that it will publish a 25 cent version of Pearl Buck's book, *The Good Earth* and *A Tale of Two Cities* by Charles Dickens. . . . The Philadelphia Opera Company invites composers to create an American opera, agreeing to produce the winner in the 1940–41 season. . . . Lake Placid weighs a winter Olympics bid, while Canada withdraws from the entire 1940 program.	Sept. 13
First Lady Eleanor Roosevelt reports no subversive gains in the United States. She doubts Communists and fascists have a strong influence on people.	Congress will meet on September 21 to discuss the arms embargo.	Five million Underwood typewriters have now been produced.	A Canadian doctor sees cancer as a deficiency disease; a high vitamin diet is recommended.	A professor declares that Negro spirituals are not from Africa, but are mere versions of white folks' songs.	Sept. 14
		Prices of meat, butter, and eggs rise in city markets, with poultry prices holding steady. . . . A price rise of about half a cent per quart of milk is anticipated, with a cut in costs seen for those on relief.	Scientists say that greater availability of heavy carbon widens their ability to study life processes of plants and animals.	Surgeons discover that half a brain is as good as the whole; removal of a small part, however, causes serious impairment.	Sept. 15

F	G	H	I	J
Includes elections, federal-state relations, civil rights and liberties, crime, the judiciary, education, healthcare, poverty, urban affairs, and population.	*Includes formation and debate of U.S. foreign and defense policies, veterans affairs, and defense spending. (Relations with specific foreign countries are usually found under the region concerned.)*	*Includes business, labor, agriculture, taxation, transportation, consumer affairs, monetary and fiscal policy, natural resources, pollution, and accidents.*	*Includes worldwide scientific, medical, and technological developments, natural phenomena, U.S. weather, and natural disasters.*	*Includes the arts, religion, scholarship, communications media, sports, entertainment, fashions, fads, and social life.*

	World Affairs	Europe	Africa & The Middle East	The Americas	Asia & The Pacific
Sept. 16	A Far East pact between Japan and Russia is seen, indicating a threat to the United States, Britain, and Nationalists in China. . . . Italy advises Japanese to leave the country. . . . The Japanese bid for U.S. friendship. . . . Russia and Japan agree on an armistice. . . . The Vatican is critical on church curbs in the Reich and disputes the Italian explanation. . . . A ceasefire is declared in the undeclared border war between Japan and its China territories, and the Soviet Union.	Britain will enlist anti-Nazi Germans. A tribunal will classify those friendly to the Allied cause. . . . The British war aim is methodical gain. Sending planes to Poland is ruled out. . . . Diplomats cross the Polish border. Envoys say the refugee situation is desperate and there is danger of famine. . . . A flank of attack on Belgium is posed; German invasion is possible. . . . France is ready if Poland collapses. Paris feels the Allied mastery of the sea assures victory in the long run.			Australia forms a war Cabinet. A new administration, heavier taxes, and recruiting are part of the plan.
Sept. 17	Experts discount air raids in the United States, holding that experience in Europe shows the sea is an effective barrier. . . . Britain envisages Soviet neutrality. A Russo-Japanese truce, viewed as a political step, has little effect on the war. . . . Gandhi urges Britain to "free" India, saying the free country would be an ally to defend democracy. . . . Greece demobilizes on the Albanian border. The move is held in exchange for Italian friendship. . . . War nerves stir the world. Modern communication makes mankind everywhere sensitive to any distant shock.	The Soviet Union invades Poland from the east. Within days, 800,000 Red Army troops are involved. . . . Italy worries about a blockade effect. Rome works on a program to get along with a minimum of imported supplies. . . . The German press presents the Reich as the champion of freedom of the seas. . . . Germans take a big lead in war publicity. The British and French censors clamp news, while Germany beats the propaganda drum. . . . Germans control more than half of Poland. . . . Germans execute an objector to the war who was a Jehovah's Witness. . . . Germany extends its 10-hour workday. . . . Nazis charge foes with inhumanity: the Poles with mustard gas and Britain with a hunger blockade. A retaliation hint is seen.		Canada's door is open to trade; no bars are raised by its belligerent status. . . . Cuba will govern the price of sugar and most likely regain the title of the world's sugar bowl. . . . Latin American countries are looking to the U.S. as a better customer.	Japan renews attacks on China following armistice with Russia. . . . The report of a double Shanghai threat brings about foreign skepticism.
Sept. 18	The Japanese disclaim Soviet pact plans. Military leaders say foreign opinion has overestimated the truce. . . . Canada feels the Soviet invasion into Poland sharply, spurring it to participation.	Russians drive 40 miles into Poland; defenses are weak. . . . Britain cuts advertising during the war; some campaigns are not to be revived until peacetime. . . . Premier Daladier cuts his trip to the front short, rushing back to Paris to confer on Russia's invasion of Poland. . . . Germany shifts troops westward. Large units come from Poland as France hurls two counterattacks. . . . The Nazi drive in the east yields three key areas. . . . The retreat of Poles changes to a rout. The Germans now face a mop-up job of its foe, crushed by mechanization.			Japan now drives for a China victory. A peace deal with Chiang Kai-shek is not ruled out. . . . Australians rush to enlist in the army.
Sept. 19	Japan warns the United States on its naval policy. The assumption of a watchdog role is really a provocation, newspapers assert. . . . President Roosevelt renews his plea on bombings, asking belligerents to spare civilian centers. . . . A Vatican City paper declares the Russian invasion of Poland a cowardly act under false pretenses.	A blast at sea sinks a British freighter. A huge blaze is reported. . . . Britain pledges to fight to the finish, despite the Soviet invasion of Poland. . . . A Czech purge is under way. The Gestapo is terrorizing leftists and intellectuals. . . . Italy is still wary of taking action, waiting to see if the Balkans, especially Romania, are under Soviet threat. . . . Lithuania guards its border strongly. Nearly full mobilization is effected as Russians take the adjoining Polish area. . . . The president asserts Polish authority, signing a proclamation before entering Romania to counter Nazi-Soviet claims. . . . Moscow outlines Polish partition. The broadcast says Germany is in accord; a buffer state plan is suggested. . . . Poland may become a socialist republic; the Reich's price for the Soviet pact is thought to be high.		Canada will depend upon the U.S. for trans-sea air mail.	
Sept. 20	Canada prepares for war overseas. . . . The Chinese are confident of Russia's help. They do not believe that the invasion of Poland changes its favorable policy. . . . Japan bars arms for German ships, promising Britain that none will be fit out as raiders in Japanese ports. . . . Japan and Italy censor messages; 40 nations now restrict communications. . . . A Vatican City paper fears Soviet designs on Europe.	The Allied chiefs meet. British will hold the Belgian line; Germans mass troops and an invasion is feared. . . . A Baltic grab is predicted. The Soviet wish for a port is thought to be behind the action of the fleet. . . . The British admit the loss of three more ships. . . . Hitler tells Allies that it is his peace or a fight to the finish. . . . Nazis execute a 71-year-old farmer for setting his grain on fire. . . . Italy strengthens its neutral stand; Hitler's failure to mention the Axis is noted in Rome. . . . Poles resist the siege, making a heroic stand against hopeless odds.		Canada prepares for the war overseas.	

A	B	C	D	E
Includes developments that affect more than one world region, international organizations, and important meetings of world leaders.	*Includes all domestic and regional developments in Europe, including the Soviet Union.*	*Includes all domestic and regional developments in Africa and the Middle East.*	*Includes all domestic and regional developments in Latin America, the Caribbean, and Canada.*	*Includes all domestic and regional developments in Asian and Pacific nations (and colonies).*

U.S. Politics & Social Issues	U.S. Foreign Policy & Defense	Economics & Great Depression	Science, Technology & Nature	Culture, Leisure & Lifestyle	
A $200,000 monastery is dedicated in New Jersey and will be maintained by the Dominican sisters.	President Roosevelt wants a limited Congressional session confined to the embargo issue. . . . Charles Lindbergh urges that the United States shun war. If we fight for democracy there, he says, we could possibly lose it here.	The CIO sets the Armour strike for Tuesday if demands are not met.	A new blood test can detect cancer. . . . Scientists find the missing link in rubber production. . . . Chemists learn that extracts from bone marrow may help the body fight infection. . . . Engineers measure a lightning bolt, discovering that its force could power 40,000 household lamps.	Giovanni Martinelli will arrive from Europe today and will perform at the Chicago City Opera Company. . . . Paramount completes its casting for *Safari* today, a movie that will star Douglas Fairbanks, Jr. . . . The Sons of the American Revolution will commemorate the 152nd anniversary of the adoption of the Constitution. . . . The Museum of Natural History will exhibit Stone Age items from New Guinea.	Sept. 16
	Army divisions are cut to 10,000 men each. This reduction from units of 20,000 is called a step towards efficiency and mobilization.	The numbers of foreclosures drops across the nation. Bank loan reports show a continued drop in a seven-month period. . . . Grocers are expected to ask that the food stamp plan continue, regardless of war developments. . . . Banks consider giving aid to financially troubled home owners to help them retain their homes. . . . By the time that actress Deanna Durbin turns 21, she is expected to have $1 million in the bank.	The doctor of the Dionne quints speaks out against kissing babies during the first month of life, saying that increases the chance of infection. . . . New research provides paint pigments with improved retention on glossy surfaces.	1939 is a big year for documentaries. . . . David Loth publishes a full-length biography on Alexander Hamilton. . . . Public libraries will host nine art exhibitions funded by the New York Art Project and the WPA. . . . Chic fashions now include laced-up corsets. . . . Autumn home decoration trends include floral printed curtains and lighter colors.	Sept. 17
Nine diseases caused the majority of US deaths, with heart disease responsible for 72 percent of those deaths. . . . Gipsy Smith, internationally known evangelist, arrives from England to begin a revival campaign. . . . A shortage of architects is predicted.		The Farm Security Administration encourages low-income farmers to churn their own butter, mill their own flour, and weave their own cloth. . . . The United States Brewers Association anticipates that beer production will be curtailed because of a shortage of hops. . . . Normalcy returns to the wheat market, with supply and demand factors in balance. . . . Pace accelerates in the steel industry. . . . New York's State Labor Department sends representatives to 21 cities to survey cost of living figures.		John Steinbeck's book *The Grapes of Wrath* tops best-seller lists. . . . A costume fête with the theme of Hollywood History will aid the Federation for the Crippled and Disabled. . . . Boxer Joe Louis recovers from a head cold and returns to training for his next fight.	Sept. 18
Poor turnout is likely in the primary election today. The rank and file of both major parties seem lukewarm about the election. . . . Divorced singer and actress Marion Talley receives custody of her daughter for nine months of the year.	A general declares that the United States is unprepared for defense, saying it is not equipped for modern war.	Accountants urge the formation of a tax study agency with a nonpartisan committee in charge of formulating policies for federal levies. . . . Married teachers will be asked to give up jobs to single young women in need of employment. In the event of financial crises in their families, their jobs could be restored. . . . Plymouth adds two models for 1940, including a car with folding seats.		The United States seeks the 1940 Olympics if Finland backs out. . . . Actresses model autumn fashions with peg skirts receiving applause. . . . Houghton Mifflin is reprinting *The Fireside Sphinx*, a collection of cat lore originally published in 1901. . . . Joe Louis finishes his training for a 20-round fight with Bob Pastor.	Sept. 19
Police arrest 15 at primary polls. A Democratic committeeman is accused of getting a voter to sign a false name. . . . Drunk driving declines by 21 percent. . . . San Antonio's mayor describes Vice President Garner as a "fine, water drinking, Christian gentleman with a fine past," adding that he is too old to run for president. . . . The American Red Cross sets up a program to help Americans stranded in war zones. . . . Schools drop fear tactics as a curb for truancy, focusing on sympathy and individualized instruction for "bad" boys and girls.				Friends row across the Mississippi Sound to celebrate the 100th birthday of a woman who had 8 children and then adopted 25 more. . . . Joe Louis beats Bob Pastor in a world class bout before a crowd of 50,000. . . . Stores show suits with hour glass figure designs. . . . The Cincinnati Reds begin selling World Series tickets even though the National League pennant has not been decided. They are swamped with sales. . . . The New York Yankees win their 100th game of the season.	Sept. 20
F *Includes elections, federal-state relations, civil rights and liberties, crime, the judiciary, education, healthcare, poverty, urban affairs, and population.*	**G** *Includes formation and debate of U.S. foreign and defense policies, veterans affairs, and defense spending. (Relations with specific foreign countries are usually found under the region concerned.)*	**H** *Includes business, labor, agriculture, taxation, transportation, consumer affairs, monetary and fiscal policy, natural resources, pollution, and accidents.*	**I** *Includes worldwide scientific, medical, and technological developments, natural phenomena, U.S. weather, and natural disasters.*	**J** *Includes the arts, religion, scholarship, communications media, sports, entertainment, fashions, fads, and social life.*	

	World Affairs	Europe	Africa & The Middle East	The Americas	Asia & The Pacific
Sept. 21	An envoy from Japan denies Soviet ties. He says the truce has no bearing on Europe and was not inspired by the Reich. . . . The armed *Mauretania* arrives in the United States with 698 passengers. It reports seeing no submarines. . . . The extra U.S. Congressional session worries Germans. . . . Pope Pius XII acts to aid Polish Catholics.	Britain rations fuel; consumers get 75 percent of last year's supply. . . . Whole populations are being moved from war zones in France. . . . A defiant Warsaw still repels its foe. Defenders bury the dead in parks as broadcasts warn Nazis that they will not yield. . . . German officers arrive in Moscow to plan military zones for the two countries. . . . Romanians discover a plot to have Bukovina joined to the Reich. . . . Italy urges peace on Hitler's terms; the press advises Allies that the defeat of Poland renders further war useless. . . . Critics of Prime Minister Neville Chamberlain decry inadequate support to Poland. . . . Refugees swarm to neutral land; thousands pour from Poland to Hungary and Romania for safety. . . . Russians advance, taking more ground.		Canada's exports to the U.S. increase from $39,600 in 1938 to $61,200 in 1939.	Chiang Kai-shek assumes rule in Szechwan province, ending the feud among militants.
Sept. 22		The fascist Iron Guard slays the Romanian premier Armand Calinescu. Romanians publicly execute nine pro-Nazi Iron Guards in retribution for the assassination. . . . The Gestapo is on alert for a Czech revolt. . . . Nazi minister Joseph Goebbels denies aiming at Belgium. . . . Poles still resist Nazis in four sectors. . . . Bands of Ukrainians battle for a small Polish territory at the base of the mountains.			
Sept. 23	British is cautious on U.S. neutrality and reticent on Roosevelt's message. . . . The Chinese ask for French aid, seeking the release of war shipments impounded in Indo-China. . . . Japan gives a Shanghai plan. The proposal is studied by the United States, Britain, and Italy. . . . The Soviets deny a peace move in China. The Chinese feel steps taken by Russia will be to their ultimate benefit.	Allied war chiefs meet in England and establish complete agreement on the course of action. . . . The army demarcation line gives Russians a large area won by Nazis. Germans withdraw to zones fixed in the deal as the Red Army takes over fighting. . . . The division of Poland upsets Italy. The Nazi-Soviet partition is held to be military, not ethnic, and a rebuff to Premier Mussolini. . . . The Dutch and Belgians open dikes, seeing a threat in German moves. . . . The Reich takes the most in the division of Poland. . . . The Romanian government executes scores of Iron Guards after the premier's assassination.		The Americas guard their safety. Each of 21 republics is set to defend itself against threat. . . . Canadians seek the purchase of 500,000 blankets from the United States. The order is too big for any American concern. . . . Chileans endorse President Roosevelt's views, believing the Neutrality Act is unsafe as is.	
Sept. 24	The French remove the ban on Chinese supplies. Burmese and Indo-Chinese routes open. . . . Greeks fear Soviet pressure may weaken Turkey's tie with the Allies. . . . A U.S. professor says that Italy is cashing in on war, and is engaged in a "scandalous profiteering" venture. . . . Pope Pius XII is deeply anxious about the Polish situation and worries about Catholics there.	Allies gird for the fourth week of war. The partition of Poland casts a shadow over Europe. . . . The British see Germany checked in the east. Soviet Russia's entry into the game of diplomatic moves may hold gains for the Allies.			
Sept. 25	The U.S. Ambassador to Poland says Nazis used 5,000 planes in their attack.	Belgium is prepared, but its army is small. The force is organized for quick action. . . . British censors release the first eyewitness accounts of movements in France. . . . Romanian King Carol disregards government wishes, attending the funeral of Premier Calinescu. . . . Christian X, King of Denmark suffers a mild heart attack. . . . French observers reject Premier Mussolini's proposal to base peace on the conquest of Poland. . . . Nazi guns and planes raze Warsaw; half of the city is in flames. . . . Nazis cite the power of Reich industry. Their capacity is greater than that of France and Britain combined, they say. . . . Russia shuts the Neva River as Finns dig trenches.			The Japanese launch a major drive in China. Tokyo says its forces are making steady gains, but the Chinese say defenses are sturdy.

A	B	C	D	E
Includes developments that affect more than one world region, international organizations, and important meetings of world leaders.	*Includes all domestic and regional developments in Europe, including the Soviet Union.*	*Includes all domestic and regional developments in Africa and the Middle East.*	*Includes all domestic and regional developments in Latin America, the Caribbean, and Canada.*	*Includes all domestic and regional developments in Asian and Pacific nations (and colonies).*

U.S. Politics & Social Issues	U.S. Foreign Policy & Defense	Economics & Great Depression	Science, Technology & Nature	Culture, Leisure & Lifestyle	
A judge rules against a teacher holding two positions, which will affect those who teach in day and night school.		An economist for the Federal Reserve Bank finds banks healthier and attributes that to less competition and stress. . . . Job placements rise as 43 percent more youth were placed in private jobs in 1939 than in 1938. . . . The continuing conflict between the AFL and CIO causes a rising hostility of the general public towards labor, some labor leaders fear. . . . Relief cases rise 3 percent in August.	Temperatures in California reach 100 for the fifth day in a row, while rain and lightning add to the discomfort of residents. . . . Electric power output sets a record this week.	Finland will not yield the 1940 Olympics to the United States. . . . Joe Louis keeps his boxing title in a thrilling bout. . . . Estelle Hamburger publishes It's a Woman's Business, a book that discusses her life in the fashion industry. . . . The Carnegie International Exhibition of Paintings will begin in October. . . . Joe Louis praises his opponent after winning last night's fight. . . . Romance styles will be popular in 1940 fashion, as gowns with wide hoopskirts gain applause at the World Fair.	Sept. 21
A jury of eight men and four women doom the "arsenic widow" to the electric chair. The judge praises the verdict, calling it courageous and saying it proves women can decide on evidence. . . . Secret service and police surround President Roosevelt. . . . Roosevelt nears his 1936 popularity as 61 percent of voters endorse the President.	Editorials back President Roosevelt's plea. Commendation on his stand on neutrality crosses the lines of major parties. . . . President Roosevelt asks Congress to repeal the arms embargo. A hard fight is indicated as 24 Senators map resistance.			Paramount buys The Monster for $50,000. . . . Twentieth-Century Fox casts Russell Simpson as Pa Joad in The Grapes of Wrath. . . . A London writer ranks US tennis stars Robert Riggs and Alice Marble as the best players in the world.	Sept. 22
A contract is signed, settling the dispute between actors unions. The American Guild of Variety Artists absorbs members of the discredited American Federation of Actors.	The Army speeds its defense program.	The followers of evangelist Father Divine support striking workers of the Shack Sandwich Shops by staging a sit down strike. . . . Milk sales increase by 5.65 percent in August.	California heat causes 65 deaths. Schools and shops close as temperatures reach 103 degrees and only slight relief is in sight.	The World Fair presents its first Mardi Gras in swing to boost autumn attendance. . . . Bob Feller pitches his 22nd win of the season for the Cleveland Indians. . . . Paramount seeks Carole Lombard as the lead in F.O.B. Detroit.	Sept. 23
	The Army creates a new mobile corps. The main unit of the force will deliver swift, hard blows.		Experiments producing 100 mice may answer pre-natal influence questions. . . . A multi-view stereoscope allows up to eight doctors to view X-rays at one time. . . . The British doctor credited with finding thyroid treatments dies.	Paul Corey publishes Three Miles Square, a "fine novel of the rural scene." . . . Americans approve the Parisian silhouette, with swing and pegtop skirts. . . . Connie Mack says that winning baseball teams need good pitching and good team work.	Sept. 24
Proctor and Gamble agree to modify their advertising based on objections by the Federal Trade Commission. They will stop claiming that their soap contains a special ingredient that allows it to be the only brand that can remove "deep down" dirt. . . . Film pioneer Carl Laemmle, Sr., dies. He organized independent film companies into Universal with its vast studio. . . . Evangelist Father Divine plays host at a 24-hour feast, with 200 items on the menu tempting his followers known as "angels" . . . Earhart monument to aid women fliers; pilots plan to raise $2,000 to give a training award. . . . A grandmother is sought in the slaying of a child.	A new draft of the Neutrality Act ends the ban on arms.		Doctor discovers that adrenal glands produce sex hormones. . . . A rat suffers from infantile paralysis. This discovery hints at the source of human epidemics.	Dr. Sigmund Freud dies. His body will be cremated. The war prevented him from becoming a British citizen. . . . The Grapes of Wrath continues to top bestseller lists. . . . Work begins on the film adaptation of Our Town. . . . Jean Arthur's refusal to play the lead role in Columbia's His Girl Friday leads to her suspension. . . . New York Yankees make a triple play in their 3-2 win over the Senators.	Sept. 25

F	G	H	I	J
Includes elections, federal-state relations, civil rights and liberties, crime, the judiciary, education, healthcare, poverty, urban affairs, and population.	Includes formation and debate of U.S. foreign and defense policies, veterans affairs, and defense spending. (Relations with specific foreign countries are usually found under the region concerned.)	Includes business, labor, agriculture, taxation, transportation, consumer affairs, monetary and fiscal policy, natural resources, pollution, and accidents.	Includes worldwide scientific, medical, and technological developments, natural phenomena, U.S. weather, and natural disasters.	Includes the arts, religion, scholarship, communications media, sports, entertainment, fashions, fads, and social life.

	World Affairs	Europe	Africa & The Middle East	The Americas	Asia & The Pacific
Sept. 26		The conflict upsets British-Balkan trade. A serious stoppage of commerce by sea is feared. . . . The Soviet Union bars a buffer-state idea in Poland. . . . The French shell Reich forts on the Rhine as Nazis mass troops near Basel. . . . Germans expect additional Soviet aid. The division of spoils is foreseen in Poland this week. Nazis think the Russians are with them wholeheartedly in the crushing of Britain. . . . Britain stages a new leaflet raid; messages tell the Reich that hope for a quick war is gone. . . . All Reich restaurants must serve a "one pot meal" that all can afford. . . . The Reich seizes radios of Jews in Prague; compulsory work service is hinted.		American nations consider a ban on the search of coastal shipping. They favor asking belligerents to respect American commerce.	Twenty thousand die in the Japanese drive. Each side loses 10,000 in battle as Chinese cities are being bombed anew.
Sept. 27		Poland surrenders to Germany. . . . Winston Churchill reports that U-boats are on the run, saying seized cargoes exceed British losses. . . . The French artillery pounds Westwall; the German raid is repulsed in a dawn battle. . . . Italy asks Allies not to risk defeat; the peace campaign emphasizes Rome's belief that the Reich would be the victor. . . . The Communist Party and propaganda are outlawed in France by a decree aimed at the Soviet Union. . . . Romania announces the execution of an alleged leader in the premier's assassination. . . . Russians advance to land won by Nazis. Germans leave the scene of bitter battle for the western front.			Japanese forces near Changsha. One column is said to be only 20 miles from the capital of the Hunan province.
Sept. 28	A big Japanese force is still in Manchukuo. Transfers will not be made until the border is fixed. . . . Britain and Japan resume talks. The Japanese are bitter at Germany. Advocates of the Axis admit they are backing the wrong horse. . . . A U.S. professor puts the issues to the Reich people; they alone can save the world by wrecking its mad tyrant, he says at a Columbia University speech. . . . China suggests U.S. mediation. The basis for peace would be a return to a nine-nation treaty, says the foreign minister.	The Allies are seen as the losers in the Soviet parley. Turkey is expected to remain a friendly neutral. . . . The British are taxed at 37 percent of income for war. . . . France raids Communist centers; Reds in the suburbs do not seem disturbed by the outlawing of the party. . . . The 20-day siege ends. Polish defenders yield their last stronghold to the Nazis. The blazing capital is faced with famine and pestilence. . . . France buries its first war dead. . . . Nazi planes raid a British fleet. . . . A Soviet ship is sunk.		Foreign ministers discuss the American protest against reduced sea commerce. They would condemn British and French blacklist items.	
Sept. 29	Efforts for peace in Rome parallel; in approaches to Germany, Pope Pius XII seems to be working through the Italian government. . . . Gandhi asks Britain to state its India aims. . . . Six leaders plea for aid to China. Continued aid by the United States is needed despite the European war. . . . The Nazi press differs on U.S. neutrality. Reports from Washington say the embargo is to be lifted, but German editorials disagree.	The British press reports that a German attack on Scotland is averted. . . . The last Warsaw fort yields to Germany. . . . The Reich denies taking part in an Estonia move. Russian procedures are not part of talks held in Moscow, it is said. . . . A Swedish ship is sunk on its way to Belgium. . . . Threatening action, Moscow and Berlin will respond if Britain and France reject peace moves.		Canadian convoys elude submarines. . . . Argentina offers a contraband plan, proposing the Americas insist on trading with belligerents in non-military goods.	Japan reduces the Manchukuo army.
Sept. 30	The Japanese stress a ban on U.S. mediation. They say the Sino-Chinese conflict is strictly a two-country issue. . . . Pope Pius XII is to address Poles today; he hopes for an end to Nazi occupation.	France offers amnesty to deserters and evaders who register now. . . . Britain launches a ration roll call; 11 million homes will be visited to determine the food needs of the nation. . . . Hitler gets new guards; a fourth group charged with protecting him is formed. . . . Italians display growing anxiety; the Reich-Soviet peace movement will be backed in hope of gaining a settlement. . . . London shuns Nazi bait; the press and people say no to a peace compromise. . . . British planes raid the Nazi fleet. . . . Nazis say a Soviet trade pact allows for a long war. . . . The Russian people worry about being dragged into war.			

A	B	C	D	E
Includes developments that affect more than one world region, international organizations, and important meetings of world leaders.	*Includes all domestic and regional developments in Europe, including the Soviet Union.*	*Includes all domestic and regional developments in Africa and the Middle East.*	*Includes all domestic and regional developments in Latin America, the Caribbean, and Canada.*	*Includes all domestic and regional developments in Asian and Pacific nations (and colonies).*

U.S. Politics & Social Issues	U.S. Foreign Policy & Defense	Economics & Great Depression	Science, Technology & Nature	Culture, Leisure & Lifestyle	
Four convicts flee a prison in Michigan, shielding themselves with two jail officials and two parole board members.		The Agriculture Department issues a revised list of farm surpluses that can be purchased through the food stamp program. . . .1940 Studebaker prices start at $660 for the Custom Coupe.		The board of the World Fair is expected to approve the continuation of the fair on its present site for 1940. . . . A new comedy, *The Man Who Came to Dinner*, opens in Boston. . . . Paris fashions rich in Spanish influence are shown as originals and as interpretations. . . . Jackie Cooper will star in Universal's *No Power on Earth*.	Sept. 26
Elliot Roosevelt says his father has not given the 1940 presidential election a thought. . . . Wisconsin officials fight higher water content in cheese.	An AFL group urges an arms ban revision. A metal trade unit asks Congress to permit the sale of goods to all nations. A report says the ban discriminates against democracies and aids dictatorships. . . . Laura Ingalls drops peace fliers over the capital; she may lose her license. . . . The Navy dispatches a force to Hawaii. The detachment will go for training and decentralization. . . . Citizens meet war propaganda with skepticism.	No lasting good is seen in the war boom. A policy group holds that the effect on trade will be unfavorable. . . . Boys' suits will rise in price from $2 to $3.50. An intermediate line may appear for spring.		The body of Sigmund Freud is cremated. There is no religious service; leaders pay tribute. . . . The World Fair cuts admission to a flat 50-cent rate for all of October. . . . New corsets are on display. Designs to induce a svelte figure interest women. . . . Brilliant array of dahlias goes on view. Over 10,000 blooms are displayed at the annual American Dahlia Society exhibit. . . . The "house of genius" needs a new tenant. Formerly rented by Theodore Dreiser, Eugene O'Neill, and other writers of note, this home is now vacant and available for a new resident.	Sept. 27
A World War I draft dodger swears he hid in the United States for seven years. He returned twice while the nation thought he was in the Reich.	First Lady Eleanor Roosevelt urges the repeal of the arms embargo. She holds that neutrality and a third term for President Roosevelt are unrelated.	CIO officers warn that the war may affect government jobs. Curtailment of services may be the result.		Paramount purchases a romantic film, *In Old Virginia*, and Joel McCrea will star in the movie. . . . Lillian Gish may return to the studio to film *Silver Nights*. Gish co-wrote the script. . . . The New York Yankees will play three doubleheaders and then the World Series will begin.	Sept. 28
A survey finds the United States fears a Nazi attack; 63 percent in a Gallup study believe Hitler will extend the war if he defeats the Allies.	Republicans put neutrality first.	Unemployment dropped 4.3 percent in August, the lowest rate since December 1937.	A Cleveland physician opposes counting sheep at night, saying that it keeps a person awake.	Metro-Goldwyn-Mayer will feature Spencer Tracy and Mickey Rooney in two different films on the life of Thomas Edison. . . . The Cincinnati Reds clinch their first National League pennant in twenty years after beating the Cardinals. . . . The New York Historical Society will exhibit a show about the history of photography.	Sept. 29
A grandmother is charged in a four-year-old's death after she admits strangling the child. She insists the death was accidental, and that she choked the child while adjusting a ribbon. . . . Ninety percent of those in high school lack medical care. A survey shows that 9 out of ten students suffer from an ailment. . . . Traffic fatalities fall 6 percent in August. . . . The Christian front replies, making a blunt denial that the group is anti-Semitic. . . . Traffic fatalities fall 6 percent in August.				The bearded lady at the World Fair is found out to be a man. The fair showman is held as a perjurer for misrepresenting his sex. . . . President Roosevelt is neutral over his favorite in the World Series: the Yankees or Reds. . . . The first biography of Christopher Columbus is on exhibit at the Jewish Theological Seminary of America. . . . Significant contrast exists in evening gowns, with bold extremes in dimensions, materials, and colors. . . . MGM tentatively assigns William Powell to *Susan and God*.	Sept. 30

F	G	H	I	J
Includes elections, federal-state relations, civil rights and liberties, crime, the judiciary, education, healthcare, poverty, urban affairs, and population.	*Includes formation and debate of U.S. foreign and defense policies, veterans affairs, and defense spending. (Relations with specific foreign countries are usually found under the region concerned.)*	*Includes business, labor, agriculture, taxation, transportation, consumer affairs, monetary and fiscal policy, natural resources, pollution, and accidents.*	*Includes worldwide scientific, medical, and technological developments, natural phenomena, U.S. weather, and natural disasters.*	*Includes the arts, religion, scholarship, communications media, sports, entertainment, fashions, fads, and social life.*

	World Affairs	Europe	Africa & The Middle East	The Americas	Asia & The Pacific
Oct. 1	Canada interns scores of Germans.... The Nazi-Soviet pact amazes the Japanese. Intensely anti-Communist, they do not understand Hitler's handing over 15 million Poles to "Reds."	The Allies adapt tactics to a new kind of war. "Science and prudence" is the motto when masses of troops come up against modern fortifications.... Britain arms big liners. Winston Churchill says 2,000 ships are to receive guns.... The British sing "Adolf," a marching song written during London's first air raid.... The British are in an air fight over the Reich.... Churchill takes up where he left off—he is back at his Admiralty job....With Poland crushed, Hitler will offer peace to France and Britain, hinting that Russia will help him if the answer is no.		Canada prepares for long warfare. ...Labor and business groups call on the Mexican government to address food shortages.	
Oct. 2	Hitler and Italian Foreign Minister Ciano discuss a seven-nation peace parlay. The United States is included. ... The Japanese are angry over U.S. naval activity. Moves in the Pacific are attacked by a retired admiral.	Winston Churchill says Allies hold the advantage at sea and in manpower. ... Four British planes are shot down in battle.... Czechs ask the Allies for the right to fight.... Many Poles blame the government for the military collapse.... Turks fear Nazis are inciting "Reds," suspecting an attempt to embroil Russia with the Allies by menacing the Balkans.... The vast Soviet army holds Polish area; more than 1 million troops are stationed there with full equipment.		Mexico sets up free international ports, restricting only the carrying of arms on these ships.	Hong Kong sees attacks by the Chinese. The Japanese infantry is fighting to hold the line 300 yards from the British colony's border.
Oct. 3	Japan stresses that peace is the aim in its policy. It wishes to stay out of the European war.... Poland continues to legally exist in the eyes of the United States. ... Pope Pius XII deplores moral decadence; he sees the trend reflected in pleas for annulments of marriage.... Soviets pour men into China, menacing either British India or Japan.	Britain's first war ditty plays in night clubs, called "We're Going to Hang out the Washing on the Siegfried Line."... Britain calls up more men. Those up to age 23 are to be summoned next.... The British relate their flight over Berlin. A squadron of bombers in full moonlight is reported to have made the trip undetected.... The French map advances in detail. Paris gives the official version of the gradual penetration of the German frontier.... Nazis are in Warsaw; the city is still on fire.... The Reich intensifies seizures in the Baltic; at least eight Swedish ships are held.		The Americas set up a safety sea zone. Belligerents are asked to avoid warlike acts in the sea of their hemisphere.... Canada's exports increase in August, largely because of meat, fish, wood products, and metals.	The Japanese report a major victory. Nineteen Chinese divisions are said to be smashed in battle. Casualties are put at 10,000.
Oct. 4	Former U.S. president Herbert Hoover says the Allies cannot lose. They control the seas and can wait until their enemies are exhausted.... Ethiopia ousts aliens. Italians seize an American hospital there. ... Tokyo admits defeat by the Soviets, calling the Mongol battle disastrous. ... A Tokyo newspaper lays blame for the war on President Roosevelt.... Leon Trotsky says the United States will join the European conflict, saying only they can shift Russian support from Germany.	Berlin assails the British war song, citing bad taste. ... Britain enlists aliens. The order permits Czechs and Poles in the armed forces. ... The division of the French is held to be Hitler's aim. The head of the army committee says the real Reich offensive lies behind Pacific moves.... Franco offers aid to restore peace. He calls this war absurd and sees little hope for quick peace.... Hopes rise in the Reich; Hitler is drafting a conciliatory speech.	Ethiopia ousts foreigners. Many of the expelled are Greek businessmen who lived in the African country for forty years.		The Chinese bomb a Japanese air base, as the defenders turn the tables on the invaders.
Oct. 5	The Americans study Polish relief plans. They will use Hoover's operations in Belgium after World War I as a pattern. ... An agent for the Americas tells belligerents about the sea safety belt zone, informing Britain, France, and Germany.... More U.S. citizens come home from Europe. A Maryland doctor says he was beaten by Nazis in Vienna. ... The Soviet Union increases purchases in the United States.	Britain taxes parents six shillings per week for the care of evacuated children.... Premier Edouard Daladier rejects an imposed peace. He says France wants more than a truce between two aggressions. ... The French rout Nazis in a battle of tanks. ...The French work 45-hour weeks. Overtime pay goes to a National Solidarity fund.... Germany suffers a soap shortage; women wash clothes with well-soaked potato peels. ... The Poles are still fighting, says the Reich command. The water supply is exhausted and food is low.... Turkey resists Russian pressure for a dominant role in the Balkans.			China balks at a drive on Changsha, claiming the defeat of the invader. The Japanese say the city has no great importance.

A	B	C	D	E
Includes developments that affect more than one world region, international organizations, and important meetings of world leaders.	*Includes all domestic and regional developments in Europe, including the Soviet Union.*	*Includes all domestic and regional developments in Africa and the Middle East.*	*Includes all domestic and regional developments in Latin America, the Caribbean, and Canada.*	*Includes all domestic and regional developments in Asian and Pacific nations (and colonies).*

U.S. Politics & Social Issues	U.S. Foreign Policy & Defense	Economics & Great Depression	Science, Technology & Nature	Culture, Leisure & Lifestyle	
Fifty-two percent of voters support a third term for President Roosevelt if strife continues. . . . The nation spreads its net for spies.	Both sides in Congress evade the real neutrality act issue. Tactical points in the debate overlook the defensive objectives in the repeal of the arms embargo.	The U.S. Chamber of Commerce urges longer work hours as the key to recovery.	Sprouted grain assists in the resistance of illness, an Ohio State University researcher says. Regular use of this food has shown positive results in animals and humans. . . . Science has improved the detection of hurricanes and the building of shelters. . . . Girls around the nation show a zest for aeronautics.	The Boston Museum of Fine Arts buys *The Virgin and Child*. This medieval work, restored for months, was purchased for an undisclosed amount. . . . Prentiss Mournian publishes *In Those Days*, a retrospective look at American life more than a century ago.	Oct. 1
The National Committee to Uphold Constitutional Government finds that Roosevelt holds too much power, calling it "shocking" and they urge Congress to repeal any powers that might allow the President to pull the United States into the war.	The rate of Army recruitment is at a peacetime high. . . . The AFL intends to recommend that the United States act as mediator for warring countries in the world. . . . The government studies new ocean flying aids. This process is speeded because the war is interfering with the reporting of weather conditions. . . . The War Department sends sealed orders to more than 10,000 plants with instructions in case of war.	Steel production is pushed to maximum levels. . . . A union leader asks for cost of living increases for workers during the war. . . . Women in the U.S. spent approximately $200,000,000 in beauty shops in 1939, with the overwhelming majority of the money paid for hair care. . . . A consumers' protection group sets up a public meeting to fight increases in milk prices. . . . New York's welfare bureau asks for testing of the food stamp program in rural areas.		Fred Apostoli loses his middleweight boxing title to Ceferino Garcia. . . . . The American Society of Composers, Authors, and Publishers hosts a musical festival to honor American creative artists and to provide relief from the burden of war news. . . . Deputies seize fishing rods and reels, guns, and drawings from John Barrymore. He is being sued by his former secretary. . . . Bing Crosby hits a 73 in an exhibition golf match. . . . Joe DiMaggio wins baseball's batting title.	Oct. 2
Congressman Martin Dies directs attacks on Reds in Chicago, seeing it as a radical hotbed. . . . A ten-year-old is expelled from school for the second time for refusing to salute the flag. The child does so because her family belongs to the Jehovah Witness faith and they do not participate in this ritual.			The Radio Corporation of America and the Farnsworth Television and Radio Corporation agree to share patents and the right to use each other's inventions. . . . A Connecticut fisherman catches a lobster with a light blue shell and bright blue spots on its claws. He sends this creature to the Peabody Museum at Yale. . . . Columbia University builds new laboratories that cost $50,000. These structures will aid oil research.	Fans present Joe DiMaggio with a gift of an automobile. He predicts the Yankees will win the World Series. . . . Modern children are seen as strangers to work. Homes and schools are urged to give needed training by chores and crafts. . . . Harlow Galleries exhibits the work of British artist, Gerald Brockhurst. A large portrait of the Duchess of Windsor is included in the displays.	Oct. 3
Three Illinois sisters admit a fatal prank. After placing spikes on railroad tracks, two men were killed in an accident. Because the girls admitted their involvement, no action will be taken against them.	President Roosevelt ignores military budgets. He orders the Army and Navy to push their present expansion; Congress can approve it later.	President Roosevelt urges labor peace; his plea is sent to the AFL convention. . . . The volume of cocoa trading is the third highest on record, with over 87,000 recorded contracts by the end of September. . . . Two hundred fifty corporations are invited to financially support the World Fair, asking them to allow their 300,000 employees to have one half or a full day off work with pay to attend the festivities. . . . The federal deficit, at the end of September, is over $976,000,000.	The majority of the female freshman college students studying at Barnard who have settled upon a field of study choose science.	Rival teams are set for the World Series. The Yankees are going after their fourth title in a row. . . . Actor John Barrymore withdraws his suit of separation against his wife. When asked if this indicates a reconciliation, the answer is no, that the action is a legal technicality. . . . Louis Bromfield publishes *It Takes All Kinds*, which includes three full-length novels and two novellas. . . . Actress Faye Temple dies. A star of the 1890s, she began her acting career at age 3.	Oct. 4
Congressman Martin Dies says he will unmask Reds in high office, saying he doesn't mean "small fry." . . . A woman is charged with $1 million in fraud. The widow is accused of selling worthless stock to prominent people. . . . Schools in New York plan to expand their tolerance program that includes two monthly assemblies.	The Army orders $6 million worth of light tanks for defense.	Thirteen thousand people with WPA jobs receive pay cuts. . . . An early dip in wheat prices attracts buyers. . . . Ford Motor Company pledges its participation in the 1940 World Fair, the first major industrial exhibitor to make this commitment.	Johns Hopkins University scientists say that the polio virus can be transmitted through the eyes. Tests on monkeys preceded this announcement.	The World Fair in San Francisco will close on October 29 rather than December 2 because of low gate receipts. . . . A new dance group, known as the Ballet Theatre, will begin work on January 4. Eight choreographers will revive old works and create new ones. . . . MGM announces the purchase of *Remember the Day* as a vehicle for Margaret Sullavan. . . . Martha Raye co-stars in Paramount's *$1,000 a Touchdown*.	Oct. 5

F	G	H	I	J
Includes elections, federal-state relations, civil rights and liberties, crime, the judiciary, education, healthcare, poverty, urban affairs, and population.	Includes formation and debate of U.S. foreign and defense policies, veterans affairs, and defense spending. (Relations with specific foreign countries are usually found under the region concerned.)	Includes business, labor, agriculture, taxation, transportation, consumer affairs, monetary and fiscal policy, natural resources, pollution, and accidents.	Includes worldwide scientific, medical, and technological developments, natural phenomena, U.S. weather, and natural disasters.	Includes the arts, religion, scholarship, communications media, sports, entertainment, fashions, fads, and social life.

	World Affairs	Europe	Africa & The Middle East	The Americas	Asia & The Pacific
Oct. 6	The *Iroquois* report amazes the United States. Officials disbelieve the German story of the possible sinking of the liner. . . . The United States sends out warships to protect the *Iroquois*. The White House is skeptical about the report, but the Cabinet decides to take precautions to avoid harm.	Belgium fears a German attack. . . . France begins a Communist purge. . . . Hitler cites Warsaw as a warning. The city's fate is termed a lesson to certain statesmen. . . . Romania resumes Iron Guard arrests. A manifesto assailing King Carol is found on a worker in the army bureau. . . . The mayor of Warsaw commits suicide. . . . Nazis seek trade with Scandinavians, proposing a pact for Germany to take all the goods the blockade keeps from Britain.		A Quebec minister resigns from his post, in protest over the premier's position on the war. . . . Canada's economic outlook changes. Since the war began, a bank review report finds that prices of primary products have risen by 21 percent.	Chinese continue gains at Changsha. Two cities are believed to be recovered from the Japanese.
Oct. 7	The British hold the League of Nations as dead. The peace machinery has collapsed, they inform the Secretary General. . . . U.S. Senators believe the Hitler peace plea is futile; pessimism marks the reaction to his speech. . . . The menaced *Iroquois* liner reports no harm and finds no explosives.	Gigantic Nazi emblems are in the background as Hitler speaks; he commands people to follow, as he demands peace or a war of destruction. . . . British finds the German peace proposal flawed, as something more reliable than Hitler's promise is declared necessary. . . . Premier Daladier rejects Hitler's proposals. French soldiers and guns are on the fighting line in Germany. . . . Hitler is said to favor a Jewish colony in Poland. . . . Hungary likes the Hitler speech; the reference to minorities, though, causes misgivings.			China celebrates the Changsha victory. The biggest single gain of war is considered to be won against the Japanese.
Oct. 8	The high toll of aerial warfare is beginning to be felt. . . . Nazi propaganda fails among Arabs. Muslims fear suppression of religion if dominated by Stalin or Hitler; democracies are their only hope. . . . Pope Pius XII recognizes the Polish regime. He is seen as aligning the Vatican with Britain, France, and the United States against Hitler.	The Balkan states worry over Soviet policy. They want to know if they are next on the expansion list, hoping to keep their 20-year reputation for peace. . . . Belgium prepares for the worst. . . . Winston Churchill awakens Britons. He rouses confidence and the fighting spirit of the people. . . . Finland is anxious about a Soviet bid. Sweden is alarmed too as advances bring Russian bombers within easy range.		Canadians adjusts life to a war pattern: East Coast cities have trial blackouts, and women exchange bridge for knitting. . . . Mexico denies giving aid to a German submarine.	
Oct. 9	Australians deride Hitler's "blustering." They declare that the Reich fails to answer even basic questions. . . . The Polish Consul to Canada predicts a revolution in the Reich and Russia, and declares the Allies will win.	Finns are said to seek Nazi aid with the Soviets. . . . Germany tightens its internal economy. The government is resolved to keep people on minimum rations during wartime. . . . Italy offers a pact for Balkan peace. . . . Nazi chiefs scorn the rebuff of the peace plan. . . . The Soviet Union agrees to rush goods to the Reich. . . . The Soviet oil supply for the Reich is doubted; Berlin is forced to drop its plan for self-sufficiency in motor fuels by 1942.	Egypt plans to sell cotton to Britain.	Canadian life falls into a war pattern, with trial blackouts and with women dropping the game of bridge for knitting.	
Oct. 10	U.S. experts belittle the Nazi-Soviet pact. It is called "window dressing" for Hitler's peace bid, as the pact is seen mostly as an exchange of goods. . . . France is said to be urging China to negotiate with Japan. . . . Vatican sources accuse Russia of acts in Poland. . . . Portugal reaffirms loyalty to Britain. Premier Antonio de Oliviera Salazar stresses amity and does not call for participation in the war. . . . The International Red Cross requires clothing for Poles. Warm underwear and medicine are needed for refugee relief.	British children return to cities. The evacuation scheme seems to be breaking down and school facilities are lacking; the industrial areas are worst. . . . French Premier Edouard Daladier will insist on a free Europe. In a radio reply to Hitler, he is expected to say the war must go on. . . . Germans in the Baltic states rush to repatriate. The families feverishly prepare to migrate to the Reich as the Red Vanguard moves in. . . . Italy modifies its South Tyrol exodus plan. Austrian-born may stay; Germans must go. . . . German planes make repeated attacks off the coast of Norway. No ships are damaged.			A spokesman admits the Japanese retreat, saying troops have withdrawn from Changsha.
Oct. 11	Nazis may accept a coup in Bessarabia. Washington hears Berlin will not resist Moscow's taking part of Romania. . . . President Roosevelt acclaims the world service program of the YMCA. . . . President Roosevelt denies mediation moves. He implies he takes little stock in press reports of Nazi hints that he should intervene.	Berlin cheers an armistice rumor. Officials are obliged to deny that the British government was forced to resign. Nazis say the Secret Service spread the story that had the public hysterical with joy. . . . French Premier Daladier cites broken pledges as proof of Nazi instability. . . . Hitler reiterates his cry for peace. Germans learn for the first time that war may last all winter. . . . Soviet aid to the Reich is thought difficult; the surplus of commodities for export has fallen off dramatically since 1931.			Disruption threatens Tokyo's Foreign Office; 120 officials pledge to resign.

A	B	C	D	E
Includes developments that affect more than one world region, international organizations, and important meetings of world leaders.	Includes all domestic and regional developments in Europe, including the Soviet Union.	Includes all domestic and regional developments in Africa and the Middle East.	Includes all domestic and regional developments in Latin America, the Caribbean, and Canada.	Includes all domestic and regional developments in Asian and Pacific nations (and colonies).

U.S. Politics & Social Issues	U.S. Foreign Policy & Defense	Economics & Great Depression	Science, Technology & Nature	Culture, Leisure & Lifestyle	
A jury finds a pastor guilty in the murder of his daughter. He is sentenced to die in the electric chair; two out of five women on the jury are near collapse. . . . Actress Joan Manners finds herself without a country. Giving up her British citizenship when she married an American actor, she discovers, during her divorce, that she is now not a citizen of either country. . . . A 20-year-old dancer who performed "A Merry Widow" for Hitler cannot recall whether he looked grim or not.	Eighteen Congressmen are in the Army reserves, subject to call up for war duty. . . . The Army's recruiting rate rises to 750 men per day.	AFL denies a seat to a printers union. The refusal of the typographical union to pay one cent a month ends a 59-year affiliation. . . . Garment prices increase by 40 cents for spring. Linings are also sure to rise.	Harvard University and the Massachusetts Institute of Technology stress the importance of cooperation between scientific researchers and the press, stating that publicity helps the general public understand science.	Ingrid Bergman of Sweden makes her Hollywood debut with Intermezzo. . . . Paramount signs Brian Donlevy to three films over the next year, including Down Went McGinty. . . . Frances Maule publishes a book on how to find—and keep—a job.	Oct. 6
Congressman Martin Dies reports a list of Reds in the capital. He says the document links high Navy yard and printing office workers to Communists. . . . A woman confesses to a murder and then changes her mind. The accused is a fortune teller who was charged with selling witch powders that contain arsenic.	President Roosevelt will guard ships as needed. The action to protect the Iroquois sets no precedent, he says, emphasizing the value of neutrality patrol at sea.	After Frederick Prince retires from Armour as its chairman of the board, the company may eliminate that position altogether. . . . The output of new automobiles continues to rise. Over the past week, 76,000 cars were built, compared to approximately 36,000 a year ago. . . . Cigarette sales decreased 50 percent in New York City. Merchants blame the combined state and city taxes with a 3-cent-per-pack increase.		Thirty thousand line the streets to cheer the Cincinnati Reds, World Series contenders. . . . An art group, the National Art Society, forms to educate the public. The group shall offer scholarships and help sponsor a radio series. . . . A retired general publishes a book about bombing from the air.	Oct. 7
To celebrate Business Week, career women will attend a series of seminars that discuss their rise in fortune over the century. . . . New York plans to dedicate its new and modern airport next week.	As a neutral nation, the United States may appeal to a large body of principles established by treaties and customs of the sea. . . . Officials at Fort Dix test chemical warfare. Three hundred officers see demonstrations of smoke screens and gases.		Waldemar Kaempffert publishes a book, Science Today and Tomorrow, where he discusses the modern day miracles and the shape of the future. . . . Dr. Harvey Williams Cushing, a brain surgeon noted as the founder of a new philosophy on neurosurgery, dies. . . . The President seeks the help of science in determining the best way to conduct blind landings. . . . A new weather project provides clues to cloud formations.	An amateur photographer says that men are much more vain than women about their photos. . . . Actress Merle Oberon encourages all actresses to knit socks for the soldiers on the front. . . . Americans create new fall fashions, with sculptured silhouettes. . . . Rutgers University begins an art lending program so that students can hang up art in their rooms. . . . A ballet show benefits church building funds.	Oct. 8
Police arrest a deluxe hermit for theft. He has a radio and six suits in his pup tent, and stole forceps to pull his own teeth. . . . The Dies inquiry office is raided in the Capitol and the loss of evidence is feared. The entry was made through a smashed window.			A professor challenges the distance to stars. The 5,000 nearest are considered less than half as far away as was previously calculated. . . . Dr. George Washington Carver, noted Negro agricultural chemist, receives one of three Roosevelt medals awarded for 1939.	The Yankees win another championship to set the baseball world record. . . . Cincinnati Reds fans show their chagrin at another loss by tossing cushions on the field. . . . The journey of Christopher Columbus will be celebrated in an opera. . . . Joe DiMaggio plans his wedding to Dorothy Arnold. . . . An incautious hawk crashes through a window and becomes tangled up in a towel. The bird survives and now lives in the zoo.	Oct. 9
A beverage importer head asserts that war may help the forces of "Drys" and that Prohibition may return. . . . Adoption figures are studied. It is determined that most people who adopt earn between $2,000 and $4,000 annually. . . . A woman leaves a $25,000 platinum ring in a beauty shop. After it is recovered from a two-ton refuse truck, the owner does not return to reclaim the ring. . . . The Guild for the Blind begins its 25th annual pencil drive.	A Congress recess is suggested so that President Roosevelt can mediate. The Senate majority chiefs give little chance to a plan to seek peace in Europe.	Economists see a rise despite the war and agree that recovery has begun. . . . President Roosevelt urges a wide charity drive. The alleviation of poverty and distress is the nation's home front, he declares. . . . Officials close all Dodge plants in Detroit, laying off 18,300 workers. . . . Macy's "cash time" plan receives an enthusiastic response, as credit sales were spread out throughout the departments of the store.		Lou Gehrig considers offers of a new job, and he may sever ties with the Yankees. . . . The Boys' Mural is unveiled. It will serve as a permanent feature of the Children's Aid Society's Children's Center. . . . Six of the players in the musical, Very Warm for May, will reprise their roles for a television program.	Oct. 10
First Lady Eleanor Roosevelt explains her "Red Tea." She never inquires about the politics of her guests, she declares. . . . Robert G. Elliot, executioner, dies. He executed nearly 400 people during his career, the most notable being Bruno Richard Hauptmann, the convicted kidnapper and murderer of Charles Lindbergh's baby. . . . The "slot machine king" is free on $50,000 bail. He is under indictment for tax evasion and is accused of adjusting his income to fit advantageous brackets.	Albert Einstein's letter on the topic of an atomic bomb is presented to the President.	The government extends the food stamp program. Citrus fruits and pork are the next additions. . . . Department store sales increased 8 percent in September. Over the first nine months of 1939, sales are 4 percent higher than in 1938. . . . Speakers laud women in business, saying their accomplishments are the most significant feats of modern times.		A China pageant enlivens the fair. This nation's freedom is hailed even though war still exists on her soil. . . . "Cover up" bonnets are decreed fashionable by the French. Milliners swing far away from the tiny hats of last season. . . . A former Swedish prince, now a professional silverware designer, exhibits his work in the United States. . . . The World Fair will be free to babies who are still carried by their mothers or who ride in baby carriages still.	Oct. 11

F	G	H	I	J
Includes elections, federal-state relations, civil rights and liberties, crime, the judiciary, education, healthcare, poverty, urban affairs, and population.	Includes formation and debate of U.S. foreign and defense policies, veterans affairs, and defense spending. (Relations with specific foreign countries are usually found under the region concerned.)	Includes business, labor, agriculture, taxation, transportation, consumer affairs, monetary and fiscal policy, natural resources, pollution, and accidents.	Includes worldwide scientific, medical, and technological developments, natural phenomena, U.S. weather, and natural disasters.	Includes the arts, religion, scholarship, communications media, sports, entertainment, fashions, fads, and social life.

	World Affairs	Europe	Africa & The Middle East	The Americas	Asia & The Pacific
Oct. 12	Japanese in China hold a U.S. Marine. Repercussions are feared. . . . The United States will not feed European armies. Argentina will get the meat business, Chicago packers say.	Albania will supply iron; asbestos, chrome, copper and tar are found in the new Italian colony. . . . Britain will get Russian lumber in exchange for rubber and tin. The deal is a blow for the Reich. . . . Communists oust their leader in Britain. The party, embarrassed by its switch to pacifism, deposes the general secretary. . . . Germans charge that Britain sold mustard gas to Poland. . . . Jews flee from Poland, crossing over into Russia to escape Nazi rule. . . . A Moscow anti-religious paper reports "liquidation" of Polish priests by Red troops.	Egypt is approached by Bulgaria for cotton sales.		The Chinese push forward in a Hunan attack, and report that the counter-offensive has regained territory held by the Japanese for nearly a year.
Oct. 13	Sweden, Denmark, Norway, and the United States enter pleas on behalf of Finland to Moscow. . . . Germany blocks Finland's talk with the United States, declining to transmit the speech of Foreign Minister Elias Erkko after consenting earlier. . . . Lithuania wants the return of Memel. It is reportedly planning with Soviet backing to ask Germany to yield the territory. . . . A papal paper sees Soviet demands increasing. Its policy toward Finland is called an attempt by Russia to dominate Scandinavia. . . . The Soviet Union is said to ask for Finnish bases.	Prime Minister Chamberlain's defiance is well received. Britons expect to hear war sirens at any time. . . . First-line fighting is intense in the west. The greatest action is reported south of Saarbruecken and east of the Moselle River. . . . The French act to bar the crossing of the Rhine. A surprise attack is feared; a rise in the river level fails to endanger fortifications on the opposite shore. . . . Hitler's plan worries Yugoslav Germans. A pro-Nazi paper seeks to allay the anxiety of repatriation. . . . Polish prisoners and civilians work Reich farms and factories; most men are only lightly guarded in camps. . . . The British capture a Reich liner near the Bahamas.		Juan Tripppe, President of Pan-American Airways meets with President Roosevelt to discuss ways to improve commercial trade between the United States and Latin American countries. . . . Canadian stocks advance sharply. . . . Cubans honor Christopher Columbus.	Chinese Reds claim victory; they repel 40,000 Japanese, killing 2,000.
Oct. 14	The Anglo-Turk accord holds curbs on the Reich. The agreement with Allies is said to freeze Italy as neutral and leave Russia free in the east. . . . U.S. Marines apologize to Japan and give compensation for the shooting of a policeman at Tientsin. . . . The Red Cross grants $1 million in war aid.	French Communist deputies stand by the peace note; five approve a call to accept Hitler's terms. . . . Finland mobilizes citizens for duty. An emergency law is invoked after the Soviet demands are studied. . . . Moscow defends the Reich's Baltic step. . . . Nazis urge the Soviets to pressure Finland; the scare of Reds in Scandinavia would force pleas to the Allies to call off the war.			
Oct. 15		The Berlin-Moscow tie looks unstable. Germans foresee the day when interests will clash. . . . Danzig Nazis demand the ousting of all Jews. . . . Fighting in the west is impeded by mud; motorized vehicles are having trouble. . . . The German *blitzkrieg* is slow in starting. Hitler's warning of a war of destruction is not immediately followed up by attack. . . . Kremlin parleys speed a Turk pact; the conclusion of the Moscow-Angora agreement is indicated in a night conference.		Americans offer to enlist in Canada; highly qualified citizens write to Ottawa. . . . Canada's air effort will cost a vast sum. The first-year estimate is $700 million.	Chinese planes bomb Hankow; many Japanese buildings and machines are destroyed.
Oct. 16	The London press berates Charles Lindbergh; Hitler's medal has gone to the colonel's head, London says.	Quiet in the west puzzles Berlin; an accelerated attack on a British blockade indicates their wrath at London. . . . German submarines sink French and British boats; many are injured. . . . Germans await more restrictions as peace hopes vanish. Fish is now unobtainable.		Coffee imports into the United States from Latin American countries reach a new peak and will exceed last year's record numbers.	Japan gives its plan for the Chinese regime.
Oct. 17	A Costa Rican Nazi official asks the government to censure the newspaper and demands punishment for a Hitler cartoon. . . . The Chinese Premier H.H. Kung sees a threat to the United States from Japan. He believes that their dream of domination will cross the Pacific, and makes a plea for U.S. aid. . . . Russian pressure on Iran is revealed. Washington hears the Soviet Union is seeking concessions and possibly a sea base. It also is interested in the oil-rich fields of Iraq.	Allies gain in building planes; France hopes to produce at thrice Germany's rate. . . . Nazis cross the frontier into French Apach, but are thrown back. Heavy losses are reported. . . . Finland weighs the Kremlin's demands. The reply to secret terms awaits the session of Nordic kings in Sweden tomorrow. A readiness to give up islands is indicated. . . . The Nazis bomb a navy base in Scotland. They hit a cruiser, killing 15.		Two Canadian army pilots die when their plane crashes.	Chinese soldiers attack Hangchow and set fire to an ammunition dump.

A	B	C	D	E
Includes developments that affect more than one world region, international organizations, and important meetings of world leaders.	*Includes all domestic and regional developments in Europe, including the Soviet Union.*	*Includes all domestic and regional developments in Africa and the Middle East.*	*Includes all domestic and regional developments in Latin America, the Caribbean, and Canada.*	*Includes all domestic and regional developments in Asian and Pacific nations (and colonies).*

U.S. Politics & Social Issues	U.S. Foreign Policy & Defense	Economics & Great Depression	Science, Technology & Nature	Culture, Leisure & Lifestyle	
A witness reports the existence of Red spies in the Army and Navy. . . . A former museum aide is charged in the theft of 22 Texas paintings. . . . The Women's National Radio Committee launches a movement to prevent hysteria from occurring over news reporting. Their goal is to reduce the reporting of unsubstantiated stories and to increase the amount of news editing.	The AFL is against the United States joining the war. They believe that the use of armed forces should be reserved in case of invasion only.	President Roosevelt appeals to the CIO for peace. He says the country wants an end to separation in the labor movement. . . . The sale of cotton maintains steady undertones. Active buying causes an increase of 3 to 6 points. . . . Food chains back ads in newspapers, to support both the press and the communities that they serve. The chains also approve the federal food stamp plan. . . . Jobs increase by 4 percent in state factories.	A few days before his death, noted neurologist Dr. Harvey Cushing delivers a manuscript to his publishers, titled *The Medical Career*. This book will appear in 1940.	Actress Betty Grable and actor Jackie Coogan divorce. Grable states that Coogan was quarrelsome, adversely affecting her acting career, and that he once sold their furniture to buy a car to leave town. . . . Selznick International attempts to buy *Waterloo Bridge* as a new vehicle for actress Vivien Leigh, but negotiations are halted by a British censor.	Oct. 12
A key Republican says that the war is a boon to them as the "peace party." . . . The Associated Press receives praise for its coverage of the war in Europe. The editor reports laudatory messages from 150 member newspapers.	The House appropriations head asks President Roosevelt to specify his defense fund aims. Committee members believe Congress would promptly grant money. . . . AP war coverage receives praise. Laudatory messages arrive from 150 newspapers around the nation. . . . James Roosevelt drops his Marine rank. He demotes himself to captain as the post is more suited to his experience. . . . The Senate tries to speed up a vote on the embargo issue.	A big war boom is held to be unlikely.	A new tool to check blood clots is found in heparin. A doctor reports the new method as giving hope in fighting heart disease. . . . New York's governor decries the idea that opportunities are limited for youth today, citing the growth of science.	As 3,000 people wait in line to see the Futurama exhibit at the World Fair, the moving chair breaks down. The exhibit remains out of order for two hours, causing visitors delay in seeing the superhighways projected for the 1960s. . . . Former president Herbert Hoover publishes *Shall We Send Our Youth*, a discussion of America and war. . . . The World Fair throng sets a weekday record.	Oct. 13
A former Communist testifies that Red workers spy on factories for Russia. . . . Bail is set at $5,000 for a father's mercy killing of an imbecile son . . . Perjury charges are dropped against the man pretending to be the bearded lady from the World Fair. . . . Col. William Hazel, Confederate veteran of the Civil War, dies at 94. He created the world's largest pipe organ, displayed in St. Louis in 1904.	The arms exemption divides Senators. The problem of lifting the ban on Pacific ports creates a new question on the embargo. . . . Col. Charles Lindbergh favors split arms sales. He would bar the sale of offensive weapons but sell defensive guns. . . . The Army names the heads of five new divisions.	General Motors will hold an exhibition of their 1940 models today.	The battle against bacteria is further extended. A new method is reported that mathematically calculates pure and potent serums.	The American Museum of Natural History receives a model of the largest salmon ever caught. This fish weighs 55 pounds. . . . Two different publishers intend to release books detailing the history of AT & T. . . . Ford Sterling, movie comic, dies at 55. Known as the "chief of the Keystone Cops," Sterling was a contemporary of Charlie Chaplin and Gloria Swanson.	Oct. 14
The Nazi-Soviet pact bolsters the Dies investigation. The committee, sharply criticized a year ago, finds itself in public favor with witnesses ready to tell all. . . . Three billion passengers ride the nation's 135,000 buses.	The Army formulates a profiteering curb. An appeals board would weigh disputes over costs. . . . A repeal of the arms embargo is expected soon. . . . An aviator is killed while testing a war plane. Formerly a Navy pilot, his neck breaks as the craft noses over.	A bumper corn crop cheers those in the northwest. This lends zest to husking contests.	A doctor recommends air-conditioned schools for the health of children. Many children, he says, suffer from respiratory diseases brought about by breathing improper air. . . . Aurora borealis is seen by an amateur astronomer. . . . New York's Municipal Airport opens.	*The Torguts* is a "prose epic with a mighty theme." Published by WL River, the book discusses far-off lands, strange people, and intimate human relationships. . . . Radio listeners choose Beethoven as the master composer, with the C Minor Symphony their favorite song.	Oct. 15
A stepfather slays a five-year-old by drowning. He says he feared the boy was going crazy. . . . Three hundred twenty five thousand spectators see New York's mayor dedicate the new airport to world service; 150 planes perform in a show at the opening ceremony. . . . A man hikes 50 miles on his 83rd birthday.	The Army and Navy add billions to their plans.	The wheat market stabilizes. . . . Steel production is up 90 percent. A shortage of pig iron prevents operations at some finishing mills.	A leg bone of a mammoth is discovered in upstate New York.	Clarinet player Benny Goodman will appear in the jazz version of *A Midsummer's Night Dream*. This is Goodman's stage debut and some of his players may appear with him . . . Religious significance has been found wanting at the World Fair.	Oct. 16
Government officials and police smash a huge bootleg ring. They hold 51 said to be operating in the metropolitan New York area. . . . Lou Gehrig takes an oath as a member of the Municipal Parole Commission. New York Mayor Fiorello LaGuardia asks him to use common sense. . . . Parents in Oklahoma give up triplets, saying that they cannot provide them with appropriate care.		Mayor LaGuardia charges that milk farmers have been betrayed by a federal-state agreement on pricing. A milk strike looms.	Surgeons remove a lung when treating cancer. They say the method is 90 percent successful. . . . Prehistoric bones are found in a cave in Rome near where a Homeric myth suggests that sailors were turned into swine.	Ethel Vance's book, *Escape*, tops many best-seller lists as it goes into its 7th printing. . . . Fair attendance sets a record for the highest week. . . . John Martin's watercolor art appears in two exhibitions. . . . Mayor LaGuardia encourages the film industry to return to New York, where it started. He points out that the city has everything in nature to serve as film locales.	Oct. 17

F	**G**	**H**	**I**	**J**
Includes elections, federal-state relations, civil rights and liberties, crime, the judiciary, education, healthcare, poverty, urban affairs, and population.	*Includes formation and debate of U.S. foreign and defense policies, veterans affairs, and defense spending. (Relations with specific foreign countries are usually found under the region concerned.)*	*Includes business, labor, agriculture, taxation, transportation, consumer affairs, monetary and fiscal policy, natural resources, pollution, and accidents.*	*Includes worldwide scientific, medical, and technological developments, natural phenomena, U.S. weather, and natural disasters.*	*Includes the arts, religion, scholarship, communications media, sports, entertainment, fashions, fads, and social life.*

	World Affairs	Europe	Africa & The Middle East	The Americas	Asia & The Pacific
Oct. 18	South Africa fights Reich propaganda and will raise funds to promote true unity. . . . German Catholics defy a Nazi order. The Vatican learns of the refusal of some priests to ring bells after Warsaw fell. . . . Neutrals in China get new pledges. Japanese army chiefs assert an order to protect American missions.	The British attempt to bomb Emden. The attack on Germany's base for minesweepers is beaten off, the mayor of the town says. . . . Franco restores Madrid as the capital; all government bureaus except the Foreign Ministry are back in the old quarters. . . . Hitler is held duped by his own propaganda. The British envoy says Nazis fed their leader Polish atrocity tales whenever he weakened. . . . Nordic solidarity will uphold Finland. . . . A Soviet writer lauds the Nazi use of U-boats.	Egypt votes itself in a "state of siege."	Canada describes extensive war activity. The Department of Defense tells of convoy and anti-submarine work.	
Oct. 19	The British tell India to develop unity; then, after war, it can become a dominion. . . . Pope Pius XII will defend Christian Europe. Shunning temporal disputes, he pledges resistance to "enemies of God." . . . Red Army experts fly to help China. Tokyo sees a military alliance; Japan is under pressure from Germany and Russia.	Britain aids refugees. A governmental agency is being formed to help the Polish. . . . Death by accident doubles in Britain, but ministers are opposed to easing up on the blackout. . . . Estonia is cut off as Red troops enter. The populace is advised to submit quietly to the quartering of soldiers in homes. . . . Germans are advised to leave Finland. The legation suggests they return to the Reich voluntarily before they get ordered to do so. . . . The Moscow impasse encourages Italy. A check to Communism in the Near East is seen in the failure of Turkey talks. . . . The Red Army hunts Polish spies.			
Oct. 20	The German Consul General defends German strength in a New York speech. He says the nation is not nearing collapse. . . . An Oxford specialist holds that Hitler is insane. He says the dictator is paranoiac and his mind is disintegrating; persecution mania is cited. . . . The Japanese say China faces Soviet claims. Russians deny a Moscow mission at Chungking.	Turkey signs a 15-year treaty with the Allies. Berlin, Moscow, and Rome are perturbed. . . . The Bulgarian Cabinet resigns as a body. The King asks members to carry on pending the formation of a new government. . . . Estonia welcomes the Red Army cordially. . . . France expresses elation over the Turk treaty. The rebuff to Germany is held to have large and immediate consequences. . . . Germany annexes sections of Poland. Districts lost in World War I are reincorporated into the Reich; the rest is a buffer. . . . Nazis warn Turks, saying they might share the Poles' fate.		Those in Canada and the East Coast of the United States feel a sharp quake. It is one of the four heaviest in the past 200 years.	
Oct. 21	Australia widens military service; compulsory training is to begin in January. . . . Japan rejects U.S. interference in the China war. The foreign minister says a third party cannot interfere with the plan. . . . Mail for Germany will go via Italy. Washington adopts a new route to avoid interception and international disputes.	Belgium feels the pinch of blockade and will need to start food rationing soon. . . . Hitler confers on retaliation for the Allied pact. . . . The last Russian troops are now in Estonia. . . . Nazi scout planes fly over Scotland. They escape British pursuers as alarms sound. . . . Nazis plan to use gas in the war, the British say. The technique is similar to 1915. . . . Poles bar the cessation of any territory. . . . The Soviet Foreign Office receives a British envoy for the first time since the three-nation pact failed; the purpose is not revealed.			China sees its foe halted for three months after the defeat suffered at Changsha. The invaders surrendered when hard pressed; others gave up when good treatment was promised. . . . Mass resignations occur in India today.
Oct. 22	Argentina keeps its curbs on U.S. trade. France, Norway, Bohemia, and Moravia are added to most-favored-nation status. . . . Civilians in Tokyo heed a U.S. warning. The military is angered. The U.S. Ambassador's speech gives the Japanese public the first idea of hostility.	The Allied Turkish treaty has large importance, as Angora swings toward the Allies. . . . The Berlin-Rome pact sets a Tyrol shift. Ten thousand Germans must move to the Reich. . . . The Czechs baffle Nazis by tactics of resistance. . . . Finns send a reply to the Soviet terms; a new trade offer is the likely response. . . . French bombard an area of 20 miles, hoping to hit the Nazi headquarters. . . . Germans are ordered to speed the sea war and Hitler calls for intensified raids. . . . A Netherlands coup by the Reich is anticipated.			The Chinese claim victories. They say they have retaken many key points near the Hunan line. . . . Three die in Shanghai in another clash. Forces of the puppet city regime fight British and Italian settlement units.

A Includes developments that affect more than one world region, international organizations, and important meetings of world leaders.

B Includes all domestic and regional developments in Europe, including the Soviet Union.

C Includes all domestic and regional developments in Africa and the Middle East.

D Includes all domestic and regional developments in Latin America, the Caribbean, and Canada.

E Includes all domestic and regional developments in Asian and Pacific nations (and colonies).

U.S. Politics & Social Issues	U.S. Foreign Policy & Defense	Economics & Great Depression	Science, Technology & Nature	Culture, Leisure & Lifestyle	
The CIO president loses a plea for free speech. The California Supreme Court, in a contempt case, rules that the right is not absolute and abuse may be punished. . . . Drinking drivers face new curbs as chemical tests are hailed. . . . An early cold spell hits New York City. Temperatures may drop to 32 degrees. . . . Fewer pupils fail in schools. Individualized instruction is seen as the key to improvement. . . . 56 percent of ex-convicts go back to prison, reports the head of U.S. Penal Institutions.	President Roosevelt doubts the adequacy of the Navy.		Experts urge vitamin build-up before surgery. . . . Movie engineers aim at audience contact. They want to make spectators feel part of the story. Pneumonia cases rise, but deaths decline. Better control of the disease is reported.	Massachusetts Women of the Moose ask that divorced people be banned from appearing in movies. The World Fair will shorten its season for 1940. . . . Mantle coats are in style, replacing fur jackets. . . . Anna Neagle will star in Irene, a Broadway musical comedy that first appeared in 1919.	Oct. 18
Pioneer autoists recall early days and share amusing stories. One shares how his car could not buck the wind. . . . The Presbyterian Church has too few candidates for clergy. . . . Road betterment is linked to increased safety.	President Roosevelt bars U.S. ports and waters to war submarines.	Cadillac-LaSalle orders increase by 40 percent over one year ago. . . . Deliveries of sugar increase, the largest total since March, 1937. . . . Retail sales increase by 7.3 percent, led by sales figures in San Francisco. . . . A shortage of scotch whiskey is feared because of the war and because of shortages during the Depression.	Doctors set up committees to study healthcare issues after they are warned that, if physicians do not take on this task, politicians will. . . . Movie engineers honor Dr. L.A. Jones for advancing the techniques of motion picture creation.	Eddie Cantor, wearing a short skirt and blonde wig in a Shirley Temple impersonation, tells the audience that his first grandson was born. . . . Leon Trotsky publishes a book titled Karl Marx. . . . Costume fête aids the disabled. Attendees appear as film characters to fit Hollywood History theme. . . . Cecil B. DeMille plans The Sun of Glory as his next project. . . . Finland hopes to stage the Olympics on a more limited basis. . . . Painter Diego Rivera will divorce.	Oct. 19
First Lady Eleanor Roosevelt urges aid for convicts. She asks for sympathy for those who have paid their debt to society and says medical care is also needed. . . . The "slot machine king" agrees to face charges of tax evasion as he gives up his fight to avoid a trial in the south. . . . A doctor wins $100,000 after a jury awards him damages for an X-ray machine injury. . . . The head of Alcatraz suggests that children need more role models such as Joe DiMaggio and Lou Gehrig.		Broad advances in men's clothing sales keep offices the busiest since 1937. . . . Chrysler delays government mediation as it continues conversations with its union. . . . New York City welfare workers will receive raises. . . . Farmers receive 40 cents of each dollar spent on 58 different foodstuffs. . . . A consumer guide assures Americans of plentiful food supplies during this winter. More meat will be available than any year since 1934.	A pioneer wireless inventor predicts "ghost" planes. He says radio will guide bombers.	Belgium will participate in the 1940 World Fair. This is the first foreign nation to give a definitive answer. . . . PWA Administrator Harold Ickes publishes a book, America's House of Lords. He also writes an introduction to a PWA publication, America Builds. . . . Somerset Maugham publishes Christmas Holiday.	Oct. 20
Actor Jackie Coogan hires a youth for protection to make sure that he doesn't get "rolled," but then the youth robs him himself. The youth pled guilty to the charge. . . . A feminine touch aids the National Auto Show as more females serve as demonstrators and lecturers. They hold the interest of visitors. . . . Temperatures reach 73 degrees for a summer-like day in New York. . . . Safety men study the problem of bicycles. They find many hazards due to the phenomenal increase in the use of this vehicle for transportation.	President Roosevelt warns that the U.S. sea frontier expands with need. The three-mile submarine limit does not establish territorial waters, he says.		The American College of Surgeons reports advances in a remedy used for the ills of women. Estrogenic synthesis is stronger and less costly than natural hormones.	Max Baer agrees to box Tony Galento in 1940. . . . Yale University bans the use of portable radios at Bowl games. . . . Eddie Cantor dedicates a mural of Pinnochio at the Jewish Hospital of Brooklyn. . . . An 11-year-old pianist makes a Town Hall debut. She performs Chopin as part of a lengthy program. . . . Lon Chaney, Jr., signs up for a role in 1,000,000 BC. . . . Eddie Albert stars in On Your Toes. . . . The World Fair aspires to be the People's Playground next year.	Oct. 21
	A survey finds a basic fear of war; 95 percent of those surveyed want to keep out of the European conflict. . . . The Army Air Corps seeks college youth as pilots. They hope to get those between ages 20 and 26 to train, as hundreds are needed.	The U.S. Chamber of Commerce assails a cut in work hours. A 42-hour workweek means hardship for many, it declares.	The Amateur Astronomers Association will conduct a seminar on telescope mirror making. . . . New emergency "iron lungs" are made of rubber and transparent material and are much less cumbersome than previous models.	Monica Dickens, the great-granddaughter of Charles Dickens, publishes One Pair of Hands. . . . The original Pennsylvania section of the famous Lincoln Highway celebrates its heritage. . . . The Battle of the Bangboards—or the annual corn husking contest—has become our biggest sports event, based upon the crowds it draws. . . . Sweatshirts and pullovers will appear in sheer materials. . . . The World Fair loses Sweden as a 1940 exhibitor. The war makes its position too precarious for participation.	Oct. 22

F	**G**	**H**	**I**	**J**
Includes elections, federal-state relations, civil rights and liberties, crime, the judiciary, education, healthcare, poverty, urban affairs, and population.	Includes formation and debate of U.S. foreign and defense policies, veterans affairs, and defense spending. (Relations with specific foreign countries are usually found under the region concerned.)	Includes business, labor, agriculture, taxation, transportation, consumer affairs, monetary and fiscal policy, natural resources, pollution, and accidents.	Includes worldwide scientific, medical, and technological developments, natural phenomena, U.S. weather, and natural disasters.	Includes the arts, religion, scholarship, communications media, sports, entertainment, fashions, fads, and social life.

	World Affairs	Europe	Africa & The Middle East	The Americas	Asia & The Pacific
Oct. 23	Argentina moves to get the Falklands. A committee is formed to press for reclamation while the British recruit a defense force. . . . Nazi minister Joseph Goebbels's speech is cleansed for broadcast in English; furious adjectives are removed. He attacks Churchill as a liar and accuses Britain of sinking *Athenia* to get the United States into war. . . . Hitler is not the only foe, the Australian premier says; the fight must go on until the Nazi system is gone.	The French quit Warndt forest where they hold only a few outposts. . . . The British rout air raiders. . . . Germany considers revising the financing of war. Loans are hinted, a policy formerly foreign to the Reich. . . . Italy reaffirms its friendship with the Reich. . . . Norwegian ports are considered to be the Soviet aim.			The fight in Shanghai imperils the puppet regime. Gangsters are linked to the Japanese and Wang Ching-wei, who plan a new Nanking regime. . . . Gandhi's party orders eight Indian ministers to quit over Britain's policies.
Oct. 24	Britain suggests U.S. shipping aids, listing ways to shorten delays in putting vessels through contraband control. . . . The Japanese see the need for negotiations with the United States. . . . Nazis seize a U.S. ship on the high seas and sail it to Russia. . . . Russia increases support to China. Recent air successes are held to be due to new planes and pilots.	A Balkan peace bloc begins to take form. Romania and Italy are said to be taking the initiative in negotiations. . . . Paris eases blackouts; Premier Daladier permits unmenaced areas to light up again. . . . Finns watch Estonia policy, fearing a change following Soviet occupation of the land. . . . Finns see Stalin; the secrecy veiling the talks gives an ominous note to negotiations. . . . Italian Premier Benito Mussolini is said to aim at being the supreme industrial power in Europe while the war lasts. . . . Nazis raise the tax on Jews to 25 percent of property. . . . One Swedish and two British ships sink after being hit by bombs.			The British Commons to weighs the new blow to India after Gandhi tells eight ministers to quit.
Oct. 25	The anti-Christian drive increases in China. Japanese and Communists put pressure on missions. . . . Japan awaits a U.S. move in China.	The French expect new tactics. A stalemate on the western front is believed likely to force new German action. . . . Germans experiment with armor for men. . . . Poland recruits troops in Britain. . . . Rapid Sovietizing occurs in Poland; living standards are lowered.		The conscription issue is voted on in Quebec today. The premier holds that rights are infringed by a federal war measure.	
Oct. 26	The Soviet Union challenges Britain's blockade. The contraband list is declared to be illegal and destructive to international trade.	Czechs stage an anti-German riot. Stores are smashed when the city is left temporarily without troops. . . . The British Commons ignores the German foreign minister's speech; it is not even mentioned during a foreign affairs debate. . . . Finns mine waters off the Soviet coast. . . . Hungarians doubt the strength of the Romanian defense. . . . The Reich will not return Memel to Lithuania. . . . Older Britons will serve; the new army supply corps invites men age 35–50. . . . The French, believing the Reich will not attack, release men for civilian tasks.		The Chile Popular Front marks its anniversary. Huge crowds confirm support of the regime elected a year ago. . . . Dominicans open doors to refugees. The island republic will waive its immigration fee to help 500 families.	
Oct. 27	Hadassah asks the United States to aid Palestine. The government is urged to use its influence after war to get justice for minorities. . . . Russia and Japan agree to release seized ships. Some were held for nearly a year. . . . Forty-one Americans are believed to be prisoners on their own ship, headed for Germany.	An Alsatian leader and French soldier receive the death penalty for giving aid to the Reich. . . . The Reich sends Czech Jews to Poland. . . . Nazis tighten censorship; telephone calls and telegrams abroad are restricted. . . . Nazi troops mass along a 650-mile front. Positions face Belgium, France, Switzerland, and the Netherlands; the German forces are placed to attack at any point.		Bolivian Army commander in Chief General Rioja is exiled for attempting to start a rebellion.	
Oct. 28	Danes report a sea fight. Copenhagen doubts the islanders' story of engagement. . . . Vatican police take extreme steps to keep the contents of the Pope's encyclical secret. . . . Pope Pius XII calls upon rulers to follow Christian ideals in governing. He decries totalitarianism.	Intensive German patrolling on the western front signals an upcoming offensive. . . . Britain confirms pocket ship raids. Two German craft have sunk three merchant vessels in one month. . . . The Reich forbids any Czech celebration of their national day. Leaders of patriotic groups in Prague urge all to secretly mourn independence. . . . Franco orders Republican soldiers to court by November 1 or face arrest. . . . German minorities fear a return to the Reich. . . . Flags and flowers welcome troops entering Lithuania. The province is restored by Russia; soldiers bring food. . . . Western Ukraine votes for Soviet rule.			

A	B	C	D	E
Includes developments that affect more than one world region, international organizations, and important meetings of world leaders.	Includes all domestic and regional developments in Europe, including the Soviet Union.	Includes all domestic and regional developments in Africa and the Middle East.	Includes all domestic and regional developments in Latin America, the Caribbean, and Canada.	Includes all domestic and regional developments in Asian and Pacific nations (and colonies).

U.S. Politics & Social Issues	U.S. Foreign Policy & Defense	Economics & Great Depression	Science, Technology & Nature	Culture, Leisure & Lifestyle	
A missionary Bishop of Idaho finds the United States to be pagan. He calls for greater efforts to evangelize the nation that is 50 percent unchurched.		The 40th National Automobile Show ends a successful run with 30 percent more attendance and twice as many direct sales. . . . Cotton continues its upward trend.	A scientist disputes that evidence points to a lifeless Mars without oxygen.	The final week of the World Fair will feature a carnival. . . . Columbia is looking for Cary Grant and Vivien Leigh to star in *Tree of Liberty*. . . . *Witness Vanishes* debuts in theaters today. . . . Author Zane Grey dies suddenly. He wrote more than 50 novels, most dealing with western adventure.	Oct. 23
Congressman Martin Dies urges action against Reds. He asks the Department of Justice to prosecute them under registration laws. . . . Eleanor Roosevelt receives a parents' medal for her outstanding service to children. She is commended for her advancement efforts toward learning. . . . Five babies in a hospital die from steam. A worn valve on a radiator blows out. . . . America's tallest police officer stands 6 feet, 11 inches tall and works in Cincinnati, Ohio. . . . Three people are shot over a Reno, Nev. divorce. An ex-sea captain kills his wife, then her nurse, and then himself.		The Institute of Meat Packers comes up with a "turkeyfurter" for a low-income solution to Thanksgiving dinner. With two potential dates to celebrate this year, an economical solution is even more important. . . . 73.3 percent of furniture was sold on credit over the last year.	Seventeen booths will be set up throughout New York during Cancer Week to aid the fund drive. . . . A huge new atom gun will tear the world's veil. Radium by transmutation is also possible, a professor tells the Academy of Sciences. . . . Doctors are urged to further study the glands.	Majority Leader Senator Barkley assails a movie, *Mr. Smith Goes to Washington*, calling it "silly and stupid." . . . The World Fair goes "slightly mad" during its last days. A Super Mardi Gras celebration gets off to a roaring start even after six "colossal" acts are canceled. . . . Universal will feature Bing Crosby in *If I Had My Way*. . . . Trainers will begin working with racehorse Seabiscuit to prepare for the horse's return.	Oct. 24
Elliot Roosevelt says the Dies Committee deserves lasting gratitude. . . . Teachers are asked to retire at age 65. . . . A female pilot is found guilty of flying over prohibited areas in the capital, dropping anti-war leaflets. A reprimand is recommended.	Fifty-four percent of people polled believe the United States will shun war. . . . Army enlistment reaches a seven-year high under the President's recruitment program.	Factories take on 700,000 workers.	Diphtheria cases increase with 14 new cases in one week. Immunizations are stressed.	The president of the U.S. Olympic Committee says that if the 1940 Olympics cannot be held in Finland because of the European crisis, they will not be held at all. . . . Joe DiMaggio wins the Most Valuable Player award in the American League.	Oct. 25
The Dies Committee puts out a list naming 563 federal aides as part of the "Red Front." The list is met with protests. . . . Alcoholic deaths are halved over the past 30 years, according to census bureau information. . . . The "Arizona trunk murderer" escapes from an asylum after stuffing her bed to fool guards. . . . Studies show a wide range of IQs for children, as much as 100 points. An expert says this points to the need for individualized study and the avoidance of putting children into pigeonholes.	Herbert Hoover urges the United States to prepare for peace, not war. He says that assuring a just settlement, not joining the fight, is our task. . . . The Senate supports giving Roosevelt power in the Neutrality Bill, rejecting an amendment to deny the President any discretion in the state of war. . . . A Senator says war means a third term for Roosevelt, pointing out the President's 45 years of contacts abroad.	A cut in relief rolls brings no benefit to New York City; 53 percent reduction of expenditures by the federal government offsets economies. . . . The dairy union votes to start a boycott.	General Electric develops a new sun lamp.	A book sale garners $6,016. One item, printed by Benjamin Franklin in 1744, sells for $185. . . . The Schools Motion-Picture Committee selects films suitable for children. . . . Singer and actor Al Jolson reports that his wife, Ruby Keeler, has filed for a separation. He is broken-hearted and hopes for reconciliation.	Oct. 26
President Roosevelt's gains are at a five-year high; 64.9 percent of voters approve of the President . . . A letter written by George Washington sells for $475. . . . An escaped Arizona murderer is ignoring pleas by relatives that she turn herself in to authorities.		The federal government has 700,000 barrels of flour for those on relief programs.	German doctor Gerhard Domagk wins the Nobel Prize in Medicine of Physiology for his development of sulfamilinide compounds (Prontosil).	Thumb sucking reveals unhappiness in a child, an expert reveals. . . . Margaret Mead publishes *From the South Seas*, a study of adolescence and sex in primitive societies. . . . Chick Evans retires from professional golf. . . . The New York Giants add their name to the list of teams wishing to play night baseball next season. . . . Burgess Meredith will star in *Young Man With a Horn*.	Oct. 27
President Roosevelt assails the question of a "Red list," calling it a sordid procedure. . . . Congressman Martin Dies defends his Red list as fair. Responding to President Roosevelt, he calls it his duty to name U.S. employees favoring aliens.		Chrysler forbids turmoil in its manufacturing plants.	An adrenal hormone is isolated in the heart. Scientists believe that this substance will be found in nearly all neurons of the sympathetic system. . . . The moon eclipse was covered by clouds. Museum observers need to go up 18,200 feet in a plane to study this blackout.	Ruby Keeler asks for a divorce from Al Jolson. . . . Marjorie Kinnan Rawlings' book, *The Yearling*, is now available for the blind as a talking book. . . . Hordes of children give the World Fair its wildest day as 150,000 stream through its gates. . . . The Grouch Club of America incorporates so that every "sourpuss" can "vent his spleen."	Oct. 28

F	G	H	I	J
Includes elections, federal-state relations, civil rights and liberties, crime, the judiciary, education, healthcare, poverty, urban affairs, and population.	*Includes formation and debate of U.S. foreign and defense policies, veterans affairs, and defense spending. (Relations with specific foreign countries are usually found under the region concerned.)*	*Includes business, labor, agriculture, taxation, transportation, consumer affairs, monetary and fiscal policy, natural resources, pollution, and accidents.*	*Includes worldwide scientific, medical, and technological developments, natural phenomena, U.S. weather, and natural disasters.*	*Includes the arts, religion, scholarship, communications media, sports, entertainment, fashions, fads, and social life.*

	World Affairs	Europe	Africa & The Middle East	The Americas	Asia & The Pacific
Oct. 29	Nazis show anger at the U.S. Senate vote. Spokesmen accept passage of the embargo repeal as reflecting sympathy for the Allies.	Balkan heads try to counter the Soviet threat. . . . Moscow paints a dark picture of war conditions in Britain. . . . British ship loss is vast, Nazis say. . . . French repulse the propaganda drive; guns answer German loudspeakers set up on the western front. . . . German shelling is now systematic. . . . Italy hears little of the Pope's encyclical. Only a 1,000-word summary is issued, and commentary is forbidden.		Bolivia ends the revolt of military cadets.	Gandhi stresses his demands, questioning whether an India dominion will be independent.
Oct. 30	The route of the U.S. ship *Flint* is held a military secret by Nazi officials. Berlin admits only that a ship, flying the swastika, is en route to a Reich port. . . . The Moscow press condemns the United States. Washington takes the place of Berlin as the victim of attacks in leading journals.	An eerie calm prevails in the west. Extreme quiet causes greater expectation of a German drive in the near future and Allies are still digging in. . . . The blockade will fail, the press tells the people of the Reich. The trade pact with Russia is cited to prove that Britain cannot starve Germany. . . . Britain expects a Russian peace bid. . . . Important figures are jailed in Slovenia. The head of railways, party chiefs, and former ministers are said to be under arrest. . . . Soviet troops enter Latvia. The forces are greeted at the border.			
Oct. 31	Japan denies a plan to talk to the United States. A spokesman repudiates the idea of parleys. . . . The Japanese are blamed for bias in China. Evidence shows anti-foreign agitations are staged in occupied districts. . . . The Reich scores the U.S. Senate's vote on the arms embargo. Newspapers interpret the move as weakening the position of neutrality of President Roosevelt. . . . Nazis threaten to blow up the *Flint* if Americans "try anything," Britons say.	Activity resumes on the western front. Clearing weather allows air-scouting patrols to resume. . . . All of Finland backs the reply to the Soviet Union. Parliamentary groups are united in the stand against concessions. . . . Baltic Germans arrive in Danzig. . . . The British guard against parachute attacks. Troops in the rear await Nazi suicide squads. . . . Britain details Nazi tortures. Concentration camp horrors are told; the practices recall the "darkest ages" with floggings and killings by guards.			
Nov. 1	Arrests in Poland alarm labor in the United States. Socialist and union leaders are reportedly taken to the Soviet Union by Russian leaders. . . . Canada liquidates German concerns. . . . The Reich press sees a divided America. The government is seen as taking steps toward war against the wishes of the people.	Belgium is guarded by a rolling gate. Obstacles are planned to snare tanks. . . . Britain modifies war restrictions. The measures must be essential and defined to avoid abuse. . . . The Dutch doubt a Nazi attack and troop moves cause no alarm. . . . Jews must leave Vienna by March 1. Authorities set the final date as 4,000 move from the city to a reservation in Poland and property is confiscated. . . . Premier Mussolini drops pro-German aides. Six are replaced in the shake-up. . . . The Rome shift is a blow to the Reich. London and Paris point out that the officials dropped had close contacts with Nazis.			
Nov. 2	The United States sees the army's hand in Tokyo's reversal on talks. . . . Australia drafts a huge war budget. . . . The United States chides Moscow, suggesting the premier sought to influence the arms embargo vote by the timing of his speech. . . . Nazis scuttle a ship in the Caribbean when stopped by a British cruiser.	Army officers await pay; some Britons have received nothing since the call to duty. . . . Britain rations butter and bacon. . . . The Finns defy the Soviet Union. They mine the Hangoe port and firmly resist the Kremlin's demand for defense base sites and a demilitarized border. . . . The British are expected not to try to take the U.S. ship *Flint* lest the Nazis scuttle it. . . . The Italian Princess of Piedmont is expecting another heir. . . . Forty Russian tanks arrive at Vilna after anti-Semitic riots and a clash between Reds and Polish nationalists.			Japan establishes its fourth naval base.
Nov. 3	Britain is gratified that the United States has lifted its arms embargo and now awaits U.S. arms. . . . The League of Nations denies that Russia ended its membership. . . . The Japanese declare that the peace asked by the United States in the East is impossible, saying Washington's aims perpetuate inequality. . . . The U.S. Senate vote angers the Reich. The end of the arms embargo is held to mean direct support to foes of Nazis.	Slovakians stage anti-Hungary riots; newspaper offices are sacked as protest against acquisitions. . . . The defeat of Germany is the primary war aim, Britain says; security is next. . . . Czechs threaten to strike over Independence Day arrests and demand the release of all celebrants. . . . Finns are in Moscow with their final offer, unyielding on questions of national integrity. . . . Italy and Greece form a closer bond; damage to the Axis is denied. . . . Allies liaison improves. . . . The White Russia zone joins the Soviet Union.		A conservative leader in Canada accuses the government of deficiency in the army, which he says lacks defense equipment, clothing, and shoes.	
	A *Includes developments that affect more than one world region, international organizations, and important meetings of world leaders.*	**B** *Includes all domestic and regional developments in Europe, including the Soviet Union.*	**C** *Includes all domestic and regional developments in Africa and the Middle East.*	**D** *Includes all domestic and regional developments in Latin America, the Caribbean, and Canada.*	**E** *Includes all domestic and regional developments in Asian and Pacific nations (and colonies).*

U.S. Politics & Social Issues	U.S. Foreign Policy & Defense	Economics & Great Depression	Science, Technology & Nature	Culture, Leisure & Lifestyle	
A building contractor announces the birth of his 24th child. After having twelve children with his first wife, he duplicates the feat with his second wife.		Oklahoma extends its foodstamp program to low-income families as well as those on relief.	A curb on cancer is urged. Recognition of its early symptoms is held to be important in its cure.	Sholem Asch publishes *The Nazarene*, telling a "great story in a memorable manner." . . . An Oxford professor of history publishes *On the Writing of History*, his 25th book. . . . The New York World Fair ends in two days, with more than 25,000,000 people visiting its exhibits. . . . A pianist teaches her canary to sing songs as she accompanies her pet bird.	Oct. 29
The Peace League declares war on Congressman Martin Dies. An emergency session authorizes the scrutiny of his speeches, with a view to libel action. . . . A captain dies at the wheel as his ferry docks. The ship smashes a pier. . . . Droughts in the west and southwest intensify. . . . A cowboy is trampled as 13,000 watch the rodeo.	The War Department organizes the shape of the future Army, a peace force of 600,000 including the National Guard.			Paris sees a change in fashion. Wartime styles feature comfortable clothes that avoid the sensational. . . . Stage and film star Alice Brady dies after a long illness. Her last work was in the screenplay *The Young Mr. Lincoln* for which she won an Academy Award in 1938. . . . *Escape* by Ethel Vance and *The Grapes of Wrath* by John Steinbeck still top best-seller lists. . . . The Princeton University Library Chronicle will begin publication, appearing four times annually.	Oct. 30
	The arms ban repeal meets its first real test in the House today. The Rules Committee adopts a resolution to send the neutrality measure to conference.				Oct. 31
Dr. George Gallup answers critics; his surveys are for factfinding only, he says.	Roosevelt adds $275,000,000 to the country's defense budget.	The pay of waitresses is inadequate, totaled at less than the welfare assistance budget. . . . Beer production drops by 4 percent and consumption drops by a similar amount.	Cancer Week starts today. This disease stands as the second biggest killer of people in the nation and Mayor LaGuardia stresses the importance of early detection. . . . Dr. Otto Rank, an associate of Sigmund Freud, dies. His opinions differed from Freud's on the matter of psychotherapy.	The New York World Fair closes at 2 a.m. and will reopen in May 1940. . . . Exactly ten years ago this month, Houghton Mifflin published a book called *Magnificent Obsession* about a doctor's journal. Readers wanted more about this character and so the author, Lloyd C. Douglas, publishes *Dr. Hudson's Secret Journal*. . . . Debutants model the Chinese costumes that they will wear to tonight's Bowl of Rice party. The fabric in many dresses is said to be decades old.	Nov. 1
A 15-year-old male wins a bread-baking contest. . . . A couple in financial distress leap 22 stories from a hotel window. . . . Stage and screen star Claude Gillingwater commits suicide rather than face his illness. He acted in movies with Mary Pickford. . . . An application bureau for Negro foster children forms.			A mammal is created without a father. A rabbit is the first to be produced by the artificial activation of an ovum. . . . The Zenith Radio Corporation is making more than 12,500 radios daily.	*Gentlemen Behave* is a book on male etiquette that is intended as counterpart to Emily Post's *Blue Book*. The book is written by Charles Hanson Towne. . . . Richardson Wright publishes *Grandfather was Queer*, in which he discusses the eccentricities of early America. . . . The price of admission for the 1940 World Fair is set at 50 cents. Brazil has agreed to return to next year's fair. . . . Fashionable shoes contain fabric, including gabardine. The wedge heel is applauded for its grace.	Nov. 2
Congressman Martin Dies says he will trace Reds in shipping unions. . . . The World Fair Railroad carries more than 7 million passengers to this year's festivities. This accounts for about 54 percent of the fair attendees.		Former president Herbert Hoover urges aid to jobless youth; dejected, they are easy prey for gangs.	Two doctors report success with hibernation treatment in battling cancer. . . . The General Motors World Fair Science Exhibit will continue to be shown throughout the winter. More than 1 million spectators saw the exhibit during one of the 12 daily demonstrations.	John Dickson Carr publishes *The Problem of the Wire Cage* and Georgette Heyer releases *No Wind of Blame*. . . . Boxer Bob Troman dies a few hours after losing a fight by a technical knockout. . . . Clare Booth's play, *Margin for Error*, will appear at the Plymouth tonight. . . . NBC will present the opera, *The Outcasts of Poker Flat*. . . . Famous humorist, Opie Read, dies. He wrote more than 50 books.	Nov. 3

F	G	H	I	J
Includes elections, federal-state relations, civil rights and liberties, crime, the judiciary, education, healthcare, poverty, urban affairs, and population.	*Includes formation and debate of U.S. foreign and defense policies, veterans affairs, and defense spending. (Relations with specific foreign countries are usually found under the region concerned.)*	*Includes business, labor, agriculture, taxation, transportation, consumer affairs, monetary and fiscal policy, natural resources, pollution, and accidents.*	*Includes worldwide scientific, medical, and technological developments, natural phenomena, U.S. weather, and natural disasters.*	*Includes the arts, religion, scholarship, communications media, sports, entertainment, fashions, fads, and social life.*

	World Affairs	Europe	Africa & The Middle East	The Americas	Asia & The Pacific
Nov. 4	All are safe on the U.S. ship *Flint*, say Nazis aboard. . . . Balkan states hail the end to the U.S. arms embargo. The Yugoslav press says it will end the fear of small nations. . . . The Nazi press charges the British with an attempt to rush the U.S. repeal of the arms embargo; Churchill is blamed. . . . China hails the U.S. vote against the embargo. . . . The *Flint* sails again. The American commander gains command; a neutrality breach is charged. . . . Germans execute an American citizen, put to death on a concealed weapons charge.	Allies expect a long winter lull. . . . Scandinavians fear attack; Sweden's anxiety increases as the U.S. envoy prepares to evacuate Americans. . . . An anxious Reich woos Bulgaria. . . . Jews in Sudetenland are deported to Poland. A mass exodus is feared. . . . The Soviet Union and Reich shift peoples; a minorities agreement provides for repatriating Germans in Ukraine and White Russia.		Canada is ready to buy U.S. planes. . . . Panama celebrates its 36th anniversary of freedom from Colombia.	
Nov. 5	The new U.S. embargo law does not affect the moral embargo placed on Japan, President Roosevelt says. . . . A British economist holds that the war will reduce the Reich and most of Europe to privation; a trade threat is paramount.	Calm continues on the western front. A Nazi raid is checked in the interior by French fliers and the likelihood of an offensive diminishes. . . . Finland's resistance irks Russians. *Pravda* sees the little republic in the role of warmonger, threatening Soviets who seek strategic concessions. . . . Italy strengthens its neutral front; Mussolini's Cabinet shakeup is designed to build defensive arms.		Hundreds are homeless after floods in Cuba. . . . Canadian housewives continue to stock up on food, as prices increase only slightly.	
Nov. 6	A German offensive is indicated. Evidence in Berlin points to an attack before Allies get the help of U.S. supplies. . . . The Japanese suggest payments to the United States. Two ex-ministers believe indemnities for damage would help the situation. . . . A Nazi grievance aim at Norway is hinted.	Britons break up a fascist meeting. Crowds stone a bus and scuffle with fascists after their rally. . . . Nazi minister Joseph Goebbels instructs the young in war duties and ridicules British propaganda. . . . Jews face famine in Poland. The 1.5 million in German-held areas are reported to be condemned to starve. . . . Mussolini orders an increase in the army. . . . The Reich shows signs of tax weariness as revenue slackens. The situation is termed ominous.		Canada is expected to buy U.S. planes. Rush orders are coming from training schools.	India talks have failed, the viceroy declares; a setback to the new constitution is seen.
Nov. 7	Berlin questions the motives of the U.S. embargo repeal, crediting "profiteers." . . . Nazi propaganda is mailed to the United States. The flood of circulars from Berlin causes the FBI to investigate. . . . Reds urge world revolt, including against the capitalist Reich.	British deny the abuse of three Nazis. They say the men hid their consular status. . . . Finns draft a reply to Soviet demands; 150,000 square miles of border land plus Hangoe is believed to be the subject of talks. . . . Seven invasion routes are indicated in the west. The terrain will determine Nazi choice; the French have prepared appropriately. . . . King Leopold of Belgium sees the British Queen on war matters. The Belgian-Dutch position in case of an offensive is believed to be the subject. . . . Paris says nine of its U.S. planes shot down nine of 27 invaders.			Gandhi talks hint at disobedience; a veiled threat of reversion to his former policy in India causes concern in London.
Nov. 8	Many previous patrons shun the Soviet fête in Washington. Roosevelt omits goodwill wishes to the Kremlin.	The Belgium-Netherlands peace proposal surprises the Reich. The Nazis' blast at neutrals is seen as a disguise for the desire to end the war on its own terms. . . . A British ship says it is chased by a U-boat. The armed freighter, with more than 100 passengers, signals from the mid-Atlantic. . . . France confers on the two neutrals' bid. Some believe the Netherlands and Belgium seek peace because of fear of a Nazi attack. . . . A German declaration says the Reich is invincible.		Air training costs worry Canada. . . . Cuba and Haiti are shaken by earthquakes of sharp intensity, but they suffer little damage.	London bars an independent India.
Nov. 9		A time bomb explodes in a shrine in Munich after Hitler leaves early. Six are killed and 60 wounded. Britain is accused. . . . Belgium and the Netherlands are said to prepare a pact against the Nazis. It will enable either country to defend the other. . . . British aviators win North Sea battles. Two German planes are shot down; another is disabled. . . . Finns seize a German ship. . . . Yugoslavs resist German demands; they refuse to speed deliveries or let the armed forces use rivers.		Argentina will buy 200 tank cars from the United States. . . . Baseball is so popular in Nicaragua that the government forms a league.	Afghanistan foils an invasion attempt. Three thousand supporters of the former king attempt to stir revolt.

A	B	C	D	E
Includes developments that affect more than one world region, international organizations, and important meetings of world leaders.	*Includes all domestic and regional developments in Europe, including the Soviet Union.*	*Includes all domestic and regional developments in Africa and the Middle East.*	*Includes all domestic and regional developments in Latin America, the Caribbean, and Canada.*	*Includes all domestic and regional developments in Asian and Pacific nations (and colonies).*

U.S. Politics & Social Issues	U.S. Foreign Policy & Defense	Economics & Great Depression	Science, Technology & Nature	Culture, Leisure & Lifestyle	
Al Capone pays his fines. He will quit prison soon. . . . The Dies group investigating un-American activities takes a surprise recess.	The U.S. adopts the Cash-and-Carry Neutrality Act, lifting automatic embargoes on arms shipments, and allowing arms shipments when paid for in cash and not carried on U.S.-registered ships.	Business leaders deny knowledge of large war orders since the arms embargo repeal.	Histories sail from Spain, intending to duplicate the route of Christopher Columbus. . . . "Frozen sleep" aids narcotics addicts. Originators of the treatment tell of apparent cures under refrigeration. Thirty cancer patients have also benefited from this treatment.	Little, Brown publishes a book entitled, *Liquor, The Servant of Man*, that studies the history of liquor drinking and the effects it has on the human body. . . . Rose Bowl choices are expected to emerge soon.	Nov. 4
Domestic politics are absent from the neutrality victory. The vote for full repeal of the embargo was joined by Democrats who fought other New Deal measures.		A federal pension drive is unshaken by rebuffs. . . . The cost of living is up 2 percent after last year's decline.	Blood can be kept for a long time if rapidly cooled, experiments by a physicist and his wife prove. This means that blood for transfusions may help many more wounded soldiers. . . . The American Chemical Society lists twelve men nominated to be its next president.	Charlie Chaplin's upcoming movie is clearly a spoof on Hitler. . . . Frances Griswold's *A Sea Island Lady* is said to be a thoughtful and moving novel about the post-war south. . . . A ball is scheduled to aid those in kindergarten. It is called the Yuletide Ball. . . . Many shows on Broadway are surprise hits this season.	Nov. 5
Congressional leaders drop their advisory plan. They quit Washington instead of staying through the recess to confer with the President. . . . Congressman Martin Dies asks the House for $100,000 more. A one-year extension, not two, is needed for his committee. . . . A U.S. Palestine group seeks $1 million. They vote to raise funds to build a homeland for Jews. . . . Automobile horns and fire engines are the noises that annoy the most hotel guests.		The Department of Agriculture predicts a rise in farm income in 1940. War exports and industrial gains at home are cited as factors. . . . U.S. Lines seeks a new flag to stay in European trade, and plans to ask permission to operate under a Panamanian registry. . . . The food stamp program continues to grow, as two more cities in Pennsylvania will participate.		The Jules S. Bache collection of paintings is once again available for view. Many of these paintings had been loaned to the World Fair. . . . Doubleday, Doran has already determined its list of winter and spring books. . . . Dr. Fritz Sternberg publishes *From Nazi Sources*, a book that purports to show why Hitler cannot win the war. . . . The New York Giants lose their first game in 20 starts when they play against the Detroit Lions.	Nov. 6
The AFL plans a drive for new members. Eight hundred committees around the United States will attempt to spread unionization. . . . The U.S. envoy confers with the *Flint* crew; the future course of the vessel is discussed. . . . A boy thanks the judge who lifts his parole and he keeps his promises. . . . An epidemic kills one dozen elderly females who were living in an asylum. . . . The Catholic Church considers ways to be fair to the Negro. . . . A former boxing champion is held on immigration charges.		Coca-Cola's business is at a new peak. . . . The United States weighs a plan to shift eight ships to Panama's flag. . . . Borden's raises its milk prices by one cent.	A new treatment of latex rubber is announced.	Somerset Maugham writes *Books and You* for Doubleday, Duran. A release date of March 22 is announced. . . . Italy agrees to return to the World Fair in 1940. Britain is still uncertain. . . . Actor Leslie Howard feels somewhat better after his automobile accident this past Saturday. His jaw is fractured, three front teeth are broken, and his chest and forehead are injured. . . . Max Schmeling, boxer, cannot come to the United States. He says that transportation problems are the issue.	Nov. 7
Stomach ulcers are fatal to a youth just ten days after he marries. . . . A fencing match is fatal. A youth dies of a fall after being wounded accidentally. . . . A college student arrested for drunkenness explains that he was conducting research for his thesis on alcohol and that he was overcome during his research. The judge gives the youth ten days in jail to recover and to "correlate his data." . . . A 75 MPH "joy ride" for four miles causes a youth to be jailed.		A two-quart container cuts the price of milk, a savings of 1.5 cents per quart. . . . President Roosevelt halts the transfer of ships to Panama's flags.		A la carte menus are now considered outdated, the president of Waldorf says. Food is wasted that way, and so a more selective form of service is encouraged. . . . Philosopher and author Will Durant calls a wife a "luxury" rather than a useful half of an economic unit. . . . Mozart is played at Carnegie Hall. . . . George Raft and James Cagney will appear together in *City of Conquest*. . . . *Rulers of the Seas* with Douglas Fairbanks, Jr. debuts.	Nov. 8
The American Medical Association is drafting a health plan for the United States, to be ready in one month. . . . Both parties hail the pension defeat. Observers in the capital discern a swing from socialist to conservative ideas. . . . First Lady Eleanor Roosevelt urges caution in reform. She advises making changes in the social order slowly. . . . A witness in a gem ring case is jailed to protect his life. . . . The Negro vote shifts in Philadelphia as three Republican wards win.		The Department of Agriculture forecasts an abundant supply of meat and dairy products. . . . More cars have sold in the first ten months of 1939 than during the entire year of 1938.	Charles Sumner Banks, a U.S. scientist living in the Philippines since 1900, dies. . . . The first bit of heavy carbon pried from nature is on exhibit for selected scientists and engineers as the Columbia Engineering School celebrates its 75th anniversary.	Retired actress Anna Bates dies. She played many roles from 1890 to 1927, with the most recent being Mammy Lou in the operetta *My Maryland*. . . . Zora Neale Hurston publishes *Moses, Man of the Mountain*. . . . Greta Garbo appears at the Music Hall in her first comedy role. . . . Twentieth Century Fox purchases a Louis Bromfield property for $75,000.	Nov. 9

F	G	H	I	J
Includes elections, federal-state relations, civil rights and liberties, crime, the judiciary, education, healthcare, poverty, urban affairs, and population.	Includes formation and debate of U.S. foreign and defense policies, veterans affairs, and defense spending. (Relations with specific foreign countries are usually found under the region concerned.)	Includes business, labor, agriculture, taxation, transportation, consumer affairs, monetary and fiscal policy, natural resources, pollution, and accidents.	Includes worldwide scientific, medical, and technological developments, natural phenomena, U.S. weather, and natural disasters.	Includes the arts, religion, scholarship, communications media, sports, entertainment, fashions, fads, and social life.

	World Affairs	Europe	Africa & The Middle East	The Americas	Asia & The Pacific
Nov. 10	Chinese-Soviet amity grows. People fear a Japanese-Russian deal. . . . France is pleased by U.S. neutrality; Paris needs war materials, not men. . . . U.S. ships reopen service to Norway, avoiding the war zone.	The Reich extends its ban on Czech Jews. . . . A British freighter sinks off the coast of England. . . . Prime Minister Chamberlain is abed with a gout attack; the war Cabinet meets in his bedroom. . . . A fatal border clash stirs the Dutch. Defense measures are rushed as a German offensive is anticipated. . . . Germany is tense. Shocked by the Munich blast, people feel a blow at Britain is near. . . . Yugoslavia balks at German planes. Belgrade tells Nazis that goods will be shipped only for those actually received.		Canadian wheat piles up and the government must look at adjusting its exporting policies with Britain.	The 77th generation descendent of Confucius is born in Chunking, China. The boy weighs eight pounds.
Nov. 11	Americans obtain Japanese amends. The embassy in Washington lists settlements in China after war damage. . . . The United States urges citizens to leave Holland. . . . The Japanese see the United States as a foe.	The Dutch ask for an inquiry on the border clash. A coastal blackout is ordered. . . . The Reich delays a response to the Belgian-Dutch peace offer.	The King of Egypt escapes from a benzene bottle attack. The King suffered no harm.	Canada tightens its wartime economy, setting up a system of priorities that will help with military facilitation. . . . Brazil begins a five-day celebration to commemorate the anniversary of its republic.	
Nov. 12	Brazil sees trade with the Reich halted. Berlin is said to bar the filling of orders unless Rio de Janeiro provides ships. . . . Burma feels India's unrest. Sympathy with England's war aims fails to still agitation for independence. . . . The Greeks try to bar a war of words. Requests are made to the Reich and Britain to curb propaganda. . . . Moscow condemns Britain's policy on India. The press says London faces violent shocks. . . . The League of Nations abandons its session. The bitter opposition of neutral states halts plans.	Britain tightens its air defenses. The people grumble at blackouts, but the army believes the precaution is necessary. . . . The Gestapo is blamed for the Dutch clash. Witnesses say the German Secret Service shot a Netherlander and kidnapped five men. . . . Nazis fear limits on Soviet aid. . . . Italy acclaims the birthday of the King, age 70. Military ceremonies are held and the press extols his reign.			
Nov. 13	Britain removes its north China force. The situation in Europe is cited.	An air-raid scare takes place in Paris. The seventh alarm lasts nearly an hour. . . . A big potato crop is a boon to Germany. The product is a mainstay to the working class and an offset to fodder shortage. . . . Holland is exposed to an aerial attack. The country sounds defenses on the ground. . . . Mussolini increases the Italian army by 23,000; specialists are enrolled to strengthen units. . . . Dutch Nazis back the defense plans. The party of 25,000 is ready to join the invasion resistance.		Argentina's exports have increased by 43 percent over the past ten months.	Australia splits its war department. Separate ministers are named for the army, navy, and air force in a Cabinet expansion.
Nov. 14	The Vatican and Italy aim for Balkan peace. . . . France cuts its garrison in China. The Japanese hail victory, but the British in Tokyo minimize the importance of the move. . . . Germany promises not to harm the U.S. ship Flint; the freighter is expected to sail from Norway today.	A British naval device aids war on U-boats. A secret listening apparatus is praised by officers. . . . A Singapore mine sinks a British liner. Twenty people, mostly children, are reported lost. . . . The Dutch put faith in the Reich pledge; the premier denies the nation is menaced. . . . Latvia orders aliens out of certain areas. Foreigners get until December 15 to leave leading cities. . . . Nazi planes bomb the Shetland Islands. . . . Nazis sink two ships to avoid seizure. . . . Nazi air scouting increases in the west. . . . Soviet troops are due in Lithuania today; they agree to admit 1,500 Jews expelled by Germany.			
Nov. 15	Allies coordinate economic policies. France and Britain are likely to save a supply of dollars for U.S. purchases.	A Nazi mine sinks a British destroyer. Four other ships are lost. . . . Czech Jews lose their real estate income. A decree blocks the use of earnings from land and mortgage. . . . Germany speeds output in Poland; 73 employment offices open to revive industry and to keep up agricultural work. . . . Nazis claim victory in the Shetland Island raid. . . . Nazis turn down peace proposals, saying the Allies rejected them first.		Air patrols guard Canada far out to sea. Planes go out hundreds of miles to watch for raiders. . . . The Americas take up the economy unity bid. Ten republics, including the United States, respond favorably to Guatemala's plan . . . Ecuador names a new Cabinet chief.	The Japanese attack near Indo-China. A major landing is made; the U.S. stand causes anxiety.

A	B	C	D	E
Includes developments that affect more than one world region, international organizations, and important meetings of world leaders.	*Includes all domestic and regional developments in Europe, including the Soviet Union.*	*Includes all domestic and regional developments in Africa and the Middle East.*	*Includes all domestic and regional developments in Latin America, the Caribbean, and Canada.*	*Includes all domestic and regional developments in Asian and Pacific nations (and colonies).*

U.S. Politics & Social Issues	U.S. Foreign Policy & Defense	Economics & Great Depression	Science, Technology & Nature	Culture, Leisure & Lifestyle	
A jury awards a 9-year-old boy the sum of $12,500. He suffered from burns when a bonfire was left unattended. . . . A pilot loses his license after telling others that he was flying to Mars. . . . An actor receives a $37,000 breach of contract settlement.	Armistice pleas will stress defense; speakers tomorrow will point to the conflict abroad.	A sharp drop in tobacco exports is anticipated. . . . Paramount Pictures shows a net profit of $710,000 for the quarter. . . . The profit of PepsiCo. Is estimated to be $4.6 million.	A clock called the "most accurate in the world" is invented. Displayed at the AT&T on Broadway, it shows the times of other countries of the world, as well.	The Canadiens beat the United States at hockey, 2–0. . . . Irwin Edman publishes Arts and the Man, an exploration of the artistic process. . . . Helen Keller expresses her delight at receiving a model-sized version of her house that allows her to "see" her home. . . . Life With Father is a hit on the stage. Next week, theater parties have booked the entire theater for two days. . . . Paramount offers Every Day is Sunday to actress Janet Gaynor.	Nov. 10
The Institute of Women's Professional Relations urges women to train for public service. Working wives are defended. . . . President Roosevelt urges all to join the Red Cross. The organization aids humanity, he says. . . . Three people receive jail sentences for a wife-swapping arrangement.	The Navy tells of faults in new destroyers. Adequate measures are taken to correct them.	The corn crop is 2 percent higher than in 1938. . . . Stores widen their sales gain by 13 percent.	Dr. R.E. Wilson, an inventor with 88 patents, receives a special chemistry award.	According to Publishers Weekly, 772 new books were published last month, a decrease of 302 since last year. . . . Modern Age Books will grant a $1,000 award to the best book dealing with American youth. The deadline for the contest is May 1, 1940. . . . Buddy Doyle, the singing comedian, dies at 38 after an appendicitis operation.	Nov. 11
Some leaders favor avoidance of controversial issues at the next session of Congress. A democratic truce through 1940 is urged. . . . Election results raise Republican hopes; they see a swing to the right in the pension plan defeat. . . . A man cites his ex-wife for not paying the second month of alimony. She is to pay him $15 per month. . . . Two hundred colleges now offer courses in public housing.		The Economy League figures the cost of war entry. It says the expense would be half of the 1917–18 outlay to date.	Admiral Richard Byrd will bottle Antarctic air for study and will test temperature effects on the earth's atmosphere. . . . An education expert says that engineering studies need liberalizing. Social studies and the humanities will assist engineering students in taking leadership roles, he says. . . . CBS plans to test two radio systems. One system will be "static-less," relying upon ultra-short waves.	The Museum of Costume Art shows an exhibit of immigrants' dress. This completes a cycle of shows that focus on the clothing of our nation. . . . Claude M. Fuess publishes a biography of former president Calvin Coolidge.	Nov. 12
City College in New York City reports that only 2 percent of its 1936 graduates are currently unemployed. . . . A great-grandmother shoots a deer on her golden anniversary. . . . A hunter is shot by his own dog who accidentally steps on a gun's trigger.	The United States keeps many air devices secret. Bomb sights, detectors, and some searchlights will not be sold to foreign buyers. . . . Twenty-three U.S. plants are currently working on military planes.	Oat prices are slightly weaker, as rye prices also recede. . . . Steel operations are high at 93 percent production. . . . Wheat crops are hit hard by the drought and the welcome rains provide little relief. . . . Wool prices increase by 50 percent.		City College is now using John Steinbeck's novel, The Grapes of Wrath, as a textbook for introductory sociology classes. This novel has been on the best-selling lists for several weeks. . . . Dodd, Mead will publish Enchanting Jenny Lind to its fall list. . . . More than 27,000 people visit the flower show at the American Museum of Natural History. Major attractions include rare South African blooms. . . . Helen Howe will perform monologue satires called Washington: All Change.	Nov. 13
Officials refuse to reveal Al Capone's location; his release is due on Sunday. . . . A counterman at a roadside clam bar is fined $50 for refusing to serve Negros. . . . Judge J.E. Walsh, who sentenced Al Capone to jail in 1929, dies at age 59.		Republicans ask to ban partisanship in the trade act fight. They request the adjournment of politics on the issue to force the law's death. . . . The Coast Guard aids "beached" soldiers. The training school will take only those made idle by the Neutrality Act; 4,000 are affected. . . . U.S. finances are found weak for a new war. The status is precarious when compared to 1914. . . . Butter holdings drop by more than 26 million pounds, nearly a record. . . . Christmas Clubs set a six-year record with 7 million members saving $350,000,000.		Fifteen big exhibitors sign up for the 1940 World Fair. They include General Motors, Edison Consolidated, du Pont, AT & T and Petroleum Group. . . . Macmillan will release a book called How Criminals are Caught. . . . William Geoffrey publishes The Compleat Lover. . . . A car crash kills movie director George Nicholls, Jr. as his car plunges 700 feet into a canyon by Hollywood. . . . George Jessel will film Before I Die in New York City. This is because of Mayor LaGuardia's efforts to bring motion pictures to New York. . . . Ranger Bill Miller, an early screen cowboy, dies at age 61.	Nov. 14
Earthquake tremors rock Philadelphia. The shock is felt from New Jersey to Maryland. . . . President Roosevelt is silent on the 1940 election despite the drive for Vice President John Garner. . . . Al Capone is allegedly on his way to Atlanta, Ga. . . . The sheriff of Essex County is arraigned on drunk driving charges.		Farm milk prices sharply increase. . . . Seven hundred movie operators will receive a ten cent raise.	A huge radio system is set up at the airport at LaGuardia Field. . . . A new low temperature oven burner for gas ranges is announced. The temperatures can go as low as 250 degrees.	One thousand four hundred guests attend the Barnard jubilee celebration. . . . Will Durant's book, The Life of Greece, is going into its second printing of 7,500. . . . RCA Victor has created a Mother Goose record. . . . The Postmaster General James Farley guest stars on the radio show, Information, Please. . . . Dorothy Gish will replace Lillian Foster in Mornings at Seven.	Nov. 15

F	G	H	I	J
Includes elections, federal-state relations, civil rights and liberties, crime, the judiciary, education, healthcare, poverty, urban affairs, and population.	Includes formation and debate of U.S. foreign and defense policies, veterans affairs, and defense spending. (Relations with specific foreign countries are usually found under the region concerned.)	Includes business, labor, agriculture, taxation, transportation, consumer affairs, monetary and fiscal policy, natural resources, pollution, and accidents.	Includes worldwide scientific, medical, and technological developments, natural phenomena, U.S. weather, and natural disasters.	Includes the arts, religion, scholarship, communications media, sports, entertainment, fashions, fads, and social life.

	World Affairs	Europe	Africa & The Middle East	The Americas	Asia & The Pacific
Nov. 16	A well-known Bolshevik says that war will aid communism. He sees the collapse of imperialism in the struggle. . . . The Japanese strike at supply routes; they are believed to be cutting off roads to Indo-China. . . . The Japanese sharpen their anti-British drive. The Tientsin blockade is tightened.	British censorship aids in war at sea. Silence on naval operations makes U-boat crews nervous and easier to catch. . . . Bulgaria is wary of a triple menace: Russian expansion, German domination, and unemployment. . . . Nazi troops with rifles charge into a group of Czech students five times to disperse them. . . . Russians berate Helsinki leaders. Radio reports charge the ruling class with inciting hatred for Soviets and exploiting the masses.			Chinese Reds fight the forces of Chiang Kai-shek.
Nov. 17	A British ship is sunk by a surface raider near east Africa. The attacker is not identified.	Al Capone excites London. Newspapers give his prison release graphic front page coverage. . . . Czechs riot again; the regime is assailed. . . . Germany proclaims that the end of Britain as a world power is their war goal. . . . The French intensify civilian discipline. Workers are forbidden to change jobs.		Canadian industrial buying returns to normal with price increases averaging 10 percent. . . . The Archbishop of Quebec praises the relationship between Canada and the United States, calling it a model for other countries. . . . The President of Ecuador, Aurelio Mosquera, dies of pneumonia and hepatic poisoning.	Japan claims the capture of Pakhoi. An air base near the city is thought to portend raids on south China roads.
Nov. 18	The African east coast prepares for attack. British areas worry over the nearness of the German raider. . . . Winston Churchill denies slurring the U.S. south. He says his broadcast was misunderstood. . . . Japanese groups urge a Russian pact of nonaggression, saying Tokyo should ignore the displeasure of Britain and the United States.	U-boats are seen aiding Russia, setting up a blockade of Finland. The Reich, on behalf of the Soviet Union, stops Finnish ships. Fifteen vessels with cargoes for neutrals are held in German ports. . . . Nine Czech students are executed. . . . The Crown Prince and Princess of Denmark expect their first child in April. . . . The Reich closes Prague University for three years as punishment for protests. . . . A lone Nazi bomber crosses England. The daring flight over an industrial area is carried out despite heavy anti-aircraft fire.	Africa's east coast prepares for an attack. British areas of the country worry about the nearness of German raider.	Canada's exports to the U.S. rise.	Japan adds to its south China gains.
Nov. 19	The Japanese attest that the United States stiffened Britain, saying the blockade could have ended three months ago. . . . The Pope's solicitude heartens Negroes. Both Catholic and non-Catholic leaders in the United States praise the encyclical on welfare and better race relations.	Artillery pounds German defenses. Nazis report only minor damage. . . . Germany renews its ship list warning. The notice is served in the press and by broadcast on the arming of merchantmen. . . . More Czechs are shot; three are executed for an act of violence against a German, Nazis say. . . . Nazis admit to a British raid on Wilhelmshaven but assert German gunfire drove them off.		Ecuador seeks economic revival. The country is struggling to overcome the disastrous effects of military regimes.	Japan looks for peace; China sees a long war. . . . Gandhi warns Britain against a long delay. He implies civil disobedience will begin again soon if deadlock continues.
Nov. 20	A Japanese journalist in Rome says that the Reich is buying 20 Soviet submarines.	Mussolini urges self-sufficiency. Gains in agriculture and industry are already cited. . . . The Balkan strategy revives the Axis link. Fitful Rome-Berlin cooperation is hinted on common ground in press dispatches. . . . Czechs abandon protest strikes as Nazis threaten more executions. . . . The French turn back fresh Reich raids. . . . The Soviets may supply the Reich with 800,000 tons of oil.		Brazil sets up steps to create a central bank using its own resources. . . . A Canadian cardinal urges the United States to stay out of the war, saying that it can best serve peace as a neutral nation.	Floods in China ruin grain. Hopeh is stricken.
Nov. 21	Finns seek funds to keep up defenses. The United States is said to favor credit. . . . Moscow urges a Soviet accord. Eagerness for a trade treaty is revealed in the emphasis on preliminary talks. . . . Victims denounce the new use of mines. They say ships sink so quickly they do not have time to launch boats.	The French report that their foe is harried by flood, saying the rising Rhine has forced Nazis from advance posts and has curtailed operations. . . . Heinrich Himmler is reportedly on his way to Prague. Hitler is said to demand that order be restored. . . . Six more ships are sunk; Britain weighs a ban on Reich exports. . . . A Nazi flier pierces London outskirts, causing wide alarm. . . . The Netherlands guns down a Reich plane; the incident is the third in three days. . . . Nazis condemn a Pole to death; he is charged with complicity in the lynching of two Germans.		A labor parley is set for Havana today. Social insurance, immigration, and women's and children's work feature on the agenda. . . . Canadian newsprint remains at $50 a ton.	The Japanese strengthen their south China forces. . . . More power is given to Chiang Kai-shek. The party makes him premier. . . . The India riot toll is now 23. The Hindu-Muslim feud spreads, and military rule is hinted.

A	B	C	D	E
Includes developments that affect more than one world region, international organizations, and important meetings of world leaders.	*Includes all domestic and regional developments in Europe, including the Soviet Union.*	*Includes all domestic and regional developments in Africa and the Middle East.*	*Includes all domestic and regional developments in Latin America, the Caribbean, and Canada.*	*Includes all domestic and regional developments in Asian and Pacific nations (and colonies).*

U.S. Politics & Social Issues	U.S. Foreign Policy & Defense	Economics & Great Depression	Science, Technology & Nature	Culture, Leisure & Lifestyle	
Al Capone is a patient in a Philadelphia hospital. Police say he suffers from paresis. . . . Thomas Dewey's presidential campaign is scheduled to start in the west on December 6. . . . A policeman kills the Long Beach mayor and shoots his bodyguard over a personal grudge.		Economists weigh war effects in the United States. They hold that private enterprise is needed and warn about public debt. . . . The Federal Reserve marks its 25th year. . . . A $60,000-a-ton gold lode is discovered in Georgia and it is comparable to the Comstock vein.	In a new book, *Excursions into Science*, 30 scientists talk about their specialties.	Macmillan is set to release *Hitler's Germany: The Nazi Background to War*. . . . Borden signs up for the 1940 World Fair, pleased with the success of its 1939 exhibit. . . . An artist scorns the taste of most Americans, saying that they're influenced by the calendar art available at grocery stores. . . . French actor Charles Boyer is expected to arrive in the United States. Some say that he is here on a propaganda mission for his country.	Nov. 16
Al Capone is free from prison. The former gangster will have three weeks of hospital treatment, then leave for Miami under police surveillance. . . . A federal jury finds General Motors guilty in a monopoly case. The company's financing method violates antitrust laws. . . . President Roosevelt returns to his Hyde Park home to lay the cornerstone of the building that will house his papers.		Massachusetts boasts a large cranberry crop this year. It is estimated that the country will produce 668,000 barrels.	Micrurgy studies occupy scientists. Bacteriologists begin a two-day study of minute, one-celled organisms and "pure" bacteria is obtained.	James Thurber publishes *The Last Flower*, a parable in pictures. . . . The New York Boxing Association watches a film of Jack Dempsey and Jess Willard. The group then discusses whether Dempsey or Joe Louis was the better fighter, with votes evenly split between the two champions. . . . F.A. Stokes, book publisher, dies at age 82.	Nov. 17
Al Capone starts brain treatment. He is considered chronically but not acutely ill. . . . An expert finds child-rearing fads evil, advising common sense instead of psychiatric frills. . . . President Roosevelt puts a third-term hint in his speech, laughing at speculation. . . . A gas explosion in Kansas City lifts a building from its foundation. . . . A 13-year-old boy sees his father slain and he picks up a gun and shoots the bandit. . . . The official portrait of Carrie Chapman Catt now hangs in the Smithsonian, the fourth feminist to be given such an honor.		Another blast is made in the Georgia gold mine. This bares a vein with a value of $160,000 per ton. . . . FSA will provide help for 2,000 farm houses. . . . Store sales were up 7 percent this week, nationwide.	Chemists give a special award to a Russian scientist who came to the United States in 1931. . . . The Smithsonian honors the British scientist, Julian Huxley. The keynote speech will be "Science, Social and Unsocial." . . . The American Association of Scientific Workers discusses the impact of science in the news.	Mothers gather to demand better films. Crime pictures and inferior second-rate films are held to be unfit for children. . . . Safe sports plan is urged on schools. Athletic supervisors are advised to study this issue. . . . Madeleine Carroll gets the lead in *My Son, My Son* and *Northwest Mounted Police*.	Nov. 18
Parents criticize newer education. Progressive methods are teacher centered, they say, and the aim is to teach students to get what they want. . . . Actor Charlie Chaplin successfully defends himself in court. He was accused of purloining the plot of *Modern Times*, but he persuaded a judge that the idea belonged to him. . . . States are encouraged to ban fireworks.	The Army reverses its decision to switch to slate blue uniforms, bringing back the drab olive color.		William Morton Wheeler publishes *Essays in Philosophical Biology*. This book bears the stamp of scholarship, humor, and integrity.	Ivan T. Sanderson publishes *Caribbean Treasure*, detailing this naturalist's experiences. . . . The Metropolitan Museum of Art displays an exceptional suit of 17th-century armor. . . . Raymond Holden publishes *Believe the Heart*, a lushly detailed novel that analyzes feminine psychology.	Nov. 19
The government lists punishable acts by labor unions. Anti-trust laws are violated if "unreasonable restraints" are used. . . . President Roosevelt mocks third-term talk at a library dedication.	Most of the college men joining the Army prefer air service.	Steel producers are swamped with a backlog of orders. . . . Negro federal workers ask for $1 billion to be given to WPA for relief of the unemployed. . . . The corn supply is held to be ample for 1939–1940, with 800,000,000 more bushels available than what is needed.		Joe DiMaggio marries film actress Dorothy Arnold. Crowds storm the church. . . . *Kitty Foyle* by Christopher Morley tops many best selling lists. . . . Simon & Schuster plans to publish a book titled *Those Were the Days*, that covers the manners and morals of Americans as determined through the pages of the Sears & Roebuck catalogues from 1905 through 1935.	Nov. 20
First Lady Eleanor Roosevelt recommends a post for former president Herbert Hoover, suggesting he head a refugee agency. . . . Congressman Martin Dies widens his committee's inquiry into Reds and Nazis. The full committee is called when the chairman sees evidence of a subversive plot. . . . A detective is held in the shooting of his wife. During seven hours of questioning, his story did not remain cohesive. . . . A girl with two guns slays her foe in a crowd. She empties one and then takes a second one out of her purse and fires at a lawyer.		A nationally known garment-trade arbitrator and labor mediator, Abraham Rothstein, dies at age 81. He settled one dispute that involved more than 4,000 workers. . . . An airline opens a pilot school in Queens. . . . A blind man will head a house for the sightless. . . . New York prisoners will make soap. . . . The grocery store is pushed as a locale to sell beer. Chicago wholesalers hear of success stories in three states.	The City Hospital receives funding for a hibernation room for treatment of cancer. Made possible by a private gift, its services can be used by the poor for free. . . . Essential protein can now be synthesized. A Purdue expert talks about making his own at a low cost.	Simon & Schuster orders a second printing of *Wacky, the Small Boy*. . . . A speech expert asks radio officials to ban stuttering as a form of comedy. . . . Thirty-seven internationally known figure skaters arrive in the United States. They will tour, putting on shows.	Nov. 21

F	G	H	I	J
Includes elections, federal-state relations, civil rights and liberties, crime, the judiciary, education, healthcare, poverty, urban affairs, and population.	Includes formation and debate of U.S. foreign and defense policies, veterans affairs, and defense spending. (Relations with specific foreign countries are usually found under the region concerned.)	Includes business, labor, agriculture, taxation, transportation, consumer affairs, monetary and fiscal policy, natural resources, pollution, and accidents.	Includes worldwide scientific, medical, and technological developments, natural phenomena, U.S. weather, and natural disasters.	Includes the arts, religion, scholarship, communications media, sports, entertainment, fashions, fads, and social life.

	World Affairs	Europe	Africa & The Middle East	The Americas	Asia & The Pacific
Nov. 22	Argentina limits its buying to Allies. Imports will be confined, if possible, to principal customers in the war period. . . . U.S. banks press Germany for a pact. Efforts are redoubled to obtain a substitute for an agreement on credits ended by war. . . . Britain will certify U.S. ship cargoes. Ships will pass goods through the blockade without visiting the control port. . . . Gandhi warns the British on India's war role. Complete freedom for India is demanded as the price.	A British prize crew takes a German ship. . . . A duel of artillery wages at the front. Continued massing of troops supports the view that Hitler must feed people victories. . . . Four Germans escape from a British camp. The seamen defied floodlights, sentries, and the high barbed-wire fences of the prison. . . . Germany seeks more diesel fuel. . . . Hungary stresses a rift with Romania. . . . The House of Commons cheers Prime Minister Chamberlain for his step to halt German sales. He says the brutal sinkings cannot be excused. . . . Nazis in Prague end martial law.		Canada bars "Red" newspapers. The French and British journals of Toronto Communists are banned.	China lays plans for three new ministries.
Nov. 23	The Reich gains in the air arms race. U.S. aid is not expected to put the Allies ahead until next fall or 1941.	Anti-Reich feeling grows in Estonia. Nazis are said to ask $20 million for the property of repatriates. . . . Artillery is active on the western front. Clearing weather enables both sides to get observations for big guns. . . . Britain trains one million soldiers. . . . France adds a ban on Reich exports, joining the British in its reprisal to cut off foreign credits in Germany. . . . Eight German planes are shot down in one day. . . . A minor row leads to three Prague executions. Nazis understood a menacing remark made in Czech. . . . Rome abandons the Balkan bloc idea.			
Nov. 24	Canada favors a British food pact. The plan would mean control by London of Canada's wheat and other products. . . . A German ship, covering the escape of a raider, is scuttled to avoid capture off the coast of Africa. . . . War perils have eased, says the U.S. Assistant Secretary of State. Only unendurable acts of violence will get the United States involved, he declares.	Air battles rage over the western front. . . . Nazis see the British coast as a military zone. Germans deny it is a commercial shipping lane. . . . Holland and Belgium protest to the Allies their objection to the project to seize German exports. German pressure is seen. . . . Rome expects a split in the Balkans. The new Cabinet in Romania is seen as linking it to the Allies; Hungary leans to the Reich.		Canadians favor a food pact with Britain. . . . Mexico ends the tax on capital exports.	A Shanghai spokesman says the new Chinese regime is soon to be established. . . . The Japanese are at the gates of Nanning, which is afire from many bombs. The south China city is reportedly devastated by the attacks of invaders' planes.
Nov. 25	The Italian foreign minister sees envoys. He says the Allied plan to seize Reich exports would hurt Italian trade. Japan is also protesting. . . . Japan and Russia open talks; peace in China is sought.	An explosive parachuted by a Reich plane shuts a British harbor for a few hours. . . . German Catholics fix war duties; large attendance at religious services is reported since the beginning of hostilities. . . . The French repulse Germans in a Moselle attack. The French report the capture of several prisoners. . . . Italy and Hungary form a new trade pact. The announcement is held significant after the switch by Romania to a pro-French government.		A Mexican labor chief urges autarchy for all Americans, calling it the basis of all social justice. . . . Brazilians must marry or pay a bachelor tax. . . . Canada's war costs exceed 1914. . . . Mexico may sell surplus oil in the United States, amounting to 2 million barrels monthly. . . . Argentina gains in the trade balance.	Nanning is captured, the Japanese report. A new push is expected. . . . Twenty-one are condemned for plotting a revolt in Thailand. The two grandsons of the late ruler are doomed.
Nov. 26	The British change their minds on the U.S. role in the war. As the French, they prefer to run the war and make the peace. . . . Neutrals expand arms buying in the United States. China becomes a significant purchaser. . . . Belligerents' crews ask for Bibles at the U.S. harbor. The New York Society says sailors have a "real desire" for them.	Food laws vary in nations at war. Germany is stinted, Britain is watchful, and France is liberal. . . . The French reveal a 35-mile range gun; the weapon awaits Nazi attack for its baptism. . . . Czech protests halt a health drive. Women fear that inoculations are a German plot to kill. . . . The Polish former envoy is reported slain. Many leaders have been executed by Nazis for "persecution" of Germany.		Brazil institutes new trade rules, designed to prevent harmful effects from the war on its economy. . . . Canada is puzzled by its flow of exports. Those to the United States increase while those sent to Britain decrease.	Chinese concede the loss of Nanning. They call the Japanese victory a "barren prize," as invaders must get food by plane. . . . . . . India is advanced in equal rights; a female politician tells how men and women cooperate.
Nov. 27	A missionary reveals cannibalism in Australia. . . . Two Americans who were arrested in France for insulting an admiral are home safe.	Nazis say the British are on the defensive in the sea war, and assert Germans can attack in any part of the North Sea. . . . Citizenship is speeded for Baltic people in Germany. Most are accepted after a four-hour inquiry. . . . The Allies choose an economic director. A London committee will coordinate world activities. . . . Germany relies on Balkan goods. Pressure is being put on states to plug wartime gaps. . . . Helsinki rules out unilateral action, saying the withdrawal of troops must be done jointly. There are 300,000 troops on the border. . . . The Reich grants respite to Teschen Jews, allowing two more weeks before mass transport to Poland. . . . Soviets charge attack by Finns who defy the demand to quit the border.		Joint labor steps in the Americas are urged. Workers' delegates stress keeping out of the war and taking action for their rights. . . . Canada sets a price of 45 cents per pound for wool during the war.	The new regime will not end the conflict, the Japanese premier says. He expects a long fight in China.
	A *Includes developments that affect more than one world region, international organizations, and important meetings of world leaders.*	**B** *Includes all domestic and regional developments in Europe, including the Soviet Union.*	**C** *Includes all domestic and regional developments in Africa and the Middle East.*	**D** *Includes all domestic and regional developments in Latin America, the Caribbean, and Canada.*	**E** *Includes all domestic and regional developments in Asian and Pacific nations (and colonies).*

U.S. Politics & Social Issues	U.S. Foreign Policy & Defense	Economics & Great Depression	Science, Technology & Nature	Culture, Leisure & Lifestyle	
A brokerage worker admits to stealing $57,000 and he returns $52,000. . . . Artie Shaw, orchestra leader and critic of the jitterbug movement, severs all ties with his musical group because of illness and he leaves for Mexico. . . . Vice President Garner will spend his 71st birthday hunting and then cooking his own dinner over a campfire.		Radio entertainers Andy 'n Amos help the Red Cross with a $7,500 donation.	Twelve engineers receive prestigious Columbia Awards.	Al Jolson is hospitalized. Friends say that he has been unable to recover from a cold after his wife left him. . . . Cartoonist Art Young publishes his autobiography. . . . Gone With the Wind is scheduled to premiere on December 19. . . . A city affairs group asks Mayor LaGuardia to push for a higher moral tone at next year's World Fair. . . . Ice stars will appear in a show tonight.	Nov. 22
Chrysler foremen cause a new crisis. The status of the CIO union of supervisors relegates the wage dispute to the background. . . . The court awards $33,500 to a child run over by a milk wagon in 1937. . . . A man writes three notes and gives them a pedestrian before jumping off a bridge. His body was recovered. . . . Negro schoolteachers win a court case, whereby Maryland County must pay them the same as white teachers. . . . No walrus meat is available for Eskimos in Alaska, so they must substitute polar bear meat for their Thanksgiving dinner.	The Army organizes a scouting regiment. The use of motorcycles is included for first time to gain speed. . . . Envoys return to give President Roosevelt war reports. The ambassadors to Britain, Belgium, and Poland share their views with the President.		The Academy of Natural Sciences announces the discovery of a horned turkey.	French actor Charles Boyer arrives in the United States. with his English wife. He denies any propaganda purpose to his travels. . . . Parades will brighten Thanksgiving fêtes, with floats, bands, and balloons and bright colors. . . . William Powell returns to the screen after a year's absence, starring in Another Thin Man with Myrna Loy. . . . Paramount finds humor with The Cat and the Canary.	Nov. 23
A divided holiday, with two different dates for Thanksgiving, fails to dim the spirit of the occasion. . . . A man held as a vagrant has $5,775 in the bank. . . . A Hollywood slaying is called a gang revenge killing.		Elliot Roosevelt says that labor is in peril. He warns unions of a "frightful beating" in Congress unless the AFL and CIO can heal their split. . . . 70 percent of the people surveyed say that they approve of the food stamp program. . . . Job placements set a record pace in October, with more than 308,000 people placed in private industry jobs.	The first air-conditioning system for cars has been announced.		Nov. 24
	President Roosevelt plans a $500 million rise in defense costs. . . . The U.S. Navy regards mine planting from planes as an effective from of attack.	The broken toy quest for the needy lags. Police and firemen plead for gifts to be repaired for children in time for Christmas. . . . Bethlehem Steel plans to raise pensions.	Archaeologists uncover new treasures in Ostia, including 12 bronze friezes of the 12 labors of Hercules. . . . Two hundred flee landslides on an Alaskan mountain.	Film comedian Stan Laurel divorces. The judge hints perjury in his ex-wife's testimony. . . . Shades of French blue grace fashions. . . . Czech art works are on display. A painting intended for Prague museum—once the country is free—is included in this exhibit. . . . Actress Simone Simon debuts on the American stage with Three After Three.	Nov. 25
	Americans man war ambulances. Field service is revived to recruit volunteers and solicit funds.	Employment rises in the building trades as September is the sixth month in a row to show such an increase. . . . The food stamp program thrives in eleven cities.	A chemistry report sees jobs in that field limited and competitive. . . . Cornell University expands its engineering work as they add a significant amount of equipment to test materials under all conditions. . . . Dr. E.E. Free dies. Former head of the "Scientific America," he was credited with the discovery of potash on the coast.	Experts face a second season of questioning on the radio on the program, Information Please. . . . Actor Wallace Beery adopts a second child. He brings home a 7-month-old girl to be a sister to his 8-year-old adopted daughter.	Nov. 26
A study shows that the speech of high school students worsens.		Amish people plan a trek to Maryland. The fertile Pennsylvania land is too costly for many after 150 years of toil. . . . Capacity rises 3 percent in power plants. . . . Elliot Roosevelt expects to start a new radio network by January 1. . . . Enthusiasm fades in cotton buying. . . . Hotel guests' list of noise complaints fuels drive for silence. . . . Duties of principals expand over the past 40 years, with the current job list equaling 400 percent of the original set of tasks.	Gerald Wendt publishes a book, Science for the World of Tomorrow.	Paramount schedules Miami, a modern musical romance set in Florida, as Mary Martin's next vehicle.	Nov. 27

F	G	H	I	J
Includes elections, federal-state relations, civil rights and liberties, crime, the judiciary, education, healthcare, poverty, urban affairs, and population.	Includes formation and debate of U.S. foreign and defense policies, veterans affairs, and defense spending. (Relations with specific foreign countries are usually found under the region concerned.)	Includes business, labor, agriculture, taxation, transportation, consumer affairs, monetary and fiscal policy, natural resources, pollution, and accidents.	Includes worldwide scientific, medical, and technological developments, natural phenomena, U.S. weather, and natural disasters.	Includes the arts, religion, scholarship, communications media, sports, entertainment, fashions, fads, and social life.

	World Affairs	Europe	Africa & The Middle East	The Americas	Asia & The Pacific
Nov. 28	The head of a German refugee camp hopes to send 25,000 Jews to Palestine, and asks for aid. . . . The Empire completes air training plans. Britain, Canada, New Zealand, and Australia agree on terms.	The Allies embargo German exports. The King signs the order and the ban takes effect today. . . . The British tell Soviets of their peace hope. London wants to see the Finnish dispute settled. . . . Finns are indignant at the Soviet charge; the idea that the little nation wants war is called ludicrous. . . . Germany supports an attack on Finland. A news service justifies the claim of Russia as the natural right of a big power. . . . Moscow is rebuffed as the Finns refuse to leave their border. They deny firing on Russians.		Argentina will cut imports, and it is expected that the sale of U.S. automobiles to the country will be halved.	
Nov. 29	The U.S. Library of Congress gets the Magna Carta. The British ambassador puts one of four copies there for safekeeping during war. . . . The Japanese ease the Tientsin blockade. American protests are the chief factor in the milder policy. . . . Germany aids Red Cross relief for the Polish. U.S. and Reich agents join together for supervision of the work. . . . The Vatican is disturbed by the threat to Finns.	Russia scraps its pact with Finland; three border clashes are reported. Moscow charges the Finnish massing of troops is hostile, sharpening the crisis. . . . Finland prepares a reply to Moscow; the Cabinet meets in an urgent night session. . . . Nazis use smoke to cover an attack; the French frontline troops resist the thrust from Germans using the new technique. . . . Turks fear a Reich-Soviet attack on the Balkans and Near East soon. . . . The British issue a warning to the Soviet Union: an attack on Finland would end trade pact talks.	The Egyptian police discover an opium cache in the stomachs of camels.	Canada increases its newsprint trade, saying that the war would not affect this venture.	
Nov. 30	Britain holds two U.S. ships. The vessels left their home ports before the designation of combat zones by President Roosevelt. . . . The Australian force will fight in Europe. . . . Japan may seize cargo of the Allies. It plans for reprisals if the Anglo-Franco ban on Reich exports continues. . . . The Reich oil situation is critical. Germany is isolated from great sources of supply, and U.S. imports have virtually ended.	Soviet artillery opens fire as troops cross the Finnish border. People run to shelters as Helsinki sees Russian planes. . . . Premier Edouard Daladier asks for renewal of powers; the French parliament is expected to vote confidence. . . . Students denounce France in rioting in Belgrade. Yugoslavia curbs the university as students back the Soviet Union. . . . Nazis back the Soviet Union on the Finnish threat.		The Havana parley recommends an immigration body in the Americas, and urges the establishment of official bodies in each country. . . . A Canadian bomber crashes, killing four.	
Dec. 1	Japan insists on a blockade cap, pressing the British to allow passage of oil extraction machinery from the Reich. . . . Finns in the United States are angry over the Soviet move.	Belgrade jails 50 Reds; action against students follows the riot in which many are injured. . . . Britain denounces Russian invaders; Prime Minister Chamberlain leads the attack on "unjustified" aggression. . . . The Finnish premier quits despite a vote of confidence. The Russian ultimatum is said to ask surrender or threatens pain of a worse blow. . . . The Finnish Cabinet resigns as the Soviet Union bombs cities. The new government will seek a truce with Russia. . . . Moscow is receptive to armistice talks.		Canada plans a Red curb. Federal officials, investigating pamphlets, hesitate to make martyrs out of Communists.	Chinese supplies are cut by the loss of Nanning. Japanese now control access to Indo-China.
Dec. 2	A Canadian air unit forms in Britain. . . . President Roosevelt's response is stern. The Soviet invasion of Finland is denounced in his strongest words since the war began. A "moral" ban is hinted. . . . A Soviet air threat to Japan is seen; bases across Asia are said to beeline for a potential attack in the spring. . . . Japan avoids taking a stand on Finland. . . . The United States takes steps to bar planes to the Soviet Union.	Moscow recognizes the new "democratic republic" founded in Finland. Its Cabinet asks for aid. . . . French Premier Edouard Daladier warns "bomb for bomb" in answering the German raid threat. . . . Fighting in Finland is intense. . . . Finland's new Cabinet says it will fight for independence. . . . Italian hostility to Russia stiffens; the press condemns the invasion of Finland. Officials are silent. . . . The Reich army chief leaves for the front to inspect troops. . . . The British show skill at sweeping mines.		The Brazilian government has decided to assist union factory workers in getting home loans.	
Dec. 3	A moral embargo of the Soviets is put in place by the United States. Roosevelt assails the "obviously guilty." . . . The Chinese are silent on the invasion of Finland. Tokyo sees an Axis break. . . . The attack on Finland arouses the French. The Russian actions clarify war issues and the U.S. response is hailed.	The Allies gain power through economic unity. The coordination plan is seen by some diplomats as the basis for a new Europe. . . . The Reich approves of the attack on Finland. The press insists the British and Swedish ministers inspired resistance to the Soviets. . . . The Balkans are in an economic trap, forced to trade with the Reich. . . . The Finnish defense line is firm and Russian losses are heavy. The government orders citizens to evacuate cities as greater air raids are feared. . . . Italians protest at the Soviet legation. Demonstrators boo and jeer Stalin.		An Ontario couple seeks to adopt the 16-year-old who accidentally shot and killed their own 15-year-old son. They are attempting to persuade the boy's mother to grant permission for the adoption.	

A	B	C	D	E
Includes developments that affect more than one world region, international organizations, and important meetings of world leaders.	*Includes all domestic and regional developments in Europe, including the Soviet Union.*	*Includes all domestic and regional developments in Africa and the Middle East.*	*Includes all domestic and regional developments in Latin America, the Caribbean, and Canada.*	*Includes all domestic and regional developments in Asian and Pacific nations (and colonies).*

U.S. Politics & Social Issues	U.S. Foreign Policy & Defense	Economics & Great Depression	Science, Technology & Nature	Culture, Leisure & Lifestyle	
Congressman Martin Dies is told that Reds run the teachers' union. Their control is called strong; First Lady Eleanor Roosevelt is willing to testify. . . . Princeton students vote Hitler as the greatest living person; Einstein second; and Chamberlain third. . . . Four people confess to selling civil service tests. It is said that they received $75 to $400 for the questions. . . . A former follower—or angel—of evangelist Father Divine sues him for peace mission funds.			Julian S. Huxley, noted British biologist and writer, wants the scientific research cooperation between the United States and England to continue.	Author Alexander Harkavy dies at age 76. He aided many immigrants with his Yiddish-English dictionaries and he founded a newspaper. . . . Larry Nixon publishes a book, "American Vacations," that talks about potential travel destinations. . . . The Metropolitan Opera season begins its 55th season, as notables of society, the arts, diplomacy, and military fill the "golden horseshoe." . . . Ethel Barrymore appears in a premiere as an eccentric 97-year-old.	Nov. 28
Reds in the United States are seen as ruled by Russia. U.S. voters believe that the Communist Party is merely an arm of the Soviet Union, a survey says. . . . The vice chairman of the Dies Committee says he doubts the group will question the First Lady, despite her offer. . . . Twenty-three get jail sentences for voter fraud, including four women. . . . Five hundred women spend the day discussing how to get a maid, as there is a labor shortage problem. . . . A committee studying sex education in the schools disbands without action.		President Roosevelt decides to have two budgets. He tells the press he wants a clear label on items set up for added defenses. . . . Cost of living increases for those in large cities are significant at 1.2 percent. New York is the hardest hit, with an increase of 2.5 percent. . . . Employers urge a change in wage laws that doesn't place such a burden on business. . . . Harvard University shows a school year-end surplus of $843 after taking in income of $14,000,000. . . . Overtime police work is rewarded with two days off work.			Nov. 29
Congressman Martin Dies attends a rally and warns the United States to stop its "aping" of Europe. Ten thousand cheer his plea for national unity and a fight on all alien forces.		Chrysler workers ratify an agreement, including a pay raise of three cents per hour for all.		Pearl Buck berates the best-seller lists, declaring they "sheep herd" thinking and calling them a book dictatorship. . . . William Saroyan publishes The Time of Your Life.	Nov. 30
An ancestor of 200 people dies at age 115. . . . New Jersey will no longer recognize new common law marriages, a measure taken to curb the spread of syphilis. The state will continue to recognize the legality of those marriages that occurred before December 1, 1939.	The Army limits the use of thermite bombs, as experts explain the incendiary problems.	Baseball executives meet in Cincinnati. Leo Durocher is one of the earliest to arrive. . . . Dollar values of engineering contracts already exceed those of the entire year of 1938. . . . The Bureau of Weights and Measures will guard against frauds intended to raise the weight—and therefore the price—of their products. An example is bricks being wrapped in satin to increase the weight of eggs. . . . Grain prices soar, with wheat on top.		The Dionne quintuplets lose their nurse. They bid farewell in the gowns worn when they met the King of England. . . . Ankle-length gowns are shown in Parisian fashions. Other clothing also hits a somber note. . . . Carl Sandburg's biography, Abraham Lincoln: The War Years, is a vast and entertaining chronicle. . . . The coach of the Navy football team is confident that his men will play over their heads to capture the game that they want so badly over the Army team. . . . There is a scalping ban on Army-Navy tickets, worth $4.40 each.	Dec. 1
Drought menaces the TVA power supply. A fall in electric current and rise in home and factory use presents a challenge. . . . Hazing is on the wane in fraternities. The use of paddles is dying on campuses. . . . President Roosevelt finds electricity ample, saying there is no emergency. . . . A court penalizes three for tarring and feathering a writer. . . . Men are accused of using a game of bingo for charity for personal gain. They defend themselves in court. . . . A burlesque satire of the civil service test circulates among workers. . . . Thomas Dewey uses the recovery issue in his bid for the Presidency.		The hungry in Cleveland, Ohio, wait for relief in patience. Their diet is insufficient but the program does prevent actual starvation.	Lorin Wright dies. The brother of the inventors helped choose Kitty Hawk as the site of their first successful flight. . . . University of Minnesota researchers take a photo in one-hundredth-millionth of one second, a record speed.	Dolores Costello, the ex-wife of actor John Barrymore, marries a Beverly Hills physician, friends say. The couple was often seen together after their divorce, but they denied plans to marry. . . . Joe Cook plans work on his next comedy, Buggy Ride. Rehearsals should begin in 30 days. . . . Marlene Dietrich intends to return to Paramount as the lead in Northwest Mounted. . . . Advance tickets for Gone With the Wind sell out.	Dec. 2
President Roosevelt misses the Army-Navy football game. International affairs prompt a change in plans. . . . An acrobat on wires delays the trains. He leads police on a wild chase for six hours before being roped and brought to earth in a daring maneuver. . . . The healthiest baby boy and the healthiest baby girl from a 1917 contest meet again as adults, fall in love, and decide to marry. He is an automobile salesman who saved pennies in his silver cup award and she is a nurse who also kept her silver cup prize.	The Army's average recruit is labeled a "superior fellow."		British scientist Julian Huxley sees all mankind as underdeveloped, learning from primitive newspapers, books, radio programs, and educational structures. Man faces an unlimited future under social planning, he tells an audience. . . . The dean of Columbia University's School of Medicine urges more cultural training for students before they enter college.	Bob Feller signs for the 1940 season. Pay for the Cleveland Indians' ace hurler is $23,000. . . . Felix Salten translates the sequel to Bambi from its original German. Published as Bambi's Children: the Story of a Forest Family, the book is called a fine sequel to a modern classic. . . . Discussion occurs over whether television viewers will accept breaks in the story-telling for commercials, as it happens with radio programming.	Dec. 3

F	G	H	I	J
Includes elections, federal-state relations, civil rights and liberties, crime, the judiciary, education, healthcare, poverty, urban affairs, and population.	Includes formation and debate of U.S. foreign and defense policies, veterans affairs, and defense spending. (Relations with specific foreign countries are usually found under the region concerned.)	Includes business, labor, agriculture, taxation, transportation, consumer affairs, monetary and fiscal policy, natural resources, pollution, and accidents.	Includes worldwide scientific, medical, and technological developments, natural phenomena, U.S. weather, and natural disasters.	Includes the arts, religion, scholarship, communications media, sports, entertainment, fashions, fads, and social life.

	World Affairs	Europe	Africa & The Middle East	The Americas	Asia & The Pacific
Dec. 4	The British cut the strength of the Tientsin garrison. The first units depart; their destination is unknown. . . . Events in Europe disturb markets. The Russo-Finnish conflict and more intense naval warfare create a nervous week. . . . A former Soviet premier assails Stalin's invasion, appealing to the United States not to confuse the attack on Finns with real Russian wishes. . . . South Americans condemn Russia.	The Finns hold their foe; the invasion on the 750-mile front is reportedly at a standstill, repulsed at the Arctic. . . . London claims hits on a Reich base. . . . The oldest of Queen Victoria's surviving children dies at 91. Princess Louise was the first to marry a commoner in 350 years.		Costa Rica ends its use of a secret radio station. Messages sent were said to be in code, but the government refuses to comment.	Japan worries about a rice shortage. Eighty thousand bushels are sent home by the army in China to allay fears of soldiers at the front.
Dec. 5	Anti-Soviet feeling grows in Japan. The press hopes Russia becomes the world's most hated nation. . . . Britain asks Canada for a big bacon supply: 4,480,000 pounds weekly. . . . Argentina and Uruguay call for punishment of the Soviet Union for the invasion of Finland. . . . The U.S. envoy in Tokyo resumes parleys. The Japanese foreign minister is said to have pledged no curb on rights in China. . . . The United States avoids a break with the Soviet Union. The peril in such a step is stressed.	Finland's peace bid is rejected. . . . Russians at the front denounce the Finnish defenders for their "base and tricky cunning," as traps take a heavy toll. . . . France is surprised by Russia's pace, expecting a swifter advance in Finland. . . . Gas rumors alarm Helsinki; most foreigners leave the city. . . . Italy hints that the League of Nations should aid Finland. . . . Three hundred Polish hostages are reportedly executed. . . . The Russians are halted. Finns report taking 1,500 as a snowstorm hinders their foe. . . . Sweden forms a coalition regime and defense preparations are spurred. . . . Greece dissolves the YMCA. Its properties and equipment are to be used by a new youth body.		Descendents of Montezuma, an Aztec ruler, sue Mexico for patrimony. . . . An angry crowd chases Chile's ex-president, injuring his son as the two return from a tour. . . . The Bolivian Cabinet resigns, stating a desire to seek other opportunities.	The Chinese retake Patang. Guerillas threaten Nanning as the Japanese extend their defense line. . . . The Chinese soldier-poet Marshal Wu dies of a tooth infection at age 61.
Dec. 6		Finns report 60 Soviet planes and scores of tanks destroyed. The Russian aim to cut Finland into two is indicated by troop moves. . . . The Balkans draw closer; the Russian invasion of Finland unites them. . . . The House of Commons meets in a secret session—the first since the last war—to debate opposition criticism. . . . The Nazis cite Finland as an example, warning neutrals of penalties for those who take the advice of democracies. . . . Hungarians decide to fight the spread of Communism with their armed forces. . . . Italian aviators aid Finland, urging Finns to resist the Soviets. . . . Britain urges Romania to cut trade with the Reich.		Experts will place a price on Mexican oil land.	War causes India to industrialize, though the process will be slow. . . . The death of Wu Pei-Fu is a blow to the Japanese. The retired warlord had been an object of steady pressure to take the puppet post. . . . Japan puts a tax on pets, Geisha girls, soap, and amusements.
Dec. 7	Allies are silent on League of Nations plans. Argentina's proposal to oust Russia will have a big majority, it is asserted. . . . Finns celebrate independence day, encouraged by President Roosevelt's supportive message. . . . Tokyo denies a Soviet pact plan. The Foreign Office answers a U.S. query with a public negative response. . . . The United States will reserve blockade rights.	Britain sends arms to Finland. Planes, ammunition, and fuel are dispatched. . . . The Reich admits the force of the blockade. An economist says Britain has brought overseas trade to a complete standstill. . . . Italian anxiety over the Balkans is acute, but it is believed doubtful that Rome would rush to protect Romania from Russia. . . . The Soviets drive on; part of Finland's defense is said to be pierced.		Canada's trade balance rises.	
Dec. 8	The Fascist Council cautions the Soviets, reaffirms the Axis, and defies the Allies. It terms the events in southeastern Europe as Italy's direct concern and pledges the safeguarding of trade in the face of the Reich blockade. . . . Pope Pius XII bids priests to obey army orders. He deplores military duty for the clergy, but counsels faithful performance. . . . Leon Trotsky gives testimony to the U.S. Dies Committee investigating un-American activities. He will talk on Stalinism.	Eight Reich raiders lose the battle over the North Sea. . . . Britain declines to act on Finland, watching with concern but playing a passive role. . . . The Dutch are ready to fight invaders. They will sacrifice everything to resist alien domination, an envoy declares. . . . The French complete new forts in France. The announcement coincides with increased German activity. . . . Helsinki expects an attack. Shop windows are boarded up and a blackout is now effective. . . . Two thousand in Budapest denounce Russia. A demonstration is staged a few hours after Hungary renews relations with the Soviet Union. . . . Romania, awake to a double threat, seeks the friendship of its neighbors. Bulgaria is ready to side with Russia, Hungary with Germany.		Dumping of pelts upsets the trade balance in fur. A new Canadian trade treaty would reduce its imports.	

A	B	C	D	E
Includes developments that affect more than one world region, international organizations, and important meetings of world leaders.	Includes all domestic and regional developments in Europe, including the Soviet Union.	Includes all domestic and regional developments in Africa and the Middle East.	Includes all domestic and regional developments in Latin America, the Caribbean, and Canada.	Includes all domestic and regional developments in Asian and Pacific nations (and colonies).

U.S. Politics & Social Issues	U.S. Foreign Policy & Defense	Economics & Great Depression	Science, Technology & Nature	Culture, Leisure & Lifestyle	
Six were arrested for "tractor fishing," where they use a tractor pump to empty a pond and then take the 2,000 pounds of fish living in those waters. . . . The Episcopal Actors Guild holds their annual memorial service for actors who have died during the year. . . . The trunk slayer escapes from the asylum for the second time within six weeks. Inside help is suspected.		Theatrical unions are moving so that they are under one roof. The screen and musical guilds, plus the theatre authority will all be together. . . . Washington hurries its approval of three Cleveland-based WPA jobs, okaying them over the telephone. . . . The chief power engineer denies that the TVA lacks basic water needs. He discounts the auxiliary use of steam in drought.		Bestselling lists still feature *The Grapes of Wrath, Christmas Holiday, Kitty Foyle, The Nazarene* and *Escape.* . . . Victor Linlahr publishes *Eat and Reduce,* a book that shows how to lose weight while eating three meals a day.	Dec. 4
The First Lady clears the Youth Congress. She investigates the group and finds no trace of outside control and sees no un-Americanism. . . . The Indian population rises rapidly. The "vanishing race" now leads all groups in its rate of increase. . . . AT&T adds nearly 700,000 new phones in 1939. . . . A decrease in drunkenness is reported in New York, six years after repeal of anti-alcohol laws. More women drinkers are suspected, in large part because of the popularity of cocktail parties. . . . Arizona officials fear that the female murderer who escaped from the insane asylum will commit suicide if feeling trapped.			Noted radiologist, Charles Vaillant, dies at age 67. Called a "martyr to science," he received worldwide honors. He is best known for allowing experimental surgeries to be done on his own body to further research.	Minor league baseball teams record attendance of 18,500,000, although the real figures may be half a million higher. The minor league chief suspects some deliberate falsification of attendance numbers. . . . David Daiches publishes a book, *The Novel and the Modern World,* where he analyzes the work of six novelists. . . . Comedians steal the show at the Madison Square Garden's ice skating revue in front of a crowd of 10,000. . . . Goldwyn selects Alice Faye for a featured role in *Natchez.* Olivia de Havilland will replace Ann Sheridan in *Married, Pretty, and Poor.* Although Sheridan could perform this role, de Havilland's popularity should rise with the release of *Gone With the Wind.*	Dec. 5
Baseball chains rile over Commissioner Kenesaw Landis. The Minor League votes for a curb on the judge's power to rule against them; the Major League is expected to follow suit. . . . President Roosevelt urges a great power grid. A system similar to that in England is advised. . . . A deer hunter captures a horned doe.	The Army and Navy vie for defense funds. Each seeks a major part of the extra $500 million proposed by the president for defense.	Cleveland sees some relief in sight. WPA will add 2,200 men to its rolls, food surpluses pour in, and a bond sales plan is pushed.		Columbia University Press releases a book that analyzes relief programs, entitled, *Financing Economic Security in the United States.* . . . A book that praises Adolph Hitler for his rare mental qualities is published in the United States. Called *European Jungle,* this book also attacks Zionists. . . . A French designer sends his styles to the United States. These include clothing with slim silhouette with waistlines slightly below the typical. . . . Paramount plans an ambitious film about Davy Crockett and the founding of the state of Texas.	Dec. 6
Presidential candidate Thomas Dewey urges the United States to end "defeatism" as a national enemy. He tells 12,000 in Minnesota that Roosevelt and his New Deal policies help create a spirit of despair.		Free enterprise is vital to recovery, industry is told. The nation's economic welfare and political liberties are linked to private business. . . . Equity demands a $10 raise in pay minimums for all those employed on Broadway.	A new science laboratory will be dedicated at Queens College.	The Amateur Comedy Club begins its 56th season tonight, reviving the melodrama, *The Jest.* . . . Roger Payne publishes, *Why Work,* a treatise on leisure. . . . Colors contrast in new suit jackets. Black dresses are seen and chamois beige will be popular for daytime wear. . . . *Hellzapoppin II* will open on Monday. It will be shown at the Winter Garden, where the original version is on its 541st presentation.	Dec. 7
Republicans move to set the date for their party convention. All want the Democrats to nominate first, but some fear a trap if they wait. . . . The Attorney General requests more judges for New York, saying that they are definitely needed to help drives against corruption and monopolies. . . . A 32-year-old woman gives birth to her fourth set of consecutive twins in five years. All are healthy. . . . Thomas Dewey is pleased by the results of his speeches, and his associates are happy with the crowds at his Minnesota address.		Curbs on industry are found unpopular. A survey for manufacturers shows that the majority of the public has faith in business. . . . Cincinnati joins in the protest over relief policies, saying that Ohio's governor must see that the state lives up to its moral obligations. . . . A Columbia University professor calls economics a neglected study, and educators encourage the addition of courses to remedy this situation.	Chemists and models display clothing made in laboratories. Hats and dresses worn were created from cellulose. The stockings, jewelry, bags, and walking sticks are made from coal, water, and air. . . . A new device detects spikes in logs. The machine is electronically operated and can be handled easily by one man, and it lets off a howl when metal is found.	The deadline nears to apply for the 1940 Knopf Literary Fellowships. Three grants of $1,200 each are available for those who wish to pursue writing in biography, fiction, or history. . . . Ethel Vance's book, *Escape,* is ready to go into its 10th printing, says Little, Brown. . . . Fans give the New York Giants a grand send-off for their title match against the Green Bay Packers. This game will decide the 1939 football championship.	Dec. 8

F	**G**	**H**	**I**	**J**
Includes elections, federal-state relations, civil rights and liberties, crime, the judiciary, education, healthcare, poverty, urban affairs, and population.	*Includes formation and debate of U.S. foreign and defense policies, veterans affairs, and defense spending. (Relations with specific foreign countries are usually found under the region concerned.)*	*Includes business, labor, agriculture, taxation, transportation, consumer affairs, monetary and fiscal policy, natural resources, pollution, and accidents.*	*Includes worldwide scientific, medical, and technological developments, natural phenomena, U.S. weather, and natural disasters.*	*Includes the arts, religion, scholarship, communications media, sports, entertainment, fashions, fads, and social life.*

	World Affairs	Europe	Africa & The Middle East	The Americas	Asia & The Pacific
Dec. 9	Former U.S. president Herbert Hoover opens a drive to aid the Finns. He issues a relief appeal to the United States. . . . The U.S. Embassy in London protests the blockade on exports as affecting U.S. trade rights. A note to Britain challenges the control of goods from Germany to the United States. . . . The League of Nations receives Finland's plea. . . . A Chinese report says that U.S. property was attacked by the Japanese 150 times.	The blockade is illegal, Finns tell Russians. Helsinki argues that the action lacks justification without a declaration of war. . . . Italy sees danger in the Balkans as fear of Russia increases. . . . Moscow disavows a threat to Romania. . . . Spain condemns the Soviet attack on Finland in the first rift of Franco's neutrality policy.			
Dec. 10	Fifty Finnish recruits sail from the United States to join the Army. Volunteers, many long-time U.S. residents, go to Finland by way of Sweden. . . . A mysterious warship is seen off Veracruz. Reports connect it to German ships in the harbor.	Walther Funk, Economics Minister, urges the Reich to save for war, saying the use of private accounts will avoid inflation. . . . Italy's Axis stand pleases Germany. The reaffirmation of solidarity measures up to all Nazi expectations, they say. . . . The plight of Jews in Poland is critical. All live in terror of the Gestapo. . . . London hears of a Polish revolt—an insurrection against the Soviets in the oil fields.		Brazil seizes 100 in a Communist plot said to be attempting to undermine the army. Plotters also want to subvert workers.	
Dec. 11	American prisoners in Spain get gifts. The U.S. Ambassador sends clothing, blankets, and food. . . . Finland stresses its right to help from the "civilized world." A broadcast says Finns fight as an outpost of western Europe. . . . Gandhi bars undermining Britain, but he also urges India to show no enthusiasm for war. . . . The Japanese see the United States as forcing a Soviet tie. A Tokyo publication warns that a Russian pact on China would aid the Communist cause. . . . The League of Nations loses face in South America. Even if Russia is expelled, four more states talk of quitting the organization.	Confidence holds in the London market. A review of the sea-war position by Winston Churchill proves a useful topic to trading interests. . . . Finland's "waist" is held to be a crucial area. Moscow sees this narrow spot as the logical place for an invasion, but transportation hits a snag. . . . Finns harass foes by primitive means. The native dagger, light machine gun, and skis are combined to offset Soviet might in the dark and icy Arctic. . . . Germany denies helping Finland. . . . Romania sees hints of Soviet approval. Russian circles in Bucharest combat British influence.		Argentina's cotton crop increases by 38 percent. . . . Canada's fertilizer exports are up. . . . Canada sets rigid wartime regulations to control all flying by civil aircraft.	
Dec. 12	A Red Cross chairman doubts the need for a war drive, pointing out the help already given France, Britain, and Poland. The group will honor the wishes of donors who mark interest in Finland. . . . A U.S. Rear Admiral calls the Japanese bombing of China "stupid." He says the attacks on cities have been a major factor of Chinese unification. . . . Soviets bring pressure on the Chinese. Adverse votes in Geneva will endanger a major source of arms for self-defense. . . . Reprisal by Japan for the blockade is seen. Nazis report they have been assured that Tokyo would seize Allied cargo in the East.	The British at the frontlines await a Reich drive. Nazis are expected to make a special assault as a mark of animosity. . . . A Finnish "white book" clarifies its position, listing the Soviet demands and rejected counter-proposals leading to war.	Four ships disappear near the tip of Africa. Long overdue, they are believed to have run afoul of a raider.	U.S. officials hint at arbitration over Mexico's oil.	
Dec. 13	The Japanese say the Nazis have new weapons. A general hints at chemical warfare in the spring. . . . The Soviets debate leaving the League of Nations. The issue is seen as a question of integrity versus gain. . . . Nazi ships are seen in Latin American ports.	The Finnish mass to bar the slicing of the nation. They report that 2,000 of their foe are slain as the Soviets push a three-way drive from the east. . . . Nazis renew their drive on the Forbach sector. Outposts are assaulted in a sharp offensive, but the French hold. . . . The Nazi white book accuses the British; 482 documents are published in an effort to prove London's "will to war."		Canadian warships patrol their Atlantic coast.	
Dec. 14	American funds aid victims of war in belligerent countries. . . . Japan assures the United States; a spokesman says Tokyo seeks "constructive adjustment" of future relations. . . . Germany releases two U.S. pulp cargoes; importers regarded the seizure as a test. . . . The League of Nations is certain to expel Russia as the committee of 13 labels it the aggressor. . . . A crew describes the seizure of U.S. mail. The British took 700 pounds bound for Germany.	A British freighter sinks off Norway; warships go to her aid. . . . The British defeat Nazi raiders in an all-day fight. . . . The House of Commons secretly debates supplies. The galleries are cleared on Prime Minister Chamberlain's motion. . . . Allied success is reported in the North Sea. Planes patrol a Nazi base to prevent the laying of mines at night. . . . Nazis capture a French outpost.		An earthquake strikes Salvador, with a strong shake at San Vicente. This city was badly damaged during an earthquake three years ago.	The Chinese start a drive in three provinces; steady gains are reported. . . . Indian Moslem leader Mohamed Ali Jinnah demands that a Royal Commission to investigate Moslem complaints of repression.

A	B	C	D	E
Includes developments that affect more than one world region, international organizations, and important meetings of world leaders.	*Includes all domestic and regional developments in Europe, including the Soviet Union.*	*Includes all domestic and regional developments in Africa and the Middle East.*	*Includes all domestic and regional developments in Latin America, the Caribbean, and Canada.*	*Includes all domestic and regional developments in Asian and Pacific nations (and colonies).*

U.S. Politics & Social Issues	U.S. Foreign Policy & Defense	Economics & Great Depression	Science, Technology & Nature	Culture, Leisure & Lifestyle	
Baseball commissioner Kenesaw Landis rejects a plan to limit his control and make minor clubs separate units. . . . A barrage of fruit misses its intended target, an editor of a Red publication. Oranges and pennies were tossed at him.	U.S. Ambassador Joseph Kennedy presents to President Roosevelt a plan for idle ships. Vessels will go in routes vacated by Britain and other belligerents.	President Roosevelt blames the governor of Ohio for the relief crisis. . . . Auto production jumps, with last week's figures the highest since July 1937. . . . Auto unions ban wildcat strikes. Temporary replacement of "outlaws" who cause walkouts is ordered.	Macmillan publishes *Cosmic Rays*, a look at the contributions of research in pure sciences before turning its focus on the effects of cosmic rays.	Work of 80 artists appears in a new exhibit. This display is the second in a series, with the first one honoring the World Fair. Peter Mendelssohn's new novel draws attention. Titled *Across the Dark River*, this book has been called remarkably taut and moving. . . . A new book from the Federal Writers Project appears: *Tennessee: A Guide to the Volunteer State*.	Dec. 9
The vast majority of voters urges peace between the AFL and CIO, a Gallup survey says. Union rights are supported, but there is also a strong sentiment for the federal regulation of workers' groups. . . . Three Civil War veterans die. Two of them—one Confederate and one Union soldier—were present at Lee's surrender. . . . A poster contest begins. The art is to be used in a drive against venereal diseases.			A chemistry professor makes several predictions about the future, including that science will continue to make plastics and fabrics. Others include further work in light metallic alloys, conquests in medicine and nutrition — and longer life spans because of those last two factors. . . . Electric cables heat soil to temperatures where seeds can germinate off season. . . . The University of Delaware sets up a fellowship.	Amateur tennis star Bobby Riggs marries. . . . Harper plans to publish a new book by Aldous Huxley called *After Many a Summer Dies a Swan*. . . . For this holiday season, the American Booksellers Association will allow gift givers to buy a token that can be exchanged for a book of a comparable price. This system has worked well in Britain.	Dec. 10
A Dies Committee investigator claims that Reds use consumer groups. Communists try to stir discontent among shoppers, he says. . . . Vice President John Garner's aim is to win or quit. Friends say he will retire if not named for the presidency. . . . The Republican national party reapportions convention votes, dividing nine among eight states and lopping three votes each off four states. . . . Father Divine, a Negro evangelist in the United States, has a plan to unite the Americas. He says he would combine the United States, Central and South America into one giant democracy.		Thomas Dewey declines to amplify upon his statement about the need for a balanced budget. . . . Mills welcome a let down in steel. This gives them time for renovation. . . . The outlook for wheat is the worst in its history because of the long drought.	Bears delay hibernation and wild ducks still linger by Bear Mountain Lake. Park officials say this may indicate that cold weather is not yet imminent.	After Carl Sandburg finishes the biography of President Abraham Lincoln, he says that he can relax. He talks about the letdown after the completion of the book and he says that the biggest difficulty was giving the right amount of space to events. . . . Warner Bros. chooses Errol Flynn for *Out of Gas*, a movie about life in modern Tahiti. . . . Dale Burnett of the New York Giants retires.	Dec. 11
An employer is upheld in refusing to hire a member of a union. The court rules that either union or non-union employees may be engaged. . . . The Supreme Court widens a wiretapping ban, barring indirect use. . . . The indictment of 100 people from data collected by the Dies Committee is foreseen. . . . Mayor LaGuardia proclaims "Children's Museum Day." . . . C. Walgreen, head of the drug store chain, dies. He began work as a factory hand, but turned to pharmacy after losing a finger. There are now about 500 Walgreens in 39 states . . . Three groups work together for truth in advertising. This is believed to be the first joint advertising committee with national influence and scope.		Cleveland renews full relief. Bond sales are planned and Roosevelt approves three WPA projects.	A conference displays plastics that can be used in the home. Sponsors say that acceptance of these products must precede general use.	Atlanta plans a four-day fête to celebrate *Gone With the Wind*. Employees in downtown Atlanta will dress up in Civil War-era garb and buildings are being modified to give them a historic appearance. . . . Nile Clarke Kinnick is chosen as the number one sports star, edging out Joe DiMaggio of the New York Yankees and boxer Joe Louis. . . . John Barrymore will bring his stage hit, *My Dear Children*, from Chicago to New York. . . . NBC will broadcast a prelude to *Gone With the Wind*.	Dec. 12
Congressman Carl Mapes dies at age 64. This Michigan Representative was in New Orleans listening to oil regulation bill hearings. . . . Thirty colleges vote to end subsidies. This ban would be on any scholarships or financial assistance based on sports prowess. . . . An 80-year-old man fathers his 23rd child. His current wife is 35 and this is their fourth child together. Twenty of the children are still living.		Shoe manufacturers agree that 35 cents per hour is a reasonable minimum wage for their workers. . . . The job shortage is held by many to be the worst problem in the United States. . . . A liquor price war is feared. The threat of national distillers to cancel price contracts on scotch is seen as the provocation.	Influenza and pneumonia begin their seasonal increase.	Douglas Fairbanks dies in his sleep. The stage and screen actor is the victim of a heart attack. . . . Actress Fay Wray gets a divorce. . . . Alice Marble is named the outstanding female athlete of 1939. Fifty-four experts place this tennis star at the top. . . . Irene Dunne will have the lead in *First Woman Doctor*, the story of Elizabeth Blackwell who graduated from medical school in 1849.	Dec. 13
Congress is urged to set Thanksgiving Day by law. . . . Dr. J.G. Thomas, a physician who made his rounds in a horse and buggy, dies at age 95. A Civil War bullet remained in his leg, post war, and he kept making rounds until he was 93. . . . Funeral services for actor Douglas Fairbanks, Jr., will be held tomorrow. Fewer than 200 are invited because the church only holds 150. Crowds will be kept away from the cemetery. . . . The Controller General of the United States suffers a stroke.	The air corps will train 400 more cadets.	New York Mayor Fiorello LaGuardia suggests a federal tax rule. He recommends that Washington fixes rate and does all collecting, giving states credits. . . . A consumer research group indicates an anti-Red stance and an opposition to that party's programs.		An x-ray revives a Shakespeare row. The study of three supposed portraits of the bard show they are actually the Earl of Oxford. . . . Pearl Metzilthin publishes *The World-Wide Cook Book*, where she includes recipes from 72 countries. . . . Thomas Craven's *A Treasury of Art Masterpieces* is bringing in about $1 million. He calls this book a difficult undertaking and he gives his publishers credit for the success of this project.	Dec. 14

F	G	H	I	J
Includes elections, federal-state relations, civil rights and liberties, crime, the judiciary, education, healthcare, poverty, urban affairs, and population.	Includes formation and debate of U.S. foreign and defense policies, veterans affairs, and defense spending. (Relations with specific foreign countries are usually found under the region concerned.)	Includes business, labor, agriculture, taxation, transportation, consumer affairs, monetary and fiscal policy, natural resources, pollution, and accidents.	Includes worldwide scientific, medical, and technological developments, natural phenomena, U.S. weather, and natural disasters.	Includes the arts, religion, scholarship, communications media, sports, entertainment, fashions, fads, and social life.

	World Affairs	Europe	Africa & The Middle East	The Americas	Asia & The Pacific
Dec. 15	An American scans data on a sea fight. Facts are sought as to whether German and British vessels met within a neutral zone. . . . Geneva is unanimous; not one voice is raised in defense of the Soviet Union. The Allies promise to aid Finland. . . . Tokyo envisages an anti-Red front, believing that almost all nations except Germany would join.	Belgium asks for aid, wanting help in caring for thousands of Jewish refugees. . . . Broadcasts in Berlin and London give different versions of a sea battle. . . . A British destroyer sinks in a crash; 120 go down in a collision with the warship. . . . Britain is jubilant on the victory against the German *Spee*; it is the cause of the greatest rejoicing so far in the conflict. . . . Prime Minister Chamberlain names Nazis as the foremost foe; Britain does not want to fight Russia. Some aid will be given to Finland. . . . Finland recaptures two cities.		Canada calls its sixth—and probably last—session of the 18th Parliament. . . . Chile expands it textile industry.	
Dec. 16	The Communist Party drops its boycott of German goods. Workers have no interest in either side of the "imperialist war." . . . The League of Nations rushes plans to help Finland. . . . The French ambassador to the United States warns of the Soviet menace, calling it the gravest aspect of war. . . . Uruguay sets a time limit; the Reich warship must leave or be interned throughout the war.	Germans say the *Spee* eluded torpedoes. . . . London gets news of its sea fight loss. The British Admiralty strengthens its force to meet the *Spee* at sea again. . . . Moscow accepts League expulsion quietly. The Russian public receives a minimized version; the Geneva body is said to have degenerated into a body of Allied imperialism. . . . The Reich halts aid from Rome to the Finns.		American nations consult on the battle off Uruguay. The significance of the sea fight in relation to the safety belt is to be determined. . . . Argentina's crops decrease.	
Dec. 17	Finland aids Iran by halting the Soviets. Stalin is believed to have been ready to push to the Baku oil fields. . . . Moscow ridicules League expulsion and rejects the rights of "aggressors," such as Britain and France, to champion the Finns.	An attack on Romania is held unlikely, despite a Soviet press campaign. Mud is considered to be a deterrent. . . . The French hurl back a massive Nazi attack. Losses are heavy. . . . Moscow suffers a food shortage. Demand for vodka continues because of lack of consumer goods.		German crew scuttles the pocket battleship *Graf Spee* off Montevideo, Uruguay. . . . The Americas support a bar on warring craft. The U.S. and other envoys in Buenos Aires draft a sea declaration in response to the *Spee* battle. . . . A delegate calls Chile a virtual utopia due to its advances and lack of unemployment.	
Dec. 18	The National Congress assails Britain for the plight of India. A member of congress urges the end of feudalism. . . . The Japanese foreign minister asks the U.S. envoy to discuss relations. Japan is anxious to improve relations in the face of Soviet pressure. . . . Hitler consults naval heads; his plea to stay in Uruguay failed. . . . Finland appeals for greater help. . . . The French plan to lend $2.5 million to China to help build a railway.	Rome supports adherence to the Axis. The press stresses that the alliance with Germany remains unimpaired. . . . The Balkan union considers possibilities for peace. A report pictures an invasion by the Reich if the British continue to cut off supplies. . . . Seventy-two Britons die in the *Spee* fight. . . . An escaped Pole reports that many prisoners die in Russia of typhus and scurvy. . . . A Hamburg port is dead from the blockade. Tied up vessels and empty export houses show the halt to the Reich's overseas trade.		The *Spee* incident gives Latin America unity. Uruguay's action in protesting to Britain and Germany is hailed by sister nations. . . . Mining companies in Canada report record outputs.	The Chinese capture part of Kaifeng. Buildings are reportedly burned in the ancient capital as the drive on the Japanese sees gains. . . . The Tokyo rice crisis ends as reserves accumulate in large cities.
Dec. 19	Canadian troops arrive in Britain. One hundred U.S. volunteers are also part of the force. . . . The Viceroy ties India's fate to war, holding that the country's future welfare hinges on the success of the Allied forces.	Twelve Reich planes are crippled in the biggest air battle of the war. London admits a loss of seven. . . . A German Labor Front leader asserts the Nazis' divine right to rule. The Reich's mission to dominate is among the war aims, he says, also demanding the annihilation of Britain, the obstacle to German success. . . . Poles hear Hitler plans a buffer zone; 20 million Poles and Jews would be amassed along the new Soviet border. . . . Russians capture Finland's Arctic strip.		Latin America importers complain about U.S. packing and ask for better work. . . . A Latin peace pact is hailed, with the Colombia-Venezuela treaty seen as extra security.	
Dec. 20	Former president Herbert Hoover forwards $100,000 for Finnish relief, to be used for children's clothes and evacuation purposes. . . . Japan is optimistic about a pact with the United States. The foreign minister says progress is being made. . . . The Soviet Union sees profit as the U.S. aim in Finland.	Few Reich troops are found in Slovakia. Germans are now respecting military zones defined by the pact that was ignored in Poland. . . . Finnish Red troops wear uniforms of the 1700s. . . . Five ports are bombed. Soviet attacks are beaten off by Finnish guns. . . . The Russian advance is made at a high cost. A correspondent watches Finns impose heavy losses.		Censors muddle Canadian reports. The newspapers obey orders and keep quiet, but the Admiralty tells the world of war stories. . . . Canadians are elated by the progress of war, both in Europe and at home.	The Chinese recapture Nanning positions. A counter-attack is said to have isolated the Japanese garrison in the south.

A	B	C	D	E
Includes developments that affect more than one world region, international organizations, and important meetings of world leaders.	Includes all domestic and regional developments in Europe, including the Soviet Union.	Includes all domestic and regional developments in Africa and the Middle East.	Includes all domestic and regional developments in Latin America, the Caribbean, and Canada.	Includes all domestic and regional developments in Asian and Pacific nations (and colonies).

U.S. Politics & Social Issues	U.S. Foreign Policy & Defense	Economics & Great Depression	Science, Technology & Nature	Culture, Leisure & Lifestyle	
Boston asks to host the 1940 Democratic National Convention. . . . The cemetery will not bar the public from the burial of Douglas Fairbanks, Jr. . . . A fake reporter steals a fur coat. The "journalist" posed as an expert and then took a $1,000 coat after slitting 15 others to determine their value. . . . Mayor LaGuardia opens war on drunk drivers and he instructs police to watch cars closely during the cocktail hour.		Aid for the neediest should not be considered a holiday gesture, *The New York Times* states. . . . Christmas buying increases by 4 percent for ten days. . . . Cotton use sets a November record. . . . Millions of pounds of squash is sent to Cleveland's neediest. . . . Mortgage frauds are being attempted on women.		*Gone With the Wind* premiers in Atlanta, and thousands relive its stirring war days. . . . Hans Mueller publishes a book about the art of Pablo Picasso. . . . *Cassell's German and English Dictionary* is released by Funk & Wagnells. . . . Ann Rutherford, who plays Scarlett O'Hara's little sister Careen in *Gone With the Wind*, visited six men who live in the Confederate Soldiers Home. . . . James Roosevelt sets up his own film unit and he will have access to the stars of Goldwyn studios.	Dec. 15
Arrested for the 50th time, a woman receives a 60-day jail term. Seventeen of the judges who had previously sent her to prison have already died. . . . Boston bans pitchforking as a form of fishing. This practice has occurred for 300 years in the city.		The Ohio governor criticizes the U.S. relief program. The federal government created the situation, he tells an insurance group. . . . The National Women's Party demands equal rights. An amendment is needed, they say, to end discriminatory statutes. . . . President Roosevelt dodges questions about his candidacy in 1940. . . . Big battles loom with trade treaties in Washington. Republicans are active.		Atlanta is won over by the film of the south. A rebel yell for Miss Mitchell mingles with applause following the first showings of *Gone with the Wind*. . . . The Metropolitan Museum of Art receives an ancient Tintoretto, *The Finding of Moses*. . . . Brazil intends to expand its exhibits at the 1940 World Fair. . . . Rose M.E. MacDonald publishes a biography, *Mrs. Robert E. Lee* about the Confederate general's wife.	Dec. 16
The drive to boycott Nazi products is intensified. Leaders plan to redouble efforts. . . . First Lady Eleanor Roosevelt warns about jobless youth; the nation must guide 4 million to careers, she says. . . . A baron agrees to be questioned over the death of a 21-year-old actress who fell or jumped.	The Army requests $4 million to build five bombers with double the speed and power of the current flying fortresses.	The Ohio governor demands reform of the WPA. He calls the agency, run under the New Deal, a "political racket." . . . Presidential candidate Thomas Dewey denounces the New Deal "zigzag" in economic policy, charging shifts on budgets, prices, and trust laws. He asks for the end of uncertainty.	Cornell University sees a connection between electrical currents in the brain and intelligence.	Attendance at professional football games rises by 12.3 percent. . . . Basketball, America's indoor winter sport, booms and provides infinite thrills. . . . The Dionne quintuplets send a Christmas card to the King and Queen of England and they also include the Princesses in their holiday wishes.	Dec. 17
An extortion ring is broken. Thirty-four are said to have taken hundreds of thousands of dollars from wealthy men. . . . Friends of Vice President Garner say that he is not anti-Roosevelt or anti-New Deal. Rather, he does not believe in a third presidential term for any one. . . . Dr. William Irving Sirovich, Congressional Representative, is found dead at home at age 57.		The president of the National Boot and Shoe Manufacturer's Association points out that a minimum wage of 35 cents per hour will cost consumers $28 million more a year. . . . Christmas mail is up 7 percent over the same time last year. . . . The liquor price wars cross new lines. Gin, rye, bourbon, cognac, and champagne prices will be cut today, while scotch continues to have its prices slashed.		Dorothy Dort Adams publishes, *My Mother Told Me*. In her book, Adams shares the humorous tale of a girl who wanted to be a poet. When grown up, she persisted in this quest.	Dec. 18
The first all-female jury is seated. The judge orders the group to avoid embarrassment when discussing a morals charge. . . . A special prosecutor says bail bond racket charges may reach high into the police department. . . . A Senator upholds private insurance. He sees a "politician's paradise" if the federal government can enter the field.		The CIO contradicts the claim of a labor shortage. Thousands of mechanics lack work. . . . Auto output increase counters the trend. The war is decreasing the number of U.S. exports. . . . The final rush begins for holiday trade. Customers have waited for a dip in prices, with men's clothing and liquor items that are selling.		Film producer Samuel Goldwyn cancels his distribution plan and announces the termination of his contract with United Artists. . . . Columnist Heywood Broun dies at 51 of pneumonia. Broun was a reporter, sports writer, drama critic, and president of the newspaper guild.	Dec. 19
Boxer Ernie Hass admits to murder and is being brought back from Toronto. He denies any political motive to the crime, saying that it resulted after a fight due to abnormal behavior of the victim. . . . New York is widening its drive to prevent the waste of water.	A review declares the United States can meet war demands without any dislocation and with no chemical shortages.	The government posts the final crop results for the year. Production is 4 percent higher than 1923–32, but 1 percent less than last year's production.	Explorer Admiral Richard Byrd wires the story of the Pitcairn plight, relating how the North Star gave food and medicine to war-hit islanders. Nearly two months without a visit left the mutineer descendents nearly starved.	Abraham Heller publishes *Jewish Survival*, a series of sermons and addresses. . . . Charley Gehringer signs with the Detroit Tigers for the 15h season.	Dec. 20

F	**G**	**H**	**I**	**J**
Includes elections, federal-state relations, civil rights and liberties, crime, the judiciary, education, healthcare, poverty, urban affairs, and population.	*Includes formation and debate of U.S. foreign and defense policies, veterans affairs, and defense spending. (Relations with specific foreign countries are usually found under the region concerned.)*	*Includes business, labor, agriculture, taxation, transportation, consumer affairs, monetary and fiscal policy, natural resources, pollution, and accidents.*	*Includes worldwide scientific, medical, and technological developments, natural phenomena, U.S. weather, and natural disasters.*	*Includes the arts, religion, scholarship, communications media, sports, entertainment, fashions, fads, and social life.*

	World Affairs	Europe	Africa & The Middle East	The Americas	Asia & The Pacific
Dec. 21	The sons and daughters of diplomats in the United States broadcast greetings to the youth of the world. The German and Russian embassies fail to participate in the annual tradition from Washington. . . . The Japanese are in a hurry to talk with the United States. The Cabinet is anxious for a temporary trade pact that does not need Senate approval. . . . President Roosevelt obtains data on the China war. The ambassador calls on the President to spread the news of the widespread offensive. . . . The United States asks the Reich to heed the neutral sea zone.	Allies recognize the Czech committee. Action by the war council will allow the former president to recruit nationals for the army. . . . Berlin Jews take the most menial jobs; still the number of unemployed doubles in one month. . . . Big shipments of French iron ore to Belgium are believed to be on the way to Germany. . . . France and Spain halt trade talks after Madrid suddenly increases its original demands. . . . The commander of the *Graf Spree* ends his life with a gunshot. . . . Signs of Nazi rule are fewer in Slovakia. . . . Stalin's 60th birthday eclipses the war, but fails to prevent murmurs of the people about Finland.		Canadian airmen are chosen for the front lines. The first squadron selected is now training in England. . . . Chile will patrol its straits.	
Dec. 22	League of Nations peace efforts are hurt by budget cuts. Staff economies are likely to impair services.	Air wars resume on the western front. . . . Britain seizes 10 percent of Reich imports. Germany's sea trade declines because of strict control by the British and French. . . . Britain gives the Czechs formal recognition; every aid is put at the disposal of the national body's war aims. . . . Hitler felicitates Stalin on his birthday. . . . Nazis jail a radio listener. The man gets 15 months for tuning to foreign broadcasts. . . . Ruthenians are unmoved by the status change. The people, apathetic and poor, are equally ready to be Hungarians. . . . Soviet fliers bomb civilians in waves, destroying a hospital area and attacking refugees.		A hard quake is felt in Costa Rica. The whole republic is rocked by the most severe tremor since 1923. . . . The United States has ruled out a trade concession on copper with Chile. . . . Nicaragua aids coffee sales by cutting exports by 20 percent.	The Chinese close in on their foe in Nanning. They report the occupation of a key pass and say the recapture of the city is near.
Dec. 23	A Finnish general asks for U.S. war aid. He scoffs at Soviet bombs but fears their greater manpower. . . . The French prepare to attack if the Soviets move toward Iraq, Iran, and Afghanistan.	Russia learns of big Soviet losses. Thirty thousand is the estimate as the injured fill hospitals. . . . The British information ministry announces a very large secret reserve of planes. . . . A British-owned paper honors the captain of the German *Graf Spree* ship, paying tribute to a "gallant officer." . . . Finns continue to press their retreating Soviet foe. . . . France approves its biggest war bill; the chamber unanimously grants 55 billion francs for first the 90 days of 1940.		Canadians prepare for its first war loan, the terms of which will be announced after the holidays. . . . Mexico boosts a levy on excess profits.	India acts to curb excesses in the silver market
Dec. 24	Christmas Eve brings feeble peace rumors; reports fly about Heinrich Himmler's trip to Rome and the Pope's expected plea to Cardinals. . . . A U.S. peace envoy to the Vatican ends a 72-year gap. . . . The Finnish war stirs a stormy Reich echo. World opinion produces moral isolation among Germans. . . . The Japanese push to Indo-China and seize Chinese war supplies. The French report their arrival at the frontier.	Britain puts its sea power to manifold uses. The fleet ensures supplies for the Allies and keeps up pressure on foes. . . . The European conflict is a blow to athletes, as it ends the last chance for Olympic glory for a generation. . . . The Finnish check on the Red Army indicates that they can be held while outside nations rally to Finland's aid. . . . Nazis encourage unwed parentage; children born out of wedlock will receive state aid.		The Americas find war uncomfortably close, causing nations to implement the Declaration of Panama. . . . Canada takes the Empire burden, assuming direction of great air defenses and also sending troops abroad. . . . The United States and Canada celebrate the Treaty of Ghent, the 125th anniversary of the end of the War of 1812. . . . Canada's Yuletide is sobered by the war, although no regret is expressed over actions.	Gains by Chinese Reds trouble the Japanese. . . . China's war songs are widely distributed and people are singing them.
Dec. 25	The head of Jewish veterans asks President Roosevelt to rebuke Russia; he urges the President to remove the U.S. envoy. . . . A U.S. Senator asks that trade with Japan continue after the pact expires in January; peace interests are cited.	French Premier Edouard Daladier exhorts people to courage. France will wage war to bar Germans from its soil, he says. . . . The Reich faces fiscal overhaul. A widening gap between buying power and consumer goods poses a problem. . . . Irish terrorists raid a Dublin fort, stealing munitions. . . . Soviet Christmas is only an illusion. Decorated trees are for the New Year fête. . . . Stalin stresses Soviet-Reich ties, saying they are cemented in blood.		Canada's Eskimos quit their hunt to celebrate Yule. . . . A Canadian government official lists the effects of the war so far.	Chungking celebrates Christmas widely. The holiday is observed by Chinese Nationalists as well as Christians. . . . The Japanese push propaganda. Reports spread from Hong Kong attempt to undermine the unity of the Chinese. . . . A bomb kills Chiang's first wife.
Dec. 26	The French call steps for peace a help; they view President Roosevelt and the Pope as seeking viable terms for the Allies to press. . . . The British Empire hears King George hail unity in war. . . . Tokyo will consult its army on U.S. policy. Generals in China must agree on any trade policy.	A silent Christmas passes on the western front. The holiday truce is unbroken despite the massing of troops. . . . Seamen of combatant nations feast aboard ships and with friends ashore. . . . The Czech envoy leaves his Moscow post. Reich pressure is seen as the Soviet Union abandons its diplomat. . . . The Finns push the battle over their foe's border and menace a rail line. . . . The *Graf Spee* wreckage washes up on a beach.	Erzinona, Turkey suffers a 7.8 earthquake. Over thirty thousand die.	The wife of Nicaragua's president gives presents to 1,000 poor children.	

A	B	C	D	E
Includes developments that affect more than one world region, international organizations, and important meetings of world leaders.	*Includes all domestic and regional developments in Europe, including the Soviet Union.*	*Includes all domestic and regional developments in Africa and the Middle East.*	*Includes all domestic and regional developments in Latin America, the Caribbean, and Canada.*	*Includes all domestic and regional developments in Asian and Pacific nations (and colonies).*

U.S. Politics & Social Issues	U.S. Foreign Policy & Defense	Economics & Great Depression	Science, Technology & Nature	Culture, Leisure & Lifestyle	
A gangster who gained control of a $10 million conspiracy is stoic at hearing his guilty verdict. . . . Blue-coated Santas hand out Christmas presents. Police officers and firemen begin distributing 226,800 toys. . . . New York lights its Christmas trees in parks. LaGuardia's daughter Jean pulls the switch that illuminates the evergreen at City Hall. . . . Three thousand people mourn the death of Heywood Broun. The story of his conversion to Catholicism stirs the crowd.	An air defense force is set for the northeast. The Army coordinates all units.	There is no law that limits daily work hours, but a federal bulletin states that the weekly aggregate cannot exceed 42 hours. . . . Fur prices decline as demand slows. . . . The last in, first out inventory style is becoming more popular.	A baby health clinic opens in the Bronx. This is its ninth clinic and is jointly funded by the WPA and the city. . . . Three hundred fifty psychologists hear news about studies of the hypothalamus.	Warner Bros. suspends Olivia de Havilland for refusing her role in Married, Pretty and Poor. . . . Albert Rosenthal, portrait painter, dies at age 76. He created etchings of Thomas Jefferson, Abraham Lincoln, John Paul Jones, and others. . . . Max Berges publishes Cold Pogrom, a novel about a powerful Jewish family in pre-Nazi Germany and what happens to them when the National Socialists come to power.	Dec. 21
Secretary of State Cordell Hull endorses a parley of liberals for the 1940 election. He depicts peril to the country if a conservative is chosen as president. . . . The motion picture reviewer of The Daily Worker loses his job because he refuses to attack Gone With the Wind in accordance with the paper's Communist beliefs.	Another step is taken to make Pearl Harbor in Hawaii the most powerful base in the western Pacific. The two largest dry docks in the world will be built there.	President Roosevelt will send soup kitchen aid if Ohioans famish. He and the governor clash once more. . . . Relief rolls were cut by 1 million during the year.	A chemist has created a method to determine the levels of arsenic in metals. . . . Scientists will hear presentations on the mixing of chemicals.	Philadelphia Athletics manager Connie Mack, who turns 77 today, hopes for a 10th pennant win with the 1941 club. . . . Christmas dinner suggestions, both festive and economical, are made by The New York Times. One menu can serve six for $2.48.	Dec. 22
Babe Ruth, Bud Abbott, and Lou Costello play Santa Claus for the needy. . . . Churches make their preparations for Christmas worship services. Catholics in the city will honor the holiday with midnight masses. . . . New York's first snow slows traffic causing holiday travelers to be delayed. . . . A prisoner, known as "Broadway Harry," escapes from court. Half an hour later, he changes his mind and turns himself back in.	The Army speeds up its recruiting efforts. It needs 243 recruits a day for 9 days to meet its quota.	President Roosevelt expects a $3 billion deficit. The capital hears he has revised a recent estimate of $2 billion as the shortage of the next budget. . . . President Roosevelt plans to build hospitals in needy areas. . . . The cost of living dropped in November.		Henry C. Wolfe, author of The German Octopus, is working on a second book: The Russian Octopus. This second book will forecast Stalin moves. . . . Indoor baseball cancels its schedule. The league formed about two months ago and game attendance has been poor. . . . Babe Ruth's daughter Julia becomes engaged. . . . Charlie McCarthy, Detective, is slated to open today with Edgar Bergen and Charlie.	Dec. 23
Christmas gaiety for New York's millions reaches its peak. Hundreds of thousands of needy enjoy gifts and parties. . . . Congressman Martin Dies predicts a step to oust 7 million. If his inquiry receives funding, he will move against aliens in industry. . . . President Roosevelt's silence about a third term affects the Republican primary race. . . . Liberals in the House back Roosevelt for a third term.	The Navy denies that captains must go down with their ships. . . . Americans find the war uncomfortably close. . . . Big Navy air boats will patrol the Pacific.	1939 marks outstanding developments and sales with the automobile. . . . A doctor cancels all outstanding bills as a gift to his patients.		A Red paper condemns Gone with the Wind, calling the movie a glorification of the Ku Klux Klan. . . . A quiet season for collegiate rugby, Princeton and Harvard universities number among the most successful.	Dec. 24
President Roosevelt exalts the neighborly spirit in a holiday rite. . . . The United States, at peace, unites in thanks on Christmas. . . . Fifteen Christmas stockings hang in the White House, as the President and First Lady take their grandchildren to church. . . . Roosevelt reviews the year.		A miner, 80, digs coal for Christmas gifts. He gives sacks of fuel to needy neighbors. . . . Cotton activity declines in the south. . . . A week without rain takes a further toll on the winter wheat crop.		A blind girl, Lillian Hillman, gets her dream fulfilled when she gets a bit part in The World We Make. Miss Hillman says that she has been living in the clouds since getting this part and she has taken her practices very seriously. . . . Confessions of a Nazi Spy, starring Edward G. Robinson, was selected as the best English-speaking film of the year. Wuthering Heights comes in second.	Dec. 25
		Efficiency gains kill farm jobs. The WPA report says the trend is not greater leisure, but migration to cities. . . . The Cabinet reports all-around gains in the economy, as industry, agriculture, and trade improve. . . . Conservation is the key to farm jobs. . . . A Denver packer sends 10 pounds of meat to 6,000 families.	High pitch deafness is held to be a danger signal, experts say. This malady is more common than what is realized.	Joe Louis ranks top in the world of boxers. . . . The Dionne quintuplets slide all over the place on their new Christmas skates. . . . Lily Pons performs in Rigoletto. Pons, in her first performance of the year, plays the role of Gilda.	Dec. 26

F	G	H	I	J
Includes elections, federal-state relations, civil rights and liberties, crime, the judiciary, education, healthcare, poverty, urban affairs, and population.	Includes formation and debate of U.S. foreign and defense policies, veterans affairs, and defense spending. (Relations with specific foreign countries are usually found under the region concerned.)	Includes business, labor, agriculture, taxation, transportation, consumer affairs, monetary and fiscal policy, natural resources, pollution, and accidents.	Includes worldwide scientific, medical, and technological developments, natural phenomena, U.S. weather, and natural disasters.	Includes the arts, religion, scholarship, communications media, sports, entertainment, fashions, fads, and social life.

	World Affairs	Europe	Africa & The Middle East	The Americas	Asia & The Pacific
Dec. 27	Australian fliers arrive in England.... The Red Cross vice chairman pictures a Europe full of migrants. He says the dislocation of populations is a major war problem. . . . The Pope sends funds to Catholic Finns.	The Allies increase their help to Finland. . . . The bombing of Viborg misses objectives, as the railway remains unscathed.... Brisk skirmishes take place on the western front. The new intensity of fighting is thought to portend heavier drives soon. . . . Hitler sets foot on French soil, visiting an advanced German patrol. . . . The Reich will transfer 80,000 Galician Jews. The group is to be exchanged for Germans in Soviet Poland.... Romania appeals for neutral unity. . . . A ship is torpedoed off the coast of England. . . . The Soviet people are irked at the failure of the Red Army to conquer Finland. Sharper food shortages cause grumbling.		Cuba delays its presidential elections until March 30. . . . No damage has been reported after a severe quake in Nicaragua.	The majority demands that the Tokyo Cabinet quit.
Dec. 28	Argentina rejects a Nazi plea on the *Spee*; the demand that the crew of the warship be classed as "distressed seamen" is denied.... Tokyo renews attacks on the United States. The press shifts from optimism on the possibility of a treaty to complaints of American coercion. . . . Finns seek to get new U.S. anti-tank and anti-aircraft guns. . . . War supplies jam free ports; they are booked six months ahead as planes, trench diggers, truck foodstuffs, and fibers fill five docks. . . . The Italian press says Soviet forces imperil Iran, Afghanistan, and India.	An Allied pledge to Sweden is expected; Finland's stand against Russia is regarded by France and Britain as equivalent to the blockade of Germany. . . . Finns again cross the Soviet border, threatening a Soviet railroad. The Soviet Union calls in more troops.... The first Indian troops arrive in France. They bring special food.... A London paper reports that Field Marshal Hermann Goering is in disfavor with Hitler.... The Reich gets Soviet goods, receiving the first shipment of oils, minerals, and grains. . . . Reich rationing tightens; fruits and vegetables may soon be curtailed.	Six thousand die in Turkey in quakes felt around the world. Successive shocks take a heavy toll on life and property.	The Mexican Chamber passes a school bill that prohibits religious instruction in institutions throughout the country.	
Dec. 29	The Pope visits the Italian King Vittorio Emmanuel III and solidifies ties. He will also receive Premier Mussolini.	Norway bars military aid to Finland. . . . New restrictions are decreed in Britain as the Nazi "guns before butter" theory is followed. . . . The British doubt Soviets plan an eastern drive. The story of troops along the Afghan border is attributed to German propaganda. . . . The Finns demolish the Soviet patrol in a fierce battle amid Arctic snow. Daylight lasts only two hours and even the slightly wounded freeze to death. . . . Finns report gains on Soviet soil and advances in two sections. . . . Nazis and Allies will trade interned civilians. The plan bars those of military age. . . . Russia reimposes news censorship.	Casualties from the Turkey quake are estimated at 110,000.	Mexico patrols its waters as British ships wait for German craft.	China reports a deficit in trade to Japan. A favorable balance is maintained in sections outside the invader's control.
Dec. 30	Japan and Russia agree on rail debt. Tokyo will make a final payment on the Chinese eastern line, long demanded by the Soviet Union. . . . The Japanese deny the Shanghai beating of a U.S. woman. A naval spokesman sees a plot against Tokyo in the woman's charge. The Embassy is apologetic.	The British accelerate war weapons output, speeding up to three to five times the starting rate. . . . A torpedoed British warship reaches port. The armor blisters are believed to have saved the vessel. . . . Patrols in the west track each other by footprints in the snow.... A new Allied pact blocks Reich trade. The Yugoslav, Turkish, and Spanish agreement bars vital war supplies to Germany. . . . The Reich says Allies are violating mandates, charging former colonies are being used for war. . . . Three thousand Russians die as Finns beat off attacks.	A starvation threat faces thousands in the Turkish quake zone. Shattered communications, snow, and ice hinder efforts.	Canada sees gains in employment.	The invaders have been halted, the Chinese declare. Three drives north are said to face mountainous terrain.
Dec. 31	The outcome of the Finnish war is vital to Tokyo. Russia encounters many difficulties in war.	All of Europe goes on short rations. Shortages vary greatly. . . . Travelers report a Bolshevist spirit in the Reich. Germans show bitter animosity toward well-dressed persons. . . . Finns drive Russians back over the border for a third time.... Foreign aid for Finns alters the war's outlook.... Hermann Goering threatens terror for Britain. Nazis will unleash the worst air raids and smash the blockade, he says. . . . New Year celebrations in London will be restrained. Large gatherings are frowned upon, but the hours are extended at public houses.	New quakes add to the Turkish death toll.	The Brazilian foreign minister again asks for a neutral zone curb.	China sees the ousting of invaders in 1940, saying Japan is significantly weakened, militarily and economically.

A	B	C	D	E
Includes developments that affect more than one world region, international organizations, and important meetings of world leaders.	*Includes all domestic and regional developments in Europe, including the Soviet Union.*	*Includes all domestic and regional developments in Africa and the Middle East.*	*Includes all domestic and regional developments in Latin America, the Caribbean, and Canada.*	*Includes all domestic and regional developments in Asian and Pacific nations (and colonies).*

U.S. Politics & Social Issues	U.S. Foreign Policy & Defense	Economics & Great Depression	Science, Technology & Nature	Culture, Leisure & Lifestyle	
Economizers face a test in the election year. The question is how far proponents of less spending will get in an inhibited Congress. . . . A popularity gain is shown for President Roosevelt; 63 percent favor him now as compared to 62 percent at the 1936 election. . . . A barber interrupts giving a customer a shave to commit suicide. . . . More patents were granted in 1939 than any other year since 1934. . . . One thousand police officers have been assigned to Times Square for New Year's celebrations. . . . School children shun fairy tales for facts, librarians report.	The Army outfits itself with weapons to defend against air attack.	Many ineligibles apply for pensions. The public is not fully aware of the old-age act rules. . . . Social agencies tell of ravages in Cleveland, saying hunger causes and aggravates disease. . . . Ninety thousand bids were filed for 2,000 city jobs in New York.	The United States charts the skies for ocean flying. . . . Scientists discuss the cellulose factory located in plants. This discovery is an advance toward the artificial creation of limitless food and fuel.	Ruby Keeler divorces Al Jolson, telling the court he called her "stupid." . . . Clark Gable's ex-wife becomes the head of a drama department of a Christian college. . . . Greek styles appear at a fashion show that was using an ancient sculpture motif.	Dec. 27
Temperatures of 11.9 degrees sets a new record low in New York. . . . Mayor LaGuardia will promote a Negro magistrate.	A glamorized army intends to use air drive for recruiting purposes.	A professor predicts pensions for the aged in a decade. Chair rockers will rule, he surmises. . . . Mayor LaGuardia acts to end city check cashing at usury rates.		Ticket scalpers ask $10 for a Rose Bowl seat. . . . The Metropolitan Opera will return to Atlanta after a ten-year lapse. . . . L.P. Senarens, dime novel author, dies. He wrote over 1,500 books under 27 pseudonyms. . . . Martha Graham performs in a dance festival, making her first appearance of the season. . . . James Roosevelt buys *The Bat*, a mystery thriller. . . . *The Hunchback of Notre Dame* will open Saturday.	Dec. 28
Baptists protest the U.S. link to the Vatican. Leaders of 10,250,000 members approve a letter to be sent to President Roosevelt today. . . . A professor decries "insane" college athletes, pleading for higher mental requirements. . . . Manufacturers are complying with new regulations about food labels.		The phone company tries a "leave word service." For a fee, operators will interrupt incoming messages.		*Meditations of an American Patriot* is published today. Its aim is to encourage the unemployed towards permanent employment. . . . This season's hats are intended to blend with modern hairstyles. . . . The first volume of a Jewish encyclopedia is published. . . . *Swanee River*, the biography of composer Stephen Foster, opens today.	Dec. 29
The Democrats set the date of their party convention. On February 5, 10 days before the Republicans meet, the Democratic National Committee will convene.	A lack of doctors is seen as a wartime peril.	President Roosevelt finishes his budget. Believed to be at $8 billion, a deficit of $2 billion is expected, more than $1 billion more than the current shortfall. . . . Home building was up 37 percent from 1938 to 1939, and 1940 figures are expected to be even higher.	Prof. Albert Einstein inspires new philosophy. An association hears his outline of a system applying relativity to fields outside physics.	*The Man Who Killed Lincoln* premieres in Rochester, N.Y.	Dec. 30
Congress is ready to take up election-year battles.	President Roosevelt appoints the son of inventor Thomas Edison as Secretary of the Navy.	Changes in taxes for 1939 are reviewed. Remedial legislation is found to have eliminated levies of punitive character. . . . Farmers fear 1940, the Secretary of Agriculture asserts, saying they will watch Congress for any hamstring. . . . Jobless payments were on time 99 percent of the time in 1939.	In 1939 there were 43,030 inventions patented, an increase of 4,054.		Dec. 31

F	**G**	**H**	**I**	**J**
Includes elections, federal-state relations, civil rights and liberties, crime, the judiciary, education, healthcare, poverty, urban affairs, and population.	*Includes formation and debate of U.S. foreign and defense policies, veterans affairs, and defense spending. (Relations with specific foreign countries are usually found under the region concerned.)*	*Includes business, labor, agriculture, taxation, transportation, consumer affairs, monetary and fiscal policy, natural resources, pollution, and accidents.*	*Includes worldwide scientific, medical, and technological developments, natural phenomena, U.S. weather, and natural disasters.*	*Includes the arts, religion, scholarship, communications media, sports, entertainment, fashions, fads, and social life.*

INDEX

The index refers to all daily entries, which are keyed to page numbers and column headings.

538B, 540A, 540B, 543J, 546B, 554B, 558B

Germany, 1936
572B, 580B, 588B, 596B, 600B, 610B, 644B, 654B, 672B

Germany, 1937
696B, 704A, 706B, 716B, 718B, 720B, 724B, 738A, 750B, 752B, 762B, 766B, 772A, 772B, 776B, 784B, 794B, 800B

Germany, 1938
820B, 822B, 838B, 846B, 848B, 849G, 854B, 856B, 858B, 864B, 868B, 874B, 876B, 878B, 879G, 883G, 886B, 888B, 890B, 892A, 892B, 896A, 896B, 898A, 898D, 900B, 901G, 902B, 904B, 905G, 906A, 906B, 907G, 909G, 910A, 910B, 912B, 913G

Germany, 1939
920A, 920B, 932B, 936B, 938B, 956B, 958B, 962B, 964B, 970B, 974B, 978B, 980B, 1002B, 1008B, 1018B, 1028B, 1038B, 1040B

Hungary 102B, 374B, 700B, 820B, 832B, 846B, 852B, 880B, 900B, 910B, 958B, 970B, 976B, 984A

Iran 540A

Iraq 540A

Italy 674B, 734B, 862B, 868B, 870B, 876B, 878B, 887H, 888B, 890B, 891G, 894B, 904B, 909G, 940B, 956B, 968B, 982B, 988B

Kristallnacht 776B, 896B

League of Nations response 826B

Mexico 172D, 452E, 802D, 810D, 860D, 864D, 888D, 894D

Poland 216A, 218B, 298B, 452B, 458B, 474B, 538B, 578B, 622B, 686B, 692A, 692B, 694B, 696B, 700A, 708B, 712B, 720B, 724B, 730B, 734B, 770B, 772B, 778B, 780B, 784B, 786B, 788B, 790B, 792B, 794B, 800B, 810B, 812B, 822B, 838B, 908B, 1014B, 1020B, 1022B, 1034B

Refugees, treatment of 398C, 420C, 426B, 430C, 440C, 444D, 448E, 450D, 452C, 454C, 464A, 464C, 466C, 468A, 476C, 480B, 559F, 573F, 578B, 580A, 600C, 618B, 656C, 870C, 872B, 874B, 878B, 878C, 888D, 890B, 892A, 892B, 894B, 894D, 895G, 896B, 898B, 898D, 899G, 900A, 900B, 902A, 902B, 902D, 902E, 903J, 904B, 906A, 906B, 908B, 909G, 912A, 912B, 920A, 920C, 922A, 922C, 923F, 924A, 930A, 939F, 960A, 966A, 968A, 970B, 971F, 972A, 972B, 974A, 974B, 978B, 982A, 1030A, 1036B. See also LEAGUE of Nations, Jewish refugees; NAZI Germany, Jewish refugees

Romania 50B, 62B, 64B, 66B, 154B, 356B, 474B, 620B, 660B, 698B, 810B, 812B, 820B, 822B, 824B, 826A, 826B, 828B, 848A, 902B, 906B

Shanghai 990A
Slovakia 986B, 990B
South Africa 900C
Soviet Union 806B, 878B
Suicides 944A, 966A, 968A
Trans-Jordan 320C

U.S. 225F, 267J, 465F, 473F, 481F, 663G, 899J, 963F, 967G, 969F, 971F

Vom Rath assassination 896B

ANTON, Archduke of Hapsburg
410B

ANTONESCU, Foreign Minister
666B

ANTWERP Chamber of Commerce
98A

ANTWERP Neptune (newspaper)
162B

APANA, Chang
379J

APEX Hosiery
745F, 783H

APHRODITE (Louys)
57J

APOSTOLI, Fred
1011J

APPLEBY, Edgar T.
111J

APPLETON, Edward Victor
543I

APPONYI, Count Albert
34B, 50B

AQUINO, Benigno
316E

AQUIRRE, Basque President
726B

ARAB Defense Party
926A

ARABELLA (opera)
351J

ARAB High Committee
684C, 752A, 782C, 822C, 898C

ARAB Inter-Parliamentary Congress, 1938 888C

ARAB National League
694A

ARAB Women's Congress for Palestine
890C

ARAFAT (Groseclose)
999J

ARAGONÉS, Sergio
775J

ARAKI, Sadao
258E, 270E, 330E, 342E, 360E, 364A, 364E, 370E, 372A, 394E

ARANDA, General
810B, 862B

ARANHA, Oswaldo
348D, 374D, 392D, 498D

ARANITAS, Gen.
748B

ARAS, Turkish Foreign Minister
744A

ARAUJO, Arturo
132D, 140D

ARAYA, Prince Lij
416C

ARBEITER-Zeitung (newspaper)
178B

ARBO, Higinio
252D

ARBOR Day
37F

ARBUCKLE, Roscoe "Fatty"
149J, 351J

ARCARO, Eddie
295J, 347J

ARCAYA, Dr. Pedro M.
56D

ARCHITECTURAL Record
63I

ARE These Our Children (film)
219J

ARE You Listening? (film)
259J

ARGENTINE-American Chamber of Commerce
140A

ARGENTINEAN Confederation of Commerce, Industry, and Production
50D

ARGENTINEAN Gold Conversion Office
131H

ARGENTINEAN Senate
366A, 428D

ARGENTINE Anti-War Pact
482A

ARGENTINE Association of Electro-Technicians
59I

ARGENTINE Bank of the Nation
138D, 174A

ARGENTINE Bureau of National Statistics
130D

ARGENTINE Bureau of Rural Statistics
114D, 162D, 186D

ARGENTINE Central Bank
216D, 526D

ARGENTINE Chamber of Deputies
290A

ARGENTINE Finance Ministry
88D

ARGENTINE Ministry of Agriculture
78D

ARGENTINE Ministry of Finance
67H, 75H

ARGENTINE National Mortgage
34D

ARGENTINE National Statistics Bureau
195H

ARGENTINE Senate
284D, 288D

ARGENTINE Women's Tennis Doubles Championship
104D

ARGOSY (ocean liner)
65I

ARIAS, Harmodio
184A, 220D, 279G, 369F, 370D, 382D, 396D, 482D, 532D, 544D, 614D, 640D

ARIAS, Justice Ricardo Leoncio Elias
146D

ARITA, Gen. Encarnacion
792D

ARITA, Hachiro
684E, 690E, 909G

ARIYOSHI, Akira
422E, 496E

ARIZONA, USS
349G

ARLEN, Richard
221J

ARLISS, George
101J, 249J

ARLOSOROFF, Dr. Chaim
348C, 422C, 434C

ARMAMENTS Yearbook (League of Nations)
250A

ARMENIAN Genocide
168C

ARMER, Laura Adams
265J

ARMISTICE Day
102A, 216A, 472A, 663G, 851G, 897J

ARMITAGE, Norman
271J

ARMORY Board
539G

ARMOUR, Norman
289G

ARMOUR, Tommy
69J, 85J

ARMOUR & Company
296D, 993H, 1005H, 1013H

ARMOUX, Maurice
645I

ARMSTRONG, Edward R.
377I

ARMSTRONG, Edwin H.
465I

ARMSTRONG, Sir Harry
114B

ARMSTRONG, Henry
875J

ARMSTRONG, James
57J

ARMSTRONG, Robert
521J

ARMSTRONG Cork Company
637H

ARMY Athletic Association
129J

ARMY Bill, 1933
321G

ARMY Day
159G\

L

1097

MARRA, Miguel 194B

MARRAUD, Pierre
112B

MARRIED, Pretty, and Poor (film)
1033J, 1039J

MARRIED Woman and Her Job, The (pamphlet)
613F

MARRINER, James
794C

MARRINER, Theodore
787G

MARS (planet)
347I, 985I, 987I, 1019I

MARSH, Benjamin
249F

MARSH, J. A.
287I

MARSH, Dr. J. B.
367I

MARSH, Mae
221J

MARSHALL, Frank
609J

MARSHALL, James
523I

MARSHALL, Sir John
289I

MARSHALL Field & Co.
591H, 669C

MARSTON, Sir Charles
374C, 466C, 521I

MARTI, Luis
80D

MARTIN, Dave
269J

MARTIN, Judge George
957F, 967F, 969F

MARTIN, Glenn
471H

MARTIN, Homer
687H, 711H, 715H, 718D, 719H, 783H, 799H, 809H, 827H, 845H, 857H, 865H, 887H, 899H, 903F, 927H, 939F, 953H

MARTIN, James F.
31F

MARTIN, John
1015J

MARTIN, Mary
1029J

MARTIN, Papper
207J

MARTIN, Raul
146D

MARTIN, Walter Clemens
613F, 619H

MARTINELLI, Giovanni
1005J

MARTINEZ, Aniceto
213I

MARTINEZ, Maximiliano Hernandez
316D

MARX, Groucho
283J, 793J

MARX, Harpo
261J, 283J, 793J

MARX Brothers
201J, 251J, 695J, 885J

MARY, Queen of Great Britain
264B, 268B, 327J

MARYAT, HMS
856B

MARYKNOLL Missions
633J

MARYLAND, USS
285G, 321G

MARYLAND Bar Association
623F

MARYLAND Cup
425J

MARY of Scotland (play)
369J

MASARYK, Thomas
148B, 376B, 418B, 430B, 456B, 460B, 564B, 778B

MASEFIELD, John
293J, 317J

MASON, Congressman
875F

MASON and Dixon Tennis Tournament
423J

MASSACHUSETTS Institute of Technology
29I, 457I, 461I, 479I, 497J, 505I, 535I, 841I, 1013I

MASSACHUSETTS Women of the Moose
1017J

MASSERA, Charley
401J

MASSEY, Lew
127J

MASSEY, Raymond
297J

MASSEY, Vincent
220A

MASSIGLI, Rene
522C

MASSON, Robert
200A

MASTER Barbers of America
89F

MASTERS golf tournament
35J

MASTIA, Ion
398B

MASTICK, Seabury C.
23F

MATCHEK, Vladimir
688B, 790B

MATEO, Antonio
700A

MATHIEU, J. Rogers
335J

MATIN, Le (newspaper)
200B

MATSAKAS, Michael
363J

MATSUDAIRA, Japanese Ambassador
424B

MATSUI, Gen. Iwane
758E, 798E, 810E, 826E, 830E

MATSUKATA, Kojiro
284E

MATSUMORO, Col. Takayoshi
344E

MATSUMOTO, Joji
400E

MATSUOKA, Yosuke
300A, 302A, 306E, 322A, 324E, 328A, 332A, 536E

MATSUSHITA, Admiral
426E

MATTERN, James
276A, 282A, 347I, 349I, 351I, 353G, 353I, 355I, 359J

MATTHEWS, Gloria
79J

MATTHEWS, H. Freeman
430D

MATTSON, Charles
687F

MAUGHAM, Somerset
1023J

MAULE, Frances
1013J

MAUPOIL, Henri
536B

MAURER, James H.
99F

MAURETANIA (ship)
1006A

MAURY, USS
131G

MAUTHAUSEN Concentration Camp
872B

MAVERICK, Maury
583G

MAWSON, Sir Douglas
34B, 495I

MAY Day
164B, 264B, 958D

MAY Department Stores
1001H

MAYER, Helene
515J

MAYER, USS
251G

MAYFLOWER (yacht)
39G

MAYHEW, Stella
425J

MAYNARD, Ken
257J

MAYO, Archie
255J

MAYO, Dr. Charles
371I, 967I

MAYO, Dr. William
987I

MAYO Clinic
537I, 969J, 973J, 987J, 991I, 995J

MAYTAG, Frederick I.
713J

MAYTAG Company
865H, 867H, 869H, 871H, 875H

MAY Wine (play)
563J

MCADOO, Ellen
469F

MCADOO, William G.
439H, 457F, 469F, 498E

MCAVOY, May
229J

MCCABE, John
85F

MCCAFFEY, Rev. Joseph A.
587G

MCCANN Company, H. K.
105F

MCCANN-Erickson, Inc.
105F

MCCARL, John R.
461H

MCCARRAN Civil Air Authority Act, 1938
859F

MCCARRON, Senator
689F

MCCARTHY, Ellen
473J

MCCARTHY, Joe
293J, 533J, 583J

MCCAULEY, Alvan
533H

MCCAWLEY, USS
197G

MCCLELLAN, George B.
548B

MCCOMB, Rev. John
493F

MCCONNELL, Bishop Francis J.
508D

MCCOOEY, John Henry
395F, 407F

MCCOOK, Justice Philip
605F, 635F

MCCORMICK, Edith Rockefeller
391J

MCCORMICK, Col. Robert R.
35F

MCCOWN, Theodore E.
266C, 272C

MCCREA, Joel
1009J

MCDANIELS, Hattie
757J

MCDERMUT, USS
221G

MCDONALD, James G.
500B, 534D, 566A, 672B

MCDONALD, James Ramsay
492A, 795J

MCDONALD, Jeanette
449J

MCDONALD, Joseph
627F

MCDONALD, Thomas
131F

MCDONNELL, Rev. James
537J

MCDUFFE, John
207F

MCEWEN, John
902E

MCFADDEN, Daniel
761H

MCFADDEN, Louis T.
35G

MCFADDEN Bill, 1932
267G

MCFARLAND, USS
471G

MCGAHEN, Rufus E.
539G

MCGILL University
293I

MCGOLDRICK, Joseph
427F

MCGOWAN, J. P.
221J

MCGOWAN, Wilder
901F

MCGRADY, Edward E.
581F

MCGRAW, John J.
271J

MCGRAW, John T.
323J

MCGRAW-Hill Construction Daily
113F

MCGUCKEN, Father William J.
601F

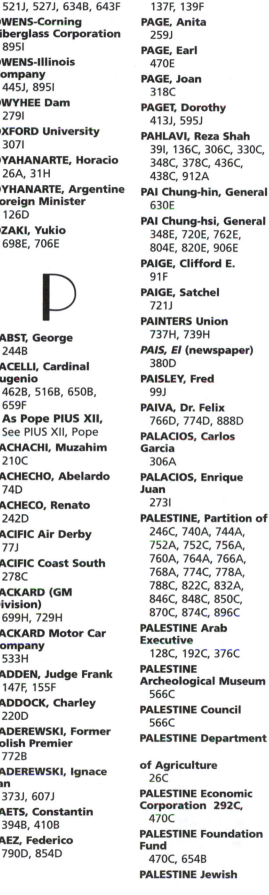

Z